Herzog , Johann Jakob; Hauck Albert

The new Schaff-Herzog Encyclopedia of religious knowledge

Vol. 1

Herzog , Johann Jakob; Hauck Albert

The new Schaff-Herzog Encyclopedia of religious knowledge

Vol. 1

Inktank publishing, 2018

www.inktank-publishing.com

ISBN/EAN: 9783747768297

THE NEW
SCHAFF-HERZOG ENCYCLOPEDIA
OF
RELIGIOUS KNOWLEDGE

EMBRACING

BIBLICAL, HISTORICAL, DOCTRINAL, AND PRACTICAL THEOLOGY AND BIBLICAL, THEOLOGICAL, AND ECCLESIASTICAL BIOGRAPHY FROM THE EARLIEST TIMES TO THE PRESENT DAY

Based on the Third Edition of the Realencyklopädie Founded by J. J. Herzog, and Edited by Albert Hauck

PREPARED BY MORE THAN SIX HUNDRED SCHOLARS AND SPECIALISTS

SAMUEL MACAULEY JACKSON, D.D., LL.D.
(Editor-in-Chief)

WITH THE ASSISTANCE OF

CHARLES COLEBROOK SHERMAN
AND
GEORGE WILLIAM GILMORE, M.A.
(Associate Editors)

AND THE FOLLOWING DEPARTMENT EDITORS

CLARENCE AUGUSTINE BECKWITH, D.D.
(Department of Systematic Theology)

HENRY KING CARROLL, LL.D.
(Department of Minor Denominations)

JOHN THOMAS CREAGH, D.D.
(Department of Liturgics and Religious Orders)
(VOL. I.)

JAMES FRANCIS DRISCOLL, D.D.
(Department of Liturgics and Religious Orders)
(VOLS. II. TO XII.)

JAMES FREDERIC McCURDY, PH.D., LL.D.
(Department of the Old Testament)

HENRY SYLVESTER NASH, D.D.
(Department of the New Testament)

ALBERT HENRY NEWMAN, D.D., LL.D.
(Department of Church History)

FRANK HORACE VIZETELLY, F.S.A.
(Department of Pronunciation and Typography)

VOLUME I
AACHEN—BASILIANS

FUNK AND WAGNALLS COMPANY
NEW YORK AND LONDON

EDITORS

SAMUEL MACAULEY JACKSON, D.D., LL.D.
(Editor-in-Chief.)
Professor of Church History, New York University.

ASSOCIATE EDITORS

CHARLES COLEBROOK SHERMAN
Editor in Biblical Criticism and Theology on "The New International Encyclopedia," New York.

GEORGE WILLIAM GILMORE, M.A.
New York, Formerly Professor of Biblical History and Lecturer on Comparative Religion, Bangor Theological Seminary.

DEPARTMENT EDITORS, VOLUME I

CLARENCE AUGUSTINE BECKWITH, D.D.
(*Department of Systematic Theology.*)
Professor of Systematic Theology, Chicago Theological Seminary.

HENRY KING CARROLL, LL.D.
(*Department of Minor Denominations.*)
One of the Corresponding Secretaries of the Board of Foreign Missions of the Methodist Episcopal Church, New York.

JOHN THOMAS CREAGH, D.D.
(*Department of Liturgics and Religious Orders.*)
Professor of Canon Law, Catholic University of America, Washington, D. C.

HUBERT EVANS, Ph.D.
(*Office Editor.*)
Member of the Editorial Staff of the Encyclopædia Britannica Company, New York City.

JAMES FREDERICK McCURDY, Ph.D., LL.D.
(*Department of the Old Testament.*)
Professor of Oriental Languages, University College, Toronto.

HENRY SYLVESTER NASH, D.D.
(*Department of the New Testament.*)
Professor of the Literature and Interpretation of the New Testament, Episcopal Theological School, Cambridge, Mass.

ALBERT HENRY NEWMAN, D.D., LL.D.
(*Department of Church History.*)
Professor of Church History, Baylor Theological Seminary (Baylor University), Waco, Tex.

FRANK HORACE VIZETELLY, F.S.A.
(*Department of Pronunciation and Typography.*)
Associate Editor of the Standard Dictionary, etc., New York City.

CONTRIBUTORS AND COLLABORATORS, VOLUME I

HANS ACHELIS, Ph.D., Th.D.,
Professor of Church History, University of Halle.

SAMUEL JAMES ANDREWS (†),
Late Pastor of the Catholic Apostolic Church, Hartford, Conn.

CARL FRANKLIN ARNOLD, Ph.D., Th.D.,
Professor of Church History, Evangelical Theological Faculty, University of Breslau.

CLARENCE AUGUSTINE BECKWITH, D.D.,
Professor of Systematic Theology, Chicago Theological Seminary.

KARL BENRATH, Ph.D., Th.D.,
Professor of Church History, University of Königsberg.

IMMANUEL GUSTAV ADOLF BENZINGER, Ph.D., Th.Lic.,
Formerly Privat-docent in Old Testament Theology, University of Berlin, Member of the Executive Committee of the German Society for the Exploration of Palestine, Jerusalem.

CARL BERTHEAU, Th.D.,
Pastor of St. Michael's Church and President of the Society for the Inner Mission, Hamburg.

EDWIN MUNSELL BLISS, D.D.,
Editor of the *Encyclopedia of Missions*, etc., Washington, D. C.

EDUARD BOEHMER (†), Ph.D., Th.D.,
Formerly Professor of Romance Languages, Universities of Halle and Strasburg.

AMY GASTON BONET-MAURY, D.D., LL.D,
Professor of Church History, Independent School of Divinity, Paris.

GOTTLIEB NATHANAEL BONWETSCH, Th.D.,
Professor of Church History, University of Göttingen.

FRIEDRICH BOSSE, Ph.D., Th.Lic.,
Professor of the New Testament and Church History, University of Greifswald.

GUSTAV BOSSERT, Ph.D., Th.D.,
Formerly Pastor at Nabern near Kirchheim, Württemberg.

JOHANN FRANZ WILHELM BOUSSET, Th.D.,
Professor of New Testament Exegesis, University of Göttingen.

JOHANNES FRIEDRICH THEODOR BRIEGER, Ph.D., Th.D.,
Professor of Church History, University of Leipsic.

CHARLES AUGUSTUS BRIGGS, D.D., D.Litt. (Oxon.),
Professor of Theological Encyclopedia and Symbolics, Union Theological Seminary, New York.

CARL VON BUCHRUCKER (†), Th.D.,
Late Supreme Consistorial Councilor, Munich.

FRANTS PEDER WILLIAM BUHL, Ph.D., Th.D.,
Professor of Oriental Languages, University of Copenhagen.

WALTER CASPARI, Ph.D., Th.Lic.,
University Preacher and Professor of Practical Theology, Pedagogics, and Didactics, University of Erlangen.

ALEXIS IRÉNÉE DU PONT COLEMAN, M.A.,
Instructor of English, College of the City of New York.

JOHN THOMAS CREAGH, D.D.,
Professor of Canon Law, Catholic University of America, Washington, D. C.

AUGUST HERMANN CREMER (†), Th.D.,
Late Professor of Systematic Theology, University of Greifswald.

GUSTAF HERMAN DALMAN, Ph.D., Th.D.,
Professor of Old Testament Exegesis, University of Leipsic, and President of the German Evangelical Archeological Institute, Jerusalem.

SAMUEL MARTIN DEUTSCH, Th.D.,
Professor of Church History, University of Berlin.

FRANZ WILHELM DIBELIUS, Ph.D., Th.D.,
Supreme Consistorial Councilor, City Superintendent, and Pastor of the Church of the Cross, Dresden.

PAUL GOTTFRIED DREWS, Th.D.,
Professor of Practical Theology, University of Giessen.

WILHELM DREXLER, Ph.D.,
Librarian, University of Greifswald.

HEINRICH DUNCKER (†), Th.D.,
Late Consistorial Councilor, Dessau.

HENRY OTIS DWIGHT, LL.D.,
Recording Secretary of the American Bible Society, New York.

DAVID ERDMANN (†), Th.D.,
Formerly General Superintendent, and Honorary Professor of Church History, Evangelical Theological Faculty, University of Breslau.

HERMANN AUGUST PAUL EWALD, Ph.D., Th.D.,
Professor of Dogmatics and New Testament Exegesis, University of Erlangen.

PAUL FEINE, Ph.D., Th.D.,
Professor of New Testament Exegesis, University of Berlin.

BARR FERREE,
Writer on Art and Architecture, New York City.

JOHANNES FICKER, Ph.D., Th.D.,
Professor of Church History, Evangelical Theological Faculty, University of Strasburg.

THEODOR FOERSTER (†), Th.D.,
Late Professor of Church History, University of Halle.

NORMAN FOX (†), D.D.,
Late Baptist Clergyman and Author, Morristown, N. J.

ALBERT FREYBE, Ph.D., Th.D.,
Gymnasial Professor, Parchim, Mecklenburg.

EMIL ALBERT FRIEDBERG, Dr.Jur.,
Professor of Ecclesiastical, Public, and German Law, University of Leipsic.

HEINRICH GELZER (†), Ph.D.,
Late Professor of Classical Philology and Ancient History, University of Jena.

GEORGE WILLIAM GILMORE, M.A.,
Formerly Lecturer on Comparative Religion, Bangor Theological Seminary.

WALTER GOETZ, Ph.D.,
Professor of History, University of Tübingen.

WILHELM GOETZ, Ph.D.,
Honorary Professor of Geography, Technical School, and Professor, Military Academy, Munich.

JOHANNES FRIEDRICH GOTTSCHICK (†), Th.D.,
Late Professor of New Testament Exegesis, Ethics, and Practical Theology, Evangelical Theological Faculty, University of Tübingen.

HERMANN GUTHE, Th.D.,
Professor of Old Testament Exegesis, University of Leipsic.

HEINRICH HAHN, Ph.D.,
Formerly Professor of History and German in the Luisenstadt Real-Gymnasium, Berlin.

ADOLF HARNACK, Ph.D., M.D., Dr.Jur., Th.D.,
Professor of Church History, University of Berlin, and General Director of the Royal Library, Berlin.

ALBERT HAUCK, Ph.D., Dr.Jur., Th.D.,
Professor of Church History, University of Leipsic; Editor of the *Realencyklopädie*, Founded by J. J. Herzog.

HERMAN HAUPT, Ph.D.,
Professor, and Director of the University Library, Giessen.

RICHARD HAUSMANN, Hist.D.,
Formerly Professor of History, Dorpat, Russia.

JOHANNES HAUSSLEITER, Ph.D., Th.D.,
Consistorial Councilor, Professor of New Testament Theology and Exegesis, University of Greifswald.

CARL FRIEDRICH GEORG HEINRICI, Ph.D., Th.D.,
Professor of New Testament Exegesis, University of Leipsic.

MAX HEROLD, Th.D.,
Dean, Neustadt-on-the-Aisch, Bavaria, Editor of *Siona*.

PAUL HINSCHIUS (†), Dr.Jur.,
Late Professor of Ecclesiastical Law, University of Berlin.

HERMANN WILHELM HEINRICH HOELSCHER, Th.D.,
Pastor of the Church of St. Nicholas, Leipsic, Editor of the *Allgemeine evangelisch-lutherische Kirchenzeitung* and of the *Theologisches Literaturblatt.*

RUDOLF HUGO HOFMANN, Ph.D., Th.D.,
Professor of Homiletics and Liturgics, University of Leipsic.

ALFRED JEREMIAS, Ph.D., Th.Lic.,
Pastor of the Luther Church and Privat-docent for the History of Religion and the Old Testament in the University, Leipsic.

FRIEDRICH WILHELM FERDINAND KATTENBUSCH, Th.D.,
Professor of Dogmatics, University of Halle.

PETER GUSTAV KAWERAU, Th.D.,
Consistorial Councilor, University Preacher, and Professor of Practical Theology, Evangelical Theological Faculty, University of Breslau.

HANS KESSLER, Th.D.,
Supreme Consistorial Councilor, Berlin.

RUDOLF KITTEL, Ph.D.,
Professor of Old Testament Exegesis, University of Leipsic.

HEINRICH AUGUST KLOSTERMANN, Th.D.,
Professor of Old Testament Exegesis, University of Kiel.

AUGUST KOEHLER (†), Ph.D., Th.D.,
Late Professor of Old Testament Exegesis, University of Erlangen.

FRIEDRICH EDUARD KOENIG, Ph.D., Th.D.,
Professor of Old Testament Exegesis, Evangelical Theological Faculty, University of Bonn.

THEODOR FRIEDRICH HERMANN KOLDE, Ph.D., Th.D.,
Professor of Church History, University of Erlangen.

HERMANN GUSTAV EDUARD KRUEGER, Ph.D., Th.D.,
Professor of Church History, University of Giessen.

JOHANNES WILHELM KUNZE, Ph.D., Th.D.,
Professor of Systematic and Practical Theology, University of Greifswald.

KARL LUDWIG LEIMBACH (†), Ph.D., Th.D.,
Late Provincial Councilor for Schools, Hanover.

LUDWIG LEMME, Th.D.,
Professor of Systematic Theology, University of Heidelberg.

EDUARD LEMPP, Ph.D.,
Chief Inspector of the Royal Orphan Asylum, Stuttgart.

FRIEDRICH LEZIUS, Th.D.,
Professor of Church History, University of Königsberg.

BRUNO LINDNER, Ph.D.,
Professor of Aryan Languages, University of Leipsic.

FRIEDRICH LIST (†), Ph.D.,
Late Studiendirektor, Munich.

GEORG LOESCHE, Ph.D., Th.D.,
Professor of Church History, Evangelical Theological Faculty, Vienna.

FRIEDRICH ARMIN LOOFS, Ph.D., Th.D.,
Professor of Church History, University of Halle.

WILHELM LOTZ, Ph.D., Th.D.,
Professor of Old Testament Exegesis, University of Erlangen.

ANDERS HERMAN LUNDSTROEM, Th.D.,
Professor of Church History, University of Upsala, Sweden.

JAMES FREDERICK McCURDY, Ph.D., LL.D.,
Professor of Oriental Languages, University College, Toronto.

GEORGE DUNCAN MATHEWS, D.D.,
Secretary of the Alliance of the Reformed Churches, London.

PHILIPP MEYER, Th.D.,
Supreme Consistorial Councilor, Member of the Royal Consistory, Hanover.

CARL THEODOR MIRBT, Th.D.,
Professor of Church History, University of Marburg.

ERNST FRIEDRICH KARL MUELLER, Th.D.,
Professor of Reformed Theology, University of Erlangen.

GEORG MUELLER, Ph.D., Th.D.,
Councilor for Schools, Leipsic.

NIKOLAUS MUELLER, Ph.D., Th.D.,
Professor of Christian Archeology, University of Berlin.

HENRY SYLVESTER NASH, D.D.,
Professor of the Literature and Interpretation of the New Testament, Episcopal Theological School, Cambridge, Mass.

CHRISTOF EBERHARD NESTLE, Ph.D., Th.D.,
Professor in the Theological Seminary (Teacher of Hebrew, New Testament Greek, and Religion), Maulbronn, Württemberg.

CARL NEUMANN, Ph.D.,
Professor of the History of Art, University of Kiel.

ALBERT HENRY NEWMAN, D.D., LL.D.,
Professor of Church History, Baylor Theological Seminary (Baylor University), Waco, Texas.

JULIUS NEY, Th.D.,
Supreme Consistorial Councilor, Speyer, Bavaria.

FREDERIK CHRISTIAN NIELSEN (†), Th.D.,
Late Bishop of Aalborg, Denmark.

HANS CONRAD VON ORELLI, Ph.D., Th.D.,
Professor of Old Testament Exegesis and History of Religion, University of Basel.

CHARLES PFENDER,
Pastor of the Evangelical Lutheran Church, Parish of St. Paul, Paris.

WILLIAM HENRY PHELEY, Ph.D.,
General Secretary of the Brotherhood of Andrew and Philip, Philadelphia.

BERNHARD PICK, Ph.D., D.D.,
Pastor of the First German Evangelical Lutheran St. John's Church, Newark, N. J.

WILLIAM PRICE,
Formerly Instructor in French, Yale College and Sheffield Scientific School, New Haven, Conn.

TRAUGOTT OTTO RADLACH,
Pastor at Gatersleben, Prussian Saxony.

GEORG CHRISTIAN RIETSCHEL, Th.D.,
University Preacher and Professor of Practical Theology, University of Leipsic.

HENDRIK CORNELIS ROGGE (†), Th.D.,
Late Professor of History, University of Amsterdam.

HUGO SACHSSE, Ph.D., Th.Lic., Dr.Jur.,
Professor of Ecclesiastical Law, University of Rostock.

KARL RUDOLF SAHRE,
Professor for Religious Instruction and Hebrew, Holy Cross Gymnasium, Dresden.

DAVID SCHLEY SCHAFF, D.D.,
Professor of Church History, Western Theological Seminary, Allegheny, Pa.

PHILIP SCHAFF (†), D.D., LL.D.,
Late Professor of Church History, Union Theological Seminary, New York.

KARL SCHMIDT, Th.D.,
Pastor at Goldberg, Mecklenburg.

EMIL SCHUERER, Ph.D., Th.D.,
Professor of New Testament Exegesis, University of Göttingen.

VICTOR SCHULTZE, Th.D.,
Professor of Church History and Christian Archeology, University of Greifswald.

LUDWIG THEODOR SCHULZE, Ph.D., Th.D.,
Professor of Systematic Theology, University of Rostock.

REINHOLD SEEBERG, Th.D.,
Professor of Systematic Theology, University of Berlin.

EMIL SEHLING, Dr.Jur.,
Professor of Ecclesiastical and Commercial Law, University of Erlangen.

FRIEDRICH ANTON EMIL SIEFFERT, Ph.D.,
Professor of Dogmatics and New Testament Exegesis, Evangelical Theological Faculty, University of Bonn.

RUDOLF STAEHELIN (†), Th.D.,
Late Professor of Church History, University of Basel.

GEORG STEINDORFF, Ph.D.,
Professor of Egyptology, University of Leipsic.

EMIL ELIAS STEINMEYER, Ph.D.,
Privy Councilor, Professor of the German Language and Literature, University of Erlangen.

ALFRED STOECKIUS, Ph.D.,
Astor Library, New York City.

PAUL TSCHACKERT, Ph.D., Th.D.,
Professor of Church History, University of Göttingen.

WILHELM VOLCK (†), Ph.D., Th.D.,
Late Professor of Old Testament Exegesis, University of Rostock.

BENJAMIN BRECKINRIDGE WARFIELD, D.D., LL.D.,
Professor of Didactic and Polemical Theology, Princeton Theological Seminary.

JOHANNES WEISS, Th.D.,
Professor of New Testament Exegesis, University of Marburg.

AUGUST WILHELM ERNST WERNER, Th.D.,
Pastor Primarius, Guben, Prussia.

EDUARD VON WOELFFLIN, Ph.D.,
Professor of Classical Philology, University of Munich.

THEODOR ZAHN, Th.D., Litt.D.,
Professor of New Testament Exegesis and Introduction, University of Erlangen.

OTTO ZOECKLER (†), Ph.D., Th.D.,
Late Professor of Church History and Apologetics, University of Greifswald.

PREFACE

This encyclopedia presents in a condensed and modified form that great body of Protestant learning called the *Realencyklopädie für protestantische Theologie und Kirche*, edited by Professor Albert Hauck, Ph.D., D.Th., D.Jur., the famous church historian of Germany. The German work is the third edition of that religious encyclopedia which was originally edited by the late Professor Johann Jakob Herzog and bore his name popularly as a convenient short title. The late Professor Philip Schaff was requested by his intimate friend Dr. Herzog to adapt the encyclopedia to the American public and this he did. To this combination of German and American scholarship the publishers gave the happy title of *The Schaff-Herzog Encyclopædia of Religious Knowledge.* This name has been familiar to thousands of the religious public on both sides of the sea for the past twenty-five years and so has been preserved as the title of this publication, with the prefix "New."

The history of this encyclopedia up to the present is this: In December, 1853, there appeared at Gotha the first part of the *Realencyklopädie für protestantische Theologie und Kirche*, which was the Protestant reply to the challenge of the Roman Catholic scholars engaged upon the *Kirchenlexikon oder Encyklopädie der katholischen Theologie und ihrer Hülfswissenschaften*, which had been appearing at Freiburg im Breisgau since 1846. The credit for suggesting the latter work must be given to Benjamin Herder (1818–88), one of the leading publishers of Germany. Its editors were Heinrich Joseph Wetzer (1801–53), professor of Oriental philology in the University of Freiburg im Breisgau, a layman, and Benedict Welte (1805–85), a priest and professor of theology in the University of Tübingen. The proposition to do as much for Protestant theology and research was mooted by a company of Protestant theologians, and Matthias Schneckenburger (1804–48), professor of theology in Bern, had been chosen editor of the projected work. But the political troubles of 1848 prevented the carrying out of the scheme and the death of Schneckenburger that year made it necessary to find another leader. At this juncture Friedrich August Tholuck (1799–1877), professor of theology in Halle, where Johann Jakob Herzog was professor from 1847 to 1854, was consulted and he named his colleague. It was an ideal choice, as Professor Herzog was a competent scholar, a friend of progress in theology, moderate in his views, and a *persona grata* to all parties among the Protestants. The publisher of the Protestant encyclopedia was Christian Friedrich Adolf Rost (1790–1856), who was carrying on the business of Johann Conrad Hinrichs, and under that name.

Both the Roman Catholic and Protestant religious encyclopedias were conspicuous successes and came to be called popularly, by the names of their editors, "Wetzer und Welte" und "Herzog" respectively. The former was finished in 1856 in twelve volumes, followed by an index volume in 1860; the latter in 1868 in twenty-two volumes including the index. In December, 1877, the Herders entrusted a new edition of "Wetzer und Welte" to Joseph Hergenröther (1824–80), at that time a professor of theology in Munich. On his elevation to the cardinalate in 1879 he transferred his editorial duties to Franz Philipp Kaulen (1827–1907), Roman Catholic professor of theology in Bonn, and under him the new edition was finished in 1901 in twelve volumes, each one much larger than those of the first edition. In September, 1903, the index volume appeared. In 1877 the first volume of the second edition of "Herzog" appeared, edited by Professor Herzog with the assistance of his colleague in the theological faculty in Erlangen, Gustav Leopold Plitt (1836–80). On Plitt's death Herzog called in another colleague, Albert Hauck (1845–), the professor of church history, who survived him and brought the work to its triumphant close in 1888 in eighteen volumes, includingthe index. In the spring of 1896 appeared the first part of the third edition of "Herzog" with Hauck, who meanwhile had gone to Leipsic as professor of church history, as sole editor. It is upon this third edition that the present work is based.

The idea of translating "Herzog" in a slightly condensed form occurred to John Henry Augustus Bomberger (1817–90), a minister of the German Reformed Church, and then president of Ursinus College, Collegeville, Pa., and in 1856 he brought out in Philadelphia the first volume, whose title-page reads thus: *The Protestant Theological and Ecclesiastical Encyclopedia: Being a Condensed Translation of Herzog's Real Encyclopedia. With Additions from Other Sources. By Rev. J. H. A. Bomberger, D.D., Assisted by Distinguished Theologians of Various Denominations. Vol. I. Philadelphia: Lindsay & Blakiston,*

1856. In this work he associated with himself twelve persons, all but one ministers. In 1860 he issued the second volume. But the Civil War breaking out the next year put a stop to so costly an enterprise and it was never resumed. The first volume included the article "Concubinage," the second "Josiah." It had been issued in numbers, of which the last was the twelfth.

In 1877 Professor Philip Schaff (1819–93) was asked by Dr. Herzog himself to undertake an English reproduction of the second edition of his encyclopedia, and this work was fairly begun when, in the autumn of 1880, Clemens Petersen and Samuel Macauley Jackson were engaged to work daily on it in Dr. Schaff's study in the Bible House, New York City. The next year Dr. Schaff's son, the Rev. David Schley Schaff, now professor of church history in the Western Theological Seminary, Allegheny, Pa., joined the staff. The original publishers were S. S. Scranton & Company, Hartford, Conn., but a change was made before the issue of the first volume and the encyclopedia was issued by Funk & Wagnalls. The title-page read thus: *A Religious Encyclopædia: or Dictionary of Biblical, Historical, Doctrinal, and Practical Theology. Based on the Real-Encyklopädie of Herzog, Plitt, and Hauck. Edited by Philip Schaff, D.D., LL.D., Professor in the Union Theological Seminary, New York. Associate editors: Rev. Samuel M. Jackson, M.A., and Rev. D. S. Schaff. Volume I. New York: Funk & Wagnalls, Publishers, 10 and 12 Dey Street.* The first volume was issued Wednesday, November 1, 1882, the second Thursday, March 1, 1883, and the third Tuesday, March 4, 1884. Volume I. had pp. xix. 1–847; volume II. pp. xvii. 848–1714; and volume III. pp. xix. 1715–2631. In November, 1886, a revised edition was issued and at the same time the *Encyclopedia of Living Divines and Christian Workers of All Denominations in Europe and America, Being a Supplement to Schaff-Herzog Encyclopedia of Religious Knowledge. Edited by Rev. Philip Schaff, D.D., LL.D., and Rev. Samuel Macauley Jackson, M. A. New York: Funk & Wagnalls, Publishers, 18 and 20 Astor Place, 1887* In 1891 the third edition of the encyclopedia was issued and with it was incorporated the *Encyclopedia of Living Divines*, with an appendix, largely the work of Rev. George William Gilmore, bringing the biographical and literary notices down to December, 1890. The entire work was repaged sufficiently to make it one of four volumes of about equal size, and it is this four-volume edition which is known to the public as the *Schaff-Herzog Encycyclopedia*, the volumes being respectively of pp. xlviii. 679 and four pages unnumbered; 680–1378; 1379–2086; iv. 2087–2629, viii. 296. As the German work at its base was overtaken by the time "S" had been reached, the "Schaff-Herzog" from that letter on was based on the first edition of "Herzog." Therefore much of its matter is now very old. Yet it has been a useful work, and in 1903 its publishers determined on a new edition based on the third edition of "Herzog," which had been appearing since 1896. But inasmuch as there was a space of ten years between the beginnings of the two works, it has been necessary to bring the matter from the German down to date. This end has been accomplished by two courses: first by securing from the German contributors to "Herzog" condensations of their contributions, in which way matter contributed to the German work has in many instances been brought down to date, and second by calling on department editors for supplementary matter.

As appears from what has been said above, this encyclopedia is not entirely a new work. It is really an old work reconstructed. Its list of titles is largely the same and it follows the same general plan as in the old work. The points of identity are: (1) that at its base lies the *Realencyklopädie für protestantische Theologie und Kirche*, once associated with the name of Herzog, now with the name of Albert Hauck, professor of church history in the University of Leipsic, and the author of the authoritative history of the Church in Germany; (2) that it gives in condensed form the information in that work, and takes such matter directly from the German work in most instances, although occasionally while the topic is the same the treatment is independent of the German contributor's; (3) that it has much matter contributed by the editorial staff and specially secured contributors; (4) that in Biblical matters it limits its titles to those of the German base, so that it should not be considered as a Bible dictionary, although the Biblical department comprehends the principal articles of such a dictionary. The points of dissimilarity are these: (1) It contains much matter furnished directly by those contributors to the German work who have kindly consented to condense their articles and bring them within prescribed limits. These limits have often been narrow, but in no other way was it possible to utilize the German matter. (2) It contains hundreds of sketches of living persons derived in almost every instance from matter furnished by themselves. In writing these sketches much help has been received, principally in the suggestion of names, from the English and American *Who's Who* and from the German *Wer ist's* (which is a similar work for Germany), and we desire to acknowledge our indebtedness with thanks. But comparison between the sketches in this book and those given of the same individual in the books referred to will reveal many differences and be so many proofs of the extensive correspondence carried on to secure the given facts. Every person sketched herein, with almost no exception, has been sent a blank for biographical data. Some thought to save themselves the trouble of filling out the blank by referring to a dictionary of living persons, but it has generally turned out that the requirements of this blank were not met by the book referred to and it has been necessary to write to the subject, and frequently more than once, before the desired information could be secured. (3) The matter in proof has been sent to persons specially chosen for eminence in their respective departments. These departments with the names of those in charge of them are: Systematic Theology, Rev. CLARENCE AUGUSTINE BECKWITH, D.D., professor of systematic theology, Chicago Theological Seminary; Minor Denominations, Rev. HENRY KING CARROLL, LL.D., one of the corresponding secretaries of the Board of Foreign Missions of the Methodist Episcopal Church, New York City; Liturgics and Religious Orders, in the first volume, Rev. JOHN THOMAS CREAGH, D.D., professor of canon law, Catholic University of America, Washington, D. C., in subsequent volumes, Very Rev. JAMES FRANCIS DRISCOLL, D.D., president of St. Joseph's Seminary, Yonkers, N. Y.; the Old Testament, Rev. JAMES FREDERICK MCCURDY, Ph.D., LL.D., professor of Oriental languages, University College, Toronto; the New Testament, Rev. HENRY SYLVESTER NASH, D.D., professor of the literature and interpretation of the New Testament, Episcopal Theological School, Cambridge, Mass.; Church History, Rev. ALBERT HENRY NEWMAN, D.D., LL.D., professor of church history, Baylor Theological Seminary (Baylor University), Waco, Texas. Besides reading the proofs they were requested to make such additions as would not only bring them up to date but represent the distinctive results of British and American scholarship. (4) A much more thorough bibliography is furnished. The attempt has been made to give sources so that students may pursue a subject to its roots; second, to supply the best literature in whatever language it occurs; third, to supply references in English for those who read only that language. (5) All articles based on German originals have been sent in proof to the writers of the original German articles when these writers were still living. Some of them had furnished the articles and they had merely been translated, but in the great majority of cases the German authors had not given that cooperation; not a few, however, have kindly read our condensations and made corrections and additions. For this cooperation thanks are due.

We here mention with gratitude the permission given by the publisher of the *Realencyklopädie für protestantische Theologie und Kirche*, Mr. HEINRICH ROST, the head of the great publishing house of J. C. HINRICHS of Leipsic, and by the editor of its third edition, Professor ALBERT HAUCK, Ph.D., D.Th., D.Jur., of the University of Leipsic, to use its contents in our discretion. Dr. Hauck has done far more than give permission. He has manifested a kindly interest in our work, has revised the condensations of his articles, and facilitated our efforts to secure from his contributors advance articles. This helpfulness is much appreciated, and we would fain give it prominent recognition.

Rev. DAVID SCHLEY SCHAFF, D.D., who holds the chair of church history in the Western Theological Seminary, Allegheny, Pa., whose father was the founder of this work and who was himself one of its original associate editors, felt unable on account of other duties to assume any editorial responsibility for the present work, as he had been asked to do by the publishers when the new edition was determined on, but he entered heartily into the arrangement whereby the sole responsibility of general editor should be lodged with his former associate editor, and has cooperated by bringing down to date almost all the articles which he and his father contributed to the first edition.

The labor of coordinating the material sent in by the many persons who have cooperated to bring out this work has fallen upon the managing editor, CHARLES COLEBROOK SHERMAN, who has discharged his difficult duties with conscientious fidelity and marked ability.

The bibliography, which is probably the greatest novelty of this encyclopedia and is a feature certain to be greatly appreciated, has been prepared by Professor GEORGE WILLIAM GILMORE, late of Bangor Theological Seminary, and the author of Hurst's *Literature of Theology*. The work of condensing and translating the articles from the contributors to the *Realencyklopädie für protestantische Theologie und Kirche* has been done by BERNHARD PICK, Ph.D., D.D., Lutheran pastor, Newark, N. J.; ALEXIS IRÉNÉE DU PONT COLEMAN, M.A. of Oxford University, instructor in English in the College of the City of New York; ALFRED STOECKIUS, Ph.D., of the Astor Library; WILLIAM PRICE; and HUBERT EVANS, Ph.D. of Leipsic. The pronunciations have been supplied by FRANK HORACE VIZETELLY, F.S.A., associate editor of the *Standard Dictionary*.

When the contributors to the *Realencyklopädie* have chosen not to condense their articles themselves, but have preferred that this work should be done by the editors of the *New Schaff-Herzog*, the fact is indicated by the use of parentheses enclosing the signature. Editorial additions or changes in the body of signed articles for which the contributors should not be held responsible are indicated by brackets. A double signature indicates that an article originally prepared by the contributor whose name appears first (in parentheses) has been revised by the contributor whose name follows. The cross (†) following the name of a contributor indicates that he is dead.

MAY 15, 1908. THE EDITOR.

CONCERNING BIBLIOGRAPHY.

For purposes of research and definite information the student is constantly under the necessity of discovering not only lists of works on a given subject, but also initials or full names of authors and place and date of publication and often the exact form of the title of a book inaccurately or partially known. To furnish this information the work which will prove useful beyond all others is the *British Museum Catalogue*, which with its *Supplement* records the books received down to 1900; accessions beyond this date are also recorded in supplementary issues. Especially valuable to the theological student are the four parts devoted to the Bibles and Bible-works in the British Museum, though the large number of entries makes it hard to consult these parts. Some help is given by the tables of arrangement. A *Subject Index* for 1881–1905, ed. G. K. Fortescue, 4 vols., London, 1902–06, makes available a very considerable part of the late literature upon all subjects. Next to this, if indeed not equally valuable so far as it is finished, is the exhaustive work doing for the French National Library and for publications in French what the work just named does for the British. This is the *Catalogue général de la Bibliothèque Nationale*, now in course of publication, Paris, 1897 sqq., of which volume xxiv., the last received, carries the list through "Catzius." The value of these two publications will be more accurately estimated when it is recalled that the two institutions are stated repositories for copyrighted books in the two countries respectively. An important feature of the first volume of the French catalogue is a helpful account of previous catalogues of the French National Library. The English work is in folio, the French in octavo. Perhaps the next best general work is that of J. C. Brunet, *Manuel du libraire*, 3 vols., Paris, 1810, superseded by the 5th ed., 6 vols., 1860–65, with *Supplément*, 2 vols., 1878–80. After these two works come in point of usefulness what may be called the national catalogues, recording the books published in Germany, France, Great Britain, Italy, and America. For Germany the work was begun in the *Allgemeines Bücher-Lexicon*, by W Heinsius, reedited and enlarged by O. A. Schulz, then by F. A. Schiller, covering the period 1700–1851 in 11 volumes, Leipsic, 1812–54, for the earlier period incomplete. This was continued by *Hinrichs' Bücher-Katalog*, covering the years 1851–65 in one volume (1875), and from that time to the present by the *Fünfjähriger Bücher-Katalog*. Half-yearly volumes are published which are superseded in course by the five-year volumes. These were accompanied by a *Repertorium* up to 1885, which arranged the entries topically. From 1883 on the *Repertorium* was superseded by a *Schlagwort-Katalog*, by Georg and L. Ost, Hanover, 1889–1904 (now complete down to 1902), serving as an index to the Hinrichs, and arranging the catch-words alphabetically.

For publications in French there is the *Catalogue général de la librairie française*, covering the period 1840–99, 15 vols., Paris, 1867–1904, begun by O. Lorenz and continued by D. Jordell, with a *Table des matières* or index published at irregular intervals, but exceedingly full and usable. The *Table systématique de la bibliographie de la France* is an annual list of copyrighted books classified according to subjects, published in Paris.

For British publications the *London Catalogue*, London, 1846, now very hard to obtain, carries the list of books from 1800 to 1846 with *Index* to the same. This was continued by the *English Catalogue*, now complete down to 1905, 7 vols., London, 1864–1905. The three volumes for 1890–1905 are arranged by authors and subjects in one alphabet. For the period 1837–89 there is an *Index of Subjects*, 4 vols., London, 1858–93. A *Yearly Catalogue* is issued, which, like the French annuals and German semiannuals, is superseded by the volume covering a series of years.

For modern Italian works the authoritative source is the *Catalogo generale della libreria Italiana, 1847–99, compilato dal Prof. Attilio Pagliaini*, 3 vols., Milan, 1901–05, a work singularly complete for the period it covers.

For American publications the period 1820–71 is inadequately covered by the *Bibliotheca Americana*, by O. A. Roorbach to 1861, and then by J. Kelly, a set of books rarely on the market. The *American Catalogue* continues this to the end of 1905 in 6 vols. folio, 2 vols. roy. 8vo, New York, 1880–1906. This was begun by F. Leypoldt and is continued by the *Publishers' Weekly*. In this series a *Yearly Catalogue* is issued, superseded like the other annuals by the larger volume. The whole is being supplemented by Charles Evans with the *American Bibliography, a Chronological Dictionary of All Publications, 1639–1820*. Of this magnificent work, vols. i.–iv. are issued, Chicago, 1903–07, bringing the titles down to 1773.

For earlier books a valuable set of volumes is L. Hain, *Repertorium bibliographicum*, 2 vols. in 4 parts and an *Index*, Stuttgart, 1826–91, giving a list of books printed from the invention of printing to 1500. To this W A. Copinger has added a *Supplement* in 2 vols., 3 parts, London, 1895-1902, and Dietrich Reichling, *Appendices*, in course of preparation and publication, containing corrections and additions, Munich, 1905 sqq.

Valuable as selected and classified lists of general literature, including theology, are Sonnenschein's *Best Books* and *Reader's Guide*, London, 1891–95. The foregoing are all in the field of general literature and are not specifically theological.

Of specifically **Theological Bibliographies,** giving lists of literature in the various departments of the science, the older ones have principally a historic value. Some of the best are: J. G. Walch, *Bibliotheca theologica selecta*, 4 vols., Jena, 1757–65, arranged topically with an index of authors; G. B. Winer, *Handbuch der theologischen Litteratur*, 3d ed., 3 vols., Leipsic, 1837–42 (gives little literature in English); E. A. Zuchold, *Bibliotheca theologica*, 2 vols., Göttingen, 1864 (an alphabetical arrangement by authors of books in German issued 1830–62); W Orme, *Bibliotheca theologica*, London, 1824 (contains critical notes). One of the older books, often referred to for its lists of editions of Scripture, is J. Le Long, *Bibliotheca sacra*, 2 vols., Paris, 1709, enlarged by A. G. Masch, 5 vols., Halle, 1778–90. T. H. Horne added to his *Introduction* a rich bibliography of the works issued before and in his time (also printed separately), London, 1839, which, however, is not found in editions of the *Introduction* later than that of 1846. An excellent work is that by James Darling, *Cyclopædia Bibliographica; a Library Manual of Theological and General Literature*, London, 1854, with supplementary volume, 1859, particularly useful as giving the contents of series and even of volumes. A modern production, noting only works in English, is J. F. Hurst, *Literature of Theology*, New York, 1896, fairly complete up to its date, arranged according to the divisions in Theology and in convenient smaller rubrics, with very full indexes. Unfortunately, it needs supplementing by the literature subsequent to 1895. It is to be hoped that the publishers will see their way to add a supplement, containing the later literature. For Roman Catholic theology consult D. Gla, *Systematisch geordnetes Repertorium der katholisch-theologischen Litteratur*, Paderborn, 1894. W T. Lowndes, *Bibliographer's Manual*, 4 vols., London, 1834, new edition by Henry G. Bohn, 1857–64, while not exclusively theological, deals largely with curious theological books and is useful for the annotations.

Among the most useful guides to theological literature are the works on Introduction to Theology or on Theological Encyclopedia and Methodology, most of which give classified lists of literature. Schleiermacher's *Kurze Darstellung des theologischen Studiums*, Berlin, 1811, 1830, was followed by K. R. Hagenbach, *Encyklopädie und Methodologie*, Leipsic, 1833, revised by M. Reischle, 1889. This last, though not in its latest form, was practically reproduced by G. R. Crooks and J. F. Hurst, New York, 1884, rev. ed., 1894, with copious lists of literature, English and American, added. Better even than this is A. Cave, *Introduction to Theology*, 2d ed., Edinburgh, 1896, in which the lists of literature are especially valuable, though the lapse of a decade since the publication makes a new edition desirable. Of very high value for its citation of literature, including Continental, English, and American, is L. Emery, *Introduction à l'étude de la théologie protestante*, Paris, 1904.

In the way of **Biblical and Theological Dictionaries and Encyclopedias** the past decade has witnessed great progress. The two great Bible Dictionaries, superseding for English readers all others, are *A Dictionary of the Bible*, by J. Hastings and J. A. Selbie, 4 vols. and extra volume, Edinburgh and New York, 1898–1904 (comprehensive and fully up to date in the Old Testament subjects, but conservative and often timid in dealing with the New Testament), and *Encyclopædia Biblica*, by T. K. Cheyne and J. S. Black, 4 vols., London and New York, 1899–1903 (also comprehensive, much more "advanced" in the Old Testament and admitting representation to the "Dutch School" in the New Testament parts, but handicapped by the Jerahmeel theory of Prof. Cheyne). F Vigouroux, *Dictionnaire de la Bible*, Paris, 1891 sqq., still in course of publication, has reached "Palestine" with part xxix., and is an excellent specimen of the conservative type of French Biblical scholarship.

In **Christian Archeology** the work of W. Smith and S. Cheetham, *Dictionary of Christian Antiquities*, 2 vols., London, 1875–80, is still valuable, and there is no later work in English to take its place. Of high value is F. X. Kraus, *Real-Encyklopädie der christlichen Alterthümer*, 2 vols., Freiburg, 1881–86. The best work, which must supersede all others because of its extraordinary completeness and fulness, but which has been only recently begun and must take many years to complete under its present plan, is F. Cabrol, *Dictionnaire d'archéologie chrétienne et de liturgie*, Paris, 1903 sqq. (parts i.–xii. are out, and bring the reader down to "Baptême"). In a different field, and worthy of high praise, is W Smith and H. Wace, *Dictionary of Christian Biography, Literature, Sects, and Doctrines*, 4 vols., London, 1877–87, representing the best English scholarship of its day, and, from the nature of its contents, not easily to be superseded. A help to this, particularly in the matter of early Christian writers, is W. Smith, *Dictionary of Greek and Roman Biography and Mythology*, 3 vols., new edition, London, 1890.

In the general field of **Historical and Doctrinal Theology** must be mentioned on the Roman Catholic side the *Kirchenlexikon* of Wetzer and Welte, 2d ed., begun by Cardinal Hergenröther, continued by F. Kaulen, 12 vols. and *Register*, Freiburg, 1880–1903. This work must be commended for its accurate scholarship, its admirable regard for proportion, and for the large range of subjects it treats with fairness and with only a suspicion of a tendency toward ultramontanism. Briefer is the *Handlexikon der katholischen Theologie*, begun by J. Schäfler (continued by J. Sax), 4 vols., Regensburg, 1880–1900. The new *Kirchliches Handlexikon* of M. Buchberger, Munich, 1904–06 (in progress), is not particularly valuable. The evangelical side of German scholarship is represented by the great work of J. J. Herzog, *Realencyklopädie für protestantische Theologie und Kirche*, 3d ed., revised under A. Hauck, Leipsic, 1896 sqq., 18 vols. issued to date. This is the great storehouse of German Protestant theology and the basis of the present work. The most ambitious work of American scholarship is J. McClintock and J. Strong, *Cyclopædia of Biblical, Theological, and Ecclesiastical Literature*, 10 vols., New York, 1867–1881, with two supplementary volumes, 1884–86 (claims to have over 50,000 titles; necessarily it is now in need of revision). Other works, each having its distinctive field, are: W F. Hook, *A Church Dictionary*, 8th ed., London, 1859, reprinted Philadelphia, 1854; J. Eadie, *The Ecclesiastical Cyclopedia*, ib., 1861; J. H. Blunt, *Dictionary of Doctrinal and Historical Theology*, 2d ed., ib., 1872; idem, *Dictionary of Sects, Heresies, and Schools of Thought*, ib., 1891 (both of considerable worth, representing "High Anglicanism"); W E. Addis and T. Arnold, *A Catholic Dictionary*, London and New York, 6th ed., 1903; J. Hamburger, *Real-Encyklopädie des Judenthums*, 3 vols., 3d ed., Leipsic, 1891–1901 (deals with both Biblical and Talmudic subjects; "by a Jew for Jews"); *The Jewish Encyclopedia*, published under the direction of an editorial board of which I. K. Funk was chairman and Isidore Singer managing editor, 12 vols., New York, 1901–06; F. Lichtenberger, *Encyclopédie des sciences religieuses*, 13 vols., Paris, 1877–82 (for French Protestants). T. P. Hughes, *Dictionary of Islam*, London, 1885, is the only encyclopedic work on the subject, but defective and unreliable. In Hymnology there are: H. A. Daniel, *Thesaurus hymnologicus*, i. Latin hymns, ii. Latin sequences, iii. Greek hymns, iv.–v. supplement to vols. i.–ii., Leipsic, 1841–55 (a storehouse of material often inaccessible elsewhere, but ill digested, inaccurate, and perplexing to consult); E. E. Koch, *Geschichte des Kirchenliedes und Kirchengesangs der christlichen Kirche*, 3d ed., partly posthumous, 8 vols. and index, 1866–77 (the greatest collection of biographies of hymnists, unfortunately not reliable); the one English cyclopedic work in hymnology is J. Julian, *Dictionary of Hymnology*, London and New York, 1907. A work of immense erudition and alone in its field, which comprehends much that is theological, is J. M. Baldwin, *Dictionary of Philosophy and Psychology*, 3 vols., New York, 1901–06 (vol. iii. in 2 parts is devoted to the bibliography of the subject, duly classified).

While most of the **Biblical Helps** are noted under the appropriate titles in the text, the following are worthy of special mention here. For the **Old Testament** all the books except Exodus to Deuteronomy were published in handy form in the Hebrew by G. Baer and F. Delitzsch, Leipsic, 1869 95 (the text, though critical, does not concern itself with readings from the versions); the best ed. so far of the complete Hebrew text is C. D. Ginsburg's *Hebrew Bible*, 2 vols., London, 1894; the text alone was reprinted in 1906 (the *Introduction to the Hebrew Bible* by Ginsburg, London, 1897, is the one indispensable handbook to the text); yet a very excellent *Biblia Hebraica* has been published by R. Kittel with the assistance of Professors G. Beer, F. Buhl, G. Dalman, S. R. Driver, M. Löhr, W. Nowack, J. W Rothstein, and V Ryssel, in 2 parts, Leipsic, 1905-06, obtainable also in smaller sections. The new series entitled *The Sacred Books of the Old Testament*, ed. Paul Haupt, now in course of publication, Leipsic, London, and Baltimore, 1894 sqq., and known generally as the "Rainbow Bible" and less widely as the "Polychrome Bible," sets forth the composite origin of the books and indicates the separate documents by printing the text on backgrounds of different tints (the critical objection to the series is that as each book is not directly the result of a consensus of scholarship, the effect in each case is the pronouncement of a single scholar and consequent indecisiveness in the verdict). The lexicons which are most worthy of confidence are: W Gesenius, *Thesaurus philologicus criticus linguæ Hebrææ*, 3 vols., Leipsic, 1826–53 (indispensable for the thorough student); idem, *Hebräisches und Aramäisches Handwörterbuch*, 14th ed. by F. Buhl, ib., 1905; and (best for the English student) F. Brown, C. A. Briggs, and S. R. Driver, *Hebrew and English Lexicon of the Old Testament*, Oxford and Boston, 1906. Besides the old Concordance of J. Fürst, Leipsic, 1848, there is now available S. Mandelkern, *Veteris Testamenti concordantiæ Hebraice et Chaldaice*, ib., 1896, which unfortunately is badly done, the errors being very numerous. The best grammar is W Gesenius, *Hebräische Grammatik*, 27th ed. by Kautzsch, 1902, Eng. transl. of 25th ed. adjusted to the 26th Germ. ed. by G. W Collins, London, 1898, along with which should be used S. R. Driver, *Treatise on the Use of the Tenses in Hebrew*, London, 1892. Related to Old Testament study is M. Jastrow, *Dictionary of the Targumim, Babli and Yerushalmi, and the Midrashic Literature*, 2 vols., London and New York, 1903. For the Greek of the Old Testament there is sadly needed a new lexicon. The only one of moment is J. F. Schleusner, *Lexici in interpretes Græcos Veteris Testamenti* , 2 vols., Leipsic, 1784–86. The *Concordantiæ Græcæ versionis*, by A. Tromm, 2 vols., Amsterdam, 1718, ought not to be discarded, even by those who possess E. Hatch and H. A. Redpath, *A Concordance to the Septuagint*, Oxford, 1892–1900, 2d ed., 2 vols. and supplement, 1906, the omissions in which make still necessary recourse to the older work.

For **New Testament** texts the student will naturally turn either to the *Editio octava critica major* of Tischendorf, 2 vols., Leipsic, 1869–72, with *Prolegomena* by C. R. Gregory, 3 vols., ib., 1884–94 (containing the most complete collection of the variant readings with description of the sources from which they are derived); to the edition by B. F. Westcott and F J. A. Hort, 2d ed., Cambridge, 1890; to R. F Weymouth's *Resultant Greek Testament*, London, 1892; to E. Nestle's *Novum Testamentum Græce*, 3d ed., Stuttgart, 1901; or to O. von Gebhardt's ed., combining the readings of Tischendorf, Tregelles, and Westcott and Hort, 16th ed., Leipsic, 1900. Of lexicons the best for general purposes is J. H. Thayer, *Greek-English Lexicon of the New Testament*, New York, 1895; but notice must be taken of H. Cremer, *Biblisch-theologisches Wörterbuch*, 9th ed., Gotha, 1902, Eng. transl. of 2d ed., Edinburgh, 1886, with supplement (a work that aims to bring out especially the theological, philosophical, and psychological elements of the New Testament vocabulary, and is not a general lexicon). A choice is given in concordances between C. H. Bruder, *Concordantiæ Novi Testamenti*, 5th ed., Göttingen, 1900, and W F Moulton and A. S. Geden, *Concordance to the Greek Testament*, Edinburgh and New York, 1897 (good for Westcott and Hort's text). For the English Bible the two concordances of value now are R. Young, *Analytical Concordance to the Bible*, 7th ed., Edinburgh and New York, 1899; and J. Strong, *Exhaustive Concordance to the Bible*, New York, 1896. The best grammar of the New Testament is F. Blass, *Grammatik des neutestamentlichen Griechisch*, Göttingen, 1902, Eng. transl. of 2d ed., London, 1905, along with which should be used E. D. Burton, *Syntax of Moods and Tenses in New Testament Greek*, Chicago, 1901 (the best work on the subject). Of H. J. Moulton's *Grammar of New Testament Greek*, only vol. i., *Prolegomena*, is published, Edinburgh, 1906. General Semitic and Oriental philology is treated in separate volumes on the individual languages in the *Porta linguarum orientalium*, ed. J. H. Petermann, H. L. Strack, and others, Berlin, 1884 sqq.

As a directory upon the geography of **Palestine** the following works represent the choicest: the latest and the standard bibliography of Palestine is R. Röhricht, *Chronologisches Verzeichniss der auf die Geographie des heiligen Landes bezüglichen Litteratur von 333 bis 1878,* Berlin, 1890. Earlier but still useful is T. Tobler, *Bibliographia geographica Palestinæ,* Leipsic, 1867 On the topography there is nothing in English, perhaps nothing in any other tongue, superior in its way to G. A. Smith, *Historical Geography of the Holy Land,* 7th ed., London, 1897 Alongside this should be put E. Robinson's *Biblical Researches in Palestine,* 3 vols., London and Boston, 1841, and in Germ. transl. at Halle the same year, and *Later Biblical Researches,* 1856 (a second ed., including both works in 3 vols., was published, Boston, 1868, but omits some things in the first edition which are sadly missed). In spite of its age this book is still useful. The Palestine Text Society of London has since 1887 been engaged in republishing the ancient itineraries and descriptions relating to Palestine, thus making available to the student material otherwise obtainable only by painful research. Special notice is deserved by the monographs published by the Palestine Exploration Fund of London, including the massive *Memoirs.* An epoch-making work was W M. Thomson's *The Land and the Book,* 3 vols., New York, 1886 (perhaps the most popular book ever written on the subject). An old classic, by no means superseded, is H. Reland, *Palæstina ex monumentis illustrata,* Utrecht 1714. On the antiquities of Israel two works with nearly the same title, *Hebräische Archäologie,* were issued in the same place and year, Freiburg, 1894, the one by I. Benzinger, in 1 vol. (new ed., Tübingen, 1907), the other by W Nowack, in 2 vols.

In the department of **Church History** the sources available to the student are growing exceedingly abundant. For a survey of early Christian literature the most detailed work is that of A. Harnack, *Geschichte der altchristlichen Litteratur bis Eusebius,* 2 vols. in 3 parts, Leipsic, 1893–1904 (a book of reference). A handbook of great value is G. Krüger, *Geschichte der altchristlichen Litteratur in den drei ersten Jahrhunderten,* Freiburg, 1895, 2d ed., 1898, Eng. transl., New York, 1897 (a model of compression and succinctness, including short lives of the writers and good lists of literature). C. T. Cruttwell, *Literary History of Early Christianity,* 2 vols., London, 1893, is also a work of merit. A massive work, doing for the Byzantine and later writers of the Greek Church what Harnack does for the early period, is K. Krumbacher, *Byzantinische Litteraturgeschichte, 527–1453,* Munich, 1897. As a guide to the use of medieval literature, and as a help to the sources and an indicator of all that is best in those sources in modern works, there is no book which can be compared with A. Potthast, *Bibliotheca historica medii ævi,* Berlin, 1896, quoted in this work as Potthast, *Wegweiser.* No student of ecclesiastical history can afford to be without this most complete guide to the MSS. and the editions of the sources of knowledge of the lives of the saints, notables, and writers down to 1500 A.D.

As a source for original investigation in **Patristics,** as well as in medieval theological writings, there is nothing so handy (because of its comprehensiveness) as the collection made under the direction of the Abbé Migne, *Patrologiæ cursus completus, Series Latina,* 221 vols., Paris, 1844–64; *Series Græca,* 162 vols., ib., 1857–66 (a set of works rarely on the market, costing about $1,200, but possessed by the principal general and theological libraries in the country; the drawback is that the text is often not critical and is very badly printed). Subsidiary to the use of Migne the following works are often quoted: J. A. Fabricius, *Bibliotheca Græca,* 14 vols., Hamburg, 1705–28, new ed., by G. C. Harles, 12 vols., 1790–1811, incomplete (quoted as Fabricius-Harles), which is a bibliographical and biographical directory to early patristic writings, and contains textual matter of great importance; J. S. Assemani, *Bibliotheca orientalis Clementino-Vaticana,* 3 vols., Rome, 1719–28 (a collection of Syriac, Arabic, Persian, Turkish, Hebrew, Samaritan, Armenian, Ethiopic, Egyptian, and other documents, with critical matter relating to them); É. Martène and N. Durand, *Veterum scriptorum et monumentorum collectio*, 9 vols., Paris, 1724–33; A. Gallandi, *Bibliotheca veterum patrum antiquorumque scriptorum ecclesiasticorum*, 14 vols., Venice, 1765–81 (contains some works otherwise difficult of access. An index of contents to Gallandi is to be found in J. G. Dowling, *Notitiæ scriptorum sanctorum patrum*, pp. 192-209, Oxford, 1839). A work of great usefulness is R. Ceillier, *Histoire générale des auteurs sacrés et ecclésiastiques*, new ed., 14 vols. in 15 and *Table générale des matières*, 2 vols., Paris, 1858–69. Noteworthy are the excellent and handy *Corpus scriptorum ecclesiasticorum Latinorum*, Vienna, 1867 sqq., appearing in parts and not in regular order (vol. xxxxvii. appeared 1906), and *Patrum apostolicorum opera*, ed. O. von Gebhardt, A. Harnack, and T. Zahn, 4 vols., Leipsic, 1876–78, the same, 5th ed. minor, 1905; and J. B. Lightfoot, *Apostolic Fathers*, 4 vols., London, 1877-89 (a work which will stand as one of the monuments of English scholarship, rich in original investigation, and with excursuses of the first rank in value and brilliancy). All these are supplemented in the case of new discoveries or by new treatment of works already in hand in the *Texte und Untersuchungen zur Geschichte der altchristlichen Litteratur*, ed. O. von Gebhardt and A. Harnack, 1st series, 15 vols., 2d series in progress (14 vols. issued), Berlin, 1883 sqq., and by the English *Texts and Studies*, ed. J. A. Robinson, 7 vols., Cambridge, 1891–1906. For the English student there are available the *Library of the Fathers*, ed. E. B. Pusey, J. Keble, and J. H. Newman, 40 vols., Oxford, 1839 sqq.; and the Ante-Nicene, and Nicene and Post-Nicene Fathers, best and handiest in the Am. ed., published as follows: *Ante-Nicene Fathers*, ed. A. Cleveland Coxe, 9 vols. and Index, Buffalo, 1887 (Index volume contains a valuable bibliography of patristics); *Select Library of the Nicene and Post-Nicene Fathers*, 1st series, ed. P Schaff, 14 vols., New York, 1887–92, 2d series, ed. P Schaff and H. Wace, 14 vols., New York, 1890-1900. The first series includes 8 vols. of Augustine's works (by far the best collection yet published in English) and 6 of Chrysostom's; the 2d series includes the church histories of Eusebius, Socrates, Sozomen, and Theodoret, and selected works of Gregory of Nyssa, Basil, Jerome, Gennadius, and others. Not to be left out of account is the *Reliquiæ sacræ* of M. J. Routh, 2d ed., 5 vols., Oxford, 1846–48, a collection of patristic and other fragments still of value and constantly employed and referred to.

Among collections of **Sources** the first place is easily held by the massive *Monumenta Germaniæ historica*, still in course of publication, of which over 60 volumes are already issued in folio and quarto, Hanover and Berlin. This series originated in the *Gesellschaft für die ältere deutsche Geschichtskunde* in Frankfort, 1819. The work was put into the hands of Dr. G. H. Pertz, to whom the great comprehensiveness of the series and its consequent value is largely due. Dr. Pertz was editor and did much of the work till in 1875 it passed into the hands of Prof. G. Waitz, at whose death in 1886 Prof. W Wattenbach took charge, and in 1888 Prof. E. Dümmler. Most of the German experts in the branches which the collected documents represent have collaborated. There are five sections, *Scriptores*, *Leges*, *Diplomata*, *Epistolæ*, *Antiquitates*, and many subsections. The documents in this royal series concern Christendom at large and not, as the title suggests, the German empire alone. There is a volume of *Indices* by O. Holder-Egger and K. Zeumer, Berlin, 1890, covering the volumes issued up to that time, and the table of contents is carried five years farther along in the work of Potthast mentioned above.

Other collections of value to the historical student are: the *Bibliotheca rerum Germanicarum*, ed. P Jaffé, 6 vols., Berlin, 1864–73; M. Bouquet, *Rerum Gallicarum et Francicarum scriptores. Recueil des historiens des Gaules et de la France*, 23 vols., Paris, 1738–1876 (begun by the Benedictines of St. Maur and continued by the Academy. A new ed. was published under L. Delisle, 1869–94. The record is carried down to 1328 A.D.); L. A. Muratori, *Rerum*

Italicarum scriptores, 25 vols. in 28, Milan, 1723–51 (covers the period 500–1500 A.D.; an elaborate new ed. under the direction of Giosuè Carducci and Vittorio Fiorini is being published by S. Lapi at Città di Castello, 1900 sqq.); *Corpus scriptorum historiæ Byzantinæ*, ed. Niebuhr, Bekker, and others, 49 vols., Bonn, 1828–78 (not so good in workmanship as is usual with German issues; a new ed. is in course of publication in 50 vols. at Bonn). In connection with this series of Byzantine historians should be noticed E. A. Sophocles, *Greek-English Dictionary*, Memorial edition, New York, 1887 (good for the Greek of the Roman and Byzantine periods). *Recueil des historiens des croisades*, 13 vols., Paris, 1841–85 (published under the care of the French Academy), is necessary for the study of the kingdoms of Jerusalem, Cyprus, and Armenia. The *Corpus Reformatorum*, begun at Halle, 1834, with the works of Melanchthon in 28 vols.; continued with Calvin's in 59; and now presenting those of Zwingli, is the indispensable source for the student of those writers. Of some value to the student, more particularly to the archeologist, are: *Corpus inscriptionum Latinarum*, Berlin, 1863 sqq., and *Corpus inscriptionum Græcarum*, Berlin, 1825 sqq. A magnificent series is in progress in the *Corpus inscriptionum Semiticarum*, Paris, 1881 sqq.

For those who have not access to large libraries a number of selections from historical documents have been printed. For church history to the time of Constantine, cf. H. M. Gwatkin, *Selection from Early Writers*, London and New York, 1893; for the medieval and modern periods one of the best is E. Reich, *Select Documents Illustrating Mediæval and Modern History*, London, 1905, with which may be compared the smaller collection by S. Mathews, *Select Mediæval Documents, 754–1254 A.D.*, Boston, 1892 (both give the selections in the original languages). For students of the medieval period O. J. Thatcher and E. H. McNeal have translated many important documents in *A Source Book for Mediæval History*, New York, 1905. Other works of this character are E. F. Henderson, *Select Documents of the Middle Ages*, London, 1892; D. C. Munro and G. C. Sellery, *Medieval Civilization*, New York, 1904 (consists of translations or condensations from European writers on important topics); J. H. Robinson, *Readings in European History*, 2 vols., Boston, 1904–06 (containing translations, condensations, and adaptations of selections, ranging from Seneca to J. A. Hobson, useful for illustration of European and American history, sacred and secular). The reader of German will receive efficient help in such publications as M. Schilling, *Quellenbuch zur Geschichte der Neuzeit*, 2d ed., Berlin, 1890; K. Noack, *Kirchengeschichtliches Lesebuch*, 2d ed., Berlin 1890; D. A. Ludwig, *Quellenbuch zur Kirchengeschichte*, Davos, 1891; P. Mehlhorn, *Aus den Quellen der Kirchengeschichte*, Berlin, 1894; C. Mirbt, *Quellen zur Geschichte des Papsttums*, 2d ed., Tübingen, 1901; H. Rinn and J. Jüngst, *Kirchengeschichtliches Lesebuch*, Tübingen, 1905.

To **English Ecclesiastical Sources** an excellent guide is C. Gross, *Sources and Literature of English History to 1485*, London, 1900. First among the collections of sources is to be mentioned A. W. Haddan and W Stubbs, *Councils and Ecclesiastical Documents relating to Great Britain and Ireland*, 3 vols. (vol. ii. in 2 parts), London, 1869–78 (covering the period 200–870 A.D.; a storehouse of original documents, unfortunately left incomplete through the death of Haddan). Of high value are David Wilkins, *Concilia Magnæ Britanniæ 446–1717*, 4 vols., London, 1737; *Monumenta historica Britannica. Materials for the History of Britain to the End of the Reign of Henry VII. Notes by H. Petrie and J Sharpe, Introduction by T D. Hardy*, vol. i. folio, London, 1848 (no more published; issued under the direction of the Record Commission); J. A. Giles, *Patres ecclesiæ Anglicani ad annum 1300*, 36 vols., Oxford, 1838–43 (the work not well done, but still useful). For the reader of English alone a large number of select sources are given in H. Gee and W. J. Hardy, *Documents Illustrative of English Church History*, London, 1896 (covers the period 314–1700). Known by the searcher after original sources as of the highest value are the publications of a number of societies. Belonging in this class, though not under the care of any society, are *Rerum Britannicarum medii ævi scriptores, published under the Direction of the Master of the Rolls*, London, 1858–91 (known as the *Rolls Series*. One of the most important of this series is No. 26, T. D. Hardy's *Descriptive Catalogue of Materials Relating to the History of Great Britain and Ireland to the End of the Reign of Henry VII.*, 3 vols. in 4, 1862–71). The Henry Bradshaw Society of London began in 1891 to publish monastic and other documents; the Camden Society exists for the purpose of publishing documents illustrative of English history (London, 1838 to date), many of which are of ecclesiastical interest; the Surtees Society of Durham, founded 1834, has issued over 100 volumes, many of which make available sources of the first rank.

In the field of **Biography** a number of works should be known to students. A monumental work begun by J. S. Ersch and J. G. Gruber, continued by A. Leskien, is *Allgemeine Encyklopädie der Wissenschaften und Künste in alphabetischer Folge*, Leipsic, 1818–89 and still receiving additions. Already 100 volumes and more have been issued, and it is to be continued from time to time. The biographical interest is so pronounced in this production that it takes a front rank in this class of works. The biographical interest is also predominant in another work to which very frequent reference is made, L. S. Le Nain de Tillemont, *Mémoires pour servir à l'histoire ecclésiastique des six premiers siècles*, 2d ed., 16 vols., Paris, 1701–12, parts of it in an English translation by T. Deacon, 2 vols., London, 1721, 1733–35. J. P Niceron, *Mémoires pour servir à l'histoire des hommes illustrés dans la republique des lettres*, 43 vols., Paris, 1729–45, is a work of reference often used; mention is due also to the *Biographie universelle, ancienne et moderne*, 45 vols., Paris, 1843 sqq., and *Nouvelle biographie universelle* of J. C. F. Hoefer, 46 vols., Paris, 1852–56, both serviceable and sometimes the only available works. Of national biographical works, for Germany there is the *Allgemeine deutsche Biographie*, 50 vols., Leipsic, 1875–1905 (still in progress; it is under the auspices of the Historical Commission of the Royal Bavarian Academy of Sciences); for France, the *Histoire littéraire de la France* begun by the Benedictines of St. Maur, 12 vols., Paris, 1733–63, and continued by members of the Academy of Inscriptions and Belles-lettres to vol. xxxii., 1898 (a new edition is in progress, completed as far as vol. xvi.); for Protestant France may be consulted E. and É. Haag, *La France protestante*, 7 vols., Paris, 1846–59, 2d ed., enlarged by H. L. Bordier, vols. i.–vi., 1887–89; also belonging here is A. C. A. Agnew, *Protestant Exiles from France*, 2 vols., Edinburgh, 1886 (printed for private circulation only). The one work of note for Holland is A. J. Van der Aa, *Biographisch Woordenboek van der Nederlanden*, Haarlem, 1852 sqq. For England there is the noble *Dictionary of National Biography*, edited by Leslie Stephen and Sidney Lee, 63 vols., and 3 supplement vols., with one of errata, London and New York, 1885–1904 (contains much of interest to Americans, especially on the founders and notables of colonial times; a cheaper ed. is promised); F. Boase, *Modern English Biography of Persons who have died since 1850*, 3 vols., Truro, 1892–1901; and J. Gillow, *Bibliographical Dictionary of English Catholics, 1534–1885*, 5 vols., London and New York, n.d. (the lists of works by the subjects of the entries are an exceedingly valuable feature, being very complete). The Danes have also a biographical dictionary like those mentioned, *Dansk biografisk lexikon, tillige omfallende Norge for tidsrummet, 1537–1814. Udgivet af* C. F. Briska, Copenhagen, 1887 sqq.

There is still needed an adequate work on American Biography which shall correspond to the English *Dictionary of National Biography* cited above. There are available the *National Cyclopædia of American Biography*, 13 vols., New York, 1892–1906 (the alphabetical order is abandoned and no consistent substitute adopted; an elaborate index volume appeared in 1906); and *Appleton's Cyclopædia of American Biography* by James Grant Wilson and John Fiske, rev. ed., 6 vols., ib., 1898–99 (the revision consists mainly of a supplement).

As a propædeutic to the study of **General Church History** an indispensable work is E. Schürer, *Geschichte des jüdischen Volkes im Zeitalter Jesu Christi*, 3d ed., 3 vols. and Index, Leipsic, 1898–1901, Eng. transl. of 2d ed., 5 vols., New York, 1891. Of works on general Church History there is a wide range of choice. A. Neander, *History of the Christian Religion and Church*, 11th Am. ed., 5 vols., Boston, 1872 (coming down to 1517 A.D.), and Index volume, 1881, is the most philosophical work on the subject yet published, superseded in parts by the discoveries made since it was written, but as a whole by no means obsolete; with this should go J. K. L. Gieseler, whose *Ecclesiastical History* in the German was in 5 vols., Darmstadt, 1824–25, Eng. transl. begun by S. Davidson and others, 5 vols., Edinburgh, 1848–56, edited and translation carried further by H. B. Smith, translation completed by Miss Mary A. Robinson, 5 vols., New York, 1857–81 (especially valuable for its citation of original documents); and J. H. Kurtz, a translation of which from the 9th German edition by J. Macpherson appeared in London, 1888–89 (condensed in form and very usable; new ed. of the German by N. Bonwetsch and P. Tschackert, 2 vols., Leipsic, 1906). P. Schaff, *History of the Christian Church*, 7 vols., New York, 1882–92, coming down through the Reformation, but omitting vol. v. on the scholastic period, is perhaps the most readable. A very compact work is W. Moeller, *History of the Christian Church*, 3 vols., London, 1892–1900 (comes down to 1648; the 2d ed. of the German original by H. von Schubert, Tübingen, 1902). J. F. Hurst, *History of the Christian Church*, 2 vols., New York, 1897–1900, is also compact; it is conservative in treatment of its subject. A. H. Newman, *Manual of Church History*, 2 vols., Philadelphia, 1900–03, is, like Hurst, compact but less conservative in tone. The reader in Church History will find three works constantly referred to; viz., J. Bingham, *Origines ecclesiasticæ, or the Antiquities of the Christian Church*, 10 vols., London, 1708–22, often reprinted, unfortunately not seldom in abbreviated form (recognized by scholars as a work of "profound learning and unprejudiced inquiry" and remaining one of the standards in this department; best ed. in 8 vols. of his complete works in 10 vols., by R. Bingham, Jun., Oxford, 1855); A. J. Binterim, *Die vorzüglichsten Denkwürdigkeiten der christ-katholischen Kirche*, 2d ed., 7 vols., Mainz, 1837–41 (a treasury of important notes on "things worthy of remembrance"); and J. C. W. Augusti, *Denkwürdigkeiten aus der christlichen Archäologie*, 12 vols., Leipsic, 1817–31. Out of the number of works on the History of Dogma the one likely to be most useful, though by no means the most philosophical, is A. Harnack, *Lehrbuch der Dogmengeschichte*, 3d ed., 3 vols., Freiburg, 1894–97, Eng. transl., 7 vols., London, 1894–99, and Boston, 1895–1900. A work of the first rank frequently referred to for the history of Europe till the fall of Constantinople is E. Gibbon, *History of the Decline and Fall of the Roman Empire*, best edition by J. B. Bury, 7 vols., London, 1896–1900 (Gibbon is said to be the only student who worked over thoroughly the Byzantine Histories; formerly regarded as an opponent of Christianity, many of his positions are now taken by church historians).

For the Church History of **Germany** three works with the same title, *Kirchengeschichte Deutschlands*, are of supereminent worth and are generally used as works of reference: A. Hauck, vol. i., 4th ed., Leipsic, 1904, vol. ii., 2d ed., 1900, vol. iii., 3d ed., 1906, vol. iv., 2d ed., 1903 (contains rich bibliography); F. W. Rettberg, 2 vols., Göttingen, 1846–48 (especially good for origins); and J. Friedrich, 2 vols., Bamberg, 1867–69 (like Hauck, good in history of the dioceses). A handy help to the early sources of German Church History is W. Wattenbach, *Deutschlands Geschichtsquellen bis zum Mittel des 13. Jahrhunderts*, 5th ed., 2 vols., Berlin, 1885, 6th ed., 1893–94 (the changes are so great that both editions are frequently quoted side by side). A work of genius, learning, and attractiveness, but avowedly from a strong Roman Catholic standpoint, is Johannes Janssen's *History of the German People at the Close of the Middle Ages*, German original ed. L. Pastor, 14th to 16th ed. completed in 8 vols., 1903, Eng. transl. by Miss Mary A. Mitchell and Miss Alice M. Christie, London, 10 vols. having appeared up to 1907

For the Church History of **France** a bibliography is furnished by A. Molinier, *Les Sources de l'histoire de France*, 2 vols., Paris, 1901-02. Besides Bouquet, already mentioned, there are available for early sources: F Guizot, *Collection des mémoires relatifs à l'histoire de France*, 31 vols., Paris, 1823-35; and *Gallia christiana*, 16 vols., ib., 1715-1865. An important work is J. N. Jager, *Histoire de l'Église catholique en France*, 20 vols., ib., 1862-78. In English there are: W H. Jervis, *The Gallican Church*, 2 vols., London, 1872; H. M. Baird, *Rise of the Huguenots*, 2 vols., New York, 1883; idem, *The Huguenots and Henry of Navarre*, 2 vols. ib., 1886-87; idem, *The Huguenots and the Revocation of the Edict of Nantes*, 2 vols., ib., 1895.

A fair survey of the course of the Church in **England** is obtained by combining W Bright, *Chapters in Early English Church History*, Oxford, 1906, with the series edited by W R. W Stephens and W Hunt, 7 vols., London, 1899-1906, as follows: W Hunt, *The English Church 597-1066* (1899); W R. W Stephens, *The English Church 1066-1272* (1901); W W Capes, *The English Church in the 14th and 15th Centuries* (1900); J. Gairdner, *The English Church in the 16th Century* (1903); W H. Frere, *The English Church in the Reigns of Elizabeth and James I.* (1904); W H. Hutton, *The English Church from the Accession of Charles I. to the Death of Anne* (1903); J. H. Overton and B. Felton, *The Church of England 1714-1800* (1906).

For the Church History of **Ireland** and **Scotland** the following are valuable: J. Colgan, *Acta sanctorum veteris et majoris Scotiæ seu Hiberniæ sanctorum insulæ* , 2 vols., Louvain, 1645-47; H. M. Luckock, *The Church in Scotland*, London, 1893; J. Lanigan, *An Ecclesiastical History of Ireland to the 13th Century*, 2d ed., 4 vols., Dublin, 1829 (a very important and essential work); J. O'Hanlon, *Lives of the Irish Saints*, 7 vols., Dublin, 1875-1877; J. Healy, *Insula sanctorum et doctorum, or Ireland's Ancient Schools and Scholars*, Dublin, 1890; and T. Olden, *The Church of Ireland*, London, 1892. Consult particularly the list of literature under CELTIC CHURCH IN BRITAIN AND IRELAND.

American Church History as a whole is treated in the *American Church History Series*, 13 vols., New York, 1893-97, issued under the auspices of the American Society of Church History. The principal denominations receive extended treatment by some of their own specialists; for the minor denominations the provision made is only that given in vol. i. by H. K. Carroll, *The Religious Forces of the United States*, new ed., 1896. It is in respect to the minor sects that most difficulty is experienced in obtaining data. Another series of a more popular character is *The Story of the Churches*, New York, 1904 sqq.

For the history of the **Papacy** an indispensable work is C. Mirbt, *Quellen zur Geschichte des Papsttums*, 2d ed., Tübingen, 1901 (a guide to the history, giving citations from original sources and a conspectus of the weightiest literature). The only work which covers nearly the entire history of the popes is that of A. Bower, *History of the Popes to 1758*, 7 vols., London, 1748-61, *with Introduction and Continuation by S. H. Cox*, 3 vols., Philadelphia, 1847 (the latter is the ed. cited in this work; the character of the *History* is poor, as was that of the author). H. H. Milman, *History of Latin Christianity*, 9 vols., new ed., London, 1883, is excellent and brings the history down to 1455; for its period (590-795, 858-891) a worthy work is R. C. Mann, *Lives of the Popes in the Early Middle Ages*, vol. i., 2 parts, London, 1902; vol. iii., 1906; of great value is L. Pastor, *Geschichte der Päpste seit dem Ausgang des Mittelalters*, 4 vols., 4th ed., Freiburg, 1901-07, Eng. transl., 6 vols., London, 1891-1902 (a most industrious and honest work, based on research in the original archives, covers the period 1305–1534; vols. i., iii., and v. of the English contain bibliographies); the period 1378–1527 is covered by M. Creighton's *History of the Papacy*, 6 vols., London, 1897 (an invaluable work); L. von Ranke, *Römische Päpste*, 9th ed., 3 vols., Leipsic, 1889, Eng. transl., 3 vols., London, 1896, is indispensable for the period 1513–1847; the story is concluded by F. Nielsen, *Geschichte des Papsttums im 19. Jahrhundert*, 2d ed., Gotha, 1880, Eng. transl., 2 vols., New York, 1906. A work which parallels part of those mentioned is F. Gregorovius, *Geschichte der Stadt Rom, 5–16 Jahrhundert*, 8 vols., Stuttgart, 1886–96, 5th ed., 1903 sqq., Eng. transl., from the 4th edition, 8 vols., London, 1901–02. The official Catholic record, covering the early and middle period, is the *Liber pontificalis*, best ed. of the whole work by L. Duchesne, containing text, introduction, and commentary, 2 vols., Paris, 1886–92, though the ed. by Mommsen, in *MGH*, *Gestorum pontificum Romanorum vol. i*, 1898, is even better so far as it goes. The bulls and briefs of the popes are best consulted in *Bullarium, privilegiorum ac diplomatum Romanorum pontificum collectio C. Cocquelines*, 14 vols., Rome, 1733–48, supplemented by *Bullarium Benedicti XIV.*, 4 vols., ib., 1754–58, and *Bullarii Romani continuatio* (Clement XIII.–Gregory XVI.) by A. Barberi and A. Spetia, 19 vols., ib., 1835–57, the whole reedited by A. Tomassetti, 24 vols., Turin, 1857–72. Consult also L. Pastor, *Acta inedita ad historiam Pontificum Romanorum*, vol. i., *1376–1464*, Freiburg, 1904.

A number of collections and discussions of the **Decrees and Proceedings of the Councils** has been made. Those most cited are P Labbe and G. Cossart, *Sacrosancta concilia*, 17 vols. in 18, Paris, 1672; J. Harduin, *Conciliorum collectio regia maxima*, 12 vols., Paris, 1715; J. D. Mansi, *Sacrorum conciliorum nova et amplissima collectio*, 31 vols., Venice, 1759–1798 (of the older collections the one most cited); C. J. von Hefele, *Conciliengeschichte*, 7 vols., Freiburg, 1855–74 (coming down to 1433; a 2d ed. was begun by the author and carried on by Cardinal Hergenröther to 1536, 9 vols. in all, 1863–90; apparently vol. vii. of the 2d ed. never appeared); the Eng. transl. of Hefele by W R. Clark includes only vols. i.–iii. of the German, down to 787 A.D., 5 vols., 1883–96. Of all these Hefele is the most accessible and now the oftenest cited.

On the subject of **Monasticism** all students are most deeply indebted to C. F de T. Montalembert, *Les Moines d'occident*, 5 vols., Paris, 1860–67, authorized Eng. transl., 7 vols., London, 1861–79. For the history of religious orders the old standard, rich in erudition, is P Helyot, *Histoire des ordres monastiques, religieux et militaires et des congrégations séculaires de l'un et de l'autre sexe*, 8 vols., Paris, 1714–19; the best modern work is M. Heimbucher, *Die Orden und Kongregationen der katholischen Kirche*, 2 vols., Paderborn, 1896–97, 2d and enlarged ed., 3 vols., 1907, utilized from Vol. IV on; the one work in English to be cited, which, however, leaves much to be desired, is C. W Currier, *History of Religious Orders*, New York, 1896.

On the history of the separate **Orders** in the Roman Catholic Church the most important are the following: for the Jesuits, A. and A. de Backer, *Bibliothèque des écrivains de la société de Jésus*, 7 vols., Liége, 1853–61, new ed. by C. Sommervogel, Paris, 1891 sqq.; the *Historiæ societatis Jesu*, by a number of hands, 6 parts in 8 vols., Rome, 1615–1759; J. A. M. Crétineau-Joly, *Histoire religieuse, politique et littéraire de la compagnie de Jésus*, 6 vols., Paris, 1844–46; for the Benedictines, J. Mabillon, *Acta ordinis sancti Benedicti*, 9 vols., Paris, 1668–1702, and his *Annales ordinis . . . Benedicti*, 6 vols., Paris, 1703–39; for the Carmelites, J. B. de Lezana, *Annales sacri prophetici et Eliani ordinis de Monte Carmelo*, 4 vols., Rome, 1651–66; for the Dominicans, *Monumenta ordinis fratrum prædicatorum*, in course of publication at Louvain since 1896 (the earlier works, now being superseded, are: A. Touron, *Histoire des hommes illustres de Saint-Dominique*, 6 vols., Paris, 1743–49, and T. M. Mamachi, *Annales ordinis* *prædicatorum*, 5 vols., Rome, 1754); for the Cistercians, A. Maurique, *Annales cisterciennes*, 4 vols., Lyons, 1642–59, and P le Nain, *Essai de l'ordre de Citeaux*, 9 vols., Paris, 1696–1697; for the Franciscans, the *Analecta Franciscana*, 3 vols., Freiburg, 1885–97, and the *Annales fratrum minorum*, begun by L. Wadding, 8 vols., Lyons, 1625 sqq., continued by J. de Luca and various hands at Naples and Rome, 26 vols., and covering the period 1208–1611.

Somewhat akin to the foregoing is the subject of **Hagiology,** in which two works stand out as preeminent. The one is the *Acta sanctorum* of J. Bolland, the issue of which was begun in 1643, continued till the dispersion of the Jesuits compelled suspension of the work from 1794 (when vol. liii. was issued) till 1845. In all 63 vols. have been published, and a new ed. has appeared, Paris, 1863–94 (see ACTA MARTYRUM, ACTA SANCTORUM). This is supplemented by the *Analecta Bollandiana*, edited by a number of Jesuits, Paris and Brussels, 1882 sqq. (still in progress; it includes documents unused or passed by in the *Acta*, newly discovered material, variant accounts, notes on the old accounts, and description of manuscripts). The other important work is the *Acta sanctorum ordinis S. Benedicti* of J. Mabillon and T. Ruinart, 9 vols., Paris, 1668–1701, and Venice, 1733–40. Mention may be made of the *Acta sanctorum Belgii* of J. Ghesquière and others, 6 vols., Brussels, 1783–94. J. Colgan's work on Scottish and Irish saints is noted above (p. xviii.). The plan of arrangement in these compilations is that of the Roman calendar, the substance is the lives and legends concerning the saints, and the value of the material varies greatly. A very large amount of the material is derived from contemporary sources and is therefore useful when sifted by the critical processes.

In the comparatively new and certainly interesting region of the **Comparison and History of Religions** the series of first importance, making available to readers of English many of the Bibles and Commentaries of the great religions, is that of the *Sacred Books of the East*, under the editorship of F Max Müller, 48 vols., Oxford, 1879–1904. A valuable set of historical expositions of the historical religions is found in the *Darstellungen aus dem Gebiete der nichtchristlichen Religionsgeschichte*, 15 vols., Münster, 1890–1903. The *Annales du Musée Guimet*, Paris, 1880 sqq., combine the features of the *Sacred Books of the East* (translations of native sources) and of the Hibbert Lectures (discussions of particular religions). The Hibbert Lectures (q.v.) are a number of series, each series amounting to a treatise on some individual religion or phase of religion, delivered in Great Britain between 1878 and 1902 by specialists of eminence. A corresponding series, known as the American Lectures on the History of Religion (q.v.), has been in progress since 1895 and is planned ahead as far as 1910. A valuable set is found in the *Handbooks on the History of Religions* edited by M. Jastrow, of which the following have appeared, Boston, 1895-1905: E. W Hopkins, *Religion of India*, 1895; M. Jastrow, *Religion of Babylonia and Assyria*, 1895; P D. Chantepie de la Saussaye, *Religion of the Ancient Teutons*, 1896; A. Wiedemann, *Religion of the Ancient Egyptians*, 1897; M. Jastrow, *Study of Religion*, 1901; and G. Steindorff, *Religion of the Ancient Egyptians*, 1905. The best individual work on the whole subject is P D. Chantepie de la Saussaye, *Lehrbuch der Religionsgeschichte*, 3d ed., 2 vols., Tübingen, 1905 (in which the author had the cooperation of numerous scholars). Next to this is C. P Tiele, *Inleiding tot de godsdienstwetenschap*, 2d ed., Amsterdam, 1900. Other important volumes are E. B. Tylor, *Primitive Culture*, 4th ed., 2 vols., London, 1903; J. G. Frazer, *The Golden Bough*, 2d ed., 3 vols., ib., 1900; F. B. Jevons, *Introduction to the History of Religion*, ib:, 1896 (all dealing with primitive religion).

GEO. W GILMORE.

BIBLIOGRAPHICAL APPENDIX

ABBEY: R. A. Cram, *Ruined Abbeys of Great Britain*, London, 1906.
T. Perkins, *Short Account of Romsey Abbey*, London and New York, 1907.

ABBOTT, E. A.: *Apologia: an Explanation and a Defense* [of the Bible], London, 1907.

ABBOTT, L.: *Christ's Secret of Happiness*, New York, 1907.
Impressions of a Careless Traveler, New York, 1907.

ABGAR: F. C. Burkitt, *Early Eastern Christianity*, pp. 11 sqq., London and New York, 1904.

ABHEDANANDA: *Vedanta Philosophy*, New York, 1907

ABRAHAMS, I.: *A Short History of Jewish Literature* [70–178 A.D.], New York, 1907.
Judaism, London, 1907.

ABYSSINIA: R. P. Skinner, *Abyssinia of To-day*, London, 1906.
Lord Hindlip, *Abyssinia*, London, 1906.
F. Rosen, *Eine deutsche Gesandschaft in Abessinien*, Leipsic, 1907.

ACTA MARTYRUM, ACTA SANCTORUM: A. Dufourcq, *Études sur les gesta martyrum romains*, Paris, 1906 sqq.
Henri Quentin, *Les Martyrologes historiques du moyen âge. Étude sur la formation du martyrologe romain*, Paris, 1907
P. Saintyves, *Les Saints, successeurs des Dieux. Essais de mythologie chrétienne*, Paris, 1907.

ACTON, LORD: *The History of Freedom and other Essays*, London, 1907.
Historical Essays and Studies, London, 1908.

ADAMS, G. M.: *Life*, by E. E. Strong, Boston, 1907.

ADDIS, W. E.: *Christianity and the Roman Empire*, new ed., London, 1906.

ADENEY, W. F.: *How to Read the Bible*, new ed., London, 1907

ADLER, C.: *Jews in the Diplomatic Correspondence of the United States*, Philadelphia, 1907.

ADRIAN IV.: *Life*, by J. Duncan Mackie, London, 1907.

AFRICA: In General: E. d'Almeida, *Historia Æthiopiæ. Libri I.–IV.*, Rome, 1907
B. Alexander, *From the Niger to the Nile*, London and New York, 1907.
A. H. S. Landor, *Across widest Africa*, London and New York, 1907
A. B. Lloyd, *In Dwarf Land and Cannibal Country*, London and New York, 1907.
C. G. Schillings, *In Wildest Africa*, New York, 1907
Algiers: Frances E. Nesbitt, *Algeria and Tunis, Painted and Described*, London, 1906.
M. W Hilton Simpson, *Algiers and Beyond*, London, 1906.
Egypt: W S. Blunt, *Secret History of the English Occupation of Egypt*, London, 1907
French Africa: G. François, *L'Afrique occidentale française*, Paris, 1907.
A. Chevalier, *L'Afrique centrale française (Mission Chari-Lac Tchad, 1902–04)*, Paris, 1907.
L. Desplagnes, *Le Plateau central Nigérien. Une Mission archéologique et ethnographique au Soudan français*, Paris, 1907
Portuguese Africa: R. C. F. Maugham, *Portuguese East Africa*, London, 1806.
G. M. Theal, *History and Ethnography of Africa South of the Zambesi. 1. The Portuguese in South Africa, from 1505–1700*, London, 1907.
South Africa: S. Passarge, *Die Buschmänner der Kalahari*, Berlin, 1907
idem, *Südafrika. Eine Landes-, Volks- und Wirtschaftskunde*, Leipsic, 1908.
J. P. Johnson, *Stone Implements of South Africa*, London, 1907.
West Africa: R. E. Dennett, *At the Back of the Black Man's Mind: or, Notes on the Kingly Office in West Africa*, London, 1907.

AGNES, SAINT: *Life*, by A. Smith, New York, 1907, and by F. Jubaru, Paris, 1907

AGNOSTICISM: W. H. Fitchett, *Beliefs of Unbelief*, Cincinnati, 1908.

AKED, C. F.: *One Hundred Responsive Readings from the Scriptures*, New York, 1908.

ALBERT OF BRANDENBURG: *Life*, by H. O. Nietschmann, Burlington, Ia., 1907

ALEXANDER IV.: *Life*, by F. Tenckhoff, Paderborn, 1907.

ALEXANDER SEVERUS: *Life*, by R. V N. Hopkins, New York, 1907.

ALFRED THE GREAT: *Proverbs*; recd. from the MSS. by W W Skeat, London and New York, 1907.

ALLARD, PAUL: Eng. transl. of *Dix leçons sur le martyre*, "Ten Lectures on the Martyrs," New York, 1907.

ALLEN, A. V. G.: *Life of Phillips Brooks*, new ed., Boston, 1907.
Freedom in the Church, Boston, 1907.
cf. J. B. Johnson, *Freedom through the Truth. An Examination of the Rev. A. V. G. Allen's "Freedom in the Church,"* New York, 1907.

ALLIES, THOMAS WILLIAM: *Life*, by Miss Mary H. Allies, London, 1907

AMBROSE, SAINT, OF MILAN: J. E. Niederhuber, *Die Eschatologie des heiligen Ambrosius*, Paderborn, 1907.

ANDREWS, L.: *Private Devotions*, new ed., London, 1907.

ANGUS, J.: *Bible Handbook*, rev. ed., 2d impression, 1907.

ANNA COMNENA: L. Du Sommerard, *Anne Comnène, témoin des croisades; Agnès de France*, Paris, 1907

APHRAATES: F. C. Burkitt, *Early Eastern Christianity*, pp. 133 sqq., London and New York, 1904.

Apocrypha, The Old Testament: *Die Weisheit des Jesus Sirach. Hebräisch und deutsch. Mit einem hebräischen Glossar*, Berlin, 1906.
R. Smend, *Griechisch-syrisch-hebräischer Index zur Weisheit des Jesus Sirach*, Berlin, 1907.
Die Weisheit des Jesus Sirach erklärt, Berlin, 1907

Apocrypha, The New Testament: *The Gospel of Barnabas, ed. and transl. from the Italian MS. in the Imperial Library of Vienna*, by Lonsdale and Laura Ragg, London, 1907.

Apollonius of Tyana: T. Whittaker, *Apollonius of Tyana and other Essays*, London, 1906.

Apologetics: Jean Rivière, *Saint Justin et les apologistes du second siècle*, Paris, 1907.
E. F. Scott, *The Apologetic of the New Testament*, London, 1907
S. Weber, *Christliche Apologetik*, Freiburg, 1907
O. Zoeckler, *Geschichte der Apologie des Christentums*, Gütersloh, 1907.

Arianism: S. Rogala, *Die Anfänge des arianischen Streites untersucht*, Paderborn, 1907.

Aristotle: Transl. of the first book of his "Metaphysics," by A. E. Taylor, Chicago, 1907.
New complete transl., ed. J. A. Smith and W. D. Ross, London and New York, 1908 sqq.

Arthur, W.: *Life*, by T. B. Stephenson, London, 1907

Asia Minor: W. M. Ramsay, *The Cities of Saint Paul; their Influence on his Life and Thought. The Cities of Eastern Asia Minor*, London and New York, 1908.

Assyria: H. Winckler, *History of Babylonia and Assyria*, London and New York, 1907

Athanasius: F. Cavallera, *S. Athanase*, Paris, 1907.

Atonement: John Scott Lidgett, *The Spiritual Principle of the Atonement as a Satisfaction made to God for the Sins of the World*, 4th ed., London, 1907.
The Atonement in Modern Thought. A Symposium, 3d ed., London, 1907.
H. C. Beeching and A. Nairne, *Bible Doctrine of the Atonement*, London and New York, 1907.
J. M. Campbell, *The Atonement the Heart of the Gospel*, London, 1907

Augustine, Saint, of Hippo: *Preaching and Teaching according to Saint Augustine. Being a new Translation of his De doctrina Christiana, Book 4, and De rudibus catechisandis. With three introductory Essays*, by Rev. W. J. Vashon Baker and Rev. Cyril Bickersteth, London, 1907.
P. Friedrich, *Die Marieologie des heiligen Augustinus*, Cologne, 1907.

Australia: N. W. Thomas, *Natives of Australia*, London, 1906.
Kinship Organizations and Group Marriage in Australia, London and New York, 1907.
K. L. Parker, *The Euahlayi Tribe. Study of Aboriginal Life in Australia*, London, 1906.
A. Buchanan, *The Real Australia*, London, 1907.

Babcock, M. D.: *Fragments that Remain; Sermons, Addresses and Prayers*, ed. Jessie B. Goetschius, New York, 1907.

Babylonia: H. Winckler, *History of Babylonia and Assyria*, London and New York, 1907.
R. J. Lau, *Old Babylonian Temple Records*, London, 1907.
J. D. Prince, *Materials for a Sumerian Lexicon*, New York, 1908.
E. Mayer, *Sumerier und Semiten in Babylonia*, Berlin, 1907.

Bampton Lectures: 1907: J. H. F. Peile, *The Reproach of the Gospel: an Enquiry into the apparent Failure of Christianity as a General Rule of Life and Conduct*, London and New York, 1907.

Banks, L. A.: *The Sinner and his Friends*, New York, 1907.

Baptism: R. Ayres, *Christian Baptism. A Treatise on the Mode of Administering the Ordinance by the Apostles and their Successors in the Early Ages of the Church*, London, 1907.
Philalethes, *Baptismon Didache; or, Scriptural Studies on Baptisms, especially Christian Baptism*, London, 1907.

Baptists: H. C. Vedder, *Short History*, new ed., Philadelphia, 1907.

Bardesanes: F. C. Burkitt, *Early Eastern Christianity*, lect. v., London and New York, 1904.

Baring-Gould: *Sermons to Children*, 2d series, London, 1907.
Tragedy of the Cæsars, new ed., London, 1907.
Nero, London, 1907.
Devonshire and Strange Events, London, 1907.
A Book of the Pyrenees, London, 1907.
Restitution of All Things, London, 1907.

Barton, W. E.: *Sweetest Story ever Told: Jesus and His Love*, Chicago, 1907.

LIST OF ABBREVIATIONS

[Abbreviations in common use or self-evident are not included here. For additional information concerning the works listed, see CONCERNING BIBLIOGRAPHY, pp. viii.–xx., above, and the appropriate articles in the body of the work. The editions named are those cited in the work.]

ADB.......... *Allgemeine deutsche Biographie*, 50 vols., Leipsic, 1875–1905
Adv.......... *adversus*, "against"
AJP.......... *American Journal of Philology*, Baltimore, 1880 sqq.
AJT.......... *American Journal of Theology*, Chicago, 1897 sqq.
AKR.......... *Archiv für katholisches Kirchenrecht*, Innsbruck, 1857–61, Mainz, 1872 sqq.
ALKG.......... *Archiv für Litteratur- und Kirchengeschichte des Mittelalters*, Freiburg, 1885 sqq.
Am.......... American
AMA.......... *Abhandlungen der Münchener Akademie*, Munich, 1763 sqq.
ANF.......... *Ante-Nicene Fathers*, American edition by A. Cleveland Coxe, 8 vols., and index, Buffalo, 1887; vol. ix., ed. Allan Menzies, New York, 1897
Apoc.......... Apocrypha, apocryphal
Apol.......... *Apologia, Apology*
Arab.......... Arabic
Aram.......... Aramaic
art.......... article
Art. Schmal.......... Schmalkald Articles
ASB.......... *Acta sanctorum*, ed. J. Bolland and others, Antwerp, 1643 sqq.
ASM.......... *Acta sanctorum ordinis S. Benedicti*, ed. J. Mabillon, 9 vols., Paris, 1668–1701
Assyr.......... Assyrian
A. T........... *Altes Testament*, "Old Testament"
Augs. Con.......... Augsburg Confession
A. V.......... Authorized Version (of the English Bible)
AZ.......... *Allgemeine Zeitung*, Augsburg, Tübingen, Stuttgart, and Tübingen, 1798 sqq.
Benzinger, *Archäologie*... I. Benzinger, *Hebräische Archäologie*, Freiburg, 1894
Bertholdt, *Einleitung*.... L. Bertholdt, *Historisch-Kritische Einleitung . . . des Alten und Neuen Testaments*, 6 vols., Erlangen, 1812–19
BFBS.......... British and Foreign Bible Society
Bingham, *Origines*..... J. Bingham, *Origines ecclesiasticæ*, 10 vols., London, 1708–22; new ed., Oxford, 1855
Bouquet, *Recueil*.... M. Bouquet, *Recueil des historiens des Gaules et de la France*, continued by various hands, 23 vols., Paris, 1738–76
Bower, *Popes*.... Archibald Bower, *History of the Popes . . . to 1758, continued by S. H. Cox*, 3 vols., Philadelphia, 1845–47
BQR.......... *Baptist Quarterly Review*, Philadelphia, 1867 sqq.
BRG.......... See Jaffé
Cant.......... Canticles, Song of Solomon
cap.......... *caput*, "chapter"
Ceillier, *Auteurs sacrés*....... R. Ceillier, *Histoire des auteurs sacrés et ecclésiastiques*, 16 vols. in 17, Paris, 1858–69
Chron.......... *Chronicon*, "Chronicle"
I Chron.......... I Chronicles
II Chron.......... II Chronicles
CIG.......... *Corpus inscriptionum Græcarum*, Berlin, 1825 sqq.
CIL.......... *Corpus inscriptionum Latinarum*, Berlin, 1863 sqq.
CIS.......... *Corpus inscriptionum Semiticarum*, Paris, 1881 sqq.
cod.......... codex
cod. D.......... *codex Bezæ*
cod. Theod.......... *codex Theodosianus*
Col.......... Epistle to the Colossians
col., cols.......... column, columns
Conf.......... *Confessiones*, "Confessions"
I Cor.......... First Epistle to the Corinthians
II Cor.......... Second Epistle to the Corinthians
COT.......... See Schrader
CR.......... *Corpus reformatorum*, begun at Halle, 1834, vol. lxxxix., Berlin, 1905
Creighton, *Papacy*...... M. Creighton, *A History of the Papacy from the Great Schism to the Sack of Rome*, new ed., 6 vols., New York and London, 1897
CSEL.......... *Corpus scriptorum ecclesiasticorum Latinorum*, Vienna, 1867 sqq.
CSHB.......... *Corpus scriptorum historiæ Byzantinæ*, 49 vols., Bonn, 1828–78
Currier, *Religious Orders*........ C. W. Currier, *History of Religious Orders*, New York, 1896
D.......... Deuteronomist
DACL.......... F. Cabrol, *Dictionnaire d'archéologie chrétienne et de liturgie*, Paris, 1903 sqq.
Dan.......... Daniel
DB.......... J. Hastings, *Dictionary of the Bible*, 4 vols. and extra vol., Edinburgh and New York, 1898–1904
DCA.......... W. Smith and S. Cheetham, *Dictionary of Christian Antiquities*, 2 vols., London, 1875–80
DCB.......... W. Smith and H. Wace, *Dictionary of Christian Biography*, 4 vols., Boston, 1877–87
Deut.......... Deuteronomy
De vir. ill.......... *De viris illustribus*
De Wette-Schrader, *Einleitung*........ W. M. L. de Wette, *Lehrbuch der historisch-kritischen Einleitung in die Bibel*, ed. E. Schrader, Berlin, 1869
DGQ.......... See Wattenbach
DNB.......... L. Stephen and S. Lee, *Dictionary of National Biography*, 63 vols. and supplement 3 vols., London, 1885–1901
Driver, *Introduction*...... S. R. Driver, *Introduction to the Literature of the Old Testament*, 5th ed., New York, 1894
E.......... Elohist
EB.......... T. K. Cheyne and J. S. Black, *Encyclopædia Biblica*, 4 vols., London and New York, 1899–1903
Eccl.......... *Ecclesia*, "Church"; *ecclesiasticus*, "ecclesiastical"
Eccles.......... Ecclesiastes
Ecclus.......... Ecclesiasticus
ed.......... edition; *edidit*, "edited by"
EJ.......... Elohist Jahvist (Yahwist)
Eph.......... Epistle to the Ephesians
Epist.......... *Epistola, Epistolæ*, "Epistle," "Epistles"
Ersch and Gruber, *Encyklopädie*........ J. S. Ersch and J. G. Gruber, *Allgemeine Encyklopädie der Wissenschaften und Künste*, Leipsic, 1818 sqq.
E. V.......... English versions (of the Bible)
Ex.......... Exodus
Ezek.......... Ezekiel
fasc.......... *fasciculus*
Friedrich, *KD*.. J. Friedrich, *Kirchengeschichte Deutschlands*, 2 vols., Bamberg, 1867–69
Fritzsche, *Exegetisches Handbuch*.......... O. F. Fritzsche and C. L. W. Grimm, *Kurzgefasstes exegetisches Handbuch zu den Apocryphen des Alten Testaments*, 6 parts, Zurich, 1851–60
Gal.......... Epistle to the Galatians
Gee and Hardy, *Documents*.... H. Gee and W. J. Hardy, *Documents Illustrative of English Church History*, London, 1896
Gen.......... Genesis
Germ.......... German
GGA.......... *Göttingische gelehrte Anzeigen*, Göttingen, 1824 sqq.
Gibbon, *Decline and Fall*...... E. Gibbon, *History of the Decline and Fall of the Roman Empire*, ed. J. B. Bury, 7 vols., London, 1896–1900
Gk.......... Greek, Grecized
Gross, *Sources*... C. Gross, *The Sources and Literature of English History . . . to 1485*, London, 1900
Hab.......... Habakkuk

Haddan and Stubbs, *Councils* .... A. W. Haddan and W. Stubbs, *Councils and Ecclesiastical Documents Relating to Great Britain and Ireland*, 3 vols., Oxford, 1869–78

Hær .... Refers to patristic works on heresies or heretics, Tertullian's *De præscriptione*, the *Pros haireseis* of Irenæus, the *Panarion* of Epiphanius, etc.

Hag.............Haggai

Harduin, *Concilia* .... J. Harduin, *Conciliorum collectio regia maxima*, 12 vols., Paris, 1715

Harnack, *Dogma* .... A. Harnack, *History of Dogma* . . . *from the 3d German edition*, 7 vols., Boston, 1895–1900

Harnack, *Litteratur* .... A. Harnack, *Geschichte der altchristlichen Litteratur bis Eusebius*, 2 vols. in 3, Leipsic, 1893–1904

Hauck, *KD* .... A. Hauck, *Kirchengeschichte Deutschlands*, vol. i., Leipsic, 1904; vol. ii., 1900; vol. iii., 1906; vol. iv., 1903

Hauck-Herzog, *RE* .... *Realencyklopädie für protestantische Theologie und Kirche*, founded by J. J. Herzog, 3d ed. by A. Hauck, Leipsic, 1896 sqq.

Heb.............Epistle to the Hebrews

Hebr.............Hebrew

Hefele, *Conciliengeschichte* .... C. J. von Hefele, *Conciliengeschichte*, continued by J. Hergenröther, 9 vols., Freiburg, 1883–93

Heimbucher, *Orden und Kongregationen* .... M. Heimbucher, *Die Orden und Kongregationen der katholischen Kirche*, 2 vols., Paderborn, 1896–97

Helyot, *Ordres monastiques* .... P. Helyot, *Histoire des ordres monastiques, religieux et militaires*, 8 vols., Paris, 1714–19; new ed., 1839–42

Henderson, *Documents* .... E. F. Henderson, *Select Historical Documents of the Middle Ages*, London, 1892

Hist.............History, *histoire, historia*

Hist. eccl. .... *Historia ecclesiastica, ecclesiæ*, "Church History"

Hom............*Homilia, homiliai*, "homily, homilies"

Hos.............Hosea

Isa.............Isaiah

Ital.............Italian

J.............Jahvist (Yahwist)

JA.............*Journal Asiatique*, Paris, 1822 sqq.

Jaffé, *BRG* .... P. Jaffé, *Bibliotheca rerum Germanicarum*, 6 vols., Berlin, 1864–73

Jaffé, *Regesta* .... P. Jaffé, *Regesta pontificum Romanorum . . . ad annum 1198*, Berlin, 1851; 2d ed., Leipsic, 1881–88

JBL .... *Journal of Biblical Literature and Exegesis*, first appeared as *Journal of the Society of Biblical Literature and Exegesis*, Middletown, 1882–88, then Boston, 1890 sqq.

JE.............*The Jewish Encyclopedia*, 12 vols., New York, 1901–06

JE ....the combined narrative of the Jahvist (Yahwist) and Elohist

Jer.............Jeremiah

Josephus, *Ant.* .... Flavius Josephus, "Antiquities of the Jews"

Josephus, *Apion*. .... Flavius Josephus, "Against Apion"

Josephus, *Life*.............Life of Flavius Josephus

Josephus, *War*... .... Flavius Josephus, "The Jewish War"

Josh.............Joshua

JPT. .... *Jahrbücher für protestantische Theologie*, Leipsic, 1875 sqq.

JQR .... *The Jewish Quarterly Review*, London, 1888 sqq.

JTS .... *Journal of Theological Studies*, London, 1899 sqq.

Julian, *Hymnology* .... J. Julian, *A Dictionary of Hymnology*, New York, 1892

KAT.............See Schrader

KB ....See Schrader

KD.............See Friedrich, Hauck, Rettberg

KL .... *Wetzer und Welte's Kirchenlexikon*, 2d ed., by J. Hergenröther and F. Kaulen, 12 vols., Freiburg, 1882–1903

Krüger, *History* .... G. Krüger, *History of Early Christian Literature in the First Three Centuries*, New York, 1897

Krumbacher, *Geschichte* .... K. Krumbacher, *Geschichte der byzantinischen Litteratur*, 2d ed., Munich, 1897

Labbe, *Concilia* .... P. Labbe, *Sacrorum conciliorum nova et amplissima collectio*, 31 vols., Florence and Venice, 1759–98

Lam.............Lamentations

Lanigan, *Eccl. Hist.* .... J. Lanigan, *Ecclesiastical History of Ireland to the 13th Century*, 4 vols., Dublin, 1829

Lat.............Latin, Latinized

Leg.............*Leges, Legum*

Lev.............Leviticus

LXX.............The Septuagint

I Macc.............I Maccabees

II Macc.............II Maccabees

Mai, *Nova collectio* .... A. Mai, *Scriptorum veterum nova collectio*, 10 vols., Rome, 1825–38

Mal.............Malachi

Mann, *Popes* .... R. C. Mann, *Lives of the Popes in the Early Middle Ages*, London, 1902 sqq.

Mansi, *Concilia* .... G. D. Mansi, *Sanctorum conciliorum collectio nova*, 31 vols., Florence and Venice, 1728

Matt.............Matthew

McClintock and Strong, *Cyclopædia* .... J. McClintock and J. Strong, *Cyclopædia of Biblical, Theological, and Ecclesiastical Literature*, 10 vols. and supplement 2 vols., New York, 1869–87

MGH .... *Monumenta Germaniæ historica*, ed. G. H. Pertz and others, Hanover and Berlin, 1826 sqq. The following abbreviations are used for the sections and subsections of this work: *Ant., Antiquitates*, "Antiquities"; *Auct. ant., Auctores antiquissimi*, "Oldest Writers"; *Chron. min., Chronica minora*, "Lesser Chronicles"; *Dip., Diplomata*, "Diplomas, Documents"; *Epist., Epistolæ*, "Letters"; *Gest. pont. Rom., Gesta pontificum Romanorum*, "Deeds of the Popes of Rome"; *Leg., Leges*, "Laws"; *Lib. de lite, Libelli de lite inter regnum et sacerdotium sæculorum xi et xii conscripti*, "Books concerning the Strife between the Civil and Ecclesiastical Authorities in the Eleventh and Twelfth Centuries"; *Nec., Necrologia Germaniæ*, "Necrology of Germany"; *Poet. Lat. ævi Car., Poetæ Latini ævi Carolini*, "Latin Poets of the Caroline Time"; *Poet. Lat. med. ævi, Poetæ Latini medii ævi*, "Latin Poets of the Middle Ages"; *Script., Scriptores*, "Writers"; *Script. rer. Germ., Scriptores rerum Germanicarum*, "Writers on German Subjects"; *Script. rer. Langob., Scriptores rerum Langobardicarum et Italicarum*, "Writers on Lombard and Italian Subjects"; *Script. rer. Merov., Scriptores rerum Merovingicarum*, "Writers on Merovingian Subjects"

Mic.............Micah

Milman, *Latin Christianity* .... H. H. Milman, *History of Latin Christianity, Including that of the Popes to . . . Nicholas V.*, 8 vols., London, 1860–61

Mirbt, *Quellen*, ... C. Mirbt, *Quellen zur Geschichte des Papsttums und des römischen Katholicismus*, Tübingen, 1901

Moeller, *Christian Church* .... W. Moeller, *History of the Christian Church*, 3 vols., London, 1892–1900

MPG .... J. P. Migne, *Patrologiæ cursus completus, series Græca*, 162 vols., Paris, 1857–66

MPL .... J. P. Migne, *Patrologiæ cursus completus, series Latina*, 221 vols., Paris, 1844–64

MS., MSS.............Manuscript, Manuscripts

Muratori, *Scriptores* .... L. A. Muratori, *Rerum Italicarum scriptores*, 28 vols., 1723–51

NA .... *Neues Archiv der Gesellschaft für ältere deutsche Geschichtskunde*, Hanover, 1876 sqq.

Nah.............Nahum

n.d.............no date of publication

Neander, *Christian Church* .... A. Neander, *General History of the Christian Religion and Church*, 6 vols. and index, Boston, 1872–81

Neh.............Nehemiah

Niceron, *Mémoires* .... R. P. Niceron, *Mémoires pour servir à l'histoire des hommes illustrés . . .*, 43 vols., Paris, 1729–45

NKZ .... *Neue kirchliche Zeitschrift*, Leipsic, 1890 sqq.

Nowack, *Archäologie* .... W. Nowack, *Lehrbuch der hebräischen Archäologie*, 2 vols., Freiburg, 1894

n.p.............no place of publication

NPNF .... *The Nicene and Post-Nicene Fathers*, 1st series, 14 vols., New York, 1887–92; 2d series, 14 vols., New York, 1890–1900

N. T. .... New Testament, *Novum Testamentum, Nouveau Testament, Neues Testament*

Num.............Numbers

Ob.............Obadiah

O.B., O.S.B. .... *Ordo sancti Benedicti*, "Order of St. Benedict"

O. T.............Old Testament

OTJC.............See Smith

P.............Priestly document

Pastor, *Popes*	L. Pastor, *The History of the Popes from the Close of the Middle Ages*, 6 vols., London, 1891–1902
PEA	*Patres ecclesiæ Anglicanæ*, ed. J. A. Giles, 34 vols., London, 1838–46
PEF	Palestine Exploration Fund
I Pet	First Epistle of Peter
II Pet	Second Epistle of Peter
Pliny, *Hist. nat.*	Pliny, *Historia naturalis*
Potthast, *Wegweiser*	A. Potthast, *Bibliotheca historica medii ævi. Wegweiser durch die Geschichtswerke*, Berlin, 1896
Prov	Proverbs
Ps	Psalms
PSBA	*Proceedings of the Society of Biblical Archeology*, London, 1880 sqq.
q.v., qq.v	quod (quæ) vide, "which see"
R	Redactor
Ranke, *Popes*	L. von Ranke, *History of the Popes*, 3 vols., London, 1896
RDM	*Revue des deux mondes*, Paris, 1831 sqq.
RE	See Hauck-Herzog
Reich, *Documents*	E. Reich, *Select Documents Illustrating Mediæval and Modern History*, London, 1905
REJ	*Revue des études Juives*, Paris, 1880 sqq
Rettberg, *KD*	F. W. Rettberg, *Kirchengeschichte Deutschlands*, 2 vols., Göttingen, 1846–48
Rev	Book of Revelation
Richter, *Kirchenrecht*	A. L. Richter, *Lehrbuch des katholischen und evangelischen Kirchenrechts*, 8th ed. by W. Kahl, Leipsic, 1886
Robinson, *European History*	J. H. Robinson, *Readings in European History*, 2 vols., Boston, 1904–06
Robinson, *Researches*, and *Later Researches*	E. Robinson, *Biblical Researches in Palestine*, Boston, 1841, and *Later Biblical Researches in Palestine*, 3d ed. of the whole, 3 vols., 1867
Rom	Epistle to the Romans
RTP	*Revue de théologie et de philosophie*, Lausanne, 1873
R. V	Revised Version (of the English Bible)
sæc	*sæculum*, "century"
I Sam	I Samuel
II Sam	II Samuel
SBOT	*Sacred Books of the Old Testament* ("Rainbow Bible"), Leipsic, London, and Baltimore, 1894 sqq.
Schaff, *Christian Church*	P. Schaff, *History of the Christian Church*, vols. i.–iv., vi., vii., New York, 1882–92
Schaff, *Creeds*	P. Schaff, *The Creeds of Christendom*, 3 vols., New York, 1877–84
Schrader, *COT*	E. Schrader, *Cuneiform Inscriptions and the Old Testament*, 2 vols., London, 1885–88
Schrader, *KAT*	E. Schrader, *Die Keilinschriften und das Alte Testament*, 2 vols., Berlin, 1902–03
Schrader, *KB*	E. Schrader, *Keilinschriftliche Bibliothek*, 6 vols., Berlin, 1889–1901
Schürer, *Geschichte*	E. Schürer, *Geschichte des jüdischen Volkes im Zeitalter Jesu Christi*, 3 vols., Leipsic, 1898–1901; Eng. transl., 5 vols., New York, 1891
Script	*Scriptores*, "writers"
Sent	*Sententiæ*, "Sentences"
S. J	*Societas Jesu*, "Society of Jesus"
SK	*Theologische Studien und Kritiken*, Hamburg, 1826 sqq.
Smith, *Kinship*	W. R. Smith, *Kinship and Marriage in Early Arabia*, London, 1903
Smith, *OTJC*	W. R. Smith, *The Old Testament in the Jewish Church*, London, 1892
Smith, *Prophets*	W. R. Smith, *Prophets of Israel . . to the Eighth Century*, London, 1895
Smith, *Rel. of Sem*	W. R. Smith, *Religion of the Semites*, London, 1894
S. P. C. K	Society for the Promotion of Christian Knowledge
S. P. G.	Society for the Propagation of the Gospel in Foreign Parts
sq., sqq	and following
Strom	*Stromata*, "Miscellanies"
s.v	sub voce, or sub verbo
Thatcher and McNeal, *Source Book*	O. J. Thatcher and E. H. McNeal, *A Source Book for Mediæval History* New York, 1905
I Thess	First Epistle to the Thessalonians
II Thess	Second Epistle to the Thessalonians
ThT	*Theologische Tijdschrift*, Amsterdam and Leyden, 1867 sqq.
Tillemont, *Mémoires*	L. S. le Nain de Tillemont, *Mémoires . . . ecclésiastiques des six premiers siècles*, 16 vols., Brussels, 1693–1712
I Tim	First Epistle to Timothy
II Tim	Second Epistle to Timothy
TJB	*Theologischer Jahresbericht*, Leipsic, 1882–1887, Freiburg, 1888, Brunswick, 1889–1897, Berlin, 1898 sqq.
TLB	*Theologisches Litteraturblatt*, Bonn, 1866 sqq.
TLZ	*Theologische Litteraturzeitung*, Leipsic, 1876 sqq.
Tob	Tobit
TQ	*Theologische Quartalschrift*, Tübingen, 1819 sqq.
TS	J. A. Robinson, *Texts and Studies*, Cambridge, 1891 sqq.
TSBA	*Transactions of the Society of Biblical Archæology*, London, 1872 sqq.
TSK	*Theologische Studien und Kritiken*, Hamburg, 1826 sqq.
TU	*Texte und Untersuchungen zur Geschichte der altchristlichen Litteratur*, ed. O. von Gebhardt and A. Harnack, Leipsic, 1882 sqq.
TZT	*Tübinger Zeitschrift für Theologie*, Tübingen, 1838–40
Ugolini, *Thesaurus*	B. Ugolinus, *Thesaurus antiquitatum sacrarum*, 34 vols., Venice, 1744–69
V.T.	*Vetus Testamentum, Vieux Testament*, "Old Testament"
Wattenbach, *DGQ*	W. Wattenbach, *Deutschlands Geschichtsquellen*, 5th ed., 2 vols., Berlin, 1885; 6th ed., 1893–94
Wellhausen, *Heidentum*	J. Wellhausen, *Reste arabischen Heidentums*, Berlin, 1887
ZA	*Zeitschrift für Assyriologie*, Leipsic, 1886–88, Berlin, 1889 sqq.
Zahn, *Kanon*	T. Zahn, *Geschichte des neutestamentlichen Kanons*, 2 vols., Leipsic, 1888–92
ZATW	*Zeitschrift für die alttestamentliche Wissenschaft*, Giessen, 1881 sqq.
ZDMG	*Zeitschrift der deutschen morgenländischen Gesellschaft*, Leipsic, 1847 sqq.
ZDPV	*Zeitschrift des deutschen Palästina-Vereins*, Leipsic, 1878 sqq.
Zech	Zechariah
Zeph	Zephaniah
ZHT	*Zeitschrift für die historische Theologie*, published successively at Leipsic, Hamburg, and Gotha, 1832–75
ZKG	*Zeitschrift für Kirchengeschichte*, Gotha, 1876 sqq.
ZKT	*Zeitschrift für katholische Theologie*, Innsbruck, 1877 sqq.
ZKW	*Zeitschrift für kirchliche Wissenschaft und kirchliches Leben*, Leipsic, 1880–89
ZWT	*Zeitschrift für wissenschaftliche Theologie*, Jena, 1858–60, Halle, 1861–67, Leipsic, 1868 sqq.

SYSTEM OF TRANSLITERATION

The following system of transliteration has been used for Hebrew:

א = ' or omitted at the beginning of a word.	ז = z	ע = '
	ח = ḥ	פּ = p
בּ = b	ט = ṭ	פ = ph or p
ב = bh or b	י = y	צ = ẓ
גּ = g	כּ = k	ק = ḳ
ג = gh or g	כ = kh or k	ר = r
דּ = d	ל = l	שׂ = s
ד = dh or d	מ = m	שׁ = sh
ה = h	נ = n	תּ = t
ו = w	ס = s	ת = th or t

The vowels are transcribed by a, e, i, o, u, without attempt to indicate quantity or quality. Arabic and other Semitic languages are transliterated according to the same system as Hebrew. Greek is written with Roman characters, the common equivalents being used.

KEY TO PRONUNCIATION

When the pronunciation is self-evident the titles are not respelled; when by mere division and accentuation it can be shown sufficiently clearly the titles have been divided into syllables, and the accented syllables indicated.

ɑ as in sof*a*	ɵ as in n*o*t	iu as in d*u*ration
ā " " *a*rm	ō " " n*o*r	c=k " " *c*at
a " " *a*t	u " " f*u*ll	ch " " *ch*urch
â " " f*a*re	ū " " r*u*le	cw=qu as in *qu*een
e " " p*e*n[1]	ʋ " " b*u*t	dh (*th*) " " *th*e
ê " " f*a*te	ʋ̄ " " b*u*rn	f " " *f*ancy
i " " t*i*n	ai " " p*i*ne	g (hard) " " *g*o
î " " mach*i*ne	au " " *ou*t	H " " lo*ch* (Scotch)
o " " *o*bey	oi " " *oi*l	hw (*wh*) " " *wh*y
ō " " n*o*	iū " " f*ew*	j " " *j*aw

[1] In accented syllables only; in unaccented syllables it approximates the sound of e in over.

THE NEW SCHAFF-HERZOG

ENCYCLOPEDIA OF RELIGIOUS KNOWLEDGE

A

AACHEN, ä'ken, **SYNODS OF:** The political importance of the town of Aachen (Latin *Aquisgranum;* French, *Aix-la-Chapelle*) under Charlemagne and his successors made it a favorite meeting-place for various assemblies. The first synod of Aachen (or Aix) is usually reckoned as having met on Mar. 23, 789, and there is no doubt that a gathering took place on that day; but its results are known only from two royal decrees, the so-called *Admonitio generalis* (*MGH*, *Leg.*, i., *Capitularia regum Francorum*, ed. A. Boretius, i., 1883, cap. 22), and the instructions for the royal representatives (cap. 23). The former repeats a summary of the earlier canonical legislation on the duties of the clergy, and adds further regulations for the improvement of clerical and social life, dealing with diligence in preaching, the education of the clergy, the observance of the Lord's Day, just judgment, equal weights and measures, hospitality, and the prevention of witchcraft and perjury. The other document treats of monastic discipline and the regulation of civil society. It is questionable if this gathering can be properly called a synod; and still less can the name be applied to that of 797 (cap. 27), which regulated the condition of the conquered Saxons. On the other hand, the assembly of June, 799, in which Alcuin disputed with Felix of Urgel (see ADOPTIONISM) may be so called, and likewise the three meetings in the years 801 and 802. Their deliberations led to a series of decrees (cap. 33–35 and 36–41) which throw light on Charlemagne's endeavors to elevate clergy and laity. The most important is the great instruction for the *missi dominici* sent out in the spring of 802, dealing with the discipline of bishops, clergy, monks, and nuns, the faithful performance of their duties by public officials, and the establishment of justice throughout the empire. Among the results of the autumn synod of 802, cap. 36 and 38 deserve special attention; they deal with the duty of intercession for the emperor and bishops, the education of the people, tithes, divine worship and the sacraments, clerical discipline, and the system of ecclesiastical visitations. The next synod (Nov. 809), was occupied with the doctrine of the procession of the Holy Ghost. In the autumn of 816, or the summer of 817, Louis le Débonnaire assembled his first synod at Aachen, when the bishops laid down new regulations for the community life, both of canons and nuns. In the summer of 817 an assembly of abbots discussed the observance of the Benedictine rule. The diets of 819 and 825 and similar later assemblies can again scarcely be counted as synods, though the one held in the sacristy of the cathedral, Feb. 6, 835, has a synodical character. It adopted a thoroughgoing pronouncement on the life and teaching of bishops and inferior clergy, and on the position of the king, his family, and his ministers, with a view to regulating the confusion which the strife between Louis and his sons had caused. It also required of Pépin of Aquitaine that he should restore the church property which he had appropriated. For the synod held at Aachen in connection with the question of Lothaire's divorce, see NICHOLAS I. The last two synods of Aachen were held under Henry II., one in the year 1000 in connection with the restoration of the bishopric of Merseburg (see WILLIGIS); the other, in 1023, when the contest between the dioceses of Cologne and Liége for the possession of the monastery of Burtscheid was decided in favor of the latter.

(A. HAUCK.)

BIBLIOGRAPHY: *Fragmentum historicum de concilio Aquisgranensi*, in Mabillon, *Analecta*, i. 52, Paris, 1723, and in Bouquet, *Recueil*, vi. 415–443; *Epistola Synodi Aquisgranensis ad Pippin*, in Labbe, *Concilia*, vii. 1728, and in Bouquet, *Recueil*, vi. 354; A. J. Binterim, *Pragmatische Geschichte der deutschen . . . Concilien*, ii., iii., Mainz, 1836–37; *MGH*, *Leg.* i. (1835) 465; ib. *Capitularia reg. Franc.*, ii. 2 (1893), 463–466; Hauck, *KD.* ii.; Hefele, *Conciliengeschichte*, vols. iii., iv.; *MGH*, *Leg. sectio iii.*, *Concilia*, i. 1 (1904).

AARON: The brother of Moses. In the Yahwistic sources of the Pentateuch he is called "Aaron, the *Levite*," i.e., the priest. He is first mentioned when Yahweh appoints him as spokesman for Moses in the mission to Pharaoh (Ex. iv. 10–17, 27–31); and consistently he always appears with Moses before the Egyptian king. Later Aaron and Hur support Moses during the battle with the Amalekites (Ex. xvii. 8–13). When the covenant was made at Sinai, Aaron, Nadab, and Abihu, with seventy elders, accompanied Moses to the mountain; but Moses alone "went up into the mount of God" (Ex. xxiv 1–2, 9–18; cf. xix. 24). While Moses delayed on the mountain Aaron made the golden calf; and later he sought to excuse himself by saying that he had acted under compulsion of the people, who were impatient at the long absence of their leader (Ex. xxxii.). In the narrative of Num. xii., Aaron again appears in an unfavorable light. He is said to have died at Mosera, in the wilderness, and Eleazar, his son took his place as priest (Deut. x. 6). Finally, he is incidentally mentioned in Josh. xxiv. 5 and 33. The significant fact in all these notices is that the Yahwistic sources recognize Aaron as *priest*. In the Priest code Aaron's genealogy and family are given in detail (Ex. vi. 20, 23). He is three years older than Moses (Ex. vii. 7). He is made Moses's "prophet" before Pharaoh (Ex. vii. 1–2), and, accordingly, plays an important part in all transactions at the Egyptian court. By means of his rod the miracles are performed (Ex. vii., viii.). During the wandering Aaron retains his prominent position, although subordinate to Moses. The hungry people murmur against both brothers, and, at Moses's command, Aaron replies to them, and later preserves a pot of manna before Yahweh (Ex. xvi.). The priesthood is instituted at Sinai and solemnly conferred upon Aaron, his four sons, and their descendants (Ex. xxviii.). Of these four sons, only Eleazar and Ithamar remain after the destruction of Nadab and Abihu (Lev. x. 1–7). Aaron is not only original ancestor and type of the priests as distinguished from the Levites, but also, in narrower sense, prototype of the high priest, who was always from his family and apparently the first-born son in direct line. A few of the laws of P are delivered to Aaron as well as Moses (Lev. xi. 1, xiii. 1, xiv. 33, xv. 1; Num. xix. 1). After the departure from Sinai, Korah and his followers rebel against Moses and Aaron; and Yahweh miraculously vindicates the supremacy of the latter (Num. xvi.–xvii.; the narrative is amplified by an account of the uprising of Dathan and Abiram and a contest between Levites and priest-[illegible] [illegible]ron dies on Mount Hor, and Eleazar becomes priest in his stead (Num. xx. 22–29, xxxiii. 38–39). Of other Old Testament passages in which Aaron is mentioned none is noteworthy except Mic. vi. 4, where he is joined with Moses and Miriam. (F Buhl.)

It is important for the history of the priesthood in Israel to notice that in the narratives of J and E (called "Yahwistic" above) the priestly function of Aaron is quite subordinate, he being mainly represented there as the spokesman and the minister of Moses and, along with Hur, as his representative—a "judge" of the people (Ex. xxiv. 13, 14). It is in the priestly tradition that the idea of Aaron's sacerdotal functions is elaborately developed.

J. F. M.

Bibliography: S. Baring-Gould, *Legends of O. T. Characters*, 2 vols., London, 1871; J. Wellhausen, *Geschichte Israels*, chap. iv., Berlin, 1878; H. van Oort, *Die Aaroneiden* in *ThT*, xviii. (1884) 289 and 235; J. Benzinger, *Hebräische Archäologie*, pp. 405–428, Freiburg, 1894; W. Nowack, *Archäologie*, ii. 87–130, ib. 1894; A. Kuenen in *ThT*, xxiv. (1890) 1–42; A. van Hoonacker, *Le Sacerdoce lévitique dans la loi et dans l'histoire des Hebreux*, Louvain, 1899; S. I. Curtiss, *The Levitical Priests*, Edinburgh, 1877.

AARON AND JULIUS: English Martyrs. See Alban, Saint, of Verulam.

ABADDON, a-bad'en ("Destruction"): In the Old Testament a poetic name for the kingdom of the dead, Hades, or Sheol (Job xxvi. 6; Prov. xv. 11, where Abaddon is parallel to Sheol). The rabbis used the name for the nethermost part of hell. In Rev. ix. 11 the "angel of the bottomless pit" is called Abaddon, which is there explained as the Greek Apollyon ("destroyer"); and he is described as king of the locusts which rose at the sounding of the fifth trumpet. In like manner, in Rev. vi. 8, Hades is personified following after death to conquer the fourth part of the earth. In rabbinical writings Abaddon and Death are also personified (cf. Job xxviii. 22).

AB'ADIM. See Talmud.

A-BAR'BA-NEL. See Abrabanel.

ABAUZIT, ā"bō"zī', **FIRMIN:** French Reformed scholar; b. of Huguenot parentage at Uzès (20 m. w.n.w. of Avignon), Languedoc, Nov. 11, 1679; d. at Geneva, Mar. 20, 1767 After the revocation of the Edict of Nantes (1685) an attempt was made to bring him up as a Roman Catholic, but it was frustrated by his mother. After some hardships and sufferings, mother and son settled in Geneva, where Abauzit was educated and where, with the exception of visits to Holland and England in 1698, he spent his long life devoted to study and the service of the city library. He was one of the most learned men of his time, possessed much versatility, and enjoyed the friendship of scholars like Bayle, Jurieu, Basnage, and Newton. Nevertheless, he published practically nothing; and after his death many of his manuscripts were destroyed by his heirs. A volume of *Œuvres diverses* appeared at Geneva in 1770; and a different edition in two volumes at London and Amsterdam in 1770–73. They include essays against the doctrine of the Trinity as commonly received, upon the Book of Daniel, and the Apocalypse. He rendered much service to a society for the translation of the New Testament into French (published 1726). Many of his theological writings are translated in E. Harwood's *Miscellanies* (London, 1774), with memoir; and seven essays are reprinted thence in Sparks's *Collection of Essays and Tracts in Theology*, vol. i. (Boston, 1823).

Bibliography: J. Senebier, *Histoire littéraire de Genève*, Geneva, 1786; E. and É. Haag, *La France protestante*, ed. H. L. Bordier, i. 2, Paris, 1877; A. Gibert, *Abauzit et sa Théologie*, Strasburg, 1865.

ABBADIE, ā"bā"dī', **JACQUES:** Protestant apologist; b. at Nay (10 m. s. by e. of Pau), France, 1654 (?); d. at Marylebone, London, 1727. He studied in the French Reformed Church academies of Saumur and Sedan, and early showed much talent. On invitation of the elector of Brandenburg, he became pastor of the French Reformed congregation in Berlin in 1680; after the death of the elector (1688), he followed Marshal Schomberg to England; and became pastor of the French church in the Savoy, London, in 1689. In 1699 he was made dean of Killaloe, Ireland. His *Traité de la vérité de la religion Chrétienne* (vols. i. and ii.,

Rotterdam, 1684; vol. iii., 1689; Eng. transl., 2 vols., London, 1694), became one of the standard apologetic works in French literature. Of his other works, *L'Art de se connaître soi-même* (Rotterdam, 1692), giving an outline of his moral system, attracted much attention and was warmly defended by Malebranche.

BIBLIOGRAPHY: For full list of his writings, consult E. and É. Haag, *La France protestante*, i., s.v., Paris, 1846; for his life, the collection of his sermons, Amsterdam, 1760, iii., and D. C. A. Agnew, *Protestant Exiles from France*, pp. 223–228, Edinburgh, 1886; on his work, R. Elliott, *The Consistent Protestant with some observations on a treatise by J. Abbadie*, London, 1777, and M. Illaire, *Étude sur J. Abbadie considéré comme prédicateur*, Strasburg, 1858.

ABBATE; ABBÉ. See ABBOT.

ABBESS: The title of the head of many monastic communities of women, even in some orders where the head of the monasteries for men does not bear the title of abbot. An abbess is commonly elected by the community. Cases of appointment by the pope on the nomination of the sovereign have occurred less frequently than in the case of abbots. By the ruling of the Council of Trent, only those are eligible who have been eight years professed and reached the age of forty, except, in exceptional circumstances, when a dispensation is granted by the pope. An absolute majority on a secret ballot is required. The election must be confirmed by the bishop (or, in certain cases of exemption, by the pope, or the head of the order), before the new abbess possesses full jurisdiction. A formal benediction, for which there is a form in the *Pontificale Romanum*, is also given by the bishop in many cases. The power thus assigned to the abbess is merely that requisite to rule her community, and in no sense a spiritual jurisdiction; she can not commute or dispense from vows, laws of the Church, or statutes of the order. She may inflict light punishments in the spirit of the rule; but the more severe ones are reserved to the ecclesiastical superior of the convent, who has jurisdiction in the *forum externum*. In general it may be said that the power of an abbess has been and is much more restricted than that of an abbot. For the peculiarly wide jurisdiction of abbesses over men as well as women in the order of Fontévraud (not without precedent in the Celtic monastic system), see FONTÉVRAUD, ORDER OF. See also ABBOT; MONASTICISM.

ABBEY: A monastic house under the rule of an abbot or an abbess. The name is strictly applicable only to the houses of those orders in which these titles are borne by the superiors. While in the East the free form of a group of scattered cells (known as a laura) continued side by side with the common dwelling of a cenobite community, the West developed a distinct style of its own in monastic architecture. The extant plan of the monastery of St. Gall (820) may be taken as typical of the construction of Western monasteries in the early Middle Ages. The center of the entire group of buildings was occupied by an open rectangular space, on the north side of which was the church, while on the other three sides ran the cloister or ambulatory, a vaulted passage open on the inner side, and serving both as a means of communication and as a place for exercise in bad weather. Connected with the cloister, on the ground floor, were the refectory and kitchen; the chapter-house, in which the reading and exposition of the rule and the chapter of faults took place; the *calefactarium* or winter dining-room; and the *parleatorium* or reception-room of outsiders. On the floor above, opening on a similar passage which connected with the choir of the church or the organ-loft, were the *vestiarium*, where the clothes were kept, the library, the dormitory, the infirmary, the rooms for the novices, and the apartments of the abbot, which were supposed to be accessible from outside without passing through the enclosure into which strangers were not allowed to penetrate. The kitchen, which lay within this enclosure, had in like manner a connection with the house for the reception of pilgrims, and with the various farm-buildings, which usually formed a separate quadrangle. The entire group of buildings was surrounded by a high, solid wall, which in some cases was fortified against the dangers of rude times by towers and strong gates. The monks' burying-ground was also within the enclosure.

This system was preserved, with slight modifications, throughout the Middle Ages, the Cistercians adhering to it with especial closeness, as may be seen at Clairvaux and Maulbronn. Sometimes it was enriched by architectural decoration, as in the high-vaulted double refectories of St. Martin at Paris and of Maulbronn, or adorned with painting, as the world-famous "Last Supper" of Leonardo da Vinci in the refectory of Santa Maria delle Grazie at Milan. In houses occupied by female religious the extensive farm-buildings were naturally lacking. The combination of hermit and community life among the Carthusians required a larger space, which was obtained by adding to the original quadrangle on the basis of the church a second larger one, commonly surrounded also by a cloister, with an open space or garden (containing a cemetery) in the cente[illegible]l with individual dwellings for the monks around it. The mendicant orders strove for simplicity in building as in other things, and were forced by their situation in towns to a more restricted plan. The teaching orders added a wing or a separate house for their pupils. The Jesuits completely abandoned the traditional plan, and built themselves large palatial houses, while modern monasteries have little to differentiate them from other large institutions. For a more detailed treatment of the structural system of abbeys and monastic buildings, consult the exhaustive monograph by Venables in the *Encyclopædia Britannica*, s.v. *Abbey*. See MONASTICISM.

BIBLIOGRAPHY: In general: *DCA*, ii. (1880) 1243–68 (gives a list of 1,481 monasteries founded before 814); *DACL*, i. 26–39; A. Ballu, *Le Monastère de Tebessa*, Paris, 1897 (valuable for detailed description of a typical abbey). AUSTRIA: G. Wolfsgruber, A. Hübl, and O. Schmidt, *Abteien und Klöster in Österreich*, Vienna, 1902. FRANCE: L. P. Hérard, *Études archéologiques sur les abbayes de l'ancien diocèse de Paris*, Paris, 1852; M. F. de Montrond, *Dictionnaire des abbayes et monastères*, ib. 1856; J. J. Bourassé, *Abbayes et monastères; histoire, monuments, souvenirs et ruines*, ib. 1869; E. P. M. Sauvage, *Histoire littéraire des abbayes Normandes*, ib. 1872; A. Peigne-Delacourt, *Tableau des abbayes et des monastères d'hommes en France* . 1768, ib. 1875; J. M. Besse, *Les premiers monastères de la Gaule*, in *Revue des questions historiques*, Apr., 1902. GERMANY: O. Grote, *Lexicon deutscher Stifte, Klöster, und Ordenshäuser*, 5 parts, Osterwick, 1874–80; H. G. Hasse, *Geschichte der sachsischen Kloster in der Mark Meissen und Oberlausitz*, Gotha, 1887; H. H. Koch, *Die Karmelitenklöster der niederdeutschen Provinz, 15–16 Jahrhundert*, Freiburg, 1889; H. Hauntinger, *Süddeutsche Klöster vor 100 Jahren*, Cologne, 1889; L. Sutter, *Die Dominican-Kloster auf die Gebiete d. heutigen deutschen Schweitz im 13 Jahrhundert*, Lucerne, 1893; A. Hohenegger, *Das Kapuziner-Kloster zu Meran*, Innsbruck, 1898; F. M. Herhagen, *Die Kloster-Ruinen zu Himmerod in der Eifel*, Treves, 1900. GREAT BRITAIN AND IRELAND: M. Archdall, *Monasticon Hibernicon*: , *the Abbeys, Priories* . *in Ireland*, London, 1786, ed. by P. F. Moran, Dublin, 1871; W. Beattie, *Castles and Abbeys of England*, 2 vols., London, 1851; M. E. C. Walcott, *Minster and Abbey Ruins of the United Kingdom*, ib. 1860; W and M. Howitt, *Ruined Abbeys and Castles of Great Britain*, 2 ser., ib. 1862–64; *Religious Houses of the United Kingdom*, ib. 1887; T. G. Bonney, *Cathedrals, Abbeys and Churches of England and Wales*, 2 vols., ib. 1888–91 (revised, 1898); W C. Lefroy, *Ruined Abbeys of Yorkshire*, ib. 1890; J. Timbs, *Abbeys, Castles and Ancient Halls of England and Wales*, 3 vols., ib. 1890; W. A. J. Archbold, *Somerset Religious Houses*, ib. 1892.

ABBO OF FLEURY, flö"rî': French abbot of the tenth century, one of the few men of that time who strove to cultivate learning and led the way for the later scholasticism; b. near Orléans; d. Nov. 13, 1004. He was brought up in the Benedictine abbey of Fleury (25 m. e.s.e. of Orléans); studied at Paris and Reims; in 985–987 was in England, on invitation of Archbishop Oswald of York, and taught in the school of the abbey of Ramsey; was chosen abbot of Fleury in 988, and brought the school there to a flourishing condition. He upheld the rights of his abbey against the Bishop of Orléans, and at the synod of St. Denis (995) took the part of the monks against the bishops. He twice represented King Robert the Pious as ambassador at Rome, and gained the favor of Pope Gregory V. He upheld strict monastic discipline; and an attempt to introduce reforms in the monastery of La Réole (in Gascony, 30 m. s.e. of Bordeaux), a dependency of Fleury, led to a mutiny by the monks in which he was fatally wounded. He wrote upon such diverse subjects as dialectics, astronomy, and canon law; and his extant letters are of much value for the history of the time.

BIBLIOGRAPHY: For his works, and his life by his pupil Aimoin, consult *MPL*, cxxxix.; for his *Epistolae*, Bouquet, *Recueil;* for his life, J. B. Pardiac, *Histoire de St. Abbon*, Paris, 1872.

ABBOT: The head of one of the larger houses in the Benedictine and other older Western monastic orders. The term originated in the East, where it was frequently used as a title of respect for any monk (being derived from the Aramaic *abba*, "father"); but there it was replaced, as the title of the superior of a monastery, by archimandrite and other titles. In the Western orders founded before the end of the eleventh century the title is still in use. According to the present system, abbots are divided into secular and regular; the former are secular clerics who are incumbents of benefices originally bearing the title of abbey but since secularized; the latter are classified according as they have authority only over the members of their house, or over certain of the faithful, or enjoy a quasi-episcopal jurisdiction over a definite territory, or are merely titular abbots, their houses having fallen into decay. They are further divided according to the term of their office, which may be either for life or for three years. A special class known as mitered abbots have permission to wear episcopal insignia. The election of an abbot is commonly by vote of the professed brothers, in most cases only those in holy orders. The candidate must be twenty-five years of age, a professed brother of the order, and a priest. Actual jurisdiction is not conferred until his confirmation either by the bishop or, in the case of exempt abbeys, by the superior in the case, frequently the pope. His benediction is the next step, which takes place according to the office in the *Pontificale Romanum*, usually at the hands of the bishop of the diocese. He has the power to regulate the entire inner life of the abbey in accordance with the rule, and to require obedience from his subordinates; according to the rule of St. Benedict, however, abbots are required not to exercise their authority in an arbitrary manner, but to seek the counsel of their brethren. In many particulars a quasi-episcopal jurisdiction has in course of time been conceded to them. Since the eighth century they have been allowed to confer the tonsure and minor orders on their subjects, to bless their churches, cemeteries, sacred vessels, etc., to take rank as prelates, and, if generals exercising quasi-episcopal jurisdiction, to sit and vote in general councils.

The practise of granting abbeys *in commendam* to deserving clerics, or even to laymen, led to the creation of a class of merely titular abbots, who had nothing of this character but the name and the revenues. This practise, which was the source of many abuses, was regulated by the Council of Trent. From it sprang the custom in France of applying the title *abbé* to any prominent clergyman who might, according to the custom of the time, lay claim to such an appointment, and then to the secular clergy in general. A somewhat analogous custom existed in Italy, where many professional men, lawyers, doctors, etc., though laymen and even married men, retained some marks of the clerical character which had earlier distinguished the majority of scholars in their dress and in the title of *abbate*. In some Protestant countries the title of abbot still clung to the heads of institutions that had grown out of monasteries suppressed at the Reformation. See MONASTICISM.

ABBOT, EZRA: Unitarian layman; b. at Jackson, Waldo County, Me., Apr. 28, 1819; d. at Cambridge, Mass., Mar. 21, 1884. He was fitted for college at Phillips Academy, Exeter, N. H., and was graduated at Bowdoin, 1840. He then taught in Maine and, after 1847, in Cambridge, Mass., also rendering service in the Harvard and Boston Athenæum libraries. In 1856 he was appointed assistant librarian of Harvard University, in 1871 he was university lecturer on the textual criticism of the New Testament, and in 1872 he became Bussey professor of New Testament criticism and interpretation in the Harvard Divinity School. From 1853 he was secretary of the American Oriental Society. He was one of the original members of the American New Testament Revision Company (1871), and in 1880 he aided in organizing the Society of Biblical Literature and Exegesis. He was a scholar of rare talents and attainments. He stood first and foremost among the textual critics of the Greek Testament in America; and for microscopic accuracy of biblical scholarship he had no superior in the world. On account of the extreme attention he paid to minute details, the number of his independent publications was small, and the results of his labors have gone into books of other writers, to which he was willing to contribute without regard to reward or adequate recognition. His *Literature of the Doctrine of a Future Life*, first published as an appendix to Alger's *History of the Doctrine of a Future Life* (Philadelphia, 1864), and afterward separately (New York, 1871), is a model of bibliographical accuracy and completeness, embracing more than 5,300 titles. He enriched Smith's *Bible Dictionary* (Am. ed., 1867–70) with careful bibliographical lists on the most important topics, besides silently correcting innumerable errors in references and in typography. His most valuable and independent labors, however, were devoted to textual criticism and are in part incorporated in Gregory's *Prolegomena* to the *Ed. viii. critica major* of Tischendorf's Greek Testament; the chapter *De versibus* (pp. 167–182) is by him, and he read the manuscript and proofs of the entire work. His services to the American Bible Revision Committee were invaluable. The critical papers which he prepared on disputed passages were uncommonly thorough, and had no small influence in determining the text finally accepted. His defense of the Johannean authorship of the fourth Gospel (*The Authorship of the Fourth Gospel; External Evidences*, Boston, 1880; reprinted by his successor in the Harvard Divinity School, J. H. Thayer, 1888) is an invaluable contribution to the solution of that question.

Of his writings, besides those already adduced, may be mentioned: an edition of *Orme's Memoir of the Controversy respecting the Three Heavenly Witnesses* (New York, 1866); work upon G. R. Noyes's (posthumous) *Translation of the New Testament from the Greek Text of Tischendorf* (1869); work upon C. F. Hudson's *Greek and English Concordance of the New Testament* (1870); *The Late Professor Tischendorf*, in *The Unitarian Review*, Mar. 1875; *On the Reading "an only begotten God," or "God only begotten," John i. 18*, ib. June 1875; *On the Reading "Church of God," Acts. xx. 28*, in the *Bibliotheca Sacra*, Apr. 1876 (like the preceding, first privately printed for the American Bible Revision Committee); *Recent Discussions of Romans ix. 5*, an exhaustive article on the punctuation of this passage in *Journal of the Society of Biblical Literature and Exegesis*, June and Dec. 1883. The four articles mentioned last, together with that on the fourth Gospel and seventeen others, were published in 1888, under the editorship of J. H. Thayer. (PHILIP SCHAFF †.) D. S. SCHAFF.

BIBLIOGRAPHY: *Ezra Abbot*, a memoir edited by S. J. Barrows, Cambridge, 1884; *Andover Review*, i. (1884) 554; *Literary World*, xv. (1884) 113.

ABBOT, GEORGE: Archbishop of Canterbury; b. at Guildford (30 m. s.w. of London) Oct. 29, 1562; d. at Croydon (10 m. s. of London) Aug. 4, 1633. He studied at Balliol College, Oxford (B.A., 1582; probationer fellow, 1583; M.A., 1585; B.D., 1593; D.D., 1597), took orders in 1585, remained at Oxford as tutor, and became known as an able preacher and lecturer with strong Puritan sympathies. He was made master of University College 1597; dean of Winchester 1600; vice-chancellor of the university 1600, 1603, 1605; bishop of Coventry and Lichfield, 1609; bishop of London 1610; archbishop of Canterbury 1611. His learning and sincerity can not be questioned; but he was austere, narrow, almost a fanatic. His one great idea was to crush "popery," not only in England, but in all Europe; and popery to him meant every theological system except that of Calvin. To further his purposes abroad, he meddled persistently in the foreign policy of the State and chose arbitrary, high-handed, and cruel means to accomplish his ends at home. His principles allowed him to flatter the king, to help him generously in money matters, and to serve him in certain political undertakings, such as the restoration of episcopacy in Scotland in 1608–10. At other times his conscience compelled him to be just, and consequently he could not retain the royal favor. A Presbyterian at heart, he accepted episcopacy only from a love of order and sense of loyalty to constituted authority; and his appointment as archbishop was displeasing to the Anglican party, who had wanted Launcelot Andrewes (q.v.). His undiplomatic course incensed his opponents, and they pursued him relentlessly and cruelly. In 1621 he killed a gamekeeper while hunting. It was purely accidental, and he was deeply shocked and grieved; nevertheless, William Laud (his successor as archbishop and his personal enemy for years) and others seized upon the incident to annoy him and weaken his influence. Charles I., after his accession, favored Laud, who brought about Abbot's sequestration for a year (1627–28) because he had refused to sanction a sermon by Dr. Robert Sibthorp, vicar of Brackley, indorsing an unlawful attempt by the king to raise money, and showing little sympathy with Abbot's favorite policy of support to the German Protestants. After this his public acts were few. But with all his faults and disappointments he was faithful to duty as he understood it; and he was generous with money, charitable to the poor, and a patron of learning. He was a member of the Oxford New Testament Company for the version of 1611; and through him Cyril Lucar (q.v.) presented the *Codex Alexandrinus* to Charles I. With other works, he published *A Brief Description of the Whole World* (London, 1599; 5th ed., 1664), a geography prepared for his pupils at Oxford, containing an interesting description of America; and *An Exposition upon the Prophet Jonah* (1600), which was reprinted in 1845 with a life by Grace Webster.

BIBLIOGRAPHY: T. Fuller, *Church History*, 6 parts, London, 1655 (ed. Brewer, 1845); *Biographia Britannica*, 6 vols., ib. 1747–66 (contains his life by W. Oldys, reprinted by Arthur Onslow, Guildford, 1777); W. F. Hook, *Ecclesiastical Biography*, 8 vols., London, 1845–52; idem, *Lives of*

Archbishops, 12 vols., ib. 1860–72; S. R. Gardiner, *History of England, 1603–1642*, 10 vols., ib. 1883–84; *DNB*, i. 5.

ABBOT, ROBERT: 1. Bishop of Salisbury; elder brother of George Abbot, Archbishop of Canterbury; b. at Guildford (30 m. s.w. of London) about 1560; d. at Salisbury Mar. 2, 1618. He studied at Balliol College, Oxford (fellow, 1581; M.A., 1582; D.D., 1597), and held several important livings. In 1609 he became master of Balliol; in 1612 regius professor of divinity at Oxford; in 1615 bishop of Salisbury. He was a learned man, an able preacher, and a prolific writer, holding in general the same views as his brother, but advocating them with more discretion and tact. His works include two treatises in reply to Bellarmine, *A Mirror of Popish Subtilties* (London, 1594), and *Antichristi demonstratio* (1603); and *A Defence of the Reformed Catholic of Mr. William Perkins* (3 parts, 1606–09), which won him royal favor and a promise of preferment.

BIBLIOGRAPHY: Thos. Fuller, *Abel Redevivus*, London, 1651 (ed. W. Nichols, 2 vols., 1867); idem, *Church History*, 6 pts., ib. 1655 (ed. by Brewer, 1845); A. Wood, *Athenæ Oxonienses*, ii. 224–227, ib. 1692; *Biographia Britannica*, 6 vols., ib. 1747–66 (life reprinted by A. Onslow, Guildford, 1777); *Criminal Trials, illustrative of British History*, ii. 366–367, ib. 1837 (deals with Abbot's part in the controversy over the Gunpowder Plot); *DNB*, i. 24.

2. Vicar of Cranbrook, Kent, 1616–43; b. probably, 1588; d. about 1657 He studied at Cambridge (college unknown), took the degree of M.A. there, and was incorporated at Oxford. Parliament having decided against pluralities of ecclesiastical offices, he resigned his Cranbrook vicarage in 1643, retaining that of Southwick, Hampshire, although much smaller. He was afterward rector of St. Austin's, London. He was a strong churchman; and engaged in many controversies, particularly with the Brownists, to whom he was not always fair. Many of his writings, as his *Milk for Babes, or a Mother's Catechism for her Children* (London, 1646), were very popular.

BIBLIOGRAPHY: A. Wood, *Fasti*, appended to *Athenæ Oxonienses*, London, 1691–92 (ed. P. Bliss, i. 323, Oxford, 1848); John Walker, *Sufferings of the Clergy*, ii. 183, London, 1714; B. Brook, *Lives of the Puritans*, iii. 182, ib. 1813; *DNB*, i. 25–26.

ABBOTT, EDWARD: Protestant Episcopalian; b. at Farmington, Me., July 15, 1841. He was educated at the University of the City of New York (B.A., 1860) and at Andover Theological Seminary (1860–62; did not graduate). In 1862–63 he was an agent of the United States Sanitary Commission, and in the latter year was ordained to the Congregational ministry. Two years later he founded the Stearns Chapel Congregational Church (now the Pilgrim Church) at Cambridge, Mass., of which he was pastor four years. In 1872–73 he was chaplain of the Massachusetts Senate. In 1879 he was ordered deacon in the Protestant Episcopal Church, and priested in 1880, his parish being that of St. James, Cambridge, which he still holds. He refused the proffered missionary bishopric of Japan in 1889. At various times he has been a member of the Board of Visitors of Wellesley College, trustee of the Society for the Relief of the Widows and Orphans of Clergymen of the Protestant Episcopal Church, director and president of the Associated Charities of Cambridge, vice-dean and dean of the Eastern Convocation of the Diocese of Massachusetts, president of the Cambridge Branch of the Indian Rights Association, member of the Missionary Council of the Protestant Episcopal Church, secretary of the Standing Committee of the Diocese of Massachusetts, member of the Provisional Committee on Church Work in Mexico, president of the Indian Industries League, president of the Cambridge City Mission, and has been active in other religious and philanthropic movements. His theological position is that of the Broad Church, sympathizing neither with the extreme of medievalism nor higher criticism. In 1869–78 he was associate editor of the Boston *Congregationalist*, and was joint proprietor and editor of the *Boston Literary World* from 1877 to 1888, again editing it in 1895–1903. His principal works are *The Baby's Things : A Story in Verse* (New York, 1871); *Paragraph History of the United States* (Boston, 1875); *Paragraph History of the American Revolution* (1876); *Revolutionary Times* (1876); *History of Cambridge* (1880); *Phillips Brooks* (Cambridge, 1900); and *Meet for the Master's Use : An Allegory* (1900).

ABBOTT, EDWIN ABBOTT: Church of England, author and educator, b. in London Dec. 20, 1838. He studied at St. John's College, Cambridge (B.A., 1861), where he was elected fellow in 1862. He was assistant master at King Edward's School, Birmingham, in 1862–64, and at Clifton College in the following year, while from 1865 to 1889 he was headmaster at City of London School. He was Hulsean lecturer at Cambridge in 1876 and select preacher at Oxford in the succeeding year. His works include *Bible Lessons* (London, 1872); *Cambridge Sermons* (1875); *Through Nature to Christ* (1877); *Oxford Sermons* (1879); the article *Gospels* in the 9th ed. of the *Encyclopædia Britannica*; *The Common Tradition of the Synoptic Gospels* (1884; in collaboration with W G. Rushbrooke); *The Good Voices, or A Child's Guide to the Bible, and Parables for Children* (1875); *Bacon and Essex* (1877); *Philochristus* (1878); *Onesimus* (1882); *Flatland, or A Romance of Many Dimensions* (1884); *Francis Bacon, an Account of his Life and Works* (1885); *The Kernel and the Husk* (1886); *The Anglican Career of Cardinal Newman* (1892); *The Spirit on the Waters* (1897); *St. Thomas of Canterbury* (Edinburgh, 1898); *Corrections of Mark Adopted by Matthew and Luke* (1901); *From Letter to Spirit* (1903); *Paradosis* (1904); *Johannine Vocabulary, A Comparison of the Words of the Fourth Gospel with Those of the Three* (1905); and *Silanus the Christian* (1906).

ABBOTT, JACOB: American Congregationalist; b. at Hallowell, Me., Nov. 14, 1803; d. at Farmington, Me., Oct. 31, 1879. He was graduated at Bowdoin, 1820; studied theology at Andover, 1822–24; was tutor and professor of mathematics and natural philosophy at Amherst, 1824–29; principal of the Mount Vernon School for Girls, Boston, 1829–33; ordained evangelist and pastor of the Eliot Congregational Church, Roxbury, Mass., 1834. In 1839 he removed to Farmington, Me., and spent the remainder of his life there and in New York devoted to literary work and teaching. He wrote many story-books which had a wide circulation, such as the *Young Christian* series (4 vols.; new edition of the *Young Christian*, with life, New York, 1882), the *Rollo Books* (14 vols.) and *Rollo's Tour in Europe* (10 vols.), the *Franconia Stories* (10 vols.), *Science for the Young* (4 vols.).

ABBOTT, JUSTIN EDWARDS: Presbyterian; b. at Portsmouth, N. H., Dec. 25, 1853. He was educated at Dartmouth College (A.B., 1876) and Union Theological Seminary, from which he was graduated in 1879. He was ordained to the Congregational ministry in the following year, and after acting as stated supply at the Presbyterian church at Norwood, N. J., in 1881–82, went to India under the auspices of the American Board of Commissioners for Foreign Missions. Since that time he has been stationed at Bombay in the Maratha Mission, and has contributed a number of monographs to scientific periodicals on the epigraphy and numismatics of India, in addition to preparing religious works in Marathi for the use of Hindu converts.

ABBOTT, LYMAN: American Congregationalist; b. at Roxbury, Mass., Dec. 18, 1835. He was educated at New York University (B.A., 1853), and after practising law for a time was ordained a minister in the Congregational Church in 1860. He was pastor in Terre Haute, Ind., from 1860 to 1865, after which he held the pastorate of the New England Church, New York City, for four years, resigning to devote himself to literary work. In 1888 he succeeded Henry Ward Beecher as pastor of Plymouth Church, Brooklyn, but resigned in 1898. He was secretary of the American Union Commission from 1865 to 1869, and later was a member of the New York Child Labor Committee and of the National Child Labor Committee. Among other societies, he is a member of the Bar Association of New York, New York State Historical Association, National Conference of Charities and Correction, Indian Rights Association, New York Association for the Blind, Association for Improving the Condition of the Poor, The Religious Education Association, American Board of Commissioners for Foreign Missions, American Institute of Sacred Literature, American Peace Society, New York State Conference of Religion, and the Universal Peace Union. His theological position is that of a Congregationalist of the Liberal Evangelical type. In addition to editing the "Literary Record" of *Harper's Magazine*, he edited *The Illustrated Christian Weekly* (1871–76) and since 1876 *The Christian Union* (with Henry Ward Beecher till 1881; name changed to *The Outlook*, 1893). He has written *Jesus of Nazareth* (New York, 1869); *Old Testament Shadows of New Testament Truth* (1870); *Illustrated Commentary on the New Testament* (New York, 1875); *Dictionary of Religious Knowledge* (Boston, 1876; in collaboration with T. J. Conant); *How to Study the Bible* (1877); *In Aid of Faith* (New York, 1886); *Evolution of Christianity* (Boston, 1896); *The Theology of an Evolutionist* (1897); *Christianity and Social Problems* (1897); *Life and Letters of Paul* (1898); *Problems of Life* (New York, 1900); *Life and Literature of the Ancient Hebrews* (Boston, 1900); *The Rights of Man* (1901); *Henry Ward Beecher* (1903); *The Other Room* (New York, 1903); *The Great Companion* (1904); *Christian Ministry* (Boston, 1905); *Personality of God* (New York, 1905); and *Industrial Problems* (Philadelphia, 1905).

ABBOTT, THOMAS KINGSMILL: Church of Ireland, author and professor; b. at Dublin Mar. 26, 1829. He was educated at Trinity College, Dublin (B.A., 1851; M.A., 1856; B.D., 1879), where he was elected fellow in 1854. From 1867 to 1872 he was professor of Moral Philosophy at Trinity College, of Biblical Greek from 1875 to 1888, and of Hebrew from 1879 to 1900, and has also been librarian of the College since 1887 He has been chairman of the Governors of Sir P. Dun's Hospital since 1897. In theology he is a Broad Churchman. His works include *Sight and Touch, an Attempt to Disprove the Berkleyan Theory of Vision* (Dublin, 1864); *Par palimpsestorum Dublinensium* (1880); *Elements of Logic* (1883); *Evangeliorum versio Antihieronymiana* (2 vols., 1884); *Theory of the Tides* (1888); *Celtic Ornaments from the Book of Kells* (1892); *Notes on St. Paul's Epistles* (1892); *Essays, Chiefly on the Original Texts of the Old and New Testaments* (Edinburgh, 1897); *Catalogue of Manuscripts in the Library of Trinity College, Dublin* (Dublin, 1900); and *Catalogue of Incunabula in the Library of Trinity College, Dublin* (1905), in addition to *Kant's Theory of Ethics*, a translation (1873).

ABBREVIATORS: Officials of the papal chancery whose duty it is to prepare apostolic letters expedited through that office. The name is derived from the fact that part of their work consists in taking minutes of the petitions addressed to the Holy See and of the answers to be returned. Formerly they were divided into two classes, *di parco maggiore* and *di parco minore*, but the latter class has long been abolished. In the College of Abbreviators at the present time there are twelve clerics and seventeen laymen. Legislation of Feb. 13, 1904, defines their duties anew. The office dates from the early part of the fourteenth century, and has been filled by many distinguished prelates. In 1466 Paul II. abolished it because it had been corrupted, but it was restored by Sixtus IV in 1471. There is also an *abbreviatore di curia* attached to the datary, who prepares minutes of papal letters addressed *motu proprio* to the entire Church.

JOHN T. CREAGH.

ABDIAS, ab'di-as: Legendary first bishop of Babylon. Under the title, *De historia certaminis apostolici* there exists a collection of myths, legends, and traditions relating to the lives and works of the apostles, and pretending to be the Latin translation of the Greek translation of the Hebrew work of Abdias. Neither the book nor its author was known to Eusebius or to Jerome, nor do they find mention before Ordericus Vitalis (12th cent.).

Bibliography: W. Lazinon, *De historia certaminis apostolici*, Paris, 1560, and often reprinted; Fabricius, *Codex apocryphus*, ii. (1st ed., 1703), and ii., iii. (2d ed., 1719); C. Oudin, *Commentarius de scriptoribus ecclesiasticis*, ii. 418–421, Leipsic, 1722; G. J. Voss, *De historicis Græcis*, p. 243. ib. 1838; J. A. Giles, *Codex apocryphus Novi Testamenti*, London, 1852; Migne, *Troisième et dernière encyclopédie théologique*, xxiv. (66 vols., Paris, 1855–66); S. C. Malan, *Conflicts of the Holy Apostles . . translated from an Ethiopic MS.*, London, 1871; *DCB*. i. 1–4.

ABEEL, DAVID: Missionary; b. at New Brunswick, N. J., June 12, 1804; d. at Albany, N. Y., Sept. 4, 1846. He was graduated at the New Brunswick Theological Seminary in 1826; in 1829 he went to Canton as chaplain of the Seaman's Friend Society; and in 1831–33 he visited Java, Singapore, and Siam for the American Board. Returning to America by way of Europe in 1833, he aided in founding in England a society for promoting the education of women in the East. He went back to China in 1838 and founded the Amoy mission in 1842. He published a *Journal* of his first residence in China (New York, 1835), *The Missionary Convention at Jerusalem* (1838), *Claims of the World to the Gospel* (1838).

Bibliography: G. R. Williamson, *David Abeel*, New York, 1849.

A'BEL ("Breath"): Second son of Adam and Eve and the brother of Cain, who, according to Gen. iv. 1–16, killed him from envy.

ABELARD, ab'e-lārd.

Abelard is a name used as the common designation of Pierre de Palais (*Petrus Palatinus*), the first notable representative of the dialectico-critical school of scholasticism founded by Anselm of Canterbury, but kept by him within the limits of the traditional orthodoxy. The meaning as well as the original form of the by-name is uncertain; it has been connected with the Latin *bajulus*, "teacher," and with the French *abeille*, "bee." The ending "-ard" is Frankish, and the entire name may be.

I. Life: Abelard was born at Palais (Le Pallet), a village of Brittany, about 12 m. e. of Nantes, in 1079; d. in the Priory of St. Marcel, near Chalon-sur-Saône (36 m. n. of Mâcon), Apr. 21, 1142. He voluntarily renounced his rights as first-born son of the knight Berengar, lord of the village, and chose a life of study. His first teacher was Roscelin, the Nominalist, at Locmenach, Brittany, now Locminé, 80 m. s. w. of Brest. Then he wandered from one teacher to another until he came to Paris, where William of Champeaux, the Realist, was head of the cathedral school and attracting great crowds. Young as he was, Abelard was bold enough to set himself up as William's rival: he lectured, first at Melun (27 m. s.s.e. of Paris), then at Corbeil (7 miles nearer Paris), and, after a few years, in Paris itself at the cathedral school. His success was sufficient to make William jealous, and he compelled Abelard to leave the city. About 1113 he betook himself to Anselm of Laon at Laon (86 m. n.e. of Paris) to study theology, having hitherto occupied himself wholly with dialectics. His stay at Laon was short and was followed by a few years at Paris, where crowds flocked to hear his lectures and brought him a considerable income.

1. Student Life and Lecturer on Philosophy.

This brilliant career was suddenly checked by the episode of Heloise, a young girl of eighteen, said to have been the natural daughter of a canon of Paris, living with her uncle, Canon Fulbert of Paris. Her education was confided to Abelard, and a passionate love sprang up between them. When Fulbert attempted to separate them, they fled toward Brittany, to the home of Abelard's sister, Dionysia, where Heloise bore a son, Astralabius. To satisfy Fulbert the lovers were married, Abelard asking that the marriage be kept secret out of regard for his ecclesiastical career. Fulbert disregarded this request and also treated his niece badly when she returned to his house. Abelard accordingly removed her to the Benedictine nunnery of Argenteuil (11 m. n.e. of Versailles), where she had been brought up, and where later she took the veil, a step which Fulbert interpreted as an attempt by her husband to get rid of her. In revenge he had Abelard attacked by night in his lodgings in Paris and mutilated, with the view probably of rendering him incapable of ever holding any ecclesiastical office. Abelard retired to the Benedictine abbey of St. Denis in Paris (probably about 1118), where he became a monk and lived undisturbed for a year or two, giving instruction in a secluded place (the "*cella*").

2. Heloise.

He received much sympathy and had many pupils. In 1121 a synod at Soissons pronounced heretical certain opinions expressed by him in a book on the Trinity (*De unitate et trinitate divina*; discovered by R. Stölzle and published, Freiburg, 1891). He was required to burn the book, and to retire to the monastery of St. Medard, near Soissons. In a short time, however, he was allowed to return to St. Denis, but was ill received there; and his assertion that the patron saint of the monastery and of France was not the same as Dionysius the Areopagite (see Denis, Saint) made more trouble with the abbot, the monks, and the court. He fled, but was compelled to return and recant his opinion concerning St. Denis. Afterward he was allowed to retire to Champagne, near Nogent-sur-Seine (60 m. s. e. of Paris) where he built an oratory to the Trinity. Pupils again gathered about him and the original building of reeds and sedges was replaced by one which he called the Paraclete. But he was still under the jurisdiction of the abbot of St. Denis and suffered much annoyance. He accepted the election as abbot of the monastery of St. Gildas in Brittany (on the peninsula of Ruis, 10 m. s. of Vannes), and stayed there ten years, but he found it impossible to control the unruly monks and they tried to poison him. He found refuge

3. Monk and Abbot.

from time to time at the Paraclete, which he had presented to Heloise after the nunnery of Argenteuil was closed (c. 1127); but his visits as spiritual director of the nuns who gathered about his wife caused scandal, and he had to give them up. Another attempt was made on his life; and once more he sought safety in flight, whither is not known.

For several years his life is obscure; it is only known that in 1136 John of Salisbury heard him lecture in the school on the hill of St. Geneviève in Paris, and that during this period he wrote his autobiography, the *Historia calamitatum*. In 1141 a council, instigated mainly by Bernard of Clairvaux, a man thoroughly antipathetic to Abelard, who had long considered his teaching wrong and his influence dangerous, met at Sens (61 m. s.s.e. of Paris). Certain extracts from Abelard's writings were pronounced erroneous and heretical (June 4, 1141).

4. Second Condemnation for Heresy.

Abelard declined to defend himself; he appealed to the pope, and with his followers left the council. His former pupil, Cardinal Guido de Castello (afterward Pope Celestine II.), took his part at Rome; but Bernard wrote a letter denouncing Arnold of Brescia, another pupil, as one of the champions of Abelard, and thereby influenced the decision of Pope Innocent II., who condemned Abelard to silence, excommunicated his followers, ordered him and Arnold to retire to a monastery, and their books to be burned (July 16, 1141). Abelard wrote an apology defending himself against the action of the council, and sent a letter to Heloise maintaining his orthodoxy. He wrote a second apology submitting to the Church, and made peace with Bernard.

By the friendly intervention of Peter the Venerable, Abbot of Cluny, permission was given him to spend the rest of his days at Cluny. He continued his studies, "read constantly, prayed often, gladly kept silence."

5. Last Days.

But, broken by his sufferings and misfortunes, he did not live long there. With a view to his physical betterment Peter sent him to the neighboring priory of St. Marcel, at Chalons and there he died. His body was taken to the Paraclete; and on the death of Heloise (May 16, 1164) her body was placed in the same coffin. In 1817 their remains were removed to the cemetery of Père Lachaise, Paris, and a monument was erected of stone from the ruins of the Paraclete.

II. System: Abelard belonged to the school of Anselm of Canterbury, but he did not follow him slavishly; and he was more critic than apologist of any system. He borrowed much from Augustine, Jerome, and older Church Fathers, as well as from Agobard, Claudius of Turin, Erigena, and Fredegis. His originality is seen in his doctrine of the Trinity and the Atonement and, as a philosopher, particularly in his teaching concerning the *principia* and his position toward the question of *universalia*.

1. Philosophy.

The latter is not quite clear; but it appears that he was neither nominalist, realist, nor conceptualist. William of Champeaux, the extreme realist, declared the *universalia* to be the very essence of all existence, and individuality only the product of incidental circumstances. To this Abelard objected that it led to pantheism; and he pursued his criticism so keenly that he forced William to modify his system. He rejected nominalism also, according to which the *universalia* are mere names, declaring that our conceptions must correspond to things which occasion them. This view is not conceptualism in so far as it does not in one-sided fashion emphasize the assertion that the general ideas are mere *conceptus mentis*, mere subjective ideas.

As theologian Abelard is noteworthy for his doctrine of revelation, his attitude toward belief on authority, and his conception of the relation between faith and knowledge.

2. Theology.

Concerning revelation he emphasizes the inner influence on the human spirit rather than its external manifestation, and does not limit inspiration to the writers of the Scriptures, but holds that it was imparted also to the Greek and Roman philosophers and to the Indian Brahmans. He teaches that the Scriptures are the result of the cooperation of the Spirit of God with the human writers, recognizes degrees of inspiration, and admits that prophets and apostles may make mistakes. He does not hesitate to disclose the contradictions in tradition, and distinguishes like a good Protestant between the authority of the Scriptures and that of the Fathers. Faith means to him a belief in things not susceptible to sense which can be grounded on rational demonstration or satisfactory authority. He opposes the compulsion of authority, will have free discussion of religious things, and everywhere follows his own conviction; but he sets narrow limits to what can be known. An adequate knowledge of the unity and trinity of God he declares impossible, as well as a scientific proof that shall compel belief in the existence of God and immortality. Here he asserts merely a possibility of belief. He condemns the acceptance of formulas of belief without knowing what they mean, and will have no one required to believe anything contrary to reason; he found nothing of the kind himself in the Scriptures or the teaching of the Church, and does not mean to exclude the supernatural. The doctrine of the Trinity he always treats in connection with the divine attributes; and in spite of all precautions the Trinity always becomes in his thought one of the attributes. He qualifies omnipotence by teaching that God does everything which he can, and therefore he could not do more than he has done. He can not prevent evil, but is able only to permit it and to turn it to good. As for his ethics, he teaches that moral good and ill inhere not in the act but in the motive. The evil propensity is not sin; it is the *pœna* merely, and not the *culpa*, which has passed from Adam upon all. His theory of the Atonement is moral. The aim of the incarnation and sufferings of Christ was to move men to love by this highest revelation of the divine love. The love thus awakened frees from the bondage of sin, enables to fulfil the law, and impels to do the will of God, no longer in fear, but in the freedom of the sons of God. By law he understands the natural law which Christ taught and fulfilled, giving thereby the highest example. By his love, faithful to death, Christ has won merit with God; and because of this merit God forgives those who enter into communion with Christ and enables them to fulfil the law. It is in personal communion with Christ, therefore, that the real Atonement consists. Only such as let themselves be impressed with the love of Christ enter into this communion. By the curse of the law from which Christ frees, Abelard understands the Mosaic religion with its hard punishments. Inasmuch as Christ made an end of the Mosaic religion, he abolished its punishments also.

III. Writings: A practically complete edition of the works of Abelard (including certain writings which are spurious or of doubtful origin) was furnished by Victor Cousin in the *Ouvrages inédits d'Abélard* (Paris, 1836) and *Petri Abelardi opera nunc primum in unum collecta* (2 vols., 1849–59); the *Opera*, from the edition of A. Duchesne and F. Amboise (Paris, 1616), with *Opuscula* published later, are in *MPL*, clxxviii. (lacks the *Sic et non*, that brilliant piece of skeptical writing). Particular works have been published as follows: the *Theologia Christiana* and the *Hexameron*, ed. Martène and Durand, in the *Thesaurus novus anecdotorum*, v. (Paris, 1717); the *Ethica* (*Scito te ipsum*), ed. B. Pez, in the *Thesaurus anecdotorum novissimus*, iii. (1721); the *Dialogus* and the *Epitome* or *Sententiæ*, ed. F. H. Rheinwald (Berlin, 1831, 1835); the *Sic et non*, ed. T. Henke and G. S. Lindenkohl (Marburg, 1851; incomplete in Cousin's edition, 1836); the *Historia calamitatum*, ed. Orelli (Zurich, 1841); the *Planctus virginum Israel super filia Jeptæ Galaditæ*, ed. W Meyer and W Brambach (Munich, 1886); the *Hymnarius paraclitensis*, ed. G. M. Dreves (Paris, 1891); the *Tractatus de unitate et trinitate divina*, ed. R. Stölzle (Freiburg, 1891). The letters have been often published in the original Latin and in translation (Latin, ed. R. Rawlinson, London, 1718; Eng., ed. H. Mills, London, 1850; ed. H. Morton, New York, 1901; Germ., with the *Historia calamitatum*, ed. P Baumgärtner, Reclam, Leipsic, 1894; French, with Latin text, ed. Grérard, Paris, 1885); and selections will be found in some of the works cited in the bibliography below.

Bibliography: J. Berington, . *Lives of Abeillard and Heloisa, with Their Letters*, 2d ed., Birmingham, 1788; C. de Rémusat, *Abélard*, 2 vols., Paris, 1845 (the standard biography); J. L. Jacobi, *Abälard und Heloise*, Berlin, 1850; F. P. G. Guizot, *Lettres d'Abailard et d'Héloise, précédées d'un essai historique*, Paris, 1839, 1853; C. Prantel, *Geschichte der Logik im Abendlande*, ii. 160–204, Leipsic, 1861; O. W Wight, *Abélard and Heloise*, New York, 1861; E. Bonnier, *Abélard et St. Bernard*, Paris, 1862; Hefele, *Conciliengeschichte*, v. 321–326, 399–435; A. Stöckl, *Geschichte der Philosophie des Mittelalters*, i. 218–272, Mainz, 1864; H. Reuter, *Geschichte der religiösen Aufklärung im Mittelalter*, i. 183–259, Berlin, 1875; E. Vacandard, *Abélard et sa lutte avec St. Bernard, sa doctrine, sa méthode*, Paris, 1881; S. M. Deutsch, *Peter Abälard*, Leipsic, 1883; A. S. Richardson, *Abélard and Heloise, with a Selection of their Letters*, New York, 1884; J. G. Compayré, *Abelard and the . History of Universities*, London, 1893; A. Hausrath, *Peter Abälard*, Leipsic, 1895; Jos. McCabe, *Peter Abélard*, New York, 1901 (an excellent book); Hauck, *KD*, iv. 409 sqq.

ABELITES, ā'bel-aits (**ABELIANS, ABELONIANS**): A sect mentioned by Augustine (*Hær.*, lxxxvii.; cf. *Prædestinatus*, i. 87) as formerly living in the neighborhood of Hippo, but already extinct when he wrote. Their name was derived from Abel, the son of Adam. Each man took a wife, but refrained from conjugal relations, and each pair adopted a boy and a girl who inherited the property of their foster-parents on condition of living together in like manner in mature life. They were probably the remnant of a Gnostic sect, tinged perhaps by Manichean influences. [The name grew out of a wide-spread belief that Abel though married had lived a life of continence.]

G. Krüger.

Bibliography: C. W. F. Walch, *Entwurf einer vollständigen Historie der Ketzereien*, i. 607–608, Leipsic, 1762.

ABELLI, a-bel'li, **LOUIS:** French Roman Catholic; b. 1603; d. at Paris Oct. 4, 1691. He was made bishop of Rhodez, southern France, in 1664, but resigned three years later and retired to the monastery of St. Lazare in Paris. He was a vehement opponent of Jansenism. His numerous works include: *Medulla theologica* (2 vols., Paris, 1651), a treatise on dogmatics; *La Tradition de l'Église touchant la dévotion envers la Sainte Vierge* (1652); *Vie de St. Vincent de Paul* (1664); *De l'obéissance et soumission due au Pape* (ed. Cheruel, 1870); and two volumes of meditations, *La Couronne de l'année chrétienne* (1657).

ABEN EZRA (Abraham ben Meir ibn Ezra): Jewish poet, grammarian, and commentator; b. in Toledo, Spain, 1092; d. Jan. 23, 1167 He left Toledo about 1138 and is known to have visited Bagdad, Rome (1140), Mantua and Lucca (1145), Dreux (45 m. w.s.w. of Paris; 1155–57), and London (1158); in 1166 he was in southern France. His poems show a mastery of the metrical art but have no inspiration, his grammatical works are not logically arranged, and his commentaries lack religious feeling. His exegetical principle was to follow the grammatical sense rather than the allegorical method of the Church; yet he resorts to figurative interpretation when the literal meaning is repugnant to reason. His critical insight is shown by hints that the Pentateuch and Isaiah contain interpolations (cf. H. Holzinger, *Einleitung in den Hexateuch*, Freiburg, 1893, pp. 28 sqq.; J. Fürst, *Der Kanon des Alten Testaments*, Leipsic, 1868, p. 16), though he lacked the courage to say so openly. His chief importance is that he made the grammatical and religio-philosophical works of the Spanish Jews, written in Arabic, known outside of Spain. His commentaries (on the Pentateuch, Isaiah, the Minor Prophets, Job, Psalms, the five Megilloth, and Daniel) are usually found in rabbinic Bibles. His introduction to the Pentateuch has been edited by W Bacher (Vienna, 1876); the commentary on Isaiah, with Eng. trans. and two volumes of *Essays on the Writings of Abraham ibn Ezra*, by M. Friedländer (4 vols., London, 1873–77). His poems have been published by D. Rosin (4 parts, Breslau, 1885–91) and J. Egers (Berlin, 1886). (G. Dalman.)

Bibliography: L. Zunz, *Die synagogale Poesie des Mittelalters*, Berlin, 1855; S. I. Kämpf, *Nichtandalusische Poesie andalusischer Dichter*, i. 213–240, Prague, 1858; M. Eisler, *Vorlesungen über die jüdische Philosophie des Mittelalters*, i. 113–120, Vienna, 1870; W. Bacher, *Abraham ibn Ezra als Grammatiker*, Strasburg, 1882; J. S. Spiegler, *Geschichte der Philosophie des Judentums*, pp. 263–265, Leipsic, 1890; H. Grätz, *Geschichte der Juden*, vi. (1894) 184–191, 289–306, 733–735; iii. (1897) 131–140, Eng. transl., London, 1891 98; J. Winter and A. Wünsche, *Die jüdische Litteratur*, ii. 184–191, 289–306, Berlin, 1894.

ABERCIUS. See AVERCIUS.

ABERCROMBIE, ab'er-crum-bi, **JOHN:** Scotch physician and writer on metaphysics; b. at Aberdeen Oct. 10, 1780; d. at Edinburgh Nov. 14, 1844. He studied medicine at Edinburgh and London, and settled in the former city as practising physician in 1804. He became one of the foremost medical men of Scotland, but is best known as the author of *Inquiries concerning the Intellectual Powers and the Investigation of Truth* (Edinburgh, 1830) and *The Philosophy of the Moral Feelings* (London, 1833), works which he wrote from a belief that his knowledge of nervous diseases fitted him to discuss mental phenomena. The books long enjoyed great popularity, but were not written in the real spirit of a truth-seeker, have little originality, and are now superseded. A volume of *Essays and Tracts*, mainly on religious subjects, was published posthumously (Edinburgh, 1847).

BIBLIOGRAPHY: W. Anderson, *Scottish Nation*, i. 2, Edinburgh, 1864; *DNB*, i. 37–38.

ABERNETHY, ab'er-neth-i, **JOHN:** Irish Presbyterian; b. at Brigh, County Tyrone, Oct. 19, 1680; d. at Dublin Dec., 1740. He studied at Glasgow (M.A.) and Edinburgh, and became minister of the Presbyterian congregation at Antrim in 1703. In 1717, following his own judgment and desire, he chose to remain at Antrim, although the synod wished him to accept a call from a Dublin congregation. To disregard an appointment of the synod was an unheard-of act for the time, and the Irish Church was split into two parties, the "Subscribers" and "Non-Subscribers," Abernethy being at the head of the latter. The Non-Subscribers were cut off from the Church in 1726. From 1730 till his death he was minister of the Wood Street Church, Dublin. Here he again showed himself in advance of his time by opposing the Test Act and "all laws that, upon account of mere differences of religious opinions and forms of worship, excluded men of integrity and ability from serving their country." His published works are: *Discourses on the Being and Perfections of God* (2 vols., London, 1740–43); *Sermons* (4 vols., 1748–51), with life by James Duchal; *Tracts and Sermons* (1751).

BIBLIOGRAPHY: J. S. Reid, *Presbyterian Church in Ireland*, 2 vols., Edinburgh, 1834–37; *DNB*., i. 48–49.

ABERT, ā'bert, **FRIEDRICH PHILIP VON:** Roman Catholic archbishop of Bamberg; b. at Münnerstadt (35 m. n.n.e. of Würzburg) May 1, 1852. He was educated at the Passau Lyceum (1870–71) and the University of Würzburg (Ph.D., 1875), and from 1875 to 1881 was active as a parish priest. In the latter year he was appointed an assistant at the episcopal clerical seminary at Würzburg, and four years later was made professor of dogmatics at the Royal Lyceum, Regensburg. In 1890 he was appointed professor of dogmatics and symbolics at Würzburg, where he was dean in 1894-95, 1899–1900, and rector in 1900–01. In 1905 he was consecrated archbishop of Bamberg. He has written *Einheit des Seins in Christus nach der Lehre des heiligen Thomas von Aquin* (Regensburg, 1889); *Von den göttlichen Eigenschaften und von der Seligkeit, zwei dem heiligen Thomas von Aquin zugeschriebene Abhandlungen* (Würzburg, 1893); *Bibliotheca Thomistica* (1895); and *Das Wesen des Christentums nach Thomas von Aquin* (1901).

ABGAR (Lat. *Abgarus*): Name (or title) of eight of the kings (toparchs) of Osrhoene who reigned at Edessa for a period of three centuries and a half ending in 217. The fifteenth of these kings, Abgar V., Uchomo ("the black," 9–46 A.D.), is noteworthy for an alleged correspondence with Jesus, first mentioned by Eusebius (*Hist. eccl.*, i. 13), who states that Abgar, suffering sorely in body and having heard of the cures of Jesus, sent him a letter professing belief in his divinity and asking him to come to Edessa and help him. Jesus wrote in reply that he must remain in Palestine, but that after his ascension he would send one of his disciples who would heal the king and bring life to him and his people. Both letters Eusebius gives in literal translation from a Syriac document which he had found in the archives of Edessa. On the same authority he adds that after the ascension the Apostle Thomas sent Thaddæus, one of the seventy, to Edessa and that, with attendant miracles, he fulfilled the promise of Jesus in the year 340 (of the Seleucidan era=29 A.D.). The *Doctrina Addæi* (Addæus = Thaddæus; edited and translated by G. Phillips, London, 1876), of the second half of the fourth century, makes Jesus reply by an oral message instead of a letter, and adds that the messenger of Abgar was a painter and made and carried back with him to Edessa a portrait of Jesus. Moses of Chorene (c. 470) repeats the story (*Hist. Armeniaca*, ii. 29–32), with additions, including a correspondence between Abgar and Tiberius, Narses of Assyria, and Ardashes of Persia, in which the "king of the Armenians" appears as champion of Christianity; the portrait, he says, was still in Edessa. Gross anachronisms stamp the story as wholly unhistorical. Pope Gelasius I. and a Roman synod about 495 pronounced the alleged correspondence with Jesus apocryphal. A few Roman Catholic scholars have tried to defend its genuineness (e.g. Tillemont, *Mémoires*, i., Brussels, 1706, pp. 990–997; Welte, in *TQ*, Tübingen, 1842, pp. 335–365), but Protestants have generally rejected it. See JESUS CHRIST, PICTURES AND IMAGES OF. (K. SCHMIDT.)

BIBLIOGRAPHY: R. A. Lipsius, *Die edessenische Abgarsage*, Brunswick, 1880; K. C. A. Matthes, *Die edessenische Abgarsage*, Leipsic, 1882; *ANF*, viii. 702 sqq.; L. J. Tixeront, *Les origines de l'eglise d'Edesse et la légende d'Abgar*, Paris, 1888; Lipsius and Bonnet, *Acta apostolorum apocrypha*, vol. i., Leipsic, 1891; W. T. Winghille, *The Letter from Jesus Christ to Abgarus and the Letter of Abgarus to Christ*, 1891; Harnack, *Litteratur*, i. 533–540, ib. 1893; *TU*, new ser. iii., 1899, 102–196.

ABHEDANANDA, ā-bed"a-nan-dā', **SWAMI:** Hindu leader of the Vedanta propaganda in America; b. at Calcutta Nov. 21, 1866. He was educated at Calcutta University, and after being professor of Hindu philosophy in India went to London in 1896 to lecture on the Vedanta. In the following year he went to New York, where he has since remained, succeeding Swami Vivekananda as head of the Vedanta Society in America. Theologically he belongs to the pantheistic and universalistic Vedanta school of Hindu philosophy. His works include, in addition to numerous single lectures, *Reincarnation* (New York, 1899); *Spiritual Unfoldment* (1901); *Philosophy of Work* (1902); *How to be a Yogi* (1902); *Divine Heritage of Man* (1903); *Self-Knowledge* (*Atma-Jnana*) (1905); *India and her People* (1906); and an edition of *The Sayings of Sri Ramakrishna* (1903).

ABIATHAR. See AHIMELECH.

ABIJAH, a-bai'jā (called **Abijam** in I Kings xiv. 31, xv. 1, 7, 8): Second king of Judah, son of Rehoboam, and, on his mother's side, probably a great grandson of David, since his mother Maachah is called a daughter of Absalom (II Chron. xi. 20; "Abishalom," in I Kings xv. 2). In I Kings xv. 10, however, Maachah, the daughter of Abishalom, appears as mother of Asa; and in II Chron. xiii. 2 the mother of Abijah is called Michaiah, the daughter of Uriel. "Michaiah" here is probably a scribal error for "Maachah," the addition "daughter of Abishalom" in I Kings xv. 10 probably a copyist's mistake; and it is possible that Uriel was son-in-law of Absalom, and Maachah, therefore, his granddaughter. Abijah reigned three years (957–955 B.C. or, according to Kamphausen, 920–918). The Book of Kings says that he walked in all the sins of his father, which probably means that he allowed idolatrous worship, and adds that the war between Judah and Israel, which followed the division, continued during his reign. According to II Chronicles xiii., Abijah gained some advantages in the war, which, though soon lost, were not unimportant. He may have been in alliance with Tabrimon of Damascus (I Kings xv. 18–19). His history is contained in I Kings xiv. 31–xv. 8, and II Chron. xiii. 1–22. (W. LOTZ.)

According to the more correct chronology Abijah reigned 918–915 B.C. J. F. M.

BIBLIOGRAPHY: See under AHAB.

ABILENE, ab"i-lī'ne: A district mentioned in Luke iii. 1 as being under the rule of the tetrarch Lysanias. It is evidently connected with a town Abila, and Josephus (*Ant.*, XVIII. vi. 10, XIX. v. 1, XX. vii. 1; *War*, II. xi. 5, xii. 8) indicates that the town in question was situated on the southern Lebanon. Old itineraries (*Itinerarium Antonini*, ed. Wesseling, Amsterdam, 1735, p. 198; *Tabula Peutingeriana*, ed. Miller, Ravensburg, 1887, x. 3) mention an Abila, eighteen Roman miles from Damascus, on the road to Heliopolis (Baalbek), the modern Suk Wady Barada, on the south bank of the river, in a fertile and luxuriant opening surrounded by precipitous cliffs. Remains of an ancient city are found on both banks of the river, and the identification is confirmed by an inscription(*CIL*, iii. 199) stating that the emperors Marcus Aurelius and Lucius Verus repaired the road, which had been damaged by the river, "at the expense of the Abilenians." The tomb of Habil (Abel, who is said to have been buried here by Cain), which is shown in the neighborhood, may also preserve a reminiscence of the ancient name, Abila. It has generally been assumed that the Lysanias intended by Luke was Lysanias, son of Ptolemy who ruled Iturea 40–36 B.C. (Josephus, *Ant.*, XIV xiii. 3; *War*, I. xiii. 1). If this be correct, Luke, is in error, since he makes Lysanias tetrarch of Abilene in 28–29 A.D. It may be noted, however, that the capital of Iturea was Chalcis, not Abila; and Josephus does not include the territory of Chalcis in the tetrarchy of Lysanias. Furthermore, there is an inscription (*CIG*, 4521) of a certain Nymphaios, "the freedman of the tetrarch Lysanias," the date of which must be between 14 and 29 A.D. Hence it is not improbable that there was an earlier and a later Lysanias and that the latter is the one who is mentioned as tetrarch of Abilene. (H. GUTHE.)

BIBLIOGRAPHY: A. Reland, *Palæstina*, 527 sqq., Utrecht, 1714; Robinson, *Later Researches*, pp. 479–484; J. L. Porter, *Giant Cities of Bashan*, i. 261, New York, 1871; C. R. Conder, *Tent-Work in Palestine*, p. 127, London, 1880; *ZDP*, viii. (1885) 40; Ebers and Guthe, *Palästina in Bild und Wort*, i. 456–460, Stuttgart, 1887; Schürer, *Geschichte*, i. 716 sqq., Eng. transl., I. ii. 335 sqq.; W. H. Waddington, *Inscriptions Grecques et Latines de la Syrie*, Paris, 1870.

ABISHAI, a-bish'a-ai: Elder brother of Joab and Asahel (I Chron. ii. 16); like them the son of Zeruiah, David's sister (or half-sister; cf. II Sam. xvii. 25, where Zeruiah's sister Abigail is called daughter of Nahash, not of Jesse). His father is not mentioned. He was David's companion in his time of persecution (I Sam. xxvi. 6 sqq.), saved his life (II Sam. xxi. 17), and served him faithfully to the end of his reign. He was the first among the "thirty" in the catalogue of David's mighty men (xxiii. 18–19, reading "thirty" instead of "three;" cf. Wellhausen, *Der Text der Bücher Samuelis*, Göttingen, 1871, and Klostermann's commentary on Samuel ad loc.). While Joab was commander-in-chief Abishai often commanded a division of the army (against the Ammonites, II Sam. x. 10–14; against Edom, I Chron. xviii. 12; against Absalom, II Sam. xviii. 2; against Sheba, II Sam. xx. 6). He was valiant and true, but severe and passionate toward David's enemies (cf. I Sam. xxvi. 8; II Sam. iii. 30, xvi. 9, xix. 21). C. VON ORELLI.

ABJURATION: A formal renunciation of heresy required of converts to the Roman Catholic Church. The First and Second Councils of Nicæa insisted on a written abjuration from those who, after having fallen into the religious errors of the time, desired to be restored to membership in the Church. The necessity of abjuration is reaffirmed in the Decree of Gratian and in the Decretals of Gregory IX., and found an important place in the procedure of the Inquisition. This tribunal distinguished four kinds of abjuration, according as the heresy to be renounced was a matter of notoriety or of varying degrees of suspicion,—*de formali, de levi, de vehementi, de violento*. Abjuration of notorious heresy or of very strongly suspected heretical inclinations took the form of a public solemn ceremony. In modern times the Roman Inquisition requires that a diligent investigation shall be conducted regarding the baptism of persons seeking admission into the Church. If it is ascertained that baptism has not been received, no abjuration is demanded; if a previous baptism was valid, or was of doubtful validity, abjuration and profession of faith are necessary preliminaries to reception into the Church. A convert under fourteen years of age is in no case bound to abjure. The act of abjuration is attended with little formality,—all that is necessary is that it be done in the presence of the parish priest and witnesses, or even without witnesses if the fact can otherwise be proved. The modern formula of abjuration found in Roman Catholic rituals is really more in the nature of a profession of faith, the only passages savoring of formal renunciation of heresy being the following, "With sincere heart and unfeigned faith I detest and abjure every error, heresy, and sect opposed to the Holy, Catholic, and Apostolic, Roman Church. I reject and condemn all that she rejects and condemns." JOHN T. CREAGH.

ABLON: Village on the left bank of the Seine, about 9 m. s. of Paris, noteworthy as the place where public worship was first conceded to the Protestants of Paris. Notwithstanding the edict of Nantes (May 2, 1598), the Protestants of the capital were not allowed a church within the city itself, but had to travel to Ablon. In 1602 they petitioned the King for a place nearer the city, alleging that during the winter forty children had died from being carried so far for baptism. In 1606 their petition was granted and the church was removed to Charenton, at the junction of the Seine and Marne, six or seven miles nearer the city. The toilsome and sometimes dangerous "expeditions" to Ablon are often spoken of by Sully and Casaubon.

ABLUTIONS OF THE MASS: The rubrics of the mass prescribe that immediately after communion the celebrant shall purify the chalice with wine, and his fingers with wine and water. These ablutions, as they are called, are drunk by the priest unless he is obliged to celebrate a second time on the same day, in which case he pours the wine and water of the last ablution into a special vessel, kept for the purpose near the tabernacle, and consumes them at the next mass. Pope Pius V. in 1570 introduced into his Missal the rubrics on this matter as they exist to-day. The first clear references to the ablutions as practised to-day are found in the eleventh century. Ablution of the hands is also prescribed before mass, before the canon, and after the distribution of communion outside of mass. JOHN T. CREAGH.

ABNER. See ISH-BOSHETH.

ABODAH ZARAH. See TALMUD.

ABOT (PIRKE ABOT). See TALMUD.

ABOT de-RABBI NATHAN. See TALMUD.

ABRABANEL, ā-brā″bā-nel′ **(ABRAVANEL, ABARBANEL), ISAAC:** The last Jewish exegete of importance; b. of distinguished family, which boasted of Davidic descent, at Lisbon 1437; d. in Venice 1509. He was treasurer of Alfonso V of Portugal, but was compelled to flee the country under his successor, John II., in 1483. He lived in Spain until the Jews were expelled thence by Ferdinand and Isabella (1492), when he went to Naples. In both countries he rendered important services to the government as financier. From 1496 till 1503 he lived at Monopoli in Apulia, southern Italy, occupied with literary work, and later settled in Venice. He wrote commentaries on the Pentateuch (Venice, 1579) and on the earlier and the later Prophets (Pesaro, 1520 [?]) which show little originality, and are valuable chiefly for the extracts he makes from his predecessors. In his Messianic treatises (*Yeshu'ot meshiḥo*, "The Salvation of his Anointed," Carlsruhe, 1828; *Ma'yene ha-yeshu'ah*, "Sources of Salvation," Ferrara, 1551; *Mashmia' Yeshu'ah*, "Proclaiming Salvation," Salonica, 1526) he criticizes Christian interpretations of prophecy, but with no great insight. His religio-philosophical writings are less important. In the interest of Jewish orthodoxy he defends the creation of the world from nothing (in *Mif'alot Elohim*, "Works of God," Venice, 1592) and advocates the thirteen articles of faith of Maimonides (in *Rosh amanah*, "The Pinnacle of Faith," Constantinople, 1505). His eschatological computations made the year of salvation due in 1503. (G. DALMAN.)

Abrabanel held a place of some importance in the history of Christian exegesis due to the facts that he appreciated and quoted freely the earlier Christian exegetes and that many of his own writings were in turn condensed and translated by Christian scholars of the next two centuries (Alting, Buddeus, the younger Buxtorf, Carpzov, and others). J. F. M.

BIBLIOGRAPHY: J. H. Majus, *Vita Don Isaac Abrabanielis*, Giessen(?), 1707(?); C. F. Bischoff, *Dissertatio . . . de . . . vita atque scriptis Isaaci Abrabanielis*, Altdorf, 1708; M. Schwab, *Abravanel et son époque*, Paris, 1865; *JQR*, i. (1888) 37–52; H. Grætz, *Geschichte der Juden*, viii. 324–334, ix. 5–7, ii. 208, 213, Eng. transl., London, 1891–98; Winter and Wünsche, *Geschichte der jüdischen Litteratur*, ii. 333, 339, 443, 451, 791–792, Berlin, 1894; D. Cassel, *Jüdische Geschichte und Litteratur*, Leipsic, 1879, pp. 321 sqq., 427, 425 sqq.

ABRAHAM, ē′bra-ham *or* ā′bra-hām.

This article will be limited to an attempt to establish the credibility of the tradition which represents Abraham as the first ancestor of the Israelites, against the arguments of those who doubt or deny the existence of the patriarch as an historical personage.

1. Sources of His Biography Analyzed.

Knowledge of Abraham's history must be derived exclusively from Gen. xi. 26–xxvi. 10. Other accounts—Josephus, *Ant.*, I. vi. 5–xvii; Philo, *De Abrahamo, De migratione Abrahami, De congressu quærendæ eruditionis causa, De profugis, Quis rerum divinarum hæres sit*; the haggadic narratives (collected by B. Beer, *Leben Abrahams nach Auffassung der jüdischen Sage*, Leipsic, 1859); the notices in Eusebius, *Præparatio evangelica*, ix. 16–20—are all excluded by their late origin. Many maintain that the Biblical narrative is also discredited for the same reason. It is true that the beginnings of the patriarchal history can not be dated later than about 1900 B.C., and even if Genesis was written by Moses (c. 1300 B.C.) its account is from 500 to 600 years later than the life of Abraham. If, as so many believe, the present Genesis originated between 500 and 400 B.C., a period of from 1,400 to 1,500 years intervenes. Whenever it may have been written, however, the Book of Genesis presents the conception of the life of Abraham current in the pious circles of Israel at the time of composition; and this conception may be shown to have been handed down from earlier periods. The narrative is a piecing together of the sources (E, J, and P) without essential additions by R. For the present purpose it matters little when P originated, since this portion of the narrative is a mere sketch, barren of details. It is generally assumed that E and J originated between the time of Jehoshaphat and Uzziah (850–750 B.C.); others think it more probable that E belongs to the time of the Judges (c. 1100 B.C.), J to that of David (c. 1000 B.C.). If the latter assumption be correct, the combination of E and J (which are supplementary rather than contradictory) gives what passed for the history of Abraham at the end of the period of the Judges and at the beginning of the monarchy. The Book of Deuteronomy contains passages which imply facts and conceptions written down in EJ (cf. vi. 3, 10, 18; vii. 7, 8, 12, 13; viii. 1, 18; ix. 5, 27; xiii. 18; xix. 8; xxvi. 3, 7, 15). If, then, Deuteronomy be Mosaic, the history of Abraham is traced back to the Mosaic time. It can not be the product of the inventive fancy of Israel during the sojourn in Egypt; for during the first half of the sojourn the patriarchal period was too near to admit of fancies, and during the oppression there was no thought of migrating to Canaan and settling there. It is thus quite improbable that fancy transformed wishes into promises once given to the fathers.

Most of the critics ascribe Deuteronomy to the last century of the monarchy of Judah. The narrative of EJ is, then, the oldest written attestation of Abraham; and the question arises, how far can this narrative be accepted as historical? If it is not historical the origin of its conception of Abraham must be explained. It has been suggested that Abraham was a deity adored in antiquity and afterward humanized (Dozy, Nöldeke, E. Meyer). But in all Semitic literature no god named Abraham is found; and no indication exists that Abraham was ever conceived of in Israel as a deity or higher being. More plausible is the view that Abraham, Isaac, and Jacob were ethnographic collective names (Wellhausen, *Prolegomena*, Berlin, 1895, pp. 322 sqq.). Abraham in particular was a combination of Israelitic, Edomitic, Moabitic, and Ammonitic nations. These collective names were afterward conceived of as names of individuals of remote antiquity, to whom fancy involuntarily ascribed a history reflecting the views and wishes of the later period. But there is little to prove that the names of the patriarchs were originally collective names; and against the supposition is the fact that the Israelites did not call themselves after the name of Abraham but after that of Isaac, Jacob, Israel. Moreover, the picture of Abraham presented by EJ is not what one would expect Israel's fancy of the time of the Prophets to paint as the portrait of a patriarch *par excellence*. Wellhausen says of the patriarchs as they appear in EJ: "They are not courageous and manly, but good house-masters, a little under the influence of their more judicious wives." It is hardly conceivable that the Israel of the monarchy should have imagined as the type of an Israelite indeed a man without courage, devoid of manliness, and ruled by his wife. Abraham's faith and obedience are emphasized and he is depicted as interceding with Yahweh; but EJ also makes him marry his half-sister, which was incest according to the Israelitic conception; he took Lot with him against Yahweh's command; though Yahweh had promised him Canaan as his abode, he went thence to Egypt; more than once he endangered the honor of his wife; his faith is occasionally, though only momentarily, not free from doubt (Gen. xv. 8, xvii. 17, 18). If, then, the origin of Abraham as a fictitious personage can not be explained and traced, nothing remains but to conclude that his history rests upon tradition. Like all tradition, that of Abraham may contain inaccuracies, amplifications, or gaps; but the less it answers the expectation of an ideal form or can be proved to be a product of later times developed from the past, the greater is its claim to credibility.

2. Historicity of Abraham Defended.

Another point raised against the historicity of the Biblical narratives of the patriarchs is that in the time of Moses, and later, Yahweh was a thunder-god dwelling on Sinai and was worshiped in a fetishistic manner by the Israelitic tribes, which at the same time were devoted to totemism. But this objection rests upon a rash inference, from single phenomena of the religious life at the time of Moses and the subsequent period, that the religious conceptions and usages of the Israelites were identical with those of the Arabs who lived two thousand years later in the time before Mohammed's appearance. The Israelites were not conscious of any special relationship with the Arabs, and the religion of the latter before Mohammed can not be proved to be a petrifaction of former millenniums.

3. Historicity of the Patriarchs Defended.

The effort to prove the patriarchs unhistorical from the narrative of the sending of the spies (Num. xiii.–xiv.)—because it appears questionable in that narrative whether it was worth while or possible for Israel to take Canaan, whereas on the basis of the history of the patriarchs both were certain—falls to the ground when it is remembered that the authors who wrote the story of the spies were fully convinced that Yahweh had promised Canaan to the fathers, and that they wrote with the supposition that no intelligent reader would see in their narrative a contradiction of this conviction. The most plausible objection to the historicity of the narratives of the patriarchs is the length of time between the events recorded and the origin of the documentary sources extant in Genesis. But that tradition may preserve a faithful record of former events especially where matters of a religious nature are concerned, will be denied only by those who judge the remote past by the conditions of the present. The Indians and the Gauls for centuries handed on their religious conceptions by means of oral tradition; and it is very possible that the authors of the documents of Genesis had records from very ancient, even pre-Mosaic, time. The possibility once admitted, that a faithful tradition concerning Abraham may have been preserved to the time when the documents of Genesis originated, the last reason for considering him a product of later Israelitic fancy, is removed.

4. Impossibility of Fully Reconstructing the Sources.

No one of the three sources which are pieced together in the present Genesis can be fully reconstructed. The document P must have contained much more material than the sum total of all the excerpts from it. The source E appears first with certainty in chapter xx.; and J, especially for Abraham's later years, is preserved only in fragments. There is thus no means of knowing all that the sources originally contained; and, furthermore, many passages of Genesis can be assigned with certainty neither to one nor another of the sources. Hence the accuracy and completeness of our knowledge of Abraham's history is dependent on the fidelity and good judgment with which the compiler of Genesis has done his work; and in attempting to delineate the true story of Abraham's life it is an imperative duty to weigh carefully the possibility and probability of each detail.

(A. Köhler†.)

The historicity of the personal as distinguished from the tribal Abraham is still held by a wide though perhaps narrowing circle of scholars. In the above article the difficulties are too lightly treated. The embarrassing question of Abraham's date is disposed of (§ 1) by the assumption that it can not have been later than 1900 B.C. But Gen. xiv., by its Babylonian synchronism, puts it in the twenty-third century B.C., at least one thousand years before Moses, and fifteen hundred years before the generally accepted date of Abraham's first biographer. Moreover, practically nothing is known of the history of his descendants until the era of Moses. When we seek for at least a substantial personality amid the vagueness, inconsistencies, and contradictions direct or inferential, that mark the several accounts, we are thrown back upon the fact of the persistent general tradition, which evidently had a very early origin, and to which great weight should in fairness be attached.

J. F. M.

Bibliography: Besides the histories of Israel and commentaries on Genesis, consult W. J. Deane, *Abraham: His Life and Times*, London, 1886; H. C. Tomkins, *Abraham and His Age*, ib. 1897; C. H. Cornill, *Geschichte des Volkes Israel*, Leipsic, 1898, Eng. transl., Chicago, 1898; P. Dornstetter, *Abraham; Studien über die Anfänge des hebräischen Volkes*, Freiburg, 1902. For the extra-Biblical traditions: G. Weil, *Biblische Legenden der Muselmänner*, Frankfort, 1845; H. Beer, *Leben Abrahams, nach Auffassung der jüdischen Sage*, Leipsic, 1859; T. P. Hughes, *Dictionary of Islam*, pp. 4–7, London, 1896 (gives Abraham passages in the Koran); B. W Bacon, *Abraham the Heir of Yahweh*, in the *New World*, vol. viii. (1899); *JE*, i. 83–92.

ABRAHAM, APOCALYPSE OF. See Pseudepigrapha, Old Testament, II., 21.

ABRAHAM A SANCTA CLARA: Monastic name by which a famous German preacher, Ulrich Megerle, is usually known; b. at Kreenheinstetten (20 m. n. of Constance), Baden, July 2, 1644; d. in Vienna Dec. 1, 1709. He was the son of an innkeeper, and received his education from the Jesuits at Ingolstadt and from the Benedictines at Salzburg. In 1662 he entered the order of the barefooted Augustinians, and rose to positions of authority, becoming prior of his house, provincial, and definitor. After 1668 or 1669, with the exception of seven years (1682–89) spent at Graz, he was attached to the Augustinian Church in Vienna. He was primarily a preacher, and his first published works were reprints of sermons. His definite literary activity dates from the plague of 1679, which called forth three small books; but these, as well as similar occasional writings—such as *Auf, auf, ihr Christen* (1683), inspired by the danger of the Turkish invasion and imitated by Schiller in the Capuchin's address in *Wallensteins Lager*, viii.; *Gack Gack* (1685), a book for pilgrims; *Heilsames Gemisch-Gemasch* (1704)—are of comparatively slight importance. His principal work, *Judas, der Erz-Schelm* (4 parts, 1686–95), is an imaginary biography of the betrayer of Christ, written from the standpoint of a satirical preacher. About the same time he wrote a compendium of moral theology, *Grammatica religiosa* (1691) in which the more dignified Latin precludes the characteristic pungent flavor of his vernacular works.

Abraham represents the Catholicism of his age not in its noblest, but in its most usual form. He is fanatical, eager to make converts, intolerant; constant in praise of the Jesuits, full of the bitterest reproaches against Protestants and Jews. He has the most childish notions of science; but he makes very skilful use of his scanty equipment of learning. He has a perfect command of every rhetorical artifice, and knows how to play upon the feelings of his hearers, to appeal to their weaknesses, and to call up vivid pictures before their minds, not disdaining to raise a laugh. Satire is his strongest weapon; and he is a direct inheritor of the old German satiric tradition. He exercises the functions of a critic with the fearlessness of a mendicant friar; neither his audience, nor the court, nor his brethren of the clergy are spared. The burlesque manner which he uses in treating the most serious subjects was popular in the fifteenth century, and may have suited that age; but it was out of place in the second half of the seventeenth. The force of the contrast becomes apparent when it is remembered that Abraham was appointed court preacher in 1677, sixteen years after the same title had been conferred on a Bossuet. It is only fair, however, to recall what the general level of education was in Roman Catholic Germany at the time, and to see in Abraham rather a popular entertainer than a preacher.

A complete edition of his works in twenty-one volumes was published at Passau and Lindau

(1835–54), and selections at Heilbronn (7 vols., 1840–44) and Vienna (2 vols., 1846). Single works are accessible in many editions (*Judas der Erz-Schelm*, Stuttgart, 1882; *Auf, auf, ihr Christen*, Vienna, 1883). (E. STEINMEYER.)

BIBLIOGRAPHY: T. G. von Karajan, *Abraham a Sancta Clara*, Vienna, 1867; W. Scherer, *Vorträge und Aufsätze zur Geschichte des geistlichen Lebens in Deutschland und Oesterreich*, Berlin, 1874; H. Mareta, *Ueber Judas den Erzschelm*, Vienna, 1875; A. Silberstein, *Denksäulen im Gebiete der Cultur und Literatur. Abraham a Sancta Clara*, ib. 1879; E. Schnell, *Pater Abraham a Sancta Clara*, Munich, 1895; C. Blanckenburg, *Studien über die Sprache Abrahams a Sancta Clara*, Halle, 1897.

ABRAHAM ECCHELLENSIS, ek″el-en′sis: A learned Maronite; b. at Eckel, Syria, in the latter part of the sixteenth century; d. at Rome in 1664. He was educated in the college of the Maronites at Rome and was promoted to doctor of philosophy and theology. For a time he was professor of Arabic and Syriac at Pisa, and afterward at Rome, where he was called by Urban III. He was one of the first to promote Syriac studies in Europe, and his Syriac grammar (Rome, 1628) was long used. In 1640 he was called to Paris by Le Jay to assist in the Paris Polyglot. The Arabic and Syriac texts for this work had been entrusted to Gabriel Sionita, a Maronite professor at Paris, who performed his work in an unsatisfactory manner. Abraham agreed to undertake the books of Ruth, Esther, Tobit, Judith, Baruch, and Maccabees, on the ground that he possessed better codices than Gabriel. The latter, however, took offense; whereupon Abraham resigned the work and returned to Rome (1642), having edited only the books of Ruth and III Maccabees. He was attacked in four letters (Paris, 1646) by Valérien de Flavigny, who wrote on the side of his friend Gabriel, and a sharp controversy ensued (cf. A. G. Masch, *Bibliotheca sacra*, Halle, 1778, p. 358). During a second residence in Paris (1645–53) Abraham taught at the Sorbonne, and published the concluding volume of an edition of the works of St. Anthony (1646; vol. i., containing the letters, had appeared in 1641), as well as *Catalogus librorum Chaldæorum auctore Hebed Jesu* (1653) and *Chronicon orientale* (1653), a history of the patriarchate of Alexandria, translated from the Arabic of Ibn al-Rahib, with an appendix treating of Arabia and the Arabs before Mohammed. In 1653 he returned to Rome. He published two works in answer to the views of John Selden (q.v.) concerning the early position of the episcopate, viz., *De origine nominis papæ* (Rome, 1660) and *Eutychius patriarcha Alexandrinus vindicatus* (1661). (A. JEREMIAS.)

BIBLIOGRAPHY: For his life consult J. S. Ersch and J. G. Gruber, *Allgemeine Encyclopädie der Wissenschaften*, i. 30, 360, Leipsic, 1818; *Biographie universelle ancienne et moderne*, xii. 457–458. Paris, 1814.

ABRAHAMITES: A deistic sect which appeared in the district of Pardubitz, eastern Bohemia, after 1782. They claimed to hold to the faith of Abraham before his circumcision; rejected most of the Christian doctrines, but professed belief in one God, and accepted, of the Scriptures, only the Decalogue and the Lord's Prayer. The government took measures against them, and they were soon suppressed. The name was also applied to the followers of one Abraham (Ibrahim) of Antioch at the beginning of the ninth century; they were charged with idolatrous and licentious practises, probably on insufficient grounds, and may have been related to the Paulicians.

BIBLIOGRAPHY: [P. A. Winkopp], *Geschichte der böhmischen Deisten*, Leipsic, 1785; J. G. Meusel, *Vermischte Nachrichten und Bemerkungen*, Erlangen, 1818; H. Grégoire, *Histoire des sectes religieuses*, v. 419 sqq., 6 vols., Paris, 1828–45.

ABRAHAMS, ISRAEL: English rabbinical scholar and author; b. at London Nov. 26, 1858. He was educated at Jews' College and University College, London (M.A., 1881). After teaching at Jews' College for several years, he was appointed senior tutor there in 1900, but in 1902 accepted a call to Cambridge as reader in Talmudic and Rabbinic Literature. He has been a member of the Committee for Training Jewish Teachers, the Committee of the Anglo-Jewish Association, was the first president of the Union of Jewish Literary Societies, and has been successively honorary secretary and president of the Jewish Historical Society.

Abrahams has been one of the editors of the *Jewish Quarterly Review* since 1889, and contributes each week to the *Jewish Chronicle*. His works include *Aspects of Judaism* (London, 1895; in collaboration with Claude G. Montefiore); *Jewish Life in the Middle Ages* (1896); *Chapters on Jewish Literature* (1899); *Maimonides* (Philadelphia, 1903; in collaboration with D. Yellin); and *Festival Thoughts* (London, 1905–06).

ABRAHAMSON, LAURENTIUS GUSTAV: Lutheran; b. at Medaker, Sweden, Mar. 2, 1856. He was educated at the public schools of his native country, and at Augustana College and Theological Seminary (Rock Island, Ill.), graduating in 1880. He entered the Lutheran ministry in the same year, and in 1886 was called to the pastorate of the Salem Lutheran Church, Chicago, where he has since remained. He was associate editor of *Augustana*, the official organ of the Augustana Synod, from 1885 to 1896, and for six years was president of the Illinois Conference of the same synod. He is also a member of the board of directors of Augustana College and Theological Seminary, president of the board of directors of Augustana Hospital, Chicago, a member of the board of missions of the Augustana Synod and the Illinois Conference, and was a delegate to the International Lutheran World's Congress at Lund, Sweden, in 1901. In 1894 he received the Swedish decoration of Knight Royal of the Order of the Polar Star from King Oscar II. In theology he belongs to the historic Evangelical Lutheran Church, and adheres to its original unaltered creeds. He has written *Jubel Album* (Chicago, 1893).

ABRASAX, ab′ra-sax (**ABRAXAS**, ab-rax′as).

Various Explanations (§ 1). The Abrasax Gems (§ 2).

Abrasax (which is far commoner in the sources than the variant form Abraxas) is a word of mystic meaning in the system of the Gnostic Basilides, being there applied to the "Great

Archon" (Gk., *megas archōn*), the *princeps*, of the 365 spheres (Gk., *ouranoi*; cf. Hippolytus, *Refutatio*, vii. 14; Irenæus, *Adversus hæreses*, I. xxiv. 7). Renan considers it a designation of the most high, unspeakable God lost in the greatness of his majesty; but he has probably been misled by erroneous statements of the Fathers, such as Jerome on Amos iii. (" Basilides, who calls the omnipotent God by the portentous name ' abraxas ' "), and pseudo-Tertullian (*Adversus omnes hæreses*, iv.: " he [Basilides] affirms that there is a supreme God by the name ' Abraxas ' ").

1. Various Explanations.

Much labor has been spent in seeking an explanation for and the etymology of the name. Salmasius thought it Egyptian, but never gave the proofs which he promised. Münter separates it into two Coptic words signifying " new-fangled title." Bellermann thinks it a compound of the Egyptian words *abrak* and *sax*, meaning " the honorable and hallowed word," or " the word is adorable." Sharpe finds in it an Egyptian invocation to the Godhead, meaning " hurt me not." Others have endeavored to find a Hebrew origin. Geiger sees in it a Grecized form of *ha-berakhah*, " the blessing," a meaning which King declares philologically untenable. Passerius derives it from *abh*, " father," *bara*, " to create," and *a*- negative—" the uncreated Father." Wendelin discovers a compound of the initial letters, amounting to 365 in numerical value, of four Hebrew and three Greek words, all written with Greek characters: *ab*, *ben*, *rouach*, *hakadōs*; *sōtēria apo xylou* (" Father, Son, Spirit, holy; salvation from the cross "). According to a note of De Beausobre's, Hardouin accepted the first three of these, taking the four others for the initials of the Greek *anthrōpous sōzōn hagiōi xylōi*, "saving mankind by the holy cross." Barzilai goes back for explanation to the first verse of the prayer attributed to Rabbi Nehunya ben ha-Kanah, the literal rendering of which is " O [God], with thy mighty right hand deliver the unhappy [people]," forming from the initial and final letters of the words the word *Abrakd* (pronounced *Abrakad*), with the meaning " the host of the winged ones," i.e., angels. But this extremely ingenious theory would at most explain only the mystic word *Abracadabra*, whose connection with *Abrasax* is by no means certain. De Beausobre derives Abrasax from the Greek *habros* and *saō*, " the beautiful, the glorious Savior." It is scarcely necessary to remark upon the lack of probability for all these interpretations; and perhaps the word may be included among those mysterious expressions discussed by Harnack (*Ueber das gnostische Buch Pistis-Sophia*, *TU*, vii. 2, 1891, 86–89), " which belong to no known speech, and by their singular collocation of vowels and consonants give evidence that they belong to some mystic dialect, or take their origin from some supposed divine inspiration." That the numerical value of the letters amounts to 365, the number of the heavens of Basilides and of the days of the year, was remarked by the early Fathers (Irenæus, Hippolytus, the pseudo-Tertullian, and others); but this does not explain the name any more than it explains *Meithras* and *Neilos*, of which the same is true. And the number 365 is made use of not only by Basilides, but by other Gnostics as well.

The Gnostic sect which comes into light in Spain and southern Gaul at the end of the fourth century and at the beginning of the fifth, which Jerome connects with Basilides, and which (according to his *Epist.*, lxxv.) used the name Abrasax, is considered by recent scholars to have nothing to do with Basilides. Moreover, the word is of frequent occurrence in the magic papyri; it is found on the Greek metal *tesseræ* among other mystic words, and still more often on carved gems. The fact that the name occurs on these gems in connection with representations of figures with the head of a cock, a lion, or an ass, and the tail of a serpent was formerly taken in the light of what Irenæus says (*Adversus hæreses*, I. xxiv. 5) about

2. The Abrasax Gems.

the followers of Basilides: " These men, moreover, practise magic, and use images, incantations, invocations, and every other kind of curious art. Coining also certain names as if they were those of the angels, they proclaim some of these as belonging to the first, and others to the second heaven; and then they strive to set forth the names, principles, angels, and powers of the 365 imagined heavens." From this an attempt was made to explain first the gems which bore the name and the figures described above, and then all gems with unintelligible inscriptions and figures not in accord with pure Greco-Roman art, as Abrasax-stones, Basilidian or Gnostic gems. Some scholars, especially Bellermann and Matter, took great pains to classify the different representations. But a protest was soon raised against this interpretation of these stones. De Beausobre, Passerius, and Caylus decisively declared them to be pagan; and Harnack has gone so far as to say that it is doubtful whether a single Abrasax-gem is Basilidian. Having due regard to the magic papyri, in which many of the unintelligible names of the Abrasax-gems reappear, besides directions for making and using gems with similar figures and formulas for magical purposes, it can scarcely be doubted that these stones are pagan amulets and instruments of magic. (W. Drexler.)

Bibliography: C. Salmasius, *De annis climactericis*, p. 572, Leyden, 1648; Wendelin, in a letter in *J. Macarii Abraxas . . . accedit Abraxas Proteus, seu multiformis gemmæ Basilidianæ portentosa varietas, exhibita . . . a J. Chifletio*, pp. 112–115, Antwerp, 1657; I. de Beausobre, *Histoire critique de Manichée et du Manichéisme*, ii. 50–69, Amsterdam, 1739; J. B. Passerius, *De gemmis Basilidianis diatriba*, in Gori, *Thesaurus gemmarum antiquarum astriferarum*, ii. 221–286, Florence, 1750; Tubières de Grimvard, Count de Caylus, *Recueil d'antiquités*, vi. 65–66, Paris, 1764; F. Münter, *Versuch über die kirchlichen Alterthümer der Gnostiker*, pp. 203–214, Anspach, 1790; J. J. Bellermann, *Versuch über die Gemmen der Alten mit dem Abraxas-Bilde*, 3 parts, Berlin, 1818–19; J. Matter, *Histoire critique du Gnosticisme*, i., Paris, 1828, and Strasburg, 1843; idem, *Abraxas* in Herzog, *RE*, 2d ed., 1877; S. Sharpe, *Egyptian Mythology*, p. 252, note, London, 1863; Geiger, *Abraxas und Elxai*, in *ZDMG*, xviii. (1864) 824–825; G. Barzilai, *Gli Abraxas, studio archeologico*, Triest, 1873; idem, *Appendice alla dissertazione sugli Abraxas*, ib. 1874; E. Renan, *Histoire des origines du Christianisme*, vi. 160, Paris, 1879; C. W. King, *The Gnostics and their Remains*, London, 1887; Harnack, *Geschichte*, i. 161. The older material is listed by Matter, ut sup., and Wessely, *Ephesia grammata*, vol. ii., Vienna, 1886. Worth consulting are B. de Monfaucon, *L'Antiquité expliquée*, ii. 356, Paris 1719–24, Eng. transl., 10 vols., London, 1721–25; R. E. Raspe, *Descriptive catalogue of . . . engraved Gems . . . cast . . . by J. Tassie . . .* 2 vols., London, 1791; J. M. A. Chabouillet, *Catalogue général et raisonné des camées et pierres gravées de la Bibliothèque Impériale*, Paris, 1858; *DACL*, i. 127–155. Plates of the so-called Abraxas-gems are to be found in the works of Count de Caylus, Matter, King, and in the *DACL*.

ABRAVANEL. See ABRABANEL.

ABSALOM. See DAVID.

ABSALON (AXEL): Archbishop of Lund (1178–1201), one of the principal figures in Scandinavian medieval history; b. on the island of Zealand, then under his father's government, probably in Oct., 1128; d. in the abbey of Sorö (on the island of Zealand, 44 m. w.s.w. of Copenhagen) Mar. 21, 1201. He was brought up with the future king Waldemar, amid surroundings which befitted his birth. When he was eighteen or nineteen, his father retired from the world to the Benedictine monastery of Sorö, which he had built, and the lad went to Paris to study theology and canon law. He came back to Denmark to find civil war raging among the partizans of three princes. As he was already a priest, he probably took no part in the bloody battle of Gradehede near Viborg (1157) which finally decided the strife in favor of his old playmate Waldemar; but in the following spring he and his retainers repelled an attack of Wendish pirates who were ravaging Zealand. When Bishop Asser of Roskilde died (on Good Friday, 1158), the chapter and the citizens quarreled over the choice of a successor, and the armed intervention of Waldemar became necessary. At an election held in his presence, Absalon was unanimously chosen, and soon showed that he considered the defense of his country not the least among his episcopal duties. The Danes now assumed the offensive against the pagan Wends, and two campaigns were made against them in 1159. The next year Waldemar joined forces with Henry the Lion, with the result that Mecklenburg was added to the German territory, and the island of Rügen to the Danish.

All this time Absalon was busy building fortresses and providing guards for the coasts, sometimes undertaking perilous winter voyages to inspect the defenses, with the aspect of a viking but the spirit of a crusader. At the same time he was laboring for internal peace by endeavoring to attach the partizans of the defeated factions to the king, and busily providing for monastic reform and extension. He brought to Denmark his old fellow student William, canon of St. Geneviève at Paris, and placed him over the canons of Eskilsö near Roskilde, whose house he later removed to Ebelholt near Arresö, helping them to build their new church and richly endowing it. After his father's death (c. 1157) discipline had decayed among the Benedictines of Sorö, and Absalon brought Cistercian monks from Esrom to restore it, making it one of the richest of Cistercian abbeys. He and his kinsfolk were buried in the great church there which he began to build after 1174. In 1162 he accompanied Waldemar to St. Jean de Laune on the Saône, where Frederick Barbarossa solemnly recognized Victor IV. as the legitimate pope and banned Alexander III. and his adherents. Absalon was much dissatisfied with this result; he desired Waldemar to refuse the oath of allegiance to the emperor, and induced him to withdraw from the sitting in which Alexander was denounced. He also protested later when Victor IV undertook to consecrate a bishop for Odense, and was supported in his attitude by the bishops of Viborg and Börglum and by most of the monastic communities, while Archbishop Eskil of Lund took the same position so strongly that he had to spend seven years in exile at Clairvaux. The bishops of Sleswick, Ribe, Aarhus, and Odense were on the side of the imperial pope.

In the fresh campaigns against the Wends, between 1164 and 1185, Absalon took an active part, winning from his contemporaries the name of *pater patriæ*. In 1167 the king gave him the town of Havn (Copenhagen), and he erected a strong fortress, which was of great importance for the development of commerce. He was active in establishing a system of tithes, which aroused much opposition. The disturbances in Eskil's jurisdiction (he had now become reconciled with the king) induced him to resign his archbishopric, naming Absalon as his successor. The latter accepted his promotion unwillingly, and was allowed to retain the see of Roskilde for thirteen years after his assumption of the higher office in 1178. As archbishop he withdrew more and more from political activity to devote himself to the interests of the Church. The part taken by the Danes in the third crusade was no doubt due to his influence. He was a strong upholder of clerical celibacy, and the purity of his own life was universally admired. He is also credited with having done much for liturgical uniformity; and it was at his wish that Saxo, one of his clergy, undertook to write his *Historia Danica*, one of the most important sources for Danish history. (F. NIELSEN.)

BIBLIOGRAPHY: J. Langebek [continued by P. F. Suhm and others], *Scriptores rerum Danicarum medii ævi*, 9 vols., Copenhagen, 1774–87; H. J. F. Estrup, *Life* (in Danish), Soröe, 1826, Germ. transl., Leipsic, 1832; Saxo Grammaticus, *Historia Danica*, part i., ed. P. E. Müller, part ii., ed. J. M. Velschow, Copenhagen, 1839–58.

ABSOLUTION. See CONFESSION OF SINS.

ABSTINENCE. See FASTING; TOTAL ABSTINENCE.

ABULFARAJ (**Abu al-Faraj ibn Harun**, commonly called *Bar Hebræus*; his real name was Gregory): Syriac writer and bishop; b. in the Cappadocian town of Melitene (200 m. n.e. of Antioch) 1226; d. at Maragha (60 m. s. of Tabriz), Azerbaijan, Persia, July 30, 1286. He belonged to a Jewish family which had gone over to Jacobite Christianity, but whether his father or a more remote ancestor made the change is uncertain. He finished his studies at Antioch and lived for a time there as a monk in a cave; he went to Tripoli, Syria, to perfect himself in medicine (his father's profession) and rhetoric; became bishop of Gubos, near Melitene (1246), of Lakabhin (1247), of Aleppo (1253); *maphrian* (primate) of the Jacobites in

Chaldea, Mesopotamia, and Assyria, with his seat at Takrit on the Tigris (1264). It was the time of the Mongol inroads under Hulaku, and the country was sorely devastated; but by his discretion and the high repute in which he was held at the Tatar court, Abulfaraj was able to do much to ameliorate the condition of the Christians. As a writer his importance is due to his wide acquaintance with the knowledge of his time; his works are exceedingly numerous upon the most diverse subjects. A few of them are in Arabic, but the greater number in Syriac.

BIBLIOGRAPHY: E. Nestle, *Syrische Grammatik*, "*Literatura*," pp. 46–50, Berlin, 1888 (gives published works of Abulfaraj); life by T. Nöldeke, in *Orientalische Skizzen*, pp. 250 sqq., Berlin, 1892, Eng. transl., London, 1892; W. Wright, *Short History of Syriac Literature*, pp. 265–281, London, 1894 (reprinted, with additions, from *Encyc. Brit.*, xxii.; gives complete list of works of Abulfaraj); Hauck-Herzog, *RE*, i. 123–124, ii. 780; E. A. W. Budge, *The Laughable Stories collected by Mar Gregory John Bar Hebræus, Syriac Text and Eng. transl.*, London, 1897.

ABUNA. See ABYSSINIA AND THE ABYSSINIAN CHURCH, §§ 2, 5.

ABYSSINIA AND THE ABYSSINIAN CHURCH.

The modern Abyssinia is a country of East Africa, between the Red Sea and the Blue Nile, to the southeast of Nubia. Its boundaries are not definite, and its area is variously given from 150,000 to 240,000 square miles. Estimates of the population vary from 3,500,000 to 8,500,000. In antiquity the term "Ethiopia" was used rather vaguely to signify Abyssinia (with somewhat wider extent than at present), Nubia, and Sennar. These were the lands of the Ethiopian Church, of which the Abyssinian Church is the modern representative. Christianity is now confined to the plateau and mountain regions of Abyssinia.

1. Worthlessness of Traditional History.

Native tradition ascribes the name of the country and the foundation of the state to Ethiops, the son of Cush, the son of Ham. The queen of Sheba who visited Solomon is identified with an Abyssinian queen, Makeda; and her visit is said to have led to the conversion of the people to Judaism. The tradition continues that she bore to Solomon a son, Menelik, who was educated in Jerusalem by his father. He then returned to the old capital, Axum, and brought with him both Jewish priests and the ark, which was carried away from the Temple in Jerusalem and deposited in the Ethiopian capital; and from that time to the present Abyssinia is said to have been ruled by a Solomonic dynasty, the succession having been broken only now and then by usurpers and conquerors. Of course, all this has no historic value. That Judaism preceded Christianity in the land is not proved by the observance of certain Jewish customs (such as circumcision, the Mosaic laws about foods, the Sabbath, etc.); these may have been introduced from ancient Egypt or the Coptic Church. A Jewish immigration, however, must have taken place, as it is proved by the presence in the land of numerous Jews, the so-called Falashas (see below, § 7); but the time, manner, and magnitude of this immigration can not be ascertained.

2. Introduction of Christianity.

There is no independent native tradition of the conversion of the Abyssinians to Christianity. According to the Greek and Roman Church historians (Rufinus, i. 9; Theodoret, i. 22; Socrates, i. 19; Sozomen, ii. 24), in the time of Constantine the Great (about 330), Frumentius and Edesius accompanied the uncle of the former from Tyre on a voyage in the Red Sea. They were shipwrecked on the Ethiopian coast and carried by the natives to the court at Axum. There they won confidence and honor, and were allowed to preach Christianity. Edesius afterward returned to Tyre; but Frumentius continued the work, went to Alexandria, where Athanasius occupied the patriarchal see, obtained missionary coworkers from him, and was himself consecrated bishop and head of the Ethiopian Church, with the title *Abba Salama*, "Father of Peace," which is still in use along with the later *Abuna*, "Our Father." It is not improbable that Christianity was known to the Abyssinians before the time of Frumentius (whose date has been fixed by Dillmann at 341); but he is properly regarded as the founder of the Ethiopian Church. In the fifth and sixth centuries the mission received a new impulse by the immigration of a number of monks (Monophysites) from upper Egypt.

3. Close Connection with Egypt in Doctrine.

The close connection between the Abyssinian Church and Egypt is very apparent in the sphere of doctrine. Like the Coptic Church, the Abyssinian holds a monophysitic view of the person of Christ. This question has long been settled; but it is still debated whether Christ had a double or threefold birth. The Abuna and the majority of the priests hold to the twofold view, which is the more purely monophysitic. The threefold view was introduced by a monk about 100 years ago, and is prevalent in Shoa (the southern and southeastern district). Also the questions of the person and dignity of Mary,—whether she really bore God, or was only the mother of Jesus; whether she is entitled to the same worship as Christ, etc.,—are eagerly debated though it seems to be the general view that an almost divine worship is due to the Virgin, and that she and the saints are indispensable mediators between Christ and man. Some even assert that the saints, who died not for their own sins, died like Christ for the sins of others.

The church books are all in the Ethiopic language, which is a dead tongue, studied only by the priests, and not understood by them. For the Ethiopic Bible translation see BIBLE VERSIONS, A, VIII. The Abyssinian canon, called *Semanya Ahadu*, "Eighty-one," because it consists of eighty-one sacred books, comprises, besides the sixty-five books of the usual canon, the Apocrypha, the

Epistles of Clement, and the Synodus (that is, the decrees of the Apostolic Council of Jerusalem; cf. W. Fell, *Canones apostolorum Æthiopice,* Leipsic, 1871).

4. The Canon and Creed. Only a very slight difference, however, is made between this canon and some other works of ecclesiastical literature,—the *Didascalia* or *Apostolic Constitutions* (text and transl. by T. P. Platt, published by the Oriental Translation Fund, London, 1834); the *Haimanot-Abo,* giving quotations from the councils and the Fathers; the writings of the Eastern Fathers, Athanasius, Cyril, and Chrysostom; and the *Fetha-Nagast,* the royal law-book. On the whole, the tradition of the Church has the same authority as the Scriptures. Of the councils, only those before the Council of Chalcedon (451) are recognized, because at Chalcedon the monophysite heresy was condemned. The Apostles' Creed is unknown; the Nicene is used.

At the head of the Church stands the Abuna, who resides in Gondar. He is appointed by the Coptic patriarch of Cairo; and,

5. Organization of the Church. according to a law, dating from the thirteenth century, no Abyssinian, but only a Copt, can be Abuna. He alone has the right to anoint the king and to ordain priests and deacons. Both in secular and in ecclesiastical affairs he has great power. The duties of the priests are to conduct divine service three or four times daily and for three or four hours on Sunday, to attend to the church business, and to purify houses and utensils. Priests, monks, and scholars celebrate the Holy Communion every morning. The deacons bake the bread for the Lord's Supper and perform menial duties. Any one who can read may be ordained deacon, and a priest is merely required to recite the Nicene Creed. To learn the long liturgies, however, is often a matter of years. It is usual to marry before ordination, as marriage is not allowed afterward. Besides priests and deacons each church has its *alaka,* who looks after church property and attends to secular business. The *debturas* sing at divine service; and the larger churches have a *komofat* who settles disputes among the clergy. Beside the secular clergy stand the monastic under the head of the *Etsh'ege,* who ranks next to the Abuna and decides many ecclesiastical and theological questions in common with him. The number of monks and nuns (living after the rule of Pachomius) is very great. At Debra Damo, one of the chief monasteries, about 300 monks live together in small huts. A part of their duties is the education of the young. The church buildings are exceedingly numerous, generally small, low, circular structures, with a conical roof of thatch and four doors, one toward each of the cardinal points. Surrounding the building is a court, occupied during service by the laymen, and often serving at night as a place of refuge to travelers. The interior, dirty and neglected, is divided into two apartments,—the holy for the priests and deacons, and the holy of holies, where stands the ark. This ark is the principal object in the whole church. Neither the deacons, laymen, nor non-Christians dare touch it; if they do, the church and the adjacent cemetery become unclean, and must be purified. Indifferent pictures of the numerous saints, the Virgin, the angels, and the devil adorn the interior; but statues are forbidden. Crosses are found, but no crucifixes.

Service consists of singing of psalms, recitals of parts of the Bible and liturgy, and prayers, especially to the Virgin and the wonder-working saints; it is undignified and unedifying. They believe that every one has a guardian spirit and therefore venerate the angels.

6. Beliefs and Practises. The archangel Michael is consdered especially holy. They divide the good angels into nine classes, of which there were originally ten, but one fell away under Satanael. Relics are preserved and venerated as by the Roman Catholic Church. Of sacraments, the Church numbers two, baptism and the Lord's Supper. Both adults and children are baptized, the former by immersion, the latter by sprinkling. For boys the rite is performed forty days after birth; for girls, eighty days. The purpose of baptism is the forgiveness of sins. The Lord's Supper is preceded by a severe fast; and offerings of incense, oil, bread, and wine are usually brought. The Jewish Sabbath is kept as well as the Christian Sunday; and altogether there are one hundred and eighty holidays in the year. Fasting, observed with great strictness, plays a prominent part in the discipline, and about half the days of the year are nominally fast-days.

Not all the inhabitants of Abyssinia are Christians; and not all Christians belong to the State Church. The Zalanes, a nomadic tribe, consider themselves to be Jews, and keep aloof from the Christians, though they are described

7. The Falashas. as being really Christians. The Chamantes are baptized, and have Christian priests; but in reality they are nearly pagans, and celebrate many thoroughly pagan rites. The real Jews, the Falashas, live along the northern shore of Lake Tsana, in the neighborhood of Gondar and Shelga, where they pursue agriculture and trade. They are more industrious than the Christians, but also more ignorant and spiritually more forlorn. Mohammedanism is steadily progressing. In order to distinguish themselves from all non-Christians, the Christians receive at baptism a cord of blue silk or cotton, called *mateb,* which they always wear around the neck.

The first missionary work which the Western Church undertook in Abyssinia was the Jesuit mission of 1555, which labored there for nearly a century; but the missionary activity of the Jesuits was deeply mixed with the politics of the country; and their main purpose seems to have been to establish there the authority of the Roman Catholic Church. At last they reached the goal. After a frightful massacre of the opposite party, King Sasneos declared the Roman Catholic Church the Church of the State. In 1640, however, the Jesuits, with their Roman archbishop, were compelled to leave the country, and the old religion with its old Church was reestablished. With the new Abuna who followed after this Roman Catholic interregnum, Peter Heyling, from Lübeck, a Protestant missionary, came into the country, but his great zeal led only to small results. The Church Missionary Society had more success in the first half of the nineteenth century. The circumstance that a pious Abyssinian monk, Abi-Ruch or Abreka, who had been guide to the traveler Bruce, translated the whole Bible into the Amharic language (1808–18), gave the first occasion to this attempt. The British and Foreign Bible Society bought and printed the translation, and in 1830

8. Christian Missions. the missionaries Gobat and Kugler were sent to Abyssinia. The latter was succeeded by Isenberg, and Gobat by Blumhardt in 1837. Later came Krapf. The work was partly spoiled by the opposition of the native priests and the intrigues of newly arrived Roman Catholics, and the missionaries were expelled in 1838. Krapf then spent three years in Shoa, but was driven thence in 1842. The Roman Catholics were expelled in 1854. In 1858 a Coptic priest who had frequented the school of a Protestant missionary in Alexandria, and favored the Protestant mission, became Abuna, and the St. Chrischona Society of Basel now sent a number of Protestant missionaries into the country. They labored with considerable success; but the disturbances of the reign of King Theodore overtook them, and almost destroyed their work. They were thrown into prison and were only released after the victory of the British.

Since that time, few missionary attempts have been made in Abyssinia. The Swedes have one or two stations in the country; and during the past ten years there has been some effort to resume work on the part of the Roman Catholics (mainly French). There is a vicar apostolic for Abyssinia with residence in Alitiena, Tigre; and a Uniat "Geez Church" is said to number 10,000 members. See AFRICA, II., ABYSSINIA.

BIBLIOGRAPHY: Makrisi (d. 1441), *Historia Coptorum Christianorum*, ed. T. Wüstenfeld, Göttingen, 1845; H. Ludolf, *Historia æthiopica* and *Commentarius*, Frankfort, 1681, 1693; J. Lobo, *Voyage d'Abyssinie* (Eng. transl., *with continuation of the history of Abyssinia . by M. Le Grand*, London, 1735; J. Stœcklein, *Allerhand so Lehr- als Geist-reiches Brief, schriften und Reis-Beschreibungen von denen Missionariis der Gesellschaft Jesu*, I. viii., Augsburg, 1728; V. de la Croze, *Histoire du Christianisme d'Ethiope*, . The Hague, 1739; J. Bruce, *Travels to Discover the Sources of the Nile, 1768–1773*, Edinburgh, 1790 (often reprinted); G. A. Hoskins, *Travels in Ethiopia*, London, 1835; C. W. Isenberg and J. L. Krapf, *Journals detailing their Proceedings in the Kingdom of Shoa*, London, 1843; C. W. Isenberg, *Abessinien und die evangelische Mission*, Bonn, 1844; J. L. Krapf, *Travels in East Africa*, London, 1860; idem, *Travels and Missionary Labours in Africa and Abyssinia*, ib. 1867; Lady Mary E. Herbert, *Abyssinia and its Apostle*, ib. 1868; J. M. Flad, *The Falashas of Abyssinia*, ib. 1869; idem, *Zwölf Jahre in Abessinien*, 2 vols., Basel, 1869–87; A. Dillmann, *Die Anfänge des axumitischen Reiches*, Berlin, 1879; A. Raffray, *Les Églises monolithes de la ville de Lalibéla*, Paris, 1882; T. Waldmeier, *Autobiography*, London, 1890; J. T. Bent, *The Sacred City of the Ethiopians*, ib. 1893; A. B. Wylde, *Modern Abyssinia*, ib. 1901; H. Vivian, *Abyssinia*, ib. 1901; M. Fowler, *Christian Egypt*, ch. vii., ib. 1901. For the liturgy, etc.: J. A. Giles, *Codex apocryphus Novi Testamenti*, ib. 1852; E. Trumpp, *Das Taufbuch der æthiopischen Kirche*, Munich, 1878; C. A. Swainson, *Greek Liturgies*, Cambridge, 1884; C. von Arnhard, *Liturgie zum Tauf-Fest der æthiopischen Kirche*, Munich, 1888.

ACACIUS, a-kê'shi-us, OF BERŒA: A monk of the monastery of Gindanus near Antioch, afterward abbot of a monastery near Berœa (Aleppo), and from 378 bishop of that city; d. about 435. He took an active part in the ecclesiastical controversies of the East, and was one of the principal complainants against Chrysostom at the synod held in 403 in a suburb of Chalcedon known as Ad Quercum. For this reason he fell out with Rome, but was acknowledged again by Innocent I. in 415. In the Nestorian controversy he occupied a mediating position. The Syrian Balæus wrote five songs in his praise. His extant writings are a letter to Cyril of Alexandria and two to Alexander of Hierapolis, as well as a confession of faith (*MPG*, lxxvii. 1445–48). G. KRÜGER.

BIBLIOGRAPHY: M. Le Quien, *Oriens Christianus*, ii. 782–783, Paris, 1763; G. Bickell, *Ausgewählte Gedichte der syrischen Kirchenväter Cyrillonas, Balæus*, in *Bibliothek der Kirchenväter*, pp. 83–89, Kempten, 1872–73; Hefele, *Conciliengeschichte*, ii. passim; *DCB*, i. 12–14.

ACACIUS OF CÆSAREA: One of the most influential bishops in the large middle party which opposed the Nicene Creed during the Arian controversy. He was the disciple of Eusebius, and his successor in the bishopric of Cæsarea. He took part in the Eusebian synod at Antioch in the spring of 341, and in another at Philippopolis in 343. By the orthodox council of Sardica in the same year he was regarded as one of the heads of the opposing party, and threatened with deposition. Common opposition to the Nicene doctrine held the party together until about 356. Thus, on the death of Maximus of Jerusalem (350 or 351), Acacius helped to get the vacant see for Cyril, who belonged rather to the opposite wing of the party, the later Homoiousians or Semi-Arians. That he fell out with Cyril and procured his deposition (357 or 358) was due partly to jealousy between the two sees, partly to the changed attitude of parties under Constantius (351–361). The two wings fell apart, and Acacius became the leader of the court party, the later Homoians, in the East. In 355 he seems to have been one of the few Easterns who represented the emperor at the Council of Milan; and, according to Jerome, his influence with Constantius was so great that he had much to do with setting up Felix as pope in the place of the banished Liberius. After the so-called Second Council of Sirmium (357) had avoided the controverted terms altogether and said nothing about the *ousia* ("substance"), it was undoubtedly Acacius who at the Council of Antioch (358) influenced Eudoxius to accept this compromise for the East. At the Synod of Seleucia (359) he took a prominent part. In obvious concert with the imperial delegates, he seemed to favor what Ursacius and Valens tried to carry in the Synod of Rimini, the acceptance of the so-called third Sirmian formula ("similar [*homoios*] according to the Scriptures similar in all things"). He and his party, it is true, expressly condemned the *anomoios* ("dissimilar") theory, but they omitted the "in all things," which agreed as little with the real views of Acacius as with those of the Western Homoians. The council ended in a schism; the Homoiousian majority, in a separate session, deposed Acacius and other leading Homoians. But he was in touch with the court; and at the discussions in Constantinople which continued those of Seleucia, the imperial wishes, represented by Acacius, Ursacius, and Valens, prevailed. He was able to celebrate his victory the next year at the Council of Constantinople, and commanded the situation in the East. With the death of Constantius the day of this imperial orthodoxy was done; and under Jovian (363–364) Acacius succeeded in accepting the Nicene orthodoxy which was now that of the court. His name appears among the signatures of those who, at the Synod of Antioch presided over by Meletius (363), accepted the Nicene formula in the sense of *homoios kat' ousian* ("similar as to substance"). With the accession of the Arian Valens (364), the situation changed once more; and apparently Acacius changed with it. He and his adherents were deposed by the Homoiousian Synod of Lampsacus (365), after which he is heard of no more; probably he soon died. He was a voluminous writer, but nothing remains except the formula of Seleucia, a fragment in Epiphanius (*Adversus hæreses*, lxxii. 6–10; *MPG*, xlii. 589–596) of his polemic against Marcellus, and scattered quotations in some of the Catenæ. (F. Loofs.)

Along with Eunomius and Aetius, Acacius may be said to have given dialectic completeness to Arianism. In their polemics against the Nicene Symbol they laid chief stress on the fact that the Father was "unbegotten," depending for his being neither upon himself nor another, which could not be said of the Son. They insisted also upon the complete comprehensibility of God. A. H. N.

Bibliography: Tillemont, *Mémoires*, vi. 1699; M. Le Quien, *Oriens Christianus*, iii. 559, Paris, 1740; Fabricius-Harles, vii. (1801) 336, ix. (1804) 254, 256; James Raine, *Priory of Hexham*, vol. i., Newcastle, 1864; Hefele, *Conciliengeschichte*, i. 677, 712, 714 sqq., 721 sqq., 734–735; *DCB*, i. 11–12.

ACACIUS OF CONSTANTINOPLE. See Monophysites.

ACACIUS OF MELITENE, mel-i-tí'ne: A bitter opponent of Nestorius in the Council of Ephesus in 431; d. after 437. A homily delivered by him at Ephesus and two letters to Cyril are in *MPG*, lxxvii. 1467–72. Melitene was a town of Armenia Secunda, the modern Malatie. G. Krüger.

Bibliography: M. Le Quien, *Oriens Christianus*, i. 441, Paris, 1762; Hefele, *Conciliengeschichte*, ii. 271, 275, 314; *DCB*, i. 14–15.

ACCA, ak'ka: Fifth bishop of Hexham (18 m. w. of Newcastle, Northumberland); d. there 740. He was the devoted friend of Wilfrid of York (q.v.), shared his missionary labors in Friesland and Sussex, accompanied him to Rome in 704, and succeeded him as bishop in 709. He was also the intimate friend of Bede, who received help and encouragement from Acca in his scholarly labors, and dedicated to him his *Hexameron* and several of his commentaries. Acca seems to have been worthy of his friends. He completed and adorned the buildings begun at Hexham by Wilfrid and collected there a large and excellent library. He was a good musician, and induced a famous singer, Maban by name, to come to Hexham and instruct the rude Northumbrians. In 732 he was expelled from his bishopric for some unknown reason, but returned before his death.

Bibliography: Bede, *Hist. eccl.*, v. 19-20; J. Raine, *Priory of Hexham*, i. pp. xxx-xxxv., 31–36, Newcastle, 1864; W. Bright, *Early English Church History*, pp. 447–448, Oxford, 1897.

ACCAD (AKKAD). See Babylonia, IV., § 11.

ACCEPTANTS: The name of that party which in the Jansenist controversy accepted the bull *Unigenitus*. See Jansen, Cornelius; Jansenism.

ACCOLTI, ak-kol'tî: The name of two cardinals who have sometimes been confused.

1. Pietro Accolti: "The Cardinal of Ancona"; b. at Florence 1455; d. at Rome Dec. 12, 1532. He studied law, but later entered the Church, and was made bishop of Ancona and cardinal by Julius II. He was the author of the famous bull of 1520 against Luther.

2. Benedetto Accolti: "The Cardinal of Ravenna," nephew of the preceding; b. at Florence, Oct. 29, 1497; d. there Sept. 21, 1549. He belonged to the college of abbreviators under Leo X., and was made a cardinal by Clement VII. in 1527. In 1535 Paul III. for some obscure reason imprisoned him in the castle of St. Angelo; and he obtained his release after some months only by payment of a large sum of money. He left some Latin writings including a few poems (published in *Quinque illustrium poetarum carmina*, Florence, 1562).

ACCOMMODATION.

The word "Accommodation" is used in theology in two senses: (1) the wider, that of a general ethical conception; and (2) the narrower, by certain writers of the latter half of the eighteenth century, in reference to a particular method of Biblical exegesis.

1. Greek Philosophical and Theological Usages. The ethical reserve denoted by this term was known to the Greek philosophers as *synkatabasis*, and the same word is used by the Greek Fathers for that method of teaching which adapts itself to the needs or to the preconceived ideas of the scholars; the expression *kat' oikonomian didaskein* is also employed, whence the word "economy" is often applied to this method by later writers.

Such accommodation or economy is required by ethics in two cases: (1) when, in a spirit of love, it spares a condition of ignorance existing in another's mind, or (2) when, in the same spirit, it keeps back some truth which the imperfect state of development of the other is not ready to receive.

2. Required by Ethics. Love bids to have patience with erring or weak consciences, so long as they are unconscious of their error or weakness, and therefore might be more injured than helped by a too hasty attack (I Cor. viii. 9-13). The aim must be improvement, not punishment—that one may "by all means save some." This consideration, however, is not due to conscious and obstinate sinners, in which case it would be a denial of duty for the sake of pleasing men. But this duty has its limits; it imports and enforces certain ethical requirements and certain spiritual truths; and in both cases its action must be adapted to the capacity of the receiver. The very nature of the human mind prescribes gradual progress in knowledge; and thus Christian teaching often requires reserve and silence, where strict enforcement of the command or full unfolding of the truth might give offense. Thus Christ kept back from his disciples certain things which they could not yet bear (John xvi. 12); and thus Paul does not exact the same requirements from all members of the churches under his care (I Cor. vii. 17, 26, 35 sqq.), feeding the "babes in Christ" with "milk, and not with meat" (I Cor. iii. 2). The Christian teacher can not, indeed, preach a different gospel to different hearers; but the manner of the preaching and the selection of material will vary with the stages in spiritual growth attained by the hearers. To this manner belong such things as the popular exposition of the truth, the use of comparisons and examples, and *argumenta ad hominem*. This kind of accommodation is not only not blameworthy, but is prescribed by the example of Christ.

The use of accommodation in matter, as distinguished from manner, is more disputable. It may be either negative, *dissimulatio*, when the teacher passes over in silence the existence of erroneous ideas in his scholars; or positive, *simulatio*, when he distinctly approves such erroneous ideas or consciously sets them forth as the truth, with the purpose in both cases of thus leading by an indirect road to the truth. Negative accommodation may be justified pedagogically by the fact that no teacher is in a position to remove all obstacles at one stroke, the gradual process being equivalent to a toleration of a certain amount of error for the time. Thus no reproach can lie against Christ because in some particulars he allowed his disciples to remain temporarily under the influence of false impressions, as long as he did this not by declared approval and with the distinct looking forward to the time when the Spirit of Truth should lead them into all truth; this covers the Jewish beliefs and practises which they were allowed to retain in his very presence. The apostles also tolerated the continued existence of numerous ancient errors in their converts, being sure that these would fall away with their gradual growth in Christian knowledge (I Cor. ix. 20 sqq.; Rom. xiv. 1 sqq.; Heb. v. 11 sqq.).

3. Negative Accommodation.

The case is quite different, however, with regard to positive accommodation in the matter of the teaching. There is no purely objective system of commandments, the same for all alike. Ethical law is subjective, varying with the individual and his circumstances—position, calling, age, sex, and the like. One is not to be a slave to prevailing customs, but is bound to take them into account, so as not to offend others. The same thing applies to prevailing beliefs and views; a man has to consider that he will be judged by his contemporaries according to the standards of the time and place; nay, that if he is to be understood by them at all, he must accommodate himself to their standpoint, and speak to a certain extent as they speak. This leads to a point which has been in the past vehemently discussed by theologians. The truth just stated was pressed by certain writers for the purpose of rendering more acceptable their doctrines in regard to revelation. It is their attitude which gave rise to the narrower meaning of the word "accommodation."

4. Positive Accommodation.

A transition to the theory that many things in the Bible are to be taken as spoken only in this accommodated sense is to be found in the treatise of Zachariä, *Erklärung der Herablassung Gottes zu den Menschen* (Schwerin, 1762): it asserted that the revelations of God in the Old Testament, the establishment of the old and new covenants, the incarnation of Christ—in other words, the facts of revelation in general—were only set forth as an "accommodation" of God to men. It was seen that this struck at the very root of the Christian faith; and the question was hotly discussed how far many Biblical expressions were mere concessions to the ideas prevalent at the time. The controversy lasted until the rise of the modern critical school, early in the nineteenth century, afforded an easier way of meeting the difficulties which these theologians had thus sought to avoid. With the help of their theory, such writers as Behn, Senf, Teller, Van Hemert, and Vogel sought to bring about a harmony between their views of reason and the Scriptural expressions. Thus, for example, they got rid of the Messianic prophecies which, they said, Jesus referred to himself merely to convince the Jews that he was the Messiah, without himself believing that they were written of the Messiah; the doctrine of angels and devils was simply a use of the common conceptions; that of the atonement becomes only a condescension of the same kind to popular ideas, intended to reconcile the Jews to the loss of their sacrifices.

5. Modern Theory of Accommodation.

In more recent times this theory has been increasingly recognized as scientifically and theologically untenable. It is. of course, obvious that many expressions of Christ and the apostles relate to merely local and temporal circumstances, and do not contain permanent rules of conduct. The apparent contradictions between revelation and the facts of physics and chemistry offer no more difficulty; Christ did not come to teach natural science; and he was obliged to adapt himself to current forms of expression in order to be understood, just as one speaks of the rising and setting of the sun, when he knows it is the motion of the earth and not that

6. Untenableness of the Theory.

of the sun which is referred to. But there is no case of concession to real error, still less of assertion of error, in any of this accommodation.

7. When Accommodation is Admissible.

As to the general ethical use of accommodation, a case may arise in which one is bound by the law of love not to make use of a liberty which in the abstract he possesses, lest the weaker brethren should be scandalized. From this point of view Paul lays down his rule in regard to the eating of meats offered to idols (I Cor. viii. 13). In like manner one may be bound, like Paul again, by the love of his neighbor to do something he would not otherwise do (Acts xvi. 3, xxi. 17 sqq.). Paul's acceptance of Timothy's circumcision was no concession to error; he did not cease to teach that the rite was unnecessary for Gentile converts; and he stoutly resisted an attempt to impose it on Titus (Gal. ii. 3–5). Limitations which he willingly imposed on his own personal liberty in the accommodation of pastoral wisdom would have been unworthy weakness if he had yielded to them when imposed by others when the circumstances did not justify them. This is the standpoint of the *Formula Concordiæ* (art. x.) in reference to the Adiaphora (q.v.). In such matters, what in itself is innocent and may be used with Christian freedom becomes, when it is sought to be imposed as an obligation, an attack on evangelical liberty which must be resisted.

(RUDOLF HOFMANN.)

8. Accommodation and the New Testament.

The theory of theological accommodation, so far as it is drawn from the New Testament, grows out of a particular conception of the knowledge of Christ and the scope of inspiration. (1) If one holds that Christ possessed complete knowledge of all matters relating to the natural world, the Old Testament, the events of his own time, and the future of the kingdom of God on earth, he may affirm either that all of Christ's teaching on these subjects is authoritative and final, or else that in many instances he fitted his teaching to the immediate needs of his hearers; in the latter case, one could not be sure as to the precise nature of the objective fact. (2) If, however, it be alleged that Jesus's intelligence followed the laws of human growth, that he shared the common scientific, historical, and critical beliefs of his day, and that for us his knowledge is restricted to the spiritual content of revelation, then his allusions to the natural world, to persons, events, books, and authors of the Old Testament, to demons, and the like are to be interpreted according to universal laws of human intelligence; thus the principle of accommodation drops away. (3) In like manner, inspiration may be conceived of either as equipping the sacred writers with an accurate knowledge concerning all things to which they refer, and yet leading them to fit their communications to the temporary prejudice or ignorance of their readers, or as quickening their consciousness concerning spiritual truth, while they were left unillumined about matters which belong to literary, historical, or scientific inquiry. It is thus evident that the question of theological accommodation in the New Testament turns in part on a solution of two previous questions—the content of our Lord's knowledge, and the scope of inspiration in the authors of the various books (cf. C. J. Ellicott, *Christus Comprobator*, London, 1892; J. Moorhouse, *The Teaching of Christ*, ib. 1892; H. C. Powell, *The Principle of the Incarnation*, ib. 1896; G. B. Stevens, *The Theology of the New Testament*, New York, 1899; L. A. Muirhead, *The Eschatology of Jesus*, London, 1904).

C. A. B.

9. Controversy in the Roman Catholic Church.

Under the title "Accommodation Controversy" is also frequently understood the long and bitter dispute between the Jesuits and the Dominicans as to the extent of lawful concessions to the prejudices of their pagan hearers by missionaries. The Jesuits were the first to preach Christianity in China—Xavier went there in 1552. They were attacked by the Dominicans and Franciscans, when, forty years later, these orders entered the same field, on the charge of having made an improper compromise with Chinese beliefs, especially in regard to the practise of ancestor worship and to the name adopted to designate the Supreme Being in Chinese. They maintained, however, that such concessions were an inevitable condition of the toleration of Christian missions in the empire. The "Chinese rites" were provisionally forbidden by Innocent X. in 1645, but were again tolerated by Alexander VII. in 1656, on the ground that they might be regarded as purely civil ceremonies. Clement IX. took a middle course in 1669; but at the end of the century the controversy broke out with renewed violence, to be terminated only by a bull of Clement XI. in 1715, absolutely prohibiting the "Chinese rites." The legate Mezzabarba attempted to mitigate the strict enforcement of this ruling; but Benedict XIV confirmed it in 1742, with the result of provoking a severe persecution which almost exterminated Christianity in China. A somewhat similar controversy raged in the eighteenth century over the so-called Malabar rites, terminated in the same sense by the bull *Omnium sollicitudinum* of Benedict XIV. (1742), the pope refusing, even at the cost of imperiling the future of missions, to permit any compromise with paganism. A heated controversy on the general subject of accommodation was provoked in England by the publication of No. 80 in the Oxford *Tracts for the Times, On Reserve in Communicating Religious Knowledge*, written by Isaac Williams (q.v.), which caused the author to be accused of Jesuitical and un-English insincerity, and provoked additional antagonism to the Oxford movement.

BIBLIOGRAPHY: On the general subject: K. F. Senff, *Versuch über die Herablassung Gottes zu den Menschen*, Leipsic, 1792; W. A. Teller, *Die Religion der Vollkommern*, Berlin, 1792; P. van Hemert, *Accommodation*, Dortmund, 1797. On the Accommodation Controversy: G. Daniel, *Histoire apologétique de la conduite des Jésuites de la Chine*, in *Recueil des divers ouvrages*, vol. iii., 3 vols., Paris, 1724; T. M. Mamachi, *Originum et antiquitatum christianarum libri xx*, ii, 373, 424, 425–426, 441–442; 6 vols., Rome, 1749–55; G. Pray, *Historia controversiarum de ritibus sinicis*, Budapest, 1789.

ACHELIS, ERNST CHRISTIAN: Reformed Church of Germany; b. at Bremen Jan. 13, 1838. He studied theology at Heidelberg and Halle from 1857 to 1860, and was pastor successively at Arsten near Bremen (1860–62), Hastedt, a suburb of Bremen (1862–75), and Barmen-Unterbarmen (1875–82). Since 1882 he has been professor of practical theology in the University of Marburg. He is president of the Marburg branch of the *Evangelischer Bund*, a member of the *Freie deutsche evangelische Konferenz*, and since 1888 has been the representative of the University of Marburg at the Hessian General Synod at Cassel, while in 1897 he was appointed a royal *Konsistorialrat*. He was created a knight of the Order of the Red Eagle, fourth class, in 1896 and of the Order of the Prussian Crown in 1905. His theological position is that of "the ancient faith, but modern theology." His writings, in addition to numerous articles in the *Allgemeine deutsche Biographie* and other standard works of reference, as well as monographs in theological magazines, include: *Die biblischen Thatsachen und die religiöse Bedeutung ihrer Geschichtlichkeit* (Gotha, 1869); *Der Krieg im Lichte der christlichen Moral* (Bremen, 1871); *Die Bergpredigt nach Matthäus und Lukas, exegetisch und kritisch untersucht* (Bielefeld, 1875); *Parteiwesen und Evangelium* (Barmen, 1878); *Die Entstehungszeit von Luthers geistlichen Liedern* (Marburg, 1884); *Die evangelische Predigt eine Grossmacht* (1887); *Aus dem akademischen Gottesdienst in Marburg* (1888; a collection of sermons delivered in 1886–88); *Die Gestaltung des evangelischen Gottesdienstes* (Herborn, 1888); *Gottfried Menkers Homilien in Auswahl und mit Einleitung* (2 vols., Gotha, 1888); *Christusreden* (3 vols., Freiburg, 1890–97; new edition, in 1 vol., Leipsic, 1898; collected sermons); *Lehrbuch der praktischen Theologie* (2 vols., Freiburg, 1890–91; revised edition, 2 vols., Leipsic, 1898); *Zur Symbolfrage* (Berlin, 1892); *Grundriss der praktischen Theologie* (Freiburg, 1893; 5th ed., 1903); *Achelis und Lachese: Die Homiletik und die Katechetik des Andreas Hyperius, verdeutscht und mit Einleitungen versehen* (Berlin, 1901); *Björnsons Ueber unsere Kraft und das Wesen des Christentums* (1902); and *Der Dekalog als katechetisches Lehrstück* (Giessen, 1905).

ACHELIS, HANS: Reformed Church of Germany; b. at Bremen Mar. 16, 1865. He studied at Erlangen, Berlin, and Marburg (Ph.D., Marburg, 1887); became privat-docent at Göttingen in 1893; was appointed professor there in 1897; went to Königsberg in 1901, and to Halle in 1907. His theological position is that of a "modern representative of the ancient faith." He has published: *Das Symbol des Fisches* (Marburg, 1888); *Acta sanctorum Nerei et Achillei* (*TU*, Leipsic, 1890); *Die ältesten Quellen des orientalischen Kirchenrechts*, I. *Canones Hippolyti* (1891), II. *Die syrischen Didaskalia, übersetzt und erklärt* (1903; in collaboration with J. Flemming); *Hippolyt-studien* (1897); *Die Martyrologien, ihre Geschichte und ihr Wert* (Berlin, 1900); *Virgines subintroductæ. Ein Beitrag zu I. Kor. vii* (Leipsic, 1902); and an edition of the works of Hippolytus, in collaboration with G. L. Bonwetsch (Leipsic, 1897).

ACHERY, ä"shê"rî', JEAN LUC d' (Dom Luc d'Achery; Lat. *Dacherius*): Benedictine; b. at St. Quentin (80 m. n.e. of Paris), Picardy, 1609; d. in Paris Apr. 29, 1685. He entered the Benedictine order while still very young, and in 1632 joined the congregation of St. Maur at Vendôme. He was of weak constitution and suffered much physically, which led his superiors to send him to Paris. There he became librarian of St. Germain-des-Prés, and for forty-five years lived solely for his books and scholarly work. He took especial delight in searching out unknown books and bringing unprinted manuscripts to publication, and was ever ready to help others from his vast store of learning. His chief work was the *Spicilegium veterum aliquot scriptorum qui in Galliæ bibliothecis, maxime Benedictinorum, latuerant* (13 vols., Paris, 1655–77; 2d ed., by De la Barre, with comparison of later-found manuscripts by Baluze and Martène, 3 vols., 1723, better arranged but less correct). He edited the first edition of the *Epistle of Barnabas* (1645), the life and works of Lanfranc (1648), the works of Guibert of Nogent (1651), and the *Regula solitariorum* of a certain priest Grimlaic (1656); he compiled a catalogue of ascetic writings (1648); and he gathered the material for the *Acta sanctorum ordinis S. Benedicti*, which was published by his scholar and assistant, Mabillon (9 vols., 1668–1701), and for which the latter has usually received the credit. (C. Pfender.)

Bibliography: L. E. Dupin, *Bibliothèque des auteurs ecclésiastiques*, xviii. 1445, Amsterdam ed.; Tassin, *Histoire littéraire de la congrégation de St. Maur*, pp. 103 sqq., Brussels, 1770.

ACHTERFELDT JOHANN HEINRICH. See Hermes, Georg.

ACŒMETI, a-sem'e-tai or ä"cei-mê'tî,-tê ("Sleepless"): An order of monks who sang the divine praises in their monasteries night and day without cessation, dividing themselves into three choirs for the purpose and undertaking the service in rotation. A certain Alexander (*ASB*, Jan., i. 1018–28) founded their first monastery on the Euphrates about the year 400, and a second at Constantinople. The abbot Marcellus spread the custom in the East. Monks from his monastery were transferred in 459 by the consular Studius to the monastery newly founded by him in Constantinople and called, after his name, the Studium, which later became famous. The members of the order are sometimes called Studites. In the controversy with the Theopaschites (q.v.) they opposed the views of the papal legate, and in 534 they were disavowed and excommunicated by Pope John II.

G. Krüger.

ACOLYTE: A member of the highest of the minor orders of the Roman Catholic Church. The order was established in the fourth or fifth decade of the third century, at the same time as the other minor orders, probably by Pope Fabian (236–250), but was not known to the East. The name (from the Gk. *akolouthos*, "a follower, attendant") indicates that the acolyte was originally the personal attendant of the bishop or of the presbyters. In this capacity he appears in Cyprian's epistles, where acolytes carry letters and fraternal gifts as directed by their bishop; and the same thing is seen in Augustine's time. This close connection with the higher clergy explains the position of the acolytes at the head of the minor orders. In the year 251 the local Roman Church had not less than forty-two acolytes (Eusebius, *Hist. eccl.*, VI. xliii. 11). When the canonical age for the different orders was fixed, acolytes were required to be under thirty (Siricius, *Ad Himerium*, xiii.; 385 A.D.). In the Middle Ages the liturgical functions of the acolyte assumed greater prominence, including the charge of the altar-lights and the eucharistic wine. In Rome the acolytes were divided by special assignment among the various churches and *regiones* of the city. Since the close of the Middle Ages, the order has had only a nominal existence, though the Council of Trent (Session xxiii., *De reform.*, xvii.) expressed a desire to see it restored to its former practical activity. In his investigation of the origin of the minor orders, Harnack has given Fabian as the founder of that of the acolytes; but he considers that it was an imitation of the pagan ritual system, in which special attendants (*calatores*) were assigned to the priests. However, this and the other minor orders may perfectly well have grown out of the needs of the Church without any copying of the pagan system. H. ACHELIS.

Since the Middle Ages the order has been understood as conferring the right to act as official assistant of the subdeacon in a solemn mass. No canonical age is now explicitly prescribed, but the requirement of a knowledge of Latin excludes the very young. J. T. C.

BIBLIOGRAPHY: Bingham, *Origines*, book i.; J. Mabillon, *Museum Italicum*, ii. 84, Paris, 1687-89; L. A. Muratori, *Liturgia Romana vetus*, ii. 407, Venice, 1748; A. Harnack, *Die Quellen der sogenannten apostolischen Kirchenordnung nebst einer Untersuchung über die Ursprung des Lectorats und der anderen niederen Weihen*, *TU*. ii. 5 (1886), 94 sqq.; R. Sohm, *Kirchenrecht*, i. 128-137, Leipsic, 1892.

ACOSTA, JOSÉ DE: Jesuit; b. at Medina del Campo (26 m. s.s.w. of Valladolid), Spain, about 1539; d. at Salamanca as rector of the university Feb. 11, 1600. He joined the Jesuits as early as 1553. In 1571 he went to the West Indies and later became second provincial of Peru. He wrote *Confessionario para los curas de Indios*, in Kechua and Aymara (1583), perhaps the first book printed at Lima; a catechism in Spanish and the native tongues (Lima, 1585); *De natura novi orbis et de promulgatione evangelii apud barbaros* (Salamanca, 1589), which he afterward translated into Spanish and incorporated in the *Historia natural y moral de las Indias* (Seville, 1590; Eng. transl., *The Natural and Moral History of the East and West Indies*, London, 1604), one of the most valuable of the early works on America; *De Christo revelato et de temporibus novissimis* (Rome, 1590); *Concilium provinciale Limense in anno MDLXXXIII.* (Madrid, 1590); *Concionum tomi iii.* (Salamanca, 1596).

ACOSTA, URIEL (originally Gabriel da Costa): Jewish rationalist; b. at Oporto, Portugal, 1594; d. at Amsterdam 1647. He belonged to a noble family of Jewish origin but Christian confession, and was educated as a Roman Catholic. In early manhood he wished to return to the faith of his fathers; and, as an open change from Christianity to Judaism was not allowed in Portugal, he fled to Amsterdam, where he was circumcised and admitted to the synagogue. Disappointed in the teaching and practise of the Amsterdam Jews, he criticized them unsparingly; in particular he aroused their resentment by declaring that the Law made no mention of the immortality of the soul or a future life. After the publication of his *Examen dos tradiçoens phariseas conferidas con a ley escrita* (1624) they put him out of the synagogue and brought him to trial before the magistrates on a charge of atheism. He was imprisoned, fined, and his book was burned. After some years he made public recantation of his alleged errors, was scourged in the synagogue, and trampled upon at the door. According to rumor, he died by his own hand. He left an autobiography, *Exemplar humanæ vitæ*, published by Philip Limborch (Gouda, 1687; republished in Latin and German, with introduction, Leipsic, 1847).

BIBLIOGRAPHY: T. Whiston, *The Remarkable Life of Uriel Acosta, an Eminent Free-Thinker*, London, 1740; H. Jellinek, *U. Acosta's Leben und Lehre*, Zerbst, 1847; I. da Costa, *Israel en de volke*, Haarlem, 1849, Eng. transl., London, 1850; H. Graetz, *Geschichte der Juden*, 3d ed., x. 120-128, 399-401.

ACTA MARTYRUM, ACTA SANCTORUM,

ac'ta mār'ter-um, ac'ta sanc"tō'rum.

By *Acta Martyrum* and *Acta Sanctorum* are meant collections of biographies of holy persons, especially of the older Church. The former title refers particularly to those who have suffered death for the faith; the latter is more general, including all "saints," i.e., Christians canonized by the Church on account of their eminently pious and pure lives.

I. Acts of Martyrs (*Acta sive passiones martyrum; Martyrologia*): The oldest authentic sources for the history of the early martyrs are the court records of the Roman empire (*Acta proconsularia, præsidialia*). They are not preserved in their original form, but more or less complete extracts from them constitute the kernel of the passion histories recorded by Christian hands; and they are acknowledged to be the authentic bases of these histories (cf. the works of Le Blant and Egli cited below), which, so far as they are based upon these official documents and thus demonstrate that they belong to the class of *acta martyrum sincera*, are either written in the form of a letter or are devotional narratives without the epistolary character (*passiones, gesta martyrum*). The former class includes the oldest of these histories; the chief examples are: the *Passio Polycarpi*, in a letter of the congregation of Smyrna, of which extracts are given by Eusebius (*Hist. eccl.*, IV. xv.), while the complete text is handed down in five Greek manuscripts; the letter of the churches of Lyons and Vienne to the Chris-

1. Acta Martyrum Sincera.

tians of Asia and Phrygia concerning their sufferings under Marcus Aurelius in 177 (Eusebius, *Hist. eccl.*, V. i.–iii.); the report of the Alexandrian bishop Dionysius to the Antiochian Fabianus on the sufferings of the Christians of his church during the persecutions under Decius (Eusebius, *Hist. eccl.*, VI. xli.–xlii.); and certain reports concerning North-African martyrs and confessors of the same time, in Cyprian's collection of epistles (xx., xxi., xxii., xxvii., xxxix., xl., etc.).

Passions in narrative form are more numerous. Among the oldest and historically most important are: From the second century, the *Acta Justini philosophi et martyris* ; the *Acta Carpi, Papyli, et Agathonicæ* (cf. Eusebius, IV. xv. 48); the *Passio sanctorum Scilitanorum* of the year 180, a report of the martyrdom at Carthage of six Numidian Christians under the proconsul Vigellius Saturninus' July 17, 180, distinguished by its strictly objective form, reproducing the official proconsular acts without Christian additions; the *Acta Apollonii*, belonging to the time of Commodus (cf. Eusebius, V. xxi.). To the third century belong the *Passio Perpetuæ et Felicitatis*, covering the martyrdom of certain Carthaginian Christians, belonging probably to Tertullian's congregation, Mar. 7, 203; the martyrdom of Pionius (cf. Eusebius, IV xv. 47), of Achatius, and of Conon, all three belonging to the epoch of Decius; the *Acta proconsularia* which record the trial and execution of Cyprian of Carthage under Valerianus, Sept. 14, 258. Finally, belonging to the beginning of the fourth century (the time of persecution under Diocletian and his coemperors, 303–323), there are the records collected by Eusebius, which now form an appendix to book VIII. of his church history, and treat of the Palestinian martyrs of that time, as well as somewhat numerous *martyria* of the period, to which must be ascribed a greater or less historical value (such as the *Testamentum xl martyrum* from Sebaste in Armenia, belonging to the time of Licinius, the newly discovered Greek text of which has full documentary value).

2. Legendary Acts. Much greater than the number of such *acta martyrum sincera sive genuina* is that of the non-authentic histories of martyrs which contain little or nothing of contemporaneous notices and have an essentially legendary character. To these belong, among others: two accounts of the martyrdom of Ignatius of Antioch; the *Martyrium Colbertinum* and the *Martyrium Vaticanum* ; the *Acta Nerei et Achillei* ; the *Passio Felicitatis et septem filiorum* ; the *Acta S. Cypriani et Justinæ* ; the legends of St. Agnes, St. Cecilia, St. Catherine, St. Maurice (qq. v.), and others.

After the cessation of persecutions the memory of the martyrs was cherished mainly by two kinds of written records: (1) *calendaria*, i.e., lists of the names of martyrs in calendar form for the purpose of fixing their memorial days for the liturgical use of individual congregations or greater church dioceses; (2) more detailed memorial books (*gesta martyrum*) for the purpose of private devotion and instruction, incorporating also longer passion narratives, and avoiding as much as possible the putting together of mere names in calendary statistical form. Of the latter kind may have been that copious collection of martyrological material from all branches of the Church which Eusebius composed in addition to the booklet on the Palestinian martyrs already mentioned (cf. his references to this collection, *Hist. eccl.*, IV xv. 47; V. *Proem.*, iv. 3; also V xxi. 5), but which was lost at a very early period (cf. Gregory the Great, *Epist.*, viii. 29).

3. Calendaria and Gesta Martyrum. Biographical and other notices were gradually added to the names of the martyrs in many of the *calendaria;* and by such inclusion of general hagiological matter they somewhat approached the character of the devotional reading-books. This enrichment of the *calendaria* with material not strictly martyrological in its nature (i.e., additions of a narrative character, not mere names) commenced in the West. While a *calendarium* of the Syriac Church from the year 412 (ed. W Wright, 1865) still shows a strictly martyrological character, the old calendar of the Roman congregation from the year 354 (ed. Ægidius Bucher, Antwerp, 1633; T. Mommsen, in *Abhandlungen der sächsischen Gesellschaft der Wissenschaften*, 1850) gives, besides the names of martyrs, those of Roman bishops (twelve in number). The same is true of the *Calendarium Africanum vetus* from the year 500, edited by Mabillon (*Vetera Analecta*, iii. 398 sqq.). The *martyrologium* of the Church of Rome mentioned by Gregory the Great in his epistle to Eulogius of Alexandria (*Epist.*, viii. 29) consisted of martyrological and non-martyrological (especially papal) elements, and had even admitted the older Roman festival calendar. The so-called *Martyrologium Hieronymianum* is an enlarged revision of this Roman calendar. In its present form it is a compilation edited about the year 600 at Auxerre in Gaul; but it was previously recast in upper Italy, as is indicated in the correspondence of the alleged author Jerome, with the bishops Chromatius of Aquileia and Heliodorus of Altinum, which stands at the beginning. It is a medley of names of places and saints, data of martyrs, and the like, collected from older local and provincial calendars. The Syriac *calendarium* already mentioned was used (in a somewhat enlarged form) by the compiler as a source of information for the East; for North Africa a *Calendarium Carthaginense* (probably from pre-Vandalic times) was used; and for Rome, no doubt, the Roman *martyrologium* to which Gregory the Great referred. Jerome probably contributed nothing to the collection (cf. the critical edition of the work, ed. J. B. de Rossi and L. Duchesne, from numerous manuscripts, in *ASB*, Nov., ii., 1894, and the criticism of B. Krusch in *Neues Archiv für ältere deutsche Geschichtskunde*, xx., 1895, 437–440). To still later times belong similar compilations ascribed to the Venerable Bede, to Florus Magister of Lyons (c. 840), to the abbot Wandelbert of Prüm (848), and others (see below, II., 2).

II. Histories of the Saints (*Acta sive vitæ sanctorum*) : From the end of the fourth century, under the influence of the *Vitæ patrum*, disseminated at first from the Eastern but soon also from the Western monasteries, true biographies of the saints became much more numerous. The biographies contained in the *Historia monachorum* of Rufinus, the *Historia Lausiaca* of Palladius, the *Historia religiosa* of Theodoret, as well as in other works like the *Pratum spirituale* of Johannes Moschus, and the *Vitæ patrum* and *Libri miraculorum* of Gregory of Tours, furnish much more devotional matter than the histories of martyrs of former centuries. This hagiological literature, of monastic origin, had the advantage that it was not so much exposed to suspicion of falsification by heretics or the incompetent (*idiotæ*) as were productions of the older passion literature (the reading of which in divine service in the Roman Church was forbidden by edict of Gelasius I. in 494). Under the influence of the new kind of biographies of monks and hermits a general hagiological element entered also to an ever-increasing degree into the martyrological collections of the older type, and thus brought about their constant expansion.

1. In the Churches of the East.

In the Churches of the East, the older calendary statistical form of the compilations, confining itself to martyrological material proper and serving only liturgical purposes, was still cultivated, especially in the so-called *menologia*, or monthly registers, as well as in the liturgical *anthologia* ("collections"). But besides these arose hagiological collections of considerable copiousness: the *menæa* arranged in a calendary form and divided according to months; and shorter, condensed *synaxaria* (from *synaxis*, "religious gathering") or extracts. In the Byzantine Church the large collection of legends by Simeon Metaphrastes (10th cent.), which is preserved in a greatly revised and corrupt form, exercised much influence (see SIMEON METAPHRASTES). Of the editors of the martyrologies and *menæa* literature of the Syriac Church in the earlier time, Stephan Evodius Assemani (q.v.) deserves mention, more recently Paul Bedjan (*Acta martyrum et sanctorum Syriace*, 7 vols., Paris, 1890–97); of those of the Russian Orthodox Church, Joseph Simonius Assemani (q.v.), and in recent times J. E. Martinov (*Annus ecclesiasticus Græco-Slavicus*, Brussels, 1863, —*ASB*, Oct., xi. 1–385) and V. Jagic ("The Menæa of the Russian Church from Manuscripts of 1095–97," St. Petersburg, 1886, Russian); of those of the Armenian Church, the Mekhitarists (q.v.), who published a *martyrologium* in two volumes at Venice in 1874; and of those of the Coptic Church, H. Hyvernat (*Les Actes des martyrs de l'Égypte*, Paris, 1886 sqq.).

In the Western Church, during the Middle Ages the hagiological literature, critically considered, deteriorated. Ado of Vienne and Usuardus (both c. 870); the author of the *Martyrologium Sangalense* (c. 900); Wolfard of Herrieden (c. 910); later, especially Jacobus de Voragine (d. 1298), author of the so-called "Golden Legend," and Petrus de Natalibus (d. 1382), author of a *Catalogus sanctorum* (often reprinted since 1493), are the main representatives of the writers of this legendary literature, of whose eccentricities and extravagancies humanists and reformers often complain.

2. In the Western Church.

Since the end of the fifteenth century efforts have been made to publish critically genuine and older texts. Early attempts were: the *Sanctuarium* of Boninus Mombritius (Venice, 1474; Rome, 1497); the first (and only) volume of the *Martyrum agones* of Jacobus Faber Stapulensis (1525); and the *De probatis sanctorum historiis* of the Carthusian Laurentius Surius (d. 1578; arranged according to the calendar; 6 vols. folio, Cologne, 1570 sqq.; 2d ed., 7 vols., 1581 sqq.). As concerns the abundance of matter and critical treatment of the documents, these first labors of modern times are far surpassed by the gigantic hagiological work the *Acta Sanctorum quotquot toto orbe coluntur*, the publication of which began at Antwerp in 1643. It was conceived by the Jesuit Heribert Rosweyde (q.v.); and after his death (1629) was undertaken by Jan Bolland and others. From the name of the first actual editor it is generally known as the *Acta Sanctorum Bollandi* or *Bollandistarum* (cited in this encyclopedia as *ASB*). With the exception of a period somewhat less than fifty years, consequent upon the disturbances of the French Revolution, the labor of preparation and publication has proceeded continuously to the present time, when the editors (following the calendary arrangement) are engaged upon the month of November (see BOLLAND, JAN, BOLLANDISTS). More or less valuable are the extracts from the Bollandist main work in collections like that of Alban Butler (*The Lives of the Fathers, Martyrs, and Other Principal Saints*, 4 vols., London, 1756–59; see BUTLER, ALBAN), his French imitator, the Abbé J. F. Godescard (*Vies des Pères, des martyrs et autres principaux saints, traduit librement de l'anglais d' Alban Butler*, 12 vols., Paris, 1763 sqq.), and A. Räss and N. Weiss, the German successors of both Butler and Godescard (*Leben der Heiligen*, 23 vols., Mainz, 1823 sqq.); mention may also be made of a later French work by Paul Guérin, *Les Petits Bollandistes* (7th ed., 18 vols., Paris, 1876). In lexical form the lives of the saints are treated by the Abbé Pétin (*Dictionnaire hagiographique*, 2 vols., Paris, 1850) and J. E. Stadler and F. J. Heim (*Vollständiges Heiligen lexikon*, 5 vols., Augsburg, 1858 sqq.). There are also hagiological collections devoted to the members of particular orders, of which the *Acta Sanctorum ordinis S. Benedicti* of J. Mabillon and others (9 vols., Paris, 1668–1701) is the most important. O. ZÖCKLER†.

The best-known work in English is that of Alban Butler, already mentioned. It is written in a heavy eighteenth century style. Much pleasanter reading is the work of Sabine Baring-Gould, *The Lives of the Saints* (15 vols., London, 1872–77; new illustrated ed., revised and enlarged, 16 vols., 1897–98). The author is a High-church Anglican, not untouched by the modern critical spirit. He states in his introduction that his work is not intended to supplant Butler, being prepared on somewhat different lines. Butler "confined his attention to the historical outlines of the saintly lives, and he rarely filled them in with anecdote. Yet it is the little details of a man's life that give it character and impress themselves on the memory. People forget the age and parentage of St. Gertrude, but they remember the mouse running up her staff." The style is diversified by occasionally introducing translations and accounts by other writers. The *Sanctorale Catholicum, or Book of Saints*, by Robert Owen (London, 1880), is a single octavo volume of 516 pages, provided with critical, exegetical, and historical notes. *The Saints in Christian Art* (3 vols., London, 1901–04), by Mrs. Arthur George Bell (née Nancy Meugens, known also by the *nom de plume* " N. d'Anvers "), contains sketches of the lives of the saints treated, written with little discrimination as to sources and in an uncritical, credulous spirit. *The Saints and Servants of God* is a series of lives, original and translated, edited by Frederick William Faber and continued by the Congregation of St. Philip Neri (42 vols., London, 1847–56). A second series was begun in 1873, in which the lives for the most part are translations of those drawn up for the processes of canonization or beatification. Another series, consisting of single-volume lives of various saints, specially prepared by modern writers, is being issued in authorized English translation under the editorship of Henri Joly for the original (French) volumes, and of the Rev. Father George Tyrrell, S.J., for the translations (Paris and London, 1898 sqq.).

3. English Lives of Saints.

A number of works are devoted to saints of the British Isles. As to the older works of this character Baring-Gould remarks (Introduction, i., pp. xxix.–xxx., ed. 1897):

" With regard to England there is a Martyrology of Christ Church, Canterbury, written in the thirteenth century, and now in the British Museum; also a Martyrology written between 1220 and 1224 from the southwest of England; this also is in the British Museum. A Saxon Martyrology, incomplete, is among the Harleian MSS. in the same museum; it dates from the fourteenth century. There is a transcript among the Sloane MSS. of a Martyrology of North-English origin, but this also is incomplete. There are others, later, of less value. The most interesting is the *Martiloge in Englysshe after the use of the chirche of Salisbury*, printed by Wynkyn de Worde in 1526, reissued by the Henry Bradshaw Society in 1893. To these Martyrologies must be added the *Legenda* of John of Tynemouth, 1350; that of Capgrave, 1450, his *Nova legenda*, printed in 1516; Whitford's Martyrology, 1526; Wilson's *Martyrologe*, 1st ed., 1608, 2d. ed., 1640; and Bishop Challoner's *Memorial of Ancient British Piety*, 1761."

Bishop Challoner's larger *Britannia Sancta, or the Lives of the Most Celebrated British, English, Scottish, and Irish Saints* (2 parts, London, 1745) may also be mentioned. *The Saints and Missionaries of the Anglo-Saxon Era*, by D. C. O. Adams (2 ser., Oxford, 1897–1901), is a collection of brief and popular lives brought down to Queen Margaret of Scotland (d. 1093). *A Menology of England and Wales*, compiled by Richard Stanton, priest of the Oratory, London (London, 1887; Supplement, 1892), is probably the fullest list in existence of names of English and Welsh saints, with brief biographical notices. It is a scholarly work based upon sources (calendars, martyrologies, legends, histories, acts) many of which were previously inedited. A somewhat wide interpretation is given to the terms " English " and " saint." *The Lives of the Irish Saints, with Special Festivals and the Commemoration of Holy Persons*, by John O'Hanlon, is an exhaustive work, in somewhat florid style, arranged according to the calendar, one volume being devoted to each month (Dublin, 1875 sqq.). Scottish calendars have been edited, with brief biographies of the saints, by A. P. Forbes in his *Kalendars of Scottish Saints* (Edinburgh, 1874). For Wales there is W. J. Rees's *Lives of the Cambro-British Saints of the Fifth and Immediate Succeeding Centuries* (Llandovery, 1853). Cardinal John Henry Newman's *Lives of the English Saints* (15 vols., London, 1844–45, and often) is more interesting now for the history of the movement which called it forth than as a contribution to hagiology. See also the bibliography of the article CELTIC CHURCH IN BRITAIN AND IRELAND.

BIBLIOGRAPHY: For elaborate bibliographical lists of acts and lives of saints: A. Potthast, *Bibliotheca historica medii ævi*, pp. xxxii.–xxxv., 1131–1646, Berlin, 1896 (the most complete list yet made in which the editions are accurately given); *MGH*, Index volume, Hanover, 1890; T. Ruinart, *Acta primorum martyrum sincera et selecta*, Paris, 1689 (latest ed., Ratisbon, 1859); Gross, *Sources*, pp. 84–89, 213-222, 245–249, 390–400, 442, 517–525; R. Knopf, *Ausgewählte Märtyrakten*, Tübingen, 1901; O. von Gebhardt, *Acta Martyrum selecta*, Leipsic, 1902. For history and criticism: A. Ebert, *Allgemeine Geschichte der Literatur des Mittelalters im Abendlande*, 3 vols., ib. 1874–87 (2d ed. of vol. i., 1889, perhaps the best survey of the subject); C. Janningus, *Apologia pro Actis Sanctorum*, Antwerp, 1695; A. Scheler, *Zur Geschichte des Werkes Acta Sanctorum*, Leipsic, 1846; J. B. Pitra, *Études sur la collection des Actes des Saintés publiés par les Bollandistes*, Paris, 1850; J. Carnandet and J. Fèvre, *Les Bollandistes et l'hagiographie ancienne et moderne*, ib., 1866; Dehaisnes, *Les Origines des Acta Sanctorum et les protecteurs des Bollandistes dans le nord de France*, Douai, 1870; A. Tougard, *De l'histoire profane dans les actes grecs des Bollandistes*, Paris, 1874; C. de Smedt, *Introductio generalis ad hist. eccl.*, Ghent, 1876 (contains a bibliography in pp. 111–197); E. le Blant, *Acta Sanctorum et leur sources*, Paris, 1880; idem, *Les Actes des martyres, supplément aux Acta sincera de Dom Ruinart*, ib. 1882; E. Egli, *Altchristliche Martyrien und Martyrologien ältester Zeit*, Zurich, 1887; A. Ehrhard, *Die altchristliche Litteratur und ihre Erforschung*, i. 539–592, Freiburg, 1900; Harnack, *Litteratur*, ii. 2, 463–482.

ACTON, JOHN EMERICH EDWARD DALBERG, first Baron Acton: Roman Catholic layman; b. in Naples, Italy, Jan. 10, 1834; d. at Tegernsee (31 m. s. of Munich) June 19, 1902. He was educated at Oscott College, Birmingham, from 1843 to 1848, then at Edinburgh, finally at the University of Munich. At Oscott the president, Nicholas Wiseman, afterward archbishop and cardinal, greatly influenced him, but at Munich the greater scholar, Dr. Döllinger, still more. These men fostered his love of truth and passion for accurate historical knowledge. Being wonderfully gifted and highly trained, he set forth upon a career of learned acquisition which made him the admiration of his associates. But in his own communion he soon became unpopular because he was a pronounced liberal. He conducted the " Home and Foreign Review " from 1862 to 1864 in the interest of anti-Ultramontanism, and so was condemned by the hierarchy and his journal virtually suppressed. He then pursued the same course in the " North British Review " from 1868 to 1872. His chief object of attack was the doctrine of papal infallibility, and he did all he could to prevent its adoption, but when it was promulgated by the Vatican Council of 1870 he did not follow his preceptor and friend Dollinger into the ranks of the Old Catholics, but remained in the Roman obedience. He showed that he had neither altered his views nor would he give up his independence when in 1874 he criticized with learning and candor the views of his patron and friend Gladstone upon Vaticanism. From 1859 to 1864 he represented Carlow in Parliament. In 1869 Mr. Gladstone raised him to the peerage. In 1886 he founded "The English Historical Review," with Professor (afterward Bishop) Mandell Creighton as editor. In 1895 he was made regius professor of modern history at Cambridge. He planned the Cambridge Modern History series, but did not live to see any of it published.

Lord Acton possessed vast stores of accurate information, but he wrote very little except review articles and book-notices. So his list of separate publications is singularly short for so great a scholar. He edited *Les Matinées royales, ou l'art de regner*, the work of Frederick the Great (London, 1863); made a great sensation by his *Sendschreiben an einem deutschen Bischof des vaticanischen Concils* (Nördlingen, 1870); by his *Zur Geschichte des vaticanischen Concils* (Munich, 1871); and by his letters as correspondent of the London "Times" during the Council. His lectures, *The War of 1870* (London, 1871), and especially those masterly ones on *The History of Freedom in Antiquity* and on *The History of Freedom in Christianity* (both Bridgnorth, 1877), fragments of that complete history of freedom which he dreamed he should one day write, and finally his inaugural lecture at Cambridge on *The Study of History* (London, 1895), show his range of knowledge and love of truth. Since his death his *Letters to Mary* [now Mrs. Drew], *Daughter of the Right Honorable W. E. Gladstone* (1904), edited with a memoir by Herbert Paul, his Cambridge Lectures (1906), and *Lectures on Modern History* (1906) have been published.

Bibliography: Wm. A. Shaw's *Bibliography of Lord Acton*, London, Royal Historical Society, 1903; *Lord Acton and His Circle*, edited by F. A. Gasquet, London, 1906 (178 letters, mostly on literary subjects, by Lord Acton, with introduction by Gasquet).

ACTS OF THE APOSTLES. See Luke II. For Apocryphal Books of Acts, see Apocrypha, B, II.

ADALBERT (ADELBERT, ALDEBERT): Frankish bishop; contemporary of Boniface (q.v.). He is known only from the letters of Boniface, who was his bitter opponent, and from the accounts of the proceedings instituted against him for heresy, which represent him as a dangerous misleader of the people, a skilful impostor, and arrogant blockhead, who thought himself equal to the apostles, declared himself canonized before birth, and claimed the power of working miracles and of remitting sins. It is said that he pretended to have a letter from Jesus, which the archangel Michael had found in Jerusalem, and other relics brought to him by angels. He disregarded confession, not thinking it necessary for the remission of sins, and planted crosses and founded chapels on the hills and by the streams, inducing the people to come thither for service instead of going to the churches of the apostles and martyrs. In his prayers unknown and suspicious names of angels were found. At the instigation of Boniface two Frankish synods (744 and 745) deposed Adalbert and condemned him to penance as a "servant and forerunner of Antichrist." A Roman synod confirmed his sentence and added excommunication. In 747 a general Frankish synod received a command from the pope to apprehend Adalbert and send him to Rome. The *major domus*, Pepin, burned his crosses and chapels; but the people seem to have sympathized with their bishop, who did not acknowledge the authority of his judges and who was not allowed to defend himself. His fate is unknown. Mainz tradition relates that he was defeated in a discussion with Boniface, that he was imprisoned at Fulda, and was killed by a swineherd while trying to escape. Opinions concerning him differ. Some look upon him as mentally unsound, as an impostor, or as a fanatic. Others see in him, as in his countryman Clement (q.v.) among the East Franks, freedom from Rome, an opponent of the romanizing tendencies of his time, and a victim of the ecclesiastical policy of Boniface. A. Werner.

Bibliography: Rettberg, i. (1846) 314–317, 368–370; H. Hahn, *Jahrbücher des fränkischen Reichs*, pp. 67–82, Berlin, 1863; Boniface, *Epistolæ*, in Jaffé, *Monumenta Moguntina*, 1866; J. H. A. Ebrard, *Die iroschottische Missionskirche der sechsten, siebenten, und achten Jahrhunderten*, pp. 341, 432–434, Gütersloh, 1873; A. Werner, *Bonifatius*, pp. 279–297, Leipsic, 1875; *DCB*, i. 77–78; Hauck, *KD*, i. (1904) 507–513.

ADALBERT OF HAMBURG-BREMEN (formerly often called **Albert**): Archbishop of Hamburg-Bremen 1045 (1043?)–1072; d. at Goslar Mar. 16, 1072. He came of a noble Saxon-Thuringian family, is first heard of as canon of Halberstadt, and followed the head of his chapter, Hermann, to Bremen when the latter was made archbishop, in 1032; on Hermann's death, three years later, he returned to Halberstadt and became provost there himself. He is probably the Adalbert who early in 1045 was acting as chancellor for Henry III. in Italian affairs. Henry nominated him to the archbishopric of Hamburg, probably in 1045, though some recent historians have placed the date at 1043. He soon showed that he had a lofty conception of the dignity of his office; and his ambition was supported by many advantages—a handsome and imposing presence, intellectual force, and the reputation of singular personal purity and moderation at a time when such qualities were rare. The reign of Henry III. was the period of his success and domination. King and archbishop, endowed with similar gifts, were attracted to each other, and found it necessary to make common cause against the Saxon dukes of the Billung house, who had already troubled the Church of Hamburg. Adalbert's frequent absences from his diocese gave the Billungs opportunity to attack it; but the archbishop, often accompanied by his vassals, could not avoid spending considerable time on the king's business. He accompanied Henry on his campaign of 1045, and went to Rome with him in the next year, taking part in the synods which deposed the three rival claimants for the papal see (Benedict IX., Sylvester III., and Gregory VI., qq.v.). Henry was minded to make him pope, but he firmly declined, and suggested the candidate on whom the choice finally fell, Suidger, bishop of Bamberg (see CLEMENT II.).

Adalbert returned with Henry in May, 1047, and devoted himself to diocesan affairs. In the territories of the Abodrites (Obotrites) Gottschalk had gained supreme power, and worked with Adalbert for the introduction of Christianity (see GOTTSCHALK, 2). Norway, Sweden, and Denmark had all recognized the spiritual jurisdiction of Hamburg; but an effort was now made to break away from it. Svend Estridsen, king of Denmark after 1047, made an alliance with Henry through Adalbert's mediation, and brought forward a plan for the establishment of a separate ecclesiastical province in Denmark, with an archbishop and seven suffragans. Adalbert naturally could not look with complacency on the withdrawal of so large a part of his jurisdiction, after the sacrifices which the Church of Hamburg had made in the previous two hundred years for the evangelization of the northern kingdoms; and he feared that Sweden and Norway would follow. Yet he could not deny that there was some justification for Svend's desire. The emperor and Pope Leo IX., who took part in the Council of Mainz in 1049, seemed not indisposed to grant it. Adalbert offered to consent, on condition that he should have the rank of patriarch for the whole north. This, he thought, would solve the difficulty; one archbishop could not be subject to another, but might be to a patriarch. The project grew on him; and he planned the establishment of eleven new German sees to serve as a basis for his dignity. He did not contemplate any immediate rejection of Rome's suzerainty; but it was obvious that his plan might easily give him a position in the north not far short of that which the pope held in the south. Leo died in 1054, and Henry in 1056; and further thought of so far-reaching a scheme had to be postponed.

Deprived of Henry's support, Adalbert suffered much at the hands of the Billung dukes. Henry's son and successor (but five years old at his father's death) in 1062 fell into the power of Anno, archbishop of Cologne (q.v.); but the latter was soon forced to share his power with Adalbert, and then to see it passing more and more into his rival's hands. Of the two, Adalbert had much the better influence on the young king. He reached the height of his power when he had the king proclaimed of age at Worms (Mar. 29, 1065), and practically held the government in his own hands. But in Jan., 1066, the princes, with Anno at their head, forced Henry to banish Adalbert from court; and his remaining years were clouded by many troubles. New assaults of the Billungs forced him to flee from Hamburg. Paganism once more got the upper hand among the Wends, who laid waste the neighboring Christian lands; in Sweden the Church had to fight for its very existence. He was recalled to court in 1069, but did not succeed in restoring the prestige of his position. He still worked for the consolidation of the royal power in Germany, but had to leave the Saxon problem behind him unsolved. He bore long physical sufferings with remarkable firmness, laboring to the last for the king and for his diocese. He wished to be buried at Hamburg; but the destruction of that city by the Wends prevented this; and his body was laid in the cathedral of Bremen, the rebuilding of which he had himself completed.

(CARL BERTHEAU.)

BIBLIOGRAPHY: Bruno, *De bello Saxonico*, in *MGH*, *Script.*, v. (1844) 327–384 (2d ed., by W. Wattenbach, in *Script. rer. Germ.*, sæc. xi, 1880); Adam of Bremen, *Gesta Hammaburgensis ecclesiæ pontificum*, in *MGH*, *Script.*, vii. (1846) 267–389 (printed separately, Hanover, 1846; 2d ed., 1876), Germ. transl. by J. C. M. Laurent (2d ed., by W. Wattenbach, Leipsic, 1888); *Chronicon Gozecensis*, in *MGH*, *Script.*, x. (1852) 140–157; Colmar Grünhagen, *Adalbert Erzbischof von Hamburg*, Leipsic, 1854; Lambert, *Annales*, in *MGH*, *Script.*, xvi. (1859), 645–650 (2d ed., by Holder-Egger, in *Script. rer. Germ.*, 1894); E. Steindorff, *Jahrbücher des deutschen Reichs unter Heinrich III.*, 2 vols., Leipsic, 1874–81, and in *ADB*, i. 56–61; G. Dehio, *Geschichte des Erzbistums Hamburg-Bremen*, i. 178–277. Berlin, 1876; R. Ballheimer, *Zeittafeln zur hamburgischen Geschichte*, pp. 18–24, Hamburg, 1895; Hauck, *KD*, iii. 649–664.

ADALBERT OF PRAGUE (Czech, *Woitech*, "Comfort of the Army"): An early German missionary, sometimes improperly called "the Apostle of the Slavs" or "of the Prussians"; b. about 950; murdered Apr. 23, 997 He was the son of a rich Czech nobleman named Slavenik, connected with the royal house of Saxony. He was educated at Magdeburg, but on the death of Adalbert (981), first archbishop of that place, whose name he had taken at confirmation, he returned home and was ordained priest by Thietmar, the first bishop of Prague, whom he succeeded two years later. He received investiture at Verona from Emperor Otho II., his kinsman, and was consecrated by Willigis, archbishop of Mainz, his metropolitan. His troubles soon began. The attempt to execute strictly what he conceived to be his episcopal duties brought him into conflict with his countrymen, who were hard to wean from their heathen customs. After five years of struggle, he left his diocese, intending to make a pilgrimage to Jerusalem; but after a sojourn at Monte Cassino, he entered the monastery of St. Boniface at Rome, where he led a singularly devoted and ascetic life. In 992, however, he was required by the pope and his metropolitan to return to Prague. The conflict with stubbornly persistent heathen customs—polygamy, witchcraft, slavery—proved as hard as ever, and he once more left his diocese, returning, after a missionary tour in Hungary, to the peaceful seclusion of his Roman cloister.

In 996 Willigis visited Rome and obtained fresh orders for Adelbert to return to his see, with permission to go and preach to the heathen only in case his flock should absolutely refuse to receive him. He went north in company with the young emperor, Otho III., and in the next spring, through Poland, approached Bohemia. Things had grown worse than ever there: his family had fallen under suspicion of treason through their connections with Germany and Poland; and the greater part of them had been put to death. His offer to return to Prague having been contumeliously rejected, he felt himself free to turn to the work which he desired among the heathen Prussians. Here he was killed by a pagan priest before he had succeeded in accomplishing much. His body was brought by the Duke of Poland and buried at Gnesen, whence it was taken to Prague in 1039. (A. Hauck.)

Bibliography: J. Canaparius, *Vita Adalberti*, in *MGH, Script.*, iv. (1841) 574–620; Bruno, *Vita Adalberti*, ib. pp. 595–612; *Miracula Adelberti*, ib. 613–616; *Passio Adalberti*, ib., xv. part 2 (1888), 705–708; *De St. Adalberto*, ib. pp. 1177–84; *MPL*, cxxxvii. 859–888 (life and miracles); H. Zeissberg, *Die polnische Geschichtsschreibung des Mittelalters*, pp. 19 sqq., Leipsic, 1873; H. G. Voigt, *Adalbert von Prag*, Berlin, 1898; Hauck, *KD*, iii. (1906) 1041 sqq.

ADALBOLD, ad′al-bōld: Bishop of Utrecht; d. Nov. 27, 1026. He was born probably in the Low Countries, and received his education partly from Notker of Liége. He became a canon of Laubach, and apparently was a teacher there. The emperor Henry II., who had a great regard for him, invited him to the court, and nominated him as Bishop of Utrecht (1010), and he must be regarded as the principal founder of the territorial possessions of the diocese, especially by the acquisition in 1024 and 1026 of the counties of Thrente and Teisterbant. He was obliged to defend his bishopric not only against frequent inroads by the Normans, but also against the aggressions of neighboring nobles. He was unsuccessful in the attempt to vindicate the possession of the district of Merwede (Mirevidu), between the mouths of the Maas and the Waal, against Dietrich III. of Holland. The imperial award required the restitution of this territory to the bishop and the destruction of a castle which Dietrich had built to control the navigation of the Maas; but the expedition under Godfrey of Brabant which undertook to enforce this decision was defeated; and in the subsequent agreement the disputed land remained in Dietrich's possession. Adalbold was active in promoting the building of churches and monasteries in his diocese. His principal achievement of this kind was the completion within a few years of the great cathedral of St. Martin at Utrecht. He restored the monastery of Thiel, and completed that of Hohorst, begun by his predecessor Ansfried. To the charge of the latter he appointed Poppo of Stablo, and thus introduced the Cluniac reform into the diocese.

Adalbold is also to be mentioned as an author. A life of Henry II., carried down to 1012, has been ascribed to him; but the evidence in favor of attributing to him the extant fragment of such a life (*MGH, Script.*, iv., 1841, 679–695; *MPL*, cxl. 87–108) is not decisive. He wrote a mathematical treatise upon squaring the circle (*MPL*, cxl. 1103–08), and dedicated it to Pope Sylvester II., who was himself a noted mathematician. There is also extant a philosophical exposition of a passage of Boethius (ed. W. Moll in *Kerkhistorisch Archief*, iii., Amsterdam, 1862. pp. 198–213). The discussion *Quemadmodum indubitanter musicæ consonantiæ judicari possint* (ed. M. Gerbert, in *Scriptores ecclesiastici de musica sacra*, i., St. Blasien, 1784, pp. 303–312; *MPL*, cxl. 1109) seems to have been ascribed to him on insufficient grounds

(A. Hauck.)

Bibliography: Van der Aa, *Adelbold, bisschop van Utrecht*, Utrecht, 1862; Hauck, *KD*, iii.

ADALDAG, ad′al-dāg: Seventh archbishop of Hamburg-Bremen (937–988); d. at Bremen Apr. 28 or 29, 988. He was of noble birth, a relation and pupil of Bishop Adalward of Verden and became canon of Hildesheim. Otho I. made him his chancellor and notary immediately after his accession, and on the death of Archbishop Unni of Hamburg-Bremen (936) nominated him to the vacant see. None of the early incumbents of the see ruled so long a time; and none did so much for the diocese, though his success was partly the fruit of his predecessors' labors and of peculiarly favorable circumstances. Under Adaldag the metropolitan see obtained its first suffragans, by the erection of the bishoprics of Ripen, Sleswick, and Aarhus; and that of Aldenburg was also placed under Hamburg, though the Slavic territories of the present Oldenburg had formerly belonged to the diocese of Verden. He resisted successfully a renewal of the efforts of Cologne to claim jurisdiction over Bremen (see Adalgar). He gained many privileges for his see, in jurisdiction, possession of land, and market rights, by his close relations with the emperors, especially Otho I. He accompanied the latter on his journey to Rome, and remained with him from 961 to 965, and is mentioned as the emperor's chief counselor at the time of his coronation in Rome. Otho placed the deposed pope Benedict V in his custody. After Adaldag's return to Hamburg, he still maintained these relations, and his privileges were confirmed by Otho II. and by the regency of Otho III. The later years of his life were troubled by inroads of the Danes and Slavonians on the north, and he may have witnessed the sack of Hamburg by the latter under Mistiwoi (if its date, as Usinger and Dehio think, was 983). (Carl Bertheau.)

Bibliography: Adam of Bremen, *Gesta Hammenburgensis ecclesiæ pontificum*, in *MGH, Script.*, vii. (1846) 267–389 (issued separately, Hanover, 1846; 2d ed., 1876); W. von Giesebrecht, *Geschichte der deutschen Kaiserzeit*, i., Brunswick, 1874; R. Köpcke and E. Dümmler, *Kaiser Otto der Grosse*, Leipsic, 1876; G. Dehio, *Geschichte des Erzbistums Hamburg-Bremen*, i. 65, 104–132, Berlin, 1877; Hauck, *KD*, vol. ii.

ADALGAR, ad′al-gār: Third archbishop of Hamburg-Bremen (888–909); d. May 9, 909. When Rimbert, who was appointed in 865 to succeed Ansgar, the first archbishop of Hamburg, stopped at the abbey of Corvey on his way to his field of labor, the abbot Adalgar gave him his brother, also named Adalgar, as a companion. The younger Adalgar was then a deacon. Toward the end of Rimbert's life he was consecrated bishop to assist the latter; and he succeeded him in the archbishopric (June 11, 888). During the latter half of his twenty years' rule, age and infirmity made it necessary for him also to have a coadjutor in the person of Hoger, another monk of Corvey; and later five neighboring bishops were charged to assist the archbishop in his metropolitan duties.

Adalgar lived in troublous times. Although Arnulf's victory over the Normans (891) was a relief to his diocese, and although under Louis the Child (900–911) it suffered less from Hungarian onslaughts than the districts to the south and east of it, yet the general confusion restricted Adalgar's activity, and he was able to do very little in the northern kingdoms which were supposed to be part of his mission. There were also new contests over the relation of Bremen to the archiepiscopal see of Cologne. Bremen had originally been under the jurisdiction of Cologne; but this relation was dissolved on the reestablishment of the archbishopric of Hamburg in 848; and Pope Nicholas I. had confirmed the subordination of Bremen to Hamburg in 864 (see Ansgar; Hamburg, Archbishopric of). In 890 Archbishop Hermann of Cologne wrote to Pope Stephen VI., demanding that the archbishop of Hamburg, as bishop of Bremen be subject to him. The course of the controversy is somewhat obscure; but it is known that Stephen cited both contestants to Rome, and when Adalgar alone appeared, Hermann being represented by delegates with unsatisfactory credentials, the pope referred the matter to Archbishop Fulk of Reims, to decide in a synod at Worms. In the mean time Stephen died; and his successor Formosus placed the investigation in the hands of a synod which met at Frankfort in 892 under Hatto of Mainz. On the basis of its report, Formosus decided that Bremen should be united to Hamburg so long as the latter had no suffragan sees, but should revert to Cologne when any were erected, the archbishop of Hamburg meanwhile taking part in the provincial synods of Cologne, without thereby admitting his subordination. Little is known of Adalgar's personality. From the way in which Rimbert's biographer and Adam of Bremen speak of him, he seems to have been a man of some force, but perhaps not strong enough for the difficult times in which his activity was cast.

(Carl Bertheau.)

Bibliography: *Vita Rimberti*, in *MGH, Script.*, ii. (1829) 764–775, and in *MPL*, cxxvi. 991–1010; Adam of Bremen, *Gesta Hammenburgensis ecclesiæ pontificum*, in *MGH, Script.*, vii. (1846) 267–389 (issued separately, Hanover, 1846; 2d ed., 1876); Jaffé, *Regesta*, vol. i.; G. Dehio, *Geschichte des Erzbistums Hamburg-Bremen*, i. 97–100, Berlin, 1877; Hauck, *KD*, vol. ii.

ADALHARD AND WALA, ad'al-hārd, wā'la: Abbots of Corbie (10 m. e. of Amiens) from about 775 to 834. They were brothers, cousins of Charlemagne, pupils and friends of Alcuin and Paul the Deacon, and men of much authority and influence in both church and state. The elder, Adalhard (b. about 751; d. Jan. 2, 826), was interested in the German language and the education of the clergy, and is especially famous for the establishment of diocesan colleges and the foundation of the abbey of New Corbie (Corvey) on the Weser (see Corvey). He gave new laws to his monastery of Corbie (*MPL*, cv. 535–550), and defended against Pope Leo III. the resolutions *de exitu Spiritus Sancti* passed in the autumn of 809 by the Synod of Aachen (see Filioque Controversy). When Charlemagne's son Pepin, king of Italy, died (810), Adalhard was appointed counselor of his young son Bernard in the government of Italy.

The younger brother, Wala (d. at Bobbio in Italy Sept. 12, 836), also enjoyed the confidence of Charlemagne, and became chief of the counts of Saxony. In 812 he was sent to join Adalhard and Bernard in Italy and work for the choice of the last-named as king of the Lombards. After the death of Charlemagne and the accession of the incapable Louis (814), whom the brothers had always opposed, they returned to Corbie, and fell into disgrace for having favored Bernard. They were deprived of their estates and Adalhard was banished. After seven years, however, a reconciliation took place between them and Louis. Wala, as successor of Adalhard at Corbie, continued his brother's work and gave especial care to the mission in the north. As head of the opposition to the repeal of the law of succession of 817 and a bold defender of the rights of the Church, he was imprisoned by Louis in 830, and regained his liberty only when, in 833, Louis's eldest son, Lothair, the future emperor, came north with an army, accompanied by Pope Gregory IV Wala's counsel was gratefully received by both Lothair and Gregory; and the former rewarded him with the abbey of Bobbio in northern Italy. Just before his death Wala became reconciled with Louis, and, at the head of an embassy sent to that monarch by Lothair, made peace between father and son.

A. Werner.

Bibliography: Paschasius Radbertus, *Vita Adelhardi*, complete in *ASM*, iv. 1, pp. 308–344; *Vita Walæ*, ib. pp. 455–522; also in *MPL*, cxx. 1507–1650; extracts in *MGH, Script.*, ii. (1829) 524–569; F. Funk, *Ludwig der Fromme*, Frankfort, 1832; Himly, *Wala et Louis-le-Débonnaire*, Paris, 1849; Jaffé, *Regesta*, vol. i.; A. Enck, *De St. Adalhardo abbate Corbeiæ antiquæ et novæ*, Münster, 1873; B. E. Simson, *Jahrbücher des fränkischen Reichs unter Ludwig dem Frommen*, i., Munich, 1874; Hauck, *KD*, vol. ii.; W. Wattenbach, *DGQ*, i. (1893) 250, ii. (1894) 170; D. C. Munro and G. C. Sellery, *Mediæval Civilization*, pp. 319-320, New York, 1904.

ADAM.

I. Doctrinal.
- The Biblical Statement Interpreted Literally (§ 1).
- The Position of Adam to the Race (§ 2).
- The Orthodox Views (§ 3).
- The Evolutionary Views (§ 4).

II. Historical.
- The Use of "Adam" as a Proper Name (§ 1).
- Foreign Influence in P (§ 2).
- The Aim and Plan of P (§ 3).
- The Narrative of J (§ 4).
- Parallels in Other Literatures (§ 5).
- The Literary Material Mythical in Character (§ 6).
- New Testament References (§ 7).

I. Doctrinal: According to the literal statement of Genesis (v. 2), the name "Adam" (Heb. *adham*, "man") was given by God himself to the first human being. The important place occupied by man, according to the Biblical idea, is the close, the appointed climax, of creation. Inanimate nature looked forward to man. To *his* creation God gave special care. It was sufficient for the Creator to order the other creatures into being; but man was molded by the divine fingers out of the dust of the earth. Thus far he belonged to the created world; but into him God breathed the breath of life, and thus put him in an immeasurably higher place; for the possession of this breath made him the "image" of God. What this "image" was is learned from the Bible (Gen. i. 26, ii. 7); it was likeness to God in the government of the creatures and in the possession of

1. The Biblical Statement Interpreted Literally.

the same spirit (see IMAGE OF GOD). God, the absolute personality, reflects himself in man and, therefore, the latter becomes the lord of creation. Adam was the representative of the race—humanity in person. Opposite to the species and genera of beasts stood the single man. He was not a male, still less a man-woman; he was man. Out of him, as the progenitor of the race, Eve was taken.

But man's true position can not be comprehended until he is considered in relation to Christ, the second man, as is most clearly expressed in Rom. v. 12 sqq.; I Cor. xv. 21–22, 45–49. By Adam's fall, sin and death entered into the world, and condemnation has come upon all through him; but from the second Adam has come just the opposite—righteousness, justification, and life. Those who by sin are united to the first Adam reap all the consequences of such a union; similarly do those who by faith are united to the second Adam. Each is a representative head.

Materialism sees in man a mere product of nature. It is difficult to see how it makes place for self-consciousness. The unity of the race is also given up; and so logically Darwinism leads to belief in a plurality of race origins. Theology, on the other hand, holds fast to the personality of man, but has, from the beginning of the science, wavered in regard to the position occupied by Adam toward the race. The oldest Greek Fathers are silent upon this point. Irenæus is the first to touch it; and he maintains that the first sin was the sin of the race, since Adam was its head (III. xxiii. 3; V xii. 3; cf. R. Seeberg, *Dogmengeschichte*, i., Leipsic, 1895, p. 82). Origen, on the other hand, holds that man sinned because he had abused his liberty when in a preexistent state. In Adam seminally were the bodies of all his descendants (*Contra Celsum*, iv.; cf. C. F A. Kahnis, *Dogmatik*, ii., Leipsic, 1864, pp. 107 sqq.). Gregory Nazianzen, Gregory of Nyssa, and Chrysostom derive sin from the fall. Tertullian, Cyprian, Hilary, Ambrose, and Augustine represent the Biblical standpoint. Pelagius saw in Adam only a bad example, which his descendants followed. Semi-Pelagianism similarly regarded the first sin merely as opening the flood-gates to iniquity; but upon this point Augustinianism since it was formulated has dominated the Church—in Adam the race sinned. (CARL VON BUCHRUCKER†.)

2. The Position of Adam to the Race.

The prominent orthodox views are: (1) The Augustinian, known as realism, which is that human nature in its entirety was in Adam when he sinned, that his sin was the act of human nature, and that in this sin human nature fell; that is, lost its freedom to the good, becoming wholly sinful and producing sinners. "We sinned in that man when we were that man." This is the view of Anselm, Peter Lombard, Thomas Aquinas, and Luther. (2) The federal theory of the Dutch divines Cocceius and Witsius is that Adam became the representative of mankind and that the probation of the human race ended once for all in his trial and fall in the garden of Eden. Accordingly the guilt of Adam's sin was imputed to his posterity. This is the theory of Turretin and the Princeton theologians. (3) The theory of mediate imputation (Placæus) is that the sin of Adam is imputed to his descendants not directly, but on account of their depravity derived from him and their consent to his sin. (See IMPUTATION; SIN.)

3. The Orthodox Views.

According to the evolutionary view of man's origin, which is not necessarily materialistic, Adam may be designated as the first individual or individuals in the upward process of development in whom self-consciousness appeared or who attained such stability of life that henceforth humanity was able to survive the shock of death. By some, the first man is conceived of as a special instance of creative wisdom and power; by others, as the natural result of the evolutionary process. Whether the human race sprang from one individual or from several is, for lack of evidence, left an open question. In this position the unity of the race is in no wise compromised, since this is grounded not in derivation from a single pair but in identity of constitution and ideal ethical and spiritual aim. This view of the first man brings into prominence the dignity of human nature and its kinship with the divine, yet at the same time profoundly modifies the traditional doctrine of original sin. In the disproportion between the inherited instincts, appetites, and desires of the animal nature and the weak and struggling impulses of the moral consciousness there arises an inevitable conflict in which the higher is temporarily worsted and the sense of sin emerges. By virtue of heredity and the organic and social unity of the race, all the descendants of the earliest man are involved with him in the common struggle, the defeat, and the victory of the moral and spiritual life. This conflict is a sign that man is not simply a fallen being, but is in process of ascent. The first man, although of the earth, is a silent prophecy of the second man, the Lord from heaven.

4. The Evolutionary Views.

C. A. BECKWITH.

II. Historical: The sources of knowledge of Adam are exclusively Biblical and, indeed, wholly of the Old Testament, since the New Testament adds nothing concerning his personality and his doings to what is recorded of him in the Book of Genesis. The main inquiry, therefore, must be as to the place occupied by Adam in the Old Testament. Here several striking facts confront us: (1) There is no allusion to Adam direct or indirect after the early genealogies. In Deut. xxxii. 8 and Job xxviii. 28 the Hebrew *adham* (*adam*) means "mankind." In Hos. vi. 7 the reading should be "Admah" (a place-name). The latest references (apart from the excerpt in I Chron. i. 1) are Gen. iv. 25 (Sethite line of J) and Gen. v. 1, 3 (Sethite line of P). (2) Outside of the genealogies there is no clear instance of the use of the word as a proper name. The definite article, omitted in the Masoretic text, should be restored in Gen. iii. 17, 21 (J) in harmony with the usage of the whole context, which reads "the man" instead of "Adam."

1. The Use of "Adam" as a Proper Name.

Eve (Gen. iii. 20; iv. 1) is the first proper name of our Bible. (3) Whatever may have been the origin of the proper name "Adam," its use here seems to be derived from and based upon the original generic sense. Even in the genealogies the two significations are interchanged. Thus while Gen. v. 1 substitutes "Adam" for "the man" of i. 27, chap. v. 2 continues: "Male and female created he *them* and called *their* name Adam." It is a fair inference that the genealogies are in part at least responsible for the individual and personal usage of the name. When it is considered that all Semitic history began with genealogies, of which the standing designation in the early summaries is "generations" (Heb. *toledhoth*), the general motive of such a transference of ideas is obvious. The process was easy and natural because in the ancient type of society a community is thought of as a unit, is a proper name without the article, and is designated by a single not a plural form. The first community having been "man" ("the adam"), its head and representative was naturally spoken of as "Man" ("Adam") when there was need of referring to him. On the etymological side a partial illustration is afforded by the French *on* (Lat. *homo*) and the German *man*, which express individualization anonymously.

2. Foreign Influence in P. The secondary character of the notion of an individual Adam is also made probable by the fact that the genealogical system of P is artificial and of foreign origin or at least of foreign suggestion. The whole scheme of the ten generations of Gen. v. is modeled upon and in part borrowed from the Babylonian tradition of the first ten kings of Babylon. Of these lists of ten there are five names in either list which show striking correspondences with five in the other, ending with the tenth, which in either case is the name of the hero of the flood story. These Babylonian kings also were demigods, having lives of immense duration, two of them, moreover (the seventh and the tenth), having, like Enoch and Noah, special communications with divinity.

3. The Aim and Plan of P. In brief, as regards P, the matter stands as follows:—His first theme was the process and plan of creation according to an ascending scale of being. At the head of creation were put the first human beings, "man" or mankind (Gen. i. 26). The second leading thought in P's "generations of the heavens and the earth" was the continuance of the race or the peopling of the earth. Expression was given to it by the statement that "the man" was created "male and female" (i. 27). The third stage in the narrative is reached when the descent of Abraham from the first man is established, in order to provide a necessary and appropriate pedigree for the house of Israel. At the head of this line was placed the individual "Man" or "Adam."

4. The Narrative of J. Turning now to the story of Paradise and the Fall, which, as has been seen, speaks of the first man only as "the man" and not as "Adam," the main motive of Gen. ii.–iv. is to account for certain characteristics and habits of mankind, above all to set forth the origin, nature, and consequences of sin as disobedience to and alienation from Yahweh. Man is presented first as a single individual; next as being mated with a woman, with and for whom he has a divinely constituted affinity; then as the head of the race upon which he brings the curse due to his own disobedience. At first sight this might seem to imply a preconception of the individuality and personality of the first man, who may as well as not have borne the name "Adam," which J himself gives him in the fragmentary genealogy of Gen. iv. 25–26. But the inference is not justified. The pictures drawn by J and the conceptions they embody are not spontaneous effusions. They are the result of careful selection and of long and profound reflection, and when the problems which J sets out to solve and the incidents which convey and embody the solution be considered, it must be concluded that the answers to the questions could have been arrived at only through the study of man, not in individuals but as a social being. In other words, this "prophetic" interpreter worked his way backward through history or tradition along certain well-known lines of general human experience, and at the heart of the story appears not a single but a composite figure, not an individual but a type, while the story itself is not history or biography but in part mythical and in part allegorical. Thus the unhistorical character of Adam is even more demonstrable from the narrative of J than from that of P.

5. Parallels in Other Literatures. Some of the primitive mythical material in Genesis has analogies in other literatures. Not to mention the more remote Avesta, attention must again be called to some of the Babylonian parallels. It is now indisputable that Eden is a Babylonian name; that the whole scenery of the region is Babylonian; that the tree of life, the cherubim, and the serpent, the enemy of the gods and men, are all Babylonian. There is also the Babylonian story of how the first man came to forfeit immortality. Adapa, the human son of the good god Ea, had offended Anu, the god of heaven (see BABYLONIA, VII., 3, § 3), and was summoned to heaven to answer for his offense. Before his journey thither he was warned by his divine father to refuse the "food of death" and "water of death" which Anu would offer to him. At the trial, Anu, who had been moved by the intercession of two lesser gods, offered him instead "food of life" and "water of life." These he refused, and thus missed the immortality intended for him; for Anu when placated had wished to place him among the gods. Some such story as this by a process of reduction along monotheistic lines may have contributed its part to the framework of the narrative of the rejection of Adam. It is indeed possible that Adam and Adapa are ultimately the same name.

An important element in the whole case is the general character of the literary material of which the story of Adam forms a portion. Apart from the conceptions proper to the religion of Israel, which give them their distinctive moral value,

6. The Literary Material Mythical in Character.

the events and incidents related belong generically to the mythical stories of the beginnings of the earth and man, which have been related among many ancient and modern peoples, and specifically to the cycle of myths and legends which reached their fullest literary development in Babylonia, and which undoubtedly were originally the outgrowth of a polytheistic theory of the origin of the universe. Much weight must also be attached to the fact that the story of Adam is practically isolated in the Old Testament, above all to the consideration that prophecy and psalmody, which build so much upon actual history, ignore it altogether.

7. New Testament References.

The New Testament references show that Jesus and Paul used the earliest stories of Genesis for didactic purposes. The remark is often made in explanation that their age was not a critical one and that the sacred authors did not in their own minds question the current belief in the accuracy of the oldest documents. This is probably true, at any rate of Paul (cf. especially I Cor. xi. 8–9; I Tim. ii. 13–14). His view of the relation between the first and second Adam (I Cor. xv. 22, 45; Rom. v. 12 sqq.) is the development of an idea of rabbinical theology, and has a curious primitive analogy in the relation between Merodach, the divine son of the good god Ea, and Adapa, the human son of Ea (cf. Luke iii. 38). Jesus himself does not make any direct reference to Adam in his recorded sayings.

J. F. McCurdy.

Bibliography: I. §§ 1, 2: Jos. Butler, *Sermons on Human Nature*, in vol. ii. of his *Works*, Oxford, 1844; S. Baird, *The First Adam and the Second*, Philadelphia, 1860; J. Müller, *Christliche Lehre von der Sünde*, Breslau, 1867, Eng. transl., *Doctrine of Sin*, Edinburgh, 1868; Chas. Hodge, *Systematic Theology*, ii., ch. v., vii., viii., New York, 1872; R. W. Landis, *Original Sin and Imputation*, Richmond, 1884; W. G. T. Shedd, *Dogmatic Theology*, ii. 1–257, iii. 249–377, New York, 1888 (vol. iii. gives catena of citations from early Christian times to the middle of the eighteenth century); H. B. Smith, *System of Christian Theology*, pp. 273–301, ib. 1890; W. N. Clarke, *Outline of Christian Theology*, pp. 182–198, 227–259, ib. 1898; R. V. Foster, *Systematic Theology*, pp. 348–355, 363–381, Nashville, 1898; A. H. Strong, *Systematic Theology*, pp. 234–260, 261–272, New York, 1902.

I. § 3: H. B. Smith, *System of Christian Theology*, New York, 1886; G. P. Fisher, *Discussions in History and Theology*, pp. 355–409, ib. 1880; cf. Calvin, *Institutes*, book ii., ch. i., §§ 6–8.

I. § 4: H. Drummond, *The Ascent of Man*, New York, 1894; J. Le Conte, *Evolution and its Relation to Religious Thought*, ib. 1894; J. Fiske, *The Destiny of Man Viewed in the Light of his Origin*, Boston, 1895; idem, *Through Nature to God*, ib. 1899; J. M. Tyler, *The Whence and the Whither of Man*, ib. 1896; C. R. Darwin, *The Descent of Man*, pp. 174–180, New York, 1896; J. Deniker, *The Races of Man*, London, 1900.

II. §§ 1–7: M. Jastrow, *Religion of Babylonia and Assyria*, pp. 511, 544 sqq., Boston, 1898; idem, in *DB*, supplement vol., pp. 573–574; H. Gunkel, *Schöpfung und Chaos*, pp. 420 sqq., Göttingen, 1895; idem, *Genesis*, pp. 5 sqq., 33, 98 sqq., ib. 1902; Schrader, *KAT*, pp. 397, 520 sqq.

ADAM, BOOKS OF. See Pseudepigrapha, Old Testament, II., 39.

ADAM OF BREMEN: Author of the *Gesta Hammenburgensis ecclesiæ pontificum*, a history of the archbishops of Hamburg-Bremen extending down to the death of Adalbert (1072). The work itself tells of its author only that his name began with "A," that he came to Bremen in 1068 and ultimately became a canon there, and that he wrote the book between the death of Adalbert and that of King Svend Estridsen of Denmark (1072–76). But there is no doubt that this is the work referred to by Helmold and assigned to a *Magister Adam*; in which case the author must be the *Adam magister scholarum* who wrote and was one of the signatories to an extant document of Jan. 11, 1069, and also the same whose death on Oct. 12, year not given, is recorded in a Bremen register.

It may be conjectured from scanty indications that Adam was born in upper Saxony and educated at Magdeburg. His education was in any case a thorough one for his time. His book is one of the best historical works of the Middle Ages. Not only is it the principal source for the early history of the archbishopric and its northern missions, but it gives many valuable data both for Germany and other countries. The author was unusually well provided with documents and with the qualities necessary for their use. His general credibility and love of truth have never been seriously challenged; and his impartiality is shown by the way in which he records the weaknesses of Adalbert, with whom he was in close relations and whom he admired. The best edition of Adam's book is by J. M. Lappenberg, in *MGH*, *Script.*, vii. (1846) 267–389 (issued separately, Hanover, 1846; 2d ed., with full introduction and notes, 1876); the work is also in *MPL*, cxlvi. 451–620. There is a German translation by J. C. M. Laurent (2d ed., revised by W. Wattenbach, Leipsic, 1888).

(Carl Bertheau.)

Bibliography: J. H. a Seelen, *De Adamo Bremensi*, in his *Miscellanea*, ii. 415–493, Lübeck, 1736; L. Giesebrecht, *Historische und literarische Abhandlung der Königsberger deutschen Gesellschaft*, ed. F. W. Schubert, iii. 141, Königsberg, 1834; W. Giesebrecht, *Geschichte der deutschen Kaiserzeit*, i. 752, Brunswick, 1874; G. Dehio, *Geschichte des Erzbistums Hamburg-Bremen*, i. 176–177, Berlin, 1877; W. Wattenbach, *DGQ*, ii. (1894) 78–82; Hauck, *KD*, iii.

ADAM, MELCHIOR, mel'ki-ōr: Protestant biographer; b. at Grottkau (35 m. s.e. of Breslau), Silesia; d. at Heidelberg, where he was rector of the city school, Mar. 23, 1622. He is remembered for his series of 136 biographies, mostly of German Protestant scholars, especially theologians (5 vols., Heidelberg and Frankfort, 1615–20; 2d ed., under the title *Dignorum laude virorum immortalitas*, 1653; 3d ed., 1706).

ADAM OF SAINT VICTOR: One of the most important of the liturgical poets of the Middle Ages; his nationality is described by the Latin word *Brito* ("Breton"?), and he was canon of St. Victor of Paris in the second half of the twelfth century. From his sequence upon Thomas Becket of Canterbury it is inferred that he survived the latter's canonization (1174). His poems do not include all of his writings, but are the most important. From the ninth century it was customary to set words (called *prosa* and *sequentia*) to the melodies (*jubili, sequentia*) with which the Hallelujah of the gradual in the mass closed (see SEQUENCE). In the twelfth century a more artificial style of composition, according to strict rules, took the place of the freer rhythms of the earlier time, and for this period of sequence composition Adam has an importance comparable to that of Notker (q.v.) for the former period. He shows a real talent in his mastery of form; and his best pieces contain true poetry, although as concerns power to excite the emotions and the higher flights of the poetic fancy, his compositions are not equal to a *Salve caput*, *Stabat mater*, or *Lauda Sion*. S. M. DEUTSCH.

BIBLIOGRAPHY: L. Gautier, *Œuvres poétiques d'Adam de St. Victor*, 2 vols., Paris, 1858 (complete and critical ed., with life in vol. i.; 3d ed., 1894), reprinted in *MPL*, cxcvi. 1421–1534 (Eng. transl. by D. S. Wrangham, *The Liturgical Poetry of Adam of St. Victor*, 3 vols., London, 1881); K. Bartsch, *Die lateinischen Sequenzen des Mittelalters*, pp. 170 sqq., Rostock, 1868; *Histoire littéraire de la France*, xv. 39–45; E. Misset, *Poésie rythmique du moyen âge; essai . . . sur les œuvres poétiques d'Adam de St. Victor*, Paris, 1882.

ADAM THE SCOTCHMAN (*Adamus Scotus*, called also *Adamus Anglicus*): A mystic-ascetic author of the twelfth century. According to his biographer, the Premonstrant Godefroi Ghiselbert of the seventeenth century, he was of north-English origin, belonged to the Premonstrant order, was abbot at Whithorn (Casa Candida) in Galloway toward 1180, and about the same time also lived temporarily at Prémontré, the French parent monastery of the order. He seems to have died soon after. It is highly improbable that he was living in the thirteenth century, as Ghiselbert thinks, who identifies him with the English bishop of the Order of St. Norbert mentioned by Cæsarius of Heisterbach (*Miraculorum*, iii. 22). The first incomplete edition of Adam's works was published by Ægidius Gourmont (Paris, 1518). It contains his three principal writings of mystic-monastic content: (1) *Liber de ordine, habitu, et professione Præmonstratensium*, fourteen sermons; (2) *De tripartito tabernaculo;* (3) *De triplici genere contemplationis*. The edition of Petrus Bellerus (Antwerp, 1659) contains also Ghiselbert's life and a collection of forty-seven sermons on the festivals of the church year, which seem to have belonged to a larger collection of 100 sermons comprising the whole church year. In 1721 Bernhard Pez (*Thesaurus anecdotorum*, i. 2, 335 sqq.) published *Soliloquia de instructione discipuli, sive de instructione animæ*, which has been ascribed to Adam of St. Victor, but belongs probably to Adam the Scotchman. All of these works with Ghiselbert's life are in *MPL*, cxcviii. 9–872. O. ZÖCKLER†.

BIBLIOGRAPHY: Godefroi Ghiselbert, *Vita Adami*, in *MPL*, cxcviii.; C. Oudin, *De scriptoribus ecclesiæ*, ii. 1544 sqq., Frankfort, 1722; A. Miræus, *Chronicon ordinis Præmonstratensis*, in M. Kuen, *Collectio scriptorum variorum religiosorum ordinum*, vi. 36, 38, Ulm, 1768; G. Mackenzie, *The Lives and Characters of the most Eminent Writers of the Scots Nation*, i. 141–145, Edinburgh, 1708.

ADAMITES (ADAMIANI): 1. Epiphanius (*Hær.*, lii.) gives an account of a sect of "Adamiani," that held their religious assemblies in subterranean chambers, both men and women appearing in a state of nature to imitate Adam and Eve, and calling their meetings paradise. Since Epiphanius knew of them only from hearsay, and is himself doubtful whether to make of them a special class of heretics, their existence must be regarded as questionable. There are further unverifiable notices in John of Damascus (*Opera*, i. 88; following the *Anakephalaiosis*, attributed to Epiphanius), in Augustine (*Hær.*, lxxxi.), and in *Hæreticarum fabularum epitome*, i. 6). G. KRÜGER.

2. Charges of community of women, ritual child-murder, and nocturnal orgies were brought by the heathen world against the early Christians, and by the latter against various sects of their own number (Montanists, Manicheans, Priscillianists, etc.). Similar accusations were made against almost all medieval sects, notably the Cathari, the Waldensians, the Italian Fraticelli, the heretical flagellants of Thuringia in 1454, and the Brethren of the Free Spirit. All of these allegations are to be regarded with much suspicion. The doctrine of a sinless state, taught by the Brethren of the Free Spirit, and, in other cases, extravagant acts of overwrought mystics may have furnished a basis, which, without doubt, was often elaborated from the accounts of "Adamites" mentioned above.

3. The name "Adamites" has become the permanent designation of a sect of Bohemian Taborites, who, in Mar., 1421, established themselves on an island in the Luschnitz, near Neuhaus, and are said to have indulged in predatory forays upon the neighborhood, and to have committed wild excesses in nocturnal dances. They were suppressed by Ziska and Ulrich von Neuhaus in Oct., 1421. It is probable that they were merely a faction of the Taborites who carried to an extreme their belief in the necessity of a complete separation from the Church and resorted to violence to spread their principles. The charges against their moral character are in the highest degree suspicious. Even in the eighteenth and nineteenth centuries certain religious sectaries were persecuted in Bohemia as "Adamites."

4. An Anabaptist sect in the Netherlands about 1580 received the name "Adamites" because they required candidates for admission to appear unclothed before the congregation and thus show that physical desire had no power over them. Members of an Amsterdam congregation who in 1535 ran through the streets naked and crying wo to the godless were probably insane. The followers of Adam Pastor (q.v.) were called "Adamites" from their leader. Silly stories of orgies by so-called devil-worshipers (the "black mass") are sometimes heard at the present time. (HERMAN HAUPT.)

BIBLIOGRAPHY: (1) I. de Beausobre, *Dissertation sur les Adamites de Bohême*, in J. Lenfant, *Histoire de la guerre des Hussites*, ii. 355–358, Amsterdam, 1731; C. W. F. Walch, *Entwurf einer vollständigen Historie der Ketzereien*, i. 327–335, Leipsic, 1762. (2) J. Nider, *Formicarius*, III. vi., Cologne, 1470; C. Schmidt, *Histoire et doctrine de la secte des Cathares*, ii. 150 sqq., Paris, 1849; W. Preger, *Geschichte der deutschen Mystik*, i. 207 sqq., 461 sqq., Leipsic, 1874; A. Jundt, *Histoire du panthéisme populaire*, pp. 48–49, 56, 111 sqq., Paris, 1875; H. Haupt, in *ZKG*, vi. (1885) 552 sqq.; H. C. Lea, *History of the Inquisition*, i. 100 sqq., New York, 1888; K. Müller, *Kirchengeschichte*, i. 610, Freiburg, 1892. (3) J. Dobrowsky, *Geschichte der böhmischen Pikarden und Adamiten*, in *Abhandlungen der böhmischen Gesellschaft der Wissenschaften von 1788*, pp. 300–343; K. Höfler, *Geschichtschreiber der hussitischen Bewegung in Böhmen*, i. 452, 499 sqq. (*Fontes rerum Austriacarum*, I. ii., Vienna, 1856), ii. 336, 345 (ib. I. vi., 1865); F. Palacky, *Geschichte von Böhmen*, iii. 2, 227 sqq., 238 sqq., Prague, 1851, iv. 1 (1857), 462; A. Gindely, *Geschichte der böhmischen Brüder*, i. 18, 36, 56–57, 97–98, Prague, 1856; Beausobre, ut sup.; J. Goll, *Quellen und Untersuchungen zur Geschichte der böhmischen Brüder*, i. 119, Prague, 1878; ii. (1882) 10 sqq.; H. Haupt, *Waldenserthum und Inquisition im südostlichen Deutschland*, pp. 23, 109, note 1, Freiburg, 1890. (4) Prateolus, *De vitis hæreticorum*, l, Cologne, 1569; C. Schlüsselburg, *Catalogus hæreticorum*, xii. 29, Frankfort, 1599; F. Nippold, in *ZHT*, xxxiii. (1863) 102; C. A. Cornelius, in *Abhandlungen* of the Royal Bavarian Academy, *Historische classe*, xi. 2, 67 sqq., Munich, 1872; Natalis Alexander, *Hist. eccl.*, xvii. 183, Paris, 1699; J. Bois, *Le Satanisme et la magie*, ib. 1895.

ADAMNAN ("Little Adam"): Ninth abbot of Iona (679–704); b. probably at Drumhome in the southwest part of County Donegal, Ireland (50 m. s.w. of Londonderry), c. 625; d. on the island of Iona Sept. 23, 704. He was a relative of Columba and the greatest of the abbots of Iona after its illustrious founder, famed alike for learning (he had some knowledge of even Greek and Hebrew), piety, and practical wisdom. He was a friend (and perhaps the teacher) of Aldfrid, king of Northumbria (685–705), visited his court in 686 and again in 688, and was converted there to the Roman tonsure and Easter computation by Ceolfrid of Jarrow. He was unable, however, to win over his monks of Iona, but had more success in Ireland, where he spent considerable time, attended several synods, and warmly advocated the Roman usages. Many churches and wells are dedicated to him in Ireland and Scotland, and his name appears corrupted into various forms, as "Ownan," "Eunan" (the patron of Raphoe), "Dewnan," "Thewnan," and the like.

The extant writings of Adamnan are: (1) *Arculfi relatio de locis sanctis*, written down from information furnished personally by Arculf, a Gallic bishop who was driven to England by stress of weather when returning from a visit to Palestine, Syria, Alexandria, and Constantinople. Adamnan added notes from other sources known to him, and presented the book to King Aldfrid. Bede made it the basis of his *De locis sanctis* and gives extracts from it in the *Hist. eccl.*, v. 16, 17 (2) *Vita S. Columbæ*, written between 692 and 697, not so much a life as a presentation without order of the saint's prophecies, miracles, and visions, but important for the information it gives of the customs, the land, the Irish and Scotch tongues, and the history of the time. (3) The "Vision of Adamnan," in old Irish, describing Adamnan's journey through heaven and hell, is probably later than his time, but may present his real spiritual experiences and his teaching. Other works are ascribed to him without good reason.

H. Hahn.

Bibliography: For works consult *MPL*, lxxxviii.; *Arculfi relatio*, in *Itinera Hierosolymitana bellis sacris anteriora*, i., pp. xxx.-xxxiii., 139–210, 238–240, 392–418 (*Publications of the Société de l'Orient latin, Série géographique*, i., Geneva, 1879), and in *Itinera Hierosolymitana sæculi iiii.-viii.*, ed. P. Geyer, pp. 219–297 (*CSEL*, xxxix., 1898); Eng. transl. by J. R. Macpherson (Palestine Pilgrims' Text Society, 1889); *Vita S. Columbæ*, ed. W Reeves, Dublin, 1857 (new ed., with Eng. transl. and an unfortunate rearrangement of the notes, by W F. Skene, Edinburgh, 1874); also by J. T. Fowler, Oxford, 1894 (Eng. transl., 1895); the text of the *Vision*, with Eng. transl., has been published by Whitley Stokes, *Fis Adamnain*, Simla, 1870; E. Windisch, *Irische Texte*, pp. 165–196, Leipsic, 1880 (contains the text). For Adamnan's life: Lanigan, *Eccl. Hist.*, passim; Reeves, in his ed. of the *Vita Columbæ*, pp. xl.-lxviii., Dublin, 1857; A. P. Forbes, *Kalendars of Scottish Saints*, Edinburgh, 1872; *DCB*, i. 41–43; W F. Skene, *Celtic Scotland*, ii. 170–175, Edinburgh, 1877; *DNB*, i. 92–93; J. Healy, *Insula Sanctorum*, pp. 334–347, Dublin, 1890; P. Geyer, *Adamnan*, Augsburg, 1895; T. Olden, *Church of Ireland*, pp. 59, 77, 104, 119, London, 1895; *Cain Adamnan, an old Irish Treatise on the Law of Adamnain*, ed. Kuno Meyer, in *Anecdota Oxoniensa*, Oxford, 1905.

ADAMS, GEORGE MOULTON: Congregationalist; b. at Castine, Me., July 7, 1824; d. at Auburndale, Mass., Jan. 11, 1906. He was educated at Bowdoin College (B.A., 1844), Bangor Theological Seminary (1844–46), the universities of Leipsic, Halle, and Berlin (1847–49), and Andover Theological Seminary (1849–50). He held successive pastorates at Conway, Mass. (1851–63); Portsmouth, N. H. (1863–71); and Holliston, Mass. (1873–89), and also acted as supply at Mentham, Mass. (1890–91), and Waban, Mass. (1905), although after 1889 he was engaged chiefly in literary work. In his theological position he was a Trinitarian Congregationalist. He was historian of the New England Historic-Genealogical Society and a member of its Council, a member of the Board of Overseers of Bowdoin College, the treasurer of the Trustees of Donations for Education in Liberia and of the Mount Coffee Association for the promotion of education in Liberia, and in 1903 was made Knight Commander of the Liberian Humane Order of African Redemption. In addition to a number of briefer studies and occasional addresses, he revised the *Biblical Museum* of James Comper Gray (8 vols., New York and London, 1871–81) under the title of *The Biblical Encyclopedia* (5 vols., Cleveland, O., 1903).

ADAMS, JAMES ALONZO: Congregationalist; b. at Ashland, O., May 21, 1842. He was educated at Knox College (A.B., 1867) and Union Theological Seminary (1870), after having served in the Civil war as a member of Company D, 69th Illinois Volunteers. He was pastor of the Congregational Church at Marshfield, Mo., in 1870–71; of the Plymouth Congregational Church, St. Louis, in 1880–86; of the Millard Avenue Congregational Church, Chicago, in 1887–88; and of the Warren Avenue Congregational Church in the same city in 1889–95. In 1891 he was a delegate from the Congregational churches of Illinois to the International Congregational Council in London, and has also been their representative at a number of national councils. He was professor in Straight University, New Orleans, 1873–77, and president in 1875–77, and then became editor of the *Dallas Daily Commercial*, Dallas, Tex. From 1887 to 1903 he was editorial writer on the Chicago *Advance*, becoming its editor-in-chief in the latter year. His principal works are *Colonel Hungerford's Daughter* (Chicago, 1896) and *Life of Queen Victoria* (1901).

ADAMS, JOHN COLEMAN: Universalist; b. at Malden, Mass., Oct. 25, 1849. He was educated at the high schools of Providence, R. I., and Lowell, Mass., and at Tufts College (A.B., 1870) and Divinity School (B.D., 1872). He has held pastorates at the Newton Universalist Church, Newton, Mass. (1872-80); First Universalist Church, Lynn, Mass. (1880-84); St. Paul's Universalist Church, Chicago, Ill. (1884-90); All Souls' Universalist Church, Brooklyn, N. Y. (1890-1901); and Church of the Redeemer, Hartford, Conn., from 1901 to the present time. He has been a trustee of Tufts College since 1880 and of the Universalist General Convention since 1895. In his theological position he is a pronounced Universalist. His works include *The Fatherhood of God* (Boston, 1888); *Christian Types of Heroism* (1891); *The Leisure of God* (1895); *Nature Studies in the Berkshires* (New York, 1899); and *Life of William Hamilton Gibson* (1901).

ADAMS, SARAH (FULLER) FLOWER: English Unitarian; b. at Harlow (25 m. n.e. of London), Essex, Feb. 22, 1805; d. in London Aug. 14, 1848. Her father was Benjamin Flower (1755-1829), printer, editor, and political writer, and, Sept. 24, 1834, she married William Bridges Adams (1797-1872), an inventor and engineer of distinction, also a writer on political subjects. She was a highly gifted woman, much esteemed by a circle of friends which included, among others, W J. Linton, Harriet Martineau, Leigh Hunt, and Robert Browning. Inherited deafness and a weak constitution prevented her from following the stage as a profession, which she had chosen in the belief that "the drama is an epitome of the mind and manners of mankind, and wise men in all ages have agreed to make it, what in truth it ought to be, a supplement to the pulpit." She wrote poems on social and political subjects, chiefly for the Anti-Corn-Law League; contributed poems and articles to the *Monthly Repository* during the years 1832-53, when it was conducted by her pastor W. J. Fox (q.v.), and published a long poem, *The Royal Progress*, in the *Illuminated Magazine* in 1845. In book form she published *Vivia Perpetua, a Dramatic Poem* (London, 1841; reprinted with her hymns and a memoir by Mrs. E. F. Bridell-Fox, 1893), and *The Flock at the Fountain* (1845), a catechism. In addition, she furnished fourteen original hymns and two translations to *Hymns and Anthems* (1840), a collection for Fox's chapel at Finsbury, including her best-known production, *Nearer, my God, to thee*. Her sister, **Eliza Flower** (1803-46), possessed much musical talent and furnished the original music for this hymn as well as for others in the book.

BIBLIOGRAPHY: *DNB*, i. 101; S. W. Duffield, *English Hymns*, pp. 382-386, New York, 1886; Julian, *Hymnology*, p. 16; N. Smith, *Hymns Historically Famous*, pp. 174-182, Chicago, 1901.

ADAMS, THOMAS: English preacher and commentator of the seventeenth century, called by Southey "the prose Shakespeare of Puritan theologians . . . scarcely inferior to Fuller in wit or to Taylor in fancy." Little is known of his life beyond what may be gathered from the title-pages and dedications of his books. He was preaching in Bedfordshire in 1612; in 1614 became vicar of Wingrave, Bucks; from 1618 to 1623 preached in London; he was chaplain to Sir Henry Montagu, lord chief justice of England, in 1653 was a "necessitous and decrepit" old man, and died probably before the Restoration. He published many occasional sermons (collected into a folio volume, London, 1630), besides a commentary on the Second Epistle of Peter (1633; ed. J. Sherman, 1839). His works, ed. Thomas Smith, with life by Joseph Angus, were published in Nichol's *Series of Standard Divines* (3 vols., Edinburgh, 1862-63).

ADAMS, WILLIAM: American Presbyterian; b. at Colchester, Conn., Jan. 25, 1807; d. at Orange Mountain, N. J., Aug. 31, 1880. He was graduated at Yale (1827) and at Andover Theological Seminary (1830); was pastor at Brighton, Mass. (1831-34); of the Broome Street (Central) Presbyterian Church, New York (1834-53); and of the Madison Square Presbyterian Church, formed from the Broome Street Church (1853-73). From 1873 till his death he was president and professor of sacred rhetoric and pastoral theology in Union Theological Seminary. He was one of the leading clergymen in New York in his time, and his influence was not bounded by his own denomination or land. Besides many individual sermons he published an edition of Isaac Taylor's *Spirit of Hebrew Poetry*, with a biographical introduction (New York, 1862); *The Three Gardens* (1856); *In the World and not of the World* (1867); *Conversations of Jesus Christ with Representative Men* (1868); *Thanksgiving* (1869).

ADAMS, WILLIAM FORBES: Protestant Episcopal bishop of Easton (Md.); b. at Enniskillen (70 m. s.w. of Belfast), County Fermanagh, Ireland, Jan. 2, 1833. He came to America at the age of eight, was educated at the University of the South, and was admitted to the Mississippi bar in 1854, but subsequently studied theology, and was ordained deacon in 1859, and priest in the following year. He was rector of St. Paul's Church, Woodville, Mass., from 1860 to 1866, when he was called to the rectorate of St. Peter's, New Orleans, but went in the following year to St. Paul's in the same city, where he remained until 1875. In that year he was consecrated first missionary bishop of New Mexico and Arizona, but was compelled by illness to resign. He then accepted the rectorate of Holy Trinity Church, Vicksburg, Miss., where he remained from 1876 to 1887, when he was consecrated bishop of Easton.

ADAMSON, PATRICK: Scotch prelate; b. in Perth Mar. 15, 1537 (according to another account, 1543); d. at St. Andrews Feb. 19, 1592. He was educated at the University of St. Andrews; preached for two or three years in Scotland; was in France as private tutor at the time of the Massacre of St. Bartholomew; returned to Scotland and to the ministry; and was made archbishop of St. Andrews in 1576. Thenceforth his life was a continual struggle with the Presbyterian party, and he died in poverty. His enemies have assailed his character, but all agree that he was a scholar and an able preacher and writer. He composed a Latin catechism for the young King James, translated the Book of Job into Latin hexameters, and wrote a tragedy on the subject of Herod. His collected works were published by his son-in-law, Thomas Wilson (London, 1619), who also added a life to an edition of his treatise *De pastoris munere*, published separately the same year.

ADAMSON, WILLIAM: Evangelical Union; b. at New Galloway (20 m. w. of Dumfries), Kirkcudbrightshire, Aug. 29, 1830. He was educated at Glasgow and St. Andrews Universities and at Evangelical Union Theological Hall. He was pastor in Perth eleven years and in Edinburgh twenty-seven years, and also conducted a public theological class in the latter city for eighteen years. He was for several years a member of the Edinburgh School Board, and took an active interest in politics and movements for reform. He is now pastor of the Carver Memorial Church, Windermere, Westmorelandshire. His writings include *The Righteousness of God* (London, 1870); *The Nature of the Atonement* (1880); *Religious Anecdotes of Scotland* (1885); *Knowledge and Faith* (1886); *Robert Milligan: A Story* (Glasgow, 1891); *Missionary Anecdotes* (1896); *Argument of Adaptation* (London, 1897); *Life of the Rev. James Morison* (1898); *Life of the Rev. Fergus Ferguson* (1900); and *Life of the Rev. Joseph Parker* (1902). He is also the editor of *The Christian News*.

ADDICKS, GEORGE B.: Methodist Episcopalian; b. at Hampton, Ill., Sept. 9, 1854. He was educated at the Central Wesleyan College, Warrenton, Mo., and at the Garrett Bible Institute, Evanston, Ill. (1876–77). He taught in the preparatory department of the Central Wesleyan College in 1875–76, and in 1877–78 preached at Geneseo, Ill., being ordained to the Methodist Episcopal ministry in the latter year. From 1878 to 1885 he taught the German language and literature in Iowa Wesleyan University and German College, Mount Pleasant, Ia., and from 1885 to 1890 held a pastorate at Pekin, Ill. In 1890 he returned to the Central Wesleyan College as professor of practical theology and philosophy, and since 1895 has been president and professor of philosophy of the same institution. In 1900 he was a delegate to the General Conference of the Methodist Episcopal Church and was a member of the University Senate of the same denomination from 1896 to 1904.

ADDIS, WILLIAM EDWARD: Church of England; b. at Edinburgh May 9, 1844. He was educated at Glasgow University and Balliol College, Oxford (B.A., 1866). Originally a member of the Church of England, he became a convert to the Roman Catholic Church in 1866, and was ordained to the priesthood in 1872 at the London Oratory, being parish priest of Sydenham from 1878 to 1888. In the latter year he renounced this faith and became minister of the Australian Church, Melbourne, Australia, an undenominational institution, where he remained until 1892, when he took a similar position at the High Pavement Chapel, Nottingham (1893–98). In 1899 he was appointed Old Testament lecturer at Manchester College, Oxford, and shortly afterward returned to the Church of England. His college accordingly attempted to expel him and to declare itself officially non-conformist, but the movement was proved illegal, and he still retains his position, although the hostile attitude of the trustees of Manchester College prevents him from resuming his work as a priest of the Church of England. He has written *A Catholic Dictionary* (London, 1883; in collaboration with Thomas Arnold); *Christianity and the Roman Empire* (1893); *Documents of the Hexateuch* (2 vols., 1893–98); and *Hebrew Religion to the Establishment of Judaism Under Ezra* (1906).

ADDISON, DANIEL DULANY: Protestant Episcopalian; b. at Wheeling, W Va., Mar. 11, 1863. He received his education at Union College and the Episcopal Theological School, Cambridge, Mass. (1886). He was curate of Christ Church, Springfield, Mass., in 1886–89 and rector of St. Peter's Church, Beverly, Mass., in 1889–95, while since 1895 he has been rector of All Saints' Church, Brookline, Mass. He is examining chaplain to the bishop of Massachusetts, director of the Church Temperance Society, member of the executive committee of the archdeaconry of Boston, president of the New England Home for Deaf-Mutes and the Brookline Education Society, vice-president of the Trustees of Donations for Education in Liberia, and a trustee of the College of Monrovia, Liberia, and of the Brookline public library. In 1904 he was made Knight Commander of the Liberian Humane Order of African Redemption. He has written: *Lucy Larcom, Life, Letters and Diary* (Boston, 1894); *Phillips Brooks* (1894); *Life and Times of Edward Bass, First Bishop of Massachusetts* (1897); *All Saints' Church, Brookline* (Cambridge, 1896); *The Clergy in American Life and Letters* (New York, 1900); and *The Episcopalians* (1904).

ADELBERT. See ADALBERT.

ADELMANN: Bishop of Brescia in the eleventh century. The time and place of his birth are unknown, and the date of his death, as well as that of his consecration as bishop, is uncertain. Gams (*Series episcoporum*, Regensburg, 1872, p. 779) assigns the latter two events to 1053 and 1048, respectively. Adelmann himself states that he was not a German; he has been commonly taken for a Frenchman, but may have been a Lombard. The first certain fact of his life is that, together with Berengar of Tours, he studied under Fulbert at Chartres. Afterward he studied, and later taught (probably from 1042), in the school of Liége, then at Speyer. The works which have made him known are: (1) a collection of *Rhythmi alphabetici de viris illustribus sui temporis*, devoted to the praise of Fulbert and his school, and (2) a letter to Berengar on his eucharistic teaching; the letter was written before Berengar's first condemnation, but after his departure from the traditional doctrine was notorious (both works in *MPL*, cxliii. 1289–98). The letter is not so much an independent investigation as a solemn warning to his friend against the danger of falling into heresy. Adelmann treats the subject from the purely traditional standpoint, and considers it settled by the words of institution.

The change (he uses the words *transferre, transmutare*) of the bread and wine into the body and blood of Christ takes place invisibly in order to afford an opportunity for the exercise of faith; such occurrences, accordingly, can not be investigated by reason, but must be believed.

(A. HAUCK.)

BIBLIOGRAPHY: *Histoire littéraire de la France*, vii. 542; Hauck, *KD*, vol. iii., p. 963.

ADELOPHAGI, ad″el-of′a-jai or -gî ("Not Eating in Public"): Certain people, mentioned in *Prædestinatus* (i. 71), as thinking it unseemly for a Christian to eat while another looked on. They are also referred to by Augustine (*Hær.*, lxxi.), who copies Philastrius (*Hær.*, lxxvi.) and is uncertain whether their scruple included members of their own sect or applied only to others. Further statements in *Prædestinatus* are to be accepted with extreme caution. G. KRÜGER.

ADENEY, WALTER FREDERIC: Congregationalist; b. at Ealing (9 m. w. of London), Middlesex, Eng., Mar. 14, 1849. He received his education at New College and University College, London. He was minister of the Congregational Church at Acton, London, from 1872 to 1889, and from 1887 to the same year was lecturer in Biblical and systematic theology at New College, London. In 1889 he was appointed professor of New Testament exegesis and church history in the same institution, holding this position until 1903, as well as a lectureship on church history in Hackney College, London, after 1898. In 1903 he was chosen principal of Lancastershire College, in the University of Manchester, and two years later was appointed lecturer on the history of doctrine in the same university. As a theologian, he accepts the results of Biblical criticism which he feels to be warranted, and welcomes scientific and philosophic investigation and criticism of religion, although he seeks to adhere firmly to basal Christian truths and to harmonize them with what he holds to be other ascertained verities. His works include, in addition to numerous articles in magazines and Hastings's *Dictionary of the Bible*, as well as in nine volumes of the *Pulpit Commentary* (1881–90), *The Hebrew Utopia* (London, 1877); *From Christ to Constantine* (1886); *From Constantine to Charles the Great* (1888); two volumes in the *Expositor's Bible* (1893-94; the first on Ezra, Nehemiah, and Esther; and the second on Ecclesiastes and the Song of Solomon); *The Theology of the New Testament* (1894); *How to Read the Bible* (1896); *Women of the New Testament* (1899); the section on the New Testament in the *Biblical Introduction* written by him in collaboration with W. H. Bennett (1899); and *A Century's Progress* (1901). He is likewise editor of *The Century Bible*, to which he himself has contributed the volumes on Luke (London, 1901) and the Epistles to the Thessalonians (1902).

ADEODATUS, ad″î-ō-dē′tus: Bishop of Rome from Apr. 11, 672, to his death, June 16, 676. His pontificate was unimportant. The *Liber pontificalis* (ed. Duchesne, i. 346) ascribes to him the restoration of the basilica of St. Peter at Campo di Merlo, near La Magliana (7½ m. from Rome), and the enlargement of the monastery of St. Erasmus in Rome, where he had been a monk. The only documents of his extant (*MPL*, lxxxvii. 1139–46) are concessions of privileges to the churches of St. Peter at Canterbury and St. Martin at Tours. For his participation in the Monothelite controversy, see MONOTHELITES. He is sometimes known as **Adeodatus II.**, because the form "Adeodatus" is used also for the name of a former pope, Deusdedit (615–618).

ADIAPHORA, ad″i-af′o-ra, **AND THE ADIAPHORISTIC CONTROVERSIES.**

In the history of Christian ethics the term "adiaphora" (pl. of Gk., *adiaphoron*, "indifferent") signifies actions which God neither bids nor forbids, the performance or omission of which is accordingly left as a matter of indifference. The term was employed by the Cynics, and borrowed by the Stoics. To the latter that only was good or evil which was always so and which man could control. Such matters as health, riches, etc., and their opposites were classed as adiaphora, being regarded for this purpose, not as actions, but as things or conditions. Adiaphora were divided into absolute and relative; the former being such as had to do with meaningless distinctions, while the latter involved preference, as in the case of sickness versus health. The Stoics did not, however, from the adiaphoristic nature of external things deduce that of the actions connected therewith.

1. Classical Greek Usage.

Jesus's ideal of righteousness as devotion of the entire person to God revealed as perfect moral character, signified, on the one side, freedom from every obligation to a statutory law, particularly precepts concerning worship. He regarded the observance of external rites as a matter of indifference so far as real personal purity was concerned, and, with his disciples observed the Jewish rites as a means to the fulfilment of his mission to Israel when they did not interfere with doing good (Mark iii. 4). Yet this ideal involved such a sharpening of moral obligation that in the presence of its unqualified earnestness and comprehensive scope there was no room for the question, so important to legalistic Judaism, how much one might do or leave undone without transgressing the Law. The slightest act, like the individual word, had the highest ethical significance to the extent that it was an expression of the "abundance of the heart" (Matt. xii. 25–37).

2. Christ's Usage.

Paul emphasizes, on the one hand, the comprehensive character of Christian ethics and, on the other, the freedom which is the Christian's; and he concludes that the observance or disregard of dicta pertaining to external things is a matter of indifference in its bearing on the kingdom of God (Rom. xiv. 17; I Cor. vi. 12, viii. 8; Gal. v. 6; Col. ii. 20). He recognizes, with the exception of the Lord's Supper, no forms for Christian worship, but merely counsels that "all things be done decently and in order" (I Cor. xiv. 40). From the fact that the Christian belongs to God, the Lord of the world, Paul deduces the authority (Gk. *exousia*) of Christians over all things (I Cor. iii. 21-23), especially the right freely to make use of the free gifts of God (I Cor. x. 23, 26; Rom. xiv 14, 20). Ability to return thanks for them is made the subjective criterion of their purity (Rom. xiv. 6; I Cor. x. 30). Those things also are permissible which are left free by implication in the ordinances of the Church, or are expressly allowed. But action in the domain of the permissible is restricted for the individual by ethical principles according to which he must be bound (Rom. xiv. 2 sqq.; I Cor. vi. 12, viii. 9, x. 23). Concrete action in all such cases he regards as not at the pleasure of the individual, but as bidden or forbidden for the sake of God.

3. Paul's Usage.

In place of this view of freedom, combining obligation with unconstraint, there soon arose one of a more legal cast. At the time of Tertullian there was in connection with concrete questions a conflict between the two principles (1) that what is not expressly permitted by Scripture is forbidden; and (2) that what is not expressly forbidden is permitted. The restriction of the idea of duty by that of the permissible, and the recognition of an adiaphoristic sphere were further confirmed by the distinction between *præcepta* and *consilia* and by the doctrine of supererogatory merits. The question of adiaphora was argued by the schoolmen. Thomas Aquinas and his followers held that there were certain actions which, so far as being intrinsically capable of subserving a good or an ill purpose, were matters of indifference; but they recognized no act proceeding from conscious consideration which was not either disposed toward a fitting end or not so disposed, and hence good or bad. Duns Scotus and his adherents recognized actions indifferent *in individuo*, i.e., those not to be deemed wrong though without reference, actual or virtual, to God. The early Church at first appropriated the Cynic and Stoic opposition to culture, holding that it interfered with the contemplation of God and divine things. But with large heathen accessions, this attitude was no longer maintained. The primitive Christian ideal was, to be sure, preserved; but its complete fulfilment was required of only those bound thereto by the nature of their calling.

4. Patristic and Medieval Usage.

Luther based his position on that of Paul. He appears, indeed, to determine the idea of adiaphora (the expression does not occur in his works) according to a legalizing criterion when he distinguishes between things or works which are clearly bidden or forbidden by God in the New Testament and those which are left free—to neglect which is no wrong; to observe, no piety. But he further says in the same connection that under the rule of faith the conscience is free, and Christians are superior to all things, particularly externals and precepts in connection therewith. In accordance with this view he considers that an external form of divine worship is nowhere enjoined (the Lord's Supper is a *beneficium*, not an *officium*); and he distinguishes between the necessary and the free in churchly forms by their effects. Prayer, the Lord's Supper, and preaching are necessary to edification; but the time, place, and mode have no part in edification, and are free. His standpoint, then, was not simply that there were certain things left free, but that the assertion of freedom (or adiaphorism) applied to the whole realm of externals. In individual cases, however, a limitation was imposed by ethical aims and rules. Christians were to take part in the external worship of God to fulfil the duty of public confession and that they might "communicate" (Heb. xiii. 16). Ceremonial forms served to perpetuate certain effective modes of observance; but they were not to be idolatrous, superstitious, or pompous. Luther, in opposition to Carlstadt, urged that in the forms of worship for the sake of avoiding offense to some, whatever was not positively objectionable should be suffered to remain. He was ready to concede the episcopal form of church government and other matters, if urged not as necessary to salvation, but as conducive to order and peace. He wished, also, to maintain Christian freedom against stubborn adherents of the Law.

5. Luther's Usage.

The churchly adiaphora formed the subject of the first adiaphoristic controversy. The Wittenberg theologians believed that the concessions on the basis of which the Leipsic interim was concluded could be justified by the principles enunciated and exemplified at the outset of the Reformation. They held that, despite formal modifications, they had surrendered only traditional points of church government and worship, and even then only such as were unopposed by Scripture, had been so recognized in the primitive Church, and had seemed to themselves excellent arrangements, conducive to order and discipline. Further, they maintained that every idolatrous usage had been discountenanced, and that from what was retained idolatrous significance had been excluded. It may be mentioned, by way of example, that the Latin liturgy of the mass was admitted, with lights, canonicals, etc., though with communion and some German hymns; also confirmation, Corpus Christi day, extreme unction, fasting, and the jurisdiction of bishops.

6. First Adiaphoristic Controversy.

Before the interim had been authentically published there arose a controversy in which the attack was led by Flacius. In his *De veris et falsis adiaphoris* (1549), he raised the question by not only maintaining that preaching, baptism, the Lord's Supper, and absolution had been commanded by God, but even by concluding from I Cor. xiv. 40 that the ceremonial usages connected therewith had been divinely ordained *in genere*. He also sought to limit the Lutheran indifference to detail by insisting on what he deemed seriousness and dignity in the liturgy, as opposed to the canonicals, music, and spectacles of the Catholic Church. In addition he protested that what might be called the individual character of the Church was to be conserved, and that existing means of edification should be altered only in favor of better ones. Under the circumstances obtaining at the time, he said, even a matter in itself unessential could not be treated as permissible, and the concessions of the interim were an act of treachery: they were occasioned by the endeavors of the emperor to restore the Catholic Church, the promulgators being moved by fear, or at best by lack of faith; and in effect they were an admission of past errors, strengthening their opponents, while the rank and file, looking at externals only, would see in the restoration of discarded usages a reversion to the old conditions. The dispute continued after the peace of Augsburg; and the *Formula Concordiæ* not only drew the distinction (art. X.) that in time of persecution, when confession was necessary, there should be no concession to the enemies of the Gospel, even in adiaphora, since truth and Christian freedom were at stake, but to some extent appropriated Flacius's restriction of the idea of adiaphora.

7. Flacius's Restriction of Adiaphora.

In the so-called second adiaphoristic controversy the Lutheran and Calvinistic systems came into conflict. Luther had maintained the right of temperate enjoyment of secular amusements. Calvin, on the other hand, stood for fundamentally different principles, in accordance with which he enforced his Genevan code of discipline. Voetius carried these principles still further. On the Lutheran side was Meisner, who is in this respect the classic opponent of the Calvinists. He puts secular amusements under the head of adiaphora as being actions neither right nor wrong *per se* but *per aliud*,—the person and the purpose especially to be considered,—and in concrete instances becoming always either right or wrong. The controversy began at the close of the seventeenth century, when secular amusements were attacked *per se* by several writers, such as Reiser and Winkler, the Pietistic theologians of Hamburg, Vockerodt, Lange, and Zierold. Lange, for example, contended that in the light of revealed law there are no indifferent acts. Those actions alone are right which are under the influence of the Holy Spirit for the honor of God in the faith and name of Christ; and he holds that the divine will exercises a direct and immediate control. Hence actions not bidden of God are necessarily actions which profit not and are therefore collectively wrong. He enumerates nineteen separate reasons why Christians should take no part in secular amusements and would exclude from the Lord's Supper those who do. He regards the defense of adiaphora as a heresy which abrogates all evangelical doctrine. Spener's theory was equally severe, but his practise was wisely modified. He counseled that those who participated in secular amusements should be dissuaded therefrom not harshly, but by indirect exhortations to follow Christ; and he would not refuse absolution to such, since many of them did not really appreciate the wrong of those things. Rothe, Warnsdorf, and Schelwig were the principal champions of the previously existing Lutheran teaching; but their defense was far less resolute than the attack.

8. Second Controversy.

The question of adiaphora has subsequently been a subject of discussion. The first to introduce a new point of view of any considerable value was Schleiermacher (*Kritik der bisherigen Sittenlehre*, 2d ed.; *Werke zur Philosophie*, ii.), who contested the ethical right of adiaphora on the basis of the necessity in the moral life of unity and stability. Only in the realm of civil law, and in the moral judgment of others whose actions must frequently, for lack of evidence, remain unexplained, does he admit of adiaphora. Most later evangelical authorities, for example Martensen, Pfleiderer, Wuttke, and, most closely, Rothe, are in substantial agreement with this position, though introducing some variations and modifications.

9. Recent Discussion.

(J. Gottschick.)

Among British and American Christians no adiaphoristic controversy has found place; but the types of religious and ethical thought that underlay the opposing forces in the controversies above considered have been in conflict at all times and everywhere. English Puritanism and early Scottish Presbyterianism, as well as New England Puritanism, either rejected adiaphora wholly or reduced them to the smallest proportions. The English Tractarians in seeking to overcome the difficulties involved in uniting with the Church of Rome gave earnest attention to adiaphora. A sign of the times is the watchword of the Evangelical Alliance, "In essentials, unity; in nonessentials, liberty; in all things, charity." The Lambeth articles proposing the Nicene and Apostles' Creeds, the two sacraments, the open Bible, and the historic episcopate as the basis of union with non-conforming Churches treated as adiaphora the Athanasian Creed, uniformity of worship, and use of the Prayer Book. The Protestant Episcopal Church in America has settled the chief point in dispute between Churchman and Puritan by eliminating the State from necessary union with the Church. In the union of religious bodies both in Great Britain and America, for which there is a growing tendency, minor differences are ignored in favor of essential principles. In all Churches some dogmas once deemed essential to the integrity of truth are laid aside never to regain their former position (cf. the Westminster Confession with the "Brief Statement of Faith" published by authority of the Presbyterian Church in the United States). With reference to conduct prescribed by ecclesiastical bodies or recognized as belonging to personal responsibility—the "personal instance"—two diametrically opposite tendencies are evident. In the first case, the spirit of democracy and of enlightened public sentiment is rapidly withdrawing many actions once regarded as legitimately under church jurisdiction, as amusements and the like, from such supervision. In the second case, if life is to be ruled by moral maxims, many actions must be left morally indeterminate, yet when every deed is seen to be not atomistic but an integral part of self-realization, then all actions take their organic place in the serious or happy fulfilment of life's aim. In both instances alike, however, the moral adiaphora disappear. C. A. B.

Bibliography: For the ethical and theological treatment of Adiaphora consult in general: the treatises on ethics, casuistry, dogmatics, and the history of philosophy. Special treatment will be found in C. C. E. Schmid, *Adiaphora, wissenschaftlich und historisch untersucht*, Leipsic, 1809; J. Schiller, *Probleme der christlichen Ethik*, Berlin, 1888; J. H. Blunt, *Dictionary of Sects, Heresies*, . s.v., Philadelphia, 1874; *KL*, i. 223–232. On the Adiaphoristic Controversy consult: Schmid, *Controversia de adiaphoris*, Jena, 1807; J. L. v. Mosheim, *Institutes of Eccl. Hist.*, ed. W. Stubbs, ii. 574–576, London, 1863; *KL*, i. 232–235, 769; iv. 1528; v. 769; xii. 1568, 1719.

ADLER, CYRUS: American Jewish scholar; b. at Van Buren, Ark., Sept. 13, 1863. He was educated at the Philadelphia High School, the University of Pennsylvania (B.A., 1883) and Johns Hopkins (Ph.D., 1887). He was fellow in Semitics at Johns Hopkins in 1885–87, and was appointed instructor in the same subject in 1887, and associate professor five years later. In 1887 he was also made assistant curator of Oriental antiquities in the United States Museum, Washington, and custodian of the section of historic religious ceremonials in 1889. In 1905 he was appointed assistant secretary of the Smithsonian Institution. He was virtually the founder of the American Jewish Historical Society in 1892 and has been its president since 1898, and was likewise one of the reorganizers (1902) of the Jewish Theological Seminary of America (New York City), of which he is a life trustee, besides serving as president in 1902-05. He has edited the *American Jewish Year Book* since 1899, has been a member of the editorial staff of the *Jewish Encyclopedia*, in which he had charge of the departments of post-Biblical antiquities and the history of the Jews in America, and has published, in collaboration with Allan Ramsay, *Told in the Coffee House* (New York, 1898).

ADLER, FELIX: Founder of the Society for Ethical Culture; b. at Alzey (20 m. s.w. of Mainz) Aug. 13, 1851. He came to America in 1857, when his father was called to the rabbinate of Temple Emanu-El, New York City, and was educated at Columbia College (A.B., 1870), the Hochschule für die Wissenschaft des Judenthums at Berlin and the university of the same city, and the University of Heidelberg (Ph.D., 1873). From 1874 to 1876 he was professor of Hebrew and Oriental literature at Cornell, but in the latter year went to New York and established the Society for Ethical Culture, a non-religious association for the ethical improvement of its members, of which he has since been the head. He has been active in various philanthropic enterprises and in popular education, being a member of the State Tenement Committee in 1884 and of the Committee of Fifteen in 1901, and in 1902 was appointed professor of political and social ethics at Columbia University. He is a member of the editorial board of the *International Journal of Ethics* and has written *Creed and Deed* (New York, 1877); *The Moral Instruction of Children* (1898); *Life and Destiny* (1903); *Marriage and Divorce* (1905); *Religion of Duty* (1905), and *Essentials of Spirituality* (1905).

ADLER, HERMANN NATHAN: Chief rabbi of the United Hebrew Congregations of the British Empire; b. at Hanover, Germany, May 30, 1839. He was educated at the University College School and University College, London (B.A., 1859), and also at the universities of Prague and Leipsic (Ph.D., Leipsic, 1861). He received the rabbinical diploma at Prague in 1862, and in the following year was appointed principal of Jews' College, London. In 1864 he became minister of the Bayswater Synagogue, London, but continued to be tutor in theology in Jews' College until 1879, when he was appointed delegate chief rabbi to relieve his father, Nathan Marcus Adler, whom age had rendered unable to perform all the duties of chief rabbi. On the death of his father, Adler was chosen his successor as chief rabbi in 1891, and at the same time was elected president of Jews' College, where he had already been chairman of the council since 1887. He is also president of Aria College and the London *beth din*, vice-president of the National Society for the Prevention of Cruelty to Children and the Mansion House Association for Improving the Dwellings of the Poor, governor of University College, and a member of the committee of the King Edward Hospital Fund and the Metropolitan Hospital Sunday Fund. He has likewise been president of the Jewish Historical Society, vice-president of the Jewish Religious Educational Board and the Anglo-Jewish Association, and representative of the Russo-Jewish Committee at Berlin (1889) and Paris (1890). In addition to numerous briefer contributions, he has written *Solomon ibn Gabirol and his Influence upon Scholastic Philosophy* (London, 1865) and *Sermons on the Biblical Passages adduced by Christian Theologians in Support of the Dogmas of their Faith* (1869).

ADLER, NATHAN MARCUS: English chief rabbi; b. at Hanover, Germany, Jan. 15, 1803; d. at Brighton (50½ m. s. of London), Sussex, England, Jan. 21, 1890. He was educated at the universities of Göttingen, Erlangen (Ph.D., 1826), Würzburg, and Heidelberg, and in 1830 was appointed chief rabbi of Oldenburg. Before a year had passed he was made chief rabbi of the kingdom of Hanover, and in 1845 he was installed in the far more important post of chief rabbi of the British Empire. In 1845 he received the assistance of a deputy delegate chief rabbi, but retained his own position until his death. Active both in philanthropic and educational measures, he was the founder of Jews' College, London, in 1855, besides being the real originator of the Hospital Sabbath among his coreligionists. He was the author of many works in English, German, and Hebrew, including *Die Liebe zum Vaterlande* (Hanover, 1838); *The Jewish Faith* (London, 1867); and *Nethinah la-Ger* (commentary on the Targum of Onkelos, Wilna, 1875).

ADO, ā″dō′: Archbishop of Vienne 860–875; b. near Sens about 800; d. at Vienne Dec. 16, 875. He was considered one of the principal upholders of the papal hierarchy, and wrote a *Martyrologium* (best ed. by D. Giorgi, 2 vols., Rome, 1745), which surpasses all its predecessors in richness of material, and a *Chronicon de sex ætatibus mundi* (Paris, 1512; Rome, 1745 et al.; extracts in *MGH, Script.*, ii., 1829, pp. 315–323) from the creation of the world to 874. His works are in *MPL*, cxxiii. 1–452.

ADONAI. See YAHWEH.

ADONAI SHOMO. See COMMUNISM, II., 1.

ADOPTION.

Adoption is a term of theology denoting the new relation to God which Jesus experienced and into which he brings his followers. In tracing the history of this conception, attention is to be paid to the different senses in which the analogy is used in religion,—the idea of homogeneousness with God, of the relation to him, and the divine basis of both.

1. Old Testament Conception.

In the Old Testament, the people, the king, and individual pious men and women are called children of God. The people become children of God by their introduction into the promised land, the king by his election, individual persons by their physical creation. It is only with regard to the heavenly spirits that the state of being a child of God (*Gotteskindschaft*) expresses homogeneousness of being. The relation is one in which God helps, pardons, educates, even through suffering, and in which men have to obey God and trust in him. But the obedience of children is not different from that of servants, and their trust is paralyzed by God's inexplicable disposition to wrath. In later Judaism the relation became one of right,—the pious man must secure his reward, which is a matter of natural desire, by his own merits and sacrifices, and he always wavers between self-righteous security and anxiety.

2. The Conception of Jesus.

Jesus as seen in the synoptic Gospels, knows God as the lofty lord to whom men are subjected in service, and as the just judge; but by inner experiences he recognizes this God as his father who discloses to him his love, and he encourages men to believe not that they *are* God's children, but that they *become* such by conducting themselves and feeling as children. The innovation lies in the quality of the relation. In spite of God's physical and spiritual superiority, man is free from the feeling of oppression and insecurity, in the first place, before the demanding will of God. Through the recognition of God as Father, Jesus knows himself urged to the service of saving love, renouncing every worldly desire, but this service means for him freedom and blessedness (Matt. xi. 28–30), because he feels it as the fulfilment of his own desire (Matt. ix. 36–38), and even as a gain in greatness and power (Matt. xx. 25–28), because in it he is raised above the Mosaic law (Matt. v. 22). In the same way he delivers those whom he encourages to believe in God's fatherly love and forgiveness, from the oppression of the law by showing them as its innermost core (Matt. v. 9, 48) the imitation of the example of the perfect God in a love which surpasses all bounds of human love. From this conception of the divine law all hedonistic elements have been removed; it expresses a reverent and cheerful devotion to an ideal. Where Jesus also uses God's retribution as an ethical motive and thus seems to substitute a relation of right for the relation of adoption, he deepens and purifies the traditional view. Reward goes hand in hand with conduct; a childlike disposition is rewarded with the dignity due to God's children (Matt. v. 9) and with physical homogeneousness (Luke vii. 36); justice is rewarded with justice (Matt. v. 6; vi. 33). He promises the kingdom (Matt. x. 13–16) to the unassuming childlike disposition, and promises reward, not to individual performance, but to the spirit which reveals itself in it (Matt. vii. 15, xxv. 23), excludes the equivalence between work and reward (Matt. xx. 1–16), and appeals to fear not as dread of physical evil, but as anxiety lest the life with God (Matt. x. 18) be lost. In the second place, the trust in God's fatherly guidance which Jesus himself proves and encourages, is of a singular surety and joyfulness. Whoever through fear of God is kept in his way, may be certain of the acquisition of salvation (Luke x. 20) and may hope not only to gain eternal life (Luke xii. 32), but already here on earth he knows himself to be lifted above all oppression of the world since he may be sure that his prayers are granted (Matt. vii. 7) and may expect from God his daily bread and know himself protected by God in every way (Matt. x. 28–31) and may venture even that which seems impossible (Mark xi. 22) and be sure of the forgiveness of his sins and of his protection in temptation (Matt. vi. 12, 13) and triumph over all hostile powers (Luke x. 19).

In opposition to philosophy, this idea is new in so far as God in the current systems of philosophy was represented as father only as the shaper of the world, and the capacity of becoming a child of God was merely a general function of reason. The religious importance of the ideal is here only secondary; it originates rather in personal dignity and is an altruism which does not extend to the love of enemies. As faith in a fatherly providence, it believes only in an order of the world which offers an opportunity to prove one's strength of will, and thus does not attain submission as expressed in Christian adoption, but only resignation.

Jesus speaks of adoption only in the imperative, —we must *become* children of God by imitation of God and trust in God; but he admonishes to become such by pointing to God's disposition and promise. His word receives additional emphasis from his personality which lives in God; and he judges the conduct of God's child in the last analysis as an effect of God (Matt. xi. 28, xv. 3; Mark x. 27). Therefore it is the natural expression of the experience of the Christian Church when in the New Testament the awakening of the child's life by the effect of divine grace is considered fundamental (II Cor. v. 17; I Pet. i. 3, 23; John iii. 5).

This effect, according to Paul, is juridical, i.e., a real adoption, a granting of the right of children (Gal. iii. 26–27), synonymous with justification; but it is also a real change through the overwhelming influence of the Holy Spirit as an unconscious power like the impersonal powers of nature (Rom. viii. 11; Gal. v. 22). Paul bases the certainty of the right of children upon the fact that through faith and baptism believers belong to Christ, but also upon the experience of the liberating effect of the spirit. The right of children means for him the claim upon the future heritage of the kingdom of God; namely, the participation in God's fatherhood (Rom. iv. 3) and the spiritualization of the body in conforming it to the body of Christ, the first of the sons of God (Rom. viii. 29–30). These figures express the idea that the prevening grace of God establishes a personal relation of love which has an analogy in the intimate communion between father and child. As I am certain that God is on my side and that I am called to eternal life, I may surely trust that he will grant me everything (Rom. viii. 31–32), not only eternal life, but also everything in the world which is not against God (I Cor. iii. 21–22) and that he will lead me through all temptations to that sanctity which belongs to the kingdom of God (I Thess. v. 23). The faith which corresponds on our part to God's intention of love remains secure even against troubles and hostile world powers because the latter can not separate from the love of God (Rom. viii. 38–39) and the former must subserve the upbuilding of the inner man (II Cor. iv. 16–18). Thus the essential feature of this child-life is not fear, as under the Law and its curse, but rather unshakable joy which expresses itself in giving thanks as the key-note of prayer. The unconscious impulse which the ethical life of the Christian assumes if he puts the impulse of the spirit in place of the Law, he modifies by bringing to expression also conscious ethical motives; namely, the love of God as experienced by him, and his call to the kingdom of God, which demand a conduct worthy of both. Even an overpowerful desire of his nature he begins to transform into an impulse for consciousness if he guides it into the channel of experienced love (II Cor. v. 15; Gal. ii. 20). But in all joy, happiness, and freedom with relation to God, the Christian is prevented from excesses by that humility which in all progress and success gives due honor to God (I Cor. xv. 10). It seems a contradiction when Paul in spite of all speaks of a retribution on the part of God according to works and awakens fear of the judgment. The seeming relation of right is only an expression for the fact that the relation of father and children, although resting upon God's free love, is mutual. The reward is a success of mutual effort (Gal. vi. 7, 8). It is attained, not by a sum of individual works, but by a sanctified personality (Thess. v. 23) which is absorbed in a uniform activity of life (II Cor. v. 10; I Cor. iii. 13). The fear of which Paul speaks is the fear of watchfulness which takes possession of us in looking at the world and the flesh, but this disagreeable feeling is immediately conquered by the joyful trust that God will protect and perfect us (I Cor. xv. 2; Rom. xi. 20–21).

3. Paul's Conception.

The Gospel and Epistles of John trace adoption back to the testimony of God (Gospel iii. 5; First Epistle ii. 19). According to them, adoption consists in a close and intimate life in and with God by which there is vouchsafed, on the one hand, the impossibility of sinning and the self-evidence of justice and love to God and our brethren, and, on the other hand, the victory over the world and blessing and the future homogeneousness with God (I John iv. 3; v. 4, 18). However natural all this may sound, these expressions are only figures for an ethico-personal communion with God, analogous to that between father and child which has its basis in the influence of Christ upon our consciousness, not in a reflected, but spontaneous way. The knowledge of God or the word of Christ (I John ii. 3; Gospel xv. 3) is parallel to the seed of God which remains in the regenerated person and guarantees his sanctity (I John iii. 9). Unity of life with God is an analogon for that unity which on earth exists between the Father and Jesus (John xvii. 21–22), where the Father in preceding love discloses to his Son his whole work and the Son remains in the love of the Father (John xv. 10) by speaking and acting according to the commandment of the Father and being solely concerned with his Father's honor (John v. 44) and yet enjoying full satisfaction, eternal life (John iv. 34, xii. 50), and at the same time fully trusting that the Father is with him and always hears him and in spite of the world brings his work to perfection which through death leads to glory (John viii. 29, xvi. 32, xvii. 4). Correspondingly there follows for his disciples from the certainty of the love of God the duty to love one another and to show the self-evident love of children by keeping the commandments (I John iv. 11, v. 3) which are freedom and life because the disciples are not slaves, but friends of the son of God (John xv. 15) and continuators of his work (John xviii. 18). In this tendency of life they may possess joyfulness (I John ii. 28, iv. 17, 18) in a world full of temptations and enemies and in face of death and judgment and may count upon the return of their love on the part of God through the gift of the spirit and the help of God which is always near, upon the forgiveness of accidental sins, purification, hearing of their prayers, and a place in the heavenly mansion of the Father (John xiv. 2, 3; xiii. 21–22; xv. 2; xvii. 17; I John i. 9).

4. The Gospel and Epistles of John.

According to Jesus, Paul, and John, the child of God is independent of men and yet he must seek communion with men. Jesus teaches to pray "Our Father"; and according to Paul and John, the spirit communicates with the individual through baptism and makes him a member of the community.

The Church has not always maintained this ideal. When its growth necessitated a stricter inculcation of the ethical conditions of salvation, the relation of children was changed under the influence of the Jewish idea of retaliation, of philosophical moralism, and the ideas of Roman law. According to the apologetic writers, to be a child of God means subjectively the ethical resemblance with God which man realizes in himself by his free action on the basis of the knowledge of God as taught by Christ. Since ethics was absorbed in individual practise of virtue and consciousness of moral freedom, the desire for a counterbalance against the moral checks from the world was not felt so much. Irenæus follows Paul by conceiving adoption as the specific effect of redemption; but he understands it, in the first place, in a moralistic sense, as a call to the fulfilment of the deepened law of nature, not only in increased love, but fear; in the second place, in a physical sense, as the sacramental elevation of the spirit to deification or imperishableness. This combination remains a characteristic feature of the Greek Church.

5. The Apologists.

Augustine deepened the physical change into an ethical change which governs ethical actions. Because God's nature is first of all justice, and only secondarily immortal, adoption, as being deification, is in the first place justification, infusion of love (*amando Deum efficimur dii*—" by loving God we are made gods"; again—" he who justifies also deifies, because by justifying he makes sons of God"), which takes place under the influence of faith, i.e., hopeful prayer, or through baptism. Thus man faces the task—*Reddite diem, efficimini spiritus* (" Do your part, and become spirit "). Adoption becomes a reality in a process in which the capacity for it increases by continual forgiveness and inspiration of love until after death the second adoption occurs, the liberation from the body which contains the law of sin. Our life is a relation between child and father in so far as love to God, childlike fear, and hope rule in it. But the idea of the New Testament is curtailed in so far as forgiveness concerns always only past sins, and hope is bound to rely upon one's own consciousness of love to God and upon merit, and forgiveness becomes uncertain in consequence of predestination, and in so far as, with the task to serve God in the world, the New Testament manner of trusting in God is also done away with, and a holy indifference takes its place. The relation of God seems to be intensified in so far as there is added as a new element the highest stage of divine love—the mystical contemplation of God; but the apparent *plus* discloses itself as a *minus*, since love to God is now conceived of by analogy with that between man and woman instead of that between father and child. Mysticism, it is true, elevates man to freedom from the Church, but it effects also indifference toward men; however, in the premystical stage there shows itself lack of independence of the Church.

6. Augustine.

In the Occident the curtailment of the childlike in Christian life was still further indulged in by bringing to prominence the ideas of the natural, juridical, and mystical; of the natural in so far as according to the scholastics a habit of grace is infused into the secret recesses of the soul, the existence of which can only be surmised by way of inference from one's own ethical transformation; of the juridical in so far as the provenience of hope from merit (" *spes provenit ex meritis* ") is more strongly emphasized; of the mystical inasmuch as the higher stage of the love of God seems realizable only in a thorough separation from occupation with worldly matters (the lower stage is identified with childlike fear) and inasmuch as even the mysticism of calmness and resignation over against an arbitrary Lord is far inferior to trust in the Father.

7. Scholasticism.

It was Luther who again conceived the relation of Christians to God as that of children to a father in the full sense of the word. For Luther Christ is the " mirror of the fatherly heart of God," the revelation and security of God's gracious disposition, and he draws from this " image of grace " faith and individual trust. He differs from Paul in so far as he understands by the inner testimony of the Holy Spirit the personal certainty of faith which has its basis in Christ. As for Paul, so for Luther, forgiveness of sins or justification or adoption is a declaration of the will of God that he adopts us as children. It is more than the remittance of past sins, it is the reception of the whole personality into the grace of God, the transposition into a permanent state which always has to be seized again by faith. Thus it is shown to be an error that meritorious works are necessary in order to obtain grace and eternal life. In this way Luther does not destroy the ethical quality of adoption, but makes it more prominent. For secure trust unites the will with God's entire will in love and thus spontaneously produces, without needing the instruction and inculcation of the law, the free and cheerful fulfilment of the will of God which takes place without any thought of reward and in which eternal life is enjoyed. This psychological derivation of morality from the nature of faith actually invalidates Luther's other derivation from the natural or unconscious impulse of the Holy Spirit. Only his opposition to the doctrine of merits made him forget to do justice to the eschatological motives of morality as they are found in Jesus and Paul, although he might have done so, considering his premises; for will needs an aim and for the will united with God in faith and love, this aim can only be the completion of that which was begun here. Faith gives him new courage and power for trust in the guidance of the whole life by the Father in which again the joy of eternal life is anticipated, and thus lays the basis for the freedom of the Christian or his royal dominion over all things which manifests itself in fearlessness and pride and defiance of Satan, world, and death as the counterpart of humble submission to God and which through the certainty of the blessing of divine guidance surpasses mysticism—ecstasies as well as resignation in God. This attitude of children is a life which is homogeneous to that of the Father, in the first place, to his disposition, in so far as our trust is a reflex of God's disposition toward us and our love corresponds to the love of God since it is not borrowed from the amiability of men, but is spontaneous, and not a divided love like that of men, but an all-comprehending one; in the second place, to the nature

8. Luther.

of God, because this love is superhuman, divine, and because faith conquers for itself the power of divine omnipotence. This life of adoption, according to its whole character, can only originate by a birth from above which, according to Luther, takes place since adoption, as vouchsafed by Christ, produces faith and with it new life. Luther also traces back the new life to a problematic effect of the Spirit, like the working of the impersonal powers of nature, which God according to his predestination adds to the word of Christ in the inner life.

9. Later German Theology. During the period of orthodoxy in Germany trust in God on the part of his children was regarded as natural religion. Pietism subordinated adoption to regeneration. In theology as influenced by Hegel, childlike union with God after the example of mysticism was traced back to an inner self-manifestation of the absolute spirit. It was Ritschl who renewed the specific ideas of Luther. J. GOTTSCHICK.

10. Two Views Held at Present. At the present time two ideas of adoption are advocated: (1) Resting back on Calvin, it is held that the primary relation of God to man was that of Creator and Governor. Man is son of God, not by virtue of anything in his constitution as a creature of God, nor on account of a natural relation to him as subject of the divine government, but solely by reason of gracious adoption. The only essential sonship is that of Christ primarily as the eternal Son, and secondarily as his humanity shares this prerogative through union with the divine nature. Through adoption the elect in Christ become partakers of Christ's sonship. Adoption is grounded neither in justification nor in regeneration, but in God's free and sovereign grace alone. Through justification the legal and judicial disabilities caused by sin are removed; through regeneration the nature is changed so as to become filial. Thus a basis is laid for the distinction between the state of adoption and the spirit of adoption (R. S. Candlish, *The Fatherhood of God*, London, 1870; J. Macpherson, *Christian Dogmatics*, Edinburgh, 1898). (2) According to the other view, man's filial relation to God is archetypal and inalienable. Adoption, in order to be real, necessarily involves the essential and universal Fatherhood of God and the natural and inherent sonship of man to God. By becoming partaker of the spirit of Christ, who, as Son, realized the filial ideal of the race, one passes out of natural into gracious sonship; that is, is adopted into the ethical and spiritual family of God, and so enters upon his ideal filial relation to God and his brotherly relation to men (A. M. Fairbairn, *The Place of Christ in Modern Theology*, New York, 1893; J. S. Lidgett, *The Fatherhood of God*, pp. 20–21, Edinburgh, 1902; James Orr, *Progress of Dogma*, pp. 325–327, New York, 1902). C. A. B.

BIBLIOGRAPHY: J. Gerhard, *Loci Theologici*, iv. 311, 374, vii. 219–222, ix. 296–297, Berlin, 1866–75; R. L. Dabney, *Syllabus of . Systematic and Polemic Theology*, pp. 627 sqq., St. Louis, 1878; B. Weiss, *Biblical Theology of the New Testament*, §§17, 20–21, 45, 71, 83, 100, 118, 150, Edinburgh, 1882–83; W Bousset, *Jesu Predigt in ihrem Gegensatz zum Judentum*, pp. 41–42, Göttingen, 1892; H. Shultz, *Old Testament Theology*, ii. 254 sqq., Edinburgh, 1892; R. A. Lipsius, *Lehrbuch der evangelisch-protestantischen Dogmatik*, pp. 126–129, 584–596, 653–703, Brunswick, 1893; J. McL. Campbell, *Nature of the Atonement*, pp. 298 sqq., London, 1895; A. Titius, *Die neutestamentliche Lehre von der Seligkeit*, i. 103–104, ii. 27–28, 138–139, 266–267, Tübingen, 1895–1900; W. Beyschlag, *New Testament Theology*, i. 60–70, 241, 310, ii. 418–419, 480, Edinburgh, 1896; E. Hatch, *Greek Ideas and Usages, their Influence upon the Christian Church*, London, 1897; R. V. Foster, *Systematic Theology*, p. 679, Nashville, 1898; H. Cremer, *Die paulinische Rechtfertigungslehre*, pp. 71–78, 224–233, 247–248, 265–266, 369–370, Gütersloh, 1899; A. Ritschl, *Christian Doctrine of Justification and Reconciliation*, pp. 75, 96, 507, 534, 603, New York, 1900.

ADOPTIONISM (ADOPTIANISM).

1. The Controversy of the Eighth Century. Its Roots. Adoptionism—a heresy maintaining that Christ is the Son of God by adoption—is of interest chiefly for the commotion which it produced in the Spanish and Frankish Churches in the latter part of the eighth century, although the formulas around which the conflict raged can indeed be traced back to the earliest period of Western theology; but the spirit of the controversy and the result showed that the orthodoxy of the eighth century could no longer entirely accept the ancient formulas. The phrases in which such writers as Novatian, Hilary, and Isidore of Seville had spoken not merely of the assumption of human nature by the Son of God, but also of the assumption of man or the son of man, led by an easy transition to words which seemed to imply that Christ, according to his humanity, was the adopted son of God; and formulas of this kind occur not infrequently in the old Spanish liturgy.

2. Elipandus, Bishop of Toledo. The Spanish bishops of the eighth century, and especially their leader, Elipandus (b. 718; bishop of Toledo from about 780), so used such phrases as to provoke criticism and disapproval first in Asturia, then in the neighboring Frankish kingdom, and finally at Rome. A certain Migetius (q.v.), preaching in that part of Spain which was held by the Moors, had given a very gross exposition of the doctrine of the Trinity, teaching that there were three bodily persons, and a triple manifestation in history of the one God. Against him Elipandus wrote a letter vindicating the orthodox idea of the immanence of the Trinity, but at the same time establishing a very sharp distinction between the second person of the Trinity and the human nature of Christ. The person of the Son was not that made according to the flesh, in time, of the seed of David, but that begotten by the Father before all worlds; even after the incarnation, the second person of the Godhead is not the bodily, of which Christ says "My Father is greater than I," but that of which he says "I and my Father are one." Elipandus did not mean to do violence to the orthodox teaching by this distinction; but if the expression were pressed, the human nature appeared a different person from the person of the Eternal Word, and the single personality of Christ disappeared. Elipandus defended himself in letters in which he used the expression that Christ was only according to his Godhead the true and real (*proprius*) Son of God, and according to his manhood an adopted son. The opposition to this view was voiced by Beatus, a priest, and the monk Heterius of Libana. Elipandus wrote in great excitement to the Asturian abbot Fidelis, bitterly attacking his opponents, who first saw the letter when they met Fidelis in Nov., 785, on the occasion of Queen Adosinda's taking the veil. In reply they wrote a treatise, discursive and badly arranged, but strong in its patristic quotations, emphasizing the unity of Christ's personality. The conflict was complicated by political circumstances and by the efforts of Asturia to attain independence of the most powerful Spanish bishop. Complaints were carried to Rome, and Adrian I. pronounced at once against Elipandus and his supporter, Ascaricus, whom he judged guilty of Nestorianism.

At what period the most prominent representative of Adoptionism, Felix, bishop of Urgel in the Pyrenees, first took part in the strife is unknown. At the synod of Regensburg in 792, he defended the heresy in the presence of Charlemagne, but the bishops rejected it. Felix, although he had retracted his doctrine, was sent by the emperor to Rome, where Pope Adrian kept him a prisoner until he signed an orthodox confession, which on his return to Urgel he repudiated as forced, and then fled to Moorish territory. In 793 Alcuin, just back from England, wrote to Felix begging him to abandon the suspicious word "adoption," and to bring Elipandus back into the right path; and he followed this up by his controversial treatise *Adversus hæresim Felicis*. About the same time Elipandus and the Spanish bishops who belonged to his party addressed a letter to the bishops of Gaul, Aquitaine, and Asturia, and to Charlemagne himself, asking for a fair investigation and the restoration of Felix. Charlemagne communicated with the pope, and caused a new investigation of the case in the brilliant assembly at Frankfort (794). Two separate encyclicals were the result—one from the Frankish and German bishops; the other from those of northern Italy—which agreed in condemning Adoptionism. Charlemagne sent these, with one from the pope (representing also the bishops of central and southern Italy) to Elipandus, urging him not to separate himself from the authority of the apostolic see and of the universal Church. Strong efforts were put forth to recover the infected provinces. Alcuin wrote repeatedly to the monks of that region; Leidrad, bishop of Lyons, and the saintly Abbot Benedict of Aniane worked there personally, supporting Bishop Nefrid of Narbonne. In 798 Felix wrote a book and sent it to Alcuin, who replied in the following spring with his more extended treatise *Adversus Felicem*. Felix must by this time have been able to return to Urgel, as he wrote thence to Elipandus. Leo III. decisively condemned him in a Roman synod of 798 or 799. Alcuin received a

3. Felix, Bishop of Urgel.

contumelious answer, and was anxious to cross swords personally with his antagonist.

Leidrad induced Felix to appear before Charlemagne, with the promise of a fair hearing from the bishops. They met at Aix-la-Chapelle in June, 799 (others say Oct., 798). After a lengthy discussion Felix acknowledged himself defeated and was restored to communion, though not to his see, and he was placed in Leidrad's charge. Felix then composed a recantation, and called on the clergy of Urgel to imitate his example. Leidrad and Benedict renewed their endeavors, with such success that Alcuin was soon able to assert that they had reclaimed 20,000 souls. He supported them with a treatise in four books against Elipandus, and prided himself on the conversion of Felix. The heretical leader seems, however, to have quietly retained his old beliefs at Lyons for the rest of his life, and even to have pushed them logically further, since Agobard, Leidrad's successor, accused him of Agnoetism, and wrote a reply to some of his posthumous writings. In the Moorish part of Spain, Elipandus seems to have had a numerous following; but here also he found determined opponents. The belief was gradually suppressed, though Alvar of Cordova (d. about 861) found troublesome remnants of it.

4. Recantation of Felix.

With the rise of scholastic theology there was a natural tendency of rigid dialectic to lead away from the Christology of Cyril and Alcuin toward a rational distinction between the two natures, not so much with any wish to insist on this as from a devotion to the conception of the immutability of God. This caused the charge of Nestorianism to be brought against Abelard. Peter Lombard's explanations of the sense in which God became man leaned in the same direction. A German defender of this aspect of the question, Bishop Eberhard of Bamberg, in the twelfth century, accused his opponents roundly of Eutychianism. In fact, the assailants of Adoptionism, starting from their thesis that Christ is really and truly the Son of God, even according to his human nature, because this nature was appropriated by the Son of God, came ultimately, for all their intention of holding the Church's doctrine of the two natures and the two wills, to a quite distinct presentation of an altogether divine Person who has assumed impersonal human substance and nature. They really deserted the position taken by Cyril, though he was one of their main authorities. If one seeks the historical origin of this late form of Christological controversy, distinguishing it from the immediate cause, it must be found in the unsettlement of mind necessarily consequent upon the attempts of the ecclesiastical Christology to reconcile mutually exclusive propositions.

5. Later Adoptionist Tendencies.

The intellectual mood which led directly to this distinction between the Son of God and the man in Christ has been variously explained. Some ascribe it to the surrounding Mohammedanism, making it an attempt to remove as far as possible the stumbling-blocks in the doctrine of Christ's nature; but this may be doubted, since the main difficulties from the Moslem standpoint—the Trinity,

6. Explanation.

and the idea of a God who begets and is begotten—remain untouched. Others see in it a survival of the spirit of the old Germanic Arianism, which is excluded by the adherence of the Adoptionists to the orthodox Trinitarian teaching. The obvious relation with Nestorianism and the theology of the school of Antioch has led others to assume a direct influence of the writings of Theodore of Mopsuestia; but there is as little evidence for this as there is for the theory that those whom Elipandus calls his "orthodox brethren" in Cordova, and whom Alcuin supposes to be responsible for these aberrations, were a colony of eastern Christians of Nestorian tendencies who had come to Spain with the Arabs. (A. HAUCK.)

BIBLIOGRAPHY: The writings of Elipandus, Felix, and Heterius in *MPL*, xcvi.; Paulinus, *Vita et Litteræ*, ib. xcix.; Alcuin, *Opera*, ib. c.-ci.; *Monumenta Alcuiniana*, in Jaffé, *Bibliotheca rerum Germanicarum*, vol. vi., Berlin, 1873; *MGH*, *Epist.*, iv., 1895; Agobard, *Vita et Opera*, in *MPL*, civ.; the *Acta* of the Synods of Narbonne, Ratisbon, Frankfort, and Aix-la-Chapelle, in Harduin, *Concilia*, iv., in Mansi, *Concilia*, xiii., in Gallandi, *Bibliotheca*, xiii., and *MGH*, *Concilia*, ii., 1904; C. W F. Walch, *Historia Adoptianorum*, Göttingen, 1755; idem, *Entwurf einer vollständigen Historie der Ketzereien*, vol. iii., 11 vols., Leipsic, 1762-85; F. C. Baur, *Die Christliche Lehre von der Dreieinigkeit und Menschwerdung Gottes*, 3 vols., Berlin, 1841–43; Rettberg, i. (1846) 428; J. C. Robertson, *History of the Christian Church*, 590–1122, London, 1856; A. Helfferich, *Der westgothische Arianismus und die spanische Ketzergeschichte*, Berlin, 1860; J. Bach, *Dogmengeschichte des Mittelalters*, i. 102 sqq., Vienna, 1873; K. Werner, *Alcuin und sein Jahrhundert*, Paderborn, 1876; C. J. B. Gaskoin, *Alcuin*, pp. 79 sqq., London, 1904; *DCB*, i. 44–47; Hefele, *Conciliengeschichte*, iii. 642–693, 721 724; Hauck, *KD*, ii. 289 sqq.

ADORATION OF THE SACRAMENT: A term of the Roman Catholic Church, where, in consequence of the doctrine of transubstantiation which affirms the presence of Christ in the Eucharist under the species of bread and wine, divine worship is paid to the Sacrament of the altar, a worship that includes adoration. This adoration is manifested in various ways, especially in genuflexions and, if the Sacrament be solemnly exposed, in prostrations. Certain forms of devotion are intended to promote adoration of the Sacrament, notably the ceremony called Benediction of the Blessed Sacrament, the Forty Hours Devotion, and the practise of perpetual adoration which secures the presence of adorers before the altar at all hours of the day and night. A congregation of priests, the Society of Priests of the Most Holy Sacrament, is devoted particularly to the worship of Christ on the altar. JOHN T. CREAGH.

AD QUERCUM, SYNODUS. See CHRYSOSTOM.

ADRAMMELECH, a-dram'el-ec: **1.** Name of a deity worshiped with child-sacrifice by the colonists whom Sargon, king of Assyria, transplanted from Sepharvaim to Samaria (II Kings xvii. 31; cf. xviii. 34; Isa. xxxvi. 19, xxxvii. 13). Since Sepharvaim is probably the Syrian city *Shabara'in*, mentioned in a Babylonian chronicle as having been destroyed by Shalmaneser IV., the god Adrammelech is no doubt a Syrian divinity. The name has been explained as meaning "Adar the prince," "splendor of the king," and "fire-king," while others think that the original reading was "Adadmelech." Since the name is Aramaic, the last is to be preferred.

2. According to II Kings xix. 37 and Isa. xxxvii. 38, Adrammelech was the name of the son and murderer of the Assyrian king Sennacherib. The form corresponds to the "Adramelus" of Abydenus in the Armenian chronicle of Eusebius (ed. A. Schöne, i., Berlin, 1875, p. 35) and the "Ardumuzanus" of Alexander Polyhistor (p. 27).

BIBLIOGRAPHY: (1) Schrader, *KAT*, ii. 408, 450; P. Scholz, *Götzendienst und Zauberwesen bei den alten Hebräern*, pp. 401–405, Ratisbon, 1877. (2) H. Winckler, *Der Mörder Sanheribs*, in *ZA*, ii. (1887) 392–396.

ADRIAN: Author of an extant *Introduction to the Holy Scriptures*, written in Greek. He was evidently a Greek-speaking Syrian; but nothing is to be learned of his life from the book. There is no doubt, however, that he is identical with the monk and presbyter Adrian to whom St. Nilus addressed three letters (ii. 60, iii. 118, 266, in *MPG*, lxxix. 225–227, 437, 516–517), and who lived in the first half of the fifth century. This work is no introduction in the modern sense, but a piece of Biblical rhetoric and didactics, aiming to explain the figurative phraseology of the Scriptures, especially of the Old Testament, from numerous examples. It closes with hints for correct exegesis. The hermeneutical and exegetical principles of the author are those of the Antiochian school. F. Gössling edited the Greek text with German translation and an introduction (Berlin, 1887).

G. KRÜGER.

BIBLIOGRAPHY: A. Merx, *Rede vom Auslegen*, pp. 64–67, Halle, 1879.

ADRIAN: The name of six popes.

Adrian I.: Pope 772–795. A Roman of noble birth, he entered the clerical state under Paul I., and was ordained deacon by Stephen III., whom he succeeded Feb. 1, 772, not, apparently, by as unanimous a choice as the official record of his election asserts; for soon afterward he encountered vehement opposition from the Lombard party in Rome led by Paul Afiarta. His adherence to the Frankish faction, his hesitation to crown the sons of Karlman, who had fled to Pavia, and thus to set them up as pretenders against Charlemagne, and the imprisonment of Afiarta by Archbishop Leo of Ravenna at his orders incited the Lombard king Desiderius to invade the Roman territory, and finally to march on Rome itself. Adrian appealed for help to Charlemagne, who arrived in Italy in Sept., 773, and forced Desiderius to shut himself up in Pavia.

During the siege of that town, which lasted till the following June, Charlemagne suddenly appeared unannounced in Rome. Adrian, though alarmed, gave him a brilliant reception. On Apr. 6 a meeting took place in St. Peter's, at which, according

Aided by Charlemagne.

to the *Vita Hadriani*, the emperor was exhorted by the pope to confirm the donation of his father, Pepin, and did so, even making some additions of territory. This donation, which rests solely upon the authority of the *Vita* (xli.-xliii.), if substantiated, has a great importance for the development of the temporal sovereignty of the popes. The question has received much attention, and its literature is scarcely exceeded in bulk by that of any other medieval controversy. No sure and universally recognized result, however, has been reached. Some modern historians (Sybel, Ranke, Martens) consider the story a pure invention; others (Ficker, Duchesne) accept it; and a middle theory of partial interpolation has also been upheld (Scheffer-Boichorst). All that can be maintained with certainty is that Charlemagne gave a promise of a donation, and the geographical delimitations give rise to difficult problems.

Disagreements with Charlemagne.

In the years immediately following Charlemagne's return from Italy, his friendly relations with Adrian were disturbed by more than one occurrence. Archbishop Leo of Ravenna seized some cities from the pope, who complained to Charlemagne; but Leo visited the Frankish court to defend himself, and met with a not unfavorable reception. Charlemagne's keen insight can not have failed to read imperfectly masked covetousness between the lines of Adrian's repeated requests for the final fulfilment of the promise of 774; e.g., in the hope held out of a heavenly reward if he should enlarge the Church's possessions; in the profuse congratulations on his victory over the Saxons, which was attributed to the intercession of St. Peter, grateful for the restitution of his domain; in the comparison drawn by Adrian between Charlemagne and "the most God-fearing emperor Constantine the Great," who "out of his great liberality exalted the Church of God in Rome and gave her power in Hesperia [Italy]"—expressions which have caused a subordinate controversy as to whether the so-called Donation of Constantine (q.v.) is referred to. How far Adrian's consciousness of his own importance had grown is evident from the fact that while in the beginning of his reign he had dated his public documents by the years of the Greek emperors, from the end of 781 he dated them by the years of his own pontificate.

Charlemagne Again Helps.

Yet Adrian could not afford to despise the Greeks; they joined the Lombard dukes of Benevento and Spoleto, and forced him once more to turn for help to Charlemagne, who made a short descent into Italy in 776, put down the revolt of the duke of Friuli against both him and the pope, but did nothing more until 780. In 781 he visited Rome again when his sons were anointed as kings—Pepin of Italy and Louis of Aquitaine. Charlemagne came to Italy for the fourth time in 786 to crush Arichis of Benevento, and Adrian succeeded in obtaining from him additional territory in southern Italy. But various misunderstandings in Adrian's last years gave rise to a report that Charlemagne and Offa of Mercia had taken counsel together with a view to the pope's deposition. The iconoclastic controversy (see Images and Image-worship, II., § 3) brought fresh humiliations from Charlemagne and from the Greek emperor Constantine VI. and his mother, the empress Irene. When the last-named was taking steps to restore the veneration of images in the Eastern Church she requested Adrian to be present in person at a general council soon to be held, or at least to send suitable legates (785). In his reply, after commending Irene and her son for their determination respecting the images, Adrian asked for a restitution of the territory taken from the Roman see by the iconoclastic emperor Leo III. in 732, as well as of its patriarchal rights in Calabria, Sicily, and the Illyrian provinces which Leo had suppressed. At the same time he renewed the protest made by Gregory the Great against the assumption of the title of *universalis patriarcha* by the Patriarch of Constantinople.

Council of Nicæa in 787.

When, however, the council met at Nicæa in 787, while it removed the prohibition of images, it paid no attention to any of these demands. The acts of this council, which Adrian sent to Charlemagne in 790, provoked the emperor's vigorous opposition, and led ultimately to the drawing up of the *Caroline Books* (q.v.), in which the position of the Frankish Church with reference to both the Roman and the Greek was made plain, and the decisions of the Council of Nicæa were disavowed. Although Adrian, after receiving a copy, took up the defense of the council with vehemence, Charlemagne had the contention of the *Caroline Books* confirmed at the Synod of Frankfort in 794. It may, however, have been some consolation to Adrian's legates that the same synod publicly condemned Adoptionism (q.v.), against which the Roman as well as the Frankish Church had been struggling. Adrian died not long after (Dec. 25, 795).

Throughout his long pontificate Adrian had been too exclusively dominated by the one idea of gaining as much advantage as possible in lands and privileges from the strife between the Franks and Lombards. He rendered no slight services to the city of Rome, rebuilding the walls and aqueducts, and restoring and adorning the churches. His was not a strong personality, however, and he never succeeded in exercising a dominant or even a strongly felt influence upon the policy of western Europe. (Carl Mirbt.)

Bibliography: *Vita Hadriani*, in *Liber pontificalis*, ed. Duchesne, i. 486–523; Einhard, *Vita Caroli*, in *MGH, Script.*, ii. (1829) 426–463; *Vita Caroli*, ed. G. Waitz, in *Script. rer. Germ.*, 4th ed., 1880; also in Jaffé, *Regesta*, iv., Eng. transl. in Thatcher and McNeal, *Source Book*, pp. 38–45; *Codicis Carolini epistolæ*, in Jaffé, l.c. iv. and in *MPL*, xcvi.; one of Adrian's letters, in verse, dated 774, in *MGH, Poet. lat. ævi Caroli*, i. (1881) 90–91; Jaffé, *Regesta*, i. 289–306, Leipsic, 1885; *De sancto Hadriano papa I an III Nonantulæ in editione Mutinensi*, in *ASB*, July, viii. 643–649; P. T. Hald, *Donatio Caroli Magni*, Copenhagen, 1836; T. D. Mack, *De donatione a Carolo Magno*, Münster, 1861; J. Ficker, *Forschungen zur Reichs- und Rechts-Geschichte Italiens*, ii. 329 sqq., 347 sqq., Innsbruck, 1869; A. O. Legge, *Growth of the Temporal Power of the Papacy*, London, 1870; W. Wattenbach, *Geschichte des römischen Papstthums*, pp. 47 sqq., Berlin, 1876; O. Kuhl, *Der Verkehr Karls des Grossen mit Papst Hadrian I.*, Königsberg, 1879; R. Genelin, *Das Schenkungsversprechen und die Schenkung Pippins*, Vienna, 1880; W. Martens, *Die römische Frage unter Pippin und Karl dem Grossen*, pp. 129 sqq., 368–387, Stuttgart, 1881; idem, *Die Besetzung des päpstlichen Stuhles unter den Kaisern Heinrich III. und IV.*, Freiburg, 1886; idem, *Beleuchtung der neuesten Kontroversen über die römische Frage unter Pippin und Karl dem Grossen*, Munich, 1898; H. von Sybel, *Die Schenkungen der Karolinger an die Päpste*, in *Kleine historische Schriften*, iii. 65–115, Stuttgart, 1881; *Liber Pontificalis*, ed. Duchesne, i., pp. ccxxxiv.-ccxliii., Paris, 1884; J. von Pflugk-Harttung, *Acta pontificum Romanorum inedita*, ii. 22 sqq., Stuttgart, 1884; P. Scheffer-Boichorst, *Pippins und Karls des Grossen Schenkungsversprechung*, pp. 193–212, Innsbruck, 1884; L. von Ranke, *Weltgeschichte*, v., part 1, p. 117, Leipsic, 1885; S. Abel, *Jahrbücher des fränkischen Reiches unter Karl dem Grossen*, i. 768–788, Leipsic, 1883 (and ii. 789–814, by B. Simson, 1888), and for donation of Charlemagne, ib. i. 159 sqq.; P. Kehr, *Die sogenannte karolingischen Schenkung von 774*, in Sybel's *Historische Zeitschrift*, lxx. (new ser., 1893) xxxiv. 385–441; Hefele, *Conciliengeschichte*, vol. iii.; Eng. transl., vol. v.; Hauck, *KD*, vol. ii.; Mann, *Popes*, I., vol. ii. 395–497.

Adrian II.: Pope 867–872. He was the son of Talarus, of a Roman family which had already produced two popes, Stephen IV. (768–772) and Sergius II. (844–847). He was a married man before entering the clerical state. Gregory IV. made him a cardinal. His great benevolence won the hearts of the Romans, and he twice refused the papacy, after the death of Leo IV (855) and of Benedict III. (858). A unanimous choice by both clergy and people, however, forced him at the age of seventy-five to accept it in succession to Nicholas I. (d. Nov. 13, 867). The election was confirmed by Emperor Louis II., and Adrian's consecration followed on Dec. 14.

His predecessor had left him a number of unfinished tasks. In the first place, it was necessary to arrive at a final decision concerning a matter which had long and deeply troubled the Frankish Church; namely, the matrimonial relations of King Lothair II. Adrian firmly insisted that Lothair should take back his legitimate wife Thietberga, at the same time releasing his mistress Walrade from the excommunication pronounced against her by Nicholas, at the request of Louis II., on condition that she should have nothing more to do with Lothair. The last-named visited Rome in 869 for the purpose of gaining the pope's consent to his divorce from Thietberga. Adrian promised no more than to call a new council to investigate the matter, but restored Lothair to communion after he had sworn that he had obeyed the command of Nicholas I. to break off his relations with Walrade. The king's sudden death at Piacenza on his homeward journey, a few weeks later, was considered to be a divine judgment. The efforts of the pope to enforce the claim of Louis II. to Lorraine were fruitless; immediately after Lothair's death his uncle, Charles the Bald, had himself crowned at Metz, though less than a year later he was forced by his brother, Louis the German, to divide the inheritance of Lothair in the treaty of Meersen (Aug. 8, 870).

Forces Lothair II. to Take Back His Wife.

Adrian's attempts to interfere in Frankish affairs were stubbornly resisted by Hincmar of Reims (q.v.), who wrote (*Epist.*, xxvii.), ostensibly as the opinions of certain men friendly to the West-Frankish king, that a pope could not be bishop and king at one and the same time; that Adrian's predecessors had claimed to decide in ecclesiastical matters only; and that he who attempted to excommunicate a Christian unjustly deprived himself of the power of the keys. When a synod at Douzy near Sedan (Aug., 871) excommunicated Bishop Hincmar of Laon on grave charges brought against him both by the king and by his own uncle, the more famous Hincmar, the pope allowed an appeal to a Roman council, and brought upon himself in consequence a still sterner warning from Charles the Bald by the pen of Hincmar of Reims (*MPL*, cxxiv. 881–896), with a threat of his personal appearance in Rome. Adrian executed an inglorious retreat. He wrote to Charles praising him for his virtues and his benefits to the Church, promised him the imperial crown on Louis's death, and offered the soothing explanation that earlier less pacific letters had been either extorted from him during sickness or falsified. In the matter of Hincmar of Laon, he made partial concessions, which were completed by his successor, John VIII.

Opposed by Hincmar of Reims.

Another conflict which Nicholas I. had left to Adrian, that with Photius, patriarch of Constantinople, seemed likely to have a happier issue, when Photius was condemned first by a Roman synod (June 10, 869), and then by the general council at Constantinople in the same year, the papal legates taking a position which seemed to make good the claims of the Roman see. But Emperor Basil the Macedonian dealt these claims a severe blow when he caused the envoys of the Bulgarians (see BULGARIANS, CONVERSION OF THE) to declare to the legates that their country belonged to the patriarchate not of Rome, but of Constantinople. Adrian's protests were in vain; a Greek archbishop appeared among the Bulgarians, and the Latin missionaries had to give place. Moravia, on the other hand, was firmly attached to Rome, Adrian allowing the use of a Slavic liturgy, and naming Methodius archbishop of Sirmium. After a pontificate marked principally by defeat, Adrian died between Nov. 13 and Dec. 14, 872. (CARL MIRBT.)

Conflict with Photius.

BIBLIOGRAPHY: The Letters of Adrian in Mansi, *Collectio*, xv. 819–820; in *MPL*, cxxii., cxxix., and in Bouquet, *Recueil*, vol. vii.; *Vita Hadriani II.*, in *Liber pontificalis*, ed. Duchesne, ii. 173–174, and in L. A. Muratori, *Rerum Italicarum Scriptores*, III. ii. 300, 25 vols., Milan, 1723–51; Ado, *Chronicon*, in *MGH*, *Script.*, ii. (1829) 315–323; idem, in *MPL*, cxxiii.; *Annales Fuldenses*, in *MGH*, *Script.*, i. (1820) 375–395, and separately in *Script. rer. Germ.*, ed. F. Kurze, Hanover, 1891; Hincmar, *Annales*, in *MGH*, *Script.*, i. (1826) 455–515, and in *MPL*, cxxv.; Hincmar, *Epistolæ*, in *MPL*, cxxiv., cxxvi.; Regino, *Chronicon*, in *MGH*, *Script.*, i. (1826) 580 sqq.; idem, in *MPL*, cxxxii. (separately ed. F. Kurze, Hanover, 1890); P. Jaffé, *Regesta*, i. 368, 369, Leipsic, 1885; Bower, *Popes*, ii. 267–282; F. Maassen, *Eine Rede des Papstes Hadrian II. von Jahre 869, die erste umfassende Benutzung der falschen Decretalen*, in *Sitzungsberichte der Wiener Akademie*, lxxii. (1872) 521; Hefele, *Conciliengeschichte*, vol. iv.; P. A. Lapotre, *Hadrian II. et les fausses décrétales*, in *Revue des questions historiques*, xxvii. (1880) 377 sqq.; B. Jungmann, *Dissertationes selectæ in hist. eccl.*, iii., Ratisbon, 1882; Milman, *Latin Christianity*, iii. 35–80; H. Schrörs, *Hinkmar*, Freiburg, 1884; J. J. Böhmer, *Regesta imperii*, I. *Die Regesten des Kaiserreichs unter den Karolingern*, pp. 751–918; idem, ed. E. Mühlbacher, i. 460 sqq., Innsbruck, 1889; Hauck, *KD*, ii. 557 sqq., 699–700; J. Langen, *Geschichte der röm-*

ischen Kirche von Nikolaus I. bis Gregor VII., pp. 113–170, Bonn, 1892; E. Mühlbacher, *Deutsche Geschichte unter den Karolingern*, 1896; E. Dümmler, *Über eine Synodalrede Papst Hadrians II.*, Berlin, 1899; *Treaty of Meersen*, Eng. transl. in Thatcher and McNeal, *Source Book*, pp. 64–65.

Adrian III.: Pope 884–885. He was a Roman by birth, the son of Benedict. The story of severe punishments inflicted by him points to revolts in the city during his rule. The assertion of the untrustworthy Martinus Polonus that he decreed that a newly elected pope might proceed at once to consecration without waiting for imperial confirmation, and that the imperial crown should thenceforth be worn by an Italian prince, are confirmed by no contemporary evidence. He died near Modena Aug., 885, on his way to attend a diet at Worms on the invitation of Charles the Fat, and was buried at Nonantula. [He was the first pope to change his name on election, having previously been called *Agapetus*.] (CARL MIRBT.)

BIBLIOGRAPHY: *Epistola*, in Bouquet, *Recueil*, ix. 200, and in *MPL*, cxxvi.; *Bulla anni* 885, in *Neues Archiv der Gesellschaft für ä. d. Geschichte*, xi. (1885) 374, 376; *Vita*, in *Liber Pontificalis*, ed. Duchesne, ii. (1892) 225, and in L. A. Muratori, *Rerum Italicarum Scriptores*, III. ii. 440–446, 25 vols., Milan, 1723–51; *Annales Fuldenses*, in *MGH*, *Script.*, i. (1826) 375–395 (separately in *Script. rer. Germ.*, ed. F. Kurze, Hanover, 1891); *Chronica Benedicti*, in *MGH*, *Script.*, iii. (1839) 199; J. M. Watterich, *Pontificum Romanorum vitæ*, i. 29, 650, 718, Leipsic, 1862; P. Jaffé, *Regesta*, i. 426-427; Bower, *Popes*, ii. 293–294; R. Baxmann, *Die Politik der Päpste von Gregor I. bis auf Gregor VII.*, ii. 60 sqq., Elberfeld, 1869; E. Dümmler, *Geschichte des Ostfränkischen Reiches*, ii. 247, 248, Berlin, 1888; J. Langen, *Geschichte der römischen Kirche von Nikolaus I. bis Gregor VII.*, pp. 298 sqq., Bonn, 1892; T. R. v. Sickel, *Die Vita Hadriani Nonantulana und die Diurnus Handschrift*, in *Neues Archiv der Gesellschaft für ä. d. Geschichte*, xviii. (1892) 109–133.

Adrian IV. (Nicholas Breakspeare; the only Englishman in the list of the popes): Pope 1154–59. He was born in England about the beginning of the twelfth century. He went to France as a boy, studied at Paris and Arles, enduring severe privations, and finally settled down in the monastery of St. Rufus near Avignon. Here he became prior, then abbot (1137), but met with bitter opposition from the monks when he attempted to introduce reforms. Eugenius III. made him cardinal bishop of Albano, and chose him (1152) for the difficult mission of regulating the relations of Norway and Sweden to the archbishopric of Lund. Returning to Rome, he was welcomed with high honors by Anastasius IV., whom he succeeded on Dec. 4, 1154.

Arnold of Brescia and Frederick Barbarossa.

His first troubles came through Arnold of Brescia (q.v.), who, besides his ethical opposition to the hierarchy, aimed at reestablishing the ancient sovereignty of Rome and its independence of the papal see. Adrian strove to secure Arnold's banishment, and succeeded in 1155 only by pronouncing an interdict on the city. He made Arnold's capture and delivery to the ecclesiastical authorities a condition of crowning Frederick Barbarossa, who thus sacrificed a man who might have been a powerful auxiliary in his conflicts with this very pope. The first meeting between Frederick and Adrian (June 9, 1155) was marked by friction; but Frederick managed, in return for substantial concessions, to secure his coronation nine days later. The Romans, however, whose subjection to the papal see the new emperor had promised to enforce, refused their recognition; and when Frederick left Rome, the pope and cardinals accompanied him, practically as fugitives. Frederick had also promised to subdue William I. of Sicily, and was inclined to carry out his promise, but the pressure of the German princes forced him to recross the Alps.

William I. of Sicily.

Adrian then attempted to pursue his conflict with William, and, by the aid of the latter's discontented vassals, forced him to offer terms. When, however, these were not accepted the king rallied his forces, the tide turned, and Adrian was obliged to grant his opponent the investiture of Sicily, Apulia, and Capua, and to renounce important ecclesiastical prerogatives in Sicily (Treaty of Benevento June, 1156). In consequence of this settlement, he was enabled to return to Rome at the end of the year, but the emperor resented this apparent desertion of their alliance, as well as the injury to his suzerainty by the papal investiture. An open breach came when, at the Diet of Besançon, in Oct., 1157, the papal legates (one of them the future Alexander III.) delivered a letter from their chief which spoke of the conferring of the imperial crown by the ambiguous term *beneficium*. The chancellor, Reginald, archbishop of Cologne, in his German rendering, gave it the sense of a fief of the papal see; and the legates thought it prudent to leave the assembly and retreat speedily to Rome.

Rebuffed by Frederick Barbarossa.

Imperial letters spread the same indignation among the people; and when Adrian required the prelates of Germany to obtain satisfaction from Frederick for his treatment of the legates, he was met by the decided expression of their disapproval of the offending phrase. Adrian's position was rendered more difficult by the appearance of a Greek expedition in Italy and by a revolt in Rome; he offered the concession of a brief in which he explained the objectionable word in the innocent sense of "benefit." Frederick took this as a confession of weakness, and when he crossed the Alps to subdue the Lombard towns (1158), he required an oath of fealty to himself, as well as substantial support from the Italian bishops. Attaining the summit of his power with the conquest of Milan in September, two months later he had the imperial rights solemnly declared by the leading jurists of Bologna. This declaration constituted him the source of all secular power and dignity, and was a denial equally of the political claims of the papacy and of the aspirations of the Lombard towns. The breach with Adrian was still further widened by his hesitation to confirm the imperial nomination to the archbishopric of Ravenna; and an acute crisis was soon reached. An exchange of communications took place, whose manner was intended on both sides to be offensive; and Frederick was roused to a higher pitch of anger when the papal legates, besides accusing him of a breach of the treaty of Constance, demanded that he should thenceforth receive no oath of fealty from the Italian bishops, that he should either restore the inheritance of Countess Matilda, Spoleto, Sardinia, Corsica, Ferrara, etc., to the Roman see, or pay a tribute for those lands, and that he should recognize the right of the successor of St. Peter to complete and unlimited dominion in Rome. These claims he met by declaring roundly that on any strict interpretation of his rights the pope also would be bound to take the oath of fealty, and that all the latter's possessions were but imperial domains held in consequence of Sylvester's investiture by Constantine.

Impending Conflict Stopped by Adrian's Death.

Both the opponents sought for allies in the impending struggle. Adrian, who was the sworn foe of the Roman republic and its liberties, joined hands with the Lombard communes who were struggling for their own. The emperor, who was doing his best to abolish communal liberty in the north of Italy, aided the Romans to uphold the principles of Arnold of Brescia. Adrian was already taking counsel with the cardinals as to the advisability of pronouncing a sentence of excommunication against Frederick when death overtook him at Anagni Sept. 1, 1159.

Adrian was a ruler who grasped clearly the ideal of a papacy striving for universal domination, and contended passionately for its accomplishment; but John of Salisbury (who, as ambassador of the king of England, had opportunity to study him at close range) records that there were moments when the terrible burden of his office weighed almost unbearably upon him. (Carl Mirbt.)

Bibliography: *Epistolæ et privilegia*, in Bouquet, *Recueil*, xv. 666–693; idem, in *MPL*, clxxxviii.; *Bullæ*, in *Neues Archiv der Gesellschaft für ä. d. Geschichte*, ii. (1876) 211–213, xv. (1889) 203–206; *Vita*, in *Liber Pontificalis*, ed. Duchesne, 1892, ii. 388 sqq.; Otto of Frisengen, *Gesta Friderici I.*, in *MGH*, *Script.*, xx. (1868) 403 sqq.; Radericus of Frisengen, *Continuatio* [of Otto's *Gesta*], ib. pp. 454 sqq.; Jaffé, *Regesta*, i.; J. M. Watterich, *Romanorum pontificum vitæ*, i. 323–336, Leipsic, 1823; Bower, *Popes*, 1845, ii. 487–502; R. Raby, *Historical Sketch of Pope Adrian IV.*, London, 1849; H. Reuter, *Geschichte Alexander's III.*, vol. i., Leipsic, 1860; Fr. v. Raumer, *Geschichte der Hohenstaufen*, ii., ib. 1871; Milman, *Latin Christianity*, London, 1883; *DNB*, i. 143–146; Hefele, *Conciliengeschichte*, v. 527–566; J. Langen, *Geschichte der römischen Kirche von Gregor VII. bis Innocenz III.*, pp. 417–438, Bonn, 1893; Eng. transl. of *Letter to Barbarossa* (Sept. 20, 1157), *Manifesto of Frederick I.*, *Letter to the German Bishops* and their *Letter to Adrian*, and *Letter to the Emperor* (Feb., 1158), in E. F. Henderson, *Select Historical Documents of the Middle Ages*, London, 1892; J. Jastrow and G. Winter, *Deutsche Geschichte im Zeitalter der Hohenstaufen*, vol. i., Stuttgart, 1897; S. Malone, *Adrian IV. and Ireland*, London, 1899; O. J. Thatcher, *Studies Concerning Adrian IV.*, Chicago, 1903; Hauck, *KD*, iv. 35, 199–227; Eng. transl. of *Treaty of Constance*, *Stirrup Episode*, *Treaty of Adrian IV. and William of Sicily*, *Letters of Adrian* (1157–58), and *Manifesto of Frederick I.*, in O. J. Thatcher and E. H. McNeal, *Source Book for Mediæval History*, New York, 1905.

Adrian V. (Ottobuono de' Fieschi): Pope 1276. He was the nephew of Innocent IV., and as cardinal deacon had been sent to England by Clement IV. to mediate between Henry III. and his barons. He was elected July 12, 1276, in a conclave on which Charles of Anjou had enforced all the rigor of the regulations of Gregory X.; and one of Adrian's first acts was to abrogate them as oppressive to the cardinals. Before he could promulgate any new system, however, and even before he had been ordained priest, he died at Viterbo Aug. 18, 1276. (Carl Mirbt.)

Bibliography: A. Chroust, *Ein Brief Hadrians V.*, in *Neues Archiv der Gesellschaft für ä. d. Geschichte*, xx. (1894) 233 sqq.; Bower, *Popes*, iii. 24; A. Potthast, *Regesta pontificum Romanorum*, ii. 1709, Berlin, 1875; Milman, *Latin Christianity*, vi. 134.

Adrian VI. (Adrian Rodenburgh or Dedel, more probably the latter): Pope 1522–23. He was born in Utrecht, was educated by the Brethren of the Common Life and at Louvain, and became professor and vice-chancellor of the university. During this period he composed several theological writings, including a commentary on the *Sententiæ* of Peter Lombard. In 1507 Emperor Maximilian I. appointed him tutor to his grandson, Charles of Spain, and in 1515 Ferdinand the Catholic made him bishop of Tortosa. In 1517 he was created cardinal by Leo X. When Charles was made German emperor and went to the Netherlands in 1520, he appointed Adrian regent of Spain. In 1522 the cardinals almost unanimously elected him pope.

Friend of Reform.

The vexation of the Romans at the choice of a German, moreover a very simple man who was not inclined to continue the splendid traditions of the humanistic popes, lasted during his entire pontificate; more serious minds, however, looked forward to his reign with hope. In spite of the fact that he consented to the condemnation of Luther's writings by the Louvain theologians, and although as inquisitor-general he had shown no clemency, yet Erasmus saw in him the right pilot of the Church in those stormy times, and hoped that he would abolish many abuses in the Roman court. Luis de Vives addressed Adrian with his proposals for reform; and Pirkheimer complained to him of the opposition of the Dominicans to learning. Even in the college of cardinals, the few who favored a reformation looked up to him hopefully, and Ægidius of Viterbo (q.v.) transmitted to him a memorial which described the corruption of the Church and discussed the means of redress.

Adrian fulfilled these expectations. Concerning indulgences he even endeavored to find a way which might lead to a reconciliation with Luther's conception, viz., to make the effect of the indulgence dependent on the depth of repentance on evidence of it in a reformed life. But here Cardinal Cajetan asserted that the authority of the pope would suffer, since the chief agent would no longer be the pope, but the believer, and the majority agreed with the cardinal. Nothing was done in the matter, no dogma was revised, and the complaints of the Germans increased. Nevertheless, Adrian simplified his household, moneys given for Church purposes were no longer used for the support of scholars and artists, he sought to reform the abuse of pluralities, and opposed simony and nepotism. His effort to influence Erasmus to write against Luther and to bring Zwingli by a letter to his side shows his attitude toward the Reformation in Germany and Switzerland.

When the diet at Nuremberg was opened in Dec., 1522, he complained in a brief of the rise of heresy in Germany and asked the diet, since mild measures could not be effectual, to employ the means formerly used against Huss. But in his instructions to his legate at the diet, Bishop Chieregati, he took a different tone, and acknowledged that "wantonness," "abuses," and "excesses" were found at the curia. This is the only instance where such a confession received official sanction. An answer was prepared by a committee, which took notice of the confession, refused to execute the edict of Worms before an improvement was visible, and asked for the meeting of a council in a German city, promising to prevent Luther from publishing his polemical writings and to see to it that the preachers proclaimed the pure gospel, but "according to the teaching and interpretation of the Scriptures approved and revered by the Christian Church." Chieregati accepted neither this nor any other answer, but left Nuremberg in haste. In strict papal circles Adrian's confession has not yet been forgiven. He died at Rome Sept. 14, 1523.

His Confession.

K. BENRATH.

BIBLIOGRAPHY: P. Burmannus, *Hadrianus VI. sive analecta historica*, . . Utrecht, 1727; C. Moringus, *Vita Hadriani VI.*, Louvain, 1536; Bower, *Popes*, iii. 299–302; L. P. Gachard, *Correspondance de Charles V. et d'Adrien VI.*, Brussels, 1859; J. S. Brewer, *Letters and Papers of the Reign of Henry VIII.*, 4 vols., London, 1862–1901 (especially vol. iii.); G. A. Bergenroth, *Calendar . . . relating to the Negotiations between England and Spain*, ii., London, 1866; idem, *Supplement* to vols. i. and ii. (1868); M. Brosch, *Geschichte des Kirchenstaates*, vol. i., Hamburg, 1880; C. v. Höfler, *Papst Hadrian VI.*, Vienna, 1880; A. Lapitre, *Adrien VI.*, Paris, 1880; L. v. Ranke, *Deutsche Geschichte im Zeitalter der Reformation*, ii., Leipsic, 1880; idem, *Die römischen Päpste*, i., ib. 1889; Eng. transl., i. 71–74, London, 1896; Milman, *Latin Christianity;* Hefele, *Conciliengeschichte*, ix. 271–299; Creighton, *Papacy*, vi. 214–273.

ADSO: One of the more prominent of the reforming abbots of the tenth century. He belonged to a noble family in the Jura Mountains, became a monk at Luxeuil, and went later to the monastery of Montier-en-Der (120 m. e.s.e. of Paris), in the diocese of Châlons-sur-Marne, reformed about 935 by the abbot Albert, whom he succeeded in 967 or 968. He laid the foundation for a splendid new basilica, remains of which are still standing (cf. Sackur, *Die Cluniacenser*, ii. 391), and undertook to reform other monasteries, e.g., St. Benignus at Dijon. Like his friends Abbo of Fleury and Gerbert of Reims (cf. Havet, *Les Lettres de Gerbert*, pp. 6, 74, Paris, 1889), he was interested in learning and investigation; and his library included the writings of Aristotle, Porphyry, Terence, Cæsar, and Vergil. He was often urged to write books, especially the lives of saints, and several works of this class by him may be found in *ASM* (ii. and iv.; copied in *MPL*, cxxxvii. 597–700).

The most famous of Adso's writings is the earliest, an *Epistola ad Gerbergam reginam, de vita et tempore Antichristi*, composed before 954, in which he opposes the prevalent notion that the appearance of Antichrist was near at hand. The work was much read, and suffered greatly from mutilations and interpolations (cf. *MPL*, ci. 1289–98); its original form has been restored by E. Sackur, in *Sibyllinische Texte und Forschungen*, pp. 104–113, Halle, 1898.

S. M. DEUTSCH.

BIBLIOGRAPHY: The chief source for Adso's life is an addition of the eleventh century to his *Vita S. Bercharii*, the patron saint of Montier-en-Der, ch xi., in *MPL*, cxxxvii. 678–679, and in *MGH, Script.*, iv. (1841) 488. Consult also the *Histoire littéraire de la France*, vi. 471–492; A. Ebert, *Allgemeine Geschichte der Litteratur des Mittelalters im Abendlande*, iii. 472–484, Leipsic, 1887; and, especially, E. Sackur, *Die Cluniacenser*, vol. i., Halle, 1892.

ADULTERY. See MARRIAGE.

ADVENT: The first season of the church year. The celebration of Advent in the Western Church was instituted toward the close of the fifth century, in Gaul, Spain, and Italy [but traces of it are found in the Council of Saragossa, 380]. The term was first understood as referring to the birth of Christ, and so the Advent season was a time of preparation for Christmas. Since it commenced at different periods (e.g., at Milan with the Sunday after St. Martin [Nov. 11]; in Rome with the first in December), the number of Sundays in Advent differed in the individual churches. The term *adventus* was also taken in the wider sense of the coming of Christ in general; hence the lessons for Advent which refer to the second coming of Christ and the last judgment. With it was also connected the notion of the coming of the kingdom of heaven. Thus originated the idea of the triple coming "to man, in man, and against man" or, corresponding to the number four of the Sundays which afterward became general, the notion of the quadruple coming "in the flesh, in the mind, in death, in majesty."

In the medieval church the Advent season was a time of fasting and repentance. Hence one finds in it the figure of John the Baptist, as the precursor of Christ and the preacher of repentance. The whole season from Advent to the octave of Epiphany was a *tempus clausum* (q.v.) until the Council of Trent, which took off the last week. In the Church of Rome Advent has still the character of a penitential season. The color of the vestments then worn is violet. This character of earnest and serious devotion appears in more preaching, teaching, and insistence upon attendance at communion. Fasting during Advent is not a general ordinance of the Church of Rome [being required only on all Fridays, the vigil of Christmas, and the three ember-days in the last week of the season].

With the adoption of the medieval church calendar, the Protestants also accepted the Advent season and Advent lessons. Thus the season retained its double character, preparation for the Christmas festival and contemplation of the different ways of the coming of Christ. Since it has become customary to separate the civil and ecclesiastical chronology and to distinguish between the civil and church years, the first Sunday of Advent has been dignified as the solemn beginning of the new church year. These various relations of the first Sunday of Advent and the whole Advent season explain the variety of the contents of the Advent hymns and prayers. Among Protestants also the Advent season has a twofold character, that of holy joy and of holy repentance. The first Sunday in Advent is no church festival in a full sense, but the relations referred to lift it and the succeeding Sundays above ordinary Sundays. See CHURCH YEAR. W CASPARI.

In the present usage of the West, the season begins on the nearest Sunday to St. Andrew's day (Nov. 30), whether before or after. In the Anglican prayer-book the service for the first Sunday emphasizes the second coming; that for the second, the Holy Scriptures; that for the third, the Christian ministry; while only the fourth relates specifically to the first coming. Advent in the Eastern Church begins on Nov 14, thus making a season of forty days analogous to Lent.

BIBLIOGRAPHY: The lectionaries in *Liber comicus*, i., Oxford, 1893, and in *Sacramentarium Gelasianum* published in L. A. Muratori, *Liturgia romanum vetus*, vol. i., Venice, 1748, and in *MPL*, lxxiv.; Smaragdus, in *MPL*, cii.; Amalarius Metensis, *De ecclesiasticis officiis*, ib. cv.; Berno of Reichenau, *De celebratione adventus*, *MPL*, cxlii.; Isidore of Seville, *De officiis*, ed. Cochlæus, Leipsic, 1534, and in M. de la Bigne, *Magna bibliotheca veterum patrum*, x., Paris, 1654; E. Martène, *De antiquis ecclesiæ ritibus*, Rouen, 1700.

ADVENT CHRISTIANS. See ADVENTISTS, 3.

ADVENTISTS: The general name of a body embracing several branches, whose members look for the proximate personal coming of Christ. William Miller (q.v.), their founder, was a converted deist, who in 1816 joined the Baptist Church in Low Hampton, N. Y. He became a close student of the Bible, especially of the prophecies, and soon satisfied himself that the Advent was to be personal and premillennial, and that it was near at hand. He began these studies in 1818, but did not enter upon the work of the ministry until 1831. The year 1843 was the date agreed upon for the Advent; then, more specifically, Oct. 22, 1844, the failure of which divided a body of followers that had become quite numerous. In the year of his death (1849) they were estimated at 50,000. Many who had been drawn into the movement by the prevalent excitement left it, and returned to the churches from which they had withdrawn. After the second failure, Miller and some other leaders discouraged attempts to fix exact dates. On this question and on the doctrine of the immortality of the soul there have been divisions. There are now at least six distinct branches of Adventists, all of which agree that the second coming of Christ is to be personal and premillennial, and that it is near at hand. The Seventh-day Adventists and the Church of God are presbyterial, the others congregational in their polity. All practise immersion as the mode of baptism.

1. Evangelical Adventists: This is the oldest branch, indeed the original body. The members adopted their *Declaration of Principles* in conference in Albany, N. Y., in 1845, and in 1858 formed the American Millennial Association to print and circulate literature on eschatology from their point of view. Their organ was the weekly paper *The Signs of the Times*, which had been established in Boston in 1840; subsequently its name was changed to *The Advent Herald*, and later still to *Messiah's Herald*, its present (1906) title. The paper has always been published in Boston. The Evangelical Adventists differ from all the other branches in maintaining the consciousness of the dead in Hades and the eternal sufferings of the lost.

BIBLIOGRAPHY: H. F. Hill, *The Saint's Inheritance*, Boston, 1852; D. T. Taylor, *The Reign of Christ*, Peacedale, R. I., 1855, and Boston, 1889.

2. Seventh-day Adventists: This branch dates from 1845, in which year, at Washington, N. H., a body of Adventists adopted the belief that the seventh day of the week is the Sabbath for Christians and is obligatory upon them. In 1850 their chief organ, *The Advent Review and Sabbath Herald*, was first issued at Battle Creek, Mich., which was made the headquarters of the body; and there in 1860 a publishing association, in 1862 a general annual conference, in 1866 a health institute, and in 1874 an educational society and a foreign mission board were established. In 1903 the publishing business and the general headquarters were removed to Washington, D. C. Their organ is now styled *The Review and Herald*. Besides the tenet which gives them their name they hold that man is not immortal, that the dead sleep in unconsciousness, and that the unsaved never awake. They practise foot-washing and accept the charismata, maintain a tithing system, and pay great attention to health and total abstinence. They accept Mrs. Ellen G. White as an inspired prophetess.

BIBLIOGRAPHY: J. N. Andrews, *History of the Sabbath and First Day*, Battle Creek, 1873 (3d ed., 1887); *Life Sketches of Elder James White and his wife Mrs. Ellen G. White*, 1880; J. N. Loughborough, *Rise and Progress of the Seventh-Day Adventists*, ib. 1892.

3. Advent Christians: The organization under this name dates from 1861, when a general association was formed. The organ of these Adventists is *The World's Crisis and Second Advent Messenger*, published in Boston. Their creed is given in the *Declaration of Principles*, approved by the general conference of 1900. They believe that through sin man forfeited immortality and that only through faith in Christ can any live forever; that death is a condition of unconsciousness for all persons until the resurrection at Christ's second coming, when the righteous will enter an endless life upon this earth, and the rest will suffer complete extinction of being; that this coming is near; that church government should be congregational; that immersion is the only true baptism; and that Sunday is the Christian Sabbath.

BIBLIOGRAPHY: I. C. Wellcome, *History of the Second Advent Message*, Yarmouth, Me., 1874.

4. Life and Advent Union: This may be said to have existed since 1848, but it was not until 1862 that it was organized, at Wilbraham, Mass., under the leadership of Elder George Stores. Its organ is *The Herald of Life and of the Coming Kingdom*, published at Springfield, Mass., weekly since 1862. It holds that all hope of another life is through Jesus Christ, and that only believers in him, who have manifested in their daily lives the fruits of the Spirit, attain to the resurrection of the dead, which will take place at Christ's coming, and that such coming will be personal, visible, and literal, and is impending. The Union holds four camp-meetings annually: two in Maine, one in Connecticut, which is the principal one, and one in Virginia.

BIBLIOGRAPHY: O. S. Halsted, *The Theology of the Bible*, Newark, 1860; *Discussion between Miles Grant and J. T. Curry*, Boston, 1863.

5. Church of God: This is a branch of the Seventh-day Adventists, which seceded in 1866 because its members denied that Mrs. Ellen Gould White was an inspired prophetess. Their organ is *The Bible Advocate and Herald of the Coming Kingdom*, published at Stanberry, Mo., which is their center. Like the parent body, the Church of God has tithes, sanatoriums, and a publishing house.

BIBLIOGRAPHY: A. F. Dugger, *Points of Difference between the Church of God and Seventh-Day Adventists*, Stanberry, Mo.; J. Brinkerhoff, *Mrs. White's Visions. Comparison of the early Writings of Mrs. E. G. White with later Publications, showing the Suppressions made in them to deny their erroneous Teaching*; D. Nield, *The Good Friday Problem, showing from Scripture, Astronomy and History that the Crucifixion of Christ took Place on Wednesday, and his Resurrection on Saturday*.

6. Churches of God in Christ Jesus, popularly known as the **Age-to-come Adventists:** These have existed since 1851, when their organ, *The Restitution* (Plymouth, Ind.), was established, but they were not organized till 1888, when the general conference was formed. They believe in the restoration of Israel, the literal resurrection of the dead, the immortalization of the righteous, and the final destruction of the wicked, eternal life being through Christ alone.

BIBLIOGRAPHY: J. P. Weethee, *The Coming Age*, Chicago, 1884.

The statistics of the Adventists are thus given by H. K. Carroll in *The Christian Advocate* for Jan. 25, 1906:

Name.	Ministers.	Churches.	Communicants.
Evangelical	34	30	1,147
Seventh-day	486	1,707	60,471
Advent Christians	912	610	26,500
Life and Advent Union	60	28	3,800
Church of God	19	29	647
Churches of God in Christ Jesus	54	95	2,872
Total Adventists	1,565	2,499	95,437

ADVERTISEMENTS OF ELIZABETH: Name commonly applied to the regulations promulgated in 1566 by Matthew Parker, archbishop of Canterbury, for the purpose, as alleged, of securing uniformity and decency in public worship, against the tendencies of the extreme Protestant party (see PURITANS, PURITANISM, § 6). It is now generally admitted that, though they represented Elizabeth's policy in ritual matters, they never received her formal sanction. They assumed some importance in the ritual controversies of the nineteenth century, the High-church party contending that they were merely an archiepiscopal injunction enforcing an irreducible minimum of ritual, while their opponents attempted to show that they were a legal prescription of a positive kind, which made the surplice the only lawful vestment of the clergy in parish churches.

BIBLIOGRAPHY: The text of the Advertisements is given in Gee and Hardy, *Documents*, pp. 467-475. Consult: J. Strype, *Life and Acts of Matthew Parker*, London, 1821; *Church Quarterly Review*, xvii. (1881) 54-60.

ADVOCATE OF THE CHURCH (Lat. *Advocatus* or *Defensor Ecclesiæ*): An officer charged with the secular affairs of an ecclesiastical establishment, more especially its defense, legal or armed. The beginnings of the office appear in the Roman empire. From the end of the fifth century there were *defensores* in Italy, charged with the protection of the poor and orphans as well as with the care of Church rights and property. In the Merovingian kingdom legal representatives of the churches had the title. In the Carlovingian period, in accordance with the effort to keep the clergy as far as possible from worldly affairs, bishops, abbots, and other ecclesiastics were required to have such an official. The development of the law of immunity made such *advocati* necessary—on the one hand, to uphold Church rights against the State and in court, on the other hand to perform judicial and police duties in ecclesiastical territory. The Carlovingian kings had the right of appointment, but sometimes waived it in individual cases. These officers were at first generally clerics, later laymen, and finally the office became hereditary. Often this advocate of the Church developed into a tyrant, keeping the establishment in absolute submission, despoiling and plundering it. He usurped the whole power of administration, limited the authority of the bishop to purely spiritual affairs, absorbed the tithes and all other revenues, and doled out to the clergy a mean modicum only. Innocent III. (1198–1216), however, succeeded in checking the growing importance of this institution, and soon the office itself disappeared.

BIBLIOGRAPHY: R. Happ, *De advocatia ecclesiastica*, Bonn, 1870; H. Brunner, *Deutsche Rechtsgeschichte*, ii. 302, Leipsic, 1892.

ADVOCATES, CONSISTORIAL: Twelve lawyers who outrank all the advocates in the papal court. They trace their origin from the close of the sixth century, when Gregory the Great appointed seven *defensores* in the city of Rome to plead the cause of poor litigants who would otherwise be without legal counsel. Sixtus IV increased the number by the addition of five junior advocates, but the memory of the historical origin of the body was preserved by reserving to the seven senior members certain privileges, among them the right to constitute the college proper of consistorial advocates. This college at the present time is made up of two clerics and five laymen, one of the latter being dean. The name "consistorial" comes from the fact that their principal duties—presenting the claims of candidates for canonization and petitioning for the pallium—are performed in papal consistories. JOHN T. CREAGH.

ADVOCATES OF ST. PETER: An association of Roman Catholic jurists formed on the occasion of the episcopal jubilee of Pius IX. in 1876, for the purpose of asserting and vindicating the rights and teaching of the Church and of the Holy See. The organization, which was blessed by Pius IX., received a signal mark of approbation from Leo XIII. in 1878, when its constitution was approved in a papal brief. From Rome, where its headquarters were established, it has spread into all the countries of Europe, but is unknown in the United States. JOHN T. CREAGH.

ADVOCATUS DEI, DIABOLI. See CANONIZATION.

ADVOWSON: In the Church of England, the right of nomination to a vacant ecclesiastical benefice, vested in the crown, the bishop, one of the universities, or a private person. Such nomination, or presentation, as it is called, is the rule in England, election by the congregation being almost unknown.

ÆDITUUS, ī-dit'ū-us: A term applied to a person having the care of ecclesiastical property. Among the Romans it described one who, with the local priest, if there was one, had charge of a temple. The Roman customs in regard to this office had their influence on the development of similar functions in the Christian Church. They were at first discharged by the *ostiarius* (q.v.), to whom the term *æditius* was sometimes applied (cf. Paulinus of Nola, *Epist.*, i.). By degrees, as the major and minor orders developed, and Church property became more valuable, permanent subordinate officials were required to look after it. The functions and designations of these officials varied, however, in different provinces. The name *æditius* fell into disuse, probably from its original association with heathen worship. It was employed in the Vulgate version of Ezek. xliv. 11; Hos. x. 5; Zeph. i. 4; and Durand (*Rationale*, ii. 5) says of the *ostiarii* that their functions resemble those of the *æditui*. In the Middle Ages the execution of the less dignified functions, which were thought incompatible with the clerical office, was committed more and more to subordinates, and by the end of that period almost entirely to laymen. The name *æditius* was still used for these officials, being thus equivalent to the later sacristan. But this was principally in central Europe, especially in Germany, where conciliar decrees show that their duty was to ring the bells, to open and close the church, etc. In the more western countries the *æditui* became rather identified with the *procuratores* or *provisores* (qq.v.) who had charge of the ecclesiastical property, though this included in some degree the maintenance of the building and the provision of vestments, candles, incense, and the like. In America during the nineteenth century the name has been not infrequently employed in Roman Catholic ecclesiastical terminology for the trustees who administer the temporal concerns of a parish.
(JOHANNES FICKER.)

ÆGIDIUS, ī-jid'i-us, **SAINT.** See GILES, SAINT.

ÆGIDIUS DE COLUMNA (Egidio Colonna): A pupil of Thomas Aquinas and reputed author of the bull *Unam sanctam;* b. at Rome 1245 (?); d. at Avignon 1316. He joined the Augustinian eremite monks, studied at Paris, and taught there for many years, being called *Doctor fundatissimus*. From 1292 to 1295 he was general of his order. In 1296 he was made archbishop of Bourges, but continued to reside in Rome. He defended the election of Boniface VIII. in his *De renuntiatione papæ*, showing that the abdication of Celestine V. was not against the canon law, and followed the court to Avignon. His numerous writings (mostly unpublished) deal with philosophy (commentaries on Aristotle), exegesis (*In Canticum Canticorum; In epistolam ad Romanos*), and dogmatics (*In sententias Longobardi; Quodlibeta*). A portion of his work on ecclesiastical polity, *De potestate ecclesiastica*, was published in the *Journal de l'instruction publique* (Paris, 1858).
K. BENRATH.

BIBLIOGRAPHY: C. E. du Boulay, *Historia universitatis Parisiensis*, iii. 671–672, Paris, 1666; W. Cave, *Scriptorum ecclesiasticorum litteraria*, ii. 339–341, Oxford, 1743; J. A. Fabricius, *Bibliotheca Latina*, i. 19–20, Florence, 1858; F. X. Kraus, *Ægidius von Rom*, in *Oesterreichische Vierteljahresschrift für katholische Theologie*, i. 1–33, Vienna, 1862; F. L[ajard], *Gilles de Rome, religieux, Augustin, theologien*, in *Histoire litteraire de la France*, xxx. 421–566, Paris, 1888.

ÆGIDIUS OF VITERBO: General and protector of the order of Augustinian eremite monks to which Luther belonged; d. as cardinal at Rome 1532. Of his many theological writings (for list cf. Fabricius, *Bibliotheca Latina*, i., Florence, 1858, p. 23) but few have been published. His address at the opening of the Lateran council of 1512 may be found in Hardouin (*Conciliorum collectio*, vol. ix., Paris, 1715, p. 1576), and a memorial on the condition of the Church, which he presented to Pope Adrian VI., was published by C. Höfler (in the *Abhandlungen* of the Royal Bavarian Academy, hist. cl., iv., Munich, 1846, pp. 62–89).
K. BENRATH.

BIBLIOGRAPHY: T. Kolde, *Die deutsche Augustiner-Congregation*, Gotha, 1879.

ÆLFRED, ÆLFRIC. See ALFRED, ALFRIC.

ÆNEAS, ī-nī'as, **OF GAZA,** gē'za: A pupil of the Neoplatonist Hierocles at Alexandria, and teacher of rhetoric at Gaza. Before 534 he wrote a dialogue, *Theophrastus* (in *MPG*, lxxxv. 865–1004), in which he opposes the doctrine of the preexistence of the soul, but asserts its immortality and the resurrection of the body; the perpetuity of the world is rejected. Twenty-five of his letters may be found in R. Hercher, *Epistolographi Græci*, pp. 24–32, Paris, 1873, and several of his treatises are in M. de la Bigne, *Bibliotheca veterum patrum*, viii. (8 vols., Paris, 1609–10); *Magna bibliotheca*, v. 3 and xii. (15 vols., Paris, 1618–22); and *Maxima bibliotheca veterum patrum*, viii. (28 vols., Lyons, 1677–1707).
G. KRÜGER.

BIBLIOGRAPHY: G. Wernsdorf, *Disputatio de Ænea Gazæo*, Naumburg, 1816; K. Seitz, *Die Schule von Gaza*, pp. 23–27, Heidelberg, 1892; K. Krumbacher, *Geschichte der byzantinischen Litteratur*, p. 432, Munich, 1897; G. Schalkhauser, *Æneas von Gaza als Philosoph*, Erlangen, 1898.

ÆNEAS OF PARIS: Bishop of Paris 858–870; d. Dec. 27, 870. He is best known as the author of one of the controversial treatises against the Greeks called forth by the encyclical letters of Photius. His comprehensive *Liber adversus Græcos* (in D'Achery, *Spicilegum*, Paris, i., 1723, 113–148; *MPL*, cxxi. 681–762; cf. *MGH*, *Epist.*, vi., 1902, p. 171, no. 22) deals with the procession of the Holy Ghost, the marriage of the clergy, fasting, the *consignatio infantium*, the clerical tonsure, the Roman primacy, and the elevation of deacons to the see of Rome. He declares that the accusations brought by the Greeks against the Latins are "superfluous questions having more relation to secular matters than to spiritual." [The work is mainly a collection of quotations or "sentences," from Greek and Latin Fathers, the former translated.]
(A. HAUCK.)

ÆNEAS SYLVIUS PICCOLOMINI. See PIUS II., Pope.

ÆPINUS, ê-pi'nus, **JOHANNES (Johann Hoeck):** The first Lutheran superintendent of Hamburg; b. at Ziesar or Ziegesar (29 m. e.n.e. of Magdeburg), in the march of Brandenburg, 1499; d. in Hamburg May 13, 1553. He was a diligent student as a boy, and was under Bugenhagen's instruction, probably while the latter was rector of the monastery of Belbuck. He took his bachelor's degree at Wittenberg in 1520; here he became the friend of Luther and Melanchthon. Then he had a school in Brandenburg, but was persecuted and imprisoned for his reforming activity, and had to leave home. Partly on account of the malice of his enemies, he adopted the modified form of the Greek word *aipeinos* ("lofty"), by which he is generally known, and which he claimed was a translation of his real name (Hoeck=*hoch*). He spent some time in Pomerania, in close relations with the leaders of the Reformation there. From about 1524 to 1528 he was in Stralsund, in charge of a school (probably private). The local authorities asked him to draw up an order of ecclesiastical discipline (*Kirchenordnung*), which went into effect Nov. 5, 1525. In Oct., 1529, he succeeded Johann Boldewan as pastor of St. Peter's in Hamburg. He carried on vigorously the work of his teacher and friend, Bugenhagen, and was chiefly instrumental in introducing his order of discipline in Hamburg. His contest with the cathedral chapter, which still adhered to the old faith, gave occasion to the earliest of his extant writings, *Pinacidion de Romanæ ecclesiæ imposturis* (1530). On May 18, 1532 he was appointed to the highest office in the Lutheran Church of Hamburg, that of superintendent according to Bugenhagen's order of discipline. In 1534 he visited England at the request of Henry VIII., to advise him as to his divorce and as to the carrying forward of the Reformation there. He returned to Hamburg in the following January, and subsequently made numerous journeys as a representative of the city in important affairs. He took part in all the church movements of the time, and frequently had the deciding voice in disputed matters. Melanchthon considered his work on the interim (1548) the best that had been written, though it did not agree with his own views.

In all his writings Æpinus displays great theological learning and equal gentleness of temper. He gave weekly theological lectures, usually in Latin, which were attended by the preachers and other learned men, and spent much time on the Psalms, taking up especially the questions which at the moment were agitating men's minds. He is best known by the controversy which arose over his teaching as to the descent of Christ into Hades. In 1542, finding that the article of the creed on this subject was frequently explained as meaning no more than the going down into the grave, in his lecture on the sixteenth psalm, he put forward the view, already given in Luther's explanation of the Psalms, that Christ had really gone down into hell, to deliver men from its power. Garcæus, his successor at St. Peter's, called him to account for this teaching, but left Hamburg in the following year and did not return until 1546. Meantime Æpinus's commentary on Ps. xvi. had been published by his assistant Johann Freder, so that his view was widely known.

The controversy became a public and a bitter one after Garcæus's return, and both sides sought to gain support from Wittenberg. Melanchthon could only say that there was no agreement among the doctors on this point, and counsel peace. Æpinus's opponents in Hamburg were so turbulent that their leaders were deprived of their offices and banished from the city in 1551. The principal monument of Æpinus's activity in Hamburg is his ordinances for the church there, which he drew up in 1539 at the request of the council. It was a necessary amplification of that of Bugenhagen, and seems to have remained in force until 1603.

(CARL BERTHEAU.)

BIBLIOGRAPHY: N. Staphorst, *Hamburgische Kirchengeschichte*, II. i., Hamburg, 1729; A. Greve, *Memoria J. Æpini instaurata*, ib. 1736; N. Wilckens, *Hamburgischer Ehrentempel*, pp. 248–280, ib. 1770; F. H. R. Frank, *Theologie der Konkordienformel*, 4 vols., Erlangen, 1858–65; Schaff, *Creeds*, i. 296–298.

AERIUS, ā-ē'ri-us: Presbyter and director of the asylum for strangers, maimed, and incapable, in Sebaste in Pontus in the fourth century. He was one of the progressive men of the time who protested against the legalistic and hierarchic tendencies of the Church. Supporting his contention by the Scriptures, he objected to the inequality of presbyters and bishops, denied the value of prayers for the dead, and opposed strict ordinances concerning fasting, which he wished to leave more to individual judgment. About 360 he resigned his position. He had many followers, who constituted a party of "Aerians"; they were severely persecuted and soon disappeared. The only source is Epiphanius (*Hær.*, lxxv.; cf. Gieseler, *Church History*, i., section 106, note 3), who treats him in a very partizan spirit. PHILIPP MEYER.

BIBLIOGRAPHY: J. Glas, *Monograph on the Heresy of Aerius*, Perth, 1745; C. W. F. Walch, *Historie der Ketzereien*, iii. 321 sqq., Leipsic, 1766.

AETIUS. See ARIANISM, I., 3, § 6.

AFFRE, DENIS AUGUSTE: Archbishop of Paris; b. at St. Rome de Tarn (55 m. n.w. of Montpellier), Aveyron, France, Sept. 27, 1793; d. at Paris June 27, 1848. He studied at the Seminary of St. Sulpice and taught theology there after having been ordained priest (1818); he became vicar-general of the diocese of Luçon 1821, of Amiens 1823, of Paris 1834, archbishop of Paris 1840. As archbishop he was zealous and faithful, and lost his life in the performance of duty. During the revolution of 1848, hoping to induce the insurgents to lay down their arms, he mounted a barricade at the Faubourg St. Antoine and attempted to address the mob, but had hardly begun to speak when he was struck by a musket ball and mortally wounded. He was one of the founders of *La France chrétienne* (1820), wrote much for it and other periodicals, and published several treatises of value on educational, historical, and religious subjects.

BIBLIOGRAPHY: P. M. Cruice, *Vie de D. A. Affre*, Paris, 1849 (abridged, 1850); E. Castan, *Histoire de la vie et de la mort de Mgr. D. A. Affre*, ib. 1855.

AFRA, SAINT: An early female martyr, concerning whom all that can be confidently asserted is that she suffered at Augsburg. This fact is attested by Venantius Fortunatus (*Vita Martini*, iv. 642–643) and the mention of her name in the older martyrologies, and there is no reason to question it since the importance of Augsburg makes the early introduction of Christianity there probable. Her *Acta* (ed. B. Krusch, *MGH*, *Script.*, *Rer. Merov.*, iii., 1896, 41–64) consist of two independent parts, *Conversio* and *Passio*, of which the latter is the older. It is said that she was dedicated by her mother to the service of Venus and lived an immoral life in Augsburg until she was converted by a bishop and deacon, who, in time of persecution, took refuge in her house, not knowing her character. She boldly confessed her faith in a general onslaught on the Christians and died by fire Aug. 5.

Bibliography: Rettberg, *KD*, i. 144–149; Friedrich, *KD*, i. 186–199, 427–430, ii. 653–654; L. Duchesne, *Ste. Afra d'Augsbourg*, in *Bulletin critique*, ii. (1897) 301–305.

AFRICA.

I. The Continent as a Whole: 1. Geographical Description: Africa extends southward from the Mediterranean Sea nearly 5,000 miles. The equator crosses it nearly in the middle of its length; but by far the greater part of its mass lies north of the equator, the breadth of the continent from Cape Verde to Cape Guardafui being about 4,600 miles. Its area is about 11,500,000 sq. miles; and the adjacent islands add to this 239,000 more. Easily accessible to Europe by the Mediterranean Sea through 2,000 miles of its northern coast, and touching Asia at the Isthmus of Suez, this continent has ever invited investigation, and has received notable influences from both of its active neighbors. The Sahara Desert, however, severing the Mediterranean coast regions from the southern and equatorial regions of the continent, has proved for centuries a bar to extended intercourse. "Had it not been for the River Nile," says Sir H. H. Johnston, "the negro and the Caucasian might have existed apart even longer without coming into contact." In fact, the great rivers of Africa are quite as important as aids to foreign intercourse in these days as the Desert has been an obstruction to it in the past. The greatest of the African rivers are the Nile, the Kongo, the Niger, and the Zambesi. Closely connected with the rivers, again, are the great lakes of central Africa, namely, Victoria, Tanganyika, and Nyassa, which belong, respectively, to the Nile, the Kongo, and the Zambesi systems. A further characteristic of the continent, noteworthy for all who seek entrance to its interior districts, is the insalubrity, one might say the deadliness, of the climate of its coasts both east and west throughout its tropical zone. The low-lying coast regions, extending in some cases 200 miles inland are sown with the graves of white men, germs of strange and fatal fevers lying in wait as it were for all strangers who venture to set foot unprepared upon that black and seething soil. The greatest mountains of Africa are all in its east central section. Kilima-Njaro in German East Africa, east of the Victoria Nyanza, is 19,600 feet high; Mweru, close by, is about 16,000 feet; and Ruwenzori, west of the Victoria Nyanza and on the border of the Kongo Independent State, is over 20,000 feet. Among the high lands of the interior the most notable section is a broad causeway of elevated plateaux which stretches from Abyssinia southward almost to Cape Colony, and which offers to the white man an almost ideal residence at a height of from 5,000 to 6,000 feet through a long range that is hardly broken save by the Zambesi River.

2. The Races of Africa: The puzzle of the races in Africa which the casual visitor classes under the comprehensive term negroes is insoluble at this day. But the key to the puzzle may probably be found in the repeated mingling of Asiatic and European blood in varying degrees and at divers distinct epochs with the blood of the African of the projecting jaw and the woolly locks. The history of Africa is practically the history of Egypt and then of her Carthaginian rival until well toward the Christian era. Only then did the Mediterranean coast of North Africa begin to have a tale of its own. The mention of this is significant; it suggests the repeated entrance of Asiatics into Africa through the whole period when Egypt was a world power, and of various sorts of Europeans into North Africa during a thousand years before the Mohammedan era.

The races now inhabiting Africa are a perpetual subject of discussion and theory because of the difficulty of accounting for the resemblances as well as the differences between them. Along the Mediterranean coast of North Africa the Arab race rules; but in all the countries of this coast from the west frontier of Egypt to the Atlantic Ocean the Berber race forms the larger part of the population, and even extends into the Sahara. A little further south, negroes of a low and degraded type are found on the west of the Nile; and they appear at different points throughout the continent as far west as the Atlantic coast. In Egypt the larger part of the population is a mixture of Arabs with the ancient Egyptian race, commonly classed as Hamites. This name distinguishes this people from the Semitic races, without throwing light on their origin. Arabs appear also at intervals along the coast of East Africa as far south as Portuguese East Africa in considerable numbers. In the northern section of this coast, along with the Arabs is found a race of negroes commonly called Nubians, the result apparently of mixtures of Arab, Egyptian, and negro races. Abyssinia, the Somali coast, and the Galla country contain a large block of people of the Hamite race, divided into groups, however, by language as well as by religion. Along the Upper Nile as far as the borders of Uganda and eastward well toward the coast are found tribes of another type of negroes generally called the Nilotic group. The negroes of the western part of Africa north of the equator are not all of the degraded type that appears along the western coast. The Fulahs are of an entirely different race, resembling the Hamites, excepting in language. The Mandingoes of the interior of Sierra Leone, Liberia, and the Ivory Coast, are also of a higher type, although their languages show no traces of northern or Asiatic influence.

Throughout Africa north of the equator small detached bodies of Arabs are found at different points; and in general the religious control of this whole great region is with the Mohammedans. For this reason north Africa is frequently spoken of as "Mohammedan Africa." It should be borne in mind, nevertheless, that throughout the region, many pagan tribes exist under Mohammedan rulers. South of the equator, generally speaking, the inhabitants of central Africa, and indeed to the borders of Cape Colony, are of the Bantu stock, often warlike and of a much higher type of intelligence than the negroes of the western coast. In the southwestern part of the continent are remnants of the Hottentots and Bushmen, once numerous in Cape Colony, while throughout Cape Colony proper the natives are known as "colored people," and represent a residue of mixtures of races during centuries. A considerable number of Dutch and of British are found in South Africa; and Portuguese, as well as many Portuguese half-breeds, are numerous in Angola and Portuguese East Africa. European colonists are slowly entering the country on all sides and from all nations, but more than half of the continent can never be a fit residence for Europeans and must remain in the hands of the negro races.

This mixture of races stands in the place of a historical record concerning the people of Africa. Neither the Africans nor any others can read the record. It is the misfortune of the people of this continent to have no history except as appendages to the outside world; and the whole mass of allusions to them in ancient history has the vague quality of tradition. Even the Roman records lack precision, and remain generalities which throw little light on the history of the actual people of the continent.

3. The Opening of Africa: The Mohammedan conquest, beginning about 640, added little to knowledge of the continent, although the Arabs in time gave to the rest of the world information about the fertile negro land beyond the desert in the unlimited region to which they gave the name *Sudan*, "the Country of the Blacks." Eight hundred years later the Portuguese undertook a wonderful series of explorations of the African coasts, which between 1446 and 1510 began the process of stamping the continent as a possession of Europe.

1. The Arabs and Portuguese.

Portugal named every important feature of the African coast as though she owned the whole continent, which in fact she did as far as the coasts were concerned. She ruled the west coast and the Cape of Good Hope from Lisbon, and the east coast, as a part of India, from Goa; and there were none but the Arabs to dispute her sway. She introduced missions also into her African possessions. But, after the fashion of the times, a mission had no objections to raise against maltreatment of the people to whom the land belonged.

2. The General European Invasion.

At last in the seventeenth century began what may be called the third period of the opening of Africa, the Arab invasion and the Portuguese occupation having been the first and second. The characteristic of this third period was a rush by every European nation that could handle ships to make the most money possible out of a vast territory whose inhabitants had not the ability to object. The Dutch took the Cape of Good Hope; and the British, the French, and the Spaniards all gained foothold in different parts of the western coast, and imprinted the nature of their enterprises upon the region by names which persist to this day; such as the "Gold Coast," the "Ivory Coast," the "Grain [of Paradise] Coast" and the "Slave Coast." When the slave-trade began, in the seventeenth century, the Germans, the Swedes, and the Danes also made haste to acquire territory whence they could despoil the continent. North Africa, however, remained in the fierce grip of Islam. The history of Africa was still a history of outsiders working their will upon the country. At the end of the eighteenth century the nations of the lesser European powers had all been dispossessed. Portugal held to her ancient acquisitions about the mouths of the Kongo and the Zambesi and began to try to discover what lay back of these; Great Britain had replaced the Dutch at the Cape of Good Hope, thus securing an extensive region in which white men could live and thrive; while France and Spain had some small settlements on the northern part of the west coast of the continent.

The slave-trade, during nearly 200 years as far as Europe is concerned, and during uncounted centuries as concerns the Asiatic countries, sums up history for the African people. They know little else of their past; but they know that. That fearful traffic transported Africa westward, until from the Ohio River in the United States away southward to the valley of the Amazon in Brazil and throughout the West Indies, the population became strongly and often predominantly African.

3. Prohibition of the Slave-Trade.

A fourth era begins for Africa with the prohibition of the slave-trade by Denmark, Great Britain, Holland, France, and Sweden (1792–1819). It was the slave-trade and its horrors which turned Protestant missionary activity toward Africa in the earliest days of the nineteenth century; and it was the discussion which preceded the prohibition of slave-trading which suggested the beginning of a systematic exploration of Africa.

A fifth period of African history is that of effective exploration of the interior by Europeans between 1840 and 1875. In this period the missionary Livingstone preceded Stanley. But Stanley, following Burton and Speke and Grant and Cameron, and seeking to find Livingstone, turned the attention of the world to the vast commercial value of Africa. A sixth period is the period of partition, beginning when Great Britain, after taking possession of many of the best territories in the southern part of the continent, occupied Egypt in 1882. In the eager rush of the European powers which followed, the great continent has been parceled out as a gold-field is parceled out by prospectors who protect by men with guns the stakes they have hastily driven into the soil, and who only then sit down to estimate the value of what they have secured in the scramble. So to the present day the history of Africa is a history of what outsiders have done in the continent rather than of what the people of the country have done or thought or planned.

4. Later Explorations and the Partition of Africa.

4. Religion and Missions: A rapid survey of the modern political divisions of Africa will be given under the name of each. It seems well, however, to make here a few general remarks upon some religious and social peculiarities of the people of the continent as a whole. The religion of Africa in its untouched and natural condition is not properly idolatrous. There is almost always some sense of a supreme being, who is a spirit, and from whom all power has originally proceeded. The actual religious observances of the people, however, except where they have been affected by Mohammedanism or by Christianity, are forms of spirit-worship connected with the use of fetishes (see FETISHISM).

1. Native Religions.

Mohammedanism has become an indigenous religion in Africa. It rules absolutely the religious thought of nine-tenths of the people of the northern parts of the continent, and controls in a less degree millions south of the Sahara from the Nile to the Niger. As a civilizing force Mohammedanism has value. The first thing the awakened negro does under Mohammedan influence is to obtain a decent robe wherewith to cover himself. Islam wherever it goes ends cannibalism. Its scheme of religious motive in life is to commend religion by making it " easy " to those who find restraint hard. It teaches a certain proportion of the people to recite Arabic litanies of praise to God, and to read Arabic; but to the great mass of the negroes its effect includes neither knowledge of Arabic nor information on the dogmas of Islam. It encourages war in a positive and very real sense; its slave-raids know no amelioration through the change from the tenth to the twentieth century; and they are barely less brutalizing than the man-eating raids which they have displaced. The weakness of Mohammedanism as a civilizing force is that it can not raise men to a level higher than the old Arabian civilization which it is proud to represent. And it is a fact of the deepest meaning, from the missionary point of view, that negroes who have become Mohammedans are equipped with an assurance of righteousness and knowledge which makes them almost impervious to Christian instruction.

2. Mohammedanism.

The Protestant missions, on the other hand, bring to their converts the Christian civilization of the twentieth century with its blessings and enlightenment. The belief that the commonest man will be elevated by study of the Bible, makes the literary culture of African languages a first principle in every mission. More than 100 of the tribal dialects have been reduced to writing, and have been given an elementary Biblical study apparatus which improves as the capacity of the people develops. In the process the language itself becomes in some degree purified, and its words enriched by more profound meanings, until the language receives power to express feelings. In South Africa hundreds of native Protestant churches lead independent ecclesiastical lives under native pastors. It is perhaps too soon to claim that anything is proved by the moderate successes of a century of Protestant missions; but at least it is not out of place to emphasize the wide difference of aim between the two great branches of the Christian Church now working for the regeneration of the tribes of Africa.

3. Protestant Missions.

African missions encounter difficulty from the European colonists. Their aim is quite different from that of the colonists. This alone would make friction and mutual opposition probable. But the aim of the colonist is sometimes aggressively opposed to that of the missionary. That aim was frankly stated by the German *Koloniale Zeitschrift* early in 1904 as follows: " We have acquired this colony not for the evangelization of the blacks, not primarily for their well-being, but for us whites. Whoever hinders our object must be put out of the way." Such assumption of the right of might is found not only in German Southwest Africa; but in the Portuguese colonies, where the slave-trade is still brutally active; in some of the French colonies, where the cruelties of the local administration broke De Brazza's heart; and in the Kongo Independent State, where mutilations and other cruelties mark the Belgian rubber trade and are glossed over by the assurance that the cutting off of hands is an old native custom. The same spirit often appears in British colonies in Africa, but there it is repressed by the government. Where the colonist acts on the " might is right " principle the missionary works a stony soil.

4. Colonists and Missions.

The colonist has had occasion from the very beginning of missions in Africa to complain that one effect of them is to make the people self-assertive. This is not a fault, provided the self-assertion does not pass the limits of mutual right. During the last five or six years a movement among the native Christians of South Africa has attracted much attention. It is what is known as the " Ethiopian movement." Its watchword is " Africa for the Africans "; and its aim is to place all African churches under strictly African leader-

5. The "Ethiopian Movement."

ship. There is a political sound in some of the utterances of the "Ethiopian" leaders; and the local governments are on the alert to check any developments along that line, more especially since American Africans have taken a hand in the movement. There appears to be some connection between this movement and the revolt of the tribes in the south of German Southwest Africa. Whatever the final outcome, it appears certain that as the African tribes learn to think for themselves they must assert their manhood; and, however foolish and futile some of the manifestations of this growing manhood may be, the fact itself is a token that ought to be welcomed. Through it Africa may yet have a history of its own.

II. The Political Divisions of Africa: Abyssinia: The only Christian country of Africa which resisted the Mohammedan irruption. It consists for the most part of a mountain knot in which rise the Atbara River and the Blue Nile, and lies between the Egyptian Sudan and the Red Sea. Area about 150,000 sq. miles; population about 3,500,000; religion, a debased form of the Coptic Church with over 3,000,000 adherents. There are also between 60,000 and 100,000 Jews (called Falashas, "exiles"), and about 50,000 Mohammedans, besides 300,000 pagans. The prevailing language is the Amharic with dialects in different sections. The sacred books of the church are in Ethiopic or Geez. The Gallas in the south have a language of their own. In 1490 Portuguese explorers introduced the Roman Catholic religion into Abyssinia. In 1604 a Jesuit mission was established which finally won the adhesion of the emperor. Intrigues led to their expulsion after about thirty years. The Carmelites and Augustinians also engaged in the work, but with no lasting results; the mission was entirely abandoned in 1797 All attempts to reestablish Roman Catholic missions were thwarted until the early part of the nineteenth century. The Lazarists succeeded about 1830 in gaining a foothold in various provinces. They were again expelled from the interior provinces, and now have their headquarters in the Italian territory of Eritrea (see below). A strong missionary advance into Harrar is also being made from Jibuti.

The earliest effort to establish a Protestant mission in Abyssinia was that of Peter Heyling, a law student of Lübeck. He went there in 1640, won favor with the Abyssinian court circles, and began to translate the Bible into colloquial Amharic. He was captured by Turks in 1652, and, refusing to become a Mohammedan, was decapitated, leaving no trace of his work. In 1752 Christian Frederick William Hocker, a Moravian physician, began a persistent effort to establish a mission in Abyssinia. But the mission got no further than Egypt, and was recalled after the death of Hocker in 1782. In 1830 the Church Missionary Society established a mission in Abyssinia, which was broken up in 1838. Later the London Society for Promoting Christianity among the Jews sent missionaries to the Falashas. Suspicions of political designs hampered the missionaries; and in 1863 they were imprisoned by the emperor. A British military expedition stormed Magdala, the capital, in 1868 and freed the captives; but the mission was not again undertaken. In 1866 the Swedish National Missionary Society began a mission in the border of the province of Tigré, near Massowah. For fifteen years the mission made little progress, suffering through the hostility of the people and through attacks of disease. Then the earliest converts were baptized, the first a Galla slave, and next a Mohammedan. In 1904 the society had ten stations in Eritrea (see below) and had succeeded in sending, with the consent of the authorities, native preachers into the southern Galla country west of Gojam. The Bible has a limited circulation in Abyssinia in several versions. The old Ethiopic Church version has been revised, and printed by the British Bible Society. The whole Bible has been translated into Amharic (1824), and into the southern Galla dialect (1898). The New Testament has been rendered (1830) into the Tigré dialect of the Geez, and single Gospels into Falasha, into two Galla dialects, and into Bogos. See Abyssinia and the Abyssinian Church.

Algeria: A French possession in northern Africa extending southward from the Mediterranean a somewhat uncertain distance into the Desert of Sahara. Area about 184,474 sq. miles; population about 4,739,000. The Algerian Sahara has about 198,000 sq. miles in addition, with a population estimated at 62,000. Although Algeria is regarded as a part of France, it still remains a Mohammedan country. The Mohammedan population is rather vaguely estimated at about 4,100,000, considerable uncertainty existing as to the number of inhabitants of the military district in the hinterland. The Christian population of Algeria is chiefly Roman Catholic (527,000). There are also about 25,000 Greeks, Armenians, and Copts, and about 30,000 Protestants. The number of Jews is 57,000. The language of the country outside of the European colonies is Arabic with several dialects of the Berber language known here as *Kabyle* (i.e. "tribesman"). Algeria forms an archdiocese of the Roman Catholic Church, and is the seat of the Algerian Missionary Society organized through the energetic efforts of Cardinal Lavigerie (q.v.), for missionary enterprises on the edge of the Sahara and in Senegambia and other African districts as far south as Lake Tanganyika. Protestant missionary enterprises are represented in Algeria by the following: two French societies working among the Jews; Miss Trotter's educational mission; the Plymouth Brethren, who have ten missionaries in different cities in Algeria, but publish no statistics; a small Swedish mission; and the North Africa mission, which occupies four stations and carries on a number of small schools for Mohammedans. None of these missions has a very large following among the natives. In fact missionaries are not allowed by the French authorities to engage in open evangelization among Mohammedans. The Arabic version of the Bible has a limited circulation in Algeria. A colloquial version of some of the Gospels has been prepared for the use of the common people who have difficulty in understanding the classical Arabic. Some parts of the Bible have been translated into the Kabyle dialect; and this version, too, has a steady though small circulation. A painful historical interest attaches to the town of Bugia in Algeria as the scene of the martyrdom in 1315 of Raymond Lully (q.v.), the missionary to the Mohammedans.

Angola: A colony of Portugal in West Africa, with a coast-line extending from the mouth of the Kongo River to the borders of German Southwest Africa. It extends into the interior to the Kongo Independent State. Area 484,000 sq. miles; population about 4,000,000, of whom 1,000,000 are rated as Roman Catholics. The Portuguese carried Roman Catholic missions to Angola in the last quarter of the fifteenth century, and a century later established a full ecclesiastical hierarchy in the old kingdom of Kongo, which lay on the left bank of the Kongo. Large numbers of the people of the old kingdom were converted to Christianity, even the king of the Kongo tribes being baptized in 1490. The residence of the king was at the place now known as San Salvador, in the northern part of Angola. This was the seat of the first Roman Catholic bishops. The residence of the bishop was afterward removed to St. Paul de Loanda on the coast, and the buildings at San Salvador fell into ruin as well as the human edifice of the Church in that region. During a hundred years or more the Church gave its blessing to the slave-trade, even the missionaries engaging in it and the bishop encouraging it. This confusion of missionary and mercantile enterprises perhaps accounts for the little progress made by early Christianity in Angola. The present Roman Catholic missionary force is in connection with the Congregation of the Holy Ghost and Sacred Heart of Mary, the mission being connected with the ecclesiastical province of Lisbon (Ulysippo).

Protestant missions in Angola were commenced in 1879 by the Baptist Missionary Society of England, which occupied San Salvador and the northern part of the Loanda district as a part of its Kongo mission. The American Board opened a mission partly supported by Canadian Congregationalists, in the Benguela district in 1880. In 1882 the Livingstone Inland Mission (English) established a station, in connection with its Kongo mission, in Portuguese territory at Mukimvika on the left bank of the Kongo. This mission was turned over to the American Baptist Missionary Union two years later. In 1886 Bishop William Taylor (q.v.) opened seven missionary stations in the district of Loanda, which are now carried on by the American Methodist Episcopal Church. The Plymouth Brethren also have a mission in Angola, and the Swiss Phil-African Mission under Heli Chatelain has a single station in Benguela, called Lincoln. All of these missions make use of education, industrial training, and medical aid to the suffering as instruments for evangelizing and elevating the people. Together these various Protestant missions report (1904) 65 missionaries (men and women), 142 native workers, 50 schools of all classes, 4,235 pupils, with about 4,000 reputed Christians. These Protestant missions have the commendation of the higher and the secret execration of the lower Portuguese officials; they are also hampered by the open hostility of the Portuguese traders and colonists; but they are encouraged by the growing desire of the natives to learn to read and to be men. The native tribes of the interior are numerous, and often separated by barriers of language, although chiefly of Bantu stock. Parts of the Bible have been translated into the Kimbundu, and the Umbundu dialects, and printed respectively at the presses of the Methodist Episcopal and the American Board missions.

Basutoland: A native protectorate in South Africa, governed by native chiefs under a British commissioner. It lies north of Cape Colony, with the Orange River Colony and Natal forming its other boundaries. Area 10,293 sq. miles; population (1904) 348,500, of whom 900 are whites. No white colonists are admitted to this territory. The Basutos belong to the Bantu race; and their language is closely allied to the Zulu-Kafir language. About 300,000 of the people are pagans; about 40,000 are Protestant Christians; and about 5,000 are Roman Catholics. The capital of the territory it Maseru, where the British commissioner resides. The Protestant missions in Basutoland are maintained by the Paris Evangelical Missionary Society, which entered the country under Rolland and Semué in 1833, and by the Society for the Propagation of the Gospel, which began its work in 1875. These two societies have about twenty-eight principal stations and more than 200 outstations with schools, seminaries, printing establishments, etc. The Roman Catholic missions are erected into a prefecture apostolic. They have 6,000 converts. The missions are carried on by Oblates of Mary the Immaculate. Statistics are difficult to obtain, since the reports do not separate work in Basutoland from that of the Orange River Colony and Griqualand. The Bible has been translated by Casalis and Mabille of the Paris mission into the language of the Basutos, generally spoken of as Suto or Lessuto (1837). There is also quite a Christian literature in the same language.

Bechuanaland Protectorate: A British protectorate in South Africa, lying between the Molopo River and the Zambesi, with German Southwest Africa on the west, and Transvaal and Rhodesia on the east. Area 275,000 sq. miles, much of it being desert; population (1904) 119,772, besides 1,000 whites. It is governed by native chiefs, Khama, Sebele, and Bathoen, each ruling his own tribe. The British commissioner, who supervises all, lives at Mafeking.

The country is traversed by the railway leading from Cape Town northward. Among the regulations is one which forbids the granting of licenses to sell liquor. Somewhat over 100,000 of the people are pagans, and about 15,000 are Christians. The Bible has been translated into the language of the chief tribes, which is called Chuan or Sechuan (1831) and single Gospels into Matabele and Mashona. Roman Catholic missions in this territory are under the charge of the Jesuits connected with the Zambesi mission. Statistics are very difficult to obtain, but the Roman Catholic Church seems to have about 3,000 adherents. Protestant missions are carried on by the London Missionary Society, which extended its work to this territory in 1862, and by the Hermannsburg Missionary Society of Germany, which entered the territory in 1864. It is difficult to obtain the exact statistics of either of these societies, since the mission reports of both cover land beyond the borders of the Bechuanaland Protectorate. It is estimated, however, that the number of their adherents is not far from 12,000.

British East Africa Protectorate: A territory under British control in the eastern part of Africa, including coast lands ten miles wide nominally belonging to Zanzibar. The protectorate extends inland to the borders of Uganda. Area about 200,000 sq. miles. While the coast regions are on the whole not healthful, there is a broad belt of highland 300 miles back from the coast which is most suitable for European habitation; and it was upon this belt of highland that the British government invited the Hebrew Zionists to establish a colony. A railway has been constructed from Mombasa to Kisumu on the Victoria Nyanza. The population is estimated at 4,000,000, of whom 500 are Europeans and about 25,000 Hindus, Chinese, Goanese, and other Asiatics. Many Arabs are found in the coast districts, especially in the northern part of the territory; and with them are the mixed race called by the Arabs Suahili (" coast people "). Inland the larger part of the population is of the Bantu race; but there are some powerful tribes like the Masai and Nandi who are of Nilotic stock. In the northern part of the country Gallas and Somalis are found. The capital, Mombasa, has had a checkered history. It was founded by the Arabs, who were in possession when the Portuguese arrived in 1498. The Portuguese continued in power with various vicissitudes until their colony was destroyed 200 years later by the Arabs. The actual British acquisition of this territory dates from 1886 to 1890.

Roman Catholic missions were established on this coast by the Portuguese in the fifteenth century, the stations being treated as an outlying district of the ecclesiastical province of Goa on the west coast of India. The missions followed the fortunes of the Portuguese occupation. They were reestablished in 1860 at Zanzibar. Protestant missions began with the arrival of Johann Ludwig Krapf, of the Church Missionary Society, in 1844. They were followed by the United Methodist Free Church in 1861, the Leipsic Missionary Society in 1886, the Neukirchen Missionary Institute in 1887, the Scandinavian Alliance Mission of North America in 1892, and the African Inland Mission, an American enterprise, in 1895. The Church of Scotland Foreign Missions Committee is preparing to enter the country also. All of these societies together report 172 missionaries, 92 stations and outstations with schools and hospitals, and about 11,000 adherents. The languages of the tribes of this territory differ greatly from each other; and several versions of the Bible will have to be prepared for them. A beginning has been made in translating the Gospels into the Suahili, Nandi, Masai, Somali, and Galla languages.

The islands of *Zanzibar* and *Pemba*, lying off the coast of German East Africa, politically belong

to this territory. Area of the two islands 1,020 sq. miles; population 200,000, including 10,000 East Indians and about 200 Europeans. Zanzibar has played an important part in the history of East and Central Africa since the beginning of the seventeenth century, when the region was occupied by Arabs of Muscat. It became a great center of African trade, including the slave-trade. The domains of the Sultan of Zanzibar extended along the whole coast from Mozambique nearly to the Straits of Bab-el-Mandeb. Since the beginning of the nineteenth century the influence of Great Britain has been gradually increasing, and so leading up to the present protectorate. Germany obtained the southern part of the possessions of Zanzibar on the mainland; Italy bought in 1905 its possession on the Somali coast; and a strip ten miles wide on the coast of British East Africa alone remains to the sultan of all his domains on the mainland, he himself being under the tutelage of a British official. Zanzibar is the seat of a Roman Catholic bishop, with missions conducted by the Congregation of the Holy Ghost, in both islands and on the mainland. The mission has about 3,500 adherents. There are ten stations. Schools and hospitals, conducted by Roman Catholic sisters, have been built in the city of Zanzibar. Protestant missions are represented by the Universities Mission which, after abandoning the Shiré country in 1861, moved its headquarters to the city of Zanzibar. Here Bishops William George Tozer, Edward Steere, and Charles Alan Smythies prepared the way for advance into the interior. The mission has a very fine cathedral and hospitals and schools in the island of Zanzibar, besides a line of stations on the mainland in German East Africa, which extends to Lake Nyassa. What has already been said of versions of the Bible in British East Africa applies to Zanzibar also. The city of Zanzibar itself is a Babel of all African nations and tribes.

Cape Colony: A British colony occupying the southern part of the African continent; bounded on the north by German Southwest Africa, Bechuanaland, the Orange River Colony, Basutoland, and Natal. The colony was founded by the Dutch in 1652, was taken by the British in 1796, was again given up to Holland in 1803, was reoccupied by the British in 1806, and, finally, was ceded to Great Britain in 1814. Area (1904), including native states and Walfisch Bay on the coast of German Southwest Africa, 276,995 sq. miles; population (1904) 2,405,552, of whom 580,380 are white, and 1,825,172 are colored. Of the colored population about 250,000 are a mixture of various races; 15,000 are Malays; and the rest are Hottentots, Kafirs, Fingoes, Bechuanas, etc. About 1,118,000 of the population are Protestants; 23,000 are Roman Catholics; 20,000 are Mohammedans; 4,000 are Jews; while 1,226,000 are pagans. Roman Catholic missions were represented in the colony before the English occupation, by two priests residing in Cape Town. In 1806, when the British captured the colony, these priests were expelled. Sixteen years later two priests were again stationed at Cape Town, without liberty, however, to go into the surrounding country. The existing mission in the colony did not commence until 1837, when Raymond Griffith arrived. He had been an Irish Dominican monk, was appointed vicar apostolic and consecrated bishop by the Archbishop of Dublin, Aug. 24, 1837. Roman Catholic missions now occupy about 100 stations and outstations in the colony. There are two vicariates and a prefecture apostolic.

Protestant Christians do not seem to have worked among the native population during the Dutch period. In 1737 the Moravian George Schmidt was sent to Cape Town, at the request of certain ministers in Holland, to try to benefit the Hottentots and the Bushmen. His success only served to anger the colonists; and he was sent back to Europe in 1742. Fifty years later, in 1792, the Moravians were permitted to reopen their mission in Cape Colony and it has been continued and expanded until the present time, now extending to the east and west. From 1822 to 1867 it had charge of the leper settlement at Hemel en Aarde and Robben Island. About 20,000 native Christians are connected with the Moravian mission. The London Missionary Society began a mission in Cape Colony in 1799 with Vanderkemp as its first missionary, and with such men as Moffat, Livingstone, Philip, and Mackenzie as his successors in a long and brilliant history which through many pains has added some 70,000 natives to the Christian body within the colony. The society has moved its missions northward into Bechuanaland and Rhodesia, one single station being still retained at Hankey in Cape Colony as an educational center. The Wesleyan Methodist Missionary Society of England commenced a mission in the colony in the year 1814 with Barnabas Shaw as its first missionary. This mission afterward spread over the whole of the colony, and extended into Natal, Transvaal, Bechuanaland, and Rhodesia. The care of the native congregations within the colony now rests with the South African Methodist Church, which has connected with it native Christians to the number of 113,600. The Glasgow Missionary Society in 1821 sent two missionaries into Kaffraria which has since been annexed to Cape Colony. The Scottish missions have been greatly extended and are now conducted under the United Free Church of Scotland, having given to missionary history such names as Ross and James Stewart, the latter called by the British High Commissioner "the biggest human" in the region. They extend through Kaffraria into Natal and have a native following of some 30,000. Their most prominent work is in the great educational establishments of Lovedale and Blythwood, which have tested and proved the ability of the Kafir-Zulu race to become civilized and useful. The Society for the Propagation of the Gospel began a mission in Cape Colony in 1821. This mission is now practically merged into the diocesan work of the Anglican Church which reports some 20,000 baptized native Christians. The Paris Missionary Society felt its way into Basutoland from a station at Tulbagh (1830). The Berlin Missionary Society (1834) with 38 stations and 10,000 adherents, and the Rhenish (1829) and the Hermannsburg (1854) missionary societies of Germany also have extensive and successful missions in Cape Colony. The African Methodist Episcopal Church, the National Baptist Convention, the Seventh-day Adventists, all from the United States, the Plymouth Brethren, and the Salvation Army are also engaged in missionary work at various points in this great colony.

Among the achievements of missions must be reckoned the success of the Rev. Dr. John Philip of the London Missionary Society in securing attention on the part of the government to the infringement of ordinary rights of natives in the midst of a rush of colonists inclined to regard the natives as mere obstacles to be removed. Dr. Philip was calumniated and persecuted; but the authorities finally understood that righteous treatment of the blacks is a necessity to the prosperity of the colony. The appearance in recent years of the "Ethiopian movement" (see above, I., 4, § 5) has aroused much suspicion; nevertheless, the authorities aim to secure justice to all, and more and more rely on missions to raise the moral standard of the negro community. See Cape Colony.

Central Africa Protectorate (British): A territory lying west and south of Lake Nyassa, and popularly called Nyassaland. Its southern portion includes the Shiré highlands and extends southward along the Shiré River as far as to the mouth of the Ruo. Area 40,980 sq. miles; population estimated at 990,000. Religion chiefly fetish-worship. About 300,000 of the people are Mohammedans, and about 18,000 are Christians. There is, however, no regular census, and these figures are mere estimates. Europeans living in the protectorate number about 500; and there are about 200 East Indians connected with the military establishment. The language of the Angoni hillmen is a dialect of Zulu; that of the lake people is in several dialects of which that known as Nyanja ("lake"), is becoming prevalent; that of the eastern part of the Shiré district is Yao.

Lake Nyassa was discovered by Dr. Livingstone in 1859. The country then was a select hunting-ground of Arab slave-raiders from Zanzibar and of the Portuguese from the Zambesi. Until 1895, when the slave-raids were stopped by the British authorities, it is said that about 20,000 men, women, and children each year were seized and made to carry ivory to the coast. There they were sold along with the ivory which they had painfully borne for 500 miles. Into such an environment missionaries went at the instance of Livingstone, risking, and with disheartening frequency sacrificing, life because they believed that the people could be saved by teaching them the principles of manhood. The Arabs and the Yao savages were against them, the climate sapped their strength, and even wild beasts attacked them. Yet the missionaries won the day, with their Bible, their practical lessons in kindliness, and with their schools, their industrial training, and their high moral principles. The story of the founding of the protectorate is a story of heroism and of the power of the Bible which the devoted missionaries gave to a people whose very speech was illiterate.

The Universities Mission, established at Livingstone's request, entered the Shiré territory under

Bishop Charles Frederick Mackenzie in 1861. The hostility of the slave-raiders and the rigors of the climate broke up the mission for a time, but it is now thoroughly established at Likoma Island in Lake Nyassa, and in some sixty villages on the east shore of the lake and among the Yao tribesmen in the eastern part of the Shiré district. The Livingstonia Mission of the Free Church of Scotland, entered the country in 1875 and established its headquarters first at Cape Maclear at the south end of the lake, moving afterward to high land well toward the northern end of the lake, where the Livingstonia Institution now stands in a most salubrious spot overlooking the western shore. This mission has about 240 stations and outstations. The schools, printing-house, hospitals, and industrial training establishments of this mission are noteworthy for completeness and beneficent influence quite as much as for their conquest of the chaos which existed when the missionaries arrived on the field. The Church of Scotland founded a mission in the Shiré highlands in 1876. The site was chosen because the missionaries were too ill and exhausted to go farther than the little group of native huts which seemed a haven of rest. Close by that miserable village has arisen about the mission the little town of Blantyre, whose post-office is now a recognized station of the Universal Postal Union. This mission has about forty stations and outstations and a fine group of schools and hospitals. The Zambesi Industrial Mission has taken up a large tract of land lying to the northwest of Blantyre and is teaching the natives to cultivate coffee and other valuable crops. It has about thirty schools in connection with its various settlements. The South African (Dutch) Ministers' Union of Cape Town established a mission in 1901 in the Angoni hill-country west of Lake Nyassa. It has seven stations and is winning favor among the people. All of these missions have been greatly aided by a commercial enterprise known as the African Lakes Corporation, formed in 1878 by Scottish business men with the definite purpose of cooperating with the missions in civilizing the people of the protectorate. It has organized a regular steamboat service on the lake and the Shiré River to the coast at Chinde, and is at last on a paying business basis. The formal establishment of the British protectorate over the lake district took place in 1891. It is one of the marks of progress in the civilization of the tribes of the region that in 1904 a large section of the fierce Angoni tribe voluntarily accepted British control and British regulations. The missions named above have about 190 missionaries (men and women), 985 native preachers and teachers, 25,000 children in their schools, and about 16,000 professing Christians on their rolls. Several of the languages of the protectorate have been reduced to writing and the Bible is in process of publication in the Nyanja, several dialects of which, the Yao, the Konde, and the Tonga, are now being unified. The Angoni tribe, in the western part of the protectorate, being of Zulu race, are able to use the Zulu Bible, of which a considerable number of copies are brought from South Africa every year.

Nyassaland is carried on the lists of the Roman Catholic Church as a provicariate confided to the care of the Algerian Missionary Society. But beyond 10 missionaries, 2 schools, and 1,000 adherents little can be learned of the progress of the mission.

Dahomey: A French possession in West Africa having a coast-line of seventy miles between Togoland and the British colony of Lagos, and extending northward to the French territory of Senegambia and the Niger. The French gained their first footing on this coast in 1851. Area 60,000 sq. miles; population estimated at about 1,000,000, commonly of unmixed negro stock. Capital, Porto Novo on the coast. About sixty miles of railway have been built and 400 miles are projected. It is worth noting that of the whole value of the annual imports into Dahomey one-fourth represents the liquor traffic. A Roman Catholic mission has existed for some years under the direction of the Lyons Seminary for Missions in Africa. There are twenty-two missionaries and fifteen schools. The number of the Roman Catholics in the mission is estimated at about 5,000. The only Protestant mission is that of the Wesleyan Missionary Society with a central station at Porto Novo. It has two missionaries who are of French nationality and it occupies ten outstations in the interior. The number of professing Protestant Christians is about 1,000.

Egypt: A tributary province of the Turkish empire lying on the Mediterranean Sea east of Tripoli, and touching Arabia on the east at the Isthmus of Suez. Area (excluding the Sudan) about 400,000 sq. miles, of which the Nile Valley and Delta, comprising the most of the cultivated and inhabited land, cover only about 13,000 sq. miles. The country is ruled by a hereditary prince called the Khedive, under British tutelage and control. Population (1897) 9,734,405. Capital, Cairo. The Mohammedan population of Egypt numbers about 8,979,000. Of the Christians 648,000 belong to the Oriental Churches, 608,000 being connected with the Coptic or Old Egyptian Church. There are also 56,000 Roman Catholics and 27,000 Protestants. About 25,000 of the population are Jews. The Roman Catholic establishments in Egypt date from the beginning of the seventeenth century, being at that time connected with the orders in charge of the holy places at Jerusalem. The present apostolic vicariate of Egypt was established in 1839. Roman Catholic missions in Egypt are under the minor Franciscan friars and the Lyons Seminary for Missions. There are also Lazarists, Jesuits, and Sisters of the Order of the Good Shepherd, Sisters of the Order of the Mother of God, Sisters of the Order of San Carlo Borromeo, and Sisters of Our Lady of Sion. There are about ninety schools, besides orphanages, hospitals, and other benevolent establishments. Protestant missions are carried on by the American United Presbyterian Mission (1854), the Church Missionary Society (in its present form 1882), the North Africa Mission, the Egypt General Mission, the Church of Scotland Committee on Missions to the Jews, the London Jews Society, the American Seventh-day Adventist

Medical Missions, the (German) Sudan Pioneer Mission, and the (German) Deaconesses of Kaiserswerth (1857). The United Presbyterian Mission is the largest of these missions, occupying stations throughout the Nile Valley and in the Sudan. All together these missions report 166 stations and outstations, 151 missionaries, with 515 native workers, 171 schools, with over 14,000 pupils and students, ten hospitals and dispensaries, two publishing houses, and about 26,000 adherents. Under British control religious liberty is more or less assured. As a consequence Mohammedans are also included in small numbers among the mission converts. The Church Missionary Society's mission publishes a weekly paper in Arabic and English expressly for Mohammedans. The Bible in Arabic, translated and printed at the expense of the American Bible Society in Beirut, is circulated throughout Egpyt, Arabic being the language of the people. See EGYPT.

Eritrea: An Italian possession in Africa extending 670 miles along the coast of the Red Sea and inland to Abyssinia and the Egyptian Sudan. Area about 85,500 sq. miles; population (estimated) 450,000, of whom about 3,000 are Europeans. The capital is Asmara. The native population of Eritrea is chiefly nomadic. In religion more than 100,000 may be reckoned Mohammedans; 17,000, Roman Catholic; 12,000, of the Eastern Churches; 1,000, Protestants; and 500, Jews. The remainder of the population is pagan, belonging to different races. Roman Catholic missionaries have made this region a basis of operations in Abyssinia for nearly three centuries, having been expelled from Abyssinia proper a number of times. Their central establishments are now at Massowah (Massaua) and Keran, where they have a hospital, schools, and two or three orphanages. Protestant missions in Eritrea also directed toward the Abyssinian population are carried on by the Swedish National Society. They have 10 stations on the borders of Tigré and in the province formerly known as Bogos with about 15 schools, a hospital, a dispensary, and a small but growing band of evangelical Christians. The Swedish missions have done good service in securing a translation of the Bible into the Galla language (1898), and through trained native workers have succeeded in establishing themselves among the Galla people in the south of Abyssinia.

French Guinea: A territory forming a part of the newly organized administrative region known as French West Africa. It lies on the coast between Portuguese Guinea and the British colony of Sierra Leone, extending inland some 400 miles to the district of Senegambia and the Niger. Area about 95,000 sq. miles; population estimated at 2,200,000. About 1,000,000 are Mohammedans; more than 1,000,000 are pagans; 1,000 are Roman Catholics, and 500 are Protestants. The capital is Konakry; from which place a railway is now under construction to the Niger River. French colonization in this district began as long ago as 1685, but its development has only been of recent date (1843). The government is undertaking in this, as in all other parts of French West Africa, to introduce a uniform system of education. This, if carried out, will prove of inestimable advantage to the population. The Roman Catholic mission in French Guinea is carried on by the Lyons Congregations of the Holy Ghost and of the Immaculate Heart of Mary. There are about 10 missionaries with 12 schools. A Protestant missionary enterprise, following one commenced in 1804 by the Church Missionary Society, is carried on in the Rio Pongas region by West Indian Christians aided by the Society for the Propagation of the Gospel. The missionaries are colored men from the West Indies specially chosen for this work, which has been undertaken with the thought of making amends to Africa for the wrongs inflicted upon its people by England and her colonies. The New Testament has been translated into the Susu language (1858).

French Kongo: A French colonial possession which occupies the west coast of Africa between the Spanish possessions of the Rio Muni on the borders of the Kongo Independent State and Kamerun, and which extends inland to Lake Chad. The French occupation began in 1841 in a small colony on the Gabun River. Its extension to the Kongo River followed the explorations of De Brazza, between 1875 and 1880. Area about 450,000 sq. miles; population estimated at from 8,000,000 upward. Capital, Libreville on the Gabun. Adjoining this territory in the Lake Chad region, Bagirmi, comprising some 20,000 sq. miles, and Wadai, with 170,000 sq. miles, in 1903 submitted to the French control. These two territories are strongly Mohammedan. French Kongo proper has about 3,500,000 Mohammedans in its northern sections, the remainder of the people being pagans of the usual African type. In race the people of the coast are not of the Bantu stock found in the interior.

Roman Catholic missions are carried on by the Congregation of the Sacred Heart of Mary and the Algerian missionary order. The ecclesiastical center is Santa Maria on the Gabun, where is the vicariate, erected in 1842 under the name, at first, of "the apostolic vicariate of both Guineas." In the Roman Catholic mission there are about fifty priests and about thirty schools with about 5,000 adherents. Protestant missions were established in 1842 by missionaries of the American Board. The mission was afterward transferred to the American Presbyterian Board (North), and later for political reasons the interior stations were passed over to the French missionaries of the Paris Evangelical Missionary Society. Together these two missions have 23 missionaries and about 1,200 adherents. The languages having been reduced to writing by missionaries, the Bible has been translated into Mpongwe (1850–74) and Benga (1858–88), and various parts have been translated into Dikele, Fang (also called by the French Pahouin), Bulu, and Galwa.

Gambia: A British colony and protectorate lying on both sides of the Gambia River, extending some 250 miles inland from its mouth and closely hemmed in by the French West African territory. The colony was commenced in 1662. Area, estimated (1903), 3,061 sq. miles; population, estimated

(1903), 163,781; capital, Bathurst on the Island of Saint Mary. There are about 90,000 Mohammedans in the colony, 56,000 pagans, 4,000 Roman Catholics, and 2,000 Protestant Christians. All of these figures, however, are estimates, excepting as to the colony proper. The Roman Catholic mission is under the care of the Lyons Seminary for Missions in Africa, and carries on two or three schools. The Protestant mission is carried on by the Wesleyan Methodist Missionary Society which entered the colony in 1821. It has 7 outstations, 4 schools, and about 2,000 adherents in the colony. The Society of Friends established a mission in this colony in 1822, and schools were carried on by Hannah Kilham until her death in 1832, when the mission was given up. The history of the Protestant missions here includes a very considerable loss of life among the missionaries, due to the unhealthfulness of the country. The Arabic Bible is used to a limited extent, and parts of the Bible have been translated also into the Wolof and Mandingo languages.

German East Africa: A German colony and sphere of influence lying on the east coast of Africa, between British East Africa and Portuguese East Africa, and extending inland to Lakes Nyassa and Tanganyika. Area about 384,000 sq. miles; population (estimated) 7,000,000, including 1,437 Europeans. There are about 15,000 Arabs, Indians, Chinese, and other Asiatics in this territory. A railway has been built from Tanga on the coast about eighty miles inland to Korogwe; it is to be carried ultimately to Lake Tanganyika. In religion the people of the country are: pagans, about 6,500,000; Mohammedans, for the most part near the coast, 300,000; Hindus, Buddhists, etc., 12,000; Roman Catholics, 20,000; Protestants, 7,000. Roman Catholic missions are carried on by the Congregation of the Holy Ghost, the Trappists, the Benedictines, and the Algerian Missionary Society. They have extensive establishments about the northern and eastern shores of Lake Tanganyika, and report 58 stations, 195 missionaries, 77 nuns, and 295 schools with 17,823 scholars. It is possible that a part of the figures here given refer to missions lying beyond the border of the Kongo Independent State. Ecclesiastical jurisdiction centers at Zanzibar. The Protestant missions are carried on by the Church Missionary Society, the Universities Mission, the German East Africa Mission, the Leipsic Missionary Society, the Moravian Church, and the Berlin Missionary Society. The two last-named societies are active at the north end of Lake Nyassa; and the Moravians are extending stations thence northward. The Universities Mission has stations along the Rovuma River and on the eastern shore of Lake Nyassa. The Berlin society has a station at Dar-al-Salam on the Indian Ocean; and the other German societies have their stations mostly along the northern boundary and in the foothills of Mounts Kilima-Njaro and Mweru. All these societies together report 60 central stations, 123 missionaries, and 230 schools with about 11,000 scholars. The Leipsic society has a printing-press, and publishes a newspaper at one of the Kilima-Njaro stations. The Suahili version of the Bible is used along the coast (completed in 1892). The New Testament has been translated into Yao (1880) and Gogo (1887). Some of the Gospels have been translated into Bondei, Chagga, Kaguru, Nyamwezi, Sagalla, Shambale, and Sukuma, and the translation is progressing in several of these as the people acquire a taste for reading.

German Southwest Africa: A German colony and protectorate on the west coast of Africa, lying south of Angola and bounded on the east and south by Cape Colony and the Bechuanaland protectorate. Area 322,450 sq. miles; population about 200,000, composed of Namaquas (Hottentots) and Damaras, with Hereros and Ovambos in the north, who are of Bantu stock. The European population numbers 4,682. Walfisch Bay on this coast is a British possession belonging to Cape Colony. The seat of administration is Windhoek. The chief seaport is Swakopmund, whence a railway of 236 miles leads to Windhoek. The Hereros in the north and the Namaquas in the south have been at war against the German authorities since 1904, and the colony has suffered much in consequence. Roman Catholic missions are carried on by the Oblates of Hünfeld, and the Oblates of St. Francis of Sales (Vienna). The latter have 2 missionaries and 4 nuns. The other missions have been disturbed by the war, and statistics are not given. Protestant missions are carried on by the Rhenish Missionary Society of Germany, and the Finland Missionary Society. Together these societies had about 16,000 adherents before the war; but recent statistics are lacking, a number of the stations having been destroyed. The Bible has been translated into Namaqua (1881), and the New Testament into Herero (1877). Some Gospels have been completed in Kuanyama and Ndonga (Ovambo).

Gold Coast Colony: A British crown colony and territory stretching for 350 miles along the Gulf of Guinea, in West Africa, between the Ivory Coast and Togoland. Area 119,260 sq. miles; population 1,500,000. About 32,000 of the people are Mohammedans; 35,000, Protestants; 6,000, Roman Catholics; and the rest are pagans of the animist type with deep veneration for fetishes. The Roman Catholic missions are connected with the Lyons Seminary for African Missions, and have 16 missionaries with 13 schools. Protestant missions were commenced in 1752 by the Society for the Propagation of the Gospel. As a result of this mission an African, Philip Quaque, was taken to England, educated, ordained, and returning to the Gold Coast, preached there for some fifty years. The missions now existing are those of the Basel Missionary Society, the Wesleyan Methodist Missionary Society (England), the National Baptist Convention (U. S. A.), and, since 1905, the Society for the Propagation of the Gospel. These missions together report 875 places of regular worship, 82 missionaries (men and women), 1,088 native workers, 235 schools with 11,557 scholars, and 34,835 Christian adherents. The missions make steady progress; but, at the same time, they point out that Mohammedanism is also making progress among the pagans. Kumassi, the former capital of Ashantiland, is now connected with the coast by a railway 168 miles long; and light steamers are used on the Volta River. An artificial harbor is being constructed at Sekondi, the coast terminal of the railway. The Bible has been translated into Akra (1844–65) and Otshi (1870). The New Testament has been translated into Fanti (1884) and Ewé (1872). Progress has been made toward completing the Bible in both of these dialects.

Ivory Coast: A French territory included in the great administrative region known as French West Africa. It has its coast-line between Liberia and the British Gold Coast Colony, and extends inland to the territory of Senegambia and the Niger. The French first obtained possessions on this coast in 1843. Area 200,000 sq. miles; population about 3,000,000, of whom 300 are Europeans. In religion about 200,000 are Mohammedans; about 1,000, Roman Catholics; and the rest, pagans. The capital is Bingerville. A railway is being constructed inland from Bassam, of which 110 miles are nearly finished. The only missions in the country are carried on by the Lyons Seminary for Missions in Africa (Roman Catholic). There are said to be 16 priests, who have 7 schools and some orphanages.

Kamerun: A protectorate and colonial possession of Germany, occupying the west coast of Africa between French Kongo and Nigeria. Inland it extends in a northeasterly direction to Lake Chad. Area about 191,000 sq. miles; population (estimated) 3,500,000, of whom (in 1904) 710 were whites. The native population is largely of the Bantu race, with tribes of Sudan negroes inland. Capital, Buea. The German annexation took place in 1884. Roman Catholic missions have been active in this region since 1889, and are in charge of the Pallotin Missionary Society of Limburg. They report 7 stations, 34 missionaries, 20 nuns, 2,418 pupils in their schools, and 3,780 Roman Catholic Christians. Protestant missions were commenced by Alfred Saker of the Baptist Missionary Society (England) in 1844, he having been expelled from Fernando Po by the Spanish government. With the German colonization of Kamerun (1880–82) difficulties arose, and the Baptist mission was turned over to the Basel Missionary Society, T. J. Comber and G. Grenfell of the Baptist mission going south to found a mission on the Kongo. A considerable body of the native Baptists declined to accept the transfer, and the German Baptists of Berlin sent missionaries to care for them. The German Baptist mission reports 14 missionaries, 1,400 pupils, and 2,170 professed Christians. The Basel Society's mission, established in 1885, has extended inland, and reports (1905) 64 missionaries, 163 native workers, 6,152 pupils, and 6,422 professed Christians. The eagerness of the natives to learn to read is remarkable. The American Presbyterians (North) opened a mission in the southern part of the country in 1885–93, which has 30 missionaries, 27 stations and outstations, 15 schools, a hospital, and about 3,000 professing Christians. The entire Bible was translated into Dualla by the Baptists in 1868, and a version of the New Testament in the same language, which others than Baptists can use, was issued in 1902. The Benga Bible, used in the Rio Muni colony, is circulated to some extent in the south of Kamerun, and parts of the Bible have been translated into Isuba and Bala.

Kongo Independent State: A region occupying in general the basin of the Kongo River and its tributaries in West Central Africa. It touches the seacoast by a narrow neck that extends along the right bank of the river to its mouth. The left bank is held by Portugal. By international agreement in 1885 the state was placed under the sovereignty of King Leopold II. of Belgium. H. M. Stanley, who first explored the region, was its first administrator. International resolutions declare the navigation of the Kongo and its branches free to all, and proclaim the suppression of the slave-trade and the protection of the native inhabitants. The region has highlands well adapted to the residence of Europeans, and its natural wealth, although but slightly developed, is probably very great. The state appears to be administered upon the ancient colonial theory of deriving revenue from it at all hazards. Great tracts of its territory have been passed over to trading companies, the first condition of whose concessions is an obligation to pay the king of Belgium from 40 to 45 per cent. of their gains. The result has been abuses. The trading companies are charged with forcing the natives to work, treating them in fact as slaves, flogging and killing or mutilating them when they fail to obey orders. Missionaries made facts of this nature known, and King Leopold appointed a commission to examine the situation, with the result that many terrible outrages were found to be habitually committed by the armed guards organized by the trading companies. The commission, while inclined to justify severe measures, as necessary to lead the natives to work, recommended that the trading companies be forbidden to use armed guards or to require forced labor from the people of the districts which they administer. There is some hope of an amelioration of conditions in consequence. The capital is Boma, at the mouth of the Kongo River.

The area of the state is estimated at about 900,000 sq. miles; population estimated at from 15,000,000 to 30,000,000. The white people number 2,483. For the most part the people of the Kongo are of the Bantu race. Every tribe has its own dialect, so that the number of dialects is considerable. Roman Catholic missions were established in the Kongo region in the latter part of the fifteenth century. It should be remembered, however, that these early missions were almost entirely in what is now still Portuguese territory. Nothing seems to have been undertaken at that time in the interior of what is now Kongo State. At the present time the Roman Catholic missions extend along the river and in the Ubangi district. They have founded a number of stations also in the Tanganyika region. Schools, industrial work, and agricultural operations are carried on with considerable success. Some of the natives have been trained by the missionaries in Europe as physicians, and render good service as such. Statistics of the missions are not clearly given, but seem to show about 20,000 converts. Protestant missions in this region quickly followed the explorations of H. M. Stanley. The Livingstone Inland Mission from England commenced work on the lower Kongo in 1878, but their stations were shortly transferred to the American Baptist Missionary Union. The Baptist Missionary Society of England established a mission on the upper river in 1879 having for its pioneers Grenfell, Comber, and Bentley; the Plymouth Brethren, led by F. S. Arnot, in the Garenganze region in 1881; the Regions Beyond Missionary Union, in the Balolo district of the upper Kongo in 1889; the American Presbyterians (South), led by S. N. Lapsley, on the Kassai River in 1891; the Swedish Missionary Society on the right bank of the lower Kongo in 1882. These missionary societies have about 200 missionaries and nearly 1,000 native workers, with schools, hospitals, industrial establishments, including printing-houses, and about 15,000 adherents. Several missionary steamers ply on the great river. Educational work is rapidly expanding, the natives showing the greatest eagerness to learn to read. The Belgian commission of inquiry in its report (1905) paid a high tribute to the value of these missions in singling out the field of the Baptist Missionary Society as a district where the natives have been taught to work and are noticeably industrious. Several of the dialects of the region have been reduced to writing by the missionaries. The whole Bible has been printed in Fioti (completed 1904); the New Testament, in Kongo (1893); and parts of the New Testament, in the Teke, Laba, Bopoto, Bolegin, Bangi, Nsembo, and Balolo. These latter translations are more or less tentative, and will hardly be enlarged more rapidly than the increase of readers may demand. In the mean time the Fioti Bible can be understood by people using other dialects in ordinary speech.

Lagos: A British colony and protectorate in Western Africa lying on the coast between Dahomey and Southern Nigeria, and extending inland to the French territories of the middle Niger. Area, including Yorubaland and the protectorate, 25,450 sq. miles; population (estimated) 1,500,000. The great mass of the population are pagan fetish-worshipers. There are some 7,000 Mohammedans, 15,000 Roman Catholics, and 32,000 Protestants. A railway has been built from Lagos to Ibadan in the Yoruba country, with a branch to Abeokuta. The Yoruba chiefs are allowed to govern their land under British supervision.

Roman Catholic missions are under the Lyons Seminary for African Missions. They report 27 priests, 24 schools, and several charitable institutions. The Protestant missions are carried on by the Church Missionary Society and a native pastorate in cooperation with it; by the Wesleyan Methodist Missionary Society; by the Southern Baptist Convention (1856); and by the National Baptist Convention (U. S. A.). The whole Protestant missionary body has 189 stations and outstations, 55 missionaries (men and women), 317 native workers, 110 schools with 7,000 scholars, and 3 hospitals and dispensaries. The government maintains Mohammedan and pagan schools, but the pupils availing themselves of this privilege of non-Christian education in 1902 were only 192. Abeokuta was evangelized in the first instance about 1842 by freed slaves who had been taught Christianity in Sierra Leone, 1,000 miles to the westward, and who led the people of the city to invite the Church Missionary Society to send missionaries there. This was done in 1846. A remarkable man connected with this mission in its early days was Samuel Crowther (q. v.), rescued as a boy from a Portuguese slaver, educated, and sent as a preacher to Abeokuta where he found his relatives. He afterward was consecrated bishop of the Niger in Canterbury Cathedral, and rendered admirable service to the mission during a long life. The assistant bishop of Yorubaland, now, is a full-blooded African. In 1903 the paramount chief of Abeokuta visited London to do homage to the king, and at the same time called at the offices of the Church Missionary Society and the Bible Society to express thanks for great services rendered to his people. The Bible has been translated into Yoruban (1850), and the New Testament into Hausa (1857). One of the Gospels has been tentatively translated into Igbira.

Liberia: An independent republic in Western Africa which has grown out of an effort to colonize freed slaves from America. The first settlement was made in 1822. The republican government was organized in 1847. The coast of the republic extends from Sierra Leone to the Ivory Coast Colony. The territory extends about 200 miles inland, and is hemmed in on the east by French territory. Only a region extending about 25 or 30 miles inland from the coast, however, is effectively administered by the republic. Area about 45,000 sq. miles; population (estimated) 2,000,000, about 20,000 of whom are of American origin. The language of the republic is English. Several native dialects are found among the tribes of the interior. It is estimated that there are about 850,000 Mohammedans and somewhat over 1,000,000 pagans in Liberia, with about 500 Roman Catholics and 25,000 Protestant Christians. Roman Catholic missions are dependent upon their headquarters at Free Town in Sierra Leone. The missionaries belong to the Congregation of the Holy Ghost and Sacred Heart of Mary. Since 1903 there has been a separate missionary jurisdiction confided to the Marist Fathers. Protestant missions in Liberia were commenced by the American Baptist Convention through the Rev. Lott Carey, who went to Monrovia in 1822. After disease had carried off many victims among the missionaries the mission was given up. The Presbyterian Church (North) established a mission in Liberia in 1833, which was also given up on account of the ravages of disease among the missionaries. The American Methodist Church established a mission at Monrovia in 1833, of which the Rev. Melville B. Cox was the pioneer. This mission is still carried on with a great measure of success. The American Protestant Episcopal Church established a mission at Cape Palmas in

1834, with the Rev. John (afterward Bishop) Payne as one of the first missionaries. This mission is still carried on with considerable success, about twenty of the mission clergy being from the Grebo tribe of natives. The American Board established a mission at Cape Palmas in 1834, the Rev. J. L. Wilson being one of the earliest missionaries. On account of the unhealthfulness of the region the missionaries and a number of their adherents removed in 1842 to the Gabun district in what is now the French Kongo colony, transferring their buildings and other immovables in Liberia to the Protestant Episcopal Mission. The National Baptist Convention established a mission in Liberia in 1853, and the Evangelical Lutheran General Synod of North America also established a mission in 1860 which is doing good industrial work. These societies together report 92 missionaries and 182 native workers operating at 168 stations, with schools, hospitals, printing-presses, and industrial institutions. Parts of the New Testament have been translated into Grebo (1838). See LIBERIA.

Morocco: An independent Mohammedan empire in Northwest Africa having a coast-line on the Mediterranean and on the Atlantic Ocean. The country is gradually falling under the direction of France. Area 219,000 sq. miles (the southern frontier, however, is not definitely fixed); population (estimated) 5,000,000, being composed of Berbers, Tuaregs, and Arabs. In name, at least, the greater part of the population is reckoned as Mohammedan. There are about 150,000 Jews and about 6,000 Christians of the Roman Catholic and Eastern churches, with a few Protestants. An apostolic prefecture of the Roman Catholics was established at Tangier in 1859, and under it are about forty priests in different cities of Morocco. Protestant missions are carried on by the North Africa Mission (1881), the Gospel Mission Union (U. S. A., 1894), and the Southern Morocco Mission (1888); besides some workers among the Jews in Tangier. There is little religious liberty in Morocco, and there seems to be but little growth of the Protestant community.

Natal: A British colony in South Africa lying on the eastern coast between Cape Colony and Portuguese East Africa. It is bounded inland by the Transvaal, the Orange River Colony, and Basutoland. Area 35,306 sq. miles; population (1903) 1,039,787. Of these, 877,388 are Zulu-Kafirs; 97,857, Asiatics; and 82,542, Europeans. About 850,000 of the population are pagans, 30,000 are Hindus, 14,000 are Mohammedans, 15,000 are Buddhists or Confucians, 22,000 are Roman Catholics, and 73,000 are Protestants. The country takes its name from the whim of Vasco da Gama, the Portuguese navigator, who happened to arrive at the coast on Christmas day. Roman Catholic missions are under the care of the Oblates of Mary the Immaculate; they report 50 missionaries and 7 native clergy, with 55 schools and several orphanages and hospitals. Their ecclesiastical center is at Pietermaritzburg, the seat of a vicar apostolic. The local Anglican, Wesleyan, and Dutch Reformed congregations all carry on missionary work; and, besides these, the following eleven missionary societies are at work in Natal: the American Board (1835), whose early missionaries were, Daniel Lindley, Robert Adams, Aldin and Lewis Grout, and Josiah Tyler; the United Free Church of Scotland; the Society for the Propagation of the Gospel, both of which entered Natal as an extension of work in Kaffraria; the Berlin Missionary Society; the Hermannsburg Missionary Society; the Norwegian Missionary Society; the Swedish Evangelical Mission Covenant; the Free Methodists of North America; the South Africa General Mission; the National Baptist Convention; and the Plymouth Brethren. All these societies together report 192 stations and outstations, 106 missionaries (men and women), 612 native workers, 161 schools with 7,016 pupils, 2 hospitals, and one printing-house. Many of the native churches formerly connected with the older missions are now independent and self-supporting, and do not appear on the mission statistics because reckoned as churches of the country. Many of the tribal chiefs, who are pagans and polygamists of a rank order, but who nevertheless treat missionaries as benefactors, oppose the Christian Church with all their might as tending to make their "subjects" think for themselves and question the commands of hereditary despots. The British authorities are inclined to hamper the freedom of the missions on account of their suspicion of "Ethiopianism." At present a native preacher may not officiate in a church unless under the immediate supervision of a responsible white clergyman.

The Bible has been translated into Zulu (1851–83). This is one of the most important of the African versions published by the American Bible Society. It has a range of circulation extending to Lake Nyassa and into Bechuanaland.

Nigeria: A British territory and sphere of influence in West Africa lying on the coast between Lagos and Kamerun, and extending inland between the German and the French possessions as far as Lake Chad. It is divided into Northern and Southern Nigeria. Lagos with its protectorate is naturally a part of the region, but at present is separately administered. Area: Northern Nigeria, 315,000 sq. miles; Southern Nigeria, 49,700 sq. miles; population (estimated for the whole great region) 23,000,000. It is estimated that the Mohammedan part of the population numbers about 10,000,000, and the pagan part about 13,000,000. This is mere guesswork, since the country is not even explored. In all the coast regions the pagans, of the most degraded class of fetish-worshipers, predominate. In Northern Nigeria the Mohammedan element is the ruling one (under British restraint), but there are large sections occupied by pagan tribes. Christians are for the most part in Southern Nigeria, and their numbers are given as: Roman Catholics, 18,000; Protestants, 6,000. The seat of government in Northern Nigeria is Zungeru on the Kaduna River; that of Southern Nigeria is Old Calabar. Steamers ply on the Niger about 400 miles from its mouth. A railway is being constructed in Northern Nigeria from Zungeru toward Kano, a great trading center south of Lake Chad.

Roman Catholic missions are carried on by the Congregation of the Holy Ghost and the Sacred Heart of Mary. Ten missionaries are reported with 6 schools. Protestant missions are those of the United Free Church of Scotland in the Calabar region in Southern Nigeria (1846) and of the Church Missionary Society in the Niger delta (1857) and in Northern Nigeria (1902, after a failure in 1890), the Qua Ibo Mission on the Qua River (1887), and the African Evangelistic Mission (1901) and the Sudan United Mission (1903) in Northern Nigeria. The missions in Northern Nigeria are still in the early stage, with little more to show than the names of Wilmot Brooke, J. A. Robinson, and W. R. S. Miller who sacrificed life for that land. In Southern Nigeria there are 82 missionaries (men and women), and 157 schools with 2,482 scholars. The Anglican bishop of this region is assisted by a bishop who is a full-blooded negro. The Bible has been translated into Efik (1862); and tentative translations of single Gospels have been made into Akunakuna, into three or four dialects of Ibo, into Idzo, and into Umon. These are all dialects of Southern Nigeria. Gospels have been translated into the Igbira and Nupé languages besides the Hausa language, all in Northern Nigeria.

Orange River Colony: A British possession in South Africa. It has the Transvaal on the north, Natal and Basutoland on the east, and Cape Colony on the west and south. During forty-six years it was the Orange Free State and was annexed to the British crown in May, 1900, in consequence of its participation in the Boer attack on the adjacent British colonies. Area 50,100 sq. miles; population (1904) 385,045, of whom 143,419 are whites and 241,626 are colored. Capital, Bloemfontein. About 220,000 of the inhabitants are pagans. The predominating Christian body is the Dutch Reformed Church. The whole number of Protestants is about 100,000; of Roman Catholics, 5,000. The country is an excellent agricultural region. Diamonds and other precious stones are found in some sections; and the population tends to increase and to become more and more varied in its constituent elements. Roman Catholic missions are in charge of the Oblates of Mary the Immaculate. The statistics of their work in the colony are not separately given, but there seem to be 14 missionary priests and 2 native priests, with 13 schools. Protestant missionary activities are largely in the hands of the local churches. The Dutch Reformed Church has here shown, much more than elsewhere used to be the case, a purpose to work for the evangelization of the native pagans. The Wesleyan Church and the Anglican Church both have missions locally supported; but the work for whites and blacks is not separately reported. Besides this local church work, in beginning which the Paris Missionary Society had a part (1831), the Berlin Missionary Society (1834) is at work in the colony with 33 stations and outstations, 18 missionaries, 148 native workers, 27 schools, and about 8,000 professed Christians connected with its stations. The Society for the Propagation of the Gospel (1863) has 4 stations among the natives, but its statistics are not separately given. The Zulu Bible, the Chuana version, and the Lesuto version used in Basutoland supply the needs of the people in this colony.

Portuguese East Africa: One of the oldest Portuguese possessions in Africa, situated on the east coast between German East Africa and Natal. It extends inland to British Central Africa, and on both banks of the Zambesi River to Rhodesia. It is composed of the districts of Mozambique, Zambesia, and Lourenço Marques. Area 293,400 sq. miles; population (estimated) 3,120,000. Much of the territory is in the hands of trading companies, which administer the laws in their respective districts. Delagoa Bay is connected by railway with Pretoria in the Transvaal, and another railway runs from Beira in Zambesia to Buluwayo in Rhodesia. The Portuguese began their colonies on this coast in 1505, and the Roman Catholic Church has had strong missions in the region ever since. The ecclesiastical organization was effected in 1612. At present missions in this territory are in the hands of the Society of Jesus, with stations extending along the Zambesi River into the interior. About 30 missionaries are reported. Protestant missions are carried on by the American Methodist Episcopal Church at Inhambane, by the Wesleyan Methodists of England in the Delagoa Bay district, by the Swiss Romande Mission in the south, and by the American Board among the Gaza tribes and at Beira, the chief seaport of the district of Zambesia. The Universities Mission has one station in this territory adjoining its field in Nyassaland. These societies together have 40 missionaries (men and women), 103 native workers, and about 7,000 adherents, with hospitals and schools. A printing-press at Inhambane is beginning to form a literature in two native languages. The New Testament has been translated into Tonga (1890), and the Gospels into Shectswa (1891). A Gospel has been translated into Ronga by the Swiss Romande missionaries.

Portuguese Guinea: A Portuguese possession adjoining French Kongo on the West African coast, and surrounded by French territory on the land side. It is included in the administration of the Cape Verde Islands. Area, including the islands, 6,280 sq. miles; population, including the islands, 1,000,000. The population is generally given as including 260,000 Roman Catholics; and there are about 170,000 Mohammedans and over 500,000 pagans on the mainland. Roman Catholic missions were established on the mainland in 1832, and are connected with the ecclesiastical province of Lisbon. They comprise eight Roman Catholic parishes. No Protestant missions have been established in this territory.

Rhodesia: An immense territory in South Africa, lying between the Transvaal and the Kongo Independent State, and having as its eastern boundary Portuguese East Africa, and as its western boundary Angola and German Southwest Africa. It is administered as British territory by the British South Africa Company under a British resident commissioner. In its northeastern portion, where it touches Lake Tanganyika, police duties are cared for by the Nyassaland protectorate. It is divided into Southern Rhodesia and Northern Rhodesia by the Zambesi River. Area about 246,000 sq. miles; population about 900,000, of whom 12,000 are Europeans and about 1,100 are Asiatics. There are about 5,000 Roman Catholics and 20,000 Protestants in this country. The Roman Catholic missions are not conterminous with the boundaries of this territory, and it is impossible to give their statistics. The missionaries are of the Algerian Society with a certain number of Jesuits in the Zambesi region. Protestant missions in this region were commenced by Robert Moffat of the London Missionary Society in 1830. Livingstone explored the whole region for the same society and unsuccessfully attempted to establish stations among the Mashonas. John Mackenzie was a worthy successor of such pioneers. At present the Protestant missionary societies in Rhodesia are: the London Missionary Society in Matabeleland and at the southern end of Lake Tanganyika; the Wesleyan Methodist Missionary Society in Mashonaland and Matabeleland; and the Paris Missionary Society in Barotseland in the territory north of the Zambesi, which F. Coillard entered in 1885 as an extension of the Society's work in Basutoland, the Barotses having the same speech as the Basutos. The Methodist Episcopal Missionary Society (U. S. A.) and the American Board have missions in the eastern part of Southern Rhodesia, near the Portuguese frontier. These societies together have 112 stations and outstations, 70 missionaries (men and women), 6,000 pupils in their schools, and 15,000 professed Christians. The construction of railways, connecting Rhodesia with Cape Town and the Portuguese seaports and opening up the country beyond the Zambesi, is bringing many colonists into the country; and their advent implies that a testing time of the reality of the Christianity of the native churches is at hand. The people use the Bible in Zulu, in Sechuana, and in Lesuto. Tentative translations of Gospels have been made in the Matabele and the Mashona languages.

Rio De Oro: A Spanish possession in North Africa stretching southward along the shore to the Atlantic Ocean from the Morocco frontier and extending inland to the French possessions of the Sahara. Area about 70,000 sq. miles; population (estimated) 130,000, almost all Mohammedans. The territory is administered by the governor of the Canary Islands. Roman Catholic missions ecclesiastically connected with the Canary Islands are established at the points occupied by Spanish traders. There are no Protestant missions in the country.

Rio Muni: Spanish possession in West Africa adjoining the German Kamerun colony and surrounded on the east and south by the territory of the French Kongo. Area 9,800 sq. miles; population (estimated) 140,000, including about 300 whites. Roman Catholic missions have existed here since 1855 and are carried on by the Spanish Congregation of the Sacred Heart of Mary, being ecclesiastically connected with the island diocese of Annobon and Fernando Po. A Protestant mission has been carried on in this territory by the American Presbyterians (North) who established themselves in 1855 on the island of Corisco, and later on the Benito River. They have 4 stations and outstations, 7 schools, and about 300 professed Christians. The Bible has been translated into the Benga language (1858), which has a somewhat extensive domain in the coast regions.

Senegal: A French colony in West Africa between the Gambia and the Senegal rivers. It consists of a narrow strip of coast land, forming the colony proper, together with certain ports on the Senegal River. Area 438 sq. miles; population (1904) 107,826, of whom 2,804 are Europeans. The people of the colony proper are citizens, having the right to vote, and being represented by a deputy in the French parliament. The capital of the colony is St. Louis, on the seacoast. Roman Catholic missions have long existed in Senegal, and were placed under an ecclesiastical prefecture in 1765. There are about 5,000 native Roman Catholics in the colony. The only Protestant mission working in Senegal is that of the Paris Evangelical Missionary Society, which has a station at St. Louis (1863) and two or three small congregations in the vicinity. Besides the Arabic Bible, which is occasionally called for, some of the Gospels have been translated into the Wolof and Mandingo languages (1882).

Senegambia and the Niger: An immense French protectorate comprising the territories formerly called Western Sudan, with the larger part of the Sahara, having the colony of Senegal on the west, the colonies of the Ivory Coast, the Gold Coast, Dahomey, and Togoland on the south, and extending on the north to the Algerian Sahara. Area 2,500,000 sq. miles; population (estimated) 10,000,000. The prevailing religion is Mohammedanism. Many pagan tribes exist who serve Mohammedan rulers and furnish slaves for the markets of Tripoli and the Barbary States. The capital is Kayes, on the Senegal River. This great territory, with the French colonies of Senegal, French Guinea, Ivory Coast, and Dahomey, forms a single region known as French West Africa, of which the governor-general resides at Dakar on the coast of Senegal. Steamers run regularly on the Senegal River some 400 miles to Kayes; and a railway has been constructed from Kayes 650 miles to some important points on the upper Niger. A feature of this region is that the French government has planned a universal system of education which it is endeavoring to apply throughout the territories effectively occupied. Roman Catholic missions have been carried on for a number of years at several of the posts on the Senegal and Niger rivers; the number of converts is reported as 10,000. No Protestant missions are reported in this great region.

Sierra Leone: A British colony and protectorate in West Africa, lying on the coast between Liberia and French Guinea, and extending inland about 180 miles, limited by the boundaries of the French possessions and of Liberia. Area about 34,000 sq. miles; population about 1,100,000. Of the people about 1,000,000 are pagans, 20,000 are Mohammedans, 5,000 are Roman Catholics, and 50,000 are

Protestants. The colony proper is limited to the Sierra Leone peninsula. It was the place whence in 1562 the first slaves were taken to the West Indies under the British flag. After slaves in England had been set free, in 1772, a district in Sierra Leone was set apart to be colonized by liberated slaves. Here, from 1786 on, freed slaves were landed and almost abandoned to their own resources except as to food—a great crowd of debased creatures from all parts of Africa, knowing no common language and having no principle of life except such evil things as they had picked up during slavery among Europeans. The situation of these freed slaves had a powerful influence in turning English missionary zeal to West Africa. The Roman Catholic establishment is under an apostolic vicariate erected in 1858 at Freetown. The missionaries are of the Congregation of the Holy Ghost and the Sacred Heart of Mary. The number of Roman Catholics is 2,800.

The Protestant missionary enterprise was commenced in the latter part of the eighteenth century by missionaries from Scotland; three having died soon after their arrival, the mission was given up. The Church Missionary Society sent missionaries to Sierra Leone in 1804; but they were instructed to go north and begin their mission in the Susu country on the Rio Pongas in what is now French Guinea. They were all Germans, chosen because of the difficulty of securing ordination of Englishmen for this society. The mission came to naught through the hostility of the slave-dealers, and was finally transferred (1814-16) to Sierra Leone. Here a solid work was soon organized among the freed slaves, and has grown ever since. The Protestant missionary societies now working in that field are: the Church Missionary Society, the Wesleyan Methodist Missionary Society, the Wesleyan Methodist Connection of America, the United Brethren (U. S. A.) in the Mendi region, and the Christian and Missionary Alliance (U. S. A.) in the eastern part of the protectorate. The Church Missionary Society field is almost wholly in the protectorate, the congregations in Sierra Leone being self-supporting and independent. Together the mission stations and outstations number about 131. There are 42 missionaries (men and women), 117 schools, and about 45,000 professed Christians connected with the missions. The English Bible is used in the colony. The New Testament has been translated into Temné (1866); parts of the New Testament into Mendi; and single Gospels, into Bullom and Kuranko. The Yoruba mission of the Church Missionary Society was an outgrowth of the society's work among freed slaves at Sierra Leone. See below, III., LAGOS.

Somaliland (British): A British protectorate on the east coast of North Africa, lying between Abyssinia and the sea and between French Somaliland and Italian Somaliland. It is administered by a consul-general. Area about 60,000 sq. miles; population (estimated) 300,000; religion, Mohammedan. Most of the people of this district are nomads and very fanatical in their intolerance of Christians. The English government has been at a considerable expense in money and men to pacify the tribes of the interior, who have attempted to drive the English from the country on religious grounds. No missions are reported in this district.

Somaliland (French): A French protectorate on the eastern coast of North Africa, near the Straits of Bab-el-Mandeb, between the Italian colony of Eritrea and British Somaliland, extending inland to the Abyssinian border and including the colony of Obock. Capital, Jibuti. Area about 46,000 sq. miles; population about 200,000, mostly Mohammedans, with some 40,000 pagans, and in the colony of Obock about 8,000 Christians. A railway has been constructed from Jibuti to the Harrar frontier in Abyssinia. There has been for many years a Roman Catholic mission conducted by the French Capuchins who have two or three schools at Obock and Jibuti, and are reaching out toward Abyssinia.

Somaliland (Italian): An Italian possession on the eastern coast of North Africa, lying between the Gulf of Aden and Abyssinia, and between British Somaliland and the mouth of the Juba River, the frontier of British East Africa. The sovereign rights of the Sultan of Zanzibar over this coast region were bought by Italy in 1905. Area about 100,000 sq. miles; population (estimated) 400,000, chiefly Mohammedans, with about 50,000 pagans. There are no records of missions established in this wild territory.

Sudan: This term is here limited to the Egyptian Sudan, the Western and Central Sudan being absorbed in the main into French spheres of influence to which other names have been given (see SENEGAMBIA AND THE NIGER, above). The Egyptian Sudan is a territory extending south from the frontier of Egypt to Uganda and the Kongo Independent State, and west from the Red Sea to the unmarked boundary of the French sphere of influence. It is nominally a possession of Egypt, but in fact is ruled for Egypt by the British. English and Egyptian flags are used together throughout the territory. Area about 950,000 sq. miles; population (estimated) 2,000,000. The population of the country was much reduced during the sixteen years' rule of the Mahdi and his dervishes, who as ardent Mohammedans wished to show the world how a country ought to be governed. General Gordon having been killed by the Mahdi's party in 1885, one of the first acts of the English on recovering the land in 1898 was to found a great "Gordon Memorial" College at Khartum, the scene of his murder, and now the seat of the new administration. The majority of the people are Mohammedans, with an uncertain number of pagan tribes in the southern districts. A considerable number of Greek, Coptic, and Armenian traders is found in the Khartum district. Roman Catholic missions exist at Khartum and Omdurman and among the pagans at Fashoda; a mission of the American United Presbyterian Church has been founded on the Sobat River; and the Church Missionary Society has established missionaries (1906) at or near Bor in the vacant pagan country between the two first-named missions. All of these missions are too newly established to have any visible fruit except attendance at schools.

The Arabic Bible is circulated in the Mohammedan parts of the Sudan. Gospels have been translated into the Dinka language.

Togoland: A German colony in West Africa, occupying the coast of the Gulf of Guinea between the Gold Coast Colony and Dahomey. It extends inland to the French territory of Senegambia and the Niger. Area about 32,000 sq. miles; population (estimated) 1,500,000, chiefly pagan; capital, Lome. The German government carries on several schools for the instruction of the natives, and is training them for administrative posts. Roman Catholic missions here are conducted by the Steyl Society for Divine Work. The missionaries number 28, with 9 nuns, 52 schools, 2,119 pupils, and 2,203 Roman Catholic Christians. Protestant missionary work is carried on by the North German Missionary Society (1847), and by the Wesleyan Methodist Missionary Society, which employs German Methodists for this field. The two societies report 78 stations and outstations, 31 missionaries (men and women), 69 schools with 3,111 pupils, and 4,600 professed Christians. The Ewé New Testament is used here, and a special translation of one of the Gospels, to satisfy local variations, has been tentatively prepared.

Transvaal: A colony of Great Britain in South Africa, lying north of the Orange River Colony and Natal, and west of Portuguese East Africa. Area 111,196 sq. miles; population (1904) 1,268,716, of whom 969,389 are colored, including Chinese and Hindus, and 299,327 are whites. The colony was settled in 1836–37 by Dutch who emigrated from Cape Colony. In 1899 dissensions with Great Britain respecting sovereignty culminated in war, and in 1900 Great Britain formally annexed the territory to her South African domains, the Boers accepting the annexation after two years. The capital is Pretoria. The religious statistics show the pagans to number nearly 1,000,000; Roman Catholics, 10,000; Protestants, 256,000; Jews, 10,000; Buddhists and Confucians, 15,000. The Dutch churches form the largest single group of Protestants. Chinese laborers at the mines are a recent addition to the population. Numbers of negroes from all parts of Africa are also drawn to Johannesburg for work in the mines, about 75,000 natives and other colored people being gathered there by opportunities for work. The Anglican, Wesleyan, and Dutch Reformed local churches all carry on missions among the natives. Other Protestant missions are those of the American Board (1893), the Berlin Missionary Society (1859) opened by A. Merensky and Knothe, the Hermannsburg Missionary Society (1857), and the Swiss Romande Mission led by H. Berthoud (1875). These societies together report (not including the enterprises of the local churches) 112 missionaries (men and women), 2,344 native workers, 300 schools with 14,674 pupils, and 84,000 professing Christian adherents. Efforts to improve the character of the workers in the mining compounds of Johannesburg are meeting with some success. The Zulu Bible is much used in the Transvaal as well as the Chuana and Lesuto versions. The New Testament has been translated into Tonga and Sepedi, both in 1888.

Tripoli: A possession of Turkey on the north coast of Africa west of Egypt. It extends southward to the Sahara and includes the oasis of the Fezzan, but its southern limits are indefinite. This territory was seized by Turkey in the sixteenth century. Area about 400,000 sq. miles; population about 1,000,000, chiefly Berbers. There are about 6,000 Europeans (Maltese and Italians), who are mainly Roman Catholics; and there are also about 10,000 Jews. There is an extensive caravan trade with the Sudan and Timbuctoo; and the slave-trade is quietly fostered by this means. The only Protestant mission in Tripoli is that of the North Africa Mission, which has 1 station with 4 missionaries, a hospital, and 2 dispensaries. Arabic and Kabyle are the languages of the country.

Tunis: A French protectorate on the northern coast of Africa lying between Tripoli and Algeria. Area about 51,000 sq. miles; population (estimated) 1,900,000, mainly Berbers and Arabs, with a foreign population (1901) of 39,000 French, 67,500 Italians, and 12,000 Maltese. The Tunisian ruler, called the Bey, is from a family which has been in power since 1575, and governs the country under the control of a French resident. The Roman Catholic Church in Tunis is under direction of the archbishop of Carthage, the see having been restored in 1884. There are 53 priests, 2 bishops, and several schools. Tunis was the scene of some of Raymond Lully's efforts to convert Mohammedans in the thirteenth century. Protestant missions are carried on in Tunis by the North African Mission, the Swedish Young Women's Christian Association, and the London Jews Society. Together these societies have 5 schools, 2 hospitals or dispensaries, and about 250 persons under instruction. Arabic is the prevailing language.

Uganda: A British protectorate in East Central Africa, lying between the Egyptian Sudan on the north, German East Africa on the south, British East Africa on the east, and the Kongo Independent State on the west. Within its boundaries lie part of the Victoria Nyanza and lakes Albert and Albert Edward. It comprises the native kingdom of Uganda and several smaller districts ruled by native kinglets under British control. Area 89,400 sq. miles; population about 4,000,000, of whom about 1,000,000 are in the kingdom of Uganda. The religious divisions of the population in the whole protectorate are: pagans, 3,500,000; Mohammedans, 50,000; Roman Catholics, 146,000; and Protestants, 250,000. A railway connects Mombasa on the coast of British East Africa with Kisumu, formerly called Port Florence, on the Victoria Nyanza. The seat of the British administration is Entebbe, and that of the kingdom of Uganda is Mengo. Henry M. Stanley visited Uganda in 1875, and found the king Mutesa a recent convert to Islam but inclined to ask questions on the religion of the Christians. He gave the king some instruction and had the Lord's Prayer translated for him into Suahili written in Arabic characters. At this time Uganda was like any other African kingdom a place of superstition, degradation of women, and bloodthirsty cruelty and oppression. Stanley was really the first of Christian missionaries there; for the slight teachings that he gave the king were not forgotten, and his translation of the Lord's Prayer was copied and recopied. On leaving Uganda Stanley wrote a letter to the London *Telegraph* describing Uganda and the willingness of King Mutesa to receive Christian instruction. He then addressed the missionary societies in these words: "Here, gentlemen, is your opportunity. The people on the shores of the Nyanza call upon you." This challenge was at once taken up by the Church Missionary Society; and in 1876 its first missionaries reached Uganda. The first converts were baptized in 1882, and persecution soon set in, when a number of the Christians were burned alive. Alexander Mackay, a layman and a member of the mission, was a man of indomitable energy and wonderful devotion; and upon him rested to a great degree the responsibility for the defense of the mission. Several of the missionaries were murdered, including Bishop James Hannington (1885), by order of King Mwanga, Mutesa's successor. Roman Catholic missionaries appeared on the scene; and quarrels and strife ensued between the two denominations. Mohammedans also intervened, trying to profit by the dissensions between the Christians. The British protectorate was declared in 1894. In 1897 the Sudanese troops in British employ revolted and attempted to seize the country in the Mohammedan interest. The valor of the Christians weighed largely in deciding this fierce little war against the mutineers. In it George Laurence Pilkington, a notable lay missionary lost his life. With the defeat of the mutineers and the assignment of the Mohammedans to separate reservations peace was finally established, and the whole protectorate is in a prosperous condition.

The Church Missionary Society has now in the protectorate 90 missionaries (men and women), 2,500 native workers, 170 schools with 22,229 scholars, and 53,000 baptized Christians. It had established a considerable industrial enterprise for the development of the people; but in 1904 this department of its work was turned over to the Uganda Company, a commercial body chartered in England to develop the country. The Roman Catholic missions were established by the Algiers Society for African Missions. There are now 88 stations and about 80,000 baptized Roman Catholic Christians. At Kaimosi, about twenty-five miles north of Port Florence, is a mission of the American Society of Friends, which is instructing the people in various industries. Altogether Uganda is after thirty years of missionary labor a remarkable instance of the change in a people which can be produced by the attempt to follow the principles of the Bible. The overthrow of barbarism in the native customs was effected before any outside political forces entered upon the scene. The Bible has been translated into Ugandan (1888), and Gospels have been rendered into Nyoro and Toro.

III. African Islands:

Annobon. See Fernando Po.

Canary Islands: A group of islands lying northwest of Africa and belonging to Spain, of which they form a province. Area 2,807 sq. miles; population 358,564, reckoned as entirely Roman Catholic, the first Roman Catholic see having been erected here in 1404.

Cape Verde Islands: A group of fourteen islands lying off the west coast of Africa and belonging to Portugal. Area 1,480 sq. miles; population (1900) 147,424, of whom about two-thirds are negroes and nearly one-third of mixed blood. The religion is Roman Catholic.

Comoro Isles: A group of small islands about half way between Madagascar and the African coast. Area 620 sq. miles; population about 47,000, chiefly Mohammedans. The islands are ecclesiastically under the jurisdiction of Mayotte, but it does not appear that any mission exists upon them

Corisco. See Fernando Po.

Fernando Po, Annobon, Corisco, and Elobey: Islands in the Gulf of Guinea, belonging to Spain. The area of these islands taken together is about 780 sq. miles; population 22,000. Roman Catholic missions are carried on in the islands by the Spanish Congregation of the Sacred Heart of Mary. Nineteen clergy are reported in Fernando Po, with about 4,000 Roman Catholics. There is a Protestant mission in Fernando Po, established by the Primitive Methodist Missionary Society in 1870, a mission established by the Baptist Missionary Society of England having been driven from the country by Spanish intolerance a number of years before. One of the Gospels was translated into Adiya, a dialect of Fernando Po, in 1846. It is now obsolete. There is a station of the American Presbyterian Church on the island of Corisco (see above, under Rio Muni).

Madagascar: An island off the southeastern coast of Africa, from which it is separated by the Mozambique Channel at a distance of 240 miles, measuring between nearest points. It is 980 miles long, and 360 miles in its greatest breadth. It is a possession of France, whose claim dates from a concession made to a trading company by the king of France in 1642. The claim was not recognized by the native rulers. After a struggle lasting intermittently from 1882 to 1896 the formal annexation to France took place. Area 224,000 sq. miles; population (1901) 3,000,000, including 15,000 Europeans and some hundreds of Africans and Asiatics. The people are of Malay stock with an infusion of African blood. The principal tribe, which ruled the larger part of the island until the French occupation, is called Hova. Sakalava, Betsileo, and Sihanaka are the names of other important tribes. The history of Madagascar during many years is connected with the story of its evangelization through the London Missionary Society, beginning in 1818. The mission had great success during fifteen years. The language was reduced to writing; schools were established; the New Testament was translated and printed; and numbers of the people professed Christianity. In 1835 the reigning queen drove out the missionaries and proscribed Christianity. After bloody persecutions it was made a capital crime to profess the religion of Christ.

This proscription ended in 1861; the missionaries returned; and in 1868 the then queen made public profession of Christianity. At the time of the French occupation there were about 450,000 Protestants and 50,000 Roman Catholics in the island. Roman Catholic missions were commenced in Madagascar in 1844, having their center in the island of Nossi-Bé and the adjacent islands until 1850, when the care of the missions was entrusted to the Jesuits. There are now 348 Roman Catholic mission stations in the island with nearly 100,000 adherents. At the time of the French occupation the Protestant missions were looked upon with great suspicion. In anticipation of being obliged to withdraw from the islands, the London Missionary Society invited the Paris Evangelical Missionary Society to take over some of its stations.

After a period of misunderstanding and friction with the Jesuit missionaries, religious liberty was made effective, and difficulties have gradually been removed. The Protestant societies now laboring in the island are: the London Missionary Society (1818), the Society for the Propagation of the Gospel (1843), the Friends Foreign Missionary Association (1867), the Norwegian Society (1867), the United Norwegian Lutheran Church in America (1892), the (Free) Lutheran Board of Missions (U. S. A., 1895), and the Paris Evangelical Missionary Society (1896). These societies together report 196 missionaries, 4,914 native workers, 2,729 schools with 133,262 pupils, and about 200,000 baptized Christians. The effect of the French school laws may probably affect the higher missionary schools; but on the whole conditions are rapidly taking a satisfactory form. The Bible was translated into Malagasy in 1835 and revised in 1886.

Madeira: An island forming a province of Portugal and lying west of North Africa. Area 505 sq. miles; population 150,574. The island was colonized by the Portuguese in 1420, and has been Roman Catholic for two centuries, the ancient inhabitants being entirely extinct. The American Methodist Episcopal Church has a mission in Madeira.

Mauritius: An island colony of Great Britain, lying in the Indian Ocean 500 miles east of Madagascar. Area 705 sq. miles; population (1901) 378,195. The religious classification under the census of 1901 was as follows: Hindus, 206,131; Mohammedans, 41,208; Roman Catholics, 113,224; Protestants, 6,644. Besides the parish priests there are 6 Jesuit missionaries and 11 from the Congregation of the Holy Ghost and the Sacred Heart of Mary. Protestant missions are carried on by the Church Missionary Society, the Society for the Propagation of the Gospel, and the Church of England Zenana Missionary Society. A large section of the population is of African or mixed blood, and the number of Chinese in business in the island is increasing.

Mayotte: An island belonging to France, situated between Madagascar and the African coast. It is under the governor of Reunion. Area 140 sq. miles; population 11,640, which is diminishing. There are 6 Roman Catholic priests and about 3,000 Roman Catholics in the island.

Reunion: An island belonging to France, situated about 420 miles east of Madagascar. Area 945 sq. miles; population (1902) 173,395, of whom 13,492 are British Indians, 4,496 are natives of Madagascar, 9,457 are Africans, and 1,378 are Chinese. The rest of the inhabitants are reckoned as Roman Catholics. The island is the seat of a Roman Catholic bishop, and it forms a part of the ecclesiastical province of Bordeaux in France.

Saint Thomas (Thomé) and Principe: Two islands in the Gulf of Guinea, belonging to Portugal, of which they are reckoned as a province. Area 360 sq. miles; population (1900) 42,000, of whom 41,000 are negroes. These islands are a source of revenue to the Portuguese government, producing quantities of coffee, cocoa, and cinchona. The products are cultivated by slave labor still imported by the Portuguese "under contract" through Angola from central Africa. About 4,000 of these "laborers" are carried to the islands every year; and it is said that none return. A Roman Catholic diocese was established in these islands in 1584, and a large part of the population is reckoned as Roman Catholic. There are no Protestant missions in this colony.

Zanzibar: See British East Africa Protectorate, above.

Henry Otis Dwight.*

Bibliography: I. Collections of titles: J. Gay, *Bibliographie des ouvrages relatifs à l'Afrique et à l'Arabie*, San Remo, 1875; P. Paulitschke, *Die Afrika-Literatur in der Zeit 1500–1750*, Vienna, 1882; G. Kayser, *Bibliographie de l'Afrique*, Brussels, 1889.

Geography and Atlases: P. Paulitschke, *Die geographische Erforschung des afrikanischen Continents*, Vienna, 1880; idem, *Die geographische Erforschung der Adal-Länder in Ost-Afrika*, Leipsic, 1884; A. H. Keane, *Africa*, 2 vols., London, 1895 (a compend); A. Poskin, *L'Afrique équatoriale. Climatologie, nosologie, hygiène*, Paris, 1897 (the one book on the subject); R. Grundemann, *Neuer Missions-Atlas*, Stuttgart, 1896 (German missions only); K. Heilmann, *Missionskarte der Erde*, Gütersloh, 1897; H. P. Beach, *Geography and Atlas of Protestant Missions*, New York, 1903.

Ethnology: T. Waitz, *Anthropologie der Naturvölker*, vol. ii., Leipsic, 1860; R. Hartmann, *Die Nigritier*, Berlin, 1877 (argues for unity of African peoples); idem, *Die Völker Afrikas*, Leipsic, 1879; H. Spencer, *Descriptive Sociology*, part iv., *African Races*, London, 1882; A. Featherman, *Social History of the Races of Mankind: Nigritians*, ib. 1885; F. Ratzel, *Völkerkunde*, 2 vols., Leipsic, 1886–88, Eng. transl., *History of Mankind*, London, 1896–97; *Natives of South Africa*, London, 1901.

Languages: R. N. Cust, *A Sketch of the Modern Languages of Africa*, 2 vols., ib. 1883 (by a master); C. R. Lepsius, *Nubische Grammatik mit einer Einleitung über die Völker und Sprachen Afrikas*, Berlin, 1880.

Exploration: D. Livingstone, *Travels and Researches in South Africa*, London, 1857; J. H. Speke, *Journal of the Discovery of the Source of the Nile*, ib. 1863; R. F. Burton, *Wanderings in West Africa*, 2 vols., ib. 1864; H. M. Stanley, *How I Found Livingstone*, ib. 1874; idem, *In Darkest Africa*, ib. 1874; V. L. Cameron, *Across Africa*, ib. 1877; C. E. Bourne, *Heroes of African Discovery*, 2 vols., ib. 1882; K. Dove, *Vom Kap zum Nil*, Berlin, 1898; J. Bryce, *Impressions of South Africa, with three maps*, London, 1899; C. A. von Götzen, *Durch Afrika von Ost nach West*, Berlin, 1899; A. B. Lloyd, *In Dwarf Land and Cannibal Country*, London, 1899; L. Lanier, *L'Afrique*, Paris, 1899 (geographical, historical, bibliographical); P. B. du Chaillu, *In African Forest and Jungle*, New York, 1903; A. H. Keane, *South Africa. A Compendium of Geography and Travel*, London, 1904.

African partition and colonization: J. S. Keltie, *The Partition of Africa*, 21 maps, London, 1893 (excellent, succinct);

*Part of the information concerning Roman Catholic missions in this article has been furnished by Prof. John T. Creagh.

Holub, *Die Colonization Afrikas*, Vienna, 1882; H. H. Johnston, *History of the Colonization of Africa by Alien Races*, in *Cambridge Historical Series*, Cambridge, 1894; H. M. Stanley, *Africa; Its Partition and Its Future*, New York, 1898.

Missions: D. Macdonald, *Africana: Heathen Africa*, 2 vols., London, 1882; R. Lovett, *History of the London Missionary Society, 1795–1895*, 2 vols., ib. 1899; F. P. Noble, *Redemption of Africa*, New York, 1899; E. Stock, *History of the Church Missionary Society*, 3 vols., London, 1899; *Ecumenical Missionary Conference, New York, 1900, Reports*, New York, 1900; C. F. Pascoe, *Two Hundred Years of the SPG*, London, 1901; J. Stewart, *Dawn in the Dark Continent; or Africa and its Missions*, ib. 1903; H. O. Dwight, H. A. Tupper, E. M. Bliss, *Encyclopedia of Missions*, New York, 1904.

Catholic Missions: M. de Montroud, *Les Missions catholiques dans les parties du Monde*, Paris, 1869; L. Bethune, *Les Missions catholiques d'Afrique*, ib. 1889; O. Werner, *Orbis terrarum catholicus*, Freiburg, 1890 (geographical and statistical); *Missiones Catholicæ*, Rome, 1901.

Native religion: T. Hahn, *Tsuni-Goam, the Supreme Being of the Khoi-Khoi*, London, 1882; A. B. Ellis, *Tshi-speaking Peoples of the Gold Coast*, ib. 1887; W. Schneider, *Die Religion der afrikanischen Naturvölker*, Münster, 1891; J. Macdonald, *Religion and Myth*, London, 1893 (on religion and society); M. A. Kingsley, *Travels in West Africa*, ib. 1897; idem, *West African Studies*, ib. 1901; R. H. Nassau, *Fetichism in West Africa*, New York, 1904 (covers native religion and society).

II. Algeria: R. L. Playfair, *Bibliography of Algeria*, London, 1888 (covers 1541–1887); A. Certeux and E. H. Carnoy, *L'Algérie traditionnelle*, 3 vols., Algiers, 1884 (on customs and superstitions); Gastu, *Le Peuple Algérien*, Paris, 1884; R. L. Playfair, *The Scourge of Christendom: Annals of British Relations with Algeria*, London, 1884; E. C. E. Villot, *Mœurs et institutions des indigènes de l'Algérie*, Algiers, 1888; F. A. Bridgman, *Winters in Algeria*, New York, 1890; F. Klein, *Les Villages d'Arabes chrétiens*, Fontainebleau, 1890; A. E. Pease, *Biskra and the Oases . . . of the Zibans*, London, 1893; J. Lionel, *Races Berbères*, Paris, 1893; A. Wilkin, *Among the Berbers of Algeria*, London, 1900.

Angola: J. J. Monteiro, *Angola and the River Congo*, 2 vols., London, 1895 (the one book); F. A. Pinto, *Angola e Congo*, Lisbon, 1888; H. Chatelain, *Folk-Tales of Angola*, Boston, 1894.

Basutoland: J. Widdicombe, *Fourteen Years in Basutoland*, London, 1892; E. Casalis, *My Life in Basutoland*, ib. 1889; Mrs. Barkly, *Among Boers and Basutos*, ib. 1893; E. Jacottet, *Contes populaires des Bassoutos*, Paris, 1895; M. Martin, *Basutoland; Its Legends and Customs*, London, 1903.

Bechuanaland: L. K. Bruce, *The Story of an African Chief, Khama*, London, 1893; E. Lloyd, *Three African Chiefs, Khamé, Sebelé, and Bathoeng*, ib. 1895; J. D. Hepburn, *Twenty Years in Khama's Country and the Batauna*, ib. 1895; W. D. Mackenzie, *John Mackenzie, South African Missionary and Statesman*, ib. 1902.

British East Africa and Zanzibar: J. Thomson, *Through Masai Land*, London, 1885; *Handbook of British East Africa including Zanzibar*, ib. 1893 (English official publication); H. S. Newman, *Banani; the Transition from Slavery to Freedom in Zanzibar*, ib. 1899; S. T. and H. Hinde, *Last of the Masai*, ib. 1901.

Cape Colony: G. McC. Theall, *History of South Africa*, 4 vols., London, 1888–89 (exhaustive); E. Holub, *Seven Years in South Africa*, ib. 1881; A. Wilmot, *Story of the Expansion of South Africa*, ib. 1895; A. T. Wirgman, *History of the English Church in South Africa*, ib. 1895; *South African Year Book for 1902–3*, ib. 1902 (official); J. Stewart, *Dawn in the Dark Continent*, ib. 1903; H. A. Bryden, *History of South Africa, 1652–1903*, ib. 1904; D. Kidd, *The Essential Kafir*, ib. 1904.

Central Africa Protectorate: H. H. Johnston, *British Central Africa*, London, 1897; J. Buchanan, *The Shiré Highlands as Colony and Mission*, ib. 1885; D. J. Rankin, *Zambesi Basin and Nyassaland*, ib. 1893; A. E. M. Morshead, *History of the Universities Mission to Central Africa*, ib. 1897; W. A. Elmslie, *Among the Wild Ngoni, Chapters . . . of Livingstonia Mission*, ib. 1899; J. W. Jack, *Daybreak in Livingstonia*, New York, 1901.

Dahomey. A. Pawlowski, *Bibliographie raisonnée . . . concernant le Dahomey*, Paris, 1895; Aspe-Fleurimont, *La Guinée française*, ib. 1890; E. F. Forbes, *Dahomey and the Dahomeans*, 2 vols., London, 1851; J. A. Skertchley, *Dahomey as it is*, ib. 1874; A. L. d'Albéca, *La France au Dahomey*, Paris, 1895; E. Foà, *Le Dahomey*, ib. 1895 (on history, geography, customs, etc.); R. S. Powell, *The Downfall of Prempeh*, London, 1896.

Egypt (for missions): G. Lansing, *Egypt's Princes, A Narrative of Missionary Labor in the Valley of the Nile*, New York, 1865; M. L. Whately, *Ragged Life in Egypt*, London, 1870; idem, *Among the Huts in Egypt*, ib. 1870; A. Watson, *The American Mission in Egypt*, Pittsburg, 1898; M. Fowler, *Christian Egypt*, London, 1900; and see EGYPT.

Eritrea: *La Colonia Eritrea*, Turin, 1891; E. Q. M. Alamanni, *L'Avenire della colonia Eritrea*, Asti, 1890; M. Schveller, *Mittheilungen über meine Reise in . . . Eritrea*, Berlin, 1895.

French Kongo: A. J. Wauters and A. Buyl, *Bibliographie du Congo, 1880–95*, Paris, 1895 (3,800 titles); P. Eucher, *Le Congo, essai sur l histoire religieuse*, ib. 1895; A. Voulgre, *Le Loango et la vallée du Kouilou*, ib. 1897; and see below KONGO.

French Guinea: L. G. Binger, *Du Niger au golfe de Guinée*, 2 vols., Paris, 1891; C. Madrolle, *En Guinée*, ib. 1894; P. d'Espagnat, *Jours de Guinée*, ib. 1898.

German Africa: *Deutsch-Ost-Afrika. Wissenschaftlicher Forschungsresultate über Land und Leute*, Berlin, 1893 and later (exhaustive); P. Reichard, *Deutsch-Ostafrika, Land und Bewohner*, Leipsic, 1892; H. von Schweinitz, *Deutsch-Ost-Afrika in Krieg und Frieden*, Berlin, 1894; Ch. Römer, *Kamerun; Land, Leute und Mission*, Basel, 1895; E. Zintgraff, *Nord-Kamerun, 1886–92*, Berlin, 1895; F. J. von Bülow, *Deutsch-Südwestafrika . . . Land und Leute*, ib. 1897; K. Hörhold, *Drei Jahre under deutsche Flagge in Hinterland von Kamerun*, ib. 1897; M. Dier, *Unter den Schwarzen*, Steyl, 1901 (missionary); F. Hutter, *Wanderungen und Forschungen in Nord-Hinterland von Kamerun*, Brunswick, 1902; and see below, KAMERUN.

Gold Coast: A. B. Ellis, *History of the Gold Coast*, London, 1893; F. A. Ramseyer and J. Kühne, *Four Years in Ashantee*, New York, 1877 (missionary); C. Buhl, *Die Basler Mission an der Goldküste*, Basel, 1882; C. C. Reindorf, *History of the Gold Coast and Ashanti from c. 1500*, London, 1895; G. Macdonald, *Gold Coast, Past and Present*, ib. 1898; D. Kemp, *Nine Years at the Gold Coast*, ib. 1898.

Ivory Coast: Bonneau, *La Côte d'Ivoire*, Paris, 1899 (historical and geographical); M. Mounier, *France noire, Côte d'Ivoire et Soudan*, ib. 1894.

Kamerun: In G. Warneck, *History of Protestant Missions, transl. from seventh Germ. ed.*, London, 1901; E. B. Underhill, *Alfred Saker, Missionary to Africa*, ib. 1884; and see above, GERMAN AFRICA.

Kongo Independent State: H. M. Stanley, *Congo and the Founding of the Free State*, 2 vols., London, 1878; W. H. Bentley, *Life on the Congo*, ib. 1890; idem, *Pioneering on the Congo*, 2 vols., New York, 1903; Mrs. H. G. Guinness, *The New World of Central Africa; the Congo*, London, 1890; F. S. Arnot, *Garenganze; or Seven Years' Pioneer Mission Work in Central Africa*, ib. 1889; idem, *Bihe and Garenganze*, ib. 1893; S. P. Verner, *Pioneering in Central Africa*, New York, 1903; E. Morel, *King Leopold's Rule in Africa*, London, 1904.

Lagos: R. F. Burton, *Abeokuta and the Cameroon Mountains*, 2 vols., London, 1863; Miss C. Tucker, *Abbeokuta: the Yoruba Mission*, ib. 1858; J. A. O. Payne, *Table of Events in Yoruba History*, Lagos, 1893.

Liberia: J. H. T. McPherson, *African Colonization: History of Liberia* (*Johns Hopkins University Studies*, series 9, No. 10), Baltimore, 1891; G. S. Stockwell, *The Republic of Liberia*, New York, 1868 (historical and geographical); J. Buettikofer, *Reisebilder aus Liberia*, Leyden, 1890; F. A. Durham, *The Lone Star of Liberia*, London, 1892; E. W. Blyden, *A Chapter in the History of Liberia*, Freetown, 1892.

Morocco: R. L. Playfair and R. Brown, *Bibliography of Morocco . . . to end of 1891*, London, 1893; R. Kerr, *Pioneering in Morocco; Seven Years' Medical Mission Work*, ib. 1894; E. de Amicis, *Morocco, Its People and Places*, New York, 1892; W. B. Harris, *The Land of an African Sultan*, London, 1879; *Géographie générale de Maroc*, Paris, 1902; A. J. Dawson, *Things Seen in Morocco*, London, 1904; *Morocco painted by A. S. Forrest and described by S. L. Bensusan*, ib. 1904.

Natal: R. Russell, *Natal, the Land and Its Story*, London, 1900; L. Grout, *Zululand, or, Life among the Zulu-Kafirs*, Philadelphia, 1864; H. Brooks, *The Colony of Natal*, London, 1876; T. B. Jenkinson, *Amazulu, the Zulus*, ib. 1882 (on people and country); J. Bird, *Annals of Natal*, 2 vols., Pietermaritzburg, 1888–89; J. Tyler, *Forty Years among the Zulus*, Boston, 1891; F. W. von Wernsdorff, *Ein Jahr in Rhodesia*, Berlin, 1899; J. Robinson, *A Lifetime in South Africa*, London, 1900.

Nigeria: C. H. Robinson, *Hausaland*, London, 1897; idem, *Nigeria*, 1900 (both authoritative); H. Goldie, *Calabar and Its Mission*, ib. 1890; R. H. Bacon, *Benin, the City of Blood*, ib. 1897; H. Bindloss, *In the Niger Country*, ib. 1899; W. R. Miller, *Hausa Notes*, ib. 1901.

Orange River Colony: *South African Republic, Official Documents*, Philadelphia, 1900; G. McC. Theal, *The Boers, or Emigrant Farmers*, London, 1888; A. H. Keane, *Africa*, in E. Stanford's *Compendium of Geography*, 2 vols., ib. 1893; H. Cloete, *History of the Great Boer Trek, and the Origin of the South African Republics*, ib. 1899.

Portuguese Africa: W. B. Warfield, *Portuguese Nyassaland*, London, 1899; R. Monteiro, *Delagoa Bay, Its Natives and Natural History*, ib. 1891; P. Gillmore, *Through Gaza Land*, ib. 1891; J. P. M. Weale, *Truth about the Portuguese in Africa*, ib. 1891.

Rhodesia: H. Hensman, *History of Rhodesia*, London, 1900; E. F. Knight, *Rhodesia of To-day; Condition and Prospects of Matabeleland and Mashonaland*, ib. 1895; A. G. Leonard, *How we Made Rhodesia*, ib. 1896; A. Boggie, *History of Rhodesia and the Matabele*, ib. 1897; S. J. Du Toit, *Rhodesia Past and Present*, ib. 1897; H. L. Tangye, *In New South Africa ; . Transvaal and Rhodesia*, ib. 1900.

Sierra Leone: J. J. Crooks, *History of the Colony of Sierra Leone*, London, 1903; D. K. Flickinger, *Ethiopia, or Twenty Years of Mission Work in Western Africa*, Dayton, 1877; E. G. Ingham, *Sierra Leone after One Hundred Years*, London, 1894; T. J. Alldridge, *The Sherbro and its Hinterland*, ib. 1901; C. George, *The Rise of British West Africa*, ib. 1904.

Somaliland: H. L. Swayne, *Seventeen Trips through Somaliland*, London, 1903; C. V. A. Peel, *Somaliland . Two Expeditions into the Far Interior*, ib. 1903; F. S. Brereton, *In the Grip of the Mullah*, ib. 1903.

Sudan: A. S. White, *Expansion of Egypt under Anglo-Egyptian Condominion*, New York, 1900; C. T. Wilson and R. W Felkin, *Uganda und der ägyptische Sudan*, 2 vols., Stuttgart, 1883; Slatin Pasha, *Fire and Sword in the Sudan*, London, 1896; D. C. Boulger, *Life of Gordon*, ib. 1897; H. S. Alford and W. D. Sword, *The Egyptian Sudan, Its Loss and Its Recovery*, ib. 1898; H. H. Austin, *Among Swamps and Giants in Equatorial Africa*, ib. 1902.

Transvaal: E. Farmer, *Transvaal as a Mission Field*, London, 1903; W. C. Willoughby, *Native Life on the Transvaal Border*, ib. 1900; J. H. Bovill, *Natives under the Transvaal Flag*, ib. 1900; D. M. Wilson, *Behind the Scenes in the Transvaal*, ib. 1901.

Tripoli and Tunis: G. E. Thompson, *Life in Tripoli*, London, 1893; De H. Wartegg, *Tunis, Land and People*, ib. 1899; M. Fournel, *La Tunisie ; le christianisme et l'islam dans l'Afrique septentrionale*, Paris, 1886; V. Guerin, *La France catholique en Tunisie . . et en Tripolitaine*, ib. 1886; A. Perry, *Official Tour along the Eastern Coast of . Tunis*, Providence, 1891; D. Bruun, *The Cave Dwellers of Southern Tunisia*, Edinburgh, 1898; H. Vivian, *Tunisia and the Modern Barbary Pirates*, London, 1899; J. L. Cathcart, *Tripoli ; First War with the United States*, La Porte, 1902.

Uganda: H. H. Johnston, *Uganda Protectorate*, London, 1904; W. J. Ansorge, *Under the African Sun: A Description of Native Races in Uganda*, ib. 1899; *Mackay of Uganda; Story of his Life by his Sister*, ib. 1899; R. P. Ashe, *Two Kings of Uganda ; or Life by the Shores of Victoria Nyanza*, ib. 1890 (missionary); S. G. Stock, *Uganda and Victoria Nyanza Mission*, ib. 1892; F. J. Lugard, *Rise of our East African Empire, Nyassaland and Uganda*, 2 vols., Edinburgh, 1893; idem, *Story of the Uganda Protectorate*, London, 1900; C. F. Harford-Battersby, *Pilkington of Uganda*, ib. 1899; A. R. Cook, *A Doctor and his Dog in Uganda*, ib. 1903 (on medical missions).

III. African Islands: Madagascar: J. Sibree, *The Great African Island*, London, 1879 (the best book); idem, *Madagascar before the Conquest*, ib. 1896; W. Ellis, *The Martyr Church*, ib. 1869; W. E. Cousins, *The Madagascar of To-day*, ib. 1895; H. Hansen, *Beitrag zur Geschichte der Insel Madagaskar*, Gütersloh, 1899; J. J. K. Fletcher, *Sign of the Cross in Madagascar*, London, 1901; T. T. Matthews, *Thirty Years in Madagascar*, ib. 1904.

Other Islands: A. B. Ellis, *The West African Islands*, London, 1885; C. Keller, *Madagascar, Mauritius, and other African Islands*, ib. 1900; N. Pike, *Subtropical Rambles in the Land of the Aphanapteryx*, ib. 1873 (on Mauritius); J. C. Mellis, *St. Helena*, ib. 1875 (scientific); H. W Estridge, *Six Years in Seychelles*, ib. 1885; A. S. Brown, *Madeira and the Canary Isles*, ib. 1890.

AFRICA, THE CHURCH OF. See ABYSSINIA AND THE ABYSSINIAN CHURCH; COPTIC CHURCH; EGYPT; MISSIONS, ROMAN CATHOLIC, PROTESTANT; NORTH AFRICAN CHURCH.

AFRICAN METHODIST EPISCOPAL CHURCH. See METHODISTS.

AFRICANUS, JULIUS. See JULIUS AFRICANUS.

AGAPE, ag'a-pî or -pê.

The Greek word *agapē* ("love," pl. *agapai*, Lat. *agapæ*) was used in the early Church, both Greek and Latin, to denote definite manifestations of brotherly love between believers, and particularly certain meals taken in common which had more or less of a religious character. The earliest mention of such meals is found in Jude 12 (possibly in II Pet. ii. 13). Distinct history begins with Tertullian, in the passage (*Apologeticus*, xxxix.) commencing: "Our supper bears a name which tells exactly what it is; it is called by the word which in Greek means 'affection.'" The agape served for the refreshment of the poorer brethren, as well as for the general edification. It was opened and closed with prayer, and after its conclusion one and another gave songs of praise, either from the Bible or of their own composition. These meetings were under the direction of the clergy, to whom (with reference to I Tim. v. 17) a double portion of food and drink was allotted. They were held at the time of the principal meal, and frequently were prolonged until dark.

1. Primitive Form of Celebration.

In the period for which Tertullian bears witness, they were not connected with the sacrament of the Eucharist; he says expressly (*De corona*, iii.) that the Lord instituted the sacrament on the occasion of a meal, while the Church does not so celebrate it, but rather before daybreak. Even apart from the secret nocturnal services of the times of persecution and the observance of the paschal vigil, the Eucharist was regularly celebrated before any meal. Notably was this rule, which is found referred to in Cyprian (*Epist.*, lxiii. 16), established in Tertullian's time, but—which is decisive for the distinction between Eucharist and agape—it existed in many parts of the Church as early as that of Justin (*Apologia*, i. 65, 67). The principle, that the Eucharist should be received only fasting, which would exclude any relation with a preceding common meal, and especially with the agape, taking place toward evening, is indirectly evidenced by Tertullian (*Ad uxorem*, ii. 5); Augustine found it so universally recognized that he was inclined to refer it to one of the ordinances promised by Paul in I Cor. xi. 34; and Chrysostom was so convinced of the antiquity of the rule that he supposed the custom of following it by an ordinary meal to have prevailed in Corinth in Paul's time. In any case, in the third and fourth centuries the development of the agape was more and more away from any connection with public worship.

From the indications of the Syriac *Didascalia* and the Egyptian liturgical books, as well as the canons of the Councils of Gangra and Laodicea it may be inferred that the giving of these feasts and the inviting to them of widows and the poor was, in the East, one of the forms usually taken by the benevolence of the wealthier members of the Church. The bishop and other clergy were invited, and, if they appeared, were received with special honor and charged with the direction of the assembly. These feasts were given at irregular times and in various places, sometimes in the church itself. This was forbidden by the twenty-eighth canon of Laodicea, at the same time that the fifty-eighth prohibited their celebration in private houses. Secular festivities in connection with the agapæ, which brought upon them the condemnation of the ascetic Eustathians (against whom the Council of Gangra defended them), caused them to be regarded more and more among the orthodox also as incompatible with the dignity of divine worship, so that they gradually became entirely separate from it, and thus tended to fall into disuse.

2. Final Form of the Agape.

How popular these feasts were in Africa, in the churches, in the chapels of the martyrs, and at the graves of other Christians, may be seen from the often renewed canon of Hippo (393), which forbids clerics to eat in churches except in dispensing hospitality to travelers, and commands them as far as possible to restrain the people from such meals. The same thing appears in Augustine's descriptions as well as in the great pains he took to repress grave abuses and, with reference to the practise of the Italian and almost all the other churches, to suppress the agapæ altogether.

It is not clear what caused the disassociation of the agape from the Eucharist in the first half of the second century. It is a misunderstanding of Pliny's letter to Trajan (*Epist.*, xcvi.) to suppose that in consequence of the prohibition of *hetariæ* ("brotherhoods") the Christians then abandoned their evening feasts and transferred the Eucharist to the morning; but it is very probable that the constant accusation of impious customs which recalled the stories of Thyestes and of Œdipus were the main reason for the separation of the Eucharist, which was an essential part of their public worship, from the connection, so liable to be misunderstood, with an evening meal participated in by both sexes and all ages. The fact that at one time the two were connected is evidenced not only by Pliny, but about the same time by the *Didache*, in which, whatever one may think about the relation of the eucharistic prayers to the accompanying liturgical acts (chaps. ix.-x.), the opening passage of the second prayer (Gk. *meta de to emplēsthēnai*) shows that a full meal belonged to the rite there referred to. Just as here the Greek word *eucharistia*, which from Justin down is employed as a technical term for the sacrament, at least includes a common meal, which is found separated from the sacrament after the middle of the second century, so Ignatius, with whom *eucharistia* is a usual designation of the sacrament, also employs *agapē* and *agapan* to denote the same observance. It is accordingly safe to conclude that in the churches, from Antioch to Rome, with which Ignatius had to do, the so-called agape was connected with the Eucharist, as Pliny shows at the same time for Bithynia and the *Didache* for Alexandria. The same may be inferred of the two Scriptural passages cited above; and one is led further back by I Cor. xi. 17–34. While Paul distinguishes as sharply as possible the eating of the one bread and the drinking of the blessed chalice from common food and drink (I Cor. x. 3, 16; xi. 23–29), he shows at the same time that in Corinth the two were connected in thought. While he rebukes the disorder of one drinking too much and another going hungry, so as to injure the dignity of the following sacrament, and lays down that eating for the mere satisfaction of hunger ought to take place at home and not in the assembly of the brethren, he is not disposed (as I Cor. xi. 33 shows) to abolish altogether the connection of the sacrament with an actual meal. This connection, then, existing into the first decades of the second century, forms the basis of the history for both Eucharist and agape which diverge from that time on. (T. Zahn.)

3. Disassociation of Agape and Eucharist.

The agape or love-feast is practised at present by Mennonites, Dunkards, German Baptists of the Anglo-American type, and other religious bodies. For an able, but not wholly successful, attempt to prove that the Lord's Supper in the apostolic time was identical with the agape, i.e., that it was nothing but a social feast for the manifestation of brotherly love, consult Norman Fox, *Christ in the Daily Meal* (New York, 1898).

A. H. N.

Bibliography: See Lord's Supper.

AGAPETUS, ag″a-pî′tus: The name of two popes.

Agapetus I.: Pope 535–536. He was the son of a Roman priest named Gordianus, who had been killed in the disturbances under Symmachus. Six days after the death of John II. he was chosen to succeed him, probably by the wish of Theodahad, king of the Ostrogoths. He began his pontificate by reconciling the contending factions among the Roman clergy and annulling the anathema pronounced by Boniface II. against the antipope Dioscorus. His decision, induced by the decrees of the North African synod, forbidding the entrance of converted Arians to the priesthood, and his defense of this measure in a letter to the emperor Justinian show him to have been a zealous upholder of orthodoxy. In 536 he was sent to Constantinople by Theodahad to try to establish peace with the emperor, and was obliged to pledge the sacred vessels of the Roman Church to obtain money for his journey. He did not succeed in the ostensible purpose of his mission, but accomplished more for the orthodox cause. Anthimus, patriarch of Constantinople, a secret adherent of Monophysitism, had, by the aid of the empress Theodora, the patroness of the Monophysites, been allowed, in defiance of the canons, to exchange the see of Trapezus (Trebizond) for the patriarchal throne. Agapetus refused all communion with him, and persisted so strenuously in his attitude, in spite of threats from the court, that he finally convinced Justinian that Anthimus had deceived him, and had him deposed, and replaced by Mennas. Agapetus himself consecrated Mennas by wish of the emperor, and apparently with the assent of the principal orthodox Eastern bishops, after he had presented a confession of faith which the pope considered satisfactory. The emperor, fearing lest he himself should be accused of sympathy with the former Monophysite patriarch, placed a confession of faith in the pope's hands, which Agapetus approved in a letter plainly showing how important he felt his triumph to be. Almost immediately afterward he fell ill and died in Constantinople Apr. 22, 536, his body being brought to Rome and buried in St. Peter's. (A. HAUCK.)

BIBLIOGRAPHY: *Epistolæ*, in *MGH*, *Epist.*, iii. (1891) 54-57, in *MPL*, lxvi., and in Jaffé, *Regesta*, i. 113-115; *Liber Pontificalis*, ed. Duchesne, i. 287-289, Paris, 1886; *ASB*, vi. 163-180; Bower, *Popes*, i. 337-344; Hefele, *Conciliengeschichte*, Eng. transl., iv. 181-194.

Agapetus II.: Pope 946-955. He was a Roman by birth, and, like his predecessor Marinus II. owed his elevation to the papal throne (May 10, 946) to Alberic, the secular master of Rome. Though hampered at home by Alberic's power, he asserted the claims of his see successfully abroad. He intervened in the prolonged contest over the archbishopric of Reims, from which Heribert of Vermandois had expelled the legitimate incumbent, Artold, to give it to his own son Hugh. The contest between the friends of the two prelates attained the dimensions of a civil war, Artold being supported by Louis IV. of France. Agapetus also took Artold's side at first; but he was deceived by the representations of a cleric from Reims into reversing his decision. After Artold had succeeded in enlightening him, the affair was referred to a synod held at Ingelheim in 948, whose final verdict in favor of Artold was confirmed by Agapetus in a Roman synod (949). [When Berengar II., Marquis of Ivrea, attempted to unite all Italy under his scepter, the pope and other Italian princes appealed to Otho I., who went as far as Pavia, expecting to be crowned emperor; but Agapetus, influenced by Alberic, turned away from him.] In 954 Alberic took an oath from the Roman nobles that at the next vacancy they would elect as pope his son and heir, Octavian; and when Agapetus died in December, 955, Octavian did in fact succeed him as John XII. (A. HAUCK.)

BIBLIOGRAPHY: *Epistolæ et Privilegia*, in *MPL*, cxxxiii., in Bouquet, *Recueil*, ix. 226-234, and in Jaffé, *Regesta*, i. 459-463; Bower, *Popes*, ii. 314-315; R. Köpke and E. Dümmler, *Kaiser Otto der Grosse*, Leipsic, 1876.

AGAPIOS MONACHOS, a-gā'pi-os mo-nā'kos ("Agapios the Monk"; Athanasio Lando): Ascetic writer of the Greek Church; b. at Candia, Crete, toward the end of the sixteenth century; d. between 1657 and 1664. After a wandering life he took up his abode in the monastery on Mt. Athos, but he found it hard to submit to the strict discipline there. He is one of the most popular religious writers of the Greeks. By his excellent translations from the Latin, ancient Greek, and Italian into the vernacular he made many devotional works of the nations accessible to his people. He meant to be orthodox, but was influenced by Roman Catholicism, and in his works he unsuspectingly quotes Peter Damian and Albertus Magnus besides Ambrose, Augustine, and others. In penance he distinguishes between the *contritio*, *satisfactio*, and *confessio*; and in the Lord's Supper he accepts the doctrine of transubstantiation without using that term. The question of his orthodoxy was seriously debated in the seventeenth century by the fathers of Port Royal and representatives of the Reformed Church (cf. J. Aymon, *Monumens authentiques de la Religion des Grecs*, The Hague, 1708, pp. 475, 599).

The most important of the works of Agapios is the "Salvation of Sinners" (1641), a devotional book for the people. His "Sunday Cycle" (1675), a collection of sermons, was also much prized. His writings went through many editions, especially those containing biographies of the saints; as the "Paradise" (1641), the "New Paradise" (c. 1664), the "Selection" (1644), and the "Summertide" (1656). The first three contain translations from Symeon Metaphrastes. PHILIPP MEYER.

BIBLIOGRAPHY: Γεδεών, Ὁ Ἄθως, Constantinople, 1855; E. Legrand, *Bibliographie Hellénique*, 3 vols., Paris, 1895-1903.

AGATHA, ag'a-tha, **SAINT:** Virgin and martyr in the Roman Catholic calendar. The accounts of her given in the Latin and Greek *Acta* (*ASB*, Feb., i. 595-656) are so largely made up of legendary and poetical matter that it is impossible to extract solid historical facts from them. The fact of her martyrdom is, however, attested by her inclusion in the Carthaginian calendar of the fifth or sixth century and in the so-called *Martyrologium Hieronymianum*; and she is mentioned also by Damasus, bishop of Rome from 366 to 384 (*Carmen*, 30). There seems no reason to doubt that she suffered at Catania on Feb. 5; but the year of her death can not be determined. She is venerated particularly in southern Italy and in Sicily, where, in many places, she is invoked as a protectress against eruptions of Mount Etna. The cities of Palermo and Catania still contend for the honor of being her birthplace. (A. HAUCK.)

AGATHISTS. See CHRISTIAN DOCTRINE, SOCIETY OF

AGATHO, ag'a-tho: Pope 678-681. He was a Sicilian monk, and in June or July, 678, succeeded Donus after a vacancy in the papacy of two and one-half months. He is especially celebrated for the decisive part which he took in the Monothelite controversy (see MONOTHELITES). He succeeded also in inducing Theodore of Ravenna to acknowledge the dependence of his church on that of Rome. At a synod held in Rome at Easter, 679, he decreed the restoration of Wilfrid, archbishop of York (q.v.), who had been deposed by Theodore of Tarsus, archbishop of Canterbury. The financial resources of the Roman see appear to have been very limited during his pontificate; for he not only attempted to administer in person the office of *arcarius* or treasurer of the Roman Church, but he persuaded the emperor to renounce the payment which had been demanded for the confirmation of a pope, though the imperial approbation was still required. Agatho died Jan. 10, 681; the Roman

Church honors his memory on that day; the Greek on Feb. 20. (A. Hauck.)

Bibliography: *Literæ*, in *MPL*, lxxxvii.; *Liber pontificalis*, ed. Duchesne, i. 350–358, Paris, 1886; Bower, *Popes*, i. 469–485; H. H. Milman, *History of Latin Christianity;* Hefele, *Conciliengeschichte*, iii. passim, Eng. transl., v. 139–144; R. C. Mann, *Lives of the Popes in the Early Middle Ages*, I. ii. 24–28.

AGDE, ägd, SYNOD OF: A synod which met Sept. 11, 506, at Agde (Lat. *Agatha*), a town on the Mediterranean coast of France (90 m. w. of Marseilles, of which it was originally a colony). The town is unimportant, though it claimed to possess the relics of St. Andrew. The synod met with the permission of Alaric II., king of the West Goths, and thirty-five bishops from the south of France attended, Cæsarius of Arles presiding. It passed forty-seven canons relating to questions of discipline, the guardianship of church property, the devout life, and—a matter of no slight importance for the south of France—the position of the Jews. An attempt was made to enforce clerical celibacy; and an almost suspicious attitude was assumed in regard to female monasticism (nuns were not to take the veil before the age of 40; no new convents were to be founded without the permission of the bishop; and the solitary life was disapproved). Provision was made for the maintenance of several traditional customs, such as the strict fast in Lent, the *traditio symboli* on the Saturday before Easter, the communion of the laity at Christmas, Easter, and Pentecost; an effort was made to secure liturgical uniformity. In regard to the Jewish question, it is observable that here, as elsewhere, there was no distinction in social life between Jews and Christians, but that the Church disapproved of intercourse with the Jews, and looked with some distrust on converts from Judaism. The canons of the synod are based upon older and not exclusively Gallic foundations: Spanish and African conciliar decisions are used, as well as the letter of Pope Innocent I. to Exsuperius of Toulouse. In like manner the canons of the First Frankish Synod at Orléans (511) and the Burgundian Synod at Epao (517) depend upon those of Agde. The latter were early included in the collections of church law, and Gratian incorporated a large part of them in his *Decretum*. (A. Hauck.)

Bibliography: Mansi, *Concilia*, viii. 319; Hefele, *Conciliengeschichte*, ii. 649–660, Eng. transl., iv. 76–86; C. F. Arnold, *Cäsarius von Arelate*, Leipsic, 1894.

AGE, CANONICAL: The age required by the canons of the Church for ordination or for the performance of any particular act. The requirement of a definite age for entering the priestly order is first found in the eleventh canon of the Synod of Neocæsarea (314 or 325): "No one is to be ordained priest before he is thirty years old . . . for Jesus Christ when thirty years old was baptized and entered upon his ministry." The first canon of the second series of canons of the Synod of Hippo in 393 required the completion of the twenty-fifth year for the reception of deacon's orders. These decisions were frequently repeated, as by the Synods of Agde (506, canon xvi.), of Arles (524, canon i.), the Third Synod of Orléans (538, canon vi.), and the Fourth of Toledo (633, canon xx.), and the later repetitions were included in the canonical collections of the early Middle Ages, but in detail they were frequently changed. Urban II. at the Council of Melfi (1089, canon iv.) laid down the law that no one should be ordained subdeacon before his fourteenth year, or deacon before his twenty-fourth. For the priesthood, though the thirtieth year still remained the minimum in the written law, the practise grew of ordaining at twenty-five. The Synod of Ravenna (1314, canon ii.) fixed the sixteenth year for subdeacons, the twentieth for deacons, and the twenty-fourth for priests. Finally the Council of Trent (1563, session xxiii.) settled the minimum at twenty-two, twenty-three, and twenty-four years, respectively, for these offices. It is sufficient to have begun the year specified in the Council. For tonsure and minor orders the Council simply requires the reception of the sacrament of confirmation and a certain degree of learning. In the Protestant Churches the attainment by the candidate of his majority is usually considered sufficient, though here and there the twenty-fourth year is still required.

In the Roman Catholic Church the canonical age is reckoned from the day of birth. Canonically the age of discretion is put at seven years, and then the sacraments of penance and extreme unction may be received because the child, being supposed to be capable of conscious choice, can commit a mortal sin; also the child is then subject to the regulations of the Church respecting abstinence and attendance on mass, and may also, as far as law is concerned, contract a marriage engagement. A marriage may not be contracted before puberty (except in case of extraordinary development of mind and body), i.e., before fourteen for boys and twelve for girls; nor may confirmation and the Lord's Supper be received till the child has been properly instructed. From twenty-one to sixty is the period when fasting at certain seasons is obligatory. The lowest canonical age for a bishop is thirty years completed. The minimum age at which simple vows may be taken is sixteen years completed. Clerics may not profess solemn vows before they have entered on their twentieth year.

Bibliography: *KL*, i. 632–638; E. Friedberg, *Lehrbuch des katholischen und evangelischen Kirchenrechts*, pp. 151, 330, Leipsic, 1903; W. E. Addis and T. Arnold, *Catholic Dictionary*, London, 1903.

AGELLI, ä-jel'lî, ANTONIO (Lat. *Agellius*): Roman Catholic scholar; b. at Sorrento, s. of the Bay of Naples, 1532; d. at Acerno, 14 m. e.n.e. of Sorrento, 1608. He joined the order of the Theatins, became bishop of Acerno in 1593, but after a few years returned to his monastery. He was famed for his knowledge of the languages of the Bible, under Gregory XIII. and Sixtus V was member of the commission for the publication of the Septuagint (1587), and assisted also in the publication of the Vulgate (1590).

Agelli wrote commentaries on the Book of Lamentations (Rome, 1598); the Psalms and Canticles (1606); Proverbs (Verona, 1649); and Habakkuk (Antwerp, 1697).

AGENDA, a-jen'da.

The name Agenda (" Things to be Done "; Germ. *Agende* or *Kirchenagende*) is given, particularly in the Lutheran Church, to the official books dealing with the forms and ceremonies of divine service. It occurs twice in the ninth canon of the Second Synod of Carthage (390; Bruns, *Canones*, i., Berlin, 1839, p. 121), and in a letter of Innocent I. (d. 417; *MPL*, xx. 552). The name was frequently employed in a more specific sense, as *agenda missarum*, for the celebration of the mass; *agenda diei*, for the office of the day; *agenda mortuorum*, for the service for the dead; *agenda matutina*, and *agenda vespertina*, for morning and evening prayers. As the designation of a book of liturgical formulas it is stated by Ducange to have been used by Johannes de Janua, but in the only published work of Johannes (c. 1287) the name does not occur. There is no doubt, however, that with the development of the ritual of the Church the classification of liturgical formulas for the use of the parochial clergy became common. Such books of procedure were known by various names; e.g., *manuale, obsequiale, benedictionale, rituale*, and *agenda*. The last title was given especially to the church books of particular dioceses wherein the general ritual of the Church was supplemented by ceremonial features of local origin, as the agenda for Magdeburg of 1497, or the *Liber agendarum secundum ritum ecclesiæ et diocesis Sleswicensis* of 1512. The use of the term in the Roman Catholic Church, however, practically ceases with the Reformation, though a few instances occur in the sixteenth and seventeenth centuries. In the Evangelical Churches, on the contrary, with the title *Kirchenbuch*, it speedily came to be the accepted designation for authoritative books of ritual. In the early days of the Reformation the agenda not infrequently constituted part of the *Kirchenordnung* or general church constitutions of a state (see CHURCH ORDER); but in the course of time the separation of the formulas of worship from the legal and administrative codes of the Church was effected.

1. The Term; its Equivalents Before the Reformation.

The earliest attempts at a reformation of the Roman ritual were naturally concerned with the mass. The innovations consisted of the omission of certain parts of the Roman ceremonial and the substitution of German for Latin, instances of the use of the vernacular in the celebration of the mass occurring as early as 1521–22. In 1523 Luther published his Latin mass, revised in accordance with evangelical doctrine; and three years later he gave to the world his *Deutsche Messe und Ordnung des Gottesdiensts*, the use of which, however, was not made obligatory. In the same year appeared his " Book of Baptism," in 1529 probably his " Book of Marriage," and during the years 1535–37 the formula for the ordination of ministers. In the *Kirchenordnungen* of the time orders of worship occur, as in Thomas Münzer's *Deutzsch kirchen ampt*, of 1523, and the *Landesordnung* of the duchy of Prussia in 1525. From this time to the end of the sixteenth century the Protestant states of Germany were busied with the task of remodeling their ecclesiastical systems and formularies of worship, the work being carried on by the great theologians of the age. The church constitutions and agenda of this period may be divided into three classes: (1) those following closely the Lutheran model; (2) those in which the ideas of the Swiss Reformation were predominant; and (3) those which retained appreciable elements of the Roman ritual. Of the first type the earliest examples are the constitutions drawn up by Bugenhagen for Brunswick, 1528; Hamburg, 1529; Lübeck, 1531; Pomerania, 1535; Denmark, 1537; Sleswick-Holstein, 1542; and Hildesheim, 1544. Justus Jonas formulated the church laws of Wittenberg (in part), 1533; of the duchy of Saxony (where the name " agenda " is first adopted), 1539; and of Halle, 1541. Hanover received its laws from Urbanus Rhegius in 1536; Brandenburg-Nuremberg, from Osiander and Brenz in 1533; and Mecklenburg, from Riebling, Aurifaber, and Melanchthon in 1540 and 1552. Among the states which adopted constitutions of the Reformed type were Hesse and Nassau, between 1527 and 1576; more closely, Württemberg, 1536; the Palatinate, 1554; and Baden, 1556. In the so-called " Cologne Reformation," drawn up largely by Butzer and Melanchthon and introduced by Archbishop Hermann in 1543, the agenda of Saxony, Brandenburg-Nuremberg, and Cassel served as models. The Roman ritual was retained to some extent in the church ordinances of the electorate of Brandenburg, 1540; Pfalzneuburg, 1543; and Austria, 1571. Of this type, too, were the ordinances drawn up by Melanchthon, Bugenhagen, Major, and others, for the electorate of Saxony in 1549; but these never went into effect, giving place in 1580 to a constitution Lutheran in character.

2. Lutheran Changes in Roman Catholic Agenda.

The Thirty Years' war exercised a disastrous influence on the entire ecclesiastical system of Germany, and particularly on church discipline. The work of restoration, however, was begun almost immediately after the cessation of hostilities, but so great was the moral degradation in which the mass of the people was plunged, so low was the standard of education and general intelligence, that in the formulation of new ecclesiastical laws the governments, of necessity, assumed a far larger share of authority over the affairs of the Church than they had possessed before the war. This increased power of the government was apparent not only in a closer supervision over the ecclesiastical administration, but also in the enforcement of a stricter adherence to the formulated modes of worship. Of the agenda promulgated after the war, the most important were those of Mecklenburg, 1650; Saxony and Westphalia, 1651; Brunswick-Lüneburg, 1657; Hesse, 1657; and Halle, 1660.

The eighteenth century witnessed a marked decline in the importance of the official liturgies in the religious life of the nation—a loss of influence so great as to make the books of the Church practically obsolescent. This was due to the rise of the pietistic movement which, in its opposition to formula and rigidity in doctrine, was no less destructive of the old ritual than was the rationalistic movement of the latter half of the century. Both pietism and rationalism were wanting in respect for the element of historical evolution in religion and worship; and the former, in laying stress on the value of individual prayer and devotion without attempting any change in the forms of divine service, led to their general abandonment for the spiritual edification that was to be obtained in the societies organized for common improvement, the so-called *collegia pietatis*. Rationalism in lending its own interpretation to the ritual, deprived it of much of its practical bearing, and necessitated, in consequence, a radical reconstruction of the prayers and hymns of the Church. But a no less important cause of change in liturgical forms is to be found in the growth of social distinctions and in the rise of a courtly etiquette which sought, with success, to impose its standards of manners and speech on the ceremonies and language of the Church. The etiquette of the salon entered the Church, and the formula "Take thou and eat," at the Lord's Supper, was altered to "Take ye and eat" when the communicants were of the nobility. The consistory of Hanover in 1800 granted permission to its ministers to introduce during public worship such changes in language, costume, and gesture as would appeal to the tastes of their "refined audiences." As a result the old official agenda passed generally out of use and were replaced by books of worship representing the views of individual ministers.

3. Decline of Lutheran Agenda in the Eighteenth Century.

In the Evangelical Churches outside of Germany books of ritual were drawn up during the early years of the Reformation. In 1525 Zwingli published the order of the mass as celebrated at Zurich and a formula of baptism based on the "Book of Baptism," issued by Leo Judæ in 1523. A complete agenda, including the two Zwinglian codes, appeared at Zurich in 1525 (according to Harnack and others, but more probably in 1529), under the title *Ordnung der Christenlichen Kilchenn zū Zürich*, and was often revised during the sixteenth and seventeenth centuries. Bern received its first formulary in 1528; Schaffhausen, in 1592, and St. Gall in 1738. Neuchâtel, in 1533, was the first French-speaking community to adopt a definite ritual; its authorship has been attributed to Farel. At Geneva, Calvin published in 1542, *La Forme des prières ecclésiastiques*, based on the practises he had found among the French of Strasburg during his sojourn in that city from 1538 to 1541. The Strasburg ritual was followed also by the French in London, and by many churches in France itself. Deserving of special mention are the constitutions drawn up in 1550 by Johannes a Lasco for the fugitives from the Netherlands resident in England. They form the first comprehensive formulation of the ritual of Calvinistic Protestantism, and are still in force in the Netherland Church.

4. The Agenda in the Reformed Church.

In Germany the return to a uniform, authoritative mode of worship was begun by Frederick William III. of Prussia in the early years of the nineteenth century. After 1613 the royal family of Prussia were adherents of the Reformed creed, but the king's personal beliefs were entirely Lutheran. After the campaign of Jena (1806) he entrusted the task of drafting a ritual to Eylert, whose work, however, failed to receive the king's approval because the author had fallen into the then common error of the writers of liturgics, namely, of paying little regard to the historical development of the evangelical forms of worship. Frederick William protested vehemently against these newly fabricated rituals, and asserted the necessity of "going back to Father Luther." With this purpose he devoted many years to the personal study of ritualistic history and attained an expert knowledge of the subject, particularly of its phases in the sixteenth century. The refusal of the great mass of the clergy to lend themselves to his efforts in favor of unity, he met with the determination to make use of the power vested in him by law to bring about the desired end. In 1822 he published the agenda for the court and cathedral church of Berlin; and two years later this formulary, increased and revised with the aid of Borowsky and Bunsen, was submitted to the various consistories. Before the end of 1825, out of 7,782 churches within the Prussian dominions, 5,243 had adopted the proposed regulations. In spite of a bitter polemic, in which Schleiermacher led the assault on the king's innovations, the new regulations were introduced in all the provinces before 1838.

5. Revival of Agenda by Frederick William III.

The king's agenda, however, did not cease to be the subject of much criticism. In 1856 it was improved; and in 1879 the General Synod determined upon a thorough revision. The work was entrusted to a committee of twenty-three, among whom were the theologians Goltz, Kleinert, Hering, Meuss, Renner, Rübesamen, Kögel, and Schmalenbach; and in 1894 their draft of a new ritual was adopted with slight changes by the General Synod. The lead of Prussia was followed by the other members of the German Empire, and most of the states have now revised their agenda or have the work in progress. Bohemia and Moravia (both Lutherans and Calvinists), Denmark, Norway, Poland, Russia, Sweden, and Transylvania have also late revisions. In France, after much agitation, a book of ritual, *Liturgie des Églises reformées de France revisées par le Synode général*, was adopted in 1897.

6. The Agenda in the Modern Lutheran Church.

(GEORG RIETSCHEL.)

The Church of England adopted the Book of Common Prayer under Edward VI., which, with slight revisions, has been made universally obligatory by acts of uniformity. It is used with modifications by the Protestant Episcopal Church of the United States (see COMMON PRAYER, BOOK OF). H. M. Mühlenberg prepared a liturgy which was adopted by the Lutheran Synod that he had organized (1748) and approved by the German Lutheran authorities at Halle, whose missionary he was. It was based upon those in use in Lüneburg (1643 onward), Calenberg (1569 onward), Brandenburg-Magdeburg (1739 onward), and Saxony (1712 onward). The liturgy of the Savoy Lutheran Church of London was the only one, apparently, actually in hand, the others exerting their influence through Mühlenberg's memory (for text cf. H. E. Jacobs, *A History of the Lutheran Church in the United States*, New York, 1893, pp 269–275; cf. also Schmucker, in the *Lutheran Church Review*, i., pp. 16–27, 161–172). Forms for baptism and the marriage ceremony were taken from the Prayer-Book of the Church of England. In 1795 Kunze published *A Hymn and Prayer Book for the use of such Lutheran Churches as use the English Language*, which has by successive revisions developed into the present *English Church Book*. In 1806 the New York ministerium adopted a liturgy modified by Episcopal influence, and in 1818 the Philadelphia ministerium adopted a liturgy in which extemporaneous prayer was allowed as well as freedom in selecting the Scriptures to be read. In 1885 after much controversy and conference the General Synod adopted a "Common Service," which has been widely accepted by the Churches, but is not regarded as obligatory.

7. American Liturgies.

The Dutch Reformed Church in the United States adopted (1771) along with the Belgic Confession, the Heidelberg Catechism, and the Canons of the Synod of Dort, the liturgical forms that were at that time in use in the Netherlands. The Nicene and Athanasian creeds are appended to the liturgy, which has undergone little change. The German Reformed Church in the United States seems to have used the Palatinate liturgy, with local modifications. In 1841 the Eastern Synod published a liturgy prepared by Lewis Mayer, which, however, failed of general approval. A "Provisional Liturgy," prepared by Philip Schaff and others (1857), likewise proved unacceptable. The "Order of Worship" was allowed by the General Synod (1866) as was also the "Western Liturgy" (1869). The "Directory of Worship" was adopted in 1887 (cf. E. T. Corwin, *History of the Reformed Church, Dutch*, and J. H. Dubbs, *History of the Reformed Church, German*, New York, 1895). A book of liturgical forms, prepared by Henry Van Dyke and others appointed by the General Assembly, for use in Presbyterian Churches, but in no way obligatory, was published in 1906. It aroused considerable opposition. A. H. N.

BIBLIOGRAPHY: J. A. Schmid, *Dissertatio de Agendis sive ordinationibus ecclesiasticis*, Helmstadt, 1718; J. L. Funk, *Die Kirchenordnung der evangelisch-lutherischen Kirche Deutschlands in ihrem ersten Jahrhundert*, 1824; idem, *Historische Beleuchtung der Agenden*, Neustadt, 1827; A. E. Richter, *Die evangelischen Kirchenordnungen des sechszehnten Jahrhunderts*, 2 vols., Weimar, 1846; H. A. Daniel, *Codex liturgicus ecclesiæ universæ in epitomen redactus*, 4 vols., Leipsic, 1847–53; J. H. A. Ebrard, *Reformirtes Kirchenbuch*, Zurich, 1847; A. Nordmeier, *Protestantische Agenda*, Gera, 1879; K. A. Dächsel, *Agende für die evangelische Kirche*, Berlin, 1880; E. Sehling, *Die evangelischen Kirchenordnungen des sechszehnten Jahrhunderts*, vol. i., Leipsic, 1903.

AGE-TO-COME ADVENTISTS. See ADVENTISTS, 6.

AGIER, ā″zhyê′, PIERRE JEAN: French lawyer; b. in Paris Dec. 28, 1748, of a Jansenist family; d. there Sept. 22, 1823. He held high positions in the French courts during the Revolution and under Napoleon and the Bourbons, but was early led into comprehensive theological studies. He learned Hebrew at the age of forty. His principal work is *Les Prophètes nouvellement traduits de l'hébreu avec des explications et des notes critiques* (8 vols., Paris, 1820–23). Among his other works are: *Le Jurisconsulte national* (3 vols., 1788); *Vues sur la réformation des lois civiles* (1793); *Traité sur le mariage* (2 vols., 1800); *Psaumes nouvellement traduits* (3 vols., 1809); *Vues sur le second avènement de Jésus-Christ* (1818); *Prophéties concernant Jésus-Christ et l'Église* (1819); and *Commentaire sur l'Apocalypse* (2 vols., 1823).

AGILBERT, ā″zhîl-bār′: Second bishop of the West Saxons (Dorchester) and afterward of Paris; b. in Gaul, probably in Paris; d. at Jouarre (35 m. e. of Paris) Oct. 11, 680; he studied in Ireland, and went to Wessex about 650, where King Cenwealh appointed him bishop to succeed Birinus (he had received consecration before leaving Gaul). As he could not speak English, Cenwealh chose another bishop, Wine, whom he located (probably in 663) in his royal city, Winchester, where he had founded a church soon after his conversion in 646. Agilbert then returned to Gaul, passing through Northumbria and attending the Synod of Whitby (q.v.) on the way. He became bishop of Paris not before 666. He assisted at the consecration of Wilfrid as bishop of York (664 or 665), and entertained Theodore of Tarsus while on his way to Canterbury. After a time Cenwealh invited him to return to Wessex; but he declined, and sent his nephew Hlothhere, or Leutherius, who was consecrated in 670 by the archbishop of Canterbury.

BIBLIOGRAPHY: Bede, *Hist. eccl.*, iii. 7, 25–28; iv. 1, 12; v. 19.

AGLIARDI, ā″glî″ār′dî, ANTONIO: Cardinal; b. at Cologno al Serio (8 m. s.s.e. of Bergamo), Lombardy, Italy, Sept. 4, 1832. After a pastorate of twelve years in his native city, he was called to Rome and appointed administrator of East Indian affairs in the College of the Propaganda, as well as professor of moral theology in the Collegium Urbanum. In the former capacity he was sent to India as apostolic delegate in 1884, after being consecrated titular bishop of Cæsarea in Palestine. Ill health forced him to return to Italy, but he was soon in India once more, and made a tour of the country which lasted five months. In 1887, after finally leaving India, he was for a time secretary for extraordinary ecclesiastical affairs, and was then successively papal nuncio at Munich and Vienna. In 1896 he was sent to Russia as ambassador extraordinary to attend the coronation of the czar, and in the same year received the cardinal's hat, while in 1899 he was made suburban bishop of Albano. In 1902 he was placed in charge of the estates of the College of the Propaganda, and since 1903 has been vice-chancellor of the Holy Roman Church.

AGNELLUS, ag″nel′lus (called also **Andrew**): The historian of the Church of Ravenna; b. in that city early in the ninth century [some authorities say in 805, of a rich and noble family]; the year of his death is unknown. He entered the clerical state very early, and became abbot of the monasteries of St. Mary ad Blachernas and St. Bartholomew, both in Ravenna. He was ordained priest by Archbishop Petronacius (817–835). His reputation for learning induced his brother clergy to ask him to write the history of the local church, and he began his *Liber pontificalis Ecclesiæ Ravennatis* before 838, and finished it after 846. It follows the model of the Roman *Liber pontificalis*, giving a series of biographies of the bishops of Ravenna, beginning with Apollinaris, said to have been a disciple of St. Peter and to have died as a martyr July 23, 75 (or 78), in whose memory the Basilica in Classe at Ravenna was dedicated in the year 549. The last bishop mentioned is George, whose death falls apparently in 846. The characteristics of the work are its strong tendency to the expression of local patriotism, and the interest which it shows in buildings, monuments, and other works of art. It is one of the earliest historical works to make an extensive use of architectural monuments as sources. Agnellus had little command of written documents; he availed himself of oral tradition wherever possible, and supplied its deficiencies by a well-meaning imagination.

(A. HAUCK.)

BIBLIOGRAPHY: His history, edited by O. Holder-Egger, is in *MGH, Script. rer. Lang.*, 1878, pp. 265–391, also in the continuation to 1296 by an unknown writer and to 1410 by Paul Scordilli, in *MPL*, cvi. 429–840; A. Ebert, *Allgemeine Geschichte der Litteratur des Mittelalters*, ii. 374–377, Leipsic, 1880.

AGNES, SAINT: A saint commemorated in the Roman Church on Jan. 21 and 28 (the Gelasian Liturgy giving the former; the Gregorian, the latter date), and in the Greek Church on Jan. 14 and 21 and July 5. Since the oldest documents (the *Calendarium Romanum*, the *Calendarium Africanum*, and the Gothic and Oriental *Missale*) agree in fixing Jan. 21 as the day of her death, Bolland has rightly assigned to that day the acts of her martyrdom. The year of her death, according to Ruinart, was about 304. The cause and manner of her martyrdom are given in a very legendary manner by an undoubtedly spurious *Passion* in the older editions of the works of St. Ambrose, which states that, having made a vow of perpetual virginity while still a child, she successfully resisted the wooing of a noble youth, the son of Symphronius, the city prefect, and embellishes the narrative with many wonders. Her hair suddenly grew so long and thick as to serve for a cloak; a light from heaven struck her importunate lover lifeless to the ground; when she was bound to the stake the flames were extinguished in answer to her prayer. After she had been beheaded at the command of the prefect, and had been buried by her parents in their field on the Via Nomentana, outside of Rome, she appeared to her people in glorified form with a little lamb at her side, and continued to perform miracles, such as the healing of the princess Constantia, for which, it is said, she was honored under Constantine the Great by the erection of a basilica at her tomb (Sant' Agnese fuori le Mura). Evidence of the high antiquity of her worship is given by Ambrose in several of his genuine writings, by Jerome (*Epist.*, cxxx., *ad Demetriadem*), by Augustine, by the Christian poets Damasus and Prudentius, and by others.

In medieval art St. Agnes is usually represented with a lamb, which indicates her character as representative of youthful chastity and innocence, but may have been derived from her name, which is to be connected with the Greek *hagnē*, "chaste" (cf. Augustine, *Sermones*, cclxxiii. 6). Two lambs are blessed every year on Jan. 21 in the Agnes basilica, mentioned above (one of the principal churches of Rome, after which one of the cardinal priests is called), and their wool is used to make the archiepiscopal pallia which are consecrated by the pope (see PALLIUM). O. ZÖCKLER†.

BIBLIOGRAPHY: For life and legends: Ambrose, *Vita gloriosa virginis Agnetis*, in folio 115 of his works, Milan, 1474; *ASB*, Jan., ii. 350–363; T. Ruinart, *Acta Martyrum*, Amsterdam, 1713, Ratisbon, 1859; A. Butler, *Lives of the Saints*, under Jan. 21, London, 1847; L. Santini, *Leben der heiligen Agnes*, Ratisbon, 1884; P. Franchi de' Cavalieri, *Santa Agnese nella tradizione e nella leggenda*, Rome, 1899. For representations in Christian art: H. Detzel, *Christliche Ikonographie*, vol. ii., Freiburg, 1896. For the Catacombs of St. Agnes: J. S. Northcote and W. C. Brownlow, *Roma Sotterranea*, London, 1879–80; M. Armellini, *Il Cimiterio di S. Agnese*, Rome, 1880; W. H. Withrow, *Catacombs of Rome*, London, 1888; V. Schultze, *Archäologie der altchristlichen Kunst*, Munich, 1895. For the mystery play of St. Agnes: *Sancta Agnes, Provenzalisches geistliches Schauspiel*, Berlin, 1869.

AGNOETÆ, ag″no-ī′tī or -ē′tê (Gk. *agnoētai*, "ignorant"): **1.** Name of a sect of the fourth century, a branch of the Eunomians (q.v.), who followed the lead of Theophronius of Cappadocia. They were so named because they limited the divine omniscience to the present, maintaining that God knew the past merely by memory, and the future by divination (Socrates, *Hist. eccl.*, v. 24).

2. The name was borne also by the sect of the sixth century, founded by Themistius, a deacon of Alexandria, and sometimes called Themistians. They consisted chiefly of the Severian faction of the Monophysites, and maintained that, as the body of Christ was subject to natural conditions, so also his human soul must be thought of as not omniscient. In support of their view they quoted Mark xiii. 32 and John xi. 34. The heresy was revived by the Adoptionists in the eighth century.

AGNOSTICISM: A philologically objectionable and philosophically unnecessary but very convenient term, invented toward the end of the nineteenth century (1869) as a designation of the skeptical habit of mind then quite prevalent. It is defined in the Oxford Dictionary as the doctrine which holds that "the existence of anything beyond and behind natural phenomena is unknown, and (so far as can be judged) unknowable, and especially that a First Cause and an unseen world are subjects of which we know nothing." It is thus equivalent to the common philosophical term, skepticism, although expressing the phase of thought designated by both alike from the point of view of its outcome rather than of its method. Some have held, it is true, that the true agnostic is not he who doubts whether human powers can attain to the knowledge of what really is, or specifically to the knowledge of God and spiritual things, but he who denies this. But there is a dogmatic skepticism, and there is no reason why there may not be a more or less hesitant agnosticism. The essential element in both is that the doubt or denial rests on distrust of the power of the human mind to ascertain truth. It is common, to be sure, to speak of several types of agnosticism, differing the one from the other according as the basis of the doubt or denial of the attainability of truth is ontological, generally psychological, definitely epistemological, or logical. But useful as this discrimination may be as a rough classification of modes of presenting the same fundamental doctrine, it is misleading if it suggests that the real basis of doubt or denial is not in every case epistemological. When it is said, for example, that God and spiritual things are in their very nature unknowable, that of course means that they are unknowable to such powers as man possesses; nothing that exists can be intrinsically unknowable, and if unknowable to men must be so only because of limitations in their faculties of knowledge. And when one is told that the sole trouble is that the balance of evidence is hopelessly in equilibrium, and the mind is therefore left in suspense, that of course means only that such minds as men have are too coarse scales for weighing such delicate matters.

Agnosticism is in short a theory of the nature and limits of human intelligence. It is that particular theory which questions or denies the capacity of human intelligence to attain assured knowledge, whether with respect to all spheres of truth, or, in its religious application, with respect to the particular sphere of religious truth. As mankind has universally felt itself in possession of a body of assured knowledge, and not least in the sphere of religious truth,—nay as mankind instinctively reaches out to and grasps what it unavoidably looks upon as assured knowledge, and not least in the sphere of religious truth,—agnosticism becomes, in effect, that tendency of opinion which pronounces what men in general consider knowledge more or less misleading, and therefore more or less noxious. Sometimes, no doubt, in what we may, perhaps, call the half-agnostic, these illusions are looked upon as rough approximations to truth, and are given a place of importance in the direction of human life, under some such designation as "regulative truths" (Mansel), or "value judgments" (Ritschl), or "symbolical conceptions" (Sabatier). The consistent agnostic, however, must conceive them as a body of mere self-deceptions, from which he exhorts men to cleanse their souls as from cant (Huxley).

In effect, therefore, agnosticism impoverishes, and, in its application to religious truth, secularizes and to this degree degrades life. Felicitating itself on a peculiarly deep reverence for truth on the ground that it will admit into that category only what can make good its right to be so considered under the most stringent tests, it deprives itself of the enjoyment of this truth by leaving the category either entirely or in great part empty. Refusing to assert there is no truth, it yet misses what Bacon declares "the sovereign good of human nature," viz., "the inquiry of truth, which is the love-making or wooing of it,—the knowledge of truth, which is the presence of it,—and the belief of truth which is the enjoying of it." On the ground that certain knowledge of God and spiritual things is unattainable, it bids man think and feel and act as if there were no God and no spiritual life and no future existence. It thus degenerates into a practical atheism. Refusing to declare there is no God, it yet misses all there may be of value and profit in the recognition of God.

Benjamin B. Warfield.

Bibliography: Modern agnosticism takes its start in the philosophy of Kant and runs its course through Hamilton and Mansel to culminate in the teaching of Herbert Spencer; its most authoritative exposition is given in their writings and in those of their followers. Good select bibliographies of the subject may be found in A. B. Bruce, *Apologetics*, p. 146, London, 1892, in F. R. Beattie, *Apologetics, or the Rational Vindication of Christianity*, i. 521, 531, Richmond, 1903, and in R. Flint, *Agnosticism*, London, 1903, foot-notes, especially that on p. 643, where the titles of works on the cognoscibility of God are collected. Consult, besides the above, from the Christian dogmatic standpoint, J. Ward, *Naturalism and Agnosticism*, ib. 1903; C. Hodge, *Systematic Theology*, I. i., ch. iv., New York, 1871; B. P. Bowne, *The Philosophy of H. Spencer*, ib. 1874 (a criticism of Spencer's agnosticism); J. Owen, *Evenings with the Skeptics*, 2 vols., London, 1881; J. McCosh, *The Agnosticism of Hume and Huxley*, New York, 1884; J. Martineau, *Study of Religion*, I. i., ch. i.-iv., London, 1889; H. Wace, *Christianity and Agnosticism*, Edinburgh, 1895; J. Iverach, *Is God Knowable?* London, 1887. The agnostics' position is set forth in H. Spencer, *First Principles*, ib. 1904 (called "the Bible of Agnosticism"); J. Fiske, *Outlines of Cosmic Philosophy*, Boston, 1874; K. Pearson, *The Ethic of Freethought*, London, 1887; R. Bithell, *Agnostic Problems*, ib. 1887; idem, *The Creed of a Modern Agnostic*, ib. 1888; idem, *Handbook of Scientific Agnosticism*, ib. 1892; *Christianity and Agnosticism, a Controversy consisting of Papers by H. Wace, T. H. Huxley, Bishop Magee, and Mrs. Ward*, New York, 1889 (this discussion aroused wide interest); L. Stephen, *An Agnostic's Apology*, London, 1893; T. Huxley, *Collected Essays*, vol. v., 9 vols., ib. 1894 (contains his side of the controversy with Dr. Wace); W. Scott Palmer, *An Agnostic's Progress*, London, 1906.

AGNUS DEI, ag′nus dē′i ("Lamb of God"):

1. An ancient liturgical formula in the celebration of the Eucharist, found in some manuscripts of the Sacramentary of Gregory the Great after the Lord's Prayer and the *Libera*. The full text, based on John i. 29, is "Agnus Dei, qui tollis peccata mundi, miserere nobis." It is found also in the ancient Eastern hymn which was annexed to the *Gloria in Excelsis* (see Liturgical Formulas, II., 3) and was early introduced into the Western Church in Latin translation, where the form is "Domine Fili unigenite, Jesu Christe, Domine Deus, Agnus Dei, Filius Patris, qui tollis peccata mundi, miserere nobis; qui tollis peccata mundi, suscipe deprecationem nostram." When the Second Trullan Council (692) undertook to forbid the representation and invocation of Christ under the figure of the lamb, Pope Sergius I., to express the opposition of the Roman Church, decreed that the *Agnus* should be sung by priest and people at the Communion. After 767, under Adrian I., it was sung by the choir only. The ritual of the mass, based in this particular on a custom which can be traced to the beginning of the eleventh century,

prescribes that the priest, before taking the sacrament, shall recite the Agnus Dei three times, bowing and beating his breast to express contrition for sin, the third time with the addition of "dona nobis pacem." The consecration precedes, the Lord's Prayer is sung with the *Libera nos;* a piece of the consecrated and broken bread is then thrown into the cup, and the *Agnus* follows. At the Church festivals it is accompanied with telling effect by soft and tender music. In the mass for the dead the words "give them rest" are substituted for "have mercy upon us," the third time with the addition of "eternal."

The *Agnus* was accepted in the Evangelical Lutheran Church at the beginning, either in the translation of Nicolaus Decius, "O Lamm Gottes unschuldig," or in the more exact form, "Christe, du Lamm Gottes, der du trägst." In the days of rationalism it was often omitted, or the phrase "Son of God" was substituted for "Lamb of God," the latter being thought to imply an unchristian, Levitical sacrificial conception. It was afterward restored, and is now used in numerous musical settings. In the Church of England the *Agnus* was incorporated in the Litany, but only to be repeated twice; and the last form (ending with "grant us thy peace") was placed first. In the first prayer-book of Edward I. it was included in the communion office, but was omitted in that of 1552 and all subsequent revisions. Nevertheless, it is almost invariably sung by congregations of High-church affiliations. M. HEROLD.

BIBLIOGRAPHY: H. A. Daniel, *Codex liturgicus*, vols. i., ii., Leipsic, 1847–48; L. Schöberlein, *Schatz des liturgischen Chor- und Gemeindegesangs*, pp. 398 sqq., Göttingen, 1880; G. Rietschel, *Lehrbuch der Liturgik*, p. 386, Berlin, 1900. Musical settings, by Vittoria, Palestrina, F. Burmeister (1601), F. Decker (1604), M. Prætorius (d. 1621), Mozart, and others; consult R. von Liliencron, *Chorordnung*, Gütersloh, 1900.

2. Name given to a wax medallion, bearing the figure of a lamb, made from the remains of the paschal taper, and consecrated by the pope in the special ceremonies on the Sunday after Easter in the first year of each pontificate and every seven years thereafter. These medallions are presented to distinguished individuals or to churches, are often enclosed in cases of costly workmanship, and are carefully preserved, almost like relics.

AGOBARD, ag'o-bārd: Archbishop of Lyons 816–840 [b., probably in Spain, 779; d. in Saintonge (an old province of western France) June 6, 840]. Nothing certain is known of his youth. He went to Lyons in 792, and probably owed his education to Leidrad, archbishop of Lyons, one of the most diligent of Charlemagne's helpers in his civilizing work. Later he became Leidrad's assistant, and then his successor. When the order of succession established by Louis le Débonnaire in 817, largely through ecclesiastical influence, was set aside at the instigation of the empress Judith (829), Agobard was one of its most zealous defenders. He seems to have taken no part in the rising of 830; but in 833 he appears among the professed opponents of Louis. He approved the deposition of the emperor, and was one of the bishops who forced him to his humiliating penance at Soissons. Consequently in 835, when Louis had recovered his power, Agobard was deprived of his office. He regained it later, being reconciled with Louis.

Agobard takes a foremost place in the annals of Carolingian culture. In strictly theological treatises such as the *Liber adversus dogma Felicis*, against Adoptionism, and another, against image-worship, he is as much a mere compiler as any of his contemporaries. When, however, in a polemic against Fredegis, abbot of St. Martin at Tours, he deals with the question of inspiration, he speaks out boldly against the doctrine of verbal inspiration, while still declaring himself to be governed by the tradition of orthodox teachers. In his political writings he was less governed by traditional views. He was not afraid to touch one of the most difficult questions of the time, that of the restitution of Church property, at the diet held at Attigny in 822; and he renewed the demand in the tractate *De dispensatione ecclesiarum rerum.* His *Comparatio utriusque regiminis ecclesiastici et politici* (833) is one of the first writings in which the claim is outspokenly made that the emperor must do the bidding of the pope. He wrote a book against the popular superstition that storms could be caused by magic, basing his argument on religious grounds, yet making appeal to sound reason. In advance of his age, again, he denied absolutely the justice of the ordeal by battle, and wrote two tractates against it. He was also to some extent a liturgical scholar; and in the preface to his revised antiphonary laid down the principle that the words of Holy Scripture should alone be used. (A. HAUCK.)

BIBLIOGRAPHY: A. Cave, *Scriptorum ecclesiasticorum historia literaria*, vol. ii., London, 1688 (contains list of the works of Agobard); *Opera*, ed. E. Baluze, 2 vols., Paris, 1666, and thence in *MPL*, civ.; also in *MGH, Leges*, i. (1835) 369, *MGH, Epist.*, v. (1899) 150–239, and in *MGH, Script.*, xv. 1 (1887), 274–279.

For his life and times: Menestrier, *Histoire civile de la ville de Lyons*, 3 parts, Lyons, 1696; K. B. Hundeshagen, *Commentatio de Agobardi vita et scriptis*, Giessen, 1831; P. Chevallard, *L'Église et l'état en France au neuvième siècle, Saint Agobard*, Lyons, 1869; T. Förster, *Drei Erzbischöfe vor 1000 Jahren*, Gütersloh, 1874; B. Simson, *Jahrbücher des fränkischen Reichs unter Ludwig dem Frommen*, i. 397 sqq., Leipsic, 1874; H. Reuter, *Geschichte der religiösen Aufklärung im Mittelalter*, i. 24–41, Berlin, 1875; *DCB*, i. 63–64; A. Ebert, *Geschichte der Litteratur des Mittelalters*, ii. 209–222, Leipsic, 1880; J. F. Marcks, *Die politisch-kirchliche Wirksamkeit des . Agobard*, Viersen, 1888; Hauck, *KD*, ii. 453 sqq.; Wattenbach, *DGQ*, i. 232, Berlin, 1904; F. Wiegand, *Agobard von Lyons und die Judenfrage*, Leipsic, 1901.

AGONIZANTS (Agony Fathers; Fathers of the Good Death, Camillians, *Clerici regulares ministrantes infirmis*): A fraternity founded at Rome in 1584 to care for the sick and minister to the dying. The founder was a pious priest Camillus de Lellis (b. at Buchianico, in the Neapolitan province Abruzzo, May 25, 1550; d. at Rome July 14, 1614), who, after a wild life as a soldier, entered the hospital of St. James at Rome in 1574, suffering from an incurable wound. Becoming converted, he devoted the remainder of his life to heroic service in the hospitals of Rome, Naples, and elsewhere. He was canonized by Benedict XIV. in 1746, and his statue now stands, among those of great founders of orders, in St. Peter's between the statues of St. Peter of Alcantara and St.

Ignatius Loyola. The society was confirmed by Sixtus V. in 1586; five years later, after the members had distinguished themselves during the plague of 1590, it was created by Gregory XIV an order with Augustinian rule. It grew rapidly in numbers and wealth during the founder's lifetime, and in 1605 was divided by Paul V into five provinces, Rome, Milan, Bologna, Naples, and Sicily. Afterward the order spread beyond Italy, especially in Spain and Portugal, and later in France and America. During the nineteenth century it met with opposition in certain countries (including Italy, where it had thirty-four houses); but it was favored by Leo XIII., who made St. Camillus and St. John of God (see CHARITY, BROTHERS OF) patrons of all Roman Catholic hospitals, and inserted their names in the litany of the dying.

O. ZÖCKLER†.

BIBLIOGRAPHY: C. Solfi, *Compendio historico della religione de' chierici regolari ministri degli infermi*, Mondovi, 1689; Fèvre, *Vie de St. Camille de Lellis*, Paris, 1885; W. Bäumker, *Der heilige Camillus von Lellis und sein Orden*, Frankfort-on-the-Main, 1887; Heimbucher, *Orden und Kongregationen*, ii. 264–271.

AGRAPHA, ag′ra-fa ("Unwritten"): Name given to so-called sayings of Jesus not recorded in the Gospels, but reported by oral tradition. The term was first used by J. G. Körner in his *De sermonibus Christi ἀγράφοις* (Leipsic, 1776), in which he gives sixteen such agrapha. Since that time several collections of agrapha have been made; and the material seemed to have reached a climax in the work published by Alfred Resch, *Agrapha: aussercanonische Evangelien-Fragmente in möglichster Vollständigkeit zusammengestellt und quellenkritisch untersucht* (*TU*, v. 4, 1889; cf. J. H. Ropes, *Die Sprüche Jesu ... eine kritische Bearbeitung des von A. Resch gesammelten Materials*, xiv. 2 of the same series, 1896). In 1897 Drs. B. P. Grenfell and A. S. Hunt discovered a papyrus page containing eight "sayings of Jesus" which are known as "the Oxyrhynchus Logia." In Feb., 1903, they came upon another papyrus fragment of a somewhat similar character, containing five additional "sayings of Jesus." Ropes divides the material found in Resch into five classes: (1) sayings which tradition has not considered agrapha; (2) passages erroneously quoted as sayings of the Lord; (3) worthless agrapha; (4) eventually valuable agrapha; (5) valuable agrapha. Such a classification is arbitrary and impossible; and even as to the number of agrapha scholars differ.

Among the more noteworthy of the agrapha are:

1. The sentence, "It is more blessed to give than to receive," quoted by Paul (Acts xx. 35) as the "words of the Lord Jesus." No such saying is mentioned in the canonical Gospels. In the *Teaching of the Apostles* (i. 5) is found "happy is he that giveth according to the commandment"; and in the *Apostolical Constitutions* (iv. 3): "since even the Lord says, 'the giver was happier than the receiver.'" In Clement of Rome (*Epist.*, i. 2), the same saying seems to be referred to under the form "more willing to give than to receive."

2. "On the same day, having seen one working on the Sabbath, he said to him, 'O man, if indeed thou knowest what thou doest, thou art blessed; but if thou knowest not, thou art accursed and a transgressor of the law.'" This very remarkable saying occurs after Luke vi. 4 in Cod. D and in Cod. Græc. B. Rob. Stephani.

3. "But ye seek to increase from little, and from greater to less. When ye go and are bidden to dinner, sit not down in the highest seats, lest one grander than thou arrive, and the giver of the feast come and say to thee, 'Take a lower seat,' and thou be ashamed. But if thou sit down in the meaner place, and one meaner than thou arrive, the giver of the feast will say to thee, 'Go up higher'; and this shall be profitable to thee." This saying is found after Matt. xx. 28 in Cod. D, and in some other codices (cf. the New Testaments of Griesbach and Tischendorf ad. loc.).

4. "Jesus said to his disciples 'Ask great things, and the small shall be added unto you; and ask heavenly things and the earthly shall be added unto you'" (Clement of Alexandria, *Stromata*, i. 24; Origen, *De Orat. libell.*, ii.; cf. Ambrose, *Epist.*, xxxvi. 3).

5. "Rightly, therefore, the Scripture in its desire to make us such dialecticians, exhorts us: 'Be ye skilful money-changers,' rejecting some things, but retaining what is good" (Clement of Alexandria, *Strom.*, i. 28). This is the most frequently quoted of all traditional sayings. Resch gives sixty-nine passages.

6. "Let us resist all iniquity, and hold it in hatred," quoted as the words of Christ by Barnabas (*Epist.*, iv.). In *Epist.*, vii. is found: "They who wish to see me and lay hold of my kingdom must receive me by affliction and suffering."

7. "Our Lord Jesus Christ said, 'In whatsoever I may find you, in this will I also judge you.'" This saying, found in Justin Martyr (*Trypho*, xlvii., *ANF*, i., p. 219), is ascribed by Clement of Alexandria (*Quis dives*, xl.) to God; by Johannes Climacus (*Scala paradisi*, vii. 159; *Vita B. Antonii*, i. 15; *Vitæ patrum*, p. 41) to the prophet Ezekiel (cf. Ezek. vii. 3, 8; xviii. 30; xxiv. 14; xxxiii. 20, with Fabricius, *Cod. Apocr.*, i. 333). These passages in Ezekiel, however, do not justify the quotation, and some apocryphal gospel is probably the authority for this saying.

8. Among the sayings found in 1903 was the following: "Jesus saith, 'Let not him who seeks ... cease until he finds, and when he finds he shall be astonished; astonished he shall reach the kingdom; and having reached the kingdom he shall rest.'" Another, with conjectural restoration of missing portions, is: "Jesus saith, '[Ye ask, who are those] that draw us [to the kingdom, if] the kingdom is in heaven? ... The fowls of the air, and all beasts that are under the earth or upon the earth, and the fishes of the sea [those are they which draw] you, and the kingdom of heaven is within you; and whoever shall know himself shall find it. [Strive therefore] to know yourselves, and ye shall be aware that ye are the sons of the [almighty] Father: [and] ye shall know that ye are in [the city of God], and ye are [the city].'"

B. PICK.

BIBLIOGRAPHY: Collections of agrapha are found in J. H. Grabe, *Spicilegium*, Oxford, 1698; J. A. Fabricius, *Codex Apocryphus Novi Testamenti*, Hamburg, 1703; R. Hoffmann, *Das Leben Jesu nach den Apocryphen*, Leipsic, 1851; B. F. Westcott, *Introduction to the Study of the Gospels*, London, 1860; Schaff, *Christian Church*, i. 162–167; A. Resch, *Agrapha*, in *TU*, v. 4, 1891; J. H. Ropes, in *TU*, xiv. 2, 1896; E. Nestle, *Novi Testamenti Græci Supplementum*, pp. 89–92, Leipsic, 1896; B. Pick, *The Agrapha: or, Unrecorded Sayings of Jesus Christ*, in *The Open Court*, xi. (1897) 525–541; idem, *The Extra-Canonical Life of Christ*, pp. 250–312, New York, 1903 (including a list of articles on the Oxyrhynchus Logia published in 1897); C. Taylor, *The Oxyrhynchus Logia and the Apocryphal Gospels*, London, 1899; E. Preuschen, *Antilegomena*, pp. 43–47, Giessen, 1901; *The New Sayings of Jesus, and Fragment of a Lost Gospel* were published by B. P. Grenfell and A. S. Hunt, Oxford and New York, 1904, reviewed in *Biblical World*, xxiv. (1904) 261, in *Saturday Review*, xcviii. (1904) 133, and *Church Quarterly*, lviii. (1904) 422. For sayings of Jesus in Mohammedan writers consult D. S. Margoliouth, in *The Expository Times*, v. (1893) 59, 107, 177; W. Lock, in *The Expositor*, 4th series, ix. (1894) 97–99; and for sayings of Jesus in the Talmud consult Pick, ut sup.

AGREDA, MARIA DE. See MARIA DE AGREDA.

AGRICOLA: Pelagian writer; under the date 429 in his *Chronicon*, Prosper of Aquitaine mentions a British theologian of this name, the son of Severianus, a Pelagian bishop, saying that he corrupted the churches of Britain by his teaching, until Pope Celestine sent Germanus, Bishop of Auxerre (q.v.), to undo the mischief and bring back the

Britons to the Catholic faith (cf. Bede, *Hist. eccl.*, i. 17). Caspari has printed five unsigned letters and a tract on riches which are obviously all by the same Pelagian author, and has shown it to be probable that this is Agricola. From them it is learned that the author on his way to the East to learn the true ascetic life, heard the Pelagian ascetic teaching from a Roman lady in Sicily, and became a zealous preacher of it. The value of these writings lies in the glimpse which they give of the ethical side of Pelagianism. (A. HAUCK.)

BIBLIOGRAPHY: C. P. Caspari, *Briefe, Abhandlungen, und Predigten aus den zwei letzten Jahrhunderten des kirchlichen Altertums und dem Anfang des Mittelalters*, Christiania, 1890.

AGRICOLA, JOHANN: An associate of Luther, and the originator of the antinomian controversy of the German Reformation; b. at Eisleben Apr. 20, 1494 (according to his own account; others give 1492 or 1496); d. at Berlin Sept. 22, 1566. His real name was Schneider, first Latinized into "Sartor," then, from a corruption of "Schneider (Snider)" to "Schnitter," into "Agricola." He entered the University of Leipsic in the winter of 1509–10, with the intention of studying medicine, but Luther attracted him to theology. After taking his bachelor's degree, he went, in the winter of 1515–16, to Wittenberg, where he came wholly under Luther's influence. He witnessed the famous promulgation of the theses; and at the Leipsic disputation (1519) he acted as Luther's secretary. He soon became friendly with Melanchthon also, and an influential member of the little group of Wittenberg theologians. A modest income was provided for him by the position of teacher of grammar and the Latin classics in the Pædagogium; and before long he lectured on dialectics and rhetoric, and later on the New Testament.

Schoolmaster in Eisleben.

On the outbreak of the Peasants' War (1525), Agricola accompanied Luther to the Hartz Mountains, and gained from Count Albert of Mansfeld the nomination as head of the Latin school to be opened at Eisleben. This work, after a visit to Frankfort, as Luther's deputy, to help settle the ecclesiastical affairs of that place, he took up in Aug., 1525; and two catechetical books grew out of it, the second of which (1528) already exhibits the opposition between the Law and the Gospel which was to develop into his antinomian convictions. A commentary on the Epistle to Titus (1530) and a translation of Terence's *Andria*, with notes (1544), are doubtless other results of his school work. At Eisleben also he began his three collections of German proverbs, with explanations, which have ever since been popular. Certain critical remarks about Ulrich of Württemberg in the first of these collections involved Agricola in difficulties both with Ulrich and with his protector, Philip of Hesse, which were ended only by two successive apologies, prevented Luther from taking him to the Marburg conference, and influenced his bearing in the Schmalkald struggle. He had opportunities of preaching at St. Nicholas's church in Eisleben, and acquired the reputation of being one of the strongest pulpit orators of the Wittenberg circle, so that he was asked to attend the Diet of Speyer in 1526 and 1529 and preach before the court. At this period also he made himself useful as a translator from the Latin, rendering among other things Melanchthon's commentary on several Pauline epistles.

Controversies.

His relations with Melanchthon were seriously disturbed in 1526. Soon after his departure from Wittenberg a new theological professorship was founded there, on which, with Melanchthon's encouragement, he set his heart. When it was conferred on the latter, Agricola's vanity received a wound which put an end to the cordiality of their friendship; and it is easy to understand why he began the antinomian controversy in 1527 with an attack, not on Luther, but on Melanchthon. Luther, however, whose relations with Agricola were still friendly, succeeded in effecting an apparent agreement. Agricola now fell out with Albert of Mansfeld. Differences arose over the measures to be taken for defense against the emperor and with regard to the treatment of matrimonial questions; and in 1536 Agricola was treating with Luther to secure a recall to Wittenberg. The elector promised him a speedy appointment to a university position, and meantime invited him to come to Wittenberg to give his counsel on the question of the Schmalkald articles. Agricola removed thither at Christmas, 1536. Albert, annoyed at the manner of his departure from Eisleben, accused him to the Wittenberg group as the founder of a new sect antagonistic to Luther, and to the elector as a turbulent fellow of the Münzer type. Luther stood by him, however, and even gave him and his family shelter in his own house; and when Luther went to Schmalkald in 1537, Agricola took his place both at the university and in the pulpit. Expressions used in some of his sermons, and the rumor that he was privately circulating antinomian theses containing attacks on Luther and Melanchthon, made him an object of suspicion. His antinomian disputes with Luther himself began; and after each apparent settlement they broke out with fresh violence (for details of the controversies see ANTINOMIANISM, ANTINOMIAN CONTROVERSIES, II.). He found employment in the newly founded Wittenberg consistory until Feb., 1539, when he formally accused Luther before the elector, who practically put him under arrest. Before the matter was settled he escaped to Berlin (Aug., 1540). At Melanchthon's suggestion and through Bugenhagen's mediation, he was allowed to retract his accusation and to return to Saxony. Cordial relations between the two men could, however, no longer exist: Luther never trusted Agricola again; and the latter, on his side, held that he remained true to the original cause, from which Luther had fallen away.

Joachim II. of Brandenburg gave Agricola a position as court preacher, and took him to the Conference of Regensburg (1541), the interim drawn up at which he considered a useful basis of unity. He followed his prince in the inglorious campaign against the Turks in 1542, and gained more and more influence over him, in spite of the efforts of Joachim's mother. He became general superintendent and visitor of Brandenburg, administering confirmation and ordination, though he himself had never received any kind of ordination. When the Schmalkald League took up arms against the emperor, Agricola attacked them in his sermons as disturbers of the peace, and gave thanks for the emperor's victory at Mühlberg, utterly failing to see the danger to the evangelical cause. It flattered his vanity when he was chosen as the Protestant theologian on the commission appointed at the Diet of Augsburg (1547–48) to draw up an interim; and he had the thankless task of endeavoring to persuade his fellow Protestants to accept it. The more strongly and increasingly they rejected it, the more animosity was concentrated on Agricola, who attempted to vindicate his Lutheran standing by the part which he took in the controversy with Osiander (q.v.); and the common cause brought him once more closer to Melanchthon. It fell to him to give judgment between Stancaro and Andreas Musculus (q.v.); and he pronounced in favor of the latter. The controversy on the necessity of good works raged for years in Brandenburg, and Agricola stoutly opposed the Philippists. For a while they seemed to prevail with Joachim, but the court swung round again to Agricola's side; and in 1563 he was able to hold a thanksgiving service in Berlin for the final victory over his opponents—a victory for strict Lutheranism won mainly by the man whom Luther had despised. He died three years later, during an epidemic of the plague. He was undoubtedly a gifted man, though his rightful development was hindered by his vanity, which brought about the breach with Luther, and by the temptations of court life, which, as he himself recognized when too late, he had not sufficient strength of mind to resist.

Later Life.

(G. KAWERAU.)

BIBLIOGRAPHY: G. Kawerau, *Johann Agricola von Eisleben*, Berlin, 1881.

AGRICOLA, STEPHAN (originally **Castenpauer**): A follower of Luther; b. in Abensberg (18 m. s.w. of Regensburg), Bavaria; d. at Eisleben Easter, 1547. He studied at Vienna, joined the Augustinians, gained fame as a preacher and teacher, and was promoted doctor of theology in 1519. Imitating St. Augustine, he preached on entire books of the Bible in Vienna in 1515, as lector in the Augustinian monastery at Regensburg in 1519–20, and in other places. His sermons brought him under suspicion. He was accused of preaching heretical, inflammatory, and offensive dogmas; of having recommended Luther's writings on the Babylonian captivity and on the abolition of the mass; of having spoken offensively of the Roman see, bishops, and clergy; and of having demanded the abolition of all ceremonies. He was imprisoned in 1522; thirty-three charges were made against him; and his answer, denying dependence upon Luther and making appeal to Augustine and the Scriptures, was of no avail. He prepared for death, and wrote *Ein köstlicher gutter notwendiger Sermon vom Sterben* (1523), which his friend Wolfgang Russ published. He escaped, however, found a home with the Carmelite Johann Frosch of Augsburg in 1523, and preached there from time to time. Not long after 1523 he published under the name of "Agricola Boius" *Ein Bedencken wie der wahrhafftig Gottesdienst von Gott selbs geboten und aussgesetzt, möcht mit besserung gemeyner Christenheyt widerumb aufgericht werden*, a kind of reformation-programme. Protected by the city council, he labored with Rhegius and Frosch for the Reformation in Augsburg, and became pronounced in his adherence to Luther's views as against Zwingli. By translating into German Bugenhagen's polemical treatise against Zwingli's *Contra novum errorem de sacramentis* (1525), he won over the Augsburg congregation to the Lutheran side. At the invitation of the landgrave Philip, he took part in the Marburg Colloquy and signed the articles agreed upon. In 1531 he left Augsburg as he was opposed to Butzer's Zwinglian tendency and went to Nuremberg, where he stayed with Wenceslaus Link. In 1537 he attended the Schmalkald Diet and signed Luther's articles. When the Reformation was introduced into the Upper Palatinate, he accepted a call to Sulzbach where he preached the first evangelical sermon June 3, 1542. He afterward went to Eisleben.

(T. KOLDE.)

BIBLIOGRAPHY: C. Spangenberg, *Wider die böse Sieben in Teufels Karnöffelspiel*, Eisleben, 1562; H. W Rotermund, *Geschichte des auf dem Reichstage zu Augsburg im Jahre 1530 . Glaubensbekenntnisses*, Hanover, 1829; Datterer, *Des Kardinals und Erzbischofs von Salzburg Matthäus Lang Verhalten zur Reformation*, Erlangen, 1892.

AGRICULTURE, HEBREW: Palestine is praised in the Old Testament as a "land flowing with milk and honey"; and, indeed, with little labor it yielded what the inhabitants needed. Of cereals, wheat was and is the most important product; the Ammonite country appears to have been specially noted for it (II Chron. xxvii. 5). The best wheat to-day is that of the Hauran and Belka, and of the high table-land between Tabor and the Lake of Tiberias. Much wheat was raised by the Hebrews in the time of Solomon, and then and later it was one of the chief articles of export (I Kings v. 11; Ezek. xxvii. 17). Barley was equally common and in the earlier time was the chief material for bread (Judges vii. 13; II Kings iv. 42). With progress in culture and the settled life its use was limited to the poorer classes (John vi. 9, 13; Josephus, *War*, V. x. 2). To-day it is used for fodder only; it was also so used in the ancient time (I Kings iv. 28), and its value appears to have been about one-half that of wheat (II Kings vii. 1). There is no evidence in the Old Testament that beer was made from it. A third and less important cereal (Heb. *kussemeth;* LXX, *olyra*, Ex. ix. 32; Isa. xxviii. 25; Ezek. iv. 9; erroneously rendered "rye" in A. V.) was probably spelt. Rye and oats are not mentioned. The chief legume-bearing plants were beans (II Sam. xvii. 28; Ezek. iv. 9) and lentils (Gen. xxv. 34; II Sam. xvii. 28, xxiii. 11; Ezek. iv. 9). Both were ground into meal, and were used for bread in time of scarcity (Ezek. iv. 9). Leeks, onions, and garlic were used as seasoning and to give relish to bread. Cucum-

Field and Garden Products.

bers and melons are also mentioned as delicacies of which the Israelites were deprived in the wilderness (Num. xi. 5). Both are particularly refreshing in hot countries, and the poor live for months on bread and cucumbers or melons alone. Of condiments and spices the Old Testament mentions two varieties of cumin (Heb. *kammon*, *ḳeẓaḥ*, Isa. xxviii. 25; the former used also as medicine) and the coriander (Ex. xvi. 31; Num. xi. 7, often mentioned in the Talmud). The New Testament adds: dill (Eng. versions, "anise," Matt. xxiii. 23), mint (ib.; Luke xi. 42), rue (Luke xi. 42), and mustard (Matt. xiii. 31, xvii. 20; Mark iv. 31; Luke xiii. 19, xvii. 6). The mustard-seed was proverbial as the smallest of seeds. The mustard plant grows quickly and reaches a height of ten feet. To these food-producing plants must be added flax (Josh. ii. 6; Isa. xix. 9; Hos. ii. 5, 9, and elsewhere) and cotton. The former of these is not much cultivated to-day; but it was of great importance to the ancient Israelites, as, together with wool, it supplied the material for their clothing. In the Greco-Roman period it was one of the chief articles of trade. The importance of the flax-cultivation can be inferred from the statement of the Talmud, that it was permissible to put a flax-bed under water on semi-holy days in order to destroy injurious insects (*Mo'ed Ḳaṭan* i. 6). Linen-manufacture was carried on especially in Galilee. How early the cotton-plant was introduced into Palestine is not known. The Hebrew terms *shesh* and *buẓ* do not necessarily mean linen, but include cotton cloth, or a mixed material like the Greek *byssos*. The foreign word *karpas* (Gk. *karpasos*) is used for cotton in Esther i. 6 and in the Talmud. In Greco-Roman times cotton was grown and exported (cf. Pausanias, V. v. 2). For wine and oil see the separate articles.

Climatic Conditions.

Palestine is praised in Deut. viii. 7, xi. 10–11, as a "land of brooks of water, of fountains and depths that spring out of valleys and hills," which has no need of artificial irrigation because it "drinketh water of the rain of heaven." Compared with the neighboring countries, it can not, indeed, be called poorly watered. In normal years the natural precipitation suffices for a great part of the fields. Land thus naturally watered is called in the Mishnah "house of the Baal" or "field of the house of the Baal," and the name is kept to this day (cf. Smith, *Rel. of Sem.*, p. 97). But the ancient Israelites knew that watercourses and underground water were indispensable (cf. Ps. i.; Deut. viii. 7; Isa. xxxii. 20; Ezek. xvii. 8), and that the rain alone was not always sufficient; they therefore appreciated the pools made by the Canaanites and added to them (see WATER SUPPLY IN PALESTINE). For these favors of nature the Israelite ever felt his immediate dependence upon Yahveh (cf. Deut. xi. 14; Jer. iii. 3, v. 24; Joel ii. 23; Zech. x. 1). Yahveh's blessing shows itself in his sending the first rain and the latter rain in due season; in the rain his mercy is seen, in the drought his anger. Thus he proves himself indeed the Baal of the land, who waters and fertilizes it (cf. Smith, l.c.).

Cultivation.

The Israelites learned agriculture from the Canaanites. How rapidly they made the transition from the nomadic stage can not be determined; it seems to have been practically complete at the beginning of the regal period (cf. I Sam. xi. 5; II Sam. xiv. 30, which indicate that high and low were then engaged in the cultivation of the soil), although certain tribes of the south and the East-Jordan country retained more or less of the nomadic character till the Exile. That the religious observances, preeminently the great festivals, rest upon an agricultural basis is significant. Irrigation was not the only artificial improvement that was necessary. The land had to be cleared of thorns and weeds, and stones had to be removed (cf. Isa. v. 2; Matt. xiii. 3–7), although the fellahs to-day often allow the stones to remain because they help to retain moisture. Extensive terracing was indispensable to retain the thin soil on the steep hillsides. Manuring and burning were practised (Isa. v. 24, xxv. 10, xlvii. 14; Joel ii. 5; Ob. 18), but probably neither extensively nor annually. Dried dung is more valuable to-day as fuel, and it was so used in the ancient time (Ezek. iv. 15). The usual method of renewing the strength of the soil was fallowing (Ex. xxiii. 11, and elsewhere). The winter crops (wheat, barley, lentils, etc.) were sown as soon as the early rain had softened the ground—from the end of October to the beginning of December. The sowing of the summer crops (millet, vetches, etc.) followed, and lasted (in the case of cucumbers) till after the winter harvest. Well-watered fields bear two crops. The surface of the soil was scratched by a very primitive plow, drawn by oxen or cows (Judges xiv. 18; I Kings xix. 19; Job i. 14; Amos vi. 12), sometimes in light soils by an ass (Deut. xxii. 10; Isa. xxx. 24). The furrow to-day is from three to four inches deep. The driver's goad (Judges iii. 31) served also to break the clods. According to the usual assumption, the field which a yoke of oxen (Heb. *ẓemedh*) could plow in a day was the unit of land-measurement, as the present unit, the *feddān* (22–23 acres), represents a season's plowing. It is more probable, however, that they measured land by the amount of seed sown, as is done in the Talmud, and that *ẓemedh* is properly a measure of capacity and then designates a piece of ground of such size that it required a *ẓemedh* of seed. The surface was evened with an implement resembling a stone-boat or with a roller (Job xxxix. 10; Isa. xxviii. 24–25; Hos. x. 11). The seed was sown by hand; wheat, barley, and spelt were often carefully laid in the furrow. In the time of the Mishnah, as at present, it was plowed in. At present, seed is sown rather thinly. An estimate of the amount of land under cultivation in ancient times is impossible. Large tracts in Palestine can never have been used for anything but pasturage; the "deserts" were extensive, as their frequent mention shows; and there was more wooded land than now (Josh. xvii. 15, 18; II Kings ii. 24). These facts make it probable that the extent of cultivated land did not materially exceed that of to-day.

Harvest. In the Jordan valley the barley-harvest begins from the end of March to the first half of April; in the hill-country, on the coast, and in the highlands, from a week to a month later. The cutting of the barley opens, that of the wheat closes, the harvest season. Altogether it lasts about seven weeks and from of old it has been a time of joy and festivity (Ps. iv. 7; Isa. ix. 3). The Feast of the First-Fruits, on which, according to the Priest Code, a barley-sheaf was offered (Lev. xxiii. 9–14), ushered in this festive time; the Feast of Weeks, seven weeks after the opening of the harvest, when an offering of two wave-loaves of the new wheat (Lev. xxiii. 17–21) was made, closed it. The grain was cut with a sickle (Deut. xvi. 9, xxiii. 25; Job xxiv. 24; Jer. l. 16; Joel iii. 13). With the left hand the reaper grasped a bundle of ears (Isa. xvii. 5; Ps. cxxix. 7), and with the right he cut them fairly close to the head. The binder followed, gathering the cut grain into his arms (Ps. cxxix. 7) and making it into sheaves (Gen. xxxvii. 7; Lev. xxiii. 10; Deut. xxiv. 19; Ruth ii. 7; Ps. cxxvi. 6), which were then collected in stacks (Judges xv. 5; Ruth iii. 7; Job v. 26). The harvesters refreshed themselves during their toil by eating parched corn and bread dipped in a mixture of vinegar and water (Ruth ii. 14). According to old custom and the law, forgotten sheaves and the privilege of gleaning after the reapers belonged to the poor (Lev. xix. 9, xxiii. 22; Deut. xxiv. 19; Ruth ii. 2); the Priest Code provided also that the corners of the field were not to be wholly reaped (Lev. xix. 9, xxiii. 22). In like manner it was permissible to pluck ears from another's field to eat (Deut. xxiii. 25; Matt. xii. 1).

The reaping was immediately followed by the thrashing. Small quantities of grain, and dill, cumin, and the like, were beaten out with a flail (Judges vi. 11; Ruth ii. 17; Isa. xxviii. 27); but in most cases wheat, barley, and spelt were taken to the thrashing-floor, which, if possible, was placed on high ground so that the wind might carry off the chaff. The kernels were trodden out by cattle or were separated by means of a rude thrashing-sled or wagon (II Sam. xxiv. 22; Isa. xxviii. 27–28; Amos i. 3). Both custom and the law forbade the muzzling of an ox in treading out the grain (Deut. xxv. 4); and to-day it is commonly estimated that an ox will consume from three to four pecks of the grain daily during the thrashing-time. Winnowing was accomplished, with the help of the wind, by means of a shovel or a wooden fork having two or more tines (Isa. xxx. 24; Jer. xv. 7). The chaff is now used as fodder; according to Matt. iii. 12, it seems in ancient time to have been burned. The grain was sifted (Amos ix. 9) and shoveled into heaps. It was usually stored in cistern-like pits in the open field, carefully covered (Jer. xli. 8). Real barns are not mentioned till late times (Deut. xxviii. 8; II Chron. xxxii. 28; Jer. l. 26; Joel i. 17). In general, Palestine may be called a fertile land, but its productivity has been greatly overestimated. To-day the mountain-lands of Judea yield on an average from two- to threefold; the valleys of Hebron, with fertilization, from four- to fivefold; the very fertile Plain of Sharon, carefully cultivated by German colonists, eightfold for wheat and fifteenfold for barley. There is no reason to believe that the average return was greater in ancient times.

Laws. Some of the laws have already been mentioned. Of greater importance in their effect upon agriculture were the laws aiming to prevent the alienation of landed property. The ancestral field was sacred (cf. I Kings xxi. 3). This provision explains the law of Lev. xxv. 25, according to which, if an impoverished Israelite had to sell his field, his kinsman had the first right of purchase (cf. Jer. xxxii. 6–12). The law also gave the original owner a perpetual right of redemption, and restored the field to him in the year of jubilee without compensation to the purchaser; a city house could be redeemed only within a year, and did not return in the year of jubilee (Lev. xxv. 27–34). The underlying thought here is that the land is not the private property of the Israelites, but belongs to God, and the Israelites have only the right of use. It may be questioned how far such laws were carried out; they are closely connected with the year of jubilee (see below). The same desire to preserve family possessions shows itself in the law of inheritance. In ancient time daughters did not inherit; if there were no sons, property passed to the nearest relative of the father, with the obligation to marry the widow (cf. the Book of Ruth). The Priest Code allows daughters to inherit when there are no sons, but they must marry within the family or, at least, within the tribe of the father (Num. xxxvi.). Still more important in its effect upon agriculture was the development of the Sabbath idea. It was an old custom and a law of the Book of the Covenant that every field should lie fallow one year in seven (Ex. xxiii. 10–11). The custom fell into disuse and Deuteronomy knows nothing of it. But the Priest Code revived it, imposed it upon the entire land at the same year (cf. Josephus, *Ant.*, XII. ix. 5), and added the theoretic and impracticable year of jubilee (see SABBATICAL YEAR AND YEAR OF JUBILEE). Lastly, laws arising from ideas of ceremonial impurity must be mentioned, such as the prohibition of sowing unclean seed (Lev. xi. 37–38), of plowing with an ox and an ass together, and of sowing different kinds of seed in one field (Lev. xix. 19; Deut. xxii. 9–10). Of the age of these customs nothing is known. The Mishnah developed and added to these laws with great detail.

I. BENZINGER.

BIBLIOGRAPHY: J. L. Saalschütz, *Das mosäische Recht*, Berlin, 1853; E. Robinson, *Physical Geography of the Holy Land*, Boston, 1865; J. G. Wetzstein, in F. Delitzsch, *Commentar zu Jesaia*, pp. 389–599, 705–711, 2d ed., Leipsic, 1869 (treats of winnowing; neither in last ed. nor in Eng. transl.); idem, *Die syrische Dreschtafel*, in *Zeitschrift für Ethnologie*, v. (1873) 270–302; F. Hamilton, *La Botanique de la Bible*, Nice, 1871; H. B. Tristram, *Natural History of the Bible*, London, 1873; idem, *The Fauna and Flora of Palestine*, in *Survey of Western Palestine*, ib. 1884 (authoritative); J. Smith, *Bible Plants, their History and Identification*, ib. 1878; C. J. von Klinggräff, *Palästina und seine Vegetation*, in *Oesterreichische botanische Zeitschrift*, xxx., Vienna, 1880; W. M. Thomson, *The Land and the Book*, 2 vols., New York, 1880–82; I. Löw, *Aramäische Pflanzennamen*, Leipsic, 1881; E. Boissier, *Flora orientalis*, Geneva, 1884; J. H. Balfour, *The Plants of the Bible*, London, 1885; G. Anderlind, *Ackerbau und Tier-*

sucht in Syrien, insbesondere in Palästina, in *ZDPV*. ix. (1886) 1–73; S. Schumacher, *Der arabische Pflug*, ib. iv. (1881) 70–84, ix. (1886) 1–73, xii. (1889) 157–166; A. E. Knight, *Gleanings from Bible Lands . . Occupations of their Inhabitants*, London, 1891; V. Hehn, *Kulturpflanzen und Haustiere*, Berlin, 1894; H. Vogelstein, *Die Landwirtschaft in Palästina zur Zeit der Mischna*, ib. 1894; H. C. Trumbull, *Studies in Oriental Social Life*, Philadelphia, 1894; *DB*, i. 48–51; *EB*, i. 76–89; *JE*, i. 262–270; E. Day, *Social Life of the Hebrews*, New York, 1901 (a useful book, based largely on a study of the book of Judges). Consult also the works on antiquities and archeology by De Wette-Räbiger, Leipsic, 1864; H. Ewald, Göttingen, 1866, Eng. transl., London, 1876; C. F. Keil, Frankfort, 1875; Schegg-Wirthmüller, Freiburg, 1887; I. Benzinger, ib. 1894; W. Nowack, ib. 1894; and *PEF, Quarterly Reports*, particularly the earlier numbers.

AGRIPPA I. AND II., kings of Judea. See Herod and his Family.

AGRIPPA CASTOR: Christian author who lived in the time of Hadrian, and was perhaps an Egyptian. Eusebius (*Hist. eccl.*, iv. 7) speaks of him very highly. He wrote a refutation of the Gnostic Basilides, which, according to Eusebius, showed independent knowledge of the latter's teaching.

G. Krüger.

Bibliography: *MPG*, vi.; M. J. Routh, *Reliquiæ sacræ*, i. 85–90, Oxford, 1846.

AGRIPPA VON NETTESHEIM, net″tes″haim′, **HEINRICH CORNELIUS:** Scholar and adventurer; b. at Cologne, of noble family, Sept. 14, 1486; d. at Grenoble 1535. He studied at Cologne and Paris, and took part in some obscure enterprise in Spain (1507–08); lectured at the University of Dôle, in Franche-Comté, on Reuchlin's *De verbo mirifico* (1509), and aroused the opposition of certain monks; was sent to England on a political mission by the emperor (1510); returned to Cologne and lectured on *quæstiones quodlibetales*; served in the imperial army in Italy from 1511 to 1518, and during the same period went to the Council of Pisa as a theologian (1511), and lectured on medicine, jurisprudence, and Hermes Trismegistus in Pavia and Turin. He was appointed syndic at Metz in 1518, but had to flee from the Inquisition two years later. He entered the service of the Duke of Savoy, practised medicine at Freiburg (1523); became physician to the queen mother of France, but was expelled and fled to the Netherlands (1529); was appointed historiographer to Charles V. and lived for some years under the protection of Archbishop Hermann of Cologne, but finally returned to France, where he died. Of his two most celebrated works, the *De occulta philosophia* (written 1509–10; first printed, book i., Antwerp, 1531; books i.–iii., Cologne, 1533) is a compilation from the Neoplatonists and the Cabala and gives a plan of the world with an exposition of the "hidden powers" which the learning of the time thought it necessary to assume for the explanation of things; the other, *De incertitudine et vanitate scientiarum et artium* (written 1526; printed 1527), is a compilation from the Humanists and Reformers, and gives a skeptical criticism not only of all sciences, but of life itself. A collected edition of Agrippa's works was published at Lyons in 1600.

Bibliography: H. Morley, *The Life of Henry Cornelius Agrippa von Nettesheim*, 2 vols., London, 1856.

AGUIRRE, ā-gîr′re, **JOSEPH SAENZ**, sānz, **DE:** Spanish cardinal; b. at Logroño (60 m. e. of Burgos), Spain, Mar. 24, 1630; d. in Rome Aug. 16, 1699. At an early age he entered the Benedictine order, and became abbot of St. Vincent at Salamanca, and in 1666 professor of theology in the university there; he was also a consultor of the Spanish Inquisition, and ultimately superior-general of the Spanish congregation of his order. In 1686 Innocent XI. made him cardinal as a reward for upholding the papal authority against Gallicanism in his *Defensio cathedræ S. Petri adversus declarationem cleri Gallicani anni 1682* (Salamanca, 1683). The most important of his numerous theological and philosophical writings are his *Collectio maxima conciliorum omnium Hispaniæ et novi orbis* (4 vols., Rome, 1693; new ed. by Catalani, 6 vols., 1753) and his unfinished *Theologia S. Anselmi* (3 vols., 1679–85; 2d ed., 1688–90).

(A. Hauck.)

Bibliography: H. Hurter, *Nomenclator literarius recentioris theologiæ catholicæ*, ii. 521–552, Innsbruck, 1893.

AGUR. See Proverbs.

AHAB, ē′hab: Seventh king of Israel; son and successor of Omri. His dates are variously given—918–897 B.C., according to the older chronology; 878–857, Kamphausen; 875–853, Duncker; 874–854, Hommel; d. about 851, Wellhausen. His history in I Kings xvi. 28–xxii. 40, is based upon two main sources, from which long extracts are given; the one, which furnished the account of the wars with the Arameans (ch. xx. and xxii.), may be described as a popular history of the kings of the northern realm and their wars; the other, from which the Elijah narratives are taken, evidently originated in prophetic circles. Both were of the ninth century and of Ephraimitic origin. The Monolith Inscription of Shalmaneser II. of Assyria (see Assyria, VI., § 8) states that in the army defeated by Shalmaneser at Karkar (854 B.C.) were 10,000 men and 2,000 chariots furnished by *Akhabbu Sir'laai*, by whom in all probability Ahab of Israel is meant (for another view, cf. Kittel, 233–234; Kamphausen, 43, note). The Moabite Stone (q.v.) also states that the subjection of Moab to Israel, established by Omri, lasted for "half of his son's days." Ahab's reign was a time of prosperity. The long war with Judah was ended, and Ahab's daughter Athaliah was married to Jehoram, Jehoshaphat's son. A marriage alliance was also made with the Phenicians, Ahab taking to wife Jezebel, daughter of Ethbaal of Tyre. The Moabites remained subject to Israel and paid a considerable tribute (II Kings iii. 4). Jericho was rebuilt, and other cities were fortified or built. Ahab erected a palace at Jezreel (probably the "ivory house" of I Kings xxii. 39). In later years he had to fight with the Arameans of Damascus, who laid siege to Samaria, but were defeated and driven off. In the following year both armies met at Aphek in the plain of Jezreel, and Ben-hadad, the Syrian king, was captured and magnanimously treated by Ahab; with the promise to give up the conquests of his father and to allow Ahab's merchants to have bazaars in Damascus, he was set free. After three years Ahab undertook a new war against Damascus to capture Ramoth-gilead, which probably was to have been delivered to Israel after the covenant at Aphek. This time he had the help of Jehoshaphat of Judah, whose son may have married Ahab's daughter at this time. The battle was lost and Ahab was mortally wounded.

Ahab's reign is of great importance in the religious development of Israel, and is marked by a bitter contest between the throne and the prophets. That Ahab had no intention of apostatizing from Yahweh, the god of his people, is shown by the names he gave his children; but to rule righteously, according to the conception of the prophets, did not suit his policy. He tolerated the calf-worship instituted by Jeroboam (I Kings xii. 26–33), and, influenced by his Phenician wife, introduced into Samaria the worship of the Syrian Baal (Melkarth), for whom he built in his capital a great temple with all the necessary paraphernalia. No doubt certain circles in Israel were shocked by this heathen worship; but the great majority saw in it no inconsistency with the Mosaic religion. It fell to Elijah to rebuke the people for "halting between two opinions"; but his voice, like that of other prophets who protested, had little effect. Jezebel tried to silence them by bloody persecutions; and Elijah complained that he was the only prophet of Yahweh left. It must not be imagined, however, that all so-called prophets of Yahveh had been killed; for Ahab, who still regarded himself as a worshiper of Yahweh, would hardly have permitted such an act. Those who did not oppose the worship of Baal were doubtless left alone; but in the eyes of Elijah they were not much better than the prophets of Baal. After the event on Mount Carmel (I Kings xviii.) Jezebel saw the futility of trying to suppress the opposition to the worship of Baal, and the prophets who had kept in hiding could come and go freely. Ahab and his wife were also denounced by Elijah for the crime committed against Naboth and his family, which led to signs of contrition on the king's part and to a postponement to his son's days of the threatened retribution (I Kings xxi.; cf. II Kings ix. 21–26). Ahab's character and achievements are differently estimated. He was undoubtedly an able man, and desired to promote the welfare of his people; he was a brave warrior, and died manfully. But in the estimation of many these virtues are outweighed by his weakness toward Jezebel, his short-sighted optimism after the victory at Aphek, and his lack of deep religious conviction and earnestness. (W LOTZ.)

BIBLIOGRAPHY: On the chronology: A. Kamphausen, *Chronologie der hebräischen Könige*, Bonn, 1883; *Chronology of the Kings of Israel and Judah compared with the Monuments*, in *Church Quarterly Review*, Jan., 1886; E. Mahler, *Biblische Chronologie und Zeitrechnung der Hebräer*, Vienna, 1887; *DB*, i. 397–403; *EB*, i. 773–819; and sections on chronology in the following named works. On the history: H. Ewald, *Geschichte des Volkes Israel*, 7 vols., Gottingen, 1864–68 (Eng. transl., 8 vols., London, 1867–83); M. Duncker, *Geschichte des Alterthums*, ii., Leipsic, 1878; B. Stade, *Geschichte des Volkes Israel*, 2 vols., Berlin, 1884–89; E. Renan, *Histoire du peuple Israel*, 5 vols., Paris, 1887–94, Eng. transl., London, 1888–91; R. Kittel, *Geschichte der Hebräer*, 2 vols., Gotha, 1888–92, Eng. transl., 2 vols., London, 1895–96; H. Graetz, *Geschichte der Juden*, 11 vols., Leipsic, 1888–1900, Eng. transl., 6 vols., London, 1891; G. Rawlinson, *Kings of Israel and Judah*, London, 1889; Smith, *OTJC*; idem, *Prophets*; H. Winckler, *Geschichte Israels*, 2 vols., Leipsic, 1895–1900; C. F. Kent, *History of the Hebrew People*, 2 vols., New York, 1896–97; idem, *Students' Old Testament*, ii., ib. 1904; J. Wellhausen, *Israelitische und jüdische Geschichte*, Berlin, 1897; idem, *Prolegomena zur Geschichte Israels*, Berlin, 1899 (in Eng., *Prolegomena to the History of Israel, with a reprint of the article 'Israel' from the "Encyclopædia Britannica,"* Edinburgh, 1885); C. H. Cornill, *Geschichte des Volkes Israel*, Leipsic, 1898, Eng. transl., Chicago, 1898; *DB*, ii. 506–518; *EB*, ii. 2217–89; H. P. Smith, *Old Testament History*, New York, 1903. Further material is to be found in the commentaries on the Books of Kings and Chronicles. On indications from the monuments: Schrader, *KB*, 6 vols., Berlin, 1889–1901; idem, *KAT*, 3d ed., by H. Zimmern and H. Winckler, 2 vols., Berlin, 1903, Eng. transl. of 1st ed., London, 1885–88; H. Winckler, *Altorientalische Forschungen*, i.–vi., Leipsic, 1893–97 (new series, 3 vols., 1898–1901; 3d series, 2 vols., 1901–05); A. H. Sayce, *'Higher Criticism' and the Monuments*, London, 1894; J. F. McCurdy, *History, Prophecy and the Monuments*, 2 vols., New York, 1894–1901; W. St. C. Boscawen, *The Bible and the Monuments*, London, 1895; S. R. Driver, in D. G. Hogarth, *Authority and Archæology*, London, 1899.

AHASUERUS, a-haz'yu-î'rus: A name given in the Old Testament to two kings. **1.** The father of Darius the Mede (Dan. ix. 1). Since Darius is mentioned before Cyrus, he can be no other than Astyages, and Ahasuerus would then be Cyaxares. Phonetically the name is just as little connected as Cyaxares with the name which that king has in the Persian cuneiform inscriptions, and which must probably be read *Huvakhshtra*. It is also often found that the Median and Persian kings are differently named in the sources, a difference which is to be explained by the fact that after their accession to the throne they took new names. In Tob. xiv. 15 "Asueros" is Astyages, since he is mentioned as the conqueror of Nineveh beside Nebuchadnezzar.

2. A king mentioned in the book of Esther, the Khshayarsha of the Persian inscriptions and the Xerxes of the Greeks, who ruled from 485 to 465 B.C., and was the son of Darius Hystaspes. This is indicated by the identity of the name and the agreement in character as that is given by Herodotus. With this agrees also the mention of Shushan (Susa) as his residence, and the statement in Esther i. that the kingdom extended from India to Ethiopia—a statement which is confirmed by the enumeration of the provinces of the Persian empire in the epitaph of Darius at Nakshi Rustem, which, however, would not suit the time before Darius. With Xerxes, not with Cambyses, the Ahasuerus of Ezra iv. 6 is no doubt identical, to whom the Samaritans presented a bill of indictment against the exiles who returned to Jerusalem.

(B. LINDNER.)

BIBLIOGRAPHY: T. Benfey, *Die persischen Keilinschriften*, Leipsic, 1847; F. Spiegel, *Eranische Alterthumskunde*, 3 vols., ib. 1871–78; Schrader, *KAT*; A. H. Sayce, *Higher Criticism and the Monuments*, pp. 543 sqq., London, 1894; W. St. C. Boscawen, *The Bible and the Monuments*, ib. 1895.

AHAUS, a''hauz', **HEINRICH VON** (**Hendrik van Ahuis**): Founder of the Brethren of the Common Life in Germany; b. in the principality of Ahaus, near Münster, 1370; d. in Münster 1439. He was descended from a noble family whose ancestors dated back to the ninth century, and who took their name from their territories on the River Aa. In 1396 he took religious orders and, influenced by his aunt, formerly abbess of Vreden in

Gelderland, then a member of the Sisterhood of the Common Life at Deventer, affiliated himself with the followers of the new teaching in that town. He remained at Deventer probably till the year 1400, living in close association with the companions and successors of Groote, the founder of the fraternity, such as Florentius Radewyns, Brinckerink, Gerhard Zerbolt, and Thomas a Kempis. Having mastered the principles and the organization of the Brethren, and imbued with their zeal, he returned to Westphalia and in the year of his arrival founded a brotherhood at Münster. The death of his father left him with ample means with which he erected a house for the accommodation of the Brethren. Later he ceded to them his magnificent residence and estate at Springbrunnen, which became the seat of the general chapter of the fraternity. Living without vows or written regulations, and given up to the practise of the humble Christian virtues, the Brethren, nevertheless, met with opposition from many of the clergy and laity. The former looked askance at their close intermingling of the ascetic and spiritual with the secular life, and resented the influence which they speedily began to exert in the field of education, while the citizens of Münster regarded the activity of the fraternity in the production of beautiful books, which constituted the chief source of their livelihood, as unwelcome competition. The Dominicans were the most zealous of their opponents and at the instance of one of that order, Matthæus Grabow, complaint against the Brethren was lodged with the Council of Constance. Owing to the intercession of Gerson and Pierre d'Ailly, however, they obtained a complete vindication (1418), and the persecution served only to hasten the rapid spread of their influence. Ahaus was one of the representatives sent to Constance to defend the cause of the brotherhood.

In 1416 Ahaus established at Cologne the second great house of the fraternity; and in 1428 a union was effected between the chapters of Cologne and Münster whereby the two houses were constituted practically one body. In 1441 this union was joined by the chapter of Wesel in Cleves, which had been founded by Ahaus in 1435. To the end of his life Ahaus busied himself with the erection of new chapters and the active supervision of the established houses; and, in addition to the three great chapters mentioned, many smaller foundations were established in the dioceses of Münster and Osnabrück. Communities of Sisters of the Common Life also were established at Emmerich, Herford, Hildesheim, and other places, aside from the mother house at Münster, with the foundation of which Ahaus was not connected. The labors of Ahaus exercised a beneficent influence upon the condition of the Church in Germany. The standard of learning among the clergy was raised, and monasticism was purified of many of its evils, while its ideals of a spiritual life received wide extension through the founding of secular communities. The Brethren were also influential in the establishment of schools, in the diffusion of literature both in manuscript and in printed form, and in the extension of the use of the vernacular for religious purposes.

L. Schulze.

Bibliography: L. Schulze, *Heinrich von Ahaus*, in *ZKW*, iii., 1882.

AHAZ, ē'haz: Eleventh king of Judah, son and successor of Jotham. He ruled, according to the older computation, 742–727 B.C.; according to Köhler, 739–724; according to Kamphausen, 734–715; according to Hommel, 734–728. The most important political event of his reign was the subjugation of Judah to Assyria as a result of the Arameo- (Syro-) Ephraimitic war. Pekah, king of Israel, and Rezin of Damascus had conspired against Judah before the death of Jotham (II Kings xv. 37), but war was not actively carried on until after the accession of Ahaz. The latter could not maintain himself in the field and retired to the fortified Jerusalem. According to the Chronicler, he was defeated in pitched battle at some stage of the war. Rezin captured Elath on the Red Sea, which had been in possession of Judah since the days of Amaziah and Uzziah (Azariah, II Kings xiv. 7, 22), and restored it to the Edomites (xvi. 6, where the reading should be "Edomites" instead of "Syrians"), perhaps in return for help in the war (cf. II Chron. xxviii. 17). Judea was laid waste and partly depopulated (cf. Isa. i. 5–9). Ahaz in his need applied for help to Tiglath-pileser II. of Assyria, who forced the enemies of the Judean king to retire; but, as the price of this deliverance, Judah became an Assyrian vassal state, the king's treasure and the treasure of the Temple being carried to Nineveh, and a yearly tribute imposed. Few kings of Judah are represented as having so little inclination to the true Yahveh-religion as Ahaz. He sacrificed "on the hills, and under every green tree," and set up molten images of the Baalim. In a time of great distress he even offered his son to Molech in the Valley of Hinnom; and it may be inferred from II. Kings xxiii. 11–12 that, under Assyrian influence, he built altars for the worship of the heavenly bodies in the vicinity of the Temple. The religious and moral deterioration of the people under Ahaz is the frequent theme of Isaiah's prophecy. (W Lotz.)

It is now generally held that the reign of Ahaz extended from 735 to 719 B.C. The dates are important not merely as fixing the time of the accession of Hezekiah with his change of policy toward Assyria, but also their correlation with other events. Thus Ahaz is seen to have survived the fall of Samaria (722 B.C.) and the Assyrian expedition against Ashdod (720 B.C.) with its consequences to Judah (cf. Isa. xx.). J. F. M.

Bibliography: Consult the works mentioned under Ahab, and C. P. Caspari, *Ueber den Syrisch-ephraimitischen Krieg unter Jotham und Ahas*, Christiania, 1849.

AHAZIAH, ē"ha-zai'ā: 1. Eighth king of Israel, son and successor of Ahab. He reigned about two years (856–855 B.C., according to Kamphausen; for other views, see the dates given for the close of his father's reign in the article Ahab). Little is known of his reign. Doubtless he ended the war with Ben-hadad (see Ahab) by treaty. After Ahab's death, the Moabites rebelled successfully; but Ahaziah seems to have undertaken no war against them. He had the misfortune to fall from a window and received serious injury; being a worshiper of Baal, he sent to Ekron to seek counsel from Baal-zebub; and his messengers were met on the way by Elijah, who foretold a fatal issue of his sickness as a punishment for sending to Baal. His history is found in I Kings xxii. 49—II Kings 1. (W Lotz.)

The death of Ahab and accession of Ahaziah of Israel fell in 853 B.C. (see Ahab), as is now generally agreed. Jehu acceded in 842 B.C., for in that year he paid homage to Shalmaneser II. according to the statement of the latter on his Black Obelisk. But Joram, who comes between Ahaziah and Jehu, reigned "twelve years" (II Kings iii. 1). This term seems to fill up the whole time between 853 and 842, inclusive. Accordingly the sickness of Ahaziah and active regency of Joram began just after the accession of the former, whose very brief reign could have had no significance whatever. J. F M.

2. Sixth king of Judah, son of Jehoram. He reigned one year (884 B.C., according to the older computation; 843, according to Kamphausen; 842, according to Hommel). He married a daughter of Ahab, and it is therefore not surprising that he was a Baal-worshiper. His relation with the house of Omri caused his early death. He joined his brother-in-law, Joram of Israel, in a campaign against Hazael of Damascus, and the two allies attacked Ramoth-gilead. Joram was wounded and returned to Jezreel, whither Ahaziah went to visit him, and there he fell into the hands of Jehu, who killed him as a member of the house of Omri. The accounts of his death in Kings and Chronicles can not be reconciled. His history is found in II Kings viii. 25–ix. 29; II Chron. xxii. 1–9. (W. Lotz.)

Bibliography: Consult the works mentioned under Ahab.

AHIJAH, a-hai'jā: A prophet, living at Shiloh, mentioned in I Kings xi. 29–39, xii. 15, xiv. 1–18; II Chron. ix. 29, x. 15. All these passages in the Book of Kings are Deuteronomic, or at least have been worked over by a Deuteronomic editor. In the latter part of Solomon's reign Ahijah seems to have enjoyed great authority as Yahweh's prophet. Next to Samuel and Elisha he is the most striking example of the fact that the prophets of Israel, besides promoting the religious life, meddled with political affairs. He gave voice to the deep dissatisfaction which all true Yahweh-worshipers felt in the latter part of Solomon's reign, and foretold to Jeroboam that he would become king over ten tribes. Years later, when Ahijah was an old man, dim of eyesight, Jeroboam sent his wife to the prophet in disguise to obtain help, if possible, in the severe sickness of his son. Again the prophet declared the misfortune to be the consequence of unfaithfulness to Yahweh; he foretold the death of the prince and the extinction of the house of Jeroboam. The Chronicler, according to his custom, made Ahijah also a historian of his time.

(R. Kittel.)

AHIMELECH, a-him'e-lec: High priest at the tabernacle in Nob. He gave the showbread and Goliath's sword to David, not knowing that the latter was fleeing from Saul, and for this reason he, together with the entire priestly family of eighty-five persons (LXX, thirty-five) and the whole city of Nob, was slain by Doeg the Edomite at Saul's command (I Sam. xxi.–xxii.). Only his son Abiathar escaped and went to David. Ahimelech is called the son of Ahitub (I Sam. xxii. 9, 20), and was therefore great-grandson of Eli and a descendant of Ithamar. "Ahiah" (I Sam. xiv. 3) is probably another name for Ahimelech; if not, Ahiah must have been an older brother of the latter who officiated before him, or possibly the father of Ahimelech, who, in this case, should be called the grandson of Ahitub. Abiathar served David as priest during the latter's exile (I Sam. xxii. 20–23, xxiii. 6–12, xxx. 7–8) and throughout his reign, although Zadok of another priestly line is always mentioned first (II Sam. xv. 24, xvii. 15, xix. 11, xx. 25). He was deposed by Solomon for having favored the succession of Adonijah (I Kings ii. 26–27, 35).

C. von Orelli.

AHITHOPHEL, a-hith'o-fel: A counselor of David. He is called "the Gilonite," i.e., from Giloh, a city in the south of Judah (II Sam. xv. 12). David esteemed him highly for his great wisdom (II Sam. xvi. 23). When Absalom revolted, Ahithophel faithlessly betrayed David in the expectation that the rebellion would be successful (II Sam. xv. 12, 31, xvi. 21, xvii. 1 sqq.). He soon perceived, however, that his authority was not paramount with the young prince; and when the latter rejected his advice to attack David at once, he went home and hanged himself (II Sam. xvii. 23). Some think that Ps. xli. 9, lv. 12 sqq. have reference to David's sad experience with Ahithophel. Eliam, a son of Ahithophel, was one of David's heroes (II Sam. xxiii. 34); it is hardly possible that he was the Eliam mentioned as the father of Bath-sheba (II Sam. xi. 3). C. von Orelli.

AHLFELD, āl'feld, **JOHANN FRIEDRICH**: Lutheran; b. at Mehringen (in the Harz, near Bernburg, 25 m. n.n.w. of Halle), Anhalt, Nov. 1, 1810; d. at Leipsic Mar. 4, 1884. His father was a carpenter, and he owed some of his later power to the fact that he was brought up with an intimate knowledge of the nature and needs of the mass of the people. From 1830 to 1833 he studied at Halle. For a year he was a private tutor, and then he taught in the gymnasium at Zerbst. His preaching at this time was influenced by rationalism. At the beginning of 1837 he was appointed rector of the boys' school at Wörlitz; and here he came under the influence of Schubring, a man of simple faith, and his views changed. In 1838 he became pastor of Alsleben, on the Saale, a village of sailors where he worked hard and exercised a powerful influence, finding time, however, for literary work, and vigorously defending the old-fashioned faith against rationalism. He was called to Halle in 1847 through Tholuck's endeavors, and did his duty nobly in the troublous times of the Revolution and of the cholera epidemic of 1849. He took positions of more and more prominence, and in 1850 was chosen pastor of St. Nicholas's Church in Leipsic. In 1881 he retired from active work.

As a preacher Ahlfeld gained and maintained a remarkable popularity. Abstract speculation was not his strong point. He was at home in the concrete, and knew how to narrate with great effect stories from Holy Scripture, from the history of the Church, and from his own or others' experience. Besides preaching, he taught in the Leipsic Theological Seminary, and for many years did good service on the commission appointed to revise Luther's version of the Old Testament. He left a lasting memorial of his labors in more than one charitable foundation with whose origin he had much to do. Of the numerous collections of his discourses may be mentioned: *Predigten über die evangelischen Perikopen* (Halle, 1848; 12th ed., 1892); *Das Leben im Lichte des Wortes Gottes* (1861; 7th ed., 1886); *Predigten über die epistolischen Perikopen* (1867; 5th ed., 1899); *Confirmationsreden* (2 series, Leipsic, 1880). (A. HAUCK.)

BIBLIOGRAPHY: *Friedrich Ahlfeld, weiland Pastor zu St. Nikolai in Leipzig; ein Lebensbild*, Halle, 1885.

AICHSPALT, aik'spält **(AICHSPALTER, ASPELT):** A common designation (from his birthplace, Aspelt, near Luxembourg) for Peter, archbishop of Mainz (1306–20); b. between 1240 and 1250; d. at Mainz June 4, 1320. He is an important figure in the politics and history of his time, but of less interest for religion or theology. Of humble origin, he was ambitious and adroit, and sought his advancement with skill and success. A knowledge of medicine helped him to win the favor of princes and popes. He was chancellor to Wenceslaus II., king of Bohemia (1296-1305), and during this time quarreled with Albert of Austria and thenceforth was an opponent of the house of Hapsburg. He promoted the election of Henry of Luxembourg as emperor in 1308, and under him was all-powerful in German affairs. He was made bishop of Basel in 1296, archbishop of Mainz in 1306, and proved himself efficient and praiseworthy in his diocese.

BIBLIOGRAPHY: J. Heidemann, *Peter von Aspelt als Kirchenfürst und Staatsmann*, Berlin, 1875.

AIDAN, ai'dan, **SAINT:** First bishop of Lindisfarne; d. at Bamborough (on the coast of Northumberland, 16 m. s.e. of Berwick) Aug. 31, 651. When Oswald, king of Northumbria (634–642), wished to introduce Christianity into his dominions (see OSWALD, SAINT; CELTIC CHURCH IN BRITAIN AND IRELAND), he applied to Seghine, abbot of Iona, for missionaries, and a certain Corman was sent, who soon returned, declaring it was impossible to Christianize so rude a people. Aidan, then a monk of Iona, suggested that Corman had failed to adapt his teaching to their needs and had expected too much, forgetting the Apostle's injunction of "milk for babes." Whereupon Aidan was at once ordained and sent to Oswald in Corman's place (635). He established himself on the island of Lindisfarne, near Bamborough, brought fellow workers from Ireland, and founded a school of twelve English boys to provide future priests. Consistently exemplifying in his daily life the doctrines he taught, he gained great influence with Oswald and, after his death, with Oswin, king of Deira, while the people were won by his mildness, humility, and benevolence. He could not preach in the Saxon language at first and Oswald acted as interpreter. His work in Northumbria was continued by Finan (q.v.). All information about Aidan comes from Bede (*Hist. eccl.*, iii. 3, 5–17, 26), who praises him and tells marvelous stories about him.

BIBLIOGRAPHY: J. H. A. Ebrard, *Die iroschottische Missionskirche*, Gütersloh, 1873; A. C. Fryer, *Aidan, the Apostle of the North*, London, 1884; J. B. Lightfoot, *Leaders in the Northern Church*, ib. 1890; W. Bright, *Early English Church History*, 153–168, 188–189, Oxford, 1897.

AIKEN, CHARLES AUGUSTUS: American Presbyterian; b. at Manchester, Vt., Oct. 30, 1827; d. at Princeton, N. J., Jan. 14, 1892. He was graduated from Dartmouth College in 1846 and from Andover Theological Seminary in 1853; entered the Congregational ministry, and became pastor at Yarmouth, Me., 1854; became professor of Latin in Dartmouth 1859; in Princeton 1866, president of Union College 1869, professor of ethics and apologetics in Princeton Theological Seminary 1871; was transferred to the chair of Oriental and Old Testament literature 1882. He was a member of the Old Testament revision company, and translated Zöckler's commentary on Proverbs in the Lange series (New York, 1869).

AILLY, PIERRE D', pyär d'ä"lyi' (Lat. *Petrus de Alliaco*): Chancellor of the University of Paris, later bishop of Cambrai and cardinal, one of the distinguished churchmen who sought to restore unity to the divided Church during the great papal schism (1378–1429; see SCHISM) by means of a general council; b., probably at Ailly-le-haut-clocher (20 m. n.w. of Amiens), in the present department of Somme, 1350; d. at Avignon Aug. 9, 1420. He was brought up in Compiègne in the midst of the desolation caused by the war with England and an insurrection of the peasants (the Jacquerie); to this was no doubt in part due the strong national feeling and the prejudice against England which he showed later. He entered the University of Paris as a student of theology in the College of Navarre in 1372, and began to lecture on Peter Lombard in 1375. His lectures (printed as *Quæstiones super libros sententiarum*, Strasburg, 1490), gained for him the reputation of a clear thinker, and helped to make the nominalism of Occam predominant in the university. He also distinguished himself as a preacher.

On Apr. 11, 1380, Ailly was made doctor of theology and professor. His treatise on this occasion, and other essays written about the same time (published as appendix to the *Quæstiones;* also in *Gersonii opera*, ed. Du Pin, i. 603 sqq., Antwerp, 1706), show his position concerning the doctrine of the Church, which was brought to the front by the schism. The Christian Church, he said, is founded on the living Christ, not on the erring Peter, on the Bible, not on the canon law. The existing evils can be cured by a general council. Against those who opposed this idea of a council he wrote in 1381 a satirical epistle "from the devil to his prelates" (text in Tschackert, Appendix, pp. 15 sqq.). In 1384 he became director of the College of Navarre, where he had among his pupils Jean Gerson, who became his faithful friend. In 1389 Ailly was made chancellor of the university and almoner of Charles VI. of France, a position which brought him in close relation with the court at Paris. When the Avignonese pope, Clement VII., died (1394), Ailly's influence secured the recognition by France of his successor, the Spaniard Peter de Luna (Benedict XIII.). As a reward Benedict made Ailly bishop of Puy (1395), and two years later bishop of Cambrai. In 1398 Charles VI. of France and Wenceslaus of Germany sent him upon unsuccessful missions to both Boniface IX. and Benedict, to try to induce them to resign their office. Benedict was then kept a prisoner in Avignon by French troops till he escaped to Spain (1403). In 1398 and again in 1408 France withdrew its obedience from Benedict, without, however, declaring for his rival. The attempt to nationalize the French Church failed because the civil authorities of the time conducted Church affairs worse than the pope. In 1408 Ailly finally abandoned the cause of Benedict. The addition of a new element of discord by the choice of a third pope at the Council of Pisa (q.v.) in June, 1409, was not in accord with Ailly's wishes; but in the main he stood by the council (cf. his *Apologia concilii Pisani*, in Tschackert, pp. 31 sqq.), though he continued to write in favor of reform by another council. John XXIII. (the Roman pope) sought to conciliate him by an appointment (June 7, 1411) as cardinal, with the title *Cardinalis Sancti Chrysogoni*, though he himself preferred to be called "the Cardinal of Cambrai." He attended the council called in Rome by John in 1412, where he interested himself in a reform of the calendar. In 1413 he traveled through Germany and the Netherlands as papal legate, and at the same time was active as a writer.

Ailly's most important services in church history, however, were rendered at the Council of Constance (met Nov. 5, 1414; see CONSTANCE, COUNCIL OF). Here he maintained the superiority of a general council over the pope, but at the same time defended the privileges of the college of cardinals against the council. It was due to Gerson and Ailly that after the flight of John XXIII. from Constance (Mar. 20, 1415), the council was not adjourned. He had the courage to preside over the first popeless session (Mar. 26, 1415), and to carry out the order of business of that important gathering. The council had to decide three points: (1) The *causa unionis* (abolition of the schism); (2) the *causa reformationis* (reformation of the Church *in capite et in membris*); and (3) *causa fidei* (the case of John Huss). Ailly was very active in the last two. As president of the commission on faith, he examined Huss (June 7 and 8, 1415; *Documenta J. Hus.*, ed. F Palacky, Prague, 1869, pp. 273 sqq.), and was present at his condemnation (July 6). He expressed his ideas on reform, as deputy of the college of cardinals, in the commission on reform and in a writing of Nov., 1416, *De reformatione ecclesiæ* (in H. von der Hardt, *Magnum œcumenicum Constantiense concilium*, i., part viii., Frankfort, 1700). His views on the power of the Church he had already published (October) in his *De potestate ecclesiæ*. When, in November, the council proceeded to the choice of a new pope, Ailly was a candidate; but the opposition of the English prevented his election. He lived on good terms with his successful competitor, Otto di Colonna, and as his legate at Avignon continued influential in the French Church till his death. Ailly was always faithful to the interests of his country, although he was more churchman than Frenchman. He influenced the young Luther by his doubts concerning the doctrine of transubstantiation (cf. Luther's *De captivitate Babylonica*, Erlangen ed., *var. arg.*, v. 29). In 1410 he wrote a geographical work *Imago mundi* (n.p., n.d.), which has interest as having been one of the sources from which Columbus drew his belief in the possibility of a western passage to India (cf. Tschackert, 334 sqq.).

PAUL TSCHACKERT.

BIBLIOGRAPHY: P. Tschackert, *Peter von Ailli*, Gotha, 1877 (gives bibliography of Ailly's works, pp. 348-366); L. Salembier, *Petrus de Alliaco*, Lille, 1886 (also gives bibliography of his works, pp. 2 sqq.); C. Erler, *Dietrich von Nieheim*, Leipsic, 1887; H. Finke, *Forschungen und Quellen zur Geschichte des Konstanzer Konzils*, pp. 103-132, Paderborn, 1889 (gives the diary of Ailly's colleague, Cardinal Fillastre, pp. 163 sqq.); B. Bess, *Zur Geschichte des Konstanzer Konzils*, vol. i., Marburg, 1891.

AILRED, ēl′red (**ÆLRED, ETHELRED**): Abbot of the Cistercian abbey of Rievaulx in England (20 m. n. of York); b. at Hexham (20 m. w. of Newcastle-upon-Tyne), probably in 1109; d. at Rievaulx Jan. 12, 1166. He spent his youth at the court of Scotland, entered the abbey of Rievaulx in 1131, became abbot of Revesby, Lincolnshire and returned to Rievaulx as abbot in 1146. H wrote historical and theological works, the former of which include lives of St. Edward the Confessor and St. Ninian, while among the latter are: *Sermones; Speculum charitatis; De spirituali amicitia; De duodecimo anno Christi; Regula sive institutio inclusarum;* and *De natura animæ*. All of his printed works, with life by an anonymous author, are in *MPL*, cxcv.

BIBLIOGRAPHY: Thos. Wright, *Biographia Britannica literaria*, ii. 187-196, London, 1846; J. H. Newman, *Lives of the English Saints*, 2 vols., ib. 1845-46; A. P. Forbes, in *Lives of St. Ninian, St. Kentigern, St. Columba*, Introduction, ib. 1875; *Ethelred*, in *DNB*, xviii. 33 35 (contains list of his writings).

AIMOIN, ē″mwān′: The name of two French monks, both known as historians.

1. **Aimoin of St. Germain**: Teacher in the monastery school of Saint-Germain-des-Prés near Paris. He seems to have begun his literary career about 865, and to have died at the end of the ninth century or in the beginning of the tenth. His works, all of a hagiographical nature, are in *MPL*, cxxvi. 1009-56.

2. **Aimoin of Fleury**: A disciple of Abbo of Fleury (q.v.), at whose suggestion, and therefore not later than 1004, he wrote a *Historia Francorum*, from their origin to the time of Clovis II. (d. 657). His life of Abbo has greater historical value; and his account of the translation of the relics of St. Benedict to Fleury contains numerous data for French history of the tenth century. His works are in *MPL*, cxxxix. 375-414, 617-870; and there are extracts in *MGH*, *Script.*, ix. (1851) 374-376.

(A. HAUCK.)

BIBLIOGRAPHY: (1) A. Ebert, *Geschichte der Litteratur des Mittelalters*, ii. 352-355; W Wattenbach, *DGQ*, i. (1904) 330. (2) W. Wattenbach, ut sup., pp. 121, 466-470.

AINGER, ALFRED: Church of England; b. at London Feb. 9, 1837; d. there Feb. 8, 1904. He was educated at King's College, London, and Trinity Hall, Cambridge (B.A., 1860), and was ordered deacon in 1860 and priested in the following year. He was successively curate of Alrewas, Staffordshire, in 1860–64, assistant master of Sheffield College School in 1864–66, and reader at the Temple Church, London, in 1866–93. From 1894 until his death he was Master of the Temple. He was likewise made canon of Bristol in 1887, and was elected honorary fellow of Trinity Hall in 1898, being also select preacher at Oxford in 1891 and 1898, as well as honorary chaplain to the queen in 1895–96 and chaplain in ordinary to the king after the latter year. In addition to a number of monographs on English authors, and besides contributions to the *Dictionary of National Biography*, he wrote *Sermons preached in the Temple Church* (London, 1870). He is best known for his biography of Charles Lamb (London, 1882) and his editions of Lamb's works (1883 sqq.). His genial humor and whimsical temperament peculiarly fitted him to be the editor of Lamb, and, with his uncommon personality and exquisite literary taste, made him one of the most popular clergymen of London. He attracted to the Temple Church perhaps the most distinguished congregation in the city.

BIBLIOGRAPHY: E. Sichel, *Life and Letters of Alfred Ainger*, New York, 1906.

AINSWORTH, HENRY: English separatist; b., probably at Swanton, near Norwich, 1571; d. at Amsterdam 1622 or 1623. Driven from England, about 1593 he went to Amsterdam, and in two or three years became "teacher" of the congregation of which Francis Johnson (q.v.) was minister. He and Johnson could not agree and the congregation divided in 1610. In 1612 Johnson went to Emden, and thenceforth Ainsworth had the field to himself. It has been inferred that he lacked a university training from a statement of Roger Williams, that "he scarce set foot within a college walls" (*Bloody Tenet*, 1644, p. 174; cf. Dexter, 270, note 68); but the register of Caius College, Cambridge, shows that he was admitted there Dec. 15, 1587, and was in residence there as a scholar for four years. He was unquestionably a learned man, wrote excellent Latin, and had a knowledge of Hebrew (perfected by association with Amsterdam Jews), equaled by that of few other Christians of his time. He was earnest and sincere in his faith, conciliatory in spirit, and moderate in controversy. He had the chief part in drafting the Congregational Confession of 1596 (entitled *A True Confession of the Faith, and Humble Acknowledgment of the Allegiance which we, her Majesty's subjects, falsely called Brownists, do hold towards God, and yield to her Majesty and all other that are over us in the Lord;* cf. Walker, pp. 41–74, where the full text is given). He wrote many controversial works (for full list consult *DNB*, i. 192–193) and a series of *Annotations* upon the books of the Pentateuch, the Psalms, and the Song of Songs (1612 sqq.; collected ed., London, 1626–27; reprinted, 2 vols., Glasgow, 1843), which have still some value.

BIBLIOGRAPHY: H. M. Dexter, *Congregationalism of the Last Three Hundred Years*, New York, 1880; W. Walker, *Creeds and Platforms of Congregationalism*, p. 43, note 1, New York, 1893.

AITKEN, WILLIAM HAY MACDOWALL HUNTER: Church of England; b. at Liverpool Sept. 21, 1841. He was educated at Wadham College, Oxford (B.A., 1865, M.A., 1867). He was presented to the curacy of St. Jude's, Mildmay Park, London, in 1865, and was ordained priest in the following year. From 1871 to 1875 he was incumbent of Christ Church, Liverpool, but resigned to become a mission preacher. The next year he founded, in memory of his father, Rev. Robert Aitken, the Aitken Memorial Mission Fund, of which he was chosen general superintendent, and which later developed into the Church Parochial Missionary Society. He twice visited the United States on mission tours, first in 1886, when the noonday services for business men at Trinity Church, New York, were begun, and again in 1895–96. Since 1900 he has been canon residentiary of Norwich Cathedral. Two years later he was a member of the Fulham Conference on auricular confession. He has been a member of the Victoria Institute since 1876. In theology he is a liberal Evangelical, but has never been closely identified with any party. He adheres strongly to the doctrines of grace, although he repudiates Calvinism. While not an opponent of higher criticism in itself, he exercises a prudent conservatism in accepting its conclusions. In his eschatology he is an advocate of the theory of conditional immortality. His writings include: *Mission Sermons* (3 vols., London, 1875–76); *Newness of Life* (1877); *What is your Life?* (1879); *The School of Grace* (1879); *God's Everlasting Yea* (1881); *The Glory of the Gospel* (1882); *The Highway of Holiness* (1883); *Around the Cross* (1884); *The Revealer Revealed* (1885); *The Love of the Father* (1887); *Eastertide* (1889); *Temptation and Toil* (1895); *The Romance of Christian Work and Experience* (1898); *The Doctrine of Baptism* (1900); *The Divine Ordinance of Prayer* (1902); and *Life, Light, and Love: Studies on the First Epistle of St. John* (1905).

AIX-LA-CHAPELLE. See AACHEN.

AKED, CHARLES FREDERIC: English Baptist; b. at Nottingham Aug. 27, 1864. He was educated at Midland Baptist College and University College, Nottingham, after having passed the early part of his life as an auctioneer. He was then pastor at Syston, Leicestershire, in 1886–88, and at St. Helens and Earlstown, Lancashire, in 1888–90, and from 1890 to 1906 was minister of Pembroke Chapel, Liverpool. In the latter year he was elected pastor of the Fifth Avenue Baptist Church, New York City. From 1893 to 1906 he made yearly visits to the United States as a lecturer and preacher, and was also vice-president of the United Kingdom Alliance and one of the founders of the Passive Resistance League. In addition to numerous sermons and pamphlets, he has written *Changing Creeds and Social Struggles* (London, 1893) and *Courage of the Coward, and other Sermons in Liverpool* (1905).

AKIBA, ā-kī'bā: Jewish rabbi, said to have lived in Jerusalem in the time of the Second Temple, and to have devoted himself to the study of the law when somewhat advanced in years. After the destruction of Jerusalem he retired to the neighborhood of Jaffa and also undertook extensive travels. He was executed during the Jewish insurrection under Hadrian (c. 133); but there is no proof that he was active in the revolt, or took any part in it except to recognize Bar-Kokba as the Messiah (in accordance with Num. xxiv. 17). Jewish tradition assigns as the cause of his death, that he taught the law when it was forbidden to do so.

Many sayings are transmitted in Akiba's name. He defended the sacred character of the Song of Songs, which he interpreted allegorically (cf. F. Buhl, *Kanon und Text*, Leipsic, 1891, pp. 28–29; E. König, *Einleitung in das Alte Testament*, Bonn, 1893, p. 450). He paid special attention to the development of the traditional law; a Mishnah is known under his name; and to his school no doubt belong the fundamental elements of the present Mishnah. His exegetical method found meaning even in the particles and letters of the law (cf. M. Mielziner, *Introduction to the Talmud*, Cincinnati, 1894, pp. 125–126, 182–185; H. L. Strack, *Einleitung in den Thalmud*, Leipsic, 1894, pp. 100–104). The Greek translation of the Old Testament by Aquila (said to have been Akiba's pupil) seems to have been influenced by such an exegesis (Buhl, *Kanon und Text*, pp. 152–155). The midrashic works Siphra on Leviticus, and Siphre on Deuteronomy, contain much material from Akiba's school. (G. DALMAN.)

BIBLIOGRAPHY: H. Grätz, *Geschichte der Juden*, vol. iv., Leipsic, 1893; H. Ewald, *Geschichte des Volkes Israel*, vii. 367, Göttingen, 1868; *Akiba ben Joseph*, in *JE*, i. 304 sqq.

AKKAD. See BABYLONIA, IV., § 11.

AKOMINATOS. See NICETAS.

ALACOQUE, MARGUERITE MARIE. See SACRED HEART OF JESUS, DEVOTION TO.

ALANUS, a-lē'nus: Name of at least three writers of the twelfth century.

1. Alanus of Auxerre: Cistercian, abbot of Larivour from 1152 or 1153 to about 1167, bishop of Auxerre, and then for about twenty years monk at Clairvaux. He wrote a life of St. Bernard (in *MPL*, clxxxv.).

2. Alanus: Abbot of Tewkesbury. He wrote a life of Thomas Becket (ed. J. A. Giles, in *PEA*, 1845; *MPL*, cxc.), letters (*MPL*, cxc.), and sermons.

3. Alanus ab Insulis (Alain of Lille; often called *Magister Alanus* and *Magister universalis*): A native of Lille who taught in Paris. He was a man of wide and varied learning, and, combining philosophical studies and interests with strong adherence to the Church, forms an important connecting link between the earlier and the later scholasticism. His writings include: (1) *Regulæ cœlestis juris* (called also *Regulæ de sacra theologia* or *maximæ theologiæ*). Like other sciences which have their principles, the *supercœlestis scientia* is not lacking in maxims. These are here laid down in a series of brief sentences, partly put in paradoxical form with minute elucidations. The work has a strong leaning toward Platonism, and contains some very peculiar thoughts. (2) *Summa quadripartita adversus huius temporis hæreticos*, which indicates by its title the ecclesiastical position of the author. The first book is directed against the Cathari, opposes their dualism and docetism, and defends the sacraments of the Church. The second book denies (chap. i.) the right (claimed by the Waldensians) to preach without ecclesiastical commission; insists upon the duty of obeying implicitly the ecclesiastical superiors, and of making confession to the priest (chaps. ii.–x.); justifies indulgences and prayers for the dead (chaps. xi.–xiii.); and denies that swearing in general is prohibited and that the killing of a person is under all circumstances sinful (chap. xviii.). (3) *De arte prædicandi*, a homiletic work which starts with the definition that "preaching is plain and public instruction in morals and faith, aiming to give men information, and emanating from the way of reason and fountain of authority." It tells how to preach on certain subjects, as on mortal sins and the virtues, and how to address different classes. (4) Less certainly genuine are the five books *De arte catholicæ fidei*, whose style is somewhat different. The work makes the peculiar effort to demonstrate the ecclesiastical doctrine not only in a generally rational but by a strictly logical argumentation *in modum artis*. The fundamental thought is striking; but the execution is sometimes weak, and the definitions are so made that the inferences become what the author wishes to prove. (5) *De planctu naturæ*, in which Alanus gives, partly in prose, partly in rhyme, a picture of the darker side of the moral conditions of the time. (6) *Anticlaudianus*, a more comprehensive work, deriving its title from the fact that the author wished to show the effects of virtues as Claudian showed those of vices. It is a kind of philosophico-theological encyclopedia in tolerably correct hexameters which are not devoid of poetic feeling. S. M. DEUTSCH.

BIBLIOGRAPHY: (1) L. Janauschek, *Origines Cistercienses*, Vienna, 1877; (3) *Opera*, in *MPL*, ccx.; the oldest notices are in Otto of St. Blasien, *Chronicon*, under the year 1194, *MGH*, *Script.*, xx. (1868) 326, Alberic of Trois-Fontaines. ib. xxiii. (1874) 881, Henry of Ghent, *De scriptoribus ecclesiasticis*, ch. xxi.; cf. Oudin, *Commentarius de scriptoribus ecclesiæ*, ii. 1387 sqq., Leipsic, 1772; *Histoire littéraire de la France*, xvi. 396 sqq.; C. Bäumker, *Handschriftliches zu den Werken des Alanus*, 1894 (reprinted from the *Philosophisches Jahrbuch* of the Görres-Gesellschaft, vi. and vii., Fulda, 1893–94); M. Baumgartner, *Die Philosophie des Alanus ab Insulis*, Münster, 1896; J. E. Erdmann, *Grundriss der Geschichte der Philosophie*, § 170. 2 vols., Berlin, 1895–96.

ALARIC. See GOTHS, § 3.

A LASCO, JOHANNES. See LASCO.

ALB: A vestment worn by Roman Catholic priests in celebrating mass, and prescribed also for the Church of England by the first prayer-book of Edward VI. ("a white albe plain, with a vestment or cope"). See VESTMENTS AND INSIGNIA, ECCLESIASTICAL. The name was applied also to the white garments worn by the newly baptized in the early Church; and from this, since Easter was the usual time for baptism, came the name for the Sunday after Easter, *Dominica in albis* (sc. *depositis*).

ALBAN, SAINT, OF MAINZ: Alleged martyr of the fourth or fifth century, whose existence is somewhat doubtful. The oldest form of the story (Rabanus Maurus, *Martyrologium*, June 21; *MPL*, cx. 1152) is that he was sent by Ambrose from Milan in the reign of Theodosius I. (379–395) to preach the gospel in Gaul, and was beheaded at Mainz on the way. Numerous details were added later. On the supposed site of his burial, to the south of the city, a church was erected in his honor, which is mentioned as early as 758. In it in 794 Charlemagne buried his third wife, Fastrade. The edifice was subsequently rebuilt (796–805); and probably at this time it was made a Benedictine house. In 1419 it was changed to a knightly foundation, to which Emperor Maximilian I. in 1515 gave the privilege of coining golden florins (called "Albanusgulden"), with the effigy of the saint arrayed in eucharistic vestments and carrying his head in his hand—a not uncommon method of representing martyrs who had been beheaded, to indicate the manner of their death. The foundation was destroyed when Margrave Albert of Brandenburg ravaged Mainz in 1552. (A. HAUCK.)

BIBLIOGRAPHY: Goswin (canon of Mainz), *Ex passione S. Albani martyris Moguntini*, in *MGH, Script.*, xv. 2 (1888), 984–990; J. G. Reuter, *Albansgulden*, Mainz, 1790; Rettberg, *KD*, i. 211; Friedrich, *KD*, i. 314.

ALBAN, SAINT, OF VERULAM: A martyr of the Britons, often mistakenly called "the protomartyr of the English." Bede (*Hist. eccl.*, i. 7), doubtless following some unknown acts of St. Alban, says that while still a pagan he gave shelter to a fugitive clerk during the Diocletian persecution; impressed by his guest's personality, he embraced Christianity, and when the clerk was discovered, wrapped himself in the fugitive's cloak and gave himself up to the authorities in his stead; he was scourged and condemned to death, performed miracles on the way to execution, and suffered on June 22; the place of his martyrdom was near Verulamium (St. Albans, Hertfordshire), and after the establishment of Christianity a magnificent church was erected there to his memory. Later accounts elaborate the narrative, and confuse the saint with others named Albanus or Albinus. It is said that the martyr served seven years in the army of Diocletian, and the name of the clerk is given as Amphibalus (first by Geoffrey of Monmouth), probably from his cloak (Lat. *amphibalus*). It seems certain that a tradition of the martyrdom of some Albanus existed at Verulamium as early as the visit of Germanus in 429 (Constantius's life of Germanus, i. 25), and there is no reason to deny its truth. But that the martyrdom took place in the Diocletian persecution is first intimated by Gildas (ed. Mommsen, *MGH*, *Chronica minora*, iii. 31) and is probably a guess. For Aaron and Julius of Carleon-on-Usk, whose names are joined by Gildas with that of Alban, no local tradition can be shown earlier than the ninth century.

BIBLIOGRAPHY: Haddan and Stubbs, *Councils*, i. 5–7; Wattenbach, *DGQ*, ii. 497; W. Bright, *Chapters of Early English Church History*, pp. 6–9, Oxford, 1897.

ALBANENSES, al″ba-nen′sîz *or* -sês: A faction of the Cathari. They derived their name from Albania, and maintained, in opposition to the Bogomiles of Thracia and the Concorezenses of Bulgaria and Italy, an absolute dualism, by which good and evil were referred to two eternally opposite and equally potent principles. See NEW MANICHEANS, II.

ALBATI. See FLAGELLATION, FLAGELLANTS, II., § 5.

ALBER, al′ber, **ERASMUS:** Theologian and poet of the German Reformation; b. in the Wetterau (a district to the n.e. of Frankfort) about 1500; d. at Neubrandenburg (75 m. n. of Berlin) May 5, 1553. He studied at Mainz and Wittenberg, and was much influenced by Luther, Melanchthon, and Carlstadt. After teaching in several places, in 1527 he became pastor at Sprendlingen (15 m. s.w. of Mainz), in the Dreieich, where for eleven years he worked diligently for the extension of Reformation doctrines and made himself known as a writer. He was an extravagant admirer of Luther, and possessed a very sharp tongue, which he used as unsparingly against Reformers who did not agree with him as against Roman Catholics. Erratic tendencies grew upon him with years, and, after leaving Sprendlingen, he moved about much and was at times in want. Shortly before his death he was made pastor and superintendent at Neubrandenburg. His writings, though often rude and coarse, were forceful and popular. They include: a rhymed version of Æsop's *Fables*, made at Sprendlingen (ed. W. Braune, Halle, 1892); *Der Barfüsser Mönche Eulenspiegel und Alcoran* (with preface by Luther, Wittenberg, 1542; Eng. transl., 1550), a satire directed against the Minorites, based upon a work of Bartolomeo Albizzi (q.v.); and *Wider die verfluchte Lehre der Carlstadter, Wiedertäufer, Rottengeister, Sakramentlästerer, Eheschänder, Musicverächter, Bilderstürmer, Feyerfeinde, und Verwüster aller guten Ordnung*, published three years after his death. Of more permanent value are his hymns (ed. C. W Stromberger, Halle, 1857), of which *Nun freut euch Gottes Kinder all* is used in German hymn-books and in English translation (*O Children of your God, rejoice*). (T. KOLDE.)

BIBLIOGRAPHY: F. Schnorr von Carolsfeld, *Erasmus Alber*, Dresden, 1886; Julian, *Hymnology*, pp. 34–35; H. Barge, *Andreas Bodenstein von Karlstadt*, i. 370 sqq., 491 sqq., ii. 512 sqq., et passim, Leipsic, 1905.

ALBER, MATTHÆUS: The "Luther of Swabia"; b. at Reutlingen (20 m. s. of Stuttgart) Dec. 4, 1495; d. at Blaubeuren (30 m. s.e. of Stuttgart) Dec. 2, 1570. He was the son of a well-to-do goldsmith, took his master's degree at Tübingen in 1518, and was immediately called as pastor to his native city. On Melanchthon's recommendation he received a scholarship, enabling him to continue his studies for three years longer. Dissatisfied with the scholastic theology at Tübingen, he went to Freiburg in 1521, but soon returned to Reutlingen, where he boldly preached Luther's doctrine and established the new teaching. At Easter, 1524, he abolished the Latin mass and auricular confession. The same year he married, and when brought to account at Esslingen secured an acquittal by skilful management, although the bishop continued to trouble him because of his marriage till 1532. The Reformation made steady progress in

Reutlingen; and in 1531 a church order with presbyterial government was introduced. During the Peasant's War Reutlingen was unmolested. The fugitive Anabaptists from Esslingen were won over by instruction and mildness. Zwingli endeavored to bring over Alber to his view of the Lord's Supper, but the latter adhered to Luther, preserving his independence, however, and remaining on friendly terms with Zwingli's friends, Blarer, Butzer, Capito, and others. In 1534 Duke Ulrich of Württemberg called Alber as preacher to Stuttgart with a view of introducing the Reformation there. In 1536 Alber went to Wittenberg, where he preached (May 28) and assisted in finishing the *Concordia*. In 1537 at the Colloquy of Urach he advised cautious procedure with regard to the removal of the images. As he opposed the introduction of the interim in 1548, he was obliged to give up his office and leave the city. For a time he lived at Pfullingen, protected by Duke Ulrich who in Aug., 1549 called him as first preacher of the collegiate Church of Stuttgart and general superintendent. He took an active part in the preparation of the Württemberg *Confession* and the church order of 1553, and he attended both the latter part of the Second Colloquy at Worms (1557) and the Synod of Stuttgart. Toward the end of 1562 he was made abbot of the reformed monastery at Blaubeuren.

G. BOSSERT.

BIBLIOGRAPHY: J. Fizion, *Cronika von Reutlingen*, ed. A. Baemeister, Stuttgart, 1862; F. G. Gayler, *Denkwürdigkeiten der Reichsstadt Reutlingen*, Reutlingen, 1840; J. Hartmann, *Matthäus Alber*, Tübingen, 1863; G. Bossert, *Der Reutlinger Sieg*, 1524, Barmen, 1894; idem, *Interim in Württemberg*, Halle, 1895; R. Schmid, *Reformationsgeschichte Württembergs*, Heilbronn, 1904.

ALBERT OF AIX: A historian of the twelfth century, designated in the manuscript of his *Historia expeditionis Hierosolymitanæ* as *canonicus Aquensis*, but whether he was a canon of Aix in Provence or of Aix-la-Chapelle (Aachen) is uncertain. It is likely, however, since he dates events by the years of Henry IV., that he was a Lorrainer rather than a Provençal. He may be the *custos Adalbertus* who is mentioned for the last time in 1192, and, in this case, he must have written his history in early youth. His work tells nothing of his personality, except that he had an ardent desire, which was never fulfilled, to visit the Holy Land. As a sort of compensation, he determined to write the events of the years 1095–1121 from the narratives of actual crusaders. His credibility was generally accepted until the middle of the nineteenth century, but since then it has been seriously questioned. It is probable that the work is based upon mere hearsay. The *Historia* is in *MPL*, clxvi., and in *Recueil des historiens des Croisades, hist. occid.*, iv. (Paris, 1879) 265–713. (A. HAUCK.)

BIBLIOGRAPHY: H. von Sybel, *Geschichte des ersten Kreuzzugs*, pp. 62–107, Leipsic, 1881; B. Kugler, *Albert von Aachen*, Stuttgart, 1885; F. Vercruysse, *Essai critique sur la chronique d'Albert d'Aix*, Liége, 1889; Wattenbach, *DGQ*, ii. 178–180.

ALBERT, antipope, 1102. See PASCHAL II., pope.

ALBERT V. OF BAVARIA AND THE COUNTER-REFORMATION IN BAVARIA: Albert V., duke of Bavaria (b. Feb. 29, 1528; d. Oct. 24, 1579), was the son of Duke William IV., whom he succeeded in 1550. The rulers of Bavaria had remained faithful to the Roman Catholic Church during the progress of the Reformation; but in spite of their endeavors the new ideas gained many adherents among both the nobility and the citizen class. Albert was educated at Ingolstadt under good Catholic teachers. In 1547 he married a daughter of Emperor Ferdinand I., the union ending the political rivalry between Austria and Bavaria. Albert was now free to devote himself to the task of establishing Catholic conformity in his dominions. Incapable by nature of passionate adherence to any religious principle, and given rather to a life of idleness and pleasure, he pursued the work of repression because he was convinced that the cause of Catholicism was inseparably connected with the fortunes of the house of Wittelsbach. He took little direct share in the affairs of government and easily lent himself to the plans of his advisers, among whom during the early part of his reign were two sincere Catholics, Georg Stockhammer and Wiguleus Hundt. The latter took an important part in the events leading up to the treaty of Passau (1552) and the peace of Augsburg (1555).

The real beginning of the Counterreformation in Bavaria may be dated from 1557, when the Jesuits first established themselves in the duchy. In summoning them to Bavaria Albert and his advisers were actuated by the desire to use their services as educators in raising the mass of the clergy from their condition of moral and intellectual stagnation. The Jesuits speedily made themselves masters of the University of Ingolstadt and through the chancellor, Simon Thaddäus Eck, exercised a predominant influence at court. Eck was ably seconded by his associates, who obtained control of the education of the youth and of the clergy, and by their preaching and writings checked the spread of the reformed ideas among the masses of the people. Till 1563 concession still had a part in the programme of the leaders, who hoped that the bestowal of communion in both kinds upon the laity and the abolition of celibacy in the priesthood would bring back many to the fold. Political events, however, led to an abandonment of the conciliatory policy. In 1563 Joachim, Count of Ortenburg, introduced the Augsburg Confession in his dominions, which he held as a direct fief of the empire. Albert discerned in this act a serious menace to the integrity of Bavaria, and took possession of the principality. Thenceforth the reformed religion, as closely connected with political insubordination, was made the object of a ruthless persecution. The opposition of the nobility was speedily overcome, and conformity to the teachings of the Church was enforced under pain of exile. By means of frequent visitations among the clergy and the people, the reorganization of the school system, the establishment of a strict censorship, and the imposition upon all public officials and university professors of an oath of conformity with the decisions of the Council of Trent, heresy was completely stamped out in Bavaria before 1580. The progress of the Counterreformation in the empire was materially helped by Bavaria.

Albert made his territory a refuge for Catholic subjects of Protestant rulers and was urgent in counseling Emperor Maximilian II. against concessions to the Protestants. At his death Bavaria was the stronghold of the Catholic reaction in Germany, and next to Spain, the most formidable opponent of the Reformed faith in Europe.

WALTER GOETZ.

BIBLIOGRAPHY: J. G. J. Aretin, *Bayerns auswärtige Verhältnisse*, Passau, 1839; S. Sugenheim, *Baierns Kirchen- und Volks-Zustände*, Giessen, 1842; M. Lossen, *Kölnische Krieg*, Gotha, 1882; C. Rüpprecht, *Albrecht V. von Baiern und seine Stände*, Munich, 1883; M. Ritter, *Deutsche Geschichte im Zeitalter der Gegenreformation*, i. 238 sqq., 300 sqq., Stuttgart, 1889; A. Knöpfler, *Die Kelchbewegung in Bayern unter Herzog Albrecht V.*, Munich, 1891; S. Riezler, *Zur Würdigung Herzogs Albrechts V von Bayern*, ib. 1891; W. Goetz, *Die bayerische Politik im ersten Jahrzehnt der Regierung Albrechts V.*, ib. 1896; idem, *Beiträge zur Gesch. Herzog Albrechts V.*, ib. 1898; C. Schellhass, *Die Süddeutsche Nuntiatur des Grafen Bartholomäus von Portia*, Berlin, 1896; S. Riezler, *Geschichte Baierns*, vol. v., Gotha, 1903; K. Hartmann, *Der Prozess gegen die protestantischen Landstände in Bayern unter . . Albrecht V.*, Munich, 1904; W. Goetz, *Die angebliche Adelsverschwörung gegen Albrecht V.*, in *Forschungen zur Geschichte Baierns*, xiii., 1905.

ALBERT OF BRANDENBURG: Elector of Mainz and archbishop of Magdeburg; b. June 28, 1490; d. at Mainz Sept. 24, 1545. He was the second son of Johann Cicero, elector of Brandenburg, and brother of the future elector, Joachim I. Through family influence he became canon of Mainz, at the age of eighteen. In 1513 he was made archbishop of Magdeburg and administrator of Halberstadt, and in 1514, having received holy orders, archbishop and elector of Mainz. Having promised to pay personally the sum of at least 20,000 gold gulden for the pallium, he was forced to borrow from the Fuggers in Augsburg. To recoup himself, he obtained (Aug. 15, 1515) from Pope Leo X. the privilege of preaching indulgences—ostensibly decreed for the building of St. Peter's in Rome—in his province for eight years, making a cash payment of 10,000 gulden and promising for the future one-half of the annual revenues. He admitted that the transaction was a money-making affair, and when the preaching began commissioners representing the Fuggers accompanied the preachers to collect their share.

Albert was a child of the Renaissance, interested in art, with a decided fondness for costly buildings, and deserves praise as a patron of the new literature. He admired Erasmus, protected Reuchlin, and drew Hutten to his court. Nevertheless, on May 17, 1517, he issued an edict against the press and appointed the reactionary Jodocus Trutvetter inquisitor for his entire province. When the way indulgences were preached raised a storm, his action was characteristic. On Oct. 31, 1517, Luther sent to him a respectful letter on the subject, and his ninety-five theses. Albert put the matter aside and left the letter unanswered; he had no conception of Luther's motives and views, and desired not to be troubled. Later, when he tried to interfere, he found that his influence was gone. At the Diet of Augsburg in 1518 he was made cardinal. After the death of the Emperor Maximilian (1519) he worked effectively for the election of Charles V. As regards Luther he continued to follow the advice of Erasmus (in a letter of Nov. 1, 1519), to have as little as possible to do with him, if he cared for his own tranquillity. So long as his personal interests did not suffer, he found it easy to be tolerant. When Luther, at the wish of his elector, wrote a second letter (Feb. 4, 1520), Albert replied quite in the spirit of Erasmus. He did not interfere when Hutten issued his anonymous anti-Roman pamphlets, and he showed himself unfriendly to the mendicant friars. But when papal legates brought him (Oct., 1520) the Golden Rose and definite orders concerning Hutten and Luther, he was ready at once to expel the former from his court and to burn the latter's books.

After the Diet of Worms (1521) Albert pretended to favor certain reforms, and many, like Carlstadt, put confidence in him. Luther, however, addressed to him a letter from the Wartburg (Dec. 1, 1521), threatening to attack publicly his "false god," the indulgences, if the sale did not cease, and to expose him before the world. Albert yielded as a matter of policy, and because no other course was open to him. He was also unable to prevent the introduction of the Reformation into Erfurt and Magdeburg. He was not on good terms with his chapter in Mainz, and during the Peasants' War the city made a compact with the peasants. It was suspected that he had in mind to follow the example of his cousin in Prussia (see ALBERT OF PRUSSIA) and to secularize his bishopric—a course which Luther openly (in a letter of June 2, 1525) called upon him to take. On the same day, however, the peasants were defeated at Königshofen, and the immediate danger being over, Albert made an alliance with Luther's most determined opponents, Joachim of Brandenburg and George of Saxony, for mutual protection and for the extermination of the Lutheran sect. For a time he continued to oppose the evangelical movement in a half-hearted way, requesting his subjects to abide by the old teaching of the Church. He introduced some outward changes in opposition to the Reformation, but without effect; his territory became smaller; and his influence in the kingdom grew less. The so-called alliance of Halle with his brother Joachim and other Catholic princes in 1533 could not retard the movement. His opposition in Dessau was in vain (1534). Even in Halle, his own city, he could not hinder the victory of the Reformation proved by the call of Justus Jonas in 1541. As early as 1536 Albert anticipated coming events, by removing his valuable collections of objects of art to Mainz and Aschaffenburg; and in 1540 he left Halle forever. In 1541 he urged the emperor at Regensburg to proceed against the Protestants with arms, if he really meant to be emperor; otherwise it were better if he had stayed in Spain. Albert had become, possibly under Jesuit influence, the most violent of the princely opponents of the Reformation. He met with continual disappointments, however, and steadily became more isolated. He took a deep interest in the Council of Trent, and appointed his legates in Apr., 1545, but did not live to see its opening. His last years were harassed by quarrels with his chapter and the importunities of his creditors, and he died, after long sufferings, alone, forsaken, and almost in want. The fine buildings which he erected at Mainz and Halle and his monument by Peter Vischer, in the abbey church at Aschaffenburg were the only memorials of his life which he left to posterity. (T. Kolde.)

Bibliography: J. H. Hennes, *Albrecht von Brandenburg*, Mainz, 1858; J. May, *Der Kurfürst, Kardinal und Erzbischof Albrecht II. von Mainz und Brandenburg*, 2 vols., Munich, 1865–75; A. Wolters, *Der Abgott zu Halle*, Bonn, 1877; H. Gredy, *Kardinal und Erzbischof Albrecht II. von Brandenburg in seinem Verhältnisse zu den Glaubensneuerungen*, Mainz, 1891; G. F. Hertzberg, *Geschichte der Stadt Halle*, vol. ii., Halle, 1891; P. Redlich, *Cardinal Albrecht von Brandenburg und das neue Stift zu Halle*, Mainz, 1900.

ALBERT THE GREAT. See Albertus Magnus.

ALBERT OF PRUSSIA.

Albert, margrave of Brandenburg-Ansbach, last grand master of the Teutonic order, first duke of Prussia, founder of the Prussian national Church, was born at Ansbach (25 m. s.w. of Nuremberg) May 17, 1490; d. at Tapiau (23 m. e. of Königsberg) Mar. 20, 1568. He was the third son of the Margrave Frederick the Elder of Brandenburg-Ansbach, received a knightly education at various courts, and was made a canon of the Cologne Cathedral. In 1508, with his brother Casimir, he took part in the Emperor Maximilian's campaign against Venice. He was elected grand master of the Teutonic order Dec. 15, 1510, was invested with the dignity of his office in 1511, and made his solemn entry into Königsberg in 1512. His efforts to make his order independent of Poland (to which it had owed fealty since the peace of Thorn, 1466) involved him in a war with the Polish king, which devastated the territory of the order until a truce for four years was made in 1521. Albert then visited Germany and tried in vain to obtain the help of the German princes against Poland. While attending the Diet of Nuremberg in 1522–23 he heard the sermons of Andreas Osiander (whom he afterward called his "father in Christ"), and associated with others of the reformed faith in that city. By such influence, as well as by the writings of Luther from the year 1520, he was won to the new teaching and openly avowed his convictions.

1. Early Life and Conversion to Protestantism.

In June, 1523, he addressed a confidential letter to Luther, requesting his advice concerning the reformation of the Teutonic order and the means of bringing about a renewal of Christian life in its territory. In reply Luther advised him to convert the spiritual territory of the order into a worldly principality. In Sept., 1523, he visited the Reformer at Wittenberg, when Luther again advised him, with the concurrence of Melanchthon, to put aside the foolish and wrong law of the order, to enter himself into the estate of matrimony, and to convert the state of the order into a worldly one. This interview was the beginning of an intimate connection between Albert and the two Reformers of Wittenberg, and was immediately followed by Luther's *Ermahnung an die Herren Deutschen Ordens falsche Keuschheit zu meiden und zu rechten ehelichen Keuschheit zu greifen*. With the advice and help of Luther, Albert provided pure Gospel preaching for his capital by calling thither such men as Johann Briessmann and Paulus Speratus (qq.v.). Johannes Amandus, called about the same time as Briessmann, while a popular and gifted preacher, proved a fanatic and agitator, and was obliged to leave the city and country in 1524. His place was taken by Johannes Poliander (q.v.). Authorized by Albert, Bishop George of Polentz (q.v.), who favored the Reformation, sent learned men to preach through the country; and evangelical writings, supplied by Albert's friend, Georg Vogler, chancellor of his brother at Ansbach, were carefully disseminated. At Christmas, 1523 George of Polentz openly embraced the new faith; and the next year, with the consent of his sovereign, he advised the ministers not only to preach the pure Gospel, but also to use the German language at the administration of baptism and the Lord's Supper. At the same time he recommended the reading of Luther's writings, and declared excommunication to be abrogated.

2. Intercourse with Luther and Melanchthon and Aid to the Reformation.

The cause made steady progress in Königsberg. Briessmann delivered free lectures to the laity and ministers, aiming to promote a knowledge of the gospel; Speratus preached to large crowds; and a newly established printing-office published various evangelical writings, especially the sermons and pamphlets of Briessmann and Speratus. Abuses and unevangelical elements in divine service and in the inner constitution of the churches, images and altars serving the worship of saints, the multitude of masses and the sacrifice of the mass, were abolished. A common treasury was established for the aid of the poor. The reformatory movement acquired new impetus from the conversion of a second Prussian prelate, Erhard of Queiss, bishop of Pomesania, who, under the title *Themata* issued a Reformation-programme in his diocese for the renewal of the spiritual life on the basis of the pure Gospel. The most important of all, however, was the carrying out of Luther's advice with regard to the transformation of the territory of the order into a hereditary secular duchy under the suzerainty of Poland, after the period of the truce had expired and peace had been made with Poland. On Apr. 10, 1525, the formal investiture of Albert as duke of Prussia took place at Cracow, after he had sworn the oath of allegiance to King Sigismund. Toward the end of the following month he made his solemn entry into Königsberg and received the homage of the Prussian prelates, the knights of the order, and the states. On July 1, 1526, he was married in the castle of Königsberg to the Danish princess Dorothea, like himself a faithful adherent of the Gospel.

3. Progress of the Reformation.

A reorganization of ecclesiastical affairs on the basis of the existing episcopal constitution now took place. The two bishops, George of Polentz and Erhard of Queiss, who were separated from Rome by their evangelical faith and reformatory activity, married. As the first evangelical bishops they confined themselves to purely ecclesiastical functions—ordination, visitation, inspection, and the celebration of marriage. The duke, as evangelical sovereign, felt himself obliged in publicly professing the Reformation and reserving the right to call a diet for regulating the affairs of the Church, to issue a mandate (July 6, 1525) requesting the ministers to preach the Gospel in all purity and Christian fidelity, and to testify against the prevailing superstition, as well as against the widespread godless and immoral drunkenness, lewdness, cursing, and frivolous swearing. The first diet to regulate the affairs of the Church was held in Dec., 1525, at Königsberg. The result was the *Landesordnung*, which regulated the appointment and support of ministers, the filling of vacancies, the observance of the feast-days, the appropriation of moneys received for the churches, for pious foundations, and for the poor. The *Landesordnung* contained also regulations for divine service, drawn up by the bishops and published by Albert (Mar., 1526) under the title *Artikel der Ceremonien und andere Ordnung*.

4. Reorganization of Ecclesiastical Affairs.

For the better regulation of existing evils, Albert, in agreement with the bishops, appointed a commission of clerical and lay members, to visit the different parishes, to investigate the life and work of the ministers, and, where necessary, to give them instruction and information. The result of this visitation, the first in Prussia, was such that in a mandate dated Apr. 24, 1528, Albert recommended the two bishops to continue such visitations in their dioceses and to impress upon the ministers their task with reference to doctrine and life. That such supervision might be permanent he ordered the appointment of superintendents. For the benefit of the many non-Germans, the ministers were supplied with translators of the preached word. Albert recommended Luther's *Postilla* as pattern for the preaching of the Gospel and caused a large number of copies to be distributed among the ministers. He also ordered quarterly conferences under the presidency of the superintendents, and in July, 1529, he authorized the bishops to arrange synodical meetings, at which questions pertaining to faith, doctrine, marriage, and other matters of importance to the pastoral office were considered. He induced Speratus (who had succeeded Queiss as bishop of Pomesania) to prepare an outline of doctrines, which was published under the title *Christliche statuta synodalia*, and distributed among the ministers as the sovereign's own confession, as is indicated by the preface, dated Jan. 6, 1530. This precursor of the Augsburg Confession the bishops assigned to the ministers in 1530 as their canon of doctrine. It was of special importance during a crisis brought on by the duke. Influenced by his friend Friedrich von Heideck, he favored the teachings of the enthusiast Kaspar Schwenckfeld (q.v.), whom he met at Liegnitz, and gave appointments to his adherents. The new ordinances of the bishops were at first not heeded. A colloquy held at Rastenburg in Dec., 1531, under the presidency of Speratus brought about no satisfactory results. Luther's representations, at first unsuccessful, finally evoked the duke's prohibition of the secret or public preaching or teaching of the enthusiasts; at the same time he stated that he allowed his subjects liberty in matters of faith, since he would not force a belief upon the people. His eyes were finally opened by the Anabaptist disorders at Münster (see MÜNSTER, ANABAPTISTS IN) and he saw the political danger of such fanaticism. In Aug., 1535, he issued a mandate to Speratus enjoining him to preserve the purity and unity of doctrine. He renewed his assurance to his brother, Margrave George, "that he and his country wished to be looked upon as constant members in the line of professors of the Augsburg Confession," and to this assurance he remained faithful to the end.

5. His Visitation and Its Consequences.

In 1540 Albert issued an ordinance treating of the many evils in the life of the people and their cure, and another concerning the election and support of the ministers, their widows and orphans, as a supplement to the *Landesordnung* of 1525. Assisted by the two bishops, he made a tour of inspection in the winter of 1542–43 to obtain a true insight into the religious and moral condition of the country. Toward the end of this tour, he issued (Feb., 1543) a mandate in the German and Polish languages, exhorting the people to make diligent use of the means of grace and admonishing those of the nobility who despised the word and the sacrament. Each house had to appoint in turn an officer to keep watch, from an elevated place, over the church attendance. Besides the Sunday pericopes the minister was to spend a half-hour in explaining the catechism. During the week devotional meetings were to be held in the houses, at which the people were to be examined as to their knowledge of the word of God. To maintain the episcopal constitution Albert, in a memorandum of 1542, assured the continuance of the two ancient bishoprics with the provision that godly and learned men should always be chosen for them. To promote Church life he issued an *Ordnung vom äusserlichen Gottesdienst und Artikel der Ceremonien* (1544), supplementing the *Artikel* of 1525. To improve the service in the churches he required the schools to train the children in singing, and had a hymn-book prepared by Kugelmann, the court band-master.

6. Ordinances of 1540 and 1544.

Albert continued to correspond with Luther and Melanchthon, and many notes from his hand, remarks on the Psalms and the Pauline epistles, show how deeply he endeavored to penetrate into the Scriptures. To promote Christian culture he established a library in his castle, the basis of the public library founded by him in 1540. For the benefit of a higher evangelical education he established Latin high-schools, and founded at Königsberg a school which in 1544, with the assistance of Luther and Melanchthon, he converted into a university. As first rector he called Georg Sabinus, son-in-law of Melanchthon, but his character rather hampered the development of the institution. A still greater impediment was the appointment, in 1549, of the former Nuremberg reformer Andreas Osiander as first theological professor, his doctrine of justification calling forth controversies (see OSIANDER, ANDREAS). After Osiander's death (1552), his son-in-law Johann Funck (q.v.) gained such influence over the duke that he appointed none but followers of Osiander, whose opponents, headed by J. Mörlin, were obliged to leave the country. The political and ecclesiastical confusion finally became so great that a Polish commission was forced to interfere, and in 1566 Funck and two of his party were executed as "disturbers of the peace, traitors, and promoters of the Osiandrian heresy." The former advisers of the duke were then reinstated.

7. Later Efforts in Behalf of the Reformation.

These painful experiences caused Albert to long for rest and the restoration of peace in Church and country. He recalled Mörlin and Martin Chemnitz, and, in consequence of a resolution of the synod, which met in 1567, to abide by the *corpus doctrinæ* of the Lutheran Church, he caused them to prepare the *Corpus doctrinæ Pruthenicum* (or *Wiederholung der Summa und Inhalt der rechten allgemeinen christlichen Kirchenlehre-repetitio corporis doctrinæ christianæ*) in which the Osiandrian errors were also refuted. This symbol, which was approved by the estates, Albert published with a preface, dated July 9, 1567, in which it was stated that "no one shall be admitted to any office in Church or school who does not approve of and accept it."

After the settlement of the doctrinal questions, a revision of the former church-order was undertaken, the outcome of which was the *Kirchenordnung und Ceremonien*, published in 1568. The vacant episcopal sees of Pomesania and Samland were filled by the appointment of G. Venediger (Venetus) and J. Mörlin, respectively, after arrangements had been made with the estates as to the election, jurisdiction, and salary of the bishops, whereby the old episcopal constitution of the Prussian Church was established and assured. Thus, notwithstanding the trials of his last years, Albert saw the full development of the Evangelical Church in the duchy of Prussia, and quiet and peace restored before his death. He left a beautiful testimony of his evangelical faith in his testament for Albert Frederick, his son by his second wife, Anna of Brunswick, whom he had married in 1550. His last words were: "Into thy hands I commit my spirit, thou hast redeemed me, O Lord God of Truth."

DAVID ERDMANN†.

BIBLIOGRAPHY: Sources: M. Luther, *Briefe*, ed. by W. M. L. de Wette and J. K. Seidemann, 6 vols., Berlin, 1826-73; P. Melanchthon, *Briefe an Albrecht Herzog von Preussen*, ed. by K. Faber, Berlin, 1817; J. Voigt, *Briefwechsel der berühmtesten Gelehrten des Zeitalters der Reformation mit Herzog Albrecht von Preussen*, Königsberg, 1841; T. Kolde, *Analecta lutherana*, Gotha, 1883; P. Tschackert, *Urkundenbuch zur Reformationsgeschichte des Herzogtums Preussen*, vols. i.-iii. (vols. xliii.-xlv. of *Publikationen aus den k. preussischen Staats-Archiven*, Berlin, 1890). General Literature: D. H. Arnold, *Historie der Königsberger Universität*, vol. i., Königsberg, 1746; idem, *Kurzgefasste Kirchengeschichte von Preussen*, ib. 1769; F. S. Bock, *Leben und Thaten Albrechts des Aeltern*, ib. 1750; L. von Baczko, *Geschichte Preussens*, vol. iv., ib. 1795; A. R. Gebser and C. A. Hagen, *Der Dom zu Königsberg*, ib. 1835; L. von Ranke, *Deutsche Geschichte im Zeitalter der Reformation*, vol. ii., Berlin, 1843, Eng. transl., new ed., Robert A. Johnson, London, 1905 (very good); W. Möller, *Andreas Osiander*, Elberfeld, 1870; *ADB*, vol. i.; K. A. Hase, *Herzog Albrecht von Preussen und seine Hofprediger*, ib. 1879 (an elaborate monograph); K. Lohmeier, *Herzog Albrecht von Preussen*, Danzig, 1890; H. Prutz, *Herzog Albrecht von Preussen*, in *Preussische Jahrbücher*, lxvi. 2, Berlin, 1890; E. Joachim, *Die Politik des letzten Hochmeisters in Preussen, Albrecht von Brandenburg*, 3 vols., Leipsic, 1892-94; P. Tschackert, *Herzog Albrecht von Preussen als reformatorische Persönlichkeit*, Halle, 1894.

ALBERT OF RIGA: Founder of the German power among the Esthonians and Letts; d. at Riga Jan. 17, 1229. He was a nephew of Hartwig, archbishop of Bremen, and is first mentioned as canon in that city. In 1199 he was ordained bishop of Uexküll, in the territory of the Livonians, as the successor of Bishop Berthold (see BERTHOLD OF LIVONIA) who had perished the previous year in an uprising of the pagan inhabitants. Though organized missionary work had been carried on among the Letts and the Livonians since 1184, they had shown themselves hostile to the new creed, and it fell to Albert to maintain his episcopal title and to spread the Gospel by the sword. Aided by a papal bull he succeeded in raising a large force of crusaders, and in the year 1200 appeared on the shores of the Dwina, where he met with little resistance from the Livonians. In 1201 he founded the town of Riga, and for the protection of his dominions and the extension of his conquests organized the Order of the Brothers of the Sword (q.v.), whose grand master was made subordinate to his authority. The Christianizing of the country was promoted by the introduction of Cistercian and Premonstrant monks, and by 1206 almost the entire Livonian population had been baptized. In 1207 Albert received Livonia as a fief from the German king, together with the title of "Prince of the Empire." Three years later he was confirmed by Innocent III. as bishop of the territories of the Livonians and the Letts, and, without receiving the dignity of archbishop, was granted the right to nominate and ordain bishops for such territorial conquests as might be made from the heathen peoples to the northeast. He now met with formidable rivalry from the Brothers of the Sword, whose grand master desired to make himself independent of the bishop. The Danes, also, by the acquisition of Lübeck in 1215, became a powerful factor in the politics of the eastern Baltic. Though forced for a time to make concessions to both, Albert by courage and a wise use of circumstances, succeeded in retaining his power unimpaired. From 1211 to 1224 vigorous campaigns were carried on against the heathen Esthonians to the northeast, who, although aided by the Russian rulers of Novgorod and Pskov, were compelled to submit to the German power. The Danish influence speedily disappeared, and the

Brothers of the Sword were forced in time to take their lands in Esthonia as a fief from Albert and from his brother Hermann, whom he had made bishop of southern Esthonia, with his seat at Dorpat. In 1227 the island of Oesel, the last stronghold of the heathen resistance and the refuge of pirates who held the eastern Baltic in terror, was overrun by a crusading army, and the conversion of the country was completed. Albert is a striking type of the militant ecclesiastic of the Middle Ages. In spite of his great services in the spread of Christianity in the Baltic lands, it is as the warrior, prince, and diplomat, rather than as bishop, that he stands out most prominently. (F LEZIUS.)

BIBLIOGRAPHY: Heinricus de Lettis, *Chronicon Livoniæ*, 1125-1227, in *MGH*, *Script.*, xxiii, (1874) 231-332; K. von Schlözer, *Livland und die Anfänge deutschen Lebens im Norden*, Berlin, 1850; F. Winter, *Die Prämonstratenser des zwölften Jahrhunderts*, ib. 1865; idem, *Die Cistercienser des nordöstlichen Deutschlands*, Gotha, 1868; R. Hausmann, *Das Ringen der Deutschen und Dänen um den Besitz Estlands*, Leipsic, 1870; G. Dehio, *Geschichte des Erzbistums Hamburg-Bremen*, ii. 160 sqq., Berlin, 1877; T. Schiemann, *Russland, Polen und Livland*, in *Allgemeine Geschichte*, ii. 1 sqq., ib. 1887.

ALBERTI, ăl-bär'-tî, VALENTIN: Lutheran; b. at Lähn (60 m. w.s.w. of Breslau), Silesia, Dec. 15, 1635; d. in Leipsic Sept. 19, 1697. He studied in the latter city and spent most of his life there, being professor extraordinary of theology from 1672. As a representative of the orthodoxy of his time he wrote against Pufendorf and Scheffling (qq.v.), but is noteworthy chiefly for his part in the Pietistic controversy. In Feb., 1687, he furnished a meeting-place in his house for the *collegia philobiblica*, which brought on the controversy in Leipsic (see PIETISM). Nevertheless, in 1696 he published an *Ausführlicher Gegenantwort auf Speners sogenannte gründliche Vertheidigung seiner und der Pietisten Unschuld*.

ALBERTINI, ăl"ber-tî'nî, JOHANN BAPTIST VON: Moravian bishop; b. at Neuwied (on the Rhine; 8 m. n.n.w. of Coblenz) Feb. 17, 1769; d. at Berthelsdorf, near Herrnhut, Dec. 6, 1831. He was educated at Neuwied, at Niesky (1782–85), and at the theological seminary of Barby (1785–88). From 1788 to 1810 he taught in the school at Niesky; from 1810 to 1821 he was preacher and bishop in Niesky, Gnadenberg, and Gnadenfrei (Silesia); in 1821 he became a member, and in 1824 president, of the Elders' Conference in the department for Church and school. He published: *Predigten* (1805); *Geistliche Lieder* (1821); and *Reden* (1832). Some of his spiritual songs are of rare beauty. He was a fellow student and friend of Schleiermacher.

ALBERTUS MAGNUS ("Albert the Great"): Founder of the most flourishing period of scholasticism; b. at Lauingen (26 m. n.w. of Augsburg), Bavaria, 1193; d. at Cologne Nov. 15, 1280. He studied at Padua, entered the order of St. Dominic there in 1223, and served as lector in the various convent schools of the order in Germany, especially in Cologne. In 1245 he went to Paris to become master of theology. In 1248 he returned to Cologne as *primarius lector* and *regens* of the school in that city. In 1254 a general chapter of the Dominican order at Worms chose him general for Germany, in which capacity he traversed the country on foot from end to end, visiting the monasteries and enforcing discipline. In 1260 Alexander IV. made him bishop of Regensburg; but this office was so little in harmony with his character and habits as a teacher and writer that, after the lapse of two years, he was allowed to resign. He retired to his monastery in Cologne, where he spent the rest of his life, making many brief visits, however, to other places; as when he went to Paris after he had reached the age of 80 to vindicate the orthodoxy of his late pupil, Thomas Aquinas.

As an author Albert evinced a many-sidedness which procured for him the title of *doctor universalis*, while his knowledge of natural science and its practical applications made him a sorcerer in popular estimation. His works fill twenty-one folio volumes as published by P. Jammy (Lyons, 1651; reedited by A. Borgnet, 38 vols., Paris, 1890–1900). They embrace logic, physics, metaphysics and psychology, ethics, and theology. By the use of translations from the Arabic and Greco-Latin versions, he expounded the complete philosophical system of Aristotle, excepting the "Politics," modifying his interpretation in the interests of the Church. Thus the influence of Aristotle came to supersede Platonism and Neoplatonism in the later scholasticism. At a time when dialectic was in sore need of a new method, the introduction of the Aristotelian logic provided a subtle and searching instrument for investigation and discussion. For Albertus, logic was not properly a science, but an organon for reaching the unknown by means of the known. Following Avicenna whom he regards as the leading commentator of Aristotle, he affirms that universals exist in three modes: (1) *Before* the individuals, as ideas or types in the divine mind (Plato). (2) *In* the individuals, as that which is common to them (Aristotle). (3) *After* the individuals, as an abstraction of thought (conceptualists and nominalists). Thus he seeks to harmonize the rival teachings concerning universals. In expounding the physical theories of Aristotle, he showed that he partook of the rising scientific spirit of the age, especially in his criticism of alchemy and in *De vegetabilibus et plantis*, which abounds in brilliant observations.

The chief theological works of Albertus were a commentary (3 vols.) on the "Sentences" of Peter Lombard, and a *Summum theologiæ* in a more didactic strain. Already the "doctrine of the twofold truth" had been accepted by his contemporaries—what is truth in philosophy may not be truth in theology, and *vice versa*. Christian thinkers were, however, profoundly perplexed by the sharp opposition between ideas drawn from Greek scientific and philosophical sources and those derived from religious tradition. Albertus sought to soften this antinomy by establishing the distinction between natural and revealed religion, which became henceforth a postulate of medieval and later theology. Since the soul can know only that which is grounded in its own nature, it rises to the mystery of the Trinity, the Incarnation, and other specifically Christian doctrines through supernatural illumination alone. Hence the well-known dictum: "Revelation is above but not contrary to reason." On the one hand, the attempt to "rationalize" the contents of revelation must be abandoned; on the other hand, philosophy must be modified in the interests of faith. The merit which belongs to faith consists in its accepting truth which comes only through revelation. In his entire discussion concerning the being and attributes of God, concerning the world as created in time in opposition to the eternity of matter as maintained by Aristotle, concerning angels, miracles, the soul, sin and free-will, grace, and finally, original and actual sin, the Aristotelian logic is applied in the most rigid manner, and when this fails Albertus retires behind the distinction thrown up between philosophy and theology. With all his learning and subtlety of argument, he made it evident that with his presuppositions and by his method a final adjudication of the claims of reason and faith, that is, a unity of intelligence, is impossible. Apart from his vast erudition, his significance lay first, in his profound influence upon scholastic and the subsequent Protestant theology through his substitution of the Aristotelian logic and metaphysics for Platonic and Neoplatonic ideas, and secondly, in the fact, that to a degree never before attempted, he set in clear light and organized in the thought of the Church the ancient opposition between Jewish supernaturalism and Greek rationalism. By the false antithesis thus raised between reason and revelation, he prepared the way for the long conflict of theology and science, of reason and dogma, of naturalism and supernaturalism, of individual judgment and collective authority, which is still unsettled. C. A. BECKWITH.

BIBLIOGRAPHY: J. Sighart, *Albertus Magnus, sein Leben und seine Wissenschaft*, Ratisbon, 1857, Eng. transl., London, 1876; B. Gauslinus, *Albertus Magnus*, Venice, 1630; F. A. Pouchet, *Histoire des sciences naturelles au moyen-âge, ou Albert le Grand et son époque*, Paris, 1853; M. Joel, *Verhältniss Albert des Grossen zu Moses Maimonides*, Breslau, 1863; O. d'Assailly, *Albert le Grand*, Paris, 1870; W. Preger, *Geschichte der deutschen Mystik im Mittelalter*, Leipsic, 1874; *Albertus Magnus in Geschichte und Sage*, Cologne, 1880; G. von Hertling, *Albertus Magnus*, ib. 1880; R. de Liechty, *Albert le Grand et S. Thomas d'Aquin*, Paris, 1880; J. Bach, *Des Albertus Magnus Verhältniss zu der Erkenntnisslehre der Griechen, Lateiner, Araber und Juden*, Vienna, 1881; A. Schneider, *Die Psychologie Alberts des Grossen*, Münster, 1903. For his philosophy: A. Stöckl, *Geschichte der scholastischen Philosophie*, 3 vols., Mainz, 1864–66; J. E. Erdmann, *Grundriss der Geschichte der Philosophie*, i., 4th ed., 1895, Eng. transl., vol. i., London, 1893.

ALBIGENSES. See NEW MANICHEANS, II.

ALBIZZI, äl-bit'sî or äl-bît'sî, **ANTONIO**: Italian priest; b. in Florence Nov. 25, 1547; d. at Kempten (50 m. s.s.w. of Augsburg), Bavaria, July 17, 1626. He became secretary to Cardinal Andrew, archduke of Austria (1576), but after the death of the latter (1591) embraced Protestantism, left Italy, and resided thenceforth in Augsburg and Kempten He wrote: *Principium Christianorum stemmata* (Augsburg, 1608); *Sermones in Matthæum* (1609); *De principiis religionis Christianæ* (1612); and *Exercitationes theologicæ* (Kempten, 1616).

ALBIZZI, BARTOLOMEO (Lat. *Bartholomæus Albicius Pisanus*): Franciscan monk; b. at Rivano, Tuscany; d. at Pisa Dec. 10, 1401. He became a celebrated preacher, and taught theology in several monasteries, chiefly at Pisa. He wrote a famous book, *Liber conformitatum vitæ Sancti Francisci cum vita Jesu Christi*, which was approved by the general chapter of his order in 1399 and was first printed at Venice toward the close of the fifteenth century. It is of great value for the history of the Franciscans, but is marred by exaggerations and lack of judgment and good taste (e.g., he states that Francis was foretold in the Old Testament by prototypes and prophecies, that he performed miracles and prophesied, and that he was crucified and is exalted above the angels). In subsequent editions many passages were modified or omitted. Erasmus Alber (q.v.) made it the basis of his *Barfüsser Mönche Eulenspiegel und Alcoran* (published at Wittenberg, with an introduction by Luther, 1542). Albizzi published also sermons and a life of the Virgin Mary (Venice, 1596).

ALBO, JOSEPH: The last noteworthy Jewish religious philosopher of the Middle Ages; b. at Monreal (125 m. e.n.e. of Madrid), Spain, about 1380; d. about 1444. He was one of the principal Jewish representatives at the disputation held in 1413 and 1414 at Tortosa, under the auspices of Benedict XIII., between selected champions of the Jewish and Christian religions, with the view of convincing the Jews, from the testimony of their own literature, of the truth of Christianity. About 1425, at Soria in Old Castile, he wrote his principal work of religious philosophy, *Sepher ha-'Iḳḳarim* ("Book of the Roots," i.e., "Fundamental Principles"). He finds three ideas fundamental in any religion, viz., God, Revelation, and Retribution. [In the idea of God he finds four secondary principles, unity, incorporeality, eternity, and perfection; in the second of his fundamentals he finds three secondary principles, prophecy, Moses as the unique prophet, and the binding force of the Mosaic Law; and from his third fundamental he derives secondarily the belief in the resurrection of the body.] He discusses also the distinguishing marks of the historic religions, attempting to prove that Judaism is differentiated from Christianity by its greater credibility and consonance with reason. Belief in a Messiah he considers an essential part not of Judaism, but of Christianity. There is a German translation of his work by W and L. Schlesinger (Frankfort, 1844). (G. DALMAN.)

BIBLIOGRAPHY: M. Eisler, *Vorlesungen über die jüdische Philosophie des Mittelalters*, iii. 180–234, Vienna, 1876; H. Grätz, *Geschichte der Juden*, 3d ed., viii. 168–178, Berlin, 1890, Eng. transl., London, 1891–98; A. Tänzer, *Die Religions-Philosophie Joseph Albo's*, Frankfort, 1896; *JE*, i. 324–327.

ALBRECHT, äl'brext. See ALBERT.

ALBRECHT, OTTO WILHELM FERDINAND: German Lutheran; b. at Angermünde (42 m. n.e. of Berlin) Dec. 2, 1855. He was educated at the gymnasium in Potsdam, at the University of Halle (1873–77), and at the Wittenberg seminary for preachers. He was assistant pastor at Wittenberg in 1880–81, and pastor at Stödten in 1881–84, at Dachwig in 1884–92, and at Naumburg (Saale) from 1892 to the present time. He was elected a corresponding member of the *Königliche Akademie gemeinnütziger Wissenschaften* in 1895. His theological position is that of a modern Lutheran. His writings include *Geschichte der Magdeburger Bibelgesellschaft* (1892); *Die evangelische Gemeinde Miltenberg und ihr erster Prediger* (Halle, 1896); *Predigten* (Gotha, 1899); *Geschichte der Marien-Magdalenenkirche zu Naumburg a. S.* (1902); and *Das Enchiridion Luthers vom Jahre 1536 herausgegeben und untersucht* (1905). He has also been a collaborator on the Weimar edition of the works of Luther, to which he has contributed the fifteenth and twenty-eighth volumes, containing the reformer's writings of 1524 and his sermons on John in 1528-29 (Weimar, 1898–1903). He is likewise a collaborator on the Brunswick edition of Luther, and is the author of numerous briefer monographs and contributions.

ALBRIGHT, al'brait, **JACOB:** Founder of "the Evangelical Association of North America;" b. near Pottstown, Penn., May 1, 1759; d. at Mühlbach, Lebanon County, Penn., May 18, 1808. His parents were Pennsylvania Germans of the Lutheran Church, in which denomination he was himself trained. His education was defective, and his early surroundings were unintellectual. After marriage he moved to Lancaster County and carried on a successful tile and brick business. Grief over the death of several children in one year (1790) and the counsels of Anton Hautz, a German Reformed minister, led to his conversion, and he became a Methodist lay preacher. At length his concern for his German Lutheran brethren led him to give up business and devote himself entirely to missionary efforts. As the Methodist Church did not desire to enter upon the German field he founded a new denomination. Its members are often called the "Albright Brethren." See Evangelical Association.

ALCANTARA, al-can'ta-ra, **ORDER OF:** A spiritual order of knights, with Cistercian rule, founded for the defense of the frontier of Castile against the Moors under Alfonso VIII., the Noble (1158–1214). Its name at first was Order of San Julian del Pereiro ("of the pear-tree"), from a Castilian frontier citadel, the defense of which was entrusted to two brothers, Suarez and Gomez Barrientos, who with Bishop Ordonius (Ordosio) of Salamanca (1160–66) founded the order. When Alcantara in Estremadura was taken by King Alfonso IX. of Leon in 1213, the seat of the order was transferred to that place. Alfonso committed the defense of this important fortress at first to the knightly order of Calatrava (q.v.), but five years later he transferred the service to the Order of San Julian, which now (1218) took the name of the Order of Alcantara, being still subject, however, to the grand master of the Calatrava order. Taking advantage of a contested election, it separated from the Calatrava order, and elected its first independent grand master in the person of Diego Sanchez. During the subsequent struggles with the Moors, in which the Alcantara knights distinguished themselves by their bravery, they had on their flag the united arms of Leon and Castile, with a cross of the order and the ancient emblem of the pear-tree. The number of their commanderies in their days of prosperity was about fifty. When Juan de Zuñiga, the thirty-eighth grand master (1479–95) resigned his office to become archbishop of Seville, the grandmastership passed to the king of Castile (Ferdinand the Catholic). With its independent existence the order lost more and more its spiritual character. In consequence of the disturbances in the Spanish monarchy, it was abolished in 1873, but was reestablished in 1874 as a purely military order of merit by Alfonso XII. O. Zöckler†.

Bibliography: Rades de Andrada, *Cronica de las tres Ordines y Caballerias de Santiago, Calatrava y Alcantara*, Toledo, 1572; *Difiniciones de la orden y cavalleria de Alcantara*, Madrid, 1663; Helyot, *Ordres monastiques*, vi. 53–65; P. B. Gams, *Kirchengeschichte von Spanien*, iii. 55–56, Ratisbon, 1876.

ALCIMUS. See High Priest.

ALCUIN, al'cwin (English name, **Ealhwine;** Lat. *Flaccus Albinus*): The most prominent adviser of Charlemagne in his efforts to promote learning; b. in Northumbria (perhaps in York) 735 (730?); d. at Tours May 19, 804. He was of good birth and a relative of Willibrod. He was educated in the famous cathedral school of Archbishop Egbert of York (q.v.), under a master, Ethelbert (Albert), who seems to have been a man of many-sided learning and who is often praised by Alcuin. With him, or commissioned by him, Alcuin made several visits to Rome, and on such journeys became acquainted with Frankish monasteries and with men like Lul of Mainz and Fulrad of St. Denis. He succeeded Ethelbert as head of the school when the latter was made archbishop (766), and, after Ethelbert's retirement and the elevation of Eanbald to the archiepiscopal throne (778), was also custos of the valuable cathedral library at York. He went to Rome to obtain the pallium for Eanbald, and at Parma (781) met Charlemagne to whom he was already known. Shortly after his return to England he accepted a call from the Frankish king, who was then gathering scholars at his court, and, with the exception of a visit to his native land on political business in 790–793, spent the rest of his life on the Continent. Charlemagne gave him the income of several abbeys, and till 790 he acted as head of a court school, where not only the sons of the Frankish nobles, but Charlemagne and his family as well, profited by his instruction.

A true scholar and teacher, Alcuin seldom meddled in worldly affairs, and his letters (more than 300 in number) give little historical information, though they are rich in personal details. He took an active part in the Adoptionist controversy, wrote two treatises against Felix of Urgel, and opposed his colleague, Elipandus. At the Synod of Frankfort in 794 he assisted in the condemnation of Felix, and later, at the Synod of Aachen in 799 (800?), induced him to recant (see Adoptionism). From 793 he was the constant and efficient helper of Charlemagne in founding schools, promoting the education of the clergy, and like undertakings. He was also in close association with contemporaries like Arno of Salzburg, Angilbert, abbot of

Centula, and Adalhard of Corbie. In 796 his patron gave him the abbey of St. Martin, near Tours, and several other monasteries. Under his guidance the school of Tours became a nursery of ecclesiastical and liberal education for the whole kingdom. His distinguished pupils there included Sigulf, who supplied the information for his biography, Rabanus Maurus, and perhaps the liturgist, Amalarius of Metz. When old and feeble and almost blind, he left the management to his scholars, but he continued to be the counselor of his royal friend till his death.

Alcuin was mild in spirit, adverse to discord, orthodox in faith, equally interested in promoting the authority of Rome and the royal priesthood of Charlemagne. His great service was his part in the so-called Carolingian renaissance, his wise and efficient efforts to elevate and educate the clergy and the monks, to improve preaching, to regulate the Christian life of the people and advance the faith among the heathen, always by instruction rather than by force. His theology, while not original, rests on an intimate acquaintance with the Fathers, especially Jerome and Augustine. To ecclesiastical learning he added classical, but in such manner that it was always the servant of the former. He was able to give his master information concerning astronomy and natural science but, as he considered grammar and philosophy auxiliary to religion, so he regarded these branches of knowledge primarily as a means of knowing God.

His theological writings include a work on the Trinity which contains the germs of the later scholastic theology. His authorship of a *Libellus de processu Spiritus Sancti* and of some other works which have been attributed to him is doubtful. He wrote commentaries on Genesis, the Psalms, the Song of Songs, John, and other books of the Bible, based upon the Church Fathers and following the current moral and allegorical exposition. At Charlemagne's request he revived the text of the Vulgate according to the best available sources. His skill as a teacher is evident in text-books on grammar and orthography, as well as in treatises on rhetoric and dialectics which resemble Cicero. His Latin poems, including epigrams, friendly letters, hymns, riddles, poems for special occasions, and the like, show more skill in versification than poetic gifts. The most important, the *De pontificibus et sanctis ecclesiæ Eboracensis*, gives valuable information concerning the state of culture in his native land and his own education [and contains (ll. 1530 61) a catalogue of the cathedral library at York, which is the earliest existing catalogue of an English library]. With the exception of the hymns, all his poems are partly in heroic and partly in elegiac verse. He prepared lives of Willibrod, Vedastus, and Richarius, which are mainly recasts and amplifications of older works. Of a liturgical and devotional character are a *Liber sacramentalis* and the *De psalmorum usu*. Intended more particularly for the laity are the *De virtutibus et vitiis* and a psychologico-philosophical treatise on ethics, *De animæ ratione ad Eulaliam virginem* (i.e., Guntrade, the sister of Adalhard). H. HAHN.

BIBLIOGRAPHY: Sources: Alcuin, *Opera*, ed. by Frobenius Forster, 2 vols., Ratisbon, 1777, contains anonymous life written before 829 A.D. on data furnished by Sigulf; reprinted in *MPL*, c.-ci.; *Monumenta Alcuiniana*, ed. by W. Wattenbach and E. Dümmler, in *BRG*, vi., Berlin, 1873 (contains life of Alcuin, his life of Willibrod, and his *De pontificibus*); Alcuin, *Epistolæ*, in *MGH*, *Epist.*, iv. 1–481 (*Epist. Caroli ævi*, ii.), 1895, and in *BRG*, 1873, vi. 144–897; idem, *Carmina*, in *MGH*, *Poetæ latini ævi Caroli*, i. (1881) 160–350; idem, *De pontificibus*, in *Historians of the Church of York and its Archbishops*, ed. by J. Raine, i. 349–398 (cf. pp. lxi.-lxv. of *Rolls Series*, No. 71, London, 1879); Martinus Turonensis, *Vita Alcuini Abbatis*, in *MGH*, *Script.*, xv. 1 (1887), 182–197. General: Rivet, in *Histoire littéraire de la France*, iv. 295–347; F. Lorentz, *Alcuins Leben*, Halle, 1829, Eng. transl., London, 1837; J. C. F. Bähr, *Geschichte der römischen Literatur im karolingischen Zeitalter*, pp. 78–84, 192–196, 302–354, Carlsruhe, 1840; J. B. Laforêt, *Alcuin, restaurateur des sciences en occident sous Charlemagne*, Louvain, 1851; F. Monnier, *Alcuin et son influence littéraire, religieuse et politique chez les Franks*, 2d ed., Paris, 1864; A. Dupuy, *Alcuin et l'école de Saint-Martin de Tours*, Tours, 1876; idem, *Alcuin et la souveraineté pontificale au huitième siècle*, ib. 1872; F. Hamelin, *Essai sur la vie et les ouvrages d'Alcuin*, Rennes, 1874; *ADB*, i. 343–348; T. Sickel, *Alcuinstudien*, i. 92, Vienna, 1875; J. B. Mullinger, *The Schools of Charles the Great*, ch. i.-ii., New York, 1904; *DCB*, i. 73–76; A. Ebert, *Allgemeine Geschichte der Litteratur des Mittelalters*, ii. 12 36, Leipsic, 1880; K. Werner, *Alcuin und sein Jahrhundert*, 2d ed., Vienna, 1881; S. Abel and B. Simson, *Jahrbücher des fränkischen Reichs unter Karl dem Grossen*, 2 vols., Leipsic, 1883; A. Largeault, *Inscriptions métriques composées par Alcuin*, Poitiers, 1885; *DNB*, i. 239–240; L. Traube, *Karolingische Dichtungen*, Berlin, 1888; Hauck, *KD*, ii. 119–145; W. S. Teuffel, *Geschichte der römischen Literatur*, p. 1090, No. 8, p. 1305, No. 3, Leipsic, 1890; Wattenbach, *DGQ*, 1893, pp. 148, 152, 159–163; A. West, *Alcuin and the Rise of the Christian Schools*, New York, 1893; C. J. B. Gaskoin, *Alcuin, his Life and Work*, Cambridge, 1904.

ALDEBERT. See ADALBERT.

ALDENBURG, BISHOPRIC OF. See LÜBECK, BISHOPRIC OF.

ALDHELM (EALDHELM), ăld'helm, **SAINT**: Abbot of Malmesbury and first bishop of Sherborne; b. probably at Brokenborough (2 m. n.w of Malmesbury), Wiltshire, between 639 and 645; d. at Doulting (7 m. s.e. of Wells), Somersetshire, May 25, 709. He was of royal family on both his father's and mother's side, studied with Maildulf (Maelduib), an Irish hermit, at Malmesbury (Maildulfsburg), and remained there as monk for fourteen years. In 670 and again in 672 he attended the school of Canterbury and laid the foundations of his many-sided knowledge under the instruction of Archbishop Theodore and his associate Hadrian. In 675 he succeeded Maildulf as abbot at Malmesbury, and as such increased the possessions of the monastery, spread abroad the faith, and founded many stone churches, after the fashion of Canterbury, in place of the small wooden ones. In 705 the bishopric of the West Saxons was divided, Aldhelm being made bishop of the western part with his seat at Sherborne (in northwestern Dorsetshire, 18 m. n. of Dorchester). He retained his abbacy. He was buried at Malmesbury, but his remains were often translated. He was canonized in 1080.

Aldhelm was one of the most learned men of his time, and he occupies a distinguished place among early British scholars. He represented both the Iro-Scottish and the Roman ecclesiastical culture, and had an acquaintance with classical authors like Homer and Aristotle, as well as with neo-Christian writers such as Prudentius and Sedulius. His works abound in Greek and Latin words, and his style is bombastic. Besides philology, poetry, music, astronomical calculations, and the like occupied him, and he is said to have written popular hymns. He made Malmesbury a rival of Canterbury as a seat of learning, and princes, abbesses, monks, and nuns from far and near were among his admirers. He is said to have visited Rome during the pontificate of Sergius (687-701) and to have returned with relics, books, and a grant of privileges for his monastery. He supported Wilfrid of York (q.v.) against his enemies, and was prominent in urging the Britons to conform to the Roman tonsure and Easter.

Besides briefer letters, preserved (often only in fragments) by Lul of Mainz, Aldhelm's works include treatises in epistolary form and poems, viz.: (1) an *Epistola ad Acircium* (King Aldfrid) concerning the number seven, riddles, versification, and the like; (2) an *Epistola ad Geruntium* (a Welsh prince, Geraint) concerning the Easter question; (3 and 4) a prose work and a poem in praise of virginity, addressed to the abbess and nuns of Barking, closing with a description of eight vices, which contains thrusts at Anglo-Saxon conditions. To his treatise on riddles he added 100 specimens dealing with nature and art, which are full of a feeling for nature, being herein a prototype of such of his countrymen as Tatwin and Boniface. In his letter to Geraint he holds as worthless good works without connection with the Roman Church. His poetry is flowery, involved, and alliterative. His chief merit was the extension of the faith in the south of England, the education of his native land, and his literary influence on the Continent.

H. Hahn.

Bibliography: *Aldhelmi Opera*, in *PEA*, No. 583, Oxford, 1844, reprinted in *MPL*, lxxxix.; *Epistolæ*, in P Jaffé, *BRG*, iii. 24–28, Berlin, 1866, and in *MGH*, *Epist.*, iii. (1892) 231-247; William of Malmesbury, *De gestis pontificum Anglorum*, ed. N. E. S. A. Hamilton, in *Rolls Series*, No. 52, pp. 332-443, London, 1870, and in *MPL*, clxxix.; idem, *De Gestis Regum Anglorum*, 1887–89, in *Rolls Series*, No. 90; Faricius, *Vita Aldhelmi*, in J. A. Giles, *Vita quorundam Anglo-Saxonum*, London, 1854, and in *MPL*, lxxxix. (Faricius was an Italian, physician to Henry I. of England, a monk of Malmesbury, and abbot of Abingford); Bede, *Hist. eccl.*, v. 18; J. M. Kemble, *Codex diplomaticus ævi Saxonici*, London, 1839; T. Wright, *Biographia Britannica litteraria*, i. 209–222, ii. 47, ib. 1851; *Eulogium historiarum*, 1858, in *Rolls Series*, No. 9; *Anglo-Saxon Chronicle*, 1861, ib. No. 23; *Registrum Malmesburiense*, 1879, ib. No. 72; *DNB*, i. 78–79, 245–247; H. Hahn, *Boniface und Lul, ihre angelsächsischen Korrespondenten*, Leipsic, 1883; M. Manitius, *Zu Aldhelm und Bæda*, Vienna, 1886 (on Aldhelm's literary work); L. Traube, *Karolingische Dichtungen*, Berlin, 1888; W. S. Teuffel, *Geschichte der römischen Literatur*, 1304, § 500, No. 2, Leipsic, 1890; L. Boenhoff, *Aldhelm von Malmesbury*, Dresden, 1894; W. Bright, *Early English Church History*, pp. 294-297, 444–446, 462–469, 471–474, Oxford, 1897; W. B. Wildman, *Life of St. Ealdhelm*, Sherborne, 1905.

ALEANDRO, GIROLAMO, ā″lê-ān′drō jî-rō′lā-mō (Lat. *Hieronymus Aleander*): Italian humanist and cardinal; b. at Motta (30 m. n.e. of Venice) Feb. 13, 1480; d. in Rome Jan. 31, 1542. He studied in his native town and in Venice, settled in the latter city as a teacher in 1499, and became a contributor to the press of Aldus Manutius. In 1508 he went to Paris and there attained great reputation as a classical scholar, being chosen in 1513 rector of the university. In the following year he went to Liége where the influence of Bishop Erard made him chancellor of the see of Chartres. As Erard's representative he went to Rome in 1516 and won the favor of Cardinal Giulio de' Medici, whose private secretary he became. Later, Leo X. appointed him librarian to the Vatican. In 1520 he went as nuncio to the court of Emperor Charles V., charged with the task of combating the heretical teachings of Luther. He procured Luther's condemnation at the Diet of Worms in 1521, and is supposed to have been the author of the edict issued against the great reformer. He was made archbishop of Brindisi in 1524 and was sent as nuncio to the court of Francis I. of France, with whom he was taken prisoner at Pavia.

Till 1531 Aleandro lived without employment, in Venice for the greater part of the time, a refugee from Rome on account of his debts. In 1531 he was sent as papal representative to Charles V., whom he accompanied to the Netherlands and Italy, zealous in inciting the emperor to action against the Protestants. After residing as nuncio in Venice from 1533 to 1535 he was summoned to Rome by Pope Paul III., who, in preparation for a general council, wished to avail himself of Aleandro's historical learning. His services gained him a cardinal's hat in 1538, in which year he went as legate to Venice where the projected council was to be held. Thence he was sent to the court of the German king Ferdinand where he at first exerted himself in favor of a conciliatory policy toward the Protestants, and, when his efforts failed, demanded their ruthless destruction. Of his writings the reports covering his various diplomatic missions are of extreme value for the history of the Reformation. His letters also are of importance, among his correspondents being Aldus Manutius, Erasmus, Ulrich von Hutten, Bembo, Contarini, and Cardinal Pole. His diaries are remarkable for their frank revelation of a life of indulgence in complete contrast with his priestly character.

(T. Brieger.)

Bibliography: His papers, declarations, and letters are scattered in A. Mai, *Spicilegium Romanum*, ii. 231–240, Rome, 1839; H. Læmmer, *Monumenta Vaticana*, pp. 77 sqq., 223-241, Freiburg, 1861; J. J. I. von Döllinger, *Beiträge zur politischen, kirchlichen und Culturgeschichte*, iii. 243–284, Vienna, 1882; P. Balan, *Monumenta Reformationis Lutheranæ*, 1 sqq., 335 sqq.; P. de Nolhac, *Studi e Documenti di Storia e Diritto*, ix. 208-217, Rome, 1888; B. Morsolin, *Il Concilio di Vicenza*, Venice, 1889; W. Friedensburg, *Legation Aleanders, 1538–39*, in *Nuntiaturberichte aus Deutschland*, vols. iii.-iv., Gotha, 1893; H. Omont, *Journal autobiographique du . J. Aléandre*, pp. 35–98, 113 sqq., Paris, 1895. The foregoing are important for the history of the Reformation. For his life: W Friedensburg, ut sup., iii. 28–41, 44, and Preface, pp. v.-vii.; C. Perocco, *Biografio del cardinale G. Aleandri*, Venice, 1839. In general: K. Jansen, *Aleander am Reichstage zu Worms*, Kiel, 1883; G. M. Mazzuchelli, *Gli Scrittori d'Italia*, I. i. 408–424, Brescia, 1753; T. Brieger, *Aleander und Luther 1521*, part 1, Gotha, 1884.

ALEGAMBE, ā″lê-gāmb′, **PHILIPPE D'**: Jesuit theologian and literary historian; b. in Brussels Jan. 22, 1592; d. in Rome Sept. 6, 1652. He entered the Jesuit order at Palermo in 1613, taught theology at Graz, and accompanied the son of Prince von Eggenberg, the favorite of Ferdinand II., on his travels. Then he returned to Graz for a time, but in 1638 was called to Rome as secretary for German affairs to the general of his order. Here he remained until his death, acting in later years as spiritual director of the Roman house. Of his writings the most noteworthy is the *Bibliotheca scriptorum societatis Jesu* (Antwerp, 1643), based upon an earlier catalogue of Jesuit writers by Peter Ribadeneira (1608, 1613), but much surpassing it in learning and thoroughness. Though betraying the Jesuit spirit, it shows, on the other hand, signs of an attempt at impartiality, proving, for example, that various books against the royal power, the episcopate, and the Sorbonne, the authorship of which the French Jesuits had tried to deny, were really written by them. A new and enlarged edition by an English Jesuit, Nathaniel Southwell, appeared at Rome in 1676. The work is now superseded by the *Bibliothèque des Écrivains de la Compagnie de Jésus* of Augustin and Aloys de Backer (7 vols., Liége, 1853-61; new ed. by C. Sommervogel, 9 vols., Brussels, 1890-1900).

(A. Hauck.)

ALEMANNI, ä″lê-män′nî: An important Germanic tribe, first mentioned by Dio Cassius as fighting a battle with Caracalla near Mainz in 213. According to Asinius Quadratus, they belonged to the confederacy of the Suevi. They came from the northeast, where the Semnones held the territory between the Oder and the Elbe. They had varying success in their struggle against the Romans, but about 260-268 they occupied the Tithe Lands, north of the Danube, and advanced south as far as Ravenna and east into what is now Austria. They fought with Maximian in 290, and obtained permanent possession of the territory extending to the Alb and the Neckar about 300. By 405 or 406 they had conquered the southern plains of Upper Swabia and the neighboring lands of northern and eastern Switzerland, as far as the Vosges. In the fifth century the region from the Iller to the Vosges and from the lower Main to the St. Gothard bore the name of Alemannia. They were a fierce and stubborn race, hostile to Roman civilization, and possessing a religion closely connected with the powers of nature. In the Tithe Lands they must have met with at least weak Christian congregations, which fell with the Roman power.

Early History.

The numerous captives who were led away from Christian Gaul had little influence after they were deprived of Christian nurture. The Alemanni, however, learned Christian views. Their prince, Gibuld, was an Arian, probably converted by Goths. The Augsburg bishopric was maintained; but the Alemanni in general continued heathen till they were overcome at Strasburg in 496 by Clovis, king of the Franks. He took their northern territory and established royal residences there. A part of the people went into the country of the Ostrogoth Theodoric, probably the present German Switzerland, where the bishoprics of Windisch and Augst (Basel) existed and the Roman population was Christian. In 536 Vitiges ceded this territory to the Frankish king Theodebert. Effective missionary work was carried on by the newly converted Franks from St. Martin's Church at Tours as a center; and churches dedicated to Saints Martin, Remigius, Brictius, Medard, Lupus, Antholianus, Clement, Felix, and Adauctus indicate the Frankish influence. In the courts the Frankish priest ruled beside the royal administrator. As early as 575 the Greek Agathias hoped for a speedy victory of Christianity among the Alemanni, because the "more intelligent" of them had been won by the Franks. Duke Uncilen (588-605) was probably, and his successor Cunzo was certainly, a Christian. The oldest law of the Alemanni, the so-called *pactus* of c. 590-600 recognizes the Church as the protector of slaves. The episcopal see of Windisch was transferred to Constance, nearer Ueberlingen, the ducal seat; and the Augsburg bishopric was separated from Aquileia, that of Strasburg coming again into prominence.

Conversion to Christianity.

But heathenism was still powerful. Many of the new converts still sacrificed to the gods. The Frankish Church was not influential enough to permeate the popular life of the Alemanni. But efficient help came from the Celtic missionaries of Ireland. In 610 Columban (q.v.), on the suggestion of King Theodebert, ascended the Rhine with monks from Luxeuil and settled at Bregenz, but had to leave after two years. His pupil Gallus, however, the founder of the monastery of St. Gall (q.v.), remained, and in connection with the native priests labored for the cause of Christ. From Poitiers came the Celt Fridolin (q.v.), founder of the monastery of Säckingen. Trudpert built a cell in the Breisgau. As the Merovingians sank lower and lower the desire of the Alemanni for independence grew, and they found need of the support of the Church in their struggle for liberty. Unwilling to see themselves surpassed in devotion by the despised Franks, they made rich donations to St. Gall. The *Lex Alemannorum*, drawn up probably at a great assembly under Duke Lantfried in 719, gave the Church and its bishops a position of dignity and power, though the life of the people was still far from being thoroughly influenced by its moral teaching. The effort for independence was crushed by the strong arm of the mayor of the palace. To balance St. Gall, which had favored it, Charles Martel, with the help of Pirmin (q.v.), founded the monastery of Reichenau in 724. Pirmin was expelled in 727, and his pupil and successor Heddo a few years later. The entire people were then baptized, but they had no clear knowledge of the Christian faith and were still influenced by heathen customs. The organizing work of Boniface was at first opposed in Alemannia, but by 798 the people had begun to make pilgrimages to Rome. Several small monasteries were established, and, besides St. Gall and Reichenau, the royal monasteries of Weissenburg, Lorsch, and Fulda received rich gifts. The distinguished Alemanni who filled bishoprics under the Carolingians, and Hildegard, the queen of Charlemagne, with her brother, Gerold, evidence the ultimate triumph of Christianity.

Irish Missionaries.

G. Bossert.

BIBLIOGRAPHY: C. F. Stälin, *Württembergische Geschichte*, vol. i., Stuttgart, 1841; Rettberg, *KD;* Friedrich, *KD;* H. von Schubert, *Die Unterwerfung der Alamannen*, Strasburg, 1884; G. Bossert, *Die Anfänge des Christentums in Württemberg*, Stuttgart, 1888; A. Birlinger, *Rechtsrheinisches Alamannien; Grenzen, Sprache, Eigenart*, Stuttgart, 1890; E. Egli, *Kirchengeschichte der Schweiz bis auf Karl den Grossen*, Zürich, 1893; *Württembergische Kirchengeschichte* of the Calwer Verlagsverein, 1893; Hauck, *KD*, i. 2; F. L. Baumann, *Forschungen zur Schwabischen Geschichte, 500–585*, Kempten, 1899.

ALESIUS, a-li'shi-us, **ALEXANDER** (Latinized form of **Aless**; known also as **Alane**): Protestant reformer; b. in Edinburgh Apr. 23, 1500; d. in Leipsic Mar. 17, 1565. He studied at St. Andrews and became canon there. In 1527 he tried to induce Patrick Hamilton (q.v.) to recant, attended him at the stake the next year, and was himself converted to the reformed doctrines. To escape from the harsh treatment of the provost of St. Andrews he fled to Germany (1532). Commended to Henry VIII. and Cranmer by Melanchthon, he went to England in 1535. For a short time he lectured on divinity at Cambridge, studied and practised medicine in London, and was much esteemed by the reforming party there till 1540, when he went back to Germany and became professor at Frankfort-on-the-Oder, removing three years later to Leipsic. He was closely associated with the German reformers, especially Melanchthon, and was honored and trusted by them, although a desire to conciliate and a belief that concord was possible where differences were irreconcilable made him sometimes appear vacillating and paradoxical. He wrote several exegetical works on different books of the Bible, and a large number of dogmatic and polemical treatises, such as *De scripturis legendis in lingua materna* (Leipsic, 1533); *De autoritate verbi Dei* (Strasburg, 1542), against Bishop Stokesley of London concerning the number of the sacraments; *De justificatione contra Osiandrum* (Wittenberg, 1552); *Contra Michaelem Servetum ejusque blasphemias disputationes tres* (Leipsic, 1554).

BIBLIOGRAPHY: J. Thomasius, *Oratio de Alexandro Alesio*, in his *Orationes*, Leipsic, 1683; T. Beza, *Icones*, Geneva, 1580; C. Wordsworth, *Ecclesiastical Biography*, vol. ii., London, 1853; T. McCrie, *Life of John Knox*, Note 1, London, 1874; *DNB*, i. 254–259.

ALEXANDER: The name of eight popes.

Alexander I.: Bishop of Rome in the early years of the second century, successor of Evaristus and predecessor of Xystus I. The statement of the *Liber pontificalis* (ed. Duchesne, i. xci.–xcii., 54) and the *Acta Alexandri* (*ASB*, May, i. 371–375) that he died a martyr, with two companions, Eventius and Theodulus, and was buried on the Via Nomentana, is improbable. The excavations made on the spot designated by the *Liber pontificalis* have indeed led to the discovery of a fragment of an inscription concerning a martyr Alexander, but he is not called a bishop. The year of Alexander's consecration is variously given: Eusebius names 103 in his *Chronicon*, and 108 in his *Historia ecclesiastica;* the *Catalogus Liberianus*, 109. The year of his death is given as 114, 116, and 118. Three letters falsely ascribed to him are in the Pseudo-Isidore (ed. Hinschius, Leipsic, 1863, pp. 94–105).

(A. HAUCK.)

BIBLIOGRAPHY: *Liber pontificalis*, ed. Duchesne, i. xci. sqq., 54, Paris, 1886; Bower, *Popes*, i. 10; R. A. Lipsius, *Die Chronologie der römischen Bischöfe*, pp. 167 sqq., Kiel, 1869; B. Jungmann, *Dissertationes selectæ in Hist. eccl.*, i. 134 sqq., Regensburg, 1880; J. Langen, *Geschichte der römischen Kirche*, Bonn, 1881; Jaffé, *Regesta*, i. 5.

Alexander II. (Anselm Badagius, sometimes called **Anselm of Lucca**): Pope Sept. 30, 1061–Apr. 21, 1073. He was born of a noble family at Baggio, near Milan. When the Patarene movement for reform began in 1056 (see PATARENES), he seems to have joined it. The archbishop Guido removed him by sending him on an embassy to the imperial court. Here he won the confidence of Henry III., which gained for him the bishopric of Lucca (1057). He was sent to Milan in 1057 and 1059 as legate in connection with the questions raised by the Pataria. On the death of Nicholas II. (1061), he was elected pope through Hildebrand's influence. This was in direct contravention of the imperial rights, confirmed by Nicholas II. himself in 1059. The empress Agnes, as regent, convoked an assembly of both spiritual and temporal notables at Basel, and Cadalus of Parma was chosen pope by the German and Lombard bishops. He assumed the title of Honorius II., and had already defeated the adherents of his rival in a bloody battle under the walls of Rome, when Godfrey of Lorraine appeared and summoned both claimants to lay the election before the young king Henry IV. At a synod of German and Italian bishops held at Augsburg in Oct., 1062, Hanno of Cologne, now regent, arranged that his nephew Burchard of Halberstadt should be sent to Rome to examine the case and make a preliminary decision. Burchard decided in favor of Alexander, who returned to Rome in the beginning of 1063, and held a synod at Easter, in which he excommunicated Honorius. The final decision of the contest was to be made at a synod of German and Italian bishops called for Pentecost, 1064, at Mantua. This was in favor of Alexander. See HONORIUS II., antipope.

Honorius did not abandon his pretensions until his death in 1072, though his power was confined to his diocese of Parma. Even during the contest Alexander had exercised considerable authority over the Western Church, and after the decision at Mantua he extended his claims in Germany, and put Archbishop Hanno of Cologne to penance for having visited Cadalus on a secular errand. Henry IV. himself was made to feel the papal power. When he desired to effect a divorce from his wife Bertha, Peter Damian threatened him with the severest ecclesiastical penalties at a diet held in Frankfort Oct., 1069. Alexander also came into conflict with Henry over several ecclesiastical appointments, of which the most important was the archbishopric of Milan, and when the king persisted in having his candidate Godfrey consecrated, though the pope had adjudged the latter guilty of simony, the royal counselors were excommunicated as having endeavored to separate their master from the unity of the Church. This was but the beginning of the long struggle which was left to the next pope, Gregory VII.

Alexander dealt in a similarly determined manner with other nations. He supported the Normans, both in the north and south of Europe, in their career of conquest, and aided William the Conqueror to consolidate his newly gained power in England by directing his legate to appoint Normans to the episcopal sees of that country; the archbishopric of Canterbury was given to Lanfranc, abbot of Bec, under whom Alexander himself had received his early training. His wide claims of universal jurisdiction were in sharp contrast with his weakness within Rome itself, where the turbulent factions maintained an unceasing struggle against him as long as he lived. His letters and diplomas are in *MPL*, cxlvi. 1279–1430.

(A. HAUCK.)

BIBLIOGRAPHY: *Liber pontificalis*, ed. Duchesne, ii. 281, Paris, 1892; Jaffé, *Regesta*, i. 566–592, ii. 750; *Gesta Alexandri II.*, in Bouquet, *Recueil*, xiv. 526–531; W. Giesebrecht, *Die Kirchenspaltung nach dem Tode Nikolaus II.*, appended to his *Annales Altahenses*, Berlin, 1841; Bower, *Popes*, ii. 370–377; M. Watterich, *Romanorum pontificum . vitæ*, i. 235–236, Leipsic, 1862; C. Will, *Benzos Panegyricus auf Heinrich IV. mit . Rücksicht auf den Kirchenstreit Alexanders II. und Honorius II.*, Marburg, 1863; R. Baxmann, *Die Politik der Päpste von Gregor I. bis auf Gregor VII.*, 2 vols., Elberfeld, 1868–69; Hefele, *Conciliengeschichte*, iv. 851–893; B. Jungmann, *Dissertationes selectæ in Hist. eccl.*, iv. 242 sqq., Ratisbon, 1880; J. Langen, *Geschichte der römischen Kirche*, pp. 532 sqq., Bonn, 1892; Milman, *Latin Christianity*, iii. 321–353; W. Martens, *Die Besetzung des Päpstlichen Stuhles unter den Kaisern Heinrich III. und Heinrich IV.*, Freiburg, 1886; C. Fetzer, *Voruntersuchungen zu einer Geschichte Alexanders II.*, Strasburg, 1887; Hauck, *KD*, iii. (1906) 704–753.

Alexander III. (Roland Bandinelli): Pope 1159–81. He was born at Sienna and lectured in canon law at Bologna, leaving a memorial of this part of his career in the *Summa Magistri Rolandi*, a commentary on the *Decretum* of Gratian. Eugenius III. brought him to Rome about 1150, and made him a cardinal. In 1153 he became papal chancellor, and during the reign of Adrian IV. was the moving spirit of the antiimperial party among the cardinals, who advocated a close alliance with William of Sicily. His determined opposition to Frederick Barbarossa led to a deep personal enmity on the emperor's part, which was not appeased when Roland appeared at the Diet of Besançon in 1157 as papal legate, and boldly proclaimed that the emperor held his lordship from the pope. Adrian IV. died Sept. 1, 1159. Six days later all the cardinals but three (some say nine) voted for Roland as his successor, and he was consecrated Sept. 20. The minority chose the imperialist cardinal Octavian, who assumed the title of Victor IV. Frederick, naturally disposed toward his own partizan, called a council at Pavia which, as was to be expected, declared Octavian the lawful pope (Feb. 11, 1160), and two days later proclaimed Alexander an enemy of the empire and a schismatic. Alexander answered from Anagni on Mar. 24 by excommunicating the emperor and absolving his subjects from their allegiance; the antipope had been excommunicated a week after Alexander's consecration.

Alexander had not the power to carry his hostility further. It is true that in Oct., 1160, at a council at Toulouse, the kings of England and France and the bishops of both countries declared for him; and Spain, Ireland, and Norway followed their lead. But he was unable to maintain a foothold in Italy. By the end of 1161 he was forced to leave Rome, and in the following March fled across the Alps to take refuge in France. The conflict might have come to an end with the death of Victor IV. at Lucca in Apr., 1164, had not Reginald, archbishop of Cologne, the imperial representative in Italy, without either the emperor's sanction or a regard for canonical forms, set up another antipope, Guido, bishop of Crema, under the title of Paschal III. In the diet held at Würzburg at Pentecost, 1165, Reginald (possessed by the conception of a German national Church independent of every one but the emperor) talked Frederick and the magnates into the irrevocable step of taking an oath never to recognize Alexander III. or any pope chosen from his party, and to support Paschal III. with all their power. But on the whole Alexander's cause was gaining. In the autumn of 1165 he left France, and by Nov. 23 he was able to reenter Rome. A year later, Frederick crossed the Alps to unseat him, and by the following summer was able to take possession of St. Peter's and install Paschal there. Alexander fled once more, but Frederick's triumph was short-lived. The plague robbed him of several thousand soldiers and drove him from Rome; in December the principal Lombard cities formed a league against the oppressive dominion of the empire, and found a protector in Alexander, in whose honor they named the new city of Alessandria; finally the antipope died (Sept. 20, 1168). The Roman partizans of Frederick, without waiting for instructions, set up a new pope in the person of John, cardinal-bishop of Albano, under the name of Calixtus III. But Frederick was weary of the strife, and hardly five months had passed before he was negotiating with Alexander. Nothing resulted, however, and the emperor took up arms once more against the pope and the Lombard League; but the battle of Legnano (May 29, 1176) was so decisively against him that he was obliged to yield on any terms. He began fresh negotiations with Alexander at Anagni in October; and at Venice the disputed matters were discussed also with the cities, as well as with William II. of Sicily and the Eastern emperor, both of whom had joined Frederick's opponents. Peace was made Aug. 1, 1177, the emperor acknowledging Alexander's title and abandoning Calixtus, who was to receive an abbey in compensation. Both sides agreed to restore whatever possessions they had taken from each other.

A still greater triumph was won by Alexander over Henry II. of England. From 1163 onward the English king was involved in a more and more acute contest with Rome, growing out of his difficulties with Thomas Becket. He demanded the deposition of the archbishop, and, on the pope's refusal, opened negotiations with Frederick, and was represented at the Diet of Würzburg, with a view to supporting Reginald of Cologne's far-reaching plans. But threats of excommunication and interdict brought him back to an apparently peaceful attitude. The murder of Becket (Dec. 29, 1170) brought things to a crisis. The king was forced to do humiliating penance at Becket's tomb and to submit wholly to the papal demands. The culminating point of Alexander's success was marked by the Third Lateran Council (Mar., 1179). Besides approving the crusade against the Cathari of southern France, which had been inaugurated by Raymond of Toulouse with the support of Louis VII., the pope's friend and protector, the 300 bishops of this brilliant assembly passed an important canon regulating papal elections, which confined the electoral power to the cardinals, excluding the lower clergy and the laity and making no mention of imperial confirmation, and required a two-thirds vote to elect.

In spite of his apparently complete triumph over his enemies, Alexander never really conquered the Roman people. Soon after the close of the council they drove him once more into exile; and a month after Calixtus III. had formally renounced his pretensions, a new antipope was set up, who took the name of Innocent III. Alexander succeeded in vanquishing this rival, but never returned to Rome, and died at Civita Castellana Aug. 30, 1181, his corpse being followed to its sepulcher in the Lateran by cries of implacable hostility from the populace. His letters are in *MPL*, cc.; his *Summa* was edited by F. Thaner (Innsbruck, 1874), and his *Sententiæ* by A. M. Gietl (Freiburg, 1891).

(A. Hauck.)

Bibliography: *Liber pontificalis*, ed. Duchesne, ii. 397-446, Paris, 1892; *Gesta Alexandri III.*, in Bouquet, *Recueil*, xv. 744-977; Jaffé, *Regesta*, ii. 145 sqq., 761; M. Watterich, *Romanorum pontificum . . vitæ*, ii. 377-451, Leipsic, 1862; K. L. Ring, *Friedrich I. im Kampf gegen Alexander III.*, Stuttgart, 1838; Bower, *Popes*, ii. 502; H. Reuter, *Geschichte Alexanders III. und der Kirche seiner Zeit*, 3 vols., 2d ed., Leipsic, 1860-64; P. Scheffer-Boichorst, *Kaiser Friedrichs I. letzter Streit mit der Kurie*, Berlin, 1866; J. Langen, *Geschichte der römischen Kirche*, pp. 439 sqq., Bonn, 1893; Milman, *Latin Christianity*, iv. 288-438; G. Wolfram, *Friedrich I. und das Wormser Concordat*, Marburg, 1883; Hefele, *Conciliengeschichte*, v. 571-722; J. R. Green, *History of the English People*, vol. i., London, 1888-92; A. M. Gietl, *Die Sentenzen Rolands, nachmals Papstes Alexander III.*, Freiburg, 1891; Hauck, *KD*, iv. 227-302.

Alexander IV. (Rinaldo de Conti): Pope 1254-61. He was made a cardinal-deacon in 1227 by his uncle, Gregory IX., and in 1231 cardinal-bishop of Ostia. As a cardinal, he does not seem to have been stronglyanti-imperialistic, and Frederick II. is found in 1233 and 1242 writing in a tone of friendship to him. On the death of Innocent IV (Dec. 13, 1254), Alexander was elected to succeed him, and at once began to follow the policy of his predecessors. Conrad IV., on his death-bed, had commended to the guardianship of the Church his two-year-old son Conradin, heir to the duchy of Swabia and the kingdoms of Jerusalem and Sicily. Alexander accepted the charge with the most benevolent promises, but less than two weeks later he demanded that the Swabian nobles should desert Conradin for Alfonso of Castile. On Mar. 25, 1255, he excommunicated Manfred, Conradin's uncle, who had undertaken to defend the kingdom of Sicily in the child's name, and on Apr. 9 he concluded an alliance with Henry III. of England, on whose son Edmund he bestowed Sicily and Apulia, to be held as papal fiefs. When some of the German princes talked in 1254 of setting up Ottocar of Bohemia as a claimant of the throne in opposition to William of Holland, the papal protégé, he forbade them to take any steps for the election of a king in William's lifetime; and when William died, he forbade the archbishops of Cologne, Treves, and Mainz to place Conradin on the throne of his father. In the contest for the crown which now arose between Alfonso X. of Castile and Richard of Cornwall, brother of Henry III. of England, the pope, whose support was asked by both, took the side of the latter, promising him (Apr. 30, 1259) not merely the support of his legates in Germany, but holding out hopes of the imperial crown. In this he was influenced by the English king's money, which was necessary to him in his contest against Manfred. In Aug., 1258, on a rumor of the death of Conradin, Manfred himself assumed the crown of Sicily, and was recognized in northern and central Italy as the head of the Ghibelline party. After the decisive victory of Montaperto had put Florence, the Guelph bulwark, in Manfred's power, Alexander excommunicated every one who should help him in any way, and laid all his dominions under an interdict (Nov. 18, 1260). This was all he could do, since an appeal to the kings of England and Norway to undertake a crusade against Manfred, and a demand for a tenth of the income of the French clergy for the same purpose had both proved unsuccessful.

Alexander had better luck against the notorious Ezzelino da Romano, son-in-law of Frederick II. and leader of the Ghibellines in northern Italy. An army raised by the pope for a crusade against this monster had accomplished little, but finally in 1259 he succumbed to a combination of princes and cities. In Rome, however, the party of Manfred was gaining strength, and in 1261 he was elected to the highest office in the gift of the people, that of senator. How terribly Italy suffered from the demoralization which followed this relentless warfare is evident from the spread of the Flagellants (See Flagellation, Flagellants), whose fanatical processions took place even in Rome (1260). A council was called to meet at Viterbo for the purpose of setting on foot a crusade against the Tatars, but before it convened Alexander died in that city (May 25, 1261). (A. Hauck.)

Bibliography: Bouret de la Roncière, *Les Registres d'Alexandre IV.*, parts 1-4, Paris, 1895 sqq.; *MGH*, *Epist. sæculi xiii.*, iii. (1894) 314-473, 729-730, and *Leg.*, iv., 1896; W. H. Bliss, *Calendar of Entries in the Papal Registers relating to Great Britain and Ireland, Papal Letters*, i. 309-376, London, 1893; A. Potthast, *Regesta*, ii. 1286 sqq., Berlin, 1875; C. J. de Cherrier, *Histoire de la lutte des papes et des empereurs de la maison de Souabe*, Paris, 1858; O. Posse, *Analecta vaticana*, 1 sqq., 120 sqq., Innsbruck, 1878; G. Digard, *La Série des registres pontificaux du treizième siècle*, Paris, 1886; E. Engelmann, *Der Anspruch der Päpste auf Confirmation und Approbation, 1077-1379*, pp. 53 sqq., Breslau, 1886; Bower, *Popes*, ii. 567-571.

Alexander V. (Peter Philargi): Pope 1409-10. He was an orphan boy from Crete, brought up by the Minorites, which order he afterward entered. After traveling in Italy, England, and France, he acquired a name as a teacher of rhetoric in the University of Paris. Later he held a dignified position at the court of Gian Galeazzo Visconti in Milan, of which see he became archbishop in

1402. Innocent VII. made him a cardinal. In 1408 he was one of those who deserted Gregory XII. with a view to compelling an end of the schism, and in the same year he had invited the pope to the Council of Pisa as a representative of the cardinals. After both Gregory XII. and Benedict XIII. had been deposed, he was unanimously elected pope by the influence of cardinal Balthasar Cossa (July 26, 1409). Like all the other cardinals present, he had signed an agreement that, if he should be elected pope, he would continue the council until the Church had received a thorough reformation in head and members; but, once crowned as pope, he dismissed the members to their dioceses, there to take counsel on the points which needed reform.

The schism was not ended by his election; Benedict XIII. was still recognized by Spain, Portugal, and Scotland; Gregory XII., by Naples, Hungary, the king of the Romans, and some other German princes. The greater part of Germany, with England and France, declared for the choice of the council, as well as the reforming leaders Gerson and Pierre d'Ailly. Alexander was more concerned with the recovery of the States of the Church than with reform. Rome and Umbria were in the possession of Ladislaus of Naples, the protector of Gregory XII. Alexander excommunicated him, declared his crown forfeit, and transferred it to Louis II. of Anjou, who, with Cardinal Cossa, commanded the force sent against Rome. Though this expedition was unsuccessful, Alexander's adherents succeeded in the last few days of 1409 in getting the upper hand in the city. Alexander, however, did not return, but remained in Bologna, a pliant instrument in the hands of his Franciscan brethren and Balthasar Cossa. The friars induced him to issue a bull (Oct. 12, 1409), which confirmed all the extensive privileges of the mendicant orders in the confessional and practically crippled the jurisdiction of the parish priests. When he indicated his intention of extending this ruling to France, the University of Paris, with Gerson at its head, threatened to retaliate by excluding the friars from the platform and pulpit. Alexander died before this ultimatum reached Rome (May 3, 1410). By modern Roman Catholic historians, as the creation of the illegitimate council of Pisa, he is not considered strictly a lawful pope, though included in their lists. (A. Hauck.)

Bibliography: *Vita*, in L. A. Muratori, *Rer. Ital. script.*, iii. 2, p. 842, Milan; Bower, *Popes*, iii. 167-171; Hefele, *Conciliengeschichte*, vi. 1033; Creighton, *Papacy*, i. 257-265 (the best); Pastor, *Popes*, i. 190-191 (from the Roman Catholic side).

Alexander VI. (Rodrigo Lanzol): Pope 1492-1503. He was born at Xativa, near Valencia, in 1430 or 1431 and was adopted by his uncle, Calixtus III., into the Borgia family and endowed with rich ecclesiastical benefices. In 1455 he became apostolic notary; in 1456, a cardinal-deacon; and in 1457, vice-chancellor of the Roman curia. He held also the bishoprics of Valencia, Porto, and Cartagena. These positions brought in vast wealth, which he spent in ostentatious luxury and riotous living. A glimpse of his life at this period is afforded by a letter of Pius II. (June 11, 1460), reproaching him for his participation in an indescribable orgy at Sienna, and rebuking him for having no thought but pleasure. At least seven—possibly nine—children were born to him as cardinal, four of whom, Giovanni, Cesare, Gioffrè, and Lucrezia, the offspring of his favorite mistress Vanozza Catanei, were the objects of his special love. On the death of Innocent VIII. he reached the height of his ambition by his election to the papacy (Aug. 11, 1492), won, it was generally believed, by simony and other corrupt practises.

Alexander was unquestionably a man of great gifts, able, eloquent, versatile, strong in mind as in body; but all these gifts were defiled by the immorality of his life, which was in no respect different as pope from what it had been as cardinal. So much may be safely said, even if certain specific accusations made by his contemporaries, such as that of incest with his daughter Lucrezia, are shown to be calumnies. The remonstrances of secular powers like Spain and Portugal against the immorality of the papal court were as vain as the denunciations of Savonarola. The former were put off with promises; the latter's mouth was stopped by excommunication (May 12, 1497), when he was endeavoring to arouse all Italy against the papacy.

Alexander's main aim, outside of the gratification of his passions, was the elevation of his children to power and wealth. While still a cardinal, he had obtained the Spanish duchy of Gandia for his eldest son, Pedro Luis, who was succeeded, on his early death, by Giovanni. Alexander invested the latter with the duchy of Benevento, together with Terracina and Preticorvo; but a few days later (June 14, 1497) he was mysteriously murdered. For a moment the pope was shocked into penitence, and talked of a reform of his court and even of abdication, but no lasting change resulted. The making of a brilliant match for Lucrezia was long an important factor in his policy. The first connection attempted was with the Sforza family. Lodovico il Moro, governor of Milan for his nephew Giangaleazzo, desired the sovereignty for himself, but was hindered by the grandfather of Giangaleazzo's wife, Ferdinand of Naples. To get the better of him, Lodovico planned a league into which the Pope should be drawn by a marriage between Lucrezia and Giovanni Sforza of Pesaro. The league was founded April 25, 1493, and included, besides Lodovico and Alexander, Venice, Sienna, Ferrara, and Mantua. Ferdinand, however, succeeded in detaching the pope from this alliance, probably through the influence of Spain, and married the natural daughter of his son Alfonso to Gioffrè, Alexander's fourth son. The alliance with Naples, however, brought the pope into difficulties. Lodovico, deserted, summoned Charles VIII. of France to take the crown of Naples for himself and try a simoniacal pope at the bar of a general council. Charles descended into Italy in autumn, 1494, and on the last day of the year, Alexander being unable to oppose him, made a magnificent public entry into Rome. The pope agreed to allow his army free passage toward Naples, and to reinstate the cardinals of the opposition faction. In return Charles paid him all the outward signs of homage, and continued his journey toward Naples, where he was able to be crowned on May 12, Alfonso II. having fled. Alexander, however, joined the league founded at Venice (March 31) to drive him out of Italy and to support the house of Aragon in reconquering Naples. In return Alexander asked the hand of Carlotta, Princess of Naples, for his son Cesare, whom he had made archbishop of Valencia immediately after his own elevation and cardinal a year later. It was necessary to divorce Lucrezia from her husband Giovanni Sforza and marry her to a natural son of Alfonso II., the Duke of Bisceglia, which was accomplished in 1498. Cesare's marriage fell through, however; and, after resigning as cardinal, he married Charlotte d'Albret, sister of the King of Navarre, being made Duke of Valentinois by Louis XII., who received in return permission to divorce his wife.

Cesare went on with designs for an extensive temporal lordship by fair means and foul. The ruling families of the Romagna having been expelled or assassinated, Alexander gave him the title of Duke of Romagna in 1501. The hatred of father and son for the house of Aragon went further. Lucrezia's second husband was murdered by Cesare's orders in 1500; and a year later Alexander joined the league of Louis XII. and Ferdinand of Spain for the division of the kingdom of Naples between them. The years 1502 and 1503 mark the height of this dominion founded on blood. Alexander was already thinking of asking the emperor for Pisa, Sienna, and Lucca for his son and making him king of Romagna and the Marches, when death cut short his plans, through an attack of malarial fever (Aug. 18, 1503).

Of what his contemporaries thought Alexander capable may be seen from the story, long believed, that he was the victim of poison prepared by his orders for one of the cardinals whose estates he coveted. In recent years Alexander has been regarded by some as an unselfish pioneer of the unification of Italy, and attempts have even been made to represent him as a true follower of Christ; but his unworthiness is generally admitted, even by Roman Catholic writers. (A. Hauck.)

Bibliography: Creighton, *Papacy*, iv. 183–end, v. 1–57 (very full, valuable appendices of documents); Pastor, *Popes*, v. 375–523, vi. 1–180 (the Romanist side, with appendices of documents); A. Gordon, *The Lives of Pope Alexander VI. and Cæsar Borgia*, 2 vols., London, 1729 (has appendix of documents); Bower, *Popes*, iii. 259–277; J. Fave, *Études critiques sur l'histoire d'Alexandre VI.*, St. Brienc, 1859; M. J. H. Ollivier, *Le Pape Alexandre VI.*, Paris, 1870; F. Gregorovius, *Lucrezia Borgia*, 2 vols., Stuttgart, 1875, Eng. transl., London, 1904; Kaiser, *Der vielverleumdete Alexander VI.*, Ratisbon, 1877; V. Nemec, *Papst Alexander VI.*, Klagenfurt, 1879; J. Burchard, *Diarium sive rerum urbanarum commentarii*, 3 vols., Paris, 1883–85 (consult Index); Hefele, *Conciliengeschichte*, viii. 300; C. G. Robertson, *Cæsar Borgia*, London, 1891; Ranke, *Popes*, i. 35–36; F. Corvo, *Chronicles of the House of Borgia*, New York, 1901. On Lucrezia Borgia consult F. Gregorovius, *Lucretia Borgia*, ib. 1903.

Alexander VII. (Fabio Chigi): Pope 1655–67. He was nuncio in Cologne from 1639 to 1651, and took part in the negotiations which led up to the peace of Westphalia, but declared that he would enter into no communications with heretics, and protested against the validity of the treaties of Münster and Osnabrück. Innocent X. took a similar view, and on his return from Germany he made Chigi cardinal and finally secretary of state. It was due to the influence of Chigi that Innocent condemned the famous five propositions alleged to have been extracted from the *Augustinus* of Jansen. Innocent died Jan. 7, 1655, and a strong party in the conclave favored Chigi as one who would be likely to be free from the reproach of nepotism; but, though Spain supported him, the opposition of France (Mazarin had been for years his personal enemy) delayed the election until Apr. 7.

Alexander VII. had the satisfaction of seeing the daughter of Gustavus Adolphus, Christina of Sweden, enter the Church, though her prolonged residence in Rome became a burden to him later. He was a consistent supporter of the Jesuits, whom he succeeded in restoring to Venice, from which city they had been excluded since the conflict with Paul V He took their side wholly in the struggle with the Jansenists (see Jansen, Cornelius, Jansenism). He became embroiled with Louis XIV., first through the refusal of the French ambassador in Rome, the Duke of Créqui, to pay certain conventional civilities to the relatives of the pope, and then through an attack on the ambassador's servants and palace made by the Corsican guards of the pope. Louis was already displeased with Alexander for his consistent support of Cardinal de Retz against Mazarin, and for his retention, in spite of Louis's intercession in their behalf, of certain possessions to which the Farnese and Este families laid claim. In such a mood he took up the Corsican affair hotly, and wrote to Alexander of a breach of the law of nations, a crime whose parallel could hardly be found among barbarians. The papal nuncio was obliged to leave Paris, and French troops occupied Avignon and the Comtat Venaissin and threatened to invade the Italian states of the Church. Alexander, unable to find any allies, saw himself compelled to accede to the most humiliating demands of France in the treaty of Pisa (1664). He was obliged not only, by a special mission of two cardinals to Paris, to beg the king's pardon, but also that of the Duke de Créqui, and to erect a pyramid in a public place in Rome, with an inscription declaring the Corsicans incapable of serving the Holy See.

Since Alexander, like his predecessor, was closely allied with Spain, he was obliged to carry Innocent's policy still further when a struggle with Portugal arose. Innocent had refused to recognize Portugal as an independent monarchy when in 1640 it broke away from Spain under the house of Braganza; and had declined to confirm the bishops nominated by King John IV Alexander took the same course in regard to the bishops; the king accordingly allowed the bishoprics to remain vacant, and divided their estates and revenues among his courtiers, even thinking at one time of the extreme measure of an absolute breach with Rome and the establishment of a national Church, whose bishops should need confirmation from no one but the metropolitan. The conflict was finally settled by Clement IX. in 1669.

Much as he had had to do with affairs of state before his elevation to the papacy, Alexander found them wearisome, and left their administration as much as possible to the congregation of cardinals entrusted with their consideration. He was a cultured friend of literature and philosophy, and took much pleasure in his intercourse with learned men, among whom Pallavicini, the historian of the Council of Trent, was conspicuous. He tried his own hand at literature; a collection of his verses, under the title *Philometi labores juveniles* appeared in Paris in 1656. He died May 22, 1667.

(A. Hauck.)

Bibliography: Ranke, *Popes*, ii. 33 sqq.; J. Bargrave, *Pope Alexander VIII. and the College of Cardinals*, in *Publications of the Camden Society*, xcii., London, 1867; R. Chantelauze, *Le Cardinal de Retz et ses missions diplomatiques à Rome*, Paris, 1879; A. Gézier, *Les Dernières Années du Cardinal de Retz*, Paris, 1879; A. Reumont, *Fabio Chigi in Deutschland*, Aachen, 1885; Gérin, *L'Ambassade de Crequy à Rome et le traité de Pise, 1662–1664*, in *Revue des questions historiques*, xxviii. (1893) 570; Bower, *Popes*, iii. 331–332.

Alexander VIII. (Pietro Ottoboni): Pope 1689–91. He came of a Venetian family, was made cardinal by Innocent X., and, later, Bishop of Brescia and *datarius apostolicus*. When Innocent XI. died (Aug. 11, 1689), much depended on the choice of his successor, both for Louis XIV. and for the League of Augsburg, formed to oppose him. His ambassador, the Duke de Chaulnes, succeeded on Oct. 6 in accomplishing the election of Cardinal Ottoboni. Louis, whom the coalition had placed in a critical situation, believed that he would find the new pope more complaisant in some disputed points than his predecessor had been. He attempted to conciliate the curia by restoring Avignon, and abandoned the right of extraterritorial immunity which he had so stubbornly claimed for the palace of his ambassador in Rome. Alexander showed a friendly spirit, and made the Bishop of Beauvais a cardinal. The coalition urged the pope neither directly nor indirectly to approve the four articles of the "Gallican liberties" of 1682, on which the strife had turned between the king and the clergy of his party, on one side, and Rome, on the other. Alexander might have been willing to confirm the bishops whom Louis had nominated in return for their part in bringing about this declaration, if they would avail themselves of the pretext that they defended the articles only in their private capacity. Louis rejected this accommodation, and the pope condemned the declaration and dispensed the clergy from the oath they had taken to uphold it.

Alexander made his name memorable in Rome by many benefits to the city, and showed his love for learning by the purchase for the Vatican library of the rich collection of Christina of Sweden. He is reproached, however, for yielding completely to the inroads of nepotism, which his predecessors had driven out. He died Feb. 1, 1691.

(A. Hauck.)

Bibliography: Gérin, *Pape Alexandre VIII. et Louis XIV d'après documents inédits*, Paris, 1878; Petrucelli della Gattina, *Histoire diplomatique des conclaves*, iii. 213, Paris, 1865; A. Reumont, *Geschichte der Stadt Rom*, iii. 2, 639, Berlin, 1870; Bower, *Popes*, iii. 334–335; Ranke, *Popes*, ii. 424, iii. 461

ALEXANDER: Patriarch of Alexandria 313–328. See Arianism, I., 1.

ALEXANDER BALAS. See Seleucidæ.

ALEXANDER OF HALES (*Halensis* or *Alensis*, *Halesius* or *Alesius*; called *Doctor Irrefragabilis* and *Theologorum Monarcha*): Scholastic theologian; b. at Hales, Gloucestershire, England; d. in Paris Aug. 21, 1245. He was educated in the monastery at Hales, studied and lectured at Paris, and acquired great fame as a teacher in theology, and entered the order of St. Francis in 1222. His *Summa universæ theologiæ* (first printed at Venice, 1475) was undertaken at the request of Innocent IV., and received his approbation. It was finished by Alexander's scholars after his death. It is an independent work giving a triple series of authorities—those who say yes, those who say no, and then the reconciliation or judgment. The authorities are chosen not only from the Bible and the Fathers, but also among Greek, Latin, and Arabic poets and philosophers, and later theologians. It treats in its first part the doctrines of God and his attributes; in its second, those of creation and sin; in its third, those of redemption and atonement; and, in its fourth and last, those of the sacraments. Among the doctrines which were specially developed and, so to speak, fixed by Alexander of Hales, are those of the *thesaurus supererogationis perfectorum*, of the *character indelibilis* of baptism, confirmation, ordination, etc.

Bibliography: J. B. Hauréau, *De la philosophie scolastique*, vol. i., Paris, 1850; A. Stöckl, *Geschichte der Philosophie*, vol. ii., Mainz, 1865; A. Neander, *Christian Church*, iv. 420–519; J. E. Erdmann, *Geschichte der Philosophie*, i. 133, 431, Berlin, 1877, Eng. transl., 3 vols., London, 1893; Moeller, *Christian Church*, ii. 328, 414, 428.

ALEXANDER OF HIERAPOLIS, hai″e-rap′ō-lis: Bishop of Hierapolis and metropolitan of the province Euphratensis. He was prominent at the third ecumenical council (Ephesus, 431) as a fierce opponent of Cyril and leader of the left wing of the Antiochians. He persisted in his opposition even after the more moderate had acknowledged the orthodoxy of Cyril, and, in consequence, was finally deposed and banished to Famothis in Egypt. Suidas ascribes to him a treatise: "What Did Christ Bring New into the World?"

G. Krüger.

Bibliography: Mansi, *Concilia*, iv. 1330-31, v. 851-965 (letters from him or to him or concerning him); Hefele, *Conciliengeschichte*, ii., Eng. transl., vol. iii. passim; *DCB*, i. 83–85.

ALEXANDER JANNÆUS. See Hasmoneans.

ALEXANDER OF LYCOPOLIS, lai-kep′ō-lis or lic″ep′ō-lis: Alleged author of a work against the doctrines of the Manicheans, written in Greek, probably about 300. He was therefore contemporary with the first apostles of Manicheism in Egypt. Photius (*Contra Manichæos*, i. 11) calls him bishop of Lycopolis (in the Thebaid), but the work (which is an important source for the Manichean system) does not even justify the inference that the writer was a Christian, and nothing is known of his life. The work was published by F Combefis in his *Auctarium novissimum*, ii. (Paris, 1672) 3–21, and is reprinted in *MPG*, xviii. 409–448.

It has been edited, with a good introduction, by A. Brinkmann (Leipsic, 1895); Eng. transl. in *ANF*, vi. 239–253. G. Krüger.

ALEXANDER NEVSKI, SAINT: A saint of the Eastern Church; b. at Vladimir (110 m. e. by n. of Moscow) 1218; d. at Goroditch (360 m. s.e. of Moscow) Nov. 14, 1263. He was the second son of Grand Duke Jaroslav II. of Novgorod. In 1240 he defeated the Swedes on the Neva, whence his title, "Nevski." Two years later he repelled the Livonians, who had the support of Rome. The popes of the time were making great efforts to bring about a union with the Eastern Church, and, to further their plans, they tried to induce Alexander and Prince Daniel of Galitch to undertake a crusade against the Tatars. Innocent IV addressed letters to Alexander (Jan. 23 and Sept. 15, 1248), urging him strenuously to submit to the Roman see, to which the duke and his advisers replied: "We know what the Old and New Testaments say, and we are also acquainted with the teaching of the Church of Constantine and from the first to the seventh council; but your teaching we do not accept." Nevertheless, Innocent and his successor, Alexander IV., pursued their plans and appointed a legate for Russia, hoping that Roman bishoprics might in the course of time be established there. Grand Duke Alexander defended his Church as ably as he did his country. He won the favor of the Tatar khans, and in 1261 a bishopric was established at Sarai on the lower Volga, the residence of the Khan of the Golden Horde. Alexander died on one of his many journeys thither. He was canonized by the Church and the day of his burial (Nov. 23) was consecrated to him. His remains were transferred on Aug. 30, 1724, to the Alexander Nevski monastery in St. Petersburg, which had been founded by Peter the Great in 1711 on the supposed scene of Alexander's victory over the Swedes in 1240. Richard Hausmann.

ALEXANDER SEVERUS (Marcus Aurelius Alexander Severus): Roman emperor 222–235; b. at Arce in Phenicia, most probably 205; murdered by the army, probably near Mainz, at the beginning of a campaign against the Germans in Gaul, Mar., 235. He was a noble character, conscientious, almost scrupulous, meek, and well inclined toward all gods and men. The religious policy which he inherited was one of electicism and syncretism. Alexander and his two immediate predecessors—Caracalla, 211–217, son and successor of Septimius Severus (q.v.), and Elagabalus, 218–222, reputed son and successor of Caracalla—may be called the Syrian emperors. They were much influenced by Julia Domna, wife of Septimius and daughter of a priest of the sun at Emesa; Julia Mæsa, her sister; and the two daughters of the latter, Soæmias, mother of Elagabalus, and Julia Mamæa, mother of Alexander. About these women gathered a circle of philosophers and scholars who took a deep interest in religious questions. There was naturally here no inclination to the Roman religion and the claims of Christianity were, in part at least, recognized. There was a disposition to attempt to revive heathenism by importing the good in the new religion. Elagabalus (q.v.) had sought to unite the religions of the empire, but in fantastic manner, aiming to make all gods subordinate to the sun-god of Emesa, whose priest he was. Alexander continued his syncretism in nobler fashion. He was susceptible to all good and had respect for all religions. The image of Christ stood in his lararium with those of Orpheus, Abraham, and Apollonius of Tyana, and he is said to have wished to erect in Rome a temple to Jesus. The Christian ethics also attracted him, he often quoted the precept "what ye will not that others do to you, that do not ye to them" and had it inscribed on public buildings. Mamæa was even more favorable to Christianity; Eusebius (*Hist. eccl.*, vi. 21) calls her "a most pious woman, if there ever was one, and of religious life," but the assertion that she was a Christian (first made by Orosius, vii. 18) is unfounded.

That the Church had peace under Alexander, as under his predecessors, was the natural consequence of his training and his character. Lampridius says expressly that Alexander "suffered the Christians to exist," and Firmilian, bishop of Cæsarea in Cappadocia, in a letter to Cyprian (*Epist.*, lxxv. [lxxiv.]), written about 256, speaks of "the long peace." To be sure, individuals may have been brought to trial here and there, but the later accounts which make Alexander a cruel persecutor under whom thousands of Christians suffered death are false, and the reputed martyrdoms under him, as of the Roman bishops Callistus and Urbanus and of St. Cecilia, are unhistoric.

(A. Hauck.)

Bibliography: Original sources are: Dion Cassius, *Hist. Rom.*, lxxiv., lxxvi., lxxx.; Ælius Lampridius, *Alexander Severus*, best in M. Nisard, *Suétone*, pp. 453–482, Paris, 1883; Eusebius, *Hist. eccl.*, v. 26, vi. 1; *NPNF*, 2d series, i. 245, 249. Consult: G. Uhlhorn, *Der Kampf des Christentums*, pp. 284 sqq., Stuttgart, 1875; B. Aubé, *Les Chrétiens dans l'empire romain*, pp. 53 sqq., Paris, 1881; J. Reville, *La Religion à Rome sous les Sévères*, ib. 1885; P. Allard, *Histoire des persécutions . du iii. siècle*, pp. 79 sqq., 171 sqq., ib. 1886; W. Smith, *Dictionary of Greek and Roman Biography*, iii. 802–804, London, 1890; Neander, *Christian Church*, i. 125–127 et passim; Schaff, *Christian Church*, ii. 58–59; Moeller, *Christian Church*, i. 191, 195.

ALEXANDER, ARCHIBALD: Presbyterian clergyman, and first professor in the Princeton Theological Seminary; b. about 7 m. e. of Lexington, in Augusta (later Rockbridge) County, Virginia, Apr. 17, 1772; d. at Princeton Oct. 22, 1851. He received as good schooling as the place and time afforded, including attendance from the age of ten at the Liberty Hall Academy of the Rev. William Graham, near Lexington. He was converted in the great revival of 1789, studied theology with Mr. Graham, was licensed in 1791 and ordained in 1794, and became president of Hampden Sydney College 1796, and pastor of the Third Presbyterian Church (Pine Street), Philadelphia, 1806. In 1812 he was entrusted by the General Assembly with the organization of the Princeton Theological Seminary. For the first year he taught all departments, but as other professors were added he confined himself to pastoral and polemic theology. His chief books were: *A Brief Outline of the*

Evidences of the Christian Religion (Princeton, 1825); *The Canon of the Old and New Testaments Ascertained* (1826); *A Pocket Dictionary of the Bible* (Philadelphia, 1829); *Biographical Sketches of the Founder and Principal Alumni of the Log College* (Princeton, 1845); and *Outlines of Moral Science* (New York, 1852).

BIBLIOGRAPHY: J. W. Alexander, *Life of Archibald Alexander*, New York, 1854.

ALEXANDER, CHARLES McCALLON: Revivalist; b. at Meadow, Tenn., Oct. 24, 1867. He was educated at Maryville College, Maryville, Tenn., but left in 1887 without taking a degree, and, after being musical director for a time in the same institution, prepared himself for evangelistic work at the Moody Bible Institute, Chicago, having already been singing associate of the Quaker evangelist John Kittrell for three months. During a part of the period of study in the Moody Bible Institute he was choirmaster of the Moody Sunday-school, and in 1893 was associated with Dwight L. Moody in the revival services connected with the World's Fair at Chicago. From 1894 to 1901 he was singing associate of the revivalist Milan B. Williams, working in Iowa for the first five years and in other parts of the United States during the remainder of the time. At the conclusion of this period Mr. Williams went for a short visit to Palestine, and in the interval Alexander was asked by Rev. Dr. R. A. Torrey to accompany him to Australia. They began their work in 1902, and for six months traveled throughout Australia, Tasmania, and New Zealand, after which they conducted a revival for six weeks in Madura, Madras, Calcutta, Bombay, and Benares. They then went to England, where they remained from 1902 to 1904, and in 1905–06 conducted successful revival services in Canada and the United States. In regard to the Bible Mr. Alexander takes the most conservative position, for he declares that he "believes in the absolute reliability of every statement" in it. He has issued *Revival Songs* (Melbourne, 1901); *Revival Hymns* (London, 1903); and *Revival Hymns* (another collection; Chicago, 1906).

BIBLIOGRAPHY: G. T. B. Davis, *Torrey and Alexander*, Chicago, 1905.

ALEXANDER, GEORGE: Presbyterian; b. at West Charlton, N. Y., Oct. 12, 1843. He received his education at Union College and Princeton Theological Seminary (1870). He was pastor of the East Avenue Presbyterian Church, Schenectady, N. Y., from 1870 to 1884, and in the following year was called to the University Place Church, New York City, where he has since remained. While at Schenectady, he was likewise professor of rhetoric and logic at Union College in 1877–83. He is president of the Presbyterian Board of Foreign Missions and of the board of trustees of São Paulo College, Brazil, as well as of the New York College of Dentistry. He is also vice-president of the Council of New York University, a trustee of Union College, and a director of Princeton Theological Seminary.

ALEXANDER, GROSS: Methodist Episcopalian; b. at Scottsville, Ky., June 1, 1852. He was educated at the University of Louisville (B.A., 1871) and Drew Theological Seminary (B.D., 1877), after having been a tutor at the University of Louisville in 1871–73 and professor of classics at Warren College, Ky., in 1873–75. He held successive pastorates in New York State (1875–77) and Kentucky (1877–84), and from 1885 to 1902 was professor of New Testament exegesis in Vanderbilt University. Since the latter year he has been presiding elder of Louisville. He was also a secretary of the general conferences held at Memphis (1894), Baltimore (1898), and Dallas (1902), and has written, in addition to numerous briefer contributions, *Life of S. P. Holcombe* (Louisville, 1888); *History of the Methodist Episcopal Church, South* (New York, 1894); *The Beginnings of Methodism in the South* (Nashville, 1897); and *The Son of Man : Studies in His Life and Teaching* (1899), besides editing *Homilies of Chrysostom on Galatians and Ephesians* (New York, 1890). In 1906 he became editor of *The Methodist Quarterly Review*.

ALEXANDER, JAMES WADDELL: Presbyterian; b. near Gordonsville, Louisa County, Virginia, Mar. 13, 1804, eldest son of Archibald Alexander (q. v.); d. at Red Sweet Springs, Virginia, July 31, 1859. He was graduated at Princeton in 1820, studied theology there and served as tutor, was licensed in 1824, and was pastor in Virginia till 1828, when he became pastor at Trenton, N. J. He was editor of *The Presbyterian*, Philadelphia (1832), professor of rhetoric and belles-lettres at Princeton (1833), pastor of Duane Street Presbyterian Church, New York (1844), professor of ecclesiastical history at Princeton Seminary (1849), recalled to his old church in New York, now reorganized as the Fifth Avenue Church (1851). Perhaps the best known of his writings were the *Plain Words to a Young Communicant* (New York, 1854) and *Thoughts on Preaching* (1864). Some of his translations of German hymns (such as Gerhardt's *O Sacred Head now Wounded*), first published in Schaff's *Deutsche Kirchenfreund*, have passed into many hymn-books.

BIBLIOGRAPHY: *Forty Years' Familiar Letters of James W. Alexander*, ed. Rev. John Hall of Trenton, 2 vols., New York, 1860.

ALEXANDER, JOSEPH ADDISON: American Presbyterian; b. at Philadelphia Apr. 24, 1809, third son of Archibald Alexander (q. v.); d. at Princeton, N. J., Jan. 28, 1860. He was graduated at Princeton in 1826; became adjunct professor of ancient languages and literature there in 1830; studied and traveled in Europe in 1833 and 1834: on his return to America, became adjunct professor of Oriental and Biblical literature in Princeton Seminary. He was transferred to the chair of church history in 1851 and to that of New Testament literature in 1859. He was a remarkable linguist, assisted in preparing the first American edition of Donnegan's Greek lexicon (Boston, 1840), and did much to introduce German theological learning into America. He wrote commentaries on Isaiah (2 vols., New York, 1846–47; ed. John Eadie, Glasgow, 1875) and the Psalms (3 vols., ib. 1850); with Prof. Charles Hodge he planned a series of popular commentaries on the books of the

New Testament, of which he himself contributed those on the Acts (2 vols., 1857), Mark (1858), and Matthew. The last-cited was published posthumously (1861), as well as two volumes of sermons (1860) and *Notes on New Testament Literature* (2 vols., 1861).

Bibliography: H. C. Alexander, *Life of J. A. Alexander*, 2 vols., New York, 1869.

ALEXANDER, WILLIAM: 1. Anglican archbishop of Armagh and primate of all Ireland; b. at Londonderry, Ireland, Apr. 13, 1824. He was educated at Tunbridge School and Exeter and Brasenose Colleges, Oxford (B.A., 1854). After his graduation he was successively curate of Derry Cathedral and rector of Termonamongan, Upper Fahan, and Camus-Juxta-Mourne (all in the diocese of Derry), while in 1863 he was appointed dean of Emly. Four years later he was consecrated bishop of Derry and Raphoe, and in 1896 was elevated to the archbishopric of Armagh and the primacy of all Ireland. He was select preacher to the University of Oxford in 1870–71 and Bampton Lecturer in 1876. He has written *Leading Ideas of the Gospels* (Oxford sermons, London, 1872); *The Witness of the Psalms to Christ and Christianity* (1877); commentaries on Colossians, Thessalonians, Philemon, and the Johannine Epistles, in *The Speaker's Commentary* (1881); *The Great Question and Other Sermons* (1885); *St. Augustine's Holiday and Other Poems* (1886); *Discourses on the Epistles of St. John* (1889); *Verbum Crucis* (1892); *Primary Convictions* (1893); and *The Divinity of Our Lord* (1886).

2. American Presbyterian; b. near Shirleysburg, Pa., Dec. 18, 1831; d. at San Anselmo, Cal., June 29, 1906. He was educated at Lafayette College and Jefferson College (B.A., 1858), and at Princeton Theological Seminary (1861). He was ordained to the Presbyterian ministry in 1862 and was pastor at Lycoming Church, Williamsport, Pa., in 1862–63. From 1863 to 1865 he was president of Carroll College and stated supply at Waukesha, Wis., and then held successive pastorates at Beloit, Wis. (1865–69) and San José, Cal. (1869–71). From 1871 to 1874 he was president of the City College, San Francisco, in addition to holding the professorship of New Testament Greek and exegesis in the San Francisco Theological Seminary, of which he was one of the founders in 1871. From 1876 until his death he was professor of church history in the latter institution. He was a member of the committee to revise the Westminster Confession of Faith in 1890–93 and was one of the editors of the *Presbyterian and Reformed Review* (now the *Princeton Theological Review*). In addition to a number of contributions of minor importance, he prepared the commentaries on the International Sunday-school lessons in 1881–83.

ALEXANDER, WILLIAM LINDSAY: Scotch Congregationalist; b. at Leith Aug. 24, 1808; d. near Musselburgh (5 m. e. of Edinburgh) Dec. 20, 1884. He studied at Edinburgh and at St. Andrews (1822–27); began the study of theology at the Glasgow Theological Academy; and was classical tutor at the Blackburn (Lancashire) Theological Academy, 1827–31. He was minister in Liverpool, 1832–34; was called to the North College Street Congregational Church, Edinburgh, 1834, and remained with the same congregation until 1877. In 1854 he became professor of theology in the Congregational Theological College at Edinburgh, and was its principal 1877–81; he was made examiner in mental philosophy of St. Andrews in 1861, and was a member of the Old Testament Revision Company from its formation in 1870. He was a frequent contributor to the periodicals and edited *The Scottish Congregational Magazine* 1835–40 and 1847–51; he wrote for the eighth edition of the *Encyclopædia Britannica*; translated Hävernick's *Introduction to the Old Testament* (Edinburgh, 1852) and the first division of Dorner's *History of the Development of the Doctrine of the Person of Christ* (1864); prepared *Deuteronomy* for the *Pulpit Commentary* (London, 1880); and brought out the third edition of Kitto's *Biblical Cyclopædia* (3 vols., Edinburgh, 1862–66). His other works include: *The Connection and Harmony of the Old and New Testaments* (Congregational Lecture, 7th series, London, 1841, revised ed., 1853); *Anglo-Catholicism not Apostolical* (Edinburgh, 1843); *The Ancient British Church* (London, 1852, new ed., revised by S. G. Green, 1889); *Christ and Christianity* (Edinburgh, 1854); *Memoirs of the Life and Writings of Ralph Wardlaw* (1856); *Christian Thought and Work* (1862); *St. Paul at Athens* (1865); *Zechariah, his Visions and Warnings* (London, 1885); *A System of Biblical Theology* (published posthumously, 2 vols., Edinburgh, 1888, ed. James Ross).

Bibliography: J. Ross, *W. L. Alexander, his Life and Works, with Illustrations of his Teachings*, London, 1887.

ALEXANDRIA, PATRIARCHATE OF: One of the most important episcopal sees of the early Church, traditionally believed to have been founded by the evangelist Mark. It originally had metropolitan jurisdiction over the whole of Egypt, and gradually became recognized as holding an even wider or patriarchal authority, next to that of Rome, until Constantinople took second place in the fourth century. For its early history in this connection, see Patriarch. The rise of heresies and divisions in the Church, so zealously combated by famous incumbents of this see, such as Athanasius and Cyril, led to schisms. The Monophysites contested the see with the orthodox or occupied it through a large part of the fifth and sixth centuries, and from the seventh century the Melchites and Copts continued the same conflict. The Coptic patriarchs maintained close relations with the Jacobite patriarchs of Antioch, and enjoyed the larger share of the favor of the Mohammedan rulers. In the fourteenth century, however, they as well as their Melchite rivals were subjected to severe persecutions. When the city was conquered by the crusaders in 1365, the Melchite patriarch was living in Constantinople under the protection of the patriarch of that see, whose influence continually increased in Alexandria, until the Alexandrian patriarchs came to be regularly chosen either from the clergy of Constantinople or from Alexandrian clergy resident there.

The seat of the patriarchate was for a long while in Old Cairo, but in modern times the incumbent has usually resided in Constantinople. Since 1672 he has had only four metropolitans under him; namely, those of Ethiopia (purely titular), Cairo (the former Memphis), Damietta (transferred from Pelusium), and Rosetta. The Coptic see was transferred to Old Cairo still earlier, under Christodoulos (1045-76), and claims jurisdiction over thirteen bishoprics. See COPTIC CHURCH; EGYPT.

ALEXANDRIA, SCHOOL OF.

The term "School of Alexandria" is used in two different senses: (1) The catechetical school was an institution which grew up not later than the last half of the second century, and lasted to the end of the fourth, with a regular succession of teachers like the schools of philosophy. (2) By the same name is also understood a group of theologians of the fourth and fifth centuries, the most important of whom was Cyril of Alexandria. They were in general opposition to the school of Antioch (q.v.), and were the progenitors of Monophysitism and of the anti-Nestorian interpretation of the decrees of Chalcedon, thus originating in the order of intellectual development the decisions of the third and fifth councils. It will be convenient to treat both meanings of the term together.

1. Origin. Nothing certain is known of the origin of Christianity in Alexandria, but it is noteworthy that tradition refers the first preaching of the Gospel there and the foundation of a group of ascetic philosophers to one and the same period, and practically to the same man, Mark the Evangelist—which indicates that the school dates from the earliest days of Alexandrian Christianity. At the end of the second century, it emerges into light as an established institution under the teacher Pantænus, thus confirming the observation, generally true, that Christianity adapted itself everywhere to local characteristics. The oldest Gnostic schools are met with in Egypt, and the oldest school found in direct relation to the Church (Justin, Tatian, and others had what might be called private schools) is that of Alexandria. If one may judge from the later period, in which the relations between the school and the Church, between the bishop and the teacher, were frequently strained, the school grew only gradually into close connection with the Church; but the Alexandrian Church itself shows, at the transition from the second to the third century, a freer, less rigidly orthodox habit of thought, which gave place to the settled Catholic forms only in the episcopate of Demetrius, under Caracalla and Elagabalus.

2. Its Development from Hellenism and Judaism. The catechetical school had forerunners in the Hellenistic "Museum" on one side, and in the Jewish schools (*batte midrashot*) on the other. The development of Helleno-Judaic learning, as seen in Philo, is a direct step to the Christian, which took up its inheritance. The speculations of the Egyptian Gnostics, the schools of Basilides and Valentinus, and those of the Church theologians proceed from the same source. Its theology is the science of interpreting the written documents; it is extracted from the divine oracles by means of the exegetic-pneumatic method. But access to the highest secrets is possible only by passing through various anterooms, designated on one side by the different disciplines of Greek philosophy, and on the other by special divine revelations. This progressive enlightenment corresponds to the constitution of nature and the human organism, with their long course of progressive development. The path thus marked out leads, however, naturally to apologetics, just as the preparatory study, in metaphysics and ethics, in knowledge and in divine love, leads to the laying of a foundation for the theological gnosis. All this has appeared already in Philo; and so has the essentially Platonic attitude toward the whole world of thought, the energetic effort to surpass Plato's *idea* by a *hypernoeton* (thus offering religion access in the form of the transcendental to a lofty region peculiarly its own), and the alchemistic process with the Bible by which it is made to yield not only the highest gnosis but also, when interpreted literally and morally, the theology of the preparatory stages.

3. Christian Modifications. The Christian school made no radical change in this way of looking at things; but it modified the earlier views by giving the revelation of God in Christ precedence over the Old Testament law, which it placed practically on a level with Greek philosophy, and by accepting the Pauline-Johannean conception of the appearance of the Godhead (the Logos) on earth. The mystery of God coming down to his creature, or of the deification of the created spirit, now became the central thought of theology, and served to strengthen the long-existing conception of the essential affinity of the created spirit with its creator. The fundamental question whether the return of souls to God is only an apparent return (since really all the time they are in him), or a strictly necessary natural process, or the historical consequence of a historical event (the Incarnation), was never satisfactorily answered by the teachers of the catechetical school. The Alexandrian orthodox teachers are distinguished from the heretical by their serious attempt to save the freedom of the creature, and thus to place a boundary between God and man and to leave some scope for history; but the attitude of the Christian Gnostic, which Origen praises as the highest, leaves room neither for the historic Christ nor for the Logos, in fact for no mediator at all, but conceives everything as existing in calm immanence and blessedness—while this very teacher, as soon as he placed himself on one of the numerous steps which lie between man as a natural being and man as a blessed spirit, became the theologian of redemption, atonement, and mediation.

The catechetical school of Alexandria has a great significance as well for the internal history of the Church as for its relation to the world outside. It furnished the Church with a dogmatic theology; it taught it scientific exegesis, in the sense then understood, and gave it a scientific consciousness; it overthrew the heretical school; it laid down the main problems of future theology; and it transformed the primitive spirit of enthusiastic asceticism into one of contemplative asceticism. In regard to the outer world, it forced the Hellenic mind to take account of the message of Christianity, it led the conflict with the last phase of Greek philosophy, Neoplatonism, and defeated its enemies with their own weapons.

4. Significance and Achievements.

The school had a settled organization under a single head. A knowledge of the course of study is obtained from the great tripartite work of Clement (the "Exhortation to the Heathen," the "Instructor," and the "Miscellanies") and from accounts of Origen's teaching. The main subjects of the older philosophy were taught, but the principal thing, to which the whole course led up, was the study of Scripture. The school seems to have had no fixed domicile, at least in Origen's day, but to have met in the teacher's house. There were no fixed payments; rich friends and voluntary offerings from such as could afford them provided for its needs. The list of heads is as follows: Pantænus, Clement, Origen, Heracles, Dionysius (the latter two afterward bishops), Pierius (Achillas), Theognostus, Serapion, Peter (afterward bishop), Macarius (?) Didymus, Rhodon. The last-named, the teacher of Philippus Sidetes, migrated to Side in Pamphylia about 405, and the school, shaken already by the Arian controversy and by the unsuccessful struggle of Theophilus with the barbarous monastic orthodoxy, became extinct.

5. Organization.

The theology of the Cappadocians, especially Gregory of Nyssa, is a product of the influence of the Alexandrian school, and in so far as this theology, with its echoes of Origenistic teaching, has never wholly died out, the work of the school has remained effective. It lived on also in the learning of Jerome, Rufinus, and Ambrose, and was valuable to the Western Church. Athanasius has nothing directly to do with the catechetical school, but his teaching on the incarnation of the Logos and his conception of the relations of God and man were in touch with one side of Origenistic speculation. By carrying through the *Homoousios* he brought about at the same time a view of the person of Christ according to which the divine nature has so absorbed the human, has so made the latter its own, that a practically complete unity of nature exists. He did not work this consequence out thoroughly; there are many uncertainties both in him and in the Cappadocians, his and Origen's disciples; but his teaching and his theological attitude led up to what was later called Monophysitism, in its strictest and most logical form. This attitude did not change when the Church felt obliged to repudiate the attempt of Apollinaris of Laodicea to represent Christ as a being in whom the Godhead took the place of the reasonable human soul. On the contrary, it was felt that the theoretical assertion of the complete and perfect human nature of Christ in opposition to Apollinaris was a sufficient protection against any dangers incurred in free speculation on the "one nature of the Word made flesh." These speculations were based on the conception of the possibility of a real fusion of the divine and human natures. This conception might be regarded in a twofold aspect, either from the standpoint of historic realism (the divine plan of salvation has historically brought together the two separate natures), or from that of philosophic idealism (the divine plan of salvation declares and makes plain what lies already in the nature of things, in so far as the intellectual creature is in the last resort substantially one with the Godhead). The connection of this with the later teaching of the school is evident; this connection, rooted as it is in Platonism, comes out in the pneumatic exegesis, although Origen's expositions, which seemed to offend against the rule of faith and Biblical realism, were rejected.

6. Later Developments.

The theologians who represented this line of thought, and who from the beginning of the fifth century are found in conflict with the school of Antioch, are called the Alexandrian school. After Macarius, the most important of them is Cyril, who is known by his numerous commentaries and polemical treatises, as well as by the victorious boldness of the position which he took in these controversies. While there may be two opinions about his character, there can be no doubt of the soteriological tendency of his theology. He succeeded in following up the partial victory which he won at the Council of Ephesus (431) and converting it into a complete one. His successor, Dioscurus, accomplished the entire defeat of the theology of Antioch, and at Ephesus in 449 the "one nature of the Word made flesh" was proclaimed to the East. At Chalcedon in 451 came the reaction, but it was brought about not so much by any opposition in the Eastern mind to the formula as by the despotic bearing of its champion. That which was adopted at Chalcedon roundly contradicted, indeed, the Alexandrian theology, but inasmuch as Cyril's orthodoxy was expressly recognized there, the new Byzantine-Roman Church, in spite of its teaching on the two natures, found a place for the Alexandrian school. In the sixth century Leontius and Justinian showed (Second Council of Constantinople, 553) that its influence was not dead—that, on the contrary, the exposition of the decrees of Chalcedon must be determined in accordance with it. No fundamental difference appeared in the attitude of the sixth council (Constantinople, 680–681); and after the Adoptionist controversy the Western theology also became consciously Alexandrian. It has never been able to do more than theoretically to assert the real humanity of Christ, or to reduce it to very narrow limits; it is, after all, essentially Apollinarian and docetic. Consequently in all its phases it has left room for mystical speculations on the relation of the Godhead and humanity, in which the human factor tends to disappear and history to be forgotten. (A. Harnack.)

7. Representatives of the Later School.

BIBLIOGRAPHY: J. F Baltus, *Défense des saints pères accusés de Platonisme*, Paris, 1711; H. E. F. Guericke, *De schola quæ Alexandriæ floruit catechetica*, Halle, 1824; C. F. W. Hasselbach, *De schola quæ floruit catechetica*, Stettin, 1824; E. R. Redepenning, *Origenes*, i., Bonn, 1841; J. Simon, *Histoire critique de l'école d'Alexandrie*, Paris, 1845; E. Vacherot, *Histoire critique de l'école d'Alexandrie*, 2 vols., Paris, 1846; C. Kingsley, *Alexandria and her Schools*, Cambridge, 1854; C. Bigg, *Christian Platonists of Alexandria*, Oxford, 1886; A. Harnack, *Lehrbuch der Dogmengeschichte*, i., ii., Freiberg, 1894, Eng. transl., 7 vols., London, 1895–1900.

ALEXANDRIA, SYNODS OF. For the synods held in Alexandria in 320 or 321 and 362, see ARIANISM I., 1, § 2; I., 3, § 6; for the synod in 400, see ORIGENISTIC CONTROVERSIES; for the synod in 430, see NESTORIUS.

ALEXIANS: An order, aiming to care for the sick and bury the dead, which originated in the Netherlands at the time of the black death about the middle of the fourteenth century. The members were at first called *Cellitæ* (Dutch, *Gellebroeders*, "Cell-brothers") and Lollards, or Nollards, on account of their monotonous intoning at burials. When and where they chose St. Alexius—according to the legend, a son of rich parents who gave all his possessions to the poor, lived for many years unrecognized as a beggar in his father's house, and died July 17, 417—as patron is not known. The place may have been Antwerp, or Cologne, or elsewhere in Lower Germany. A certain Tobias is said to have had a part in their foundation, and the name *Fratres voluntarie pauperes*, which is sometimes applied to them, may have been their oldest and chosen designation. From the fifteenth century they were found in great numbers in Belgium and western Germany. In 1459 Pius II. permitted them to take the solemn vows. To avoid being taken for Beghards, and to escape persecution, they adopted the monastic rule of St. Augustine (with black cassock), and Sixtus IV confirmed the arrangement in 1472. Later they appeared in the four provinces of the Upper Rhine, Middle Rhine, Flanders, and Brabant, without central government or priests at the head of the different monasteries. Jan Busch (q.v.), the monastic reformer of the fifteenth century, took note of their illiterate and deficient lay character. A reform of the order, which was verging on decay, was undertaken in 1854 by the monastery of Mariaberg in Aachen, and was confirmed by Pius IX. in 1870. About fifteen houses, for both sexes, scattered over western Germany, are affiliated with Aachen, and there are others in Belgium. O. ZÖCKLER †.

BIBLIOGRAPHY: Helyot, *Ordres monastiques*, iii. 401–406; G. Uhlhorn, *Die christliche Liebestätigkeit im Mittelalter*, pp. 390 sqq., Stuttgart, 1884; W Moll, *Vorreformatorische Kirchengeschichte der Niederlande*, ii. 250 sqq., Leipsic, 1895; Heimbucher, *Orden und Kongregationen* i. 479–481.

ALEXIUS I., ā-lex'i-us, **COMNENUS:** Emperor of Constantinople 1081–1118, founder of the Comnenus dynasty. He was the nephew of Isaac Comnenus, who as emperor (1057–59) had tried through the army to save the state from the selfish tyranny of the official class, but had been put to death, with the result that for two decades military weakness, administrative demoralization, and the loss of provinces to Turks and Normans had brought the empire into an almost hopeless condition. During this period Alexius won considerable renown by defeating a Norman mercenary captain named Ursel, who attempted to found a kingdom in Asia Minor, and two pretenders to the imperial throne. He was adopted by the empress Maria, but found himself so zealously watched in Constantinople that his only safety was to seize the crown for himself, which he accomplished by a masterly conspiracy. New dangers, however, threatened him. Asia Minor was largely in Mohammedan hands; the sovereignty of the empire in the Balkan peninsula was scarcely more than nominal; and Robert Guiscard menaced the Adriatic provinces, having already taken the south Italian ones. Alexius summoned his forces, and ratified the burdensome treaty with Venice which his predecessor had made, but he was defeated, and the Normans occupied Durazzo, the western gate of the empire. He tried to create a diversion by inciting the German king, Henry IV., to an attack on southern Italy, which afforded only temporary relief, and nothing but Robert's death in 1085 saved him from this determined foe.

Steady pressure from the half-barbarous hordes of the Balkans made a new danger, and at one time it seemed likely that the Turkish pirates of Asia Minor and the Sultan of Iconium would join them in an attempt to effect the complete overthrow of the empire. By the aid of the Cumans, however, they were defeated with horrible slaughter (1091). The lack of military force inspired Alexius with the idea of gaining assistance from the West. The first crusade (1095–99), partly due to his appeals for the expulsion of the Turks, assumed far different proportions from those which he had expected; but he might have welcomed it, had it not been that the participation of Bohemund, Robert Guiscard's son, gave it the appearance of a mere episode in the old Norman inroads. At first all went peaceably, but mutual distrust soon showed itself. At the siege of Nicæa (1097), Alexius did not wait to see if the crusaders would fulfil their agreement to restore to him the territory which had but recently belonged to the empire, but gained the city by a secret agreement with the Turkish garrison. When Antioch fell (1098), it was not restored to the emperor. This marked the crisis of the undertaking. The Turks threatened to recapture Antioch, and Alexius was entreated to send the help he had promised. He saw that by giving it he would make the Turks his irreconcilable foes, without finding submissive vassals in the crusaders, and he drew back, seizing the opportunity to recover possession of the coasts of Asia Minor, with the large maritime cities and the islands, and then using this recovered territory as a base of operations against the new Norman principality in Syria. Bohemund found himself obliged in 1104 to seek help from the pope and the kings of England and France. He spread the belief that Alexius was the enemy of Christianity and a master of all deceits and wiles. A new crusade, led by Bohemund, sought to pass through the Eastern empire, but its purpose was perfectly understood in Constantinople. Preparations were made in time, and in the winter of 1107–08 Alexius won the greatest triumph of his reign. Bohemund was forced to submit to the humiliating conditions of the treaty of Deabolis, and to hold Antioch as a fief of the empire, without the right to transmit it. The last ten years of Alexius's reign were years of struggle for the maintenance of his recovered dominion in Asia Minor, and for the consolidation of his power at home. To gain the help of the ecclesiastics, as well as to atone for the sins of his youth, he regulated the life of his court with great strictness, and did his utmost to repress the sects (Paulicians, Armenians, Monophysites, and Bogomiles) which had flourished in the anarchy of the time immediately preceding his own.

It is difficult to arrive at an unprejudiced view of Alexius's character, so much have the one-sided views of the Western historians prevailed. His success in making the weakened empire once more a power must be admired. He was a man of infinite resource, of tremendous energy, of an indefatigable readiness to avail himself of circumstances, not wanting in physical courage, but even greater in moral steadfastness. (C. NEUMANN.)

BIBLIOGRAPHY: Sources: Nicephorus Bryennius, *Commentarii*, in *CSHB*, viii., 1836; Anna Comnena, *Alexiad*, ibid. iii., 1878, and ed. by Reifferscheid, 2 vols., Leipsic, 1884; also Theophylact, *CSHB*, iv., 1834, cf. Krumbacher, *Geschichte*, pp. 133 sqq., 463–464. Consult G. Finlay, *Hist. of the Byzantine and Greek Empires*, 2 vols., London, 1854; A. F. Gfrörer, *Byzantinische Gesch.*, 3 vols., Graz, 1872–77; B. Kugler, *Geschichte der Kreuzzuge*, Berlin, 1880; H. E. Tozer, *The Church and the Eastern Empire*, London, 1888; C. W. C. Oman, *Byzantine Empire*, New York, 1892 (popular but useful); Gibbon, *Decline and Fall*, v. 232, vi. 79, 1898; F. Harrison, *Byzantine Hist. in the Early Middle Ages*, London, 1900; F. Chalandon, *Essai sur Alexis I. Comnenus*, Paris, 1900.

ALFORD, HENRY: Dean of Canterbury; b. in London Oct. 7, 1810; d. at Canterbury Jan. 12, 1871. He studied at Trinity College, Cambridge (B.A., 1832), and was ordained deacon in 1833, priest in 1834, and elected a fellow of Trinity the same year; he became vicar of Wymeswold, Leicestershire, 1835, minister of Quebec Chapel, Marylebone, London, in 1853, and dean of Canterbury in 1857. He was a many-sided man, a good musician, a wood-carver and painter of some skill, a good preacher, and for many years a successful teacher of private pupils. His publications include sermons, lectures, essays and reviews, poems, hymns, a translation of the Odyssey in blank verse (London, 1861), an edition of the works of John Donne (6 vols., 1839), *The Queen's English* (1864), and even a novel, *Netherton on Sea* (1869), written in collaboration with his niece (Elizabeth M. Alford). He was Hulsean lecturer for 1841–42 and published his lectures under the title, *The Consistency of the Divine Conduct in Revealing the Doctrines of Redemption* (2 vols.). He was the first editor of *the Contemporary Review* (1866–70). The great work of his life, however, was his *Greek Testament* (4 vols., London, 1849–61; thoroughly revised in subsequent editions), which introduced German New Testament scholarship to English readers, and involved a vast amount of patient labor. An outcome of this work was *The New Testament for English Readers* (4 vols., 1868) and a revised English version (1869). He was one of the original members of the New Testament Revision Committee. Near the close of his life he projected a commentary on the Old Testament, and prepared the Book of Genesis and part of Exodus, which were published posthumously (1872).

BIBLIOGRAPHY: *H. Alford, his Life, Journals, and Letters, by his widow*, London, 1873; *DNB*, i. 282–284.

ALFRED (ÆLFRED) THE GREAT: King of the West Saxons 871–901; b. at Wantage (60 m. w. of London), Berkshire, 849; d. at Winchester, Hants, Oct. 28, 901. He was the youngest son of Ethelwulf and Osburga, and succeeded his brother Ethelred on the throne. His reign, with its recurring conflicts with the Danes, contained many vicissitudes; nevertheless, he succeeded in establishing his power, enlarged the borders of his realm, and advanced the spiritual and intellectual welfare of his people. He remodeled the political and ecclesiastical organization of his kingdom, rebuilt the churches, monasteries, and schools burnt by the Danes, and founded new ones. He invited learned men to his country and provided for them there, and through the intimate connection which he maintained with Rome he was able to procure books and form libraries. Of still greater import were his personal exertions to arouse among his countrymen a desire for knowledge and culture. He translated Boethius's *De consolatione philosophiæ* and the history of Orosius. Both works are treated with great freedom, much change was necessary to adapt them to the needs of the rude Saxons, and Alfred himself did not always fully understand his text. There are many omissions and additions. The work of Orosius (an attempt to write a history of the world from a Christian standpoint) is supplemented by a geographical and ethnological review of Scandinavia and the Baltic countries from the reports of Othhere and Wulfstan. Of greater importance from a religious point of view is Alfred's translation of the *Liber pastoralis curæ* of Pope Gregory I. (590–604), a book well adapted to influence the spirit of the Saxon clergy. A paraphrase of Bede's *Historia ecclesiastica gentis Anglorum* has been erroneously ascribed to Alfred; it may, however, have been prepared under his direction. Translations or paraphrases of the *Dialogus* of Gregory I. and of the "Soliloquies" of St. Augustine have also been ascribed to him. His millennary was celebrated at Winchester in 1901, and commemorative exercises were held in America also.

BIBLIOGRAPHY: The *Whole Works of King Alfred*, with preliminary essay, were published in a "Jubilee Edition," 3 vols., Oxford, 1852–53. Separate editions are: Of the Orosius, text and Latin original, ed. H. Sweet, London, 1883; of the Boethius, text and modern English, ed. W. J. Sedgefield, Oxford, 1899–1900; of the Gregory, text and translation, ed. H. Sweet, London, 1871–72; of the Bede, text and translation, ed. T. Miller, ib. 1890–98, and J. Schipper, 3 parts, Leipsic, 1897–98; of the "Soliloquies" of St. Augustine, ed. H. L. Hargrove (*Yale Studies in English*, No. 13), New York, 1902. For Alfred's laws, consult *Ancient Laws and Institutes of England*, ed. B. Thorpe, London, 1840. The chief sources for Alfred's life are: The *De rebus gestis Ælfredi* of the Welsh bishop Asser, ed. W. H. Stevenson, Oxford, 1904; the *Anglo-Saxon Chronicle*, ed. B. Thorpe (*Rolls Series*, No. 23), 1861, and C. Plummer, Oxford, 1892; translations of both Asser and the *Chronicle* by J. A. Giles in Bohn's *Antiquarian Library*, iv.; of Asser by A. S. Cook, Boston, 1906. Of the many modern lives of Alfred the following may be mentioned in German: R. Pauli, Berlin, 1851, Eng. transl., London, 1853, and J. B. Weiss, Freiburg, 1852; in English: T. Hughes, London, 1878; E. Conybeare, ib. 1900; W. Besant, *The Story of King Alfred*, ib. 1901; C. Plummer, Cambridge, 1902; and the volume of essays by different writers, ed. A. Bowker, London, 1899. Consult also Lappenberg, *Geschichte von England*, vol. i., Hamburg, 1834, Eng. transl. by B. Thorpe, ii., London, 1845; W. Stubbs, *Constitutional History of England*, vol. i., Oxford, 1880; E. A. Freeman, *History of the Norman Conquest*, vol. i., ib. 1880; A. Bowker, *The King Alfred Millenary*, London, 1902.

ALFRIC, al'fric (**ÆLFRIC**) (*Alfricus Grammaticus*): Anglo-Saxon abbot. He was a scholar and friend of Athelwold of Abingdon, afterward bishop of Winchester (c. 963), and was abbot of Cerne in Dorsetshire and of Ensham (c. 1006). He has been identified, probably with insufficient reason, with Alfric, archbishop of Canterbury (996–1006), and with Alfric, archbishop of York (1023–51). He did much for the education of clergy and people, and his name is second only to that of King Alfred as a writer of Anglo-Saxon prose. He was a strong opponent of the doctrine of transubstantiation. His writings include a grammar with glossary, a collection of homilies, and a translation of the first seven books of the Old Testament. The Ælfric Society was founded in London in 1842 to publish his works as well as others. For this society B. Thorpe edited two books of the homilies (2 vols., London, 1844–46); the third book has been edited by W. Skeat (*Ælfric's Lives of Saints*, London, 1881). The grammar may be found in the *Sammlung englischer Denkmäler*, Berlin, 1880; the *Heptateuchus*, in C. W. M. Grein, *Bibliothek der angelsächsischen Prosa*, i. (Cassel, 1872).

Bibliography: *DNB*, i. 164–166; Caroline L. White, *Ælfric* (*Yale Studies in English*, No. ii.), Boston, 1898.

ALGER, al"zhê', **OF LIÉGE (ALGER OF CLUNY**, *Algerus Scholasticus*, and *Algerus Magister*): Theological writer of the twelfth century; d. at Cluny 1131 or 1132. He enjoyed the instruction of the best teachers in the cathedral school of Liége, which was then the great school of northwestern Germany, and a nursery of high-church notions. Alger, afterward *scholasticus* at the cathedral, does not seem to have been a champion of this tendency. After the death of Bishop Frederick, in 1121, he retired to the monastery of Cluny, where he lived on very friendly terms with Abbot Peter. He is described as a man of great intellect, a wise counselor, faithful in every respect, of wide learning, yet modest and unassuming. The most noteworthy of his writings are: (1) *De sacramentis corporis et sanguinis domini libri iii.*, which occupies a prominent place among the rejoinders to Berengar's doctrine of the Eucharist. The first book treats of the doctrine of the substantial presence of Christ in the Eucharist, aiming to prove it from Scripture and tradition; it then treats of the reception of the sacrament, especially of worthy participation. The second book treats of different controversies respecting the matter, form, and efficacy of the sacraments. The third opposes especially those who make the legality and efficacy of the sacrament dependent on the worthiness of the dispenser. The difficult questions are treated clearly and acutely. In the main Alger follows Guitmund of Aversa, but not without expansion of his doctrine in some points. He was the first to assert the two propositions that the human nature of Christ because of its exaltation above all creatures has the faculty of remaining where it pleases and existing at the same sime undivided in every other place and that the sensual qualities of the elements exist after the transubstantiation as *accidentia per se*, i.e., without subject. (2) In the *Tractatus de misericordia et justitia*, important for the history of canon law and Church discipline, Alger attempts to explain and harmonize the apparent contradictions between the different laws of the Church. Each proposition is given in a brief thesis or title, followed by numerous quotations from Scripture, the Fathers, councils, and genuine and spurious papal decretals as proofs; the authorities which seem to oppose each other, are put in juxtaposition; and a reconciliation is attempted. Many patristic passages as well as many of the explanatory chapter-headings are copied from this work in the *Decretum Gratiani*. Alger, however, was not the only predecessor and pattern of Gratian, as the whole development of ecclesiastical and canonical science was in that direction. S. M. Deutsch.

Bibliography: Alger's works are in *MPL*, clxxx. Consult the *Histoire littéraire de la France*, xi. 158 sqq.; A. L. Richter, *Beiträge zur Kenntniss der Quellen des kanonischen Rechts*, pp. 7–17, Leipsic, 1834; H. Hüffer, *Beiträge zur Geschichte der Quellen des Kirchenrechts*, pp. 1–66, Münster, 1862; Wattenbach, *DGQ*, ii. (1894) 145, 513.

ALGER, al'jer, **WILLIAM ROUNSEVILLE**: Unitarian; b. at Freetown, Mass., Dec. 30, 1822; d. in Boston Feb. 7, 1905. He was a graduate of Harvard Divinity School, 1847, and held various pastorates (Roxbury, Mass., 1848–55; Boston, as successor of Theodore Parker, 1855–73), but after 1882 lived in Boston without charge. His best-known books are *The Poetry of the Orient* (Boston, 1856, 5th ed., 1883); *The Genius of Solitude* (1865, 10th ed., 1884); *Friendships of Women* (1867, 10th ed., 1884), and particularly *A Critical History of the Doctrine of a Future Life* (Philadelphia, 1863, 12th ed., Boston, 1885), to which Ezra Abbot furnished his famous bibliography of books on eschatology (see Abbot, Ezra).

ALGERIA. See Africa, II.

ALLARD, al"lar', **PAUL**: Layman, French Christian archeologist; b. at Rouen Sept. 15, 1841. He was educated at the Collège Libre de Bois-Guillaume (near Rouen) and at the Faculté de Droit of Paris. He was admitted to the bar, and for many years has been a judge in the civil court of his native city. He is a member of the Rouen Academy, as well as of the *Académie de Religion Catholique* and the *Académie Pontificale d'Archéologie*, both of Rome. He is likewise a corresponding member of the *Société des Antiquaires de France*, and the editor of the *Revue des traditions historiques* of Paris. His chief works are: *Les Esclaves chrétiens depuis les premiers temps de l'Église jusqu'à la fin de la domination romaine en Occident* (Paris, 1876; crowned by the French Academy); *L'Art païen sous les empereurs chrétiens* (1879); *Esclaves, serfs et mainmortables* (1884); *Histoire des persécutions*

(4 vols., 1882–90); *Le Christianisme et l'empire romain de Néron à Théodose* (1897); *Saint Basile* (1898); *Études d'histoire et d'archéologie* (1898); *Julian l'Apostat* (3 vols., 1900–03; crowned by the French Academy); *Les Chrétiens et l'incendie de Rome sous Néron* (1903); *Les Persécutions et la critique moderne* (1903); and *Dix leçons sur le martyre* (1906). He has also made a translation, with additions and notes, of the *Roma Sotterranea* of Northcote and Brownlow under the title *Rome souterraine* (Paris, 1873).

ALLATIUS, al-lē'shius or -shus, **LEO (LEONE ALACCI)**: Roman Catholic scholar; b. on the island of Chios 1586; d. in Rome Jan. 19, 1669. He was brought to Calabria at the age of nine, and in 1600 went to Rome, where he became one of the most distinguished pupils of the Greek College founded in 1577 by Gregory XIII. He studied philosophy and theology, and later also medicine at the Sapienza, and became a teacher in the Greek College and a scriptor in the Vatican library. When Maximilian of Bavaria presented the Heidelberg library to the pope (1622), Allatius was chosen to superintend its removal to Rome, and he spent nearly a year in the work. The death of Gregory XV. just before his return deprived him of a fitting reward; and he was even suspected of having appropriated or given away part of this charge. He was supported by the liberality of some of the cardinals, especially Francesco Barberini, who made him his private librarian (1638). Alexander VII. appointed him keeper of the Vatican library in 1661, and he lived the retired life of a scholar until his death. Allatius's contemporaries regarded him as a prodigy of learning and diligence, though apparently somewhat narrow and pedantic, and without much critical judgment. His literary productions were of the most varied kind. The interests which lay nearest to his heart were the demonstration that the Greek and Roman Churches had always been in substantial agreement, and the bringing of his fellow countrymen to acknowledge the supremacy of Rome. His principal writings, the *De ecclesiæ occidentalis et orientalis perpetua consensione* (Cologne, 1648), and the smaller *De utriusque ecclesiæ in dogmate de purgatorio consensione* (Rome, 1655), bear upon this subject; his *Confutatio fabulae de papissa* (1630) aims to vindicate the papacy. He was vigorously opposed by Protestant scholars, such as Hottinger, Veiel, and Spanheim, and some Roman Catholics (as R. Simon) admitted that his treatment of history was one-sided. He found an ardent helper in the German convert B. Neuhaus (Nihusius), the pupil and then the opponent of Calixtus. Allatius published many other works of a similar tendency, e.g., on the procession of the Holy Ghost (1658), the Athanasian Creed (1659), the Synod of Photius (1662), and the Council of Florence (1674). He also edited, annotated, or translated a number of Greek authors, both ecclesiastical and secular, and contributed to the Paris *Corpus Byzantinorum.* He left behind him plans and preliminary studies for still more extensive undertakings, such as a complete library of all the Greek authors. His literary remains, and an extensive correspondence, comprising more than 1,000 letters in Greek and Latin, came in 1803 into the possession of the library of the Oratorians in Rome. (A. HAUCK.)

BIBLIOGRAPHY: S. Gradius, *Vita Leonis Allatii*, first published in Mai, *Nova patrum bibliotheca*, vi., part 2, pp. v.-xxviii., Rome, 1853; Fabricius-Harles, *Bibliotheca Græca*, xi. 435 sqq.; J. M. Schröckh, *Kirchengeschichte seit der Reformation*, ix. 21, Leipsic, 1810; A. Theiner, *Die Schenkung der Heidelberger Bibliothek . . . mit Originalschriften*, Munich, 1844; H. Laemmer, *De L. Allatii codicibus*, Freiburg, 1864; H. Hurter, *Nomenclator literarius*, ii. 119 sqq., Innsbruck, 1893.

ALLEGORICAL INTERPRETATION. See EXEGESIS OR HERMENEUTICS, III., §§ 2–5.

ALLEGRI, āl-lē'grī, **GREGORIO**: Italian composer; b. in Rome, of the family of the Correggios, most probably about 1585; d. there Feb. 18, 1652. He studied music under Nanini (1600–07), and after 1629 belonged to the choir of the Sistine Chapel. He was one of the first to compose for stringed instruments. His most celebrated work is a *Miserere* for two choirs, one of five and the other of four voices, which, as given at Rome during Holy Week, acquired a great reputation. For a long time extraordinary efforts were made to prevent the publication of the music; but Mozart at the age of fourteen was able to write it down from memory, and Dr. Charles Burney (author of the *History of Music*) procured a copy from another source and published it in *La musica che si canta annualmente nelle funzioni della settimana santa, nella cappella pontificia* (London, 1771). The effect of the *Miserere* as given in Rome seems to be due to the associations and execution rather than to any inherent quality in the music, as presentations of it elsewhere have proved distinctly disappointing.

BIBLIOGRAPHY: F. Mendelssohn-Bartholdy, *Letters from Italy and Switzerland, transl. by Lady Wallace*, pp. 133–134, 168–191, Philadelphia, 1863.

ALLEINE, al'en, **JOSEPH**: English non-conformist; b. at Devizes (86 m. w. of London), Wiltshire, 1634; d. at Taunton, Somersetshire, Nov. 17, 1668. He was graduated at Oxford in 1653 and became chaplain to his college (Corpus Christi); in 1655 he became assistant minister at Taunton, whence he was ejected for non-conformity in 1662; he continued to preach and was twice imprisoned in consequence, and his later years were troubled by constant danger of arrest. He was a learned man, associated as an equal with the fellows of the Royal Society, and engaged in scientific study and experimentation. He is now remembered, however, as the author of *An Alarm to Unconverted Sinners* (London, 1672; republished in 1675 under the title *A Sure Guide to Heaven*). He published several other works, including an *Explanation of the Assembly's Shorter Catechism* (1656).

BIBLIOGRAPHY: C. Stanford, *Companions and Times of Joseph Alleine*, London, 1861; *DNB*, i. 299–300.

ALLEINE, RICHARD: English non-conformist; b. at Ditcheat (18 m. s. by w. of Bath) 1611; d. at Frome Selwood (11 m. s. by e. of Bath) Dec. 22, 1681. He was educated at Oxford and was rector of Batcombe (15 m. s. by w. of Bath) from 1641 till ejected for non-conformity in 1662, when he removed to Frome Selwood, only a few miles away, and there preached. His fame rests on his

Vindiciæ pietatis, or a vindication of godliness, in four parts, each with a different title (London, 1663–68).

ALLEMAND, al"mān' (ALEMAN), LOUIS D': Archbishop of Arles and cardinal; b. of noble family at the castle of Arbent (in the old district of Bugey, 55 m. n.e. of Lyons), department of Ain, 1380 or 1381; d. at Salon (28 m. w.n.w. of Marseilles), department of Bouches du Rhône, Sept. 16, 1450. While quite young he was made canon of Lyons; he became *magister* and *decretorum doctor* and as such took part in the Council of Constance; in 1418 he became bishop of Magelone, in 1423 archbishop of Arles, and in 1426 cardinal with the title of St. Cecilia. During the council at Basel, he became the center of the opposition against pope Eugenius IV., and when in 1438 the rupture occurred between the council and the pope, Allemand was the only cardinal who remained at Basel and directed the transactions. Eugenius declared that Allemand and all who had taken part in the council had forfeited their dignities, but Allemand continued to work in favor of the council and in the interest of the election of Felix V When, however, this antipope resigned (1449), and the Fathers of Basel submitted to Pope Nicholas V., Allemand also was restored. He died in the odor of sanctity, and was buried at Arles. Clement VII. beatified him in 1527. PAUL TSCHACKERT.

BIBLIOGRAPHY: *ASB*, Sept., v. 436 sqq.; G. J. Eggs, *Purpura docta*, libri iii. and iv., p. 50 sqq., Munich, 1714; D. M. Manni, *Della vita e del culto del beato Lodovico Alemanni*, Florence, 1771; *KL*, i. 473.

ALLEN, ALEXANDER VIETS GRISWOLD: Protestant Episcopalian; b. at Otis, Mass., May 4, 1841. He was educated at Kenyon College, Gambier, O. (B.A., 1862), and Andover Theological Seminary (1865), and was ordained priest in the Protestant Episcopal Church in 1865. He was the founder and first rector of St. John's Church, Lawrence, Mass., in 1865–67, and in the latter year was appointed professor of church history in the Episcopal Theological School, Cambridge, Mass., where he still remains. Since 1886 he has been a member of the Massachusetts Historical Society. His principal writings are: *Continuity of Christian Thought* (Boston, 1884); *Life of Jonathan Edwards* (1889); *Religious Progress* (1893; lecture delivered at Yale University); *Christian Institutions* (New York, 1897); and *Life and Letters of Phillips Brooks* (1900).

ALLEN, HENRY: Founder of the Allenites; b. at Newport, R. I., June 14, 1748; d. at Northhampton, N. H., Feb. 2, 1784. Without proper training he became a preacher, and while settled at Falmouth, Nova Scotia, about 1778, began to promulgate peculiar views in sermons and tracts. He held that all souls are emanations or parts of the one Great Spirit; that all were present in the Garden of Eden and took actual part in the fall; that the human body and the entire material world were only created after the fall and as a consequence of it; that in time all souls will be embodied, and when the original number have thus passed through a state of probation, all will receive eternal reward or punishment in their original unembodied state. He denied the resurrection of the body, and treated baptism, the Lord's Supper, and ordination as matters of indifference. He traveled throughout Nova Scotia and made many zealous converts. The number of these, however, dwindled away after his death.

BIBLIOGRAPHY: Hannah Adams, *View of Religions*, pp. 478–479, London, 1805.

ALLEN, JOHN: **1.** Archbishop of Dublin; b. 1476; murdered at Artaine, near Dublin, July 27, 1534, during the rebellion of Lord Thomas Fitzgerald. He studied at both Oxford and Cambridge; was sent to Rome on ecclesiastical business by Archbishop Warham, and spent several years there; held various benefices in England, and became an adherent of Cardinal Wolsey and his agent in the spoliation of religious houses; was nominated archbishop of Dublin Aug., 1528 (consecrated Mar., 1529), and a month later was made chancellor of Ireland. He was involved in Wolsey's fall, impoverished by it, and lost the chancellorship. He was a learned canonist, and wrote an *Epistola de pallii significatione*, when he received the pallium, and a treatise *De consuetudinibus ac statutis in tutoriis causis observandis*. He compiled two registers, the *Liber niger* and the *Repertorium viride*, which give valuable information regarding his diocese and the state of the churches.

BIBLIOGRAPHY: G. T. Stokes, *Calendar of the "Liber niger Alani,"* in the *Journal of the Royal Society of Antiquaries of Ireland*, ser. 5, iii. (1893) 303–320.

2. Dissenting layman; b. at Truro, Cornwall, 1771; d. June 17, 1839, at Hackney, where for thirty years he kept a private school. His chief work was *Modern Judaism: or a Brief Account of the Opinions, Traditions, Rites, and Ceremonies of the Jews in Modern Times* (London, 1816); he published also (1813) what was long the standard English translation of Calvin's *Institutes of the Christian Religion*.

ALLEN, JOSEPH HENRY: American Unitarian; b. at Northborough, Mass., Aug. 21, 1820; d. at Cambridge, Mass., Mar. 20, 1898. He was graduated at Harvard in 1840, and at the Cambridge Divinity School in 1843, and became pastor at Jamaica Plain (Roxbury), Mass. (1843), Washington, D. C. (1847), and Bangor, Me. (1850). In 1857 he returned to Jamaica Plain, and thenceforth devoted himself to teaching and literary work, often supplying the pulpits of neighboring towns, and with brief pastorates at Ann Arbor, Mich. (1877–78), Ithaca, N. Y. (1883–84), and San Diego, Cal. After 1867 he lived in Cambridge and was lecturer on ecclesiastical history in Harvard University, 1878–82. He was editor of *The Christian Examiner* (1857–69) and of *The Unitarian Review* (1887–91); with his brother, W F Allen, and J. B. Greenough he prepared the Allen and Greenough series of Latin text-books. He translated and edited an English edition of certain of the works of Renan (*History of the People of Israel*, 5 vols., Boston, 1888–95; *The Future of Science*, 1891; *The Life of Jesus*, 1895; *Antichrist*, 1897; *The Apostles*, 1898); and published, among other works, *Ten Discourses on Orthodoxy* (Boston, 1849); *Hebrew Men and Times from the Patriarchs to the Messiah* (1861); *Our Liberal Movement in Theology*, *chiefly as shown in recollections of the History of Unitarianism in New England* (1882); *Christian History in its Three Great Periods* (3 vols., 1882–83); *Positive Religion* (1892); *Historical Sketch of the Unitarian Movement since the Reformation* (*American Church History Series*, New York, 1894); *Sequel to 'Our Liberal Movement'* (Boston, 1897).

ALLEN, WILLIAM: 1. "The cardinal of England;" b. at Rossall (36 m. n. of Liverpool), Lancashire, 1532; d. at Rome Oct. 16, 1594. He entered Oriel College, Oxford, in 1547 (B.A. and fellow, 1550; M.A., 1554), and after the accession of Mary decided to devote himself to the Church. He became principal of St. Mary's Hall, Oxford, and proctor of the university in 1556, canon of York in 1558. His zeal for the Roman religion soon attracted the notice of the authorities under Elizabeth, and in 1561 he left Oxford for the University of Louvain. In 1562 he came home, much broken in health, and spent the next three years in England, constantly encouraging the Catholics and making converts. He left his native land for good in 1565, was ordained priest at Mechlin, and lectured on theology in the Benedictine college there. He conceived the idea of a college for English students on the Continent, and in 1568 opened the first and most famous of such institutions, that at Douai (q.v.). He continued to administer and serve the college till 1588, although in 1585 he had removed to Rome. Pope Sixtus V raised him to the cardinalate in 1587. Philip II. nominated him archbishop of Mechlin, 1589, but he was not preconized by the pope. Gregory XIV. made him prefect of the Vatican library.

The great aim of Allen's life was to restore England to the Church of Rome. This aim he pursued persistently. Until his fiftieth year he contented himself with persuasive measures alone ("scholastical attempts," in his own words), and met with no inconsiderable success. Had it not been for the missioners who were continually going into the country from his schools, probably the Roman Catholic religion would have perished as completely in England as it did in Scandinavian countries.

About 1582 Allen began to meditate force and to interfere in politics. He was closely associated with Robert Parsons (q.v.), was cognizant of the plots to depose Elizabeth, and became the head of the "Spanish party" in England. It was at the request of Philip II. that he was appointed cardinal; and the intention was to make him papal legate, archbishop of Canterbury, and lord chancellor, and to entrust to him the organization of the ecclesiastical affairs of the country, if the proposed invasion of England should succeed. Just before the Armada sailed he indorsed, if he did not write, *An Admonition to the Nobility and People of England and Ireland concerning the present wars, made for the execution of his Holiness's sentence, by the King Catholic of Spain* (printed at Antwerp), and an abridgment of the same, called *A Declaration of the Sentence of Deposition of Elizabeth, the Usurper and Pretensed Queen of England*, which was disseminated in the form of a broadside. Both publications were violent and scurrilous, as well as treasonable from the English point of view, and roused great indignation in England, even among the Catholics, who, unlike Allen, very generally remained true to their country and sovereign. Allen's conduct, however, it should be borne in mind, was consistent with his belief in papal supremacy and with his views concerning excommunication and the right of the spiritual authorities to punish. He is described as handsome and dignified in person, courteous in manner, and endowed with many attractive qualities. Stories concerning his wealth and the princely style in which he lived in Rome are not true.

BIBLIOGRAPHY: The more important of his many writings are: *Certain Brief Reasons Concerning Catholic Faith*, Douai, 1564; *A Defence and Declaration of the Catholic Church's Doctrine Touching Purgatory and Prayers for the Souls Departed*, Antwerp, 1565; *A Treatise Made in Defence of the Lawful Power and Authority of Priesthood to Remit Sins*, Louvain, 1567; *De sacramentis in genere, de sacramento eucharistiæ, de sacrificio missæ*, Antwerp, 1576; and *A Brief History of the Martyrdom of Twelve Reverend Priests*, 1582. He helped make the English Bible translation known as the Douai Bible, and was one of the commission of cardinals and scholars who corrected the edition (see BIBLE VERSIONS, B. IV., § 5, A, II., 2, § 5). At the time of his death he was engaged upon an edition of Augustine's works.

On his life consult: *First and Second Diaries of the English College, Douay*, London, 1878; *Letters and Memorials of William Cardinal Allen*, 1882 (constituting with the foregoing vols. i. and ii. of *Records of the English Catholics*, edited by fathers of the Congregation of the London Oratory). The *Historical Introductions* to these works, by T. F. Knox, give much valuable information, and his life (in Latin) by Nicholas Fitzherbert, published originally in *De antiquitate et continuatione catholicæ religionis in Anglia*, Rome, 1608, is reprinted in the last-named, pp. 3–20; J. Gillow, *Dictionary of English Catholics*, i. 14–24, London, 1885; *DNB*, i. 314–322, gives excellent list of sources.

2. American Congregationalist; b. at Pittsfield, Mass., Jan. 2, 1784; d. at Northhampton, Mass., July 16, 1868. He was graduated at Harvard in 1802; was licensed to preach in 1804 and soon after became assistant librarian at Harvard. He succeeded his father as pastor at Pittsfield in 1810. In 1817 he was chosen president of the reorganized Dartmouth College, but two years later the Supreme Court of the United States declared the reorganization invalid. He was president of Bowdoin College, 1820–39. He wrote much and was an industrious contributor to dictionaries and encyclopedic works. His *American Biographical and Historical Dictionary* (Cambridge, 1809, containing 700 names; 2d ed., Boston, 1832, 1,800 names; 3d ed., 1857, 7,000 names) was the first work of the kind published in America.

ALLEY, WILLIAM: Bishop of Exeter; b. about 1510 at Chipping Wycombe, Bucks, England; d. at Exeter Apr. 15, 1570. He was educated at Eton, Cambridge, and Oxford, espoused the cause of the Reformation, but kept in retirement during the reign of Mary. Elizabeth made him divinity reader in St. Paul's, and in 1560 Bishop of Exeter. He revised the Book of Deuteronomy for the Bishops' Bible, and published an exposition of I Peter, with notes which show wide reading (2 vols., London, 1565).

ALLIANCE, EVANGELICAL. See EVANGELICAL ALLIANCE.

ALLIANCE OF THE REFORMED CHURCHES: A voluntary organization formed in London in 1875, on the model of the Evangelical Alliance, but confined to Churches of presbyterial polity and more churchly in the character of its representation. The official name is "Alliance of the Reformed Churches Holding the Presbyterian System" and popularly the Alliance is known as the "Presbyterian Alliance." The calling of the Council of Trent suggested to Cranmer a synod of Protestants to make a union creed, and in the spring of 1552 he wrote to Melanchthon, Bullinger, and Calvin on the subject and received favorable responses but nothing came of it. Beza in 1561 made a similar proposition, with as little results. So also in 1578 in the Scottish *Second Book of Discipline* and in 1709 in the collection of Scottish church laws, place is given to the idea. But it was not till 1870, when President James McCosh of Princeton College, first, and Rev. Prof. William Garden Blaikie, of Edinburgh, second, proposed that the different Presbyterian and Reformed Churches should get together in a conference, that tangible results followed. In 1873 the General Assembly of the Presbtyerian Church in Ireland and that of the Presbyterian Church of the United States simultaneously appointed committees to correspond with other Churches on the subject. This led to the holding of a meeting in New York, Oct. 6, 1873, during the sessions of the Sixth General Conference of the Evangelical Alliance, at which a committee was appointed to bring the matter before the Presbyterian Churches throughout the world and to obtain their concurrence and cooperation. This committee issued an address in which they distinctly stated that what was proposed was not that the Churches "should merge their separate existence in one large organization; but that, retaining their self-government, they should meet with the other members of the Presbyterian family to consult for the good of the Church at large, and for the glory of God." The proposal met with such general approval that in July, 1875, a conference was held at the English Presbyterian College in London. At this meeting, which lasted four days, and where nearly one hundred delegates, representing many Churches, attended, a constitution for the proposed Alliance was prepared, from which the following are extracts:—

Origin.

"1. This Alliance shall be known as THE ALLIANCE OF THE REFORMED CHURCHES THROUGHOUT THE WORLD HOLDING THE PRESBYTERIAN SYSTEM.

"2. Any Church organized on Presbyterian principles, which holds the supreme authority of the Scriptures of the Old and New Testaments in matters of faith and morals, and whose creed is in harmony with the consensus of the Reformed Churches, shall be eligible for admission into the Alliance."

It was also proposed that there should be a triennial council of delegates, ministers and elders, in equal numbers, to be appointed by the different Churches in proportion to the number of their congregations; and that this council, while at liberty to consider all matters of common interest, should "not interfere with the existing creed or constitution of any Church in the Alliance, or with its internal order or external relations."

The Alliance which was thus proposed was one, not of individual church members, but of Reformed and Presbyterian Churches as such. Its constitution met with great favor. It furnished an opportunity for the different church organizations to come into close fraternal relations with each other while retaining their separate existence and independence. Since its formation, the Alliance has held a General Council in each of the following cities, Edinburgh (1877), Philadelphia (1881), Belfast (1884), London (1888), Toronto (1892), Glasgow (1896), Washington (1899), and Liverpool (1904), at all of which questions of doctrine, polity, Home and Foreign Missions, and other forms of Christian activity have been fully discussed, the papers read with the subsequent discussions being published in a volume of proceedings. The Alliance is the rallying-point of the Reformed and Presbyterian Churches of the world, all of these with one or two exceptions having joined its fellowship. Its membership thus embraces not only the English-speaking Churches of Great Britain and America and the historic Churches of the European Continent, but also the Churches in the colonial and other territories of Great Britain, with the newly formed Churches which are the fruit of missionary labor among non-Christian peoples. Through the Alliance the special conditions of each Church have become better known to sister Churches than they had been previously, and hence, not only by sympathy and counsel, but also by large financial aid, the Alliance has sought to assist the weaker communities.

Aims and Achievements.

The General Councils of the Alliance are neither mass-meetings nor conferences open to all, but consist exclusively of delegates appointed by the several Churches; yet neither are they synods or church courts, for they have no legislative authority of any kind and can only submit to all the Churches or to such as may be specially interested, any conclusions which they have reached. For administrative purposes, the Alliance has divided its Executive Commission or Business Committee into an Eastern Section located in Great Britain, and a Western Section located in the United States, but working in harmony with each other by constant intercorrespondence. As representing about thirty millions of souls, holding a common system of doctrine and adhering to a common polity and whose voluntary contributions for church purposes were reported at the Liverpool Council in 1904 as amounting in the previous year to considerably more than thirty-eight millions of dollars, the Alliance forms to-day one of the most closely united and influential organizations of Christendom.

G. D. MATHEWS.

BIBLIOGRAPHY: The *Proceedings* and *Minutes* of each of the General Councils have been published—of the first by J. Thomson, of the second by J. B. Dales and R. M. Patterson, and of the third and succeeding by G. D. Mathews. Consult also the *Quarterly Register of the Alliance*, 1886 to date.

ALLIES, THOMAS WILLIAM: English Roman Catholic; b. at Midsomer Norton (14 m. n.e. of Glastonbury), Somersetshire, Feb. 12, 1813; d. at St. John's Wood, London, June 17, 1903. He was first class in classics at Oxford, 1832. He took orders in the Anglican Church in 1838, serving for two years as chaplain to the bishop of London and for ten years as rector of Launton. In 1850 he was received into the Roman Catholic Church by his friend, Cardinal, then Father, Newman. He wrote extensively on theological subjects, his principal works being, *St. Peter, his Name and Office* (London, 1852); *The Formation of Christendom* (8 vols., 1861–95); *Per crucem ad lucem* (2 vols., 1879); *A Life's Decision* (1880); *Church and State* (1882), a continuation of *The Formation of Christendom;* and *The Throne of the Fisherman* (1887).

ALLIOLI, äl″li-ō′lī, **JOSEF FRANZ:** Roman Catholic; b. at Sulzbach, Austria, Aug. 10, 1793; d. at Augsburg May 22, 1873. He studied theology at Landshut and Regensburg, and Oriental languages at Vienna, Rome, and Paris. In 1823 he became professor of Oriental languages and Biblical exegesis and archeology at Landshut, and went to Munich when the university was removed thither in 1826. In 1835, being compelled to give up teaching through throat trouble, he became a member of the cathedral chapter at Munich and, in 1838, provost of the cathedral at Augsburg. He was active in charitable work and promoted the Franciscan Female Institute of the Star of Mary. The most noteworthy of his numerous publications was *Die heilige Schrift des Alten und Neuen Testaments aus der Vulgata mit Bezug auf den Grundtext neu übersetzt und mit kurzen Anmerkungen erläutert* (6 vols., Nuremberg, 1830–34), a third edition of an earlier work by H. Braun (ib. 1786). It far surpassed its predecessors, received papal sanction, and has been often reissued.

ALLIX, ā′līx′, **PIERRE:** Controversialist of the French Reformed Church; b. at Alençon (118 m. w.s.w. of Paris), Orne dept., 1641; d. in London Mar. 3, 1717. He was educated in the theological seminary at Sedan, and held pastoral charges at Saint-Agobile in Champagne and at Charenton. On the revocation of the Edict of Nantes (1685) he went to England, and James II. allowed him to establish a church in London for the numerous French exiles using the liturgy of the Church of England. In 1690 he was appointed canon of Salisbury. The fame of his learning was so great that both Oxford and Cambridge conferred the degree of doctor upon him, and the English clergy requested him to write a complete history of the councils. This great work was to embrace seven folio volumes, but it never appeared. His published writings, in French, English, and Latin, are mostly of a polemical or apologetic nature, and display a thorough knowledge of Christian antiquity and of the primitive and medieval ecclesiastical writers. In his two books, *Some Remarks upon the Ecclesiastical History of the Ancient Churches of Piedmont* (London, 1690), and *Remarks upon the Ecclesiastical History of the Ancient Churches of the Albigenses* (1692), he upheld against Bossuet the view that the Albigenses were not dualists, but identical with the Waldenses, and he contributed much to the upholding of this erroneous view.

(A. Hauck.)

Bibliography: E. and É. Haag, *La France protestante*, i. 61–66, Paris, 1879; *DNB*, i. 334–335; D. C. A. Agnew, *Protestant Exiles from France*, ii. 328–334, Edinburgh, 1886.

ALLON, HENRY: English Congregationalist; b. at Welton (10 m. w. of Hull), Yorkshire, Oct. 13, 1818; d. in London Apr. 16, 1892. He studied at Cheshunt College, Hertfordshire, and from Jan., 1844, till his death was minister of Union Chapel, Islington, London (for the first eight years as associate of the Rev. Thomas Lewis). During his ministry the congregation increased to a membership of nearly 2,000, and a new church building on Compton Terrace, Islington, was opened in Dec., 1877. He was chairman of the Congregational Union in 1864 and also in the Jubilee Year (1881). He was interested in the musical service of public worship and compiled hymn, anthem, and chant books, as well as a volume of hymns for children, which were largely used in the Congregational churches of England. He wrote much for the periodical press, edited the *British Quarterly Review*, 1865–87, and published *The Life of Rev. James Sherman* (London, 1863).

Bibliography: W. H. Harwood, *Henry Allon, The Story of his Ministry, with Selected Sermons and Addresses*, London, 1894 (by his successor at Islington).

ALL SAINTS' DAY (Lat. *Festum omnium sanctorum*): The first day of November. The Greek Church as early as the time of Chrysostom consecrated the Sunday after Whitsunday to the memory of all martyrs. The underlying idea of this festival is the same as that of All Saints' Day, although no connection between the two can be shown. The origin of All Saints' Day is obscure. It is said that Boniface IV (608–615) made the Pantheon at Rome a church of Mary and all martyrs and that the commemoration of this dedication was transferred from May 13 to Nov. 1 (Durand, *Rationale*, vii., chap. 34). More probable is the view that the festival is connected with the oratory which Gregory III. (731–741) erected in St. Peter's, "in which he laid the bones of the holy apostles and of all the holy martyrs and confessors, just men made perfect in all the world" (*Liber pontificalis, Vita Greg. III.*, ed. Duchesne, i. 417). Traces of the festival are found in the Frankish kingdom at the time of the Carolingians, it was commended by Alcuin (*Epist.*, lxxv.), and in the ninth century it became general. Luther did not approve of the festival, and Lutheran and Reformed churches do not observe it. The Church of England, however, and its branches retain it. W. Caspari.

ALL SOULS' DAY (Lat. *Commemoratio omnium fidelium defunctorum*): The second day of November. The ancient Church distinguishes between the dead who have died for the Church (martyrs) and those who, while they have not suffered death for the Church, yet have died as believers. All Souls' Day is dedicated to the memory of the latter. It is founded on the doctrine of the value of prayers and the Eucharist for the dead. Odilo of Cluny (d. 1049) instituted the festival for the Cluniacs (*ASM, sæc. vi.*, i. 585); and in course of time it was extended to all who had died in the faith. The *Missale Romanum* prescribes a special requiem-mass for the day. Luther demanded that the festival be given up, and it soon disappeared among Protestants. It is not observed in the Church of England. The German rationalists favored a commemoration of the dead (cf. G. C. Horst, *Mysteriosophie*, ii., Frankfort, 1817, 432). The litany of the Moravians for Easter morning is a Protestant pendant to All Souls' Day, and the rapid rise and popularity of the festival show that it satisfies a feeling of the Christian mind which the Church would do well to recognize. W. CASPARI.

ALMAIN, al″mên′, **JACQUES:** Gallican theologian; b. at Sens c. 1450; d. in Paris 1515. He was professor of theology in the College of Navarre in Paris, and at the request of Louis XII. prepared a reply to Cardinal Cajetan's work on the superiority of the pope to a general council (*Tractatus de auctoritate ecclesiæ et conciliorum generalium adversus Thomam de Vio*, Paris, 1512; see CAJETAN, CARDINAL). A similar work was his *Expositio circa decisiones magistri Guilelmi Occam super potestate Romani pontificis* (1517). He wrote also *Moralia* (1510) and *Dictata super sententias magistri Helcot* (1512).

ALMEIDA, al-mê′i-da, **MANOEL:** Jesuit missionary; b. at Vizeu (50 m. e.s.e. of Oporto), Portugal, 1580; d. at Goa 1646. He entered the Order of the Jesuits 1595; was sent to the East Indies 1602; lived in Abyssinia 1624–34; returned to Goa and became provincial of the order in the Indies. He left material for a general history of Abyssinia and of the Jesuits there, which was edited and published, in Portuguese, with additions, by Balthazar Tellez (Coimbra, 1660). Almeida's letter from Abyssinia to the general of his order for 1626–27 was published in Italian and French (Rome and Paris, 1629).

ALMONER (Fr. *aumônier*; Lat. *eleemosynarius*): An office at the French court from the thirteenth century onward, originally filled by one of the court chaplains who was entrusted with the distribution of the royal alms. Later there were several of these almoners, so that from the fifteenth century a grand almoner was named. The first to bear this title was Jean de Rely, later bishop of Angers and confessor of Charles VII. The grand almoner was one of the highest ecclesiastical dignitaries in France, and was charged with the supervision of charitable works in general, and of the court clergy. Nominations to benefices in the king's gift, including bishoprics and abbeys, were made through him. The office was abolished with the monarchy, though it was revived under both Napoleons.

Attached to the British court is the Royal Almonry, which dispenses alms for the sovereign, with these officers: hereditary grand almoner (the marquis of Exeter), lord high almoner (the lord bishop of Ely), subalmoner (subdean of chapels royal), the groom of the almonry, and the secretary to the lord high almoner. In the papal court the almoner of the pope is president of the *elimosineria apostolica*, a body composed of two clerics and four laymen. There is a similar office at the Spanish court.

ALMS: A gift to which the recipient has no claim and for which he renders no return, made purely from pity and a desire to relieve need. Such a gift has religious value in Buddhism and in Islam. But it was in Judaism that almsgiving was first highly regarded from a religio-ethical point of view. The Old Testament has a higher conception, based upon the ideas that the land belongs not to individuals but to God, whence all have equal right to its fruits, and that the regulating principle of conduct toward others among God's chosen people must be " thou shalt love thy neighbor as thyself " (Lev. xix. 18, 34). Benevolence follows as an ordinary duty. In postcanonical times almsgiving almost imperceptibly assumed the character of a voluntary act of merit and even of expiation for sin and assurance of salvation (Tobit iv. 7–11, xii. 8–9; Ecclus. iii. 30, xxix. 12–13). Such overvaluation of external acts is rebuked in Matt. vi. The New Testament revelation is a gospel of the voluntary love of God, in which good works can have no efficacy toward justification and salvation. They are, on the contrary, the inevitable result and proof of the renewed life (Matt. vii. 15–23; Luke x. 33–37). It is from this point of view that the idea of a divine reward finds application to the observance of charity in the New Testament (Matt. vi. 4, xix. 21; Luke xiv. 14; Acts x. 4; II Cor. ix. 7; Gal. vi. 9).

The Judaic conception of almsgiving as an act of merit and satisfaction came into the early Church through the Jewish Christians. A classic expression of Jewish-Christian thought is II Clement xvi. 4: "Almsgiving, therefore, is a good thing, even as repentance for sin. Fasting is better than prayer, but almsgiving than both. And love covereth a multitude of sins; but prayer out of a good conscience delivereth from death. Blessed is every man that is found full of these. For almsgiving lifteth off the burden of sin." The idea is completely dominant in Cyprian (*De opere et eleemosynis*), and was, indeed, unavoidable, if the Old Testament Apocrypha were accepted as on a par with the canon. Save that propitiatory value was afterward assigned to the sacrament of penance, the position of the Roman Catholic Church has remained essentially that of Cyprian. Augustine conceded influence in the alleviation of purgatorial suffering to almsgiving, and the "Sentences" of Peter Lombard, the dogmatic manual of the Middle Ages, emphasize the idea out of all true proportion.

Poverty was so highly prized by the early Church that the pseudo-Clementine Homilies (XV. vii. 9) declare the possession of property as defilement with the things of this world, a sin. In the fourth century poverty, through monasticism, became a factor in the Christian ideal life. And in the thirteenth century begging, through Francis of Assisi, received a religious idealization, which was in the highest degree pernicious to social good order. The mendicant monk is nothing more nor less than a grossly immoral character. The Reformation rejected all these errors, required some form of labor from the Christian as the basis of his membership in society, and sought to substitute organized care of the poor for the prevalent haphazard methods of giving and receiving alms. Protestant dogmatics grants to alms no share whatever in the doctrine of salvation. Far above any individual instance of almsgiving is the spirit of benevolence, which seeks no merit in the gift and aims at permanent benefit, not the satisfying of a temporary need. Modern humanitarian endeavor and recent legislation, which seek to prevent those incapable of work from becoming recipients of alms, are but an extension of the principles enunciated by the Reformation. Churches should accept the rational principle which avoids indiscriminate and unintelligent almsgiving, tending to pauperization and the encouragement of idleness. But it is true that organization can never fully take the place of personal benevolence or render it unnecessary. (L. LEMME.)

BIBLIOGRAPHY: On the historical side, S. Chastel, *Charity of the Primitive Churches*, Philadelphia, 1857; G. Uhlhorn, *Christliche Liebesthätigkeit*, 3 vols., Stuttgart, 1895. Eng. transl., *Christian Charity in the Ancient Church*, New York, 1883. On the practical side, P. Church, *The Philosophy of Benevolence*, New York, 1836; *Systematic Beneficence, comprising "The Great Reform" by A. Stevens, "The Great Question" by L. Wright, "Property consecrated" by B. St. J. Fry*, New York, 1856; M. W. Moggridge, *Method in Almsgiving*, London, 1882. Consult also the books on Christian Ethics and on Socialism.

ALOGI, al'o-jî (Gk. *alogoi*): A name coined by Epiphanius (*Haer.*, li.) to designate certain people whom he treats as a distinct sect. The account which he gives agrees with that of Philaster (*Haer.*, lx.), because both depend on the *Syntagma* of Hippolytus. Epiphanius can not have known of them by either oral tradition or personal contact; he speaks of them as a phenomenon of the past, of the time when Montanism vexed the Church of Asia Minor, and is unable to give any answer to the most obvious questions in regard to them. Before his time they have no more definite name than "the heretics who reject the writings of John." Epiphanius was uncertain whether they rejected the epistles of John, and Hippolytus had referred only to their criticism of the Gospel and the Apocalypse. The former justifies the name "Alogi" by the assertion that the sect did not accept the Logos proclaimed by John; but the grounds which he quotes from them for their rejection of the Johannine writings, equally with the indications of Hippolytus and Philaster, fail to support this view of their critical attitude; indeed, in another place Epiphanius contradicts himself. His consequent association of the Theodotians with the Alogi is thus only one of his groundless fancies.

Epiphanius quotes a number of their assertions, e.g., that the books in question were written not by John, but by Cerinthus, and are unworthy to be received in the Church; that they do not agree with the works of the other apostles; and that the Apocalypse is absurd in numerous particulars. The determining motive of their criticism can not be made out from his fragmentary indications. If the name "Alogi" and the notion that this motive was a rejection of the Christology of the fourth Gospel are demonstrably groundless inventions of Epiphanius, which moreover fail to explain the contemptuous tone of the sect toward the Apocalypse, it is all the more noteworthy that he not only places them in chronological and geographical relation to the Montanists of Asia Minor, but attributes to them also a denial of the existence of the charismata in the Church. If he has here, as a comparison with Irenæus (III. xi. 9) shows, repeated confusedly the thoughts of Hippolytus, it follows that the latter found in the passage of Irenæus referred to an argument against the Alogi, although Irenæus's context only requires him to deal with their rejection of the fourth Gospel and not of the Apocalypse. Thus it may be taken as the opinion of Irenæus and Hippolytus that these otherwise orthodox people, in their opposition to the Montanists, sought to withdraw from the latter the supports which they found for their doctrine of the Paraclete in the Gospel of John and for their millenarianism in the Apocalypse. The rejection of the Johannine books by the Alogi is evidence that these books were generally received; their ascription to Cerinthus, a contemporary of John, of the belief that they were written in John's lifetime. This ascription need not involve any special reference to the actual teaching of Cerinthus, which, according to the more trustworthy authority of Irenæus, Hippolytus, and the pseudo-Tertullian (*Haer.*, x.), bore no resemblance to that of the apostle. (T. ZAHN.)

BIBLIOGRAPHY: The sources are indicated in the text. Consult: Harnack, *Litteratur*, II. i. 376 sqq., 670–671, 689–691, 692, 695; T. Zahn, *Geschichte des neutestamentlichen Kanons*, i. 220–262, ii. 47, 50, 236, 967–991, 1021, Leipsic, 1890–91; idem, *Forschungen*, v. 35–43, 1892; Neander, *Christian Church*, i. 526, 583, 682; Moeller, *Christian Church*, i. 158, 223, 233; *DB*, ii. 701, iii. 537, iv. 240; G. P. Fisher, *Some Remarks on the Alogi*, in *Papers of the American Society of Church History*, vol. iii., pt. 1, pp. 1–9, New York, 1890.

ALOMBRADOS, ā''lom-brā'dez (modern spelling, **ALUMBRADOS**; Lat. *Illuminati*; "Enlightened"): Spanish mystics who first attracted the attention of the Inquisition in 1524 (Wadding, *Annales minorum*, under the year 1524), when a certain Isabella de Cruce of Toledo is mentioned as a representative of their quietistic-ascetic teachings and their enthusiastic striving for divine inspirations and revelations. About 1546 Magdalena de Cruce of Aguilar, near Cordova, a member of the Poor Clares, is said to have been accused of spreading immoral antinomian teachings and to have been forced to abjure her heresies; and there are like reports of a Carmelite nun, Catherina de Jesus of Cordova, about 1575, and of a Portuguese Dominican nun, Maria de Visitatione, in 1586. The founder of the Society of Jesus, in his student days, was accused of belonging to the Illuminati at Alcala in 1526, and at Salamanca in 1527, and the second time was imprisoned for forty-two days (cf. Gothein, p. 225; see JESUITS). A connection between the Spanish Illuminati of the sixteenth century and the German reformatory movement has often been conjectured, especially by Roman Catholics, but without good reason; nor can influence from Anabaptists like Münzer or Schwenckfeld be seriously considered.

An ordinance of the Spanish Inquisition dated Jan. 28, 1558, mentions the following heretical teachings as characteristic of the Illuminati: "Only inward prayer is well-pleasing to God and meritorious, not external prayer with the lips. The confessors who impose outward acts of repentance are not to be obeyed; the true servants of God are superior to such discipline and have no need of meritorious works in the common sense; the contortions, convulsions, and faintings, which accompany their inner devotion, are to them sufficient tokens of the divine grace. In the state of perfection the secret of the Holy Trinity is beheld while here below, and all that should be done or left undone is communicated directly by the Holy Spirit. When perfection is attained it is no longer necessary to look to images of the saints, or to hear sermons or religious conversations of the common kind" (J. A. Llorente, *Geschichte der spanischen Inquisition*, Germ. ed., ii., Stuttgart, 1824, pp. 3–4). A still fuller record of Illuminatic errors is given by Malvasia (*Catalogus omnium hæresium et conciliorum*, Rome, 1661, xvi. century, pp. 269–274), who enumerates fifty heretical propositions, including besides those already mentioned the following: "In the state of perfection the soul can neither go forward nor backward, for its own faculties have all been abolished by grace. The perfect has no more need of the intercession of the saints, even devotion to the humanity of Jesus is superfluous for him; he has no more need of the sacraments or to do good works. A perfect man can not sin; even an act which, outwardly regarded, must be looked upon as vicious, can not contaminate the soul which lives in mystical union with God."

The ecclesiastical annalist Spondanus records in the year 1623 an inquisitorial process against Illuminatic mystics in the dioceses of Seville and Granada, in which the grand inquisitor Andreas Pacheco mentions no less than seventy-six heretical propositions, many of them antinomian. Like things are told of the French sect of *Illuminés* (called also *Guérinets* from their leader the Abbé Guérin) who were prosecuted in 1634 in Flanders and Picardy. Another sect of *Illuminés* which appeared about 1722 in southern France has more resemblance to the freemasons, and seems to have been a precursor of the Order of Illuminati in south Germany, especially in Bavaria (see ILLUMINATI).

O. ZÖCKLER†.

BIBLIOGRAPHY: H. Heppe, *Geschichte der quietistischen Mystik in der katholischen Kirche*, 41 sqq., Berlin, 1875; M. Menendez y Pelayo, *Historia de los heterodoxos Españoles*, ii. 521, iii. 403, Madrid, 1880; H. C. Lea, *Chapters from the Religious History of Spain Connected with the Inquisition*, passim, Philadelphia, 1890; E. Gothein, *Ignatius von Loyola und die Gegenreformation*, pp. 61–62, 224 sqq., Halle, 1895.

ALOYSIUS, al"o-i'shius', SAINT, OF GONZAGA (LUIGI GONZAGA): Jesuit; b. in the castle of Castiglione (22 m. n.w. of Mantua), the ancestral seat of the Gonzaga family, Mar. 9, 1568; d. in Rome June 21, 1591. His father was Marquis of Castiglione and a prince of the Holy Roman Empire, but the boy turned away from the pleasures of courts and devoted himself early to a life of asceticism and piety. In 1585 he renounced his claim to the succession in order to join the Society of Jesus, and took the vows in 1587. His death was due to his self-sacrificing labors in the care of the sick during the prevalence of the plague in Rome. He was beatified by Gregory XV in 1621, and canonized by Benedict XIII. in 1726. Devotion to him is wide-spread in the modern Roman Catholic Church, in which he is regarded as a model of the virtue of purity, and an especial patron of young men, particularly those who enter the ecclesiastical state.

BIBLIOGRAPHY: V. Cepari, *De vita beati Aloysii Gonzagæ*, Cologne, 1608, Eng. transl. by F. Goldie, London, 1891; C. Papencordt, *Der heilige Aloysius*, Paderborn, 1889.

ALPHA AND OMEGA (A, Ω): The first and last letters of the Greek alphabet. They are used in a symbolic sense in three places in the Book of Revelation. In i. 8 God describes himself as "Alpha and Omega, the beginning and the ending, which is, and which was, and which is to come, the Almighty." The expression is similarly used in xxi. 6 (cf. Isa. xliv. 6, xlviii. 12). In xxii. 13 the name "Alpha and Omega, the beginning and the end, the first and the last" is the designation adopted for himself by Christ, who is also called "the first and the last" in ii. 8. If, as is apparent from the context, these passages express the same symbolic meaning, that of eternity as unlimited duration, it is plain that the use of this name is intended to guarantee the fulfilment of the prophecies mentioned in the passages. Commentators have referred, in explanation of the expression, to the use of the first and last letters of the Hebrew alphabet (א ת) in rabbinical literature, though the parallelism is not acknowledged by all scholars. A long line of early and medieval writers discuss the passages cited from Revelation. Thus Clement of Alexandria has one or more of them in mind when he says (*Stromata*, iv. 25): "For he [the Son] is the circle of all powers rolled and united into one unity. Wherefore the Word (Gk. *Logos*) is called the Alpha and the Omega, of whom alone the end becomes the beginning, and ends again at the original beginning without any break." As in this passage, so in *Stromata*, vi. 16, he explains the prophecies with reference to Christ alone. Tertullian (*De monogamia*, v.) makes a similar use of the name. Ambrose (*In septem visiones*, i. 8) says that Christ calls himself the beginning because he is the creator of the human race and the author of salvation, and the end because he is the end of the law, of death, and so on. Prudentius, in his hymn *Corde natus ex parentis*, paraphrases the words of Revelation. The Gnostics extracted from the letters their characteristic mystical play on numbers; the fact that A and Ω stood for 801, and the sum of the letters in the Greek word for dove (*peristera*) amounted to the same, was used by the Gnostic Marcus to support the assertion that Christ called himself Alpha and Omega with reference to the coming of the Spirit at his baptism in the form of a dove (Irenæus, I. xiv 6, xv. 1). Later, Primasius played on the numbers in the same way to prove the essential identity of the Holy Ghost with the Father and the Son (on Rev. xxii. 13). An evidence of the place which these letters held in Gnostic speculation is afforded by a piece of parchment and one of papyrus preserved in the Egyptian Museum at Berlin, both originally used as amulets. On the former the letters are found together with Coptic magical formulas and a cross of St. Andrew; the latter also contains Coptic formulas, divided by a cross which terminates at each extremity in A or Ω.

The letters occur much less frequently in the literary sources of Christian antiquity and of the Middle Ages than in monumental inscriptions. With the various forms of the monogram of Christ and of the cross, they belonged to the most popular symbols of early Christian art, which was never tired of reproducing them on all kinds of monuments, public and private, and in every sort of material. The fact that with but very few exceptions, A and Ω are found, as far as is known, on these monuments in connection with figures or symbols of Christ—never of God in the abstract or of God the Father—leads to the interesting conclusion that the popular exegesis of the above-named passages of the Apocalypse referred their meaning to Christ alone, and thus affords a proof that the makers of these monuments were indirectly expressing their belief in his divinity. The possibility, however, can not be denied that in certain cases motives of a superstitious nature may have led to the employment of these symbols; but it is much less easy to reason with certainty from the monumental remains than from the literature of the time. Modern Christian art, less given to symbolism, is relatively poor in examples of the use of these letters, though they have reappeared more often in the nineteenth century, as a general rule in connection with the monogram of Christ. Full and detailed descriptions of their early use, with the dates of their appearance in different countries, and classification of their employment alone, with human or animal figures, or (which is much more frequent) with other symbols, may be found in abundance in the archeological works of De Rossi, Garrucci, Hübner, Le Blant, Kraus, and others, and in the *Corpus inscriptionum Latinarum*.

(NIKOLAUS MÜLLER.)

BIBLIOGRAPHY: A vast amount has been written on the subject; the best single article is in *Dictionnaire d'archéologie chrétienne et de liturgie*, fasc. i., cols. 1–25, Paris, 1903, and contains diagrams and very full and definite references to the literature.

ALPHÆUS, al-fī'us: Father of the second James in all four of the lists of the apostles. He is interesting in so far as he may with probability be identified with the Clopas (A. V Cleophas) of John xix. 25. Of the two Marys who stood by the cross with the mother of Jesus, one is called in this passage the wife of Clopas; in Matt. xxvii. 56 and in Mark xv. 40, the mother of James, or James the Less, presumably the second apostle of this name. The question how the use of two different names, Alphæus and Clopas, is to be explained may be answered in two ways. Either Κλωπάς (=Κλεόπας, a contraction of Κλεόπατρος, as Ἀντίπας of Ἀντίπατρος) was the Greek name which Alphæus bore in addition to his Aramaic one; or there are here two alternative Grecized forms, both representing חַלְפַי. Against the former view is the fact that the contraction κλω for κλεο in Greek names is never found elsewhere; and in favor of the latter is the fact that the initial ח, commonly rendered by the smooth breathing or by X, is sometimes also represented by K. In any case the diversity of names need not prevent the identity of person. This identity would make Alphæus the uncle, and James, the son of Alphæus, the cousin, of Jesus—a result of some importance for the question as to James (q.v.). (K. SCHMIDT.)

The most probable solution of this much vexed problem seems to lie in a ground form עַלְפַי, the two modes of pronouncing the first letter of which (as in Arabic) would give rise to the variant names Alphæus and Clopas or Cleophas.

G. W G.

BIBLIOGRAPHY: J. B. Lightfoot, *Galatians*, p. 267, London, 1890; T. Keim, *Jesus of Nazara*, iii. 276, London, 1878; J. B. Mayor, *Epistle of St. James*, pp. xvi.-xvii., London, 1897; *DB*, i. 74–75; *EB*, i. 122–123.

ALSACE-LORRAINE (Germ. *Elsass-Lothringen*): An immediate "imperial territory" (*Reichsland*), forming the extreme southwest of the German empire, bounded on the north by the grand duchy of Luxemburg, Rhenish Prussia, and the Rhine Palatinate (Rhenish Bavaria), on the east by Baden, on the south by Switzerland, and on the west by France. Its area is 5,603 square miles, with a population (1905) of 1,814,630, including 1,375,300 (75.8 per cent.) Roman Catholics, 406,100 (22.3 per cent.) Protestants, and 33,130 (1.88 per cent.) Jews. The preponderance of Roman Catholics points back to the political conditions of the sixteenth century, when the territory for the most part belonged to the house of Austria, the duke of Lorraine, and the bishops of Strasburg. The Reformation found entrance only in the free city of Strasburg and in certain other cities and minor dependencies; and much of the progress there made was lost under the dragonnades and through the work of the Jesuits in the time of Louis XIV

The Lutheran Church.

Ecclesiastical matters were little changed by the transfer of Alsace-Lorraine from France to Germany after the war of 1870–71. The Church of the Augsburg Confession is still constituted according to the law of the first French republic as amended in 1852 after the *coup d'état* of Louis Napoleon. A presbyterial council, chosen by the congregation, under the presidency of the pastor, has general oversight of the spiritual and temporal concerns of each congregation. Its acts and decisions must be confirmed by the next higher ecclesiastical board, the consistory—in some cases representing a single congregation, in others a union of several—which is chosen by a highly complicated system. Its functions are in general the same as those of the presbytery—to maintain discipline, to care for the order of divine service, and to manage Church property. There are also inspection districts, each having one clerical and two lay inspectors. At the head of the Church is a directory, a standing board, and an upper consistory, which meets yearly. The directory consists of two laymen and one of the clerical inspectors appointed by the government, and two lay members chosen by the upper consistory. It has power to review all acts of presbyteries and consistories, manages all Church property, forms the intermediate body between Church and government, and appoints all ministers after consultation with presbyterial councils and consistories. It has a voice in appointing the teachers of the Protestant gymnasium, has the right of nominating the inspectors, licenses and ordains preachers, and executes the decrees of the upper consistory. The latter meets annually in regular session. The business to be brought before it must have the approval of the government and its decisions require government confirmation. Its sessions are limited to six days and a representative of the government must be present. Ministers' salaries range between 1,420 and 2,840 marks according to position and length of service. The most important foundations are under the administration of the Chapter of St. Thomas in Strasburg; they are partly ecclesiastical, partly educational, the latter being the more important.

Reformed and Other Bodies.

The Reformed Church of Alsace-Lorraine has substantially the same constitution as the Church of the Augsburg Confession. Its congregations are led and governed by similar presbyterial councils and consistories, but the latter are not united into an external administrative unity. It has a numerical strength about one-fifth that of the Lutheran Church. Of other Protestant bodies the Mennonites, with a membership of about 2,500, are the strongest. The government expenditures for salaries and other Church purposes are more than 700,000 marks yearly.

The Roman Catholic Church.

The Roman Catholic Church of Alsace-Lorraine comprises the two bishoprics of Strasburg (Alsace) and Metz (Lorraine), formerly belonging to the province of Besançon, but since 1874 independent of all archiepiscopal or metropolitan jurisdiction. The bishops are named by the reigning prince, and receive canonical institution from Rome. They select all books to be used in church services, and present priests for appointment to the prince, but name directly the lower clergy as well as the directors and professors of the diocesan seminaries, in which the clergy receive their training. They also direct these seminaries and order the instruction in them. Each bishop has two vicars-general and a chapter, which becomes influential only in the case of a vacancy in the bishopric. The salaries of priests range from 1,500 to 2,000 marks; vicars receive 540 marks. Church buildings and rectories by law belong to the civil authorities so that the latter are charged with their maintenance, if the ordinary revenues (managed by a committee of the congregation) do not suffice. Such buildings may not be diverted from their original purpose. Many of the churches are used by both Protestants and Roman Catholics. The cemeteries also are common property, and any resident may be buried in them without confessional distinction. The taking of monastic vows for life is forbidden, and the law recognizes no religious order; nevertheless, more than twenty are represented, the greater number being for females. The expenditures of the State for the Roman Catholic Church amount to more than 2,000,000 marks yearly.

The Jews are divided into three consistories, each with a chief rabbi, at Strasburg, Colmar, and Metz, respectively. Rabbis receive salaries from the State, varying from 1,500 to 1,900 marks.

WILHELM GOETZ.

ALSTED, al'sted, **JOHANN HEINRICH**: Reformed theologian; b. at Ballersbach, near Herborn (43 m. n. of Wiesbaden), Nassau, 1588; d. at Weissenburg (Karlsburg, 240 m. e.s.e. of Budapest), Siebenbürgen, Hungary, Nov. 8, 1638. He studied at Herborn and became professor there in the philosophical faculty in 1610, and in the theological faculty in 1619. In 1629 he went to the newly founded University of Weissenburg. He represented the Church of Nassau at the Synod of Dort (1618–19). He was one of the famous teachers of his time, and compiled a series of compends of pretty nearly every branch of knowledge, which are interesting as showing the scholarly and literary methods and achievements of the seventeenth century. The most remarkable were *Cursus philosophici encyclopædia* (Herborn, 1620) and *Encyclopædia septem tomis distincta* (ib. 1630). The first of these comprises two volumes; one a quarto of 3,072 pages, containing: i., *quatuor præcognita philosophica: archelogia, hexilogia, technologia, didactica;* ii., *undecim scientiæ philosophicæ theoreticæ: metaphysica, pneumatica, physica, arithmetica, geometria, cosmographia, uranoscopia, geographia, optica, musica, architectonica;* iii., *quinque prudentiæ philosophicæ practicæ: ethica, œconomica, politica, scholastica, historica;* vol. ii. gives the *septem artes liberales*. The second work, in two folios, includes as its first, third, and fourth divisions the three given above, and adds: ii., *philologia*, i.e., *lexica, grammatica, rhetorica, logica, oratoria, poetica;* v., *tres facultates principes: theologia, jurisprudentia, medicina;* vi., *artes mechanicæ;* vii., a miscellaneous section, *præcipuæ farragines disciplinarum: mnemonica, historica, chronologia, architectonica, critica, magia, alchymia, magnetographia*, etc., including even *tabacologia*, or the *doctrina de natura, usu et abusu tabaci*. Theology is divided into seven branches: *naturalis, catechetica, didactica, polemica, casuum, prophetica* (homiletics), and *moralis*. He also wrote a *Diatribe de mille annis* (Frankfort, 1627), in which he fixes the beginning of the millennium at the year 1694.

(E. F. KARL MÜLLER.)

BIBLIOGRAPHY: F. W. E. Roth, in *Monatshefte der Comenius-Gesellschaft*, 1895, pp. 29 sqq.; H. F. Criegern, *J. A. Comenius als Theolog*, pp. 365 sqq., Leipsic, 1881.

ALTAR.

I. **In Primitive Religion**: The word "altar," derived ultimately from the Latin *alere*, "to nourish," through *altus*, derived meaning "high," is usually taken to mean a raised structure; but etymology and history are against this. "Altar" is the rendering in the Old Testament of *mizbeaḥ* (Aram. *madhbaḥ*), "place of sacrifice," and in the New Testament of *thusiastērion*, having the same meaning. The Greek word *bōmos* indeed means a raised structure; but the possession of two words by the Greek suggests development and differentiation. The Latin *ara* means the seat or resting-place, not "of the victim" (so Andrews, *Latin Lexicon*, s.v.), but of the deity; and on that account the word was avoided by the Fathers. The word "altar" has its ultimate root in the actual purport of the early sacrifice (q.v.), viz., a meal of worshipers and worshiped. So far from the place of sacrifice being invariably a raised structure, it was sometimes a trench (e.g., in the celebrated sacrifice of Ulysses described in *Odyssey*, xi.), while in the famous tombs at Mycenæ there were depressions connected by small shafts with the graves, and generally explained as the places of deposit of offerings to the dead. At the present day the African places his offering of oil to the tree spirit not on an altar, but on the ground.

1. Altar not Necessarily a Raised Structure.

To understand the development of the altar it must be recalled that, as is generally conceded, religion has passed through the animistic stage. That is to say, man in his primitive state might regard any object—tree, rock, mountain, fountain, stream, sea, etc.—as the seat of divine power. His mental processes then led him to approach whatever he regarded as divinity as he approached human superiors, namely with gifts, which he applied directly to the objects of his worship, casting his offerings into fountain, stream, sea, or fire, laying them at the foot or on the top of the mountain, or smearing oil or fat, or pouring blood or wine on the divine stone. In other words, these objects were both divinity and altar.

The best Biblical example of this primitive mode of thinking and acting is in the passage Gen. xxviii. 11-18. Jacob had pillowed his head on a stone, and there resulted his dream of the ladder. In accordance with the mental processes of his time, on awakening he conceived the cause of this dream to be the divinity in (or of) the stone—note his exclamation, "this is a Bethel" (a "place or house of God")—and he "poured oil upon the stone." In this he paralleled the custom of the pre-Mohammedan Arabs, as proved by W. R. Smith (*Rel. of Sem.*, Lecture v.) and Wellhausen (*Heidentum*, pp. 99 sqq.). The passages referred to in these two authors demonstrate that such a stone was more than an altar; it was the visible embodiment of the presence of deity. The same might be shown in the customs of other peoples, as for example, the Samoans (cf. Turner, *Samoa*, London, 1884, pp. 24, 281). This anointing of sacred stones is a custom followed by the Samoyeds to this day, and was known in Russia and in the west of Ireland in the early part of the last century. The custom is entirely on a par with the superstitious practise, only recently abandoned, in remote parts of Wales and Cornwall, of putting pins and other trifles in wells and springs reputed to have healing qualities, doubtless in pagan times the seat of worship (cf. *Folk-Lore*, in which many examples are given). The Greek and Roman custom of pouring a libation to Neptune into the sea at the beginning of a voyage will occur to the reader as a survival from the time when the sea was a deity and not merely the domain of one.

2. Altar and Divinity One.

The stone (in the Old Testament the word is often rendered "pillar," q.v.) and cairn "or witness" (Gen. xxxi. 45-54; cf. Josh. xxiv. 26-27 with xxii. 26-27) were almost certainly such embodiments of the presence of deity (note the words, Gen. xxxi. 52, "This heap be witness and this pillar [stone] be witness," and, in Josh., "It [this stone] hath heard"); the covenant and oath were under the protection of the deity there present (cf. Baal-berith = "Baal [protector] of the covenant," Judges viii. 33, and El-berith = "God [protector] of the covenant," Josh. ix. 46, R. V., and the Greek Zeus orkios = "Zeus [protector] of the oath"). In the Genesis passage the covenant-making feast, at which the clan and the deity were commensals, followed the appeal to the covenant-guarding object. And while the fact is not expressly stated, that the pillar of Jacob and Laban was anointed hardly admits of question, in view of the custom attending the holding of such a feast-sacrifice. At least in early times, then, the same object was sometimes both divinity and altar.

The next step shows the differentiation between the two. The later Arabic term for altar is *nuṣb* from the same root as the Hebrew *maṣṣebah* ("pillar"). It has been shown by W. R. Smith and Wellhausen in the works already cited that the *anṣab* (pl. of *nuṣb*) were stones, the objects of worship, and later merely altars. This shows a development in conception. A similar unfolding took place in Hebrew practise (see II., below), where stones are shown to have been used as altars. But often among the Hebrews the stone pillar was retained, an altar was erected, and the two stood side by side (Hos. iii. 4; Isa. xix. 19). Then the pillars came to be more or less ornate (cf. the Greek *Hermæ* and the two pillars in Solomon's Temple, 1 Kings vii. 15-22, which last are hard to explain except as a transference to the Temple of the pillars customary at shrines). That the *maṣṣebah* represented deity is now generally granted. The old custom of applying the sacrifice to the monolith had become outworn; it was no longer deity but only deity's representative, and the altar was provided on which to place (or, in the case of fire-sacrifices, to consume) the offerings.

3. Altar and Divinity Differentiated.

That the altars were rude at first, and that the elaborate ones of later times were the product of developed esthetic perceptions, is as clear from archeological investigations as is the development of the house and temple from the simple cave or booth dwellings, and of the elaborate ritual from the simple worship of primitive ages.

The location of altars is implicitly indicated in the foregoing. Wherever deity indicated its presence either by some such subjective manifestation as a dream, or by terrestrial phenomena such as the issue of a fountain or of subterranean gases, or by such supposed interference in the sphere of human events as by a storm which changed the fortune of battle, or by aerial phenomena such as the formation of thunder-claps with resultant lightning on the crest of a mountain—thither men brought their offerings and there altars were found or placed. Naturally the tops of hills (see HIGH PLACES) and groves were universally adopted; and these passed from early to late possessors of the lands as sacred places. The one test was the supposed residence or frequent attendance of deity at the spot.

II. In the Old Testament: The altars of the oldest code were of earth, and therefore simple mounds, or of unhewn stones (Ex. xx. 24). (Were the two mules' burden of earth, II Kings v. 17, for an altar?) Sometimes a single boulder or monolith sufficed (Josh. xxiv. 26–27; cf. xxii. 26–27; Judges vi. 20; I Sam. vi. 14, xiv. 33; I Kings i. 9). For the cairn as an altar, note Gen. xxxi. 45–54, and cf. xxviii. 18. As late as the Deuteronomic code (Deut. xxvii. 5) undressed stone is specified as the material for the altar, and the height of the altar is limited. The elaboration in form and material of the altars of Solomon (I Kings viii. 64) and of Ahaz (II Kings xvi. 10–11) are directly traceable to contact with outside culture and the development of esthetic perception and desire (see ART, HEBREW). The locations correspond closely with primitive usage and with the fact that early Hebrew worship was in large part derived from or coalesced with Canaanitic practise. "High places," i.e., the tops of hills, were especially used, and there are several traces of tree and fountain altars, e.g., the Paneas source of the Jordan and the Fountain of Mary near Jerusalem.

1. Pre-Deuteronomic and Deuteronomic.

Post-Deuteronomic means exilic or postexilic and the history of the Hebrew altar is bound up with that of the Temple. The effects of contact with advanced culture are shown in the elaborated structure and equipment, while the differentiation of the altar of burnt offering and that of incense tells the story of advancing elaboration of cult. The "table of showbread" was in form and purpose an altar.

2. Post-Deuteronomic.

GEO. W GILMORE.

III. In the Christian Church: The oldest designation of the place of celebration of the "Lord's Supper" is "the Lord's table" (Gk. *trapeza kuriou*, I Cor. x. 21). This expression or "table" alone or with an adjective ("holy, sacred, mystic table;" *trapeza hiera, hagia, mystikē*, etc.) is used by the Greek Fathers. The general Greek word for altar (*thysiastērion*) is less frequently used and *bōmos* is purposely avoided. The Latin writers use *mensa, altare, altarium*, but show repugnance to *ara*.

1. Before the Reformation: a. To about the Year 1000: As the oldest meeting-places of Christian worship, rooms in ordinary dwellings, differed essentially from the Jewish sanctuary in Jerusalem and from the temples of the Greeks and Romans, so also the "table of the Lord" differed from the Jewish and heathen altars; and it is significant that the absence of altars in the Christian service was especially offensive to the heathen (Minucius Felix, *Octavius*, 10; Origen, *contra Celsum*, vii. 64, viii. 17; Cyprian, *Ad Demetrianum*, 12). The celebration of the agape and the Eucharist required a table, and it was but natural that the first disciples of the Lord, like himself, should celebrate the sacred meal about and on a table. When the religious service was transferred from private houses to special buildings, the exclusive use of tables for the celebration of the Eucharist was still continued. The frequent notices that the persecuted sought and found a safe hiding-place beneath the altar or embraced the legs of the altar as a sign of their distress (cf. Schmid, pp. 31–32, 69–70), as well as notices in Gregory of Tours (*Miraculorum libri vii.*, i. 28) and Paulus Silentiarius (*Descriptio ecclesiæ S. Sophiæ*, pp. 752 sqq.), that the altars in St. Peter's at Rome and in St. Sophia at Constantinople were supported by columns, presuppose the table-form of the altar. The recollection of this original form has never been lost in the Church, and to this day the table-altar is the rule in the Greek Church.

1. Form and Structure.

When relics first began to be transferred from their original resting-places to churches, their receptacles were placed beneath the altar—seldom before or behind it, and not until the Middle Ages above it. The space was then sometimes walled up, giving the altar a coffin- or chest-like form. Such altars are found here and there as early as the fifth century, and during the Middle Ages they became usual. The terms *martyrium* and *confessio* were applied to such tombs as well as to the crypt-like space which held the coffin (*arca*), to the coffin itself, and to the altar. To make it possible to see and touch the holy contents an opening (*fenestrella*) was left in front with a lattice of metal or marble (*transenna*) or two doors (*regiolæ*). It must not be assumed that all altars of the Middle Ages were provided with relics. A canopy (*ciborium*), supported by pillars, was frequently found as early as the time of Constantine. The material used was wood, stone, and metal; gold, silver, and precious stones were sometimes employed.

It was usual in antiquity to spread a table with a cloth in preparation for a banquet, and this custom was transferred to "the table of the Lord." Optatus of Mileve in the second half of the fourth century is the first to mention such a covering (*De schismate Donatistorum*, vi. 1, 5). Thenceforth altar-cloths are more frequently mentioned. Their size can not be determined. They seem to have been generally of linen, though other materials, as silk and gold-brocade, were used. Only one such covering was used at first, later the number varied. To this period belongs the *corporale* (called also *palla corporalis, oportorium dominici corporis*, Gk. *sindōn*), in which the bread intended for the oblation was wrapped (Isidore of Pelusium, *Epist.*, i. 123). Later there were two *corporalia* (or *pallæ*): one spread over the altar-

2. Accessories and Ornamentation.

cloths, on which the holy vessels stood; the other used to cover the cup and the paten. In time the name *corporale* was restricted to the first of these, and *palla* was used for the second. Both were of linen. Among the most elaborate and costly of altar-appendages in the Romanesque period were the *antependia* or *frontalia*, which were used as decorations for the altar-front; the back and the sides of the altar also were often adorned in like manner. When altars of gold and silver are mentioned it is probable that in most cases metal plates in the front of the altar are meant. The oldest specimens which have been preserved date from the ninth to the twelfth centuries. They represent scenes from Bible history and the lives of saints, usually with the figure of Christ in the center. Precious stones and glass are inserted. *Antependia* were also made of costly cloths with gold and silver embroidery, and mosaics and reliefs were built into the sides of the altar. Crosses are represented in these decorations, and stood near altars; they were also placed above or hung below the *ciborium*, but in the first millennium crucifixes did not stand on the altars. In like manner lamps were hung from the *ciboria* or stood about the altars, but not on them.

At first there was only one altar in the place of worship, symbolic of unity. In a basilica without transepts it stood at the center of the chord of the apse. The Eastern Church retained the single altar; but in the West the number increased under the influence of the custom of private masses and the veneration of relics. A church in Gaul in the time of Gregory the Great (d. 604) had thirteen; the cathedral at Magdeburg, forty-eight. After the year 1000 altars received different names according to their position and use.

3. Number and Varieties of Altars.

The main altar was called the *altare majus, capitaneum, cardinale, magistrum*, or *principale*, "high altar"; the others were *altaria minora*. After Alexander VI. began to grant special indulgences at certain altars the term *altare privilegiatum* came into use; a mass for the dead read at such an altar brought plenary indulgence. Abbey-churches had an altar dedicated to the holy cross (*altare sanctæ crucis*), placed between the choir and the nave, and intended for the lay brothers. Portable altars (*altaria viatica, portabilia, itineraria, gestatoria, motoria*) are mentioned from the seventh century; they were used by missionaries, prelates, and princes on journeys.

b. From the Year 1000 to 1300: The increasing veneration which was paid to relics led early in this period to a desire to place holy remains on the altar—not beneath it or near it as had been done previously. In the thirteenth century, relics on the altar were a part of its regular equipment. When the entire body of a saint was removed from its original resting-place some special provision for its shrine had to be made, and this led to an extension of the altar at the rear (*retabulum*). Wood or stone was used, and decorations similar to those of altars were provided. In some instances such *retabula* took the place of the canopies; where the latter were retained they began to be made in two stories, the relic-case being put in the upper one. Many such cases have been preserved; they are made of copper, silver, gold, and ivory, and are ornamented with enamel, filigree-work, and gems. Altars were surrounded with columns connected by cross-bars from which curtains hung. Railings fencing off the altar were known to the earlier time, but were not general. They became more common with the growing distinction between clergy and laity, and as the number of the clergy increased, the size of the chancel became greater. From the thirteenth century, crosses, crucifixes, and candles appear on the altar. The position of the cross and the lights was not fixed, and the latter numbered one or two, seldom more. Other articles which belonged to the altar furniture were gospel-books, often in costly binding, flabella, little bells, and thuribles.

c. From 1300 to the Reformation: The *ciborium* altar lasted through the period of Romanesque art and even defied the influence of the Gothic. In France the *retabulum* was retained till toward 1400, but in Germany before that time it gave way to higher structures built upon the altar. The tendency to regard such additions as mere receptacles for the relic-cases disappeared. The holy remains were again placed within the altar, or, if retained upon it, filled only a subordinate part. Wood came to be more generally used as material. Doors were provided for the shrine. Later both shrine and doors were set upon a pedestal (*predella*), which after 1475 became an integral part of the altar. The earlier altars of this period hold rigidly to the Gothic style, but later more freedom is apparent. Carving, sculpture, reliefs, and painting were freely used as decoration.

2. Since the Reformation: The Reformed Churches undertook to remove all accessories of medieval worship, including the altar, for which they substituted a simple table. The Lutheran churches, however, aiming merely to do away with that which was contrary to Scripture, opposed only the conception of the "table of the Lord" as a sacrificial altar. The secondary altars were no longer used, but were not always removed from the churches. The high altar was generally reserved for the celebration of the Lord's Supper, the relic-cases with the monstrance and host being removed, and the decorations with the crucifixes and lights, and the *antependia* and the like being retained.

1. Lutheran and Reformed Churches.

The relics beneath the altar were sometimes merely covered over, not disturbed. New altars built for evangelical churches during the first half of the sixteenth century followed the general plan and structure of those already existing. In the paintings Bible scenes or events of the Reformation took the place of incidents in saints' lives. Portraits of founders and their families were introduced. The general form and structure were made subordinate to the paintings, but in the latter half of the century the architectural features sometimes obscured the paintings. During the baroco period altars and all church furniture shared in the generally depraved taste of the time. From the middle of the seventeenth century the pulpit began to be placed behind the altar, and elevated above it, and then the organ and choir were placed above the pulpit. The result was to dwarf and degrade the altar, and the tasteless pictures and other decorations of the time do not diminish the displeasing effect. The nineteenth century brought a return to the early Christian and Gothic forms. The altars of the latest time are marked by eclecticism and by a striving after novelty which often mixes discrepant elements.

(Nikolaus Müller.)

2. The Church of England.

In the Church of England, after the Reformation much stress was laid by many Reformers on bringing the altar down into the body of the church and designating it as the "Holy Table," the name which it nearly always bears in the Prayer-book. By the eighteenth century it had usually assumed the shape of a small table, frequently concealed from sight by the immense structure of pulpit and reading-desk in front of it; but with the Tractarian and Ritualist movements of the nineteenth century and the increasing frequency and reverence of the celebration of the Eucharist, it gradually resumed its former shape and dignity. In the American Episcopal Church this change was productive of bitter controversy, and about 1850 the retention of a table *with legs* was considered a sign of unimpeachable Protestant orthodoxy.

Bibliography: On primitive altars, besides the works mentioned in the text, consult: C. Maurer, *De aris Græcorum pluribus deis in commune positis*, Darmstadt, 1885; E. B. Tylor, *Early Hist. of Mankind*, London, 1878; idem, *Hist. of Civilization*, ib. 1891; J. G. Frazer, *Golden Bough*, 3 vols., ib. 1900. On Jewish altars: P. Scholtz, *Götzendienst und Zauberwesen*, Regensburg, 1865; C. Piepenbring, *Histoire des lieux de culte et du sacerdoce en Israel*, in *RHR*, xxiv. (1891) 1–60, 133–186; Benzinger, *Archäologie*, § 52; Nowack, *Archäologie*, ii., §§ 73 sqq.; A. van Hoonacker, *Le lieu du culte dans la législation rituelle des Hebreux*, 1894; A. F. von Gall, *Altisraelitische Kultstätte*, in *ZATW*, iii. (1898). On Christian altars: J. Pocklington, *Altare Christianum*, London, 1637; Sven Bring, *Dissertatio historica de fundatione et dotatione altarium*, ib. 1751; J. Blackburne, *A Brief Historical Inquiry into the Introduction of Stone Altars into the Christian Church*, Cambridge, 1844; *On the Hist. of Christian Altars*, published by the Cambridge Camden Society, 1845; M. Meurer, *Altarschmuck*, Leipsic, 1867; A. Schmid, *Der christliche Altar und sein Schmuck*, Ratisbon, 1871; Charles Rohault de Fleury, *La Messe, études archéologiques sur ses monuments*, 8 vols., Paris, 1883–89 (the most comprehensive collection of the material, with illustrations, to the close of the Romanesque period); E. U. A. Münzenberger and S. Beisel, *Zur Kenntniss und Würdigung der mittelalterlichen Altäre Deutschlands*, 2 vols., Frankfort, 1885–1901; V. Statz, *Gothische Altäre*, Berlin, 1886; A. Hartel, *Altäre und Kanzler des Mittelalters und der Neuzeit*, Berlin, 1892; N. Müller, *Ueber das deutsch-evangelische Kirchengebäude im Jahrhundert der Reformation*, Leipsic, 1895; H. D. M. Spence, *White Robe of Churches*, pp. 210–243, New York, 1900; E. Bishop, *History of the Christian Altar*, London, 1906. Consult also works on Christian archeology and Christian art, especially Christian architecture.

ALTAR-BREAD: The bread used in the Roman Catholic and Greek churches in the Sacrament of the Eucharist. It is made from pure wheaten flour, mixed with water, and baked, all conditions being regulated by strict law. The Council of Florence, to meet the contention of Michael Cærularius that the Latins did not possess the Eucharist because of their use of unfermented bread, defined that either kind may be validly employed. Nevertheless, it is unlawful to-day for a Latin priest to use fermented, or for a Greek priest, except in the Armenian and Maronite rites, to use unfermented bread. The practise of the Greeks has always been the same, but in the Western Church both fermented and unfermented bread were employed down to the ninth century. The altar-bread is also called a host, because of the victim whom the sacramental species are destined to conceal. In the Latin Church the host is circular in form, bearing an image of the crucifixion or the letters I. H. S., and is of two sizes; the larger is consumed by the celebrant or preserved for solemn exposition, and the smaller given to the people in communion. The name "particles" given to the smaller hosts recalls the fact that down to the eleventh century communion was distributed to the faithful by breaking off portions of a large bread consecrated by the celebrant. The large host of the Greeks is rectangular in shape, and the small host triangular. Great care is taken in the preparation of altar-breads, many synodal enactments providing that it shall be committed only to clerics or to women in religious communities.

John T. Creagh.

ALTAR-CARDS: Three cards, containing certain prayers of the mass, placed on the altar in Roman Catholic churches, the central card being larger than those placed at either end. Their introduction dates from the sixteenth century, when the middle card began to be employed as an aid to the memory of the celebrant and to relieve him from the necessity of continually referring to the missal. When the reading of the beginning of St. John's Gospel was prescribed, the card on the Gospel side was added, and later, to make the arrangement appear symmetrical, the third card came into use. In masses celebrated by a bishop, the practise anterior to the sixteenth century is maintained by the substitution of a book called the canon, from which are read the prayers usually printed on altar-cards. Since most of these prayers are to be said secretly or inaudibly, altar-cards are sometimes called secret-cards. John T. Creagh.

ALTAR-CLOTHS. See Altar, III., 1, a, § 2.

ALTENBURG, COLLOQUY OF. See Philippist

ALTENSTEIN, äl″ten-stain′, **KARL FREIHERR VON STEIN ZUM:** German statesman, first minister of public worship in Prussia (1817–40); b. at Ansbach (20 m. w.s.w. of Nuremberg), Bavaria, Oct. 1, 1770; d. in Berlin May 14, 1840. He lost his father at the age of nine, and to the fact that his character was formed under the influence of his mother has been attributed his incapacity in after-life for making thoroughgoing and clear-cut decisions. He was educated in his birthplace and at the universities of Erlangen and Göttingen, where he studied law primarily, but found plenty of time for researches in philosophy, especially the philosophy of religion, and the natural sciences. In 1793 he received a minor legal appointment at Ansbach, which in the mean time had become Prussian. Here he was under Hardenberg, who recognized his ability and had him transferred to

Berlin in 1799. At the capital he gained the reputation of an authority in financial matters, and was made a privy councilor in the financial department in 1803, succeeding Stein as minister of finance in 1808. Unable to cope with the almost impossible task of satisfying the demands of Napoleon, he retired in 1810. Hardenberg, who had been compelled to join in overthrowing him, tried three years later to bring him back to public life, and in 1817 secured his appointment as head of the newly founded ministry of public worship, education, and medicine. These important branches of public administration had until then formed departments of the ministry of the interior, and had been badly managed.

Altenstein took up religious questions as a man who understood and cared for them, though his Christianity had a decidedly rationalistic tinge. Difficulties of many kinds beset him during his long tenure of office, arising partly from the determined and obstinate character of his sovereign and partly from demagogic opposition, as well as from the great Halle controversy of 1830 and from the vexed question of the Catholic attitude in regard to mixed marriages. When, in 1824, without his knowledge, the direction of education was taken from Nicolovius and given to Von Kamptz, Altenstein was on the verge of resigning his post, but he decided that it was his duty to remain. One of the great achievements of his administration was the systematic improvement to a remarkable extent of primary and secondary education. (F. Bosse.)

Bibliography: Freiherr von Stein, in *Deutsche Revue*, vol. vii., 1882; H. Treitschke, *Deutsche Geschichte in 19. Jahrhundert*, Leipsic, 1882; *ADB*, vol. xxxvi.

ALTHAMER, äl'thäm''er, **ANDREAS** (sometimes known by the Greek form of his name, **Palaiosphyra**): German Reformer; b. in the village of Brenz, near Gundelfingen (28 m. n.w. of Augsburg), Württemberg, c. 1500; d. at Ansbach, probably in 1519. He studied at Leipsic and Tübingen. In 1524 he is found settled as priest at Gmünd in Swabia, where he was the leader of the evangelical party, and he remained there after he had been deposed and had married. He escaped with difficulty in the reaction of the Swabian League, and fled to Wittenberg, remaining there nine months and proceeding to Nuremberg in the summer of 1526. His Lutheran convictions were now mature, and he maintained a constant literary activity against both the Zwinglians and the Roman Catholics. He was pastor at Eltersdorf, near Erlangen, in 1527, deacon at St. Sebaldus's, Nuremberg, in 1528; he took part as an ardent Lutheran in the disputation at Bern, and in the same year was called to Ansbach to assist in spreading the Reformation in Brandenburg. In November he published a complete catechism, remarkable not only for the clearness and precision of its teaching, but also as being the first work of the kind to take the title of catechism. For the next few years he was the soul of the Protestant party in that part of Germany, and by his untiring energy and gifts of organization did much in the development there of the evangelical religion. Of his theological works may be mentioned his *Annotationes in Jacobi Epistolam* (Strasburg, 1527), which carried still further Luther's views of that epistle, though it was modified in the edition of 1533. His notes on the *Germania* of Tacitus, published in complete form 1536, have preserved his fame as a classical scholar even where the Reformer has been forgotten. (T. Kolde.)

Bibliography: T. Kolde, *Andreas Althamer, der Humanist und Reformator in Brandenburg-Ansbach*, Erlangen, 1895 (contains a reprint of his catechism).

ALTHAUS, PAUL: German Protestant; b. at Fallersleben (17 m. n.e. of Brunswick) Dec. 29, 1861. He was educated at the universities of Erlangen and Göttingen, and held various pastorates from 1887 to 1897, when he was appointed associate professor of practical and systematic theology at the University of Göttingen, becoming full professor two years later. He has written *Die historische und dogmatische Grundlage der lutherischen Taufliturgie* (Hanover, 1893) and *Die Heilsbedeutung der Taufe im Neuen Testament* (Gütersloh, 1897).

ALTING, JOHANN HEINRICH: Reformed theologian; b. at Emden (70 m. w.n.w. of Bremen), East Friesland, Feb. 17, 1583; d. at Groningen (92 m. n.e. of Amsterdam) Aug. 25, 1644. He studied at Groningen and Herborn, acted as tutor for several German princes, and traveled as far as England. In 1613 he became professor of dogmatics at Heidelberg, and in 1616 director of the seminary in the *Collegium Sapientiæ*. Leaving Heidelberg because of the disturbances of the Thirty Years' war, he went to Holland, and in 1627 was appointed professor at Groningen. He was one of the delegates from the Palatinate to the Synod of Dort (1618–19) and was a decided but Biblical predestinarian. He collaborated on the Dutch Bible version. He published nothing during his lifetime; after his death his son, **Jacob Alting** (b. at Heidelberg 1618; d. at Groningen, where he was professor of Hebrew, 1679) published several of his works, the most noteworthy being the *Theologia historica* (Amsterdam, 1664), a pioneer work on the history of doctrine. (E. F. Karl Müller.)

ALTMANN, ält'män: Bishop of Passau 1065–91; d. at Zeiselmauer (12 m. n.w. of Vienna), Lower Austria, Aug. 8, 1091. A Westphalian of noble birth, he became first a student and then head of the school of Paderborn. Later he was provost of Aachen, then chaplain to Henry III., after whose death he was attached to the household of the Empress Agnes. In 1064 he made the pilgrimage to Jerusalem, and was chosen bishop of Passau before his return. He adhered steadfastly to Gregory VII. in his conflict with Henry IV., and was the first of the German bishops to proclaim against the king the sentence of excommunication which had been pronounced in Rome. He allied himself with the South German princes, and acted as papal legate in the assemblies at Ulm and Tribur in the autumn of 1076. Rudolf of Swabia had no more faithful partizan. As a result of this attitude, Altmann had to leave his diocese, which suffered severely (1077–78) from Henry's resentment. He went to Rome early in 1079, and was there when

Gregory VII. hurled a second anathema at Henry in the synod of 1080. He returned to Germany as permanent papal vicar. Under his influence Liutpold of Austria broke with Henry, and Altmann was able to return to Passau. After Rudolf's death (Oct. 15, 1080), he was entrusted with the pope's instructions with regard to the setting up of a new contestant for the throne, and Hermann of Luxemburg was chosen (Aug., 1081). Altmann does not appear as leader of the papal party in Germany after Liutpold's defeat by the Bohemians at Mailberg in 1082. He maintained himself for a while in the eastern part of his diocese, Passau itself being held by an opposition bishop, and rejected all compromise. In the internal administration of his diocese his policy was vigorously Hildebrandine. (Carl Mirbt.)

Bibliography: His life, by an anonymous author of the twelfth century, ed. W. Wattenbach, is in *MGH, Script.*, xii. (1856) 226–243; another life by Rupert, abbot of Gottweig (d. 1199), is in *MPL*, cxlviii.; and there are modern lives by T. Wiedemann, Augsburg, 1851, J. Stülz, Vienna, 1853, and A. Linsenmeyer, Passau, 1891. Consult C. Mirbt, *Die Publizistik im Zeitalter Gregors VII.*, Leipsic, 1894; W. Martens, *Gregor VII.*, ib. 1894; Hauck, *KD*, iii. 341.

ALTMANN, WILHELM: German librarian and historian: b. at Adelnau (65 m. s.e. of Posen) Apr. 4, 1862. He was educated at the universities of Breslau, Marburg, and Berlin (Ph.D., 1885), and was librarian successively at Breslau (1886–89), Greifswald (1889–1900), and Berlin (1900–06), being appointed chief librarian of the musical collection in the Royal Library of Berlin in 1906. In theology his position is liberal. He has written *Wahl Albrechts II. zum römischen König* (Berlin, 1886); *Der Römerzug Ludwigs des Baiern* (1886); *Studien zu Eberhart Windecke* (1891); *Die Urkunden Kaiser Sigismunds* (2 vols., Innsbruck, 1896–99); and *Richard Wagners Briefe nach Zeitfolgung und Inhalt* (Leipsic, 1905). He has also edited, among other works, *Acta N Gramis* (Breslau, 1890); *Ausgewählte Urkunden zur Erläuterung der Verfassungsgeschichte Deutschlands im Mittelalter* (Berlin, 1891; in collaboration with E. Bernheim); and *Eberhart Windeffes Denkwürdigkeiten zur Geschichte des Zeitalters Kaiser Sigismunds* (1893).

ALTRUIST COMMUNITY. See Communism, II., 2.

ALUMBRADOS. See Alombrados.

ALUMNATE: A term used to denote the position of a student in an episcopal or papal seminary. In order to enter such an institution the candidate must be capable of receiving orders and have the express intention of taking them. The seminarist receives the privileges of the clerical state as soon as he is tonsured, even before ordination. The alumni of the seminaries and colleges for the training of missionaries have special privileges, on condition that when they enter the college they solemnly swear not to join any religious order, but as secular priests to devote their whole lives to missionary work, under the general direction of the Propaganda, to which they are required to make annual reports. (E. Friedberg.)

Bibliography: P. Hinschius, *Kirchenrecht*, iv. 503 sqq. 517, Berlin, 1888; O. Mejer, *Die Propaganda*, i. 73 sqq., 225 sqq., Göttingen, 1852.

ALVAR OF CORDOVA (called also **Paul Alvar**): Spanish Christian champion against the Mohammedans; b. about 800; d. about 861. His ancestors appear to have been Jews, and his family was wealthy. He lived, highly esteemed, upon an inherited estate near Cordova, where he was educated with his lifelong friend Eulogius (q.v.) by the abbot Speraindeo (d. before 852), author of a work against Islam and of a glorification of two Christian brothers who suffered martyrdom under Abd al-Rahman II. From this teacher Alvar and his fellow pupil imbibed a feeling of hatred toward the Mohammedans. Spanish Christians at the time were filled with a fanatical longing for martyrdom and found an easy way to the attainment of their desire by publicly reviling Mohammed, which was forbidden under the penalty of death. Alvar encouraged such proceedings, while Eulogius, after some hesitation, became the soul of the movement. In Alvar's chief work, the *Indiculus luminosus* (854), he undertakes to prove that Mohammed was a precursor of Antichrist and that it was therefore permissible to revile him. That he did not himself seek a martyr's death is explained by the often-repeated assertion of Eulogius, that only such should sacrifice themselves as were ripe for eternal life through personal holiness. The movement died out after Eulogius had suffered (859), and Alvar then wrote his friend's life in a strain of extravagant glorification. His last and most mature work was a *Confessio*, imitated (but not slavishly) from the *Oratio pro correptione vitæ* of Isidore of Seville; in mystico-contemplative form it expresses deep contrition and the longing for salvation. A few of Alvar's Latin poems have been preserved, and a *Liber scintillarum*, a sort of Christian ethics in the form of a collection of quotations from Biblical and ecclesiastical writers, is ascribed to him with probability by a Gothic manuscript of Madrid (cf. *MPL*, xc. 94–95). His works are in *MPL*, cxv., cxxi.

Bibliography: W. von Baudissin, *Eulogius und Alvar*, Leipsic, 1872.

ALYPIUS, SAINT: 1. A saint of the Roman Calendar; b. of a prominent family at Thagaste, Numidia, in the fourth century. He became a pupil of Augustine in Carthage and later one of his most devoted friends, and was converted from Manicheanism by him. He preceded Augustine to Rome to study law and was assessor there to the court of the Italian treasury. When Augustine went to Milan, Alypius accompanied him, attended the preaching of Ambrose, was converted to Christianity, and baptized with Augustine on Easter, 387. With Augustine he returned to Africa and lived with him at Thagaste till in 391 Augustine became bishop of Hippo and Alypius abbot of a monastery at Thagaste. In 394 he became bishop of Thagaste and survived Augustine. His day is Aug. 15. He is mentioned many times in Augustine's "Confessions" (vi. 7–16 and elsewhere), and several of Augustine's letters to him have been preserved.

2. A saint of the Greek Calendar; b. at Adrianople about 550. In imitation of Simeon he stood upon a pillar, hence was called The Stylite. He

is said to have died at the age of 108, and to have spent his last fifty years on his pillar. His day is Nov. 26. See STYLITES.

BIBLIOGRAPHY: 1. *ASB*, Aug., iii. 201-208. 2. Simeon Metaphrastes, *Vita sancti Alypii Cionitae*, ed. L. Surius, in *De probatis sanctorum historiis*, Nov., vi. 588-595, Cologne, 1575.

ALZOG, äl'tsoн, **JOHANN BAPTIST**: Roman Catholic; b. at Ohlau (17 m. s.e. of Breslau), Silesia, June 29, 1808; d. at Freiburg-im-Breisgau Mar. 1, 1878. He studied at Breslau and Bonn, served as private tutor, and was ordained priest in 1834. He became professor of church history and exegesis at Posen (1836), Hildesheim (1845), and Freiburg (1853). While at Posen he supported his archbishop, Martin von Dunin (q.v.) in his measures against mixed marriages. In 1869 he became a member of the commission on dogma in the preparation for the Vatican Council, and was the only member of the commission who held the declaration of papal infallibility as wholly inopportune. His chief works were: *Universalgeschichte der christlichen Kirche vom katholischen Standpunkte* (Mainz, 1841; 10th ed. by F. X. Kraus, *Handbuch der allgemeinen Kirchengeschichte*, 2 vols., 1882; Eng. transl., from 9th ed., 3 vols., Cincinnati, 1874–78, new ed., 1903; it is said that the English translation does not faithfully reproduce the original, being less candid and reliable); *Grundriss der Patrologie oder die ältern christlichen Litterargeschichte* (Freiburg, 1866); *Die deutschen Plenarien im 15ten und zu Anfang des 16ten Jahrhunderts* (1874).

BIBLIOGRAPHY: F. X. Kraus, *Gedächtnissrede auf Johannes Alzog*, Freiburg, 1879.

AMADEISTS, See FRANCIS, SAINT, OF ASSISI, AND THE FRANCISCAN ORDER, III., § 7.

AMALARIUS, am-a-lē'ri-us, **OF METZ (AMALARIUS SYMPHOSIUS)**: Liturgical writer of the ninth century; b. about 780; d. 850 or 851. In his youth he enjoyed the instruction of Alcuin, and Metz has commonly been regarded as the place of his principal activity. He appears as a deacon at the Synod of Aachen in 817, and was mainly responsible for the patristic part of the *Regula Aquisgranensis*, which imposed the canonical life upon the clergy of the empire. In 825, now a *chorepiscopus*, he was in Paris for the synod called by Louis in connection with the iconoclastic controversy, and was selected by the emperor, with Halitgar of Cambrai, to accompany the papal envoys to Constantinople about this matter. The authorities do not relate whether he accomplished the mission, but it is certain that he once visited Constantinople. His principal work (written not earlier than 819) was *De ecclesiasticis officiis*, in which he discusses all liturgical usages, the festivals and offices of the Church, and the vestments of the clergy down to the smallest detail, from the standpoint of mystical symbolism. The diversities between the German antiphonaries next drew his attention, and in 831 he went to Rome to ask Gregory IV. to issue an authorized Roman antiphonary. The pope did not see his way to do this, but he called Amalarius's attention to the Roman antiphonaries at the abbey of Corbie. He came home to revise his earlier book in the light of new sources, and compile an antiphonary based on the Frankish ones together with these Roman texts; the commentary on this forms his work *De ordine antiphonarii*. After the restoration of Louis to the throne, the rebellious archbishop of Lyons, Agobard (q.v.), was deposed, and Amalarius was put in charge of his diocese. Here he used his power to bring about a sweeping change in the liturgy, but aroused strong opposition, led by the deacon Florus, a warm partizan of Agobard, who worked against Amalarius unceasingly, and finally accused him of heresy at the Synod of Quiercy in 838. The synod condemned some of his expressions, and Agobard, shortly afterward returning to Lyons, began to undo all that he had done in regard to the liturgy. Nothing is known of his later life, except that in the controversy over Gottschalk's teaching he wrote in support of Hincmar. He is said to have been buried in the abbey of St. Arnulf at Metz. His writings give an insight into the liturgical forms of the early ninth century, and are especially illuminating on the relation of the Gallican liturgies to the Roman, which was gaining steadily in the Frankish empire. To its permanent conquest over the Gallican, Amalarius's work undoubtedly contributed. He is also important from his influence on later medieval liturgiologists, many of whom follow his mystical method, and most of whom quote him extensively. He shows a wide knowledge of Scripture and the Fathers, with praiseworthy diligence and conscientiousness in the use of his authorities. His works are in *MPL*, cv. (RUDOLF SAHRE.)

BIBLIOGRAPHY: R. Mönchmeyer, *Amalar von Metz, sein Leben und seine Schriften*, Münster, 1893; *Histoire littéraire de la France*, vol. iv.; Ceillier, *Auteurs sacrés*, vols. xviii., xix., Paris, 1752, 1754; Hefele, *Conciliengeschichte*, vol. iv.; R. Sahre, *Der Liturgiker Amalarius*, Dresden, 1893.

AMALARIUS OF TREVES (AMALARIUS FORTUNATUS): Archbishop of Treves. Little is known of his life, but he is not the same as the liturgiologist Amalarius of Metz, with whom he has been identified. He became archbishop about 809, and is supposed to be the Bishop Amalharius whom Charlemagne commissioned about 811 to consecrate the newly erected church at Hamburg. In the spring of 813 he set out for Constantinople with Abbot Peter of Nonantula, to bring to a conclusion the negotiations for peace between the Frankish and Byzantine courts. The envoys, learning that Michael, to whom they were accredited, had been succeeded by Leo V., remained eighty days in Constantinople, and returned in company with two Byzantine ambassadors, to find Charlemagne's son Louis on the throne. This is the last known fact in Amalarius's life. There is no solid foundation for the assumption that he died in 814 or 816. Certain passages in a letter of his to Hilduin, abbot of Saint-Denis (ed. G. Meier, in *Neues Archiv für ältere deutsche Geschichtskunde*, xiii., 1887, 307–323), have led to the supposition that he resigned his see (his successor Hetti was in possession of it in 816) and lived some time longer as head of a monastery. His writings are a short treatise on baptism, formerly ascribed to Alcuin, in answer to a letter of inquiry addressed by Charlemagne to the archbishops of his empire (in *MPL*, xcix. 887–902), and the *Odoporicum* or *Versus marini*, a poem of eighty hexameters, giving an account of his journey to Constantinople (*MPL*, ci. 1287–88, among the works of Alcuin; ed. E. Dümmler, in *MGH*, *Poetæ lat. ævi Carol.*, i. 426–428, 1881; cf. *Addenda*, ii. 694).

(Rudolf Sahre.)

Bibliography: Rettberg, *KD*, i. 426–428; J. Marx, *Geschichte des Erzstifts Trier*, Trier, 1858–62; Hauck, *KD*, ii. 192.

AMALEK, am'a-lek, **AMALEKITES,** am'-alek-aits: A Bedouin people who are somewhat prominent in the older history of Israel. Their territory was the steppes south of the hill-country of Judea and the Sinaitic desert (the modern Tih; Gen. xiv. 7; Ex. xvii. 8; Num. xiii. 29, xiv, 25, 43, 45; I Sam. xv. 4–7, xxvii. 8). From Judges v. 14 and xii. 15 it has been conjectured that they once dwelt in Palestine and were gradually driven to the south. Neither the Old Testament nor extra-Biblical sources give satisfactory information concerning their ethnographical relations (cf. Nöldeke, *Ueber die Amalekiter und einige andere Nachbarvölker der Israeliten*, Göttingen, 1864). Israel is said to have gained a great victory over them at Rephidim while on the way to the promised land, and Yahweh then commanded the extirpation of this people (Ex. xvii. 8–16; cf. Deut. xxv 17–19; I Sam. xv. 2–3). Again when certain of the Israelites attempted, against Yahweh's command, to enter Canaan from Kadesh, they fell into the hands of the Amalekites (Num. xiv. 45). In post-Mosaic time the Kenites lived in the southern part of the wilderness of Judah among nomad Amalekites (Judges i. 16, LXX.). They are said to have made forays against Israel in the narratives of Ehud and Gideon (Judges iii. 13, vi. 3, 33, vii. 12), but it is doubtful if Amalekites were expressly named in the sources from which these narratives are drawn. At Samuel's command Saul made war upon them and gained a great victory; because he did not carry out the injunction to destroy them utterly he was rejected by the prophet (I Sam. xv.). Their king, Agag, is here named, and their sheep, oxen, and other possessions are mentioned, as well as a "city of Amalek," which is not referred to elsewhere. David attacked them after they had made a raid upon Ziklag, and only those who had camels escaped (I Sam. xxx.). Thenceforth the Amalekites disappear from history except for the notice, in I Chron. iv. 42, that a band of Simeonites (probably in the time of Hezekiah) exterminated the last remnant of them, dwelling on Mont Seir. That Haman is called an Agagite in Esther iii. 1 ("an Amalekite," Josephus, *Ant.*, XI. vi. 5) has no significance, owing to the character of the book.

(F. Buhl.)

Bibliography: A. Dillmann, *Commentary on Genesis*, on chaps. x. and xxxvi., 2 vols., Edinburgh, 1897 (best); T. Nöldeke, *Ueber die Amalekiter und einige andere Nachbarvölker der Israeliten*, Göttingen, 1864; A. H. Sayce, *Races of the Old Testament*, London, 1891; *DB*, i. 77–78; *EB*, i. 128–131.

AMALRIC, a-mal'rik (Fr. *Amaury*), **OF BENA AND THE AMALRICIANS,** a-mal-rish'ans: A notable representative of pantheism in the Middle Ages and his followers. Amalric was born at Bena, near Chartres, and toward the end of the twelfth century lectured in Paris on philosophy and theology. He enjoyed the reputation of a subtle dialectician, and the favor of the Dauphin, afterward King Louis VIII. How far he carried his pantheism in the public teaching can not now be determined; but his doctrine of the membership of believers in the body of Christ was so pantheistic in tendency that it aroused suspicion, and he was accused of heresy by the chancellor of the diocese, who exercised an official oversight over the schools of Paris. In 1204 he was summoned to Rome to give an account of his teaching before Innocent III., who decided against him. Returning to Paris, he was forced to recant. Soon afterward he died, and received churchly burial at St.-Martin-des-Champs (1 m. e. of Morlaix, Finistère). After his death traces of a sect formed by him were discovered, and a synod was called in Paris in 1209 to take measures for its suppression. Amalric's teaching was condemned, and he himself was excommunicated; nine ecclesiastics together with William the Goldsmith, one of the seven prophets of the sect, were burned at the stake. At the Fourth Lateran Council in 1215, Innocent III. renewed the condemnation of Amalric's teaching.

There is no doubt that Amalric took up the teaching of Johannes Scotus Erigena, and developed it into a thoroughgoing pantheism. Only three propositions can certainly be ascribed to Amalric himself: (1) that God is all things; (2) that every Christian is bound to believe himself a member of Christ, and that none can be saved without this faith; and (3) that no sin is imputed to those who walk in love. The teaching of his disciples is an expansion of these theses. God, they said, has revealed himself thrice, and each time more completely. With the incarnation in Abraham the epoch of the Father begins; with the incarnation in Mary, that of the Son; with the incarnation in the Amalricians, that of the Holy Spirit. As the coming of Christ set aside the Mosaic law, so the sacraments and ordinances of the second dispensation were now abolished. The sect called the veneration of the saints idolatry; the Church, the Babylon of the Apocalypse; the pope, Antichrist. The revelation of the Holy Ghost in the hearts of the believers takes the place of baptism, and is indeed the resurrection of the dead and the kingdom of heaven; no other is to be expected; nor is there any hell but the consciousness of sin. Their doctrine, that the spirit, which is God, can not be affected by the deeds of the flesh, or commit sin, became a cover for manifold excesses, proven not only by contemporary records, but also by numerous testimonials as to the Brethren of the Free Spirit, who were the direct successors of the Amalricians. (A. Hauck.)

Bibliography: Sources are: G. Armoricus, *De gestis Philippi Augusti*, in Bouquet, *Recueil*, xvii. 83; B. Guido, *Vita Innocentii papæ*, in Mansi, *Concilia*, xxii. 801–809, 980; C. Bäumker, *Ein Traktat gegen die Amalricianer aus dem Anfang des XIII. Jahrhunderts*, Paderborn, 1895. Consult

C. Hahn, *Geschichte der Ketzer im Mittelalter*, iii. 176 sqq., Stuttgart, 1845; Krönlein, *Amalrich von Bena und David von Dinart*, in *TSK*, xii. (1847) 271 sqq.; W Preger, *Geschichte der deutschen Mystik im Mittelalter*, i. 166 sqq., 173 sqq., Leipsic, 1874; A. Jundt, *Histoire du panthéisme populaire au moyen âge*, p. 20, Paris, 1875; H. Reuter, *Geschichte der religiösen Aufklärung im Mittelalter*, ii. 218 sqq., Berlin, 1877.

AMANA SOCIETY. See COMMUNISM, II., 3.

AMANDUS, a-man′dus: Bishop and missionary of the Franks; d. at the abbey of Elno, near Tournai, Feb. 6, 661 (?). He was a man of rank from Aquitania, took holy orders in early youth against the will of his father, and lived in a cell in the city-wall of Bourges till he was induced by a vision of St. Peter to give himself up to mission-work in Friesland. He preached and baptized near Ghent. The Frankish government neglected to protect the mission near the frontier, and the hostility of the haughty Frieslanders hindered the work. Amandus therefore went to Carinthia and Carniola to seek a better field among the Slavic invaders, south of the Danube. Here, however, he was not successful; and he returned to Ghent, where he founded two monasteries, Blandinium and Gundarum, and a third, Elno, near Tournai. From these the Friesian mission-work was carried on with more success. Amandus was made bishop of Maestricht, and in this position he helped to carry through the Roman resolutions against the Monothelites, and tried to reform the clergy. As the latter showed themselves obstinate, he retired from his see between 647 and 649, entered the abbey of Elno, and worked to the end of his life for the conversion of the Frankish and Basque heathen. He was said to have performed miracles, and it was believed that miracles occurred at his tomb, which became a place of pilgrimage.

A. WERNER.

BIBLIOGRAPHY: Baudemund and Milo wrote accounts of his life which with other sources are in *ASB*, Feb., i. 815–903. Consult Gosse, *Essai sur St. Amand*, 1866; J. J. de Smedt, *Vie de St. Amand*, Ghent, 1881; Rettberg, *KD*, i. 554, ii. 507–508; Friedrich, *KD*, ii. 322; J. Desilve, *De schola Elnonensi S. Amandi*, Louvain, 1890; Hauck, *KD*, i. 269 sqq.

AMANDUS, JOHANNES. See ALBERT OF PRUSSIA, § 2.

AMARNA TABLETS.

I. Tell el-Amarna: The Amarna tablets are a collection of cuneiform documents, so called from Tell el-Amarna, the name by which the place where the tablets were discovered is generally known outside of Egypt. It is really a conventionalized word, compounded of the Arab *tell*, "mound," and a word formed either from the name of the Arabic tribe Amran or from a place near Amarieh. The place is 160 miles above Cairo, between Thebes and Memphis, or, more closely, between Assiout and Beni-Hassan. The mound is the site of the city built by Amenophis IV., known otherwise as the heretic king Khu-en-aten, that he might there develop untrammeled by the hostile priesthoods his favorite cult of the disk of the sun (*aten*) with which he hoped to supersede all other cults and to unify the religion of Egypt (see EGYPT, I.). His attempt was of course opposed by all the priesthoods of all the other cults, and after his death his name was held accursed because of his efforts in that direction. His position in Egypt was very like that of Julian "the Apostate" among the Christians of Rome. The place which he built for his capital was allowed to fall into ruins, not being occupied after his death by any other king. It is this fact which accounts for the presence of the tablets there and also for their preservation. The foreign office of his reign with its archives was located there, and when the palace was disused, the chamber where the tablets were kept was covered by the débris of the disintegrating buildings. These facts constitute one of the strongest proofs of the genuineness of the documents, which indeed is established beyond all question. The mound was excavated in 1891–92 by W M. F. Petrie and a corps of assistants under the auspices of the Egypt Exploration Fund. The finds made were most valuable, although the site had been rifled by Arabs and travelers. The entire reign of the king whose capital was there was illuminated by the finds, and the activities, religious, political, and industrial, were laid bare. That excavation was the result, however, not the cause, of the finding of the tablets. One of the hopes was that other tablets would be discovered, a hope which largely stimulated the search but was not realized.

II. The Tablets: The discovery was accidental. In 1887 a peasant woman while searching in the ruins for antiquities to sell to travelers discovered the place of deposit within the palace enclosure. The tablets were all taken out, naturally without the extreme care which skilled excavators would have used, were conveyed down the river, and sold. Eighty-two letters and fragments came into the possession of the British Museum, 160 went to Berlin, the Gizeh museum has sixty, while a few are in private hands. In all, about 320 documents of the series are known. Some fragments were afterward found in the place of deposit by Petrie, verifying the location as given by the peasants, but adding hardly anything to the knowledge already gained. The tablets are different in many respects, particularly in shape, from those recovered from Babylonian and Assyrian mounds. Most of them are rectangular, a few are oval, some are flat on both sides, some convex on both, some pillow-shaped, some are kiln-dried, others sun-dried. Many of them confirm by the texture of the clay the assertions of the inscriptions as to their sources. Six of them are the largest known of this species of tablet, measuring ten inches by eight. The language, except in three of the documents, is the neo-Babylonian, closely related to Assyrian, Aramaic, Hebrew, and Arabic, approximating most closely the Assyrian. One letter is in the Hittite language but in the cuneiform script. Sometimes a Sumerian ideograph is used, of which the explanation occasionally follows either in Assyrian or in Canaanitic. In all but half a dozen tablets the general character of the writing is inferior, showing the work of unskilled scribes.

The differences are often individualistic, and mannerisms which run through a whole series combine with other details to point infallibly to identity of source for that series. The spelling is poor, and modifications of characters occur which have not been discovered in other cuneiform documents. The tablets are all to be dated within the reigns of Amenophis III. and IV., father and son, about 1500–1450 B.C. Besides the foregoing, a tablet recognized by nearly all scholars as belonging to the series was found by Bliss in his excavation of Tell el-Hesy (Lachish) in Palestine. This contains the name of Zimrida of Lachish (almost certainly the writer of letter No. 217 in Winckler's arrangement, and mentioned in Nos. 181 and 219 of the same), not to be confounded with Zimrida of Sidon, who is also a correspondent (as is apparently done by Bliss, *Mounds of Many Cities*, London, 1896, pp. 54 sqq.). Some of the letters contain Egyptian dockets mostly illegible, probably notes of date of receipt and other remarks. The condition of the tablets varies greatly; on some only a few characters remain; others lack only a few to be complete.

III. Authors and Contents: With the exception of some fragments of a bilingual dictionary, compiled by order of the Pharaoh, and a mythological fragment, the tablets are letters, most of which deal with the political situation of Syria, Palestine, and Philistia. The most noteworthy are the following: One letter is from Amenophis III. to Kallima-Sin of the Babylonian Kasshite dynasty, asking the latter for a daughter as a wife and replying to the latter's insinuation that there was no information that a former wife, sister of Kallima-Sin, was yet alive and well-treated. Four letters from Kallima-Sin to Amenophis III. complain that a Babylonian envoy was kept in Egypt six years, and when sent back brought only a small quantity of gold, and that of inferior quality. He asks more and better gold, which is needed at once for a building which he is erecting; he asks for a daughter of Amenophis as a wife, or if not that, then some one whom he can palm off as a daughter of the Pharaoh. One of the letters shows that he is sending his daughter to the harem of Amenophis. There are six letters of Burnaburiash of Babylon to Amenophis IV., assuring the latter of the former's fraternal feelings, asking presents and promising others in return, also seeking help against his "vassal" Asshur-uballit of Assyria who revolts against the suzerain power. There is also a letter of Asshur-uballit to Amenophis IV., seeking presents, including gold for the decoration of a palace, similar to those which had been sent to his father Asshur-nadin-ahi, and promising others in return. Some of the finest, longest, and best-written are from Tushratta, king of Mitanni (see ASSYRIA), to Amenophis IV., one of whose wives is a sister of Tushratta. One of these promises a daughter of the writer to the Pharaoh, but it is expected that a great deal of gold (not alloyed like the last that was sent) will be returned for her. After considerable delay and, apparently, bargaining also the daughter was sent. This series tells too, of a victory of Tushratta over the Hittites, and might be taken to prove that Mitanni was not a Hittite kingdom. Three from the same person to Amenophis IV include in their contents condolence upon the death of the Pharaoh's father, for which consolation is found by the writer in the fact that the son of that father succeeds to the throne; friendly relations are promised; two golden statuettes which have been promised are asked for (not wooden one likes those which have been sent); complaints are made about the detention of ambassadors in Egypt; and gold is requested. Tushratta also writes a letter to the queen dowager Ti, asking her good offices with the Pharaoh in urging the latter to fulfil the engagements entered into.

The rest of the tablets contain correspondence from petty kings and governors of Amoritic, Syrian, Palestinian, and Cypriote (?) cities to the Pharaohs, telling of revolts and assaults upon the Pharaoh's authority, and of invasions by the Hittites and *Ḥabiri*; or they make accusations against other of the Pharaoh's governors, or defend themselves as loyal subjects of Egypt. The most noteworthy of these are a series from *Alashia* (either a district in north Syria or Cyprus); fifty-seven from Rib-Addi of Gebal (Byblos) to the Pharaoh, and eight to Egyptian officers high in position; eight from *Abi-Milki* of Tyre (the name compounded of the name of the god for which "Moloch" was given in the Old Testament; see MOLOCH); seven from *Abd-ḫiba* of Jerusalem (the latter spelled *U-ru-sha-lim*, "city of peace"; Winckler, *Tell-el-Amarna Letters*, Letter 180, line 25), which tell of a confederation formed by Gezer, Ashkelon, and Lachish against Jerusalem, and asking help against them and the *Ḥabiri*; two are from Ammunira of Beirut.

IV. Value of the Tablets: The results gained from the study of the documents are threefold—historical, geographical, and linguistic.

The most remarkable result of the discovery is the fact that the correspondence even between Egypt and its vassals was carried on not in Egyptian, but in an Asiatic tongue, and that the cuneiform. This implies that the entire area covered by the correspondence outside Egypt was controlled in culture by Babylonia. This control was so thoroughgoing that governmental transactions and diplomatic intercourse were necessarily carried on in the tongue of the lower Euphrates.

1. Historical.

The royal correspondence reveals the relations between the court of Egypt, on the one side, and the courts of Babylonia, Assyria, and Mitanni, on the other, consisting of intermarriages, with Egypt as the haughtier power in the earlier period, this strain of superiority giving way later to one of equality. The Pharaohs entered into marriage relations with the daughters of Asiatic regal houses, but at first refused and afterward granted the request for reciprocity in this respect. This division of the documents shows the kings making requests of each other for bakshish and complaining of the quality of that formerly given. Egypt seems the source of gold, and from the plaints appears guilty of attempting to cheat by alloying heavily the metal which it sent as a present, in one case the proportion of pure gold being only six parts in twenty. The relation of Assyria to Babylonia receives side-light in the fact that the Babylonian asks help against his "vassal" Asshur-uballit of Assyria, who, however, seems to be in friendly relations with Egypt; a second point in this connection is contained in the reference in the Tushratta correspondence to the sending of the image of Ishtar of Nineveh to Egypt, which implies that Nineveh was then a part of Mitanni (see ASSYRIA, vi., 2, and cf. C. Niebuhr, *Studien zur Geschichte des alten Orients*, Leipsic, 1894, p. 92).

But the most important results historically are those which relate to the connections of Egypt with Syria and Palestine. Thothmes III. had carried the arms of Egypt as far as the Taurus Mountains. A period of Egyptian quiescence had followed, and, as a consequence, in the period of the letters Egyptian hegemony was threatened in three ways: first by revolts of the cities under governors who had been appointed by the Pharaoh or by the governors who were unfaithful; second, by a Hittite advance from the north and northeast; third, by the *Ḥabiri* from the east. The correspondence abounds in charges by governors who claim to be faithful to the Pharaoh against other governors; and again and again they beg for help from him which apparently is not sent, though the news of continuous loss of territory is the burden of the letters. Some of the men charged with rebellion protest their fidelity and make counter-charges, but in many cases practically confess their disloyalty by their excuses for not rendering service due or required. The whole situation is one of the weakening of Egyptian influence as its leadership and control slips away under the battering of the triplex adverse forces. The mention of the advance of the Hittites is most illuminating, showing the beginning of the empire established in the century following. The question raised by the frequent mention of the *Ḥabiri* has been answered in three ways: (a) they were the Hebrews of the Exodus just arriving from the wandering; (b) they were Hebrews, but not those of the Exodus, representing rather the Abrahamic-Lot tribes prior to the settlement in Egypt which is described in the last chapters of Genesis; (c) they were not Hebrews at all, but people of nomadic strain whose exact affiliations are unknown. The first of these three answers is not now supported by any prominent authority; the other two are still under debate. In favor of the second is the single Egyptian inscription (Meneptah's; see EGYPT) which plainly mentions the Hebrews as already in Canaan during the reign in which most modern scholars place the Exodus and before the tribes under Moses could have entered the land.

2. Geographical. The geographical information can not be given here at length, since almost every item would require extended discussion. A large number of known cities or localities is named, such as Tyre, Sidon, Byblos, Beirut, Ajalon, Accho, Megiddo, Kadesh, Gath, Lachish, Jerusalem, Mitanni, and Edom. Other places are mentioned in such connections that the approximate locality is recognized, such as Tunip, south of Aleppo. Still other place-names appear in the correspondence, the exact or even approximate location of which is undetermined, such as *Ḳaṭna* and *Irḳata*. One hundred and thirty towns in all are mentioned. But the existence of these places is made known and their relative importance often appears from the character of the passage in which the names occur. For the political geography of the region and the time, these tablets are of the first importance.

3. Linguistic. The linguistic data given in the letters afford a means of comparison of the Babylonian and Assyrian with earlier and with later forms, and so constitute a standard of comparison in what had been a dark period for both. For Aramean and Canaanitic the data are the earliest known and, therefore, of the highest value. These letters show the Semitic languages represented as differing only dialectically, and as in all probability mutually intelligible to the inhabitants of the different regions. GEO. W GILMORE.

BIBLIOGRAPHY: H. Winckler, *Der Thontafelfund von El-Amarna*, in Schrader, *KB*, v. 1, Berlin, 1896; idem, *Tel-el-Amarna Letters*, New York, 1896 (transliterated text and transl. in Germ. and Eng.); C. Bezold, *Oriental Diplomacy*, London, 1893; C. R. Conder, *Tel-el-Amarna Tablets*, ib. 1893 (transl. and discussion of the tablets in the British Museum); W. M. F. Petrie, *Tel-el-Amarna*, ib. 1894 (account of the excavation and its results); idem, *Tel-el-Amarna Letters*, ib. 1898; C. Niebuhr, *Die Amarna-Zeit. Ægypten und Vorderasien um 1400 vor Christus nach dem Thontafelfunde von el-Amarna*, Leipsic, 1899; *Assyrian and Babylonian Literature*, New York, 1901 (gives transl. of selected letters). The discussion in periodicals has been very full; consult *Presbyterian Review*, x. (1888) 476–481; *PSBA*, x. (1888) 540–569; *Babylonian and Oriental Record*, iii. (1889) 286–288, v. (1891) 114–119; *Bibliotheca Sacra*, l. (1893) 696; *Thinker*, ix. (1894) 408; *Nation*, lix. (Jan. 5, 1894).

AMAZIAH, am″a-zai′ā: Eighth king of Judah. He was the son of Joash, and reigned 838–810 B.C., according to the old computation; 797–792, according to Duncker; 800–792, according to Wellhausen; 796–778, according to Kamphausen; 799–773, according to Hommel. At the age of twenty-five he succeeded his father, who had been murdered by his servants, and his first act was to put the conspirators to death; in harmony with Deut. xxiv. 16, however, he spared their children. He attacked the Edomites, gained a victory over them, and captured a stronghold known as "the Rock," to which he gave the name "Joktheel." He may also have taken and destroyed Elath, which his son Uzziah rebuilt (II Kings xiv. 22). He next began war against Joash of Israel, but was defeated, and Jerusalem was taken and pillaged. Like his father, Amaziah was slain by conspirators, whose motive is not known. He was buried with royal honors at Jerusalem. The prophetic writers of the Book of Kings reckon him among the better kings of Judah, but the Chronicler ascribes his downfall to idolatry and apostasy from Yahweh.
(W. LOTZ.)

BIBLIOGRAPHY: His history is in II Kings xiv. 1–20; II Chron. xxv. Consult the works mentioned under AHAB.

AMBO: A sort of raised platform in early Christian churches, used for a variety of purposes.

The name is met with frequently in medieval works, more rarely in the older, which employ a number of synonymous expressions. Cyprian speaks of a *pulpitum*, by which he evidently means a raised place to which the lectors ascended to read to the people "the precepts and good tidings of the Lord." Eusebius relates (*Hist. eccl.*, vii. 30) that Bishop Paul of Samosata erected both a "bema" and a lofty throne to speak from; and the context shows that he is not speaking of the semicircular apse, which was sometimes called "bema" also. So, according to Sozomen (*Hist. eccl.*, viii. 5), John Chrysostom preached seated upon the platform (Gk. *bēma*) of the readers; and the same historian speaks (ix. 2) of a grave placed "beneath the ambo," adding the definition "platform of the readers." Other expressions are *analogius* or *analogium*, *suggestus*, *solea*, *pyrgus*, and *ostensorium*. Other historians besides Sozomen mention Chrysostom going up into the "ambo" to preach, so as to be heard better.

With the beginning of the Middle Ages, the mention of the ambo becomes frequent. Among the services of Pope Sixtus III. to the Church, Platina notes that he adorned the ambo or *suggestus* in the Basilica Liberiana, *ubi evangelium et epistola canitur*. The so-called liturgy of St. John Chrysostom contemplates the reading of the gospel in that place by the deacon. The use of the ambo for psalm-singing is evidenced, e.g., by the fifteenth canon of the Council of Laodicea (341?) which reads: "Besides the appointed singers, who mount the ambo and sing from the book, others shall not sing in the Church." While in primitive times the bishop was the only preacher, and taught the people from his throne or from the altar, in the succeeding centuries the cases grow more numerous in which he commits the office to other clergy, who choose the ambo from which to speak. Pastoral letters of the bishops were read from the same place. The ambo of St. Sophia in Constantinople had a special use, serving for imperial coronations. With all the variety of use the Middle Ages did not forget the original purpose of the ambo. Innocent III., commanding that the deacon shall go up into it to read the gospel, draws a parallel between it and the mountain from which the Lord taught the people. He prescribes two entrances; one for the deacon, the other for the subdeacon. It was considered proper that the gospel should be read from a higher step than the epistle, to show, as Hugh of St. Victor says, that the teaching of Christ is far higher than that of his apostles.

The early rule was to have only one ambo in each church, and this continued in the Middle Ages, except in the largest churches. The position of the ambo in the primitive and early medieval churches can not be positively determined; presumably it stood in the nave, in front of the division between nave and choir. Where there were two, they were placed one on each side against the columns dividing nave from aisles. Sometimes, as in St. Clement's at Rome, the ambo formed an integral part of the screen dividing the clergy from the laity. As to material, the ambo was frequently made of wood. That which Abbot Suger of St. Denis restored about the middle of the twelfth century was decorated with tablets of ivory, and Emperor Henry II. gave one to the cathedral of Aachen which had not only ivory, but precious stones and gilded copper-plates set in the wood. Most of the extant older ambos are of marble, frequently adorned with mosaics or reliefs on the sides toward the congregation. As far as it is possible to form a general conception of their structure, they consisted of a flat base, either square, oblong, hexagonal, or circular, supported by columns or a plinth, sometimes, however, resting on figures of lions or men. Access to the ambo was given by one or two flights of steps, and it was railed around in front and occasionally surmounted by a canopy. Decoration was mainly used on the surface of the front, and was of infinite variety, and frequently of great richness. Especially beautiful are the marble reliefs with Biblical and allegorical scenes made for the churches of northern and central Italy by the artists of the twelfth and thirteenth centuries, with Niccolò Pisano at their head. Most of the ambos now extant are in Italy; notable northern examples are that already mentioned at Aachen, one at Halberstadt, and one at Windisch-Matrei. With the developemnt of Gothic architecture the place of the ambo was taken in a general way by the rood-loft above the choir-screen, and the modern lectern and pulpit serve the same purpose. See PULPIT.

(NIKOLAUS MÜLLER.)

BIBLIOGRAPHY: R. de Fleury, *La Messe: études archéologiques sur ses monuments*, iii. 1 sqq., and plans, Paris, 188. Consult the works on Christian archeology and art.

AMBROSE OF ALEXANDRIA: Friend of Origen; d. about 250. Attracted by Origen's fame as a teacher, he visited his school about 212, and was converted by Origen from the Valentinian heresy to the orthodox faith (Eusebius, *Hist. eccl.*, VI. xviii. 1). He was a sufferer during the persecution under Maximinus in 235 (Eusebius, *Hist. eccl.*, VI. xxviii.), and is last mentioned in Origen's *Contra Celsum*, which the latter wrote at the solicitation of Ambrose. He was wealthy and provided his teacher with books for his studies and secretaries to lighten the labor of composition (Eusebius, *Hist. eccl.*, VI. xxiii. 1–2; Jerome, *De vir. ill.*, lvi.). Origen often speaks of him in terms of affection as a man of education and literary and scholarly tastes. All of his works written after 218 are dedicated to Ambrose.

AMBROSE THE CAMALDOLITE (Ambrogio Traversari, Lat. *Traversarius*): Prominent humanist; b. at Portico (30 m. n.e. of Florence) 1386; d. Oct. 20, 1439. He became general of the Order of the Camaldolites in 1431. Pope Eugenius IV. sent him to the Council of Basel, but his exertions in behalf of his master were unsuccessful, as were also his efforts at Ferrara and Florence, 1438–39, toward a union with the Greeks. As an enthusiastic humanist Traversari offers "the first example of a monk in whom the polite scholar is in conflict with the Holy Spirit" (G. Voigt, *Die Wiederbelebung des klassischen Altertums*, i., Berlin, 1893, p. 321). At the table of Cosimo de' Medici, where the most learned met, he took an active part in the conversation about the authors of antiquity. He studied especially the Greek ecclesiastical authors. K. BENRATH.

BIBLIOGRAPHY: His epistles, with life by L. Melius, were edited by P. Canneto, Florence, 1759. Consult Creighton, *Papacy*, ii. 270-272, 277-278, 379.

AMBROSE (Lat. *Ambrosius*), **SAINT, OF MILAN**: One of the great leaders and teachers of the Western Church; b. of a rich and noble Roman family at Treves c. 340; d. at Milan Apr. 4, 379. He was educated in Rome for the bar, and about 370 was appointed consular prefect for Upper Italy and took up his residence at Milan. In 374 a fierce contest arose in the city between the orthodox and the Arian parties concerning the election of a bishop to succeed Auxentius. Ambrose, as the first magistrate, repaired to the church to maintain order and was himself by unanimous vote transferred from his official position to the episcopal chair. He was as yet only a catechumen, but he was immediately baptized, and, eight days afterward (Dec. 7, 374) was consecrated bishop. As a leader of the Church Ambrose distinguished himself by his support of the orthodox faith. In 379 he succeeded in establishing an orthodox bishop at Sirmium in spite of the efforts of the Arian empress Justina. In 385–386 he refused to deliver up a basilica in Milan to the empress for Arian worship. These contests with Arianism he has reported himself in his letters to his sister Marcellina (*Epist.*, xx., xxii.) and to the Emperor Valentinian II. (*Epist.*, xxi.), and in his oration *De basilicis tradendis*. Also with the Roman monk Jovinian (q.v.) he had a sharp controversy (*Epist.*, xlii.).

Ambrose opposed paganism no less zealously than heresy. In the senate hall at Rome stood an altar to Victory on which all oaths were taken. In 382 Gratian had this altar removed, probably at the instigation of Ambrose. The senate, which favored the old religion, made repeated efforts to have the altar restored, under Gratian, Valentinian II., and Theodosius, but unsuccessfully owing to Ambrose's opposition. On the other hand, he held that the State, though it might interfere with paganism, must not interfere with the Church. In 388 the Christians burned a synagogue at Callinicum in Mesopotamia and Theodosius ordered that it be rebuilt at the expense of the bishop of the place, but Ambrose induced the emperor to recall the order. In 370 the people of Thessalonica during a riot murdered the military governor, and Theodosius retaliated with a fearful massacre; Ambrose rebuked the emperor and counseled him to do public penance (*Epist.*, li.).

As a teacher of the Church Ambrose concerned himself more with practical and ethical than with metaphysical questions; his writings are rich in striking practical remarks, but not original. Of his dogmatical works the *De mysteriis* reminds of Cyril of Jerusalem and the *De fide* and *De spiritu sancto* follow Basil very closely. Concerning the question of sin, Ambrose stands nearer to Augustine than the earlier Western Fathers or the Eastern theologians, but is more in accord with the earlier than with the later views of the great teacher. His exegetical works are mostly founded upon Basil and are marred by the allegorical method; their chief and best characteristic is their practical tendency. The same thing may be said of his sermons, which exhibit the full worth of the true Roman gentleman. Among his moral and ascetic works are *De officiis ministrorum* (modeled upon Cicero), *De virginibus, De viduis, De virginitate*, etc. The growing tendency toward asceticism shows itself in the high value he attached to celibacy, the martyr's death, and voluntary poverty; and the notion of a higher and purer Christian life to be attained by such means betrays the influence of the Stoic moral theory which he found in his model. Ambrose introduced a comprehensive reform in Church music (see AMBROSIAN CHANT); and a liturgy long used in the diocese of Milan is associated with his name by tradition. Of the hymns ascribed to him not more than four or five are genuine, and the *Te Deum* is not in this number (see TE DEUM). His extant works also include ninety-one letters.

Ambrose was buried in the Ambrosian basilica at Milan near the martyrs Gervasius and Protasius. In the ninth century Archbishop Angilbert II. placed the remains of the three in a porphyry sarcophagus, which was discovered in 1864, and opened in 1871 (cf. Biraghi, *I tre sepolchri Santambrosiani*, Milan, 1864; A. Riboldi, *Descrizione delle reliquie dei SS. Ambrogio, Gervasio, e Protasio*, 1874; F. Venosta, *Sant' Ambrogio, la sua basilica, la sepoltura e lo scoprimento del suo corpo*, 1874). (T. FÖRSTER†.)

BIBLIOGRAPHY: The works of Ambrose have been published by the Benedictines of St. Maur, 2 vols., Paris, 1686–90; often reprinted, as in *MPL*, xiv.-xvii., by Ballerini, 6 vols., Milan, 1875–86; and in *CSEL*, Vienna, 1896 sqq. Some of his principal works are translated in *NPNF*, vol. x., New York, 1896. The oldest life is by Paulinus (in the Benedictine edition of the works). Later lives are: In French, by Louis Baunard, Paris, 1871, and the Duc de Broglie, 1899, Eng. transl., London, 1899; in German, by T. Förster, Halle, 1884; in English, by Alfred Barry, London, 1896. Consult also J. Pruner, *Die Theologie des Ambrosius*, Eichstätt, 1862; P. Ewald, *Der Einfluss der stoisch-ciceronischen Moral auf die Ethik bei Ambrosius*, Leipsic, 1881; M. Ihm, *Studia Ambrosiana*, 1889; G. M. Dreves, *Aurelius Ambrosius, der Vater des Kirchengesanges*, Freiburg, 1893; J. B. Kellner, *Der heilige Ambrosius als Erklärer des Alten Testaments*, Ratisbon, 1893; R. Thamin, *St. Ambroise et la morale chrétienne au quatrième siècle*, Paris, 1895.

AMBROSE, ISAAC: Puritan; b. in Lancashire, England, 1604; d. at Preston 1664. He studied at Brasenose College, Oxford, and after 1631 became one of the king's four preachers in Lancashire with residence at Garstang. Favoring Presbyterianism, he suffered imprisonment and other hardships during the civil war, and was ejected from Garstang for non-conformity in 1662. He is described as a learned man, of quiet and retiring disposition and sincere piety. His best-known work is *Looking unto Jesus* (London, 1658). A collected edition of his works appeared in 1674 and has been often reprinted (Dundee, 1759; London, 1829, etc.).

AMBROSIAN CHANT: A lively, rhythmical, melodious congregational song, which grew out of a union of the ancient Greek musical system in four keys with the traditional Church psalmody. Whether it was introduced by Ambrose, bishop of Milan (374-397), or whether he merely regulated and improved it, is not certain. The singing had been confined to the choir (Gk. *psaltai*, Lat. *cantores*), who recited the psalms and prayers in monotonous fashion with no fixed rules. The new Ambrosian tunes were lively and joyous, all took part in the singing, and the people found pleasure and enjoyment in it. Augustine in his *Confessions* (IX. vii. 15; X. xxxiii. 50) speaks in glowing terms of the effect of this new method of singing, which was executed "with a clear voice and modulation most suitable." Antiphonal or responsive singing between men and women, congregational choirs, or congregation and choir, borrowed from the Greek Church, came particularly into use (see ANTIPHON). As text Ambrose used the Greek and Latin hymns already existing, both rimed and unrimed. He also composed hymns himself, generally without rimes, but well adapted to the melodies: as *Deus creator omnium; Jam surgit hora tertia; Æterne rerum conditor; Veni redemptor gentium;* perhaps also *O lux beata Trinitas; Splendor paternæ gloriæ.*

The Ambrosian music spread rapidly and was soon dominant throughout the West. But in course of time an artificial and profane manner crept in, which, toward the close of the sixth century, called forth the Gregorian reaction; and thus the singing in the churches was again confined to the choirs or the clergy. The popular, fresh, congregational singing of the Reformation period may be regarded as a partial revival of the ancient Ambrosian chant. M. HEROLD.

BIBLIOGRAPHY: H. A. Daniel, *Thesaurus hymnologicus*, Halle, 1841; C. Fortlage, *Gesänge christlicher Vorzeit*, Berlin, 1844; F. J. Mone, *Lateinische Hymnen des Mittelalters*, 3 vols., Freiburg, 1853-54; J. Kayser, *Beiträge zur Geschichte und Erklärung der ältesten Kirchenhymnen*, Paderborn, 1881; F. Gevært, *Les origines du chant liturgique dans l'église latine*, Paris, 1890; M. Dreves, *Aurelius Ambrosius der "Vater des Kirchengesangs,"* Freiburg, 1893; H. A. Köstlin, *Geschichte der Musik*, Berlin, 1899.

AMBROSIANS: Name of several religious societies, organized in the city or diocese of Milan after the fourteenth century, which chose St. Ambrose as their patron. The only one to attain more than local importance was the Order of the Brethren of St. Ambrose of the Grove (*Fratres S. Ambrosii ad Nemus*), founded before 1530 by three pious Milanese, Alexander Crivelli, Alberto Besuzi, and Antonio Petrasancta, and called after their meeting-place, a grove outside the Porta Cumena in Milan, to which Ambrose used at times to resort (cf. his *De bono mortis*, iii. 11). Gregory XI. confirmed the society in 1375 on the rule of St. Augustine; Eugenius IV. in 1445 united it with three other Ambrose-brotherhoods, which had originated independently at Genoa, Eugubio, and Recanati near Ancona, into a *Congregatio S. Ambrosii ad Nemus Mediolanensis.* Sixtus V brought about in 1589 the reunion of the Milanese and a non-Milanese division of the order, which was temporarily separated under the name of *Congregatio fratrum S. Ambrosii ad Nemus et S. Barnabæ.* To these combined Ambrose and Barnabas orders, Paul V. granted many privileges in 1606. But Innocent X., considering the smallness and insignificance of the order, decided upon its dissolution about 1650. The bull with respect to it is given in the *Bullarium magnum*, iii. 194.

The following societies were confined to Milan and its neighborhood: (1) The Nuns of St. Ambrose of the Grove, founded in 1475 by two ladies of Milan not far from Pallanza on Lago Maggiore. (2) The *Schola S. Ambrosii* or *Oblationarii*, a society of old men and women who undertook to assist at the Ambrosian mass in the churches of Milan, especially in bringing oblations (*oblationes*). (3) The Society of the Oblates of St. Ambrose, founded by Archbishop Carlo Borromeo and confirmed by Gregory XIII. in 1578. They were bound to strict obedience to superiors, especially the archbishop of Milan. During the seventeenth century the society was in a flourishing state and numbered about 200 members, but having decreased to only 16 in 1844 it was abolished. O. ZÖCKLER†.

BIBLIOGRAPHY: Helyot, *Ordres monastiques*, iv. 52-63, Paris, 1715; Heimbucher, *Orden und Kongregationen*, i. 488-489, 510, ii. 336 338.

AMBROSIASTER: The name commonly used for the unknown author of the *Commentaria in xiii. epistolas beati Pauli*, which, from about 850 until the time of Erasmus, were commonly ascribed to Ambrose of Milan. This opinion, which is not yet quite extinct, has no support in ancient tradition, and there are many reasons against it—such as the style, the Scripture version used, the opinion about the authorship of the Epistle to the Hebrews, and the attitude toward Greek literature. But the idea that it is a compilation made about 800 is equally baseless. The *Codex Cassinensis*, though lacking Romans, shows that the commentary had its recognized form earlier than 570. The Scripture text is consistent, belonging to a time before Jerome and to the recension known as the Itala. The anthropology is naive pre-Augustinian; the eschatology is still millenarian; the polemics against heresy point to the period about 380; the *filioque* is lacking. Numerous small details of historical allusion point to the same date.

Little success has attended the attempt to identify the author. Because Augustine in 420 quoted a passage as from *sanctus Hilarius*, some critics have been inclined to see in the Ambrosiaster's work a part of the lost commentary of Hilary of Poitiers on the Epistles. For a long time it was thought that Augustine referred to the Roman deacon Hilary, the partizan of Lucifer of Calaris. The presbyter Faustinus, the opponent of Damasus and author of a treatise on the Trinity, has also been suggested. But neither the style, the Scripture version used, nor the christology is his. The author was probably a presbyter of the Roman Church; possibly Augustine and he were both quoting Hilary. The attempt to identify him, on the ground of notable similarities, with the author of the pseudo-Augustinian *Quæstiones ex utroque testamento* has not met with general approval.

Though the work of Ambrosiaster does not, from an antiquarian standpoint, belong to the most interesting relics of Christian antiquity, its exegesis is often valuable, distinguished by soberness, clearness, and richness of thought, and singularly unbiased and objective for its period. Certain prejudices, as against the speculations and "sophistries" of the Greeks, and against the deacons, are explicable by the circumstances of the time assigned above to its composition. The author repeatedly remarks that the institutions of the Church have undergone essential alterations since the apostles' time. Of great interest are his remarks about the primitive organization, which he considers to have been very informal, all teaching and all baptizing as occasion offered. He thinks that the primitive institutions were modeled after the synagogue; that presbyters and bishops were originally the same, as indeed, he says, they still are fundamentally; that the Roman Church was founded not by the apostles, but by certain Jewish Christians, who imposed a Judaic form upon it to be corrected by better-informed later arrivals; that not Peter alone, but Paul also, had a primacy. In a manuscript written about 769 by Winitharius, a monk of St. Gall, and elsewhere, Origen is named as the author, which is explicable by the presence of certain Origenistic ideas. (F. Arnold.)

In 1899 Dom Morin (*Revue d'histoire et de littérature religieuse*) suggested as the author of the "Ambrosiaster" works Isaac the Jew, a professed convert, who prosecuted Pope Damasus on a capital charge and who was said by the friends of the pope to have relapsed to Judaism and "profaned the Christian mysteries" (382 A.D.). In 1903 Morin withdrew this identification in favor of Decimius Hilarianus Hilarius, prefect of Rome in 383, and pretorian prefect of Italy in 396. A. Souter (formerly of Caius College, Cambridge, now professor at Mansfield College, Oxford), in an article in the *Sitzungsberichte* of the Vienna Academy, 1904, and in *A Study of Ambrosiaster* (*TS*, vol. vii., No. 4, 1905) adopted the later view of Morin, and from an exhaustive study of manuscripts and comparison of the Ambrosiastrian works with contemporary writings has concluded that this view "entirely satisfies the conditions of the problem," and he advises those who may incline to a different view to "read the works of the author carefully in the forthcoming Vienna edition [part of which he is himself editing] before coming to a conclusion on the subject." C. H. Turner, fellow of Magdalen College, Oxford, expressed hearty approval of Morin's first identification and, in an article in *JTS* (Apr., 1906, pp. 355 sqq.), refuses to be convinced by the arguments of Morin or those of Souter that Decimius Hilarianus Hilarius rather than Isaac the Jew wrote the "Commentaries" and the "Questions." The writer's millenarianism, extraordinary familiarity with Jewish history and customs, and unstrongly favorable to the theory that the books usually friendly attitude toward Judaism are were written by Isaac and are as strongly inimical to the theory that the official Decimius Hilarianus Hilarius was the author. Equally in favor of Isaac's authorship are allusions by Jerome to views regarding the genealogies, ascribed to some Judaizing teacher whose name he does not deign to mention, which are identical with those of "Ambrosiaster." A young Roman Catholic scholar Joseph Wittig, has recently advocated the Isaac hypothesis, and has called attention to the fact that "Isaac" and "Hilary" both mean "laughing" as a means of accounting for the ascription of the "Commentaries" to Hilary by Augustine. Recent writers (Harnack, Jülicher, Morin, Souter, Turner, and others) are agreed in attributing the *Commentaria* and the *Quæstiones* to the same author. The *Commentaria* as "the earliest commentary on the Pauline epistles" and the *Quæstiones* as "the earliest substantial book on Biblical difficulties," are of considerable importance. Jülicher pronounces the *Commentaria* "the best commentary on St. Paul's epistles previous to the sixteenth century," and Harnack is equally appreciative. Several other extant works are attributed to the same author. A. H. Newman.

Bibliography: His work is usually included among the works of Ambrose; it is in *MPL*, xvii. and in P. A. Ballerini, *Ambrosii Opera*, iii. 349–372, 971–974, Milan, 1877. Consult A. Souter, *A Study of Ambrosiaster*, Oxford, 1905 (claims to prove finally that Ambrosiaster was Hilary the layman); C. Oudin, *Commentarius de scriptoribus ecclesiasticis*, i. 481 sqq., Leipsic, 1722; J. B. Pitra, *Spicilegium Solesmense*, i., pp. xxvi.-xxxiv., 49–159, 567, Paris, 1852; J. H. Reinkens, *Hilarius von Poitiers*, pp. 273, Schaffhausen, 1864; *DCB*, i. 89–90; J. Langen, *Commentarium in Epistolas Paulinas* , Bonn, 1880; H. B. Swete, *Theodore of Mopsuestia on the Minor Epistles of St. Paul*, i., p. lxxviii., ii., p. 351, Cambridge, 1880–82; Marold, *Der Ambrosiaster nach Inhalt und Ursprung*, *ZWT*, xxvii. (1884) 415–470.

AMEN. See Liturgical Formulas.

AMERICAN BAPTIST MISSIONARY UNION. See Baptists, II., 3, § 7.

AMERICAN BAPTIST PUBLICATION SOCIETY. See Baptists, II., 3, § 7.

AMERICAN BIBLE SOCIETY. See Bible Societies, III., 1.

AMERICAN BIBLE UNION. See Bible Societies, III., 2.

AMERICAN BOARD OF COMMISSIONERS FOR FOREIGN MISSIONS. See Congregationalists, I., 4, § 11; Missions.

AMERICAN AND FOREIGN BIBLE SOCIETY. See Bible Societies, III., 2.

AMERICAN AND FOREIGN CHRISTIAN UNION: A society organized May 10, 1849, by the *union* (as indicated by the name) of the *American* Protestant Society (founded 1843), the *Foreign* Evangelical Society (instituted 1839 as the expansion of the French Association of 1835), and the *Christian* Alliance of 1842. The purpose was to prosecute more efficiently the work of the three societies named; viz., to convert Roman Catholics to Protestantism; or, to quote its constitution, "by missions, colportage, the press, and other appropriate agencies, to diffuse the principles of religious liberty, and a pure and evangelical Christianity, both at home and abroad, where a corrupted Christianity exists."

For a number of years the society prospered, and spread its influence over Europe, North and South America, and adjacent islands. From 1849 to 1859 its yearly receipts averaged $60,000. But it was compelled gradually to contract its operations. It withdrew from France in 1866, from Italy and Europe, and other foreign stations generally, in 1873; and ultimately it limited its efforts to the support of the American Church in Paris. Its monthly periodical, *The Christian World* (35 vols., New York, 1850–84), gave an account of its work; the number for April, 1880, contains a historical sketch of the first thirty years; that for June, 1884, has the thirty-fifth annual report; consult also the last number (Nov., 1884).

AMERICAN LECTURES ON THE HISTORY OF RELIGIONS: A lectureship made possible by the union of a number of universities and theological seminaries in the United States, each of which provides a sum proportionate to the requirements of the year. The lectures are under the care of a committee consisting of representatives of the institutions which unite in furnishing the funds and hearing the lectures. The courses thus far delivered and published are:

1895: T. W. Rhys Davids, *Buddhism: Its History and Literature*, New York, 1896.

1896: D. G. Brinton, *Religions of Primitive Peoples*, ib. 1897.

1898: T. K. Cheyne, *Jewish Religious Life after the Exile*, ib. 1898.

1899: K. Budde, *The Religion of Israel to the Exile*, ib. 1899.

1903: G. Steindorff, *The Religion of the Early Egyptians*, ib. 1905.

1906: G. W. Knox, *The Development of Religion in Japan*, ib. 1906.

AMERICAN MISSIONARY ASSOCIATION. See CONGREGATIONALISTS, I., 4, § 10.

AMERICAN REFORM TRACT AND BOOK SOCIETY. See TRACT SOCIETIES.

AMERICAN SEAMEN'S FRIEND SOCIETY. See SEAMEN, MISSIONS FOR.

AMERICAN SUNDAY-SCHOOL UNION. See SUNDAY-SCHOOLS.

AMERICAN TRACT SOCIETY. See TRACT SOCIETIES.

AMES, WILLIAM (Lat. *Amesius*): Puritan; b. at Ipswich, Suffolk, England, 1576; d. at Rotterdam Nov. 14, 1633. He studied at Christ's College, Cambridge, and became fellow. From the first he was a rigid and zealous Puritan and so without hope of preferment in the Church of England. In 1611 he went to Leyden, thence to The Hague, where he became chaplain to Sir Horace Vere, commander of the English troops in the Netherlands, but lost this post through intrigues of the High-church party at home. He was paid four florins a day by the States General to attend the Synod of Dort (1618–19) and assist the president; became professor of theology at Franeker in 1622, and rector in 1626; shortly before his death he became pastor of the English church in Rotterdam. He contemplated settling in New England, and his family went thither, taking with them his library. His influence on the Continent was considerable, and his reputation is greater there than in his native land. As a decided Calvinist he was active in the Arminian and other controversies of his time, both with voice and pen. His most noteworthy books were the *Medulla theologica* (Amsterdam, 1623; Eng. transl., *The Marrow of Sacred Divinity*, London, 1642) and the *De conscientia et ejus jure vel casibus* (1632; Eng. transl., *Conscience*, 1639), an ethical treatise which was really a continuation of the old scholastic casuistry. A collected edition of his Latin works, with life by M. Nethenus, was published in five volumes at Amsterdam in 1658. (E. F. KARL MÜLLER.)

AMICE, am′is: A vestment worn by Roman Catholic priests when celebrating mass. See VESTMENTS AND INSIGNIA, ECCLESIASTICAL.

AMIOT (wrongly spelled *Amyot*), ā″mī″ō′, **JOSEPH MARIA:** Jesuit missionary; b. at Toulon Feb. 18, 1718; d. at Peking Oct. 8, 1793. He joined the Jesuits in 1737 and entered China as a missionary in 1751. The reigning emperor, Kien-Lung, was hostile to the Christians, but the missionaries were allowed to proceed to Peking and to work there, if not in the provinces. Father Amiot devoted himself assiduously for the rest of his life to the study of Chinese history, language, and literature and was one of the first to give Europe accurate information concerning Eastern Asia. The results of his work were published for the most part in the *Mémoires concernant les Chinois* (15 vols., Paris, 1776–91), in the proceedings of learned societies, and in the *Lettres édifiantes et curieuses* (34 vols., 1717–76). They include a life of Confucius (*Mémoires*, vol. xii.) and a *Dictionnaire tartare-mantchou-français* (ed. Langlès, 3 vols., 1789–90).

AMISH. See MENNONITES.

AMLING, WOLFGANG: German Reformed theologian; b. at Münnerstadt (35 m. n.n.e. of Würzburg), Franconia, in 1542; d. at Zerbst May 18, 1606. He studied at Tübingen, Wittenberg, and Jena; was appointed rector of the school of Zerbst in 1566, minister at Koswig in 1573, and, shortly after, minister and superintendent at St. Nicolai in Zerbst. He was vehemently opposed to the *Formula Concordiæ*, and led the population of Anhalt from Lutheranism to Calvinism. He wrote the *Confessio Anhaldina* (1578).

AMMIANUS MARCELLINUS, am″mi-ā′nus mār″-sel-lī′nus: Author of a Roman history (*Rerum gestarum libri xxxi.*) extending from Nerva to the death of Valens (96–378). He was a native of Antioch, and is said to have died about 400. He devoted himself to philosophical studies, entered the army under Constantius, accompanied Julian in the war against the Persians, and took part under Julian's successors in the wars both of the Orient and the Occident. He afterward retired to Rome and resumed his studies. The first thirteen books of his history are lost; the remaining eighteen, beginning with the year 353, give much valuable information concerning the general state of the Church and many important particulars—the character of Julian, his proceedings, views held by the educated concerning Christianity, etc.

The question whether Ammianus was a Christian has often been raised. At present the generally accepted view is that he was not. His work contains many caustic remarks on the doctrines of Christianity. He speaks of the martyrs, of synods, and of other details of the Christian system, in a way which points to a non-Christian author. It is, however, equally certain that he was not an adherent of the common paganism. He recognized a supreme *numen*, which curbs human arrogance and avenges human crime, and, in general, his views are those of the best Greek writers, approaching a monotheistic standpoint. It seems probable that he believed that primitive pure Christianity and the philosophy of enlightened pagans were the same. From this point of view Ammianus could consistently speak with favor of many things he found among the Christians. He censures Constantine's interference in the Arian controversy and calls it a "confusion of the absolute and plain Christian religion with old-womanish superstition," meaning by "superstition," as the connection shows, the controversy concerning the Trinity and the divinity of Christ. He censured the emperor Julian for forbidding to the Christians instruction in liberal studies, while he did not blame the restoration of pagan sacrifices at the beginning of Jovian's reign. He was not opposed to the paganism of Julian, but to the violation of religious toleration.

(E. VON WÖLFFLIN.)

BIBLIOGRAPHY: The editio princeps (books xiv.-xxvi. only), ed. Angelus Sabinus, was published in Rome, 1874; a better edition (books xvi.-xxx.) is S. Gelenius, Basil, 1533; the latest is by V. Gardthausen, Leipsic, 1874. Consult Teuffel-Schwabe, *Geschichte der römischen Litteratur*, p. 1092, Leipsic, 1890.

AMMON, CHRISTOPH FRIEDRICH VON: German theologian; b. at Baireuth Jan. 16, 1766; d. in Dresden May 21, 1850. He distinguished himself as a student at Erlangen, and became professor there in 1789. In 1794 he went to Göttingen as professor, university preacher, and director of the theological seminary; returned to Erlangen in 1804; in 1813 went to Dresden as court preacher; became member of the Saxon ministry of worship and public instruction in 1831, and vice-president of the consistory in 1835. He was a versatile and many-sided man, an accomplished scholar in diverse fields, an influential official in Church and State, a prolific writer, and much admired as preacher and orator. The most noteworthy of his theological writings were: *Entwurf einer reinen biblischen Theologie* (3 vols., Erlangen, 1792; 2d ed., 1801-02); *Handbuch der christlichen Sittenlehre* (1795; 2d ed., 3 vols., Leipsic, 1838); *Summa theologiæ christianæ* (1803; 4th ed., ib. 1850); *Die Fortbildung des Christentums zur Weltreligion* (ib. 1833; 2d ed., 4 vols., 1836–40). At first Ammon was a decided rationalist, but his tone changed in successive editions of his works, and in 1817 he surprised his friends by defending the theses of Claus Harms (q.v.) in *Bittere Arznei für die Glaubensschwäche der Zeit* (Hanover). Later he returned to his earlier views, and his vacillation subjected him to much harsh criticism. His last writings were *Die Geschichte des Leben Jesu* (3 vols., Leipsic, 1842–47) and *Die wahre und falsche Orthodoxie* (1849). From 1813 to 1822 he was editor of the *Kritisches Journal der neuesten theologischen Litteratur*.

(F. W. DIBELIUS.)

BIBLIOGRAPHY: *Ch. F. v. Ammon, nach Leben, Ansichten und Wirken*, Leipsic, 1850.

AMMONITES: A people of Palestine, allied, according to Gen. xix. 38, to Abraham through Lot, and therefore, like the brother people Moab, akin to the other Abrahamic nations, Israel, Ishmael, and Edom. The name is here explained as *ben 'ammi*, "son of my kinsman." Their territory lay east of the Jordan and north of Moab, from whom they were separated by the Arnon (Num. xxi. 13). An Amoritic king, Sihon, and, later, the Israelites are said to have excluded them from the western and richer part of this district and to have confined them to the steppe lands farther to the east (Josh. xii. 2, xiii. 10, 25; Judges xi. 22). Cities belonging to them are mentioned (Judges xi. 33; II Sam. xii. 31), whence it appears that they were in part a settled people, in part nomadic. Their chief city and the one most frequently named was Rabbah (Rabbath-ammon; Deut. iii. 11; Josh. xiii. 25; II Sam. xii. 26–27; Ezek. xxi. 20; and often), the modern Amman. They had a king in the earliest time. Their religion was doubtless like that of the Moabites; their chief divinity was Milcom (I Kings xi. 5, 33; II Kings xxiii. 13; the mention of Chemosh as god of the Ammonites in Judges xi. 24 is probably an error; see CHEMOSH). The name "Milcom" has been explained as meaning "Am is king," Am (*'Am*) being the name of an older deity (cf. *Balaam*, "Am is lord," and Gen. xix. 38). The relations between the Israelites and Ammonites were generally hostile (Judges xi.; I Sam. xi.; II Sam. x. 1-14, xii. 26–31; II Kings xxiv. 2; II Chron. xx.; Neh. ii. 10, iv. 3, vi. 1; Jer. xl. 13–14, xlix. 1–6; Ezek. xxv. 1–10; Amos i. 13; Zeph. ii. 8); and this fact is reflected in the account of their disgraceful origin in Gen. xix. 30–38. Solomon had an Ammonitish wife (I Kings xiv. 21). Assyrian inscriptions state that Baasha, king of Ammon, was among the allies defeated by Shalmaneser II. at Karkar (854 B.C.), and show that the Ammonite Puduilu, a contemporary of Manasseh of Judah, like all the west-Asiatic princes of the time, was a vassal of Esarhaddon (681–668 B.C.).

In postexilic times also the Ammonites shared the fortunes of their neighbors, and were under Persian, Egyptian, and Syrian rule. Their old capital Rabbah was made a Hellenistic city and named "Philadelphia" after Ptolemy II., Philadelphus. In 218 B.C. it was captured under Antiochus the Great. In the Maccabean period the Ammonites were under a tyrant Timotheus, whom Judas defeated in several battles (I Macc. v. 6–8). About 135 B.C. Philadelphia was ruled by a tyrant named Zeno Cotylas (Josephus, *Ant.*, XIII. viii. 1). It was included in the Decapolis by Pompey, and long remained under Roman rule. At the beginning of the Jewish wars, like most of the Hellenistic cities, it was attacked by the Jews. The name "Ammonite" occurs for the last time in Justin Martyr (d. 166), who says they were very numerous. The present extensive ruins at Amman belong to Roman times.

(F. BUHL.)

BIBLIOGRAPHY: E. Kautzsch, in Riehm, *Handwörterbuch des biblischen Altertums*, pp. 55–56, Bielefeld, 1884 (an admirable sketch); A. H. Sayce, *Races of the Old Testament*, London, 1891; A. Dillmann, *Commentary on Genesis*, on xix. 38, Edinburgh, 1897; *DB*, i. 82–83: *EB*, i. 141–145.

AMMONIUS, am-mō'ne-us, **OF ALEXANDRIA:** An Alexandrian of the third century who is thought to have made one of the earliest attempts to prepare a harmony of the Gospels. Eusebius (*Hist. eccl.*, vi. 19) and Jerome (*De vir. ill.*, lv.) strangely confuse him with Ammonius Saccas (q.v.). He may have been a younger contemporary of Origen. Of his work nothing is known except what may be gathered from a statement of Eusebius (*Epist. ad Carpianum*), that he put beside the text of the Gospel of Matthew the parallel passages from the three other Gospels. Whether he wrote out the parallels in full, or merely indicated them by some system of reference, and whether or not he also included the variants from Matthew can only be conjectured. His work was probably intended for the learned rather than for general use. The so-called Ammonian sections are contained in the edition of the "Tables" of Eusebius (i.e., his gospel harmony), using the Authorized Version as text, prepared by S. H. Turner (New York, 1860). See BIBLE TEXT, II., 1, § 4.

BIBLIOGRAPHY: McGiffert in Eusebius, *Hist. eccl.*, in *NPNF*, i. 38, 39; 267.

AMMONIUS (AMMON, AMUN) THE HERMIT. See MONASTICISM.

AMMONIUS SACCAS, sak'kas: The founder of Neoplatonism; he lived at Alexandria c. 175–242. He was of Christian parentage and education, but returned to heathenism. For a long time, it is said, he earned his living as a porter and carried the grain sacks from the ships; hence his name. Herennius, Longinus, Plotinus, and Origen the Neoplatonist, as well as the Christian Origen, were among his pupils. He wrote nothing, and it is impossible to reproduce his system from the statements of his disciples.

AMOLO, am'ō-lō: Archbishop of Lyons, 841-852. He was educated in the school of Lyons under Agobard, whom he succeeded in the archbishopric, and whom he resembled in his freedom from credulity and superstition. In a letter to Theotbold, bishop of Langres, dealing with a case of the exhibition of unauthorized relics by two men who came from Italy and pretended to be monks, he advised that they should be prohibited, citing other cases in his experience which had been mere fraud and avarice. Amolo also followed Agobard in his protest against the powerful position which the Jews were acquiring in the south of France. His book *Adversus Judæos*, dedicated to Charles the Bald, contains some interesting details as to the Messianic expectations of the Jews at the beginning of the Middle Ages. In a letter to Gottschalk, who had sought to find in him a supporter, he exhorts the imprisoned monk to submit to the judgment of the ecclesiastical authorities, and definitely repudiates several of his assertions on the subject of predestination. His works are in *MPL*, cxvi., and his letters in *MGH*, *Epist.*, v. (1899) 361 sqq. (A. HAUCK.)

AMON, EGYPTIAN DEITY: The local deity of Thebes in Upper Egypt. The etymology of the name, as in the case of most Egyptian deities, is uncertain; the theologians of the later time explained it as meaning "the concealed," from the root 'MN, "to be veiled, hidden." Amon appears to have been originally a harvest-god; but as early as the Middle Kingdom he was thought of as sun-god, according to the teaching that all Egyptian deities, whatever might be their names, were only different forms of the one sun-god. As such he was called *Amon-Ra-setn-ntēru*, "Amon the Sun God, the King of the Gods," and was later identified by the Greeks with their Zeus (hence the late Greek name for Thebes, *Diospolis*). His holy animal was a ram with horns curving downward. He is usually represented in human form, blue in color, wearing a close-fitting hat with two long upright plumes. Less often he is represented ithyphallic, in the form of the harvest-god, Min of Koptos, with whom he was often identified. Ram-headed figures of Amon are also found, especially in Nubia.

Amon gained much from the changed political conditions after the fall of the Old Kingdom. Thebes became the metropolis of Egypt and its god took the chief place in the Egyptian pantheon. The Pharaohs undertook their campaigns in Asia and Nubia in the name of Amon and naturally the lion's share of the booty fell to him. His great temple, near the present Karnak, "the throne of the world," was begun by the kings of the twentieth dynasty, and was extended and adorned by succeeding generations until it became the most imposing of Egyptian temples (see No). His worship was introduced in the conquered provinces and his sanctuaries arose all over Nubia, in the oases of the Libyan desert, and in Syria. Under the New Kingdom he was preeminently the national god of Egypt. The only check to the growth of his power and wealth was the abortive attempt of Amenophis IV., about 1400 B.C., to introduce the worship of the sun's disk. Under the Ramessids Amon's possessions were almost incredible (cf. Erman, *Life in Ancient Egypt*, London, 1894, pp. 302–303). His high priest came to be the first person in the State after the king, and eventually, toward the end of the twentieth dynasty, was able to supplant the latter. The priests of Amon did not long retain the throne, but their great wealth perpetuated their political influence until the twenty-sixth dynasty, when their power seems to have declined, and Amon gradually sank back to the position of a local deity. In the oases, however, and in Ethiopia his worship and the authority of his priests lasted till Roman times and the introduction of Christianity.

(G. STEINDORFF.)

BIBLIOGRAPHY: C. P. Tiele, *History of the Egyptian Religion*, pp. 147–150, Boston, 1882; H. Brugsch, *Religion der alten Aegypter*, pp. 87 sqq., Leipsic, 1885; A. Erman, *Life in Ancient Egypt*, passim, London, 1894; A. Wiedemann, *Religion of the Ancient Egyptians*, 109–110, New York, 1897 (authoritative); E. A. W. Budge, *Gods of the Egyptians*, i. 23, 79, 88, ii. 1–16, 324, London, 1903 (the fullest account, in a volume richly illustrated); P.D. Chantepie de la Saussaye, *Lehrbuch der Religionsgeschichte*, i. 208–209, Tübingen, 1905; G. Steindorff, *Religion of the Ancient Egyptians*, New York, 1905.

AMON, ē'men, **KING OF JUDAH:** Fourteenth king of Judah, son and successor of Manasseh. He reigned, according to the old chronology, 642–641 B.C.; according to Kamphausen, 640–639;

according to Hommel, 641–640. During his short reign nothing of importance took place. Judah, which was tributary to the Assyrians, enjoyed peace. Amon walked in the ways of his father, Manasseh, imitated the Assyrians in worshiping the heavenly bodies, and continued the Baal and Moloch cults. His servants conspired against him and slew him. The "people of the land" rose up against the conspirators, slew them, and made Josiah, his son, eight years old, king in his stead. His history is found in II Kings xxi. 18–26; II Chron. xxxiii. 20–25. (W. Lotz.)

Bibliography: Consult the works mentioned under Ahab.

AMORITES, am'ō-raits: According to Gen. x. 15–18; I Chron. i. 13–16, one of the eleven tribes descended from Canaan. They are frequently mentioned in lists of the Palestinian peoples dispossessed by Israel (Gen. xv. 21; Ex. iii. 8; Deut. vii. 1; Josh. iii. 10; etc.). As distinguished from the Canaanites, they seem to have formed the chief part of the population of the west-Jordan highlands (Num. xiii. 29; Deut. i. 7, 19–20, 44; Josh. v. 1, x. 6). In certain passages (particularly in E and D) the term is used as a general designation of the pre-Israelitic peoples of Palestine (Gen. xv. 16; Josh. vii. 7, xxiv. 15, 18; Judges vi. 10; I Sam. vii. 14; II Sam. xxi. 2; I Kings xxi. 26; II Kings xxi. 11; Isa. xvii. 9, LXX.; Ezek. xvi. 3; Amos ii. 9–10). In Judges i. 34–35 the people of the lowlands west of the mountains of Judah are called Amorites. Elsewhere (as in Gen. xiv. 7, 13, xlviii. 22, and in many passages in which the east-Jordan kings, Sihon and Og, are called Amorites) it is doubtful whether or not a particular tribe is meant. The extra-Biblical sources have raised new problems instead of throwing light on the ethnographical question. The "Amara" of the Egyptian inscriptions, who are usually identified with the Amorites, lived in the valley between Lebanon and Anti-Lebanon (cf. W. Max Müller, *Asien und Europa*, Leipsic, 1893, pp. 218–233). Hence it seems probable that the Amorites moved southward in the fifteenth century B.C.—a movement which may be referred to in the Tell el-Amarna letters (cf. H. Winckler, *Geschichte Israels*, i., Leipsic, 1895, p. 52). (F. Buhl.)

The Amorites are mentioned in the Old Testament more frequently than any other people of Palestine except the Canaanites. West of the Jordan they seem to have been confounded the one with the other; but as the Canaanites are never said to have lived east of the Jordan so the Amorites do not appear on the Mediterranean coast-land. The difficult question as to whether or not the two peoples are essentially identical is probably to be decided in the negative, though it is quite possible that the Amorites as well as the Canaanites were a Semitic people. There is, in any case, no sufficient warrant for the assumption of Sayce and others that they were akin to the Libyans. The Babylonian name for Canaan, *mat Amurê*, "land of the Amorites" shows that at least the eastern side of Palestine was Amoritic at an early date, and it is a plausible supposition that the two related peoples separated in southern Syria, the Canaanites following the coast-land (their proper home) and then spreading eastward to the hill-country, and the Amorites coming gradually southward, mainly east of the Jordan. A learned annotator intimates (Deut. iii. 9) that they were once the dominant people about Anti-Lebanon, as the "Sidonians" or Phenicians were about Lebanon. After their loss of the Moabite country (Num. xxi. 21-35) they were gradually absorbed by the Hebrews, Amorites, and Arameans.

J. F. McCurdy.

Bibliography: A. H. Sayce, *The White Race of Ancient Palestine*, in *Expositor*, July, 1888; idem, *Races of the O. T.*, London, 1891; *DB*, i. 84-85; *EB*, i. 146-147, 640-643; Meyer, in *ZATW*. i. (1881) 122 sqq.; J. F. McCurdy, *History, Prophecy and the Monuments*, §§ 130-131, 3 vols., New York, 1896-1901.

AMOS, ê'mos: The third of the minor prophets, originally a herdsman and farmer of Tekoa (a town twelve miles s.s.e. of Jerusalem), and destitute of a prophetical education (Amos i. 1, vii. 12, 14–15). The Fathers wrongly identified him with the father of Isaiah (Amoz), because his name in the Septuagint is identical with that of Isaiah's father.

Life.

He prophesied in the Northern Kingdom during the reigns of Uzziah in Judah (777–736 B.C.) and Jeroboam II. in Israel (781–741), when Israel was at the very height of its splendor (i. 1, vii. 10–11). His prophecies were apparently all given in one year, specified as "two years before the earthquake," a momentous but undatable event (i. 1; cf. Zech. xiv. 5; Josephus, *Ant.*, IX. x. 4, gives a fabulous story). The place was Beth-el, the greatest sanctuary of the Northern Kingdom. His plain speaking led to the charge of conspiracy, and he was compelled to return to Judah (Amos vii. 10–12). Nothing more is known of him.

The Book of Amos, after the opening verse, is divisible into three parts: (1) Chaps. i. 2–ii. 16, describing the judgments of God upon Damascus (i. 3–5), Philistia (i. 6–8), Tyre (i. 9–10), Edom (i. 11–12), Ammon (i. 13–15), Moab (ii. 1–3), Judah (ii. 4–5), and Israel (ii. 6–16). (2) Chaps. iii.–vi., a series of discourses against the Northern Kingdom threatening punishment and judgment. The subdivision of this section is a matter of dispute.

The Book of Amos.

The prophet sets forth in his usual rhetorical manner the moral and religious degeneracy of the people. (3) Chaps. vii.–ix., beginning with three successive threatening visions (vii. 1–3, 4–6, 7–9). These were made the basis of the complaint against Amos of Amaziah, high priest at Beth-el, to the king Jeroboam II., and hence resulted his banishment (vii. 10–13). Before he goes, however, he insists upon the reality of his call (vii. 14–15), and foretells the sad fall of the high priest and his family (vii. 16–17). Chaps. vii., viii., and ix. contain two visions and their explanations. The first is of threatening content, but the second (ix. 1–7) adds a promise of salvation for a faithful remnant and of the universal sway of religion and prosperity (ix. 8–15). The book gives only an abstract of the prophet's complete discourses.

The style of Amos is rhetorical. His figures, analogies, and similes are excellent, though at times surprising (cf. iii. 3–6; iv. 2; v. 7; xiii. 11–14). The notion that Amos borrows his similes chiefly from his early mode of life, and thus betrays his extraction, is generally accepted; but it is hardly well founded when the variety of them is observed (cf. ii. 13; iii. 4, 5, 8, 12; vi. 12; viii. 8; ix. 5; and the visions of vii. 1 and viii. 1). On the other hand, the Hebrew of Amos is abnormal, but it is uncertain how much belongs to the author himself. The integrity and genuineness of the book are generally acknowledged; only i. 9-11; ii. 4, 5; iii. 14b; iv. 13; v. 8, 9; viii. 6, 8, 11, 12; ix. 5, 6, 8–15, partly on account of the contents, partly on account of the connection, have been regarded as glosses by modern critics (Duhm, Stade, Giesebrecht, Cornill, Schwally, Smend, Wellhausen).

Its Importance.

The modern school of Biblical scholars regard the Book of Amos as the oldest written testimony to that activity of the prophets of the eighth century B.C. whereby the religion of Israel was given a more ethical and spiritual character. It is therefore important to note its contents and presuppositions. Two evils in the moral and religious conditions of the Northern Kingdom receive the prophet's severe condemnation, viz., the reprehensible conduct of the high and mighty (ii. 6–7a; iii. 10; iv. 1; v. 7, 11–12; viii. 4–6), and the perverted religious forms and observances (ii. 7b–8; v. 26; viii. 14). The latter, with their idolatrous representations of the deity, were specially offensive to a pious Judean, who believed that Yahweh dwelt on Zion and not in visible form. Reliance upon the offerings, gifts, feasts, and processions of Beth-el and the other sanctuaries as a means of securing Yahweh's favor was a terrible mistake, which could only bring the most direful consequences (iv. 4–13; v. 4–6, 21–24; ix. 1–8). The true way to serve Yahweh was to become like him and to practise goodness and righteousness (v. 14, 24). The prophet makes no claim to new ideas concerning Yahweh or his relations to the world in general and to Israel in particular. What he has to say upon these topics is all assumed as already known to the pious. It is the idolatrous worship, with its attendant evils, which he reprobates and wishes to correct. (A. KÖHLER†.)

BIBLIOGRAPHY: Besides the works mentioned in the article MINOR PROPHETS, consult: W. R. Harper, *Amos and Hosea*, in *International Critical Commentary*, New York, 1905 (gives a full list of the important literature, clxxviii. clxxxix.); G. Baur, *Der Prophet Amos erklärt*, Giessen, 1847; J. H. Gunning, *De godspraken van Amos*, Leyden, 1885; K. Hartung, *Der Prophet Amos nach dem Grundtexte erklärt*, in *Biblische Studien*, iii., Freiburg, 1898; H. G. Mitchell, *Amos, an Essay in Exegesis*, Boston, 1893, 1900; J. J. P. Valeton, *Amos en Hosea*, Nijmwegen, 1894 (Germ. transl., Giessen, 1898, an excellent work); S. R. Driver, *Joel and Amos*, in *Cambridge Bible*, 1897; S. Oettli, *Amos und Hosea, zwei Zeugen gegen die Anwendung der Evolutionstheorie auf die Religion Israels*, in *Beiträge zur Förderung Christlichen Theologie*, v. 4, Gütersloh, 1901.

AMPHILOCHIUS, am″fi-lō′ki-us, **SAINT**: Apparently a cousin of Gregory Nazianzen, and closely associated with him and with Basil the Great in directing the policy of the Church at the time of the defeat of Arianism. He was originally a lawyer, but retired to a life of devotion and asceticism. In 373 he was chosen bishop of Iconium, the metropolitan see of Lycaonia. The year of his death is uncertain; but Jerome includes him, as still living, in his *De viris illustribus* (392), and he appears as taking part in a synod at Constantinople in 394. Of the numerous works ascribed to him by Combefis (cf. *MPG*, xxxix.), not a few are doubtless not genuine. Late investigation, however, has brought to light other genuine works of Amphilochius. The *Epistola synodica* in defense of the orthodox doctrine of the Trinity (376), and the *Iambi ad Seleucum*, ascribed to Gregory Nazianzen (*MPG*, xxxvii.), not without importance for the history of the canon, are not the only works of Amphilochius which are still extant. (F. LOOFS.)

BIBLIOGRAPHY: Fabricius-Harles, *Bibliotheca Græca*, viii. 373–381, Hamburg, 1802; *DCB*, i. 103–107 (quite exhaustive); J. Fessler, *Institutiones patrologiæ*, i. 600–604, Innsbruck, 1900; K. Holl, *Amphilochius von Ikonium*, Tübingen, 1904; G. Ficker, *Amphilochiana*, part i., Leipsic, 1906.

AMPULLÆ, am-pul′lî or -lê: [Flasks or vials for holding liquids. In ecclesiastical usage they have been employed for the water and wine of the mass and for the consecrated oil used in baptism, confirmation, and extreme unction. Such vessels were sometimes of considerable size and were made of gold, silver, crystal, onyx, or glass. Specimens are preserved at Paris, Cologne, Venice, and elsewhere; and there is one at Reims said to have been miraculously provided for the baptism of Clovis in 496.] Deserving of most notice are the so-called *ampullæ sanguinolentæ, phiolæ cruentæ* or *rubricatæ* ("blood-ampullæ"), glass flasks "which contain a reddish sediment and are alleged to have once held the blood of martyrs. They have been found almost exclusively in the graves of the catacombs, near the slab with which the grave was sealed or fastened to it by mortar. They are first mentioned by Antonio Bosio, the explorer of the Roman catacombs, who relates that in certain graves as well as in glass or clay vessels, he found blood congealed and dried, which, when moistened with water, assumed its natural color (*Roma sotterranea*, Rome, 1632, p. 197). Soon afterward a certain Landucci discovered such vessels with a watery or milky fluid which, when shaken, assumed the color of blood (De Rossi, 619). The discovery of a *phiola rubricata* came to be regarded as certain proof of a martyr's grave, and the Congregation of the Sacred Rites decided accordingly in 1668 when doubts were raised concerning the *indicia martyrii* at the removal of relics from the catacombs. Doubts continued, however, and a Jesuit, Victor de Buck, made the strongest presentation of the case of the skeptics, arguing on scientific grounds (*De phiolis rubricatis*, Brussels, 1855). After a new find in the cemetery of S. Saturnino in 1872 a papal commission undertook an exact microscopical investigation, which was believed to establish the presence of blood. Roman Catholic archeologists and theologians had generally conceded a possibility that the claims might be well founded, while opposing the unsystematic and unscientific assumption that all red sediment was blood, and demanding an adequate investigation in each case.

The following weighty and conclusive objections, however, are made even to the possibility: (1) There is no literary testimony that the blood of martyrs was preserved as is presupposed, and no satisfactory reason has been given why it should have been thus saved. (2) A large percentage of these ampullæ come from the graves of children under seven years of age, who can hardly have suffered in the persecutions of the Christians; furthermore, more than one-half of them are of the time of Constantine or later. (3) Non-Christian graves furnish similar vessels with red sediment. (4) In no case has the sediment been proved to be blood by chemical and microscopic examination. The attempt made in 1872 is untrustworthy, and its results are rejected by competent judges. (5) The specimens with inscriptions (such as *sang.*, *sa.*, and the like) and the monogram of Christ or the cross are forgeries. The red sediment is probably oxid of iron produced by the decomposition of the glass. It has been suggested that it is the remains of communion wine, and the sixth canon of the Synod of Carthage of 397 lends support to the view, but the chemical analysis is against it (cf., however, Berthelot in *Revue archéologique*, new series, xxxiii., 1877, p. 396). Certain heathen burial customs in which wine (cf. Schultze, *Katakomben*, pp. 52, 54, and note 15) or oil was used offer analogies. The original purpose and significance of these ampullæ was probably not uniform.

(Victor Schultze.)

Bibliography: F. X. Kraus, *Die Blutampullen der römischen Katakomben*, Frankfort, 1868; idem, *Ueber den gegenwärtigen Stand der Frage nach dem Inhalte und der Bedeutung der römischen Blutampullen*, Freiburg, 1872; idem, *Roma sotterranea*, pp. 507 sqq., ib. 1879; "Paulinus," *Die Märtyrer der Katakomben und die römische Praxis*, Leipsic, 1871; G. B. de Rossi, *Roma sotterranea*, iii. 602 sqq., Rome, 1877; Victor Schultze, *Die sogenannten Blutgläser der römischen Katakomben*, in *ZKW*, i. (1880) 515 sqq.; idem, *Die Katakomben*, pp. 225 sqq., Leipsic, 1882.

AMRAPHEL. See Hammurabi and his Code, I., § 1.

AMSDORF, NIKOLAUS VON: German Protestant; b. at Torgau (30 m. n.e. of Leipsic) Dec. 3, 1483; d. at Eisenach May 14, 1565. He began his studies at the University of Leipsic in 1500, but two years later went to Wittenberg, being among the first students in the newly founded university in that city. There he fell under the influence of Luther, whose intimate friend he became, and to whose teachings he lent unquestioning adhesion from the very beginning. He was with Luther at the Leipsic disputation in 1519, accompanied him to Worms in 1521, and was in the secret of his sojourn at the Wartburg. In 1524 he became pastor and superintendent in Magdeburg and was active in introducing the Reformation into that city, organizing the ritual closely on the model of Wittenberg. He performed similar services in Goslar and Einbeck. From the first he was rigid in his views, opposed to the least departure from the orthodox Lutheran doctrine, and fierce in his attacks on such men as Melanchthon and Butzer who came to represent a policy of conciliation and compromise both within the Protestant Church and toward the Roman Catholic princes. Thus he was largely instrumental in the failure of the Regensburg conference of 1541, where his attitude toward the emperor was as fearless as it was narrow. In the same year the Elector John Frederick appointed him bishop of Naumburg-Zeitz against the wishes of the chapter and in spite of the protest of the emperor. The battle of Mühlberg (1547) compelled him to seek refuge in Weimar. His quarrel with Melanchthon and his supporters had grown embittered with time, and he helped to found a new university at Jena in opposition to the tendencies represented at Wittenberg. In the same spirit he assumed charge of the Jena edition of Luther's works, which was to correct the alleged faults and omissions of the Wittenberg edition.

In 1552 Amsdorf was made superintendent at Eisenach, whence, with Flacius, whom he caused to be called to Jena, he carried on a virulent polemic against the so-called Philippists and Adiaphorists. The formal break between the orthodox Lutheran party and the followers of Melanchthon at the colloquy of Worms in 1557 was largely due to Amsdorf's efforts. From 1554 to 1559 he was engaged in a violent controversy with Justus Menius, superintendent at Gotha, concerning the doctrine of good works as essential to salvation; and in the stress of conflict he was led to assume the extreme position that good works are actually detrimental to the welfare of the soul, denoting by "good works," however, those that man performs for the express purpose of attaining salvation. When, in 1561, as a result of his views on the doctrine of sin, Flacius, together with his followers, was expelled from Jena, Amsdorf was spared because of his advanced age and his great services to the Protestant cause in the early days of the Reformation.

(G. Kawerau.)

Bibliography: E. J. Meier, biography of Amsdorf in M. Meurer, *Das Leben der Altväter der lutherischen Kirche*, iii., Leipsic, 1863; Eichhorn, *Amsdorfiana*, in *ZKG*, vol. xxii., 1901.

AMULET, am'yu-let: A word first used to designate objects having a magical effect in warding off or driving away evils—the evil eye, illness, demons, etc.—and thus practically equivalent to "talisman." By degrees it came to be employed for objects worn about the person. Used down to the seventeenth century for things forbidden by the Church, it gradually acquired a more general meaning. The limits of this article preclude the discussion of the origin of amulets, of their psychological basis, or of their significance in the universal history of religion.

In the Old Testament and Judaism.

In the Old Testament, objects of the kind are mentioned among the ornaments worn by women (Isa. iii. 16–26) and by animals (Judges viii. 21); the bells on the border of the high priest's robe had no other primary significance (cf. "the bells of the horses," Zech. xiv. 20). Later Judaism completely surrounded the individual with intangible spirits, but provided numerous means of protection against the evil they might effect—the presence of angels, pronouncing the name of God, amulets containing the Holy Name, and fragments of Scripture worn on the person (the "phylacteries" of Matt. xxiii. 5) or fastened to the door-posts of houses. The special power over demons attributed to Solomon may also be mentioned; formulas of exorcism were referred to him, and the possessed were supposed to be healed, on the invocation of his name, by the methods prescribed by him.

The demonological conceptions of Judaism and the magic of the East had a very strong influence on the Greco-Roman world. Christianity, however, at first rejected these superstitious observances, and protested against every accusation of the use of magic arts. There came a change with the entrance of the pagan multitudes, with their material ideas of religion and their need for an external realization of the supernatural. The ideas about demons, found in the exorcisms of the second century (Origen, *Contra Celsum*, vi. 39, 40) were generalized, paganized, and Judaized. As the ecclesiastical writers abundantly testify (see passages quoted in Bingham, *Origines*, vii. 250), magical formulas began to be used again; mysterious objects, inscribed with characters often unintelligible, were placed upon the bodies of new-born infants and the sick; and Chrysostom (on I Cor. vii. 3) warns his hearers against love-philters. The teachers of the Church branded all this as actual apostasy from the faith; and the Christian civil government punished severely the use of amulets in sickness. To meet this tendency an attempt was made to give these methods a Christian coloring, or to employ elements susceptible to a Christian interpretation. The demons, who had been supposed to have special care of races or of individuals, now became angels, and protection was afforded by their names inscribed on amulets. In like manner the name of God was used. Even some of the clergy provided such amulets, though the Church forbade them to do so, and excommunicated those who wore them (Synod of Laodicea; Synod of Agde, 544). The cross (see CROSS AND ITS USE AS A SYMBOL, § 3) took a specially prominent place among these protecting objects. Women and children commonly wore verses from the Gospels for this purpose. Chrysostom told the people of Antioch that they ought rather to have the Gospels in their hearts. That of John was thought to be particularly efficacious; it was laid on the head to drive out fever, and Augustine commends the practise (*Tractatus vi in cap. i. Johannis evangelii*, *MPL*, xxv. 1443), "not because it is done for this purpose," but because it means the abandonment of the pagan ligatures. The whole range of sacred things was brought into service. Satyrus, the brother of Ambrose, in a shipwreck, hung the eucharistic bread, wrapped in an *orarium*, about his neck "that he might get help from his faith" (Ambrose, *De obitu fratris*, xliii.). Similar use was made of oil and wax from holy places and of water and salt that had been blessed. Relics of the saints, enclosed in costly cases, were worn. Since the Church was unable entirely and all at once to drive out every vestige of heathen superstition, it did the next best thing when it took into consideration the needs of popular, unspiritual devotion, and gradually, by the conversion of the old means, forced into the background or effaced their non-Christian elements.

In the Early Church.

Lack of space forbids the discussion in detail of the diversified forms even of Christian development of the idea, as they are found in the numerous relics of antiquity, from those of the catacombs down, or to give any account of the multiplicity of objects which are commonly used among the devout Roman Catholics at the present day, with at least some remnant of the idea of the ancient amulets underlying them—scapulars, crosses, the agnus dei, rosaries, and an endless variety of medals with pictures of the Virgin and the saints. These objects may serve different purposes; they may be tokens of sharing in a wide-spread and approved devotion, or signs of membership in some pious confraternity, or souvenirs of a visit to some holy place; but in most instances the priestly blessing which they have received is distinctly understood to give them a positive power (on condition of the proper faith and other dispositions on the part of the wearer or possessor) against the assaults of evil spirits and other ills.

Survivals.

(JOHANNES FICKER.)

BIBLIOGRAPHY: W. King, *Talisman and Amulets*, in *Archæological Journal*, xxvi. (1869) 25–34, 149–157, 225–235; J. A. Martigny, *Dictionnaire des antiquités chrétiennes*, article *Amulette*, Paris, 1877; W. R. Smith, in *Journal of Philology*, xiv. (1881) 122–123; E. C. A. Riehm, *Handwörterbuch des biblischen Altertums*, Bielefeld, 1884; J. Wellhausen, *Skizzen*, iii. 144, Berlin, 1887; M. Friedländer, *Jewish Religion*, pp. 331–338, London, 1891; J. L. André, *Talismans*, in *The Reliquary*, vii. (1893) 162–167, 195–202, viii. (1894) 13–18; *DB*, i. 88–90, iii. 869–874.

AMYOT. See AMIOT.

AMYRAUT, am″ï-rō′, **MOÏSE** (Lat. *Moses Amyraldus*): Calvinist theologian and preacher; b. at Bourgueil (27 m. w.s.w. of Tours), Touraine, 1596; d. at Saumur Jan. 8, 1664. He came of an influential family in Orleans, began the study of law at Poitiers, and received the degree of licentiate in 1616; but the reading of Calvin's *Institutio* turned his mind to theology. This he studied eagerly at Saumur, under Cameron, to whom he was much attached. After serving as pastor for a short time at Saint-Aignan, he was called in 1626 to succeed Jean Daillé at Saumur, and soon became prominent. The national synod held at Charenton in 1631 chose him to lay its requests before Louis XIII., on which occasion his tactful bearing attracted the attention and won the respect of Richelieu. In 1633 he was appointed professor of theology at Saumur with De la Place and Cappel, and the three raised the institution into a flourishing condition, students being attracted to it from foreign countries, especially from Switzerland. Theological novelties in their teaching, however, soon stirred up opposition, which came to little in France; but in Switzerland, where the professors were less known, it reached such a pitch that students were withdrawn, and in 1675 the Helvetic Consensus was drawn up against the Saumur innovations. Amyraut was specially attacked because his teaching on grace and predestination seemed to depart from that of the Synod of Dort, by adding a conditional universal grace to the unconditional particular.

Amyraut first published his ideas in his *Traité de la prédestination* (Saumur, 1634), which immediately caused great excitement. The controversy became so heated that the national synod at Alençon in 1637 had to take notice of it. Amyraut and his friend Testard were acquitted of heterodoxy, and silence was imposed on both sides. The attacks continued, however, and the question came again before the synod of Charenton in 1644–45, but with the same result. Amyraut bore himself so well under all these assaults that he succeeded in conciliating many of his opponents, even the venerable Du Moulin (1655). But at the synod of Loudun in 1659 (the last for which permission was obtained—partly through Amyraut's influence—from the crown), fresh accusations were brought, this time including Daillé, the president of the synod, because he had defended what is called "Amyraldism." This very synod, however, gave Amyraut the honorable commission to revise the order of discipline. In France the harmlessness of his teaching was generally recognized; and the controversy would soon have died out but for the continual agitation kept up abroad, especially in Holland and Switzerland.

Amyraut's doctrine has been called "hypothetical universalism"; but the term is misleading, since it might be applied also to the Arminianism which he steadfastly opposed. His main proposition is this: God wills all men to be saved, on condition that they believe—a condition which they could well fulfil in the abstract, but which in fact, owing to inherited corruption, they stubbornly reject, so that this universal will for salvation actually saves no one. God also wills in particular to save a certain number of persons, and to pass over the others with this grace. The elect will be saved as inevitably as the others will be damned. The essential point, then, of Amyraldism is the combination of real particularism with a purely ideal universalism. Though still believing it as strongly as ever, Amyraut came to see that it made little practical difference, and did not press it in his last years, devoting himself rather to non-controversial studies, especially to his system of Christian morals (*La morale chrestienne*, 6 vols., Saumur, 1652–60). The real significance of Amyraut's teaching lies in the fact that, while leaving unchanged the special doctrines of Calvinism, he brought to the front its ethical message and its points of universal human interest. See CALVINISM. (E. F. KARL MÜLLER.)

BIBLIOGRAPHY: E. and É. Haag, *La France Protestante*, i. 72–80, Paris, 1846 (gives a complete list of his voluminous works); E. Saigey, in *Revue de théologie*, pp. 178 sqq., Paris, 1849; A. Schweizer, *Tübinger theologische Jahrbücher*, 1852, pp. 41 sqq., 155 sqq.

ANABAPTISTS.

The name "Anabaptists" (meaning "Rebaptizers") was given by their opponents to a party among the Protestants in Reformation times whose distinguishing tenet was opposition to infant baptism, which they held to be unscriptural and therefore not true baptism. They baptized all who joined them; but, according to their belief, this was not a rebaptism as their opponents charged. In opposition to the Church doctrine they held that baptism should be administered only to those who were old enough to express by means of it their acceptance of the Christian faith, and hence, from their point of view, their converts were really baptized for the first time. Another epithet often applied to them was "Catahaptists," meaning pseudobaptists, as if their baptism were a mockery, and with an implication of drowning, which was considered the appropriate punishment for their conduct and frequently followed their arrest.

In studying this movement the following facts should be borne in mind: (1) The Anabaptists did not invent their rejection of infant baptism, for there have always been parties in the Church which were antipedobaptists (cf. A. H. Newman, *History of Antipedobaptism*, Philadelphia, 1897). (2) There are two kinds of Anabaptists, the sober and the fanatical. Failure to make this distinction has done mischief and caused modern Baptists to deny their connection with the Baptists of the Reformation, whereas they are the lineal descendants of the sober kind and have no reason to be ashamed of their predecessors. (3) Even among the fanatical Anabaptists there were harmless dreamers; not all the fanatics were ready to establish a Kingdom of the Saints by unsaintly deeds. (4) Information concerning the Anabaptists is largely derived from prejudiced and deficient sources.

I. The Sober Anabaptists: These were the product of the Reformation in Switzerland started by Zwingli. Shortly after he began to preach Reformation doctrine in Zurich, in 1519, some of his hearers, very humble persons mostly, gathered in private houses to discuss his sermons, and Zwingli often met with them. He had laid it down as a principle that what is not taught in the Bible is not a law of God for Christians, and had applied this principle to the payment of tithes and the observance of Lent. In 1522 these friends of Zwingli asked him where he found his plain Scripture authorizing infant baptism and whether, according to his principle he was not compelled to give it up. Zwingli, however, though he wavered at first, decided to stand by the Church, arguing that there was fair inferential support in the Bible for the practise, and that it was the Christian substitute for the Jewish rite of circumcision. Over this point an estrangement took place between him and his parishioners. The little company received accessions of a desirable character, and came to include scholars and theologians like Felix Manz and Conrad Grebel, who socially and intellectually were the peers of Zwingli's followers. Hübmaier was a visitor. In 1524 as the result of letters or visits from Thomas Münzer and Andreas Carlstadt they took very decided antipedobaptist positions; but public opinion in Zurich was against

1. In Switzerland.

them, and the magistrates on Jan. 18, 1525, after what was considered the victory of the Church party in a public debate, following many private conferences, ordered that these antipedobaptists present their children for baptism, and made it a law that any parents refusing to have their infant children baptized should be banished. On Jan. 21 they forbade the meetings of the antipedobaptists and banished all foreigners who advocated their views. Shortly after this the antipedobaptists began to practise believers' baptism. In a company composed entirely of laymen one poured water in the name of the Trinity on other members in succession, after they had expressed a desire to be baptized, and so, as they claimed, they instituted veritable Christian baptism. Like scenes were enacted in other assemblies. It is noteworthy that these first believers' baptisms were by pouring; immersion was introduced later. Also that in all the lengthy treatises of Zwingli on baptism there is no discussion as to the mode. These early Baptists practised pouring, sprinkling, and immersion as suited their convenience, and did not consider the mode as of much importance.

2. Anabaptist Tenets. Though infant baptism was the first and the main issue between the Anabaptists and the Church party, there were others of great importance. The former said that only those who had been baptized after confession of faith in Christ constituted a real Church; the latter, that all baptized persons living in a certain district constituted the State Church. The Anabaptists maintained that there should be a separation between the State and the Church; that no Christian should bear arms, take an oath, or hold public office; that there should be complete religious liberty. All this was not in accord with the times; and thus the Anabaptists were considered to be enemies of the standing order, and were treated accordingly. On Sept. 9, 1527, the cantons of Zurich, Bern, and St. Gall united in an edict which may be taken as a specimen of its class. It gives reasons for prosecuting the Anabaptists, which are manifestly prejudiced and even in part false, and then decrees the death by drowning of all of them who are teachers, baptizing preachers, itinerants, leaders of conventicles, or who had once recanted and then relapsed. Foreigners in these cantons associating with the Anabaptists were banished, and if found again were to be drowned. Simple adherents were to be fined. It was made the bounden duty of all good citizens to inform against the Anabaptists (for the full text consult S. M. Jackson, *Huldreich Zwingli*, New York, 1903, pp. 259–281). Similar laws against the Anabaptists were made and enforced in South Germany, Austria, the Tyrol, the Netherlands, England, and wherever they went. Such treatment suppressed Anabaptism, or at all events, drove it beneath the surface. How ineffectual it was to extinguish it appears from the fact that early in 1537, four Anabaptists from the Netherlands quietly stole into Geneva, and began making converts. John Calvin, who neglected no opportunity to do God service, as he conceived it, got wind of their presence and had them and their seven converts banished by the magistrates (the incident is described by Beza in his life of Calvin, ed. Neander, p. 8; cf. Calvin's *Tracts*, Eng. transl., i. xxx.; Doumergue, *Jean Calvin*, ii. 242; Herminjard, *Correspondance des Réformateurs*, iv. 272). Anabaptists persisted in great numbers in Moravia, the Palatinate, Switzerland, Poland, and elsewhere.

3. In the Netherlands and England. Only in the Netherlands did the Anabaptists escape persecution, and there they became quite numerous. They were joined in 1536 by a remarkable man, Menno Simons (q.v.), who organized them and his name has been given to the sect (see MENNONITES). From the Netherlands they passed into England; but no sooner did they make converts there than Henry VIII. included them in a decree of banishment, and those who remained he threatened to put to death. Indeed, in 1535 there is record of ten persons who were burned in London and other English towns on the charge of Anabaptism (cf. John Foxe, *Acts and Monuments*, ed. Townsend, v., London, 1843, p. 44). How little this cruel course succeeded is evidenced by the continued presence in England of the Baptist Church.

That among the sober kind of Anabaptists there were unworthy persons, that some of them held visionary views, and that a few may have been goaded into occasional violence of expression, and possibly of conduct, may be accepted as proved; but that they were as a party guilty of the charges brought against them, as in the joint edict mentioned above, is untrue. As a class they were as holy in life as their persecutors; and their leaders, in Biblical knowledge and theological acumen, were no mean antagonists.

II. The Fanatical Anabaptists: The earliest mention of Anabaptism in connection with the Lutheran Reformation is in the spring of 1521 when Niklaus Storch, Markus Stübner, and a third person, who

1. The Zwickau Prophets. was a weaver, as Storch had been, made their appearance in Wittenberg and sought to convert the professors of its university to their views, which were the familiar Anabaptist ones of opposition to military service, private property, government by those not true Christians, infant baptism, and the oath, together with the novel one that there should be a dissolution of the marriage bond in the cases where there was not agreement between the married couple in religious belief. These views they pressed with great vehemence and no little success. They also claimed to be inspired to make their deliverances. As they came from Zwickau, they are called the Zwickau Prophets (q.v.). Carlstadt was impressed by them, and characteristically allowed iconoclastic practises in his church. Melanchthon wavered, but Luther, who at the time of their visit was at the Wartburg, was so much stirred by the confusion they induced that he left his seclusion and opposed them stoutly and silenced them by ridicule rather than by arguments.

Among the leaders and followers on the peasant side in the Peasants' war which desolated Germany in 1525, were those who held antipedobaptist views. After the war Strasburg became the center of the Anabaptists and, after 1529, when it was visited by Melchior Hoffmann (q.v.), "the evil genius of the Anabaptists," it was the center of their propaganda. Hoffmann united to the usual Anabaptist views, belief in himself as the inspired interpreter of prophecy and as inspired leader generally. He declared that he was one of the "two witnesses" of Rev. xi. 3; that Strasburg was to be the New Jerusalem, and the seat of universal dominion; and that non-resistance might be given up. These views he preached with great effect through East Friesland and the Netherlands, and his followers called themselves "Melchiorites." After he had been thrown into prison (1533) Jan Matthys, a baker from Haarlem, appeared in Strasburg and claimed to be the other "witness" of the Apocalypse; but he altered the programme by transferring the capital of the kingdom of the saints to Münster, and advocating force in maintaining it. After sending four apostles, one of whom was the notorious John of Leyden, he came thither himself (Feb., 1535), and led a successful revolt against the magistracy and bishop of the city. In Apr., 1535 he was killed and was succeeded by John of Leyden who caused himself to be proclaimed king, and declared polygamy to be the law of the kingdom. Meanwhile the city was besieged by the expelled bishop aided by the neighboring princes and by the imperial troops. If half that is said to have gone on within the city be true (the reports come from very prejudiced sources), fanaticism was there the order of the day. Hence the defense was lax, owing to dependence on divine power to work deliverance. Nevertheless, the siege lasted many months, and treachery within rather than assaults without at last opened the gates on June 25, 1535 (see MÜNSTER, ANABAPTISTS IN). The fanatical Anabaptists were universally taken as typical, and to this day when Anabaptism is mentioned it is supposed to be the equivalent of absurd interpretation of Scripture, blasphemous assumption, and riotous indecency. Münster was, however, only the culminating point of fanaticism engendered by persecution, and Anabaptism in itself, strictly interpreted, is not responsible for it.

2. In Strasburg and Munster.

BIBLIOGRAPHY: The sources are the writings of Anabaptists, the official records of proceedings against them, and the writings of their opponents. Of the extensive literature, the following works may be mentioned: C. W. Bouterwek, *Zur Litteratur und Geschichte der Wiedertäufer*, Bonn, 1864; C. A. Cornelius, *Die niederländischen Wiedertäufer*, Munich, 1869; E. Egli, *Die Züricher Wiedertäufer*, Zurich, 1878; idem, *Die St. Gallen Wiedertäufer*, 1887; H. S. Burrage, *History of the Anabaptists in Switzerland*, New York, 1882; L. Keller, *Die Reformation und die älteren Reformparteien*, Leipsic, 1885; R. Nitsche, *Geschichte der Wiedertäufer in der Schweiz*, Einsiedeln, 1885; J. Loserth, *Der Anabaptismus in Tirol*, Vienna, 1892; idem, *Der Kommunismus der mährischen Wiedertäufer*, 1894; K. Kautsky, *Der Kommunismus im Mittelalter im Zeitalter der Reformation*, Stuttgart, 1894, Eng. transl., *Communism in Central Europe in the Time of the Reformation*, London, 1897; H. Lüdemann, *Reformation und Täufertum in ihrem Verhältnis zum christlichen Princip*, Bern, 1896; R. Heath, *Anabaptism from its Rise at Zwickau to 1536*, London, 1895; E. Müller, *Geschichte der bernischen Täufer*, Frauenfeld, 1895; K. Rembert, *Die Wiedertäufer im Herzogtum Jülich*, Berlin, 1899; G. Trumbült, *Die Wiedertäufer*, in *Monographien zur Weltgeschichte*, vii., Leipsic, 1899; E. C. Pike, *The Story of the Anabaptists*, in *Eras of Nonconformity*, London, 1904; the biographies of Anabaptist leaders, especially that of Balthasar Hübmaier, by H. C. Vedder, New York, 1905, and works on the Reformation. See also the works mentioned in the article, MÜNSTER, ANABAPTISTS IN.

ANACHORITE. See ANCHORET.

ANACLETUS, an″a kli′tus: The name of one pope and one antipope.

Anacletus I.: Roman presbyter at the close of the first century. The hypothesis of Volkmar, that he had no historical existence is opposed by the prevailing unanimity of the Greek and Latin lists of the popes. These differ, however, in the place which they ascribe to him, some naming him fourth and some third. The latter is the older order. As the name in Greek is sometimes written *Anenklētos* and sometimes *Klētos*, the *Catalogus Liberianus* and other early authorities were betrayed into the mistake of making two distinct persons. It is impossible to determine his date. Twelve years is the longest time assigned to his pontificate. The assertion, that he, as well as Linus and Clemens, was consecrated by St. Peter, sprang from the tendency to connect him as closely as possible with the beginnings of the Church. That he met a martyr's death under Domitian, or, as Baronius and Hausrath assert, under Trajan, can not be adequately demonstrated. His festival in the Roman Catholic Church falls on July 13.

(A. HAUCK.)

BIBLIOGRAPHY: *Liber pontificalis*, ed. Duchesne, vol. i., pp. lxix.-lxx., 52; G. Volkmar, *Ueber Eunodia, Eunodius, und Anaclet*, in Baur and Zeller, *Theologische Jahrbücher*, xvi. 147–151, Tübingen, 1857; A. Hausrath, *Neutestamentliche Zeitgeschichte*, iii. 391, Heidelberg, 1875; J. B. Lightfoot, *The Apostolic Fathers*, I. i. 201 sqq., London, 1890; A. Harnack, in *Sitzungsberichte der Berliner Akademie*, 1892, 617–658; idem, *Litteratur*, II. i. 70 sqq.

Anacletus II. (Pietro Pierleoni): Antipope, 1130-38. He was descended from a Jewish family which had grown rich and powerful under Gregory VII., studied in Paris, and later became a Cluniac monk. Paschal II. recalled him to Rome, and in 1116 made him a cardinal. He accompanied Gelasius II. on his flight to France, and after his death took a leading part in the elevation of Calixtus II., who made him legate to England and France in 1121, and, conjointly with Cardinal Gregory, who was to be his rival for the papacy, to France in 1122. It is impossible to determine how far the description of him as an immoral and avaricious prelate is based on the enmity of his later opponents; but it is certain that even under Paschal II. he was already laying his plans to be made pope. On Feb. 14, 1130, he attained his aim so far as to be chosen by a majority of the cardinals, though not to be enthroned before nine of them had elected Gregorio Papareschi as Innocent II. Anacletus used both his own resources and those of the Church to win over the Romans, and Innocent was obliged to flee. In Sept., 1130, Anacletus allied himself with Roger of Sicily, and thus made a decided enemy of Lothair the Saxon, who was already inclined to support Innocent, and now, with England and

France, declared for him. In Oct., 1131, Innocent excommunicated Anacletus at Reims; in the following spring he set out for Italy; and in Apr., 1133, entering Rome in Lothair's company, he took possession of the Lateran, while Anacletus held the Vatican. Lothair pronounced the latter an outlaw and a criminal against both the divine and the royal majesty; but he was himself forced to leave Rome in June, and Anacletus forced Innocent once more to flee to Pisa. In the autumn of 1136 Lothair returned, and succeeded in compelling southern Italy to recognize Innocent. The end of the schism was, however, due less to him than to Bernard of Clairvaux, who succeeded in separating not only the city of Milan, but many of the principal Romans from Anacletus's party (see BERNARD, SAINT, OF CLAIRVAUX). Negotiations were even opened with Roger of Sicily, his last supporter; but at this juncture Anacletus died, Jan. 25, 1138. His letters and privileges are in *MPL*, clxxix. 689–732, and in Jaffé, *Regesta*, i. 911–919. (A. HAUCK.)

BIBLIOGRAPHY: A. von Reumont, *Geschichte der Stadt Rom*, ii. 408. 3 vols., Berlin, 1867–70; P. Jaffé, *Geschichte des deutschen Reichs unter Lothar*, Berlin, 1843; Bower, *Popes*, ii. 464–470; W. Bernhardi, *Lothar von Supplinburg*, Leipsic, 1879; W. Martens, *Die Besetzung des päpstlichen Stuhls*, 323 sqq., Freiburg, 1886; Hefele, *Conciliengeschichte*, v. 406 sqq.; J. Langen, *Geschichte der römischen Kirche*, pp. 315 sqq., Bonn, 1893; Hauck, *KD*, iv. 128–138.

ANAGNOST. See LECTOR.

ANAMMELECH, a-nam'e'lec or a''nam''mê'lec: According to II Kings xvii. 31, a deity worshiped with child-sacrifice by the Sepharvites who were settled in Samaria by Sargon (see ADRAMMELECH). If Sepharvaim be sought in Babylonia, it is natural to refer the name "Anammelech" to the Babylonian god Anu (*Anu-malik* or *Anu-malku*, "King Anu"; cf. Jensen, pp. 272 sqq.; Schrader, p. 353; Bæthgen, pp. 254–255). If, however, as is more probable, Sepharvaim was a city of Syria, the Babylonian derivation is untenable. The name of a goddess Anath is found in a Greco-Phenician inscription (*CIS*, i. 95) of Lapithos in Cyprus belonging to the time of Ptolemy I. Soter (d. 283 B.C.). It occurs also on a Phenician coin with a picture of the goddess riding upon a lion, and a star above her head. The name "Anath" appears in the Old Testament towns Beth-anath (in Naphtali, Josh. xix. 38; Judges i. 33) and Beth-anoth (in Judah, Josh. xv. 59); also in the proper name "Anath" (Judges iii. 31, v. 6), and perhaps in the town Anathoth near Jerusalem. It is not impossible that the passage in II Kings is corrupt, and "Anammelech" may be merely a variant of "Adrammelech." It is wanting in Lucian's text of the Septuagint.

BIBLIOGRAPHY: P. Scholz, *Götzendienst und Zauberwesen bei den alten Hebräern und den benachborten Völkern*, pp. 405–407, Ratisbon, 1877; F. Baethgen, *Beiträge zur semitischen Religionsgeschichte*, Berlin, 1889; P. Jensen, *Die Kosmologie der Babylonier*, Strasburg, 1890; Schrader, *KAT*

ANANIAS, an''-a-nai'as: The high priest in whose time the apostle Paul was imprisoned at Jerusalem (probably 58 A.D.; Acts xxiii. 2, xxiv. 1). In the Lucan description of the conflict between Paul and Palestinian Judaism (xxi.–xxvi.; cf. K. Schmidt, *Apostelgeschichte*, i., Erlangen, 1882, pp. 240 sqq.), Ananias is represented as head of the Sadducaic hierarchical party which was dominant in the Sanhedrin, and confirmed its complete apostasy from the hope of Israel by persecution of the apostle of Christ, whereas the apostle deposes and divests of its divine authority and dignity the leadership which had become faithless to its calling. According to Josephus (*Ant.*, XX. v. 2, vi. 2, ix. 2–4; *War*, II. xii. 6, xvii. 6, 9), Ananias, son of Nebedæus, was appointed high priest about 47 A.D. by Herod of Chalcis (the twentieth in the succession of high priests from the accession of Herod the Great to the destruction of Jerusalem). In the year 52 he had to go to Rome to defend himself before Claudius against a charge made by the Samaritans against the Jews. He was not deposed at this time, however (cf. C. Wieseler, *Chronologische Synopse der vier Evangelien*, Hamburg, 1843, pp. 187–188), but held his office until Agrippa II. appointed Ishmael, son of Phabi, his successor, probably in 59 A.D. Ananias is the only high priest after Caiaphas who ruled for any length of time. He exercised considerable influence after leaving his office until he was murdered in the beginning of the Jewish war. (K. SCHMIDT.)

BIBLIOGRAPHY: Schürer, *Geschichte*, i. 584, 603, ii. 204, 219, 221, Eng. transl., I. ii. 173, 188–189, II. i. 182, 200 sqq.

ANAPHORA, an-af'o-ra: Name used in the Eastern liturgies for the later or more sacred part of the eucharistic service, answering to the *Missa fidelium* of the early times, from which the catechumens were excluded, and in the main to the canon of the Roman mass. It begins with the kiss of peace and accompanying prayers, after the "greater entrance" or solemn oblation of the elements on the altar. (GEORG RIETSCHEL.)

ANASTASIUS: Of the many bearers of this name in the Eastern Church the following three are specially deserving of notice:

1. Anastasius I.: Patriarch of Antioch, 559–599. He was a friend of Gregory I., and strongly opposed Justinian's later church policy, which favored the Aphthartodocetæ (see JULIAN OF HALICARNASSUS; JUSTINIAN; MONOPHYSITES). He was banished in 570 by Justin II., was recalled in 593 by Maurice, and died in 599. His day is Apr. 21. Of his writings there have been printed: (1) Five addresses on true dogmas; (2) four sermons (of doubtful genuineness); (3) "A Brief Exposition of the Orthodox Faith" (in Greek); (4) fragments; (5) an oration delivered Mar. 25, 593, when he resumed the patriarchal chair.

2. Anastasius II.: Patriarch of Antioch, 599–609, in which year he was murdered by Antiochian Jews. His day is Dec. 21. He translated the *Cura pastoralis* of Gregory I.

3. Anastasius Sinaita: Priest, monk, and abbot of Mount Sinai; b. before 640; d. after 700. He defended ecclesiastical theology against heretics and Jews, and composed various works which have not been fully collected and examined. They include: (1) A "Guide" in defense of the faith of the Church against the many forms of Monophysitism: (2) "Questions and Answers by Different Persons on Different Topics"; (3) "A Discourse on the Holy

Communion"; (4) anagogic observations on the six days of creation; (5) a discourse and homilies on the sixth Psalm; (6) two discourses on the creation of man in the image of God; (7) a fragment against Arianism; (8) a list of heresies; (9) "A Short and Clear Exposition of our Faith"; (10) a treatise on the celebration of Wednesday and Friday; (11) a fragment on blasphemy. The "Argument against the Jews" (*MPG*, lxxxix. 1208–82) is not earlier than the ninth century; the *Antiquorum patrum doctrina de verbi incarnatione* (ed. Mai, *Nova collectio*, vii. 1, 6–73), however, appears to be genuine. G. Krüger.

Bibliography: For the various Eastern writers named Anastasius, consult Fabricius-Harles, *Bibliotheca Græca*, x. 571–613, Hamburg, 1807. Their writings are in *MPG*, lxxxix. and in J. B. Pitra, *Juris ecclesiastici Græcorum historia et monumenta*, ii. 238–295, Rome, 1868. Also K. Krumbacher, *Geschichte der byzantinischen Litteratur*, Munich, 1897. For Anastasius Sinaita: J. B. Kumpfmüller, *De Anastasio Sinaita*, Würzburg, 1865; O. Bardenhewer, *Des heiligen Hippolytus von Rom Commentar zum Buche Daniel*, pp. 13–14, 106–107, Freiburg, 1877; A. C. McGiffert, *Dialogue between a Christian and a Jew*, 17, 35–37, New York, 1889; A. Papadopoulos-Kerameus, Ἀνάλεκτα κτλ, i., pp. 400–404, St. Petersburg, 1891; D. Serruys, *Anastasiana*, in *Mélanges d'archéologie et d'histoire*, xxii. 157–207, Rome, 1902.

ANASTASIUS, an"as-tê'shi-us or zhus: The name of four popes and one antipope.

Anastasius I.: Pope 398–401. According to the *Liber pontificalis* (ed. Duchesne, i. 218–219), he was a Roman by birth, was elected near the end of November or early in December, 398, and was pontiff three years and ten days. He is principally known for the part he took in the controversy over the teaching of Origen. He showed himself also a rigid upholder of the orthodox position against the Donatists. At the synod held in Carthage Sept. 13, 401, a letter was read from him exhorting the African bishops to expose the misrepresentations of the Donatists against the Church, and practically to hand them over to the secular arm. His letters and decrees are in *MPL*, xx. 51–80. See Origenistic Controversies. (A. Hauck.)

Bibliography: *Liber pontificalis*, ed. Duchesne, i. 218 sqq., Paris, 1886; Bower, *Popes*, i. 126–131; B. Jungmann, *Dissertationes selectæ*, ii. 205–206, Regensburg, 1881; J. Langen, *Geschichte der römischen Kirche bis Leo I.*, pp. 653 sqq., Bonn, 1881.

Anastasius II.: Pope 496–498. According to the *Liber pontificalis* (ed. Duchesne, i. 258–259), he was a Roman by birth. He was consecrated apparently on Nov. 24, 496. His pontificate fell within the period of the schism between the East and West, which lasted from 484 to 519, as a consequence of the sentence of excommunication pronounced by Pope Felix II. against Acacius, patriarch of Constantinople. Anastasius endeavored to restore communion with Constantinople, sending two bishops immediately after his consecration with a letter to the Eastern emperor offering to recognize the orders conferred by Acacius (who was now dead), at the same time asserting the justice of his condemnation. The *Liber pontificalis* (l.c.) relates that upon the arrival in Rome of the deacon Photinus of Thessalonica, Anastasius communicated with him, though he maintained the orthodoxy of Acacius and was thus, according to the Roman view, a heretic. This seems to have aroused opposition among the Roman clergy, and a suspicion arose that the pope intended to reverse the decision against Acacius. In the *Decretum* of Gratian he is said to have been "repudiated by the Roman Church" (*MPL*, clxxxvii. 111), and hence ecclesiastical writers as late as the sixteenth century usually regard him as a heretic. The baptism of Clovis, king of the Franks, fell at the beginning of his pontificate, but the letter of congratulation which the pope is supposed to have written to him is a forgery. He died in November, 498.

(A. Hauck.)

Bibliography: *Liber pontificalis*, ed. Duchesne, i. 258 sqq., Paris, 1886; Bower, *Popes*, i. 291–296; R. Baxmann, *Die Politik der Päpste von Gregor I. bis auf Gregor VII.*, i. 20 sqq., Elberfeld, 1868; J. Havet, *Questions Mérovingiennes*, Paris, 1885; J. Langen, *Geschichte der römischen Kirche bis Nicholas I.*, pp. 214 sqq., Bonn, 1885.

Anastasius III.: Pope 911–913. He was a Roman by birth. His pontificate fell in the period during which Rome and its Church were under the domination of the noble factions, and consequently little is known of his acts. Nicholas, patriarch of Constantinople, protested to him against the toleration by the legates of his predecessor, Sergius III., of the fourth marriage of the Eastern emperor, Leo VI. Before Anastasius could answer this letter, he died, probably in August, 913. Two privileges ascribed to him, one genuine, one spurious, are in *MPL*, cxxxi.

(A. Hauck.)

Bibliography: *Liber pontificalis*, ed. Duchesne, ii. 239, Paris, 1892; Bower, *Popes*, ii. 307–308; R. Baxmann, *Die Politik der Päpste*, ii. 82, Elberfeld, 1868.

Anastasius IV. (Conrad of Suburra): Pope 1153–54. He had been a canon regular and abbot of St. Rufus in the diocese of Orléans, and was made cardinal-bishop of Sabina by Honorius II. After the contested election of 1130, he had taken his stand as one of the most determined opponents of Anacletus II. He remained in Rome as the vicar of Innocent II. when the latter fled to France, and on the death of Eugenius III. (July 5, 1153), was elected to succeed him. In his short reign he ended the controversy with Frederick Barbarossa over the title to the archiepiscopal see of Magdeburg, recognizing Wichmann of Naumburg, which Eugenius III. had refused to do. The decision was looked upon in Germany as a victory for the emperor. Another long-standing dispute in England was terminated by Anastasius's final recognition of Archbishop William of York, who had been rejected by Innocent II. and Celestine II., had been confirmed by Lucius II., and had again been deposed by Eugenius III. He died Dec. 3, 1154, and was succeeded on the following day by the English cardinal Nicholas Breakspear as Adrian IV His letters and privileges are in *MPL*, clxxxviii. (A. Hauck.)

Bibliography: *Liber pontificalis*, ed. Duchesne, ii. 281, 388, 449, Paris, 1892; Bower, *Popes*, ii. 485–487; A. von Reumont, *Geschichte der Stadt Rom*, ii. 442, 3 vols., Berlin, 1867–70; Hefele, *Conciliengeschichte*, v. 537; J. Langen, *Geschichte der römischen Kirche von Gregor VII. bis Innocenz III.*, p. 414, Bonn, 1893.

Anastasius: Antipope 855. As cardinal-priest of St. Marcellus, in Rome, he had been in decided opposition to Pope Leo IV., and from 848 to 850 had been obliged to absent himself from that city. After twice inviting him to appear before a synod, Leo finally excommunicated him (Dec. 16, 850), and pronounced a still more solemn anathema against him at Ravenna (May 29, 853), repeating it in a council at Rome (June 19), and deposing him from his priestly functions (Dec. 8). Anastasius, however, relied on his wealth and his connections in Rome, and aspired to be elected pope on the death of Leo. Leo died on July 17, 855, and the Roman clergy at once chose Benedict III. to succeed him. Anastasius set himself up as a rival candidate. Accompanied by some friendly bishops and influential Romans, he intercepted the imperial ambassadors on their way to Rome, and won them over to his side. On Sept. 21 he forced his way into the Lateran, dragged Benedict from his throne, stripped him of his pontifical robes, and finally threw him into prison. These proceedings, however, caused great indignation in Rome. Not only almost all the clergy, but also the populace sided with Benedict, who was liberated and consecrated (Sept. 29) in St. Peter's. Hergenröther identifies Anastasius with the librarian of the Roman Church of the same name (see ANASTASIUS BIBLIOTHECARIUS), but this seems doubtful. The antipope relied on secular assistance, while the author was a convinced adherent of the strict ecclesiastical party. (A. HAUCK.)

BIBLIOGRAPHY: *Liber pontificalis*, ed. Duchesne, ii. 106 sqq., Paris, 1892; *MPL*, cxxviii., pp. 1331, 1345; Bower, *Popes*, ii. (1845) 227–228; J. Langen, *Geschichte der römischen Kirche bis Nicholas I.*, pp. 837, 844, Bonn, 1885; Hefele, *Conciliengeschichte*, iv. 178 sqq.

ANASTASIUS BIBLIOTHECARIUS: One of the few important men among the Roman clergy in the middle of the ninth century; d. 879. He grew up in Rome, and inherited from his uncle Arsenius (whose visits to the Carolingian courts in 865 had such an important influence on the development of the papal power) close relations with both the spiritual and secular powers of the day. He was for some time abbot of what is now Santa Maria in Trastevere, and about the end of 867 Adrian II. made him librarian of the Roman church. In 869 Emperor Louis II. sent him to Constantinople to arrange the marriage of his daughter Irmengard with the eldest son of Basil the Macedonian. Here he attended the last session of the eighth ecumenical council; and when the acts of the council, entrusted to the Roman legates, were taken from them by pirates on the homeward journey, he supplied a copy of his own. He seems to have influenced John VIII. in favor of his friend Photius. Hincmar of Reims begged his intercession, which was successful, with Adrian II. The references in Hincmar's writings seem to identify the librarian with the cardinal-priest of St. Marcellus who was the iconoclastic candidate for the papacy in 855, and was several times excommunicated. (On the question of his part in the compilation of the *Liber Pontificalis* see LIBER PONTIFICALIS.) His *Chronographia tripartita* is important for its influence on the study of general church history in the West. In a rough age, when East and West were drifting further asunder, he labored zealously to make the fruits of Eastern culture accessible to the Latins. Most of his works are in *MPL*, cxxix.; the *Chronographia tripartita* is in *Theophanis chronographia*, ed. C. de Boor, Leipsic, 1883, pp. 31–34b.

(F. ARNOLD.)

BIBLIOGRAPHY: J. Hergenröther, *Photius*, ii. 228–241, Regensburg, 1868; P. A. Lapôtre, *De Anastasio bibliothecario*, Paris, 1884; Krumbacher, *Geschichte*, pp. 122–124, 127; *Liber Pontificalis*, ed. Duchesne, ii., pp. vi., 188, Paris, 1892; Wattenbach, *DGQ*, 304, ii. 510.

ANATHEMA, a-nath'e-ma: Among the Greeks the word *anathēma* denoted an object consecrated to a divinity; a use of the word which is explained by the custom of hanging or fastening (*anatithesthai*) such objects to trees, pillars, and the like. The weaker form *anathema* was originally used side by side with *anathēma* in the same sense. The double form explains the frequent variations of manuscripts between the two, which later become confusing, since *anathema* took on a restricted signification and was used in a sense exactly opposite to *anathēma*. This later usage arose partly from the use of *anathema* in the Septuagint as an equivalent for the Hebrew *ḥerem*, which is correct enough according to the root-idea of the Hebrew word; but the latter had acquired a special meaning in the religious law of the Old Testament, designating not only that which was dedicated to God and withdrawn from ordinary use as holy, but also and more especially that which was offered to God in expiation, to be destroyed. In like manner *anathema* came to denote not only what belonged irrevocably to God, but what was abandoned to him for punishment or annihilation. This double meaning is explicable by the interrelation of law and religion under the old covenant. The declaration of *ḥerem* recognized God's right to exclusive possession of certain things and to the annihilation of whatever offended his majesty. Under this law booty taken in war was wholly or partly destroyed (Deut. xiii. 16; Josh. vi. 18, viii. 26), idolatrous peoples were put to death, and cities were razed, never to be rebuilt (Josh. vi. 26; I Kings xvi. 34). The same double sense of *ḥerem*, *anathema*, is found in the early Greek and Roman law, which has the same combination of religious and secular bearing; *devotio* in one aspect is the same as the Greek *kathierōsis*, in another as *imprecatio*, *maledictio*, *exsecratio*.

In postexilic Israel the *ḥerem* found a new use as a penal measure directed to the maintenance of the internal purity of the community. It then denoted the penalty of exclusion or excommunication, sometimes with confiscation of property (Ezra x. 8). It was developed by the synagogue into two grades, *niddui* (Luke vi. 22; John ix. 22, xii. 42) and *ḥerem*, which included the pronouncing of a curse. It was now an official act with a formal ritual. The connection between exclusion and cursing explains the use of *anathema* in the sense of simple cursing (Mark xiv. 71) or of binding by a solemn vow (Acts xxiii. 12). In the technical sense the word *anathema* occurs in four passages of Paul's epistles, all of which show that he was thinking of a definite and recognized conception and a purely spiritual one (Rom. ix. 3; I Cor. xii. 3, xvi. 22; Gal. i. 8, 9). The falling under this solemn curse is conditioned and justified by the act of the subject, in failing to love God or in preaching a false gospel. These passages show that Paul was not thinking of anathema as a disciplinary measure of the community, as under the synagogue; there is no connection between it and the penalties inflicted on moral offenders (I Cor. v. 5, 11; I Tim. i. 20). It is pronounced only against those who set themselves in treasonable opposition to God himself, to his truth and his revelation. Paul's use of the word, therefore, goes back of the practise of the synagogue to the Septuagint use. This explains the fact that in the development of ecclesiastical discipline the word "anathema" is not used as a technical term for excommunication before the fourth century. It occurs in the canons of Elvira (305) against mockers and in those of Laodicea (341?) against Judaizers; and after the Council of Chalcedon (451) it becomes a fixed formula of excommunication, used especially against heretics, as in the anathemas of the Council of Trent and later papal utterances. No settled unity of belief has, however, been arrived at in regard to it; now absolute finality of operation is claimed for it, now it is considered as revocable. And there is as little agreement as to its effects, the limits of its use, and its position in the scale of penalties. Du Cange includes the prevalent conceptions of it when he defines it as "excommunication inflicted by bishop or council, not amounting quite to the major excommunication, but still accompanied by execration and cursing." See EXCOMMUNICATION. (G. HEINRICI.)

BIBLIOGRAPHY: See under EXCOMMUNICATION.

ANATOLIUS, an"a-tō'li-us, **OF CONSTANTINOPLE**: Patriarch of Constantinople; d. 458. He belonged to the Alexandrian school, was *apocrisiarius* at Constantinople of Dioscurus of Alexandria (q.v.), and succeeded Flavian as patriarch after the "Robber Synod" of Ephesus (449). It was a time of conflict, and Anatolius was more than once accused of heresy, ambition, and injustice. At the Council of Chalcedon (451) he succeeded in having reaffirmed a canon of the second general council (Constantinople, 381) which placed Constantinople on an equal footing with Rome. He crowned the emperor Leo I. in 457, which is said by Gibbon (chap. xxxvi.) to be the first instance of the performance of such a ceremony by an ecclesiastic. Anatolius is identified by John Mason Neale (*Hymns of the Eastern Church*, London, 1862) with the author of the hymns (in Neale's translation) *Fierce was the wild billow*, and *The day is past and over*. Others think that Anatolius the hymn-writer lived at a later time.

BIBLIOGRAPHY: *DCB*, i. 111; Julian, *Hymnology*, pp. 63, 1140.

ANATOLIUS OF LAODICEA: Bishop of Laodicea in the third century. He was a native of Alexandria, and excelled in rhetoric and philosophy, the natural sciences, and mathematics. His fellow citizens requested him to establish a school of Aristotelian philosophy. In 262 he left Alexandria, acted for a time as coadjutor of Bishop Theotecnus of Cæsarea, and was made bishop of Laodicea in 268 or 269. Eusebius (*Hist. eccl.*, VII. xxxii. 14–20) gives a considerable extract from a work of his on the paschal festival, and mentions another, in ten books, on calculation. The Latin *Liber Anatoli de ratione paschali* probably belongs to the sixth century. It is in *MPG*, x., and in B. Krusch, *Studien zur mittelälterlichen Chronologie*, Leipsic, 1880, pp. 311–327; cf. *ANF*, vi. 146–153. G. KRÜGER.

BIBLIOGRAPHY: T. Zahn, *Forschungen zur Geschichte des Kanons*, iii. 177–196, Leipsic, 1884; A. Anscombe, *The Paschal Canon attributed to Anatolius of Laodicea*, in *English Historical Review*, x. (1895) 515–535; Krüger, *History*, p. 216.

ANCHIETA, ān"shî-ē'tα, **JOSÉ DE**: The apostle of Brazil; b. at La Laguna, Teneriffe, Canary Islands, 1533; d. at Retirygba, Brazil, June 15, 1597 He joined the Jesuits in 1550, and three years later went to Brazil. In 1567 he was ordained priest, and thenceforth lived as missionary in the wild interior, laboring amid great hardships for the conversion of the savages. He became provincial before his death. Both the Indians and the Portuguese believed that he worked miracles. He wrote two catechisms in the native Brazilian tongue, a dictionary of the same, and a grammar (*Arte de grammatica da lingoa mais usada na costa do Brasil*, Coimbra, 1595), which is the standard work on the subject. A treatise by him in Latin on the natural products of Brazil was published by the Academy of Sciences at Lisbon (1812).

BIBLIOGRAPHY: His life has been published in Spanish (Jerez de la Frontera, 1677), in Portuguese (Lisbon, 1672), in Latin (Cologne, 1617), and in English (London, 1849).

ANCHORET (ANCHORITE, ANACHORITE): A name applied to one of the class of early ascetics who withdrew from the world to devote themselves in solitude to the service of God and the care of their souls, practically synonymous with hermit. See ASCETICISM; MONASTICISM.

ANCILLON, ān-sî'yen: Name of an old Huguenot family of France, one of whose members resigned a high judicial position in the sixteenth century for the sake of his faith. His son, **Georges Ancillon**, was one of the founders of the Evangelical Church of Metz. Other members of the family were the following:

David Ancillon: Great-grandson of Georges Ancillon; b. at Metz Mar. 17, 1617; d. at Berlin Sept. 3, 1692. He attended the Jesuit college of his native city, studied theology at Geneva (1633–41), and was appointed preacher at Meaux (1641) and Metz (1653). In 1657 he held a conference on the traditions of the Church with Dr. Bédaciar, suffragan of the bishop of Metz; and, as a false report of this conference was spread by a monk, he published his celebrated *Traité de la Tradition* (Sedan, 1657). At the revocation of the edict of Nantes he went to Frankfort and became pastor at Hanau (1685), where he wrote an apology of Luther, Zwingli, Calvin, and Beza. Later he went to Berlin, where the Elector Frederick William appointed him preacher to the French congregation. The

Vie de Farel, which appeared at Amsterdam in 1691 under his name, is a mutilated copy of a manuscript which he had not intended for publication.

Charles Ancillon: Eldest son of David Ancillon; b. at Metz July 28, 1659; d. in Berlin July 5, 1715. He was judge and director of the French colony in Brandenburg and historiographer to Frederick I. Of his writings the following have interest for the Church historian: *Réflexions politiques* (Cologne, 1685); *Irrévocabilité de l'édit de Nantes* (Amsterdam, 1688); *Histoire de l'établissement des Français réfugiés dans les états de Brandebourg* (Berlin, 1690). He published also *Mélange critique de littérature* (3 vols., Basel, 1698), based upon conversations with his father, and containing an account of his life.

Jean Pierre Frédéric Ancillon: Great-grandson of Charles Ancillon; b. in Berlin Apr. 30, 1767; d. there Apr. 19, 1837. He was teacher in the military academy of Berlin and preacher to the French congregation, his sermons attracting much attention. In 1806 he was appointed tutor to the crown prince, and in 1825 minister of state, which position he retained till his death. He published two volumes of sermons (Berlin, 1818).

Bibliography: E. and É. Haag, *La France protestante*, i. 80–96, Paris, 1846; R. L. Poole, *A History of the Huguenots of the Dispersion*, pp. 144 sqq., London, 1880; G. de Felice, *Histoire des protestants de France*, pp. 377 378, Toulouse, 1895.

ANCYRA, an-sai'ra, **SYNOD OF:** A council held at Ancyra (the modern Angora, 215 m. e.s.e. of Constantinople), a considerable town in the center of Galatia. The year is not stated, but it was probably soon after the downfall of Maximinus had freed the Eastern Church from persecution, presumably in 314. Nine canons of the synod deal with the treatment of the lapsed. The tenth permits deacons to marry if they have expressed such an intention at their ordination. The thirteenth forbids chorepiscopi to ordain priests and deacons. From the eighteenth canon it may be inferred that the episcopate of Asia Minor was inclined to appoint bishops without regard to the right of election on the part of the people, and that the latter frequently succeeded in opposing such appointments; it also provides that bishops named for any church but not received by it must remain members of the presbytery to which they had belonged, and not seek an opportunity to exercise episcopal jurisdiction elsewhere. (A. Hauck.)

Bibliography: Hefele, *Conciliengeschichte*, i. 219–242, Eng. transl., i. 199–222.

ANDERSON, CHARLES PALMERSTON: Protestant Episcopal bishop of Chicago; b. at Kemptville, Canada, Sept. 8, 1864. He was educated at Trinity College School, Port Hope, Ont., and Trinity University, Toronto (B.D., 1888). He was ordained priest in 1888 and was rector at Beachburg, Ont., in 1888–91, and at Grace Church, Oak Park, Chicago, in 1891–1900. In the latter year he was consecrated bishop coadjutor of Chicago, and on the death of Bishop William E. McLaren in 1905 he became bishop. He is a member of the committee of the Episcopal Church on Capital and Labor and of the Sunday-School Commission, and is the author of *The Christian Ministry* (Milwaukee, 1902).

ANDERSON, GALUSHA: Baptist; b. at Clarendon, N. Y., Mar. 7, 1832 He was educated at Rochester University (B.A., 1854) and Rochester Theological Seminary (1856). He was pastor of a Baptist church at Janesville, Wis., from 1856 to 1858 and of the Second Baptist Church, St. Louis, from 1858 to 1866, when he was appointed professor of homiletics, church polity, and pastoral theology in Newton Theological Institution, Newton Centre, Mass. In 1873 he resumed the ministry and was pastor of the Strong Place Baptist Church, Brooklyn, in 1873–76 and of the Second Baptist Church, Chicago, in 1876–78. From 1878 to 1885 he was president of Chicago University, and after a pastorate of two years at the First Baptist Church, Salem, Mass. (1885–87), he occupied a similar position at Denison University until 1890. In the latter year he was appointed professor in the Baptist Union Theological Seminary, Morgan Park, Ill., and from 1892 until his retirement as professor emeritus in 1904 was professor of practical theology in the Divinity School of the University of Chicago. In collaboration with E. J. Goodspeed he translated selected homilies of Asterius, under the title *Ancient Sermons for Modern Times* (New York, 1904).

ANDERSON, JOSEPH: Congregationalist; b. at Broomtoro (a hamlet of Rossshire), Scotland, Dec. 16, 1836. He was educated at the College of the City of New York (B.A., 1854) and Union Theological Seminary (1857), and held successive pastorates at the First Congregational Church, Stamford, Conn. (1858-61), the First Congregational Church, Norwalk, Conn. (1861–64), and the First Congregational Church, Waterbury, Conn. (1865–1905), of which he is now pastor emeritus. He was moderator of the General Association of Connecticut in 1877 and 1890, and of the General Conference of Congregational Churches in 1878, and has been a member of the Yale Corporation since 1884. He was also president of the Connecticut Bible Society in 1884 1904 and a delegate to the International Congregational Council held at London in 1891. He is vice-president of the American Social Science Association and of the Mattatuck Historical Society, as well as a corporate member of the American Board of Commissioners for Foreign Missions, a director of the Missionary Society of Connecticut since 1875, and a member of the American Antiquarian Society and the American Historical Association. Among his numerous works special mention may be made of *The Town and City of Waterbury* (3 vols., Waterbury, Conn., 1896), which he edited and in great part wrote.

ANDERSON, LARS. See Andreä, Lorenz.

ANDERSON, MARTIN BREWER: American Baptist; b. at Brunswick, Me., Feb. 12, 1815; d. at Lake Helen, Fla., Feb. 26, 1890. He was graduated at Waterville College (Colby University), Me., 1840; studied at Newton Theological Institution 1840–41; was tutor in Latin, Greek, and mathematics in Waterville College 1841–43, and professor of rhetoric 1843–50. He was editor-in-chief and joint proprietor, with the Rev. James S. Dickerson, of *The New York Recorder*, a Baptist weekly newspaper (later known as *The Examiner*), 1850–53, and first president of the University of Rochester, N. Y., 1853-88. He was president of the American Baptist Home Missionary Society 1864–66, of the American Baptist Missionary Union 1870–72, and member of the New York State Board of Charities 1868-72. A volume of selections from his *Papers and Addresses*, was edited by W C. Morey (2 vols., Philadelphia, 1895).

BIBLIOGRAPHY: A. C. Kendrick and Florence Kendrick, *Martin Brewer Anderson, a Biography*, Philadelphia, 1895.

ANDERSON, RUFUS: American Congregationalist; b. at North Yarmouth, Me., Aug. 17, 1796; d. in Boston May 30, 1880. He was graduated at Bowdoin College 1818; studied at Andover Theological Seminary 1819–22; became assistant to the corresponding secretary of the American Board 1822, assistant secretary 1824, and foreign secretary 1832, which last position he filled till 1866, resigning then because he was convinced that the age of seventy years constitutes "a limit beyond which it would not be wise to remain in so arduous a position." He visited officially the missions of the Board in the Mediterranean 1828–29 and again in 1843–44, in India 1854–55, and in the Sandwich Islands 1863. His published works include: *Observations on the Peloponnesus and Greek Islands* (Boston, 1830); *Foreign Missions, their Relations and Claims* (New York, 1869); *A Heathen Nation* [the Sandwich Islanders] *Evangelized* (1870); a history of the missions of the American Board to the Oriental churches (2 vols., 1872) and in India (1874).

ANDERSON, WILLIAM FRANKLIN: Methodist Episcopalian; b. at Morgantown, W Va., Apr. 22, 1860. He was educated at the State University of West Virginia, Morgantown, W Va., Ohio Wesleyan University, Delaware, O. (B.A., 1884), Drew Theological Seminary (B.D., 1887), and New York University (M.A., 1897). He has held successive pastorates at the Mott Avenue Methodist Episcopal Church (1887–89), St. James's Church, Kingston, N. Y. (1890–94), Washington Square, New York (1895–98), and Highland Avenue Church, Ossining, N. Y. (1899–1904). He was recording secretary of the Board of Education of the Methodist Episcopal Church from 1898 to 1904, when he was elected corresponding secretary. In 1898 he was made a member of the Board of Managers of the Missionary Society of the Methodist Episcopal Church, and was a member of the General Missionary Committee in 1901–02. In theology he is progressively conservative. He is the editor of *The Christian Student*, and in addition to numerous contributions to religious magazines has written *The Compulsion of Love* (Cincinnati, 1904).

ANDRADA, an-drā'da, **ANTONIO D':** Jesuit missionary; b. at Villa de Oleiros, Alemtejo, Portugal, about 1580; d. at Goa Mar. 16, 1634. He went to the missions in the East Indies, became superior of the missions of Mongolia, and made two journeys into Tibet, being one of the first Europeans to penetrate that land. He published an account of his first journey (1624) under the title *Novo descubrimento do Graõ Catayo o dos Reynos de Tibet* (Lisbon, 1626). His letter from Tibet for 1626 was published in Italian (Rome, 1626) and French (Paris, 1629).

ANDRADA, DIDACUS, did'a-cus **(DIOGO) PAYVA D':** Theologian; b. at Coimbra, Portugal, July 26, 1528; d. at Lisbon Dec. 1, 1575. He joined the Jesuits, taught theology at Coimbra, and was one of the Portuguese delegates to the Council of Trent. He replied to Martin Chemnitz's attack on the Jesuits (*Theologiæ Jesuitarum præcipua capita*, Leipsic, 1562), in his *Explicationum orthodoxarum de controversis religionis capitibus libri decem* (Venice and Cologne, 1564; the first book, *De origine Societatis Jesu*, was published separately at Louvain, 1566, and, in French at Lyons, 1565). Chemnitz then wrote his celebrated *Examen concilii Tridentini quadripartitum* (Frankfort, 1565–73). Andrada was prevented by death from finishing his reply, but what he had prepared was published under the title, *Defensio Tridentinæ fidei catholicæ quinque libri* (Lisbon, 1578). See CHEMNITZ. He was a brother of the Augustinian monk known as Thomas a Jesu (q.v.).

BIBLIOGRAPHY: H. Hurter, *Nomenclator literarius recentioris theologiæ catholicæ*, i. 43 sqq., Innsbruck, 1892.

ANDREÄ, an'drê-a, **JAKOB:** Lutheran; b. at Waiblingen (7 m. n.e. of Stuttgart), Württemberg, Mar. 25, 1528; d. at Tübingen Jan. 7, 1590. He was educated at the Pædagogium at Stuttgart, and studied theology at Tübingen from 1541 to 1546. In the latter year he became deacon at Stuttgart, but had to leave in 1548, after the introduction of the Interim (q.v.), and went to Tübingen, where he was appointed deacon at the *Stiftskirche*. In 1553 he took the degree of doctor of theology, was appointed city pastor and afterward superintendent-general at Göppingen. He now developed activity in behalf of the Evangelical Church at large, helping to introduce the Reformation in many places. In 1557 he attended the diets of Frankfort and Regensburg, and was present at the Conference of Worms. In 1559 he attended the Diet of Augsburg; in 1560 he held a church-visitation in Lauingen; in 1561 he was at Erfurt; and in the fall of the same year, in company with the Tübingen chancellor Jakob Beurlin and the Stuttgart court-preacher Balthasar Bidembach, he went to Paris to attend the religious colloquy in Poissy.

Beurlin having died at Paris, Andreä was appointed professor of theology, provost, and chancellor in Tübingen. In 1563 he went to Strasburg to settle a dispute caused by Zanchi on the *inamissibilitas gratiæ*, in 1564 he attended the conference in Bebenhausen to examine the Heidelberg Catechism, and the colloquy in Maulbronn. In 1568 his prince sent him to Brunswick-Wolfenbüttel to assist in the introduction of the Reformation and in framing an Evangelical Church ordinance; at the same time also he joined with Chemnitz, Selnekker, and other theologians of northern Germany, in paving the way for a consensus of the Saxon and other Evangelical Churches. Therewith began the most important period in Andreä's life, his activity in behalf of the Formula of Concord.

Andreä's first plan was to neutralize the differences by means of formulas so general that they could be accepted by all. Two years were spent in traveling, during which he visited every Evangelical Church, university, and city in northern and southern Germany, and conferred with all important theologians. But neither the Flacians nor the Philippists, the two extreme parties among the Lutherans, had full confidence in him; and in the convention at Zerbst, May, 1570, his attempt proved a failure. Andreä now changed his plan. There was to be no more attempt at compromise, but the line was to be sharply drawn between Lutherans and the adherents of Zwingli and Calvin; and thus the Philippists and all other individual shades of Lutheranism were to be destroyed. Andreä preached six sermons on the points in controversy in 1572 and published them in the two following years. Copies were sent to Duke Julius, Chemnitz, Chyträus, and others. He then sent an epitome of these sermons, with the approval of the Tübingen faculty and the Stuttgart consistory, to the theologians of north Germany, for examination and criticism, who introduced some changes and produced the so-called Swabian-Saxon *Concordia*. A comparison of this Swabian-Saxon *Concordia* with Andreä's original Swabian *Concordia* and the Maulbronn Formula by a convention at Torgau, May 28, 1576, resulted in the *Liber Torgensis*, which was again revised by Andreä, Chemnitz, and Selnekker at the monastery of Bergen in March, 1577. Three further conferences were held at Bergen, May 19–28, 1580, at which Chyträus, Musculus, and Körner were present besides Andreä, Chemnitz, and Selnekker. The outcome was the *Bergische Buch* or *Formula Concordiæ*, which appeared June 25, 1580, and which became the symbolical book of the Lutheran Church (see FORMULA OF CONCORD). Andreä received much abuse—even Selnekker, Chyträus, and Chemnitz were dissatisfied—but he bore it patiently, convinced that he had worked for the truth and the peace of the Church. He continued his reformatory work, visited churches, and took part in controversies; at the request of Duke Frederick of Württemberg he spoke against Beza at the colloquy of Mümpelgart in March, 1586, discussing the Lord's Supper, the person of Christ, predestination, baptism, etc.

There is no collected edition of Andreä's writings, which numbered more than one hundred and fifty. Among the more noteworthy were: *Refutatio criminationum Hosii* (Tübingen, 1560); *De duabus naturis in Christo* (1565); *Bericht von der Ubiquität* (1589); *De instauratione studii theologici*, *De studio sacrarum literarum*, published posthumously (1591 sqq.). His sermons have been often published (cf. *Zwanzig Predigten von den Jahren 1557, 1559, 1560*, ed. Schmoller, Gütersloh, 1890). (T. KOLDE.)

BIBLIOGRAPHY: J. V. Andreä, *Fama Andreana reflorescens*, Strasburg, 1630 (an autobiography written in 1562, edited by his grandson, the main source for Andreä's life); C. M. Fittbogen, *Jacob Andreä, der Verfasser des Concordienbuches. Sein Leben und seine theologische Bedeutung*, Leipsic, 1881 (not altogether satisfactory); *KL*, i. 818-821.

ANDREÄ, JOHANN VALENTIN: Theologian and satirist, grandson of Jakob Andreä; b. at Herrenberg, near Tübingen, Württemberg, Aug. 17, 1586; d. at Stuttgart June 27, 1654. In 1601 he entered the University of Tübingen, where his reading covered a vast range on the mathematical sciences, language, philosophy, theology, music, and art. After living for a number of years as tutor in noble families and traveling extensively in France, Switzerland, Austria, and Italy, he became deacon at Vaihingen, Württemberg, in 1614. His duties gave him leisure for prolific authorship, and forty of his writings (numbering about 100 in all) were produced during his six years' sojourn in Vaihingen. In 1612 he published *De christiani cosmoxeni genitura*, a eulogy of early Christianity, and *Die Christenburg*, an epic allegory dealing with the struggles and ultimate triumph of the Christian soul. These were followed by *Turbo* (1616), a comedy in which pedantry was wittily satirized, and *Menippus* (1618), of which worldly folly was the subject. In 1619 he published *Reipublicæ christianopolitanæ descriptio*, an account of an ideal Christian state after the manner of More's *Utopia* and Campanella's *City of the Sun*. In all of these Andreä appears as a foe of sectarianism and intolerance, and with wit and energy pleads for a union of denominations on the basis of the fundamental Christian teachings. In 1614 there appeared anonymously *Fama fraternitatis Roseæ Crucis*, followed the next year by *Confessio fraternitatis Roseæ Crucis*, satires on the astrological and mystic agitations of the time. Andreä, whose authorship of the two pamphlets is more than probable, though not established beyond doubt, later declared that the Order of the Rosicrucians (q.v.) was a myth and a product of his own brain; nevertheless he has been spoken of as the founder or restorer of that fraternity.

From 1620 to 1639 Andreä was superintendent at Calw, displaying in the unhappy days of the Thirty Years' war heroic devotion to duty. In 1634 Calw was sacked, and of its 4,000 inhabitants only 1,500 escaped the sword, while the plague carried off nearly one-half of the remainder. Andreä worked unceasingly among the dying, uniting in himself the duties of physician, minister, and grave-digger, and when the progress of the infection had been checked he set to work resolutely to restore law and order in the devastated city. In 1639 he was called to Stuttgart as court preacher with a seat in the Consistorium. Upon him fell the task of reorganizing the church system and the schools which had shared in the ruin that the war had brought. An admirer of the Genevan system of government, he attempted to introduce its principal features into the country, but failed because of the opposition of his fellow members in the Consistorium. He was partially successful, however, in establishing general and local conventions composed of government officials and members of the clergy for the enforcement of the church laws. The public regulation of private morals was a cardinal principle with him through life, and found expression in his *Theophilus*, written in 1622 and published in 1649. This work contains also a dissertation on the education of the young that entitles Andreä to serious consideration as a predecessor of Pestalozzi. In 1650 Andreä became general superintendent in Württemberg, but was compelled by failing health to resign his office.

(H. Hölscher.)

Bibliography: His autobiography was published in Germ. by D. C. Seybold in 1799, and in the original Latin by F. H. Rheinwald, Berlin, 1849. Consult also W. Hossbach, *J. V Andreä und sein Zeitalter*, Berlin, 1819; K. Hüllemann, *V. Andreae als Pädagog*, 2 vols., Leipsic, 1884–93; J. P. Glöckler, *J. V Andreä*, Stuttgart, 1886; A. Landenberger, *J. V Andreae*, Barmen, 1886; P. Wurm, *J. V. Andreä*, Calw, 1887.

ANDREÄ, LORENZ (LARS ANDERSON): The great ecclesiastico-political Swedish reformer; b. probably at Strengnäs (40 m. e. of Stockholm) about 1480; d. there Apr. 29, 1552. He was archdeacon of Strengnäs when through Olaus Petri (q.v.) he was converted to the Lutheran views. In 1523 the newly chosen king Gustavus Vasa chose him to be his chancellor. As such he aided Olaus and Laurentius Petri in their reformatory activity and contributed largely to bring about the religious liberty granted at the Diet of Vesterås in 1527, and the full introduction of the Reformation at the Council of Oerebo in 1529. In 1540 he and Olaus Petri opposed the effort of Vasa to transform the Swedish Church in the direction of presbyterianism and thus roused the king's anger. On trumped up charges of high treason Andreä was sentenced to death. The king pardoned him but deprived him of his offices and he lived the rest of his life in retirement. He wrote *Tro och Gerningar* ("Faith and Good-Works"), reprinted Stockholm, 1857. See Sweden.

ANDREW THE APOSTLE: One of the twelve apostles, brother of Peter; born, like him, in Bethsaida (John i. 40, 44), and a member of Peter's family in Capernaum (Mark i. 29). According to John i. 35–42, Andrew was one of the first to follow Jesus in consequence of the testimony of the Baptist, and he brought Peter to the Lord. In Jesus's later choice of disciples in Galilee Peter and Andrew were the first whom he called to follow him permanently and intimately (Matt. iv. 18–20; Mark i. 16–18). It is not therefore without good reason that the Greeks give to Andrew the epithet "the first called." According to the *Acta Andreæ* (Tischendorf, *Acta apostolorum apocrypha*, Leipsic, 1851, pp. xl. sqq., 105 sqq.; R. A. Lipsius, *Die apokryphen Apostelgeschichten*, i., Brunswick, 1883, 543 sqq.), he labored in Greece; according to Eusebius (*Hist. eccl.*, iii. 1), in Scythia, whence the Russians worship him as their apostle. His day is Nov. 30, because, according to tradition, he was crucified on that day at Patræ in Achaia by the proconsul Ægeas upon a *crux decussata* (X, hence known as St. Andrew's cross; cf. Fabricius, *Codex apocryphus*, Hamburg, 1703, pp. 456 sqq.). The name Andrew, although Greek, was common among Jews (Dio Cassius, lxviii. 32).

(K. Schmidt.)

Bibliography: *DB*, i. (1898) 92–93, contains a résumé of the contents of apocryphal literature; the reference to Lipsius in the text points to the fullest discussion of this literature; Harnack, *Litteratur*, i. 127–128; *DCB*, i. 30.

ANDREW OF CÆSAREA: Metropolitan of Cæsarea in Cappadocia, author of a commentary on the Apocalypse which has some importance in exegetical history. He has been variously thought to have flourished between the fifth and the ninth centuries. His time was certainly after the Persian persecutions and the strife between Arians and the orthodox "New Rome." A reference of the prophecy of Gog and Magog to the Scythian peoples of the extreme north, "whom we call Huns," has been thought to indicate the period before the rule of the Huns was broken; but the parallel in Arethas (*MPG*, cvi. 756) shows that "Huns" was used as a generic name for barbarian invaders. The only sure criterion by which the earliest possible date may be determined is Andrew's citation of authorities. The latest of these is the so-called Dionysius the Areopagite, whose writings are first certainly mentioned in 533; so that Andrew can not have written before the middle of the sixth century. He cites as witnesses to the inspiration of the Apocalypse, Papias, Irenæus, Methodius, Hippolytus, Gregory Nazianzen, and Cyril of Alexandria. His striking omission of Origen is explicable, in the light of his dependence on the latter's bitter opponent Methodius, by the recrudescence of Origenistic controversy in the sixth century. Other authorities are Epiphanius, Basil, Eusebius, and Justin; of non-Christian writers, he once cites Josephus.

Andrew's expository method is set forth in the introductory dedication to his brother and fellow worker Macarius The Apocalypse, he says, like any other inspired Scripture, is at once historical, tropological, and anagogical; but the last aspect is most prominent in it, and requires unfolding. The expositor must, however, observe his limits. God has made his revelation in Christ susceptible by the human intellect; and so history and mystery are not to be treated alike. But the explanation may at least console and edify the reader by showing the transitoriness of all earthly things and by teaching him to long for the glories of the future. Andrew's exposition is accordingly characterized by the effort to arrive at a Christian interpretation of history, by an interest in its facts, and by a cautious restraint in the elucidation of prophecy. But in spite of this, his conception that the Apocalypse as a whole offers a clear revelation of the divine government of the world colors his exposition throughout. His style is usually glossarial, though here and there he adds an edifying excursus. Where necessary, he gives different views, leaving the reader to take his choice; but his commentary is much more than a mere catena, the quotations occupying a relatively small space. From the standpoint of textual criticism, as was first recognized by Bengel, the commentary has an importance of its own. Matthæi noticed that the glosses of Andrew had not seldom crept into the manuscripts; and F. Delitzsch was inclined to attribute the uncertainty of the cursive texts of the Apocalypse to the influence of the commentaries of Andrew and Arethas (q.v.). The commentary is in *MPG*, cvi. (G. Heinrici.)

Bibliography: *DCB*, i. 154–155; *KL*, i. 830–832.

ANDREW OF CARNIOLA: Archbishop of Carniola (Krain) in the fifteenth century. He was a Slavonian, and became a Dominican monk. Through the favor of the Emperor Frederick III. he was made archbishop of Carniola with residence at Laibach. He assumed the title "Cardinal of San Sisto." In 1482 he went to Switzerland and tried to get a general council convened at Basel. On July 21 he nailed a formal arraignment of Pope Sixtus IV to the doors of the cathedral, accompanying it with a demand for a council. The pope excommunicated him, and the local authorities put him in prison, where he was found dead on Nov. 13, 1484. probably having committed suicide. His secretary, Peter Numagen of Treves, thought him crazy.

Bibliography: Peter Numagen, *Gesta archiepiscopi Craynensis*, in J. H. Hottinger, *Historiæ ecclesiasticæ Novi Testamenti*, iv. 347–604, Zurich, 1654; J. Burckhardt, *Erzbischof Andreas von Krain und der letzte Concilsversuch in Basel, 1482–84*, Basel, 1852; E. Frantz, *Sixtus IV und die Republik Florenz*, pp. 433 sqq., Regensburg, 1880.

ANDREW OF CRETE: Archbishop of Crete; b. at Damascus; d. not earlier than 726. He became a monk at Jerusalem (whence he is sometimes called Andrew of Jerusalem), and was sent by the Patriarch Theodore to the sixth general council (Constantinople, 680). Later he was made archbishop. He was inclined to Monothelitism, but was able to restore his reputation for orthodoxy by zeal for image-worship. He is commemorated as a saint in the Greek Church on July 7. Among Greek hymn-writers he occupies a prominent place as the inventor of the so-called canons (see Canon). His penitential canon ("the great canon") of 250 strophes is especially famous. It is still sung on the Thursday before Palm Sunday and on some other days of Lent. Andrew was also the author of many homilies, some of them very long.

G. Krüger.

Bibliography: Andrew's works are in *MPG*, xcvii.; *Anthologia Græca*, ed. W. Christ and M. Paranikas, 147–161, Leipsic, 1871; Πατμιακὴ βιβλιοθήκη, pp. 330–331, Athens, 1890; A. Papadopoulos-Kerameus, Ἀνάλεκτα κτλ, i. 1–14, St. Petersburg, 1891; A. Maltzew, *Andachtsbuch der orthodox-katholischen Kirche des Morgenlandes*, 176–277, Berlin, 1895. A few stanzas of the Great Canon, with two or three other hymns are translated in J. M. Neale's *Hymns of the Eastern Church*, pp. 73–84, London, 1876, where a brief sketch of his life is given. Consult Fabricius-Harles, *Bibliotheca Græca*, xi. 62–64, 68–75, Hamburg, 1808; *Analecta sacra*, ed. J. B. Pitra, i. 626–627, Paris, 1876; A. Ehrhard, in Krumbacher's *Geschichte*, p. 165; F. Diekamp, *Hippolytos von Theben*, p. 108, Münster, 1898.

ANDREW OF LUND (ANDERS SUNESÖN): Archbishop of Lund; b. at Knarthorp (3 m. n.w. of Copenhagen) about 1160; d. on the island of Ivö (in Lake Ivö, near Lund) June 24, 1228. He came of the noble family of Hvide whose members filled the highest offices in Church and State. In 1182 he went to Paris, completed his studies there, and, returning in 1190, was made dean of the cathedral of Roeskilde, where his elder brother was bishop. Canute VI. made him at the same time court-chancellor. In 1194–96 he was on mission to Rome and Paris in regard to the repudiation, by Philip Augustus of France, of his wife Ingeborg, a sister of the Danish king. In 1201 Andrew succeeded Absalon as archbishop of Lund, an office which carried with it the dignities of primate and papal legate.

Andrew was zealous in the suppression of concubinage among the priesthood, active in raising the standard of learning among them, and an enemy to the sale of indulgences. In 1206 he preached a crusade against the heathen inhabitants of the island of Oesel off the coast of Esthonia. When Albert of Riga (q.v.) was compelled to seek the aid of the Danes against the Russians and Esthonians in 1218, he agreed to place the bishopric of Esthonia under the authority of the archbishop of Lund, and in the following year Andrew was engaged in regulating the affairs of that see. In 1223 he resigned his office and retired to the island of Ivö in the lake of the same name, achieving a reputation for wonder-working sanctity. He was the author of *Lex Scandiæ provincialis* (ed. P. G. Thorsen, Copenhagen, 1853) and *Hexaëmeron* (ed. M. C. Gertz, ib. 1892), a dogmatic poem in twelve books, expository of the theology of Peter Lombard.

(F. Nielsen.)

Bibliography: P. E. Müller, *Vita Andreæ Sunonis, Archiepiscopi Lundensis*, Copenhagen, 1830; F. Hammerich, *En skolastiker og en Bibeltheolog fra Norden*, ib. 1865.

ANDREW AND PHILIP, BROTHERHOOD OF: An interdenominational religious society for men of all ages. The sole object, as declared by the constitution, is to spread Christ's kingdom among men. The brotherhood was founded by the Rev. Rufus Wilder Miller, of the Reformed Church, who organized the first local chapter at Reading, Pa., May 4, 1888. Other chapters were formed in the same denomination, conventions began to be held, and the *Brotherhood Star*, the monthly bulletin of the association was established. At the convention of Reformed chapters at Bethlehem, Pa., in 1890, the formation of brotherhood chapters in other denominations was recommended, the chapters in each denomination to be under the control of that denomination, and all to be united in a federation of brotherhoods. In this way the work was extended, until to-day there are 921 chapters in the United States, Canada, Japan, Australia, India, and other lands, with about 40,000 members, representing some twenty-three denominations; there are also fifty-eight brotherhoods for boys.

Each local chapter is subjected to the supervision and control of the pastor and governing body of the congregation, and chapters of each denomination are associated in a denominational executive council. From these councils representatives are elected to a body known as the federal council of the brotherhood of Andrew and Philip. It is through this larger body that the literature of the association is issued. Denominational Councils are now organized in the Baptist, Congregational, Methodist Episcopal, Presbyterian, and Reformed Churches.

The distinctive characteristic of the brotherhood is the emphasis it places upon personal work. There are two rules of prayer and service. The rule of service is to make personal efforts to bring men and boys within the hearing of the Gospel, as set forth in the service of the church, men's Bible-classes, and prayer-meetings. The rule of prayer is to pray daily for the spread of Christ's kingdom among men, and God's blessing upon the labors of the brotherhood. Chapters sustain a weekly Bible-class, or men's prayer-meeting, and engage in a great variety of good works, as ushering, work in Sunday-schools, visiting jails, hospitals, etc.—all as the needs of the church may require. Chapters also maintain free reading-rooms and gymnasiums, organize boys' clubs and cottage prayer-meetings, provide for the evening church service, assist in the orchestra or choir, support home and foreign missions, and do other work of a similar character. WILLIAM H. PHELEY.

BIBLIOGRAPHY: *Manual of the Brotherhood of Andrew and Philip*, New York, n. d.; *Brotherhood Star*, Philadelphia (a monthly); Booklets published by the Federal Council, 25 E. 22 St., New York; W. B. Carpenter, *Religious Brotherhoods*, in *Contemporary Review*, lvii. (1889) 29 sqq.; L. W. Bacon and C. W. Northrop, *Young People's Societies*, pp. 48–50, and cf. Index, New York, 1900.

ANDREWES, LANCELOT: English bishop; b. at Barking (7 m. e. of London) 1555; d. at Winchester House, Southwark, Sept. 26, 1626. He entered Pembroke Hall, Cambridge, in 1571, was graduated B.A. 1575, was ordained 1580, and became catechist at Pembroke; he was master of Pembroke from 1589 to 1605. He also held the living of St. Giles's, Cripplegate, and was prebendary of St. Paul's; he became chaplain to the queen and dean of Westminster in the latter part of Elizabeth's reign. Under James I. he was made bishop of Chichester in 1605, of Ely in 1609, and of Winchester in 1619. He was a man of austere piety, rigorous in the performance of private devotion, liberal in charities, one of the most learned men of his time, and enjoys a well-deserved reputation as prelate, as preacher, and as writer. He was thought by many to be the natural successor to Bancroft as archbishop of Canterbury in 1611; but George Abbot (q.v.) was appointed instead. Andrewes was a member of the Hampton Court Conference (q.v.), and his name heads the list of scholars appointed in 1607 to prepare the Authorized Version; he belonged to the first company of translators, to whom were assigned the books of the Old Testament as far as II Kings.

The only writings of Bishop Andrewes published during his life were the *Tortura Torti sive ad Matthæi Torti responsio* (1609) and one or two subsequent treatises, all written in reply to Cardinal Bellarmine, who had attacked King James because of the oath of allegiance imposed upon Roman Catholics in England after the Gunpowder Plot. In 1629 ninety-six of his sermons were published, edited by Bishops Buckeridge and Laud; certain sermons have been many times reedited and reprinted. A number of volumes based upon his works (such as *The Pattern of Catechistical Doctrine, or an Exposition of the Ten Commandments*, 1642) pass under his name. His prayers, composed in Greek and Latin for his own use, are famous, and have been often translated (cf. *The Greek Devotions of Lancelot Andrewes, from the manuscript given by him to William Laud and recently discovered*, ed. P. G. Medd, London, 1892; *The Devotions of Bishop Andrewes, Græce et Latine*, ed. H. Veale, 1895; *The Private Devotions of Lancelot Andrewes*, ed. E. Venables, 1883).

BIBLIOGRAPHY: His works, with his life by H. Isaacson (first published 1650) and other notices, are collected in the *Library of Anglo-Catholic Theology*, 11 vols., Oxford, 1841–54. There are many later memoirs and essays, as: A. T. Russell, *Memoirs of the Life and Works of L. Andrewes*, London, 1863; *St. James's Lectures*, 2d ser., Lecture 3, ib. 1876; *DNB*, i. 401–405; R. L. Ottley, *Lancelot Andrewes*, ib. 1894; A. Whyte, *Lancelot Andrewes and his Private Devotions*, Edinburgh, 1896.

ANDREWS, EDWARD GAYER: Methodist Episcopal bishop; b. at New Hartford, N. Y., Aug. 7, 1825. He was educated at Cazenovia Seminary, Cazenovia, N. Y., and Wesleyan University, Middletown, Conn. (B.A., 1847). He held various pastorates in Methodist Episcopal churches in Central New York from 1848 to 1854, when he was appointed teacher and principal in Cazenovia Seminary, where he remained until 1864. He was then pastor in Stamford, Conn., from 1864 to 1867 and in Brooklyn, N. Y., from 1867 to 1872. In the latter year he was elected bishop. He visited Methodist Episcopal missions in Europe and India in 1876–77, in Mexico in 1881, and in Japan, Korea, and China in 1889–90, while in 1894 he was a delegate to the British and Irish Methodist Conference. In theology he holds the faith of his denomination for essentials of doctrine, but with deference to the results of recent Biblical investigations.

ANDREWS, ELISHA BENJAMIN: Baptist; b. at Hinsdale, N. H., Jan. 10, 1844. He was educated at Brown University (B.A., 1870), Newton Theological Institution (1874), and the Massachusetts Institute of Technology (1879–80), and also studied in the universities of Berlin and Munich (1882–83). He served in the Union army in the Civil War, being promoted from private to second lieutenant. He was principal of the Connecticut Literary Institute, Suffield, Conn., 1870–72, and pastor of the First Baptist Church, Beverly, Mass., 1874–75. In the latter year he was appointed president of Denison University, Granville, Ill., and held this position until 1879, when he accepted a call to Newton Theological Institution as professor of homiletics and practical theology. In 1882 he became professor of history and political economy at Brown University, and in 1888 of political economy and finance at Cornell. In 1889 he was chosen president of Brown University, where he remained until 1898. He then became superintendent of the Chicago schools until 1900, when he was made chancellor of the University of Nebraska, at Lincoln, a position which he still occupies. He was a member of the United States delegation to the Brussels International Monetary Commission in 1892, and is also a member of the Grand Army of the Republic, the Loyal Legion, and the American Economic Association. In theology he is a liberal evangelical Baptist. His works include *Brief Institutes of Constitutional History, English and American* (New York, 1886); *Brief Institutes of General History* (1887); *Institutes of Economics* (1889); *The Problem of Cosmology* (1891); *Eternal Words* (1893; a volume of sermons); *Wealth and*

Moral Law (1894); *An Honest Dollar, with seven Other Essays on Bimetallism* (1894); *History of the United States* (2 vols., 1894; revised and enlarged, 5 vols., 1905); and *History of the United States in the last Quarter Century* (1896). He has also published *Outlines of the Principles of History* (New York, 1893), a translation of J. G. Droysen's *Grundris der Historik* (3d ed., Leipsic, 1882).

ANDREWS, SAMUEL JAMES: Catholic Apostolic Church: b. at Danbury, Conn., July 30, 1817; d. at Hartford Oct. 11, 1906. He was educated at Williams College (B.A., 1839), and studied law in Hartford, Boston, and New York, being admitted to the Connecticut bar in 1842 and to the Ohio bar in 1844. In the following year, however, he gave up law and studied theology at Lane Theological Seminary, Cincinnati. He was licensed as a Congregational clergyman in Connecticut in 1846, and two years later was ordained pastor of the Congregational church at East Windsor, Conn. Loss of voice compelled him to retire from the ministry in 1855, although he still preached occasionally. In 1865 he was appointed an instructor in Trinity College, Hartford, and three years later took charge of a Catholic Apostolic (Irvingite) church in the same city. In theology he was a consistent follower of the creed which he professed. His chief writings were: *Life of Our Lord Upon the Earth* (New York, 1862); *God's Revelations of Himself to Man* (1885); *Christianity and Anti-Christianity in Their Final Conflict* (1898); *The Church and its Organic Ministries* (1899); *William Watson Andrews, a Religious Biography* (1900; life, letters, and writings of his brother, William Watson Andrews, q.v.); and *Man and the Incarnation* (1905).

ANDREWS, WILLIAM WATSON: Catholic Apostolic Church, brother of Samuel James Andrews; b. at Windham, Conn., July 26, 1810; d. at Wethersfield, Conn., Oct. 17, 1897. He was graduated at Yale in 1831. During this year his attention was drawn to the religious movement then going on in England which culminated in the Catholic Apostolic Church. The point that seems at first to have interested him most was whether the gifts of the Spirit as originally given were or were not to abide in the Church, and his study of the Scriptures led him to the conclusion that they are a permanent endowment, and, if not still possessed, it was because of unbelief. Closely connected with the work of the Spirit in the Church was another question: Was the return of the Lord to be desired, and the Church to be ever praying and looking for it? Believing this return to be an object of hope, he was led to ask if any preparation was needed; and, if so, might not the work in England be the preparation? In 1833 he was licensed to preach, and in May, 1834, was ordained pastor of a Congregational church in Kent, Conn. Here he continued fifteen years, declining invitations to go to larger spheres of labor, preferring his quiet country life, which gave him time for study and reflection. In 1842, partly for his health, and partly to learn from personal observation the progress of the religious movement which interested him, he went to England and became fully convinced that the movement was of God. He offered himself to its leaders as ready to take part in it, but was directed by them to return to his parish and continue his work there. This he did, but on the death of his wife in 1848, he was released from his charge by the North Association of Litchfield County, and soon entered the Apostolic communion. In 1849 he was appointed pastor of a small congregation at Potsdam, N. Y., and remained there for six years, doing some work elsewhere as an evangelist. In 1856 he left Potsdam and entered upon his evangelistic work in which he continued till his death. From 1858 his home was in Wethersfield, Conn.

The only book published by Mr. Andrews was *The Miscellanies and Correspondence of Hon. John Cotton Smith* (New York, 1847). Of his numerous addresses, articles, and pamphlets mention may be made of his sermon at Kent, May 1849, on withdrawing from the Congregational ministry; *The True Constitution of the Church*, read before the North Association of Litchfield County, 1855; *Review of Mrs. Oliphant's Life of Edward Irving*, in *The New Englander*, 1863 (reprinted in Scotland, 1864 and 1900); *Remarks on Dr. Bushnell's "Vicarious Sacrifice,"* published at the request of the Hartford Fourth Association, 1866; *The Catholic Apostolic Church*, in the *Bibliotheca Sacra*, 1866; *The Catholic Apostolic Church*, in Schaff's *Creeds of Christendom*, i., New York, 1884, 905-915; and an address at Kent, his old parish, on the sixtieth anniversary of his ordination, May 27, 1894.

Samuel J. Andrews†.

Bibliography: *William Watson Andrews, a Religious Biography, with Extracts from his Letters and other Writings prepared by his Brother, Samuel J. Andrews*, New York, 1900 (contains the sermon at Kent, May, 1849, and the address, 1894, mentioned above, pp. 206-265).

ANGARIÆ: Certain taxes or services usually rendered on the Ember Days (q.v.), whence the name was transferred to the latter. Consult Du Cange, s.v.

ANGEL.

The name "Angel" as a designation for spiritual beings of the supernatural world, has come into modern languages with Christianity from the Greek *angelos* ("messenger"), which is itself a rendering of the Hebrew *mal'akh*. The latter, in form an abstract noun ("mission," "message"), occurs only as a concrete ("messenger"), and acquired a special meaning, particularly in the singular, as the designation of a supernatural bearer of a divine revelation. The transition was then easy to the sense of a generic name for the beings of the heavenly world, from whom the God of Israel is called "Yahweh, God of Hosts," or "Yahweh of Hosts." To distinguish angels from men, they are called "sons of God" (Gen. vi. 2, 4; Job i. 6, ii. 1, xxxviii. 7) or "sons of the mighty" (Ps. xxix. 1, margin, lxxxix. 6). A special connection with God is always implied, as well as a certain superiority over men (I Sam. xxix. 9; II Sam. xiv. 17, 20). This connection is emphasized by the epithet "holy" (A. V., "saints"; Job v. 1, xv. 15; Ps. lxxxix. 5, 7; Dan. viii. 13; Zech. xiv. 5). In I Kings xxii. 19-24 and Acts xxiii. 9 a distinction is made between angels and spirits, and in the Talmud the latter name is used for demons only. With reference to their duties angels are called "watchers" in Dan. iv. 13, 17, 23.

I. Biblical Conceptions: As concerns their function, it is not the Biblical conception that angels are the indispensable means of communication between the higher and lower worlds, nor are they a personification of nature powers. Yet they are consistently represented as serving God's purposes in revelation and salvation, and are his "ministering spirits" (Heb. i. 14) from the appointment of the cherubim to guard Eden (Gen. iii. 24) to their activity at the second coming and the end of the world (Matt. xiii. 41, xxiv. 29-31; cf. Gen. xxiv. 7, 40, xlviii. 16; Ex. xiv. 19, xxiii. 20, 23; Luke xvi. 22). Sometimes they appear in companies (Gen. xxviii. 12, xxxii. 1–2; II Kings vi. 16–17; Matt. xxv. 31; Luke ii. 13; Rev. xix. 14), but usually it is one angel who executes God's command; he is called the "angel of God" or "angel of Yahweh" (Gen. xvi. 7, 9–11, xxi. 17; Ex. iii. 2, xiv. 19; Judges vi. 20; and often). The relation of the "angel of Yahweh" to Yahweh himself is a difficult question. One of the three who appear in Gen. xviii. 2, 22 (cf. xix. 1) is evidently Yahweh, and Yahweh and his angel are both called the guide of Israel (Ex. xiii. 21, xiv. 19). Similar identification apparently occurs elsewhere, while in Zech. i. 9, 12–14, and other passages there is a sharp distinction.

1. Angels are God's Servants.

In the New Testament *the* angel of the Lord occurs only when *an* angel has been previously mentioned (Matt. i. 24; Luke i. 11, 13, ii. 9, 10, 13; Acts xii. 7, 11, vii. 30, 38, Gk. text). There is no thought of an identification of the angel with the Lord. That the conception is different from that of the Old Testament can not be proved, and such an assumption is not in accord with Stephen's references (Acts vii. 30–35) to the appearance in the burning bush (Ex. iii.). But the distinction between the angel and Yahweh does not hinder from making the angel speak as Yahweh or from speaking of the angel as of Yahweh. It follows that the distinction can not be a product of later times. The angel is not the Logos, the second person of the Trinity, as assumed by the Greek Fathers, the older Lutheran dogmaticians, and Hengstenberg; nor is he merely a theophany (Vatke, De Wette, Wellhausen, Kosters, and others). The former view is not consistent with the New Testament revelation, which makes it impossible to find in the Old Testament a knowledge of the threefold character of God; and the latter falls because a "mission," not an "appearance," of God is always spoken of. The true Biblical conception of the "angel of Yahweh" is that of a created being (Neh. ix. 6), belonging to the heavenly hosts (Augustine, Jerome, Hofmann, Riehm), who represents God, but is in no way identified with God. The fact, that in the New Testament the angel of Yahweh recedes, does not justify the assumption that he is a type of Christ. A realization of God's presence through angels and the communication of his revelation by them was as necessary in the old covenant as the revelation and presence of God in Christ or in the Holy Spirit are in the new (cf. Acts vii. 38; Gal. iii. 19; Heb. ii. 2). The angel has no more place in the new covenant because the first has been made old and is "ready to vanish away" (Heb. viii 13).

2. The New Testament Conception not Different from the Old.

From the beginning the appearance of an angel is looked upon as a sign of God's favor (Gen. xxiv. 7, 40, xlviii. 16; Ex. xxiii. 20; II Kings xix. 35; Isa. lxiii. 9), and the belief that God's angels guard his servants finds expression in the Psalms (Ps. xxxiv. 7, xci. 11). From the unity of God arises the conception of a multiplicity of angels (Gen. xxviii. 12, xxxii. 2); and then it is only a step to that of Yahweh's hosts (Josh. v. 14–15), with which he comes to the help of Israel (Isa. xxxi. 4–5), which surround his throne, offering him praise and adoration (I Kings xxii. 19; Ps. cxlviii. 2), and constitute, in the language of the synagogue, "the family above." Apocalyptic literature develops the thought, depicting in symbolic narratives the part of the angels in the history of Israel (cf. the visions of Zechariah, Ezekiel, and Daniel). In the Book of Daniel (viii. 16, ix. 21, x. 13, xii. 1) two angels are named—Gabriel and Michael. The fact that names are given (cf. Judges xiii. 18) and the names themselves indicate Babylonian influence, which later tradition recognizes by ascribing the many angels' names which it knows to Babylon (*Genesis, Rabbah* xlviii.). What is said of these two angels does not contradict existing views, but is merely a development of them, influenced by contact with Babylonian and Persian ideas. The fantastic and bizarre conceptions of later Judaism, however, can not deny their origin from this heathenism (cf. Tobit iii. 17, v. 6, 21, vi. 4-17, viii. 2–3). That which is really new in the Book of Daniel concerns the participation of the angels in the sin of the world. In the New Testament the apocalyptic symbolism appears in the Book of Revelation only (cf. xii. 7 sqq.; Jude 9). All allusions to angels in New Testament history and in the Epistles can be explained as in full accord with Old Testament conceptions, and if new ideas are found by any it is only because of the desire to find them. It requires great art of eisegesis to ascribe to Paul (as does Everling) the angel doctrine of Jewish legend and rabbinic theology.

3. Later Developments.

4. Distinctions among Angels. Cherubim and Seraphim. Fallen Angels.

There are evidently distinctions among angels, based on differences of duties, not of rank. In this way passages like Dan. x. 13, xii. 1; I Thess. iv. 16; Jude 9 are to be explained. The same observation holds with regard to the cherubim and seraphim, who belong to the angels. The signification of the latter name (only in Isa. vi.) is not certain. From comparison with the Arabic it has been thought to mean *nobilis*, whence the signification would be "angel-leader" (cf. Josh. v. 13–15; Dan. x. 13, xii. 1). Another derivation is from the Hebrew *saraph*, "to burn," and the name is then thought to be given to these beings because of their peculiar relation to the divine holiness, of which they are the heralds and guards. Whether the prophet coined the name with reference to the act attributed to the seraph in verses 6–7, or found it already in use, can not be determined. In any case it is the name only and not the representation that is new. The description of their form is different from that of the cherubim. In the latter case the description is symbolic, and the symbolism is more and more richly developed from the cherubim that guard Eden, in the figures of the Tabernacle (Ex. xxv. 17–22) and the Temple (I Kings vi. 23–28), and the visions of Ezekiel (Ezek. i. 4–14, iii. 12–14, ix. 3, x. 6–22, xi. 22, xli. 18), to the description of the Apocalypse (Rev. iv. 6–11). In that way they unite in themselves all excellencies, they typify the exaltation of God above every creature, as well as the purpose that every creature shall be a bearer of the majesty of God. Sin is found among the angels (Gen. vi. 1–4; II Pet. ii. 4; Jude 6), but not, as among men, as something affecting all. Since Satan appears among the "sons of God" (Job i. 6; cf. I Chron. xxi. 1; Zech. iii. 2), he is reckoned among the angels. The interest which he shows in the sin of men in these passages justifies the assumption (first in Wisdom, ii. 24; cf. Rev. xii. 9, xx. 2) that he is the serpent of Gen. iii. He is therefore the first fallen, to whom the other fallen angels (or demons) join themselves as his angels (Matt. xxv. 41). "Evil angels" (Ps. lxxviii. 49) are angels who do ill at God's command, not wicked angels.

As concerns the origin of the Biblical conception of angels, the view that they represent the natural powers of old Semitic heathenism stands or falls with the representation of Deut. iv. 19 (also in Paul) that heathenism is an apostasy from the true God. It may be noted that angels never serve as an explanation of the events of nature, but appear only in connection with a divine revelation. The decision depends also on the question as to the reality of angels. That they, as well as Satan and the demons, actually exist is held to be indubitably proved by the words and conduct of Jesus. The upper world, to which we are striving, is full of life and needs not to be peopled by us, but is prepared for us with all that is proper to it, freed from the limitations of the present.

(H. Cremer†.)

II. Judaic Notions:

1. Names and Classes.

To the two names known to Daniel the Book of Tobit (iii. 17) adds that of Raphael, while the Book of Enoch (xxi.) knows seven archangels—Uriel, Raphael, Raguel, Michael, Sariel, Gabriel, Jerahmeel—and seven classes of angels (lxi. 10), namely, the cherubim, seraphim, ophanim, all the angels of power, principalities, the Elect One (Messiah), and the (elementary) powers of the earth and water. They have seven angelic virtues (lxi. 11): the spirit of faith, of wisdom, of patience, of mercy, of judgment, of peace, and of goodness.

2. Functions, Duties, etc.

In the Slavonic Enoch and rabbinic literature, the further development of the heavenly hierarchy introduces the seven heavens, and tells of the food of angels, the hours at which they worship God, their language, and their knowledge. They mediate between God and man, carry prayers to the throne of God (Tobit xii. 12–15; Gk. Apoc. Baruch xi.), and accompany the dead on their departure from this world. Angels are also the guardians of the nations. In Enoch xxxix. 59 the seventy shepherds are the guardian angels of the seventy nations, over whom rules Michael, as Israel's angel-prince. With these God sits in council when holding judgment over the world, each angel pleading the cause of his nation. It was these angel-princes whom Jacob saw in his dream (*Gen. Rabbah* lxviii.). There is also a special angel-prince set over the world, *Sar ha-'olam* (Talmud, *Yebamot* 16b; *Ḥullin* 60a; *Sanhedrin* 94a), who is said to have composed Ps. xxxvii. 25, civ. 31, and, partly, Isa. xxiv. 16. Besides the guardian angels of the nations, sixty-three angels are mentioned as janitors of the seven heavens, and at each of these heavens stand other angels as seal-bearers. The head and chief of all these is Asriel. Angels protect the pious and help them in their transactions. Every man has a special guardian angel, and there are accompanying angels. Thus two angels—one good and one evil—accompany man as he leaves the synagogue on Sabbath eve. Three good angels receive the souls of the pious, and three evil angels those of the wicked, who testify for them (Talmud, *Shabbat* 119a; *Ketubot* 104a). Great as is the number and influence of the angels, yet in many respects they are inferior to man. Enoch (xv. 2) intercedes on behalf of the angels, instead of having them intercede for him; and none of the angels could see what he saw of God's glory (xiv 21), or learn the secrets of God as he knew them (Slavonic *Enoch* xxiv. 3; *Ascensio Isaiæ* ix. 27 38). Adam was to be worshiped by the angels as the image of God (*Vita Adæ et Evæ*, p. 14; *Gen. Rabbah* viii.); before his fall his place was within the precincts of God's own majesty, where the angels can not stay (*Gen. Rabbah* xxi.). They were inferior in intelligence to Adam, when names were given to all things (*Pirḳe Rabbi Eli'ezer* xiii.). Adam reclined in Paradise, and the ministering angels roasted meat and strained wine for him (Talmud, *Sanhedrin* 59b). Every man that does not practise magic enters a department of heaven to which even the ministering angels have no access (Talmud, *Nedarim* 32a).

The essence of the angels is fire; they sustain themselves in fire; their fiery breath consumes men, and no man can endure the sound of their voices (Talmud, *Shabbat* 88b; *Ḥagigah* 14b). Another theory is that they are half fire and half water, and that God makes peace between the opposing elements (Jerusalem Talmud, *Rosh ha-Shanah* ii. 58a). According to one tradition, each angel was one-third of a world in size: according to another, 2,000 parasangs, his hand reaching from heaven to earth. The angels, numbering either 496,000 or 499,000, are said to have been created either on the first day (*Book of Jubilees* ii. 2), the second day (Slavonic *Enoch*), or on the fifth day (*Gen. Rabbah* iii.). Their food is manna, of which Adam and Eve ate before they sinned (*Vita Adæ et Evæ*, p. 4).

As a rule, the angels are represented as good, and as not subject to evil impulses (*Gen. Rabbah* xlviii. 14); nevertheless, two were expelled from heaven for 138 years on account of prematurely disclosing the decree of Sodom's destruction (ib.). Two narratives are given in Enoch vi.–xv., of the fall of the angels. According to one, Azazel was the leader of the rebellion, and the chief debaucher of women; according to the other, Samiaza, or Shamhazai, was the chief seducer. Each has ten chieftains and 100 angels at his command. They are punished at the hands of Michael, Gabriel, Raphael, and Uriel (Enoch ix. 1, xl. 2).

B. Pick.

III. Development of the Scriptural Angelology: The nature of Holy Scripture forbids any attempt to build upon its text a systematic angelology. The Bible covers a wide field of time, and, for anything save its main purpose, it is a book of imperfect record. Moreover, its evidence on this question is less apt to be direct than indirect. An elaborate angelology can therefore be derived from the Bible only by doing violence to sound exegesis. Yet it is possible to detect a general movement of thought and to deduce a conclusion, touching the weight to be given to the scriptural doctrine of angels.

1. The Belief in Angels Common to All Antiquity.

The belief in angels is not an original element in the Scriptures; the Bible holds it in common with all the men of antiquity, who lacked a unifying conception of law and made the poet and the theologian one and the same person. So the mind instinctively peopled space with personal forces both good and evil. The field of reality, being governed neither by the scientific idea of law nor by the monotheistic idea of God, was inevitably broken up and parceled out by a kind of spiritual feudalism. The belief in angels being thus instinctive, it follows that, so far as the Scriptures are concerned, the doctrine in question is not a primary one; on the contrary, it is a subordinate element. To be true to the Bible itself, the emphasis must be put on the relation between that belief in angels which the men of the Bible inherited from antiquity and that saving knowledge of the divine unity which is the heart of God's word. The center of gravity and interest is not in angelology as such.

2. The Hexateuch.

The central and controlling element in the Old Testament is the self-revelation of God in his holy and creative unity. The pith of prophecy is God's manifestation of himself in terms of the moral order in the experience of the chosen nation. It is significant, then, that in the Hexateuch the angels in their plurality play a small part (Gen. xix. 15, xxxii. 1). The "angel of Yahweh," "the angel of the presence," on the other hand, are constantly in evidence. The unity of God, dominating the religious consciousness, has given a monarchical turn to the angelology of antiquity.

3. The Prophets.

In the preexilic prophets the angels appear but twice. In both cases (Hosea xii. 4, Isa. xxxvii. 36) the usage is unitary. This fact, taken with the extreme rarity of the term on the one hand, and, on the other hand, with the fact that the existence of heavenly hosts is taken for granted (Isa. vi. 1–6), gives a weighty piece of evidence. Even in exilic prophecy as a whole there is no emphasis. The "angel of the presence" appears once (Isa. lxiii. 9). The angels in their plurality do not appear. The prophetic passion spends itself upon God's presence in the crises of the nation's history, and upon his power to guide it toward a supreme moral end (the day of Yahweh). Even in Ezekiel, in whom the apocalyptic tendency begins to be strongly marked, the angels are not named.

But in Zechariah a new turn is taken. The angel of Yahweh appears incessantly. Moreover, the angels in their plurality appear (Zech. ii. 3). The apocalyptic tendency is becoming dominant. The moral passion of prophetism is declining. And from Zechariah's time on, there seems to be a steady increase in the amount of attention given to the angels. How far this is due to the influence of Parseeism and how far to the inherent tendency of Judaism, it may be impossible to determine with precision. But certain it is that as Judaism abounds in its own sense and its difference from prophetism develops, the angels play a larger and yet larger part. The climax is reached when the Essenes impose upon those entering the order a terrible oath not to betray the names of the angels (Josephus, *War*, II. viii. 7). At this point, Judaism comes close to Chaldean magic.

4. The New Testament.

Davidson has said (*DB*, i., p. 97) that in the New Testament there is no advance. The statement is misleading. There is not nor can there be any advance beyond the Jewish angelology. The Jewish mystic knew a great deal about the angelic hosts, their hierarchical order, and their names. In truth, he knew more than there was to know. "Advance" in this direction would have meant a fuller exposition of unreality. But the New Testament is the literary product of a magnificent revival of Hebrew prophetism. The clarity of the moral and spiritual consciousness relegates the angels to a secondary position. Even in the New Testament Apocalypse the angels are wholly subsidiary to the Kingdom of God. Thus in xix. 10, xxi. 17, and xxii. 9 a view appears fundamentally opposed to that of mystical Judaism. Angels and men are citizens of one divine commonwealth. Worship of the angels is not to be thought of. So, again, in the synoptic gospels and the Acts, the existence of the angels, while taken for granted, is not a primary element of consciousness.

In the Pauline and Petrine letters, the angels play an even more subordinate part. The Christians of Corinth, in danger of falling below their dignity, are informed that the disciples of Christ will be his coassessors in judging the angels (I Cor. vi. 3). Peter, dwelling on the consummation of prophecy, declares that angels desire to understand the mystery of the gospel (I Pet. i. 12). In Heb. i. 14 their function is clearly described. They are spirits worshiping God and sent from God to serve the followers of Jesus.

5. Conclusion.

When, therefore, the Scriptures are placed against the background of antiquity, a certain unity of movement and thought is found. The doctrine of angels is inherited, not created. And it is controlled and utilized by the saving word, the self-revelation of God as the creative unity within human consciousness and society, the moralizing power in history, and the moral end toward which nature and history are being guided (Rom. xi. 36). From this point of view the ecclesiastical discussion over the worship of angels and the careful distinction between dulia and latria is more or less a reversion of type. HENRY S. NASH.

BIBLIOGRAPHY: J. Ode, *Commentarius de angelis*, Utrecht, 1739; E. C. A. Riehm, *De natura et notione symbolica Cheruborum*, Basel, 1864; idem, *Die Cherubim in der Stiftshütte und im Tempel*, in *TSK*, xliv. (1871) 399 sqq.; A. Kohut, *Ueber die jüdische Angelologie und Dämonologie in ihrer Abhängigkeit vom Parsismus*, Leipsic, 1866; F. Godet, *Études bibliques*, i. 1–34, Paris, 1873; W. H. Kosters, *De Mal'ach Jahwe* and *Het ontstaan en de ontwikkeling der angelologie onder Israel*, in *ThT*, ix. (1875) 367–415, x. (1876) 34–69, 113–141; J. H. Oswald, *Angelologie, im Sinne der katholischen Kirche dargestellt*, Paderborn, 1883; O. Everling, *Die paulinischen Angelologie und Dämonologie*, Göttingen, 1888; J. M. Fuller, *Angelology and Demonology*, Excursus II. to *Tobit*, in Wace's *Apocrypha*, i. 171–183, London, 1888; T. K. Cheyne, *Origin and Religious Contents of the Psalter*, pp. 322–327, 334–337, London, 1891 (very valuable); C. H. Toy, *Judaism and Christianity*, pp. 141–172, Boston, 1891; C. G. Montefiore, *Hibbert Lectures*, pp. 429 sqq., London, 1892 (characterized by G. B. Gray as valuable); R. Stübe, *Jüdisch-babylonische Zaubertexte*, Halle, 1895 (a work of special interest); F. Weber, *Jüdische Theologie auf Grund des Talmud*, pp. 166 sqq., Leipsic, 1897; M. Schwab, *Vocabulaire de l'angélologie d'après manuscrits hébreux*, Paris, 1897; H. Oehler, *Die Engelwelt*, Stuttgart, 1898; W. Lücken, *Michael*, Göttingen, 1898; *DCB*, i. 93–97; *EB*, i. 165–170; *JE*, i. 583–597 (deals with biblical, talmudic, and post-talmudic angelology); and the works on Old and New Testament theology (including R. Smend, *Alttestamentliche Religionsgeschichte*, Freiburg, 1893) and dogmatics; W. Bousset, *Die Religion des Judenthums*, pp. 313–325, Berlin, 1903.

ANGELA OF BRESCIA. See MERICI, ANGELA.

ANGELICALS: A sisterhood founded about 1530 by Ludovica di Torelli, Countess of Guastalla (then, at the age of twenty-five, for the second time a widow), to care for sick and reformed women. The members were to lead lives of angelic purity (whence the name) and self-denial, indicated by coarse clothing, a wooden cross on the breast, and a cord about the neck. The foundress placed them under the supervision of Antonia Maria Zaccaria, founder and director of the Barnabites (q.v.); and herself labored, under the monastic name of Paola Maria, as manager of the main convent of her society near Milan till her death (Oct. 29, 1569). The order was first confirmed by Paul III. (1534) with the rule of St. Augustine, with the provision that the Angelicals were to assist the Barnabites in their missionary work among women. The obligation to live in seclusion was adopted in 1557. Archbishop Borromeo of Milan subjected the statutes of the order to a stricter revision, which was confirmed by Urban VIII. (1625). The order never spread outside of Lombardy (especially Milan and Cremona) and was dissolved at the beginning of the nineteenth century. A branch, however, still exists, the Society of the Guastallinæ founded by the same Countess Torelli, devoted to the education of girls of noble birth (the number being limited to 18); they occupy a building outside the Porta Romana at Milan, and are under the supervision of the Barnabites.

O. ZÖCKLER†.

BIBLIOGRAPHY: C. G. Rosignoli, *Vita e virtù della contessa di Guastalla L. Torella*, Milan, 1686; Helyot, *Ordres monastiques*, iv. 116–223; Heimbucher, *Orden und Kongregationen*, i. 519–520.

ANGELIS, an'je-lis, **GIROLAMO**, ji-rō'l-ūmō: Jesuit missionary; b. at Castro Giovanni, Sicily, 1567; d. in Japan Dec. 24, 1623. He joined the Jesuits at the age of eighteen, and in 1602 went to Japan. When the Jesuits were expelled from the country in 1614, he assumed Japanese dress and remained for nine years without discovery. He was then imprisoned and burned alive with two other Jesuits and forty-two native Christians. He wrote *Relazione del regno di Iezo*, printed with letters of other Jesuits at Rome in 1624, and separately the next year. He was canonized by Pius IX.

ANGELUS, an'je-lʊs: The ordinary name (taken from its opening word in Latin) of a Roman Catholic prayer, recited three times a day, when the church bells ring at 6 a.m., at noon, and at 6 p.m. It consists of three versicles and responses, each followed by a "Hail Mary!" and a collect, which is the same as that for the Annunciation in the Anglican Prayer Book, the whole forming a devotion in honor of the incarnation of Christ. In its present form it dates from the middle of the sixteenth century, though the custom of ringing bells at certain times of the day to remind the faithful of certain prayers is at least as old as the thirteenth.

ANGILBERT, an-gil'bert, or **ENGELBERT** (Fr. pron. ān"zhîl-bār'), **SAINT**: Friend and counselor of Charlemagne, whose daughter Bertha he is said to have married, and by her had two sons, Harnid and Nithard (the historian); d. Feb. 19, 814. He enjoyed the confidence of Charlemagne till the end of the latter's life, and was employed in many difficult negotiations. That he entered the monastery of Centula (the modern St. Riquier, about 25 m. n.w. of Amiens) in 790 is not probable; he was abbot of the monastery later, however, and rebuilt it with much splendor. He was named the "Homer" of the literary circle at Charlemagne's court, and a few Latin lyrics and a fragment of an epic ascribed to him are extant (in *MPL*, xcix. 825–854; *MGH*, *Script.*, xv. 1, 1887, 173–181; *Poetæ Latini ævi carolini*, i., 1881, 355–381).

ANGILRAM, an″gil-rum (Fr. pron. ān″zhîl-rām′): Bishop of Metz 768, after 787 with the title of archbishop; d. 791. In 784 he was made court chaplain by Charlemagne, who obtained from the pope a dispensation freeing Angilram from the obligation of residing at the seat of his bishopric. Most codices of the pseudo-Isidorian decretals contain a minor collection of statutes, consisting of seventy-one, seventy-two, or eighty chapters relating to suits against the clergy, especially bishops, and generally bearing the name *Capitula Angilramni*. In some manuscripts the superscription states that Angilram presented these *capitula* to Pope Adrian; in others (the older and better) that the pope presented them to Angilram when he was in Rome in connection with his affair. In either version the story is improbable, and it is generally agreed that Angilram had nothing to do with these *capitula*. They were probably written by the author of the pseudo-Isidorian decretals (q.v.).

BIBLIOGRAPHY: Rettberg, *KD*, i. 501 sqq.; Hinschius, *Decretales Pseudo-Isidorianæ*, Leipsic, 1863; Richter-Dove, *Lehrbuch des Kirchenrechts*, p. 87, ib. 1886.

ANGLICAN CHURCH or **COMMUNION**: A comprehensive name for the Reformation churches of English origin, including the Church of England and its branches in Ireland, Scotland, the colonies, and India, with the various missionary jurisdictions, and the Protestant Episcopal Church of the United States. The liturgy in all is the Book of Common Prayer with modifications (see COMMON PRAYER, BOOK OF), and the Thirty-nine Articles are accepted with changes necessary to fit local conditions (see THIRTY-NINE ARTICLES). All have episcopal organization and hold to the "historic episcopate" (see APOSTOLIC SUCCESSION). The Lambeth Conference (q.v.) is a meeting of bishops of the Anglican communion intended to promote the unity and fellowship of its members. See ENGLAND, CHURCH OF; IRELAND; SCOTLAND; PROTESTANT EPISCOPAL CHURCH.

ANGLO-SAXONS, CONVERSION OF THE: The Angles, Saxons, and kindred peoples who by the end of the sixth century were established in the east of Britain from the Forth southward and in the greater part of the south, in their Continental homes were all worshipers of Woden, whom they considered their ancestor. They dispossessed in England a fully Christianized people, but did not adopt their religion (see CELTIC CHURCH IN BRITAIN AND IRELAND). The first Christian church among them was Frankish in origin and was established in Kent, whose king, Ethelbert (c. 560–616), married a Christian princess, Bertha, daughter of Charibert, king of Paris. She was granted full freedom of religion in her new home, and brought with her to England a Christian chaplain, Liudhard by name. A ruined church near Canterbury, dating from Roman times (St. Martin's, three quarters of a mile east of the present cathedral), was repaired for her use. The real conversion of the Anglo-Saxons, however, is properly regarded as begun by Pope Gregory the Great (590–604).

Gregory the Great Sends a Mission to Kent.

As the story goes (Bede, *Hist. eccl.*, ii. 1), while Gregory was still a deacon, either in 578 or 585, he saw one day in the slave-market at Rome certain boys whose fair complexion, bright faces, and golden hair excited his admiration. Inquiring about them, he was told that they were Angles; whereupon he exclaimed "No wonder, for they have the faces of angels." Informed that they were heathen and from Deira, he remarked "From wrath [*de ira*] they must be saved and called to the mercy of Christ. Who is their king?" "Ælle," was the reply; and the pun-loving Italian concluded, "Alleluia! the praises of God must be sung in those parts." Betaking himself to the pope, Gregory asked that he be allowed to go in person as missionary to the land of the captives, but the Romans would not permit him at that time to leave their city. When he became pope, Gregory remembered the beautiful captives. He tried to find English boys whom he could instruct at Rome and then send to their people; and in 596 he despatched a mission of monks to England under the lead of Augustine (see AUGUSTINE, SAINT, OF CANTERBURY). When Augustine died (604 or 605) Kent had been converted and the gospel had found entrance into Essex. Justus and Mellitus had been established as bishops at Rochester (for West Kent) and London (for the East-Saxons), respectively. With the consent of his witan, Ethelbert promulgated laws recognizing the Church as an institution and Christian obligations. A heathen reaction followed Ethelbert's death (616), which for a time checked further advances from Canterbury (see JUSTUS; LAURENCE; MELLITUS).

As in Kent, so in Northumbria the way for the introduction of Christianity was prepared by the marriage (625) of the king, Edwin,

Northumbria and Wessex.

with a Christian princess, Ethelburga, daughter of Ethelbert of Kent. She was accompanied to the North by Paulinus, who became first bishop of York and converted King Edwin and many of his people (see EDWIN; PAULINUS). The work was interrupted and many of its results destroyed in 633, when Penda, king of Mercia, a heathen champion, in alliance with the Britons of Wales, overthrew and slew Edwin. It was resumed in 635 by Aidan supported by King Oswald, and was completed by their successors (see AIDAN, SAINT; OSWALD, SAINT; OSWY). At the same time the West-Saxons were gained for Christianity by Birinus (q.v.). The church of Aidan and Oswald, however, had no connection with Canterbury or Rome, but was organized as a part of the old British or Celtic Church, and continued such till the synod of Whitby in 664.

A marriage between Peada, son of Penda and under-king of the Middle-Angles, with a Northumbrian princess, daughter of Oswy, led to his conversion. He was baptized by Finan, Aidan's successor at Lindisfarne, in 653. Finan also baptized (probably at the same time) Sigbert, king of Essex, which had relapsed into heathenism after the time of Augustine. Peada's conversion was followed by that of his people. Four priests of the Northumbrian Church, Cedd (q.v.), Adda, Betti, and Diuma, settled in his kingdom, and even Penda did not restrict their preaching. Penda, the last powerful pagan ruler, was slain in battle with Oswy of Northumbria in 655, and the complete Christianization of Mercia soon followed. Diuma was consecrated bishop of Mercia by Finan, probably in 656. His see was at Lichfield. About ten years later Diuma's third successor, Jaruman, supported by Wulfhere, king of Mercia, and Penda's son, completed the conversion of Essex, a part of whose people had a second time relapsed into heathenism.

Mercia and Essex.

Christianity was introduced into East Anglia from Kent; but the only result was that the king, Redwald, set up Christian and heathen altars side by side. An obscure story connected with the conversion of Edwin of Northumbria (Bede, *Hist. eccl.*, ii. 12) has led to the conjecture that Paulinus (q.v.) may have been sent on a mission to East Anglia before 616. Eorpwald, Redwald's son, became a Christian through the influence of Edwin in 627 or 628, but in the same year he was killed by a heathen. After three years his brother, Sigbert, who had accepted Christianity in Gaul, gained the throne, and with the help of Felix (q.v.), who became bishop of Dunwich in 631, evangelized the land.

East Anglia.

Sussex received the Gospel through the labors of Wilfrid of York (q.v.) between 681 and 686, although its king, Ethelwalh, had been baptized earlier in Mercia and had made some unsuccessful efforts to introduce the Gospel. Its first bishop was Eadbert (709).

Sussex.

The Anglo-Saxon Church, like all churches of the early Middle Ages, had in many respects a national character. The wishes of the kings determined the appointment of bishops, if indeed the kings did not directly name them. Princes and rulers took part in synods, and bishops attended the councils of the rulers. Kings issued ecclesiastical orders. The Anglo-Saxon tongue was heard in divine service, and the baptismal formula also was Anglo-Saxon. The Old and New Testaments were read in Anglo-Saxon, and old homilies were translated into the vernacular. Dioceses were formed according to political divisions and were named after peoples rather than towns.

The Anglo-Saxon Church.

BIBLIOGRAPHY: *Anglo-Saxon Chronicle*, ed. B. Thorpe, in *Rolls Series*, No. 23, 2 vols., 1861; also ed. C. Plummer, Oxford, 1892; Bede, historical works, particularly *Hist. eccl.*, ed. C. Plummer, 2 vols., Oxford, 1896; Gildas, *De excidio et conquestu Britanniæ*, ed. T. Mommsen, in *MGH*, *Chronica minora*, iii. (1898) 1–85; also ed. H. Williams, with transl., London, 1899; the letters of Gregory the Great, ed. P. Ewald and L. M. Hartmann, in *MGH*, *Epistolæ*, i.-ii., 1887–93; those relating to the mission to England, with other material pertaining to St. Augustine, in *The Mission of St. Augustine*, ed. A. J. Mason, Cambridge, 1897; Haddan and Stubbs, *Councils*, vol. iii.; J. M. Lappenberg, *Geschichte von England*, i., Hamburg, 1834, Eng. transl., *A History of England, under the Anglo-Saxon Kings*, 2 vols., London, 1845; B. Thorpe, *Ancient Laws and Institutes of England*, ib. 1840; R. Schmid, *Die Gesetze der Angelsachsen*, Leipsic, 1858; J. M. Kemble, *The Saxons in England*, ii. 342–496, London, 1876; J. R. Green, *History of the English People*, vol. i., book i., ib. 1877; idem, *The Making of England*, ib. 1882; W. Stubbs, *The Constitutional History of England*, i., ch. viii., Oxford, 1883; E. Winkelmann, *Geschichte der Angelsachsen bis zum Tode König Alfreds*, Berlin, 1884; W. Bright, *Early English Church History*, Oxford, 1897; W. Hunt, *The English Church from its Foundation to the Norman Conquest*, London, 1899.

ANGLUS, THOMAS. See WHITE, THOMAS.

ANGOLA. See AFRICA, II.

ANGUS, JOSEPH: English Baptist; b. at Bolam (15 m. n.w. of Newcastle), Northumberland, Jan. 16, 1816; d. at Hampstead, London, Aug. 28, 1902. He studied at King's College, London, at Stepney Baptist College, and at Edinburgh University (M.A., 1838), and became pastor of the New Park Street Baptist Church, Southwark, London (1838), cosecretary of the Baptist Missionary Society (1840), sole secretary (1842), and president of Stepney College (1849), which position he held till 1893. During his administration the College was removed to Regent's Park and affiliated with the University of London, its attendance doubled, its endowment was augmented by a professorial fund of £30,000, and scholarships were provided for missionary and other students. He was a member of the first London School Board, and of the New Testament Revision Company. He published: *The Voluntary System* (London, 1839), a prize essay in reply to the lectures of Dr. Chalmers on Church establishments; *Christ our Life* (1853), which won a prize for an essay on the life of Christ adapted to missionary purposes and suitable for translation into the languages of India; *Christian Churches* (1862); *Lectures on Future Punishment* (1870); *Apostolic Missions* (1871; new ed. 1892); *Six Lectures on Regeneration* (1897). He wrote the commentary on Hebrews for Schaff's *International Commentary on the New Testament*, New York and Edinburgh (1883); and for the Religious Tract Society he prepared: *Handbooks of the Bible* (1854; partly rewritten by Samuel G. Green 1904), the *English Tongue* (1862), *English Literature* (1865); and *Specimens of English Literature* (1866; new ed. 1880). For the same society he edited Butler's *Analogy* (1855), and *Sermons* (1882), and Wayland's *Elements of Moral Science* (1858).

ANHALT: Duchy of the German empire, surrounded, except for a short distance on the west, where it touches the duchy of Brunswick, by Prussian territory (government districts of Magdeburg, Potsdam, Merseburg). Its area is 906 square miles; population (1900), 316,000; capital, Dessau. Ninety-six per cent. of the people are Protestants; 3½ per cent. are Roman Catholics; while the Jews comprise little more than one-half of 1 per cent. Among the minor Protestant bodies are Irvingite congregations in Bernburg and Coswig. The Evangelical State Church is a product of the Wittenberg Reformation. During the controversies of the later sixteenth century it held fast to the original formulas, but remained free from the one-sided tendency represented in the *Formula of Concord*. Attempts to introduce certain church practises from the Palatinate, with the Heidelberg catechism, toward the close of the sixteenth century were ineffectual. The political division into four principalities after 1606 favored certain divergencies,—for example in Anhalt-Bernburg and Anhalt-Cöthen there was a stronger tendency toward Reformed usages and teachings. But in 1880 a united Church in a united land was formally established; and that the union is not nominal but real is shown by the freest Christian fellowship, by the adoption of a uniform form of divine service, and by the use of the same church books. To-day the distinction between Lutheran and Reformed is not thought of.

The Church is legally recognized as a distinct institution, independent of the secular government, and the management of its internal affairs is entrusted to the consistory, which reports directly to the duke. A synod, consisting of the superintendents of the five circles into which the land is divided, five members named by the duke, and twenty-nine members elected in the circles, meets every three years; it has a share in ecclesiastical legislation, considers church needs and conditions in general, and exercises a control over the funds under the administration and at the disposal of the consistory. Previous to 1874 the consistory had the chief direction and administration of the schools, but in that year a state board of education was created. The consistory, however, is represented in this board, and the local pastors are generally the inspectors of the lower schools. With very few exceptions the duke is patron of churches and livings.

The number of livings in the duchy is 155 with eight secondary ones, and there are 212 parishes and 215 churches. A legally established pastors' association has three endowed libraries. Church music is promoted by an annual course in organ-playing in Dessau. Seventy-nine parishes have Sunday-schools. The contributions for foreign missions average 14,000 marks yearly, and for the *Gustav Adolf Verein* (q.v.) 10,000 marks. The work of the *Innere Mission* (q.v.) is also well supported, and a deaconesses' house has been established in Dessau. (H. Dunckert†.)

ANICETUS, an-i-sí'tus: Pope from about 154 to about 165. According to the *Liber pontificalis* (ed. Duchesne, i. 58, 134), he was a Syrian by birth. Irenæus (*Adversus hæreses*, III. iii. 3–4) mentions him as the successor of Pius I. and the predecessor of Soter, and refers to the journey of Polycarp to Rome, which took place in Anicetus' pontificate. A fuller account of it is given in Irenæus' letter to Victor, of which Eusebius has preserved a considerable fragment (*Hist. eccl.*, V. xxiv. 12–17; see Polycarp). The dates of Anicetus are uncertain. If Polycarp died in 155, the accession of Anicetus must be placed in 154, and the assignment of eleven years to his pontificate would bring its termination to 165. He is called a martyr in the Roman martyrology, as well as by Rabanus Maurus, Florus, and others, and is commemorated on Apr. 17. (A. Hauck.)

Bibliography: *Liber pontificalis*, ed. Duchesne, i. 58, 134, Paris, 1886; Bower, *Popes*, i. 13–14; Jaffé, *Regesta*, i. 9; J. B. Lightfoot, *Apostolic Fathers*, i. 201 sqq., London, 1890; A. Harnack, in *Sitzungsberichte der Berliner Akademie*, pp. 617–658, 1892; idem, *Litteratur*, ii. 1, pp. 70 sqq.

ANIMALS: I. Regulations Respecting Their Use. 1. For Food: According to the lists (Lev. xi. 1–31, 46–47; Deut. xiv. 1–19), the clean animals (i.e., those whose flesh might be eaten) were ruminant quadrupeds which parted the hoof, were cloven-footed, and chewed the cud; aquatic animals that had fins and scales; all birds except the nineteen species specified, which were birds of prey or carrion; only those flying insects which, like the grasshopper, have two long legs for leaping. No vermin was clean, nor was the carcass of any clean animal, if it had died naturally, or been torn to death. Everything was unclean that touched the unclean; so was the kid seethed in its mother's milk, and the heathen sacrifices in all their parts. See Dietary Laws of the Hebrews.

2. For Sacrifice: The general rule was, that only the clean animals could be offered; this dates back to the pre-Mosaic period (Gen. viii. 20). Asses, camels, and horses were not offered by the Hebrews. But only the *tame* among even the clean animals could be sacrificed; therefore, no animal of the chase. Doves were not regarded as wild. Every animal offered must be without blemish (Lev. xxii. 20), at least seven days old (verse 27; Ex. xxii. 30), because too young flesh is disgusting, and therefore unclean. Nor must it be too old; for bovines three years, for small cattle one, was usual (Ex. xxix. 38; Lev. ix. 3; Num. xxviii. 9; Lev. i. 5, "bullock," a young ox). What man might not eat, it was profanation to sacrifice. See Defilement and Purification, Ceremonial.

II. The Emblematic Use of Animals.—1. In the Old Testament: Locusts were used as the symbol of the divine judgments. The twelve oxen which bore the brazen sea in the court of the temple (I Kings vii. 25) were doubtless symbolic; the animal shapes which appeared in prophetic visions were also symbolic (Ezek. i. 5–14), and seem to be identified with the cherubim (Ezek. x. 1).

2. In the New Testament: Peter uses a lion as the emblem of Satan (I Pet. v. 8); on the other hand, a lion is the emblem of Christ (Rev. v. 5). The ass symbolizes peace (Matt. xxi. 5); the dove, innocence and the Holy Ghost; the dog and swine, uncleanness and vulgarity (Matt. vii. 6; II Pet. ii. 22). But the emblematic use of beasts is much greater in Revelation than in all the other books of the Bible combined. Constant mention is made of the four living creatures (iv. 6, etc.) who were from the fifth century considered as symbolizing the four evangelists. Christ is constantly called the Lamb; the Devil, the dragon (xii. 3, etc.). There are, besides, a beast who comes out of the bottomless pit (xi. 7), horses (vi. 2, etc.), locusts (ix. 3), birds (xix. 17), and frogs (xvi. 13).

3. The Ecclesiastical Use of Animals: This was very varied. There was not only the lamb for Christ but also dolphins, hens, pelicans, apes, and centaurs. The old Gothic churches exhibit these fanciful and really heathen designs. Bernard of Clairvaux raised his voice against them. In the catacombs one finds the drawing of a fish to symbolize Christ, because the initials of the title of Christ (Gk. *Iēsous Christos Theou Uios Sōtēr*) spell the Greek word for "fish" (*ichthus*). See SYMBOLISM.

III. The Use of Emblematic Animals in Worship: Among the Hebrews there are two spoken of. The brazen serpent which Moses made, which was at last destroyed by Hezekiah, because it was worshiped (II Kings xviii. 4). The golden calf was not intended as a substitute for the Yahweh worship, but as an aid; but it became a snare to Israel in the wilderness before Sinai (Ex. xxxii.) and in the days of Jeroboam I. and his successors on the throne of Israel (I Kings xii. 28–30).

ANIMISM. See COMPARATIVE RELIGION, V., 1, a, §§ 1–4; HEATHENISM, §§ 2, 6.

ANNA: 1. Mother of the Virgin Mary. See ANNE, SAINT. **2.** A "prophetess," mentioned in Luke ii. 36–38. See HANNAH.

ANNA COMNENA, com-nī'na: A Byzantine princess of both literary and political importance, daughter of Alexius Comnenus (q.v.); b. Dec. 2, 1083; d. after 1148. Brought up in a circle of highly cultivated women, and betrothed in early youth to the heir-presumptive of the empire, the son of the last emperor of the house of Ducas, she seemed to have a brilliant future before her. But the prince died, and his place was taken later by Nicephorus Bryennius, the son of a conquered pretender. It became plain that the emperor intended to make Anna's brother John his heir, instead of his daughter or her husband. When Alexius died (1118), Anna was the soul of a conspiracy against John. It failed, and military rule suppressed the court cabals. Anna recovered her confiscated property; but on the death of her husband, ten years later, she fell gradually into disfavor at court and lived much alone, solacing herself by literary interests, her taste for which was the result of the brilliant literary epoch of which Michael Psellus was the chief representative. She wrote a remarkable history of her father's reign, with the title *Alexias*, which professes to be a continuation of the unfinished history of the Comneni by her husband. Her style is typical of literary classicism, being full of quotations from standard authors, and affecting to despise the barbarisms of the living tongue. This affectation is carried so far that she apologizes for mentioning barbarian names as for an offense against the customs of polite society. Allied to this is the haughty assertion of the primacy of Byzantium over all uncivilized foreigners, whether popes, Turks, or crusaders. Its strong personal bias, its prejudice against the two successors of Alexius, and its constant revelation of the bitterness of disappointed ambition detract from the historical value of the work. Yet the wealth of information contained in it makes it the principal source for the history of Byzantium at the epoch of the first crusade. It is in *MPG*, cxxxi.; the best edition is by A. Reifferscheid, in the *Bibliotheca Teubneriana* (2 vols., Leipsic, 1884). (C. NEUMANN.)

BIBLIOGRAPHY: Gibbon, *Decline and Fall*, vols. v. and vi., passim (by the only thorough student of Byzantine literature as a whole); H. von Sybel, *Geschichte des ersten Kreuzzuges*, pp. 460–468, Leipsic, 1881 (on the chronology of Anna Comnena); C. Neumann, *Griechische Geschichtschreiber im 12 Jahrhundert*, Leipsic, 1888; T. A. Archer and C. L. Kingsford, *The Crusades*, pp. 49, 52, 191–192, 358, New York, 1895; Dieter, *Zur Glaubenswürdigkeit der Anna Komnena*, in *Byzantinische Zeitschrift*, iii. (1894) 386–390; Krumbacher, *Geschichte*, pp. 274–279.

ANNAS (called **Ananos** by Josephus): Jewish high priest, son of Seth. He was appointed high priest in 7 A.D. by Quirinius, governor of Syria, and retained his office under three successive governors, till he was deposed in the year 14 by Valerius Gratus. His second successor in the high-priesthood was his son Eleazar; the fourth, his son-in-law (John xviii. 13) Joseph, called Caiaphas (Matt. xxvi. 3 sqq.), who held the office from 18 to 36 A.D. Four other sons of Annas officiated as high priests; and as he was called happy for this reason, it may be inferred that he lived to see the installation of most of them. He was dead at the time of the siege of Jerusalem, and his tomb was then shown. According to the New Testament, Annas acted as high priest after his deposition; he occupied an influential position, and presided at the trial of Jesus. These statements are not to be rejected as unhistorical, since high priests who were no longer active retained not only their official title but also many of the prerogatives of office. That Annas was held in high repute beside the acting Caiaphas can be explained from the length of his life and from his family relations. The form of expression in Luke iii. 2 and Acts iv. 6, where Annas appears as an acting high priest, is somewhat incorrect. Like most members of the aristocratic high-priestly line, he was a Sadducee (Acts iv. 1, 6, v. 17) and Josephus calls his son Annas the Younger, a rigid Sadducee. [Josephus (with John xviii. 13) seems to show that Annas was the most influential man in Jerusalem for a generation.] F. SIEFFERT.

BIBLIOGRAPHY: Josephus, *Ant.*, XVIII. ii. 1–2, iv. 3, XX. ix. 1; Schürer, *Geschichte*, ii. 217, 221, Eng. transl. II. i. 182–183, 198, 202–204; *DB*, i. 99–100; *EB*, i. 171–172; *JE*, i. 610–611.

ANNATS (ANNATES). See TAXATION, ECCLESIASTICAL.

ANNE (ANNA), SAINT: Mother of the Virgin Mary. According to apocryphal tradition (*Evangelium de nativitate Mariæ* and *Protevangelium Jacobi*), she is said to have been born at Bethlehem, the daughter of the priest Matthan. She was married to the pious Joachim of the tribe of Judah, and for twenty years was childless. At her assiduous supplication, an angel foretold "that she should conceive and bring forth, and that her seed should be praised in the whole world." Joachim too received comforting promises from the angel. When the daughter was one year old the parents prepared a banquet, and Anna sang a song of praise similar to the *Magnificat*. When three years of age, Mary, having been dedicated before her birth to the service of God, was brought to Jerusalem by her parents and given to the priests to be educated in the Temple. According to later apocryphal legends, Joachim died soon after Mary's birth, and Anna, "not out of sensual lusts, but at the prompting of the Holy Spirit," married first Cleophas, to whom she bore Mary, the wife of Alphæus, and after his death Salomas, by whom she became the mother of a third Mary, the wife of Zebedæus. The legend in this form, which owes its development to the luxuriant Anne cult of the later medieval period, was known to Jean Gerson (d. 1429; cf. his *Oratio de nativitate virginis Mariæ, Opera*, iii. 59). Conrad Wimpina (in his *Oratio de divæ Annæ trinubio*, 1518), as well as Johann Eck (in a sermon in vol. iii. of his *Homiliæ*, Paris, 1579), defended the legend.

Thus the most fantastic excesses of the Anne cult coincide with the Reformation epoch, and were defended by Roman Catholic theologians of the most different schools,—not only immaculistic Franciscans, but also Dominicans, Carmelites, and Augustinian hermits. Even Luther, in his youth, when overtaken by a thunderstorm, cried to Anne for help, and vowed, if delivered, to become a monk (Köstlin, *Leben Luthers*, i. 49, Berlin, 1893). It was a firm belief in the popular mind of the time that Christ's grandmother preserved health, made rich, and protected in death. The pictorial representations of the fifteenth to the seventeenth century dedicated to Anne are almost innumerable as well as the Anne churches. In post-Reformation times popes promoted the Anne cult; thus Gregory XIII. in 1584 ordered that on July 26, the supposed day of Anne's death, a double mass should be said throughout the whole Church; and Benedict XIV. in his *De festis Mariæ Virginis* (ii. 9), recommends the veneration of St. Anne. In the Greek church St. Anne is also celebrated, partly by festivals (July 25 in commemoration of her death; Dec. 9, as the day of her conception; Sept. 9, as the day of her marriage with Joachim), partly by a rich ascetic-homiletical literature, which reaches back to Gregory of Nyssa, but without following the later medieval legends of Western tradition.

O. ZÖCKLER†.

BIBLIOGRAPHY: J. Trithemius, *De laudibus S. Annæ*, Mainz, 1494; P. Canisius, S. J., *De Maria deipara virgine*, i. 4, Ingolstadt, 1577; C. Frantz, *Geschichte des Marien- und Annen-Cultus*, Halberstadt, 1854; H. Samson, *Die Schutzheiligen*, pp. 1 sqq., Paderborn, 1889. From the Protestant standpoint: G. Kawerau, *Caspar Güttel*, pp. 16 sqq., Halle, 1882; E. Schaumkell, *Der Cultus der heiligen Anna am Ausgang des Mittelalters*, Freiburg, 1893; G. Bossert, *St. Anna Cultus in Württemberg*, in *Blätter für württembergische Kirchengeschichte*, i. (1886) 17, 64 sqq. For Anne in art: H. Detzel, *Christliche Ikonographie*, i. 66–80, Freiburg, 1894.

ANNET, PETER. See DEISM.

ANNI CLERI: A method of repaying loans for the erection of a church or parsonage, whereby succeeding pastors contribute a portion of their income in fixed instalments.

ANNIHILATIONISM.

1. Definition and Classification of Theories.

A term designating broadly a large body of theories which unite in contending that human beings pass, or are put, out of existence altogether. These theories fall logically into three classes, according as they hold that all souls, being mortal, actually cease to exist at death; or that, souls being naturally mortal, only those persist in life to which immortality is given by God; or that, though souls are naturally immortal and persist in existence unless destroyed by a force working upon them from without, wicked souls are actually thus destroyed. These three classes of theories may be conveniently called respectively, (1) pure mortalism, (2) conditional immortality, and (3) annihilationism proper.

2. Pure Mortalism.

The common contention of the theories which form the first of these classes is that human life is bound up with the organism, and that therefore the entire man passes out of being with the dissolution of the organism. The usual basis of this contention is either materialistic or pantheistic or at least pantheizing (e.g., realistic); the soul being conceived in the former case as but a function of organized matter and necessarily ceasing to exist with the dissolution of the organism, in the latter case as but the individualized manifestation of a much more extensive entity, back into which it sinks with the dissolution of the organism in connection with which the individualization takes place. Rarely, however, the contention in question is based on the notion that the soul, although a spiritual entity distinct from the material body, is incapable of maintaining its existence separate from the body. The promise of eternal life is too essential an element of Christianity for theories like these to thrive in a Christian atmosphere. It is even admitted now by Stade, Oort, Schwally, and others that the Old Testament, even in its oldest strata, presupposes the persistence of life after death,—which used to be very commonly denied. Nevertheless, the materialists (e.g., Feuerbach, Vogt, Moleschott, Büchner, Häckel), and pantheists (Spinoza, Fichte, Schelling, Hegel, Strauss; cf. S. Davidson, *Doctrine of the Last Things*, London, 1882, pp. 132–133), still deny the possibility of immortality; and in exceedingly wide circles, even among those who would not wholly break with Christianity, men permit themselves to cherish nothing more than a "hope" of it (S. Hoekstra, *De hoop der onsterfelijkheid*, Amsterdam, 1867; L. W E. Rauwenhoff, *Wijsbegeerte van den Godsdienst*, Leyden, 1887, p. 811; cf. the "Ingersoll Lectures").

The class of theories to which the designation of "conditional immortality" is most properly applicable, agree with the theories of pure mortalism in teaching the natural mortality of man in his entirety, but separate from them in maintaining that this mortal may, and in many cases does, put on immortality

3. Conditional Immortality.

Immortality in their view is a gift of God, conferred on those who have entered into living communion with him. Many theorists of this class adopt frankly the materialistic doctrine of the soul, and deny that it is a distinct entity; they therefore teach that the soul necessarily dies with the body, and identify life beyond death with the resurrection, conceived as essentially a recreation of the entire man. Whether all men are subjects of this recreative resurrection is a mooted question among themselves. Some deny it, and affirm therefore that the wicked perish finally at death, the children of God alone attaining to resurrection. The greater part, however, teach a resurrection for all, and a "second death," which is annihilation, for the wicked (e.g., Jacob Blain, *Death not Life*, Buffalo, 1857, pp. 39–42; Aaron Ellis and Thomas Read, *Bible versus Tradition*, New York, 1853, pp. 13–121; George Storrs, *Six Sermons*, ib. 1856, p. 29; Zenas Campbell, *The Age of Gospel Light*, Hartford, 1854). There are many, on the other hand, who recognize that the soul is a spiritual entity, disparate to, though conjoined in personal union with, the body. In their view, however, ordinarily at least, the soul requires the body either for its existence, or certainly for its activity. C. F. Hudson, for example (*Debt and Grace*, New York, 1861, pp. 263–264), teaches that the soul lies unconscious, or at least inactive, from death to the resurrection; then the just rise to an ecstasy of bliss; the unjust, however, start up at the voice of God to become extinct in the very act. Most, perhaps, prolong the second life of the wicked for the purpose of the infliction of their merited punishment; and some make their extinction a protracted process (e.g., H. L. Hastings, *Retribution or the Doom of the Ungodly*, Providence, 1861, pp. 77, 153; cf. Horace Bushnell, *Forgiveness and Law*, New York, 1874, p. 147, notes 5 and 6; James Martineau, *A Study of Religion*, ii., Oxford, 1888, p. 114). For further discussion of the theory of conditional immortality, see IMMORTALITY.

Already, however, in speaking of extinction we are passing beyond the limits of "conditionalism" pure and simple and entering the region of annihilationism proper. Whether we think of this extinction as the result of the punishment or as the gradual dying out of the personality under the enfeebling effects of sin, we are no longer looking at the soul as naturally mortal and requiring a new gift of grace to keep it in existence, but as naturally immortal and suffering destruction at the hands of an inimical power. And this becomes even more apparent when the assumed mortalism of the soul is grounded not in its nature but in its sinfulness; so that the theory deals not with souls as such, but with sinful souls, and it is a question of salvation by a gift of grace to everlasting life or of being left to the disintegrating effects of sin. The point of distinction between theories of this class and "conditionalism" is that these theories with more or less consistency or heartiness recognize what is called the "natural immortality of the soul," and are not tempted therefore to think of the soul as by nature passing out of being at death (or at any time), and yet teach that the actual punishment inflicted upon or suffered by the wicked results in extinction of being. They may differ among themselves, as to the time when this extinction takes place,—whether at death, or at the general judgment,—or as to the more or less extended or intense punishment accorded to the varying guilt of each soul. They may differ also as to the means by which the annihilation of the wicked soul is accomplished,—whether by a mere act of divine power, cutting off the sinful life, or by the destructive fury of the punishment inflicted, or by the gradual enervating and sapping working of sin itself on the personality. They retain their common character as theories of annihilation proper so long as they conceive the extinction of the soul as an effect wrought on it to which it succumbs, rather than as the natural exit of the soul from a life which could be continued to it only by some operation upon it raising it to a higher than its natural potency.

4. Annihilationism Proper.

It must be borne in mind that the adherents of these two classes of theories are not very careful to keep strictly within the logical limits of one of the classes. Convenient as it is to approach their study with a definite schematization in hand, it is not always easy to assign individual writers with definiteness to one or the other of them. It has become usual, therefore, to speak of them all as annihilationists or of them all as conditionalists; annihilationists because they all agree that the souls of the wicked cease to exist; conditionalists because they all agree that therefore persistence in life is conditioned on a right relation to God. Perhaps the majority of those who call themselves conditionalists allow that the mortality of the soul, which is the prime postulate of the conditionalist theory, is in one way or another connected with sin; that the souls of the wicked persist in existence after death and even after the judgment, in order to receive the punishment due their sin; and that this punishment, whether it be conceived as infliction from without or as the simple consequence of sin, has much to do with their extinction. When so held, conditionalism certainly falls little short of annihilationism proper.

5. Mingling of Theories.

Some confusion has arisen, in tracing the history of the annihilationist theories, from confounding with them enunciations by the earlier Church Fathers of the essential Christian doctrine that the soul is not self-existent, but owes, as its existence, so its continuance in being, to the will of God. The earliest appearance of a genuinely annihilationist theory in extant Christian literature is to be found apparently in the African apologist Arnobius, at

6. Early History of Annihilationistic Theories.

the opening of the fourth century (cf. Salmond, pp. 473-474; Falke, pp. 27-28). It seemed to him impossible that beings such as men could either owe their being directly to God or persist in being without a special gift of God; the unrighteous must therefore be gradually consumed in the fires of Gehenna. A somewhat similar idea was announced by the Socinians in the sixteenth century (O. Fock, *Der Socinianismus*, Kiel, 1847, pp. 714 sqq.). On the positive side, Faustus Socinus himself thought that man is mortal by nature and attains immortality only by grace. On the negative side, his followers (Crell, Schwaltz, and especially Ernst Sohner) taught explicitly that the second death consists in annihilation, which takes place, however, only after the general resurrection, at the final judgment. From the Socinians this general view passed over to England where it was adopted, not merely, as might have been anticipated, by men like Locke (*Reasonableness of Christianity*, § 1), Hobbes (*Leviathan*), and Whiston, but also by Churchmen like Hammond and Warburton, and was at least played with by non-conformist leaders like Isaac Watts. The most remarkable example of its utilization in this age, however, is supplied by the non-juror Henry Dodwell (1706). Insisting that the "soul is a principle naturally mortal," Dodwell refused to allow the benefit of this mortality to any but those who lived and died without the limits of the proclamation of the Gospel; no "adult person whatever," he insisted, "living where Christianity is professed, and the motives of its credibility are sufficiently proposed, can hope for the benefit of actual mortality." Those living in Christian lands are therefore all immortalized, but in two classes: some "by the pleasure of God to punishment," some "to reward by their union with the divine baptismal Spirit." It was part of his contention that "none have the power of giving this divine immortalizing Spirit since the apostles but the bishops only," so that his book was rather a blast against the antiprelatists than a plea for annihilationism; and it was replied to as such by Samuel Clarke (1706), Richard Baxter (1707), and Daniel Whitby (1707). During the eighteenth century the theory was advocated also on the continent of Europe (e.g., E. J. E. Walter, *Prüfung einiger wichtigen Lehren theologisches und philosophisches Inhalts*, Berlin, 1782), and almost found a martyr in the Neuchatel pastor, Ferdinand Olivier Petitpierre, commonly spoken of by the nickname of "No Eternity" (cf. C. Berthoud, *Les Quatre Petitpierres*, Neuchatel, 1875). In the first half of the nineteenth century also it found sporadic adherents, as e.g., C. H. Weisse in Germany (*TSK*, ix., 1836, 271-340) and H. H. Dobney in England (*Notes of Lectures on Future Punishment*, London, 1844; new ed., *On the Scripture Doctrine of Future Punishment*, 1846).

The real extension of the theory belongs, however, only to the second half of the nineteenth century. During this period it attained, chiefly through the able advocacy of it by C. F. Hudson and E. White, something like a popular vogue in English-speaking lands. In French-speaking countries, while never becoming really popular, it has commanded the attention of an influential circle of theologians and philosophers (as J. Rognon, *L'Immortalité native et l'enseignement biblique*, Paris, 1894, p. 7; but cf. A. Gretillat, *Exposé de théologie systématique*, IV., 1892, p. 602). In Germany, on the other hand, it has met with less acceptance, although it is precisely there that it has been most scientifically developed, and has received the adherence of the most outstanding names.

7. Nineteenth Century Theories.

Before the opening of this half century in fact it had gained the great support of Richard Rothe's advocacy (*Theologische Ethik*, 2 vols., Wittenberg, 1845-47; 2d ed., 1867-72, §§ 470-472; *Dogmatik*, iii., Heidelberg, 1870, §§ 47-48, especially p. 158), and never since has it ceased to find adherents of mark, who base their acceptance of it sometimes on general grounds, but increasingly on the view that the Scriptures teach, not a doctrine of the immortality of the soul, but a reanimation by resurrection of God's people. The chief names in this series are C. H. Weisse (*Philosophische Dogmatik*, Leipsic, 1853-62, § 970); Hermann Schultz (*Voraussetzungen der christlichen Lehre der Unsterblichkeit*, Göttingen, 1861, p. 155; cf. *Grundriss der evangelischen Dogmatik*, 1892, p. 154: "This condemnation of the second death may in itself, according to the Bible, be thought of as existence in torment, or as painful cessation of existence. Dogmatics without venturing to decide, will find the second conception the more probable, biblically and dogmatically"); H. Plitt (*Evangelische Glaubenslehre*, Gotha, 1863); F. Brandes, (*TSK*, 1872, pp. 545, 550); A. Schäffer (*Auf der Neige des Lebens*, Gotha, 1884; *Was ist Glück?* 1891, pp. 290-294); G. Runze (*Unsterblichkeit und Auferstehung*, i., Berlin, 1894, pp. 167, 204: "Christian Eschatology teaches not a natural immortality for the soul, but a reanimation by God's almighty power. The Christian hope of reanimation makes the actualization of a future blessed existence depend entirely on faith in God"); L. Lemme (*Endlosigkeit der Verdammnis*, Berlin, 1898, pp. 31-32, 60-61); cf. R. Kabisch (*Die Eschatologie des Paulus*, Göttingen, 1893).

The same general standpoint has been occupied in Holland, e.g., by Jonker (*Theologische Studien*, i.). The first advocate of conditionalism in French was the Swiss pastor, E. Pétavel-Olliff, whose first book, *La Fin du mal*, appeared in 1872 (Paris), followed by many articles in the French theological journals and by *Le Problème de l'immortalité* (1891; Eng. transl., London, 1892), and *The Extinction of Evil* (Eng., 1889). In 1880 C. Byse issued a translation of E. White's chief book. The theory not only had already been presented by A. Bost, (*Le Sort des méchants*, 1861), but had been taken up by philosophers of such standing as C. Lambert (*Système du monde moral*, 1862), P Janet (*RDM*, 1863), and C. Renouvier (*La Critique philosophique*, 1878); and soon afterward Charles Sécretan and C. Ribot (*RT*, 1885, no. 1) expressed their general adherence to it. Perhaps the more distinguished advocacy of it on French ground has come, however, from the two professors Sabatier, Auguste and Armand, the one from the point of view of exegetical, the other from that of natural science. Says the one (*L'Origine du péché dans le système théologique de Paul,* Paris, 1887, p. 38): "The impenitent sinner never emerges from the fleshly state, and consequently remains subject to the law of corruption and destruction, which rules fleshly beings; they perish and are as if they had never been." Says the other (*Essai sur l'immortalité au point de vue du naturalisme évolutionniste,* 2d ed., Paris, 1895, pp. 198, 229): "The immortality of man is not universal and necessary; it is subject to certain conditions, it is conditional, to use an established expression." "Ultraterrestrial immortality will be the exclusive lot of souls which have arrived at a sufficient degree of integrity and cohesion to escape absorption or disintegration."

8. English Advocates.

The chief English advocate of conditional immortality has undoubtedly been Edward White whose *Life in Christ* was published first in 1846 (London), rewritten in 1875 (3d ed., 1878). His labors were seconded, however, not only by older works of similar tendency such as George Storrs's *Are the Wicked Immortal?* (21st ed., New York, 1852), but by later teaching from men of the standing of Archbishop Whately (*Scripture Revelation Respecting the Future State,* 8th ed., London, 1859), Bishop Hampden, J. B. Heard (*The Tripartite Nature of Man,* 5th ed., Edinburgh, 1852), Prebendary Constable (*The Duration and Nature of Future Punishment,* London, 1868), Prebendary Row (*Future Retribution,* London, 1887), J. M. Denniston (*The Perishing Soul,* 2d ed., London, 1874), S. Minton (*The Glory of Christ,* London, 1868), J. W Barlow (*Eternal Punishment,* Cambridge, 1865), and T. Davis (*Endless Suffering not the Doctrine of Scripture,* London, 1866). Less decisive but not less influential advocacy has been given to the theory also by men like Joseph Parker, R. W. Dale, and J. A. Beet (*The Last Things,* London, 1897). Mr. Beet (who quotes Clemance, *Future Punishment,* London, 1880, as much of his way of thinking) occupies essentially the position of Schultz. "The sacred writers," he says, "while apparently inclining sometimes to one and sometimes to the other, do not pronounce decisive judgment" between eternal punishment and annihilation (p. 216), while annihilation is free from speculative objections. In America C. F. Hudson's initial efforts (*Debt and Grace,* Boston, 1857, 5th ed., 1889; *Christ Our Life,* 1860) were ably seconded by W R. Huntington (*Conditional Immortality,* New York, 1878) and J. H. Pettingell (*The Life Everlasting,* Philadelphia, 1882, combining two previously published tractates; *The Unspeakable Gift,* Yarmouth, Me., 1884). Views of much the same character have been expressed also by Horace Bushnell, L. W Bacon, L. C. Baker, Lyman Abbott, and without much insistence on them by Henry C. Sheldon (*System of Christian Doctrine,* Cincinnati, 1903, pp. 573 sqq.).

9. Modifications of the Theory.

There is a particular form of conditionalism requiring special mention which seeks to avoid the difficulties of annihilationism, by teaching, not the total extinction of the souls of the wicked, but rather, as it is commonly phrased, their "transformation" into impersonal beings incapable of moral action, or indeed of any feeling. This is the form of conditionalism which is suggested by James Martineau (*A Study of Religion,* ii., Oxford, 1888, p. 114) and by Horace Bushnell (*Forgiveness and Law,* New York, 1874, p. 147, notes 5 and 6). It is also hinted by Henry Drummond (*Natural Law in the Spiritual World,* London, 1874), when he supposes the lost soul to lose not salvation merely but the capacity for it and for God; so that what is left is no longer fit to be called a soul, but is a shrunken, useless organ ready to fall away like a rotten twig. The Alsatian theologian A. Schäffer (*Was ist Glück?,* Gotha, 1891, pp. 290–294) similarly speaks of the wicked soul losing the light from heaven, the divine spark which gave it its value, and the human personality thereby becoming obliterated. "The forces out of which it arises break up and become at last again impersonal. They do not pass away, but they are transformed." One sees the conception here put forward at its highest level in such a view as that presented by Prof. O. A. Curtis (*The Christian Faith,* New York, 1905, p. 467), which thinks of the lost not, to be sure, as "crushed into mere thinghood" but as sunk into a condition "below the possibility of any moral action or moral concern like persons in this life whose personality is entirely overwhelmed by the base sense of what we call physical fear." There is no annihilation in Prof. Curtis's view; not even relief for the lost from suffering; but it may perhaps be looked at as marking the point where the theories of annihilationism reach up to and melt at last into the doctrine of eternal punishment.

BENJAMIN B. WARFIELD.

BIBLIOGRAPHY: An exhaustive bibliography of the subject up to 1863 is given in Ezra Abbot's Appendix to W. R. Alger's *History of the Doctrine of a Future Life,* also published separately, New York, 1871; consult also W. Reid, *Everlasting Punishment and Modern Speculation,* pp. 311–313, Boston, 1874. Special works on annihilationism are J. C. Killam, *Annihilationism Examined,* Syracuse, 1859; I. P. Warren, *The Wicked not Annihilated,* New York, 1867; N. D. George, *Annihilationism not of the Bible,* ib. 1874; J. B. Brown, *Doctrine of Annihilation in the Light of the Gospel of Love,* London, 1875; S. C. Bartlett, *Life and Death Eternal. A Refutation of the Theory of Annihilationism,* Boston, 1878. The subject is treated in S. D. F. Salmond, *Christian Doctrine of Immortality,* pp. 473–499, Edinburgh, 1901; R. W. Landis, *Immortality,* pp. 422 sqq., New York, 1860; A. Hovey, *State of the Impenitent Dead,* pp. 93 sqq., Boston, 1875; C. M. Mead, *The Soul Here and Hereafter,* Boston, 1879; G. Godet, in *Chrétienne Evangélique,* 1881–82; F. Godet, in *Revue Théologique,* 1886; J. Fyfe, *The Hereafter,* Edinburgh, 1889; R. Falke, *Die Lehre von der ewigen Verdamniss,* pp. 25–38, Eisenach, 1892. On conditional immortality, consult W. R. Huntington, *Conditional Immortality,* New York, 1878; J. H. Pettingell, *Theological Tri-lemma,* ib. 1878; idem, *Life Everlasting. What is it? Whence is it? Whose is it? A Symposium,* Philadelphia, 1882; E. White, *Life and Death: A Reply to J. B. Brown's Lectures on Conditional Immortality,* London, 1877; idem, *Life in Christ. A Study of the Scripture Doctrine on the Conditions of Human Immortality,* New York, 1892. Further discussions may be found in the appropriate sections of most works on systematic theology and also in works on eschatology and future punishment. See, besides the works mentioned in the text, the literature under IMMORTALITY.

ANNIVERSARIUS (sc. *dies*), **ANNIVERSARIUM:** A day or service in memory of a deceased person. From the second century it was usual in Christian congregations to celebrate the death-days of their martyrs with divine service as they recurred annually. Families also used to commemorate their departed members on their death-days. From this custom arose the festivals of the martyrs and saints, as also those anniversaries for departed members of the congregations which are still held in the Roman Catholic Church, and consist in masses and alms provided for by special endowments.

ANNO: Archbishop of Cologne; b. probably 1010; d. at Cologne Dec. 4, 1075. He came of a noble Swabian family, received his education at Bamberg, and, through the favor of Emperor Henry III., attained the dignities of dean of Goslar and archbishop of Cologne (1056). After the death of Henry III. (1056) and the accession of his infant son, Henry IV., under the regency of his mother Agnes of Poitou, Anno exercised considerable influence at court, and took part in the contest which broke out between the empire and Rome. The lack of capacity for the duties of government revealed by the queen-regent led to the formation of a conspiracy in 1062, under the leadership of Anno, who in the same year made himself master of the young king's person and thereby became virtual ruler of the empire. Desire for personal aggrandizement restrained him from making use of his power for the interests of Germany in the quarrel with the papacy, which now entered upon an acute phase. Upon the death of Pope Nicholas II. (1061) the party hostile to German influence, under the leadership of Hildebrand, had chosen as his successor Anselm of Lucca, who assumed the title of Alexander II. In opposition the imperial party had raised to the papal office Cadalus of Parma under the name of Honorius II. A synod at Augsburg, summoned in 1062 to decide on the conflicting claims of the two candidates, rendered a temporary decision in favor of Alexander II.; and two years later a second synod, at Mantua, made formal acknowledgment of Alexander's rights. Anno, who was in complete control at Augsburg, was actuated in this course, so seemingly hostile to the welfare of the empire, by the desire to preserve in his hands the balance of power between the papal and imperial forces and thus to secure for himself the rôle of arbiter between the two. When the council of Mantua assembled, however, his influence had undergone serious diminution and he was unable to prevent the confirmation of the Italian pope. A strong rival for power now appeared in the person of Adalbert, archbishop of Hamburg-Bremen (see ADALBERT OF HAMBURG-BREMEN), with whom Anno was compelled to share his authority over the young king (1063). Two years later the archbishop of Cologne found himself almost entirely superseded.

The fall of Adalbert in 1066 brought Anno once more to the front for a brief time, but he never again exercised the authority he had formerly possessed. The last years of his life were embittered by quarrels with Rome, by a rising of the citizens of Cologne which he suppressed with extreme severity, and by charges of treasonable correspondence with William I. of England, for which there seems to have been little foundation. There was not wanting in the worldly prelate a certain ascetic austerity which the misfortunes of his later years tended to accentuate, giving him a posthumous reputation of great holiness, and in 1183 he was canonized. (CARL MIRBT.)

BIBLIOGRAPHY: Sources for biography are: *Vita sancti Annonis*, by a monk of Siegburg (c. 1100), in *MGH*, *Script.*, xi. (1854) 465–514 and in *MPL*, cxliii.; *Vita minor sancti Annonis* by another monk (c. 1186), ed. F. W. E. Roth in *NA*, xii. (1887) 209–215; a poem by an unknown author ed. J. Kehrein, Frankfort, 1865. Consult T. Lindner, *Anno II. der Heilige*, Leipsic, 1869; E. Steindorff, *Jahrbücher des deutschen Reichs unter Heinrich III.*, 2 vols., ib. 1874–81; W. von Giesebrecht, *Geschichte der deutschen Kaiserzeit*, vol. iii., ib. 1890; G. Meyer von Knonau, *Jahrbücher des deutschen Reichs unter Heinrich IV.*, 2 vols., ib. 1890–94; Wattenbach, *DGQ*, ii. 107–109, 137, 140, 146, 183; Hauck, *KD*, vol. iii.

ANNOTATED BIBLES. See BIBLES, ANNOTATED.

ANNULUS PISCATORIS, an'yu-lus pis-ka-tō'ris: The official ring worn by the popes. Every Roman Catholic bishop wears a ring, which symbolizes that he is wedded to his diocese. This custom dates from very early times, and is mentioned by Isidore of Seville, who calls the ring *signum pontificalis honoris*. The ring worn by a pope is engraved with a representation of St. Peter fishing—whence its special name—and with the title of the pontiff. From the fifteenth century papal briefs have been sealed with this ring, and are accordingly said to be given "under the seal of the fisherman." At the present time, instead of this seal, an imprint of the same device in red ink is more commonly used. The ring is given to the newly elected pontiff in the conclave by the cardinal camerlingo, and is broken on the death of the pope.

ANNUNCIATION, FEAST OF THE: A festival celebrated in the Greek, Roman Catholic, and Anglican churches on Mar. 25, in commemoration of the beginning of the incarnation (Luke i. 26–38). Though Augustine mentions the date of the event as nine months before Christmas, the earliest indisputable evidence for the celebration of the feast is furnished by Proclus, patriarch of Constantinople, who died before the middle of the fifth century. The probable date of its origin is about the end of the fourth century. The Council of Toledo (656) ordered its observance on Dec. 18, objecting to its celebration in the mournful season of Lent; and the church of Milan kept it on the fourth Sunday in Advent; but the Roman date finally prevailed throughout the West. The ancient Roman year having commenced with March, on the twenty-fifth of which month the vernal equinox fell in the Julian calendar, it was natural for Christian countries to date their years from the feast which commemorated the initial step in the work of redemption; in some parts of England and the United States this date is still the legal term from which leases, etc. are reckoned.

ANNUNCIATION, ORDERS OF THE (ANNUNCIADES): Five Roman Catholic congregations, two for men and three for women, have their name from the annunciation to the Virgin Mary (Luke i.

26–38). (1) The highest knightly order of the house of Savoy (now the ruling house of Italy): As the spiritual order of the "Knights of the Collar" it was founded by Count Amadeus VI. in 1362, and was specially favored by Amadeus VIII. (Pope Felix V.; d. 1451). In 1518 under Charles III. it was dedicated to Santa Maria Annunziata. Later it became a secular order of merit and nobility. (2) The "Archbrothers of the Annunciation": Founded about 1460 by Cardinal Johannes de Turrecremata (Juan de Torquemada) in the Church of Santa Maria sopra Minerva at Rome; it had importance only for that church. (3) The "Annunciades of Santa Marcellina" (or of St. Ambrose): Founded in Genoa in 1408 for the care of the sick and the performance of like deeds of charity. Their most famous member was the ascetic and mystical writer Catharina Fieschi-Adorno who died in 1510 (see CATHARINE, SAINT, OF GENOA). (4) The "Blue Annunciades" (*Annuntiatæ cœlestes*; Italian, *Turchine*, from *turchina*, "turquoise"; so called from the color of their cloak): Founded in 1604 by the pious Maria Vittoria Fornari, a widow of Genoa. In the seventeenth century they had more than fifty convents, mostly in upper Italy. (5) The *Religieuses Annonciades* (known also as the "Order of the Ten Virtues of the Holy Virgin"): Founded about 1498 by Jeanne de Valois, Queen of France, and her confessor, Gilbert Nicolai. At one time they had forty-five convents in France and Belgium. The order was destroyed by the French Revolution.

O. ZÖCKLER†.

BIBLIOGRAPHY: Helyot, *Ordres monastiques*, iv. 62–63, 297–309, vii. 239–250, viii. 322–325, Paris, 1715; Heimbucher, *Orden und Kongregationen*, i. 521–523.

ANNUS CARENTIÆ, an'us kā-ren'shi-ī: The term during which a canon or other prebendary must renounce part of his revenues to the pope, the bishop, the church buildings or furniture, or for some other ecclesiastical purpose. In some countries a certain percentage is annually paid to an ecclesiastical fund.

ANNUS CLAUSTRALIS, clos-tra'lis: The first year in which a canon holds his benefice, and during which he is bound to be in strictest residence.

ANNUS DECRETORIUS, dec"re-tō'ri-us: The year 1624, which by the peace of Westphalia (1648) was taken as the basis for the division between the Roman Catholic and the Protestant churches in German territory.

ANNUS DESERVITUS, des-er-vī'tus, or **ANNUS GRATIÆ**, grē'shi-ī or -ē: The term, varying in length in different countries, during which the heirs of an ecclesiastic are entitled to enjoy his revenues after his death.

ANNUS LUCTUS: The year of mourning, in some countries an obstacle to marriage (q.v.).

ANOINTING. See OINTMENT; SACRAMENTALS.

ANOMOIOS, ANOMOIANS (ANOMŒANS). See ARIANISM.

ANRICH, GUSTAV ADOLF: German Lutheran; b. at Runzenheim (a village of Lower Alsace) Dec. 2, 1867. He was educated at the universities of Strasburg, Marburg, and Berlin, and in 1894 became privat docent at Strasburg. He was pastor at Lingolsheim, Lower Alsace, from 1896 to 1901, when he became director of the Theologischer Studienstift, Strasburg. Since 1903 he has been associate professor of church history at Strasburg. He has written *Das antike Mysterienwesen in seinem Verhältniss zum Christentum* (Göttingen, 1894); *Clemens und Origenes als Begründer der Lehre vom Fegefeuer* (Tübingen, 1902); and has edited *Die Anfänge des Heiligenkults in der christlichen Kirche* of E. Lucius (1904).

ANSEGIS, an-sē'jis (abbreviated form of **Ansegisil**): **1. The Elder Ansegis:** Abbot of Fontanella (St. Wandrille, 15 m. n.n.w. of Rouen); b. in the latter part of the eighth century; d. at Fontanella July 20, 833. He received his first instruction in a cloister-school in the diocese of Lyons, became a monk in the monastery of Fontanella, and was made abbot of St. Germain de Flay, in the diocese of Beauvais, in 807 His energy and good management attracted the notice of Charlemagne, who called him to his court of Aix-la-Chapelle, and put him with Einhard in charge of his building operations. Louis the Pious also held him in great favor, and endowed him in 817 with the abbey of Luxeuil, and in 823 with that of Fontanella. Here he published his collection of Frankish laws, *Libri iv. capitularium regum Francorum*, which in 829 obtained official authority. Most of these *capitularia* can be compared with the original documents, and the comparison shows that Ansegis altered very little in the text; but Benedict of Mainz (Benedictus Levita), who, twenty years later, continued the work, made arbitrary, not to say fraudulent, alterations. In the ninth century the work was translated into German, and up to the thirteenth century the German kings took an oath on the book as containing the rights of the realm.

BIBLIOGRAPHY: Sources are: *Vita Sancti Ansegisi*, by an unknown contemporary, in *MPL*, cv.; of the *Capitularium collectio* the best edition is by A. Boretius in *MGH*, *Leg.*, ii., *Capitularia Regum Francorum*, i. (1883) 382–450. Consult H. Brunner, *Deutsche Rechtsgeschichte*, i. 382–384, Leipsic, 1887.

2. The **Younger Ansegis** became archbishop of Sens in 872; d. Nov. 25, 882. In 876 he was appointed papal vicar in Gaul and Germany, with the right to convoke synods and to act as the representative of the pope in all affairs of the Church. At the synod of Ponthion (876), however, a number of the Frankish bishops refused to acknowledge his authority, and nothing is heard of a real activity on his part as papal vicar. In 877 he seems to have lost the confidence of the pope, and in the following year another papal vicar was appointed. On his tombstone he is called *Primus Gallorum Papa*, and up to the fifteenth century the Archbishop of Sens was styled *Galliæ et Germanorum Primas*.

(P. HINSCHIUS†.)

BIBLIOGRAPHY: E. L. Dümmler, *Geschichte des ostfränkischen Reichs*, i. 748, 767, 795, 837, 845 sqq., ii. 40, 70, 81, 122, Leipsic, 1862–65; P. Hinschius, *Kirchenrecht*, i. 597, Berlin, 1869.

ANSELM, SAINT, OF CANTERBURY: The father of medieval scholasticism and one of the most eminent of English prelates; b. at Aosta.

Piedmont, 1033; d. at Canterbury, England, Apr. 21, 1109. He was well-born and his parents were wealthy. While still a boy he wished to be a monk, but his father—a harsh man and unkind to his son— forbade; his mother, a good and devout woman, had died early. When about twenty-three Anselm left home, and, after three years in Burgundy and France, went to Bec in Normandy, where his celebrated countryman, Lanfranc, was prior. Here he became a monk (1060). He succeeded Lanfranc as prior in 1063, and became abbot in 1078. The abbey had possessions in England, which called Anselm frequently to that country. He was the general choice for archbishop of Canterbury when Lanfranc died (1089), but the king, William Rufus, preferred to keep the office vacant, and apply its revenues to his own use. In 1093 William fell ill and, thinking his end near, literally forced Anselm to receive an appointment at his hands. He was consecrated Dec. 4 of that year. The next four years witnessed a continual struggle between king and archbishop over money matters, rights, and privileges. Anselm wished to carry his case to Rome, and in 1097, with much difficulty, obtained permission from the king to go. At Rome he was honored and flattered, but he obtained little practical help in his struggle with the king. He returned to England as soon as he heard of the death of William (1100), and at the earnest request of the new king, Henry. But a difficulty at once arose over lay investiture and homage from clerics for their benefices. Though a mild and meek man, Anselm had adopted the Gregorian views of the relation between Church and State, and adhered to them with the steadiness of conscientious conviction. The king, though inclined to be conciliatory, was equally firm from motives of self-interest. He had a high regard for Anselm, always treated him with much consideration, and personal relations between them were generally friendly. Nevertheless there was much vexatious disputing, several fruitless embassies were sent to Rome, and Anselm himself went thither in 1103, remaining abroad till 1106. His quarrel with the king was settled by compromise in 1107, and the brief remaining period of his life was peaceful, though clouded by failing bodily powers. He was canonized in 1494.

Anselm is one of the most attractive characters of the medieval Church. He was preeminently a scholar, and considered the monastic life the happiest and best. When duty called, however, he did not shrink from assuming the burdens of administration and from mixing in the turmoils of statecraft, and he proved that steadfast rectitude is as efficacious as the devious ways of politicians. His honesty and simplicity were sometimes found embarrassing by diplomatic pontiffs and time-serving bishops. He was unfeignedly humble, kind of heart, and charitable in judgment, of spotless integrity, as zealous in good works as in the performance of duty, patient under trial and adversity. He was skilful in winning and training the young, achieved marked success as a teacher, and the common people were always on his side. In the history of theology he stands as the father of orthodox scholasticism, and has been called "the second Augustine." His mind was keen and logical, and his writings display profundity, originality, and masterly grasp of intellect. Of the two theological tendencies occupying the field in his time—the one, more free and rational, represented by Berengar of Tours; the other, confining itself more closely to the tradition of the Church, and represented by Lanfranc—he chose the latter; and he defines the object of scholastic theology to be the logical development and dialectic demonstration of the doctrines of the Church as handed down through the Fathers. The dogmas of the Church are to him identical with revelation itself; and their truth surpasses the conceptions of reason so far that it is mere vanity to doubt a dogma on account of its unintelligibility. *Credo ut intelligam, non quæro intelligere ut credam*, is the principle on which he proceeds; and after him it has become the principle of all orthodox theology. As a metaphysician Anselm was a realist, and one of his earliest works, *De fide Trinitatis*, was an attack on the doctrine of the Trinity as expounded by the nominalist Roscelin. His most celebrated works are the *Monologium* and *Proslogium*, both aiming to prove the existence and nature of God; and the *Cur deus homo*, in which he develops views of atonement and satisfaction which are still held by orthodox theologians. The two first-named were written at Bec; the last was begun in England "in great tribulation of heart," and finished at Schiavi, a mountain village of Apulia, where Anselm enjoyed a few months of rest in 1098. His meditations and prayers are edifying and often highly impressive.

[In the *Monologium* he argues that from the idea of being there follows the idea of a highest and absolute, i.e. self-existent Being, from which all other being derives its existence—a revival of the ancient cosmological argument. In the *Proslogium* the idea of the perfect being—"than which nothing greater can be thought"—can not be separated from its reality as existing. For if the idea of the perfect Being, thus present in consciousness, lacked existence, a still more perfect Being could be thought, of which existence would be a necessary metaphysical predicate, and thus the most perfect Being would be the absolutely Real. The argument is significant, partly as showing the profound influence of Realism over Anselm's thought, and partly as revealing him to be the first to enter upon the perilous transcendent pathway of the ontological argument, to be followed by Descartes (*Meditationes*), Hegel and his school, and especially J. Caird (*Philosophy of Religion*, New York, 1881, pp. 153–159. For criticism of the ontological argument, cf. Kant, *Critique of the Pure Reason*, New York, 1881, pp. 500 sqq., Ueberweg, *History of Philosophy*, i., New York, 1873, pp. 383–386).

The key to Anselm's theory of the Atonement (see ATONEMENT) was the idea of "satisfaction." In justice to himself and to the creation, God, whose honor had suffered injury by man's sin, must react against it either by punishing men, or, since he was merciful, by an equivalent satisfaction, viz., the death of the God-man, which will more than compensate for the injury to his honor, on the ground of which he forgives sin. Incidental features of his theory are—sin as a violation of a private relation between God and man, the interaction of the divine righteousness and grace, and the necessity of a representative suffering. In the Reformed doctrine, sin and the Atonement took on more of a public character, the active obedience of Christ was also emphasized, and the representative relation of Christ to the law brought to the front. In the seventeenth century the forensic and penal justice of God came into prominence; Christ was conceived of as suffering the punishment of our sin,—a complete equivalent of the punishment which we must have suffered,—on the ground of which our guilt and punishment are pardoned. In the following century, Owen (*Works*, ix. 253–254) held that the sufferings of Christ for sinners were not *tantidem* but *idem*. In more recent discussions along this line, Hodge (*Systematic Theology*, ii. 480–495) maintains that Christ suffered neither the kind nor degree of that which sinners must have suffered, but any kind and degree of suffering which is judicially inflicted in satisfaction of justice and law. There has indeed been no theory of the work of Christ which has not conceived of it as a satisfaction; even the so-called moral influence theories center in this idea (cf. W. N. Clarke, *Outline of Christian Theology*, New York, 1898, pp. 348, 349). It is therefore evident how fundamental is the idea of satisfaction presented by Anselm. Only it must be observed first that in the evolution of the Christian doctrine of salvation the particular way in which the satisfaction was realized has been differently conceived; and secondly, if the forgiveness of sin in Jesus Christ takes place only when the ethical nature of God is satisfied, the special form in which the satisfaction is accomplished is of subordinate importance. In one class of views—the representative or juridical—the satisfaction was conditioned on a unique and isolated divine-human deed—the death or the life and death of Christ; in the other theories, the satisfaction is threefold—in the expression of the divine good-will, through the life and death of Christ, in the initial response of sinners to forgiving grace, and in the final bringing of all souls to perfect union with the Father. Cf. C. A. Beckwith, *Realities of Christian Theology*, Boston, 1906, pp. 220–229. For criticism of Anselm on the Atonement, cf. Harnack, *Dogmengeschichte*, iii., Freiburg, 1890, pp. 351–358, Eng. transl., vi. 67–78.] C. A. Beckwith.

Bibliography: The best edition of Anselm's works is by G. Gerberon, a monk of the Congregation of St. Maur, Paris, 1675 (2d ed., 1721; reprinted at Venice, 1744, and, with corrections and additions, in *MPL*, clviii.-clix.). The *Monologium* and *Proslogium* were published by C. Haas, Tübingen, 1863; the *Cur deus homo*, by H. Lämmer, Berlin, 1857, and by O. F. Fritzsche (3d ed., Zurich, 1893). The *Monologium* and *Proslogium* were translated into French by H. Bouchitté, *Le Rationalisme chrétien*, Paris, 1842; the *Cur deus homo*, into German by B. Schirlitz, Quedlinburg, 1861. In English are: The *Cur deus homo*, with selections from his letters, London, 1889; his *Book of Meditations and Prayers*, with preface by Cardinal Manning, 1872; and the *Proslogium, Monologium*, and *Cur deus homo*, transl. by S. N. Deane, with introduction, bibliography, etc., Chicago, 1903.

The sources for Anselm's life are the *Historia novorum* and *Vita Anselmi* of his chaplain and friend, Eadmer, printed in Gerberon and Migne, ut sup., and edited for the *Rolls Series* by M. Rule, London, 1884; the *Vita alia* by John of Salisbury, in *MPL*, cxcix., and the *Vita brevior*, ib. clviii. Of modern works the following may be mentioned: R. W. Church, *The Life of St. Anselm*, London, 1870 (" masterly, accurate, vigorous "); F. R. Hasse, *Anselm von Canterbury*, 2 parts, part i., *Leben*, Leipsic, 1843, part ii., *Lehre*, ib. 1852, abridged Eng. transl. by W. Turner, London; 1850: C. de Rémusat, *St. Anselme de Cantorbéry*, Paris, 1868 (contains able criticism of Anselm's philosophy, with which cf. E. Saisset in *Mélange d'histoire, de morale, et de critique*, Paris, 1859); M. Rule, *Life and Times of St. Anselm*, 2 vols., London, 1883 (the result of long study, but marred by prejudice); *DNB*, ii. 10–30; P. Ragey, *Histoire de St. Anselme*, Paris, 1889; J. M. W. Rigg, *St. Anselm of Canterbury, a Chapter in the Hist. of Religion*, London, 1896; A. C. Welch, *Anselm and his Work*, London, 1901; E. A. Freeman, *History of the Norman Conquest*, passim; idem, *History of the Reign of William Rufus*, vol. i., chap. iv., and vol. ii., chap. vii. (valuable for references to authorities).

ANSELM OF HAVELBERG: Bishop of Havelberg, later archbishop of Ravenna; d. 1158. He took an active part in ecclesiastical and still more in political affairs under the emperors from Lothair III. to Frederick I. Having joined the Premonstrants he went to Magdeburg, probably influenced by Norbert, who consecrated him in 1129 bishop of Havelberg. As such he labored zealously for the order, to whose duties especially belonged the organization of the church in the Wendic countries, and founded a Premonstrant chapter in Havelberg. In 1135 Lothair III. sent him as ambassador to Constantinople in the hope of effecting a union against Roger of Sicily. He held a friendly conference on the principal points of controversy between the Eastern and the Western Churches, with the archbishop of Nicomedia, and afterward at the request of Pope Eugenius III. wrote three "Dialogues," descriptive of it. In 1147 he took part as papal legate in the crusade against the Wends, and then devoted several years to the affairs of his bishopric. The Emperor Frederick I. employed him again on political missions; he sent him to Constantinople in 1154, when he wished to secure a Greek princess for his wife, and in 1155 caused him to be chosen archbishop of Ravenna. In the same year Anselm was successful in mediating between Frederick and the Pope (Giesebrecht, v. 59, 64). His writings, besides the one mentioned above, treat especially of the relation between canons and monks, which was much discussed in his time. They are in *MPL*, clxxxviii.

S. M. Deutsch.

Bibliography: Spieker, *Anselm von Havelberg*, in *ZHT*, vol. x., part ii. (1840) 1–94; W. von Giesebrecht, *Geschichte der deutschen Kaiserzeit*, iv.-v., Brunswick, 1874; Hauck, *KD*, vol. iv. passim.

ANSELM OF LAON (Lat. *Laudunensis;* called also *Scholasticus*): Archdeacon of Laon; b. at Laon about the middle of the eleventh century; d. there July 15, 1117. He enjoyed the instruction of Anselm of Canterbury at Bec, and from 1076 was teacher of scholastic theology at Paris, where he gathered around him a number of prominent pupils. With the most notable of them, the genial William of Champeaux (q.v.), he laid the foundation of the later University of Paris. Toward the end of the century he became archdeacon and cathedral *scholasticus* in his native city. His reputation as the foremost Biblical exegete made the school renowned and induced young Abelard to attend his lectures. His influence on posterity was mainly due to his *Glossa interlinearis*, a paraphrastic commentary on the Vulgate, which far surpassed the popular *Glossa ordinaria* of Walafrid Strabo, but was not able to displace entirely this older work. He also wrote exegetical notes on the Song of Songs, Matthew, and Revelation.

O. Zöckler†.

Bibliography: Anselm's works are in *MPL*, clxii. (includes an interesting letter on the problem of evil, *Num Deus vult malum?*). A number of previously unprinted sentences were published by G. Lefèvre in *Anselmi Laudunensis et Radulfi fratris ejus sententiæ*, Evreux, 1894. Consult *Histoire littéraire de la France*, x. 182 sqq.; P. Feret, *La Faculté de théologie de Paris*, i. 25–33, Paris, 1894; H. Hurter, *Theologia catholica tempore medii ævi*, pp. 17–18, Innsbruck, 1899.

ANSELM OF LUCCA: 1. Anselm Badagius (Badagio): Bishop of Lucca 1057–73, also pope (Alexander II.) 1061–73. See Alexander II., pope.

2. Bishop of Lucca 1073–86; d. at Mantua Mar. 18, 1086. He was nephew and successor of the preceding, and bore the same family name. In 1073 he is designated *electus Lucensis* by Gregory VII., whom he consulted as to whether he should receive investiture from the king. The pope decided that it should be postponed until Henry IV. had cleared himself of association with his excommunicated counselors and had made his peace with Rome. Henry especially requested that Anselm's consecration should not take place until after his investiture; and in fact he received the ring and staff from the king's hand before he was consecrated, Apr. 28, 1075. Soon after, troubled in conscience by this relation, he wished to resign his see and retired to a monastery, but was recalled by Gregory, whom he afterward supported with a more ardent loyalty than any other Italian bishop. His personality counted for much when Guibert of Ravenna had been set up as an antipope, and the struggle of Gregory with Henry IV and the Lombard bishops reached its height. With Countess Matilda, Anselm was the principal upholder of the papal cause in the north of Italy. He was driven from his diocese, but was entrusted with a vicariate covering the whole of Lombardy. When Gregory felt death approaching, he commended Anselm to Otto of Ostia and Hugh of Lyons as his choice for successor; but Anselm died while still an exile. His most notable literary work was his *Collectio canonum*, which was incorporated almost bodily in the *Decretum Gratiani*. Other important writings of his were directed to the ending of the schism; the principal one preserved is the *Liber contra Wibertum et sequaces ejus*, written in 1085–86 after Gregory's death. Fragments of a commentary on the Psalms and some devotional treatises attributed to Anselm have also been preserved.

(Carl Mirbt.)

Bibliography: The *Liber contra Wibertum* and *Collectio canonica*, with spurious works, etc., are in *MPL*, cxlix.; the former, ed. E. Bernheim, also in *MGH*, *Libelli de lite*, i. (1891) 519–528 (cf. Preface, pp. 65–66). His life, written immediately after his death, at the request of Matilda, by Bardo, a priest who had been his close associate, is in *MPL*, cxlviii. and, with extracts from some of his works, ed. R. Wilmans, in *MGH*, *Script.*, xii. (1856) 1–35. Consult A. Overmann, *Die vita Anselmi Lucensis episcopi des Rangerius*, in *NA*, vol. xxi., 1896; W. von Giesebrecht, *Geschichte der deutschen Kaiserzeit*, vol. iii., Leipsic, 1890; J. Langen, *Geschichte der römischen Kirche von Gregor VII. bis Innocenz III.*, Bonn, 1893; C. Mirbt, *Die Publizistik im Zeitalter Gregors VII.*, Leipsic, 1894; W. Martens, *Gregor VII.*, 2 vols., ib. 1894; G. Meyer von Knonau, *Jahrbücher des deutschen Reichs unter Heinrich IV. und Heinrich V.*, vol. ii., ib. 1894; Wattenbach, *DGQ*, ii. (1894).

ANSGAR or **ANSKAR** (*Aasgejr*, *Osgejr*, "God's Spear"; the modern **Oscar**): The apostle of Scandinavia, first archbishop of Hamburg (831–865); b. of prominent Frankish parents near the monastery of Corbie (9 m. e. of Amiens), probably in 801; d. at Bremen Feb. 3, 865. After his mother's early death he was brought up at Corbie, and made rapid progress in the learning of the time. In 822 he was one of a colony sent to found the abbey of Corvey (New Corbie) in Westphalia, and became there a teacher and preacher. When, four years later, Harold, king of Denmark, made an alliance with the Franks which included the acceptance of their religion, Ansgar was among those chosen to accompany the king to Denmark to evangelize the people. He and his companion Autbert founded a school at Harold's court after the Frankish model, but their work had to be abandoned on account of the downfall of Harold (827) and the illness and death of Autbert. In the autumn of 829, probably, Swedish ambassadors appeared at the imperial court and asked that Christian missionaries be sent to their country. Again Ansgar was selected, and with him, Witmar, his former colleague in the abbey-school at Corvey. After a perilous journey, they reached Sweden and were allowed to preach freely, with considerable success, at Björkö (Birka) on an island in Lake Mälar.

Ansgar spent two years in Sweden, returning home in 831 to report to the emperor. The time was now ripe for the accomplishment of a plan of great importance for the northern missions, which Charlemagne had had in mind, and for which his son had now found the right man, viz., the establishment of a bishopric of Hamburg. Besides a diocese formed from those of Bremen and Verden, the new metropolitan was to have the right to send missions into all the northern lands and to consecrate bishops for them. Ansgar was consecrated in Nov., 831, and, the arrangements having been at once approved by Gregory IV., went to Rome to receive the pallium directly at the hands of the pope and to be named legate for the northern lands. This commission had previously been bestowed upon Ebo, archbishop of Reims; but an amicable agreement was reached by which the jurisdiction was divided, Ebo retaining Sweden for himself. For a time Ansgar devoted himself to the needs of his own diocese, which was still missionary territory with but a few churches. He founded in Hamburg a monastery and a school; the latter was to serve the Danish mission, but accomplished little.

After the death of Louis le Débonnaire (840), Ansgar lost the abbey of Turholt, which had been given as an endowment for his work, and in 845

Hamburg was destroyed by the Danes, so that he was a bishop without either see or revenue. Many of his helpers deserted him, and his work was in danger of extinction. The new king, Louis the German, came to his aid; after failing to recover Turholt for him, he planned to bestow upon him the vacant diocese of Bremen. There were many canonical and other difficulties in the way; but after prolonged negotiations Nicholas I. approved the union of the two dioceses (864). From 848 Ansgar resided in Bremen, and did what he could to revive the Danish mission. When he was established in a position of dignity once more, he succeeded in gaining permission from King Haarik to build a church in Sleswick, and secured the recognition of Christianity as a tolerated religion. He did not forget the Swedish mission, and spent two years there in person (848–850), at the critical moment when a pagan reaction was threatened, which he succeeded in averting. In his own diocese he showed himself a model bishop, forward in all works of charity, and of a prayerful and ascetic life. His humility was most marked; when people attempted to venerate him as a wonder-worker, he reproved them, saying that it would be the greatest of miracles if God should deign to make him a really devout man. He was canonized by Nicholas I. not long after his death. A collection of brief prayers from his hand is extant with the title *Pigmenta* (ed. J. M. Lappenberg, Hamburg, 1844). The *Vita et miracula* of Willehad, first bishop of Bremen (*MGH, Script.*, ii., 1829, 378–390; also in *MPL*, cxviii. 1013–32) is attributed to Ansgar by Adam of Bremen; the life, however, is by another. (A. Hauck.)

Bibliography: Rimbert (disciple and successor of Ansgar), *Vita Anskarii*, ed. C. F. Dahlmann, in *MGH*, *Script.*, ii. (1829) 683–725, and *MPL*, cxviii.; Adam of Bremen, *Gesta Hammenburgensis ecclesiæ*, i. 17–36 et passim; there are modern lives by G. H. Klippel, *Lebensbeschreibung des Erzbischofs Ansgar*, Bremen, 1843; A. Tappehorn, *Leben des heiligen Ansgar, Apostels von Dänemark und Schweden*, Münster, 1863, and others. Consult also G. Dehio, *Geschichte des Erzbistums Hamburg-Bremen*, i. 42 sqq., ii. 51–52, Berlin, 1877; G. F. Maclear, *Apostles of Mediæval Europe*, pp. 151–171, London, 1888; Wattenbach, *DGQ*, 1904, i. 297, ii. 79, 508; Hauck, *KD*, ii. 350, 602, 618, 624, 660, 673 sqq., 726, 765; T. von Schubert, *Ansgar*, Kiel, 1901.

ANSO: A monk and abbot (776–800) of Lobbes (35 m. s. of Brussels), but not, like his predecessors, also a bishop. He was considered a worthy, zealous man, but no scholar; nevertheless, while a monk, he compiled from the sources biographies of the first two of the abbot bishops of Lobbes,—the *Vita S. Ursmari* (in *ASB*, April, ii. 560–562, and *ASM*, iii. 1, 248–250) and the *Vita S. Ermini* or *Erminonis* (*ASB*, April, iii. 375–377; *ASM*, iii. 1, 564–568).

Bibliography: *Histoire littéraire de la France*, iv. 203.

ANTERUS, an′te-rus: Bishop of Rome in the third century, successor of Pontianus. According to the *Catalogus Liberianus*, he was consecrated Nov. 21, 235; the divergent account of Eusebius (*Hist. eccl.*, VI. xxix. 1), which makes him enter upon his office in the reign of Gordianus, is of less authority. After a pontificate of little over a month, he died Jan. 3, 236. The stone placed over his grave in the cemetery of Calixtus was discovered in 1854. (A. Hauck.)

Bibliography: *Liber pontificalis*, ed. Duchesne, i. 147, Paris, 1886.

ANTHONISTS. See Anthony, Saint, Orders of.

ANTHONY, ALFRED WILLIAMS: Free Baptist; b. at Providence, R. I., Jan. 13, 1860. He was educated at Brown University (B.A., 1883), Cobb Divinity School (1883–86), and the University of Berlin (1888–90), and was pastor of the Essex Street Free Baptist Church, Bangor, Me., from 1885 to 1888. On his return from Germany he was appointed professor of New Testament exegesis at Cobb Divinity School, a position which he still holds. He is also a member of the conference board of the General Conference of Free Baptists, the chairman of the Free Baptist committee of conference on union with other bodies, a member of the Interdenominational Commission of Maine since its organization in 1891 and secretary since 1904, trustee and secretary of the board of the Maine Industrial School for Girls since 1899, and member of the school committee of Lewiston since 1906. Among the societies to which he belongs are the American Philological Association, the American Institute of Sacred Literature, the Society of Biblical Literature and Exegesis, and the Maine Academy of Medicine and Science. In theology he is a moderate progressive. He has written: *An Introduction to the Life of Jesus* (New York, 1896); *The Method of Jesus* (1899); *The Sunday-School—Its Progress in Method and Scope* (1899); and *The Higher Criticism in the New Testament* (1901); and has edited *Preachers and Preaching* (1900), and *New Wine Skins* (1901).

ANTHONY, SAINT, THE HERMIT. See Monasticism.

ANTHONY, SAINT, ORDERS OF: The oldest and most important of the religious orders named after St. Anthony, the father of monasticism, is that of the Hospitalers of St. Anthony, founded about the time of the first crusade (1095–99) by a nobleman of St. Didier la Mothe in Dauphiné, Gaston by name. According to the traditions of the order, Gaston's son, Guérin, was cured of the disease known as St. Anthony's fire (*morbus sacer*), whereupon the father founded a hospital for those suffering from this and similar maladies, near the great church of St. Didier, and, with his son and eight knightly comrades, undertook the part of nurses in the institution. St. Anthony appeared to the founder, gave him his staff (shaped like the letter "T"), and encouraged him in the work. Urban II. is said to have confirmed the order at the synod at Clermont in 1095. Calixtus II. in 1118 dedicated the church belonging to the Benedictine monastery Mons Major at St. Didier to St. Anthony, and so made it the chief sanctuary of the order, which was subject to the Benedictines. From the end of the twelfth century the order spread through the foundation of many houses (as at Rome in 1194; at Acco in 1208; and many in central and north Germany), and it acquired considerable wealth through the persistent zeal of its almsgatherers. They wore a black robe with a light blue "T" (St. Anthony's cross), and a little bell on the neck announced their coming. After a hard struggle the Hospitalers freed themselves from the Benedictines, and in 1286, by adopting the rule of St. Augustine, they became regular canons (popularly known as *Tönniesherrn*). In 1297 Boniface VIII. freed them from all episcopal jurisdiction and made their head master, the general abbot of St. Didier, directly subject to the papal see. At the beginning of the sixteenth century the number of houses amounted to 364. The order had suffered a moral deterioration, which the general abbot, Brunel de Gramont, with papal support, vainly endeavored to correct in the seventeenth century. In 1774 the order was united with the Knights of Malta (see JOHN, SAINT, ORDER OF HOSPITALERS OF). O. ZÖCKLER†.

BIBLIOGRAPHY: Heimbucher, *Orden und Kongregationen*, i. 401–402; Helyot, *Ordres monastiques*, ii. 108–114; Seifart, *Die Tönnesherrn und der ehrsame Rat in Hildesheim*, in *Zeitschrift für deutsche Culturgeschichte*, 1872, pp. 121, 384; G. Uhlhorn, *Die christliche Liebesthätigkeit im Mittelalter*, pp. 178, 432, 478, Stuttgart, 1884.

ANTHONY, SAINT, OF PADUA: The most celebrated of the followers of St. Francis of Assisi; b. at Lisbon, of a distinguished, knightly family, about 1195; d. at Padua June 13, 1231. When fifteen years of age he joined the Augustinian canons at Lisbon. Afterward he went to Coimbra and by zealous study made himself master of the theology of his time. The translation of the bones of the first martyred Franciscans from Morocco to Coimbra awakened in Anthony a desire for martyrdom; to accomplish his purpose in 1220 he joined the Minorites and sailed to Africa; being confined to his bed by sickness throughout the winter, he resolved to return home. On the way he was driven to Messina and with the brethren there went to the chapter at Assisi in 1221, where he was taken to a hermitage in the Romagna. By accident his oratorical gifts became known when he was ordained priest at Forli; and he was made preacher of the order. Of his public activity, which now commenced, very little is known. For a time he acted as lector to the Minorites at Bologna, although Francis of Assisi, influenced by Elias of Cortona, who wished to introduce scientific study into the order, gave his permission very reluctantly. Anthony next went to France, and was guardian at Puy and custos in Limousin. As in the Romagna, he showed himself an indefatigable persecutor of heretics in the struggle with the Cathari. At Rimini he converted some of them by his persuasive powers, and he united the converts at Padua into a brotherhood of penitents. Finally he was made provincial, and in 1229 went to Padua.

In 1230 Anthony took part in the general chapter at Assisi, and he was released from his office as provincial in order that he might devote himself entirely to preaching. He, however, took a prominent part in the controversy of the parties which developed among the Minorites. He sided with Elias and was among the delegates sent to Rome to have the differences decided by the pope, who accordingly issued the bull *Quo elongati*, Sept. 28, 1230 (see FRANCIS, SAINT, OF ASSISI, AND THE FRANCISCAN ORDER).

Anthony's fame rests solely upon his ability as a preacher, which produced a great impression, especially in the district of Treviso. The Latin sketches of his sermons convey little impression of his manner, but they show him to have been a strict preacher of repentance and of contempt of the world, who urged indefatigably the use of the means of grace provided by the Church. It is said that 30,000 auditors listened to him in an open field at Padua. His restless activity wore him out, and, suffering from dropsy, he vainly sought relief by retiring to solitude, taking up his abode in a tree. He was canonized for political reasons by Gregory IX., May 30, 1232. [There is a curious story that on one occasion, disgusted with the indifference of his audience, Anthony betook himself to the seashore and addressed his discourse to the fishes, which came in shoals to listen. Joseph Addison, *Remarks on Italy*, at the end of "Brescia, Verona and Padua," gives the Italian text and an English translation.] E. LEMPP.

BIBLIOGRAPHY: Of the works ascribed to Anthony only the sermons preserved at Padua are certainly genuine. Those which have been published will be found in A. Pagi, *Sermones S. Antonii Paduani de Sanctis*, Avignon, 1684; A. Josa, *Legenda seu vita et miracula S. Antonii de Padua*, Bologna, 1883; idem, *Sermones*, Padua, 1885. The edition (Padua, 1895 sqq.) begun by A. M. Locatelli (d. 1902) does not state what MSS. are followed. Other collections are not genuine or very doubtful. The sources and most important literature for Anthony are gathered in Leon de Kerval, *S. Antonii de Padua vitæ duæ, etc.*, in *Collection d'études et des documents sur l'histoire religieuse et littéraire du moyen âge*, vol. v., Paris, 1904. For his life: E. de Azevedo, *Vita del glorioso taumaturgo portoghese sant' Antonio di Padova*, Bologna, 1790, last ed., Venice, 1865; H. J. Coleridge, S. J., *The Chronicle of St. Antony of Padua*, London, 1876; E. Lempp, in *ZKG*, xi. (1890) 177–211, 503–538, xii. (1891), 414–451, xiii. (1892) 1–46; J. Rigauld, *La Vie de Saint Antoine de Padua, publiée pour la première fois avec une introduction sur les sources*, par Ferdinand-Marie d'Araules, Bordeaux, 1899; Mrs. A. Bell, *Saint Antony of Padua; Seven full-page Reproductions from Old Masters of Scenes in the Life of St. Antony*, London, 1900; A. Lepitre, *Antoine de Padoue* (in the Joly series), Paris, 1901, Eng. transl. by Edith Guest, London, 1902.

ANTHROPOLOGY. See THEOLOGY.

ANTHROPOMORPHISM and **ANTHROPOPATHISM** (Gk. *anthrōpos*, "man," + *morphē*, "form," and *pathos*, "passion, suffering"): Terms designating views of God which represent him as possessed of a human form or members, human attributes, or human passions. Such views arise from the natural tendency or necessity of man to conceive of higher beings by analogy with himself, and are incidental to all religions at a certain stage of their development. Many passages of the Bible easily lend themselves to an anthropomorphic interpretation. The Audians (q.v.) of the fourth and fifth centuries taught that all references to God's hands, ears, eyes, etc., are to be interpreted literally. Some philosophers believe the conception of God as a personal spirit to be anthropomorphic. Scholars who accept the compilatory theory of the origin of the Pentateuch consider anthropomorphism a marked characteristic of the Elohist, usually cited as E. Others maintain that the Scriptures, rightly interpreted, lend no support to such views. See COMPARATIVE RELIGION, VI., 1, a, § 3.

Anthropomorphism is inseparable from any conception of supernatural powers or God. This fact has received two interpretations. (1) Religion never outgrows the essential characteristics of its origin, whether this is conceived of as mythological (Comte), animistic (Tylor), or through dreams (Spencer). In the lower stages of religion, the gods are only larger men. According to Feuerbach, following Xenophanes and Lucretius (*De rerum natura*, v. 121), man creates God in his own image (cf. Feuerbach, *Wesen des Christenthums*, chap. 1, § 2). In the progress from polytheism to monotheism, the human qualities are indefinitely enlarged, concentrated, and united in one being, but the being is still human. Between the mode of human intelligence and omniscience, the human will and omnipotence, between human goodness and divine perfection, between personality and the Infinite is not only an immeasurable but an irreconcilable difference. The result for thought is either that there is no God (Comte), or, if such a being exists, we are compelled to distrust all anthropomorphic notions and take refuge in the Unknown and the Unknowable (Spencer, *First Principles*, New York, 1892, pp. 108–123). The latter alternative leaves room for the religious sentiments, but only in the form of awe. To rid the idea of God of every trace of anthropomorphism, however, simply abolishes the idea itself. (2) According to the second view—which is met with under many variations—religious ideas are not only incurably anthropomorphic, but they share this property with all other ideas. They contain objective truth, even if this is lacking in scientific accuracy of expression. Either rational and moral qualities are to be ascribed to God, on the ground that these are essential to the perfection of personality (S. Harris, *The Self-Revelation of God*, New York, 1887, pp. 433–440), or, since they are derived from the human consciousness and the region of the finite, they may be interpreted only analogically and symbolically; e.g., force, cause, energy, the eternal, the infinite, the power not ourselves that makes for righteousness, even personality and fatherhood have a real meaning for religious feeling and thought, although their full significance transcends both definition and comprehension. The Scriptures, which are marked by definite stages of anthropomorphic representations of God, contain a corrective for an undue reliance on this mode of conception.

C. A. Beckwith.

Bibliography: John Fiske, *Outlines of Cosmic Philosophy*, part 1, chap. vii., part 3, chap. ii., Boston, 1891; idem, *Idea of God*, pp. 111–118, Boston, 1886; F. Paulsen, *Einleitung in die Philosophie*, pp. 275–281, Berlin, 1895, Eng. transl., pp. 252–256, New York, 1898.

ANTICHRIST.

The name "Antichrist" is first found in the Epistles of John (I. ii. 18, 22, iv. 3; II. 7). The idea, however, is in earlier New Testament writings, and its roots are in the Old Testament. According to a modern supposition they are even to be sought in the Babylonian chaos-myth,—a native myth of the springtime, which narrates how Tiamat, the ruler over the deeps of darkness and the waters, aided by her powers, rebelled against the upper gods, but was overcome by Marduk, the son of the gods, who had been elevated to the throne, and then created the heavenly lights. It has been supposed that the Old Testament writings indicate that this myth migrated to Canaan in very ancient times, was transferred by the Israelites to the latter end of the world, and was applied in various forms also to political enemies of the people; and herein is sought the origin of the Old Testament idea of a rise and conquest of evil powers, which preceded the establishment of the kingdom of God (Gunkel, *Schöpfung und Chaos*, Göttingen, 1895, pp. 221 sqq.). But influence of old Oriental thoughts upon the figurative style of Biblical writings can be admitted only in a very limited degree.

1. The Idea Possibly of Babylonian Origin.

Neither the sources of the eschatological ideas which meet in the notion of Antichrist, nor the characteristic features of their development can be traced back to extra-Biblical elements. The belief in the election of Israel as a people of God, sanctified unto him and blessed by him, received a rude shock by the experience of a reality apparently opposed to such choice. Hence arose the prophecy, that, because of its faithlessness Israel is given over to heathen powers, but that it shall be delivered from them, their presumption being punished for exceeding their divine commission as God's scourges. Thus the opinion was formed that before the kingdom of God is completed it is to be attacked by the godless world. As the representative of the latter, Ezekiel (xxxviii. 2, xxxix. 1–6) mentions Magog, the land of King Gog, a comprehensive designation of the nations of the north. Zechariah (xii.–xiv.) describes more minutely the oppression of the people of God by hostile powers. When Antiochus IV. Epiphanes of Syria undertook with cruel severity to supplant the religion of Israel by Greek heathenism, these ideas found a further development. The heathen world-power then appeared not as an instrument of punishment in the hand of God, but as his adversary, attacking with destructive purpose the very center of his kingdom. The history of the godless world-kingdom, which reaches its climax in the person of the proud king, is thus represented in the Book of Daniel.

2. Old Testament Conceptions.

Gradually the last enemy of the kingdom of God came to be thought of as the antitype of the Messiah; at least such is the representation of the later Hellenistic Jewish literature (cf. Num. xxiv. 7, LXX.; *Sibyllines*, iii. 652 sqq.). In the extant pre-Christian Palestinian literature no indication is found of a personal antitype of the Messiah. In the older portions of the Book of Enoch the appearance of the Messiah is spoken of as taking place at the end of all struggles

3. Later Hellenistic Jewish Literature.

and judgments (Enoch xc. 37). In the pseudo-Solomonic Psalms (xvii. 27-39) of the time of Pompey, and in the Fourth Book of Ezra, of the time of the Flavian emperors, it is the godless powers or the heathen nations who are overpowered by the Messiah. In the almost contemporary Apocalypse of Baruch (xl. 1-2) this passage is applied to the destruction of a last impious king by the Messiah. The conception here is not yet influenced by Christianity; and thus the expectation of a personal opponent to the Messiah is found in pre-Christian Judaism.

4. In the New Testament.

In the New Testament writings the thought seems to be influenced by ideas which originated in the Christian revelation. The great struggle against sin as selfishness revived the idea of a final culmination of the enmity against God. On the other hand, by the separation of the religious life from the national-political life, the idea is divested of its natural form and is more spiritualized. In his eschatological discourse where the abomination of desolation in the holy place is spoken of as expressive of the tribulation of the approaching end (Matt. xxiv. 15), Jesus quoted the Book of Daniel. But the Messianic son of man is here not opposed, as in Daniel, by a ruler who at the same time destroys the religious and national side of the theocracy, but by a great number of pseudo-prophets and pseudo-Messiahs (Matt. xxiv. 5), who are thought of as fanatical representatives of a Jewish natural Messianic idea. The apostle Paul, when he declares that the appearance of the man of sin, the opponent who rises against everything which contains good and God's service, will precede the coming of Christ (II Thess. ii. 3-4), no doubt also thought in the first place of a pseudo-Messiah in personal recollection of the bitter opposition to the Gospel by Judaism filled with politico-Messianic thoughts (I Thess. ii. 15). For his picture of the adversary he doubtless took some traits from the description of Antiochus Epiphanes in the Book of Daniel and that of Caligula in history, who had his image in the form of Jupiter set up in the Temple at Jerusalem. Furthermore, Paul's high conception of the superhuman virtue of Christ, is reflected in the description of his antitype. In John's Apocalypse the counterpart of the kingdom of God in the last times, besides the nations Gog and Magog, which are to march against the holy city after the completion of the millennium (Rev. xx. 8), includes also the Roman power, personified (xvii. 11) in the incendiary, matricide, and persecutor of the Christians on the imperial throne, Nero (xvii. 9 sqq.), as well as a multitude of false prophets who mislead to the cult of the world-kingdom and its rule (xiii. 11-17, xvi. 13, xix. 20, xx. 10), representing no doubt the heathenish Roman practises of augury and necromancy. The last development of the idea within the New Testament is found in the Epistles of John, where the thought is of an opponent to the true Christ, putting himself in his place, brought about by doctrinal necessities to characterize heretics who destroy the unity of the historical Jesus and the bearer of the revelation of God, Christ. In these persons, according to the clear statement of the epistles (I John ii. 22; II John 7), the idea and the character of the Antichrist are realized.

5. In Post-Christian Judaism and in the Church.

In post-Christian Judaism the early national conception was enhanced. The name "Antichrist," borrowed from Christianity, does not become current until late (e.g., in Abrabanel). But in the first Christian centuries there is found in Jewish literature the notion of a perpetrator of outrages upon the Jewish people in the last days. Sporadically, the figure of a powerful woman after the manner of Cleopatra appears (*Sibyllines*, iii. 77, v. 18, viii. 200); oftener that of an imperial Roman anti-Messiah. In later times Antichrist was represented in Jewish theology as victor over the suffering Messiah, and was called Romulus, also Armillus. In the Christian Church of the first centuries the main types of the Biblical Antichrist reappear. Origen identified the notion in an abstract sense with that of false doctrine. Certain contemporaneous representatives of heretical teaching were called by the name, without thereby excluding the expectation of an Antichrist as a future individual (cf. *Didache*, xvi.). Very often the latter was thought of as a false Jewish Messiah —hence circumcised and compelling circumcision— and it was expected that he would come from the tribe of Dan and from the East. The connection of Antichrist with Nero in the Apocalypse of John was also developed by representing him as the resuscitated Nero (Lactantius, *De mortibus persecutorum*, ii.; Jerome, on Dan, xi. 17; Augustine, *De civitate Dei*, xx. 13). Both conceptions were strangely fused (Victorinus, *Comment. ad Apoc.*) or outwardly connected with each other into the notion of a double Antichrist, a Western (Roman) and an Eastern, appearing in Jerusalem. In relation to Satan, the Antichrist was thought of as a man working his will, as his son, and even as his incarnation.

The idea receded in the Middle Ages, and when it again appeared it was mostly applied to phenomena of the present. It has often been applied to the papacy, an interpretation which was adopted by Luther (*Adversus execrabilem Antichristi bullam*) and other Reformers, and taken into the symbolical books of the Lutheran Church (*Art. Schmal.*, ii. 4; *Tract. de pot. Papæ*). On the other hand, Roman Catholics have referred the Antichrist to Luther and Protestantism. F. SIEFFERT.

As Bousset (*Antichrist*) has so convincingly shown, a tradition was evidently current in Jewish thought which underlay the teaching both of Paul and the Apocalypse concerning the Antichrist. The tradition appears to have contained the following features. The coming of Antichrist was prevented by the Roman power. When this power should fall, the Antichrist, not of foreign birth but a Jewish false Messiah, would establish himself in the temple at Jerusalem and require men to worship him. His reign would last for three and one-half years. By means of his miraculous power he would convert the world to his side. Later, his real character would be exposed; the believing Jews having fled into the wilderness would be pursued by him, and then he would be slain by the true Messiah with the breath of his mouth. This tradition is in part followed and in part contradicted by the Apocalypse and by Paul. In its background is the Book of Daniel with its fierce foreign oppressor; the Apocalyptic Belial, a supernatural spirit who will antagonize God at the end of time (*Sybillines*, bk. iii.); the doctrine of Satan (Rev. xx. 2); the Babylonian dragon-myth (Gunkel, *Schöpfung und Chaos*); and a man filled with satanic might. The doctrine of Antichrist contains one of the solutions which the early Church had to offer for two problems of the religious consciousness—the origin and overthrow of evil, and theodicy. C. A. B.

Bibliography: McClintock and Strong, *Cyclopædia*, i. 254–261 (able historical review, but omits survey of the Pseudepigrapha, a lack supplied in R. F. Charles, *Critical History of the Doctrine of a Future Life*, London, 1899); J. G. Walch, *Bibliotheca theologica*, ii. 217 sqq., 4 vols., Jena, 1757–66 (gives bibliography of controversy between Protestants and Catholics); T. Malvenda, *De Antichristo*, Rome, 1604; J. H. Newman, *The Protestant Idea of Anti-Christ*, in his *Critical and Historical Essays*, ii. 112–185, London, 1871; *DCB*. i. 120–122; S. Huntingford, *The Apocalypse and the Antichrist of St. Paul and St. John*, London, 1881; *Computation of 666 . the Coming of Anti-Christ*, ib. 1891; W. Bousset, *Der Antichrist in der Ueberlieferung des Judenthums, des Neuen Testaments und der alten Kirche*, Göttingen, 1895, Eng. transl., London, 1896; H. Gunkel, *Schöpfung und Chaos*, Göttingen, 1895; E. Wadstein, *Antichrist*, in *ZWT*, xxxviii.-xxxix. (new series, iii.-iv., 1895–96), 79–157, 251–293; M. Friedländer, *Der Antichrist in den vorchristlichen jüdischen Quellen*, Göttingen, 1901.

ANTIDICOMARIANITES, an″ti-dic″o-mê′ri-an-aits: A name applied by Epiphanius (*Hær.*, lxxviii.) to opponents of the belief in the perpetual virginity of Mary, the mother of Christ. The New Testament speaks of the "brethren" of Jesus; and in Tertullian's time the opinion was still prevalent that Mary's marriage with Joseph was a true marriage. Thus he writes (*De monogamia*, viii.): "Truly it was a virgin who bore Christ, but after doing so she married, in order that the last title of sanctity might be checked off in the inventory of Christ; a mother who was both a virgin and a once married woman." But by the fourth century it was considered as established that there had not been a real marriage. The older belief had not, however, altogether disappeared. Epiphanius found the opinion current in Arabia that Mary, after the birth of Christ, had lived with Joseph as his wife and had children by him. He classed the adherents of this view as a sect, bestowed upon them a name of his own composition, meaning "opponents of Mary," and controverted their belief in a lengthy treatise, which he gives in the passage cited above. (A. Hauck.)

ANTILEGOMENA. See Canon of Scripture.

ANTIMENSIUM, an″ti-men′si-um: A name applied in the Greek Church to a linen cloth spread upon the altar before the beginning of the eucharistic service, and considered as making it an altar ready for the sacrifice. Since the Greek Church, like the Roman Catholic, holds that the eucharistic sacrifice may be offered only on a consecrated altar, and since this consecration can be performed only by the bishop (taking place usually at the time of the consecration of the church), the mass could not be celebrated in churches not yet consecrated, if the use of this consecrated cloth—in the Roman Catholic Church, of a portable altar-stone (see Altar)—were not held to supply the deficiency. Georg Rietschel.)

ANTINOMIANISM AND ANTINOMIAN CONTROVERSIES.

I. Antinomianism in General: The name antinomianism is a comparatively modern designation of several types of ethical thought in which hostility to the Mosaic law (including the decalogue) and to the principles therein embodied has led to immoral teaching and practise. Traces of such thought are evident in the New Testament. The spiritualization of the law into the one precept of love to God taught and exemplified by Jesus encouraged some overenthusiastic devotees to believe that they had been exalted to such a height of spirituality and such an overmastering love to God that they needed to have no regard to moral precepts or to outward conduct; while Paul's insistence on the goodness, holiness, and spirituality of the law did not suffice to convince all of those who considered themselves his disciples that, as being utterly ineffectual for human salvation and as occasioning and inciting to sin, it was not itself sin and worthy to be treated with abhorrence. Paul's sharp conflict with Judaizers in regard to the observance of Jewish ceremonies could hardly fail to convince his more radical anti-Judaistic followers that the effort to keep the law perfectly was not only vain but involved the setting at naught of the gospel of free grace in Christ Jesus. Some such perversion of Paul's teaching was probably in the mind of the writer of II Pet. iii. 16. The members of the Corinthian Church who were puffed up and did not mourn over the incestuous person, as well as the parties guilty of the abominable union (I Cor. v. 1–6), were probably antinomian, and of like tendency were doubtless the Nicolaitans (Rev. ii. 2, 15; see Nicolaitans), those that held the teaching of Balaam (Rev. ii. 14), and those that suffered the woman Jezebel (Rev. ii. 20).

1. New Testament Antinomianism.

Many Gnostics objected to the Mosaic law as being too formal and not sufficiently spiritual, on the one hand, and as giving too much place to carnal indulgence, on the other (see Gnosticism). Holding the flesh in contempt as an evil product of the demiurge, some thought it their duty to practise a rigorous asceticism, while others are represented by their Christian assailants as thinking it right to destroy the body by vicious practises.

2. Gnostic Antinomianism.

The Cainites (q.v.) regarded with approval Cain, Esau, Korah, the Sodomites, and all other characters reprobated in the Old Testament, and presumably supposed that they were doing God service in themselves defying the authority of Jehovah (the demiurge) and doing the things forbidden in the law. Carpocrates (q.v.) and Epiphanes appear to have disseminated antinomian teachings. The followers of Marcion (q.v.) and the Manicheans (q.v.) were antinomian in the sense that they rejected the Mosaic law because of its permission of marriage and even polygamy and concubinage, of capital punishment, etc.; but did not, so far as appears, make repudiation of the law an excuse for fleshly indulgence. The followers of Priscillian (q.v.), a strong ascetic party in Spain with Gnostic tendencies (fourth and fifth centuries), were tortured into confessing the most immoral practises; but there is no good reason for crediting the calumnies of their persecutors. The Messalians (q.v.), a mystical sect that flourished in Syria, Mesopotamia, and Armenia from the fourth century onward, are said to have practised a squalid kind of asceticism, mendicancy, promiscuous sleeping together of men and women, and prayer to the devil. On account of the last-named practise they were sometimes called Satanites. It seems probable that they were antinomian. Of like character, or worse, were the Adamites referred to by Epiphanius, and the same may be said of medieval parties known by this name (see Adamites).

The Bogomiles and kindred sects (see New Manicheans) are accused by their enemies of the most immoral practises. Amalric of Bena (d. 1204) carried pantheistic ideas so far as to maintain that "to those constituted in love no sin is imputed" (see Amalric of Bena). His followers are said to have maintained that harlotry and other carnal vices are not sinful for the spiritual man, because the spirit in him, which is God, is not affected by the flesh and can not sin, and because the man, who is nothing, can not sin so long as the spirit, which is God, is in him.

3. Antinomianism of the Middle Ages.

Such teachings were carried to the most immoral consequences by the Brethren of the Free Spirit and the Beghards (qq.v.), if the inquisitorial records of the fifteenth century can be believed. Johann Hartmann in the diocese of Mainz claimed that by contemplation he had become so completely one with God and God so completely one with him that an angel could not tell the difference; that a man free in spirit is rendered impeccable and can do whatever he will and whatever pleases him. He carried these doctrines to the most extreme and revolting consequences (cf. the documents in Döllinger, *Beiträge zur Sektengeschichte des Mittelalters*, ii., Munich, 1890, pp. 384 sqq.). This type of antinomianism seems to have been widespread during the later Middle Ages and was perpetuated in some of the parties of the Reformation time.

The pantheistic sect of the "Libertines," who appeared in the Netherlands about 1525 and thence spread into France and were combated by Calvin (see Libertines, 3; Loists) were Antinomians. They disregarded the Mosaic law and law in general as inapplicable to the spiritual man and felt free to lie, steal, and indulge the passions. David Joris (q.v.), the mystic, was accused by his opponents of antinomian teachings, but apparently without sufficient reason.

4. Of the Sixteenth and Seventeenth Centuries.

It would be easy to point out antinomian tendencies in a number of continental parties of the sixteenth and seventeenth centuries not commonly reckoned among Antinomians. The hyper-Calvinistic (supralapsarian) teaching of men like Piscator (d. 1625) and Gomar (d. 1641) in the Netherlands, as that "sins take place, God procuring and himself willing that they take place, nay, absolutely so willing" and that in giving the law and commanding its observance He made its observance absolutely impossible, really struck at the root of human responsibility and discouraged any effort to control the natural impulses. So, too, the Jesuit casuists of the more reckless type in substituting for the Mosaic law the Canon Law and in making the violation of the latter easy by their doctrines of "philosophical sin," "direction of attention," "mental reservation," and "probabilism," etc., were constructively antinomian. Mystics of the later time, so far as they pantheistically identified themselves with God and supposed that by virtue of such spiritual exaltation they were subject to no ordinances human or divine, were antinomian in the sense in which the Brethren of the Free Spirit were.

Of special importance in this connection, because of the wide-spread influence exerted by his teachings on English and American thought and life, is Hendrik Niklaes, founder of the Familists (q.v.). In 1577 several of his works were published in English and called forth a considerable body of polemical literature. At this time there are said to have been one thousand Familists in England, and they were making an active and successful propaganda.

5. In England.

To counteract their influence the privy council issued a form of abjuration to be applied to members of the party arraigned for heresy. Their principles were too nearly identical with those of the Brethren of the Free Spirit not to be subversive of morality as well as of Scriptural authority and historical Christianity, and their errors were all the more insidious because of the fact that they allowed themselves to conform outwardly to any required ecclesiastical or civil usages, and by the use of ambiguous language to profess the acceptance of any doctrine.

During the Civil War and Commonwealth times almost every imaginable type of religious propagandism went forward with astonishing zeal and success. Familism (with other important influences) produced a relatively pure and evangelical mysticism in the Society of Friends and a grosser form of antinomianism in the Ranters (see below). The first, as far as known, to propagate distinctively antinomian principles in England at this time was John Eaton, who wrote *The Honeycomb of Free Justification by Christ Alone* (London, 1642). He distinguished the time of the law, the time of John the Baptist, and the Christian dispensation, as glorious, more glorious, and most glorious. Under the Mosaic law "sin was severely taken hold of, and punished sharply in God's children. John laid open their sins, and the danger of them, yet we read not of any punishment inflicted on God's children. The third time, the most glorious, is since Christ groaned out his blood and life upon the cross, by which sin itself, and guilt, and punishment are so utterly and infinitely abolished that there is no sin in the Church of God, and that now God sees no sin in us; and whosoever believeth not this point is undoubtedly damned" (quoted by E. Pagitt, *Heresiography*, London, 1662, p. 122). The following summary of teachings of seventeenth-century Antinomians from Thomas Gataker's *Antinomianism Discovered and Confuted* (London, 1652; quoted by Pagitt, p. 123) may be accepted as substantially trustworthy:

1. That the Moral Law is of no use at all to a believer, nor a rule for him to walk in, nor to examine his life by, and that Christians are free from the mandatory power of it: whence one of them [Antinomians] cried out in the pulpit, "Away with the Law, which cuts off a mans legs and then bids him walk." 2. That it is as possible for Christ to sin as for a child of God to sin. 3. That the child of God need not nor ought not to ask pardon for sin, and that it is no less than blasphemy for him so to do. 4. That God doth not chasten any of his children for sin, nor is it for the sins of God's people that the land is punished. 5. That if a man know himself to be in a state of grace, though he be drunk, or commit murder, God sees no sin in him. 6. That when Abraham denied his wife, and in outward appearance seemed to lie in his distrust, lying, dissembling, and equivocating that his wife was his sister, yea, then all his thoughts, words, and deeds were perfectly holy and righteous from all spot of sin in the eyes of God.

6. The Ranters.

By far the most unattractive of the sectaries of this time are the Ranters, who seem to have been almost identical in doctrine and practise with the Brethren of the Free Spirit and who, by their enthusiastic propagandism, seduced multitudes from the fellowship of the evangelical denominations. According to Samuel Fisher (*Baby Baptism Mere Babism*, London, 1653), "Some Ranters are not ashamed to say that they are Christ and God, and there is no other God than they, and what's in them, and such like blasphemies." They denied the existence of the devil, heaven, and hell. Moses they declared to be a conjurer and Christ a deceiver of the people. Prayer is useless. Preaching and lying are all one. The Scriptures they regarded as cast-off fables, and when they condescended to use them at all they practised the most absurd allegorizing. They claimed that nothing is sin but what a man thinks to be so. Their practise is represented as corresponding with their immoral teaching.

7. Later Phases of Antinomianism.

A large proportion of the Particular Baptists of England during the latter half of the eighteenth century, by way of reaction against Socinianism and the missionary movement, became involved in a hyper-Calvinistic (supralapsarian) type of thought that involved making God responsible for evil, complete denial of human initiative or part in salvation and conduct, renunciation of the law as a rule of life, and the disowning of human agency and responsibility in the extension of the kingdom of Christ. This Baptist antinomianism was combated in England by Andrew Fuller, John Ryland, and others. A still more virulent type of antinomianism appeared among American Baptists in the nineteenth century by way of reaction against the missionary and educational work of the denomination. Here as in England leaders and led were illiterate and deeply prejudiced against human institutions and agencies, which they regarded as an impertinent interference with God's sovereignty. These antinomian Baptist parties are still extant. See BAPTISTS, I., 4, §§ 4–5; II., 3, §§ 3, 4.

A. H. NEWMAN.

II. Antinomian Controversies:

1. Of the German Reformation: Antinomian doctrines were vigorously discussed in Germany during the Reformation period until the Formula of Concord made a final adjustment of the matter in 1577. Luther had held that the Mosaic law, as an ancient code devised under special conditions for a particular people, was superseded by the civil law of modern states, and no longer possessed for Christians a juridical or ceremonial force.[1] Furthermore, the whole law, even the decalogue included, was in no wise to be employed by Christians in the spirit of justification by works, since that involved a superficial and mercenary idea of divine justice. There was, however, need to preach the law from a spiritual standpoint, emphasizing a realization of sin by which the conscience should be humbled before the divine wrath; though the preaching of the law exclusively led to

1. Luther's Earlier Teachings about the Law.

[1] In combating the legalistic element in medieval Roman Catholic teaching and in the radical religious parties of the early Reformation time, Luther allowed himself to use language in disparagement of the Mosaic law so strong and unqualified as to give great encouragement to those that were eager for fleshly freedom. A few sentences should be quoted: "Christ is not harsh, severe, biting as Moses. . . . Therefore, away with Moses forever, who shall not terrify deluded hearts." Again: "The gospel is heavenly and divine, the law earthly and human; the righteousness of the gospel is just as distinct from that of the law as heaven from earth, as light from darkness. The gospel is light and day, the law darkness and night." In his polemic "against the Heavenly Prophets" (Erl. ed., xxix. 150) he says: "We will take our stand on the right ground and say that these sin-teachers and Mosaic prophets shall leave us unconfounded by Moses; we will neither see nor hear Moses. How does this please you, dear revolutionists? And we say further that all such Mosaic teachers [i.e., the Zwickau prophets, q.v.] deny the gospel, banish Christ, and overthrow the whole New Testament. I speak now as a Christian and for Christians, since Moses was given to the Jewish people alone and has nothing to do with us Gentiles and Christians. We have our gospel and New Testament; if they will prove from this that pictures are to be done away with, we will gladly follow them. But if they wish by means of Moses to make Jews of us, we will not suffer it." Of course, he did not mean utterly to repudiate Moses, but rather by a *tour de force* to repudiate what he considered an unauthorized use of Moses. (A. H. N.)

either hypocrisy or despair. In his emphasis on justification by faith, Luther asserted that true repentance proceeded from a realizing sense of the work of Christ. The preaching of faith was to take precedence of all else, since, faith having been attained, contrition and consolation spontaneously followed. Nevertheless, more frequently and in entire consistency with the formal definition of his position in 1520, the process of salvation was described by him as beginning with the operation of the law upon the soul, which in repentance casts about for aid and is met with the promise of remission of sins through Christ.

2. Agricola's Controversy with Melanchthon, 1527.

The antinomian controversy was preluded by the complaints preferred in Bohemia in 1524 against one Dominicus Beyer, who strictly adhered to Luther's doctrine, but was accused by some of reversion to the Roman view in preaching, as it was said, the approach to faith through works of merit. Luther, Melanchthon, and Bugenhagen completely exonerated Beyer and clearly enunciated the Wittenberg position. Later Melanchthon's *Articuli de quibus egerunt per visitatores* (1527; *CR*, xxvi. 7 sqq.) placed the preaching of the law at the portal of Christian instruction, asserting that it led to repentance, which was the antecedent of faith, and without which the preaching of the gospel was unintelligible. Johann Agricola, who had eagerly emphasized Luther's earlier statements of repentance as a consequence of the gospel of divine grace, chose to regard Melanchthon's declaration as a personal affront. After addressing to Luther several memorials on the subject, he made specific complaints and circulated in manuscript a censure of Melanchthon's teaching. In a conference at Torgau (Nov. 26–28, 1527) an adjustment was finally effected by Luther, who distinguished between faith in the general sense (*fides generalis*), as indeed antedating repentance, and the justifying faith which, impelled by conscience, apprehends divine grace.

3. Agricola's Controversy with Luther, 1537 sqq.

Agricola, though professing satisfaction, nevertheless continued in his antinomian position; repentance, consciousness of sin, and the fear of God were to be based upon the gospel and not upon the law. He began even to gather a party about himself as the Paul of the Reformation, who must set right Peter (Luther). Reports to this effect having gained currency, three published discourses of his were examined and found to contain antinomian views. In July, 1537, and again in September, Luther preached against such error, though without mention of Agricola, declaring in the latter instance that the gospel could no more be preached independently of the law than could the law independently of the gospel. At the close of October, Agricola came to an agreement with Luther whereby unanimity was recognized in the substance of doctrine. But now Agricola undertook to publish his *Summarien über die Evangelien*, the imprimatur of the rector being dispensed with on the ground that Luther had already seen and approved of the work. Luther thereupon forbade its completion, and determined upon an unsparing conflict. He published some antinomian theses of Agricola which had been privately circulated, and on Dec. 18 held his first disputation against them.[1] Agricola did not put in an appearance, and Luther accordingly challenged him to a second disputation (Jan. 12, 1538), at which a solemn reconciliation took place. Agricola even authorized Luther to draw up a retraction in his name, which the latter did in damaging fashion in a letter to Caspar Güttel of Eisleben. The conflict seemed over, and in Feb., 1539, Agricola was appointed to the Wittenberg consistory. The dispute was, however, revived through reflections made against Luther by Agricola in a disputation at the University. Luther responded, and proceeded to vigorous attacks on the antinomians. He considered even the excommunication of Agricola. The latter, on his side, thought himself calumniated and collected material for his justification. In Mar., 1540, he submitted his complaints to the Elector. To these complaints Luther responded that what Agricola termed calumnies were but conclusions inevitably to be drawn from the latter's propositions. The Elector instituted formal proceedings against Agricola, who, though under pledge not to leave Wittenberg, withdrew

[1] The more important of Agricola's eighteen propositions are: i. Repentance is to be taught not from the decalogue or any law of Moses, but from the suffering and death of the Son through the gospel. ii. For Christ says in the last chapter of Luke: "Thus it behooved Christ to die and in this manner to enter into his glory, that repentance and remission of sins might be preached in his name." iii. And Christ, in John, says that the Spirit, not the law, convicts the world of sin. iv. The last discourse of Christ teaches the same thing: 'Go, preach the gospel to every creature." vii. Without anything whatever the Holy Spirit is given and men are justified: this thing [the law] is not necessary to be taught either for the beginning, the middle, or the end of justification. viii. But the Holy Spirit having been given of old is also given perpetually, and men are justified without the law through the gospel concerning Christ alone. xiii. Wherefore, for conserving purity of doctrine we must resist those who teach that the gospel is not to be preached except to those who have been crushed and made contrite through the law. xvi. The law only convicts of sin and that, too, without the Holy Spirit; therefore it convicts unto damnation. xvii. But there is need of a doctrine that not only with great efficacy condemns, but also at the same time saves: but that is the gospel, which teaches conjointly repentance and remission of sins. xviii. For the gospel of Christ teaches the wrath from heaven and at the same time the justice of God, Rom. i. For it is the preaching of repentance joined to a promise which reason does not naturally apprehend, but which comes through divine revelation.

Luther added to these acknowledged articles of Agricola several other statements of doubtful authenticity which Agricola was supposed to have made: The law is not worthy to be called the word of God. Art thou a harlot, a knave, an adulterer, or any other sort of sinner if thou believest thou art in the way of salvation. The decalogue belongs to the town hall, and not to the pulpit. All who go about with Moses must go to the devil. To the gallows with Moses! To hear the word and live accordingly is the consequence of the law. To hear the word and feel it in the heart is the proper consequence of the gospel. Peter knew nothing about Christian freedom. His declaration "making your calling sure through good works" is good for nothing. As soon as thou thinkest it must go thus and so in Christendom, everybody is to be refined, honorable, discreet, holy, and chaste, thou hast already prostituted the gospel. Agricola disowned the most manifestly immoral of these propositions, and there is no reason to believe that he practised or approved of the immorality that seems involved in his teachings.

A. H. N.

in August to Berlin. From there he recalled his complaints and at Luther's demand prepared a letter of retraction. For a time he modified his views to some extent so that they approximated in a measure to those of Luther; but Luther's distrust was not removed, nor was Agricola really convinced of error.

After Agricola it was especially Jakob Schenk, court-preacher of Duke Henry and the Reformer of Freiberg, who came under suspicion of Antinomianism; he is said to have declared that "all who preached the law were possessed with the devil; do what you will, if you only believe, you are saved," and "to the gallows with Moses!" An inquiry instituted against him (June, 1538) ended in his being called by the Elector to Weimar as court-preacher. In 1541 Duke Henry summoned him to Leipsic as preacher and university lecturer, but council, clergy, and theological faculty were all strongly opposed to him. Objection was made to the publication of his sermons, and they were found in several points to be at variance with the Augsburg Confession. In the indictment appears the old charge of antinomian doctrine, resting, indeed, on very slight foundations. In 1543 he finally left the duchy. The contents of his published writings furnish no adequate basis for calling him an Antinomian. But there is no doubt that his sermons erred repeatedly in that direction.

4. Jakob Schenk.

In connection with the Majoristic dispute over the necessity of good works, Luther's pupils, Andreas Poach of Erfurt and Anton Otho (Otto) of Nordhausen denied that the law had any significance whatever for believers, and thus arose the dispute *de tertio usu legis*. Otho directed his contention immediately against Melanchthon, though the latter had merely repeated Luther's statements. Against Otho and those of similar views arose several leaders, in particular Morlin and Wigand. On the other hand, Melanchthon and his more immediate school was accused of antinomian doctrine in declaring the gospel to be the proclamation of repentance.

5. Later Controversies.

The Formula of Concord fixed the terminology of the whole matter by deciding that the law was a special revelation teaching what is just and pleasing in the sight of God, and refuting whatever is opposed to the divine will; while the gospel, on the other hand, taught what it was necessary to believe, especially the doctrine of forgiveness of sin through Christ. All that pertained to the punishment of sin belonged to the preaching of the law, though it was conceded that it might be said the gospel discoursed of repentance and the remission of sin, if gospel were understood to mean the sum of Christian doctrine. The preaching of the law became effective to a consciousness of sin only when the law was spiritually expounded by Christ. (G. KAWERAU.)

6. Settlement of the Controversy.

2. The Antinomian Controversy in New England: The Puritans of New England, following in the footsteps of Calvin and Knox, were theocratic in their ideas of Christianity and were inclined to make the legalistic system of the Old Testament their model. The enforcement of rigorous regulations pertaining to every department of life (strict observance of Sunday as Sabbath, regular attendance at church, avoidance of every form of frivolity in dress or demeanor) provoked reaction here as it had done in Geneva. Mrs. Anne (Marbury) Hutchinson (b. in Lincolnshire 1590 or 1591; married about 1612 to William Hutchinson of Alford, Lincolnshire), who had been under the ministry of John Cotton (q.v.) at Boston, Lincolnshire, had imbibed antinomian views, probably from Familists, and, on her arrival in New England (whither she followed her eldest son, Edward, arriving in Sept., 1634), while she continued to enjoy the ministrations of Cotton, now pastor of the Boston (Mass.) church, soon began to express in strong language her aversion to the preaching of a "covenant of works" in contradistinction to a "covenant of grace," by most of the Massachusetts preachers. She regarded Cotton as a preacher of a "covenant of grace," and he was no doubt considerably influenced by her views; when the agitation of the question seemed likely to wreck the colony, he found difficulty in convincing the dominant party of the soundness of his opinions. Rev. John Wheelwright, Mrs. Hutchinson's brother-in-law, a Cambridge graduate (arrived in New England May, 1636), accepted her views. Sir Henry Vane (arrived Oct., 1635; chosen governor May, 1636; see VANE, SIR HENRY) became a zealous advocate of the "covenant of grace." Mrs. Hutchinson expounded her views to large gatherings of women, who twice a week resorted to her house, and thus propagated them widely. She claimed that after a year of prayer it had been revealed to her that she had trusted in a covenant of works; under like divine impulse she had come to New England, there being no one in England that she durst hear. She was the daughter of an English clergyman and combined considerable theological information and argumentative effectiveness with a steadfastness and persistence worthy of a better cause. Like most religious reformers of the time she had wrought herself into the conviction that the few dogmas she held represented the whole truth and that all other teaching was diabolical and abominable. The chief opponents of Mrs. Hutchinson were John Wilson, pastor of the Charlestown church, Hugh Peters, pastor of the Salem church, and John Winthrop (qq.v.). In Dec., 1636, the ministers censured Vane as responsible for the hurtful agitation, and sought to convince Mrs. Hutchinson of her errors. The Boston church of which Vane was a member undertook to censure Wilson, but could not secure the required unanimity, and Cotton was content publicly to admonish him. In Jan., 1637, Wheelwright, in a sermon, denounced the "covenant of works" people as "antichrists" and thus added fuel to the flames. In March the Court by a majority vote censured Wheelwright, and, in the gubernatorial election in May, Vane was defeated and Winthrop was elected. Coercive measures soon removed the disturbing element from Massachusetts. Vane returned to England. Wheelwright founded the town of

Exeter in New Hampshire. The Hutchinsons went to Rhode Island (1638), and most of the party ultimately settled near Newport. After the death of her husband in 1642, Mrs. Hutchinson moved into Dutch territory in Westchester County, New York, and was murdered there by Indians in August or September, 1643.

The character of this movement may best be set forth by quoting a contemporary summary of Mrs. Hutchinson's teachings:

1. That the Law, and the preaching of it, is of no use at all to drive a man to Christ. 2. That a man is united to Christ and justified without faith, yea from eternity. 3. That faith is not a receiving of Christ, but a man's discerning that he hath received him already. 4. That a man is united to Christ only by the work of the Spirit upon him, without any act of his. 5. That a man is never effectually Christ's till he hath assurance. 6. This assurance is only from the witness of the Spirit. 7. This witness of the Spirit is merely immediate, without any respect of the Word, or any concurrence with it. 8. When a man hath once this witness, he never doubts more. 9. To question my assurance, though I fall into murder or adultery, proves that I never had true assurance. 10. Sanctification can be no evidence of a man's good estate. 11. No comfort can be had from any conditional promise. 12. Poverty in spirit . is only this, to see I have no grace at all. 13. To see I have no grace in me will give me comfort; but to take comfort from sight or grace is legal [legalistic]. 14. An hypocrite may have Adam's graces that he had in innocency. 15. The graces of saints and hypocrites differ not. 16. All graces are in Christ, as in the subject, and none in us, so that Christ believes, Christ loves, etc. 17. Christ is the new creature. 18. God loves a man never the better for any holiness in him, and never the less be he never so unholy. 19. Sin in a child of God must never trouble him. 20. Trouble in conscience for sins of commission, or for neglect of duty, shows a man to be under a covenant of works. 21. All covenants of God expressed in works are legal works. 22. A Christian is not bound to the Law as the rule of his conversation. 23. A Christian is not bound to pray, except the Spirit moves him. 24. A minister that hath not this (new) light is not able to edify others that have it. 25. The whole letter of the Scripture is a covenant of works. 26. No Christian must be pressed to duties of holiness. 27 No Christian must be exhorted to faith, love, and prayer etc., except we know he hath the Spirit. 28. A man may have all graces and yet want Christ. 29. All a believer's activity is only to act sin. (Pagitt, ut sup., 124–126.) The following utterances ascribed to Mrs. Hutchinson and her followers are also significant: "In the saving conversion of a sinner the faculties of the soul and working thereof are destroyed and made to cease; and the Holy Ghost agitates instead of them. . That God the Father, Son, and Holy Ghost may give themselves to the soul, and that the soul may have true union with Christ, true remission of sins, . true sanctification from the blood of Christ, and yet be an hypocrite. That the Spirit doth work in hypocrites by gifts and graces, but in God's children immediately. That it is a soul-damning error to make sanctification an evidence of justification. . That the devil and nature may be the cause of good works."

A. H. Newman.

Bibliography: The subject of early Antinomianism is treated in such works on N. T. Theology as that of W. Beyschlag, 2 vols., Edinburgh, 1894 96, and in treatises on Gnosticism (q.v.). Consult Neander, *Christian Church*, i. 447 454 et passim, ii. 769, iii. 588; *KL*, i. 357–358, 928–940, v. 1527, ix. 1157 (covers the whole subject); C. Schlusselburg, *Catalogus hereticorum*, Frankfort, 1597.

On the German Antinomian Controversy consult: G. J. Planck, '*Geschichte der Entstehung . des protestantischen Lehrbegriffs*, vo . iv., 6 vols., Leipsic, 1791 1800; J. J. I. Döllinger, *Die Reformation*, iii. 387 sqq., Regensburg, 1846; F. H. R. Frank, *Die Theologie der Concordienformel*, ii. 243 sqq., Erlangen, 1861; J. K. Seidemann, *Dr. Jacob Schenk*, Leipsic, 1875; G. Müller, *Paul Lindenau*, ib. 1880; K. R. Hagenbach, *History of Christian Doctrines*, ii. 418, iii. 67, Edinburgh, 1880–81; G. Kawerau, *Agricola*, Berlin, 1881; J. Seehawer, *Zur Lehre vom Gebrauch des Gesetzes und zur Geschichte des späteren Antinomismus*, Rostock, 1887; T. Kolde, *Martin Luther*, ii. 463 sqq., Gotha, 1893; F. Loofs, *Dogmengeschichte*, Halle, 1893; J. Köstlin, *Martin Luther*, ii. 125, 134, 418, 438, 448–452 et passim, Berlin, 1903.

On the later English and American Antinomianism consult: *Story of the Rise, Reign, and Ruine of the Antinomians, Familists and Libertines that infected the Churches of New England*, London, 1644; Tobias Crisp, *Works*, ib. 1690; John Fletcher, *Checks to Antinomianism*, in *Works*, vols. ii.-vi., 8 vols., ib. 1803; D. Bogue, *History of Dissenters*, 4 vols., ib. 1808–12; W. Orme, *Life of Baxter*, ii. 232 and chap. ix., ib. 1830; D. Neal, *History of Puritans*, 2 vols., New York, 1848; C. F. Adams, *Three Episodes of Massachusetts . . . History*, the *Antinomian Controversy*, Boston, 1892; B. Adams, *The Emancipation of Massachusetts*, ib. 1887 (on Puritanism and the various conflicts of New England); and further the works of Wesley and Andrew Fuller.

ANTIOCH, PATRIARCHATE OF. See Patriarch; Syria.

ANTIOCH, an'ti-oc, **SCHOOL OF**: A term designating, not an educational institution like the catechetical school of Alexandria, but a theological tendency deriving its influence from a number of prominent teachers. [The name is from Antioch on the Orontes, 16 m. from the Mediterranean, the famous city, the third in point of population in the Roman empire, and no mean rival of Rome in splendor. There were the groves of Daphne, where the sensual was pandered to in all ways. Yet there the first preachers of Christianity came, and it was there that the converts to the new faith were first called Christians.] A distinction must be made between an old and a new school—the former from about 270 to 360, the latter (to which the name is confined by some), after 360. The presbyter and martyr Lucian (q.v.; d. 311), who had great influence as an exegete and a metaphysician, and his contemporary the presbyter Dorotheus are generally mentioned as the founders of this school, but it may even go back as far as Paul of Samosata; at least, Lucian seems to have refused his assent to Paul's condemnation. Under altered circumstances, the cool intellectuality of the Antiochians, which shrank from the "mystery" of the incarnation, became Arianism. Arius himself, Eusebius of Nicomedia, and Asterius were disciples of Lucian; and the name of the last was frequently used by the Eusebian party to countenance their attempts at compromise. Most important, however, was Lucian's activity in Biblical criticism. In this field his influence was directly opposed to the dogmatico-allegorical expositions of the school of Origen, and it made for historical investigation.

Of Lucian's scholars, Arius as a presbyter in Alexandria had performed for some time the function of expounding the Scriptures, and the clever "sophist" Asterius is said to have written commentaries on the Gospels, the Psalms, and the Epistle to the Romans, of which only an unimportant fragment remains. The semi-Arian bishop Eusebius of Emesa (q.v.) is of more importance. Jerome attests the influence of his exegetical method on Diodorus, and calls Chrysostom "the follower of Eusebius of Emesa and Diodorus" (*De vir. ill.*, cxix., cxxix.). Eustathius of Antioch (q.v.) must be mentioned, not only for his dogmatic connection with the school (though a strict adherent of the Council of Nicæa, he met the Arian conclusion from the finite qualities of Christ against the fulness of his Godhead by a sharp distinction between the divine and human natures in him, between the eternal Son and his temple), but even more for his exegesis. His celebrated treatise on the witch of Endor (*De Engastrimytho*) is directly opposed to the method of Origen. Diodorus of Tarsus (q.v.; d. 378) may be considered the father of the school in the narrower sense. Chrysostom and Theodore of Mopsuestia were among his pupils, and the latter became the classical representative of the school. His theology is vigorous and original, a genuine offspring of the old Greek theology as seen in Origen, emphasizing strongly the freedom of the will as against the Augustinianism characteristic of Western thought. Both Diodorus and Theodore, in unison with the great doctors of their age as regards the Nicene faith, combated not only Arianism but Apollinarism. In exegesis Diodorus declares that he prefers the historical to the allegorical method; and Theodore strives with great energy for a true grammatico-historical exposition, and makes remarkable strides toward true Biblical criticism.

Theodore's brother, Polychronius, first a monk in the cloister of St. Zebinas near Kyros, then bishop of Apamea (d. 430), was superior to Theodore as a Hebrew and Syriac scholar; his commentary on Daniel, of which considerable fragments were published by Mai in his *Nova collectio*, i., is distinguished by its study of the history of the period. The principles of the school of Antioch bore their fairest fruit in the thoughtful, practically edifying expositions of John Chrysostom (q.v.), though both he and another distinguished writer closely akin to him, Isidore of Pelusium (q.v.), make concessions to the allegorical method, or do not distinguish sharply between type and allegory. The latest writer who properly belongs to the school is the many-sided, clever, learned, but somewhat wavering Theodoret. In spite of his great dependence on and reverence for Theodore, he not only leaned in dogma to compromise, but in his exegesis he drifted away from Theodore's principles and bowed to ecclesiastical traditionalism, abandoning a large part of the exegetical conquests of the school.

The polemical activity of the school is of no small importance. There were many of the old heretics still left in the region of its influence, as well as numerous Jews and pagans; and it fought the battles of the Church against them at a time when the other provinces were able to enjoy a large measure of peace. (A. Harnack.)

Bibliography: L. Diestel, *Geschichte des Alten Testaments in der christlichen Kirche*, pp. 126–141, Jena, 1869; H. Kihn, *Die Bedeutung der antiochischen Schule*, Weissenburg, 1866, idem, *Theodor von Mopsuestia und Junilius Africanus*, Freiburg, 1879, idem, in *Tubinger TQ*, 1880; C. Hornung, *Schola Antiochensis*, Neustadt, 1864; P. Hergenröther, *Die antiochische Schule*, Würzburg, 1866; F. A. Specht, *Der exegetische Standpunkt des Theodor und Theodoret*, Munich, 1871; Neander, *Christian Church*, i. 674, 722, ii. 182, 346, 388–394, 493–504, 542–544, 712–722, 726–733, 737–739; O. Bardenhewer, *Polychronius*, Freiburg, 1879; Möller, *Christian Church*, i. 406–409.

ANTIOCH, SYNOD OF, 341 A.D.: Records of more than thirty synods held at Antioch in Syria in the early days of the Church are preserved. Of these the more important fall within the period of the controversy about the person of Christ, and are treated in connection with it. That of the year 341 requires separate treatment. It was held in connection with the consecration of the so-called Golden Basilica begun by Constantine and completed by Constantius. Athanasius says that ninety bishops were present; Hilary says ninety-seven. The synod passed twenty-five canons, and promulgated three creeds with a design to remove the Nicænum. The first canon confirmed the decision of the Nicene council on the celebration of Easter, and the second enforced participation in the complete liturgy. Most of the others dealt with questions of ecclesiastical organization, such as the relations of dioceses and the development of the metropolitan system. Priests were forbidden to wander from one diocese into another; schismatic assemblies were prohibited; persons excommunicated by one bishop were not to be reconciled by another; and strangers were not to be received without "letters of peace." The provincial system gained a firmer foothold by the reiteration of the fifth canon of Nicæa, requiring synods to be held twice a year. The position of the *chorepiscopus* suffered a corresponding depression in the eighth and tenth canons. Abstinence from interference with other dioceses and strict guardianship of church property are enjoined upon the bishops, who are also forbidden to name their successors. These canons formed an element of ecclesiastical law for both East and West, and were included in the *Codex canonum* used by the Council of Chalcedon. (A. Hauck.)

Bibliography: Neander, *Christian Church*, i. 605–606, ii. 187, 193, 205, 432–434, 436, 761; Hefele, *Conciliengeschichte*, i. 502–530, Eng. transl., ii. 56–82; F. Maassen, *Geschichte der Quellen des kanonischen Rechts*, i. 65 sqq., Gratz, 1870.

ANTIOCHUS, an-tai'o-kus: The name of thirteen kings of Syria, belonging to the dynasty founded by Seleucus I., Nicator (312–280 B.C.), after the death of Alexander the Great. See Seleucidæ.

ANTIOCHUS: Abbot of Mar Saba (about 3 hours s.w. of Jerusalem), early in the seventh century, a Galatian by birth. He wrote a work entitled in Greek "Pandect of the Holy Scriptures," a collection of moral sayings from the Bible and the older Church Fathers. An introductory epistle describes the martyrdom of forty-four monks of Mar Saba and the capture of Jerusalem when the Persian king Chosroes II. conquered Palestine (614), and the last chapter gives a list of heretics beginning with Simon Magus. Another of his works, *Exomologesis*, also depicts the sufferings of Jerusalem.

Bibliography: *MPG*, lxxxix.

ANTIPAS: Son of Herod the Great. See Herod and his Family.

ANTIPATER (an-tip'a-ter) **OF BOSTRA:** Bishop of Bostra (70 m. s. of Damascus) soon after 450. As a theologian he belongs to the opponents of the

Origenists, against whom he wrote his chief work (in Greek), the "Refutation." Only a few fragments of it are preserved, in the "Parallels" of John of Damascus. Most of the homilies ascribed to Antipater are not his. Even the two on John the Baptist and Annunciation Day, which Migne claims for him, are doubtful; the first supposes a fully developed veneration of the Baptist, and its diction is suggestive of Byzantine rhetoric; the other address is more simple. The question as to the genuineness of the homilies can not be decided until more of them shall have been published. His works are in *MPG*, lxxxv., xcvi. (the quotations in John of Damascus). PHILIPP MEYER.

BIBLIOGRAPHY: Fabricius-Harles, *Bibliotheca Græca*, x. 518 sqq., Hamburg, 1807.

ANTIPHON, an'ti-fon: A term denoting primarily alternating song or chanting, one voice or choir answering another. It was a Jewish custom (Ezra iii. 11; I Chron. xxix. 20; Ps. cvi. 45; Matt. xxvi. 30) and was early introduced into the Christian Church. Basil (*Epist.*, ccvii.), in writing to the clergy of Neocæsarea, mentions the two commonest methods: "Now, divided into two parts, they sing antiphonally with one another. . . Afterward they again commit the prelude of the strain to one, and the rest take it up." The latter method could be either hypophonic, when the response consisted of the closing words of each verse or section; epiphonic, when an expression like "Amen," "Alleluia," "Gloria Patri" was repeated at the end of a psalm; or antiphonic in the strict sense, when the second body of singers responded to the first half of each verse with the second half, or the two bodies repeated verses alternately. Later the term "antiphon" came to mean merely a verse or formula with which the precentor, or precentors, began, and which was repeated by the entire choir at the end of the song. It determines the mode of the piece, and closes with the key-note followed by the dominant and the *euouæ* (the last notes of the piece; the name is made up of the vowels of *seculorum, amen*). The whole antiphon (abbreviated into *ana*) is now sung both at the beginning and at the end of psalms at lauds and vespers on double feast-days; at other times, only at the end. A collection of antiphons is called an *antiphonarium* or *antiphonale*.

The *Breviarium Romanum* has many excellent antiphons, and the Evangelical Lutheran Church has also made use of them. They are chosen with reference to the content of the psalm or hymn to which they are joined, or they indicate its relation to special days and times. For example, an antiphon to Ps. lxiii. for Christmas is: "And the angel said unto them, fear not, for behold I bring you good tidings"; for Trinity Sunday, "*Gloria tibi, Trinitas*"; for apostles' days, "Ye are my friends." The music of the ancient antiphons is generally appropriate, beautiful, and powerful.

M. HEROLD.

BIBLIOGRAPHY: F. Armknecht, *Die heilige Psalmodie*, Göttingen, 1855; L. Schöberlein, *Schatz des liturgischen Chor- und Gemeinde-Gesangs*, i. 550 sqq., ib. 1880; W. Löhe, *Agende*, Nördlingen, 1884; M. Herold, *Vesperale*, 2 vols., Gütersloh, 1893; F. Hommel, *Antiphonen und Psalmentöne*, ib. 1896; R. von Liliencron, *Chorordnung*, ib. 1900.

ANTIPOPE: A papal usurper, not elected in the canonical way, but resting his claims on fraud or force. Political intrigues, the ambitions of sovereigns, and the action of a minority of the cardinals have generally been responsible for rival popes. In 1046 there were four claimants of the papacy: Sylvester III., Benedict IX., Gregory VI., and Clement II. It has not always been easy to decide which of the rivals was the true pope, and in such cases schism has been the result. The longest schism (known as "the Great Schism") succeeded the death of Gregory XI. (1378) and lasted fifty years (see SCHISM). For the names of the antipopes, see the list given in the article POPE, PAPACY, AND PAPAL SYSTEM.

ANTITACTÆ, an"ti-tac'tî or -tê: The name given by Clement of Alexandria (*Strom.*, iii. 34–39; followed by Theodoret, *Hæreticarum fabularum epitome*, i. 16) to a branch of Gnostic libertines, who rejected the demiurge. See CARPOCRATES AND THE CARPOCRATIANS. G. KRÜGER.

ANTITRINITARIANISM.

Antitrinitarianism is the general name for a number of very different views which agree only in rejecting the Christian doctrine of the Triune God. This doctrine did not originate in the extra-Christian world, but, with whatever adumbrations in the Old Testament revelation (cf. Dorner, *System of Christian Doctrine*, i., Edinburgh, 1880, pp. 345 sqq.), was first distinctly revealed in the missions of the Son and Spirit, and first clearly taught by Jesus (cf. W Sanday, *The Criticism of the Fourth Gospel*, London, 1905, pp. 218 sqq.) and his apostles. It naturally, therefore, as a purely Christian doctrine, had to establish itself against both Jewish and heathen conceptions; and throughout its history it has met with more or less contradiction from the two opposite points of view of modalism (which tends to sink the persons in the unity of the Godhead) and subordinationism (which tends to degrade the second and third persons into creatures).

The earliest antitrinitarians were those Jews who in the first age of the Church were convinced, indeed, that Jesus was the promised Messiah, but, in their jealously guarded monotheism, could not admit him to be God, and taught therefore a purely humanitarian Christology. They bear the name in history of Ebionites (q.v.). The emanationism of the Gnostic sects, which swarmed throughout the second century, tended to subordinationism; and this tendency is inherent also in the Logos speculation by which the Christological thought of the Church teachers through the second and third centuries was dominated. The Logos speculation was not, however, consciously antitrinitarian; its purpose was, on the contrary, to construe the Church's immanent faith in the Trinity to thought, and to that end it suggested a descending series of gradations of deity by which the transcendent God (the Father)

1. The Earliest Antitrinitarianism.

stretched out to the creation and government of the world (Son and Spirit). This subordinationism, however, bore bitter fruit in the early fourth century in the Arian degradation of the Son to a creature and of the Spirit to the creature of a creature.

The ripening of this fruit was retarded by the outbreak, as the second century melted into the third, of the first great consciously antitrinitarian movement in the bosom of the Church. This movement, which is known in history as Monarchianism (q.v.) arose in Asia Minor and rapidly spread over the whole Church. In its earliest form as taught by the two Theodoti and Artemon, and in its highest development by Paul of Samosata, it conceived of Jesus as a mere man. In this form it was too alien to Christian feeling to make much headway; and it was quickly followed by another wave which went to the other extreme and made the Father, Son, and Spirit but three modes of being, manifestations, or actions of the one person which God was conceived to be. In this form it was taught first by Praxeas and Noetus and found its fullest expression in Sabellius, who has given his name to it. The lower form is commonly called Ebionitic or dynamistic Monarchianism; the higher, modalistic Monarchianism or, to use the nickname employed by Tertullian, Patripassianism. Modalistic Monarchianism came forward in the interests of the true deity of Christ, and, appearing to offer a clear and easy solution of the antinomy of the unity of God and the deity of the Son and Spirit, made its way with great rapidity, and early in the third century seemed to threaten to become the faith of the Church. It was partly in reaction from it that the Arians in the early fourth century pressed the subordinationism of much early church teaching to the extreme of removing the Son and Spirit out of the category of deity altogether, and thus created the greatest and most dangerous antitrinitarian movement the Church has ever known. The interaction of the modalistic and Arian factors brought it about that the statement of the doctrine of the Trinity wrought out in the ensuing controversies was guarded on both sides; and so well was the work done that the Church was little troubled by antitrinitarian opposition for a thousand years thereafter. During the Middle Ages the obscure dualistic and pantheistic sects, it is true, held to antitrinitarian doctrines of God; but within the Church itself defective conceptions of the Trinity, resting commonly on a pantheistic basis, manifested themselves rather in theological tendencies than in distinct parties (e.g., Johannes Scotus Erigena; other tendencies in Roscelin and Abelard). In the great upheaval of the Reformation the antitrinitarianism of the obscure sects came into open view in the Anabaptist movement (Denk, Hätzer, Melchior Hofmann, David Joris, Johannes Campanus). At the head of the pantheistic antitrinitarianism of the Reformation era, however, stands Michael Servetus, and though his type of thought soon passed into the background, it was destined to be revived whenever mystical tendencies waxed strong (Boehme, Zinzendorf, Swedenborg). Meanwhile Laelius and Faustus Socinus succeeded in forming an organized sect of rationalistic antitrinitarians who found a refuge in Poland, established a famous university, issued symbolical documents (the chief of which is the Racovian Catechism, 1605), and created an influential literature (Schlichting, Völkel, the two Crells, Ostorodt, Schmalz, Wolzogen, Wiszowati).

2. Monarchianism and Other Forms to the Reformation.

By the middle of the seventeenth century the Socinian establishment at Racow was broken up, but the influence of the type of thought it represented has continued until the present day. In Transylvania, indeed, the old Unitarian organization dating from the labors of Blandrata and David still exists. Elsewhere antitrinitarianism has crept in by way of more or less covert innovations representing themselves as "liberal," and running commonly through the stages of Arminianism and Arianism to Socinianism. In England, for example, a wide-spread hesitancy with regard to the doctrine of the Trinity was observable before the end of the seventeenth century, manifesting itself no less in the high subordinationism of writers like George Bull than in the frank Arianism of others like Samuel Clarke. It was not until 1774, however, that the first Unitarian chapel distinctly known as such was founded (Theophilus Lindsey), though this type of thought was rapidly permeating the community under the influence of men of genius like Joseph Priestly and men of learning like Nathaniel Lardner; and before the end of the second decade of the nineteenth century, a large body of the foremost Presbyterian congregations had become avowedly Unitarian. A somewhat similar history was wrought out in Ireland, where after a protracted controversy the Synod of Ulster was divided in 1827 on this question, W Bruce leading the Unitarian party.

3. Antitrinitarianism in Great Britain.

By the middle of the eighteenth century, the prevalent attitude of suspicion with regard to the doctrine of the Trinity had communicated itself to the New England churches, and soon an antitrinitarian movement, developing out of the lingering Arminianism, was in full swing, which from 1815 received the name of Unitarianism. The consequent controversy reached its height in 1819, the date of the publication of W E. Channing's sermon at the ordination of Jared Sparks at Baltimore, and was virtually over by 1833. The result was a body of definitely antitrinitarian churches bound together on this general basis, whose leaders have illustrated, on every possible philosophical foundation, every possible variety of antitrinitarianism from the highest modalism or Arianism down (and increasingly universally so as time has passed) to the lowest Socinianism.

4. In New England.

Meanwhile the "liberal" tendencies of modern theological thought have produced throughout Christendom a very large number of theological teachers who, while not separating themselves from the trinitarian churches, are definitely antitrinitarian in their doctrine of God. Accordingly, although the organized Unitarian churches, which were earlier not unproductive of men of high quality (e.g., John James Tayler, James Martineau, James Drummond, in England; Theodore Parker, Andrews Norton, Ezra Abbot, A. P. Peabody, F. H. Hedge, James Freeman Clarke, in America), show no large power of growth, it is probable that at no period in the history of the Christian Church has there been a more distinguished body of antitrinitarian teachers within its fold. Every variety of antitrinitarianism finds its representatives among them. The Arian tendency is, indeed, discoverable chiefly in the high subordinationism of men who do not wish to break with the church doctrine of the Trinity (Franck, Twesten, Kahnis, Meyer, Beck, Doedes, Van Oosterzee), though a true Arianism is not unexampled (Hofstede de Groot). In sequence to the constructions of Kant and his idealistic successors, a great number of recent theologians from Schleiermacher down have stated their doctrine of God in terms of one or another form of modalism (De Wette, Hase, Nitzsch, Rothe, Biedermann, Lipsius, Pfleiderer, Kaftan), though sometimes, or of late ordinarily, this modalism is indistinguishable from Socinianism, allowing only a "Trinity of revelation"—of God in nature (the Creation), in history (Christ), and in the conscience (the Church). Consonant with the general drift of modern thought this recent antitrinitarianism is commonly, however, frankly Socinian, and recognizes only a monadistic Godhead and only a human Jesus (cf. A. B. Bruce, *The Humiliation of Christ*, Edinburgh, 1881, Lecture v.; James Orr, *The Christian View of God and the World*, Edinburgh, 1903, Lecture vii., and notes). The most striking instance of this bald Socinianism is furnished probably by A. Ritschl, but a no less characteristic example is afforded by W Beyschlag, who admits only an ideal preexistence in the thought of God for Jesus Christ, and affirms of the Holy Spirit that the representation that he is a third divine person "is one of the most disastrous importations into the Holy Scriptures." See RITSCHL, ALBRECHT BENJAMIN; TRINITY. BENJAMIN B. WARFIELD.

5. Antitrinitarianism of the Present.

BIBLIOGRAPHY: J. H. Allen, *Historical Sketch of the Unitarian Movement since the Reformation*, New York, 1894 (in American Church History Series); F. S. Bock, *Historia Antitrinitariorum*, 2 vols., Königsberg, 1774–84; L. Lange, *Geschichte und Entwickelung der Systeme der Unitarier vor der Nicänischen Synode*, Leipsic, 1831; F. Trechsel, *Die protestantischen Antitrinitarier vor Socin*, Heidelberg, 1839–44; O. Fock, *Der Socinianismus nach seiner Stellung in der Gesammtentwickelung des christlichen Geistes*, Kiel, 1847; R. Wallace, *Antitrinitarian Biography*, 3 vols., London, 1850. See also under ARIANISM; EBIONITES; MONARCHIANISM; SOCINUS (FAUSTUS), SOCINIANS; UNITARIANS; and cf. the treatment of these movements in the Church histories.

ANTON, PAUL: Lutheran; b. at Hirschfelde (near Zittau, 50 m. e.s.e. of Dresden), in Upper Lausitz, Feb. 2, 1661; d. at Halle Oct. 20, 1730. He studied at Leipsic, became tutor there, and helped to found Francke's *Collegia biblica* (see PIETISM). In 1687–89 he traveled in southern Europe as chaplain to the future Elector of Saxony Frederick Augustus, and on his return became superintendent at Rochlitz. In 1693 he was summoned as court chaplain to Eisenach, and two years later was appointed professor in the newly established university at Halle. With J. J. Breithaupt and A. H. Francke (qq.v.), Anton gave to the Hallensian theology its pietistic character, and he helped largely to make the university one of the leading schools of Protestant theology in Germany. He adhered more closely than his colleagues to the orthodox Lutheran doctrine. His peculiar activity was in the field of practical theology. As professor of polemics, he sought to ground that study upon psychological principles. "Every one," he was accustomed to say, "carries within himself the seeds of unbelief and heresy; and introspection is a more fruitful means for ascertaining the true principles of belief than personal or sectarian controversy." The Lord, he taught, would forgive a thousand faults and transgressions, but not hypocrisy or unfaithfulness to duty. The consciousness of sin was always present with him, and he impressed himself upon his auditors by his evident sincerity. Anton's lectures were edited in part by Schwenzel in 1732 under the title *Collegium antitheticum*. His devotional works—such as *Evangelische Hausgespräch von der Erlösung* (Halle, 1723) and *Erbauliche Betrachtung über die sieben Worte Christi am Kreuz* (1727)—attained great popularity. (GEORG MÜLLER.)

BIBLIOGRAPHY: An autobiography to 1725 was published in *Denkmal des Herrn Paul Anton*, Halle, 1731.

ANTONELLI, ān"to-nel'lī, **GIACOMO,** jā'cō-mō: Cardinal secretary of state under Pius IX. and chief political adviser of that pope; b. at Sonnino (64 m. s.e. of Rome), in the then Papal States, Apr. 2, 1806; d. in Rome Nov. 6, 1876. He received his earlier education at the Roman Seminary, then studied law at the Sapienza, and, after holding several minor posts in the papal government, was appointed delegate or governor successively of Orvieto, Viterbo, and Macerata. He showed so much force and judgment at the outbreak of the revolution of 1831 that Gregory XVI. found a place for him in the Ministry of the Interior, transferring him in 1845 to the position of treasurer of the *Camera Apostolica* or minister of finance. On his appointment in 1840 as canon of St. Peter's he received deacon's orders, but he never became a priest. Pius IX. made him a cardinal in 1847, and on the organization of the municipal council, in the autumn of that year, named him as its president. A few months later, on the establishment of a ministry on modern lines, he was again placed at the head (as president of the council, though Recchi was nominally prime minister), but soon resigned the position, becoming prefect of the pontifical palaces, in which position he organized the flight to Gaeta. Thence, as secretary of state, he conducted the negotiations which led to the pope's return (Apr. 12, 1850), from which date till his death he remained at the head of public affairs under Pius IX.

As the strongest supporter of the reactionary policy, Antonelli was regarded by the Liberals as an incarnation of evil; but materials are not yet at hand for the formation of a final judgment on his career. His opponents, however, admit that he was a man of genius in diplomacy and of unswerving constancy in the defense of his principles. His private life has been bitterly attacked, and it is true that he was more statesman than cleric. Whatever may be thought of his character, however, he was one of the strong men of the nineteenth century; and his name will be indissolubly connected in history with that of the pontiff whom he served so faithfully. See PIUS IX.

BIBLIOGRAPHY: A. de Waal, *Cardinal Antonelli*, Bonn, 1876; *Tres hombres ilustres, Pío IX., Lamoricière y Antonelli*, Madrid, 1860; E. Veuillot, *Célébrités catholiques contemporaines*, Paris, 1870; *KL*, i. 978-979.

ANTONIANS, an-tō'ni-ans, or **ANTONINES**, an"tō-nainz': **1.** Religious orders among the Roman Catholic Chaldeans, Maronites, and Armenians, which follow a rule called the rule of St. Anthony. In reality St. Anthony (251-356), although he is justly styled the father of cenobitic life, left no rule to his followers save those scattered directions found in his writings. The so-called rule of St. Anthony is, therefore, the work of some later writer who took its substance, however, from the teachings of the saint. At the present time the Antonians are grouped in four congregations; the Chaldean Antonians of St. Hormisdas, founded in Mesopotamia in 1809 for missionary work, with about one hundred members; the Maronite Antonians of Aleppo, with 120 members; the Maronite Baladite Antonians, the most numerous of all, with 700 members; and the Maronite Congregation of St. Isaiah, with 240 members. JOHN T. CREAGH.

A fifth congregation called after St. Anthony, now almost extinct, was founded among the Roman Catholic Armenians by Abraham Attar-Muradian, a merchant, who in 1705, with his brother James, a priest, retired to Mount Lebanon to lead an ascetic life. Here, in 1721, they established the monastery of Kerem, followed by another at Beit-Khasbo near Beirut. In 1761 a third community was founded in Rome, near the Vatican. About 1740 the exiled bishop of Haleb (Aleppo), Abraham Ardzivian, who had found refuge at Kerem, took advantage of a long vacancy in the Cilician patriarchate to set himself up as catholicos of Cilicia, and secured papal confirmation in 1742. His first successor was the above-mentioned James, who was followed by Michael and Basil, also Antonians. In 1866 the patriarch of the Catholic Armenians, Anthony Hasun, residing in Constantinople, adopted the title " Patriarch of Cilicia," and put an end to the nominal Antonian patriarchate. The Antonians usually numbered fifty or sixty, and served the Roman Catholic mission in Turkey. In 1834 they transferred their novitiate and school to Rome, only the abbot and a few brothers remaining in the Lebanon. In 1865 Sukias Gazanjian was chosen abbot and was consecrated by the last Lebanon patriarch. He lived in Constantinople as head of the anti-Hasun party. On Hasun's charges, he was summoned to Rome in 1869; but before his case could be heard, the Vatican council met. He and his monks were among the first to reject papal infallibility, and were obliged to escape by night, with the help of the French ambassador. In 1876 Malachi Ormanian, the best-known and best-educated of the Antonians, went to Rome and finally closed their house there. (He afterward joined the Armenian Church, and has published *Le Vatican et les Arméniens* and other works.) The present members of the congregation, having made their submission to the pope, are concentrated in one community in Constantinople.

2. An antinomian sect which originated in the canton of Bern, Switzerland, early in the nineteenth century, founded by Anton Unternährer (b. at Schüpfheim, in the canton of Lucerne, Sept. 5, 1759; d. in the jail of Lucerne June 29, 1824). Unternährer was educated and confirmed in the Roman Catholic Church; after a varied career as cowherd, cabinet-maker, private teacher, and quack doctor, he settled in 1800 at Amsoldingen, near Thun, and began to hold religious meetings, to preach, and to issue books. He announced himself as the Son of God, come to fulfil the incomplete work of Jesus, to judge mankind (especially rulers and judges, who were all to be abolished), and to cancel all debts. On Apr. 16, 1802, he appeared before the Minster of Bern with a crowd of adherents, to whom he had predicted the occurrence of some great event. The tumult was suppressed, and Unternährer was condemned to two years' imprisonment. On his release he was received by his adherents with enthusiasm, and riots again occurred. For five years Unternährer was confined in Lucerne as a lunatic. He returned to the world more collected and more serious, but by no means cured, and in 1820 he was permanently confined in the jail.

Unternährer's publications comprise about fifteen pamphlets, including, with others, *Gerichtsbüchlein; Buch der Erfüllung;* and *Geheimniss der Liebe*. He taught that the primitive relation between God and man was expressed in the two commandments, to love and multiply, and to abstain from the tree of knowledge. Tempted by Satan, man violated the second commandment and attained great wisdom, which is the curse of mankind. It began with the distinction between good and evil, and ends in institutions innumerable—State, Church, courts, schools, and the like. From the curse there is only one means of salvation; namely, through the fulfilment of the first commandment, to love and multiply; and for this purpose all restraints arising from such ideas as marriage, family, etc., must be thrown off. The principal seat of the sect was Amsoldingen, whence it spread to Gsteig, near Interlaken. Suppressed here in 1821, it reappeared at Wohlen, near Bern, in 1830, under the leadership of Benedict Schori, and again at Gsteig, in 1838-40, under the leadership of Christian Michel. Severe measures were necessary to suppress its excesses.

BIBLIOGRAPHY: J. Ziegler, *Aktenmässige Nachrichten über die sogenannten Antonisekte im Kanton Bern*, in Trechsel, *Beiträge zur Geschichte der schweizerischen reformirten Kirche*, iii. 70 sqq., Bern, 1842; G. Joss, *Das Sektenwesen im Kanton Bern*, ib. 1881.

ANTONINUS, an″to-nai′nus, **PIUS**: Roman emperor 138-161; b. near Lanuvium (Civita Lavigna, 18 m. s.s.e. of Rome) Sept. 19, 86; d. at Lorium (in southern Etruria, 12 Roman miles from Rome) Mar. 7, 161. He was made consul in 120 and was adopted by Hadrian in 138, after he had distinguished himself by his administration of the province of Asia. On his accession as emperor he took the name Titus Ælius Hadrianus Antoninus Pius, his original one having been Titus Aurelius Fulvius Boionius Arrius Antoninus. Under his just and gentle rule the empire enjoyed almost unbroken peace. In his last years he left the government more and more in the hands of his associate, Marcus Aurelius (q.v.), with whom he was on terms of the closest friendship. For the Christian Church his reign is marked by the flourishing of Marcion and the Gnostic schools, by the apology of Aristides and the writings of Justin, probably by the *Oratio* of Tatian, and possibly by the final edition of the *Shepherd* of Hermas. Within the same period fall the beginning of the Easter controversy, the visit of Polycarp and Hegesippus to Rome, the rise of the monarchical episcopate in that city, and the early stages of the consolidation against Gnosticism of the Roman Church. The civil magistrates observed the same policy of tolerance toward the Church as under Trajan and Hadrian. Practically, however, by forbidding or rendering difficult the delation of the Christians on a charge of atheism by the excited population of Asia Minor, as well as by his edicts addressed "to the people of Larissa, Thessalonica, Athens, and all the Greeks," Antoninus so far protected them that he was considered by many ecclesiastical writers as a positive friend of the new religion. His prohibition of denunciation by fanatical private citizens, however, can not be taken as equivalent to an official sanction for the practise of Christianity. (A. Harnack.)

Bibliography: E. E. Bryant, *Reign of Antoninus Pius*, Cambridge, 1895 (a scholarship-essay); Neander, *Christian Church*, i. passim; B. Aubé, *Histoire des persécutions*, pp. 297-341, Paris, 1875; W. W. Capes, *The Age of the Antonines*, London, 1876; Schaff, *Church History*, ii. 51-52; also, on the period, C. Merivale, *History of the Romans under the Empire*, 8 vols., London, 1865.

ANTONINUS, SAINT, OF FLORENCE (ANTONIO PIEROZZI): Archbishop of Florence; b. in that city 1389; d. there May 2, 1459. In 1404 he joined the Dominicans, and in 1436 was made prior of the monastery of San Marco in Florence. In 1439 he took part in the negotiations for union with the Greeks. In 1446, against his wish but at the express behest of Pope Eugenius IV., he was chosen archbishop. His blameless life and devotion to duty rendered him beloved by all, and his canonization by Adrian VI. in 1523 was looked upon as the just due of an untiring, humble, and exemplary bishop. He has been a favorite subject of Florentine art.

The humanistic tendency of the time had no effect upon Antoninus. He wrote certain works quite in the scholastic spirit, as: *Summa theologica* (4 parts, Venice and Nuremberg, 1477; ed. P and B. Ballerini, Verona, 1740), based upon Thomas Aquinas, the first text-book of ethics, and still esteemed in Italy; *Summa confessionalis* or *Summula confessionum* (Mondovi, 1472); and *Summa historialis* or *Chronicon ab orbe condita bipartitum* (3 vols., Venice, 1480, and often; ed. P Maturus, S. J., Lyons, 1587), a world-chronicle to 1457, uncritical and full of fables and legends, but showing industry and systematic arrangement. Here and there, as in judging of the great schism, he ventures to advance his own opinion and he questions the genuineness of the Donation of Constantine. A complete edition of Antoninus' works, in four volumes, was published at Venice, 1474-75, and a second edition, in eight volumes, at Florence, 1741. In later years have appeared: *Opera a ben vivere di Sant' Antonino* (Florence, 1858) and *Lettere* (1859). K. Benrath.

Bibliography: A life, by Franciscus Castilionensis, and another by Leonardus de Serubertis are in *ASB*, May, i. 314-362; Quétif-Echard, *Scriptores ordinis prædicatorum*, i. 817-819, Paris, 1719; Æneas Silvius, *Commentarii*, p. 50, Frankfort, 1614; Creighton, *Papacy*, i. 504; A. von Reumont, *Briefe heiliger und gottesfürchtiger Italiener*, pp. 135-150, Freiburg, 1877; idem, *Lorenzo de' Medici*, i. 148, 176, 562-564, Leipsic, 1874, Eng. transl., i. 123, 151, 463-465, London, 1876.

ANTONIO DE LEBRIJA, an-tō′ni-ō dê lê-bri′ha, (Lat. *Ælius Antonius Nebrissensis*, i.e., "of Lebrija," the ancient Nebrissa, on the Guadalquivir, 34 m. s. of Seville): Spanish humanist; b. 1442 (1444?); d. at Alcala July 2, 1522. He studied in his native land, and for about ten years in Italy, and returned to Spain with a plan for reforming the schools and studies. As professor in Salamanca and by his *Introductiones in Latinam grammaticam* (1481; innumerable editions, translations, and adaptations, even as late as Paris, 1858; an Eng. ed., London, 1631), he led the way to a knowledge of the classics. Retiring from the university, he spent eight or ten years in the preparation of a Latin-Spanish and Spanish-Latin lexicon (Seville, n.d.; Alcala, 1532; and often), a pioneer work at that time. He published also archeological works and a grammar of Greek and of Castilian, and labored to improve the text of the Vulgate. He was one of the chief workers on the Complutensian polyglot, and spent his last years as teacher at Alcala, protected by Cardinal Ximenes from the attacks of the adherents of the old scholastic school. As historiographer to Ferdinand the Catholic he wrote a history of two decades of the reign of Ferdinand and Isabella (Granada, 1545) [by some assigned to Hernando da Pulgar rather than to Antonio; cf. Potthast, *Wegweiser*, Berlin, 1896, p. 946]. K. Benrath.

Bibliography: Nicholaus Antonius, *Bibliotheca Hispana nova*, i. 132-139, Madrid, 1783; J. B. Muñoz, in *Memorias de la real academia de la historia*, iii. 1-30, Madrid, 1799; C. J. Hefele, *Cardinal Ximenes*, pp. 116-117, 124, 379, 458, Tübingen, 1844.

ANTWERP POLYGLOT. See Bibles, Polyglot.

APHARSACHITES, a-fār′sa-kaits, **APHARSATHCHITES**, a-fār″sath′kaits, **APHARSITES**, a-fār′-saits: Words occurring only in the Book of Ezra (Apharsachites, v. 6; Apharsathchites and Apharsites, iv. 9). Most translators and commentators have regarded them as names of peoples, including them among the tribes settled in Samaria by the Assyrians (II Kings xvii. 24), and have made unsatisfactory attempts to identify them (e.g., the

Apharsites with the Parrhasii of East Media—so M. Hiller, *Onomasticum sacrum*, Tübingen, 1706—or with the Persians—Gesenius, *Thesaurus;* Ewald, *Geschichte Israels;* E. Bertheau, commentary on Ezra, Göttingen, 1838). The best explanation has been given by Eduard Meyer (*Entstehung des Judenthums*, Halle, 1896, pp. 37 sqq.), following a hint of G. Hoffmann (in *ZA*, ii., 1887, pp. 54 sqq.). He regards "Apharsachites" and "Apharsathchites" as equivalent, the "th" (the Hebrew letter *tau*) having been inserted in the latter by mistake, and gives to all three words the same meaning, "Persians." The passage Ezra iv. 9, accordingly, he reads: "Rehum the commissioner and Shimshai the scribe, and the rest of their colleagues the Persian magistracy, the Persian *tarpelaye*, the people of Erech, Babylon, and Shushan, that is, the Elamites." The word *tarpelaye* (English versions "Tarpelites") is left untranslated as necessarily meaning an official class of some unknown sort and not the name of a people. It is possible, however, that the "Apharsites" are not "Persians," but that the form arose by dittography, the word for scribe (*saphera*) just above being first copied by mistake and then assimilated to the form for "Persians." If "Apharsites" were to be thus ruled out of the verse and the Bible, the "Tarpelites" would be an unknown people heading the list like those that follow, and not the name of a class of officials. J. F. McCurdy.

APHRAATES, a-frä'tîz: The "Persian sage." He is known as the author of twenty-two homilies, arranged according to the letters of the Syriac alphabet, and a treatise, *De acino benedicto* (Isa. lxv. 8), in Syriac. The first ten homilies were written in the years 336–337, the others in 344–345; the treatise in Aug., 345. The latter is mentioned in Armenian lists of the apocryphal books. In the life of Julianus Saba (P. Bedjan, *Acta martyrum et sanctorum*, vi., Paris, 1896, p. 386) it is said that Aphraates was a pupil of Julianus and that he died, according to some, at the age of 104 years. If this be true, he may have been the Aphraates mentioned by Theodoret (*Hist. eccl.*, iv. 22–23), who had an interview with Valens. The name occurs again in the Syriac martyrology of the year 411. Its form in modern Persian is *Farhad.* The name Jacobus seems to have been adopted by Aphraates as bishop of the monastery of Mar Mattai, near Mosul (cf. G. P. Badger, *The Nestorians*, i., London, 1852, p. 97).

With Ephraem Syrus, Aphraates may be called the first classic writer of the Syrian Church. His style is pure, and he shows deep knowledge of the Scriptures, with earnest zeal for the welfare of the Church. There is no trace of the christological controversies of Arius, a single polemical passage against Valentinians, Marcionites, and Manicheans, but many against the Jews, from whose traditions Aphraates draws richly (cf. S. Funk, *Die haggadischen Elemente in Aphraates*, Vienna, 1891). He used the *Diatessaron* of Tatian instead of the single Gospels. The sixth homily shows that monks and eremites were already organized in his time and place. His psychology is peculiar, especially his doctrine of the sleep of the soul. His days are Jan. 29 (Greek calendar) and Apr. 7

Gennadius of Marseilles, in his *De viris illustribus* (c. 495), confounded Aphraates with Jacob of Nisibis, under whose name nineteen of the homilies were published in an Armenian translation by N. Antonelli (Rome, 1756). George, bishop of the Arabians, in a letter about 714 (P. de Lagarde, *Analecta Syriaca*, Leipsic, 1858; German transl. by V. Ryssel, ib. 1891), is better informed. The Syriac original was first made accessible by W. Wright (*The Homilies of Aphraates, the Persian Sage*, i., text, London, 1869; the translation did not appear). With Latin translation the homilies are in *Patrologia Syriaca*, i. (Paris, 1894). There is a German translation by G. Bert (*TU*, iii. 3, Leipsic, 1888), and an English translation of selections in *NPNF*, 2d ser., vol. xiii. E. Nestle.

Bibliography: J. B. F. Sasse, *Prolegomena in Aphraatis sermones*, Leipsic, 1878; J. Forget, *De vita et scriptis Aphraatis*, Louvain, 1882; W. Wright, *A Short History of Syriac Literature*, London, 1894; and the preface to Wright's ed. of the *Homilies;* F. C. Burkitt, *Early Eastern Christianity*, pp. 132–140, London, 1904.

APHTHARTODOCETÆ, af'thar"tō-do-sî'tî. See Monophysites.

APION, ê'pe-on: Alexandrian grammarian of the first century. He was born in the Great Oasis of Egypt, was educated in Alexandria, and gained repute there as teacher and lecturer; during the reigns of Tiberius and Claudius he lectured on rhetoric and grammar in Rome; under Caligula he traveled through Greece and Italy lecturing on Homer. He seems to have been vain and superficial, with a touch of the charlatan in his character. Among other works, he wrote a glossary on Homer, a eulogy of Alexander the Great, and a history of Egypt. But it is as an early anti-Semite that Apion is remembered; his hatred of the Jews was bitter and extreme and led him to record slanders in his history of Egypt which are refuted by Josephus in his work known as *Contra Apionem*, although but a part of it is directed against Apion. In the year 40 A.D. Apion headed a delegation sent from Alexandria to Caligula at Rome to make charges against the Jews; the counterdelegation, sent by the Jews for their defense, was led by Philo (q.v.). The extant fragments of Apion's historical works are collected in C. O. Müller's *Fragmenta historicorum Græcorum*, iii. (Paris, 1849), pp. 506–516.

Bibliography: *DCB*, i. 128–130; Schürer, *Geschichte*, iii. 406–411, Leipsic, 1898, Eng. transl., II. iii. 257–261 (contains full references to literature); *JE*, i. 666–668.

APOCALYPSE, THE. See John the Apostle, II., 1. For apocryphal apocalypses, see Apocrypha, B, IV.; see also Pseudepigrapha, Old Testament, II., 4–21, and Apocalyptic Literature, Jewish.

APOCALYPTIC LITERATURE, JEWISH: The latest type of Jewish prophetic writing. The literature generally called "apocalyptic" commences with Daniel (for date, see Daniel, Book of) and closes with IV Ezra-Baruch. On the one side, the limit is the time of the Maccabean rising; on the other, the downfall of the Jewish nationality.

Fundamental Characteristics. The notion of two ages following each other (this age and the coming one; cf. IV Ezra, vii. 50, "The Most High made not one age, but two"), which stands also in the background of New Testament literature, governs apocalyptic conceptions. The underlying idea here is dualism, the thought being that God alone is not in full control of "this age," since diabolic might finds exercise therein. It is interesting to observe how through Jewish apocalyptic the idea of "world" as a whole, developing itself according to certain laws, is made familiar to later Judaism (cf. Dan. vii. 1 sqq.; Enoch lxxxv. sqq.; Baruch xxvii. sqq.), and how the inner, significant, religious-historical development of Judaism is conditioned by its external history. In its developed form apocalyptic literature originated in a period when a civilized power, the Hellenic, ruling the world by external might and inner mental superiority, entered upon a contest with Judaism, in which the latter, aroused to national consciousness, accepted the gage of battle. The Greek power, and afterward the Roman, supplied the apocalyptic seer with the material for the formation of his conceptions. Thus the time of the Maccabees is the natal hour of the Jewish apocalyptic, and Daniel is its mental creator.

Two other thoughts permeate Jewish apocalyptic: the idea of a world-judgment and the hope of resurrection from the dead. The idea of the great judgment and of God as judge of the world permeates Jewish literature subsequent to the writing of Dan. vii. In their entire purity and complete ethical power these thoughts come out only in the gospel; but the two thoughts, that in this age God is an absentee and that at its end he will destroy his world-adversaries in the great judgment, rule the Jewish idea of God. The belief in the resurrection of the dead, which is still greatly limited in Daniel, only gradually took hold of the Jewish national soul. The Psalms of Solomon know little of it (xvii. 44); it prevailed in the time of Jesus, when denial of the doctrine was regarded as disloyalty. The hope of a resurrection of the dead gave a strongly individualistic character to apocalyptic piety: it suggested inquiry about the final lot of the individual—how the individual could stand in judgment before God. This individualism was a consequence of the piety of Jeremiah and the Psalms; but the thought of individual responsibility in the final judgment nowhere developed in Judaism its full ethical force, and it was stifled again and again by the fanciful expectations of national greatness on earth, or was applied in Pharisaic party polemic against the "impious and apostates."

In general it must be emphasized that, when compared with the preceding epoch, this apocalyptic does not imply an advance of religious individualism; it reveals rather a stronger influx of national elements into the piety of Judaism. In the Maccabean period the piety of later Judaism became again national piety. The temper of apocalyptic was thoroughly particularistic and narrowly national. God's kingdom involved only mercy to Israel and judgment to the heathen (Psalms of Solomon xvii. 2). In spite of the transcendental and ideal character which the apocalyptic picture gradually assumed (cf. the idea of a "coming age," world-judgment, waking from the dead), the old, earthly hopes of Israel of a kingdom of Davidic glory, a Messiah bearing David's name, an earthly empire, and a gloriously renewed Jerusalem are closely bound up with it. This divergence shows itself especially in the position which the expected Messiah occupied in this literature. With the world-judgment, the destruction of the world, and the awaking from the dead, the expected Davidic king was to have little to do; consequently his form occasionally disappeared entirely (so in Daniel and the Assumption of Moses). On the whole, however, the transcendental retained its position; at one time it was only partly pushed aside (Enoch xc. 4; IV Ezra vii. 28; Baruch xxix.); at another, it partly corresponded to the picture of hope which involved an ideal transfiguration (cf. Psalms of Solomon xvii., and the "similitudes" in Enoch). This divergence led finally to the assumption of a double finale: first, the intermediate Messianic realm (Rev. xx.; Book of the Secrets of Enoch xxxiii.), in which earthly expectations were to be realized; and, second, the "coming age," ushered in by the world-judgment and the resurrection from the dead which should satisfy the more transcendental aspirations (cf. Enoch xciii., xci. 12-19; IV Ezra vii. 28-29; Baruch xl. 3; Rev. xx.; Book of the Secrets of Enoch xxxiii.).

With this fundamental character of Jewish apocalyptic a number of external qualities are connected. All apocalyptic writers indulged in fanciful computation of the end. The apocalyptic seer lived in a time when all felt that the prophetic spirit had departed, when important decisions awaited the coming of a prophet (I Macc. iv. 40; cf. ix. 27, xiv. 41) and the judgment of prophecy (Zech. xiii. 2 sqq.). Apocalyptic arithmetic took the place of prophecy; thus in the center of Daniel's prophecies (Dan. ix.) the seventy years of Jeremiah are interpreted as seventy year-weeks (i.e., 70 × 7 years), which interpretation is followed by Enoch lxxxix. sqq.; or the duration of the world was estimated on the basis of some hidden

External Qualities. wisdom (Assumption of Moses i. 1, x. 12; Enoch xc., xci.; IV Ezra xiv. 11; Baruch liii.), for only the wise and intelligent could understand these secrets (Rev. xiii. 18, xvii. 9; Mark xiii. 14). A consequence of the foregoing is the non-creative character of this literature; it followed closely the older literature of Israel, especially the idea of theophanies (Isa. vi. and Ezek. i.), the prophecies concerning Babylon (Isa. xiii., xiv.; Jer. l.-li.), Tyre (Ezek. xxvii., xxviii.), and Gog and Magog (Ezek. xxxviii., xxxix.). The most promiscuous notions and views from other religious departments crept in, and these, understood only in part or not at all, were circulated as coins stamped once for all. Behemoth and Leviathan, the dragon, the beast

I.—14

with seven heads, the four ages, the seven spirits, the twenty-four elders, the candlestick with seven branches, the two witnesses, and the woman clothed with the sun—all these imply great religious-historical connections which can not now be fully understood, but which nevertheless existed. A necessary rule for the interpretation of apocalyptic literature is that a single apocalypse can not be explained in itself, but only from a survey comprising, if possible, all related works. The fantastic element in Jewish apocalyptic literature is not due to an excess of imagination in these authors, who were so poor in spirit; the impression of strangeness is due to the use of abnormal religious images. For discussion of the several books, see APOCRYPHA, B, IV.; PSEUDEPIGRAPHA, OLD TESTAMENT, II., 4–21. (W. BOUSSET.)

BIBLIOGRAPHY: The best treatment is to be found in R. H. Charles's editions of apocalyptic writings, e.g., his *Enoch*, London, 1893, *Apocalypse of Baruch*, 1896, *Ascension of Isaiah*, 1900, *Jubilees*, 1902, and in his *Critical History of the Doctrine of a Future Life*, 1899; A. Hilgenfeld, *Die jüdische Apokalyptik*, Jena, 1857; J. Drummond, *Jewish Messiah*, London, 1877; R. Smend, in *ZATW*, v. (1885) 222–250; *DB*, i. 109–110; Schürer, *Geschichte*, iii. 181-185, Eng. transl., II. iii. 44 sqq.; M. S. Terry, *Biblical Apocalyptics*, New York, 1898; *EB*, i. 213–250 (reviews the important apocalyptic literature); *JE*, i. 669–685 (treats of late Jewish productions); W. Bousset, *Die jüdische Apokalyptik*, Berlin, 1903; F. C. Porter, *The Messages of the Apocalyptical Writers*, New York, 1905.

APOCATASTASIS, ap″o-ca-tas′ta-sis.

By Apocatastasis ("restoration") is meant the ultimate restitution of all things, including the doctrine that eventually all men will be saved. The term comes from the Greek of Acts iii. 21, but is given a wider meaning than it has in that passage. The doctrine first appears in Clement of Alexandria (flourished 200) in the declaration that the punishments of God are "saving and disciplinary, leading to conversion" (*Strom.*, vi. 6). His successor at the head of the Alexandrian

1. Earliest Advocates.

catechetical school, Origen (186–253), taught that all the wicked would be restored after they had undergone severe punishment and had received instruction from angels and then from those of higher grade (*De principiis*, I. vi. 1–3). He also raised the question whether after this world there perhaps would be another or others in which this instruction would be given (*De principiis*, II. iii. 1), and interpreted Paul's teaching respecting the subjection of all things to God as implying the salvation of the "lost" (*De principiis*, III. v. 7). These beliefs and speculations he based on Bible statements(especially on Ps. cx. 1; I Cor. xv. 25 sqq.), but declared that the doctrine would be dangerous to disseminate (*Contra Celsum*, vi. 26). He, and it would seem, Clement of Alexandria also, advocated the Apocatastasis as part of a theory of the divine attributes which subordinated righteousness to mercy; of human freedom, which made the will never finally fixed; and of sin, which represented it rather as weakness and ignorance.

Similar ideas of the divine goodness, human freedom, and sin led to the advocacy of the Apocatastasis by Gregory Nazianzen (328–389), but not openly; by Gregory of Nyssa (332–398), publicly, as in his treatise "On the Soul and the Resurrection" (*MPG*, xlvi. 104); by Didymus of Alexandria (308–395), in his commentary on I Peter iii. (in Galland, *Bibliotheca patrum*, vi. 292 sqq.); and by Diodorus of Tarsus (flourished 375), in his treatise "On the Divine Economy" (in J. S. Assemanus, *Bibliotheca orientalis*, III. i. 324). Even Chrysostom (347–407), when commenting on I Cor. xv. 28, quoted without contradiction the view that by the expression "God shall be all in all" was meant universal cessation of opposition to God (*MPG*, lxi. 342). So also the Monophysite, Stephen bar-Sudaili, abbot of a monastery at Edessa in the sixth century, advocated the Apocatastasis in a treatise which he wrote on the subject under the name of Hierotheus (as is stated in Assemanus, ut sup., ii. 290 sqq.). It was taught also by Maximus Confessor (580–662), called by the Greeks *Theologos* and revered as the leader of the Orthodox against the Monothelites, drawing from Gregory of Nyssa, as in his answer to the thirteenth question of his "Questions and Doubts" (*MPG*, xc. 796). The existence of this belief in the eighth century is shown by the warning against it given in 718 by Pope Gregory II., when sending out missionaries (*MPL*, lxxxix. 534). In the ninth century it was roundly asserted by that very independent speculative theologian Johannes Scotus Erigena, in the third book of his treatise "On the Division of Nature" (*MPL*, cxxii. 619–742). He drew from Origen, pseudo-Dionysius Areopagita, Gregory of Nyssa, and still more directly, from Maximus Confessor.

But the writers defending the Apocatastasis are decidedly in the minority; and so bad was the repute of Origen for sound thinking that any theory known to be derived from him was looked at askance by the sober-minded. Jerome (d. 420), for example, reckoned the Apocatastasis among the "abhorrent" heresies of Origen (*Epist.*, cxxxiv.).

2. Opponents.

The emperor Justinian, in his edict against Origen, issued in 545, made it the ninth of the ten doctrines for which the latter should be anathematized; and when, at Justinian's call, a council met in Constantinople that same year to condemn Origen, the doctrine appears as the fourteenth of the fifteen for which he was cursed (Hefele, *Conciliengeschichte*, ii. 789, 797, Eng. transl., iv. 220, 228).

In the West, Augustine (354–430) threw his influence against the Apocatastasis, teaching in the most unmistakable language the absolute endlessness of future punishment (e.g., "City of God," xxi. 11–23).

At a later period the doctrine appears in the teachings of the great pantheistic thinker Amalric of Bena (d. 1204), only to be again condemned by the Western Church; for it was one of the counts upon which Amalric was declared a heretic by Pope Innocent III., and for which his followers, the Brethren and Sisters of the Free Spirit, after his death, were condemned by the Fourth Lateran Council, in 1215 (Hefele, ut sup., pp. 863, 881).

3. In the Middle Ages. It appears also among the mystics. Jan Ruysbroeck (1293–1381), Johann Tauler (1300–61), and Johann von Goch (d. 1475) are said to have accepted it; but it was rejected by Eckhart (flourished 1300), Suso (1300–65), and their followers (cf. C. Ullmann, *Reformers before the Reformation*, i., Edinburgh, 1855). Still later it is found as one of the 900 theses which that brilliant scholar Giovanni Pico della Mirandola proposed to defend in public debate in Rome in 1487, and was thus expressed: "A mortal sin of finite duration is not deserving of eternal but only of temporal punishment." But it was among the theses pronounced heretical by Pope Innocent VIII. in his bull of Aug. 4, 1484; and the debate was never held (cf. *Giovanni Pico della Mirandola*, ed. J. M. Rigg, London, 1890, pp. vii. sqq.).

4. The Reformation. The Apocatastasis emerged in the Protestant Church of the earliest days. Thus Luther, writing on Aug. 18, 1522, to Hans von Rechenberg, who had asked him if there was any salvation for those out of Christ at death, states that a belief in the ultimate salvation of all men, and even of the devil and his angels, was held among the sect of Free Spirits in the Netherlands, one of whom was then in Wittenberg. They based it on Ps. lxxvii. 9, 10 and on 1 Tim. ii. 4. He then proceeds to refute it. Again Luther warns against this belief when writing to the Christians in Antwerp in 1525 (cf. de Wette's ed. of Luther's letters, ii. 453 and iii. 62). The doctrine was held among the Anabaptists. Hans Denk taught it in its extreme form, saying that not only all men, but even the devil and his angels, would ultimately be saved; and another Anabaptist leader, Jacob Kautz (Cucius), in 1527 at Worms put as the fifth of seven articles he propounded for debate: "All that was lost in the first Adam is and will be found more richly restored in the Second Adam, Christ; yea, in Christ shall all men be quickened and blessed forever" (Zwingli, *Opera*, viii. 77; cf. S. M. Jackson, *Selections from Zwingli*, p. 148). So, too, Zwingli asserts that it was part of the Anabaptist creed that the devil and all the impious will be blessed (*Opera*, iii. 435; cf. Jackson, ut sup., p. 256). Indeed, while perhaps not universally accepted by Anabaptists, it was held by so many of the party in Switzerland, Upper Germany, and Alsace that in Article xvii. of the Augsburg Confession are these words: "They [the Lutherans] condemn the Anabaptists, who think that to condemned men and the devils shall be an end of torments." It is, however, not put in the *Formula of Concord* among the erroneous teachings of the Anabaptists.

5. In Modern Times. Toward the end of the seventeenth century the doctrine of the Apocatastasis again appeared, and ever since it has found numerous defenders. The earliest were Mrs. Jane Lead, of London (1623–1704), Johann Wilhelm Petersen (1649–1727), and the Philadelphian Society which Mrs. Lead founded. With them the doctrine was established not only on the Bible, but also on personal revelations. It is noteworthy that Jakob Boehme (1575–1624), who so greatly influenced them, did not teach it (cf. his *Beschreibung der drei Prinzipien göttlichen Wesens;* Eng. transl., *Concerning the Three Principles of the Divine Essence*, London, 1648, chap. xxvii. § 20). There is an elaborate defense of the Apocatastasis by Ludwig Gerhard, *Vollständiger Lehrbegriff der ewigen Evangelii von der Widerbringung aller Dinge* (Hamburg, 1727). The Philadelphians won over the authors of the *Berleburg Bibel* (1726–42; see BIBLES, ANNOTATED, AND BIBLE SUMMARIES); but their chief convert was Friedrich Christoph Oetinger (q.v.; 1702–82), who wove this tenet into his theological system, depending chiefly upon I Cor. xv. and Eph. i. 9–11. It is said that Bengel (1687–1752), the father of modern exegesis, believed in it, but thought it dangerous to teach publicly.

The rationalists of Germany, after the second half of the eighteenth century, commonly and supernaturalists frequently have upon various grounds advocated the Apocatastasis. Thus, Schleiermacher (1768–1834) was pronounced in its favor, deriving his principal arguments from his doctrines of the will and of the atonement, and remarking that the sensitiveness of conscience in the damned, as revealed in the parable of the rich man and Lazarus, shows that they may be better in the next life than in this, and also that if a portion of God's creatures were forever debarred from participation in the redemption of Christ, then there would be an inexplicable dissonance in God's universe. Martensen and Dorner considered the probability that between death and the last judgment there might be a fresh offer of the gospel, but put a rejection and consequent exclusion from salvation among the possibilities. The difficulties of the estate of the "lost" have driven others, as Rothe, Hermann Plitt, and Edward White, to the theory of annihilationism (q.v.). Ritschl thought that such information as the New Testament gives hardly admits of a decision between the theories of endless punishment and complete annihilation. Friedrich Nitzsch considered belief in a final restoration as well founded as the opposite view, and admitted the hypothesis of annihilationism as a third possibility. In America opposition to the orthodox teaching as to the absolute endlessness of conscious suffering after death of those excluded from heaven has led to the formation of the Universalist denomination (see UNIVERSALISTS); and there are many of other religious connections in the United States, England, and other countries who favor the doctrine of an Apocatastasis in more or less modified form. For further discussion consult the histories of Christian doctrine and the works mentioned in the article UNIVERSALISTS. The teaching of the Roman Catholic Church, which is flatly against the doctrine, is presented by J. B. Kraus in *Die Apokatastasis der unfreien Kreatur* (Regensburg, 1850).

[Many significant facts indicate a relaxing of the traditional rigidity of belief with reference to this subject. There is an unwillingness on the part of many to assume any dogmatic attitude concerning God's dealing with those who die impenitent. Again, there is a refusal to limit probation to the earthly life merely, fixing, instead, the decisive moment at the judgment, thus making room for those to whom an adequate offer of the gospel has been wanting here (cf. *Progressive Orthodoxy*, by professors of Andover Theological Seminary, Boston, 1886). Further, denominational approval or disapproval of the theory of an Apocatastasis is not so much in evidence as wide and influential advocacy of it by distinguished writers and preachers in many communions—the attitude partly of dogmatic belief, and partly of the "larger hope." It has been represented in Great Britain in the Established Church by F. D. Maurice (*The Word "Eternal" and the Punishment of the Wicked*, Cambridge, 1853), F. W. Farrar (*Eternal Hope*, London, 1878; *Mercy and Judgment*, 1881), E. H. Plumptre (*The Spirits in Prison*, London, 1886); among Baptists by Samuel Cox (*Salvator Mundi*, London, 1877; *The Larger Hope*, 1883); among Independents by J. Baldwin Brown (*The Doctrine of Annihilation in the Light of the Gospel of Love*, London, 1875) and R. J. Campbell of the London City Temple. In America it has found expression among Congregationalists by George A. Gordon (*Immortality and the New Theodicy*, Boston, 1896), and among Baptists the grounds for it have been suggested by W. N. Clarke (*Outline of Christian Theology*, New York, 1898, pp. 476–480). Important theoretical considerations have influenced this result: (1) The tendency toward a monistic theory of the universe. (2) A change in the idea of God from that of sovereign and judge to that of father. (3) Election conceived of not as limited to a definite portion of mankind but, with Schleiermacher, as a historical process, therefore in this world only partially, in the world to come to be completely, realized. (4) The universal immanence of God and hence the presence of ethical and redemptive relations wherever the moral consciousness exists. (5) Life regarded less as probation than as discipline. (6) Sin defined not so much as wilful and incorrigible perversity as natural defect, ignorance, and emotional excess, as well as result of unfortunate heredity and unworthy environment.

C. A. B.]

Bibliography: In favor of the doctrine may be mentioned: F. Delitzsch, *Biblische Psychologie*, pp. 469–476, Leipsic, 1855, Eng. transl., Edinburgh, 1865; T. R. Birks, *Victory of Divine Goodness*, London, 1870; A. Jukes, *Second Death and Restitution of All Things*, ib. 1878; I. A. Dorner, *Eschatology*, ed. by Newman Smyth, New York, 1883; F. W. Farrar, *Eternal Hope*, London, 1892; Tennyson, *In Memoriam*, § liv. Against it: A. A. Hodge, *Popular Lectures on Theological Themes*, Philadelphia, 1887; A. Hovey, *Biblical Eschatology*, ib. 1888; and in general the orthodox writers on systematic theology. The subject may be studied in the various histories of doctrine and in the compends and systems of divinity in the sections on "Eschatology."

APOCRISIARIUS, ap″o-cris″i-ê′ri-us: A general designation in early times for ecclesiastical ambassadors, derived from the Greek *apokrinesthai* "to answer" (hence the Latin term *responsales* for the same class). The name is found applied to the legates sent by the pope to guard his metropolitan rights in Sicily until the Mohammedan invasion, and to episcopal representatives in Rome. The office assumed its most formal and important character in the Eastern Church, where the patriarchs were represented at the imperial court by *apocrisiarii*, and bishops maintained similar diplomatic agents in the residences of the patriarchs. The popes also, at least from Leo the Great to the time of the iconoclastic controversy, regularly had *apocrisiarii* in Constantinople; they were sometimes called also *diaconi*, because usually chosen from the order of deacons. The officials described here have nothing but the name in common with the *apocrisiarius* of the Frankish ecclesiastical system (see Archicapellanus).

(A. Friedberg.)

APOCRYPHA.

Apocrypha is a Greek word meaning "hidden," which, when applied to writings, may signify either those which are kept in concealment or those the origin of which is unknown. The word is used in both senses in patristic literature. When the followers of Prodicus, according to Clement of Alexandria (*Strom.*, I. xv. 69), boasted of possessing the "apocryphal books" of Zoroaster, they called these works "apocryphal" not because they did not know their origin (since they ascribed them to

Zoroaster), but because they regarded the books as not to be made public. The reason in this case for keeping the writings concealed was the special value attached to them. But writings may also be withdrawn from general use because they are inferior. With this thought in mind Origen and Didymus of Alexandria make a distinction between the "common and widely circulated books" (Gk. *koina kai dedēmeumena* or *dedēmosieumena biblia*) and the apocryphal books of Scripture (Origen on Matt. xiii, 57, *ANF*, ix, 425; Didymus of Alexandria on Acts viii, 39, *MPG*, xxxix, 1669). In like manner Eusebius calls the canonical books which were used in the churches *dedēmosieumena* (*Hist. eccl.*, III, iii, 6, and elsewhere). Similarly Jerome (*Epist.*, xcvi) explains the Greek *apokryphos* by the Latin *absconditus*. (For further illustration cf. T. Zahn, *Geschichte des neutestamentlichen Kanons*, i, Leipsic, 1888, 126 sqq.)

1. Writings Withheld from Public Use.

The Christian usage is clearly derived from a Jewish custom. The Jews, because they hesitated actually to destroy copies of sacred writings, were in the habit of either depositing in a secret place (*genizah*) or of burying such as had become defective or were no longer fit for public use. The new-Hebrew word for this "concealing" is *ganaz*, "to save, hoard." Writings which were withdrawn from public use because of questionable contents were treated in the same way; thus King Hezekiah is said to have "stored up" the "Book of Remedies" because it prejudiced faith and trust in God (*Pesaḥim* iv, 9). Hence *ganaz* came to mean "to declare uncanonical" (*Shabbat* 30b; cf. Fürst, *Der Kanon des Alten Testaments*, Leipsic, 1868, pp. 91-93). Since the Christian phraseology undoubtedly followed the Jewish, it can not be questioned that "apocryphal" in ecclesiastical usage according to its original and proper signification means nothing else than "excluded from public use in the Church."

But "apocryphal" in both Greek and Latin may be applied also to writings the origin of which is unknown, and this meaning led to that of "forged, spurious." In this sense Augustine speaks of "the fables of those scriptures which are called apocryphal because their origin, being obscure, was unknown to the fathers" (*De civitate dei*, XV, xxiii, 4, *NPNF*, 1st ser. ii, 305); and again he says the apocryphal books "are so called, not because of any mysterious regard paid to them, but because they are mysterious in their origin, and in the absence of clear evidence have only some obscure presumption to rest upon" (*Contra Faustum*, xi, 2, *NPNF*, 1st ser. iv, 178). In many cases it can not be decided which meaning was intended (cf. Hegesippus in Eusebius, *Hist. eccl.*, IV, xxii, 8; Clement of Alexandria, *Strom.*, III, iv, 29; *Apostolic Constitutions*, vi, 16). It seems, however, that the original meaning, so sharply and consistently expressed in Origen, was not that generally given to the word before his time. At any rate, it is questionable whether it was clearly present to the mind of Irenæus and Tertullian in the following passages. The former, speaking of the Marcosians, says: "They adduce an unspeakable number of apocryphal and spurious writings, which they themselves have forged" (*Hær.*, I, xx, 1, *ANF*, i, 344); and Tertullian says: "I would yield my ground to you, if the scripture of the *Shepherd* [of Hermas] . had deserved to find a place in the divine canon; if it had not been habitually judged by every council of churches among apocryphal and false writings" (*De pudicitia*, x, *ANF*, iv, 85). After the word was once introduced, its ambiguity easily led to a notion differing from the original meaning. In the case of Augustine this is certain. Jerome, too, seems to use the word in the sense of "obscure in origin" when he says that all apocryphal writings "are not really written by those to whom they are ascribed" (*Epist.*, cvii, 12, *NPNF*, 2d ser. xi, 194) The two senses—"exclusion from public use in the Church" and "obscure in origin"—are often combined in the same passage. The meaning became finally so generalized that the word signifies simply what is wrong and bad, as in the Latin adaptation of Origen's "Preface to the Song of Solomon" at the end: "Those writings which are called apocryphal (which contain much that is corrupt and contrary to the true faith) should not be given place or admitted to authority;"—the words in parentheses appear to be added by the Latin editor. (For further information cf. C. A. Credner, *Geschichte des neutestamentlichen Kanons*, Berlin, 1860, pp. 110 sqq.; A. Hilgenfeld, *Der Kanon und die Kritik des Neuen Testaments*, Halle, 1863, pp. 6 sqq.; H. J. Holtzmann, *Einleitung in das Neue Testament*, Freiburg, 1892, pp. 145 sqq.; T. Zahn, *Geschichte des neutestamentlichen Kanons*, I, i, Leipsic, 1888, pp. 123 sqq.)

2. Writings of Uncertain Origin.

In the ancient Church and in the Middle Ages the term "apocryphal" was almost never applied, as in the Protestant Church, to those portions of the Greek and Latin Bibles which were foreign to the Hebrew canon. Indeed, it could not be so applied, for those books have always been a part of the Greek and Latin Bibles. Jerome alone once made a statement (in the *Prologus galeatus*) implying that these writings do indeed fall into the category of apocrypha. During the Middle Ages there were at the most a very few isolated voices which spoke to that effect (Hugo of St. Cher; cf. de Wette-Schrader, *Einleitung in das Alte Testament*, Berlin, 1869, p. 66). It was in the Protestant Church that this nomenclature first became customary. The earliest to introduce it, appealing expressly to Jerome, was Carlstadt in his *De canonicis scripturis libellus* (Wittenberg, 1520; reprinted in Credner, *Zur Geschichte des Kanons*, Halle, 1847, pp. 291 sqq.). He there expressly stated that by "apocryphal" he understood "non-canonical"; and in this sense the Protestant Church has always understood the word. The first edition of the Bible in which the writings in question were expressly called apocryphal was that of Frankfort, 1534, which was followed in the same year by Luther's first edition (cf. G. W.

3. Use of the Term by Protestants.

Panzer, *Geschichte der deutschen Bibelübersetzung*, Nuremberg, 1783, pp. 294 sqq.).

A. Old Testament Apocrypha: Those portions of the Greek and Latin Old Testaments which are not found in the Hebrew Canon,—the term "apocrypha" being used in this article with the meaning given to it by the Protestant Church (see § 3, above).

I. Position in the Canon: The Hebrew canon of the Bible in the first century of the Christian era comprised about the same books as at present, though the canonicity of the books of Ecclesiastes and the Song of Songs was disputed (Mishnah, *Eduyot*, v, 3; *Yadayim*, iii, 5; J. Fürst, *Der Kanon des Alten Testaments nach den Ueberlieferungen in Talmud und Midrasch*, Leipsic, 1868; see CANON OF SCRIPTURE, I). But it was otherwise with the Hellenistic Jews. As far as the extent of the Greek canon of the Bible can be traced, it included a number of writings which are wanting in the Hebrew canon. No clear proofs of this from pre-Christian times exist; but the fact that Christians using the Greek Bible received these other writings also makes it highly probable that these belonged to the canon of the Hellenistic Jews.

1. Apocrypha in the Greek Canon.

While it may be conceded to the opponents of this view that Hellenistic Jews had no strict conception of a canon, it can not be denied that certain writings were received into the Greek Bible-collection which were foreign to the Hebrew canon (cf. De Wette-Schrader, *Einleitung*, pp. 311 sqq.; Bleek, *TSK*, 1853, pp. 323 sqq.). The fact that Philo did not quote these other writings proves nothing, since Philo was interested mainly in the Pentateuch.

In the New Testament there are no express references to the so-called Apocrypha, a fact the more remarkable since most of the New Testament authors took their quotations from the Greek translation of the Old Testament. But to understand this rightly, one must not forget that a number of canonical writings of the Old Testament are never cited in the New Testament; others only seldom. The Pentateuch, the Prophets, and the Psalms are frequently quoted; the historical books not so often; while the Song of Songs, Ecclesiastes, Esther, Ezra, and Nehemiah are never cited. The lack of express citations can therefore not be emphasized; and on the other hand, it can not be denied that at least in some writings of the New Testament the Apocrypha are used. This applies particularly to the Epistle of James and that to the Hebrews. That Ecclesiasticus was known to the author of the Epistle of James can not be denied in the face of the many parallels (cf. Werner in *TQ*, 1872, pp. 265 sqq.). The author of the Epistle to the Hebrews doubtless refers in xi, 34 sqq. to the story of the Maccabees (cf. II Macc. vi, 18–vii, 42). Striking agreements with the Wisdom of Solomon are also found (thus Heb. i, 3=Wisdom vii, 26; Heb. iv, 12–13=Wisdom vii, 22–24); and there can be no doubt that Paul made use of this book (cf. in general Bleek, *TSK*, 1853, pp. 325 sqq., especially 337–349).

2. Used in Some New Testament Writings.

Among the Church Fathers the Apocrypha were in common use from the earliest times. Clement of Rome puts "the blessed" Judith beside Esther as an example of female heroism (*Epist.*, lv, *ANF*, ix, 245). Barnabas (xix, 9) goes back to Ecclus. iv, 31 when he quotes "Be not ready to stretch forth thy hands to take whilst thou withdrawest them from giving." Justin Martyr (*Apol.*, i, 46, *ANF*, i, 178) refers to the additions to Daniel. That none of these passages has the form of a true Scripture citation may be viewed as accidental and may be explained from the small extent of this oldest literature. But from the time of Athenagoras true citations can be proved. Athenagoras ("Plea for the Christians," i, 9, *ANF*, ii, 133) quotes among the "voices of the prophets," as divinely inspired, Baruch iii, 25 upon an equality with Isa. xliv, 6; Irenæus (*Hær.*, IV, xxvi, 3, *ANF*, i, 497) cites as the words of "Daniel the Prophet" the history of Susanna, and (*Hær.*, V, xxxv, 1, *ANF*, i, 565) the Book of Baruch as the work of Jeremiah; Tertullian quotes the history of Susanna (*De corona*, iv, *ANF*, iii, 95), Bel and the Dragon (*De idololatria*, xviii, *ANF*, iii, 72), and the Wisdom of Solomon (*Adversus Valentinos*, ii, *ANF*, iii, 504) as canonical Scripture. Clement of Alexandria quotes Ecclesiasticus very often with the formula "Scripture," "Holy Scripture," "Wisdom says," and the like, and not so frequently, but with the same formulas, Wisdom of Solomon, Baruch, and Tobit. Abundant examples of the same practise can be cited from Hippolytus, Cyprian, and others.

3. By the Church Fathers.

In view of these facts it may be asserted that the Church of the first centuries made no essential difference between the writings of the Hebrew canon and the so-called Apocrypha. Only in an isolated way and evidently as the result of learned inquiry does an express limitation of the canon to the extent of the Hebrew Bible appear; for example, Melito of Sardis, according to Eusebius (*Hist. eccl.*, IV, xxvi, 14), mentions only the books of the Hebrew canon as canonical, but he gives this list expressly as the result of learned inquiry in Palestine. When Origen gives a list which comprises only the Hebrew canon (Eusebius, *Hist. eccl.*, vi, 25), he gives it as the canon of the Hebrews, and his own view can not be deduced from the passage given by Eusebius. On the other hand, from Origen's correspondence with Julius Africanus it is deducible that he was by no means in favor of excluding those parts which were wanting in the Hebrew canon, because he defends the Greek additions to Daniel, and he likewise cites some Apocryphal writings (Maccabees, Wisdom, Ecclesiasticus, Tobit, Baruch) as "Scriptural authority," "the Holy Word," "Scripture," etc. (cf. De Wette-Schrader, *Einleitung*, p. 53). The critique which Julius Africanus wrote on the Greek text of the Book of Daniel, trying to remove the portions not found in the Hebrew-Aramaic text (*Epist. ad Origenem*), evidently remained an isolated phenomenon.

The learned disquisitions of men like Origen resulted, however, in this, that stricter regard was paid to the difference between the Hebrew and the Greek canon. Wherever the purpose was to fix theoretically the range of the canon, recourse was had to the Hebrew canon as to something settled over against the fluctuations of the Greek canon. Thus there are a number of lists of the canonical books from the fourth century which confine themselves to the Hebrew canon and either do not mention the other writings or assign to them a lower value. Athanasius is most instructive in this respect. In his *Epistola festalis*, xxxix (*NPNF*, 2d ser. iv, 552), after mentioning the canonical writings of the Old and New Testaments, he adds Wisdom of Solomon, Ecclesiasticus, Esther, Judith, Tobit, Teaching of the Apostles, and the Shepherd of Hermas as "not included in the canon, but appointed by the Fathers to be read by those who newly join us and wish for instruction in the word of godliness." The specified writings were to be read in the Church, and are expressly differentiated by Athanasius from the "Apocrypha"; they are not mentioned at all in the lists of Cyril of Jerusalem, Gregory Nazianzen, and Amphilochius (cf. T. Zahn, *Geschichte*, II, i, 172–180, 212–219). The usage of Epiphanius varies: in one place he gives only the Hebrew canon; in another he mentions also Tobit and Judith as in the canon, while Ecclesiasticus and Wisdom of Solomon seem to him "doubtful." That he expresses only his own opinion is proved by still a third passage (*Hær.*, lxxvi), where after the canonical writings, which are not named individually, he mentions Wisdom of Solomon and Ecclesiasticus as "Holy Scripture." His wavering was due to the fact that, on the one hand, he used the canon of the Jews as the norm, while, on the other hand, he was unwilling to give up his Greek Bible (cf. T. Zahn, *Geschichte*, II, i, 219–226). The only one who in the ancient Church opposed the Apocrypha was Jerome; and this was no doubt due to his Hebrew studies and his zeal for the "body of truth in the Hebrew." The principal passage is in the *Prologus galeatus* (*NPNF*, 2d ser. vi, 489), in which he says that the books not on the list he gives must be reckoned among the Apocrypha.

4. The Beginning of Exclusion.

All these declarations, more or less unfavorable to the Apocrypha, lose much of their importance from the fact that the men who excluded the Apocrypha from the canon use them in an impartial manner as though canonical; so Athanasius, Cyril, Epiphanius, and even Jerome, who in spite of his theory is not afraid to quote Ecclesiasticus as "Sacred Scripture." Roman theologians have rightly laid great stress upon this fact; for it proves that, notwithstanding opposite theories, ecclesiastical practise on the whole was to use the Apocryphal like the canonical writings. Moreover, the West decided in their favor. Augustine (*De doctrina Christiana*, ii, 8) counted the Apocrypha as canonical, and the same was the case with the synods at Hippo (393) and Carthage (397), held under his influence (cf. T. Zahn, *Geschichte*, II, i, 246–259). This position was prevalent down to the time of the Reformation, though in the Middle Ages there were not lacking voices which sided with Jerome (cf. De Wette-Schrader, *Einleitung*, pp. 64 sqq.). In the Greek Church of the Middle Ages the Apocrypha were as a rule included in the canon.

5. Accepted by the Roman Catholic Church.

In the Church of Rome the question concerning the Apocrypha was definitively settled by the Council of Trent, which in its fourth session fixed the extent of the canon in such a manner that it included the Apocrypha. Hence the official edition of the Vulgate (that of 1592) includes the Apocrypha with the other writings, and in the following order: Nehemiah (numbered as II Ezra) is followed by Tobit, Judith, Esther (with the additions), Job, Psalms, Proverbs, Ecclesiastes, Song of Solomon, Wisdom of Solomon, Ecclesiasticus, Isaiah, Jeremiah, Lamentations, Baruch with the Epistle of Jeremiah, Ezekiel, Daniel with the additions, the Twelve Minor Prophets, I and II Maccabees. As an appendix (in smaller type and with the explicit statement that they stand "outside the series of canonical books"), the Old Testament is followed by the Prayer of Manasses, III and IV Ezra. From this official canon of the Church of Rome the manuscripts and editions of the Greek Bible differ mainly in this, that in them III Ezra (which, however, is here always numbered as I Ezra) is put on a par with the other writings, IV Ezra (as a rule also the Prayer of Manasses) is wanting, III Maccabees being substituted for it; some few manuscripts and editions contain also IV Maccabees. The arrangement is generally this: I Ezra stands before the canonical Ezra; Judith and Tobit stand together with Esther; Wisdom, and Ecclesiasticus with the Solomonic writings; Baruch and the Epistle of Jeremiah with Jeremiah. The position of the books of the Maccabees is the most uncertain; in the (printed) editions they generally stand at the end of the Old Testament.

6. Rejected by Protestants.

In the Protestant Church, Carlstadt (*De canonicis scripturis*, Wittenberg, 1520) was the first to pay special attention to the theory of the canon. He sided with Jerome in designating the writings in question as "apocrypha," that is, as non-canonical writings (cf. Credner, *Zur Geschichte des Kanons*, p. 364). Yet he distinguished within them two classes. On Wisdom, Ecclesiasticus, Judith, Tobit, I and II Maccabees, he remarked: "These are apocrypha, i.e., outside of the Hebrew canon, nevertheless they are holy writings." The others, however, were for him "plainly apocrypha, deservedly exposed to the strictures of the censor (Credner, 389)." Though this discrimination has found no favor, Carlstadt's position is on the whole that of the Protestant Church. In the first complete original edition of Luther's translation (1534) the Apocrypha formed a supplement to the Old Testament with the heading "Apocrypha; that is, books which, although not estimated equal to the Holy Scriptures, are yet useful and good to read." As to the number of received writings, Luther's Bible agreed with the Vulgate, with the modification, however, that of the three books found in the appendix to the Vulgate the Prayer of Manasses was received, and both books of Ezra were excluded. In the Reformed Church the apocryphal books have received the same treatment as in the Lutheran, except that usually a stricter sentence has been passed upon them. In modern times, opposition has twice been raised against them, each time in England (1825 and 1850); and the result has been a substantial augmentation of information about them.

II. Manuscripts of the Greek Text: As the Apocrypha form an integral part of the Greek Old Testament, they are included in the Septuagint manuscripts, of which the most important are: (1) the *Codex Vaticanus*, in which the books of Maccabees do not appear; (2) the *Codex Sinaiticus*, containing Esther, Tobit, Judith, I and IV Maccabees, Wisdom, Ecclesiasticus; (3) the *Codex Alexandrinus*, containing all the Apocrypha. (For particulars cf. the prolegomena to O. F Fritzsche, *Libri Apocryphi Veteris Testamenti Græce*, Leipsic, 1871. On the manuscripts of the Septuagint in general cf. Swete, *Introduction to the Old Testament in Greek*, Cambridge, 1900, pp. 122-170; see also BIBLE TEXT, I, 4, § 2.)

III. Ancient Versions: Mention is made here of only the Latin and Syriac because they are the most important in point of age and circulation.

1. Latin: Various Old Latin texts of most Apocrypha exist, the interrelations of which have not yet been fully investigated (cf. Schürer, *Geschichte*, vol. iii). These must be distinguished from Jerome's translation, and an estimate of the amount of the Old Latin that has been preserved can be obtained only by inference from what is known concerning Jerome's labors. He undertook a twofold translation of the Old Testament. At first he was satisfied with revising the Old Latin translation on the basis of the Septuagint; after that he translated the Old Testament anew from the original text (cf. Kaulen, *Geschichte der Vulgata*, Mainz, 1868, pp. 153 sqq.; see BIBLE VERSIONS, A, II, 2), necessarily omitting the Apocrypha, because they were not in the original text. Jerome says expressly concerning some that he passes them by. In response to special requests he worked over two of the apocryphal books, Tobit and Judith, but he performed the work hastily and reluctantly and evidently not in connection with his great Bible version (cf. the preface to both books, *Opera*, ed. Vallarsi, 11 vols., Verona, 1734-42 x, 1, sqq., 21 sqq.). The Vulgate texts of the additions to Esther and Daniel are also Jerome's work. He received these into his translation from the original text, but marked them with the obelus (cf. his remarks on Esther, *Opera*, ed. Vallarsi, ix, 1581). The translation of the additions to Esther is so free that in some passages it gives merely the general sense. The additions to Daniel are translated with greater fidelity, but from the text of Theodotion, as noted by Jerome himself. The version of these four books passed into the Vulgate. The Vulgate contains also the books of Ezra (put into the appendix since the Council of Trent), Baruch, and the Epistle of Jeremiah, I and II Maccabees, Ecclesiasticus, and Wisdom. Since Jerome did not translate these, the Vulgate text is to be regarded as essentially the same as that of the Old Latin. The question is only whether some of these texts have not undergone correction at the hand of Jerome. It is to be regretted that information is very meager as to the extent of Jerome's revision of the Old Latin which was originally made from the Septuagint. But on two Apocrypha, the Wisdom of Solomon and Ecclesiasticus, there is a valuable notice in the extant "Preface to the Edition of the Books of Solomon according to the LXX" (Vallarsi, x, 436), from which it is learned that in Ecclesiasticus and Wisdom of Solomon, Jerome "saved the pen," i.e., he did not emend them since he "desired to correct only the canonical writings." As by "canonical writings" here he refers only to the Solomonic literature, it remains a possibility that he nevertheless emended the non-Solomonic Apocrypha, Ezra, Baruch, I and II Maccabees. And it is at any rate worthy of notice that these four books are extant in the Latin in double texts, whereas Ecclesiasticus and Wisdom are extant only in the text of the Vulgate. The presumption is obvious: that one of each of these four double texts embodies the revision of Jerome. (The chief collection of Old Latin texts is P. Sabatier, *Bibliorum sacrorum latinæ versiones antiquæ*, 3 vols., Paris, 1751; cf. also S. Berger, *Notices et extraits des manuscrits de la Bibliothèque Nationale et autres bibliothèques*, Paris, 1893, xxxiv, 2, pp. 141-152; idem, *Histoire de la Vulgate pendant les premiers siècles du moyen âge*, Paris, 1893; Thielmann, *Bericht über das gesammelte handschriftliche Material zu einer kritischen Ausgabe der lateinischen Uebersetzungen des Alten Testaments*, in *Sitzungsberichte der Münchener Akademie, hist. Klasse*, 1899, vol. ii, pp. 205-243.)

1. The Old Latin and Jerome's Versions.

2. Syriac: Here also distinction must be made between the common Syriac (Peshito) and the Hexaplar Syriac version. The former was printed by Walton in the London Polyglot, and, from examination of six manuscripts in the British Museum, by P de Lagarde (*Libri Veteris Testamenti apocrypha Syriace*, Leipsic, 1861). The most important manuscript is the *Codex Ambrosianus* B. 21 Inf. of the sixth century, which contains the whole of the Old Testament and the following Apocrypha: Wisdom, Epistle of Jeremiah, I and II Epistles of Baruch, additions to Daniel, Judith, Ecclesiasticus, Apocalypse of Baruch, IV Ezra, I-V Maccabees (V Maccabees = Josephus, *War*, vi). Only Ezra and Tobit are wanting. The character of this Syriac translation is different in the different books, some being quite literal and faithful, others free and inaccurate. The Hexaplar Syriac is the Syriac translation prepared after the text of Origen's Hexapla, and is for the most part extant in manuscripts at Milan, Paris, and London. The most important manuscript is the *Codex Ambrosianus* C. 313 Inf. It contains Wisdom, Ecclesiasticus, Baruch, Epistle of Jeremiah, and the additions to Daniel. To the Hexaplar translation belongs

2. The Peshito and Hexaplar Syriac Versions.

also the Syriac text of Tobit i–xii. The rest of the book is from the Peshito.

IV. Origin and Contents of the Individual Writings.

1. **The Apocryphal Ezra** (I Esdras; for II Esdras see PSEUDEPIGRAPHA, OLD TESTAMENT, II, 7): In the Greek Bibles this book is called II Ezra; in the Latin, III Ezra (Nehemiah = II Ezra). The whole is a worthless compilation, the main part of which is identical with the canonical Ezra. The mutual relations may be seen from the following:

Chap. i = II Chron. xxxv-xxxvi: The restoration of the temple worship under Josiah (639–609 B.C.), and the history of Josiah's successors till the destruction of the Temple (588). Chap. ii, 1–14 = Ezra i: Cyrus in the first year of his reign (537 B.C.) allows the exiles to return, and restores to them the vessels of the Temple. Chap. ii, 15–25 = Ezra iv, 7–24: In consequence of an accusation against the Jews, Artaxerxes (465–425 B.C.) forbids the continuation of the building of the Temple and the walls of Jerusalem. Chap. iii-v, 6, independent: Zerubbabel obtains the favor of Darius (521–485 B.C.), and secures permission to lead the exiles back. Chap. v, 7–70 = Ezra ii, 1-iv, 5: List of those who returned with Zerubbabel, the activities of Zerubbabel, and the interruption of the building of the Temple during the time of Cyrus (536–529 B.C.) and till the second year of Darius (520 B.C.). Chap. vi-vii = Ezra v-vi: Resumption and completion of the building of the Temple in the sixth year of Darius (516 B.C.). Chap. viii-ix, 36 = Ezra vii-x: Ezra returns with a caravan of exiles in the seventh year of Artaxerxes (458 B.C.); the beginning of Ezra's activities. Chap. ix, 37–55 = Neh. vii, 73–viii, 13: Ezra proclaims the Law.

The apocryphal differs from the canonical Ezra in the following four points: (1) The passage iv, 7-24 of the canonical Ezra is placed first; (2) the passage iii–v, 6 of the apocryphal Ezra is inserted from an unknown source; (3) II Chron. xxxv–xxxvi serves as a preface; (4) Neh. vii, 73–viii, 13 is added at the end. In the canonical Ezra, iv, 6-23 is in the wrong place; it belongs to a later period and treats not of the interruption of the building of the Temple but of the interruption of the building of the walls. The redactor of the apocryphal Ezra has indeed taken it out of its wrong surroundings, but he has increased the confusion by locating the passage wrongly and by adding as supplement the account of the interruption of work on the Temple. Not satisfied with this he inserted also the piece iii–v, 6, which transfers the action into the time of Darius, whereas in v, 7-70 events in the reign of Cyrus are discussed. Thus the history goes backward; first (ii, 15–25) Artaxerxes, then (iii–v, 6) Darius, finally (v, 7–70) Cyrus. And in the last passage it is told very ingenuously how Zerubbabel had already returned with the exiles under Cyrus (cf. v, 8, 67–70), after the statement has been made expressly that Zerubbabel through a special favor of Darius obtained permission to return. The opinion of Howorth that the apocryphal Ezra is more original than the canonical is a reversal of the actual state of the case, as is sufficiently shown by Kosters. Concerning the sources used by the compiler two facts appear: (a) The canonical Ezra which he used was not that of the Septuagint, but was the Hebrew-Aramaic original (cf. Nestle, *Marginalien und Materialien*, Tübingen, 1893, pp. 23–29); (b) the portion iii–v, 6 he certainly found ready to hand, since it stands in the directest opposition to the rest of the narrative. It seems to be from a Greek original, not a translation from the Hebrew. The purpose of the entire compilation was correctly stated by Bertholdt (*Historisch-kritische Einleitung in die Bücher des Alten Testaments*, 6 vols., Erlangen, 1812–19, iii, 1011) in the following words: "He intended to compile from older works a history of the Temple from the last epoch of the legal worship to its rebuilding and of the reestablishment of the prescribed divine service." The compiler evidently purposed to quote further from Nehemiah; for the abrupt close can not possibly have been intended. As to the date of compilation all that can be said is that the book was used by Josephus (*Ant.*, xi, 1–5).

2. **Additions to Esther** (The Rest of Esther): The Book of Esther narrates how Esther, the foster-daughter of a Jew named Mordecai at the court of King Ahasuerus (Xerxes) in Shushan, becomes the wife of the king; how Haman, the prime minister who intended to destroy Mordecai and all Jews, is himself brought to the gallows; and how by her intercession Esther finally induces the king to revoke the edict issued under Haman's influence, and thus saves her people. Into this narrative the following pieces are inserted in the Greek Bible: (a) Before i, 1, Mordecai's dream of the miraculous deliverance of his people; (b) after iii, 13, the text of the first edict of Artaxerxes (thus the king is named in this section) which decrees the extermination of the Jews; (c) after iv, 17, the text of the prayers of Mordecai and Esther for the salvation of their people; (d) in place of v, 1–2, the reception of Esther by the king; (e) in place of viii, 13, the text of the second edict of Artaxerxes, which recalls the first; (f) after x, 3, Mordecai perceives the significance of his dream. It is difficult to decide whether these pieces were interpolated by the translator of the Septuagint version of Esther or by a later hand. There is no reason for assuming for them a Hebrew original. It is true that Hebrew and Aramaic texts exist, but they are late in origin, and most likely were made directly or indirectly from the Greek, as were other Hebrew and Aramaic texts of the Apocrypha. For these additions Josephus is the oldest witness (*Ant.*, VI, vi, 6 sqq.), since the annotation to Esther according to which Dositheus and his son Ptolemy brought the book (to Egypt) in the fourth year of the reign of King Ptolemy and Cleopatra, refers to the book as a whole and can not be used as testimony for the antiquity of the interpolated passages. Moreover, this testimony is very indecisive, since there were no less than four Ptolemies, each of whom had a wife named Cleopatra. In this book, especially interesting is the text-recension which is extant in Codices 19, 93A, 108B, the latter two containing both texts, the common and the revised. The revision of the common text, which on the whole characterizes the readings of these manuscripts, is more radical in Esther than is usual, on which account Fritzsche published both texts side by side in his edition of 1848 as well as in his collection of the Apocrypha. Lagarde did the same in his edition of the Septuagint (i, 1883).

3. **Additions to Daniel**: (a) *The Song of the Three Children*: In the third chapter of Daniel it

is told how the three children Shadrach, Meshach, and Abednego (or, as their Hebrew names are given in i, 7, Hananiah, Mishael, and Azariah), refusing to fall down before the image of the king, were punished by being thrown into the furnace, but were miraculously saved. In the Greek text of Daniel an insertion is made after iii, 23, in which it is told that Azariah when in the furnace prayed to God to be saved, and when his prayer was heard, that the three sang a song of praise, the text of the prayer as well as of the song being given. (b) *The History of Susanna:* In the Greek text this passage generally stands at the beginning of Daniel, and Daniel is introduced as still a boy. Susanna, the wife of a prominent Jew of Babylon, named Joacim, is wrongly accused of adultery, and condemned to death, but is saved by the young Daniel's wisdom and prophetic gift. (c) *Bel and the Dragon:* Daniel proves to the king of Babylon (whom Theodotion calls Cyrus) that the god Bel neither eats nor drinks the offerings put before him. The destruction of a dragon, which is an object of worship, Daniel brings about by feeding it with indigestible cakes. Being cast into the lion's den at the instigation of the enraged populace, Daniel is not touched by the lion, and is miraculously fed by the prophet Habakkuk.

Of these three insertions the first only is a proper supplement to the canonical book of Daniel. The other two are independent and probably originated independently. There is no certain reason for assuming that either of the three insertions was originally written in Hebrew or Aramaic. The history of Susanna is certainly a Greek original, as was inferred by Julius Africanus and Porphyry from plays on words possible only in Greek (cf. Bertholdt, *Einleitung*, iv, 1575 sqq.; a thorough but nevertheless abortive effort to put aside the force of these plays was made by Wiederholt in *TQ*, 1869, pp. 290–321). Of the Song of the Three Children in the furnace and the story of the dragon, Gaster published an Aramaic text from a Jewish chronicle of the Middle Ages, which he regards as the original (Gaster, *The Unknown Aramaic Original of Theodotion's Additions to the Book of Daniel*, in *PSBA*, xvi, 1894, pp. 280–290, 312–317; xvii, 1895, pp. 75–94). But the author of the chronicle says that he gives the insertions, "which Thodos found; and this is the section which was inserted into his text by Thodos, the wise man, who translated in the days of Commodus, King of the Romans" (*PSBA*, xvi, 283, 312). Since Symmachus and Aquila are also mentioned as Bible translators, Thodos is no doubt Theodotion, as Gaster also states. The chronicler himself thus declares that the insertions are later than Theodotion. Still less originality can be claimed by another Aramaic (Syriac) reproduction of the story of the dragon, which Raymundus Martini quoted in his *Pugio fidei*, and which was published by Neubauer (*The Book of Tobit*, London, 1878, pp. xci–xcii, 39–43); the same can also be said of the Hebrew recension of the History of Susanna in Jellinek, *Bet ha-Midrash* (6 vols., Vienna, 1877, vi, 126–128). On account of the linguistic agreement of the insertions with the translation of the rest of the book, Fritzsche is led to the assumption that they are united with the book by the translator [of the Septuagint], and were recast by him (*Exegetisches Handbuch*, i, 114). This is improbable if the Greek origin of the insertions is maintained. Before the Daniel legend could produce new formations in the Greek language, a Greek book of Daniel had to exist. On the History of Susanna there is an interesting correspondence between Julius Africanus and Origen, in which the former denies the genuineness of the story and the latter defends it (*Julii Africani de historia Susannæ epistola ad Origenem et Origenis ad illum responsio*, ed. J. R. Wetstenius, Basel, 1674, Eng. transl., *ANF*, iv, 385–392). The text of the Septuagint of the Book of Daniel, together with its additions, was early displaced from ecclesiastical use by the version of Theodotion; consequently all manuscripts and editions of the Septuagint contain Theodotion's version of Daniel. The text of the Septuagint is extant in only one manuscript, which is in the library of Prince Chigi at Rome (*Codex Chisianus*, no. 88 in Holmes's *Vetus Testamentum;* Tischendorf dates it in the eleventh century), and was first edited by Simon de Magistris (*Daniel secundum LXX ex tetraplis Origenis nunc primum editus e singulari Chisiano codice*, Rome, 1772). A correct reprint of the *Codex Chisianus* was first published by Cozza (*Sacrorum bibliorum vetustissima fragmenta Græca et Latina*, part iii, Rome, 1877), and after him by Swete (*The Old Testament in Greek*, iii, Cambridge, 1894). Wherever Theodotion could not revise after a Hebrew original, his text in the additions is nothing but a revision of the Septuagint. The text of the Septuagint is the basis of the Hexaplar-Syriac version.

4. The Prayer of Manasses: After King Manasseh had been taken to Babylon by the Assyrians, and while in captivity, he repented and besought God to be delivered; God heard his prayer and brought him back again to Jerusalem (II Chron. xxxiii, 11–13). According to II Chron. xxxiii, 18–19, this prayer was written in the "Book of the Kings of Israel" and in the "History of Hozai" and "among the sayings of the seers." This reference suggested the composition of a prayer which should correspond to the situation. It is found in some manuscripts of the Septuagint (e.g., *Codex Alexandrinus*) among the hymns given at the head of the Psalms; and is also quoted in full in the Apostolic Constitutions, ii, 22. The latter furnishes the earliest trace of the existence of the prayer; it may be, as Nestle supposes, that it was transferred from this passage into the manuscripts of the Septuagint. It is nowhere found in the text of Chronicles. The Latin translation in the Vulgate (since the Council of Trent put into the appendix) is entirely different from the Old Latin, and is of very late origin.

5. Baruch: Under the name of Baruch, the faithful friend and companion of the prophet Jeremiah, whose prophecies he wrote down (Jer. xxxvi, 4, 17 sqq., 27, 32; xlv, 1) and with whom he shared the involuntary abode in Egypt (Jer. xliii, 5–7), a work is extant which consists of the following three parts, rather loosely connected: (a) i, 2–iii, 8: In the fifth year after the destruction of Jerusalem by the Chaldeans (586 B.C.), the Jews in Babylon send messages to Jerusalem to the high priest Joiakim, forward money to provide sacrifices for the Temple, and ask prayers for the life of King Nebuchadnezzar and his son Belshazzar. In the letter which the messengers bring to Jerusalem the point is especially emphasized that the present misfortune is but a punishment for the people's sin and their disobedience to God's commandments, especially because they did not obey the king of Babylon, as God desired them; (b) iii, 9–iv, 4: Israel is exhorted to return to the source of all wisdom, who is God alone; (c) iv, 5–v, 9: The discouraged people are exhorted to take heart. Though Jerusalem is devastated and the people scattered, God will bring them back into the holy city.

Opinions differ much as to the date of composition. It is the more difficult to decide because the three pieces of which the work is composed are of different character and come from at least two, possibly three, authors. The position of Roman Catholic theologians that the book really belongs to Baruch is untenable. The author was unacquainted with the circumstances of the times (cf. Fritzsche, *Exegetisches Handbuch*, i, 170), and was in the dark as to the situation invented by himself, not having pictured it clearly to his own consciousness. On the one hand, he presupposed the destruction of the city by the Chaldeans (i, 2), yet spoke as if the ritual and the Temple itself still existed (i, 10, 14). Even Ewald's view, that the book originated in the latter Persian and first Greek period, is far from the truth. There are parallels with the Book of Daniel which make certain literary dependence of one upon the other. Daniel ix, 7–10 corresponds almost literally to Baruch i, 15–18. But it is hardly conceivable that such a very original and creative mind as the author of Daniel copied from Baruch. This brings the book down into the later Maccabean times, on account of the necessary interval between Baruch and Daniel. With this date most of the Protestant critics seem to be satisfied (so Fritzsche, *Exegetisches Handbuch*, i, 173, and De Wette-Schrader, *Einleitung*, p. 603). But it is very questionable whether this is correct, whether, with Hitzig (*ZWT*, 1860, pp. 262 sqq.) and Kneucker (*Das Buch Baruch*, Leipsic, 1879), the date should not be brought down to the time of Vespasian.

Mention should be made of the fact, first noted by P. E. E. Geiger (*Der Psalter Salomos*, Augsburg, 1871, p. 137), that Baruch v has the same view-point as the Psalter of Solomon xi. The thoughts are in part derived from Isaiah. A literary relationship between Pseudo-Solomon and Pseudo-Baruch can hardly be denied. Considering the psalmlike character of Baruch, it seems more appropriate to grant priority to the psalms than to Baruch. This would lead at least into the time of Pompey, in which the psalms originated (cf. Schürer, *Geschichte*, iii, 150 sqq.). Besides, the first as well as the third part of the book presupposes the destruction of Jerusalem and of the Temple, the devastation and ruin of the country, and the removal of the inhabitants into captivity (i, 2; ii, 23, 26; iv, 10–16). To be sure, according to the author's plan, the action is placed in the time of the Chaldeans; but the whole work, with all its exhortations and consolations, suits a similar situation, and is not sufficiently motived, unless the contemporaries of the author lived under the pressure of like conditions (cf. Fritzsche, *Exegetisches Handbuch*, i, 172 sqq.). Circumstances similar to those of the time of the Chaldeans existed again in consequence of the great war of 66–70 A.D. Such a destruction of city and Temple took place neither in the time of the Maccabeans nor in the time of Pompey (to which Graetz assigns the book). Finally, some striking peculiarities suggest the war from 66 to 70. The author considers the misfortune of Israel a punishment for its rebellion against the king of Babylon, and exhorts the people to offer sacrifice and prayer to Nebuchadnezzar and Belshazzar (ii, 21 sqq., i, 10 sqq.). In like manner Josephus (*War*, II, xvii, 2–4) saw the real cause of the war in the abolition of the sacrifice for the Roman emperor. The entire unhistorical juxtaposition of Nebuchadnezzar and Belshazzar suggests Vespasian and Titus. That parents might eat the flesh of their children during a famine (ii, 3) was already threatened (Lev. xxvi, 29; Deut. xxviii, 53; Jer. xix, 9; Ezek. v, 10), and is stated as a fact (II Kings vi, 28 sqq.; Lam. ii, 20, iv, 10). It may be recalled that the very same thing is also narrated of the war under Vespasian (Josephus, *War*, VI, iii, 4). In view of these facts the inference is allowable that the Book of Baruch originated in the time of Vespasian. It is first quoted by Athenagoras ("Plea for the Christians," ix, where Baruch iii, 35 is quoted as the utterance of a prophet), and is also quoted by Irenæus (*Hær.*, IV, xx, 4; V, xxxv, 1), and Clement of Alexandria (*Pædagogus*, I, x, 91–92; II, iii, 36).

The question of the unity of authorship can be treated only in connection with the question of the original language. In the latter respect Jerome says (*Prolegomena in Jer.*), "It is neither found nor read among the Hebrews." Over against this in the Hexaplar-Syriac there occurs three times (in i, 17 and ii, 3) the remark "This does not exist in the Hebrew" (cf. Ceriani's notes to his edition in the *Monumenta sacra et profana*, i, 1, Milan, 1861–1871). According to this, it may be assumed that a Hebrew Baruch, corresponding to the Greek which has been preserved, was known to antiquity; and the linguistic character, at least of the first part, confirms this assumption. But the diction from iii, 9 is perceptibly different. Accordingly the view of Fritzsche has much in its favor; viz., that the first part is a translation from the Hebrew; the rest, however, is from a Greek original (*Exegetisches Handbuch*, i, 171 sqq.). With this it is also decided that there were two authors; the translator of the first part added the rest from his own resources, but both are to be dated in the time of Vespasian. Finally it is worthy of remark that the use of Theodotion's version of Daniel can be shown (cf. L. E. T. André, *Les Apocryphes de l'Ancien Testament*, Paris, 1904, pp. 251 sqq.;

TLZ. 1904, p. 255). From this it must be inferred that this version is much older than is generally supposed.

6. The Epistle of Jeremiah: As an addition to the Book of Baruch there is often found the so-called Epistle of Jeremiah (occurring as chap. vi in the Vulgate, in Luther's Bible, and in the English). Originally it had nothing to do with the Book of Baruch, and in older manuscripts is separated from it. But without any valid reason the two were united at a very early period. The letter is addressed to the exiles designated by Nebuchadnezzar to be led to Babylon. In contents it is a somewhat diffusive and rhetorical exhortation, though in good Greek, against the Babylonian deities, together with an ironical description of their nothingness. Its genuineness is out of the question; for the epistle was certainly originally written in Greek. Besides, the duration of the exile (verse 3) is given as lasting seven generations in opposition to Jer. xxix, 10. Many find in II Macc. ii, 1 sqq. direct reference to this epistle. But what is said there has nothing to do with it. Still less can it be regarded as a reference to the epistle, when the fact is taken into account that in one Targum to Jer. x, 11, this Aramaic verse is designated a "copy" from an epistle of Jeremiah (cf. Nestle, *Marginalien und Materialien*, 1893, pp. 42 sqq.).

7. Tobit: The name of this book and of its hero is read in the Vulgate *Tobias*; but in the Greek text *Tobit* (or *Tobith*), in the English translation "Tobit," where "Tobias" is only the name of the son of Tobit. According to the Greek text, in the first part of the book Tobit himself tells his story, speaking in the first person; from iii, 7, the narrator speaks in the third person. Tobit, a son of Tobiel of the tribe of Naphtali belonged to the exiles who were led away to Nineveh into captivity by the Assyrian king Shalmaneser. He lived there also under the kings Sennacherib and Esarhaddon and always distinguished himself by an exemplary piety. Since in spite of this piety he still experienced misfortune, he was derided and ridiculed (i, 1-iii, 6). A similar experience was that of a pious woman named Sara, the daughter of Raguel in Ecbatana (iii, 7-15). Because both prayed to God in their distress, the angel Raphael was sent to deliver both from the sufferings which befell them in their innocence, and to unite Sara and Tobias, the son of Tobit, in marriage (iii, 16-xii, 22). Tobit sang a psalm of praise in honor of God, and lived to be a hundred and forty-eight, and Tobias lived to be a hundred and twenty-seven (xiii, xiv). This is the course of the narrative, which is adorned with many details, exhibits a good talent for composition, and also displays the spirit of the strictly Pharisaic legality. Older theology down to the nineteenth century regarded the story as history; but the narrative is no doubt pure fiction. Its object is obvious; it is to prove that God never forsakes the pious and righteous; on the contrary, he always takes care of them, though they seem to be forsaken; finally that he richly rewards their piety. On this account those who, like Tobit, dwell among the Gentiles should not suffer themselves by the hardships of their external circumstances to become faithless to God.

The contents being so general, it is impossible to fix the time of composition. But with some probability it may be said that the book originated during the last two centuries B.C. There is no reason to go down to the post-Vespasian time, as Hitzig does (*ZWT*, 1860, pp. 250 sqq.); for here the case is essentially different from that of Baruch. While it is true that from the standpoint of the Assyrian times the destruction of Jerusalem and, conformably to it, its rebuilding also are prophesied (xiv, 4-5; xiii, 9-10, 16 sqq.), the entire book is by no means intended to comfort the readers for the destruction of Jerusalem. It is true that Hitzig infers, from the fact that the author depicts the rebuilding of city and Temple with more extravagant colors than would apply to the historical building, that he did not live while this historical building stood. But a careful consideration of the principal passage sets us right. Chap. xiv, 5 reads: "And they shall build the house but not like to the former, until the times of that age be fulfilled; and afterward they shall return from the places of their captivity, and build up Jerusalem gloriously, and the house of God shall be built in it forever with a glorious building, even as the prophets spake concerning it." Here two things are plainly distinguished: (a) the historical building of Zerubbabel, which is insignificant ("not like to the former"); and (b) the beautiful building of eternity, which is to follow this at the end of this age, which is still in the future even for the author. The very fact that the writer knew nothing of a repeated catastrophe between the two would indicate that he lived in pre-Vespasian or even in pre-Herodian times. Clear signs of a use of the book are lacking till the second century of the Christian era. Reference is made in xiv, 10 to the legend of Achikar or Achiachar, which is extant in different late recensions (cf. Conybeare, Harris, and Lewis, *The Story of Ahikar from the Syriac, Arabic, Armenian, Greek, and Slavonic Versions*, London, 1898). No Hebrew (or Aramaic) copy of the book was known to Origen and his Jewish advisers (*Epist. ad Africanum*, xiii: "The Jews neither use Tobit nor Judith, nor do they have them in Hebrew"). It is therefore probable that the extant Semitic texts are late. An Aramaic text was edited by A. Neubauer (*The Book of Tobit, a Chaldee Text from a Unique MS. in the Bodleian Library*, Oxford, 1878; cf. G. Bicknell, in *ZKT*, 1878, pp. 216-222; T. Nöldeke, in *Monatsberichte der Berliner Akademie*, 1879, pp. 45-69; and G. H. Dalman, *Grammatik des Jüdisch-palästinischen Aramäisch*, Leipsic, 1894, pp. 27-29). There exist also two Hebrew compositions generally acknowledged to be of late date (cf. C. D. Ilgen, *Die Geschichte Tobi's*, Jena, 1800, cxxxviii sqq., ccxvii sqq.; Fritzsche, *Exegetisches Handbuch*, ii, 5, 9 sqq., xiv; T. Nöldeke, *Die Alttestamentliche Litteratur*, Leipsic, 1868, pp. 108 sqq.). The Aramaic text has this in common with the Latin revision of Jerome (and with this only), that the story of Tobit is narrated from the beginning in the third person, whereas in all other texts, in i, 1-iii, 6, Tobit speaks in the first person. The Aramaic text is thus perhaps identical with, or at any rate nearly related to, that used by Jerome. Dalman for linguistic reasons declares it to be later. But a decision is difficult, since Jerome actually leans more upon the Old Latin. Since the uniform adoption of the third person is evidently secondary, the originality of the Aramaic as against the Greek is out of the question. It is probable that in the Aramaic text also the first person in chap. i, 1–iii, 6 was originally preserved; for it is still used in the so-called *Hebræus Munsteri*, which, according to other indications, was made from the Aramaic. But even with this supposition there is no reason to assume an Aramaic text as the original of the Greek (so Fuller in Wace's *Apocrypha*, i, 152–155, 164–171). The style of the Greek text makes its originality rather probable. Of the Greek text there are three recensions: (a) the common text contained also in the Vatican and Alexandrian manuscripts and followed by the Syriac version to vii, 9; (b) that preserved in the Sinaitic codex upon which the Old Latin leans for the most part; (c) the text of codices 44, 106, 107, which are the basis of the Syriac from vii, 10. The manuscripts named represent in the beginning the common recension, so that this text is preserved only for vi, 9–xiii, 8. In his edition of the Apocrypha, Fritzsche gives all three texts. Swete gives the text of the Vatican and Sinaitic.

8. Judith: The contents of this book are briefly as follows: Nebuchadnezzar, king of Assyria (sic), overcomes Arphaxad, king of Media, and sends his general, Holofernes, against the Western nations which did not take the field with him against Arphaxad. They are subdued, and their places of worship destroyed (i–iii). Holofernes now attacks the Jewish people, who had recently returned from the captivity and rededicated their temple. In the face of the imminent danger of having their sanctuary profaned, the whole people are bent upon resistance to the utmost, and the high priest Joiakim makes the necessary arrangements. Holofernes directs his main attack upon the fortress Bethulia, which he hopes to conquer by famine (iv–vii). The distress having become very great, a beautiful widow, Judith by name, offers to become the savior of her people. Having been admitted to the hostile camp, she contrives to gain the confidence of Holofernes. While Holofernes lies in a drunken stupor, Judith kills him and then hastens back into the city. The Jews make a sally, put the enemy to flight, and all Israel is saved (viii–xiv). Judith is praised as the savior of the people, and at her death at the advanced age of 105 years is greatly lamented by all the nation (xv–xvi).

As is the case in the Book of Tobit, so here there can be no doubt that the contents is not history but a didactic narrative. The historical details are so incredibly confused, and the parenetic object is so manifest, that only by wilfully closing the eyes can one fail to see that the book is fiction. What the parenetic object is, is plain enough: The Jewish people was to be encouraged to fight with the sword boldly and resolutely, for the continuance of its faith and worship, even against a superior enemy. This points clearly to Maccabean times. It may be admitted that the presupposed historical background would fit well the time of Artaxerxes Ochus, for this king in one of his campaigns against Phenicia and Egypt (c. 350 B.C.) made prisoners among the Jews; and Holofernes of Cappadocia and the eunuch Bagoes were the most prominent generals in these campaigns. Since, in the history of Judith, both Holofernes and the eunuch Bagoes play parts (xii, 11 sqq., xiii, 1 sqq., xiv, 14), it seems easy to locate the Judith story in the time of Ochus.

But the author mentions also Nebuchadnezzar. All that can be said is that in his literary license the author took a part of his material from events in the time of Ochus (T. Nöldeke, *Die alttestamentliche Litteratur*, Leipsic, 1868, p. 96; and *Aufsätze zur persischen Geschichte*, Leipsic, 1887, p. 78). But he certainly wrote later. And, since the story deals with a time of religious oppression, Maccabean times are indicated as the date of composition (cf. Fritzsche, Ewald, Hilgenfeld, and Nöldeke). Volkmar, Hitzig, and Graetz date it in the time of Trajan. Volkmar especially has vainly expended much learning and fancy to prove that the history of the campaigns of Nebuchadnezzar and Holofernes is merely a disguised representation of the campaigns of Trajan and his generals against the Parthians and the Jews. The fact that Clement of Rome (lv) mentions Judith forbids this late dating. It is generally agreed that the Greek text is a translation of a Hebrew original, as is evident from the entire coloring of the language and from mistakes in the translation (i, 8; ii, 2; iii, 1, 9, 10; cf. Fritzsche, *Exegetisches Handbuch*, ii, 115 sqq.). The Aramaic recension which Jerome perused is not to be regarded as the original, since neither Origen nor his Jewish advisers knew of a Hebrew (or Aramaic) text (*Epist. ad Africanum*, xiii, quoted above). It appears that the original was lost before Origen's time, and that the Aramaic translation used by Jerome originated after that time. The extant paraphrastic Hebrew recensions are still later products (cf. Zunz, *Die gottesdienstlichen Vorträge der Juden*, Berlin, 1832, pp. 124 sqq.; Lipsius, in *ZWT*, 1867, pp. 337–366; Ball, in Wace's *Apocrypha*, i, 252–257; Gaster, in *PSBA*, xvi, 1894, pp. 156–163). Of the Greek text three recensions are extant: (a) the common and original one; (b) that of the codices 19, 108; (c) that of 58, which was followed by the Syriac and the Old Latin.

9. I Maccabees: The name Maccabeus was originally only the surname of Judas, the son of Mattathias (I Macc. ii, 4: "Judas who was called Maccabeus"). By it Judas was at all events to be characterized as a valiant hero. The assured meaning of the name is yet to be found. From Judas the name was afterward applied to the whole family, even to the whole party of which Judas became leader. So, generally, the Maccabeans were the believing Israelites, who, in defense of the faith of their fathers, undertook the struggle against the Syrian overlords. I Maccabees tells the story of these struggles and the history of the independent Jewish community which was the fruit of these struggles up to the time of the death of the high priest Simon (135 B.C.). It commences with the beginning of the reign of Antiochus Epiphanes (175 B.C.), narrates how his efforts at a forcible suppression of the Jewish religion became the cause of the open revolt against Syrian overlordship, describes the changing results of this revolt under the leadership of Judas Maccabeus until his death (161 B.C.); then the further course of the Maccabean efforts under the guidance of Jonathan, brother of Judas, who, by adroitly taking advantage of circumstances, was able to obtain from the Syrian kings recognition of his status as prince and high priest of the Jews (161–143 B.C.); finally the history of the high priest Simon, a third brother (143–135 B.C.). The narrative is rich in detail and by its unadorned simplicity wins a confidence which, so far as Jewish history is concerned, is not shaken by the fact that the author shows himself badly informed on matters concerning foreign nations, such as the Romans. The exaggerated numbers even do not detract from its credibility in other things. That a narrative which enters so into detail must be based upon other sources is a matter of course, though nothing more definite can be stated concerning the character of the sources. A reference to these seems to be indicated in ix, 22 (cf. Grimm, in Fritzsche, *Exegetisches Handbuch*, iii, 22 sqq.). The book compares to good advantage with other historical books in that it fixes all important events according to an established chronology, the Seleucidan era, which begins in the autumn of 312 B.C. But I Maccabees apparently makes the era begin in the spring of that year. The time of composition can be fixed with great probability within very narrow limits. On the one hand the author knew a chronicle of the acts of John Hyrcanus (135–105 B.C.; cf. xvi, 24). From this can be inferred that he wrote after John's reign. On the other hand, he certainly wrote before the expedition of Pompey, since the Romans were for him friends and protectors of the Jewish people. The composition belongs therefore to an early decade of the first pre-Christian century. That the book was originally written in Hebrew is evident from its linguistic character, a conclusion confirmed by the testimony of Origen and Jerome; the former (in Eusebius, *Hist. eccl.*, VI, xxv, 3) gives the Hebrew title of the book, the meaning of which, on account of the uncertainty of the text-tradition, is difficult to ascertain. Jerome says in the *Prologus galeatus*: "I Maccabees I found in Hebrew; II Maccabees is Greek, as can be proved from the very language." The Greek translation was used by Josephus (cf. Grimm, in Fritzsche, *Exegetisches Handbuch*, p. 28; H. Bloch, *Die Quellen des Flavius Josephus*, Leipsic, 1879, pp. 80–90). It is strange that Josephus knows hardly anything of chaps. xiv–xvi. J. von Destinon (*Die Quellen des Flavius Josephus*, Kiel, 1882, pp. 60–91) supposed therefore that the book originally did not have these chapters and that the first copy differed also in other respects from the present. But the very free use made by Josephus offers no sufficient support for this theory. A Hebrew recension which A. Schweizer (*Untersuchungen über die Reste eines hebräischen Textes vom ersten Makkabäerbuch*, Berlin, 1901) considers original was made in the Middle Ages from the Latin (cf. *TLZ*, 1901, p. 605; *REJ*, xliii, 1901, pp. 215–221).

10. II Maccabees: This book is parallel with I Maccabees except that it begins a little earlier; viz., with the last year of Seleucus IV, Philopator, brother and predecessor of Antiochus Epiphanes, and closes much earlier; viz., with the victory of Judas Maccabeus over Nicanor (161 B.C.). It therefore covers a much shorter period than the first. In its literary, historical, and religious character it differs much from I Maccabees. It is more rhetorical, and its language and style prove that it was originally produced in Greek. In credibility it stands far below I Maccabees. It narrates in part the same events, in part different events, and in a different order. On the whole, in cases of conflict between the two, it is better to follow I Maccabees, though it may be admitted that in some details the second may here and there follow a better tradition. The means by which to decide with certainty in every case no longer exist; and the second book deserves a less degree of confidence, because its purpose is by no means exclusively historical. The author's interest was evidently more narrowly religious than that of the first. His immediate object was not to narrate the deeds of a glorious past, but to influence the present religiously.

Of the sources, the author himself says (ii, 19 sqq.) that his book is only an epitome of the large work of Jason of Cyrene, which in five books narrated the history of the Maccabean struggles in the times of Antiochus Epiphanes and his son Antiochus Eupator. Unfortunately, this Jason of Cyrene is otherwise wholly unknown. This much can be said of the time of the epitomist with some certainty, that he wrote before the destruction of Jerusalem, as may be inferred from the purpose of the book and also from xv, 37. Josephus seems to have read neither the work of Jason nor that of the epitomist. It is possible that the description of the tyrants who persecuted the pious and virtuous, given in Philo, *Quod omnis probus liber*, xiii, depends upon II Maccabees (so P. E. Lucius, *Der Essenismus*, Strasburg, 1881, pp. 36–39). Heb. xi, 35 sqq. seems to refer to II Macc. vi and vii. The first express quotation is found in Clement of Alexandria (*Strom.*, V, xiv, *ANF*, ii, 467): "Aristobulus, who is mentioned by the composer of the epitome of the books of the Maccabees" (cf. II Macc. i, 10).

11. III Maccabees: If II Maccabees falls short of credibility when compared with the first, the third can lay still less claim to the character of a historical document. It has the name "Book of the Maccabees" very improperly and only because it treats also of the oppression and deliverance of believing Israelites. It has nothing to do with the time of the Maccabees. The contents are as follows: Ptolemy IV, Philopator (222–205 B.C.) visits the temple at Jerusalem after his victory over Antiochus the Great at Raphia (217 B.C.). Being seized with a desire to penetrate into the Holy of Holies, and not heeding the entreaties of the people to forego his outrageous purpose, the king is punished when about to carry out his design by falling paralyzed to the ground. Enraged at this, on his arrival in Egypt, he wreaks his vengeance on the Alexandrian Jews. But all his decrees are frustrated by God's miraculous intervention. The king now becomes a friend and benefactor of the Jews, whom he permits to kill the apostates, a privilege of which they make much use.

The style in which this narrative is written corresponds closely to the insipidity of the contents. The book is more bombastic and unnatural than II Maccabees. Since the narrative evinces its unhistorical character, it is necessary only to inquire what facts possibly form the basis of or induced its composition. To begin with, it is to be remembered here that Josephus transfers the story of the confinement of Jews in the Hippodrome to be trodden down by elephants to the reign of Ptolemy VII, Physcon (*Apion* ii, 5); like III Maccabees (vi, 36), he remarks that in remembrance of the deliverance experienced, the Alexandrian Jews annually celebrated a festival. According to this the narrative seems to have some historical foundation; and as concerns the chronology, Josephus is to be followed rather than III Maccabees. At all events this work is a late production. The author knows the Apocryphal additions to Daniel (cf. vi, 6). The book is mentioned by Eusebius (*Chron.*, ed. Schöne, ii, 122 sqq.) in the *Canones Apostolorum* (lxxxv), by Theodoret, and others (Grimm, in Fritzsche, *Exegetisches Handbuch*, p. 21). The abrupt beginning shows the book has not come down complete.

12. Jesus Sirach (Ecclesiasticus): The Book of Proverbs by Jesus the son of Sirach is the extracanonical double of the canonical Book of Proverbs. Like that, it gives the results of practical wisdom in poetical form. It comprises the whole range of human life in all directions and relations, and aims at giving the correct point of view for all human enterprises so they may be correct as concerns conduct. The highest as well as the lowest, the greatest as well as the smallest, are brought within the sphere of the author's reflections and counsels. He speaks of the fear of God and of divine wisdom, of friendship and mercy, of self-control and moderation, and of other virtues; he speaks also of the contrary vices. He speaks of the special tasks which differences in age, sex, calling, and in civic and social position make obligatory upon the individual. He speaks of the mutual relations between parents and children, masters and servants, high and low, rich and poor. He gives maxims of prudence for social intercourse and political behavior. The form in which he clothes his thoughts is throughout that of Hebrew poetry. No plan for the book is discernible. The writer arranges his ideas in groups, but these groups are not arranged with reference to any scheme. The morality which runs through the whole is indeed somewhat homely, sometimes purely utilitarian. But on the whole there is a solid, seriously moral disposition expressed in the book, combined with a rational and practical contemplation of the world. What the author offers is the ripe fruit of a many-sided education and of a long experience.

The extant Greek text is, as may be seen from the preface, only a translation. Jerome asserts that he had seen a Hebrew exemplar (cf. the Preface to his translation of the Solomonic books, ed. Vallarsi, ix, 1293 sqq.): "There is a right praiseworthy book of Jesus the son of Sirach and a pseudepigraphical one which is called the Wisdom of Solomon. The first I found in the Hebrew called 'Proverbs,' and not 'Ecclesiasticus,' as among the Latins, to which are added Ecclesiastes and Song of Songs; so that they agreed with the books of Solomon not only in number, but also in the kind of matter."

Prior to 1896, only a few sayings of the Hebrew original, which are quoted in Rabbinic literature, were known (collected by Schechter in *JQR*, iii, 1891, pp. 682–706; still more completely by Cowley and Neubauer, *The Original Hebrew of a Portion of Ecclesiasticus*, London, 1897, pp. xix–xxviii). Since 1896 large portions of the Hebrew text have been discovered. They all come from the *genizah* ("lumber-room") of the ancient synagogue at Cairo. The fragments are remains of four different manuscripts, and supplement each other in such a way that, on the whole, two-thirds of the Hebrew text has been recovered. Of the flood of literature which these finds have induced the principal text-publications are mentioned below (especially important are *The Book of Ecclesiasticus in Hebrew*, London, 1901, a facsimile of all the leaves; the condensed work of N. Peters, *Der jüngst wiederaufgefundene hebräische Text des Buches Ecclesiasticus*, Freiburg, 1902; and R. Smend, *Die Weisheit des Jesus Sirach erklärt*, 1906, and *Die Weisheit des Jesus Sirach hebräisch und deutsch herausgegeben*, 1906). The denial of the originality of the Hebrew text by Margoliouth, Bickell, and formerly also by Levi, must be called an aberration. Almost all competent scholars regard this as beyond doubt. Besides the Greek versions and the Hebrew fragments, there is still another witness, the Syriac translation. This was not made from the Greek, like the other Syriac texts of the Apocrypha, but directly from the Hebrew. From the passage quoted above from Jerome, it is seen that the book was called "Proverbs" in the Hebrew. In Greek manuscripts the standing title is "The Wisdom of Jesus the Son of Sirach." In the Latin Church the title *Ecclesiasticus* has become customary since the time of Cyprian.

The author calls himself "Jesus the Son of Sirach the Jerusalemite" (l, 27). The preface of his grandson, the translator, gives his date. He says of himself that he came into Egypt "in the thirty-eighth year of King Euergetes." This cannot mean the translator's thirty-eighth year of life, but the thirty-eighth year of the reign of Euergetes. Of the two Ptolemies who had the name "Euergetes" the first ruled only twenty-five years. Consequently, only the second, whose full name was Ptolemæus VII, Physcon Euergetes II, can be meant. He ruled conjointly with his brother from 170 B.C. and was sole king from 145 B.C. But his regnal years were reckoned from the former date. According to this, the thirty-eighth year in which the grandson of Jesus Sirach came into Egypt was 132 B.C. The grandfather, the author of the book, may have lived and written about 190–170 B.C. It is singular that in the Latin Church the book has usually been regarded as a work of Solomon, on which account some Western canonical lists reckon five Solomonic writings (T. Zahn, *Geschichte des neutestamentlichen Kanons*, ii, 151, 245, 251, 272, 1007 sqq.).

13. The Wisdom of Solomon: In some books of the Old Testament, wisdom, that is, the wisdom resting in God and coming from him, is praised as the highest good, as the source of all perfection and the giver of all happiness and blessing (cf. Prov. viii–ix and Job xxviii, 12 sqq.). In later literature this was a favorite thought, and was further developed. It is met with again in Jesus Sirach and in the Wisdom of Solomon. The author of this book, who assumes the name of Solomon, reproaches his royal colleagues, the Gentile rulers (i, 1; vi, 1), with the folly of impiety and especially of idolatry. Only the pious and righteous is truly happy; the impious falls under divine judgment. Idolatry is the height of folly. In opposition to it the author recommends true wisdom, using the idea in its fullest possible content. For he understands by the word "wisdom" subjective as well as objective, human as well as divine. Both have one meaning, and are identical in essence. Human wisdom adjusts true knowledge to all spheres of life. It instructs man in the ways of God and teaches him God's holy will. On this account it is the source of all happiness and all true joy to him who gives himself to it. It imparts not only honor and glory but also eternal life and everlasting salvation. And this it can do only because human wisdom is but an emanation from the divine wisdom, or, rather, is identical with it. Originally it was joint possessor with God of his throne (ix, 4); it was present when God created the world (ix, 9); it is most intimately connected with God and initiated into God's knowledge (viii, 3–4); it is a breathing of the power of God, an effulgence from the glory of the Almighty (vii, 25–26); its action is identical with God's; it works all things (viii, 5), orders all things (viii, 1), and renews all things (vii, 27). From these fundamental thoughts the standpoint of the author is evident; he was a Jewish philosopher. On the one hand, he occupied throughout the standpoint of Old Testament revelation; on the other hand, he had acquired also a peculiar philosophical culture. He had learned not only from the sages of his people, but also from the Hellenes, from Plato and the Stoics. He thus belongs to that school, the classical representative of which is Philo, which can be designated as a marriage of Jewish faith with Greek philosophical culture. With this everything is said that can be said of the author of the book. The book stands between Jesus Sirach and Philo, and is the bridge from the one to the other. As to its date, it can be put with some probability between the two, 150–50 B.C. (cf. Grimm, in Fritzsche, *Exegetisches Handbuch*, vi, 32–34), though the inference from priority in thought to priority in time is not cogent. It is certainly wrong to think, like Weisse and others, of a Christian author. Clear traces of an acquaintance with the book are found in the New Testament (cf. W. Sanday and A. C. Headlam, *Commentary on Romans*, 1895, pp. 51–52, 267–269). It is first quoted in the time of Irenæus (Eusebius, *Hist eccl.*, v, 26). That the book was originally written in Greek is a matter of course, considering its lofty rhetoric, which is somewhat artificial and overdone. Jerome says, "The very style betrays Greek eloquence."

E. SCHÜRER.

BIBLIOGRAPHY: Texts, Greek, along with the Septuagint: *Codex A*, by Grabe, 4 vols., Oxford, 1707–20; by H. H. Baber, 3 vols., London, 1812–26; facsimile ed., by E. M. Thompson, ib. 1881. *Vatican Codex* and *Codex Friderico-Augustanus*, by Tischendorf, Leipsic, 1846, and 4 vols., Rome, 1862. *Codex B*, by Mai, 5 vols., Rome, 1857; by C. Vercellone and J. Cozza, 6 vols., ib. 1868–81 (a corrected ed. of Mai); photographic reproduction, 6 vols., ib. 1889–90. Critical and comparative text: H. B. Swete, *Old Testament in Greek according to the Septuagint*, 3 vols., 8vo, Cambridge, 1895–99 (a 4to ed. is in preparation).

Separate editions of the Apocrypha: A. Fabricius, *Codex pseudepigraphus veteris testamenti*, 2 vols., Hamburg, 1722–23; by Augusti, Leipsic, 1804; and by Apel, ib. 1804; O. F. Fritzsche, *Libri Apocryphi*, ib. 1871 (apart from Swete's, the best edition). Latin: by Stephens, Geneva, 1556–57; the Sixtine ed., 3 vols., Rome, 1590 (corrected, 1592, from which all Roman Catholic editions are copied). P. Sabatier, *Bibliorum sacrorum . . . vetus italica*, Reims, 1739–49 (Old Latin text). Syriac: P. de Lagarde, *Libri veteris testamenti apocryphi Syriace*, Leipsic, 1861; by Ceriani, *Codex Ambrosianus B 21*, photolithographic ed., 2 vols., Milan, 1876–83, and *Codex Ambrosianus C 313*, photolithographic ed., Milan, 1874, also Baruch and Letter of Jeremiah, Milan, 1861; by C. Bugati, in Syriac the additions to the Book of Daniel, Milan, 1788. German: E. Kautzsch, with the help of numerous scholars, *Die Apocryphen und Pseudepigraphen des Alten Testaments*, 2 vols., Tübingen, 1900 (contains introduction, notes, and brief bibliographies). English: The older Bibles usually contained the Apocrypha; besides these, the Variorum ed. by C. J. Ball, London, 1892 (contains full notes); the Bagster ed., London, n.d. (authorized text; the Revised Version was issued at Cambridge, 1895); consult also: W. R. Churton, *Uncanonical and Apocryphal Scriptures*, London, 1884. Lexicon: Wahl, *Clavis . . . apocryphorum*, Leipsic, 1853.

Introductions: L. E. T. André, *Les Apocryphes de l'Ancien Testament*, Florence, 1903; B. Welte, *Die deuterokanonischen Bucher*, in J. G. Herbst, *Einleitung*, II, iii, Freiburg, 1844; W. M. L. de Wette, *Einleitung in die kanonischen und apokryphischen Bücher*, 8th ed. by Schrader, Berlin, 1869; S. J. Cornely, *Introductio in veteris testamenti libros . . .*, ii, 1–2, Paris, 1887; F. Buhl, *Kanon und Text des Alten Testaments*, Leipsic, 1891 (Eng. transl., London, 1892); F. E. König, *Einleitung in das Alte Testament, mit Einschluss der Apokryphen*, Bonn, 1893; Schürer, *Geschichte*, iii, 1898 (Eng. transl., II, iii, 1891; contains general and special introduction and notes of literature); K. Budde, *Geschichte der althebräischen Litteratur: Apocryphen*, von A. Bertholet, Leipsic, 1906; S. N. Sedgwick, *The Story of the Apocrypha*, London, 1906.

Exegetical literature on the entire Apocrypha: O. Zöckler, in *Kurzgefasster Kommentar*, *Die Apokryphen*, Munich, 1891; O. F. Fritzsche and C. L. W. Grimm, *Kurzgefasstes exegetisches Handbuch zu den Apokryphen*, Leipsic, 1851-60; H. J. von Holtzmann, *Die apokryphischen Bücher*, ib. 1869; E. Reuss, *La Bible, Ancien Testament*, vi, vii, Paris, 1878–79; E. C. Bissell, *Apocrypha of the Old Testament*, New York, 1880, addition to the Eng. transl. of Lange's commentary; *The Old Testament, Authorized Version, with Brief Commentary, Apocryphal Books*, London, S.P.C.K., 1881; H. Wace, *Holy Bible, with . . . Commentary, Apocrypha*, 2 vols., London, 1888, in the *Speaker's Commentary*.

On the individual books: The Apocryphal Ezra; the text and notes by Bensly and James in *TS*, iii, 2, Cambridge, 1895; R. L. Bensly, *Missing Fragment of the Fourth Book of Ezra*, London, 1875; *DB*, s. v. *Esdras*, i (1898), 758–766; R. Basset, *Les Apocryphes éthiopiens traduites en français*, Paris, 1899; H. Gunkel, *Der Prophet Ezra*, Tübingen, 1900; *EB*, s. v. *Ezra, the Greek*, ii, 1488–94. *JE*, s. v. *Esdras*, v. 219–222.

Apocryphal Esther: A. Scholtz, *Kommentar über das Buch Esther mit . . . Zusätzen und über Susanna*, Würzburg, 1892, also *Die Namen im Buche Esther*, in *TQ*, 1890, pp. 209–264; Jacob, *Das Buch Esther bei den LXX*, in *ZATW*, x (1890), 241–298; *JE*, v, 237–241.

Apocryphal additions to Daniel: O. Bardenhewer, *Biblische Studien*, ii, 2–3, pp. 155–204, Freiburg, 1897; vi, 3–4, ib. 1901; Wiederholt, in *TQ*, 1869, 287 sqq., 377 sqq., 1871, 373 sqq., 1872, 554 sqq.; Brill, in *Jahrbücher für jüdische Geschichte und Litteratur*, iii (1877), 1–69, viii (1887), 22 sqq.; A. Scholz, see above under Esther; *EB*, i, 1013–1015; *DB*, i, 267–268, iv, 630–632, 754–756; W. H. Daubney, *The Three Additions to Daniel; A Study*, Cambridge, 1906.

Prayer of Manasseh: E. Nestle, *Septuagintastudien*, iii, 4, p. 6 sqq., and iv, Stuttgart, 1899.

Baruch: J. J. Kneucker, *Das Buch Baruch*, Leipsic, 1879 (the best book on the subject); H. A. C. Hävernick, *De libro Baruchi commentarius criticus*, Königsberg, 1843; F. H. Reusch, *Erklärung des Buches Baruch*, Freiburg, 1853; Grätz, in *Monatsschrift für Geschichte und Wissenschaft des Judentums*, 1887, pp. 385–401; *DB*, i, 251–254; *EB*, i, 492–494; *JE*, ii, 556–557.

Epistle of Jeremiah: *DB*, ii, 578–579; *EB*, ii, 2395.

Tobit: *Semitic Studies in Memory of A. Kohut, ed. by G. A. Kohut*, 264–338, Berlin, 1897; F. H. Reusch, *Das Buch Tobias*, Freiburg, 1857; A. Neubauer, *Tobit, a Chaldee Text*, Oxford, 1878; A. Scholz, *Commentar zum Buche Tobias*, Würzburg, 1889; M. Rosenmann, *Studien zum Buche Tobit*, Berlin, 1894; F. C. Conybeare, J. R. Harris, and L. Lewis, *Story of Ahikar from the Syriac, Arabic . . . Versions*, London, 1898; E. Cosquin, *Le Livre de Tobie et l'histoire du Ahikar*, in *Revue Biblique*, Jan., 1899; *DB*, iv, 785–789; *JE*, xii, 171–172.

Judith: A. Scholz, *Das Buch Judith, eine Prophetie*, Würzburg, 1885; idem, *Commentar zum Buche Judith*, ib. 1887; Vigouroux, *Dictionnaire de la Bible*, iii, 1822–33; *JE*, vii, 388–390.

The Books of Maccabees: K. F. Keil, *Commentar*, Leipsic, 1875 (still the best); C. Bertheau, *De secundo libro Maccabæorum*, Göttingen, 1829 (quite useful); H. Ewald, *Geschichte*, iv, 602 sqq., Göttingen, 1864; H. Graetz, *Geschichte der Juden*, iii, 613–615, 671–684, Leipsic, 1884; A. Schlatten, *Jason von Cyrene*, Munich, 1891; G. A. Deissmann, *Bibelstudien*, pp. 258 sqq., Marburg, 1895, Eng. transl., pp. 341–345, Edinburgh, 1901; H. Willrich, *Juden und Griechen vor der makkabäischen Erhebung*, pp. 64–65, Göttingen, 1895; W. Fairweather and J. S. Black, in *Cambridge Bible for Schools*, Cambridge, 1897; Abrahams, in *JQR*, 1896, pp. 39–58, 1897, pp. 39 sqq.; A. Büchler, *Die Tobiaden und die Oniaden im II Makkabäerbuche*, Vienna, 1899; B. Niese, *Kritik der beiden Makkabäerbücher*, Berlin, 1900; *DB*, iii, 187–196; *EB*, iii, 2857–81; Stuys, *De Maccabæorum libris*, Amsterdam, 1904; *JE*, viii, 239 sqq.

Ecclesiasticus: C. Seligmann, *Das Buch der Weisheit des Jesus Sirach*, Breslau, 1883; A. Astier, *Introduction au livre de l'Ecclésiastique*, Strasburg, 1861; T. K. Cheyne, *Job and Solomon, or the Wisdom of the Old Testament*, London, 1887; E. Hatch, *Essays in Biblical Greek*, pp. 246–282, ib. 1889 (text-critical); H. Bois, *Essai sur les origines de la philosophie Judéo-Alexandrine*, pp. 160–210, 313–372, Paris, 1890; D. S. Margoliouth, *The Place of Ecclesiasticus in Hebrew Literature*, Oxford, 1890; E. Nestle, *Marginalien und Materialien*, pp. 48–59, Tübingen, 1893; I. Levi, *L'Ecclésiastique, ou la Sagesse de Jésus, fils de Sira*, Paris, 1898; H. Herkenne, *De veteris Latinæ ecclesiastici capitibus*, i–xliii, Leipsic, 1899 (important for the text); also in Bardenhewer's *Biblische Studien*, vi, 1, 2, pp. 129–14, 1901; N. Peters, ib. iii, 3, 1895; *EB*, i, 1164–1179, iv, 4640–51; *DB*, iv, 539–551; *JE*, xi, 388–397. On the recently discovered Hebrew text consult: *Facsimiles of the Fragments recovered of the Book of Ecclus.* in Hebrew, Oxford, 1901 (a complete edition); A. E. Cowley and A. Neubauer, *Original Hebrew of a Portion of Ecclesiasticus*, Oxford, 1897 (text and discussion); A. Schlatter, *Das neugefundene hebräische Stück des Sirach*, Gütersloh, 1897; R. Smend, *Das hebräische Fragment . . . des Jesus Sirach*, Berlin, 1897; F. E. König, *Die Originalität des neulich entdeckten Sirach Textes*, Freiburg, 1899; D. S. Margoliouth, *Origin of the "Original Hebrew" of Ecclus.*, London, 1899 (combats originality of the Hebrew text); S. Schechter and C. Taylor, *The Wisdom of Ben Sira . . . from Heb. MSS. in the Cairo Genizah Collection*, Cambridge, 1899 (chiefly textual); H. L. Strack, *Die Sprüche Jesus des Sohnes Sirach*, Leipsic, 1903; I. Levi, *The Hebrew Text of the Book of Ecclesiasticus, with Notes and Glossary*, Leyden, 1904; most of the literature on the new text appeared in periodicals of the year 1900; cf. *Theologischer Jahresbericht* for 1900 (gives 51 titles).

Wisdom of Solomon: W. J. Deane, *Book of Wisdom*, London, 1881; E. Pfleiderer, *Die Philosophie des Heraklit von Ephesus*, Berlin, 1886; J. Drummond, *Philo Judæus*, i, 177–229, London, 1888; P. Menzel, *Der griechische Einfluss auf . . . Weisheit Salomos*, Halle, 1889; H. Bois, *Essai sur les origines de la philosophie Judéo-Alexandrine*, pp. 201–307, 373–412, Paris, 1890; *DB*, iv, 928–931; *EB*, iv, 5336–49; *JE*, xii, 538–540.

B. New Testament Apocrypha: The relation between the canonical and the apocryphal writings of the New Testament is quite different from that between the same classes of books of the Old Testament. The Old Testament Apocrypha aim simply at a continuation of sacred history and strive to accomplish their purpose in a legitimate manner though without divine authority. The apocryphal writings connected with the New Testament, on the contrary, aim to introduce spurious sources among the genuine. They are writings which by name and contents pretend to be canonical, though the Church, because of their dubious origin and contents, has not given them a place in the canon. Like the canonical books of the New Testament, they may be divided into four classes: I. Gospels; II. Acts of the Apostles; III. Epistles of the Apostles; IV. Apocalypses.

These writings are of very unequal value. The apocryphal Acts seem to have had the most influence in the Church; for they, more than the Gospels, were looked upon as "the source and mother of all heresy." Of course, not all of these writings were composed directly for heretical purposes. Many of them, no doubt, had more innocent motives, such as mere "pious fraud." But from their first appearance a suspicion of heresy clung to them all and contributed much to put the whole literature under ban.

When the canon of the New Testament was fixed and the apocryphal books thereby became outlawed, they ceased to be read; and in the Middle Ages, even their names were forgotten. Nevertheless, although the books themselves were delivered over to contempt and oblivion, it was not so with their contents. From their fables sprang sacred legends, which were kept alive in the Church during the Middle Ages as "ecclesiastical tradition," which was often utilized in the development of its dogma. Indeed, numerous dogmas, usages, and traditions hark back to these apocryphal writings; and it was consequently of as much moment to the Protestant Church to subject this whole literature to a thorough investigation as it was to the Roman Church to keep the whole matter in convenient obscurity. The careful study of these writings in modern times has proved of great value, revealing a wealth of material usable for the elucidation of archeological and dogmatic problems. Study of them has become a distinct department of the theological curriculum.

I. Apocryphal Gospels: Of the many apocryphal Gospels (J. A. Fabricius, in his *Codex apocryphus Novi Testamenti*, 2 vols., Hamburg, 1703, reckons over fifty), some have come down entire, others only in fragments; and of a few only the names are known. The method employed in these compositions is always the same, whether the author intended simply to collect and arrange what was floating in the general tradition or intended to produce a definite dogmatic effect. He rarely relied on his own invention; but generally elaborated what was hinted at in the canonical Gospels, transformed words of Jesus into deeds, described the fulfilment of an Old Testament prophecy in a slavishly literal manner, or represented Jesus as working marvels closely resembling but surpassing Old Testament miracles. The work done, the author took care to conceal his own name, and inscribed his book with the name of some apostle or disciple, in order to give it authority. In the following list those Gospels are first mentioned the texts of which have been preserved.

1. The Protevangelium of James: This was ascribed to James, the brother of the Lord; in the index of Gelasius and Hormisdas it is called the "Gospel of James the Less [Younger]." It has twenty-five chapters, and covers the period from the announcement of the birth of Mary to the murder of the innocents. It is very old, perhaps of the second century, was widely circulated, and shows traces of Ebionitic origin. The text is given by Tischendorf (*Evangelia Apocrypha,* 2d ed., Leipsic, 1876; Eng. transl. by A. Walker, *ANF,* viii, 361-367), also by Conybeare from an Armenian manuscript (*AJT,* i, 1897, pp. 424 sqq.).

2. The Gospel of Pseudo-Matthew, or Book of the Origin of the Blessed Mary and the Infancy of the Savior: This begins with the announcement of the birth of Mary, and closes with the youth of Jesus, and is contained in forty-two chapters. It seems to be of Latin origin, and to have been drawn from the Protevangelium of James and the Gospel of Thomas (Eng. transl., *ANF,* viii, 368–383).

3. The Gospel of the Nativity of Mary: This contains in ten chapters the history of Mary before the birth of Jesus. It covers therefore nearly the same ground as the Gospel of Pseudo-Matthew, but is a little later in date (Eng. transl., *ANF,* viii, 384–387).

4. The History of Joseph the Carpenter: This contains in thirty-two chapters a biography of Joseph, and gives an elaborate description of his death. It was evidently written in glorification of Joseph, and was intended for recital on the day of his festival. It probably belongs to the fourth century; and, as Joseph was a favorite of the Monophysite Copts, Coptic (and not Arabic) was most likely the language of the original (Eng. transl., *ANF,* viii, 388-394).

5. The Gospel of Thomas: This, next to the Protevangelium of James, was the oldest and most popular of the Apocryphal Gospels. It was in use as early as the middle of the second century, among the Gnostics with whom it originated, especially among those who held Docetic views of the person of Christ. It is extant in two Greek recensions, in a Latin and in a Syriac version; all of which have somewhat expanded titles. The two Greek recensions and the Latin version are given by Tischendorf (pp. 140–180); English translation of the three by Walker (*ANF,* viii, 395–404).

6. The Arabic Gospel of the Infancy: This comprises in fifty-five chapters the period from the birth of Jesus to his twelfth year, and consists mostly of stories dealing with the residence in Egypt. The first nine chapters follow very closely the Protevangelium of James; the last twenty chapters follow the Gospel of Thomas; the part between seems to rest on some national tradition, which explains the favor it found among the Arabs, as well as the circumstance that several of its details were incorporated into the Koran. The whole work has an Oriental character, and shows contact with magic and demonology and with Zoroastrian ideas. No more definite date for its composition can be fixed than that it antedated the Koran. The Arabic text is probably a translation from the Syriac; and no manuscript is earlier than the thirteenth century. Tischendorf published a revised Latin translation; English version by Walker (*ANF,* viii, 405–415).

7. The Gospel of Nicodemus: This consists of two separate works, the *Deeds [or Acts] of Pilate* and *The Descent of Christ to the Underworld,* which were united at an early date, and the whole did not receive the title "Gospel of Nicodemus" until after the time of Charlemagne. The former of these two works is of some importance for the explanation and further elucidation of the canonical Gospels (cf. Lipsius, *Die Pilatusakten,* 2 ed., Kiel, 1886), while the latter is of very little interest. The former contains a detailed account of the trial of Jesus before Pilate, and of the action of the Sanhedrin subsequent to his death, which was intended to furnish proof of the resurrection and ascension. The latter contains an account by two men, Carinus and Leucius, who had been raised from the dead. The text of the Gospel of Nicodemus is given by J. C. Thilo (*Codex apocryphus Novi Testamenti,* Leipsic, 1832), who furnishes a list of translations into English, French, Italian, and German, and by Tischendorf; English translation by Walker (*ANF,* viii, 416–458).

In most of the manuscripts containing these two works and in close connection with them occur other writings; namely: (a) An *Epistle of Pilate* to the emperor, containing a report on the resurrection of Christ. (b) An *Epistle of Pontius Pilate,* another letter, in which he excuses the injustice of his decision by the impossibility of resisting the prevailing excitement. It was widely diffused in early times. (c) The *Report of Pilate* on the trial, execution, death, and resurrection of Jesus. (d) The *Judgment of Pilate,* a report of the examination of Pilate before the emperor, his condemnation and execution. Others which deserve nothing more than mention of their titles are: (e) The *Death of Pilate;* (f) The *Narrative of Joseph of Arimathea;* (g) The *Avenging of the Savior;* (h) The *Reply of Tiberius to Pilate* (Eng. transls., *ANF,* viii, 459–476).

8-37. Apocryphal Gospels Preserved only in Fragments or Known only by Name: Besides the Gospels mentioned above there were others, of which there remain only a few fragments or only the names: **(8) The Gospel according to the Egyptians:** Quoted by Clement of Rome and

Clement of Alexandria, and mentioned by Origen, Epiphanius, and Jerome. It was used by the Encratites and Sabellians [and composed either at Antioch (Zahn) or in Egypt (Harnack) in the middle of the second century]. (9) **The Eternal Gospel:** The work of a Minorite of the thirteenth century, based upon Rev. xiv, 6. It was condemned by Pope Alexander IV. It is mentioned here solely because of its name and is not properly reckoned among the apocryphal Gospels (see JOACHIM OF FIORE). (10) **The Gospel of Andrew:** Perhaps the same as the Acts of Andrew (see below II, 6). (11) **The Gospel of Apelles:** Possibly a mutilated version of a canonical Gospel like that of Marcion (cf. A. Harnack, *De Apellis gnosi monarchia*, Leipsic, 1874, p. 75). (12) **The Gospel of the Twelve Apostles:** Jerome identified this with what he calls the Gospel among the Hebrews. (13) **The Gospel of Barnabas.** (14) **The Gospel of Bartholomew:** On the tradition that Bartholomew brought the *Hebrew Gospel of Matthew* to India, where it was found by Pantænus, cf. Fabricius, i, 341. (15) **The Gospel of Basilides.** (16) **The Gospel of Cerinthus:** Mentioned by Epiphanius (*Hær.*, li, 7); perhaps a mutilated version of the Gospel according to Matthew, similar to that used by the Carpocratians. (17) **The Gospel of the Ebionites:** Epiphanius (*Hær.*, xxx, 13, 16, 21) has preserved fragments of this Gospel which he says was a mutilated *Gospel of Matthew* called by the Ebionites *The Hebrew Gospel*. It is not identical with the *Gospel of the Nazarenes*. (18) **The Gospel of Eve:** Mentioned by Epiphanius as in use among certain Gnostics (*Hær.*, xxvi, 2, 3, and 5). [Preuschen prints the extracts quoted by Epiphanius as a fragment of an Ophite Gospel (*Antilegomena*, Giessen, 1901, p. 80). Jesus is represented as saying in a voice of thunder: "I am thou, and thou art I, and wherever thou art there am I, and in all things I am sown. And from whencesoever thou gatherest me, in gathering me thou gatherest thyself." Cf. J. H. Ropes, *Die Sprüche Jesu*, Leipsic, 1896, p. 56.] (19) **The Gospel according to the Hebrews:** According to the testimony of Jerome, this book was identical with the Gospel of the Twelve Apostles and the Gospel of the Nazarenes, and was written in Aramaic in Hebrew characters, used among the Nazarenes, and translated by himself into Greek and Latin. (20) **The Gospel of James the Elder:** Said to have been discovered in 1595 in Spain, where, according to tradition, James labored. (21) **John's Account of the Departure of Mary:** It exists in Greek, in two Latin versions (all three translated into English by Walker, *ANF*, viii, 587–598), also in Syriac, Sahidic, and Arabic versions. (22) **The Gospel of Judas Iscariot:** According to Irenæus, Epiphanius, and Theodoret, used among the Cainites, a Gnostic sect. (23) **The Gospel of Leucius.** (24) **The Gospel of Lucian and Hesychius:** Mentioned as forgeries by the *Decretum Gelasii* (VI, xiv, 15). Jerome ("Prologue to the Gospels") believes that they were only the first recensions of the Gospel text, though he also charges the two men with unauthorized tampering with the text. Lucian was a presbyter at Antioch; Hesychius was a bishop in Egypt toward the end of the third century. (25) **The Gospels of the Manicheans:** These were four in number. (*a*) The *Gospel of Thomas*, a disciple of Manes (this Gospel must be distinguished from the other *Gospel of Thomas*, see 5 above); (*b*) *The Living Gospel*; (*c*) *The Gospel of Philip*; (*d*) *The Gospel of Abdas.* (26) **The Gospel of Marcion:** Marcion (q.v.), the founder of the famous anti-Jewish sect known as Marcionites, admitted only Pauline writings into his canon. He lived in the first half of the second century. The passages in which Paul speaks of his Gospel (Rom. ii, 16; Gal. i, 8; II Tim. ii, 9) obviously suggested the attribution to him of a special Gospel. Marcion regarded the Gospel of Luke as Paul's, but he obtained this Gospel only by eliminating from Luke all Jewish elements, as is attested by Irenæus, Origen, and Tertullian. The latter two quote the corrupted passages. (27) **The Questions, Greater and Lesser, of Mary:** Two works of obscene contents, used by some Gnostics, according to Epiphanius (*Hær.*, xxvi, 8). (28) **The Apocryphal Gospel of Matthew.** (29) **The Narrative of the Legal Priesthood of Christ.** (30) **The Gospel of Perfection:** Used by the Basilidians and other Gnostics, not the same as the *Gospel of Philip* or the *Gospel of Eve* (cf. Fabricius, i, 373; ii, 550). (31) **The Gospel of Peter:** Mentioned by Origen, Eusebius, and Jerome, and used by the congregation at Rhossus in Cilicia toward the end of the second century. Serapion, bishop of Antioch, found it there (c. 191 A.D.) and after examination condemned it (Eusebius, *Hist. eccl.*, vi, 12). An important fragment of the *Gospel of Peter* was discovered in 1886 in a grave, supposed to be that of a monk, in an ancient cemetery at Akhmim, the ancient Panopolis in Upper Egypt. It was published in 1892 (*Memoirs of the French Archeological Mission at Cairo*, IX, i). *The Gospel of Peter* was edited by Harnack (2d ed., 1893), Zahn (1893), Von Schubert (1893), and Von Gebhardt (1893). [For English translation cf. *ANF*, ix, 7–8. It has been the subject of numerous able articles in the theological journals since its publication in 1892.] (32) **The Gospel of Philip:** Mentioned and quoted by Epiphanius (*Hær.*, xxvi, 13) as being in use among the Gnostics. Possibly it is the same as was in use among the Manicheans (see above 25, c). (33) **The Gospel of the Simonites,** or, as it was also called by themselves, *The Book of the Four Corners and Hinges of the World*: Mentioned in the *Arabic Preface to the Council of Nicæa.* (34) **The Gospel according to the Syrians:** Possibly identical with the *Gospel according to the Hebrews.* (35) **The Gospel of Tatian:** Mentioned by Epiphanius (*Hær.*, XLVI, i, 47, 4) as being used by the Encratites and by Catholic Christians in Syria. Being a compilation from the four Gospels, it was called also "The Diatessaron"; see HARMONY OF THE GOSPELS; TATIAN. (36) **The Gospel of Thaddæus:** Mentioned in the Gelasian Decree. The name may have been intended for that of the apostle Judas Thaddæus, or for that of one of the Seventy who, according to tradition, was sent to King Abgar of Edessa (see ABGAR; and cf. Eusebius, *Hist. eccl.*, i, iii). (37) **The Gospel of Valen-**

tinus: Usually identified with the *Gospel of Truth* on the authority of Irenæus, who says that the *Gospel of Truth* was used by the Valentinians, and that it was very dissonant from the canonical Gospels.

II. Apocryphal Acts of the Apostles: This class of writings originated through the operation of the same causes that produced the apocryphal Gospels, though the heretical tendency in the Acts is generally more prominent. For this reason they were as much feared in the early Church as the apocryphal Gospels; and it appears from references in Eusebius, Epiphanius, and Augustine that they had great influence. Since they were often worked over for dogmatic purposes, criticism has to inquire into the antiquity and originality of the existing codices. Among those who manufactured apocryphal Acts one Lucius (or Leucius) Charinus, a Manichean, is especially mentioned. His collection is said to have comprised the Acts of Peter, John, Andrew, Thomas, and Paul. Of these a few fragments only are preserved in the original form, which were afterward revised to accord with catholic dogma; in an enlarged form the collection became known as the **Acts of the Twelve Apostles,** which, according to Photius, was used by the Manichean Agapios. It must not be overlooked that some of these revised Acts are of a very high antiquity; thus the *Acts of Peter* were in use in the second century and the *Journeys of Thomas* in the third century A collection entitled the **Acts of the Holy Apostles** is mentioned by Greek chroniclers from the sixth century. Toward the end of the sixth century a Latin collection became known, ascribed to Abdias (q.v.), the supposed bishop of Babylon. In its original form the collection comprised the "passions" of all the twelve apostles (including Paul instead of Matthias), in its revised form the "virtues" or "miracles" of Peter, Paul, John, Andrew, and Thomas, and the "passions" of Matthew, Bartholomew, Philip, the two Jameses, both Simons, and Jude, of the older collection. A third collection was in use in the Coptic Church, and is extant in the Ethiopic language as the **Contest of the Apostles** [best edition by E. A.W. Budge, *The Contendings of the Apostles*, 2 vols., London, 1899–1901]. There are also numerous Syriac recensions.

The most notable of these apocryphal Acts are (1) **Acts of Peter and Paul,** the oldest testimony for which is Eusebius, with possibly Clement of Alexandria; (2) **Acts of Paul and Thecla,** known to Tertullian, ascribed to a presbyter in Asia, and belonging to the first half of the second century; (3) **Acts of Barnabas, Told by John Mark,** which has another title in some Greek manuscripts, *Journeys and Martyrdom of the Holy Barnabas the Apostle;* (4) **Acts of Philip,** possessing high antiquity and having been much used in the literature of both branches of the early Church; (5) **Acts of Philip in Greece,** later than the last-mentioned; (6) **Acts of Andrew,** a very early composition; (7) **Acts of Andrew and Matthew in the City of the Anthropophagi,** much used by the Gnostics and Manicheans; (8) **Acts and Martyrdom of Matthew,** to be connected with the last-named as its continuation; (9) **Acts of Thomas,** also a work of high antiquity; (10) **Consummation of Thomas,** the completion of the story begun in the foregoing *Acts of Thomas;* (11) **Martyrdom of Bartholomew;** (12) **Acts of Thaddeus** (the Syriac reads "of Addas"), built upon the very old tradition of the exchange of letters between Abgar (q.v.) of Edessa and Christ; (13) **Acts of John,** likewise very old, and esteemed highly by Gnostics and Manicheans; the "History of Prochor" mentions the *Acts of John,* but (14) **a History of John** (in Syriac), and (15) **Passion of John** have no connection with Prochor; while (16) **On the Life of John** adds nothing to the last three. Besides the foregoing, there are many fragments of Acts, which do not call for mention. English translations of these apocryphal Acts will be found in *ANF*, viii, 477–564.

III. Apocryphal Epistles: Besides the fictitious correspondence between Christ and Abgar (see Abgar), other alleged writings of Christ are known which belong to the realm of mythology (collected by Fabricius, i, 303–321; iii, 439, 511–512). There are letters from the Virgin Mary to Ignatius, and letters to Mary which are of a very late date (given in Fabricius, i, 834, 844, 851). Two letters of Peter to James are also known. From Col. iv, 16 it is learned that Paul wrote a letter to the Laodiceans which is lost; it is not to be wondered at that this lost letter soon found an apocryphal substitute, which was in circulation in Jerome's time (*De vir. ill.*, v), and was published in many languages (cf. Zahn, *Kanon*, ii, 566 sqq., 584–585; Zahn treats also [ii, 612 sqq.] of the spurious correspondence between Paul and Seneca). Since in I Cor. v, 9, Paul speaks of an earlier letter to the Church of Corinth (which has been lost), care was taken to substitute another letter to the Corinthians in place of the lost one. A Latin text recently discovered was published and discussed by Carrière and Berger (*La Correspondance apocryphe de St. Paul et des Corinthiens*, Paris, 1891); cf. A. Harnack (*TLZ*, 1892, 2 sqq.), T. Zahn (*TLB*, 1892, 185 sqq., 193 sqq.), Bratke (*TLZ*, 1892, 585 sqq.).

IV. Apocryphal Apocalypses: Although the names of a considerable number of apocryphal apocalypses are known, the texts or fragments of texts of only a few are extant (collected by Tischendorf, *Apocalypses Apocryphæ*, Leipsic, 1866), viz.: (1) **Apocalypse of John:** Differed from the canonical book of the same name. (2) **Apocalypse of Peter:** Mentioned in the Muratorian Canon and by Clement of Alexandria, Methodius, Eusebius, and others. A fragment of this apocalypse was recently discovered together with the *Gospel of Peter* (see I [31] above), and published at Paris in 1892 (cf. *ANF*, ix, 141 sqq.). (3) **Ascension of Paul:** Is based on II Cor. xii, 2–4, where Paul tells of being caught up into heaven. (4) **Apocalypse of Paul:** Spoken of by Augustine and Sozomen (cf. *ANF*, viii, 149 sqq.). (5) **Apocalypse of Bartholomew:** Extant only in fragments in a Coptic manuscript in the Paris library. (6) **Apocalypse of Mary:** Exists only in fragments of late manuscripts. (7) **Apocalypse of Thomas:** Mentioned in the *Decretum Gelasii.* (8) **Apocalypse of Stephen:**

Based on Acts vii, 55: said to have been in use among the Manicheans. For English translations, consult *ANF*, viii, 575–586; ix, 141–174.

(RUDOLF HOFMANN.)

BIBLIOGRAPHY: Collections of Apocrypha: J. A. Fabricius, *Codex Apocryphus Novi Testamenti*, 2 vols., Hamburg, 1703, vol. iii, 1743; J. C. Thilo, *Codex Apocryphus Novi Testamenti*, Leipsic, 1832; W. Giles, *Codex Apocryphus Novi Testamenti*, 2 vols., London, 1852; W. Wright, *Contributions to the Apocryphal Literature of the New Testament from Syrian MSS.*, ib. 1865; M. Bonnet, *Supplementum codicis apocryphi*, 2 vols., Paris, 1883–95 (of great value); M. R. James, *Apocrypha Anecdota . . Thirteen Apocryphal Books and Fragments*, in *TS*, ii, 3, and v, 1, Cambridge, 1893–97; E. Nestle, *Novi Testamenti Græci Supplementum*, Berlin, 1896; *ANF*, viii-ix; *Apocryphal New Testament*, London, Boston, and New York, n. d. (out of print); E. Hennecke, *Neutestamentliche Apokryphen . in deutscher Uebersetzung und mit Einleitungen*, Tübingen, 1904.

Collections of Gospels: C. Tischendorf, *Evangelia Apocrypha*, Leipsic, 1876; G. Brunet, *Les Évangiles apocryphes*, Paris, 1863; B. H. Cowper, *Apocryphal Gospels and Documents Relating to Christ*, London, 1870; Jos. Variot, *Des Évangiles apocryphes*, Paris, 1878; A. Resch, *Ausserkanonische Paralleltexte zu den Evangelien*, 3 vols., Leipsic, 1892-97; E. Preuschen, *Antilegomena. Die Reste der ausserkanonischen Evangelien*, Giessen, 1901.

Collections of Apocryphal Acts: C. Tischendorf, *Acta Apostolorum Apocrypha*, revised ed. by Lipsius and Bonnet, 3 vols., Leipsic, 1891, 1898, 1903 (essential for texts); R. A. Lipsius, *Die Apocryphen Apostelgeschichten und Apostellegenden*, 4 vols., Brunswick, 1883–90 (exceedingly important); W. Wright, *Apocryphal Acts of the Apostles from Syriac MSS.*, London, 1871; A. S. Lewis, *Mythological Acts of the Apostles from an Arabic MS.*, ib. 1904.

Apocalypses: C. Tischendorf, *Apocalypses apocryphæ*, Leipsic, 1866.

Treatises covering the subject: A. Harnack, *Geschichte der altchristlichen Litteratur*, Leipsic, 1893 (exhaustive); J. Pons, *Recherches sur les apocryphes du nouveau Testament*, Montauban, 1850; R. Hofmann, *Das Leben Jesu nach den Apokryphen*, ib. 1851; M. Nicolas, *Études sur les évangiles apocryphes*, Paris, 1866; S. Baring-Gould, *Lost and Hostile Gospels*, London, 1874; B. F. Westcott, *Introduction to the Study of the Gospels*, ib. 1888; T. Zahn, *Geschichte des neutestamentlichen Kanons*, 2 vols., Leipsic, 1888–92 (from the conservative standpoint); W. E. Barnes, *Canonical and Uncanonical Gospels*, ib. 1893 (clear and useful); G. Krüger, *Geschichte der altchristlichen Litteratur in den ersten drei Jahrhunderten*, Freiburg, 1895, Eng. transl., New York, 1897.

On individual Gospels: W. Wright, *Evangelium Thomæ*, London, 1875; R. Reinsch, *Die Pseudo-Evangelien von Jesu und Maria's Kindheit in der romanischen und germanischen Litteratur*, Halle, 1879; R. A. Lipsius, *Die edessenische Abgar-Sage*, Brunswick, 1880; F. Robinson, *Coptic Apocryphal Gospels*, in *TS*, iv, 2, Cambridge, 1896; F. C. Conybeare, *Protevangelium of James*, in *AJT*, i (1897), 424 sqq.; Ragg, *Italian Version of the Lost Apocryphal Gospel of Barnabas*, Oxford, 1905. On the Gospel of the Hebrews: E. B. Nicholson, *Gospel According to the Hebrews*, London, 1897; R. Handmann, *Das Hebräer-Evangelium*, Leipsic, 1888; G. Salmon, *Historical Introduction to the Study of the New Testament*, pp. 161–170, London, 1894. On the Logia Jesu: B. P. Grenfell and A. S. Hunt, *Logia Jesu, Sayings of our Lord*, London, 1897; A. Harnack, *Ueber die jüngst entdeckten Sprüche Jesu*, Freiburg, 1897; W. Lock and W. Sanday, *Two Lectures on the Sayings of Jesus*, London, 1897; C. Bruston, *Les Paroles de Jésus récemment découvertes et remarques sur le texte . de l'Évangile de Pierre*, Paris, 1898; A. Jacoby, *Ein neues Evangelienfragment*, Strasburg, 1900; J. H. Ropes, *Die Sprüche Jesu*, Leipsic, 1896.

The Peter Fragments were issued, translated, or discussed by: J. R. Harris, London, 1892; J. A. Robinson and M. R. James, ib. 1892; O. Von Gebhardt, Leipsic, 1893; A. Harnack, ib. 1893; A. Lods, in three works, Paris, 1892, 1893, 1895; A. Sabatier, ib. 1893; H. von Schubert, two works, Berlin, 1893, Eng. transl. of one, Edinburgh, 1893; D. Völter, Tübingen, 1893; T. Zahn, Leipsic, 1893; and C. Bruston, see above under Logia Jesu.

Apocryphal Acts: S. C. Malan, *The Conflicts of the Holy Apostles*, London, 1871; R. A. Lipsius, *Die Quellen der Petrussage*, Kiel, 1872; C. Schlau, *Die Acten des Paulus und der Thecla*, Leipsic, 1877; T. Zahn, *Acta Johannis*, Erlangen, 1880; M. Bonnet, *Acta Thomæ*, Leipsic, 1883; A. E. Medlycott, *India and the Apostle Thomas. Critical Analysis of Acta Thomæ*, London, 1905. On the Acts of Pilate: R. A. Lipsius, *Pilatusakten*, Kiel, 1886; C. Tischendorf, *Pilati circa Christum judicio quid lucis in Actis Pilati*, Leipsic, 1855; Geo. Sluter, *Acta Pilati*, Shelbyville, Ind., 1879; W. O. Clough, *Gesta Pilati*, Indianapolis, 1880; J. R. Harris, *Homeric Centones and the Acts of Pilate*, London, 1889.

Other works: W. F. Rinck, *Das Sendschreiben der Korinther an den Apostel Paulus*, Heidelberg, 1823 (argues for genuineness), answered by C. Ullmann, *Ueber den dritten Brief Pauli an die Korinther*, ib. 1823; E. Dulaurier, *Fragment des Révélations apocryphes de St. Barthélémy*, Paris, 1835; A. Harnack, *De Apellis Gnosi Monarchia*, Leipsic, 1874.

APOLLINARIS, α-pol″li-nē′ris (**APOLLINARIUS**), **CLAUDIUS**: Bishop of Hierapolis in Phrygia. He was a contemporary of Melito, and flourished in the reign of Marcus Aurelius (161–180), occupying a prominent position as an apologist and an opponent of Montanism, which took its rise in the ecclesiastical province to which he belonged. He was a prolific writer, but of his numerous works, still much read in the time of Eusebius, only a few, and of these little more than the titles, are known. Eusebius (*Hist. eccl.*, iv, 27) mentions an apology addressed to the emperor; since the story of the "thundering legion" (q.v.) seems to have been told in this, it can not have been written before 171, though Eusebius, in his *Chronicon*, assigns it to 170. The same historian mentions an apology against the Greeks in five books, two books "Concerning Truth," and a letter against the Montanists, which is also referred to by Serapion, bishop of Antioch, in his letter to Caricus and Pontius. This, according to Eusebius, was written later than the apologetic works mentioned above, and contained a report of the proceedings of a synod held against the Montanists, with a list of signatures of the members of the synod. Photius also names a treatise "On Piety." The *Chronicon Paschale* (ed. Dindorf, i, 13) preserves two fragments of a work on the Passover, all that has been preserved of the work of Apollinaris; these have been questioned, but without good reason. Two books against the Jews and one against the Severians have been erroneously attributed to him. In the catenæ numerous fragments are found with the name of Apollinaris attached to them, which have never been carefully examined; but it is probable that most, if not all, belong to the younger Apollinaris of Laodicea.

(A. HARNACK.)

BIBLIOGRAPHY: Fabricius-Harles, *Bibliotheca Græca*, vii (1801), 160–162; *ANF*, viii, 772–773; Harnack, *Litteratur*, i, 243–246; idem, *TU*, i (1882), 232–239.

APOLLINARIS OF LAODICEA: The name of two men, father and son, known to Church history. **Apollinaris the Elder** was an Alexandrian, taught grammar at Berytus, and then at Laodicea in Syria, and was made a presbyter at the latter place. What Socrates (*Hist. eccl.*, ii, 46) says of his literary activity belongs probably to the son (cf. Sozomen, *Hist. eccl.*, v, 18). **Apollinaris the Younger** was born presumably about 310, and was likewise a teacher of rhetoric. About 346 he became acquainted with **Athanasius**; and they remained warm friends, notwithstanding theological differences. Athanasius calls him a bishop in 362; and, as he was at first an energetic representative of Homoousianism in Syria, he was presumably the Homoousian antibishop of Pelagius of Laodicea, who belonged to the right wing of the middle party. When he proclaimed his peculiar views openly can not be stated with certainty. The synod at Alexandria in 362 seems to declare against them, and he was considered a heretic at the beginning of the seventies. Roman synods in 377 and 382 and one at Antioch in 378 testified against his doctrine. The second ecumenical council (Constantinople, 381) condemned the Apollinarians as the last heretics who issued from the Trinitarian controversy, and the emperor Theodosius set the great seal upon this condemnation in 388. Apollinaris was dead when Jerome wrote his *Viri illustres* in 392.

Life.

Great as is the confusion concerning the life of the man, it is still greater as regards his literary activity, which is the more to be regretted, as Apollinaris was evidently one of the most prominent ecclesiastical writers of the fourth century. This may be seen from the high esteem in which he was held during his lifetime by friend and foe and from the expressions of later writers. According to Philostorgius (*Hist. eccl.*, viii. 11; cf. xii. 15), Athanasius as a theologian was a child when compared with Apollinaris; and as concerns "experience" (e.g., knowledge of Hebrew) he would give the preference to the Laodicean above Gregory and Basil. Apollinaris was famous not only as a theological author but also as a poet. As a new Homer he treated the Old Testament history from the Creation to Saul in twenty-four books, wrote comedies after the pattern of Menander, tragedies in the style of Euripides, and odes after Pindaric models. There is extant only a "Paraphrase upon the Psalter," which fails to exhibit the poetic genius ascribed to the author. Of his exegetical efforts there have been preserved only fragments on Proverbs, Ezekiel, Isaiah, and the Epistle to the Romans; the exegesis is sober, sensible, and avoids allegory. As Christian apologist Apollinaris is said to have surpassed his predecessors in his thirty books against Porphyry (Philostorgius, viii. 4; Jerome, *De vir. ill.*, civ.; idem, *Epist.*, xlviii. 13, lxx. 3; Vincent of Lerins, *Commonitorium*, xi.); he wrote a work, "On Truth," against Julian and the philosophy of the time, and opposed the Arians in a work against Eunomius of Cyzicus; he wrote also against Marcellus of Ancyra. All these writings seem to have been lost. It is also impossible to form a correct estimate of his dogmatic writings. All that has been directly transmitted are seven larger and some short fragments from an "Exposition of the Divine Incarnation in the Likeness of Man" (in the rejoinder of Gregory of Nyssa to Apollinaris). But it is known that the Apollinarians and Monophysites circulated some of the productions of Apollinaris under the names of Gregory Thaumaturgus, Athanasius, and Julius of Rome to deceive innocent readers as to their true origin and nature, and Caspari has proved that the "Sectional Confession of Faith," ascribed to Thaumaturgus, belongs to Apollinaris. The same may be said of the treatise "On the Incarnation of the Word of God," ascribed to Athanasius, and of the alleged epistles of Felix of Alexandria and Julius of Rome to Dionysius of Alexandria. Attempts (especially of Dräseke) to ascribe other works to Apollinaris have been unsuccessful.

Writings.

The tendency of the Athanasian doctrine of redemption to the deification of humanity, little as Athanasius himself doubted that the Logos had assumed the perfect humanity, was not fitted for reviving interest in the human personality of the Redeemer. Thus it is not strange that so zealous a champion of the homoousios as Apollinaris, with his logical and dialectic training, started with doubts upon this point. Perfect God and perfect man is, according to his opinion, a monstrosity, contradicting all laws of reason. In this way would originate a "man-god," a "horse-deer," a "goat-stag," —fabulous beings like the Minotaur. This proves true not only logically, but also on comparing the notion of the perfect man with the demands to be made upon the Redeemer in the interest of redemption. Supposing him to be perfect man, how could Christ be without sin? If, as the apostle knew, man consists of spirit (mind), soul, and body, the human mind can not be adjudicated to Christ, for this is changeable; but the Redeemer has an unchanging mind. Since he can not be composed of four parts, he has indeed assumed a human body and a human soul, but not a human spirit. The *logos homoousios* rather takes its place. Thus originated the *μία φύσις τοῦ θεοῦ λόγου σεσαρκωμένη* (not *σεσαρκωμένου*), in which the flesh is deified and which as a whole becomes an object of adoration. The consequence is obvious, that all passive conditions [the susceptibility to suffering] of the historical Jesus are referred to the Logos and consequently to the Deity itself, though Apollinaris and some of his adherents recoiled from it. The Apollinarian Christology, which made great advances to the consciousness of the believers, which in the first line is always directed to the divine in Christ, and which seemed to lead away farthest from the generally detested thought of the "mere man" (Paul of Samosata), has exercised great influence on the further development of the Christological doctrine in the Eastern Church. With a certain right, one can even say with Harnack (*Dogmengeschichte*, p. 314) that the view of Apollinaris, when compared with the presuppositions and aims of the Greek conception of Christianity as religion, is perfect; but one can only do so by regarding the extremest consequences as the correct expression of what is intended. On the further development of Apollinarianism see the articles treating of the Christological controversies of the fifth and sixth centuries.

His Christology.

G. Krüger.

That Apollinaris, side by side with Paul of Samosata and Arius, should have come to be regarded as an archheretic, nay as in a certain sense the archheretic, is thoroughly intelligible. All three with their theories came in violent conflict with essential postulates of the Christian piety of the Church; Paul destroyed the complete Deity, Apollinaris the complete humanity, Arius both. The pious Christian consciousness required in the person of Christ ideal humanity and absolute Deity and was content to regard the manner of the union of the two as a mystery, i.e., as transcending the comprehension of the human mind. Yet in so far as it tended to set aside the conception of Christ as a "mere man" (Paul of Samosata), the theory of Apollinaris was for the time acceptable to many. A. H. N.

Bibliography: The best collection of the writings of Apollinaris and his pupils is that by H. Lietzmann, *Apollinaris von Laodicea und seine Schule*, *TU*, i., Tübingen, 1904. Cf. also I. Flemming and H. Lietzmann, *Apollinarische Schriften* (Syriae), in the *Abhandlungen der königlichen Gesellschaft der Wissenschaften zu Göttingen*, vol. vii., Berlin, 1904. Apollinaris' paraphrase of the Psalms is in *MPG*, xxxiii.; the remains of his dogmatic works are in *TU*, vii. 3, 4, Leipsic, 1892; of his exegetical writings, in A. Mai, *Nova patrum bibliotheca*, vii. 2, pp. 76–80, 82–91, 128–130; in A. Ludwich, *Probe einer kritischen Ausgabe*, Königsberg, 1880–81; The *Sectional Confession of Faith* is in *ANF*, vi. 40–47; cf. C. P. Caspari, *Alte und neue Quellen*, Christiania, 1879.

On the name: T. Zahn, *Forschungen zur Geschichte des Kanons*, v. 99–109, Leipsic, 1893. For life: J. Dräseke, *Apollinaris von Laodicea, sein Leben und seine Schriften*, in *TU*, vii. 3, 4, ib. 1892. On his writings: A. Ludwich, in *Hermes*, xiii. (1878) 335–350, and in *ZWT*, xxxi. (1888) 477–487, xxxii. (1889) 108–120. On his theology: A. Dorner, *Die Lehre von der Person Christi*, i. 975–1036, Stuttgart, 1846; A. Harnack, *Lehrbuch der Dogmengeschichte*, ii. 309–321, Freiburg, 1895; J. Schwane, *Dogmengeschichte der patristischen Zeit*, pp. 277–283, ib. 1895; G. Voisin, *L'Apollinarisme*, Paris, 1901. On literary and theological problems: C. W. F. Walch, *Entwurf einer vollständigen Historie der Ketzereien*, iii. 119–229, Leipsic, 1766.

APOLLONIA, ă″pol-lō′nî-a, SAINT: A martyr of Alexandria, according to a letter from Dionysius, bishop of Alexandria, to Fabian of Antioch, preserved by Eusebius (*Hist. eccl.*, vi. 41), and giving an account of a persecution of the Alexandrian Christians in the winter of 248–249. This persecution was the work of the populace, stirred up by the celebration of the one-thousandth anniversary of the founding of Rome, but was connived at by the authorities. As victims of this outburst Dionysius names Metras, Quinta, Sarapion, and Apollonia, whom he calls in Greek *parthenon presbutin*, probably signifying a deaconess. Because in her martyrdom all her teeth were knocked out, she is popularly regarded in Roman Catholic countries as a patroness against toothache. Her festival falls on Feb. 9. A. Hauck.

Bibliography: K. J. Neumann, *Der römische Staat*, i. 331, Leipsic, 1890.

APOLLONIUS, ap″ol-lō′ni-us: 1. A Roman martyr under Commodus. Eusebius (*Hist. eccl.*, v. 21) states that he was renowned for his learning and wisdom; he was accused by an "instrument of the devil" at a time when the government did not favor religious persecution, and consequently the accuser suffered the death penalty; the judge, Perennis, wished to save Apollonius, allowed him to make an eloquent defense before the senate, but was ultimately compelled by the law to condemn the Christian to death by beheading. Jerome expands these notices (*De vir. ill.*, xlii., liii.; *Epist.* lxx., *ad Magnum*). As the downfall of Perennis took place in 185, the martyrdom must be dated between 181 and that year, probably in 184. N. Bonwetsch.

Bibliography: (1) *Apology and Acts of Apollonius*, ed. and transl. from the Armenian by F. C. Conybeare, London, 1894 (cf. *The Guardian*, June 21, 1893); Greek transl. of the same in *Analecta Bollandiana*, xiv. (1895) 284–294, and cf. xxiii. (1899) 50, and E. T. Klette, *Der Process und die Acta S. Apollonii*, in *TU*, xv. 2, Leipsic, 1897; O. von Gebhardt, *Acta martyrum selecta*, pp. 44 sqq., Berlin, 1902. Also A. Harnack, in *Sitzungsberichte der Berliner Akademie*, 1893, pp. 721–746, and in *TLZ*, xx. (1895) 590 sqq.; Seeberg, *NKZ*, iv. (1893) 836 sqq.; E. G. Hardy, *Christianity and the Roman Empire*, London, 1894; Max, Prinz von Sachsen, *Der heilige Märtyrer Apollonius von Rom*, Mainz, 1903; O. Bardenhewer, *Geschichte der altkirchlichen Litteratur*, vol. ii., Freiburg, 1903.

2. Author of a work against the Montanists, of which Eusebius gives a fragment (*Hist. eccl.*, v. 18). It was written forty years after the appearance of Montanus and shows that the deliverances of the new prophets were false and that the conduct of the Montanist authorities was opposed to the manner of true prophets. According to Jerome (*De vir ill.*, l., liii.), Tertullian added to his six books *De ecstasi*, a seventh against the charges of Apollonius; but he is mistaken (*De vir. ill.*, xl.) in ascribing to Apollonius what is related by Eusebius in *Hist. eccl.*, v. 16. The designation of Apollonius as "leader of the Ephesians," in *Prædestinatus*, xxvi. is a fiction. N. Bonwetsch.

Bibliography: N. Bonwetsch, *Geschichte des Montanismus*, pp. 30, 49, Erlangen, 1881; G. Voigt, *Eine antimontanistische Urkunde*, Leipsic, 1891; T. Zahn, *Forschungen zur Geschichte des neutestamentlichen Kanons*, pp. 21 sqq., Leipsic, 1893.

APOLLONIUS OF TYANA: Neo-Pythagorean philosopher, elevated by non-Christians to a place by the side of Christ; b. at Tyana in Cappadocia, the modern Kiz-Hissar (80 m. n.w. of Tarsus); d. at Ephesus, probably, 98 A.D. He was educated at Ephesus and at Tarsus, but, disgusted by the immorality of the latter city, he went to Ægææ (the modern Ayas, on the Gulf of Iskanderun, 50 m. s.e. of Adana). In its temple of Æsculapius he studied medicine and philosophy, and became an ardent and lifelong adherent of Pythagoras. He observed the five years of absolute silence enjoined by the Pythagoreans, and then started on his memorable and extensive travels, which took him into all parts of the known world, made him acquainted with many prominent persons, and gave him a great reputation for wisdom. He seems to have exerted a virtuous example and to have been a religious reformer. Falling under the suspicion of Domitian, he went to Rome for his trial and was acquitted after he had endured a brief imprisonment (94 A.D.). The last ten years of his life were passed in Greece, where he had many disciples.

The importance of Apollonius as a religious reformer was more and more magnified, and shortly after his death statues and even temples were erected in his honor by emperors, and he was worshiped as a god. Among his prominent admirers was the talented and learned Julia Domna, wife of the emperor Severus, who requested one of her literary men, Flavius Philostratus, to write for her a biography of Apollonius and for this purpose supplied him with data, including the travel-journal of his companion, the Assyrian Damis, and a collection of his letters. On the basis of these, with large additions of legendary matter and notices of every description, the book was prepared; but it was not published till after the death of the empress (217). It bears every evidence of being a historical novel, and its miraculous details are not deserving of analysis; but non-Christians ever since have pretended to find in Apollonius a pagan Christ, and in the stories told about him, counterparts of those related of Christ and his apostles.

The earliest person named who made this use of Philostratus's novel is Hierocles, governor of Bithynia during the Diocletian persecution (303), who wrote a work against the Christians in which he instituted a comparison between Apollonius and Christ. This stirred up the church historian Eusebius, to write a refutation, in which he shows how unreliable as a source the romance of Philostratus is. The deist Charles Blount (see DEISM) and Voltaire revived this use of Philostratus in the interest of their paganism, while in the nineteenth century Ferdinand Christian Baur called attention afresh to Philostratus's work and elaborated the thesis that Philostratus had purposely modeled his narrative on that of the Gospels. Edward Zeller followed him in this advocacy, the Frenchman Albert Réville also. But there is no evidence that Philostratus had any knowledge of the Gospels and the Acts, and the life of the Apostle Paul is a much closer parallel to Apollonius than that of Christ, who was no peripatetic philosopher.

BIBLIOGRAPHY: Sources: C. L. Kayser's ed. of *Fl. Philostrati Opera*, 2 vols., Leipsic, 1871, contains also *Apollonii Epistolæ* and *Eusebius adv. Hieroclem;* the latter is also in *MPG*, iv.; Eng. transl. of first two books of Philostratus, by C. Blount, London, 1680, and of all by E. Berwick, 1809; French transl. by J. F. Salvemini de Castillon, Paris, 1774, and by A. Chassang, 1862, with transl. of the letters of Apollonius; Germ. transl. by E. Baltzer. Consult also: E. Müller, *War Apollonius . ein Weiser, . Betrüger, . Schwärmer und Fanatiker*, Breslau, 1861; A. Réville, *Apollonius of Tyana*, London, 1866; J. H. Newman, in *Historical Sketches*, ii., London, 1872 (noteworthy); O. de B. Priaulx, *Indian Travels of Apollonius*, ib. 1873; F. C. Baur, *Apollonius von Tyana und Christus*, in *Drei Abhandlungen*, Leipsic, 1876; C. Mönckeberg, *Apollonius von Tyana*, Hamburg, 1877; C. H. Pettersch, *Apollonius von Tyana*, Reichenberg, 1879; C. L. Nielsen, *Apollonius fra Tyana*, Copenhagen, 1879; J. Jessen, *Apollonius . und sein Biograph*, Hamburg, 1885; D. M. Tredwell, *Sketch of the Life of Apollonius of Tyana*, New York, 1886; K. S. Guthrie, *The Gospel of Apollonius of Tyana*, Medford, 1900; G. R. S. Mead, *Apollonius of Tyana*, London, 1901; T. Whittaker, in *The Monist*, xiii. (1903) 161–217.

APOLLOS, a-pel′es (probably a contraction from Apollonius): A man eminent in New Testament history. His special gifts in presenting Christian doctrine made him an important person in the congregation at Corinth, and his name came to be attached to a faction there (I Cor. i. 12), but there is no indication that he favored or approved an overestimation of his person. Nor can it be said that Paul objected to his work of presenting the way of salvation; on the contrary he thinks Apollos a valuable helper in carrying on his work in the important Corinthian congregation (I Cor. iii. 6, iv. 6, xvi. 12). In harmony with Paul's notices are the statements of the Acts of the Apostles (xviii. 24–28) that Apollos was a highly educated Alexandrian Jew, who came to Ephesus (probably in 54 A.D.), was instructed in the gospel there by Aquila and Priscilla, and afterward settled in Achaia, where, by the grace of God he showed himself useful to the Church. The rest of this notice to the effect that he came to Ephesus as a disciple of the Lord and preached Jesus in the synagogues, when he knew only of John's baptism, is odd.

It is difficult to get a correct idea of his religious standpoint; but it probably was that of the so-called disciples of John, of whom mention is made in Acts xix. 1–7. Taken all in all, it may be said that Apollos was a zealous missionary, who, while confessing Jesus, did not have the full New Testament revelation, and stood in danger of becoming antagonistic to the apostolic message to all the world; he became, however, an adherent of the Pauline doctrine, and the author of the Acts of the Apostles thought this fact of sufficient importance to be included in his history. In the Epistle to Titus (iii. 13) Apollos is mentioned, with Zenas, as bearer of the letter to Crete. The Epistle to the Hebrews (q.v.) has often been ascribed to Apollos, beginning with Luther, and he has been suggested as the author of the fourth Gospel ([Tobler], *Die Evangelienfrage*, Zurich, 1858). (K. SCHMIDT.)

BIBLIOGRAPHY: E. Renan, *St. Paul*, pp. 240, 372 sqq., Paris, 1869; Conybeare and Howson, *St. Paul*, ii., chap. xiv., London, 1888; C. von Weizsäcker, *The Apostolic Age*, 2 vols., London, 1894-95; A. C. McGiffert, *Hist. of Christianity in the Apostolic Age*, New York, 1897; W. Baldensperger, *Der Prolog des vierten Evangeliums*, pp. 93-99, Freiburg, 1898.

APOLOGETICS.

Significance of the Term (§ 1).
Place Among the Theological Disciplines (§ 2).
Source of Divergent Views (§ 3).
The True Task of Apologetics (§ 4).
Division of Apologetics (§ 5).
The Conception of Theology as a Science (§ 6).
The Five Subdivisions of Apologetics (§ 7).
The Value of Apologetics (§ 8).
Relation of Apologetics to Christian Faith (§ 9).
The Earliest Apologetics (§ 10).
The Later Apologetics (§ 11).

1. Significance of the Term.

Since Planck (1794) and Schleiermacher (1811), "apologetics" has been the accepted name of one of the theological disciplines or departments of theological science. The term is derived from the Greek *apologeisthai*, which embodies as its central notion the idea of "defense." In its present application, however, it has somewhat shifted its meaning, and we speak accordingly of apologetics and apologies in contrast with each other. The relation between these two is not that of theory and practise (so, e.g., Düsterdieck), nor yet that of genus and species (so, e.g., Kübel). That is to say, apologetics is not a formal science in which the principles exemplified in apologies are investigated, as the principles of sermonizing are investigated in homiletics. Nor is it merely the sum of all existing or all possible apologies, or their quintessence, or their scientific exhibition, as dogmatics is the scientific statement of dogmas. Apologies are defenses of Christianity, in its entirety, in its essence, or in some one or other of its elements or presuppositions, as against either all assailants, actual or conceivable, or some particular form or instance of attack; though, of course, as good defenses they may rise above mere defenses and become vindications. Apologetics undertakes not the defense, not even the vindication, but the establishment, not, strictly speaking, of Christianity, but rather of that knowledge of God which Christianity professes to embody and seeks to make efficient in the world, and which it is the business of theology scientifically to explicate. It may, of course, enter into defense and vindication when in the prosecution of its task it meets with opposing points of view and requires to establish its own standpoint or conclusions. Apologies may, therefore, be embraced in apologetics, and form ancillary portions of its structure, as they may also do in the case of every other theological discipline. It is, moreover, inevitable that this or that element or aspect of apologetics will be more or less emphasized and cultivated, as the need of it is from time to time more or less felt. But apologetics does not derive its contents or take its form or borrow its value from the prevailing opposition; but preserves through all varying circumstances its essential character as a positive and constructive science which has to do with opposition only—like any other constructive science—as the refutation of opposing views becomes from time to time incident to construction. So little is defense or vindication of the essence of apologetics that there would be the same reason for its existence and the same necessity for its work, were there no opposition in the world to be encountered and no contradiction to be overcome. It finds its deepest ground, in other words, not in the accidents which accompany the efforts of true religion to plant, sustain, and propagate itself in this world; not even in that most pervasive and most portentous of all these accidents, the accident of sin; but in the fundamental needs of the human spirit. If it is incumbent on the believer to be able to give a reason for the faith that is in him, it is impossible for him to be a believer without a reason for the faith that is in him; and it is the task of apologetics to bring this reason clearly out in his consciousness, and make its validity plain. It is, in other words, the function of apologetics to investigate, explicate, and establish the grounds on which a theology—a science, or systematized knowledge of God—is possible; and on the basis of which every science which has God for its object must rest, if it be a true science with claims to a place within the circle of the sciences. It necessarily takes its place, therefore, at the head of the departments of theological science and finds its task in the establishment of the validity of that knowledge of God which forms the subject-matter of these departments; that we may then proceed through the succeeding departments of exegetical, historical, systematic, and practical theology, to explicate, appreciate, systematize, and propagate it in the world.

It must be admitted that considerable confusion has reigned with respect to the conception and function of apologetics, and its place among the theological disciplines. Nearly every writer has a definition of his own, and describes the task of the discipline in a fashion more or less peculiar to himself; and there is scarcely a corner in the theological encyclopedia into which it has not been thrust. Planck gave it a place among the exegetical disciplines; others contend that its essence is historical; most wish to assign it either to systematic or practical theology. Nösselt denies it all right of existence; Palmer confesses inability to classify it; Räbiger casts it formally out of the encyclopedia, but reintroduces it under the different name of "theory of religion." Tholuck proposed that it should be apportioned through the several departments; and Cave actually distributes its material through three separate departments.

2. Place Among the Theological Disciplines.

Much of this confusion is due to a persistent confusion of apologetics with apologies. If apologetics is the theory of apology, and its function is to teach men how to defend Christianity, its place is, of course, alongside of homiletics, catechetics, and poimenics in practical theology. If it is simply, by way of eminence, the apology of Christianity, the systematically organized vindication of Christianity in all its elements and details, against all opposition—or in its essential core against the only destructive opposition—it of course presupposes the complete development of Christianity through the exegetical, historical, and systematic disciplines, and must take its place either as the culminating department of systematic theology, or as the intellectualistic side of practical theology, or as an independent discipline between the two. In this case it can be only artificially separated from polemic theology and other similar disciplines—if the analysis is pushed so far as to create these, as is done by F. Duilhé de Saint-Projet who distinguishes between apologetical, controversial, and polemic theology, directed respectively against unbelievers, heretics, and fellow believers, and by A. Kuyper who distinguishes between polemics, elenchtics, and apologetics, opposing respectively heterodoxy, paganism, and false philosophy. It will not be strange, then, if, though separated from these kindred disciplines it, or some of it, should be again united with them, or some of them, to form a larger whole to which is given the same encyclopedic position. This is done for example by Kuyper who joins polemics, elenchtics, and apologetics together to form his "antithetic dogmatological" group of disciplines; and by F. L. Patton who, after having distributed the material of apologetics into the two separate disciplines of rational or philosophical theology, to which as a thetic discipline a place is given at the outset of the system, and apologetics, joins the latter with polemics to constitute the antithetical disciplines, while systematic theology succeeds both as part of the synthetic disciplines.

Much of the diversity in question is due also, however, to varying views of the thing which apologetics undertakes to establish; whether it be, for example, the truth of the Christian religion, or the validity of that knowledge of God which theology presents in systematized form. And more of it still is due to profoundly differing conceptions of the nature and subject-matter of that "theology," a department of which apologetics is. If we think of apologetics as undertaking the defense or the vindication or even the justification of the "Christian religion," that is one thing; if we think of it as undertaking the establishment of the validity of that knowledge of God, which "theology" systematizes, that may be a very different thing. And even if agreement exists upon the latter conception, there remain the deeply cutting divergences which beset the definition of "theology" itself. Shall it be defined as the "science of faith"? or as the "science of religion"? or as the "science of the Christian religion"? or as the "science of God"? In other words, shall it be regarded as a branch of psychology, or as a branch of history, or as a branch of science? Manifestly those who differ thus widely as to what theology is, can not be expected to agree as to the nature and function of any one of its disciplines. If "theology" is the science of faith or of religion, its subject-matter is the subjective experiences of the human heart; and the function of apologetics is to inquire whether these subjective experiences have any objective validity. Of course, therefore, it follows upon the systematic elucidation of these subjective experiences and constitutes the culminating discipline of "theology." Similarly, if "theology" is the science of the Christian religion, it investigates the purely historical question of what those who are called Christians believe; and of course the function of apologetics is to follow this investigation with an inquiry whether Christians are justified in believing these things. But if theology is the science of God, it deals not with a mass of subjective experiences, nor with a section of the history of thought, but with a body of objective facts; and it is absurd to say that these facts must be assumed and developed unto their utmost implications before we stop to ask whether they are facts. So soon as it is agreed that theology is a scientific discipline and has as its subject-matter the knowledge of God, we must recognize that it must begin by establishing the reality as objective facts of the data upon which it is based. One may indeed call the department of theology to which this task is committed by any name which appears to him appropriate: it may be called "general theology," or "fundamental theology," or "principial theology," or "philosophical theology," or "rational theology," or "natural theology," or any other of the innumerable names which have been used to describe it. Apologetics is the name which most naturally suggests itself, and it is the name which, with more or less accuracy of view as to the nature and compass of the discipline, has been consecrated to this purpose by a large number of writers from Schleiermacher down (e.g., Pelt, Twesten, Baumstark, Swetz, Ottiger, Knoll, Maissoneuve). It powerfully commends itself as plainly indicating the nature of the discipline, while equally applicable to it whatever may be the scope of the theology which it undertakes to plant on a secure basis. Whether this theology recognizes no other knowledge of God than that given in the constitution and course of nature, or derives its data from the full revelation of God as documented in the Christian scriptures, apologetics offers itself with equal readiness to designate the discipline by which the validity of the knowledge of God set forth is established. It need imply no more than natural theology requires for its basis; when the theology which it serves is, however, the complete theology of the Christian revelation, it guards its unity and protects from the fatally dualistic conception which sets natural and revealed theology over against each other as separable entities, each with its own separate presuppositions requiring establishment—by which apologetics would be split into two quite diverse disciplines, given very different places in the theological encyclopedia.

3. Source of Divergent Views.

It will already have appeared how far apologetics may be defined, in accordance with a very prevalent custom (e.g., Sack, Lechler, Ebrard, Kübel, Lemme) as "the science which establishes the truth of Christianity as the absolute religion." Apologetics certainly does establish the truth of Christianity as the absolute religion. But the question of importance here is how it does this.

4. The True Task of Apologetics.

It certainly is not the business of apologetics to take up each tenet of Christianity in turn and seek to establish its truth by a direct appeal to reason. Any attempt to do this, no matter on what philosophical basis the work of demonstration be begun or by what methods it be pursued, would transfer us at once into the atmosphere and betray us into the devious devices of the old vulgar rationalism, the primary fault of which was that it asked for a direct rational demonstration of the truth of each Christian teaching in turn. The business of apologetics is to establish the truth of Christianity as the absolute religion directly only as a whole, and in its details only indirectly. That is to say, we are not to begin by developing Christianity into all its details, and only after this task has been performed, tardily ask whether there is any truth in all this. We are to begin by establishing the truth of Christianity as a whole, and only then proceed to explicate it into its details, each of which, if soundly explicated, has its truth guaranteed by its place as a detail in an entity already established in its entirety. Thus we are delivered from what is perhaps the most distracting question which has vexed the whole history of the discipline. In establishing the truth of Christianity, it has been perennially asked, are we to deal with all its details (e.g., H. B. Smith), or merely with the essence of Christianity (e.g., Kübel). The true answer is, neither. Apologetics does not presuppose either the development of Christianity into its details, or the extraction from it of its essence. The details of Christianity are all contained in Christianity: the minimum of Christianity is just Christianity itself. What apologetics undertakes to establish is just this Christianity itself—including all its "details" and involving its "essence"—in its unexplicated and uncompressed entirety, as the absolute religion. It has for its object the laying of the foundations on which the temple of theology is built, and by which the whole structure of theology is determined. It is the department of theology which establishes the constitutive and regulative principles of theology as a science; and in establishing these it establishes all the details which are derived from them by the succeeding departments, in their sound explication and systematization. Thus it establishes the whole, though it establishes the whole in the mass, so to speak, and not in its details, but yet in its entirety and not in some single element deemed by us its core, its essence, or its minimum expression.

5. Division of Apologetics.

The subject-matter of apologetics being determined, its distribution into its parts becomes very much a matter of course. Having defined apologetics as the proof of the truth of the Christian religion, many writers naturally confine it to what is commonly known somewhat loosely as the "evidences of Christianity." Others, defining it as "fundamental theology," equally naturally confine it to the primary principles of religion in general. Others more justly combine the two conceptions and thus obtain at least two main divisions. Thus Hermann Schultz makes it prove "the right of the religious conception of the world, as over against the tendencies to the denial of religion, and the right of Christianity as the absolutely perfect manifestation of religion, as over against the opponents of its permanent significance." He then divides it into two great sections with a third interposed between them: the first, "the apology of the religious conception of the world;" the last, "the apology of Christianity;" while between the two stands "the philosophy of religion, religion in its historical manifestation." Somewhat less satisfactorily, because with a less firm hold upon the idea of the discipline, Henry B. Smith, viewing apologetics as "historico-philosophical dogmatics," charged with the defense of "the whole contents and substance of the Christian faith," divided the material to much the same effect into what he calls fundamental, historical, and philosophical apologetics. The first of these undertakes to demonstrate the being and nature of God; the second, the divine origin and authority of Christianity; and the third, somewhat lamely as a conclusion to so high an argument, the superiority of Christianity to all other systems. Quite similarly Francis R. Beattie divided into (1) fundamental or philosophical apologetics, which deals with the problem of God and religion; (2) Christian or historical apologetics, which deals with the problem of revelation and the Scriptures; and (3) applied or practical apologetics, which deals with the practical efficiency of Christianity in the world. The fundamental truth of these schematizations lies in the perception that the subject-matter of apologetics embraces the two great facts of God and Christianity. There is some failure in unity of conception, however, arising apparently from a deficient grasp of the peculiarity of apologetics as a department of theological science, and a consequent inability to permit it as such to determine its own contents and the natural order of its constituent parts.

6. The Conception of Theology as a Science.

If theology be a science at all, there is involved in that fact, as in the case of all other sciences, at least these three things: the reality of its subject-matter, the capacity of the human mind to receive into itself and rationally to reflect this subject-matter, the existence of media of communication between the subject-matter and the percipient and understanding mind. There could be no psychology were there not a mind to be investigated, a mind to investigate, and a self-consciousness by means of which the mind as an object can be brought under the inspection of the mind as subject. There could be no astronomy were there no heavenly bodies to be investigated, no mind capable of comprehending the laws of their existence and movements, or no means of observing their structure and motion. Similarly there can be no theology, conceived according to its very name as the science of God, unless there is a God to form its subject-matter, a capacity in the human mind to apprehend and so far to comprehend God, and some media by which God is made known to man. That a theology, as the science of God, may exist, therefore, it must begin by establishing the existence of God, the capacity of the human mind to know him, and the accessibility of knowledge concerning him. In other words, the very idea of theology as the science of God gives these three great topics which must be dealt with in its fundamental department, by which the foundations for the whole structure are laid,—God, religion, revelation. With these three facts established, a theology as the science of God becomes possible; with them, therefore, an apologetic might be complete. But that, only provided that in these three topics all the underlying presuppositions of the science of God actually built up in our theology are established; for example, provided that all the accessible sources and means of knowing God are exhausted. No science can arbitrarily limit the data lying within its sphere to which it will attend. On pain of ceasing to be the science it professes to be, it must exhaust the means of information open to it, and reduce to a unitary system the entire body of knowledge in its sphere. No science can represent itself as astronomy, for example, which arbitrarily confines itself to the information concerning the heavenly bodies obtainable by the unaided eye, or which discards, without sound ground duly adduced, the aid of, say, the spectroscope. In the presence of Christianity in the world making claim to present a revelation of God adapted to the condition and needs of sinners, and documented in Scriptures, theology can not proceed a step until it has examined this claim; and if the claim be substantiated, this substantiation must form a part of the fundamental department of theology in which are laid the foundations for the systematization of the knowledge of God. In that case, two new topics are added to the subject-matter with which apologetics must constructively deal, Christianity—and the Bible. It thus lies in the very nature of apologetics as the fundamental department of theology, conceived as the science of God, that it should find its task in establishing the existence of a God who is capable of being known by man and who has made himself known, not only in nature but in revelations of his grace to lost sinners, documented in the Christian Scriptures. When apologetics has placed these great facts in our hands—God, religion, revelation, Christianity, the Bible—and not till then are we prepared to go on and explicate the knowledge of God thus brought to us, trace the history of its workings in the world, systematize it, and propagate it in the world.

The primary subdivisions of apologetics are therefore five, unless for convenience of treatment it is preferred to sink the third into its most closely related fellow. (1) The first, which may perhaps be called philosophical apologetics, undertakes the establishment of the being of God, as a personal spirit, the Creator, preserver, and governor of all things. To it belongs the great problem of theism, with the involved discussion of the antitheistic theories. (2) The second, which may perhaps be called psychological apologetics, undertakes the establishment of the religious nature of man and the validity of his religious sense. It involves the discussion alike of the psychology, the philosophy, and the phenomenology of religion, and therefore includes what is loosely called "comparative religion" or the "history of religions." (3) To the third falls the establishment of the reality of the supernatural factor in history, with the involved determination of the actual relations in which God stands to his world, and the method of his government of his rational creatures, and especially his mode of making himself known to them. It issues in the establishment of the fact of revelation as the condition of all knowledge of God, who as a personal Spirit can be known only so far as he expresses himself; so that theology differs from all other sciences in that in it the object is not at the disposal of the subject, but vice versa. (4) The fourth, which may be called historical apologetics, undertakes to establish the divine origin of Christianity as the religion of revelation in the special sense of that word. It discusses all the topics which naturally fall under the popular caption of the "evidences of Christianity." (5) The fifth, which may be called bibliological apologetics, undertakes to establish the trustworthiness of the Christian Scriptures as the documentation of the revelation of God for the redemption of sinners. It is engaged especially with such topics as the divine origin of the Scriptures; the methods of the divine operation in their origination; their place in the series of redemptive acts of God, and in the process of revelation; the nature, mode, and effect of inspiration; and the like.

7. The Five Subdivisions of Apologetics.

The estimate which is put upon apologetics by scholars naturally varies with the conception which is entertained of its nature and function. In the wake of the subjectivism introduced by Schleiermacher, it has become very common to speak of such an apologetic as has just been outlined with no little scorn. It is an evil inheritance, we are told, from the old *supranaturalismus vulgaris*, which "took its standpoint not in the Scriptures but above the Scriptures, and imagined it could, with formal conceptions, develop a "ground for the divine authority of Christianity" (Heubner), and therefore offered proofs for the divine origin of Christianity, the necessity of revelation, and the credibility of the Scriptures" (Lemme). To recognize that we can take our standpoint in the Scriptures only after we have Scriptures, authenticated as such, to take our standpoint in, is, it seems, an outworn prejudice. The subjective experience of faith is conceived to be the ultimate fact; and the only legitimate apologetic, just the self-justification of this faith itself. For faith, it seems, after Kant, can no longer be looked upon as a matter of reasoning and does not rest on rational grounds, but is an affair of the heart, and manifests itself most powerfully when it has no reason out of itself (Brunetière). If repetition had probative force, it would long ago have been established that faith, religion, theology, lie wholly outside of the realm of reason, proof, and demonstration.

8. The Value of Apologetics.

It is, however, from the point of view of rationalism and mysticism that the value of apologetics is most decried. Wherever rationalistic preconceptions have penetrated, there, of course, the validity of the apologetic proofs has been in more or less of their extent questioned. Wherever mystical sentiment has seeped in, there the validity of apologetics has been with more or less emphasis doubted. At the present moment, the rationalistic tendency is most active, perhaps, in the form given it by Albrecht Ritschl. In this form it strikes at the very roots of apologetics, by the distinction it erects between theoretical and religious knowledge. Religious knowledge is not the knowledge of fact, but a perception of utility; and therefore positive religion, while it may be historically conditioned, has no theoretical basis, and is accordingly not the object of rational proof. In significant parallelism with this, the mystical tendency is manifesting itself at the present day most distinctly in a wide-spread inclination to set aside apologetics in favor of the "witness of the Spirit." The convictions of the Christian man, we are told, are not the product of reason addressed to the intellect, but the immediate creation of the Holy Spirit in the heart. Therefore, it is intimated, we may do very well without these reasons, if indeed they are not positively noxious, because tending to substitute a barren intellectualism for a vital faith. It seems to be forgotten that though faith be a moral act and the gift of God, it is yet formally conviction passing into confidence; and that all forms of convictions must rest on evidence as their ground, and it is not faith but reason which investigates the nature and validity of this ground. "He who believes," says Thomas Aquinas, in words which have become current as an axiom, "would not believe unless he saw that what he believes is worthy of belief." Though faith is the gift of God, it does not in the least follow that the faith which God gives is an irrational faith, that is, a faith without cognizable ground in right reason. We believe in Christ because it is rational to believe in him, not even though it be irrational. Of course mere reasoning can not make a Christian; but that is not because faith is not the result of evidence, but because a dead soul can not respond to evidence. The action of the Holy Spirit in giving faith is not apart from evidence, but along with evidence; and in the first instance consists in preparing the soul for the reception of the evidence.

This is not to argue that it is by apologetics that men are made Christians, but that apologetics supplies to Christian men the systematically organized basis on which the faith of Christian men must rest. All that apologetics explicates in the forms of systematic proof is implicit in every act of Christian faith. Whenever a sinner accepts Jesus Christ as his savior, there is

9. Relation of Apologetics to Christian Faith.

implicated in that act a living conviction that there is a God, knowable to man, who has made himself known in a revelation of himself for redemption in Jesus Christ, as is set down in the Scriptures. It is not necessary for his act of faith that all the grounds of this conviction should be drawn into full consciousness and given the explicit assent of his understanding, though it is necessary for his faith that sufficient ground for his conviction be actively present and working in his spirit. But it is necessary for the vindication of his faith to reason in the form of scientific judgment, that the grounds on which it rests be explicated and established. Theology as a science, though it includes in its culminating discipline, that of practical theology, an exposition of how that knowledge of God with which it deals objectively may best be made the subjective possession of man, is not itself the instrument of propaganda; what it undertakes to do is systematically to set forth this knowledge of God as the object of rational contemplation. And as it has to set it forth as knowledge, it must of course begin by establishing its right to rank as such. Did it not do so, the whole of its work would hang in the air, and theology would present the odd spectacle among the sciences of claiming a place among a series of systems of knowledge for an elaboration of pure assumptions.

Seeing that it thus supplies an insistent need of the human spirit, the world has, of course, never been without its apologetics. Whenever men have thought at all they have thought about God and the supernatural order; and whenever they have thought of God and the supernatural order, there has been present to their minds a variety of more or less solid reasons for believing in their reality. The enucleation of these reasons into a systematically organized body of proofs waited of course upon advancing culture. But

10. The Earliest Apologetics.

the advent of apologetics did not wait for the advent of Christianity; nor are traces of this department of thought discoverable only in the regions lit up by special revelation. The philosophical systems of antiquity, especially those which derive from Plato, are far from empty of apologetical elements; and when in the later stages of its development, classical philosophy became peculiarly religious, express apologetical material became almost predominant. With the coming of Christianity into the world, however, as the contents of the theology to be stated became richer, so the efforts to substantiate it became more fertile in apologetical elements. We must not confuse the apologies of the early Christian ages with formal apologetics. Like the sermons of the day, they contributed to apologetics without being it. The apologetic material developed by what one may call the more philosophical of the apologists (Aristides, Athenagoras, Tatian, Theophilus, Hermias, Tertullian) was already considerable; it was largely supplemented by the theological labors of their successors. In the first instance Christianity, plunged into a polytheistic environment and called upon to contend with systems of thought grounded in pantheistic or dualistic assumptions, required to establish its theistic standpoint; and as over against the bitterness of the Jews and the mockery of the heathen (e.g., Tacitus, Fronto, Crescens, Lucian), to evince its own divine origin as a gift of grace to sinful man. Along with Tertullian, the great Alexandrians, Clement and Origen, are the richest depositaries of the apologetic thought of the first period. The greatest apologists of the patristic age were, however, Eusebius of Cæsarea and Augustine. The former was the most learned and the latter the most profound of all the defenders of Christianity among the Fathers. And Augustine, in particular, not merely in his "City of God" but in his controversial writings, accumulated a vast mass of apologetical material which is far from having lost its significance even yet.

It was not, however, until the scholastic age that apologetics came to its rights as a constructive science. The whole theological activity of the Middle Ages was so far ancillary to apologetics, that its primary effort was the justification of faith to reason. It was not only rich in apologists (Agobard, Abelard, Raymund Martini), but every theologian was in a sense an apologist. Anselm at its beginning, Aquinas at its culmina-

11. The Later Apologetics.

tion, are types of the whole series; types in which all its excellencies are summed up. The Renaissance with its repristination of heathenism, naturally called out a series of new apologists (Savonarola, Marsilius Ficinus, Ludovicus Vives) but the Reformation forced polemics into the foreground and drove apologetics out of sight, although, of course, the great theologians of the Reformation era brought their rich contribution to the accumulating apologetical material. When, in the exhaustion of the seventeenth century, irreligion began to spread among the people and indifferentism ripening into naturalism among the leaders of thought, the stream of apologetical thought was once more started flowing, to swell into a great flood as the prevalent unbelief intensified and spread. With a forerunner in Philippe de Mornay (1581), Hugo Grotius (1627) became the typical apologist of the earlier portion of this period, while its middle portion was illuminated by the genius of Pascal

(d. 1662) and the unexampled richness of apologetical labor in its later years culminated in Butler's great *Analogy* (1736) and Paley's plain but powerful argumentation. As the assault against Christianity shifted its basis from the English deism of the early half of the eighteenth century through the German rationalism of its later half, the idealism which dominated the first half of the nineteenth century, and thence to the materialism of its later years, period after period was marked in the history of apology, and the particular elements of apologetics which were especially cultivated changed with the changing thought. But no epoch was marked in the history of apologetics itself, until under the guidance of Schleiermacher's attempt to trace the organism of the departments of theology, K. H. Sack essayed to set forth a scientifically organized "Christian Apologetics" (Hamburg, 1829; 2d ed., 1841). Since then an unbroken series of scientific systems of apologetics has flowed from the press. These differ from one another in almost every conceivable way; in their conception of the nature, task, compass, and encyclopedic place of the science; in their methods of dealing with its material; in their conception of Christianity itself; and of religion and of God and of the nature of the evidence on which belief in one or the other must rest. But they agree in the fundamental point that apologetics is conceived by all alike as a special department of theological science, capable of and demanding separate treatment. In this sense apologetics has come at last, in the last two-thirds of the nineteenth century, to its rights. The significant names in its development are such as, perhaps, among the Germans, Sack, Steudel, Delitzsch, Ebrard, Baumstark, Tölle, Kratz, Kübel, Steude, Franck, Kaftan, Vogel, Schultz, Kähler; to whom may be added such Romanists as Drey, Dieringer, Staudenmeyer, Hettinger, Schanz, and such English-speaking writers as Hetherington, H. B. Smith, Bruce, Rishell, and Beattie.

BENJAMIN B. WARFIELD.

BIBLIOGRAPHY: Lists of literature will be found in F. R. Beattie's *Apologetics*, Richmond, 1903; in A. Cave, *Introduction to Theology*, Edinburgh, 1896; in G. R. Crooks and J. F. Hurst, *Theological Encyclopedia and Theology*, pp. 434–437, New York, 1894; in P. Schaff, *Theological Propædeutic*, ib. 1893. Consult F. L. Patton, in *Princeton Theological Review*, ii. 110 sqq.; *Presbyterian and Reformed Review*, vii. (1896), pp. 243 sqq. On the history of apologetics and apologetic method: H. E. Tzschirmer, *Geschichte der Apologetik*, Leipsic, 1805; G. H. van Senden, *Geschichte der Apologetik*, 2 vols., Stuttgart, 1846; K. Werner, *Geschichte der apologetischen und polemischen Literatur*, 5 vols., Schaffhausen, 1861–67 (Roman Catholic); W Haan, *Geschichte der Vertheidigung des Christentums*, Frankenberg, 1882 (popular). For early Christian apologies consult *ANF* and *NPNF*, Am. ed., New York, 1884–1900; for discussions of these, F. Watson, *The Ante-Nicene Apologies, their Character and Value*, Cambridge, 1870 (Hulsean essay); W. J. Bolton, *Evidences of Christianity as exhibited in the . . Apologists down to Augustine*, London, 1853; F. R. Wynne, *The Literature of the Second Century*, London, 1891 (popular but scholarly); A. Seitz, *Apologie des Christentums bei den Griechen des IV. und V. Jahrhunderten*, Würzburg, 1895. On special phases in the history of apologetics: L. Noack, *Die Freidenker in der Religion, oder die Repräsentanten der religiösen Aufklärung in England, Frankreich und Deutschland*, 3 vols., Bern, 1853–55; A. S. Farrar, *Critical History of Free Thought*, London, 1863; C. R. Hagenbach, *German Rationalism in its Rise, Progress, and Decline*, Edinburgh, 1865; A. Viguié, *Histoire de l'apologétique dans l'église reformée française*, Geneva, 1858; H. B. Smith, *Apologetics*, New York, 1882 (appendix contains sketches of German apologetic works); J. F. Hurst, *History of Rationalism*, ib. 1902; A. H. Huizinga, *Some Recent Phases of Evidences of Christianity*, in *Presbyterian and Reformed Review*, vii. (1896) 34 sqq. Apologetical literature: F. R. Beattie, *Apologetics, or the Rational Vindication of Christianity*, i., Richmond, 1903 (to be completed in 3 vols.); W. M. Hetherington, *Apologetics of the Christian Faith*, Edinburgh, 1867; J. H. A. Ebrard, *Apologetik*, Gütersloh, 1880 (Eng. transl., *Apologetics, or the Scientific Vindication of Christianity*, 2 vols., Edinburgh, 1886–87); A. Mair, *Studies in the Christian Evidences*, Edinburgh, 1883; G. F. Wright, *Logic of Christian Evidences*, Andover, 1884; F. H. R. Frank, *System der christlichen Gewissheit*, Erlangen, 1884, Eng. transl., *Christian Certainty*, Edinburgh, 1886; P. Schanz, *Apologie des Christentums*, 3 vols., Freiburg, 1887–88, Eng. transl., *Christian Apology*, New York, 1894 (Roman Catholic); L. F. Stearns, *The Evidence of Christian Experience*, New York, 1891 (the best book on the subject); A. B. Bruce, *Apologetics, or Christianity defensively stated*, Edinburgh, 1892; H. Wace, *Students' Manual of the Evidences of Christianity*, London, 1892; J. Kaftan, *Wahrheit der christlichen Religion*, Bielefeld, 1888, Eng. transl., 2 vols., Edinburgh, 1894; C. W. Rishell, *Foundations of the Christian Faith*, New York, 1899; W. Devivier, *Cours d'apologétique chrétienne*, Paris, 1889, Eng. transl., *Christian apologetics*, 2 vols., New York, 1903; A. Harnack, *What is Christianity?* London, 1901; J. T. Bergen, *Evidences of Christianity*, Holland, Mich., 1902; A. M. Randolph, *Reason, Faith, and Authority in Christianity*, New York, 1903; the Boyle and Bampton lecture series deal exclusively with subjects in apologetics; see also under AGNOSTICISM; ANTITRINITARIANISM, and ATHEISM.

APORTANUS, ap"ōr-tā'nus, **GEORG** (**Jurien, or Jürjen, van der Dare, Daere, or Dure**): Early follower of Luther in East Friesland; b. at Zwolle; d. in the autumn of 1530. He was brought up in Zwolle by the Brethren of the Common Life, and became teacher in their school. In 1518 Count Edzard of East Friesland called him to Emden to educate his sons. With the support of the count, he began to preach Luther's doctrines at Norden in 1519, was excluded from the pulpit in consequence, and then preached in the open air till the importunity of the people brought him back as chief pastor. In 1529 he held a disputation at Oldersum, presided over by the influential Ulrich of Dornum, and induced many to adopt Luther's teachings. L. SCHULZE.

APOSTASY (Gk. *Apostasia*, "Revolt"): According to the teaching of the earlier ages, apostasy might be either *apostasia perfidiæ, inobedientiæ*, or *irregularitatis* (i.e., revolt agains the faith, authority, or the rules). The two latter classes often ran into each other, and have been reduced by later theologians to two distinct though still related kinds of desertion, namely, *apostasia a monachatu* and *a clericatu*, which of course occur only in non-Protestant churches, while the *apostasia a fide* or *perfidiæ* is contemplated in Protestant church law also. *Apostasia a monachatu*, the abandonment of the monastic life, takes place when a member of a religious order leaves it and returns to the world, whether as a cleric or as a layman, without permission of the proper authority. *Apostasia a clericatu*, the abandonment of orders, is in like manner the unauthorized return to the world of a person in holy orders; the minor orders which require no irrevocable self-dedication do not come under the same head. As early as the Council of

Chalcedon (451) such offenders were excommunicated; and later ecclesiastical law maintains this position even more strongly, requiring the offender's diocesan to arrest and imprison him, if a cleric, or, if a monk, to deliver him to the authorities of his order, to be punished according to its own laws. In non-Catholic countries both classes of apostates may commonly be forgiven on condition of voluntary return to obedience; and the bishops possess various faculties for the purpose. Neither of these forms of apostasy is punished by the State.

Apostasia a fide is the deliberate denial, expressed by outward acts, of the Christian faith, whether connected or not with the adoption of a non-Christian religion. This is allied to heresy, of which, in fact, it forms a higher degree. The passages of Scripture on which the treatment of this form of apostasy is based are Heb. iii. 12, vi. 4–9, x. 16–29; II Pet. ii. 15–21; II John 9–11; Luke xii. 9. During the epoch of persecution such apostasy was of course far commoner than in later times; but the primitive Church made a distinction, calling apostates only those who had abandoned the faith of their own free will, distinguishing them from those who had yielded to violence or seduction. According to the various manners of denying Christ, they were classified as *libellatici*, *sacrificati*, *traditores*, etc. (see LAPSED). All were by the very nature of the case excommunicated, and at first some churches felt bound, in accordance with the passages cited above, to refuse absolution altogether or withhold it until the hour of death. Afterward this severity decreased, and apostates, like other excommunicated persons, were restored to communion on fitting penance. Among later enactments, the decree of Boniface VIII. (1294–1303) prescribing the same procedure for apostates to Judaism as for heretics has been of special influence not only in ecclesiastical, but in civil legislation.

Under the first Christian emperors, the Roman state considered apostasy as a civil crime, to be punished by confiscation of goods, inability to make wills or serve as a witness, and infamy. During the Middle Ages the Empire had no occasion to adopt special legislation against apostasy, but was content to adhere to the ecclesiastical view of it as a qualified heresy. Since in the countries for which the Protestant legal codes were designed apostasy to Judaism or idolatry was not looked for, they make no mention of such a crime. It is, however, in the very nature of a State Church, that it can not tolerate desertion of its communion, but must mark its sense of the evil by such means as are in its power. Nowadays, of course, the aid of the State can no longer be called in to punish such offenders. (E. FRIEDBERG.)

BIBLIOGRAPHY: G. M. Amthor, *De apostasia*, Coburg, 1833; E. Platner, *Quæstiones de jure criminum Romano*, Marburg, 1842; N. München, *Das kanonische Gerichtsverfahren und Strafrecht*, ii. 357, Cologne, 1865.

APOSTLE ("One Sent [of God]"): A name applied in the Old Testament to the chosen organs of the divine revelation (Num. xvi. 28; Isa. vi. 8; Jer. xxvi. 5). In the New Testament it is used not only in a special sense for Jesus himself, but also for John the Baptist (John i. 6) and for those whom Jesus sent forth (cf. Luke xi. 49 with Matt. xxiii. 34, 37). It would seem that the name was chosen by Jesus himself for the Twelve, since it came so early into use as a definite term for a definite body of men, and then for others who held or claimed a similar position (Acts xiv. 4, 14; II Cor. xi. 5, xii. 11; I Thess. ii. 6; Rev. ii. 2).

The Twelve.

The training of the Twelve shows that they had a future mission, which was fully opened to them by the appearance and teaching of the risen Christ (Acts i. 2–11); they are to be witnesses to him, and especially to his resurrection, before all peoples. Their number, corresponding to that of the twelve tribes, shows that they are destined primarily to work among the children of Israel, to whom, accordingly, they make their first appeal in Jerusalem. By degrees they collect around them a distinct community, in which they hold the position of appointed leaders (Acts ii. 42, iv. 35, v. 1–2, vi. 1–2), and after persecution begins to spread the Gospel throughout Palestine and its neighborhood, they remain mostly in Jerusalem, thence exercising supervision over the Church of the Circumcision (Acts viii. 14, ix. 32–43), and providing for the performance of some of their internal duties by the choice of deacons and the formation of the college of presbyters under James.

The original apostles are still occupied with the Jews when their number receives an addition; the manner of Saul's conversion shows that he is destined to a similar work, but especially among the Gentiles (Acts ix. 1–31; Gal. i. 11–24).

Paul.

This involves, despite Paul's consciousness of equal authority and independence, no breach with the earlier organization. His ministry, begun by a miracle, develops itself in perfect continuity and in unity with that of the older apostles. His very conversion and call do not take place without the intervention of a member of the existing community (Acts ix. 10–18, xxii. 12–16); only after an unsuccessful attempt to work among the Jews does he turn to the Gentiles (Acts ix. 20–31, xxii. 17–21), and even then he enters the work already founded from Jerusalem as an auxiliary of Barnabas, who is sent thence (Acts xi. 25); he is sent out only with Barnabas by the combined Jewish and Gentile community, with his attention directed first to the conversion of the Jews (Acts xiii.), and only the stubborn opposition of the synagogues causes him to decide in favor of the direct mission to the Gentiles (verse 46). He is, however, fully recognized at the Apostolic Council at Jerusalem (q.v.) by the older apostles and the representatives of Jewish Christianity as an independent apostle to the Gentiles; and no opposition from Jewish Christians in Galatia or at Corinth makes them recede from this attitude. In all his far-reaching activity as head of the Gentile Church, he never forgets the welfare and the future of his own countrymen (Rom. xi. 13–14); nor is there any division between the Gentile Church and the older apostles, to his unity with whom Paul constantly appeals in teaching his converts (I Cor. xv. 3; Eph. ii. 20, iii. 5).

The work of the Twelve was by no means confined to the Circumcision. At the end of the Pauline period Peter was still, both in person and by letters, exercising apostolic influence among the Gentiles, and after Paul's death, John took the place of leader among them.

Later Use of the Term.

Yet the special relation of the Twelve to the work among the twelve tribes is emphasized by the promise for the future in Matt. xix. 28. Though the word "apostle" is used in the New Testament in a wider sense, properly it is limited to the first and highest office in the Church, distinct from all other offices (I Cor. xii. 28; Eph. iv. 11), to be filled only by those personally chosen by the Lord; and after their death no others filled exactly the same place. [The word was used also in the early Church as a convenient term by which to refer to the epistolary literature of the New Testament (see EVANGELIARIUM). It has been employed to designate the first or the principal missionary to a people, as Columba, Augustine of Canterbury, and others. It is used also in some modern Churches as the title of high dignitaries, as among the Mormons.]

(K. SCHMIDT.)

BIBLIOGRAPHY: J. B. Lightfoot, *Galatians*, Excursus on *The Name and Office of an Apostle*, London, 1887 (opened up new views on the subject, and should be supplemented by A. Harnack in *TU*, ii. 1, pp. 93–118, Leipsic, 1884); C. Weizsäcker, *Apostolisches Zeitalter*, pp. 584–590, Tübingen, 1901, Eng. transl. of earlier ed., 2 vols., Edinburgh, 1894; J. F. A. Hort, *The Christian Ecclesia*, London, 1897 (contains important contributions); E. Haupt, *Zum Verständniss des Apostolats*, Halle, 1896; A. V. G. Allen, *Christian Institutions*, consult Index, New York, 1897; A. C. McGiffert, *Hist. of Christianity in the Apostolic Age*, New York, 1897; A. Harnack, *Mission und Ausbreitung des Christentums*, book iii., chap. 1, § 1, Berlin, 1902, Eng., transl., *Expansion of Christianity*, New York, 1904; *DB*, i. 126; *EB*, i. 264 sqq.

APOSTLES' CREED.

The Apostles' Creed or Apostolicum (i.e., *apostolicum symbolum*) is the briefest of the so-called ecumenical creeds (see SYMBOLICS). With the Nicæno-Constantinopolitan and Athanasian creeds, for more than five centuries preceding the Protestant Reformation it was in use in the West and enjoyed especial authority (cf. E. Köllner, *Symbolik*, Hamburg, 1857, p. 5). The Eastern Church has never traced any symbol to the apostles, or designated any as apostolic in the strict sense of the word; and here and there in the West the Nicæno-Constantinopolitan creed has been called apostolic (cf. Caspari, i. 242, note 45; ii. 115, note 88; iii. 12, note 22). The three chief branches of the Church in the West, however, have the so called *symbolum apostolicum* in essentially the same form (*textus receptus*).

1. The First Ecumenical Creeds.

Apart from details the *textus receptus* can be traced with some degree of certainty to the beginning of the sixth or the end of the fifth century. On the other hand, it can be proved that before that time this form of the symbol was nowhere used officially in any Church whether among the *interrogationes de fide* or the *traditio* and *redditio symboli;* nor can any traces of it be discovered before the middle of the fifth century. Since it by no means came to the West from the East, and in the Western provincial Churches symbols were in use which differ greatly from the *textus receptus* of the Apostolicum, it follows that the latter could hardly have existed before the middle of the fifth century, and most likely originated about 500.

2. Present Form not Earlier than Fifth Century.

In its present form the Apostolicum is first found in a sermon of Cæsarius of Arles (d. 542; Pseudo-Augustine, 244; cf. Kattenbusch, i. 164 sqq.), with which may be compared *Sermo*, 240, 241 (texts in Hahn, §§ 47–49), and the symbol in the *Missale Gallicanum vetus* (Hahn, § 36). The immediate predecessor of Cæsarius' and, consequently, of our "apostles' creed" is most likely the symbol of Faustus of Riez of about 460 (Hahn, § 38; Kattenbusch, pp. 158 sqq.), but its reconstruction is difficult. On the other hand, the stage succeeding that of the old Roman symbol (see below) in the direction of our Apostolicum is represented by the highly interesting symbol discovered by Bratke in the Bern Codex n. 645 sæc. vii. (*SK*, lxviii., 1895, 153 sqq.), which is to be regarded as a Gallican, or rather Gallico-British, symbol belonging to the fourth century. It differs from the ancient Roman symbol only by the additions of *passus, descendit ad inferos, catholicam*, and *vitam æternam.* These four additions all tend in the direction of our Apostolicum and at the same time prove that they are the four older additions, while *conceptus, etc.*, and *communionem sanctorum* are the later ones (but *creatorem cœli et terræ* and *mortuus* are also older).

3. Earliest Appearance.

Two considerations are against a Roman origin of the Apostolicum: (1) It is not found in Rome until the Middle Ages, i.e., many centuries after its attestation by Cæsarius of Arles; (2) From the end of the fifth, or the beginning of the sixth century until the tenth the Nicæno-Constantinopolitan creed in Greek was used in Rome in the *traditio symboli*, and not the Apostolicum (Caspari, iii. 201–202, 226; ii. 114–115, note 88); a shorter symbol was also in use in Rome (see below), but it was not identical with the Apostolicum. With the spread of the *textus receptus* in western Europe during the sixth century, the legend of its wondrous origin also spread (cf. Hahn, § 46β). The fact that such a late symbol is called from the very beginning "the Apostolic," still more, that, as concerns its origin, it is traced back to a "bringing together" (Gk. *symbolē*, Lat. *collatio*)

4. Legend of its Origin.

because each of the twelve apostles in a meeting before their separation is said to have contributed a sentence to it, supposes that the history of the symbol did not commence with the end of the fifth century, but that the *textus receptus* was preceded by another form, the attributes of which were transferred to the new text and supplanted it. This supposition which the very simple contents and the brief, precise form of the symbol suggest, is also sufficiently confirmed by history. By the investigations of Ussher, and more especially by those of Caspari, it has become evident that between 250 and 460 a symbol was used in the religious service of the Roman Church, which was highly esteemed, and to which no additions were permitted; as early as the fourth century this symbol was held to be derived directly from the twelve apostles in the form in which it was used, and it was supposed to have been brought to Rome by Peter. This symbol, the older, shorter Roman (in distinction from the Apostolicum, which is sometimes called the later, longer Roman, because it owes its general authority in the West to Rome), is completely extant in a number of texts (Hahn, §§ 14–20; Caspari, ii. 48; iii. 4, 5, 28–203). In its original Greek text it runs thus:

5. Greek Text of the Roman Symbol.

Πιστεύω εἰς θεὸν πατέρα παντοκράτορα· καὶ εἰς Χριστὸν Ἰησοῦν (τὸν) υἱὸν αὐτοῦ τὸν μονογενῆ, τὸν κύριον ἡμῶν, τὸν γεννηθέντα ἐκ πνεύματος ἁγίου καὶ Μαρίας τῆς παρθένου, τὸν ἐπὶ Ποντίου Πιλάτου σταυρωθέντα καὶ ταφέντα, τῇ τρίτῃ ἡμέρᾳ ἀναστάντα ἐκ (τῶν) νεκρῶν, ἀναβάντα εἰς τοὺς οὐρανούς, καθήμενον ἐν δεξιᾷ τοῦ πατρὸς ὅθεν ἔρχεται κρῖναι ζῶντας καὶ νεκρούς· καὶ εἰς πνεῦμα ἅγιον, ἁγίαν ἐκκλησίαν, ἄφεσιν ἁμαρτιῶν, σαρκὸς ἀνάστασιν.

"I believe in God the Father Almighty and in Christ Jesus, his only-begotten Son, our Lord, born of the Holy Ghost and of Mary, the Virgin, who was crucified under Pontius Pilate and buried; on the third day he rose from the dead, ascended into heaven, sitteth on the right hand of the Father from whence he shall come to judge the quick and the dead; and in the Holy Ghost, the holy church, the remission of sins, the resurrection of the flesh."

6. Earliest Appearance of the Legend of its Origin.

The legend that this symbol was composed by the apostles, appears as early as the *Explanatio symboli* of Ambrose. The fact that the writer was aware of its being divided into twelve articles, perhaps indicates that the legend that each apostle had contributed one of them was already known. But Rufinus, who wrote later, knows only of a common composition of the Roman symbol by the apostles soon after Pentecost and before the separation. This legend he refers to a *traditio majorum.* It doubtless existed as early as the beginning of the fourth century. Both Ambrose and Rufinus testify that the wording of this symbol was most scrupulously preserved in the Roman Church. The apostolic origin of this symbol is also attested by Jerome, by the Roman bishops Celestine I. (422–431), Sixtus III. (431–440), and Leo I. (440–461), by Vigilius of Thapsus, and in the *Sacramentarium Gelasianum* (cf. Caspari, ii. 108–109, note 78, iii. 94–95; Hahn, § 46, note 163).

The fact that Augustine in his eight expositions of the creed follows the Roman symbol, leaves no doubt that in the fourth century and in the first half of the fifth the Roman Church made extensive use in the *redditio* of a symbol identical with the one mentioned above, and allowed of absolutely no additions to it. Ambrose was certainly not the only one to protest against many antiheretical additions. The epistle of Marcellus to Julius shows that between the years 330 and 340 this symbol was the official one in use in Rome; but other testimonies like Novatian's tractate *De trinitate* (Hahn, § 7) and the fragments from the epistles and writings of Bishop Dionysius of Rome point with certainty to the middle of the third century. That the shorter Roman symbol as represented in the Epistle of Marcellus and in the *Psalterium Æthelstani* (Hahn, § 16; Caspari, iii. 161–203), was already the predominant one in the Roman Church about the year 250, can by no means be doubted. But here a series of questions arises, the answers to which involve very complicated investigations and combinations: (1) How is the shorter Roman symbol related to the Western symbols which were used, between 250 and 500 (or 800), in the religious services of the provincial churches until they were superseded by the (Gallican) *Symbolum apostolicum* and the Nicæno-Constantinopolitan creed? (2) How is the shorter Roman symbol related to the longer (i.e., the Apostolicum as it is now known) from the time of Cæsarius, and why was it displaced by the latter? (3) When and where did the shorter symbol originate? (4) How is the shorter Roman symbol related to the Eastern, pre-Constantinopolitan symbols? (5) How is the shorter Roman symbol related to the different forms of the rule of faith which are known from the first three centuries? These five questions can be separated only *in abstracto.* A definite and separate answer to each of them is impossible. In what follows they will be discussed together and only a general answer attempted.

7. Age of the Roman Symbol.

In surveying the very numerous provincial and private confessions which remain from the Western Church, belonging to the period from the fourth to the sixth (seventh) century (cf. Hahn, 20–45; Caspari, ii., iii.; Kattenbusch, 59–215, 392 sqq.), six important observations may be made: (1) In the choice and arrangement of the single parts the confessions all exhibit the same fundamental type as the shorter Roman symbol. (2) The shorter a Western symbol is, the more closely it approaches the shorter Roman symbol. The shortest symbols of the provincial Churches of the West are almost, if not altogether, identical with it. (3) The later a Western symbol is, the more does it deviate by additions (hardly ever by omissions) from the shorter Roman. These additions are not of a directly polemical nature, but are to be regarded as completions and extensions held to be necessary in the interest of elucidation. Such additions by no means alter the fundamental character of the symbol, since they are not of a speculative dogmatic nature. (4) The majority of the additions which the Western symbols exhibit

8. Comparison of Western Symbols.

may be regarded as a kind of intermediate step between the shorter and longer Roman symbols. This consideration, however, is not so important as the fact that during the third and fourth centuries the great provincial Churches of the West produced different types. Four such types can be readily distinguished, the Italian, African, Gallican (including the Irish), and Spanish. As for the Gallican type, which is seen in our Apostolicum, it is characterized by such historical additions as are to be found in Oriental forms of faith or symbols (viz., " maker of heaven and earth," " suffered," " died," " descended into hell"; " catholic "). In its final form the Gallican type is not in every respect the richest or the longest of the Western symbols, but it is so as to its historical contents. In this important respect the final form of the Gallican type has completely preserved the distinguishing features of the old Roman symbol. It exhibits the same brief and severe style, and, nevertheless, also preserves all the significant historical features which became attached to the *Symbolum Romanum* in the course of its history. The Gallican *Apostolicum* also exhibits the same classical elaboration and ecumenical tendency as its Roman copy. (5) The less any Church was influenced by the Roman, the more did its symbol differ from the shorter Roman. The symbols of the Gallican Church differ relatively much from it. (6) In reducing all Western symbols to one archetype, without regard to the differences, the shorter Roman symbol is obtained without difficulty. From these observations it may be inferred with certainty (*a*) that the shorter Roman symbol was the source of all Western confessions of faith; (*b*) that the longer Roman symbol practically proceeded from the other, though not at Rome, and as a result received also the same attributes, which originally belonged to the shorter symbol.

The supposition is also justified that the shorter Roman symbol must have already existed before the middle of the third century, otherwise the facts that all Western Churches originally used this very symbol, and that, e.g., the African Church had already developed before the year 250 its special type on the basis of the *Symbolum vetus Romanum* can not be explained (cf. Cyprian in Hahn, §§ 28, 29). The Roman symbol must therefore have originated at least about the year 300; and this can be proved from the writings of Tertullian, as well as from a comparison of the shorter Roman symbol with the Eastern symbols, which are rich in additions, introductions, dogmatic remarks, etc., besides omissions. The Nicæno-Constantinopolitan creed made an end to this fluctuating state of the confession, and from about 430 superseded the other Eastern confessions, and to this day the Constantinopolitan creed has remained the symbol of the Byzantine Church.

Considering the state of affairs which existed in the East till the middle of the fifth century, it is difficult to characterize the fundamental type of the Eastern symbols. But, in spite of the many deviations, there exists a certain affinity with the shorter Roman symbol, the acceptance of which was hindered by (1) the circumstance that the Christological section of the Roman symbol came into conflict with a Christological type already established; (2) by the desire to give fuller expression to the " higher " Christology in the creed.

9. Assumption of an Asia Minor Original of the Roman Symbol.

It was not till the time of the Arian controversy that fixed symbols in the East began to be formed. From an examination of the Rules of Faith, and the fragments of those rules and formula-like sentences which are now familiar as belonging to the Eastern half of the Church from the middle of the first to the middle of the third century, scholars like Caspari, Zahn, Loofs, and others have inferred that there must have existed an Eastern symbol or, to be more precise, a symbol from Asia Minor, to which the old Roman symbol was related as daughter or sister. The assumption rests principally, if not exclusively, on what is found in Clement of Alexandria, Irenæus, Justin, and Ignatius; and the inference drawn therefrom is that in the East there existed in the second century a fixed symbol, or, rather, many symbols, related to the Roman symbol but independent of it. At best the Roman symbol is contemporaneous with the Asiatic or Syrian; more probably it is later. Harnack, who formerly shared this view, is now of opinion that the fact that single sentences seem to be echoes of the symbol, or tally with it, offers no guaranty that they themselves derive from one symbol. Before any symbol existed God was " almighty "; Jesus Christ was called " the only-begotten son, our Lord "; he was proclaimed as " begotten by the Holy Ghost, born of the Virgin Mary," as having " suffered under Pontius Pilate," and as coming to " judge the quick and the dead." Without following the argument in refutation of the testimonies derived from early Fathers in detail, it can be stated that, while the existence of a primitive typical Eastern form up to a certain point is admitted, nevertheless it is insisted that the great feat of forming the symbol, and of therewith laying the foundation of all ecclesiastical symbols, remains the glory of the community at Rome. To this Roman symbol which is unhesitatingly to be traced back to about the middle of the second century, no doubt Tertullian refers (*Hær.*, xxxvi.). Had a symbol been established in Rome at the time of the fierce struggle with Gnosticism and Marcionitism (about 145–190), it would have run differently. On the other hand, it is not advisable to go back too far beyond the middle of the second century.

10. Summary.

To sum up: The symbol originated in Rome about the middle of the second century. It was based upon the baptismal formula and on confessional formulas of a summarizing character (such as may be identified from the New Testament and from Ignatius, Justin, and Irenæus), which had been generally handed down, including Eastern formulas (Asia Minor, Syria), and was largely under the influence of the New Testament writings. In Rome itself the symbol was never altered. It made its way into the Western provinces from the end of the second century onward, without claiming to have been, in the strictest sense, composed by the apostles. This accounts for the different modifications in those provinces (whereas at Rome it was designated as apostolic in the strict sense of the word sometime between 250 and 350). Among these modifications, those became historically the most important which were derived from the primitive confessional formulas or *mathēma* (i.e., substance of instruction) of the East; namely, "creator of heaven and earth," "suffered," "died," "descended into hell," "life everlasting," besides the *catholicam*—these are just the modifications traceable in the Gallican symbols which issue in our Apostolicum—in addition, the *conceptus*, which is obscure in its origin and otherwise of little importance, and, most perplexing of all, the *communionem sanctorum*. In this connection may rightly be borne in mind the particularly close relations existing between southern Gaul and the East.

11. The Old Roman Symbol Displaced.

That the Roman Church after the beginning of the sixth century gradually allowed itself to be separated from and finally robbed of the symbol which it had previously guarded so faithfully, is a phenomenon not yet fully explained, although Caspari (ii. 114 sqq.; iii. 201 sqq., 230 sqq.) has made some very important contributions toward a solution of the problem. What is most decisive is the fact that it was not the longer (Gallican) daughter recension which displaced the mother, but that at Rome from the beginning of the sixth century the Nicæno-Constantinopolitan symbol took the place of the shorter symbol in the *traditio* and *redditio symboli*, whereas in the baptismal questions the old Roman symbol still remained in use. The displacement of the old Roman symbol by the Constantinopolitan becomes very intelligible, when one considers the conditions of the time. The rule of the Ostrogoths in Italy brought the Church of Rome in dangerous proximity to Arianism, and, in order to emphasize its attitude with respect to this heresy, the Church felt compelled to adopt a more explicit, so to speak polemically formed, symbol. Then, again, when this necessity ceased to press on the Church, and a return to a simpler creed became possible, the old symbol had grown dim in memory; while the new Roman, which was in fact the Gallican, the *Symbolum Apostolicum*, recommended itself by its more complete form. The differences were overlooked, or else not regarded as considerable; and the legend which had invested the old symbol with a halo of glory awoke again around the new one, and again and for a long time became a power in the Church, till it was exploded in the age of the Renaissance and the Reformation.

12. Interpretation of the Symbol.

In interpreting the apostolic symbol historically, it must be remembered that those portions of the same which belonged to the old Roman confession must be explained from the theology of the later apostolic and postapostolic ages (not simply, as some claim, "according to the New Testament"). This explanation must take into consideration that the symbol is an elaborated baptismal formula and that in its primitive form it must therefore not be regarded as an expression of intrachurch polemics, but rather as a Christian confession, composed for the purpose of instructing in Christianity as distinguished from Judaism and heathenism. In the course of history the theological explanation of the symbol on the whole keeps pace with the general development of dogmatics and theology. But the distinction between theological rules of faith and a confession serving for Christian instruction remains in the consciousness of the West, and is characteristically reflected in the *Explanationes symboli*.

13. Clauses not Found in the Old Roman Symbol.

As concerns the expressions of the apostolic symbol which are not in the old Roman, it is necessary to ascertain when, where, and under what conditions they first appear. Of most of them it may be said that they are a natural explication of the ancient symbol, that they do not alter its character, that they contain only the common faith of the Church—even of the Church of the second century—and that at the end of the second century they were known in the West, though they had not yet found a stable place in any of the provincial symbols. Two only of the additions can not be so regarded, namely the phrases *descendit ad inferos*, in the second article, and *sanctorum communionem* in the third. But both additions, on account of their dubious meaning, must be allowed to be failures. Even in modern times they are explained quite differently by different parties in the Church (cf. Kattenbusch, i. 1 sqq.). (A. Harnack.)

Bibliography: The general works, A. Hahn, *Bibliothek der Symbole*, 3d ed. by G. L. Hahn, Breslau, 1897; C. P. Caspari, *Ungedruckte, unbeachtete, und wenig beachtete Quellen zur Geschichte des Taufsymbols und der Glaubensregel*, 3 vols., Christiania, 1866–75; J. R. Lumby, *History of the Creeds*, London, 1880; Schaff, *Creeds*, i. 14–23, ii. 45–55. Particularly on the Apostles' Creed are: J. Pearson, *Exposition of the Creed*, London, 1659, and constantly reprinted (the English classic on the subject); M. Nicolas, *Le Symbole des Apôtres*, Paris, 1867; J. Baron, *The Greek Origin of the Apostles' Creed*, London, 1885; L. de Grenade, *Le Symbole des Apôtres*, Paris, 1890; A. Harnack, *Das apostolische Glaubensbekenntnis*, Berlin, 1896; idem, *The Apostles' Creed*, transl. of *Apostolisches Symbolum* in the *Protestantische Realencyklopädie*, Leipsic, 1896, by S. Means, ed. T. B. Saunders, London, 1901; S. Bäumer, *Das apostolische Glaubensbekenntnis*, Mainz, 1893; C. Blume, *Das apostolische Glaubensbekenntnis*, Freiburg, 1893; J. Haussleiter, *Zur Vorgeschichte des apostolischen Glaubensbekenntnisses*, Munich, 1893; T. Zahn, *Das apostolische Symbolum*, Leipsic, 1893; F. Kattenbusch, *Das apostolische Symbolum*, 2 vols., ib. 1894–1900; H. B. Swete, *The Apostles' Creed and Primitive Christianity*, Cambridge, 1894; C. M. Schneider, *Das apostolische Glaubensbekenntnis*, Ratisbon, 1901; A. C. McGiffert, *The Apostles' Creed, its Origin, its Purpose, and its Historical Interpretation*, New York, 1902; W. R. Richards, *Apostles' Creed in Modern Worship*, ib. 1906; H. C. Beeching, *Apostles' Creed*, London, 1906; and see under Symbolics.

APOSTLES, TEACHING OF THE TWELVE. See Didache.

APOSTLESHIP OF PRAYER. See Confraternities, Religious; Sacred Heart of Jesus, Devotion to.

APOSTOLIC BRETHREN: A sect founded in northern Italy in the latter half of the thirteenth century by Gherardo Segarelli, a native of Alzano in the territory of Parma. He was of low birth and without education, applied for membership in the Franciscan order at Parma, and was rejected. Ultimately he resolved to devote himself to the restoration of what he conceived to be the apostolic manner of life. About 1260 he assumed a costume patterned after representations which he had seen of the apostles, sold his house, scattered the price in the market-place, and went out to preach repentance as a mendicant brother. He found disciples, and the new order of penitents spread throughout Lombardy and beyond it. At first the Franciscans and other churchmen only scoffed at Segarelli's eccentric ways; but about 1280 the Bishop of Parma threw him into prison, then kept him awhile in his palace as a source of amusement, and in 1286 banished him from the diocese. All new mendicant orders without papal sanction having been prohibited by the Council of Lyons in 1274, Honorius IV issued a severe reprobation of the Apostolic Brethren in 1286, and Nicholas IV renewed it in 1290. A time of persecution followed. At Parma in 1294 four members of the sect were burned, and Segarelli was condemned to perpetual imprisonment. Six years later he was made to confess a relapse into heresies which he had abjured, and was burned in Parma July 18, 1300. A man of much greater gifts now took the lead of the sect. This was Dolcino (q.v.), the son of a priest in the diocese of Novara, and a member of the order since 1291, an eloquent, enthusiastic utterer of apocalyptic prophecies. At the head of a fanatical horde, who were in daily expectation of seeing the judgment of God on the Church, he maintained in the mountainous districts of Novara and Vercelli a guerrilla warfare against the crusaders who had been summoned to put him down. Cold and hunger were still more dangerous enemies; and finally the remnant of his forces were captured by the bishop of Vercelli—about 150 persons in all, including Dolcino himself and his "spiritual sister," Margareta, both of whom, refusing to recant, were burned at the stake June 1, 1307. This was really the end of the sect's history. It is true that even later than the middle of the century traces of their activity are found, especially in northern Italy, Spain, and France; but these are only isolated survivals.

The ideal which the Apostolic Brethren strove to realize was a life of supposed perfect sanctity, in complete poverty, with no fixed domicil, no care for the morrow, and no vows. It was a protest against the invasion of the Church by the spirit of worldliness, as well as against the manner in which the other orders kept their vows, particularly that of poverty. In itself the project might have seemed harmless enough, not differing greatly from the way in which other founders had begun. When the order was prohibited, however, the refusal to submit to ecclesiastical authority stamped its members as heretics. Persecution embittered their opposition; the Church, in their eyes, had fallen completely away from apostolic holiness, and become Babylon the Great, the persecutor of the saints. Their apocalyptic utterances and expectations are a link with the Joachimites (see JOACHIM OF FIORE); in fact, parallels to their teaching, mostly founded on literal interpretations of Scripture texts, may be found in many heretical bodies. They forbade the taking of oaths, apparently permitting perjury in case of need, and rejected capital punishment; their close intercourse with their "apostolic sisters" gave rise to serious accusations against their morals, though they themselves boasted of their purity, and considered the conquest of temptation so close at hand as especially meritorious. (HUGO SACHSSE.)

BIBLIOGRAPHY: J. L. Mosheim, *Versuch einer unparteiischen Ketzergeschichte*, i. 193–400, Helmstadt, 1746; Helyot, *Ordres monastiques*, iv. 54 sqq., 8 vols.; L. Ferraris, *Prompta bibliotheca canonica, juridica moralis*, . vi. 634, 7 vols., Rome, 1844–55; H. C. Lea, *History of the Inquisition*, iii. 103 sqq., New York, 1887.

APOSTOLIC CHURCH DIRECTORY: A work of Egyptian origin, probably of the third century. It appears in early times to have had no fixed title, although it was generally received as apostolic. The title given above is a translation of that (*Apostolische Kirchenordnung*) used for it by Bickell, its first modern editor. It professes to have been delivered word for word by the apostles, whose names are given as John, Matthew, Peter, Andrew, Philip, Simon, James, Nathanael, Thomas, Cephas (!), Bartholomew, and Jude, the brother of James. John is represented as the first to speak and, after the apostles, Mary and Martha also say something. The precepts given by the apostles fall into two sections, one dealing with the moral and the other with the ecclesiastical law (chaps. i.–xiv., and xvi.–xxx.). The first part is almost a literal transcription of the *Didache* (i.–iv. 8), the observations at the close of it are borrowed from the Epistle of Barnabas (xxi. 2–4, xix. 11). The precepts relating to ecclesiastical organization deal with the choice of bishops and with presbyters, lectors, deacons, widows, lay people, and deaconesses. The canon referring to deacons occurs twice, in chaps. xx. and xxii., one being apparently a later insertion.

The work was evidently written for a very small community. It imposes on the clergy limitations in regard to marriage which go far for that period. The section on deaconesses is interesting, in regard to both the foundation and the regulations of the institution. A wider field of activity is assigned to the lector than one is accustomed to; but no minor orders in the later sense are known, nor is there any approach to metropolitan organization. These primitive traits induced Harnack to attempt to distinguish two sources belonging to the second century, represented by chaps. xvi.–xxi., and xxii.–xxviii.; but this is unnecessary, as primitive customs persisted for a long time in certain parts of the Church. H. ACHELIS.

BIBLIOGRAPHY: Editions from the Greek: J. W. Bickell, *Geschichte des Kirchenrechts*, i. 87–97, 107–132, 178 sqq., Giessen, 1843; P. de Lagarde, in C. C. J. Bunsen, *Christianity and Mankind*, vi. 449–460, London, 1854; A. Hilgenfeld, *Novum Testamentum extra canonem receptum*, part iv., pp. 93–106, Leipsic, 1884; A. Harnack, in *TU*, ii. 2, pp. 225–237, and ii. 5, pp. 7–31, ib. 1886. Editions from the Coptic: H. Tattam, *The Apostolical Constitutions or Canons of the Apostles in Coptic with an Eng. Transl.*, London, 1848; P. de Lagarde, *Ægyptiaca*, pp. 239–248, Göttingen, 1883; U. Bouriant, *Recueil de travaux*, v. 202–261, Paris, 1883; consult also Harnack, *Litteratur*, pp. 451 sqq. and cf. *TU*, vi. 4, pp. 39 sqq., Leipsic, 1891.

APOSTOLIC CONSTITUTIONS AND CANONS.

Apostolic Constitutions and Canons is the name applied to an ancient collection of ecclesiastical precepts. The Constitutions profess to be regulations for the organization of the Church put forth by the apostles themselves and published to the faithful by Clement of Rome. In reality they are of Syrian origin, and were composed by a cleric from older sources in the latter half of the fourth century. They consist of eight books. The eighty-five Canons have the form of synodal decisions, and proceeded from the same source not much later. The fate of the two collections, so nearly allied in their origin, has been different. The Constitutions can never have been received outside of a narrow circle. They were considered spurious even in an extremely uncritical age, and thus never came as a whole into any of the great collections of ecclesiastical law in the East, though a part of the eighth book is frequently met with in these. They were unknown in the West until the sixteenth century, at which time neither Baronius nor Bellarmine made any attempt to vindicate their authenticity, though Anglican theologians took a great interest in them and frequently upheld their apostolic origin. The Canons, on the other hand, were generally received as genuine, included in many collections of Church law, and translated into several Oriental languages; to this day they stand at the beginning of the canonical system of the Eastern Church. The first fifty were made known to the West by Dionysius Exiguus (d. before 544), from whom they passed into a number of Latin collections, e.g., the pseudo-Isidorian Decretals, the *Decretum Gratiani*, and the Decretals of Gregory IX.

1. Origin and History.

The criticism of the Constitutions was placed upon secure foundations for the first time when their sources were definitely assigned—the first six books (by Lagarde) to the *Didascalia*, the seventh to the *Didache*, and the eighth to the writings of Hippolytus of Rome.

2. The Constitutions, Books i.-vi.

The first of these sources is a constitution of the third century, written by a bishop of Cœle-Syria and attributed by him to the twelve apostles. Its unique value lies in the fact that it gives a picture down to the minutest details, of the life of a Christian community of the third century. The daily life of the individual and the family, the public worship, the wide practical charity and the strict moral discipline, the relation of the Church to the State and to the surrounding world, in science, art, and literature—all this is vividly depicted in the *Didascalia*. It throws a great deal of light on the origin of the order of deaconesses. Some things are peculiar; thus the New Testament canon includes, besides the four canonical Gospels, that of Peter and probably that according to the Hebrews, and some apocryphal *Acta* in addition to the canonical Acts. Striking characteristics are the friendly tone toward the Jews, in contrast with a hostile feeling toward the Jewish Christians; apparently the author was at the head of a community of Gentile Christians, and found that a neighboring Jewish-Christian community had a greater influence upon his flock than he approved. Ascetic directions in regard to mastery over the flesh are entirely wanting.

The first thirty-two chapters of the seventh book of the Constitutions are a mere recasting of the *Didache*. Noteworthy liturgical prayers (xxxiii.-xxxviii.) and directions as to baptism (xxxix.-xlv.) follow; the baptismal creed in chapter xli. played a not unimportant part in the councils of the fourth century. The eighth book is a compilation from various sources. Chapters i. and ii. contain an independent treatise on the charismata, which, since Hippolytus is known to have written on this subject, is supposed with great probability to be his. With chap iv. begins a liturgical directory which is ascribed directly to the apostles; chaps. v.-xv. form the well-known "Clementine" liturgy. Achelis has tried to demonstrate that the source of this part is the Egyptian church directory, which in its turn is derived from the *Canones Hippolyti* (preserved in an Arabic version). If this theory is correct, this part of the eighth book also would be ultimately due to Hippolytus. The Egyptian directory was a Greek work of the third century, which is preserved only in the Oriental versions. In opposition to Achelis, Funk, of Tübingen, maintained that the Apostolic Constitutions were the original work, the Egyptian directory derived from them, and the *Canones Hippolyti* from that again. The compiler of the Constitutions acted as an editor in dealing with his sources, attempting by revision and addition to fuse the various sources into a serviceable whole. He was an inhabitant of Syria, possibly a neighbor of the earlier author of the *Didascalia*. A connection can be traced between him and the pseudo-Ignatius, the Syrian forger who made twelve letters out of the seven genuine ones of Ignatius; certainly allied in time and thought with this man, he may have been identical with him. His date has been variously given, from c. 350 to c. 400, and can probably never be accurately determined, as the Constitutions have clearly been retouched later, especially the eighth book, which was the most used.

3. Books vii. and viii.

The Apostolic Canons grew up in the same surroundings, probably with the view of covering the lack of authenticity of the Constitutions by a new forgery. Their numbering varies; the division into eighty-five seems to be the oldest. Outside of the Constitutions, their sources are the decrees of the Dedication Synod of Antioch in 341 and other councils. Canon lxxxv. is the interesting Bible canon of both the Old and New Testaments, which omits the Apocalypse, but includes the two Clementine epistles and the Constitutions as Scripture.

4. The Canons.

Information as to other Oriental writings more or less connected with the Constitutions and their sources may be found in W Riedel, *Die Kirchen-*

rechtsquellen des Patriarchats Alexandrien (Leipsic, 1900), which treats among others the *Thirty Traditions of the Apostles*, the Arabic *Didascalia*, and a version of this, the Ethiopic *Didascalia*—a comparatively late work which has nothing to do with the Syriac *Didascalia*, but is probably related to the *Testamentum Jesu Christi*. An Oriental corpus, the *Clementina*, consists of the *Testamentum*, the Apostolic and Egyptian directories, an extract from the Constitutions, and the Apostolic Canons. It is divided into eight books by the Arabic and Syriac copyists. The title and introduction are taken from the Constitutions, to which the *Clementina* was intended as a supplement. H. ACHELIS.

BIBLIOGRAPHY: Editions: The Constitutions are in Cotelerius-Clericus, *Sanctorum patrum . . opera*, i. 190–482, Amsterdam, 1724 (reproduced in *MPG*, i.); W. Ültzen, *Constitutiones apostolicæ*, Schwerin, 1853; P. de Lagarde, *Constitutiones apostolorum*, Leipsic, 1862, and in C. C. J. Bunsen, *Analecta Ante-Nicæna*, ii., London, 1854 (the first critical ed.). The Canons are included in most council collections, in the *Corpus juris civilis* and *Corpus juris canonici*. For the Syriac consult: P. de Lagarde, *Didascalia apostolorum syriace*, Leipsic, 1854; M. D. Gibson, in *Horæ Semiticæ*, i.-ii., London, 1903 (with Eng. transl., from recently discovered MSS.). From the Latin: E. Hauler, *Didascaliæ apostolorum fragmenta Veronensia Latina*, Leipsic, 1900; H. Achelis and J. Flemming, in *TU*, new ser., x. 2, ib. 1904, cf. H. Achelis, in *TU*, vi. 4, ib. 1891, and in *ZKG*, xv. (1894) 1 sqq. The Eng. transl. of Whiston is given with notes in *ANF*, vii. 391–505 (reproduced from the second volume of his *Primitive Christianity*). Consult also F. X. Funk, *Die apostolischen Konstitutionen*, Rottenburg, 1891; W. Riedel, in *Römische Quartalschrift*, xiv. (1900) 3 sqq.; J. Leypoldt, *Saidische Auszüge aus dem achten Buche der apostolischen Konstitutionen*, in *TU*, new ser., xi. 1, Leipsic, 1904; G. Horner, *The Statutes of the Apostles; or, Canones ecclesiastici, ed. with Transl. from Ethiopic and Arabic MSS.* . London, 1905; D. L. O'Leary, *Apostolical Constitutions*, ib. 1906. The discussions upon the *Didache* and the *Apostolical Church Directory* involve the *Constitutions and Canons*.

APOSTOLIC COUNCIL AT JERUSALEM.

The Apostolic Council is the common designation of the meeting described in Acts xv. It took place in 51 or 52 A.D., between the missionary journey of Paul and Barnabas and that of Paul alone, and marks a distinct stage in the proclamation of the apostles' message to the Gentile world; viz., the recognition of the right of the Gentiles to a place in the Christian community, without subjection to the Mosaic law.

1. New Testament Statements and Allusions.

Interest in Luke's report of the proceedings is increased by the fact that Paul himself refers to the Council in Gal. ii. 1–10 from a controversial standpoint. The comparison of the two accounts has led some recent theologians to assert that the account in Acts is essentially different from that of Paul, and that the author of Acts has made the facts fit the views which he takes of the whole period (see below, § 5). In earlier time this council was the special point used as a fulcrum for the attempt of the Tübingen school to overthrow the received tradition as to the history and literature of the time. Although the objections of Baur, especially as to the irreconcilability of Acts xv. and Gal. ii., have few extreme representatives nowadays, yet their results are seen in recent attempts to deny the unity of the Acts, regarding the book as a composite of various sources, which do not always agree in material and in tendency.

In the following treatment of the Apostolic Council the Book of Acts is assumed to be the work of Luke of Antioch, the companion of Paul, who (xvi. 10 sqq.) narrates in the first person; and the events detailed in chap. xv. are believed to be given partly from his own knowledge, partly from the testimony of the participants. There is no a priori reason to suppose that for chap. xv., or generally for any part of the Antiochian-Pauline period, Luke was working over written authorities;

2. Luke the Author of the Account in Acts.

he undoubtedly had seen the Jerusalem letter (verses 23–29), but probably gives it here freely from memory. For a long time Paul's most trusted coadjutor, he would naturally enter intelligently into the Pauline attitude; and this is precisely what is found in his presentation of Paul's labors. His standpoint is that found in the Pauline theodicy of Rom. ix.–xi., which excludes any tendency contrary to history, and allows the writer to consider historical facts in a perfectly objective manner. One may thus expect with confidence to find Luke's report of the Council historically accurate. Of this accuracy Paul's expressions must of course serve as a criterion; since, however, Paul is not, like Luke, writing from the standpoint of general history, but to enforce a special point of dispute, Luke's account must be taken as the basis of any later treatment professing to be historical.

It is learned from Luke's account that some time after Paul and Barnabas had returned to Antioch from their missionary journey, there appeared certain Jewish Christians who taught the hitherto unheard-of doctrine that converts from heathenism could not be saved without circumcision, thus denying the equality prevailing for some ten years (or since Acts xi. 20) between the circumcised and uncircumcised members of the Church of Antioch.

3. Occasion for the Council.

This caused great disturbance among the Gentile Christians, whose liberty was threatened, and Paul and Barnabas opposed it strongly and were deputed to lay the question before the apostles and elders in Jerusalem. This mission implies no doubt in their minds of their own position, which had been approved all along; but they wished to be positively assured that they were in harmony with the source of their Christianity, for the quieting of their own minds and the suppression of further attacks from the Judaizing party. Luke gives with care the serious discussion which led up to the decision. The Jerusalem community at first received the tidings of Gentile conversions not with unqualified joy; some Pharisaic members of the Church put forward a definite demand that the Gentile Christians should be bound to the observance of the Mosaic law. It is to be noticed, however, that this demand was not put forward, as at Antioch, on the theory that they could not otherwise be saved. The practical demand was the same, and was so strongly pressed that the decision was postponed to another meeting, in which again a long discussion took place without result. Since the extreme thesis of the disturbers at Antioch was not put forward here, there must have been other weighty grounds which induced no inconsiderable portion of the Church to press for the subjection of the Gentiles to the Mosaic law—apparently based on the idea that the law was God's ordinance for the lives of men far more universally than merely among the Jews.

4. The Outcome. Four Prohibitions.

It was Peter, the head of the Church of the Circumcision, who silenced this party by the unequivocal declaration of the principle of salvation by grace alone through faith. He appealed, as to something they all knew, to the fact that God had long before proclaimed salvation by his ministry to Cornelius and his household; he declared that the people of God in Israel had not been able to bear the law as a means of salvation, but were equally dependent with the Gentiles upon divine grace, showing that this fundamental principle would be endangered if they insisted upon the observance of the law. This argument reduced the opposition to silence; no one was willing to attack the truth that salvation was to be obtained without the law through faith. The time was now ripe for Barnabas and Paul to show how God had attested their ministry by signs and wonders, which proved also their apostolic independence (cf. II Cor. xii. 12). The final verdict was rendered by James, showing that the prophets had foreshadowed the upbuilding of a Church without the law, and proposing instead of its enforcement to emphasize four prohibitions, which are connected with the rules laid down in Lev. xvii. and xviii. equally for the children of Israel and for the strangers sojourning among them, as also with those imposed by later Jewish tradition on the "proselytes of the gate"; they are possibly nothing but these rules in the form in which they were observed among proselytes in the apostolic times, in the districts here affected (Syria and Cilicia). They are derived originally from the Mosaic law, and forbid what to the Jewish ethical consciousness was highly offensive. Neither of these points is made, however, but they are forbidden as things in themselves morally reprehensible—their prohibition is necessary in order to separate Gentile morality from Gentile immorality and superstition. By the word "fornication" (Gk. *porneia*) is signified the unrestricted sexual intercourse which was practically tolerated in the heathen world. The words "to abstain from meats offered to idols" refer to both private and public meals on the flesh of the victims of sacrifices, which connected the social life of the people with pagan worship. The prohibition of "blood" and "things strangled," while not so easily understood, may be taken to stamp with disapproval the habits in regard to food which prevailed among barbarous tribes, but were rejected by the more civilized Greeks and Romans, though they must have been known among the populations to whom the first recipients of the letter belonged. In a word, the whole purpose of the decree was to mark off by a sharp line of division the life of the Gentile Christians from that of the heathen around them.

5. Alleged Contradiction between Acts and Gal. ii.

The account in the Acts has been assailed by numerous critics as a more or less consciously biased presentation of the real story, as it may be taken from Gal. ii. The accusations are mainly these: the account in Acts minimizes the fundamental opposition which existed between Paul and the Jerusalem Church by ascribing to the latter a Pauline standpoint which it had not; the account gives as a result of the Council a limitation of the Gentiles' liberty and equal title to which Paul could never have consented; in defiance of history, it attributes to Paul a position of subordination to the Jerusalem apostles. The first point scarcely needs further discussion after what has been said. The Pauline expressions in Gal. ii. must be taken in connection with the explanatory preface in chap. i. His Galatian opponents asserted that his preaching to the Gentiles needed correction and completion, supporting this by the statement that he had formerly subordinated himself to the Twelve. He appeals to the superhuman origin of his mission and the fact that he had sought no confirmation of his gospel from men, not even from the Twelve (Gal. i. 11–20). But with verse 21 another point of view begins; the remaining verses are written to demonstrate that no relation existed between him and the Palestinian Christianity, the older apostles, which would give his opponents any right to appeal to them against him. When in Gal. ii. 1 he mentions going up to Jerusalem fourteen years later, it is in order to demonstrate that after so long a time the original concord remains undisturbed. The situation is thus exactly that described in Acts xv. What Paul designates "that gospel which I preach among the Gentiles" is the very thing opposed by the disturbers and brought up in Jerusalem. In both cases uncertainty exists as to the position of Jerusalem toward it, and certainty is sought. In both Paul appears with Barnabas; and if he mentions that he took with him Titus, who was uncircumcised (meaning thereby to test the attitude of the Jerusalem Church toward Gentile Christians), Luke also relates that certain of the Gentile converts from Antioch were sent with him. Paul is stating facts to repel a personal attack on himself; Luke mentions the matter in its bearing on the history of the Church as a whole. Thus there was no need to mention in the Acts the revelation which (in addition to the desire of the community) decided Paul's journey, while Paul speaks of it apparently to emphasize the importance of the proceeding. That Paul omits any notice of the decree is not surprising when one considers that its purpose was not in any way to limit the freedom of the Gentiles from the law, and that he had no motive to enter on the subject here. On the other hand, he does narrate something which Luke omits, in verses 6–10. Certain prominent leaders, especially the three "pillars," recognizing the grace given to him, explicitly agreed that he and Barnabas should go to the heathen, and they to the circumcision. By this he means to confirm what must have been denied in Galatia—that his independent position involved no breach with Jerusalem, but had been distinctly sanctioned by the leaders of the Church there. Luke might have been expected to mention this less public discussion and agreement, of which he must have known, and, as a matter of fact, Acts xv. 4, 12, 26 may be taken to refer indirectly to it; not to mention that, according to his narrative alone, it would seem likely that the leaders had had their minds settled as to the position of Paul and Barnabas, and in some such way as Gal. ii. describes. The same process of intelligent comparison will also show that the account of the conflict at Antioch in Gal. ii. 11 sqq. is by no means (as has been frequently asserted) irreconcilable with the narrative of the Acts.

6. Later History of the Decision of the Council.

A word must be said about the later history of the decree. Originally it was addressed to that part of the Gentile Christians who had been in relation with Jerusalem. On his own motion Paul extended it to other Gentile communities already existing. Neither his own writings nor the Acts show that he enforced it upon communities formed later as a decree of the Jerusalem Council: but in regard at least to the first two points, the manner in which they are referred to in I Cor. v., vi., viii.–x. and in Rev. ii. shows that the prohibition was held to be of universal obligation among the Gentile Churches; and in the second century they played an important part in connection with the Gnostic controversy. Singularly enough, no trace of the other two prohibitions is found either in apostolic or in subapostolic times; if the view of them given above is correct, this would be explained by the fact that there was no need to enforce them in the civilized Hellenic world. Later passages in Tertullian (*Apol.*, ix.), Minucius Felix (*Octavius*, xii.), and the *Clementine Homilies* (vii. 4, 8) and *Recognitions* (iv. 36), point to an avoiding of blood even in cooked meats, which must have been based on a misunderstanding of the decree. (K. Schmidt.)

Bibliography: The subject is treated in the appropriate sections in works on the Apostolic Age, in commentaries on the Acts, and in works on the Apostles Peter and Paul; of especial value are: J. B. Lightfoot, *Galatians*, pp. 283–355, London, 1866; O. Pfleiderer, *Der Paulinismus*, pp. 278 sqq., 500 sqq., Leipsic, 1873. Eng. transl. London, 1877; C. von Weizsäcker, *Das Apostelconcil*, in *Jahrbücher für deutsche Theologie*, 1873, pp. 191–246; T. Keim, *Aus dem Urchristentum*, pp. 64–89, Zurich, 1879; F. W. Farrar, *Paul*, chaps. xxi.–xxiii., London, 1883; idem, *Early Days of Christianity*, i. 294–297, ib. 1882; J. G. Sommer, *Das Aposteldekret*, 2 parts, Königsberg, 1888–89; W. F. Slater, *Faith and Life of the Early Church*, London, 1892 (exceedingly valuable).

APOSTOLIC FATHERS: A common designation for those writers of the ancient Church who were scholars of apostles, or supposed to be such; viz., Barnabas, Hermas, Clement of Rome, Ignatius, Polycarp, Papias, and the author of the epistle to Diognetus (qq.v.).

Bibliography: The first collection of the writings of these Fathers was by J. B. Cotelerius, Paris, 1672 (reedited with notes by J. Clericus, Antwerp, 1698, 2d ed., Amsterdam, 1724). Other editions are by L. T. Ittig, Leipsic, 1699; J. L. Frey, Basel, 1742; R. Russell, London, 1746; W. Jacobson, Oxford, 1838; C. J. Hefele, Tübingen, 1855; E. de Muralto, *Barnabæ et Clementis epistolæ*, vol. i., Zurich, 1847; A. R. M. Dressel, Leipsic, 1863; A. Hilgenfeld, ib. 1876–81; O. von Gebhardt, A. Harnack, and T. Zahn, ib. 1894; F. X. Funk, Tübingen, 1901; J. B. Lightfoot, London, 1869–90 (than which there is nothing finer). Eng. translations are by W. Wake, London, 1693 (rev. ed., Oxford, 1861); in vol. i. of *ANF*, Edinburgh, 1867, American ed., Buffalo, 1887; C. H. Hoole, London, 1872; and J. B. Lightfoot, in ed. mentioned above. Germ. transl. by H. Scholz, Gütersloh, 1865, and by J. C. Mayer in *Bibliothek der Kirchenväter*, 80 vols., Kempten, 1869–88. Consult A. Harnack, *Litteratur* (exhaustive); J. Donaldson, *Critical History of Christian Literature and Doctrine*, London, 1894; J. Nirschl, *Lehrbuch der Patrologie und Patristik*, 3 vols., Mainz, 1881–85; J. Alzog, *Grundriss der Patrologie oder der älteren christlichen Literaturgeschichte*, Freiburg, 1888; O. Zöckler, *Geschichte der theologischen Litteratur*, Gotha, 1890; C. T. Cruttwell, *Literary History of Early Christianity*, 2 vols., London, 1893; G. Krüger, *Geschichte der altchristlichen Litteratur*, Freiburg, 1895, Eng. transl., New York, 1897 (altogether the handiest book, and useful because of its notices of the literature on the separate subjects).

APOSTOLIC KING: An honorary title of the kings of Hungary, said to have been given originally to Stephen, the first Christian king of that country, by Pope Sylvester II. (999–1003), on account of his religious zeal. It was renewed and confirmed to Maria Theresa, for the Austro-Hungarian royal family, by a brief of Clement XIII., Aug. 19, 1758.

APOSTOLIC MENNONITES. See Mennonites.

APOSTOLIC SUCCESSION: According to the theory of supporters of the episcopal form of church polity, the uninterrupted succession, from the apostles to the present day, of bishops and priests set apart by the laying on of hands. The Greek, Roman Catholic, and Anglican Churches maintain that this succession is essential to the validity of sacramental ministrations, and allow no one not thus ordained to minister in their churches. The last-named body asserts its possession by all three; the Roman Catholic concedes it to the Greek but not to the Anglican; while the Greeks regard its possession by either of the other two as at best exceedingly doubtful. See Episcopacy; Ordination; Polity.

Bibliography: A. W. Haddan, *Apostolical Succession in the Church of England*, London, 1869; E. McCrady, *Apostolical Succession and the Problem of Unity*, Sewanee, 1905.

APOSTOLICI (called by themselves **Apotactici**, "Renuntiants"): A heretical sect of the third and fourth centuries which renounced private property and marriage. They existed in Asia Minor and are mentioned by Epiphanius (*Hær.*, lxi.). They accepted as Scripture the apocryphal Acts of Andrew and of Thomas.

APPEALS TO THE POPE: Appeals from lower officials or courts, which, considered as an ordinary process of law, with effect of suspension and devolution, may be based upon the pope's capacity of bishop and metropolitan, or upon his supposed primacy over the entire Catholic world. Those of the former class have nothing peculiar about them. As concerns the latter class, the third and fourth canons of the Council of Sardica (343) do not, as asserted by Roman Catholic canonists, recognize such an appellate jurisdiction; and no such jurisdiction existed earlier. The council indeed lays down the law that in case of the deposition of a bishop the matter may be referred to the pope, who may either decline to act (in which case the deposition holds good), or may order an investigation by neighboring bishops and certain specially appointed priests. But, apart from the fact that the Council of Sardica is not recognized as ecumenical, and that its decrees were long ago known to have been interpolated to bring them into harmony with the Nicene canons, every true appeal presupposes a review of the formalities and a decision on the validity of the grounds for the lower court's sentence, neither of which is mentioned in the Sardican canons. The claim by the Roman See of a supreme judicial power was only made possible by the victory of the orthodox party, always represented by Rome, over Arianism, and the imperial decision (380) that the faith of the Roman pontiff was the standard, and that he should have precedence over all other bishops. This claim was first made by Innocent I. (402–417) in his letter to Victricius of Rouen; attempts to enforce it met with the determined opposition of the primates, and failed until a firm foundation for them was laid under Leo I. by a law of the emperor Valentinian III. in 445.

The Roman view is set forth in more than one passage of the pseudo-Isidorian decretals. These assert that, in conformity with the decrees of Sardica, bishops may appeal to Rome in all causes, and that the more serious ones must be decided by the Roman See, not by the bishops; and then that not only in such cases, but in all, and by any injured person, appeal may be made to the pope. These claims were in accord with the ideas of the twelfth century, and gave definite form to the concurrent jurisdiction of the pope, by which he might either immediately or through his legates decide or call up questions otherwise belonging to the ordinary. This is not the same thing as the appellate jurisdiction; but the conceptions belonging to the latter are touched by the assertion that in cases where failure of justice occurs in the secular courts, recourse may be had from any tribunal to the Church, that is, eventually to the curia. Although Alexander III. (1159 81) had admitted that appeals from civil tribunals, while customary, were not in accordance with strict legal principles, Innocent III. (1198–1216) affirmed the principle that the Church had the right to take measures against any sin, and thus against denial of justice by secular courts. A reaction against the abuse of appeals to Rome was evidenced in Germany by the "Golden Bull" [issued by the emperor Charles IV. in 1356; for text cf. O. Harnack, *Das Kurfürsten-Kollegium*, Giessen, 1883], which forbade them to be made from secular tribunals; by the Concordat of Constance (1418); and by the thirty-first session of the Council of Basel, to which corresponds the twenty-sixth section of the Pragmatic Sanction of 1439. The Concordat established the principle that appeals should be decided not in Rome, but by *judices in partibus;* and this provision was repeated in the latter two documents, which also forbade appeals *per saltum* and before the definitive sentence of the lower tribunal. The Council of Trent (sessions 13, chaps. 1–3, and 24, chap. 20 [held in 1551 and 1563]) decreed that only *causæ majores* should be taken to Rome, the others being decided by *judices synodales*, papal delegates so called because their nomination was left to the diocesan and provincial synods. When it appeared that these bodies did not act successfully, Pope Benedict XIV (1740–58) transferred the nomination to bishops and chapters (*judices prosynodales*) by the constitution *Quamvis paternæ* of 1741. At present the bishops receive faculties enabling them to delegate these nominees in the pope's name for a certain number of years. Appeals which do go to Rome are referred to two congregations, that of the council and that of bishops and regulars.

In modern times, even earlier than the period of the emperor Joseph II. (1765–90), both Catholic and Protestant governments have either abolished these appeals or very strictly limited them; but these limitations are considered by the curia as only *de facto;* not *de jure*, and the extensive medieval claims are still upheld in theory.

(E. Friedberg.)

Bibliography: For Golden Bull in Eng. consult: Henderson, *Documents*, pp. 220–221; Thatcher and McNeal, *Source Book*, pp. 283 sqq. (cf. pp. 329–332 on the general subject of appeals). On appeals: G. Phillips, *Kirchenrecht*, v. 215 sqq., Ratisbon, 1857; P. Hinschius, *Kirchenrecht*, v. 773 sqq., v. 281, Berlin, 1888–95.

APPEL, THEODORE: German Reformed clergyman; b. at Easton, Pa., Apr. 30, 1823. He was educated at Marshall College, Mercersburg, Pa. (B.A., 1842), and at the German Reformed Seminary in the same town (1845). He was tutor in Greek in Marshall College in 1842–45, and pastor of German Reformed churches at Cavetown, Md. (1845–51), and Mercersburg, Pa. (1851–53). He also held the professorship of mathematics at Marshall College from 1851 to 1853, and was professor of mathematics, physics, and astronomy at Franklin and Marshall College from 1853 to 1877, while from 1878 to 1886 he was superintendent of home missions in the Reformed Church. He is secretary of the Board of Visitors of the Reformed Theological Seminary and holds a similar office on the Board of Home and Foreign Missions of the Reformed Church. From 1878 to 1886 he edited the *Reformed Missionary Herald* and from 1889 to 1893 the *Reformed Church Messenger*. He retired from active life in 1897. In theology he adheres to the Mercersburg type of doctrine of the German Reformed Church. In addition to numerous contributions to periodicals, he has written *College Recollections* (Reading, Pa., 1886); *The Beginnings of the Theological Seminary of the Reformed Church* (Philadelphia, 1886); and *The Life and Work of Rev. John W Nevin* (1889). He has likewise edited Nevin's lectures on the history of the English language (Lancaster, Pa., 1895).

APPELLANTS: The name of that party, which, in the controversy between the Jansenists and the Jesuits, rejected the bull *Unigenitus*, and appealed to a general council. See Jansen, Cornelius, Jansenism.

APPLETON, JESSE: American Congregationalist; b. at New Ipswich, N. H., Nov. 17, 1772; d. at Brunswick, Me., Nov. 12, 1819. He was graduated at Dartmouth 1792; ordained minister at Hampton, N. H., Feb., 1797; chosen second president of Bowdoin College, 1807. During the greater part of his term he acted as professor of philosophy and rhetoric and was pastor of the Congregational Church at Brunswick. His theological lectures and academic addresses, and a selection from his sermons, with memoir, were published at Andover (2 vols., 1836).

APPONIUS, ap-pō'ni-us: The author of an exposition of the Song of Solomon. He names himself in his preface, addressed to the presbyter Armenius, but neither the time nor the place of his activity can be determined with certainty. An approximation to his date may be reached by means of the facts that he mentions Macedonius, Photinus, and Bonosus among heretics, and that Bede (d. 735) quotes him, which places him between the beginning of the fifth century and the middle of the seventh—probably nearer the beginning than the end of this period, since he does not mention Nestorius and Eutyches among his heretics. Mai identified Armenius with the personage of that name associated with Agnellus, and accordingly fixed the middle of the sixth century as Apponius's date. His insistence on the position of Peter as vicar of Christ has been thought to point to Rome or its vicinity as the place of his residence. His interpretation of the Canticles is entirely mystical and spiritual, regarding it as an exposition of the relations of God with his Church. (A. HAUCK.)

BIBLIOGRAPHY: Books i.-vi. of Apponius's work are in the *Bibliotheca maxima patrum Lugdunensis*, xiv. 98 sqq., 1677, and in the *Bibliotheca patrum*, of De la Bigne, i. 763 sqq., Paris, 1589; books vii., viii., and the first half of ix., in Mai, *Spicilegium Romanum*, v. 1 sqq.; the complete work is edited by H. Bottina and I. Martins, Rome, 1843.

APPROBATION OF BOOKS. See CENSORSHIP.

APSE (APSIS): The semicircular or semioctagonal enclosure with which the choir of the older Christian churches generally terminates. The ground-plan of this enclosure is an arc, on the chord of which the altar is raised, while the bishop's throne is placed in the center, against the wall, with rows of benches for the clergy on both sides, sometimes one row above the other (*apsides gradatæ*). In the Roman *basilica*, or hall of justice, which in numerous cases was actually turned into a Christian church with very slight modifications, while its ground-plan formed the starting-point for all Christian church architecture, the exterior form of the building was perfectly rectangular, and the apse, with its seats for the magistrate and the officers of the court, was formed internally.

There are still churches extant on this plan, and they are the oldest; such as the Sta. Croce in Gerusalemme in Rome, and several others in Africa and Asia Minor, all of the third century. In churches of the fifth century, such as Sant' Apollinare in Classe at Ravenna, etc., the apse has generally become visible also in the exterior form; and not only the choir, but also the aisles, terminate in apses. In St. Sophia in Constantinople, and in churches built after that model, the transepts are provided with apses; and, in some few cases in Germany, such as the Church of Reichenau on the Lake of Constance, the choir has apses at both ends. See ARCHITECTURE, ECCLESIASTICAL.

AQUARII, a-cwê'ri-ai ("Water People"): The name given by Philastrius (*Hær.*, lxxvii.; cf. Augustine, *Hær.*, lxiv.; *Prædestinatus*, lxiv.) to certain Christians who used water instead of wine in the Lord's Supper (q.v.). G. KRÜGER.

AQUAVIVA, ā''cwa-vī'va, **CLAUDIO:** Fifth general of the Jesuits; b. at Naples Sept. 14, 1543; d. at Rome Jan. 31, 1615. He studied at Rome, joined the order in 1567, and was chosen its general in 1581. He showed himself a highly capable ruler in the midst of difficulties both within the order and without. The Spanish Jesuits organized a revolt against him and had the support of the Inquisition, King Philip II., and Pope Clement VIII., but he ultimately established himself all the firmer from the very attacks which were intended to overthrow him. In the dispute between the Dominicans and the Jesuits following the publication of Molina's book on free will (see MOLINA) he supported the latter skilfully and successfully. It was under Aquaviva's leadership that the order reached its assured position in the world. He wrote *Industriæ pro superioribus ad curandos animæ morbos* (Florence, 1600), and compiled the oldest *Ratio studiorum* (Rome, 1586) and the *Directorium exercitiorum sancti Ignatii* (1591). His letters addressed to the members of the order are in the *Epistolæ præpositorum generalium societatis Jesu*, Antwerp, 1635, and have been printed in other editions.

AQUILA, ac'wi-la: **1.** Translator of the Old Testament into Greek; see BIBLE VERSIONS, A, I., 2, § 1.

2. A Jewish Christian from Pontus, who was intimately connected with Paul, and is always mentioned in connection with his wife, Prisca (so in Paul according to the best readings) or Priscilla (Luke), whose name is usually put first. When the first epistle to the Corinthians was written the pair lived at Ephesus (I Cor. xvi. 19), and their house was a meeting-place for the congregation there. It may be inferred that they were well known to the Corinthians, probably from a residence at Corinth, and this is confirmed by the Acts, according to which Aquila and Priscilla, being driven from Rome by the order of Claudius, settled at Corinth shortly before Paul's arrival there (xviii. 1-3). If this expulsion is connected with disturbances among the Roman Jews due to Christianity, it is not impossible that the pair were already Christians, and this view is favored by the fact that Paul stayed with them. From Corinth they went to Ephesus with Paul (Acts xviii. 18), and here Apollos was instructed in Christianity by them (xviii. 26). From Rom. xvi. 3–5 they seem to have been in Rome when that epistle was written; but this passage is thought by some to be out of place and properly to belong to an epistle directed to the Ephesians; II Tim. iv. 19 puts them again at

Ephesus. According to later tradition, Aquila became bishop of Heraclea; according to another tradition, he suffered martyrdom with his wife (cf. *ASB*, July 8). (P EWALD.)

AQUILA (ADLER) KASPAR: Lutheran; b. at Augsburg Aug. 7, 1488; d. at Saalfeld (65 m. s.w. of Leipsic), Thuringia, Nov. 12, 1560. He studied at Leipsic (1510) and, after 1513, at Wittenberg. In 1515–16 he appears to have been chaplain to Franz von Sickingen during his campaigns against Worms and Metz; from 1517 to 1521 he officiated as pastor at Jengen, near Augsburg, where, influenced by the writings of Luther, he became an adherent of the Reformation. In Jan., 1521, he went to Wittenberg to obtain his master's degree. During the next two years (1522–23) he was again with Sickingen; then he returned to his home, and was imprisoned at Dillingen by the bishop of Augsburg (Sept., 1523). He was soon liberated, however, and went to Wittenberg, where he rendered Luther valuable aid in the translation of the Old Testament. Through Luther's influence he became minister at Saalfeld (1527) and was present at the Diet of Augsburg in 1530. In 1548 he published a virulent attack against his former friend, Agricola, because of the latter's support of the Interim of 1548. The emperor set a price on his head and Aquila sought refuge with the counts of Henneberg. In 1550 he became dean of the Collegiate Institute at Schmalkald but returned two years later to Saalfeld.

(G. KAWERAU.)

BIBLIOGRAPHY: His life is given by J. Avenarius, *Kurze Lebenbeschreibung*, Meiningen, 1718; C. Schlegel, *Leben und Tod Caspari Aquilæ*, Leipsic, 1737 (especially rich); F. Gensler, *Vita*, Jena, 1816; F Roth, *Augsburgs Reformationsgeschichte*, Munich, 1901.

AQUILEIA, ä″cwi-lê′yä, PATRIARCHATE AND SYNODS: Aquileia, or Aglar, a town at the north end of the Adriatic (45 m. e.n.e. of Venice), was originally a Roman outpost against the Celts and Istrians and was a place of commercial importance as early as the reign of Augustus. Tradition ascribes the founding of its church to Mark the Evangelist, who is said to have come from Rome and consecrated St. Hermagoras (alleged to have died as a martyr) as its first bishop. Somewhat less legendary is the tradition that its bishop, Helarus or Hilarius, suffered martyrdom there about 285. Its bishop, Valerianus (369–388), the fellow combatant of Ambrose against the Arians, appears as metropolitan, and presided at the first Aquileian provincial council (381), which was attended by thirty-two bishops from Upper Italy, Gaul, and Africa; it excommunicated and deposed the Illyric bishop Palladius who leaned toward Arianism. When the Lombards invaded Upper Italy, the metropolitan Paul transferred his seat from Aquileia to the isle of Grado (568). The Aquileian metropolitans residing there refused to acknowledge the fifth ecumenical council of 553, convened by Justinian I., and remained in this schismatic opposition nearly 150 years. An effort of Gregory the Great to bring them back to the Roman Church failed, since the synod convened by the metropolitan Severus (586–607) at Grado (c. 600) still refused to acknowledge the council. The successor of Severus, Candidianus (died c. 612), accepted the catholic orthodox tradition, but the schism continued, nevertheless. Under the protection of the Lombards a number of schismatic antibishops were created, who resumed their seat in Aquileia and took the title of Patriarch, and the bishops of Grado soon followed their example. The controversy did not cease when in 698 the Aquileian Patriarch Peter (induced by Sergius I. of Rome) abjured his schism. On the contrary, both patriarchates, that of Aquileia and that of Grado, maintained themselves side by side till the middle of the eighteenth century. Repeated efforts of the popes (such as that of Leo IX. by the *bulla circumscriptionis* of 1053) to effect a reconciliation were unsuccessful. When Nicolaus V in 1451 abolished the patriarchate of Grado, and established one for Venice, the incumbents of the Aquileian see were placed in a difficult position; both Venice and Austria, to whose territory Aquileia belonged, as well as Udine and Cividale, where the Aquileians had commonly resided since the early Middle Ages, obtained the right of appointment. The difficulties were finally adjusted 300 years later by Benedict XIV., who abolished the Aquileian patriarchate by the bull *Injunctum* (1751) and founded in its place two archbishoprics, one at Udine for Venetian Friuli to be filled by Venice, and the other at Görz for Austrian Friuli to be filled by Vienna. Several synods more or less noteworthy were called by the Aquileian patriarchs during the Middle Ages. One at Friuli (Forum Julii) in 796 under Paulinus (787–802), the friend of Alcuin and theological counselor of Charlemagne, declared against the Greek dogma of the procession of the Holy Spirit. There were several in the fourteenth century (1305, 1311, 1339, etc.). The last of importance met in Cividale in 1409 at the call of Gregory XII. in opposition to the reform-council at Pisa. O. ZÖCKLER†.

BIBLIOGRAPHY: B. M. de Rubeis, *Monumenta ecclesiæ Aquilejensis*, Strasburg, 1740; G. Fontanini, *Historia litteraria Aquilejensis*, Rome, 1742; Hefele, *Conciliengeschichte*, ii. and vi.; P. B. Gams, *Series episcoporum ecclesiæ catholicæ*, pp. 772 sqq., 791 sqq., Regensburg, 1873; Meister, *Das Concilium von Cividale*, in *Historisches Jahrbuch der Görres Gesellschaft*, xiv. 320 sqq., Munich, 1893.

AQUILEIAN CREED: The creed of the Church of Aquileia as given by the Aquileian Rufinus (*Expositio symboli apostolorum*, *MPL*, xxi.) forms a parallel to the older, shorter Roman baptismal formula with three interesting variants: (1) At the end of the first article it adds to *Deo Patre omnipotente* the words *invisibili et impassibili* (probably as explanation against Patripassianism); (2) In the second article, between the words *sepultus* and *tertia die resurrexit* it puts a reference to Christ's descent into Hades (I Pet. iii. 19; Eph. iv. 9) by the words *descendit ad inferna*—the oldest catholic orthodox confession of this article of faith, since the synod at Sirmium in 358 and Nicæa 359 which mention the same fact were semi-Arian; (3) In article iii. it inserts *hujus* before *carnis resurrectionem*, thus emphasizing the identity of the resurrection-body with the earthly body of man. The creed of the ancient churches of Friuli published by B. M. de Rubeis (*Dissertatio de liturgicis*, Venice, 1754) from a *scrutinium catechumenorum*

Forojuliense of the sixth century (cf. the text in Hahn, 43–44) differs from that of Rufinus, and the three characteristic formulas of the latter mentioned above, are wanting. One of these formulas at least, the *descendit ad inferna* is also found in the parallel text transmitted by Venantius Fortunatus (*Expositio symboli*, xi. 1), which must be regarded as an excerpt from the text of Rufinus (Hahn, 45–46). The *Explanatio symboli* of Bishop Nicetas (or Niceta), which has often been regarded as a parallel text to the Aquileian confession, has nothing to do with it, since the bishop in question had his see not at Romatiana (or Portus Romatianus) near Aquileia, but at Remesiana in Dacia (see NICETAS OF REMESIANA). O. ZÖCKLER†.

BIBLIOGRAPHY: A. Hahn, *Bibliothek der Symbole und Glaubensregeln der alten Kirche*, Breslau, 1897; F. Kattenbusch, *Das apostolische Symbol*, i. 102–132, Leipsic, 1894; Schaff, *Creeds*, ii. 49–50 (gives sources and the text with notes).

AQUINAS. See THOMAS AQUINAS.

ARABIA.

I. Use of the Name.
II. Geography and Topography.
III. History.
IV. Religion.

I. Use of the Name: The root-meaning of the Semitic word is "dry" or "sterile"; as a noun it means "desert." (1) *Old Testament Usage.* The term occurs first as a place name, Jer. xxv. 24 (Isa. xiii. 20, where it is equivalent to "nomad," is exilic or later). In earlier passages it is simply "desert." Ezekiel (xxvii. 21) and the Chronicler (II Chron. xvii. 11; xxi. 16; xxii. 1; xxvi. 7; Neh. ii. 19; iv. 7; vi. 1) use it as a national appellative. In the early parts of the Bible the Arabs are called Amalekites, Ishmaelites, Midianites, the *Me'onim* (=Minæans, see III. below), and the like. (2) *New Testament Usage.* In Acts ii. 11 the use corresponds to that of late passages in the Old Testament. The Arabia of Paul's retirement (Gal. i. 17), usually taken as the Syrian desert, is rather the Sinaitic peninsula (cf. Gal. iv. 25). (3) *Assyrian Usage.* The inscriptions later than the ninth century B.C. contain frequent allusions to Arabs, but generally mean only those of the Syrian desert. With these contact was frequent. Tiglath Pileser III. invaded the peninsula, as did Esarhaddon. In earlier times the country was known to Babylonians as Magan, and is often mentioned. (4) *The Arabic Usage.* According to Nöldeke (*Encyclopædia Biblica*, i. 274) the term "Arab" was in early (pre-Christian?) use by the Arabs themselves as a general term denoting the inhabitants of the peninsula. It was so employed during Mohammed's lifetime, though several passages in the Koran apply the term to nomads as distinct from inhabitants of towns. (5) *Greek Usage* employs the word inexactly of the nomads of the Syrian desert, but Herodotus (ii. 11; iii. 107–113; iv. 39) means by "Arabia" the peninsula. (6) In the following discussion "Arabia" will mean only the peninsula south of a line drawn from the head of the Persian Gulf to the southeast extremity of the Mediterranean, thus excluding the region commonly known as the Syrian desert.

II. Geography and Topography: Only the edges of the peninsula have been explored by Europeans. (For a history of exploration, cf. the chapter by Hommel in Hilprecht, *Explorations in Bible Lands*, Philadelphia, 1903, 691–752; D. G. Hogarth, *The Penetration of Arabia*, London, 1904.) For information about the central regions dependence must be placed upon Arab geographers; "mostly unexplored" is Hommel's significant phrase (Hilprecht, 697). (1) *Physical Features.* The shape is that of a thick-legged boot, with the toe toward the east. The peninsula is about 1,400 miles in length by from 600 to 1,200 in width. It consists of a narrow belt of fertile sea-plain around the east, south, and west sides, terminated by a chain of mountains, practically continuous, rising abruptly to a height of 4,000 to 10,000 feet, through which passes give access to a central plateau, which in its highest parts is 8,000 feet above the sea. Arabia has no river system, only a system of wadies or valleys. In these, during the dry season, the waters sink below the surface to be found only by digging; and the waters of the interior, collected temporarily in the wadies, lose themselves in the sand. (2) *Climate.* Lying as Arabia does between 12° 40′ and 32° n. lat., its prevailing temperature is high, notwithstanding its elevation. The interior is also very dry, owing to the fact that the mountains intercept the moisture from the sea. Different parts of the coast region have a rainy season which differs curiously in time; Yemen (the southwestern corner) has its rains between June and September. Oman (the southeastern projection), between February and April, and Hadramaut (the southern coast district), between April and September. (3) *The fringing sea-plain* possesses great fertility, though generally untilled. The most of the interior plateau is desert, either of sand or of gravel and stone. But there are areas of surprising fertility, some of considerable extent, as is involved in the existence of the kingdoms owning sway over settled populations (see III. below). A smaller area is under cultivation now than in early times owing to the decay of works of irrigation. (4) *Fauna and Flora.* The animal life as conditioned by the climate includes of course the camel; the lion, leopard, wolf, fox, hyena, and jackal are the beasts of prey and carrion; the antelope, gazelle, ibex, and hare are the game animals; the jerboa represents the rodents; and the marmot and ostrich are natives. The qualities of the Arab horse (not a native) will be at once recalled. The flora is characterized by the date-palm, fig-tree, aromatic herbs, and the coffee-berry. (5) *Inhabitants.* The statement has generally passed muster that the inhabitants of the peninsula are the purest type of Semites. The isolation of the country makes this a priori reasonable. The mental characteristics of the race are depth and strength of emotion, consequent warmth of feeling and brilliancy of expression, philosophical shallowness and metaphysical ineptitude, imagination of great power, a tremendous fixedness of will leading to fanatical intensity, and temperance in all but sexual relations. (6) *Commerce.* The products of Arabia have been remarkable for concentration rather than for bulk. Incense, spices, aromatic herbs, essences, gold, emeralds, agate, and onyx have been the staples of its trade. Before 1000 B.C., the Arabs were the common carriers of Eastern trade.

III. History: The function of Arabia in world-history has been to serve as the cradle, if not the birth-place, of the Semitic race. For this it was well fitted, isolated as it is by three seas and a trackless desert. At almost regular intervals it has sent forth hordes of Semites in waves of migration to become makers of history. The first of these made the initial conquest of the pre-Semitic civilization of the lower Tigris and Euphrates, and is represented by the great names of Sargon I. and his son Naram-Sin, about 3800 B.C. It was possibly the second wave which gave to Babylonia the Arabic dynasty which began to rule about 2400 B.C., represented best by the renowed Hammurabi (q.v ; possibly the Amraphel of Gen. xiv.), the codifier of Babylonian law. The third wave was the Aramean migration, assigned to about the seventeenth pre-Christian century, of which the Hebrews were an offshoot. The Nabatæans (fifth to third centuries B.C.) were the fourth, and the Mohammedan exodus made the last of this remarkable series of migrations. It looks as though Arabia's function had been to nourish her sons for a millennium and then to send them forth to conquer an empire. The general conception that Arabia was wholly a country of nomads is not true. Recent exploration, partial though it is, has proved that not only are there regions of thickly settled populations and numerous well-built cities in the present, but that there were several kingdoms of considerable importance at least as early as 1000 B.C. Three of the most noted are the Minæan, Sabean, and Hadramautic, situated in the south, but on the plateau; and those of Meluhha, Cush, and Mizri in the north, southeast from the Edomitic territory. The last two are referred to in the Old Testament, but are there confused with Ethiopia and Egypt, since the Hebrew name of the former is Cush and of the latter Mizraim. The investigations of Doughty, Halévy, and Glaser, to mention only these among a host of authorities, and the inscriptions now in the hands of scholars, render incontrovertible the existence of a Minæan realm as early as Solomon's time, and make it probable that this kingdom was subdued by a sovereign of the Sabean power (the Sheba of Scripture), which latter continued down to 500 B.C. or later. About the Christian era the Himyaritic or Ethiopian kingdom ruled in southern Arabia. While there are traces of Minæan and Sabean domination in northern Arabia, it is unlikely that the peninsula was unified governmentally before Mohammed's day. In spite of what has been said of the kingdoms of Arabia, the general idea that the Arab is a nomad is nearly correct. Tribal life is to him the normal one. Mohammed's miracle, therefore, was not, as he claimed, the Koran, but a united Arabia. Before him, Arabia was one great battle-ground of the tribes. The occupations of the people were commerce and pasturage; their pastimes were the feast, the chase, or the pursuit of vengeance in the blood-feud or of war for plunder or glory. A striking feature was the month of truce during which feud and war were suspended that the tribes might in peace revisit and worship at the shrines of their tribal deities. For the rest of the year, fighting was legal and normal.

IV. Religion: When Mohammed chose Allah as his god, he took one whose name was already common property throughout the country. The three goddesses who were daughters of Allah (cf. Wellhausen, *Reste arabischen Heidenthums*, Berlin, 1897, 24 sqq.) and were widely worshiped, testify to this fact. But the Koran testifies to the dominance of idolatry; the Kaaba was a home of idols. W. R. Smith has demonstrated the existence of animism, with the consequent or accompanying totemism, as native and persistent among Arabs. Stone-worship, the cults of local gods, the bloody and the mystic sacrifice, especially the primitive sacrifice in which god and worshipers were clan-brothers and commensals, are proved facts for this region. All of which is to say that the gods of Arabia were many. Yet the civilization of cities implies the supereminence of some gods with a prestige which lifted them above the horde of little deities. These greater gods were heaven-gods, a consequence of the clear atmosphere and brilliant skies. Examples of these are Athtar, a male deity, the evening or morning star (north-Semitic, Ishtar, female), and Wadd, the moon-god, known also as Amm and regnant over love. Sun-deities of different names were numerous and were often feminine. But underlying the cult of these more prominent gods was that of the local divinities, the more cherished favorites of the tribes and clans. Sometimes the images or symbols of tribal gods were collected in some shrine which then became the goal of pilgrimage,—the case of the Kaaba at Mecca. The "Black Stone" in the Kaaba, the only official relic of ancient Arabia, is pronounced meteoric. It is a remainder of a once dominant fetishism.

Owing to the difficulties offered by the physical character of the country and the rigid Mohammedanism of the people Arabia is not a promising field for Christian missionary enterprise. A few sporadic attempts have been made, however, in some of the coast towns, where foreign influence most readily finds entrance. There is a Roman Catholic vicar apostolic for Arabia with residence at Aden.

GEO. W GILMORE.

BIBLIOGRAPHY: For the geography résumés of the results of travelers are found in the chapter of Hommel and the work by Hogarth mentioned in the text. For a view of the facts gleaned from native sources consult R. Ritter, *Erdkunde von Arabien*, 8th double volume or xii.-xiii. of his collected works, Berlin, 1846-47; A. Sprenger, *Die alte Geographie Arabiens*, Bern, 1875; E. Glaser, *Skizze der Geschichte und Geographie Arabiens*, 2 vols., Berlin, 1890. For reports of travels, J. L. Burckhardt, *Travels in Arabia*, 2 vols., London, 1829 (a classic); C. Niebuhr, *Reisebeschreibung nach Arabien*, 2 vols., Copenhagen, 1774–78, French ed., Amsterdam, 1776–80; T. R. Wellsted, *Travels in Arabia*, London, 1838; W. G. Palgrave, *Narrative of a Year's Journey through Central and Eastern Arabia*, 2 vols., London, 1862–63; A. Zehme, *Arabien und die Araber seit hundert Jahren*, Halle, 1875; C. M. Doughty, *Travels in Arabia Deserta*, 2 vols., Cambridge, 1888; E. Nolde, *Reise nach Innerarabien*, Brunswick, 1895; R. E. Brunnow and A. von Domaszewski, *Die Provincia Arabia*, vols. i.–ii., Strasburg, 1904-06, 80 mks. per vol. For history C. de Perceval, *Essai sur l'histoire des Arabes avant l'Islamisme*, Paris, 1847–49; Ahmed Khan Bahadur, *The Historical Geography of Arabia*, 1840 (deals with the history and geography of pre-Islamic times); L. A. Sedillot, *Histoire générale des Arabes*, Paris, 1876; E. Glaser, *Die Abes-*

sinier in *Arabia und Africa*, Munich, 1889; H. Winckler, *Altorientalische Forschungen*, 2d series, i. 2, Leipsic, 1898. For inscriptions and the language: Osiander, in *ZDMG*, xix. (1865), 159–293, xx. (1866) 205–287; F Hommel, *Sudarabische Chrestomathie*, Munich, 1893; idem, *ZDMG*, liii. (1899), pt. 1; J. Halévy, in *JA*, series 6, xix. For the people: J. L. Burckhardt *Notes on the Bedouins and Wahabies*, 2 vols., London, 1831; S. M. Zwemer, *Arabia the Cradle of Islam*, New York, 1900 (deals also with missionary work). For the religion: Ahmed Khan Bahadur, u.s.; Smith, *Rel. of Sem.*; idem, *Kinship*; J. Wellhausen, *Reste arabischen Heidentums*, Berlin, 1897; G. A. Barton, *A Sketch of Semitic Origins*, New York, 1902; D. Nielsen, *Die altarabische Mondreligion*, Strasburg, 1904.

ARABIANS (Lat. *Arabici*): A name given by Augustine (*Hær.*, lxxxiii.) to sectaries in Arabia, mentioned by Eusebius (*Hist. eccl.*, vi 37), who says that they held that the human soul dies with the body and will rise with it on the Day of Resurrection. Origen combated this opinion at an Arabian synod about 246. Consult Walch, *Historie der Ketzereien*, ii 167–171; E. R. Redepenning, *Origenes*, ii. (Bonn, 1846) 105 sqq G. KRÜGER.

ARABIC GOSPEL OF THE INFANCY. See APOCRYPHA, B, I., 6.

ARAKIN. See TALMUD.

ARAM, ā'ram, ARAMEANS, ar"a-mī'anz, AND THE ARAMAIC LANGUAGE.

Aram is the Old Testament designation for the Semitic Arameans or Syrians settled in Syria and Mesopotamia, north to the Taurus and east to the Tigris; but, as these peoples never formed a political unit, the name is used only with reference to some particular tribe region, or state. Thus the Old Testament distinguishes. (1) *Aram Naharaim*, "Aram of the two rivers," i.e , the Euphrates and Tigris (or Khabur; Gen. xxiv 10; Deut. xxiii. 4, Judges iii 8; Ps. lx. title); in the Amarna Tablets (q v.) it is called *Na'rima* (*ZA*, vi., 1891, p. 258); in Egyptian inscriptions, *Nahrina* (W Max Müller, *Asien und Europa*, Leipsic, 1893, pp. 219 sqq.). The Pentateuch priest-code reads *Padan* (*Paddan*)-

1. The Name. Old Testament Usage. *Aram* (Gen. xxv 20; xxviii. 2, 5–7; xxxi 18; xxxiii. 18; xxxv 9, 26; xlvi. 15), "fields of Aram,"—a name which may be preserved in the Tell Feddan of Arabic geographers (see below, § 7). (2) *Aram Dammesek*, named from its chief city, Damascus, often called simply Aram because it was the people best known, and of most importance to Israel (II Sam. viii. 5–6; Isa. vii. 8; xvii. 3; Amos i. 5) (3) *Aram Zobah*, at the time of Saul and David the most powerful realm in Syria (I Sam xiv. 47; II Sam. viii. 3; x 6, 8; Ps. lx title; I Chron. xviii. 3; II Chron. viii. 3). Schrader (*KAT*. 135) identifies Zobah with the Subit of the inscriptions, which he puts south of Damascus; Halévy identifies it with the later Chalcis on the slopes of Lebanon. (4) *Aram Beth-Rehob* (II Sam. x. 6), a city not far from Dan (Judges xviii. 28) in the upper part of the lowlands of Lake Huleh, watered by the Leddan, the middle source of the Jordan. (5) *Aram Maachah* (I Chron. xix. 6), and (6) *Geshur in Aram* (II Sam. xv. 8), independent kingdoms in the time of David. (See below, § 9.)

In the list of nations in Gen. x., four descendants of Aram are mentioned: Uz, Hul, Gether, and Mash (verse 23). The first name is also found in Gen. xxii. 21 among the descendants of Nahor, and in xxxvi. 28 and I Chron. i. 42 among the Horites. In Jer. xxv. 20 "the kings of the land of Uz" are mentioned among those to whom Yahweh gives the wine-cup of his wrath; they are followed by the Philistines and the latter by Edom. Finally in Lam. iv. 21 the daughter of Edom is mentioned as dwelling in the land of Uz, i.e., having possession of the same. A comparison of these passages, including Job i. 1–3, shows that the Uzites as an Aramaic tribe must be looked for in the Hauran. Hul without doubt is the inhabitants of the Huleh low-country, mentioned above. Gether can not be identified. Mash, for which the Chronicler (i. 17) reads Meshech (cf. Ps. cxx. 5), has been connected since Bochart with Mt. Masius (cf. Strabo, xi., p. 541), now Tur Abdin, north of Nisibis. When Aram is made a descendant of Kemuel (Gen. xxii. 21) and a grandson of Nahor, a younger branch of the Aramaic people is probably meant.

As to the original home of the Arameans, the prophecy of Amos (ix 7) states that they were

2. Origin of the Arameans. brought from Kir and should go back thither in captivity (i. 5). The location of Kir is uncertain; some identify it with Cyrrhestica, between the Orontes and Euphrates; others think it means South Babylonia. The name has not as yet been found in inscriptions. Moses of Chorene (*Hist. armen.*, i., p. 12) mentions Aram among the ancestors of the Armenian people; but Aram has as little to do with Armenia as with Homer's *Eremboi* or *Arimoi*. The name may signify "elevation," "highland." In the cuneiform inscriptions it appears as *Arumu* and *Arimi*, the "land of the Khatti" also comprises the Arameans. Schrader thinks that the Khatti were the Western and Southern Arameans, the Arumu the Eastern and Northern. The Greeks called the Arameans Syrians, which is an abbreviation of Assyrians. Those Greeks who were settled along the southern coast of the Black Sea first applied the name to their Cappadocian neighbors, who were Assyrian subjects. Thence it was extended to the whole population of the Assyrian Empire, and thus it became synonymous with Aramea. Afterward the Christian Arameans adopted the name Syrian, because among the Jews Aramean meant heathen.

The religion of the Arameans was polytheistic (Judges x. 6; II Chron. xxviii. 23) and like all cults

3. Religion. of Nearer Asia was symbolic nature-worship. Owing to the dispersion of the Arameans, an Aramean pantheon is not known, but only individual gods. Furthermore, at a very early period, Babylonian, Arabian, and probably other deities were adopted by the Arameans; the Syrian god Tammuz (Ezek. viii. 14) is of Assyrian origin.

The Aramaic language belongs to the northern division of the Semitic family; it includes an Eastern and a Western branch. To the latter belongs the so-called Biblical Aramaic (Jer. x. 2; Dan. ii. 4–vii. 28; Ezra iv.–8, vi. 18; vii. 12–26; cf. Gen. xxxi. 47), which since the time of Jerome (*ad Dan.*, ii. 4) has been erroneously called "Chaldaic." According to II Kings xviii. 26, Aramaic was understood in Jerusalem in the time of the kings, though not by the common people. At an early time it was the *lingua franca* of Nearer Asia, and occupied a position similar to that of the English or French languages of to-day. About the middle of the second century B.C., the Aramaic had become the vernacular in Syria, Palestine, and the neighboring countries. To the Western Aramaic belongs also a great part of Jewish literature (Targums, Palestinian Gemara, etc.), the Samaritan, the idiom of the so-called Nabatæan inscriptions of the Sinaitic peninsula, the Palmyrene inscriptions, etc. The most important branch of the Eastern Aramaic is the so-called Syriac, usually designated as the "Edessene language"; its literature is almost exclusively Christian, and spread even into Persia. The division of these Syriac-speaking Christians into Nestorians and Monophysites resulted in the cultivation of an East Syriac (Nestorian, Persian) and West Syriac (Jacobitic, Roman) dialect. The oldest Syriac document still extant is the translation of the Old and New Testaments which probably belongs to the end of the second Christian century. (See BIBLE VERSIONS, A, III.) To the Eastern Aramaic belongs also the language of the Babylonian Talmud, a Jewish transformation of the Syriac; the Mandæan (called also Sabian), the dialects in which the holy writings of the Mandæans (q.v.) are written; and certain dialects, still spoken about Tur Abdin on the upper Tigris, in certain parts east and north of Mosul, in the neighboring mountains of Kurdistan, and on the Western side of Lake Urumiah. The Western Aramaic dialects are more closely allied to the Hebrew than the Eastern Aramaic, and not only strongly influenced the Hebrew, but finally displaced it. Just when this took place can not be determined, but at the time of Jesus the vernacular in Palestine was exclusively Aramaic. Also see MESOPOTAMIA.

4. The Aramaic Language.

W. VOLCK†.

The Arameans were the most widely distributed of the Semitic families in their permanent settlements in pre-Christian times. Till the end of the seventh century B.C. they were found as seminomads with enormous herds of cattle on both sides of the lower Tigris east of Babylonia. As shepherds and as traders they moved west and north from time immemorial along the course of the Euphrates as far as the mountains, also crossing the river into Syria in occasional bands. After the downfall of the Egyptian and Hittite régimes in Syria they occupied that region in large numbers in the twelfth century B.C., and soon became there the controlling power, a position which, as far as race and language were concerned, they maintained till many centuries after the Christian era. They thus extended from the western border of Elam, as far as the Mediterranean; anywhere in this immense area the Arameans were at home. They had the instinct and the habit of travel and trade. Even as shepherds they were not like the Bedouin Arabs, for they kept their flocks and herds mainly for sale in the markets of the cities, near which they were usually found. As traders they were for land traffic what the Phenicians were on the sea. The range of their activity and enterprise is indicated by the fact that in the eighth century B.C. Aramaic inscriptions were written in Assyria east of the middle Tigris, and in the extreme northwest of Syria; that Aramaic was then understood in Palestine (II Kings xviii. 26); and that soon thereafter the Semitic alphabet, with Aramaic endings to the names of the letters, was introduced into Greece from Asia Minor. The Arameans were, in fact, the successors of the old Babylonians in the control of the business and commerce of western Asia, and it was from their system of writing (not from the Phenician) that the later alphabets of most of the civilized world were derived.

5. Extent of Aramean Settlements.

6. Activity and Enterprise of the Arameans.

For Biblical history the most important Aramean settlements were those about the middle Euphrates in upper Mesopotamia, and those in southern Syria and northern Palestine which are usually represented in modern versions by the name "Syrian." The former region was Aramean from very early times, even when under Babylonian control in the fourth and third millenniums B.C. The center of the community was Charran (Haran), on the river Balich, one of the greatest trading cities of the ancient East. It was a seat of the worship of the moon-god, corresponding to Ur on the lower Euphrates. Hence the clan of Terah, to which Abraham belonged, when on its western migration from Ur halted at Charran and settled in its neighborhood, between that city and the Euphrates. This district is the *Paddan-Aram* of P, which is shown by Gen. xxxi. 21 to have been east of the Euphrates. *Aram Naharaim*, used by other writers for the same region, does not mean "Aram of the two rivers" (Euphrates and Tigris), but merely "Aram of the rivers," and therefore does not include Mesopotamia in the wider sense as the Septuagint translates it. Probably the right reading is *Naharim* ("rivers"), in accordance with the Amarna form *Na'rima*.

7. The Arameans of Mesopotamia.

This region was the ancestral home of Israel, as is indicated in the traditions of Rebecca and Laban, of Leah and Rachel, as well as in the saying "a wandering Aramean was thy father" (Deut. xxvi. 5, R. V., margin). After the establishment of Israel in Palestine and of the southern Arameans in the intervening Syrian territory, little is heard from the sa-

8. Their Place in Biblical History.

cred writers of the Mesopotamian Arameans. According to Judges iii. 8, 10 a king, Cushan-rishathaim, overran the whole western country including the land of Israel, which he held for eight years. Another brief notice is to the effect that Hadarezer king of the Arameans of Zobah, had the assistance of troops from beyond the river against King David (II Sam. x. 16).

9. Cities and States in Southern Syria.

Much more important for Israel was the group of communities on the northeast of Palestine, of which the most famous was Damascus, the greatest city and state ever controlled by the Arameans. Damascus, however, as a city, was much older than the Aramean immigration of the twelfth and eleventh centuries B.C., and was doubtless an Amorite trading-post in the old days of Babylonian supremacy. Indeed, it is doubtless true that the Arameans occupied Amorite settlements, just as the contemporary Israelites occupied those of the Canaanites. These "Syrian" states, southwest of Damascus, and on the lower slopes of Hermon, are first heard of in connection with the wars of David about 980 B.C. (II Sam. viii. and x.), the passage referring to the wars of Saul (I Sam. xiv. 47) being based on a confused reminiscence of later conditions. To Zobah (at first the most powerful state), Geshur, and Beth-Rehob on the east of the upper Jordan must be added Tob (Judges xi. 3, 5; II Sam. x. 6, 8); and to Maachah on the west must be added Hamath, to be distinguished from "Hamath the Great" (Amos vi. 2), the more famous city on the Orontes in Middle Syria. This Hamath lay northwest of the city of Dan, and beside it ran the road leading west and north to the valley of the Litany and Orontes (Cœlesyria). Hence the "entering in of Hamath" marked the northern boundary of Israel, as did also the neighboring city of Dan. All of these cities and petty states were long debatable ground between Damascus and northern Israel. They lay, however, within the natural domain of Damascus, and ultimately became Syrian.

10. The Arameans of Damascus and Israel.

Israel's relations with the kingdom of Damascus did much to determine its destiny After Damascus and the sister states had been made tributary to David, a new régime in Damascus put that city at the head of the Syrian Arameans in the days of Solomon (c. 945 B.C.), and threw off the yoke of Israel (I Kings xi. 23 sqq.). The next step was the annexation of northern Naphtali (already, as above stated, in large part Aramean), in the reign of Baasha, by Benhadad I. (about 890 B.C.). This was the beginning of a war which lasted a century, and which would certainly have resulted in the ruin of Israel, if it had not been for the repeated attacks made upon Damascus by the great Assyrian power. Israel suffered most from Benhadad II. and Hazael of Damascus. Only once is a truce mentioned between the two countries (I Kings xx. 34; xxii. 1), which lasted over two years (855–853 B.C.) and was favored by an exceptional combination of the western states against an Assyrian invasion under Shalmaneser II., so that in 854 B.C. Benhadad and Ahab were found fighting side by side in defense of the West-land. The war, when resumed, was for a time disastrous to the Hebrews, so that in the reigns of Jehu and Jehoahaz, Hazael of Damascus and his successor held not only northern but probably also southern Israel in subjection. At length in the reign of Joash of Israel in 797 B.C. Damascus was taken by Adad-nirari III., of Assyria, and Aramean domination came to an end. Damascus, however, retained its independence, which it held till it was converted into a Roman province after the capture of the city by Tiglath-Pileser III. in 732 B.C.

11. Spread of Aramean Influence in Later Times.

Damascus, however, still retained its commercial importance and remained the business and social center of Aramean influence in southern Syria, which increased with the extinction of the small western nationalities. Indeed, the unifying process through which the whole of western Asia passed under the domination of Assyria, the later Babylonian, and the Persian empires, was materially hastened by the trade and commerce of the ubiquitous Arameans. Palestine itself gradually became Aramean in speech, if not materially so in population. The prevalence of the Aramaic language for many centuries after the Arameans had ceased to have any great political importance is the most striking proof of the manifold activity of the people. Originally one of the three great north Semitic dialects, along with the Babylonian (Assyrian) and Canaanitic (Hebrew), it had practically displaced the other two as a living speech by the second century B.C. Thus it happens that not only were considerable portions of two Old Testament books written in Aramaic but also all of these books had to be popularly explained in Aramaic and translated into that language, in the form of the Targums, before and after the Christian era. Moreover, the language of the later Old Testament books generally is more or less colored by Aramaic, and Jesus and his disciples spoke an Aramaic dialect (Matt. xxvii. 46, and elsewhere). But the chief literary use of Aramaic came after the close of the canon, Edessa (modern Orfa) in upper Mesopotamia having succeeded to much of the business and importance of the neighboring Charran which remained pagan. A great Christian school was founded there in the second century, and this became the center of the vast "Syriac" literature.

J. F. McCurdy.

Bibliography: For history, etc., consult C. von Lengerke, *Kenaan*, i. 218 sqq., Königsberg, 1844; C. Ritter, *Erdkunde*, parts x. and xvi., Berlin, 1843, 1852; T. Nöldeke, *Namen und Wohnsitze der Aramäer*, in *Ausland*, xl. (1867), nos. 33–34, also 'Ασσύριος, Σύριος, Σύρος, in *Hermes*, v. (1871) 443–468, and *Die Namen der aramäischen Nation und Sprache*, in *ZDMG*, xxv. (1871) 113–131. For the people, A. Featherman, *Social History of the Races of Mankind*, ii., London, 1881; H. Spencer, *Descriptive Sociology*, v. *Asiatic Races*, London, 1876. For the religion, F. Bäthgen, *Beiträge zur semitischen Religionsgeschichte*, Berlin, 1888, and Nöldeke's review of the same in *ZDMG*, xlii. (1888) 470–487. For the Aramaic language, E. Renan, *Histoire générale et système comparé des langues sémitiques*, Paris, 1863; T. Nöldeke, *Die semitischen Sprachen*, pp. 31–47, Leipsic, 1889; idem, *Grammatik der neu-syrischen Spra-*

che am Urmia-See und in Kurdistan, Leipsic, 1868; idem, *Kurzgefasste syrische Grammatik*, Leipsic, 1898; S. D. Luzzato, *Elementi grammaticali del Caldeo biblico e del dialetto talmudico babilonese*, Padua, 1865, Eng. transl. by G. Goldammer, New York, 1877; E. Kautzsch, *Grammatik des biblischen Aramäischen*, Leipsic, 1884; J. Levy, *Chaldäisches Wörterbuch über die Targumim und einen grossen Theil des rabbinischen Schriftthums*, 2 vols., Leipsic, 1867–68; C. Brockelmann, *Lexicon Syriacum*, Berlin, 1895; R. Payne Smith and J. Payne Smith (Mrs. Margoliouth), *Compendious Syriac Dictionary*, Oxford, 1903; A. Meyer, *Jesu Muttersprache*, Freiburg, 1896. For the Aramaic and Nabatæan inscriptions, *CIS*, i. and ii. For the important inscriptions of Senjirli in northern Syria, D. H. Müller, *Die alten semitischen Inschriften von Sendschirli*, Vienna, 1893; *Ausgrabungen in Sendschirli*, in *Mittheilungen des königlichen Museums*, Berlin, 1893 sqq. On the extent of the Aramean settlements and their possessions in northern Palestine consult: Schrader, *KAT*, pp. 28–29, 36, 182, 232, 239; and H. Winckler, *Orientalische Forschungen*, vol. iii., part 3, Leipsic, 1905.

ARATOR, a-rē′-ter: Christian poet of the middle of the sixth century. He was a Ligurian of noble family, and was educated by the archbishop Laurentius at Milan; the poet Ennodius was his friend, and the latter's nephew Parthenius was Arator's fellow student at Ravenna. He chose a diplomatic career and for a time acted as *comes domesticorum*, and afterward as *comes privatorum* of the Ostrogothic king Athalaric. He then entered the priesthood and was made subdeacon at Rome by Pope Vigilius, to whom he dedicated his epico-didactic poem, *De actibus apostolorum libri ii.* (read in public in 544). In 1076 and 1250 hexameters he describes the deeds of the apostles to the martyrdom of Peter and Paul, taking the Acts of Luke as a basis. He treats his subject with some poetical skill and with rich allegorical expositions, which are often in bad taste. He aims to show the superiority of Peter to Paul, and the work contains traces of Mariolatry, hagiolatry, and relic-worship. An epistle of Arator's to Vigilius, a second to an abbot Florianus, and a third to his early friend Parthenius are also extant. His main work was much read in the Middle Ages, and exists in many manuscripts of the tenth and eleventh centuries. It and the letters are in *MPL*, lxviii. 46–252, and there is an edition by A. Hübner, Neisse, 1850.

K. Leimbach.

Bibliography: K. Leimbach, *Ueber den Dichter Arator*, in *TSK*, xlvi. (1873) 225 sqq., and the works on Latin literature.

ARCADIUS, ār-kē′-di-us, **FLAVIUS**: Eastern Roman emperor 383–408; b. in Spain, about 377; d. at Constantinople May 1, 408. He was the elder son of the emperor Theodosius and the empress Ælia Flavilla, and was educated in secular sciences at Constantinople by the sophist Themistius, and by Arsenius, an ascetic, in the Christian religion. In 383 his father conferred upon him the title of Augustus, and in 384 he was made consul. When in 394 Theodosius went to the West to overthrow the usurper Eugenius, the government was left in care of Arcadius, with the assistance of the minister Rufinus. By the unexpected death of the emperor, Jan. 17, 395, at Milan, Arcadius became emperor of the East. By nature good-hearted and yielding, also without energy and narrow-minded, he became the weak tool of those who knew how to obtain his favor, above all of Rufinus, a cunning and unprincipled Gaul, and, after his murder, of the eunuch Eutropius, who covered his selfish atrocities with the name of the lawful ruler, and finally till his fall (399) united all power in himself. Arcadius was also influenced by his wife Eudocia, the beautiful daughter of Bauto, a Frank. Under him the Byzantine empire assumed that oriental character, which it subsequently retained. His piety was sincere, and he worshiped the relics of saints and martyrs devoutly. Even before he was sole regent he interdicted the public worship, instruction, and organization of the heretics (*Cod. Theod.*, XVI. v. 24; a. 394), and in the following year withdrew all former privileges (XVI. v. 25). Investigations had to be made for heretics in the imperial chancery, and among the court-officials (XVI. v. 29). Closely connected with this was his procedure against polytheism. In 397 he ordered that the material from temples in Syria should be used for the repair or construction of public roads, bridges, aqueducts, and walls (XV. i. 36), and in 399 he issued an order to the prefect of the East to destroy all rural sanctuaries. In all this Chrysostom was his hearty supporter. The most important result was probably the destruction of the Marneion and of seven other temples in Gaza in 401 (cf. the interesting account in Marcus's life of Porphyrius, bishop of Gaza, and J. Dräseke, *Gesammelte patristische Untersuchungen*, Leipsic, 1889, pp. 208 sqq.). Yet it can not be said that Hellenism suffered much under Arcadius; compared with the policy of Theodosius, there was even a certain relaxation (cf. V. Schultze, *Geschichte des Unterganges des griechisch-römischen Heidentums*, i., Jena, 1887, 353 sqq., ii., 1892, passim). Toward the Jews Arcadius was surprisingly friendly, and it has been suspected that they secured the favor of Eutropius by money. They had a jurisdiction of their own similar to that of the bishops, and the right of sanctuary analogous to the ecclesiastical (*Cod. Theod.*, II. i. 10; IX. xlv 2; cf. Grætz, *Geschichte der Juden*, iv. 387 sqq.). Seditions from within, and inroads of the barbarians from without, made the rule of the weak emperor a sad chapter of Byzantine history, which, however, must not be judged wholly according to the unfriendly or hostile heathen sources (especially Eunapius and Zosimus). Quite a number of reforms were decreed during his government which is also not lacking in other good measures.

Victor Schultze.

Bibliography: The sources are in the writings of Zosimus, Philostorgius, Socrates, Sozomen, and Chrysostom; consult further Gibbon, *Decline and Fall*, chap. xxxi.; S. R. Sievers, *Studien zur Geschichte der römischen Kaiser*, 335 sqq., Berlin, 1870; F. W. Unger, *Quellen zur byzantinischen Kunstgeschichte*, vol. i., Vienna, 1878; A. Güldenpenning, *Geschichte des oströmischen Reiches unter den Kaisern Arcadius und Theodosius II.*, Halle, 1885; A. Puech, *St. Jean Chrysostome et les mœurs de son temps*, Paris, 1891, C. W. C. Oman, *Story of the Byzantine Empire*, London, 1892.

ARCANI DISCIPLINA ("Instruction in the [Sacred] Secret," i.e., initiation into the mystery): A term first applied by Dallæus and G. T. Meier to the practise of maintaining a studied reticence (*fides silentii*) concerning the form and character of introduction into the Church, as if this were something analogous to initiation into the mysteries of the heathen world. The practise is especially observed in the fourth and fifth centuries. Baptism and the Lord's Supper, with the baptismal formula and the Lord's Prayer, in so far as these had an essential part in the introduction, were made the center of the supposed mysteries. In accordance with this idea, after the sermon, to which all could listen, at the beginning of the so called *missa fidelium*, the deacon warned all uninitiated away from divine service with the words: "Let no one of the catechumens, let no one of the hearers, let no one of the unbelievers, let no one of the heterodox, be present" (*Apostolic Constitutions*, viii. 12).

The *arcani disciplina* became a subject of confessional polemics through the attempt of the Jesuit Emanuel von Schelstrate to prove that it was instituted by Jesus and followed by the apostles; and that for this reason the Roman doctrine of the sacraments (especially transubstantiation), the veneration of images and saints, and other teachings of the Roman Catholic Church do not appear in the early Church. In reply Tentzel proved conclusively that until toward the year 200 the Church knew of no mysteries to be kept secret. Nevertheless, Roman Catholic scholars with few exceptions (e.g., Batiffol) have endeavored to defend Schelstrate's position. Justin's detailed exposition of the act of baptism and the celebration of the eucharist, however (*Apol.*, i. 61, 66, 67), is decisive. The exclusion of the unbaptized was an inner necessity (cf *Didache*, ix. 5) and does not imply a mysterious character of the cult; the secrecy also concerned not the dogma directly, but the symbols and performance.

Various Theories.

Thus far Protestants are agreed, but not concerning the nature and origin of the *disciplina*. Casaubon assigned its beginnings to the influence of the heathen mysteries and a borrowing of their forms for purposes of instruction, and scholars immediately following him accepted his views. Frommann sought the root in an imitation of the Jewish practise with regard to proselytes. Rothe called attention to a connection with the catechumenate of the early Church, and Credner to a relation with the twofold division of the cult resulting from the dogmatic-mystic conception of the Lord's Supper. T. Harnack recognized in the discipline a systematic transformation of the divine service into a form of mystery,—a phenomenon which has a parallel in the fact that the Roman Catholic Church to-day finds the secret of its power in the mystic-theurgic act of its priests (cf. Bonwetsch). Zezschwitz maintained, more in accord with the views of Rothe, that the cult acquired an exclusive character and the *fides silentii* arose in the Church from prudential motives because of persecution; when persecution ceased, the sermon sufficed for the needs of the catechumens (*audientes*) and full knowledge of the higher Christian secrets, as well as participation in the vital part of the service, was reserved for a final grade of maturity (attained only by the *competentes*); references to these matters naturally ceased. It may confidently be asserted, however, that the *arcani disciplina* was not founded in the external condition of the Church or in pedagogic considerations, but was a real, though unconscious, assimilation to the ruling ideas of the mysteries. The notion that communion with God was possible only by assimilation to God in a future state of incorruption through the medium of sacred acts, led as naturally to the formation of a hierarchy, differing from the laity and bringing divine essence into it by sacred acts, as to a transformation of the divine service into a celebration of mysteries which were supposed to include the divine in symbols and symbolic acts. Anrich is correct, therefore, in designating the *disciplina* as an analogy within the Church of the system of efficacious initiations among the Gnostics and the natural outcome of the theology of a Clement and an Origen, influenced by the Greek mysteries (against this view, however, cf. Batiffol).

Not Earlier than the Third Century.

Zahn (p. 326) has demonstrated that the beginnings of the *arcani disciplina* can not be traced earlier than the third century. When Irenæus (*Hær.*, III. iv. 1–2) demands that the baptismal confession be transmitted orally it is only to the end that, being written in the memory, it may become an inner possession. Tertullian (*Apol.*, vii.; *Ad nat.*, i. 7) speaks of a *fides silentii* with reference to the Christian mysteries, but from the standpoint of an opponent. Hippolytus (*Ad Dan.*, i. 16, 18) speaks of baptism without pointing out the duty of silence. Phrases like "the initiated know" in Origen do not establish the existence of the *disciplina*, since it can not be proven that Origen represented general usage. In *Contra Celsum*, iii. 59–61, he has no cultic acts in view; when he remarks (*Levit. hom.*, 9, 10; ix. 364, ed. Lommatsch), "He who is imbued with the mysteries knows the flesh and the blood of the Word of God," he is thinking of the mysteries of the gnosis (Anrich, 129, n. 2). His reference to the anxiety lest some of the consecrated bread should be dropped (*Exod. hom.*, xiii. 3; ix. 156) is a warning against the inattentive hearing of the Word; and his reference (*Lev. hom.*, xiii. 3; ix. 403) to *ecclesiastica mysteria* proves nothing. Methodius does not apply Matt. vii. 6 to sacred acts (Photius, *Bibl.*, cod. 235), nor are such acts "the orgies of our mysteries, the mystic rites of those who are initiated" (*Sympos.*, vi. 6).

In the fourth and fifth centuries the *arcani disciplina* was in its bloom; the frequent occurrence in the sermon of "the initiated know," "the initiated," is characteristic, and the transference of the phraseology of the mysteries into the Church is evident. "To initiate" (Gk. *myeisthai*) and "to instruct" (*katēcheisthai*) become interchangeable terms. Baptism is called "the seal of the mystic perfection" and "a mystic purification (*katharmos*) and lustration (*katharsion*)"; the Lord's Supper is "the mystery"; its elements are "symbols." "To be initiated" (*mystagōgeisthai*) signifies to be competent to partake of the sacraments, and to betray the mysteries is expressed by the corresponding *exorcheisthai*.

It is characteristic of the *disciplina* that the immediate object of the mystery was not the dogma and sacramental gift, but the elements and the ritual performance. In Theodoret's dialogue *Inconfusus* (iv. 125, ed. Schultze), the orthodox shrinks from openly naming bread and cup lest "some one uninitiated be present," and vaguely calls the body and blood of the Lord a gift. The desire was, of course, to withhold even from the eyes of the initiated the act and the "mystic symbols"; hence the exclusion of the unbaptized from the *missa fidelium* and the watch at the door by the ostiaries. Baptism and the Lord's Supper were the real object of the *disciplina*. To keep people in actual ignorance was, of course, impossible, but the silence observed produced the impression of a mystery. The Lord's Prayer at the Supper held the same position as the confession in baptism; the character of secret objects was given to both (cf. Sozomen, *Hist. eccl.*, i. 20; Ambrose, *De Cain et Abel*, I. ix. 37). The opposite to the confession of the neophyte was the renunciation, which was also kept secret. Everything which preceded and followed baptism necessarily partook of the secrecy. The eucharist as the climax of the whole mystagogy is the mystery *par excellence*. Dogmas were mysteries (Basil, *De spir. sanc.*, xxvii. 66) only in so far as the Church generally claimed to possess wonderful mysteries, especially the dogma of the Trinity on account of its relation to the baptismal symbol; but no secrecy of the dogma was intended. With the disappearance of the catechumenate the *arcani disciplina* ceased, although in the Greek liturgy the formula for dismissing the catechumens remained; but the cult of the Greek Church now actually assumed the character of a mystico-allegorical drama, a mystery of the heathen kind, though of a higher type. N. BONWETSCH.

The Immediate Object of the Disciplina.

BIBLIOGRAPHY: I. Casaubon, *De rebus sacris et ecclesiasticis*, Geneva, 1654; G. T. Meier, *De recondita veteris ecclesiæ theologia*, Helmstedt, 1670; E. von Schelstrate, *Antiquitas illustrata circa concilia generalia et provincialia* and *Commentatio de s. Antiocheno concilio*, Antwerp, 1678, 1681; W. E. Tentzel, *Exercitationes selectæ*, ii., Leipsic, 1692, contains Tentzel's *Dissertatio de disciplina arcani*, 1683; Schelstrate's *Dissertatio apologetica de disciplina arcani contra disputationem E. Tentzelii*, 1685; and Tentzel's reply, *Animadversiones;* G. C. L. T. Frommann, *De disciplina arcani*, Jena, 1833; R. Rothe, *De disciplinæ arcani origine*, Heidelberg, 1841; K. A. Credner, in the *Jenaer allgemeine Litteraturzeitung*, 653 sqq., 1844; T. Harnack, *Der christliche Gemeindegottesdienst im apostolischen und altkatholischen Zeitalter*, pp. 1–66, Erlangen, 1854; G. von Zezschwitz, *System der Katechetik*, i. 154–209, Leipsic, 1863; N. Bonwetsch, *Wesen, Entstehung, und Fortgang der Arkan-disciplin*, in *ZHT*, xliii. (1873) 203–299; T. Zahn, *Glaubensregel and Taufbekenntnis in der alten Kirche*, in *ZKW*, i. (1880) 315 sqq.; E. Bratke, *Die Stellung des Clemens Alexandrinus zum antiken Mysterienwesen*, in *TSK*, lx. (1887) 647–708; E. Hatch, *The Influence of Greek Ideas and Usages upon the Christian Church*, chap. x., London, 1890; H. Holtzmann, *Die Katechese der alten Kirche*, in *Theologische Abhandlungen Weissäcker gewidmet*, pp. 68–76, Freiburg, 1892; G. Anrich, *Das antike Mysterienwesen in seinem Einfluss auf das Christentum*, Göttingen, 1894; G. Wobbermin, *Religionsgeschichtliche Studien zur Frage der Beeinflussung des Urchristentums durch das antike Mysterienwesen*, Berlin, 1896; P. Batiffol, *Études d'histoire et de théologie positive*, Paris, 1902; H. Gravel, *Die Arkandisciplin*, part i., Münster, 1902.

ARCHBISHOP: A bishop in the Roman Catholic and some parts of the Anglican Church, who has not only the charge of his own diocese like any other bishop, but also certain rights of oversight and precedence over several other bishops whose dioceses are included in his province. In the third century, by analogy with the political divisions of the Empire (see EPARCHY), there grew up an organization of several bishoprics under the leadership of a metropolitan, the bishop of the provincial capital; it was his place to conduct episcopal elections, to confirm the choice and to consecrate the one chosen, and to convoke the bishops of his province in an annual synod. In concert with them, he regulated the affairs of the province, and the synod formed a court of appeal from the decisions of individual bishops, as well as one of first instance for charges brought against them. In the following centuries the metropolitan system was adopted by the Christian countries of the West as well. In the Merovingian period, however, the joint power claimed by the princes in filling episcopal sees and the importance attained by national councils robbed the position of the metropolitans of much of its independence; nor were they able to recover it in the Carolingian era, between the domination assumed by Charlemagne and the papal claims to an immediate decision in weighty matters, for which the pseudo-Isidorian decretals had furnished a basis. The rights of a metropolitan were accordingly limited in the thirteenth century legal compilations of the *Corpus Juris Canonici* to the following particulars: (1) The confirmation of episcopal elections and consecration of bishops in his province; (2) calling and presiding over provincial councils; (3) general oversight of his suffragans, visitation of their dioceses, and imposition of censures and penalties on them, though not of deposition; (4) hearing of appeals from episcopal courts; and (5) the so-called *Jus devolutionis* (q.v.). The first of these he lost in the fifteenth century, when confirmation and consecration of bishops were reserved to the pope. The Council of Trent confirmed the second, but limited the third by requiring the assent of the provincial council. At the same time, however, he was charged with the erection, maintenance, and direction of seminaries in the dioceses of his suffragans, and with the enforcement of their obligation of residence. An archbishop has the title of "Most Reverend," and ranks immediately after patriarchs. He wears the pallium (q.v.) as a special symbol of his jurisdiction, and a particular kind of cross (*crux erecta* or *gestatoria*) is carried before him within his own province. The title ἀρχιεπίσκοπος is frequently applied in the fourth century to the metropolitan of Alexandria, but after the development of the great patriarchates it came to denote other bishops of large cities who were undistinguishable in rank from metropolitans; and the titles have been practically synonymous in the West—though there are a few Roman Catholic archbishops (such as those of Amalfi, Lucca, and Udine) who are not metropolitans, and in the case of titular archbishops (see BISHOP, TITULAR) it follows from the nature of their office that there is no metropolitan jurisdiction. In the Anglican communion, the title of archbishop was for a long time confined to the metropolitans of England and Ireland, owing to legal difficulties in the way of its use in the colonial churches; but of late years there has been an increasing tendency to its use, and the proposal has even been made to establish archbishops with metropolitan jurisdiction in the Episcopal Church of the United States. In the evangelical churches of Germany the dignity of an archbishop has been conferred only in individual instances on general superintendents, as by Frederick William III. on Borowski at Königsberg in 1829 (see BOROWSKI, LUDWIG ERNEST VON). (P. HINSCHIUS†.)

BIBLIOGRAPHY: Bingham, *Origines*, books i., iv., xvii.; C. W. Augusti, *Denkwürdigkeiten aus der christlichen Archäologie*, Leipsic 1820; A. J. Binterim, *Denkwürdigkeiten der christkatholischen Kirche*, V. i. 465 sqq., Mainz, 1829; A. Nicolovius, *Die bischöfliche Würde in Preussens evangelischer Kirche*, Königsberg, 1834; E. Löning, *Geschichte des deutschen Kirchenrechts*, i. 362, ii. 197, Strasburg, 1878; J. Mast, *Abhandlungen über die rechtliche Stellung der Erzbischöfe in der katholischen Kirche*, Freiburg, 1878; Hauck, *KD*, iii. 16 sqq.

ARCHDALL, MERVYN: Anglican bishop of Killaloe, Ireland; b. Feb. 16, 1833. He was educated at Trinity College, Dublin (B.A., 1856), and was successively curate of Templecrone (1856–57), Trinity Church, Dublin (1857–62), Lislee (1862–63), vicar of Templebready (1863–72), and rector of St. Luke's, Cork (1872–94). He was archdeacon of Cork from 1878 to 1894, canon of St. Patrick's Cathedral, Cork, in 1891, and examining chaplain to bishops Meade and Gregg of Cork from 1872 to 1894. He was dean of Cork from the latter year until 1897, when he was consecrated bishop of Killaloe.

ARCHDEACON and **ARCHPRIEST:** Officials who are mentioned very early as heads of the lower or ministering clergy and of the other priests. Both are assistants and sometimes representatives of the bishop, the archpriest more in liturgical functions, the archdeacon in those of church government. In the early history of the dioceses of northern and western Europe, which were originally much larger than the older ones of the East and South, we find a number of archpriests whose functions are different from those indicated. The diocese is divided into parishes (much larger than the modern parishes), frequently following political divisions in their boundaries. The inhabitants of a parish, considered as a single community, have one church, often on the site of a heathen temple, set apart for the principal ecclesiastical functions. This is the church for Sunday service, baptism, funerals, and the payment of church taxes. Through the surrounding country are scattered other smaller churches used for less important functions, and served by clergy who are representatives of the parish priest. With the increase in the number of principal or " baptismal " churches, the importance of the archpriests diminished. From the ninth century their place was taken by rural deans, who had the oversight of more than one archpresbyterate, and, as they were generally taken from among the archpriests, frequently retained that title. The archdeacons did not hold everywhere the same relation to the archpriests. Under Leo the Great (440–461) they appear in charge of church property and jurisdiction in the dioceses. By the ninth century, priests began to be named to this office, and finally none but priests held it, who were placed over the archpriests. About the same time in France, somewhat later in Germany, the custom arose of dividing the dioceses into several of these archdeaconries. With the development of the cathedral chapters, it became usual for the head of the chapter to be archdeacon, or, if there were several archdeacons in the diocese, the office was held also by canons or other heads of collegiate bodies. The power of the archdeacon gradually increased; by the beginning of the thirteenth century he is already known as *judex ordinarius*, and has an independent right to make canonical visitations, to decide many cases (especially matrimonial), to examine candidates for ordination, and to install beneficed clergy. The bishops found it necessary to repress the presumption of the archdeacons, and in some cases (as at Tours 1239, Liége 1287, Mainz 1310) they obtained legislation in councils against further growth of these powers; in other cases they set up officials of their own to exercise the jurisdiction which the archdeacons either had or claimed. Among these latter are the *officiales foranei*, with a concurrent jurisdiction, and above both, for the exercise of appellate jurisdiction and of the rights reserved to the bishops, the *officiales principales* and vicars-general. Since neither the archdeacons nor the archpriests gave ready submission to these new officials, a great number of local differences of usage grew up, which were first reduced to some sort of uniformity by the Council of Trent in the sixteenth century. By it the archdeacons were finally deprived of all criminal and matrimonial jurisdiction, and their right to hold visitations made dependent on the bishop's permission. Since that time they have declined in importance or disappeared entirely in many dioceses, and their functions are nowadays discharged usually by the vicar-general and his assistants. At Rome the archdeacon developed into the cardinal-camerlingo and the cathedral-archpriest into the cardinal-vicar, while in the other dioceses their place has been frequently taken by coadjutor or assistant bishops. (E. FRIEDBERG.)

In the Church of England the archidiaconal office has been retained in vigor. There are seventy-one archdeacons in all, each diocese having a plurality. They are members of the cathedral chapters and often hold separate benefices. Appointed by the bishop, the archdeacon assists the bishop in visitation and in looking after the temporalities of the parishes entrusted to his care. He has the privilege and duty of holding court from time to time and from place to place for the trial of minor ecclesiastical causes both disciplinary and financial. A. H. N.

BIBLIOGRAPHY: J. G. Pertsch, *Vom Ursprung der Archdiakone*, Hildesheim, 1743; Kranold, *Das apostolische Alter der Archdiaconalwürde*, Wittenberg, 1768; A. J. Binterim, *Denkwürdigkeiten der christ-katholischen Kirche*, I. i. 386–434, Mainz, 1825; *DCA*, i. 135–138; A. Schröder, *Die Entwickelung des Archidiakonats*, Augsburg, 1890; and the works on canon law.

ARCHELAUS, är″ke-lē′us. See HEROD AND HIS FAMILY.

ARCHEOLOGY, BIBLICAL: The term archeology has become current through the work of Josephus bearing that name (Gk. *Archaiologia*; Lat. *Antiquitates*),—a presentation of Hebrew and Jewish history from the Creation to the time of Nero. Before Josephus, Dionysius of Halicarnassus (i. 4; iv. 1) and others applied the name to ancient histories and mythologies. Biblical archeology in this sense should treat Biblical history in all its relations. The term is now restricted, however, to a certain section of Biblical history, and means the scientific description of the relations, institutions, and customs of the civil and religious life of Israel in Bible times. The science is thus distinguished from Biblical history in the common sense, from Biblical theology, and from Christian archeology and church history. It would be more exact to speak of Hebrew-Jewish archeology based on Biblical sources; but the old name is too firmly established to be superseded.

Meaning and Scope.

The science is one of the most important helps to the understanding of the Old Testament and such parts of the New as have a Jewish background; it acquaints both the scholar and the Bible-reader with the conditions which must be known if the events recorded and the religious views set forth are to be rightly appreciated. But its aim can only be attained when sought in the right way. The method must be historical and the study must begin with a critical examination of the sources; the customs and institutions described can not be considered isolated phenomena, but must be treated as parts of the organic whole of world history; their historical development must be traced. It may here be remarked that in the present state of knowledge of the history of Hebrew literature many points of archeology do not admit of a final decision. A topical arrangement on the whole seems preferable to an attempt to present the matter chronologically. The most natural subdivision draws the line between religious and secular things. The former division will include the holy places (the ark of the covenant, the tabernacle, high places, the temple, synagogues), holy actions (sacrifice, prayer, vows, oracles, purification), holy seasons (Sabbath, new moon, festivals), and holy persons (priests, Levites, seers, prophets, Nazirites, hierodules, etc.). The latter head subdivides into things of public and private life, and includes arts and sciences, weights, measures, divisions of time, and the like. A description of land and people forms a fitting introduction.

Aim, Method, and Subdivisions.

Of the sources of Biblical archeology, the most important are, of course, monuments, inscriptions, and coins. As to monuments, Palestine is well known to be poorer than most other lands of civilized antiquity. The most important now known are certain remains of buildings, walls, and aqueducts in Jerusalem. Here and there graves have been opened which throw some light upon burial customs. Pottery and weights may be mentioned here, though specimens are few. The triumphal arch of Titus in Rome has sculptures of articles of temple furniture, and various Assyrian, Egyptian, and Phenician monuments and sculptures illustrate Israelitic architecture (temples, palaces, altars, etc.), explain Israelitic customs (dress, war, etc.), or furnish pictures of Israelitic things or persons. Inscriptions relating to Hebrew and Jewish history are also surprisingly few. The only important ones thus far found are the Moabite Stone, the Siloam inscription (qq.v.), and the tablet on the temple of Herod. Certain Phenician inscriptions (such as the sarcophagus inscription of Eshmunezer and the votive tablet of Massilia), and some Greek and Latin inscriptions from Palestine touch upon Jewish history. The Assyrian and Egyptian inscriptions and those of Nearer Asia in general, as well as all monuments of these peoples, now and then furnish material of more or less importance (see INSCRIPTIONS). Such coins as we have belong to Maccabean and later times. The written sources are: (1) The books of the Old and New Testaments and the Old Testament apocrypha; (2) the writings of Josephus, especially the *Bellum Judaicum*, the *Antiquitates*, and the *Contra Apionem*, which are not altogether free from partizanship; (3) Philo's great allegorical commentary on the Pentateuch, which likewise has an apologetic tendency and betrays the fact that the author did not know Hebrew; (4) the rabbinic writings, Midrash, Targums, and Talmud, which are obscure and in their present form are hardly older than the second Christian century. Lastly, owing to the tenacity with which nomad Bedouins hold to their customs and religious conceptions for centuries, the accounts of travelers in Palestine and neighboring lands from the Middle Ages to the present time, as well as the descriptions of pre-Islamic Arabia, furnish an important source and one which has only lately begun to receive the attention which it deserves. (R. KITTEL.)

Sources.

The definition given above may be better appreciated if certain distinctions are pointed out and explained: (1) The distinction between Biblical history and Biblical archeology. The archeology of a country or a people is an essential preparation for the intelligent study of its history. But archeology also includes a related branch of historical study, namely the history and antiquities of the related peoples, and neither the beginnings nor progress of Hebrew history can be understood without a good knowledge of the older and of the contemporary Semites out of whom Israel grew, by whom its fortunes were determined, and whose genius influenced vitally its religious and social character. For example, in the first order of value for Biblical study must be placed the history and religion of Babylonia and Assyria, and the religious and social institutions of the ancient Arabians and Arameans. (2) The distinction between the relevant and the irrelevant in the history and antiquities of the related or neighboring peoples. Here the vaguest notions are encouraged by a loose application of the term archeology. For example, Egypt is constantly looked to for illustration of the Bible and for confirmation of its records, and a large part of the material pub-

Certain Distinctions.

lished by the Society of Biblical Archeology, and the greater portion of many separate works upon the same theme are devoted to Egyptian research, which has yielded very little for the understanding of Biblical history, and virtually nothing for the illustration of the religious and social life of the Hebrews. The reason therefor lies partly in the unique and unsympathetic character of Egyptian culture, partly in the fact that Egypt had very seldom any controlling influence on Palestine during the formative period of Israel, and partly in the circumstance that the Egyptian records are not so businesslike and accurate as, for example, those of Assyria and Babylonia, which form an indispensable supplement to Biblical history. (3) The distinction between ancient and modern conditions. It is a common error to suppose that the study of Bible lands and the manners and customs of their present habitants furnish Biblical archeology accurately reproduced. As a matter of fact such a study is informing only along the line of external resemblance. The outward life of the Semitic peoples has remained in many respects like its ancient past because of a similarity of occupation and the slow march of civilization. Occasional Bible texts here and there are illumined by a reference to modern customs. But there is a world-wide difference in the Nearer East, as elsewhere, between the life and spirit of the past and the present. The Bible itself, regarded in the light of its own political, social, and religious atmosphere, is the great handbook of Biblical archeology, whose primary elements, moreover, are not so much facts as conditions and principles, such as the inseparable relation between God and his people, between the people and the land, and between God and the land; the immediate and direct action of the Deity in all events and in all phenomena; the unity and actual identity of what are called the sacred and the secular, of religion and life, or of religion and morals; the solidarity of the community as the basis of the State and the ground of the responsibility of the individual; and a world-consciousness without abstract ideas and to which even God himself was the most concrete of realities. J. F. M.

Bibliography: Of works on Biblical archeology or useful as sources, the more important of ancient time are: Eusebius, "On the Names of Places in the Holy Scripture," commonly called the *Onomasticon*, translated into Latin by Jerome, with title, *De situ et nominibus locorum Hebraicorum*, both in P. de Lagarde, *Onomastica sacra*, Göttingen, 1870, 1887; Epiphanius, "On Weights and Measures," ed. Lagarde, *Symmicta*, ii. 149–216, Göttingen, 1880. More modern works: C. Sigonius, *De republica Hebraica*, Bologna, 1582; B. Arias Montanus, *Antiquitates Judaicæ*, Leyden, 1593; T. Godwin, *Moses et Aaron*, Oxford, 1616; ed. J. H. Hottinger, Frankfort, 1710; P. Cunæus, *De republica Hebraica*, Lyons, 1617; J. Spencer, *De legibus Hebræorum ritualibus*, Cambridge, 1685; rev. ed. by L. Chappelow, 1727, by C. M. Pfaff, Tübingen, 1732; J. Lund, *Die alten jüdischen Heiligthümer, Gottesdienste, und Gewohnheiten*, Hamburg, 1695; M. Leydekker, *De republica Hebræorum*, Amsterdam, 1704; A. Reland, *Palæstina ex monumentis veteribus illustrata*, Utrecht, 1714; A. G. Wähner, *Antiquitates Ebræorum*, Göttingen, 1743; J. D. Michaelis, *Mosaisches Recht*, Frankfort, 1771–75, Biehl. 1777, Eng transl., London, 1814; H. E. Warnekros, *Entwurf der hebräischen Alterthümer*, Weimar, 1782, 1794, 1832. Most of the works which had appeared at the time were collected by B. Ugolino in his *Thesaurus antiquitatum sacrarum*, 34 vols., Venice, 1744–69. From this time on there are numerous works, such as those of G. L. Baur, *Gottesdienstliche Verfassung*, Leipsic, 1805; J. Jahn, Vienna, 1817–25, Eng. transl., Andover, 1827; W. M. L. de Wette, 4th ed. by F. J. Räbiger, Leipsic, 1864; J. H. Pareau, Utrecht, 1817; J. M. A. Scholz, Bonn, 1834; E. W. Hengstenberg, *Bücher Mose's und Ægypten*, Berlin, 1841, Eng. transl. by R. D. C. Robbins, Andover, 1843; C. von Lengerke, *Kenaan*, Königsberg, 1844; H. Ewald, Appendix to vol. ii. of *Geschichte des Volkes Israel*, Göttingen, 1848, 1866, Eng. transl. by H. S. Solly, London, 1876; J. L. Saalschütz, *Mosaisches Recht*, Berlin, 1853; idem, *Archäologie*, Königsberg, 1855–56; K. F. Keil, Frankfort, 1858–59, 1875, Eng. transl., Edinburgh, 1887–88; D. B. von Haneberg, Munich, 1869; H. J. Van Lennep, *Bible Lands; their modern Customs and Manners illustrative of Scripture*, New York, 1875. The latest works are E. C. Bissell, *Biblical Antiquities*, Philadelphia, 1888 (conservative); E. Babelon, *Manual of Oriental Antiquities . Chaldæa, Assyria, Persia, Syria, Judæa, Phœnicia, and Carthage*, London, 1889, new ed., 1906 (valuable for purposes of comparison); J. T. de Visser, *Hebreeuwsche Archæologie*, 2 vols., Utrecht, 1891–98; J. Benzinger, *Hebräische Archäologie*, Freiburg, 1894 (an excellent handbook); W Nowack, *Hebräische Archäologie*, Freiburg, 1894 (goes well with Benzinger); C. Clermont-Ganneau, *Recueil des monuments inédits ou peu connus, art, archéologie, epigraphie*, 3 vols., Paris, 1897–1900; *Recent Research in Bible Lands*, ed. H. V Hilprecht, Philadelphia, 1898; T. Nicol, *Recent Archæology and the Bible*, London, 1899; a useful book is H. V. Hilprecht, *Explorations in Bible Lands*, Philadelphia, 1903; the various histories of Israel by Wellhausen, Stade, Kittel, and others are also important. For Arabian Antiquities see under Arabia, and for Egypt and Asia Minor see those articles. For the medieval itineraries and modern works of travel, consult R. Röhricht, *Bibliotheca geographica Palæstinæ*, Berlin, 1890; a useful bibliography will be found in J. F. Hurst, *Literature of Theology*, 118–130, New York, 1896.

ARCHEOLOGY, CHRISTIAN: The science which investigates and exhibits the ecclesiastical and religious forms of life and conditions of the Christian community for the period terminating with the Middle Ages. It may be divided into: (1) Law and government, including such topics as constitution, the clergy, monasticism, discipline, church law, synods, relations to the State, etc.; (2) worship—the various forms of divine service, festivals, such acts as baptism, confirmation, the marriage ceremony, burial, consecrations (of churches, altars, bells, holy water, etc.), benedictions and maledictions, exorcism, etc.; (3) art—architecture, painting, sculpture, church furniture, burial arrangements, etc.; (4) private and public life—the giving of names, marriage, position of women, prayer, education, slavery, occupations, corporations and societies, amusements, pilgrimages, superstitions, benevolent institutions, etc. Church music and books are better treated, it would seem, under the head of worship than of art. The sources of Christian archeology are the same as for church history. One of the most important and the last to receive the attention it deserves is furnished by monumental remains.

The history of the science begins with the first work of Protestantism on church history, the "Magdeburg Centuries" (1559–74; see Magdeburg Centuries), which, however, makes no distinction between archeology and history; the same is true of the work of the Roman Catholic scholar, Cæsar Baronius (cf. the epitome of Baronius's *Annales* by C. Schulting, Cologne, 1601). As an independent science Christian archeology may be said to have originated with Joseph Bingham's massive work, *Origines ecclesiasticæ, or the Antiquities of the Christian Church* (10 vols., London, 1708–22; see

BINGHAM, JOSEPH). A number of monographs followed during the eighteenth century, and during the nineteenth the study was pursued with new vigor. C. W. Augusti's *Denkwürdigkeiten aus der christlichen Archäologie* (12 vols., Leipsic, 1817-31), *Lehrbuch der christlichen Alterthümer für akademische Vorlesungen* (1819), and *Handbuch der christlichen Archäologie* (3 vols., 1836-37; cf. J. E. Riddle, *A Manual of Christian Antiquities, Compiled from the Works of Augusti and Other Sources*, London, 1839, 1843; L. Coleman, *The Antiquities of the Christian Church, Translated and Compiled from the Works of Augusti, with Numerous Additions from Rheinwald, Siegel, and Others*, Andover, 1841), were works of value. A. J. Binterim in his *Vorzüglichste Denkwürdigkeiten der kristkatholischen Kirche* (7 vols., Mainz, 1825-37) purposely ignored Protestant researches and contributed little to the subject. Other works worthy of mention are G. F H. Rheinwald, *Kirchliche Archäologie* (Berlin, 1830); H. E. F. Guericke, *Lehrbuch der christlich-kirchlichen Alterthümer* (Leipsic, 1847, Berlin, 1859; Eng. transl., London, 1851); V. Schultze, *Archäologie der christlichen Kirche*, in Zöckler's *Handbuch der theologischen Wissenschaften*, ii. (Munich, 1889). Lexical works are: W. Smith and S. Cheetham, *Dictionary of Christian Antiquities* (2 vols., London, 1875-80); F. X. Kraus, *Real-Encyklopädie der christlichen Alterthümer* (2 vols., Freiburg, 1880-86); Orazio Marnecchi, *Elements d'Archéologie chrétienne* (3 vols., Rome and Paris, 1890); F. Cabrol, *Dictionnaire d'archéologie chrétienne et de liturgie* (Paris, 1903 sqq.). A useful and readable book is Walter Lowrie's *Monuments of the Early Church* (New York, 1901). For works on Christian art, see ART AND CHURCH. VICTOR SCHULTZE.

BIBLIOGRAPHY: F. Piper, *Einleitung in die monumentale Theologie*, Gotha, 1867; F. X. Kraus, *Ueber Begriff, Umfang, Geschichte der christlichen Archäologie*, Freiburg, 1879.

ARCHES, COURT OF: The court of appeal of the archbishop of Canterbury. Its name comes from the original place of the court in the vestry of the Church of St. Mary of the Arches, which was in the crypt. The judge was originally called the Official Principal of the Arches Court, but now is called the Dean of the Arches, because the functions of dean and principal have been united. The dean once was set over thirteen churches in London, which were exempt from the bishop of London's jurisdiction, but now he has no such authority as the churches are no longer exempt. The office is only titular and the court itself has no regular place of meeting but sits in the library of Lambeth Palace or in the church house. The court is rarely convened. The judge is the only ecclesiastical judge authorized to sentence clergymen of the Church of England to deprivation. Appeals from the decision of the court are heard by the judicial committee of the Privy Council. The present judge (1906) is Sir Arthur Charles, appointed by the archbishop of Canterbury in 1899 and holding a life office.

ARCHEVITES, ăr'ke-vaits: The name of a people mentioned only in Ezra iv. 9, possibly one of the tribes settled by the Assyrians in Samaria (II Kings xvii. 24). While it is possible that the name was an official designation, it is better taken as meaning "inhabitants of Erech" (see APHARSACHITES).

ARCHICAPELLANUS, ăr"ki-ka-pel'lā-nus (also called *capellanus sacri palatii*, and by Hincmar of Reims *apocrisiarius*): The title of the principal ecclesiastical dignitary at the court of the Frankish sovereigns, who not only presided over the other court chaplains but also had the oversight of the court school, and from the reign of Louis le Débonnaire (814-840) adjudicated all matters of justice at court which affected ecclesiastics. It was thus a very influential position. In 856 the *archicapellanus* was put at the head of the court chancery, which had been managed under the Merovingian line by a secular commission and under the Carolingians by a *cancellarius*. The combined functions were entrusted to Archbishop Liudhard of Mainz in 870, and the title *archicancellarius* became commonly applied to the office, which under the Ottos was definitely attached to the see of Mainz. But from 1044 the archbishop only bore the latter title, while that of *archicapellanus* once more designated a strictly court functionary, whose place was taken after the thirteenth century by the almoner (q.v.). (E. FRIEDBERG.)

BIBLIOGRAPHY: A. J. Binterim, *Denkwürdigkeiten der christkatholischen Kirche*, I ii. 83 sqq., Mainz, 1825; G. Waitz, *Deutsche Verfassungsgeschichte*, iii. 516 sqq., iv. 415, Kiel, 1860-61.

ARCHIEREUS, ar"ki-ĕr'e-us: A common designation in the Greek Orthodox Church for the higher clergy in distinction from the other from presbyter down.

ARCHIMANDRITE, ăr"ki-man'drait (Gk. *archimandritēs*, "ruler of the fold," *mandra*, "fold," being applied to a monastic association as consisting of the sheep of Christ): A name given to the head of a larger monastic community, either the abbot of a single monastery or, more in accord with the meaning of the word, the general abbot of several monasteries belonging to one congregation. The title was in general use in the East as early as the fifth century. In the West it is found in the rules of Isidore of Seville (vi.) and Columban (vii.), of the latter part of the same century. From the tenth century it served as a general designation of prelates, even of archbishops. In 1094 Roger of Sicily put all Basilian monks of Sicily and Calabria under an archimandrite, who was later superseded by a secular prelate. By a brief of Urban VIII., Feb. 23, 1635, the archimandrite of Messina was granted quasiepiscopal jurisdiction, the use of the pontificals, and other privileges. The abbots of the Greek Uniate Churches in Poland, Galicia, Transylvania, Hungary, Slavonia, and Venice also have the title "archimandrite." In the Russian Church the archimandrites enjoy high honor and wear marks of respect which elsewhere belong only to bishops—infulæ, staves, crosses, and the like. They are generally under the diocesan bishop, though many had become immediately subject to the patriarch of Constantinople or the Russian metropolitan previous to the formation of the Holy Synod. Consult Du Cange and, for a most exhaustive treatment, *ACL*, s.v.

ARCHITECTURE, ECCLESIASTICAL.

I. General Treatment: Christian architecture, as a separate and independent thing, exists no more than a Christian state. The conception of a state is not altered by the fact that its citizens happen to be Christians; nor does architecture receive its essential form from being used for Christian or non-Christian purposes. Some of the problems of architecture were altered with the advent of Christianity, as it had now to build churches instead of temples, one of the most important tasks ever laid upon architecture, and in fact for many centuries almost the only important one. The first question to be considered is the origin of this problem, the origin, that is, of specially designed church buildings.

1. The First Places of Christian Worship.

The oldest documents referring to Christian worship show that the faithful assembled in the house of some member of the Church. At Jerusalem they met from house to house (Acts ii. 46); at Troas in an upper room (Acts xx. 7-8); Paul designated Gaius as the host of the whole church of Corinth (Rom. xvi. 23), implying that when they came together as a church, they met in his house. The mention of upper rooms does not prove that such were the only parts of the houses in which these gatherings took place; and we must remember that these houses were usually the small houses of poor people, constructed in the usual manner of the Greco-Roman world. Since the rooms were generally small, there would be no place for the assembly as soon as it got beyond a small number, except in the *atrium* or court-yard; the contention that divine worship could not have been held there, because the sacred mysteries would have been exposed to profane eyes, can not be upheld, as the *arcani disciplina* (q.v.) is of later growth. This domestic worship was in harmony with the spirit of early Christianity, full as it was of ideas of one family of brethren. A Christian house was the ideal place for it. The primitive Church, therefore, lacked not only the means but the motive to erect any special building for divine worship; it had no temples, and expressly rejected the idea of building them (cf., e.g., Minucius Felix, *Octavius*, x., xxxii.).

2. The First Special Buildings.

Nevertheless, it was not long before special buildings were erected for worship, and considered holy. To understand the change, it is necessary to try to fix the date at which this took place. Unquestionably special places existed in Alexandria in the time of Origen (cf. his "On Prayer," xxxi. 5, Berlin ed., p. 398); but the date may be put further back by observation of the popular use of the term *ekklēsia*. In classical Greek meaning an assembly of citizens, it came in Christian use to denote, first the gathering of the believers, then the Christian community either local or universal, and finally the meeting-place. This last use is common by the beginning of the fourth century; it is found in Eusebius and in his Latin contemporary Lactantius (*De mort. persec.*, xii., p. 186, ed. Brandt and Laubmann). But still earlier, Clement of Alexandria (*Strom.*, vii. 5, p. 846, ed. Potter), Hippolytus (*In Dan.*, i. 20, p. 32), and Tertullian (*De idol.*, p. 36), shortly before or shortly after the year 200, all apply the word to a distinctly recognized place of worship. The two latter also call it "the house of God." The Greek term *kyriakon* (Eng. "church"), with its Latin equivalent *dominicum*, appears somewhat later. But by about 200 there were at least two recognized names for a Christian place of worship, and the existence of a name demonstrates the prior existence of the thing. Whether these buildings belonged to the community or to individual Christians can scarcely be answered with certainty for the third century; the theory of corporate ownership is doubtful at the beginning of this period, though it becomes demonstrable toward the close. The edict of Constantine and Licinius, given in Eusebius, *Hist. eccl.*, x. 5, in 313 assumes a generally recognized corporate possession of many Christian meeting-places.

3. Changes Demanded by Altered Circumstances of Christians.

Between the spring of 58, when Gaius was receiving the church of Corinth in his house, and the time about 200, when a Christian goes into a special "house of God," Christianity had ceased to be the close brotherhood which it was at first; it had developed a complicated organization, with a marked distinction between clergy and laity; the conceptions of priest and sacrifice had won a place. And as the body changed, so did its worship; the place which had sufficed for the simple, informal gatherings of the first Christians was no longer adequate.

The next question, as to the form of these earliest distinct churches, is one which it is impossible to answer certainly from direct tradition. But it can not be avoided, because on it depends another, as to the origin of the Christian basilica, than which there is none more important in the whole range of ecclesiastical archeology.

4. Origin of the Christian Basilica.

The basilica has an influence on the development of church architecture to the present day, and this development is unintelligible without an attempt to arrive at a theory of the origin of this structural form. Its definition is not matter of controversy; it is an oblong building, divided by rows of pillars into three (or sometimes five) aisles, the central one the highest and covered with a flat roof, with a projecting addition, generally semicircular, more rarely square, at one end. When, however, it is asked how such a building came to be constructed for Christian worship, there is no such possibility of agreement. It has been held to have originated from the forensic basilica or the so called private basilica; from the Roman dwelling-house or the *cella cimiterialis;* and from the demands of Christian worship by a new creation. The limits of an article like the present preclude minute examination of these various theories; but obvious objections lie against all of them, as they are expressed by their defenders. The most certain fact in this whole discussion is that when the Church was established under Constantine, it did not need to go in search of a form for its buildings; the form already existed, substantially the same in all parts of the empire. It is not too much to say that we are forced to consider the form found in the beginning of the fourth century as the product of a long course of development. From what has been said, it follows that this development took place approximately from 180 to 300. Eusebius (*Hist. eccl.*, viii. 1, 5) indicates that before 260 the churches were what we might call small oratories, but increased in size after that date—though this increase must not be exaggerated; the facts that the famous church of Nicomedia could be razed to the ground in a few hours (Lactantius, *De mort. persec.*, xii., p. 187; Athanasius, *Apol. ad Const.*, xv., ed. Maur, i. 1, p. 241), and that the churches of Treves and Aquileia needed to be replaced by larger buildings as early as 336, show that it was only relative. Thus, though the hypothesis of a development from the private house of the earliest age is attractive, it does not lead directly to the basilican form, which in its essence requires a considerable size; a basilica for one or even two hundred people could not have been constructed. What we need, and what these various theories do not provide, is an intermediate stage.

5. First Step toward a Church Building.

A direct prescription as to church-building is found for the first time in a fourth century passage incorporated with the Apostolic Constitutions (II. lvii. 3), which shows what was then regarded as essential. This was very little; it is limited to a marking of the distinction between clergy and laity, and a special place for the bishop. Accordingly, the place set apart for the clergy was a more or less fixed dimension; its form might vary—it might be made either by the cutting off of one end, or by the addition of a semicircular or oblong space, in the middle of which was the bishop's seat. That the semicircular or apsidal form finally prevailed is due partly to acoustic considerations—the bishop preached from his throne—and partly to the esthetic motive which made this form a popular one in the architecture of the imperial period. The space assigned to the laity, as long as they were comparatively few in number, could only be a simple oblong, the form which appears as normal in the Apostolic Constitutions. This general type, of a simple oblong room with an apse at one end, may safely be taken as that of the churches which after 260 were demolished or abandoned. None of them is preserved; but churches like Santa Balbina in Rome and that of Hidra in Africa show that this form did not at once disappear even when the basilica became the recognized type. The Hidra church is particularly instructive; it is square and small—if the measurements given by Kraus are correct, the sides are only about 20 feet, with a corresponding apsidal *presbyterium*. This is the church for not more than 100 people which we need for our intermediate stage.

6. Second Step.

The development from this to the basilica falls probably in the period between 260 and 303, which was marked by great activity in building. The motive of the change was the need for more space; the problem was, how to attain this end without upsetting the recognized plan of an oblong auditorium with an added apse for the clergy. The proportional lengthening of the main hall could not go far, as the extension of the width was limited. The only thing to do was to break up the width, and thus came a division of aisles. The final solution, that of a wide central division with narrower side aisles, does not seem to have been reached at once; the basilica at Hidra shows the singular arrangement of side aisles wider than the middle section. A period of experiment must have come first; but, given the division, both esthetic and practical considerations inevitably suggested the plan finally adopted. The middle section being the main division, its raising to a greater height followed, for purposes of lighting, especially since other buildings must have frequently stood on each side of the church. This arrangement was not new; it has been found, for example, in the temples of Hierapolis and Samothrace: and thus it is not surprising that the same or a similar solution of the problem was found simultaneously in different places—though it probably required some time for this solution to be universally recognized as the best, as it was in the fourth century. The designation of churches as basilicas must have begun in the third century, since it is already a familiar term at the beginning of the fourth. This transition was the easier because the original meaning of the word had been practically superseded by what was nearly the sense of our word " hall."

With the reign of Constantine begins the building of large and splendid churches, through his encouragement and the activity of the bishops, first in the East, later in Rome and the West. The earliest was the church at Tyre under Licinius; then follow, under Constantine, the buildings at Jerusalem, Bethlehem, Mamre, Constantinople, Nicomedia, Heliopolis, and perhaps St. Peter's in Rome. None of these remains; the oldest large basilicas extant, Santa Maria Maggiore in Rome and the churches of Ravenna, belong to the fifth and sixth centuries. Thus we are dependent on the descriptions of the lost buildings, the first of which is the unfortunately too rhetorical account given by Eusebius (*Hist. eccl.*, x. 4) of the church at Tyre. According to this picture, it corresponded in essential details to the type of basilica found in Africa and the West; but we learn from the latter not to suppose that everything described by Eusebius was uniformly present.

7. Church-Building Activity after 313.

Though the adoption of the basilican style did not exclude creative freedom on the part of the architect, no further development of the idea ever took place in the Roman empire. Here, as in other things, we see the powerless despair which contented itself with endless reproductions of an accepted type, and reproductions which were successively poorer. The basilican style in itself, however, was capable of development to a marked degree. Among the artistic creations of the ancient world, it was the one which was destined to have the greatest future. It is conceived wholly in the ancient spirit, as is shown particularly in the feeling for space which regulated its dimensions. The relation of height to length and breadth shows that the beauty of the building was sought in broad, dignified extent. That it grew up in an era of decaying art is evident on the face of it. Only in the rows of columns which divide the aisles is constructive necessity made to minister to beauty; nowhere in the rest of the building is there any attempt to please. There is nothing more depressing in the history of architecture than the straight brick walls, only broken here and there by a few small windows, that enclose it. Decoration of a sumptuous kind partly makes us forget this poverty; but the decoration is purely arbitrary, extraneous, not required by the nature of the plan.

8. Basilica Style Reproduced.

The basilica, then, was the normal type of churches built to hold congregations assembled for worship. But these were not the only ecclesiastical buildings thought of after the fourth century. Special ritual observances or the desire to display princely pomp brought about the use of the circular structure, which became the normal one for baptisteries and memorial chapels. As to the former, when we remember that adult baptism was frequent, that immersion was customary, and that the observance of regular seasons for baptism made the number of candidates large, we see that a comparatively large pool was required; and the building constructed to enclose it naturally allowed for placing it in the center, and so could be only circular. The building of memorial churches was begun by Constantine with that of the Holy Sepulcher at Jerusalem, and again the circular or polygonal form was prescribed by its relation to the sacred object or the tomb which they were intended to enshrine. The simple structure might be enriched by a number of small chapels or niches, or surrounded by a corridor; a cupola or dome necessarily covered it. Here it was not so much the working out of a new form as the adaptation of one already existing; even when the chapels were prolonged so as to make the ground-plan into a Greek cross, it was scarcely a new form. Examples are the Lateran baptistery and the two at Ravenna, the tombs of Galla Placidia and Theodoric at Ravenna, and the church of Santa Costanza in Rome.

9. Change to Circular Buildings.

When an attempt was made to use these buildings for general purposes of worship, a new problem arose in the laying out of the approved places for clergy and people. Churches of this type were used in the East for congregational purposes as early as Constantine's reign; according to Eusebius's description (*Vita Const.*, iii. 50, p. 207), that which the emperor built at Antioch was apparently an octagonal building surmounted by a cupola, and so was the one put up by the father of Gregory Nazianzen in his see city (*Orat.*, xviii. 39, *MPG*, xxxv. 1037), while Gregory of Nyssa (*Epist.*, xxv., *MPG*, xlvi. 1093) describes a similar one. But we know nothing of the interior arrangements of these. Later (not before the second half of the fifth century) comes the puzzling church of Santo Stefano Rotondo on the Celian Hill, whose size proves that it was meant for public worship. This, the ugliest building of the kind ever constructed, only shows how far the Roman architect was from understanding his task; he built a church as he would have built a memorial chapel, without realizing the total difference in requirements. Yet, in spite of all the difficulties presented by this form, especially by the absence of perspective when the altar was placed in the middle, a certain number of churches were built with which no basilica can compare in beauty—really the highest achievements of the older ecclesiastical architecture. The best of these is San Vitale at Ravenna (early sixth century). Here one of the eight chapels is removed, and a longer apse put in its place, which gives a certain effect of length—though only by a disturbance of the harmony of the original plan. Much more admirable is the solution found in the church of Sts. Sergius and Bacchus, and, more completely, in St. Sophia, both in Constantinople. But here the essence of this central form of structure is not only disturbed, as in San Vitale—it is absolutely abandoned. In the Greek and Russian churches the domed church became the accepted type, after the model of St. Sophia. The ground-plan of the latter was not commonly followed, the cruciform being preferred; and thus, when each arm of the cross was surmounted with its cupola, as well as the central space, they became simply a number of similar connecting rooms, and the main attraction of the type, its impressive unity, was lost.

10. Memorial Churches.

The new peoples who were to carry on the work of civilization during the Middle Ages inherited in the basilica a type capable of great development, though not, as it came to them, much developed.

It was the only type which had great influence on medieval architecture. The men of the Middle Ages were by no means blind to the attractions of the style which we call the Byzantine; but the attempts made in that style, as by Charlemagne at Aachen in imitation of San Vitale, and by others after the Church of the Holy Sepulcher had aroused the admiration of the crusaders, were only sporadic; they did not determine the future progress of ecclesiastical architecture, which has the basilica for its true starting-point.

11. Basilica the Accepted Type of Western Medieval Churches.

It is worth while to examine the attitude of the different modern nations toward this inheritance of the past. In Rome building activity was never at a standstill, though a large part of it was mere restoration. But for six centuries after Gregory the Great (d. 604), people did not conceive the idea that they could build otherwise than as their fathers had built. The new churches of the twelfth and early thirteenth centuries, Santa Maria in Trastevere and San Lorenzo fuori le Mura, simply reproduce the scheme of the basilica; yet when Honorius III. (1216-27) began the latter, Gothic churches had been building in France for more than fifty years. Rome, then, has nothing to do with the history of medieval church architecture. The rest of Italy was not quite so unfruitful. Tuscany is far from poor in admirable medieval buildings. These are partly in the old line of development—San Miniato at Florence, for all its attractive features, shows no trace of new constructive ideas—and partly carry it further. This is especially the case with the cathedral of Pisa, which is not only the most successful example of what Tuscan artists could do in the handling of large masses and in richness of decoration, but carries the basilican principle a distinct step further. It is enlarged into a frankly cruciform shape, and carries the principal feature of the Byzantine style, the dome. But, however celebrated are the beauties of this cathedral, one can not deny that the combination of these two widely different forms is less successful here than in San Vitale and St. Sophia. There is an especially irreconcilable antagonism between the dome and the flat roof of the nave. The cathedral of Pisa does not unfold the possibilities latent in the basilican type—it merely attaches to this type a foreign element. In the north of Italy a more decisive forward step was taken, when its architects boldly faced the problem of the vaulting of the basilica. The answer was not found at once. In Sant' Ambrogio at Milan the execution of the vaulting is at the expense of the lighting of the nave, and the church is gloomy in spite of Italian suns. San Michele at Pavia and the cathedral of Parma were the first to succeed in obviating this defect.

12. Combination of Basilica and Domed Styles.

But the progress of wide development of the basilican scheme is not connected with the Lombard churches; it goes on across the Alps, where from the Frankish period its course is uninterrupted. Its first effort was the so called Romanesque basilica, though the name is modern and not very satisfactory. The development of this second important type is not as obscure as that of the original basilica but here, too, difficulties abound. The weakest feature of the old basilica was the arrangement of the transverse section; and it was here that the innovators took up the task. Cruciform basilicas had been built in the Frankish kingdom even before Charlemagne; and the emphasis laid upon this shape leads us to think that symbolic more than artistic considerations determined its adoption. Yet the esthetic gain was considerable. It led to the lengthening of the choir or chancel into a harmonious proportion to the total length of the church. The raising of the choir above the level of the nave has been thought to have originated in the increasing veneration of relics; altars had long been erected over the graves of the martyrs, but now the narrow crypts of the earlier period gave place to larger chapels, with the result indicated. Possibly the same motive led to the addition of a second apse at the western end of the church, which was, in any case, a step toward connecting the church and the tower. Towers had not been a part of the original basilica, except in some cases in Syria. At the very beginning of the Middle Ages, without, it would seem, any influence from the East, the oldest towers begin to appear in Italy—unlovely erections in the shape of a cylinder or a parallelepiped, which display the inability of the period to construct an architectural work divided into well-related parts. No attempt was made to connect them with the church. In the Frankish kingdom the construction of towers is at least as old as in Italy—in any case pre-Carolingian; but here we meet with attempts to break up the unwieldy mass and to place it in relation to the church. Another change was in the supports of the roof. The old columns were replaced by heavier pillars, capable of bearing a greater weight; and this was again a step in advance. The use of columns in the basilicas was a degradation of this fine element of classical architecture, which was not designed to support the lofty walls of the nave of the Christian church. The architects of the fourth and fifth centuries were insensible to the discordance between their form and their use; but whether or not the German innovators felt it, they removed it. The tendency to go beyond tradition thus showed itself in the most various ways in the Frankish empire; how far it had gone by the first half of the ninth century may be seen in the plans of St. Gall. The final result was the Romanesque basilica which dominated all the Christian countries north of the Alps.

13. The Romanesque Basilica.

Though, however, there is this general agreement in type, each country developed along its own lines. The most instructive illustrations may be taken from France and Germany. In the latter country the plan of the old basilica was preserved in these particulars: The threefold division of the congregation's part, the raising and direct lighting of the nave, the flat roof, and the termination of the whole building in an apse or choir. Four main features were new. The first is the preference for

14. Variations in the Detail of the Romanesque Basilica.

the cruciform structure, from which sprang the establishment of fixed proportions for the whole church; the square formed by the intersection of the two arms of the cross was taken as the unit, to be repeated once on each of three sides, and twice or three times on the other. The second new feature is the connection of the tower or towers with the church, so that under various arrangements, with one, two, or more towers, the aim was always to present them as an integral part of the building. The third point is that the attention was no longer concentrated on the interior; by the development of façades and doorways, by the breaking up and diversifying of the wall-surface, the exterior of the church took on a new character of imposing beauty. Fourthly, the individual elements of the whole were freely worked over and transformed. The old models were not cast aside—the acanthus capital was imitated for a long time—but new forms, appropriate both to the material and to the special end in view, were boldly created. Outside, however, of these general characteristics, there was the greatest freedom in design. In one place an apse was added on the eastern side of each transept, forming a termination to the side aisles. In another, the side aisles were carried out beyond the transept, and then terminated each by an apse. In a third, these aisles were curved around the main apse, and relieved by smaller apsidal formations projecting from the curve. Here the semicircular apse was employed; there the polygonal shape was preferred, or the old rectangular preserved. The same freedom is found in the supports; sometimes columns still uphold the roof of the nave, sometimes pillars, or an alternation of both. The presence or absence of galleries afforded scope for infinite variety. This is what gives the Romanesque basilica not the least of its charms. No style excludes mere slavish copying of models more than this; none offered greater opportunities to the artistic imagination.

And yet the flat-roofed basilica was only a preparation for a still higher form—the vaulted church.

15. The Vaulted Church.

It was probably less artistic dissatisfaction with the flat roof that brought about the change than a desire to secure protection against fire by substituting stone vaulting for a wooden roof. Medieval histories are full of accounts of devastating conflagrations in the principal churches. The change was made gradually; after architects had tried their hands at vaulting the side aisles, they came in 1097 to carry a vault over the broad nave of the cathedral of Spires. Cross-vaulting was here employed, thus distributing the weight of the vault among four supporting pillars. The example was soon followed in Mainz and Worms, in the abbey church of Laach, and elsewhere: and the advantages of this style were speedily recognized.

Besides the new possibility of reaching a strictly symmetrical disposition of the ground-plan, other changes came in. The great Romanesque churches were usually monastic or collegiate, and thus served not only for the worship of the laity in general but also for the daily offices of canons or monks. Consequently, in opposition to the natural arrangement of the building, the choir was cut off from the nave by a high stone screen in many of these churches, and served for the offices, a special altar for the worship of the laity being often erected at the east end of the nave. The rood-screen sometimes bore a lofty platform for reading the Scriptures to the congregation assembled in the nave, the *lectorium*. The connection of the monastic or collegiate buildings with the church led to the laying out of cloisters, around a rectangular court, one side of which was frequently formed by the church.

If the Romanesque basilica in its final form is compared with the ancient, a notable difference will be observed.

16. Differences between the Ancient and Romanesque Basilica.

The idea of length prevailed in the earlier conception; the eye was led on entering at once to the altar and the *presbyterium* behind it. The later style did not abandon the idea of length, but modified it greatly; the disposition of all spaces is conditioned by the principle of grouping. The place for the congregation is not a single unbroken space like the central division of the old basilica, but a group of small rectangular spaces; the eye does not go directly, but by a succession of steps, to the altar. So the small apses were grouped about the main apse, the side aisles about the nave, the place for the congregation with the place for the clergy. The same idea of grouping prevails equally in the exterior. It is upon this quality that the picturesque character of the Romanesque basilica and its real superiority over the ancient rests, for art requires rhythm rather than mere uniformity.

If we turn to France, the story is different in a number of particulars.

17. French Ecclesiastical Development.

Instead of the gradual, almost logical development of Germany, we see there a bewildering richness of forms and motives. The tendency there also was from the flat roof to the vaulted; not only the date of the change, however, varies in diffferent parts of France—this was so also in Germany—but the final result also differs in different places. In the south, to render vaulting possible, they abandoned the path followed since the third century, and went back to the single hall, covering it with barrel-vaulting (cathedral of Orange), and went from that to a cruciform plan (Montmajour); or they retained the threefold division, but gave up the raising of the central section, making three barrel-vaulted sections of nearly equal height (St. Martin d'Ainay at Lyons, nave of St. Nazaire, Carcassonne). Besides barrel-vaulting the cupola was frequently employed, without, however, adopting the ground-plan of the centralized structures; in some places a long nave was covered with a succession of equal cupolas (Cahors, Angoulême). The north, however, held firmly to the basilica. As in Germany, the way to vaulting was prepared by the strengthening of the supports; columns gave way to round or square pillars. Cross-vaulting was frequently used, but not as exclusively as in Germany; the half-barrel was especially used in Burgundy (Cluny, Paray-le-Monial, Autun). Barrel-vaulting really answered more nearly to the original plan, adapted as it is to the preservation of the impression of length. But since the ground-plan was generally similar to the German, the result was not altogether harmonious.

After the twelfth century, the predominance of the Romanesque basilica was first endangered and then altogether broken down by the introduction of the Gothic style. This name again, invented by the ignorant vanity of the Italians, is admittedly unsatisfactory, but there is no accepted substitute for it. The origin of the Gothic style may be traced in the simplest way to the effort to find the best manner of forming the cross-vaulting; but its universal acceptance throughout so large a part of Europe shows that it must have provided what the age was unconsciously seeking. The north of France is its birthplace. The preliminary steps were taken at Saint-Denis under Abbot Suger (1140–44); here first the walls lost all significance as supporting elements, and were only retained to enclose the space. This is really the essential point of the Gothic style—so to construct the vaulting, and so to support the superstructure by buttresses as to render the roof independent of the walls, and also, by the use of pointed arches, of the rectangular floor-space. Free disposition of space was won, but little use was made of it. The relation of the middle to the side aisles remained the same as in the Romanesque; so did the enrichment of the choir by radiating chapels, and the greater height of the nave. But while the main features of both ground-plan and elevation were still the same, all the individual parts were new and harmonious with each other. The introduction of the pointed arch in the vaulting led to its adoption for all arches. It has been said that in this style the vertical principle reached its extreme development; but this is misleading. The Gothic cathedral is essentially a structure of length, as much as the churches that went before it. The choir which terminates it is as much as ever the principal member, to which the arches of the nave lead the eye. The fact that in the façades of the French cathedrals the vertical lines are everywhere broken by horizontal elements can not be taken as an inconsistency—these most perfect specimens of Gothic art are not likely to have violated a Gothic principle. All we can say is that the development of height which was present in the Romanesque is continued in the Gothic. This bold soaring into the air was taken as symbolic of spiritual aspiration; it was a logical consequence which fitted the age of the schoolmen. Growing wealth and luxury also found their satisfaction in the increased beauty of the design.

18. Introduction of the Gothic Style.

The enthusiastic approval of the new style showed itself first in France. Simultaneously with Saint-Denis the rebuilding of the cathedral of Sens was begun; that of Notre Dame in Paris followed in 1163, that of Reims in 1210, and a few years later that of Amiens. In less than a century the most perfect works of the new style were completed or under way. From France it passed almost immediately across the Channel, though in England it took on a distinct character by the infusion of Norman elements. In Germany there was a period of transition. Certain elements were gradually introduced, as in the nave of Bamberg and the choir of Magdeburg. Its complete victory dates from the beginning of the thirteenth century; by the middle of that century was begun the cathedral of Cologne, of which it must at least be said that it carries out Gothic principles with an unsurpassed logical fulness. But this very completeness was a reason why the ambitious architects of those ages were unwilling to rest in it. Numerous variations were afterward introduced, many of which really led away from Gothic principles while they retained Gothic features. By the suppression of the triforium the wall regained its place; the abandonment of side aisles in other places, the construction of a single large hall, even sometimes with a flat roof, vindicated once more the claims of breadth as against height, in a way which seems to appeal to modern feeling, if one may judge from the praise bestowed upon these buildings of really very varying artistic value.

19. Its Adoption in France and Germany.

Italy never did more than play with the Gothic style. Unlike the northern architects, who looked upon it as a solution of a problem which had long puzzled them, the Italians merely imported it as a foreign fashion, partly under the influence of the mendicant orders. It opened new possibilities to the fancy of Italian architects, but they never made it their own.

After the downfall of Gothic predominance, there is no longer any unity of development. The tendencies of the Renaissance led away from Romanesque and Gothic, rather in the direction of the early basilica; and one of its great services to ecclesiastical architecture is its conquest of the domed or circular church, displayed most fully in St. Peter's at Rome. But the artists of this period also succeeded in using this form for parochial and smaller churches. It was one of the weakest points about Gothic that it was incapable of producing a masterpiece on a small scale. Here the Renaissance masters excelled it; in the Badia at Florence, San Giovanni delle Monache at Pistoia, and especially the Madonna di San Biagio at Montepulciano they gave evidence that greatness of line was possible with moderate dimensions. This was a distinct gain; but the further development is not pleasant to record, either on the Catholic or the Protestant side. The former, after the Counterreformation, is characterized by display, by a struggle after magnificence, and a loss of feeling for the beauty of simplicity and quiet grandeur. The development of general art in the baroco and rococo styles corresponded to this weakness, and produced the eighteenth century barbarities of vulgar ostentation. Modern styles have also had their influence on Protestant church-building, but no one form has attained a recognized mastery. (A. Hauck.)

20. No Present Single Predominant Type.

II. English Ecclesiastical Architecture: Some able attempts have been made in recent years to limit the term "Gothic" to buildings of the highest and most developed type, churches, in short, erected within the narrow confines of the Royal Domain of France. The contention is perhaps one of terms rather than of facts. At least it is certain that if the highest type of Gothic is that of the Royal Domain—which is unquestionably true—the art had a very wide distribution throughout Europe. This was brought about partly by the bands of traveling craftsmen, who journeyed from city to city, from country to country, and by the natural desire to build in the new style, which was copied wherever its beauties and structural qualities were known.

But while it is not difficult to trace the new style to its point of origin in the Royal Domain, it speedily lost its essentially French characteristics in taking root in new soil. The Gothic of the various countries of Europe exhibits distinctive characteristics of its own, which not only differentiate it from the Gothic of the Royal Domain, but give it a character and feeling, almost a form thoroughly national and individual. Of few countries is this more clearly the case than England, whose Gothic monuments are among the most splendid in Europe and exhibit some of the most remarkable manifestations of this beautiful style.

1. Romanesque Architecture.

Normandy Romanesque appeared in England before the Conquest. It began with the commencement of Westminster Abbey by Edward the Confessor in 1065. For the next hundred years the building art of England was a development of the art of Normandy, but richer, more complete, more varied, and with a much more numerous series of monuments. Most of the Anglo-Saxon churches were rebuilt completely, and many wholly new churches and foundations erected, many of them of great size.

A new epoch in English architecture was occasioned by the introduction of the Cistercian Order about 1140. Between 1125 and the end of the twelfth century more than a hundred Cistercian abbeys were founded in England. Until about 1175 the larger share of the work was done by the monks and canons regular; at that date the secular canons became the leaders in building, and the English Gothic monuments were chiefly built by them. Hence the larger number of English Romanesque churches was due to the regular orders, while the Gothic churches are chiefly the work of the secular canons. Yet England saw no such wholesale destruction of Romanesque monuments as happened in France. There, many great Romanesque churches were completely rebuilt in the newer Gothic. In England, on the contrary, many extensive Romanesque parts were retained to which Gothic additions were made at various periods. The great churches of England, therefore, offer very much more variety in style than the great churches of France. And this is as true of the smaller churches as of the larger. Another interesting fact concerning English churches is that most of the greatest churches have either always been cathedral churches or are now cathedrals. A number of English bishops had their seats in monks' churches, while many other monastic churches became cathedrals in the time of Henry VIII. or were made so later. The English cathedrals, therefore, comprise nearly all of the largest medieval churches remaining in England.

2. Introduction of Gothic.

3. Three Periods.

The classification of English Gothic monuments by periods has been a subject of much study. The determinating feature is the window tracery, always an essential and characteristic element. In a general way three leading periods may be distinguished: Early English or Lancet, from 1175 or 1180 to 1280, indicated by simplicity, dignity, and purity of design; Decorated or Geometric, from 1280 to 1380, characterized by decorative richness and greater lightness of construction; Perpendicular, from 1380 into the sixteenth century, distinguished by fan-vaulting, four-centered arches, and tracery in which vertical and horizontal lines strongly predominate.

4. Characteristics of English Gothic.

Apart from the special features indicated by this classification, English Gothic had certain other general characteristics all of which helped materially in producing a characteristic style of building. Compared with the churches of France those of England were low and long. While the French builders delighted in structural experiments, and in the cathedral of Beauvais attempted a lightness and delicacy of construction which was never surpassed in Europe, those of England avoided such dangerous efforts. Their use of the flying buttress, a leading and typical feature of French Gothic, was of the slightest. But while they did not, because of this, build high vaults, they displayed in their vaulting a much greater variety and richness than did the French, whose vaults are, in a measure, of uniform character. The splendid English vaults are, in truth, one of the most notable characteristics of English Gothic architecture. The earliest English efforts at decorative vaulting are the ribbed vaults, with many ribs rising from a common point of origin, presenting many small faces easily filled in. The next stage shows minor ribs, called liernes, connecting the main ribs and forming star-shaped and other patterns. The final type, and the most complex and the most beautiful, was the fan-vault, in which the ribs are multiplied indefinitely; the vaults are elaborately paneled, and often supplied with pendants decorated with ribs. The structural significance of the vault is almost lost sight of in these enrichments, and the fan-vaulting is a splendid stone ceiling rather than a structural roof-covering as is the case with the purer earlier vaults or the more logical vaults of France.

The English builders of the medieval period appear to have always had a special predilection toward enriched and decorative ceilings. The most beautiful, even if the least structural form of stone roofing, was reached in their fan-vaults. Their wooden ceilings were equally notable. Many English open-timbered ceilings, with decorated trusses and paneled surfaces, are works of extraordinary beauty and thoroughly characteristic of early and late English Gothic.

While the history of English Gothic architecture is largely written in its cathedrals, the great churches are very far from completing the record of English medieval building. The English parish church is a thoroughly interesting and highly characteristic form of building, often very mixed as to styles and dates, most generally small and low in proportions, but almost always beautiful in design and charmingly environed. Some few of them are churches of great size, but the larger number are of modest proportions. The royal and college chapels also constitute an important group of typical English churches. The royal chapels at Windsor and Westminster, King's College Chapel at Cambridge, and Merton College Chapel at Oxford are among the most notable achievements of English Gothic architecture. Nor should the lesser monuments, the chapels within churches, the screens and tombs, be neglected by the student of English medieval architecture, for the architectural and sculptured parts of these minor structures often exhibit an exquisite delicacy of design and remarkable command of decorative forms.

5. The Smaller English Churches.

Of churches built in the Renaissance style England has but few. The most notable is St. Paul's Cathedral in London. This great and splendid church is the masterpiece of Sir Christopher Wren. It was begun in 1675 and the uppermost stone was placed on the lantern of the dome in 1710. The dome is one of the most impressive in Europe and ranks among the greatest domes of the world. Wren's churches in the city of London are an important group of English churches. Designed in a characterized rendering of the classic style, they constitute the last original contribution to English church architecture.

6. Renaissance Architecture.

Modern English church architecture is almost wholly a restudy of the architecture of the past. Up to within the last quarter of the nineteenth century this study, while often zealously made, was without real understanding of the nature of either Romanesque or Gothic architecture. Gothic models were copied with avidity, and the designers imagined that in copying Gothic forms, they were doing all that was necessary to obtain a genuinely Gothic building. But the spirit, the feeling, the truth of the older art was forgotten or ignored in the new. Even the old forms were unintelligently used and the spirit was completely wanting.

7. Modern English Architecture.

Toward the close of the nineteenth century, however, a group of London architects attacked the problem of church-building in a new way. The old forms were restudied and used as the old builders might have used them. A new spirit of reverence in church architecture was developed, and a number of notable churches built which illustrated a genuine mastery of Gothic forms and uses that make the best of recent English churches structures truly worthy of attention.

III. Ecclesiastical Architecture in America: Ecclesiastical architecture in America is much more a reproductive architecture than in any other country. Alone of all the great countries of modern times the United States has no historic architecture of its own. Great Britain and the Continent abound in historic examples of building of every sort, but America has nothing that is old save what it itself has created. The earliest architecture of America was necessarily purely constructive, that is to say, without artistic intent or purpose. As the colonies developed, more attention was given to the building of churches and meeting-houses, and some of the structures erected in this period have genuine interest and real merit. But colonial architecture was but the copying of English forms, in most cases by untrained men who hardly understood what they were copying. The interest which attaches to these buildings, which were confined to New England, the eastern, and some of the southern States, is often very real, but they offer little material for the modern architect, who, even at his best, is scarcely more than a copier or a modifier.

The later history of church architecture in America affords little occasion for congratulation. Being without historic models of their own, American architects have been forced to use the models of Europe as a basis for their church designs. For many years this translation of architectural materials was accomplished with little credit to all concerned. As in England, American architects copied forms without understanding their meaning, with results little removed from the commonplace. In the last few years a more enlightened conception of the meaning and purpose of church architecture has taken root among American architects, and some few churches have been built worthy of our time and the purpose to which Christian structures are dedicated.

BARR FERREE.

BIBLIOGRAPHY: Dictionaries: A. Cates, *Dictionary of Architecture*, 22 parts, London, 1852–92 (a monumental work); Viollet-le-Duc, *Dictionnaire raisonné de l'architecture française*, 10 vols., Paris, 1854–69; W. J. and G. A. Audsley, *Dictionary of Architectural and Allied Arts*, 10 vols., London, 1880–83; J. W. Mollett, *Dictionary of . Art and Architecture*, ib. 1883; J. Gwilt, *Encyclopedia of Architecture*, ib. 1888; P. Planat, *Encyclopédie de l'architecture*, 6 vols., Paris, 1886–92 (a standard); H. Louppen, *Dictionnaire d'architecture*, Paris, 1891; Russell Sturgis, *Dictionary of Architecture and Building*, 3 vols., New York, 1901.

History of architecture: C. J. Bunsen, *Die Basiliken des christlichen Roms, mit Atlas*, 2 vols., Munich, 1842; A. A. Lenoir, *Architecture monastique*, 2 vols., Paris, 1852–56; J. A. Messmer, *Ursprung, Entwickelung und Bedeutung der Basilica*, Leipsic, 1854; C. von Lützow, *Die Meisterwerke der Kirchenbaukunst*, Leipsic, 1862; E. Hübsch, *Monuments de l'architecture chrétienne*, Paris, 1866; J. Fergusson, *History of Architecture in all Countries*, i., ii., iv., 4 vols., London, 1874–76 (the standard work); C. E. Norton, *Studies of Church Buildings in the Middle Ages*, New York, 1880; T. R. Smith and J. Slater, *Classic and Early Christian Architecture*, London, 1882; G. Dehio and G. von Bezold, *Die kirchliche Baukunst des Abendlandes*, 2 vols. text, 8 vols. plates, Stuttgart, 1884; G. B. Brown, *From Schola to Cathedral*, Edinburgh, 1886 (on the relation of architecture to the life of the church); W. Lübke, *Geschichte der Architektur*, Leipsic, 1886; A. Gosset, *Évolution historique de la construction des églises chrétiennes*, Paris, 1887; *Great Cathedrals of the World*, 100 photographs, Boston, 1888; J. Ruskin, *Stones of Venice*, 3 vols., London, 1886; idem, *Seven Lamps of Architecture*, London, 1888; H. Holzinger, *Die altchristliche Architektur*, Stuttgart, 1889; G. Clausse, *Basiliques et mosaiques chrétiennes*, 2 vols., Paris, 1893; *Der Kirchenbau des Protestantismus*, Berlin, 1893; J. T. Perry, *Chronology of Mediæval and Renaissance Architecture*, London, 1893 (careful and trustworthy); R. P.

Spiers, *The Orders of Architecture, Greek, Roman, Italian*, London, 1893; A. D. F. Hamlin, *History of Architecture*, New York, 1896; A Choisy, *Histoire de l'architecture*, 2 vols Paris, 1899; J. C. Ayer, *Rise and Development of Christian Archæology*, Milwaukee, 1902; W. Durandus, *Symbolism of Churches and Church Ornaments*, notes by J. M. Neale and B. Webb, London, 1906.

Architecture in various lands: Great Britain, England. G. A. Poole, *History of Architecture in England*, London, 1848; J. F. Hunnewell, *England's Chronicle in Stone*, London, 1887; *Cathedrals, Abbeys and Churches of England and Wales*, 2 vols., London, 1891; J. A. Gotch and W. T. Brown, *Architecture of the Renaissance in England*, 2 vols., London, 1891–94 (accurate, deals with the period 1560–1630); W. J. Loftie, *Inigo Jones and Wren; the Rise and Decline of Modern Architecture in England*, London, 1893; M. G. van Rensselær, *English Cathedrals*, New York, 1893; T. S. Robertson, *Progress of Art in English Church Architecture*, London, 1898; R. Blomfield, *Renaissance Architecture in England*, London, 1901; *Cathedral Churches of England*, New York, 1901; H. Muthesius, *Die neuere kirchliche Baukunst in England*, Berlin, 1901; E. S. Prior, *Gothic Art in England*, London, 1900; idem, *Cathedral Builders in England*, ib. 1905; F. Bond, *English Cathedrals*, ib. 1903; idem, *Gothic Architecture in England*, ib. 1906.

Scotland: D. MacGibbon and T. Ross, *Ecclesiastical Architecture of Scotland . . . to the Seventeenth Century*, 3 vols., New York, 1896–97; M. E. L. Addis, *Cathedrals and Abbeys of Presbyterian Scotland*, Philadelphia, 1901.

Ireland: G. Petrie, *Ecclesiastical Architecture in Ireland Anterior to the Norman Invasion*, Dublin, 1845 (rich in illustrations); R. R. Bras, *Ecclesiastical Architecture of Ireland*, Dublin, 1874; M. Stokes, *Early Christian Architecture in Ireland*, London, 1878.

France: E. E. Viollet-le-Duc, *Dictionnaire raisonné de l'architecture française*, ut sup.; H. A. Revoil, *Architecture romane du midi de la France*, 3 vols., Paris, 1873; J. F. Hunnewell, *Historical Monuments of France*, Boston, 1884; C. Enlart, *Monuments religieux de l'architecture romane et de transition dans la région picarde*, Paris, 1895; A. St. Paul, *Histoire monumentale de la France*, Paris, 1895; F. Miltoun, *Cathedrals of France*, 2 vols., Boston, 1903–04.

Germany: W. Lübke, *Ecclesiastical Art in Germany*, Edinburgh, 1870; H. Otto, *Handbuch der kirchlichen Kunstarchitektur des deutschen Mittelalters*, 2 vols., Leipsic, 1883–85; Th. Kutschmann, *Romanesque Architecture and Ornamentik in Germany*, New York, 1901.

Italy: Waring and McQuoid, *Examples of Architectural Art in Italy and Spain*, London, 1850; E. A. Freeman, *Historical and Architectural Sketches*, London, 1876, chiefly on Italy; O. Nothes, *Die Baukunst des Mittelalters in Italien*, Jena, 1884; J. Ruskin, *Examples of the Architecture of Venice*, London, 1887 and often; W. J. Anderson, *Architecture of the Renaissance in Italy*, New York 1901; C. A. Cummings, *History of Architecture in Italy from Constantine to the Renaissance*, Boston, 1901; C. Salvatore, *Italian Architecture During the Fourteenth to the Sixteenth Century*, Boston, 1904; C. H. Moore, *Character of Renaissance Architecture*, London, 1905.

Other lands: Owen Jones, *Plans . . . of the Alhambra*, 2 vols., London, 1842–45, 100 plates; C. Rudy, *The Cathedrals of Northern Spain*, London, 1906; A. F. Calvert, *Alhambra: Mohammedan Architecture*, ib. 1906; A. Heales, *Churches of Gottland*, London, 1890; idem, *Architecture of the Churches of Denmark*, ib. 1892; M. Schuyler, *American Architecture*, New York, 1892.

Gothic architecture: J. K. Colling, *Details of Gothic Architecture*, 2 vols., London, 1852–56, republished New York, 1900 (from measurements of twelfth to fourteenth century examples, 190 lithographs); *Gothic Ornament*, 3 vols., London, 1855; G. E. Street, *Gothic Architecture in Spain and in Italy*, 2 vols., London, 1869–74; M. H. Bloxam, *Principles of Gothic Ecclesiastical Architecture*, i., ii., London, 1882; L. Gonse, *L'Art gothique*, Paris, 1890; E. Corroyer, *L'Architecture gothique*, Paris, 1892, Eng. transl., London, 1893; C. Englart, *Origines françaises de l'architecture gothique en Italie*, Paris, 1894; C. H. Moore, *Development and Character of Gothic Architecture*, London, 1899.

ARCHITECTURE, HEBREW: Before David and Solomon the Israelites had no architecture. The present village of Siloah (*Silwân*) on the Mount of Olives furnishes a type of their oldest houses and towns; it lies on the steep hillside, and the houses are not detached but half caves, the slope of the land making it possible to utilize the natural rock for one or more walls. Because their subjects did not know how to build houses David and Solomon had to import Phenician workmen for their palaces. This was probably the beginning of Hebrew architecture. It is not probable that a Jeroboam II. did not adorn his capital with a palace and temple. In Jerusalem, however, Solomon's structures seem to have been the first and last of any size (but cf. Jer. xxii. 14), and his operations were too great for the financial resources of his land (I Kings ix. 10–23). The prophet Amos (v. 11) looks upon the building of houses of hewn stone by the rich of Israel as something new and reprehensible (cf. Isa. ix. 10). After the Exile the Temple was rebuilt with help from Phenicia (Ezra iii. 7), but the new structure fell far short of Solomon's in splendor and impressiveness. The community was too poor for great secular buildings. Not until the days of Hellenism was there any building activity, and then the Greco-Roman style dominated. It is therefore correct to say that architecture as an art never existed among the Hebrews; whenever their building was more than a mere mechanical trade they had foreign help.

Accordingly it is impossible to speak of a Hebrew architectural style or school. Nevertheless, Hebrew building had certain characteristics, imposed first of all by natural conditions. Wood in Palestine was and is scarce and expensive (the beams for Solomon's temple had to be imported from Lebanon, I Kings v. 6–10), and the most available material was the easily worked limestone in the mountains, and clay in the lowlands. The house, developed from the cave, consisted generally of but one room; it was low and had few windows or doors. The clay houses were roofed by means of a few unhewn tree trunks, branches, and brush, over which a layer of earth was placed and the whole covered with a mixture of clay and straw. The stone houses had domed roofs; the earliest were made by placing stones on the corners and others upon these until the space was covered. But the Hebrews early learned to construct arches, probably from the Babylonians or Phenicians.

Solomon's temple was a stone building, wood being used only for decoration and the roof. Its massive walls, the absence of pillars (the two columns at the entrance bore no weight), and the use of great squared stones (I Kings v. 17–18; vii. 9–12) are characteristic, and show that wooden structures did not furnish the pattern. The Syrians and Phenicians attained great skill in building with squared stones; a noteworthy feature is a smoothly chiseled or sunken border from two to four inches wide about the outer face of each stone. In Solomon's palaces wood was more freely used; the "house of the forest of Lebanon" (I Kings vii. 2–5) has its name from the fact. Here foreign models were evidently followed, which are naturally to be sought in the land from which the wood was brought.

I. Benzinger.

BIBLIOGRAPHY: Perrot and Chipiez, *Histoire de l'art dans l'antiquité*, iv., *Judée, Syrie*, etc., 176–218, Paris, 1887, Eng. transl., 2 vols., London, 1890; idem, *Le Temple de Jérusalem et la maison du Bois-Liban*, Paris, 1889; C. C. W. F. Bähr, *Der salomonische Tempel mit Beschreibung seines Verhältnisses zu heiliger Architektur*, Carlsruhe, 1848; M. de Vogüé, *Le Temple de Jérusalem*, Paris, 1864; J. Fergusson, *The Temple of the Jews and other Buildings in the Harem Area at Jerusalem*, London, 1879; F. O. Paine, *Solomon's Temple and Capital*, London, 1886; T. Friedrich, *Tempel und Palast Salomo's*, Innsbruck, 1887; idem, *Die vorderasiatische Holztektonik*, 1891; E. C. Robins, *The Temple of Solomon*, London, 1887; O. Wolff, *Der Tempel von Jerusalem und seine Maasse*, Graz, 1887; Benzinger, *Archäologie;* Nowack, *Archäologie*, i. 251–259; *DB*, i. 142–144; Schürer, *Geschichte*, i. 392, Eng. transl., I. i. 437–438.

ARCHIVES, ECCLESIASTICAL.

I. Europe: The great value and also the extreme importance of ecclesiastical records, for historical inquiry as well as in the daily life of the minister and other church officials, in former times were not properly perceived and appreciated. Works on canon law have usually little to say on the subject. Within the last few decades, however, the representatives of historical theology have pointed out the duty of the Church to attend to a careful administration and preservation of its archival treasures. A number of provincial synods in Germany, including the Austrian general synod, have passed important resolutions in that direction, and the later ecclesiastical legislation has provided for reorganization of the ecclesiastical archives and registry. The archival system of the Moravian Brethren is excellent. In 1888–89 a fire-proof building was erected for the archives at Herrnhut (cf. A. Glitsch, *Versuch einer Geschichte der historischen Sammlungen der Brüder-Unitat*, Herrnhut, 1891). The archives collected in Coblenz in consequence of a resolution passed by the eighth Rhenish provincial synod in 1853 are arranged in a model way. The interest in the same has steadily grown, and since the publication of a catalogue, they have been constantly consulted. Those Reformed Dutchmen, who as fugitives from Spanish persecution fled from the Netherlands to the countries of the Rhine, brought thither their Presbyterian church-order and synodical institutions, and taught Germany to take care of its ecclesiastical archives.

1. Germany.

The first national synod of the Reformed Church of France held at Paris in 1559 enjoined that in every church all important matters relating to religion should be registered, that the material should be collected by a pastor at each district synod, and that the material gathered by each provincial synod was to be brought to the general synod. Since that time ecclesiastical archives, especially in those parts where the oldest constitution after Calvin's idea had been adopted, have been carefully kept. The *Société pour l'histoire du Protestantisme français* (founded in 1852) has contributed largely toward their preservation and revision.

2. France.

In Holland, the Walloon general synod appointed in 1878 a *Commission de l'histoire et de la bibliothèque des églises Wallones*, which publishes bulletins containing an account of its work. The Dutch Reformed Church has adopted some good rules, and its archives are in the Willem's Church in the Hague; a catalogue is published.

3. Holland.

[The archives of the Classis of Amsterdam, which had charge of about twenty colonies in different parts of the world, are kept in the Consistory Room of the *Oude Kerck*. There are here about 100 volumes in manuscript, and twenty-five portfolios of letters from the different colonies. The letters of the classis to the colonies are recorded in a succession of volumes, numbered xx.–xxxii. (For a full account of these archives, cf. *Ecclesiastical Records of the State of New York*, 6 vols., printed at the expense of the State of New York, 1901–06, vol. i., pp. 18–24.) In the same room are found complete sets of the minutes of the Synod of North Holland, in many manuscript volumes; also minutes of many of the other provincial synods, more or less complete (*Ecclesiastical Records*, i. 24–25). The minutes of the General Synod of Holland are found at 100 Java Street, in The Hague. Here also are the original minutes of the Synod of Dort, 1618–19; the reports on the translation of the Bible, 1637; and the minutes of most of the provincial synods of Holland. Consult *Ecclesiastical Records*, i. 26–27, which give many references; also *Catalogus van het Oud Synodaal Archief*, prepared by H. Q. Janssen, minister at St. Anna ter Muiden; with the indexes of the Old Provincial Ecclesiastical Archives, published by the General Synod of the Netherlands Reformed Church, 1878, p. 198. This gives a list of all the books and papers in these archives of the General Synod.]

In Switzerland the different cantons look after their archives more or less independently (cf. *Inventur der Schweizer Archiv, herausgegeben auf Veranlassung der allgemeinen geschichtsforschenden Gesellschaft der Schweiz*, Bern, 1895 sqq.). In Scandinavian countries the ecclesiastical archives are not separated from those of the State, but of late special attention has been paid to the former. In England the *Reports* of the Historical Manuscripts Commission (appointed in 1869) contain much that is derived from the archives of the Established Church. The Huguenot Society of London (founded 1885) issues valuable publications, and the General Assembly of Scotland also pays attention to archival matters.

4. Switzerland, Scandinavia, and England.

After the Magdeburg Centuries proved that the so called Isidorian decretals were forgeries, he papal archives became almost inaccessible for scientific research until Pope Leo XIII. opened them to scholars of all nations, and appointed

5. The Papal Archives.

a historical commission to edit and publish them. The subarchivists, however, may deny access to works of a familiar character or those which it does not seem opportune to publish.

T. O. RADLACH.

II. America: The American Baptist Historical Society has its headquarters in Philadelphia with the American Baptist Publication Society and is gathering much valuable material. The Samuel Colgate Collection of Baptist documents in connection with Colgate University, Hamilton, N. Y., is large and, supported by a good endowment, is likely to grow. Several of the States have their own Baptist Historical Societies and are collecting documents. There is a good deal of material on Texas Baptist history in the library of Baylor University at Waco, and the librarian is seeking to enlarge the collection. Most of the State Baptist colleges and the Southern Baptist Theological Seminary at Louisville, Ky., have collections of greater or less importance. Regents Park Baptist College, London, probably has more material on English Baptist history than any other one institution. A collection is also being made at the Baptist Church House, Southampton Row, London. The Mennonite library at Amsterdam is said to be rich in materials relating to the Mennonites and other antipedobaptists.

1. Baptists.

The polity of the Congregationalists makes each congregation a law unto itself and the archives are kept in the congregations. In this way much valuable material has never found its way into print or even into general knowledge. The Congregational Library was founded in Boston in 1853 to be a repository of such material, and much has been gathered there. Other valuable repositories are Yale University library, which has Henry Martyn Dexter's collection; the Massachusetts Historical Society and the Prince Library in Boston; and the library of the American Antiquarian Society at Worcester. The various state bodies and the National Assemblies held at Albany, N. Y., in 1852, in Boston in 1865, and triennially since 1871, publish their minutes. Since 1854 a Year Book (Boston: Congregational Publishing Society) has been published, which gives statistics and a list of ministers, etc.

2. Congregationalists.

Among the Lutherans the Historical Society of the General Synod has its collection of documents in the library of the Gettysburg (Pa.) Theological Seminary; there is an archivarius of the General Council and the archives are in the Krauth library, Mount Airy, Philadelphia. By resolution of the Synod of Pennsylvania all congregations are requested to have their history written up to date and copies deposited in the synodical archives; also biographical sketches of all deceased clerical members. Valuable material is preserved in Amsterdam; at the Gloria Dei Church, Philadelphia; Old Swedes' Church, Wilmington, Delaware, and in St. Matthew's German Church, New York City. The great source of information relating to the early Lutheran history in Pennsylvania is the so called *Hallesche Nachrichten*, or more exactly *Nachrichten von den vereinigten deutschen evangelisch-lutheranischen Gemeinden in Nord America, absonderlich in Pennsylvanien* (2 vols., Halle, 1750–87; new ed. by Mann, Schmucker, and Germann, vol. i., Allentown, 1886).

3. Lutherans.

The archives of the various branches of Methodists are to be sought in the published journals of the General Conferences and minutes of the Annual Conferences, also in the written minutes of the minor bodies. Collections are in the libraries of the denominational publishing houses. The archives of the Moravian Church are at Bethlehem, Pa., and embrace the minutes of various synods, conferences, etc.

4. Methodists and Moravians.

The constitution of the Presbyterian Church in the United States requires each one of the church courts, in their regular gradation (viz., the church session, presbytery, synod, and general assembly) to keep fair and full records of its proceedings. Further, the church session, composed of the pastor and the ruling elders of a particular congregation, is required to submit its records to the next higher judicatory, the presbytery; the presbytery submits its records to the synod; and each synod submits its records to the general assembly. This system secures a proper record in the first place; then corrects errors, both as to fact and law; and also introduces uniformity of both record and action into all church procedure. The first Presbyterian congregations in America were founded early in the seventeenth century and the written records of some of them go back into that century. The first presbytery was formed in Philadelphia in 1706 and its manuscript records are in existence with the exception of the first page. The General Synod was established in 1717, and its manuscript records are complete. The first general assembly met in 1789, and its records are likewise intact. Many of the records of the presbyteries and synods are published regularly in printed form from year to year, and the minutes of the proceedings of the general assembly have been published from 1789 to the present time. The complete records of the General Presbytery, General Synod, and General Assembly from 1706 to 1869 have been reprinted in eleven volumes, edited by Rev. Dr. Wm. H. Roberts, stated clerk of the General Assembly. The volumes from 1870 to date are issued separately. The Presbyterian Historical Society, located in the Witherspoon Building, Philadelphia, renders invaluable service to all Presbyterian and Reformed Churches in the United States by providing proper accommodations for historical records of all description.

5. Presbyterians.

In the matter of the preservation of its archives, the Protestant Episcopal Church has always been careful, having had for a number of years a joint commission on archives, consisting of prominent members of both houses of the General Convention. In addition, there is a historiographer, a custodian of the standard Bible and of the standard prayer-book, and, further, a

6. The Protestant Episcopal Church.

recorder of ordinations. Reports from these several officials are submitted and published triennially, and efforts are made from time to time to add to the already valuable collection of archives such material as may appear to be worthy of preservation.

7. The Reformed Churches, Dutch and German.

The Reformed Church in America (Dutch Reformed Church) has a special fire-proof room set apart for its archives in the Sage Library at New Brunswick, N. J. Here are deposited all the minutes of the coetus, 1737–71; of the old provisional synods, 1771–99; of the general synod, 1794 to present time; of the four particular synods, except the volumes yet in use; of many of the classes, all having been invited to deposit their records here; and of many of the churches; also, in part, of the benevolent boards. Here also are to be found the original documents and letters, or transcripts of the same (about 2,000 pages), secured by the historian, J. Romeyn Brodhead, in Holland in 1841–43; also transcripts of the minutes of the Classis of Amsterdam, and of the Synod of North Holland, so far as these relate to America; and transcripts of the correspondence between these Holland bodies and the churches and early ecclesiastical bodies in America, secured by the Rev. Dr. E. T. Corwin, in Holland, in 1897–98, bound in fifteen volumes, and amounting to about 4,000 pages. A large part of this material has been printed at the expense of the State of New York, in the six volumes styled *Ecclesiastical Records of the State of New York* (1901–06). Consult the article *Amsterdam Correspondence* in the *Papers of the American Society of Church Hist.*, viii. (1897), pp. 81–107; the introduction to *Ecclesiastical Records of New York*, vol. i., pp. 5–48; the *Journal of the Presbyterian Historical Society*, vol. i., No. 2 (Dec., 1901), pp. 161–188; *Digest of Constitutional and Synodical Legislation of the Reformed Church in America* (1906), articles *Archives, Amsterdam Correspondence, General Synod, Synodical Archives*, etc. The Reformed Church in the United States (German Reformed Church) has preserved in the library of the Historical Society of Lancaster, Pa., transcripts of original documents, embracing correspondence with Holland. The various synods and classes have also their manuscript minutes. Many official documents have been published by the several States.

Bibliography: For list of early works consult the article "Archivwesen, kirchliches" in Hauck-Herzog, *RE*, i. 785. General works: G. Holtzinger, *Katechismus der Registratur und Archivkunde*, Leipsic, 1883; F. Frisch, *Anleitung zur Einrichtung und Führung der Gemeinde-Registraturen*, Stuttgart, 1885; K. A. H. Burkhardt, *Handbuch und Adressbuch der deutschen Archive*, Leipsic, 1887; H. Bresslau, *Urkundenlehre*, i., chap. v., *Die Archive*, Leipsic, 1889; F. von Löher, *Archivkunde*, Paderborn, 1890; F. von Helfert, *Staatliches Archivwesen*, Vienna, 1893; the *Archivale Zeitschrift*, vols. i.–xiii., ed. F. von Löher, Munich, 1876–89, new series ed. L. von Rockinger, 1889 sqq. For the Evangelical Church of Germany, E. W. Kühnert, *Praktische Winke zur Einrichtung einer Pfarrregistratur*, Hanover, 1893–94; A. Kluge, *Das Kirchenarchiv*, Barmen, 1895. For the papal archives: P. Hinschius, *Das Kirchenrecht*, i. 432 sqq., Berlin, 1869; L. P. Gachard, *Les Archives du Vatican*, Brussels, 1874; G. B. de Rossi, *De origine, historia, indicibus, scrinii et bibliothecæ sedis apostolicæ*, Rome, 1886; S. Löwenfeld, *Geschichte des päpstlichen Archivs bis zum Jahre 1817* and *Zur neuesten Geschichte des päpstlichen Archivs*, in *Historisches Taschenbuch*, ed. W Maurenbrecher, 6th ser. 5–6, Leipsic, 1886–87; A. Pieper, *Römische Archive*, in the *Römische Quartalschrift*, i., Rome, 1887; Von Pflugk-Hartung, *Ueber Archive und Register der Päpste*, in *ZKG*, xii., Gotha, 1890

ARCHONTICI (ār-con'ti-sai *or* -sî). See Gnosticism.

ARCHPRESBYTER. See Archdeacon.

ARCIMBOLDI, ār"chîm-bol'dî, **GIOVANNI ANGELO:** Archbishop of Milan 1550–55; d. at Milan Apr. 6, 1555. He belonged to an old and famous family in Milan, where his father was senator and councilor and his uncle archbishop. Before reaching his thirtieth year, he was apostolic protonotary and referendary to Leo X., who employed him in various financial matters connected with the building of St. Peter's, and on Dec. 2, 1514, named him commissary-general of the indulgence for a large part of Germany and for Scandinavia, with the rank and powers of a legate *a latere*. Another document of September, 1516, entrusted him with the functions of a political peacemaker in Sweden. He spent some time in North Germany, especially at Lübeck and Hamburg, and made full use of his powers, which included various means of raising money by the sale of titles and privileges. He then went through the diocese of Ratzeburg to Holstein, and came in 1516 or 1517 to Copenhagen. In return for a payment of 1100 Rhenish florins, King Christian granted him license to proclaim his indulgences in Denmark. He reached Sweden in March, 1518, having promised Christian to work for him and his policy of union between the three Scandinavian kingdoms. Sten Sture the younger, then viceroy, as leader of the national party, was striving for the complete independence of Sweden, and at this time was especially involved in a struggle with the prelates of the union party; he had forced, sword in hand, the resignation of the ambitious and stubborn archbishop Gustav Trolle. At the end of the year, Arcimboldi was in Stockholm and Upsala; and Sten Sture spared no pains to win over the clever and powerful legate, and fully succeeded. At the assembly of Arboga in December, 1518, the appointed peacemaker confirmed the canonically unjust sentence of the Swedish Diet against Gustav Trolle, induced probably by the rich presents he received and by the hope of gaining the metropolitan dignity. Meantime he took in large sums of money from all Sweden and Norway in return for his indulgences. But Christian II. was naturally little pleased with the behavior of the legate; besides complaining to the pope, he seized his treasures, imprisoned his brother Antonio, and threatened to do the same to him. Arcimboldi saved himself by flight to Lund, then in Danish territory, whence he passed through Sweden again and so back to Lübeck, where the difference in his reception showed the approach of the Reformation, and where he found affixed to the church-doors a bull obtained from the pope by Christian, excommunicating Sten Sture and all who had aided him in the deposition of Trolle. He returned to Rome and succeeded in changing the pope's views, which was the easier as Christian had shown an inclination toward the Reformation, and had also (1520) aroused the horror of Europe by beheading a large number of Swedish nobles in order to strengthen his position. Arcimboldi was not, however, fully restored to favor for some years. In return for the influence of his family, exerted to win Milan for Charles V., he was made bishop of Novara in 1525, and archbishop of Milan in 1550.

(Herman Lundström.)

Bibliography: B. Zimmermann, *De J. A. Arcimboldo*, Upsala, 1761; J. M. Schröck, *Christliche Kirchengeschichte seit der Reformation*, ii. 11, Leipsic, 1805; F. L. G. Raumer, *Geschichte Europas seit dem Ende des fünfzehnten Jahrhunderts*, ii. 103, Leipsic, 1833; J. Weidling, *Schwedische Geschichte im Zeitalter der Reformation*, Gotha, 1882; K. Hamann, *Ein Ablassbrief Arcimboldi aus dem Jahre 1516*, Hamburg, 1884; and literature on the Reformation in Sweden.

AREOPAGUS (Gk. *Areios Pagos*, "Mars's Hill"). See Greece, I.

ARETAS, ăr′e-tas (later Gk. form **Arethas**, on coins and inscriptions *Charethath*): The name of four princes of the Nabatæan kingdom in the s. and e. of Palestine, whose capital was Petra. In the Bible (according to correct readings) only two of them are named—in II Macc. v. 8, the earliest of the name whom we know, or Aretas I., with whom in 169 B.C. the high priest Jason sought refuge from Antiochus Epiphanes; and the one who is probably to be designated Aretas IV., mentioned in II Cor. xi. 32. According to Josephus (*Ant.*, xviii. 5) his daughter was the first wife of Herod Antipas, who was put away to make room for Herodias (Matt. xiv. 3 and parallels). This divorce caused enmity between him and Herod, and disputes over boundaries brought on a war, in which Aretas was victorious (c. 36 A.D.). At the command of Tiberius, the proconsul of Syria, Vitellius, took the field against him; but while the expedition was on its way toward Petra, it was recalled by the news of Tiberius's death (Mar. 16, 37). It is difficult to determine how a "governor" (Gk. *ethnarchēs*) under Aretas came to have power at Damascus about the same time, as mentioned in II Cor. xi. It is unlikely that, as Marquardt and Mommsen conjecture, the city had belonged to the Nabatæan territory since the days of Aretas III. More probable is the widely held view that Aretas IV. took forcible possession of it temporarily before, during, or after the expedition of Vitellius, at least during the winter of 36-37 Another theory is that Caligula, who (unlike his predecessors) was unfriendly to Herod, conceded to Herod's opponent the sovereignty of the city which had once belonged to the Nabatæan princes. Zahn has sought to solve the problem in a surprising way by trying to show that this "governor" or ethnarch of King Aretas was a Bedouin chief subject to him (cf. Schürer, in *TSK*, lxxii., 1899, pp. 95 sqq.), who had no authority in Damascus, but watched the gates of the city, from the outside. Another difficulty is offered by the fact that Luke (Acts ix. 23-25) attributes the peril of Paul at Damascus not to the ethnarch under Aretas, but to the Jews. It is possible, however, that the Jews caused the ethnarch's action and also watched the gates themselves, but the simplest explanation is that Luke mentions them merely as the original instigators. In any case the notices give no certain date for Pauline chronology; but the event can be approximately fixed in the winter of 36-37. if the hypothesis of forcible occupation be correct, or after March, 37, if that of investiture by Caligula is preferred. But Zahn has made clear that an earlier date is not impossible.

(P. Ewald.)

Bibliography: Schürer, *Geschichte*, i. 726-744, Eng. transl., I. i. 345-362 (contains history of the Nabatæan kings and a very full bibliography); K. Wieseler, *Chronologie des apostolischen Zeitalter*, 142-143, 167-175, Gottingen, 1848; Gutschmid, in J. Euting, *Nabatäische Inschriften*, Berlin, 1885; Conybeare and Howson, *Paul*, i., chap. iii., appendix, London, 1888; C. Clemen. *Chronologie der paulinischen Briefe*, § 22, Halle, 1893; T. Zahn, in *NKZ*, 1904, 39 sqq.

ARETHAS: Archbishop of Cæsarea; b. at Patræ about 860. In the light of recent investigations and discoveries he appears as a vigorous ecclesiastical ruler in the Byzantine empire, and as a powerful promoter of learning, who took up and carried on the traditions of the school of Photius. The period of his life was one of great interest in scholarship and in the collection of the surviving treasures of antiquity. He became archbishop of Cæsarea under the Emperor Leo VI. (d. 912), and as such was next in rank to the patriarch of Constantinople. He must have lived to a good old age, as we have a manuscript letter of his to the emperor Romanus (d. 944). In his episcopal capacity, he was a defender of orthodoxy as it was understood by Photius. He despised both the Nestorians and the "insane" Eutychians, whom he classed with the Manicheans; he rejected Tatian's doctrine of the Logos as equally heretical with the Arian. The tendency to the veneration of relics and of the Virgin Mary appears here and there in his works. Both these and his actions display a passionate temperament, with an unswerving steadfastness when he has once taken a side. Leo VI. came into conflict with the canon law by his decision to marry for the fourth time, probably induced by the desire for a male heir. The story of this conflict (901-907) unfolds a remarkable picture of Byzantine politics, as conditioned by the mutual relations of Church and State. While the Saracens were threatening the frontier of the empire, Leo labored diligently to gain the consent of the patriarch Nicholas to his fourth marriage; but Nicholas was reluctant to give it, and appealed to the disapproval of Arethas in support of his action in refusing to admit the emperor to the Church. When the patriarch showed a more conciliatory temper, Arethas refused to follow him, and was banished after the downfall of Nicholas. He won the latter's successor, Euthymius, to his way of thinking, and adhered to his support when Nicholas was restored after the death of Leo. Euthymius, after an outward reconciliation with his competitor, retired to a life of asceticism, dying in 917. The hatred of his enemies pursued him even to the grave; but three years later Arethas was able to show his constancy by accomplishing the reverential translation of his remains. These data for the biography of Arethas are illustrated by a number of letters and occasional writings collected in the unpublished

Moscow Codex 315 (called 302 by Matthæi). These show that he held a position of great influence in relation not only to the emperors but to all the principal political, military, and ecclesiastical leaders. That his life was full of controversy appears from the number of his polemical writings, directed sometimes to his own vindication from personal charges, but more often against the Iconoclasts, the Armenian Monophysites, the Jews, or the "babblings" of Lucian and Julian. Especially noteworthy is that against his former pupil Nicetas of Paphlagonia. But his interests were by no means exclusively ecclesiastical, as is shown by a number of beautifully written manuscripts which he had prepared for his library, and himself completed by introductions, notes, and appendices. The most valuable contain works of Euclid, Aristides, Plato, Lucian, and Marcus Aurelius, as well as a collection of Christian apologists down to Eusebius, which in many cases supplies the primary text. The notes vary in value, but show a wide knowledge of Greek and Alexandrian literature, and contain many remarks of historical, antiquarian, and lexicographic importance. The principal work of Arethas's own composition is his commentary on the Apocalypse, written probably after 913, and based upon the earlier commentary of Andrew of Cæsarea. It is not, however, a mere compilation, but contains a large amount of new observations and quotations from other sources, increasing it, for the early chapters, to more than double the length found in Andrew. The exegetical standpoint is the same; Arethas takes it for granted that the Apocalypse contains revelations from the world beyond, and finds in each prominent word the possibility of manifold references to past and future history, though holding firmly that these interpretations must be justified by the rest of Scripture and by pure Christian thought. The text of his commentary is in *MPG*, cvi. 487–786, and in Cramer, *Catena Græcorum patrum in Novum Testamentum*, viii. (Oxford, 1844), pp. 176–582. Few of his other works have been published. (G. Heinrici.)

Bibliography: J. C. T. Otto, *Des Patriarchen Gennadius . . Confession . . nebst Excurs über Arethas' Zeitalter*, Vienna, 1864; Rettig, in *TSK*, iv. (1831) 755–756; C. de Boor, *Vita Euthymii, Anekdoton zur Geschichte Leos des Weisen*, chaps. xii., xv., xvi., xviii., xx., Berlin, 1888; Krumbacher, *Geschichte*, pp. 233–234.

ARETIUS, a-rē′-shî-us (Grecized from *Marti*), **BENEDICTUS:** Scientist and theologian; b. at Bätterkinden, in the canton of Bern, Switzerland, 1505; d. at Bern March 22, 1574. He studied at Strasburg and at Marburg, where he became professor of logic; was called to Bern as school-teacher, 1548, and became professor of theology, 1564. His chief work, *Theologiæ problemata* (Bern, 1573), was a compendium of the knowledge of the time and was highly valued. His *Examen theologicum* (1557) ran through six editions in fourteen years. His works also include a commentary on the New Testament (1580 and 1616) and on the Pentateuch (1602; 2d ed., with commentary on the Psalms added, 1618), a commentary on Pindar (1587), a description of the flora of two mountains of the Bernese Oberland, Stockhorn and Niesen (Strasburg, 1561), a Hebrew method for schools (Basel, 1561), and a defense of the execution (in 1566) of the Antitrinitarian Valentin Gentilis (Geneva, 1567).

Bibliography: J. H. Graf, *Geschichte der Mathematik und der Naturwissenschaften in Bernischen Landen*, i. 25–29, Bern, 1888.

ARGENTINA: A South American republic, bounded on the north by Bolivia and Paraguay, on the east by Paraguay, Brazil, Uruguay, and the Atlantic Ocean, on the south by the Atlantic, and on the west by the Andes, which separate it from Chile. It is divided into fourteen provinces and nine territories (*gobernaciones*), and has an area of 1,125,100 square miles and a population of about 4,200,000. The capital is Buenos Ayres (permanently founded, 1580). The republic had its origin in a struggle against Spain which broke out in 1810 and was an outcome of the Napoleonic interference in the mother country. The constitutive assembly was replaced in 1818 by a constitution, although the war with Spain did not end until 1824. This constitution, as amended in 1860, provides for a congress of two chambers, the Senate and the Deputies, and each province has also an elected assembly for its own government.

The constitution declares the state religion to be Roman Catholic and requires the president or his substitute to be of that faith, but establishes the right of governmental exequatur for all papal mandates, and grants other creeds the free exercise of their religion. The hierarchic organization of the Roman Catholic Church naturally began soon after the Spanish conquest, but did not receive its present form until 1865. The archbishop of Buenos Ayres, which was an episcopal see as early as 1582, has the capital under his control, which contains nearly 800,000 inhabitants. The suffragan bishoprics are those of Paraguay (founded 1547), Cordoba (1570), Salta (1806), San Juan de Cuyo (1834), Paraná (1859), La Plata (1897), Santa Fé (1897), and Tucuman (1897). Cordoba, the first city of the country to have a cathedral, is also the richest in religious buildings.

In 1884 a Vicar-Apostolic of Carmen de Patagones was appointed with jurisdiction over southern Argentina and northern Patagonia. He draws his priests from the Salesians, as does also the apostolic prefecture for southern Patagonia, erected in 1883. Throughout Patagonia an active missionary propaganda is carried on among the aborigines, of whom some 30,000 are estimated to be unbaptized.

Although almost half the inhabitants of Argentina are either immigrants or the children of immigrants, and come from the most varied countries of Europe, the great majority of these newcomers belong to the Roman Catholic Church, on account of the predominance of Italians (about 500,000), Spaniards (about 200,000), and Roman Catholic Swiss. For decades the latter have flocked in great numbers to northern Argentina. The relatively small number of Protestants in the republic is estimated at about 33,000. Of these between 23,000 and 24,000 belong to the German synod of La Plata, which also includes the Evangelicals of Paraguay and Uruguay. To them must be added a group of congregations of the Swiss Reformed, the Anglican Church (with a number of places of worship in Buenos Ayres), and North American Presbyterians, who are most numerous in the capital, as well as in Rosario and Bahia Blanca.

Education is under the control of the State by a law of 1868, and the number of public schools, which has steadily increased, is now 3,400, in addition to parochial schools. The high schools consist of sixteen "lyceums," and there are likewise two universities, of which that at Cordoba is the more distinguished.

WILHELM GOETZ.

BIBLIOGRAPHY: T. A. Turner, *Argentina and the Argentines*, New York, 1892; Comte A. de Gubernatis, *L'Argentina*, Florence, 1898; *Annuario de la dirección general de estadistica*, Buenos Ayres, 1899; C. Wiener, *La République Argentine*, Paris, 1899; *Encyclopædia Britannica, Supplement*, s.v.

ARIANISM.

Arianism is a heresy, named from its most prominent representative, Arius, a presbyter of Alexandria (d. 336; see ARIUS). It denied that the Son was of the same substance (Gk. *homoousios*) with the Father and reduced him to the rank of a creature, though preexistent before the world. No Christological heresy of ancient Christianity was more widely accepted or tenacious. During a part of the fourth century it was the ruling creed in the Eastern Church, though there were constant and vigorous protests by the orthodox party. It was also the form of Christianity to which most of the barbarian Teutonic races were at first converted.

I. History: The roots of the Arian conflict lie deep in the differences of the ante-Nicene doctrine of the Logos, especially in the contradictory elements of Origen's Christology, which was claimed by both parties. Origen attributed to Christ eternity and other divine attributes, which lead to the Nicene doctrine of the identity of substance, but, on the other hand, in his zeal for the personal distinctions in the Godhead, he taught with equal emphasis a separate essence and the subordination of the Son to the Father, calling him "a secondary God," while the Father is "*the* God"; the Logos was a creature and occupies a position between the nature of the unbegotten (Gk. *agennētos*) God and the nature of all begotten things (*Contra Celsum*, iii. 34). He taught the eternal generation of the Son from the will of the Father, but represented it as the communication of a secondary divine substance. In the East these different representations were discussed and found advocates, and a synod at Antioch (268) rejected the doctrine of identity of substance. Through the Antiochian School the doctrine of the subordination of the Son was worked out. Lucian, the teacher of Arius (see LUCIAN THE MARTYR) and of Eusebius of Nicomedia, exercised a controlling influence on the views of Arius; Harnack (*History of Dogma*, iv. 3) calls him "the Arius before Arius." The first opponent of Arius was Alexander, bishop of Alexandria, and the greatest doctrinal opponent of the Arian Christology was Athanasius.

1. Origin of the Heresy.

1. From 318 to the Council of Nicæa, 325: The origin of the controversy is involved in some obscurity, and the accounts are not easy to reconcile. The earliest date for the clash of views is 318. The Christological question had become a burning one in Egypt. Alexander both in church and presbyterial gatherings had taken it up and refuted false views, as Arius afterward reminded him (Epiphanius, *Epist. Arii ad Alex.*). According to Socrates (i. 5), Alexander gave the first impulse to the controversy by insisting, in a meeting of presbyters and other clergy, on the eternity of the Son; whereupon Arius openly opposed, and charged him with Sabellianism. He reasoned thus: "If the Father begat the Son, he must be older than the Son, and there was a time when the Son was not; from this it further follows that the Son has his subsistence (Gk. *hypostasis*) from nothing." The accounts of Sozomen (i. 15) and Epiphanius differ in dating the conflict from discussions among the presbyters and laymen, and Sozomen represents Alexander as at first taking no decided position between the two opinions. In 320 or 321 Alexander convened a synod of about a hundred Egyptian and Lybian bishops at Alexandria, which excommunicated Arius and his followers. Arius found powerful friends in Eusebius of Nicomedia, Eusebius of Cæsarea, Paulinus of Tyre, Gregory of Berytus, Aetius of Lydda, and other bishops who either shared his view, or at least considered it innocent. He took refuge with Eusebius at Nicomedia, which had been the imperial residence since Diocletian, and spread his views in a half-poetic work, *Thalia* ("The Banquet"), of which Athanasius has preserved fragments. Alexander defended himself and warned against Arius in a letter which he sent to many bishops (Epiphanius, lxix. 4, says 70; Socrates gives the letter, i. 6). Arius made appeal to Eusebius of Cæsarea and others to secure his reinstatement as presbyter, and a Palestinian synod went so far as to authorize him to labor in Alexandria, subject to the authority of the bishop, Alexander. In a short time the whole Eastern Church became a metaphysical battle-field. The

2. Outbreak of the Controversy.

attention of the Emperor Constantine was called to the controversy, and in a letter to Alexander and Arius he pronounced it a mere logomachy, a wrangle over things incomprehensible; he also sent Hosius of Cordova to Egypt to mediate between the contending parties (Socrates, i. 7, gives the letter, as does also Eusebius, *Vita Const.*, ii.). From political considerations, however, at the suggestion of certain bishops, he called the first ecumenical council of the Church, to settle the Arian controversy together with the question of the time of celebrating Easter and the Meletian schism in Egypt.

2. The Council of Nicæa, 325: The council met at Nicæa in Bithynia. It consisted of three hundred and eighteen bishops (about one-sixth of all the bishops of the Greco-Roman Empire), resulted in the formal condemnation of Arius, and the adoption of the "Nicene Creed," which affirms in unequivocal terms the doctrine of the eternal deity of

3. The Nicene Creed.

Christ in these words: "[We believe] in one Lord Jesus Christ, the only Son of God, begotten of the Father, Light of Light, very God of very God, begotten, not made, being of one substance with the Father, by whom all things were made; who for us men, and for our salvation, came down and was incarnate, and was made man; he suffered, and the third day he rose again, and ascended into heaven; from thence he cometh to judge the quick and the dead." To the original Nicene Creed is added the following anathema: "And those who say there was a time when he [the Son] was not; and he was made out of nothing, or out of another substance or thing, or the Son of God is created, or changeable, or alterable; —they are condemned by the holy catholic and apostolic Church." This anathema was omitted in that form of the Nicene Creed which is usually, though incorrectly, traced to the Constantinopolitan Synod of 381, and which after the Council of Chalcedon, in 451, entirely superseded the Nicene Creed of 325, in its primitive form. (See below, § 8.)

It is possible that Alexander and Hosius had come to an understanding, before the council met, concerning the use of the term *homoousios* (Socrates, i. 7, says they discussed the *ousia* and *hypostasis*); Harnack positively takes this position, Loofs hesitates. The creed was signed by nearly all the

4. Acceptance of the Creed.

bishops, Hosius at the head, even by Eusebius of Cæsarea, who, before and afterward, occupied a middle position between Athanasius and Arius. This is the first instance of such signing of a doctrinal symbol. Eusebius of Nicomedia and Theognis of Nicæa signed the creed, but not the condemnatory formula appended, and for this they were deposed, and banished for a short time. Two Egyptian bishops—Theonas and Secundus—persistently refused to sign, and were banished, with Arius, to Illyria. This is the first example of the civil punishment of heresy, and opened the long and dark era of persecution for all departures from the catholic or orthodox faith. The books of Arius were burnt, and his followers branded as enemies of Christianity. The Nicene Creed has outlived all the subsequent storms, and, in the improved form recognized at Constantinople in 381, it remains to this day the most generally received creed of Christendom; and, if the later Latin insertion, the *filioque*, be omitted, a bond of union between the Greek, the Roman, and the orthodox Protestant Churches.

3. From the Council of Nicæa, 325, to the Council of Constantinople, 381: Not long after the Nicene Council an Arian and semi-Arian reaction took place, and acquired for a time the ascendency in the empire. Arianism now entered the stage of its political power. This was a period of the greatest excitement in Church and State: Council was held against council; creed was set up against creed; anathema was hurled against anathema. "The highways," says the impartial heathen historian, Ammianus Marcellinus, "were covered with galloping bishops." The churches, the theaters,

5. Arian Reaction. Athanasius.

the hippodromes, the feasts, the markets, the streets, the baths, and the shops of Constantinople and other large cities were filled with dogmatic disputes. In intolerance and violence the Arians even exceeded the orthodox.) The interference of emperors and their courts only poured oil on the flames, and heightened the bitterness of contest by adding confiscation and exile to the spiritual punishment of synodical excommunication. The unflinching leader of the orthodox party was Athanasius (q.v.), a pure and sublime character, who had figured at the Council of Nicæa as a youthful archdeacon, in company with Alexander, whom he succeeded as bishop (326); but he was again and again deposed by imperial despotism, and spent twenty years in exile. (He sacrificed everything to his conviction, and had the courage to face the empire in arms (hence the motto: *Athanasius contra mundum*). He was a man of one idea and one passion,—the eternal divinity of Christ,—which he considered the corner-stone of the Christian system. The politico-ecclesiastical leader of the Arian party was Eusebius of Nicomedia who, probably owing to the influence of the Emperor Constantine (Socrates, i. 25 etc.), was recalled from exile and baptized Constantine on his death-bed. Constantine was turned favorably to Arius, accepted a confession he prepared, recalled him from exile, and ordered him to be solemnly restored to the communion of the catholic Church at Constantinople; he even demanded his restoration in Alexandria by Athanasius; but, on the day preceding his intended restoration, the heretic suddenly died (336). In the year following, Constantine himself died, and his son Constantine II. recalled Athanasius from his first exile. In the West the Nicene statement found universal acceptance. But in the East, where Constantius, the second son of Constantine the Great, ruled, opposition to the Nicene formula was well-nigh universal, and was maintained with fanatical zeal by the court and by Eusebius of Nicomedia, who was transferred to Constantinople in 338. Athanasius was attacked on personal charges with great vehemence by the Eusebians, who sought to supersede the doctrine of the *homoousia* by indirect methods. He was banished to Gaul in 335. Eustathius of Antioch, a supporter of Athanasius, had been deposed at a synod at Antioch in 330 (Socrates, i. 23), the charge being that he advocated Sabellianism. Marcellus of Ancyra, another vigorous defender of the Nicene symbol, was also deposed at a synod in Constantinople. Arius's death occurred a little later, but the work of punishing his opponents went on. Athanasius was deposed a second time (339), and took refuge with Julius of Rome, who, with the great body of the Western Church, believed him a martyr.

It is unnecessary to follow the varying fortunes of the two parties, and the history of councils, which neutralized one another, without materially advancing the points in dispute. The most important are the synod of Antioch, 341 (q.v.), which set forth an orthodox creed, but deposed Athanasius; the orthodox synod of Sardica, which declared Athanasius and Marcellus orthodox, and the Arian counter-synod of Philippopolis, 343; the synods of Sirmium, 351, which protested against Athanasius's reinstatement at Alexandria; Arles, 353; Milan, 355, which condemned Athanasius in obedience to Constantine; the second synod at Sirmium, 357; the third, 358; at Antioch, 358; at Ancyra, 358; at Constantinople, 360; at Alexandria, 362. Aided by Constantius, Arianism, under the modified form represented by the term *homoiousios* ("similar in essence," as distinct from the Nicene *homoousios* and the strictly Arian *heteroousios*), gained the power in the empire; and even the papal chair in Rome was for a while desecrated by heresy during the Arian interregnum of Felix II. But the death of Constantius in 361, the indifference of his successor, the Emperor Julian, to all theological disputes (the exiled bishops were at liberty to return to their sees, though he afterward banished Athanasius), the toleration of Jovian (d. 364), and especially the internal dissensions of the Arians, prepared the way for a new triumph of orthodoxy. The Eusebians, or semi-Arians, taught that the Son was similar in substance (*homoiousios*) to the Father; while the Aetians (from Aetius, a deacon of Antioch who revived Arianism) and the Eunomians (from Eunomius, Bishop of Cyzicus in Mysia) taught that he was of a different substance (*heteroousios*), and unlike (*anomoios*) the Father in everything as also in substance (hence the names Heteroousiasts and Anomoians or Anomœans). A number of compromising synods and creeds undertook to heal these dissensions, but without permanent effect.

6. Various Synods and Parties.

On the other hand, the defenders of the Nicene Creed, Athanasius, and, after his death in 373, the three Cappadocian bishops,—Basil the Great, Gregory of Nazianzus, and Gregory of Nyssa,—triumphantly vindicated the catholic doctrine against all the arguments of the opposition. The Cappadocians made the *homoousios* the starting-point of their discussions, as is apparent from the correspondence of Basil with Apollinaris. Damasus, the Roman bishop, true to the general policy of his predecessors and of Julius in particular, had Arianism condemned at two Roman synods, 369, 377. When Gregory of Nazianzus was called to Constantinople in 379, there was but one small congregation in the city which had not become Arian; but his able and eloquent sermons on the deity of Christ, which won him the title of "the Theologian," contributed powerfully to the resurrection of the catholic faith. The rising influence of monasticism, especially in Egypt and Syria, was bound up with the cause of Athanasius and the Cappadocians; and the more conservative portion of the semi-Arians gradually approached the orthodox in spite of the persecutions of the violent Arian emperor, Valens.

7. Vindication of Orthodoxy.

4. The Final Triumph of the Nicene Orthodoxy under Theodosius the Great, 381: Theodosius was a Spaniard by birth, and reared in the Nicene faith. On entering Constantinople he removed the Arians from the charge of the churches and substituted the orthodox party. During his reign (379–395) he completed externally the spiritual and intellectual victory of orthodoxy already achieved. He convened the second ecumenical council at Constantinople in 381, which consisted of only one hundred and fifty bishops, and was presided over successively by Meletius, Gregory of Nazianzus, and Nectarius of Constantinople. The council condemned the Pneumatomachian heresy (which denied the divinity of the Holy Spirit), the Sabellians, Eunomians, Apollinarians, etc., and virtually completed the orthodox dogma of the Holy Trinity. The Nicene Creed now in common use (with the exception of the Latin clause *filioque*, which is of much later date and rejected by the Greek Church) can not be traced to this synod of Constantinople, but existed at an earlier date; it is found in the *Ancoratus* of Epiphanius (373), and derived by him from a still older source, namely, the baptismal creed of the Church of Jerusalem. It is not in the original acts of the Council of Constantinople, but was afterward incorporated in them and may have been approved by the Council. Dr. Hort derives it mainly from Cyril of Jerusalem, about 362–364 (cf. his *Dissertations* and see the article CONSTANTINOPOLITAN CREED). The emperor gave legal effect to the doctrinal decisions and disciplinary canons, and in July, 381, he enacted a law that all church property should be given up to those who believed in the equal divinity of the Father, the Son, and the Holy Spirit. Bishops like Ambrose of Milan supported the emperor and did much to bring the Nicene doctrine into complete acceptance.

8. The Council of Constantinople, 381.

After Theodosius, Arianism ceased to exist as an organized moving force in theology and church history; but it reappeared from time to time as an isolated theological opinion, especially in England. Emlyn, Whiston, Whitby, Samuel Clarke, Lardner, and many who are ranked among Socinians and Unitarians, held Arian sentiments; but Milton and Isaac Newton, though approaching the Arian view on the relation of the Son to the Father, differed widely from Arianism in spirit and aim.

9. The Later Arianism.

5. Arianism among the Barbarians: The church legislation of Theodosius was confined, of course, to the limits of the Roman Empire. Beyond it, among the barbarians of the West, who had received Christianity in the form of Arianism during the reign of the Emperor Valens, it maintained itself for two centuries longer, though more as a matter of accident than choice and conviction. The Ostrogoths remained Arians till 553; the Visigoths, till the Synod of Toledo in 589; the Suevi in Spain, till 560; the Vandals, who conquered North Africa in 429, and furiously persecuted the catholics, till 530, when they were expelled by Belisarius; the Burgundians, till their incorporation in the Frank Empire in 534; the Lombards in Italy, till the middle of the seventh century. Alaric, the first conqueror of Rome, Genseric, the conqueror of North Africa, Theodoric the Great, King of Italy, were Arians; and the first Teutonic translation of the Scriptures of which important fragments remain came from the Arian or semi-Arian missionary Ulfilas.

II. The Creed of Arianism: The Father alone is God; he alone is unbegotten, eternal, wise, good, unchangeable. He is separated by an infinite chasm from man. God can not communicate his essence. The Son of God is preexistent, "before time and before the world," and "before all creatures." He is a middle being between God and the world, the perfect image of the Father, the executor of his thoughts, yea, even the Creator of the world. In a secondary or metaphorical sense he may be called "God." But, on the other hand, Christ is himself a "creature,"—the first creature of God, through whom the Father called other creatures into existence. He is "made," not of "the essence" of the Father, but "out of nothing," by "the will" of the Father, before all conceivable time, yet in time. He is not eternal, and there "was a time when he was not." Neither was he unchangeable by creation, but subject to the vicissitudes of a created being. By following the good uninterruptedly, he became unchangeable. With the limitation of Christ's duration is necessarily connected a limitation of his power, wisdom, and knowledge. It was expressly asserted by the Arians that the Son does not perfectly know the Father, and therefore can not perfectly reveal him. He is *essentially different* from the Father (*heteroousios*, in opposition to the orthodox formula, *homoousios*, "coequal," and the semi-Arian *homoiousios*, "similar in essence"). Aetius and Eunomius afterward more strongly expressed this by calling him *unlike* the Father (*anomoios*). As to the humanity of Christ, Arius ascribed to him only a human body with an animal soul, not a rational soul. He anticipated Apollinaris of Laodicea (q.v.), who substituted the divine Logos for the human reason, but from the opposite motive,—to save the unity of the divine personality of Christ.

1. The Arian Teaching.

The subsequent development of Arianism by Aetius and Eunomius brought out no new features, except many inconsistencies and contradictions. The controversy degenerated into a heartless and barren metaphysical war. The eighteen or more creeds which Arianism and semi-Arianism produced between the first and the second ecumenical councils (325-381) are leaves without blossoms, and branches without fruit.

The Arians supported their doctrine from those passages of the Bible which seem to place Christ on a par with the creature (Prov. viii. 22-25; Acts ii. 36; Col. i. 15), or which ascribe to the incarnate Christ (not the preexistent Logos) in his state of humiliation lack of knowledge, weariness, sorrow, and other changing affections and states of mind (Luke ii. 52; Mark xiii. 32; Heb. v. 8, 9; John xii. 27, 28; Matt. xxvi. 39), or which teach some kind of subordination of the Son to the Father (especially John xiv. 28: "The Father is greater than I," which refers, not to the essential nature, but to the state of humiliation). Arius was forced to admit, in his first letter to Eusebius of Nicomedia, that Christ was called *God* (even "the full, only-begotten *God*," according to the famous disputed reading for "only-begotten *Son*," in John i. 18. Cf. Hort's first dissertation). But he reduced this expression to the idea of a subordinate, secondary, created divinity. The dogmatic and philosophical arguments were chiefly negative and rationalistic, amounting to this: The Nicene view of the essential deity of Christ is unreasonable, inconsistent with monotheism, with the dignity and absoluteness of the Father, and of necessity leads to Sabellianism, or the Gnostic dreams of emanation.

2. Arguments of the Arians.

On the other hand, Arianism was refuted by Scriptural passages, which teach directly or indirectly the divinity of Christ, and his essential equality with the Father. The conception of a created Creator, who existed before the world, and yet himself began to exist, was shown to be self-contradictory and untenable. There can be no middle being between Creator and creature; no time before the world, as time is itself a part of the world, or the form under which it exists successively; nor can the unchangeableness of the Father, on which Arius laid great stress, be maintained, except on the ground of the eternity of his Fatherhood, which, of course, implies the eternity of the Sonship. Athanasius charges Arianism with dualism, and even polytheism, and with destroying the whole doctrine of salvation. For if the Son is a creature, man still remains separated, as before, from God: no creature can redeem other creatures, and unite them with God. If Christ is not divine, much less can *we* be partakers of the divine nature, and in any real sense children of God.

3. Refutation of Arianism.

(PHILIP SCHAFF †) D. S. SCHAFF.

BIBLIOGRAPHY: Sources (1) on the orthodox side, the church histories of Rufinus, Socrates, Sozomen, and Theodoret, and most of the Fathers of the fourth century, especially the dogmatic and polemic works of Athanasius (*Orationes contra Arianos*, etc.), Basil (*Adv. Eunomium*), Gregory of Nazianzus (*Orationes theologicæ*), Gregory of Nyssa (*Contra Eunomium*), Epiphanius (*Ancoratus*), Hilary (*De trinitate*), Ambrose (*De fide*), Augustine (*De trinitate* and *Contra Maximum Arianum*). (2) On the Arian side, the fragments of the *Thalia*, and epistles of Arius to Eusebius of Nicomedia and Alexander of Alexandria, preserved in Athanasius, Epiphanius, Socrates, and Theodoret; the fragments of the church history of Philostorgius; Eusebius, *Vita Constantini; Fragmenta Arianorum*, in Mai, *Nova collectio*, iii., Rome, 1828. For the synodical transactions, Mansi, *Concilia*, vols. ii.-iii. Later literature: L. Maimbourg, *Histoire de l'Arianisme*, Paris, 1675; G. Bull, *Defensio fidei Nicænæ*, Oxford, 1703, Eng. transl., 1851; C. W F. Walch, *Vollständige Historie der Ketzereien*, vols.

ii.-iii., 11 vols., Leipsic, 1762 sqq.; F. C. Baur, *Die christliche Lehre von der Dreieinigkeit und Menschwerdung Gottes*, i. 306–825, Tübingen, 1841; J. A. Möhler, *Athanasius der Grosse*, books ii.-vi., Mainz, 1844; J. A. Dorner, *Entwickelungsgeschichte der Lehre von der Person Christi*, i. 773–1080, Stuttgart, 1854, Eng. transl., Edinburgh, 1861; E. Revillout, *Le Concile de Nicée*, Paris, 1861; H. Voigt, *Die Lehre des Athanasius*, Bremen, 1861; Neander, *Christian Church*, ii. 403–473; F. Böhringer, *Athanasius und Arius*, Leipsic, 1874; W. Kölling, *Geschichte der arianischen Häresie bis zur Entscheidung in Nicäa*, 2 vols., Gütersloh, 1874–83; F. J. A. Hort, *Two Dissertations on μονογενὴς Θεὸς* and on *the "Constantinopolitan" Creed and other Eastern Creeds of the Fourth Century*, Cambridge, 1876; J. H. Newman, *The Arians of the Fourth Century*, London, 1876; A. P. Stanley, *The Council and Creed of Constantinople in Christian Institutions*, London, 1881; Schaff, *Christian Church*, iii. 616–649; H. M. Gwatkin, *Studies of Arianism*, Cambridge, new ed., 1900, earlier ed., popularized in *The Arian Controversy*, London, 1891; A. von Gutschmid, *Kleine Schriften*, ii. 427–449, Leipsic, 1890 (valuable for chronology); O. Seeck, in *ZKG*, xvii. (1896) 1–71; K. Künstle, *Eine Bibliothek der Symbole und theologischen Tractate zur Bekämpfung des Priscillianismus und westgothischen Arianismus*, Mainz, 1900; R. Rainy, *The Ancient Catholic Church*, 323–357, London, 1902; W. Bright, *The Age of the Fathers*, i. 53–246, London, 1903. Consult also Gibbon, *Decline and Fall*, chap. xxi., Hefele, *Conciliengeschichte*, i.-ii., also in Eng. transl., the histories of Christian doctrine, such as Harnack, Eng. transl., iv., Loofs, Fisher, and Seeburg, and J. Chrystal, *Authoritative Christianity*, vol. i., Jersey City, 1891.

ARIAS, ā″rī′ɑs, **BENEDICTUS** (Called Montanus): Spanish scholar; b. probably at Fregenal de la Sierra (215 m. s.w. of Madrid), Estremadura, Spain, Nov. 12, 1527; d. at Seville July 6, 1598. He studied in Seville and Alcala and became especially proficient in languages; became a priest of the knightly order of St. Iago and accompanied Bishop Martin Perez Ajala of Segovia to the Council of Trent. King Philip II. called him from a life of scholastic retirement at Aracena near Seville and sent him to Belgium in 1568 to superintend the preparation of the Antwerp Polyglot (see Bibles, Polyglot, II.), and when the work was completed (1572) he went to Rome to present it to the pope. On his return to Spain the king rewarded him with a pension and several remunerative appointments, such as court chaplain and librarian at the Escorial. He was blamed for preferring the Hebrew text to the Vulgate and for introducing the Targums into the Polyglot. The Jesuits, to whom he was opposed, were particularly active with charges against him, but he succeeded in clearing himself at Rome. Besides the *Apparatus* to the Antwerp Polyglot (containing dissertations *De Hebraicis idiotismis, De arcano sermone*, etc.), he wrote commentaries on many of the books of the Bible, *Antiquitatum Judaicarum libri ix.* (Leyden, 1593), *Liber generationis et regenerationis Adam* (Antwerp, 1593), translated into Latin Benjamin of Tudela's travels (1575), and wrote Latin poems.

Bibliography: *Memorias de la real academia de la historia*, vii. 1–199, Madrid, 1832.

ARIBO, ā″rī′bō: Bishop of Freising 764–784. If, as is probable, he is the boy whose story he tells in the *Vita Corbiniani*, xxxiv., he was born at Mais near Meran, and educated by Bishop Erembert of Freising. His signature appears first as witness to a document of 748. Under Bishop Joseph he was ordained and filled the office of notary, soon afterward of archpriest, and later of abbot of Scharnitz. After Joseph's death (Jan. 17, 764), he was raised to the bishopric of Freising, whose possessions he increased considerably. The opposition of Tassilo, duke of Bavaria, to Frankish rule made trouble for him; he took the Frankish side, and appears to have been deprived of his bishopric by Tassilo, since in 782 Abbot Atto of Schledorf was in charge of the diocese, while Aribo did not die until May 4, 784. He wrote two biographies, one of St. Corbinian, whose relics he translated to Freising, probably in 768 (not fully completed; afterward retouched by the monk Hrotroc), and one of Emmeram, abbot and bishop of Regensburg. The former in its original form, ed. S. Riezler, was published at Munich in 1888; as completed, in C. Meichelbeck, *Historia Frisingensis*, i. (Augsburg, 1724), and in *ASB*, Sept., iii. 281–296; the latter is in *Analecta Bollandiana*, viii. (1889) 220–255, and in *MGH, Script. rer. Merov.*, iv. (1902), pp. 452–524, and *ASB*, Sept., vi. 474–486.

(A. Hauck.)

Bibliography: Rettberg, *KD*, ii. 258–259; Wattenbach, *DGQ*, i. 138, 171; Hauck, *KD*, ii. 387.

ARISTEAS, ar″is-tī′ɑs: The name assumed by the author of a letter professing to give the history of the translation into Greek of the Hebrew Pentateuch for Ptolemy II. Philadelphus. The letter states that, at the suggestion of Demetrius Phalereus, Ptolemy sent Aristeas to the high priest Eleazar to obtain experienced men to render the Hebrew Law into Greek for the library at Alexandria. Eleazar chose seventy-two men, six from each of the tribes, who went to Egypt, were received with great honor, completed their task, and were sent back with presents for themselves and the high priest. There is a legend that five were Samaritans and that their copies were preserved.

This narrative was for centuries the account accepted by Jews and Christians of the origin of the Septuagint. It appears in Aristobulus (as quoted by Eusebius, *Præparatio evangelica*, xiii. 12), Philo (*Vita Mosis*, ii.), Josephus (*Ant.*, XII. ii. 2 sqq.), Justin Martyr, Irenæus, Clement of Alexandria, Tertullian, and so on down to Whiston. The letter has been shown to be unhistorical, e.g., Demetrius Phalereus was banished from Alexandria at the beginning of the reign of Ptolemy Philadelphus. Its purpose was the glorification of the Hebrew race, religion, and literature. Its statements are entirely discredited by modern criticism, and its author is entirely unknown.

Bibliography: The letter was printed with a number of editions of the Bible, e.g., that of J. Andreas, 1471; was translated into English by J. Done, London, 1633, was edited in Greek with English translation, London, 1715; it is appended to Swete's *Introduction to the Septuagint*, London, 1902; and was translated with notes by H. St. J. Thackeray, London, 1904. H. Hody wrote in 1685, *Contra Historiam Aristeæ de LXX Interpretibus Dissertatio*, and followed it in 1705 with his great *De bibliorum textibus originalibus*, which completely demolished the letter as a foundation for history. C. Hayes vainly attempted a defense in 1736. Consult also: E. Nestle, *Septuagintastudien*, vol. ii., Ulm, 1896; J. E. H. Thomson, in *PEF*, Quarterly Statement, p. 82, Jan., 1902 (on the legend which includes Samaritans among the Seventy).

ARISTIDES, ar″is-tai′dîz, **MARCIANUS**: An Athenian philosopher, who, according to Eusebius (*Hist. eccl.*, iv. 3), wrote a popular Christian apology. Little was known of the work till 1891, when Harris and Robinson published a complete Syriac version and proved at the same time that the greater part of the apology is contained in the legend of Barlaam and Josaphat (q.v.), extant in many Greek manuscripts and numerous translations. Since that time much attention has been paid to the work. It is addressed to Antoninus Pius and has points of contact with the *Kerygma* of Peter, the *Shepherd* of Hermas, the *Didache*, and Justin, but more especially with the letter to Diognetus. After speaking of the true idea of God (chap. i.), it takes up the origin of the nations which followed error and those which followed the truth. The barbarians are treated in chapters iii.-vii., the errors of the Hellenes in viii.-xiii. with an excursus on the Egyptians (xii.), chapter xiv. is devoted to the Jews, and xv.-xvii. speak of the Christians, especially of their life and customs, in an attractive and instructive manner. Through the apology the name Aristides obtained a certain literary popularity among the Armenians. A homily "On the Call of the Thief and the Answer of the Crucified" (Luke xxiii. 42-43) and a fragment of a letter "To All Philosophers" are ascribed to him. Other names from old Christian literature besides that of Aristides were applied to literary frauds in Armenia from the fifth to the seventh century (cf. F. C. Conybeare, in *The Guardian*, July 18, 1894).

(A. HARNACK.)

BIBLIOGRAPHY: The Greek and Syriac texts (the latter from a manuscript of Mount Sinai), with introduction and translation, were published by J. R. Harris and J. A. Robinson in *TS*, i., Cambridge, 1891; there is a translation by D. M. Kay in *ANF*, ix. 259-279; the Armenian text was published by the Mechitarists at Venice in 1878. Consult Harnack, *Litteratur*, i. 96, 1893; J. R. Harris, *The newly recovered Apology of Aristides, its Doctrine and Ethics*, London, 1891; M. Picard, *L'Apologie d'Aristide*, Paris, 1892; R. Raabe, in *TU*, ix., 1892; P. Pape, in *TU*, xii., 1894; R. Seeberg, *Der Apologet Aristides*, Erlangen, 1894; J. A. Robinson, *Apology of Aristides*, Edinburgh, 1896; Krüger, *History*, where a bibliography of the principal contributions to periodical literature up to 1897 is given.

ARISTO OF PELLA: Reputed author of a "Dialogue between Jason and Papiscus concerning Christ." The work was known to Celsus, and Origen (*Contra Celsum*, iv. 52) defends it against his contemptuous opinion without naming the author. Maximus Confessor in his scholia to the "Mystic Theology" of Dionysius the Areopagite (chap. i., p. 17, ed. Corderius) ascribes it to Aristo of Pella, and Eusebius (*Hist. eccl.*, iv. 6) quotes from Aristo (without naming the work) concerning the war of Bar-Kokba. Citations in Jerome show that the author used the Bible-version of Aquila. A letter, wrongly attributed to Cyprian (*Opera*, iii. 119-120, ed. Hartel), states that a certain Celsus made a Latin translation of the Dialogue, probably in the fifth century, and tells that Jason was a Jewish Christian and Papiscus an Alexandrian Jew and that the former converted the latter. The work was probably written between 140 and 170 and was used by Tertullian and Cyprian, and made the basis of other works of a similar character.

(A. HARNACK.)

BIBLIOGRAPHY: A. C. McGiffert, *Dialogue between a Christian and a Jew*, New York, 1889; Harnack, *Litteratur*, i. 92-95; Krüger, *History*, 104-105; Schürer, *Geschichte*, i. 63-65, Eng. transl., I. i. 69-72.

ARISTOBULUS, ar″is-to-biū′lus: **1.** The name of several notable persons in the last period of Jewish history, belonging to the Hasmonean and Herodian families. See HASMONEANS; HEROD AND HIS FAMILY.

2. A Jewish Alexandrian writer of the time of Ptolemy VI. Philometor, according to Clement of Alexandria (*Stromata*, II. xv. 72; xxii. 50; V. xiv. 97; VI. iii. 32), Origen (*Contra Celsum*, iv. 17), Anatolius (in Eusebius, *Hist. eccl.*, vii. 32), and Eusebius (*Præp. evan.*, vii. 14; viii. 10; xiii. 12; *Chron.*, ed. Schoene, ii. 124-125). In II Macc. i. 10 an Aristobulus is mentioned as teacher of one of the Ptolemies and the most influential member of the Jewish Alexandrian diaspora, and a letter is addressed to him written under Philometor. Clement and Eusebius identify the author quoted by them with the one mentioned here. Accordingly Aristobulus flourished about 170-150 B.C. Clement (V xiv. 97) states that he wrote "abundant books to show that the peripatetic philosophy was derived from the law of Moses and from the other prophets," and Eusebius (*Chron.*) that he wrote expositions of the writings of Moses, which he dedicated to Philometor. Fragments are found in Eusebius (*Præp.*, viii. 10 and xiii. 12; cf. *Hist. eccl.*, VII. xxxii. 16-19). They express two of the fundamental thoughts of the Alexandrian Jewish apologists,—that the heathen writers derived their wisdom from the writings of Moses, and that the anthropomorphisms of the Old Testament must not be taken literally. It is questionable, however, whether this Aristobulus is a historical person. Hody, Willrich, and others have brought forward weighty reasons for thinking him a Jewish fiction. Whether the instructor of Philometor was first invented and afterward the apologist or *vice versa* must be left undecided.

(W BOUSSET.)

BIBLIOGRAPHY: H. Willrich, *Juden und Griechen vor der makkabäischen Erhebung*, Göttingen, 1895; M. Joel, *Blicke in die Religionsgeschichte zu Anfang des zweiten Jahrhunderts*, 79-100, Breslau, 1880; Elter, *De Aristobulo Judæo*, Bonn, 1894-95 (of value); Schürer, *Geschichte*, iii. 384-392, 1898, Eng. transl., II. iii. 237-243 (very full in its list of books, for which the article in *KL* is also worth consulting).

ARISTOTLE, ar′is-tet-l: Greek philosopher; b. at Stagira, in Thrace, 384 B.C.; d. at Chalcis, on the island of Eubœa, 322 B.C. At the age of seventeen he became a scholar of Plato in Athens and remained with him twenty years; after Plato's death (347 B.C.) he went to the court of Hermias, at Atarneus in Mysia; in 343 B.C. he was summoned by King Philip of Macedon to become teacher of his son Alexander. After the latter became king, Aristotle opened a school in Athens (probably in 334 B.C.) near the temple of Apollo Lykeios (whence it was called the Lyceum, while from his habit of giving instruction while walking back and forth the school has been called peripatetic, from Gk.

peripateo). After Alexander's death the anti-Macedonian party in Athens forced him to retire to Chalcis.

The philosophy of Aristotle is a strongly pronounced dualism; matter and form, God and the world, are distinct though inseparable existences. The harmony of this duality is an equally pronounced pantheism; God is an act rather than a will, a process and not a person. But the dualism of Aristotle is not materialistic; the form, God, is the principal constituent, and his pantheism is absolutely monotheistic, directly opposed to every form of polytheism. Therefore it may be inferred that he would win sympathy in the Christian Church; and while some of the Fathers attack him vehemently (as Irenæus) and others (as Justin Martyr) pass him by in silence, there are those among them (as Clement of Alexandria) who consider him a precursor of Christ, holding the truth in so far as it could be held before Christ came. Then, when the dialectical elaboration of the Christian dogmas began, his great labors on logic were by no means neglected. The heretics used them in the fourth and fifth centuries, and the catholics followed the example in the sixth and seventh.

In the Latin Church Aristotle was introduced by Boëthius and Cassiodorus. His study received a powerful impulse from the Jewish and Arabic doctors, who translated his works into Syriac and Arabic; and the anxiety which the Roman Church felt with respect to his metaphysical works, and which led to their condemnation and exclusion from the universities, disappeared after the time of Albertus Magnus and Thomas Aquinas. The Renaissance, which brought the works of Aristotle to the West in the original Greek text, developed an Aristotelian and a Platonic school; but when the Renaissance grew into the Reformation, and the splendid edifice which had been built up on Plato and Aristotle—the medieval scholasticism—tumbled down, Aristotle lost at once his influence on Christian theology (see SCHOLASTICISM; also ALBERTUS MAGNUS; THOMAS AQUINAS). At present, however, he is an increasing force in theology. His "Metaphysics" is the inspiration of all who seek for the ultimate meaning of reality—matter, form, efficient cause, final cause or end, and God. His "Ethics" and "Politics" remain the most original and stimulating source for the study of those personal and social virtues which Christianity has to train. His principle of attention to the individual and the concrete, his minute and unwearied investigation of phenomena, his analytic insight to which these disclose their secret, profoundly affect the spirit and method of ethical and religious thinkers who study his works.

BIBLIOGRAPHY: Aristotle's works were very numerous and are imperfectly preserved. The standard complete edition is by Immanuel Bekker, 5 vols., Berlin, 1831–71; single works have been published by many editors. There is an English translation by different hands in Bohn's "Classical Library," 7 vols.; of English books devoted to separate works the following may be mentioned: The *Constitution of Athens*, by T. J. Dynes, London, 1891; F. G. Kenyon, London, 1891; E. Poste, London, 1891–92; J. E. Sandys, London, 1893. The *Psychology*, by E. Wallace, London, 1882; W. A. Hammond, London, 1902. The *Ethics*, by F. H. Peters, London, 1881; A. Grant, London, 1885; I. Bywater, Oxford, 1892; J. E. C. Welldon, London, 1892; F. Harvey, Oxford, 1897; and St. J. Stock, Oxford, 1897. The *Poetics*, by S. H. Butcher, London, 1903, and H. Morley, London, 1901. The *Politics*, by W. E. Bolland, with introductory essays by Andrew Lang, London, 1877; B. Jowett, Oxford, 1885; J. E. C. Welldon, London, 1888; J. E. Sandys, London, 1893; W. L. Newman, 1902. The *Rhetoric*, by J. E. Sandys, Cambridge, 1877. *Youth and Old Age, Life and Death*, by W. Ogle, London, 1897. The *Posterior Analytics* by E. Poste, Oxford, 1850; E. S. Bouchier, London, 1901. The *Parts of Animals*, by W. Ogle, London, 1882. On the general subject, valuable works are: G. H. Lewes, *Aristotle*, London, 1864; G. Grote, *Aristotle*, 2 vols., London, 1879. An edition of the ancient commentators is in course of publication by the Berlin Academy (1882 sqq.). For bibliography, consult M. Schwab, *Bibliographie d'Aristote*, Paris, 1896; J. M. Baldwin, *Dictionary of Philosophy and Psychology*, vol. iii., part 1, pp. 75–99 (indispensable); for special lexicon, M. Kappes, *Aristoteles Lexikon, Erklärung der philosophischen termini technici des Aristoteles*, Paderborn, 1894; the histories of philosophy should be consulted for the system and influence of Aristotle.

ARIUS, a-rai'us or ê'ri-us: One of the most famous of heretics; b. in Libya (according to others, in Alexandria) about 256; d. at Constantinople 336. He was educated by Lucian, presbyter in Antioch (see LUCIAN THE MARTYR), and became presbyter in Alexandria. The bishop of that city, Alexander, took exception to his views concerning the eternal deity of Christ and his equality with the Father and thus, about 318, began the great controversy which bears the name of Arius. He is described as a tall, lean man, with a downcast brow, austere habits, considerable learning, and a smooth, winning address, but quarrelsome disposition. The silence of his enemies conclusively proves that his general moral character was irreproachable. His opponents said that he cherished a personal grudge against Alexander, because he was not himself elected bishop; but the subordination views which he had imbibed in the Antiochian school are sufficient to explain the direction of his development and the course of his life. Condemned by a synod at Alexandria in 320 or 321, he left the city, but was kindly received both by Eusebius of Cæsarea and Eusebius of Nicomedia, and it was evident that not a few of the Asiatic churches favored his ideas. A reconciliation was brought about between him and Alexander; but hardly had he returned to Alexandria before the strife broke out again, and with still greater violence. In spite of his many and powerful friends, Arius was defeated at the Council of Nicæa (325), and banished to Illyria. Soon, however, a reaction in his favor set in. The Eusebian party espoused his cause more openly, and through Constantia, the sister of the emperor, he got access to the court. He was formally recalled from banishment; and all the chiefs of the Eusebians were assembled in Constantinople to receive him back into the bosom of the Church, when he suddenly died the day before the solemnity at the age of over eighty years, at a time and in a manner that seemed to the orthodox to be a direct interposition of Providence, and a condemnation of his doctrine; while his friends attributed his death to poison. Athanasius relates the fact in a letter to Serapion (*De morte Arii*) on the authority of a priest, Macarius of Constantinople.

Epiphanius (*Hær.*, lxviii. 7) compares his death to that of Judas the traitor. Socrates (*Hist. eccl.*, i. 38) and Sozomen (*Hist. eccl.*, ii. 30) give minute accounts with disgusting details. Arius's principal work, called *Thalia* (" the Banquet "), which he wrote during his stay with Eusebius at Nicomedia, was a defense of his doctrine in an entertaining popular form, half poetry, half prose; with the exception of a few fragments in the tracts of Athanasius, it is lost. A letter to Eusebius of Nicomedia, and one to Alexander of Alexandria, are extant (cf. Fabricius-Harles, viii., Hamburg, 1802, p. 309). It should be borne in mind that all knowledge of Arius is derived from the accounts of his enemies and opponents, written during the course of an exceedingly bitter controversy. See ARIANISM; ATHANASIUS; and consult the works there mentioned.

ARK OF THE COVENANT.

According to the Pentateuchal narrative, the ark of the covenant was the receptacle of the tables of the law (called " tables of the covenant," Deut. ix. 9, 11, 15; " tables of the testimony," Ex. xxxi. 18, xxxii. 15, xxxiv. 29), attesting the divine will, the foundation of the community between God and Israel. It is so called in Num. x. 33, xiv. 44; Deut. x. 8. (cf. Heb. ix. 4); in Ex. xxv. 22, xxvi. 33–34 " ark of the testimony " is found. According to the description of Ex. xxv. 10–22, xxvi. 33–34, xxxvii. 1–9, xl. 20–21, it was a chest of shittim (acacia) wood, standing on four feet, two cubits and a half (three feet nine inches) long, a cubit and a half (two feet three inches) wide and high; it was overlaid with gold inside and out, decorated with a golden crown (rim or molding), and had a gold ring at each of the four corners above the feet, through which passed staves overlaid with gold that the ark might be carried; these staves were never to be removed. The cover was a massive golden plate, at the end of which figures of cherubim were placed, facing each other and looking toward the cover, while their outspread wings extended over the latter. The place of the ark was at the rear of the Holy of Holies of the tabernacle.

1. Description.

These cherubic figures direct the thought to Yahweh as enthroned over the ark (Ps. lxxx. 1; Jer. iii. 16–17). As it contained the tables of stone upon which were written the ten commandments, God was enthroned over that which was binding upon the people to which nothing could be added and from which nothing could be taken away. The Hebrew word *kapporeth* is best taken in the sense of " cover," not as " expiatory vessel," as is often done after the Septuagint, which translates it by *hilastērion* (Vulg. *propitiatorium*). Passages like Lev. xvi. 14–15; I Chron. xxviii. 11, do not necessarily require the latter interpretation. For when on the great day of atonement, according to the first passage, the high priest sprinkled the blood of atonement upon the first part of the *kapporeth*, he did it because it bore the throne of God, to which the blood was to be brought near; and in the same manner the designation of the Holy of Holies as *beth ha-kapporeth* in the passage in Chronicles, can be rejected as unsuitable to this interpretation only by those who overlook that the *kapporeth* is not to be thought of without the cherubim which bear the presence of God, which presence it is which makes the place of the ark the Holy of Holies.

2. Meaning of Kapporeth.

With the chests used in the idol worship of some nations of antiquity, the ark of the covenant had nothing at all in common. For those chests contained either images of gods or a mysterious symbolism like the mystic chests used in the service of the mysteries of Dionysius, Demeter, and Venus. In the strongest contrast to the heathen mystery, that which the ark contained was known and revealed to all the world; but it was also known to every one that it was as holy as the Word of God, spoken to Israel, and the protodocument of the fundamental conditions of the communion-relation existing between him and his chosen people.

3. Chests Used in Other Cults.

According to the explicit statement in I Kings viii. 9, a passage which precludes the idea that Solomon made any change in the old Mosaic sanctuary, there was nothing in the ark save the two tables of stone. When the author of the Epistle to the Hebrews (ix. 4) says that in the ark of the covenant were the golden pot that had manna (Ex. xvi. 33) and Aaron's rod that budded (Num. xvii. 10), he follows a tradition which proceeded from an inaccurate conception of these passages. For when Aaron is commanded (Ex. xvi. 33) to put the pot with manna " before Yahweh," and when Moses is told (Num. xvii. 10) to bring Aaron's rod again " before the testimony," it does not follow that these things were kept inside of the ark. A comparison with other passages where similar expressions are used does not lead to the inference that the pot of manna and the rod were kept in the Holy of Holies, but rather that they were in the sanctuary.

4. Contents of the Ark.

At the destruction of Solomon's temple the ark seems to have been burned; at least the second temple had an empty Holy of Holies. According to the Talmudic treatise *Yoma* (53*b*), a stone three fingers above the ground was in the place of the ark, on which the high priest put his censer on the yearly day of atonement. It is this stone to which, according to some expositors, Zech. iii. 9 refers. The prophet Jeremiah refers to a time of which he says (iii. 16–17) " in those days, said the Lord, they shall say no more, the ark of the covenant of the Lord, neither shall it come to mind; neither shall they remember it; neither shall they visit it; neither shall that be done any more. At that time they shall call

5. The Second Temple.

Jerusalem the throne of the Lord." This utterance reminds of the description of the new temple, which Ezekiel gives in the last chapters of his book (xl. sqq.), in which nothing is read of an ark of the covenant, where the living cherubim carrying the glory of God take the place of the cherubim of the tabernacle and of the Solomonic temple, made by the hand of men,—a reference to the time of the true dwelling of God in his congregation made perfect, in whose heart he wrote his law (Jer. xxxi. 33), a time when shall be fulfilled what the ark of the covenant of the Mosaic legislature together with the tabernacle prophetically prefigured as "a shadow of the good things to come" (Heb. x. 1).

W VOLCK†.

6. Character of the Accounts in Exodus.

In the preprophetic age, "the ark" was the most important symbol of the Hebrew religion, and its functions belonged almost wholly to that period. The preceding sketch takes for granted that the descriptions of it given in Exodus correspond to its form, condition, and contents as it actually appeared throughout its many vicissitudes. But it is now generally admitted that they are an idealization, like the accounts in the same priestly code of the tabernacle itself. The tradition, however, that the ark was transported from Sinai to Palestine, and was moved from place to place till it was finally lodged in the shrine of David in Jerusalem and thence naturally transferred to the temple of Solomon, is doubtless based on fact.

7. The First Period of the Ark's History.

The chief significance of the ark in the history of religion is that it represents in unique fashion the transition stage between the primitive conceptions of the Deity and those announced by the prophets. The advance made by the Mosaic revelation upon the previous beliefs of the Hebrews is signally shown in its representation of Yahweh as more than a mere local deity. He was, indeed, still thought of as inseparable from his chosen people; but wherever they went he might go with them. He did not, it is true, forsake Sinai at once; in great emergencies he came thence in his full power and majesty to the new home of his worshipers (Judges v. 4 sqq., cf. I Kings xix. 8 sqq., Deut. xxxiii. 2). The ark, however, was to be a constant and unfailing proof that he was among them as their champion and protector. This is the original meaning of Ex. xxxiii. (cf. R. Smend, *Alttestamentliche Religionsgeschichte*, Leipsic, 1893, pp. 12–13). The question of the literal accuracy of the statement that the two tablets of the law were placed in the ark at Sinai and were thenceforward kept there will be settled according to the view taken by each inquirer of the character of the Mosaic teaching. It is perhaps easier to believe that they were placed there at first than to suppose that they were kept there during the whole early history of Israel. The guardians of the ark were then very little concerned about the commandments of Yahweh; what they wanted was to have him fight their battles; they cared more for his *numen* than for his *nomen*. Moreover, it is not said whether the version of the decalogue contained in Ex. xx. (E) or that of xxxiv. (J) was the one that was laid in the ark. So long as both versions were in vogue neither could have been regarded as exclusively sacrosanct. Possibly some sacred stone was first placed in the ark as a talisman. It is noteworthy that the place in the Jordan where the ark stood when the waters were divided was marked by a heap of stones—a sacred memorial (Josh. iii.–iv.). The first period in the history of the ark came to an end with its capture by the Philistines when it was demonstrated that the power of Yahweh did not necessarily accompany those who trusted to its presence for victory (I Sam. iv.). This was doubtless a wholesome lesson; but the moral of it was weakened in later times by the sacerdotalists who added to the genuine tradition stories of the terrible punishments inflicted both upon the Philistines and Hebrews who failed, though unwittingly, fully to appreciate the sanctity of the ark (I Sam. v., vi.).

8. The Second Period.

In the next period the ark, instead of being itself an object of worship and an instrument of blessing or cursing, became a sacred relic in a permanent sanctuary. The transition stage was the time between its return from the Philistine country and its triumphal transportation to Jerusalem (I Sam. vii. 1–2; II Sam. vi. 1–11). The circumstances are obscure. But this much seems plain: That there was no fitting sanctuary for the ark now that Shiloh, the national religious center, had been destroyed; that the ark itself, having ceased to be a beneficent wonder-worker, was kept in seclusion; and that during the whole of the unsettled reigns of Saul and of David in Hebron it was never regarded or appealed to as a national palladium, not even in the most anxious days of battle. When a permanent seat of worship and of central government had been provided by David, it was natural that the most venerable monument of the national religion (cf. Jer. iii. 16) should be securely housed and guarded. But it had lost its practical efficiency. We do not read of its being again taken forth with the army (II Sam. xi. 11 merely implies that it had not as yet a fitting temple of its own); and David himself in his utmost peril refused to have it carried with him when he left Jerusalem before Absalom (II Sam. xv. 24 sqq.). With its removal to the temple of Solomon it disappears from the record of Israel's religion. It was superseded by the living word of Revelation.

J. F. MCCURDY.

BIBLIOGRAPHY: The best treatment is found in *EB*, i. 300–310, with that in *DB*, i. 149–151 perhaps next; J. H. Kurtz, *Beiträge zur Symbolik des alttestamentlichen Kultus*, in *Zeitschrift für lutherische Theologie*, xii. (1851) 27 sqq.; idem, *Der alttestamentliche Opferkultus*, §§ 11, 15, Leipsic, 1862; A. Köhler, *Lehrbuch der biblischen Geschichte*, i. 368–369, Erlangen, 1875; Sehring, *Der alttestamentliche Sprachgebrauch in Betreff des Namens der Bundeslade*, in *ZATW* xi. (1891) 114–115; Couard, *Die religiöse nationale Bedeutung der Lade*, in *ZATW*, xii., 1892; W. H. Kosters, in *ThT*, xxvii., 1893 (brilliant); H. Winckler, *Geschichte Israels*, i. 70–77, Leipsic, 1895; R. Kraetzschmar, *Die Bundesvorstellung im Alten Testament*, pp. 208–220, Marburg, 1896; C. von Schick, *Die Stiftshütte des Tempel in Jerusalem, und der Tempelplatz der Jetztzeit*, Berlin, 1896; W. Lotz, *Die Bundeslade*, Leipsic,

1901; M. Debelius, *Die Lade Jahves*, in *Forschungen zur Religion und Litteratur des Alten und Neuen Testaments*, Leipsic, 1906. On other arks, C. C. W. F Bähr, *Symbolik der Mosäischen Stiftshütte*, Heidelberg, 1841; Simpson, *Ark-shrines of Japan*, in *TSBA*, v. 550–554; C. J. Ball, in *TSBA*, xiv. 4.

ARKITES, ärk'aitz: A people mentioned in Gen. x. 17 and I Chron. i. 15 as descendants of Canaan. Since Josephus (*Ant.*, I. vi. 2) the name has been connected with a town Arca (modern *'Arka* and *Tell 'Arka*), at the foot of Lebanon, about 12 m. n. of Tripoli. It is mentioned in Assyrian inscriptions and in the Tell el-Amarna tablets (Schrader, 42, 55, 194), and was an important place in late Roman times. The emperor Alexander Severus was born there in a temple dedicated to Alexander the Great, and from this fact the town was called Cæsarea Libani. It was an important fortress during the crusades and a flourishing commercial town in the twelfth century. The ruins which remain belong to Roman times.

Bibliography: E. Robinson, *Later Biblical Researches*, 375–381, Boston, 1856; Schürer, *Geschichte*, i. 594, note 36, Eng. transl., I. ii. 201, note 35.

ARLES, ärl, **ARCHBISHOPRIC OF**: An ancient see in southern France (44 m. n.w. of Marseilles), whose incumbents from the early part of the fifth century to the early part of the seventh, bore the title of primate, descriptive of their position as representatives of the Roman curia in that country and first among the bishops of the Gallic Church. The gospel was brought to Arles from Marseilles about the beginning, probably, of the third century and the first mention of a bishop of Arles occurs about 255. With the division of the empire by Diocletian and the subsequent rapid decline of Lyons, Arles rose to an eminent position as a commercial and administrative center and a stronghold of Roman civilization in Gaul. Its bishops, however, were formally under the authority of the bishop of Vienne as metropolitan till about the year 400 when Arles succeeded Treves as the residence of the prefect of Gaul, becoming, thereby, the capital of the Roman power in western Europe. The metropolitan rights of Vienne were thereupon brought into question, and, after a synod at Turin (401) had failed to arrive at a decision in the matter, a grant of extensive privileges was obtained in the year 417 from Pope Zosimus by Patroclus, bishop of Arles since 412. The territory of the see of Arles was increased at the expense of Marseilles, and upon Patroclus was conferred the title of metropolitan of the Viennois with authority over the episcopal sees of Narbonne and Aix. To raise the ecclesiastical authority of Arles to a degree commensurate with its political importance the pope conferred upon its bishop the title of primate, and with it, the power to intervene as arbiter in such disputed church questions as were not reserved for the decision of the bishop of Rome.

The primacy of Arles had some justification and much of the authority which it rapidly gained from a legend which makes its appearance about this time connecting Arles with the name of Trophimus who, sent by the Apostle Peter to preach the gospel in Gaul, was reputed to have made that city the scene of his first labors. Subsequently the legendary Trophimus was identified with the person of that name mentioned in the New Testament (Acts xx. 4, xxi. 29; II Tim. iv 12). As a result of the dispute between Hilary, Bishop of Arles from 429 (see Hilary, St., of Arles), and Pope Leo the Great, the primatial dignity was abolished in 445 and the office of metropolitan was transferred to Vienne. So firmly grounded, however, was the authority of Arles by this time that in 450 the claims of the church of Trophimus to the primacy and the vicariate were brought before the pope by nineteen bishops of Gaul, and though Leo refused to admit the validity of these claims he receded so far from his position as to divide the metropolitan dignity between Vienne and Arles. Actually, Arles retained such preeminence as to make it still the first of Gallic episcopates. The incursion of the Visigoths into Provence in 466 severed all relations between Arles and Rome for nearly thirty years, but the rise of the Arian power in southern France and in the north of Italy, led to a reestablishment of the Roman connection, in defense of the threatened cause of orthodoxy. Upon Cæsarius, bishop of Arles, was conferred, in 513, the pallium as token of the vicarial office (for the first time in the history of the Western Church) together with the right of exercising pastoral supervision over the churches in Gaul and Spain. As administrator and, more important still, as a formulator of ecclesiastical legislation Cæsarius made his influence felt throughout the country and traces of his work were to be found in Spain, Ireland, Italy, and Germany (see Cæsarius of Arles). But with the rise of the national Frankish Church and the removal of the political center of the kingdom to the north the authority of the bishops of Arles rapidly declined. As late as 613 they appear in the character of papal vicars but their importance soon became second to that of the bishops of Lyons. In 794 the number of suffragans under the authority of the Archbishop of Arles was eight; in 1475 they numbered only four. The bishopric was abolished in 1802 but the title of *primat des primats des Gaules* is still borne by the archbishop of Vienne. [Among the ninety-six incumbents of the see the most distinguished, besides those already mentioned, were Vigilius (588–610), who was apostolic vicar under Gregory the Great over all the bishops of Burgundy and Austrasia, Cardinal Peter de Foix (1450–62), an important ecclesiastical statesman, and the last archbishop, Jean Marie Dulan (1775–92), who was guillotined at the age of eighty-seven by the revolutionary authorities.]

(F. Arnold.)

Bibliography: For sources consult *Epistolæ Arelatenses genuinæ* and *Epistolæ Viennenses spuriæ*, in *MGH, Epist.*, iii. (1891) 1–109. On the general subject, M. Trichaud, *Histoire de la sainte église d'Arles*, 4 vols., Paris, 1858–65; E. Löning, *Geschichte des deutschen Kirchenrechts*, i. 436–498, Strasburg, 1878; J. Langen, *Geschichte der römischen Kirche*, i. 742–785, Bonn, 1881; W. Gundlach, *Der Streit der Bistümer Arles und Vienne*, Hanover, 1890; D. Bernard, *La Basilique primatiale de St. Trophime d'Arles*, Paris, 1893; L. Duchesne, *Fastes épiscopaux de l'ancienne Gaule*, i., chap. ii. 84–144, Paris, 1894.

ARLES, SYNODS OF: The first great western synod was held at Arles, in the presence of the emperor Constantine, who called it, and under the presidency of Marinus, the bishop of the place, in 314 (316?). Thirty-three bishops were present, representing almost all the western provinces, from Africa to Britain. The significance of the synod in regard to the Donatist controversy will be treated under DONATISM. The canons are principally interesting as showing how the Church endeavored to adapt itself to the alteration in its circumstances brought about by the recognition of Christianity. They declare that the acceptance of a government office is no reason for forsaking the fellowship of the Church, and that those who refused to serve in the army when summoned should be excommunicated, while they refused to consider charioteers and actors as members of the Church unless they renounced their professions. The principal enactments, however, related to clerical and lay discipline. Important regulations as to ecclesiastical usages were the prescription of unanimity in keeping Easter, the forbidding of the African custom of rebaptizing heretics, and the requirement of the presence of three bishops at least for an episcopal consecration. Another synod was held at Arles in 353 during the Arian controversy; it is not included in the usual enumeration. What is called the second synod was held in the fifth century, not before 443. Its 56 canons are mostly reaffirmations of older decrees. It is called in question by Duchesne (*Fastes episcopaux*, Paris, 1894, p. 141). The next synod, in 451, declared its adhesion to the "Tome of St. Leo" on the Incarnation. What is usually called the third, a few years later, decided a local dispute between a bishop and an abbot. After two more synods, in 463 and about 475 (for the latter see LUCIDUS), the so called fourth met under the presidency of Cæsarius in 524, and was largely concerned with means for increasing the number of the clergy. The fifth was held in 554, to establish more firmly the episcopal authority. No others worth mentioning occur until the reforming synod of 813, held under Charlemagne's auspices and expressing his views. Another was held in 1234 in connection with the crusade against the Albigenses. (A. HAUCK.)

BIBLIOGRAPHY: The acts are in Mansi, *Concilia*, the canons of 1, 2, 4, and 5 in H. P. Bruns, *Canones apostolorum et conciliorum*, ii., Berlin, 1839; of 4 and 5 in *MGH, Concilia*, i. (1893), ii. (1904); consult Hefele, *Conciliengeschichte*, passim.

ARMAGH, BISHOPRIC OF: An ancient episcopal see in Ireland, traditionally reputed to have been founded by St. Patrick about 445, and now existing in connection with both the Roman Catholic and the Anglican Churches. It had exclusive metropolitan jurisdiction over the whole of Ireland until 1152, when a national council at Kells provided for the elevation of three other sees, those of Cashel, Dublin, and Tuam, to archiepiscopal rank, Armagh still holding the primacy. Of the earlier archbishops the most famous was St. Malachy (d. 1148; see MALACHY O'MORGAIR, ST.), the friend of St. Bernard and reformer of the Irish Church. Edward VI., in the course of his efforts to establish Protestantism, attempted to transfer the primacy to Dublin, and the Protestant Archbishop of Dublin is at present designated as "primate of Ireland," while his colleague of Armagh has been known as "primate of all Ireland" since the beginning of the eighteenth century. The Roman Catholic succession was maintained with the greatest difficulty in the later sixteenth and seventeenth centuries; one archbishop was assassinated, another died in the Tower of London, and a third (Plunket) was executed in 1681 on the charge of complicity in the "Popish Plot." The diocese comprises Louth, the greater part of Armagh and Tyrone, and a section of Derry. The Anglican diocese included that of Clogher from 1850 to 1886 when Clogher was restored as a separate jurisdiction. For additional details on the earlier history, see CELTIC CHURCH IN BRITAIN AND IRELAND.

ARMENIA.

I. History.
 The Old Armenian Kingdom—to 600 B.C. (§ 1).
 Indo-Germanic Immigration—the Armenians (§ 2).
 The Persian Period, 226-642 (§ 3).
 The Califs and the Inroads of the Turks—to 1381 (§ 4).
II. Literature.
 Begins in the Fourth Century (§ 1).
 The Armenian Alphabet. Translations (§ 2).
 Original Armenian Literature. Moses of Chorene (§ 3).
 The Eighth and Succeeding Centuries (§ 4).
III. The Armenian Church.
 Legends (§ 1).
 Gregory the Illuminator (§ 2).
 History to 600 (§ 3).
 To 1166 (§ 4).
 Negotiations for Union with Rome and the Greek Church (§ 5).
 From 1600 (§ 6).
 The Armenian Uniates (§ 7).
 The Evangelical Armenians (§ 8).
 Armenians in America (§ 9).

Armenia is a country situated in western Asia between the Black and Caspian Seas and the Taurus and Caucasus Mountains. In its widest extent it lay between 37 and 49° east longitude, 37° 30′ and 41° 45′ north latitude. The Euphrates divided it into Great and Little Armenia, respectively east and west of the river. It is a lofty mountain-land with extensive plains, including the head waters of the Cyrus (Kur) and Araxes (Aras), which flow northward to the Caspian Sea, as well as of the Euphrates and Tigris. The mountains are well wooded and enclose deep and fruitful valleys. The winters are severe with much snow, the summers dry and hot. The native geographers regarded their land as the middle of the world.

I. History: The older history of Armenia is learned from Assyrian accounts and native cuneiform inscriptions. The Assyrians called the country *Urarṭu* (see ASSYRIA), corresponding to the Biblical land or kingdom of Ararat (II Kings xix. 37; Isa. xxxvii. 38; Jer. li. 27). The native name for the people is Chaldini from Chaldis, their chief god. The oldest inhabitants are distinguished from the later by their language, which is allied to the Ural-Altaic family. Originally living east of Lake Van, the Urarteans pressed to the south and east and founded a kingdom as rivals of the Assyrians. Their capital was the well-fortified garden-city Van-Tuspa. The temple of the national god Chaldis became the center of the theocratically organized kingdom.

1. The Old Armenian Kingdom—to 600 B.C.

By means of the Menuas canal (at present the Shamiram Su), King Menuas supplied his city with water. Under his son, Argistis I., against whom Shalmaneser III. (783–773 B.C.) had to fight six times, the kingdom reached its height, but Tiglath-Pileser soon made an end to its glory and in 735 B.C. the capital Tuspa was destroyed. The weakened kingdom, nevertheless, continued in constant enmity with the Assyrians. Thither the sons and murderers of Sennacherib fled in 681. B.C. In the course of time better relations were brought about between the two kingdoms, and till 640 B.C. ambassadors of the king of Urartu went to Nineveh. The prophet Jeremiah is the last who mentions the kingdom, and after this it disappears from history (cf. C. F. Lehmann, *Das vorarmenische Reich von Van*, in the *Deutsche Rundschau*, 1894–95, pp. 353–369; also articles by Lehmann and W. Belck in *Zeitschrift für Ethnologie*, xxiv., 1892, 122–152, *Zeitschrift für Assyriologie*, vii., 1892, 255–267, *Verhandlungen der Berliner Gesellschaft für Anthropologie*, xxv., 1893, (61)–(82), and following years).

2. Indo-Germanic Immigration. The Armenians.

The advance of Indo-Germanic tribes in the sixth century B.C. added greatly to the population of Armenia. The Persians and Greeks called this new element Armenians, whereas the people call themselves *Hayk*, (plural of *Hay*) and their country *Hayastan*, claiming a mythical Hayk as their ancestor. The newly immigrated Indo-Germanic tribes absorbed the aborigines. The Armenians were at first under Median, afterward under Persian sway. They took part in the general revolt under Darius I. (after 521 B.C.), but, five times defeated, they remained quiet under the Achæmenidæ. In the time of Xenophon, Armenia was divided into an eastern and western satrapy. It reached the zenith of its power under Tigranes I. (about 90–55 B.C.), a descendant of Artaxias. He extended the bounds of his kingdom, and took the title of King of Kings, but in 66 B.C. Armenia was reduced to its old limits. From that time on the kingdom leaned either toward the Parthians or Romans, till it became a Roman province under Trajan (114–117).

3. The Persian Period, 226–642.

The overthrow of the Parthian Arsacidæ and the establishment of the rule of the Sassanidæ in Persia in 226 was of great importance for Armenia. As relatives of the dethroned legitimate heirs, the Armenian princes were the sworn enemies of the Persian kings. In 238 the Armenian King Chosrov was murdered at the instigation of the Persians. During the following disturbances the latter succeeded in occupying the country temporarily and forcing upon it the hated Mazdaism, till in 261, by the victory of Odenathus of Palmyra, the country received its freedom. The king's son Trdat (Tiridates), who had fled to Roman territory, restored the kingdom and maintained it in the closest connection wth Rome and in continual struggle with the Persians. The conversion of the king and people to Christianity necessitated a policy friendly to Rome, which came to an end by the unhappy issue of Julian's campaign and the disgraceful peace of Jovian, 363. The Persians occupied Armenia and King Arsaces (Arshak) was made a prisoner. Valens, perceiving the great mistake, made Arshak's son Pap king (367–374). But the nobility and priests had the upper hand. From 378 to 385 the kingdom was governed by the clerically inclined Manuel the Mamikonian. In 387 Theodosius the Great divided the kingdom with the Persians; the Romans received a piece of the West with Garin (Theodosiopolis), but four-fifths of Armenia came to Persia. Till 428 nominal Armenian kings ruled under Persian supremacy; then marzbans ("frontier-governors") were appointed, some of whom were Armenians. On the whole, the Persians showed great consideration for the country. Many revolts favoring the Byzantines were unsuccessful, but after the Emperor Maurice reinstalled Chosrov Parvez in 591, the latter peacefully ceded almost all Armenia to the empire. With the rise of the Mohammedan power it fell under Arab rule.

4. The Califs and the Inroads of the Turks—to 1381.

The first century of the califs was an epoch of national and literary development, and Ashot I., Bagratuni, belonging to an ancient Armenian dynasty, succeeded in 855 in becoming the prince of princes and in obtaining in 885 the royal crown from the calif. The new kingdom comprised not only Armenia, but also Albania and Iberia (Georgia). In 913 it became free, but was divided into petty kingdoms, of which that of the Artsrunians of Vaspurakan was the most important. Afraid of the aggressive Seljuks, Senekherim, the last Artsrunian, ceded his kingdom in 1021, and Gagik the Bagratunian in 1041, to the Byzantines, but they, too, could not withstand the great danger. The systematic cruel devastation of the country by the hordes of the Seljuks gave the deathblow to the political life and civilization of the Armenians at home. During these campaigns many Armenians withdrew to the Taurus and Cilicia. In 1080 a certain Rupen, probably a Bagratide, founded a small kingdom and a new dynasty (Rupenides). His brave successors conquered all Cilicia. With Byzantium they were not on friendly terms, but their relation to the states of the crusaders was close. Levon II. was crowned king in 1198. The Rupenides were followed in 1342 by the Lusinians of Cyprus. In connection with the Mongols and the West, the kingdom tried to withstand the assault of the Egyptian Mamelukes. But in 1375 King Levon VI. had to give up his last fortress. He died at Paris in 1381. From that time on the Armenians have never had an independent kingdom.

II. Literature: An Armenian literature commences with the introduction of the Armenian writing. Until the fourth century they wrote Syriac, Greek, or Persian. Armenian works said to belong to this early time, are partly translations,

I.—19

1. Begins in the Fourth Century.

partly later forgeries. The orations of Gregory the Illuminator (Venice, 1838; ed. Ter Mikelian, Vagharshabad, 1896; German, by J. F Schmid, Regensburg, 1872) belong to a much later time. To his contemporary, Zenop Glak, a Syrian bishop and afterward abbot of the monastery Surp Garabed in Taron, a history of the conversion of his province is ascribed, said to have been originally written in Syriac. It is extant in an Armenian translation, "History of Taron," and is continued by Bishop John the Mamikonian, said to have lived in the seventh century. Both works are historically worthless, legendary writings of the eighth and ninth centuries. Under the name of Agathangelos, secretary of the Armenian king Trdat, a history of the conversion of the king and the introduction of Christianity is extant in Armenian and in Greek translation. It consists of independent writings relating to St. Gregory, united after 456 (cf. A. von Gutschmid, *Kleine Schriften*, iii., Leipsic, 1892, 394 sqq., 420). Of great value is the historical work of Faustus of Byzantium, containing the history of Armenia from 317 to 390 and written in Greek. Fragments are extant in Procopius (*De bello Persico*, i. 5), and the entire work—four books—in an Armenian translation.

2. The Armenian Alphabet. Translations.

The founders of the Armenian national literature are the catholicos Sahag (d. 439) and his friend and helper, Mesrob (d. 440), the inventor of the Armenian alphabet. Till their time there existed no Armenian translation of the Holy Scriptures, and the Bible lessons and prayers were read either in Syriac or Greek. Mesrob's plan for a special alphabet for the Armenians was favored by Sahag and by King Vramshapuh (395–416). With the help of the Greek hermit and calligrapher Rufinus, the alphabet, mostly following the Greek, was produced (cf. H. Hübschmann, *Ueber Aussprache und Umschreibung des Altarmenischen*, in *ZDMG*, xxx., 1876, 53 sqq.; V Gardthausen, *Ueber dem griechischen Ursprung der armenischen Schrift*, ibid. 74 sqq.). For the Iberians and Albanians, two neighboring nations but dependent upon Armenian culture, Mesrob also invented alphabets. The Armenian alphabet was first applied to the translation of the Bible. But as all Greek books had been destroyed, and the study of Greek was interdicted in the schools, the translation was made from the Syriac version, and not from the original text. Men were sent, however, to Constantinople to study the Greek language and examine authentic copies of the Scriptures; and the result of these exertions was a truly admirable translation, produced after 432 (see BIBLE VERSIONS, A, VI.). The liturgical books for the church service, the church history of Eusebius, and the life of St. Anthony by Athanasius, were also translated into Armenian. Of translations, the Greek text of which has perished, the following may be mentioned: Certain treatises of Philo; the chronicle of Eusebius; the apology of Aristides; homilies of Severianus of Gabala; the commentaries of Ephraem Syrus on the Bible; and certain writings of Basil the Great, Chrysostom, Cyril of Jerusalem, Athanasius, and others. All these works belong to the golden period. To the later school of translators are attributed translations of Plato's works, Aristotle's categories, and Porphyry's commentary on them, Ignatius' shorter epistles, writings of Hippolytus, Epiphanius, Gregorius Thaumaturgus, Euthalius, and others.

3. Original Armenian Literature. Moses of Chorene.

The original literature of the Armenians is almost exclusively historical and theological. To Mesrob's pupil, Eznik of Kulb, is due a work against heretics, and Mesrob's biographer, Koriun, wrote an authentic record of the beginnings of Armenian literature. More famous is Moses of Chorene (*Moses Chorenensis*), author of a history of Armenia to the death of Mesrob (440), the only native source for the pre-Christian period of the country. It probably originated in the seventh or early eighth century and was first published at Amsterdam, 1695, and with a Latin translation by W and G. Whiston, London, 1736; the best edition is that of the Mekhitarists (Venice, 1843) in the complete edition of Moses's works; French transl., in Langlois, ii. 45 sqq., German by M. Lauer (Regensburg, 1869). To Moses is also ascribed a rhetoric and geography, edited with the history by the Whistons; a better recension is offered by A. Soukry, in his French and Armenian edition (Venice, 1881; cf. von Gutschmid, ut sup., 282 sqq., 322 sqq.; A. Carrière, *Moïse de Khoren et les généalogies patriarcales*, Paris, 1891, and *Nouvelles sources de Moïse de Khoren*, Vienna, 1893).

One of the most eminent of Armenian historians is Eghishe (Elisæus) Vartabed, author of a history of the religious war of the Armenians against the Persians under Yezdigerd II., 439–451 (Eng. transl., by C. F Neumann, London, 1830). His junior contemporary, Lazar of Parpi, wrote a history of Armenia from 388 to 405. John Mandakuni, catholicos 480–487, wrote homilies and prayers. To the seventh century belongs Bishop Sebeos's history of Heraclius. Toward the end of the century the church history of Socrates was translated into Armenian, and an orthodox Armenian wrote in Greek an important but partial sketch of Armenian church history from Gregory the Illuminator to his own time.

4. The Eighth and Succeeding Centuries.

To the eighth century belong John of Odzun, surnamed the Philosopher, and Stephen, archbishop of Siunik, who translated the writings of Dionysius Areopagita, Cyril of Alexandria, Nemesius, Athanasius, Gregory of Nyssa, and others; also the epistle of the patriarch Germanus to the Armenians. In the same century Armenian translations were made of the writings of Georgius Pisida, Hesychius of Jerusalem, Theodore of Ancyra, Evagrius, Antipater of Bostra, Johannes Climacus, and Titus of Crete. Toward the end of the century Levond (Leontius), "the great Vartabed," wrote a history of the Arabian inroads into Armenia and the wars with the Empire, 661–788

To the tenth century belong two historical works, one by the catholicos John, an Armenian history from the beginning to the year 925; the other by Thomas Artsruni, giving the history of the Artsrunians to 936. In the same century lived Chosrov the Great, who wrote an exposition of the Armenian breviary; Mesrob the Priest, the biographer of Nerses the Great and author of a history of the Georgians and Armenians; and Gregory of Narek, a celebrated writer of hymns, prayers, homilies, etc. Historians include Uchtanes, Bishop (of Urha, i.e., Edessa?), and Moses of Kalankaituk. To the eleventh century belong Stephen Asolik of Taron, author of a history to the year 1004; Aristakes of Lazdiverd, who in his history from 989 to 1071 describes the catastrophe of Armenia caused by the Seljuks; and Gregorios Magistros (1058), whose letters are important for contemporary history.

Another flourishing period is the twelfth century under the reign of the dynasty of the Rupenides. To this time belong Nerses Klayetsi or Shnorhali, catholicos 1166–73, who wrote poems and prayers, the latter translated into thirty-six languages; Ignatius, author of a commentary on Luke; Sarkis Shnorhali, who wrote on the catholic epistles; Matthew of Edessa, whose history, comprising the period from 952 to 1132, and continued by Gregory the Priest to 1162, contains many interesting notices concerning the crusades; Samuel of Ani, author of a chronicle to the year 1179, continued later to 1664; Nerses of Lambron, Archbishop of Tarsus, whose dogmatic works and spiritual addresses are published with the dogmatic letters of Gregory Tla, catholicos 1173–80; Michael the Great, patriarch of the Syrians 1166–99, who wrote a chronicle to the year 1198; and Mekhitar Gosh (d. 1213), author of 190 fables.

The thirteenth century was also rich in authors. Vartan the Great wrote a chronicle to the year 1268, and an exposition of Biblical passages. Giragos of Gandzak wrote a history consisting of two parts: one comprising the older Armenian history to 1165; the other contemporaneous, treating of the Mongols, Iberians, and the author's country, Albania, to 1265. His contemporary, the monk Maghakia wrote a history of the Mongolian inroads to 1272. Stephen Orbelian, archbishop of Siunik 1287–1304, wrote a history of Siunik. Sempad, brother of King Hetum I. (1224–69), composed a chronicle to 1274, continued to 1331. Mekhitar of Ayrivank wrote a chronography to 1289. To the period of decay belong Thomas of Metsop, of the fifteenth century, author of a history of Timur and his successors. To the seventeenth century belongs Arakel of Tabriz, author of a history from 1602 to 1661. With the eighteenth century commences the literary activity of the Mekhitarists (q.v.) and an entirely new era, animated by Western science.

III. The Armenian Church: Armenia has the glory of being the first land which made Christianity the religion of the country. Later legend places the first preaching of Christian doctrine there in the apostolic time and claims for the land the graves of the four apostles, Bartholomew, Thaddæus (Lebbæus), Simon, and Judas. The most prominent and important are Bartholomew and Thaddæus, and they are often mentioned alone. Sometimes two Thaddæi are distinguished—the apostle, and one of the seventy.

1. Legends. These are the apostles whose activity the older legend has placed in the East, and these legends, mostly of Greek or Syriac origin, were worked over and enlarged by the Armenians in a relatively late time; the product can be seen in the historical work of Moses of Chorene. The Bartholomew legend is evidently the oldest; Greek testimonies of the fifth century know of his death by martyrdom in Urbanopolis (Albanopolis, Nerbanopolis, etc.), an otherwise unknown city of Great Armenia. But the importance of Bartholomew does not come up to that of Thaddæus. The legend of Abgar, King of Edessa (see ABGAR), of his correspondence with Jesus and the sending of Thaddæus to Edessa, enjoyed at an early period great popularity in Armenia. The Armenian form of the legend is extant in a translation of the *Doctrina Addæi* (" Labubna of Edessa, Abgar's letter, or History of the Conversion of the Edessenes," Armen., Venice and Jerusalem, 1868, French by Alishan, Venice, 1868, by Emin in Langlois, ii. 313 sqq.).

There can be no doubt that Christianity was introduced in Armenia very early. Before Gregory the Illuminator, the true apostle of

2. Gregory the Illuminator. Armenia, Merujan, the bishop of the Armenians, wrote a letter on repentance (Eusebius, *Hist. eccl.*, VI. xlvi. 2) to Dionysius of Alexandria (248–265). A new epoch begins with Gregory. According to unreliable tradition, Anak, a scion of the noble house of Suren Pahlav, the murderer of King Chosrov (d. 238), was his father. Like many other Armenian princes he sought refuge on Roman territory during the Persian occupation. At Cæsarea he received a Christian and Greek education, which was of the utmost importance for the entire ecclesiastical development of Armenia. When the Armenian kingdom was retaken and reorganized, Gregory was one of the most zealous helpers of the king. But with the restoration of the kingdom was also connected the restitution of the national religion, which had been supplanted by Persian fire-worship. As a Christian, Gregory refused to offer chaplets upon the altar of the great goddess Anahid on the national festival arranged by the king, and professed to be a Christian. The enraged king subjected him to cruel tortures; legend speaks of his confinement in a pit for thirteen years. At last the king was converted by a miracle (Sozomen, ii. 8), and then the Christianizing of the country was undertaken by both. At the head of the army, Trdat and Gregory marched to the ancient capital Artaxata; the temple of Anahid and the oracle of Tiur with its school of priests were destroyed after a stout resistance, and all the temple property was given to the Christian churches. In the same manner they acted in West Armenia. At the request of the king, Gregory, accompanied by a retinue of Armenian feudal princes, went to Cæsarea, and was consecrated primate of Armenia by Leontius. From Cappadocia Gregory brought the relics of John the Baptist (Surp Garabed) and

Athenogenes (Atanagines), who were now made the national saints. Gregory then went south and at Ashtishat in the country of Taron destroyed the most celebrated sanctuary of the country, the temple of Vahagn, Anahid, and Astghik, and in its place the splendid Christ-Church, "the first and great church, the mother of all Armenian churches," was erected. From Taron Gregory went to the province of Ararat, where stood the famous sanctuary of the god Vanatur of Bagavan. This, too, was turned into a church of St. John and St. Athenogenes, and the people who had gathered there from the northeast were baptized.

Three things may be noticed in this newly constituted Armenian Church. First, its national character. Gregory preached in the native tongue; the sons of the former idolatrous priests were educated in a Christian school, which formed the seminary for future bishops; pupils of this school gradually occupied the twelve episcopal sees, established by Gregory. The second feature is the compulsory conversion, and the third the Judaic character of the church.

3. History to 600.

The patriarchate has its parallel rather in the Jewish high-priesthood than in specific Christian distinctions; like the episcopate, it became hereditary in some families. The superior clergy, as a rule, were married. Gregory was followed by his younger son, Aristakes, who in 325 attended the Council of Nicæa; then by his elder son Vrtanes, who made his elder son Gregory catholicos of the Iberians and Albanians. Nerses, great-grandson of Vrtanes, ordained catholicos at the urgent wish of king and people, in 365 convened a synod at Ashtishat, which regulated marriages between relatives, limited the excessive mourning over the dead, and founded the first monasteries, the first asylums for widows, orphans, and the sick, and the first caravansaries for travelers. King Arshag, displeased with the order of things, appointed an anticatholicos, but when Arshag was made prisoner by the Persians, Nerses acted as regent for the minor king Pap (367–374). As soon as the latter became of age he abolished many things introduced by Nerses, and poisoned him before 374. Basil of Cæsarea anathematized the Armenian kingdom and refused to consecrate a new catholicos. But King Pap found pliant clerics who were willing to receive ordination from native bishops. After Nerses's death Armenia was definitely freed from all spiritual connection with Cæsarea and made ecclesiastically independent. About 390 Sahag the Great, the Parthian, Nerses' son, was made catholicos. His government forms the most important turning-point of the Armenian Church. Like his father he promoted monasticism; he opposed the deposition of the last king Ardashes and the turning of Armenia into a Persian satrapy (428). But the nobility had its way and the Persian government, by making use of this opposition, deposed the influential Sahag and appointed two Syrians in succession as catholicoi. Through the efforts of Sahag and Mesrob, the Syrian language was now superseded by the Armenian. The continued connection with Greece preserved the Armenian Church from being crippled and isolated. At the request of the nobility, Sahag was again made catholicos before he died (Sept. 15, 439). He was the last in the male line of the family of Gregory the Illuminator. The family estate went to his daughter's sons, the Mamikonians, whereas the dignity of catholicos, after Greco-Oriental custom, was now given to monks. Sahag's successor, Joseph, held a synod at Sahapivan to remove certain abuses. The Council of Chalcedon (451), which later Armenians condemned, had no effect upon the contemporaries, because King Yezdigerd II. (438–457) endeavored to make Mazdaism the ruling religion in Armenia. The princes yielded at first, but soon the people revolted, and the magi and their temples had to suffer. Vartan the Mamikonian stood at the head, but the Armenians were defeated in 451 and many of the nobles and clerics were deported to Persia, where they suffered martyrdom after many years of imprisonment. One of these martyrs was Joseph the catholicos (454). The persecution ceased in 484, and during the time of peace which now followed, the Armenians were wholly influenced by the ruling Greek-Oriental theology, and Zeno's Henotikon (482) became their rule of faith. The synod at Vagharshabad, which was convened in 491 by the catholicos Babken and which was attended not only by the Armenian bishops but also by the Albanian and Iberian, solemnly condemned the Council of Chalcedon. This synod is epoch-making in the Armenian Church. From now on the Armenians, as well as the Syrians and Egyptians accept only the strict Monophysitic doctrine as orthodox (cf. A. Ter Mikelian, *Die armenische Kirche in ihren Beziehungen zur byzantinischen*, Leipsic, 1892). With the Persian government the clergy had thus far lived in peace. But an effort to erect a temple of fire in the capital Duin in 571 led to a massacre of the magi and Persians. The Armenians for the time being attached themselves to the Romans. Many priests and the catholicos fled to Constantinople, where the latter died. Armenia remained under Persian sway.

4. To 1166.

A new epoch in the Armenian Church begins under Emperor Heraclius. After he had restored the cross to Jerusalem in 629, he opened negotiations with the Monophysites of Syria, which seemed to favor a union. The Armenian catholicos Ezr also shared in them, and partook with the emperor in the celebration of the eucharist. The union lasted during the lifetime of Heraclius. The rise of Islam changed the country's policy toward Rome. The national hatred between Armenians and Greeks became most violent. The Greek soldiers stationed in Armenia complained that they were treated like infidels. Nerses III., Ezr's successor, had been educated in Greece and secretly favored the Chalcedonian Council (i.e., the Monothelite doctrine), but the synod at Duin, which met at the wish of the emperor under the presidency of Nerses, condemned again in the most solemn manner the Council of Chalcedon. But when in 652 the emperor Constantine appeared at Duin, the decisions of Chalcedon were solemnly proclaimed on Sunday in the main church; the catholicos and the bishops received the sacrament from a Greek priest. Justinian II. (689–690) succeeded in making a new union with the catholicos Sahag III. (677–703) and his bishop, whom he had called to Constantinople; but having returned to their homes, they repudiated it. Under the patriarchate of Elia (703–713), Nerses Bakur, catholicos of the Albanians, and Queen Sparam tried to introduce the Chalcedonian belief into their country. But the Armenian catholicos protested against them to the calif Abd al-Malik and with the help of Arabian soldiers the two leaders were taken to Damascus bound in chains and the Albanian orthodoxy was saved. During the ninth and tenth centuries under the rule of the Bagratunians the Church became again influential. Many monasteries were built, and many theologians and famous ascetics are mentioned. Even Monophysitic coreligionists from Colchis and the Roman empire entered the Armenian monasteries. But this growth of religious life also developed hatred of the Greeks. In vain was the correspondence between the patriarch Photius and the catholicos Zakaria (853–876). The very friendly letters of Nicolaus Mysticus and of the catholicos John the Historian (897–925), touched merely upon the oppressed condition of the Armenian empire, avoiding all theological questions. Anania (943–965), however, following the counsel of "the deep thinkers" advised to rebaptize the Greeks. His mild successor, Vahanik, being suspected of heresy, was deposed. An effort of the zealous metropolitan of Sebastia to discuss again the question of the two natures, was frustrated by the catholicos Khachik (971–990) in a long letter still extant (Stephanus Asolik, iii. 21) and the orthodox Armenian doctrine was defended by quotation from the Fathers. Khachik's successor, Sargis (992–1019) resided at Ani, the famous residence of the Bagratunians, where Queen Katramide, wife of Gagik (989–1020) had built a splendid cathedral. A hard time began for the Armenian Church when in the ninth century the realm was annexed by the Byzantine empire. A large orthodox hierarchy was established in the new provinces. At the head stood a metropolitan with the title of Keltzene, Kortzene, and Taron, besides twenty-one bishops. Of course, they were shepherds without sheep. The Greeks continued their efforts to force upon the Armenians the Chalcedonian faith. The opposition was much strengthened by the ill-treatment of the higher clergy. Khachik II. (1058–65) was kept a prisoner at Constantinople for three years. The revenues of the catholicos decreased to such a degree that the incumbent often was in want. But with Vahram, the son of Krikor, catholicos 1065–1105, the patriarchate became again hereditary, as in the beginning. Krikor's seven successors till 1202 were his relatives on either the father's or mother's side. They were called Pahlavuni, because they traced back their supposed pedigree to Gregory the Illuminator and the Suren Pahlav. There is no doubt that this family rendered great services to the Armenian Church in different times. Jealousy and self-interests were sometimes the cause of anticatholicoi, whose number at times was four. But the people only considered those as lawful who belonged to Gregory's house. In 1147 Gregory III. Pahlavuni (1113–66) bought of the widow of Count Jocelin of Edessa the fortress Hromkla, which remained the residence of the Armenian catholicoi till 1293.

The close relation between the Armenian kingdom of Cilicia and the Latin states of Syria and Palestine, soon brought the Armenian Church into closer contact with Rome. At first the Armenians welcomed the crusaders as enemies of the Greeks. But they soon changed their minds when they had to suffer (as, e.g., in Edessa) under their rule. Negotiations for a union were soon resumed. From political motives the kings especially, sometimes also the catholicoi, favored these ineffectual negotiations. Levon II., "because he ascribed his greatness to the apostles Peter and Paul in Rome," wished to obtain a royal crown from Pope Celestine III. and Emperor Henry VI. Conrad of Wittelsbach, Archbishop of Mainz, brought the crown in 1198 with three papal injunctions: (1) To celebrate the principal festivals on the same days as the Roman Church; (2) Continual devotion by day and night; (3) To fast on Christmas-eve and Easter-eve. The king pacified the nobles and the clergy with the words: "Be not disturbed, I will play the hypocrite." During the fourteenth and fifteenth centuries a small fraction of the Armenian nation had become definitely united with Rome. The Vartabed John of Cherni learned the Latin language from the Dominican Bartholomew and in connection with him founded a special branch of the Dominicans, the Unitores. He introduced the Latin language into the service of the Church, declared the Armenian sacraments invalid, rebaptized the laymen, and reordained the ministers who followed him. One of his adherents, Nerses Balienz, bishop of Urmia, who with others had been expelled from the Church and driven from Armenia, in order to revenge himself went to Avignon and calumniated the Armenian Church before the pope, charging it with one hundred and seventeen errors. They were communicated to the catholicos, refuted at a synod in Sis in 1342, and the pope was satisfied by this thorough refutation. The fanatical action of the Unitores generally effected the very opposite result. With the Greeks, too, negotiations concerning union took place. Emperor Manuel Comnenus after 1165 corresponded with Nerses IV. Shnorhali (catholicos 1166–73). This correspondence was continued by Nerses' successor Gregory IV (1173–80); but the Synod of Hromkla (1179) rejected all proposals of the Greeks. The death of Manuel (1180) and of the catholicos Gregory, who was disposed toward a union, made an end to all union endeavors. Another effort made in 1196 by the "ecumenical" council at Tarsus in the interest of King Levon II. was also fruitless. During the Persian persecutions the Armenians migrated to the West. Rich mercantile colonies existed, especially in Poland. The escaped catholicos Melkiseth died at Lemberg in 1625, after having

5. Negotiations for Union with Rome and the Greek Church.

founded a bishopric there for which he had consecrated Nikolaios. At the instance of the Jesuits the latter joined the union.

6. From 1600. With the seventeenth century a new period begins for the Armenians. From Echmiadzin (Vagharshabad), the seat of the catholicos, clerics were sent out to establish Armenian printing offices. Such were established at Lemberg 1616, at Julfa and Leghorn 1640, at Amsterdam 1660 (transferred to Marseilles in 1672), at Constantinople 1677, and elsewhere. Till then the Armenians were little better educated than the Syrians or Copts. The merit of making them acquainted with European culture belongs to Mekhitar and his order, the Mekhitarists (q.v.). In 1828 Persian Armenia came under Russian sway, and again a new period commenced for the national Church.

The national Armenian Church, whose adherents are erroneously called Gregorians, considers as its head the "supreme patriarch and catholicos of all Armenians," residing at Echmiadzin, who is elected by a national council consisting of members of all Armenian eparchies. Connected with the patriarchal see is a theological-philosophical academy An incomplete catalogue of the library at Echmiadzin was published by Brosset (*Catalogue de la bibliothèque d'Edschmiadzin publié par M. Brosset*, St. Petersburg, 1840). Besides the supreme patriarchate there are two lower ones, those of Jerusalem and Constantinople.

7. The Armenian Uniates. The Armenians who are united with the Roman See (the so called Uniates or United Armenians) have maintained themselves since the times of the crusaders and the Unitores, and gradually increased in numbers. Several catholicoi negotiated with Rome, but the clergy and people remained anti-Roman. When, however, the order of Mekhitarists was established, a catholicate in connection with Rome was founded. Abraham Attar-Muradian in 1721 founded in the Lebanon the monastery of Kerem, which accepted the rule of St. Anthony (see ANTONIANS, 1). His successors besides their own names take also that of the prince of the apostles. For the better regulation of the affairs of the Catholic and United Armenians, Pius IX. issued, July 12, 1867, the bull *Reversurus*. But a great portion of the United, protected by the Turkish government, did not recognize the injunctions of the bull, and in 1870 they renounced the Roman See, calling themselves Oriental Catholics. The most prominent men among the United and most of the Venetian Mekhitarists sided with them. On May 20, 1870, Pope Pius IX. suspended many priests, and when they did not yield, he excommunicated four bishops and forty-five other priests. The result was that the separatists now formed an independent organization under the civil patriarch John Kapelian, who, however, submitted to Pope Leo XIII. in 1879. In 1880 Anton Hassun was made the first Armenian cardinal. He died at Rome in 1884. His successor as patriarch of Cilicia with residence at Constantinople was Stephen Azarian, surnamed Stephanus Petrus X., to whom the pope sent an encyclical in 1888, in which the preservation of the Armenian language and liturgy for religious purposes is guaranteed to the Armenians, and everything is confirmed which Benedict XIV enjoined concerning their own and other Oriental liturgies (cf. D. Vernier, *Histoire du patriarchat Arménien catholique*, Paris, 1890).

According to *Missiones catholicæ cura S. Congregationis de propaganda fide descriptæ anno 1901*, the present status of the Armenians united with Rome is as follows: The seat of the Armenian patriarch of Cilicia is Constantinople. The diocese comprises 16,000 Catholic Armenians; 13 congregations; 85 priests (including 16 Mekhitarists of Venice, 10 of Vienna, and 14 Antonians); 5 boys' and 7 girls' schools; 2 colleges besides the seminary of the patriarch and 1 lyceum; the convent of the Mekhitarists of Venice at Kadikeuy, of those of Vienna at Pancaldi, of the Antonians at Ortakeuy; one monastery of the Sisters of the Immaculate Conception. To the jurisdiction of the patriarch belong also 15 bishoprics. Excluded from this supervision are the dioceses of Alexandria in Egypt, Artuin in Russia, and Lemberg in Austria, whose archbishop has been named since 1819 by the emperor of Austria. The United Armenians, not including those in Hungary, in Russia outside of the eparchy of Artuin, and in Persia, number about 100,000 according to the lists of the propaganda. (H. GELZER.)

8. The Evangelical Armenians. The evangelical movement among Armenians had its origin early in the nineteenth century in several attempts to revive religion in the Eastern Churches. A large number of Armenians in Turkey, inhabiting Cilicia and central and southern Asia Minor, have lost their own language, speaking Turkish, but writing it with Armenian letters. They are quite unable to understand the Armenian church books. In 1815 two Armenian ecclesiastics prepared a version of the New Testament in Turkish for these people, which was afterward printed (1819) at St. Petersburg. About the same time the Church Missionary Society of London sent a mission to Malta to advance the cause of religion in the Greek and other Oriental Churches. This mission came in contact with Armenians before its abandonment in 1830. In 1823 the Basel Mission Institute sent two of its graduates, Mr. Zaremba (who was a Russian count by birth) and Mr. Pfander (afterward renowned as a missionary to Mohammedans in India and in Turkey). These men, driven from the Caucasus by the Czar Nicholas I., left a strong evangelical Armenian body, which still perseveres, at Shushi, Shemakhi, and Baku. About this time an Armenian scholar of Constantinople, acting for the British Bible Society, translated the New Testament into modern, or colloquial Armenian, the ancient and ecclesiastical language being unintelligible to the common people. This was published at Paris in 1823, and became another of the influences vaguely at work for reform.

The chief advance in this direction came through the American Board, of Boston, Mass., which sent missionaries to Turkey in 1819 and has steadily prosecuted its purpose of enlightening the members of the Oriental Churches up to this time. Turkey being in turmoil at this time, the mission printing-press was established at Malta; explorations were made throughout Syria, Greece, Egypt, Asia Minor, and finally, in 1830–31, through a large part of Eastern Turkey besides the Caucasus and Persia. As a result, stations of the American Board were founded among the Armenians at Smyrna (1820), Constantinople (1831), Brousa, and Trebizond (1833). The printing plant for Armenian, Turkish, and Greek was removed from Malta to Smyrna in 1835 and there Bible work was pressed forward. A translation of the Bible into modern Armenian, by Elias Riggs, was published in 1852, and the translation of the Bible into Turkish written with Armenian letters by William Goodell was published in 1841—the first translation of the Old Testament into this language. These two translations placed the Bible within reach of all the Armenians of the Turkish empire. In 1904 the circulation of the Scriptures among Armenians in Turkey amounted to nearly 30,000 copies.

The purpose of the American Board in entering the field of the Armenian Church was by no means hostile to it. Not the Armenians but the assurance of the Mohammedans that they had tested Christianity and found it wanting was the real objective. The first missionaries at Constantinople laid their plans before the Armenian patriarch, and during twelve years had his friendly approval, especially for their schools. A less liberal patriarch punished with severe persecution from 1845 to 1847 Armenians who had adopted the idea of individual study of the Bible. Finally the British Government interfered in behalf of religious liberty, solemnly proclaimed by the Sultan in the Hatti Sherif of 1839. All Armenians who chose to escape the pains of the ban by declaring themselves Protestants were protected by Turkish police against the rancor of the patriarch; and in 1852–54 the "Protestant Community" as it is officially called, or the "Evangelical Community" as it is called by its members, was formally recognized, with a layman as its representative before the throne, and with all the rights of a separate religious organization. Since then evangelical Greeks, Bulgarians, Syrians, Jews, etc., have been added to this body.

The American Board's missions among the Armenians have extended throughout Asiatic Turkey, to the Persian frontier on the east, and to the Arabic-speaking provinces of Syria and Mesopotamia on the south. The central stations number 13 and the outstations 241, with 161 missionaries (of whom 63 are unmarried women) and 956 native workers. The communicants in its congregations (1905) number 14,542, and the adherents 50,738. It should be noted, however, that separate statistics of the Armenians in these congregations are not kept. It is perhaps safe to estimate them at about seventy per cent of the whole number. Educational work is extensive and effective. There are 22,152 scholars of all grades and both sexes in the 529 primary and intermediate schools, the six colleges for men and women, and the four theological seminaries, which receive candidates for the ministry of the Old Armenian Church as well as those of the Evangelical body. Robert College at Constantinople, founded by Christopher Robert of New York with Cyrus Hamlin for its first president, is not included in these statistics. It is not connected with the mission, nor is it in any sense propagandist. Yet its liberal education of Armenians has tended to strengthen the position of the Evangelical Armenian body. A publishing house at Constantinople, removed from Smyrna in 1853, and with uninterrupted productiveness since it was founded in Malta in 1822, issues school books, religious books, hymnals, commentaries, and other helps to the study of the Bible, besides a family newspaper that appears in an Armenian and a Turkish edition.

A small number of Armenians have joined the evangelical movement through the mission of the (American) Disciples of Christ. Many, whose statistics are not separately kept, have connected themselves with the American Presbyterian missions in Persia. Reckoning all these together, and adding to them the evangelical Armenians in the Russian Caucasus and in the territory taken from Turkey in the war of 1877–78, the total number of Evangelical Armenians may be estimated in these countries at about 80,000.

HENRY OTIS DWIGHT.

9. Armenians in America.

Armenian immigration to the United States practically commenced in 1895 after the massacres of that time. A few had come earlier for education, business, or manufacturing, and there were small communities in a few of the larger cities. After that the number increased rapidly. The census of 1900 makes no distinction of races from Turkey, though the later immigration reports do. It thus follows that exact figures are scarcely obtainable. The best estimates place the total (1906) at not far from 30,000, of whom from 7,500 to 10,000 may be considered as Protestants or Evangelicals, the remainder belonging to the Gregorian or Orthodox Church. The largest single community, practically a colony, is at Fresno, Cal., where at least 4,000 are located. The other centers are New York City (3,500–4,000), Boston (2,500), Worcester, Mass. (1,200), Providence. R. I. (1,200), and Philadelphia (500). In the immediate suburbs of Boston and the manufacturing towns of Eastern Massachusetts and New Hampshire, in Hartford, and in New Jersey there are a number of communities of varying size and changing from year to year.

The Protestant Armenians have organized churches in New York City, Troy, N. Y., Worcester, Mass., Providence, R. I., and Fresno, Cal., besides a number of missions, or places where services, more or less regular, are held. The great majority are connected with the Congregational denomination, but there are Presbyterians. The Gregorians have an archbishop at Worcester, and vartabeds or priests at New York, Worcester, Providence, Boston, and Fresno. These visit other places in their vicinity to perform rites or ceremonies that may be desired. They have church buildings at Worcester and Fresno. The attendance upon church services is said to be on the whole excellent in those communities where there are regular organizations. It is to be noted that there are many small communities where members identify themselves with the local churches.

In general character the Armenians in the United States show much the same characteristics as in their own country. They are industrious, frugal, peaceable. They retain a close connection with their relatives and friends in the home-land as is shown by the sums annually remitted to them. With the exception of the Fresno colony, chiefly agricultural, they are for the most part traders, manufacturers, or laborers in the large factories. They preserve to a considerable degree their distinctive nationalism and were the conditions in Turkey to change, would probably return in large numbers. EDWIN MUNSELL BLISS.

BIBLIOGRAPHY: Descriptive and geographical works: H. Hyvernat and P. Müller-Simonis, *Relation des missions scientifiques , , notes sur la géographie et l'histoire ancienne de l'Arménie et les inscriptions du bassin de Van*, Paris, 1892; H. F. Tozer, *Turkish Armenia and Eastern Asia Minor*, London, 1881; E. Noguères, *Arménie. Géographie, histoire, religion, mœurs, littérature*, Paris, 1897; H. F. B. Lynch, *Armenian Travels and Studies*, London, 1901. On the people: A. Megorovian, *Étude ethnographique et juridique sur la famille et le mariage arménien*, Paris, 1895; J. Creagh, *Armenians, Koords and Turks*, 2 vols., London, 1880; J. B. Telfer, *Armenia and its People*, London, 1891; G. H. Filian, *Armenia and her people*, New York, 1896. On the language and literature: F. J. B. Ananian, *Dictionary of Modern Armenian Language*, Venice, 1869; F. M. Bedrossian, *Eng.-Armenian and Armenian-Eng. Dictionary*, 2 vols., London, 1875–79; J. H. Petermann, *Brevis linguæ Armenicæ grammatica*, Berlin, 1872; K. H. Gulian, *Elementary Modern Armenian Grammar*, London, 1902; P. Sukias Somal, *Quadro delle opere di vari autori anticamente tradotti in Armeno*, Venice, 1825, and *Quadro della storia letteraria di Armenia*, Venice, 1829; C. F. Neumann, *Versuch einer Geschichte der armenischen Litteratur*, Leipsic, 1836, a German adaptation of the preceding; M. Patcanian, *Catalogue de la littérature arménienne depuis le commencement du iv. siècle jusque vers le milieu du xvii.*, in *Mélanges asiatiques*, iv. 1., St. Petersburg, 1860; F. Nève, *L'Arménie chrétienne et sa littérature*, Louvain, 1886.

For the history the sources accessible in European languages are: M. Chamchian, *History of Armenia from B.C. 2247 to A.D. 1780, translated from the original Armenian by J. Avdall, with continuation to date*, 2 vols., Calcutta, 1827; J. Saint-Martin, *Mémoires historiques et géographiques sur l'Arménie*, 2 vols., Paris, 1818–19; M. Brosset, *Les Ruines d'Ani*, 2 parts, St. Petersburg, 1860–61; idem, *Collection d'historiens arméniens*, 2 vols., St. Petersburg, 1874–76; V. Langlois, *Collection des historiens anciens et modernes de l'Arménie*, 2 vols., Paris, 1867–69; E. Dulaurier, *Le Royaume de la Petite-Arménie*, in *Recueil des historiens des croisades; documents arméniens*, i., Paris, 1869; idem, *Étude sur l'organisation politique, religieuse, et administrative du royaume de la Petite-Arménie*, in *JA*, ser. v., xvii. (1861) 377 sqq., xviii. (1861) 289 sqq. Consult N. T. Gregor, *Hist. of Armenia from Earliest Ages*, London, 1897 (a handy manual); Nerses Ter-Mikaelian, *Das armenische Hymnarium*, Leipsic, 1905 (a hist. of the development of hymnology in the Armenian Church).

For the native religion of Armenia, consult H. Gelzer, *Zur armenischen Götterlehre*, in the *Berichte der königlichen sächsischen Gesellschaft der Wissenschaften zu Leipzig*, phil.-hist. *Classe*, xlviii. (1896) 99–148; A. Carrière, *Les Huit Sanctuaires de l'Arménie païenne*, Paris, 1899. The works mentioned in the text have all been printed, either by the Mekhitarists, at St. Petersburg, or elsewhere; some are accessible in translation, either independently or in collective works like those of Brosset and Langlois, mentioned above. For the history of the Armenian Church, missions, and modern religious conditions consult: E. Dulaurier, *Histoire, dogmes, traditions, et liturgie de l'église arménienne orientale*, Paris, 1855; S. C. Malan, *Life and Times of St. Gregory the Illuminator*, London, 1868, a transl. from the Armenian; idem, *The Divine Liturgy of the Orthodox Armenian Church of St. Gregory*, ib. 1870, transl. from the Armenian; idem, *Confession of Faith of the Holy Armenian Church*, ib. 1872; C. H. Wheeler, *Ten Years on the Euphrates*, New York, 1868; R. Anderson, *History of the Missions of the American Board to the Oriental Churches*, 2 vols., Boston, 1870; E. F. K. Fortescue, *The Armenian Church*, London, 1872; F. Nève, *L'Arménie chrétienne*, Louvain, 1886; D. Vernier, *Histoire du patriarcat arménien catholique*, Lyons, 1891; F. C. Conybeare, *The Armenian Church*, in *Religious Systems of the World*, London, 1893, and *The Key of Truth: a Manual of the Paulician Church of Armenia. Text and transl.*, London, 1898; H. Gelzer, *Die Anfänge der armenischen Kirche*, in the *Berichte der königlich sächsischen Gesellschaft der Wissenschaften zu Leipzig, phil.-hist. Classe*, xlvii. (1895) 109–174; W. St. C. Tisdall, *Conversion of Armenia to the Christian Faith*, London, 1896; *Melodies of the Holy Apostolic Church of Armenia*, the liturgy, etc., translated by J. B. Melik-Belgar, Calcutta, 1897; E. Lohmann, *Im Kloster zu Sis, ein Beitrag zu der Geschichte der Beziehungen zwischen dem deutschen Reiche und Armenien im Mittelalter*, Striegau, 1901; K. Beth, *Die orientalische Christenheit der Mittelmeerländer. Reisestudien zur Statistik und Symbolik der . armenischen Kirchen*, Berlin, 1902; A. Harnack, *Die Mission und Ausbreitung des Christentums in den ersten drei Jahrhunderten*, Leipsic, 1902, Eng. transl., London, 1904, passim; S. Weber, *Die katholische Kirche in Armenien*, Freiburg, 1903 (the most complete account of Armenian church history to the beginning of the sixth century from the Roman Catholic standpoint); E. Ter-Minassiantz, *Die armenische Kirche in ihren Beziehungen zu den syrischen Kirchen bis zum Ende des dreizehnten Jahrhunderts*, *TU*, new series, xi. 4. The recent disturbances in Armenia have called forth a number of works (some of them to be used with caution), such as F. D. Greene, *The Armenian Crisis and the Rule of the Turk*, London, 1895; G. Godet, *Les Souffrances de l'Arménie*, Neuchâtel, 1896 (containing a list of churches, monasteries, and villages destroyed, and names of ministers murdered); J. Lepsius, *Armenien und Europa*, Berlin, 1896; J. R. and H. B. Harris, *Letters from Armenia*, New York, 1897; A. Nazarbek, *Through the Storm, Picture of Life in Armenia*, New York, 1899; H. O. Dwight, *Constantinople and its Problems*, New York, 1901.

ARMINIUS, JACOBUS (Jakob Hermanss), AND ARMINIANISM: A Dutch theologian and the theological system he is supposed to have held. Arminius was born at Oudewater (18 m. e.n.e. of Rotterdam) Oct. 10, 1560; d. at Leyden Oct. 19, 1609. After his father's early death he lived with Rudolphus Snellius, professor in Marburg. In 1576 he returned home and studied theology at Leyden under Lambertus Danæus. Here he spent six years, till he was enabled by the burgomasters of Amsterdam to continue his studies at Geneva and Basel under Beza and Grynæus. He lectured on the philosophy of Petrus Ramus and the Epistle to the Romans. Being recalled by the government of Amsterdam, in 1588 he was appointed preacher of the Reformed congregation. During the fifteen years which he spent here, he gained the general respect, but his views underwent a change. His exposition of Rom. vii. and ix., and his utterances on election and reprobation gave offense. His learned but hot-headed colleague, Petrus Plancius, in particular opposed him. Disputes arose in the consistory, which for the time being were stopped by the burgomasters.

Arminius was suspected of heresy because he regarded the subscription to the symbolical books as not binding and was ready to grant to the State more power in ecclesiastical matters than the strict Calvinists would admit. When two of the professors of the University of Leyden, Junius and

Trelcatius, died (1602), the curators called Arminius; and Franciscus Gomarus (q.v.), the only surviving theological professor, protested, but he became reconciled after an interview with Arminius. The latter entered upon his duties in 1603 with an address on the high-priestly office of Christ, and was made doctor of theology. But the dogmatic disputes were renewed when Arminius undertook public lectures on predestination. Gomarus opposed him and published other theses. A great excitement ensued in the university and the students were divided into two parties. The ministers in Leyden and other places took part in the controversy, which became general. The Calvinists wanted the matter settled by a general synod, but the States General would not have it. Oldenbarneveldt, the Dutch liberal statesman, in 1608 gave both opponents opportunity to defend their views before the supreme court, and a verdict was pronounced that since the controversy had no bearing upon the main points pertaining to salvation, each should bear with the other. But Gomarus would not yield. Even the States of Holland tried to bring about a reconciliation between the two, and in Aug., 1609, both professors and four ministers for each were invited to undertake new negotiations. The deliberations were first held orally, afterward continued in writing, but were terminated in October by the death of Arminius.

In his *Disputationes*, which were partly published during his lifetime, partly after his death, and which included the entire department of theology, as well as in some discourses and other writings, Arminius had clearly and pointedly defined his position and expressed his conviction. On the whole these writings are a fine testimony to his learning and acumen. The doctrine of predestination belonged to the fundamental teachings of the Reformed Church; but the conception of it asserted by Calvin and his adherents, Arminius could not make his own. He would not follow a doctrinal development which made God the author of sin and of the condemnation of men. He taught conditional predestination and attached more importance to faith. He denied neither God's omnipotence nor his free grace, but he thought it his duty to save the honor of God, and to emphasize, on the basis of the clear expressions of the Bible, the free will of man as well as the truth of the doctrine of sin. In these things he was more on the side of Luther than of Calvin and Beza, but it can not be denied that he expressed other opinions which were violently controverted as departures from the confession and catechism. His followers expressed their convictions in the famous five articles which they laid before the States as their justification. Called Remonstrants from these *Remonstrantiæ*, they always refused to be called Arminians. See REMONSTRANTS. For the Arminianism of John Wesley and the Methodists, see METHODISTS.

H. C. ROGGE†.

Arminianism in its later development has entered widely into the thought of the Church, both on the Continent, in Great Britain, and in America. It was welcomed in the Lutheran Church as a relief from the teachings of Augustine and the Reformed Churches. In Holland it became allied with the more liberal tendencies,—Socinian, rationalistic, universalistic,—thus withdrawing itself from the traditional interpretation of Christianity. The number of its professed adherents in that country (most of them in Amsterdam) is not large (see REMONSTRANTS). In England also it developed a strong affinity with Socinianism in its doctrine of God and the person of Christ, and with Pelagianism in its conception of human nature. About the time of the Restoration, according to Hallam (*Literary History of Europe*, ii., London, 1855, p. 131), the Arminians were called Latitude-men or Latitudinarians (q.v.) and were addicted to Greek philosophy and natural religion. During the eighteenth century Arminianism was advocated by many of the leading writers of Great Britain,—Tillotson, Jeremy Taylor, Chillingworth, Burnet; by Hoadly, a Socinian; and by Whitby, John Taylor; and Samuel Clarke, Arians. With many others it was rather a repudiation of Calvinism than a definitely formed theory. In America Arminianism showed itself now as an advocacy of freedom of thought and thus of toleration; now as emphasis on natural human duties rather than on speculative theology; now as silent, now as outspoken protest against the tenets of Calvinism. Owing to the writings of Whitby, John Taylor, and Samuel Clarke, its influence greatly increased in the eighteenth century. To Jonathan Edwards its menace formed the motive for his greatest work, *The Freedom of the Will*. The name itself was made to cover many things for which Arminianism proper was not responsible—rationalistic tendencies of thought, depreciation of the serious nature of sin, indifference to vital piety, and laxity of morals. Arminianism became more a condition than a theory. In spite of opposition, however, in part on account of its later profound spirit through Wesley, and in part by virtue of its essential truth, it has thoroughly leavened the Christian thought of America. A sign of the times is, that theological schools confessedly Arminian educate young men for Churches which are traditionally Calvinistic, and ministers holding Arminian views are received by such Churches as thoroughly "orthodox."

C. A. B.

BIBLIOGRAPHY: The works of Arminius were published Frankfurt, 1631, Eng. transl., by J. and W. Nichols, London, 1825–28; the latter contains life by Brandt and the oration by P. Bertius; best Am. ed. of the works and life, New York, 1842; the life is published separately, London, 1854. On the original doctrines, *The Confession of Faith of those called Armenians*, . . . *the Doctrines of the Ministers* . . . *known by the name of Remonstrants, transl. out of the Original*, London, 1684. The official *Acts* are in *Acta synodi nationalis Dordrechti*, Dordrecht, 1620, Fr. transl., 1624, and in J. A. Fabricius, *Bibliotheca Græca*, xi. 723, Hamburg, 1705; the *Canons* are in P. Schaff, *Creeds of Christendom*, iii. 550–597, New York, 1877; the collection of minutes in *Acta et scripta synodalia Dordracena*, Harderwyck, 1620; consult: M. Graf, *Beitrag zur Geschichte der Synode von Dortrecht*, Basel, 1825. On the earlier Arminianism, G. Brandt, *Historia reformationis Belgicæ*, 3 vols., The Hague, 1700, Eng. transl., 4 vols., London, 1720; J. Nichols, *Calvinism and Arminianism compared in their Principles and Tendency*, 2 vols., London, 1824; *KL*, i. 1375–84. On later phases, W Cunningham, *Reformers and Theology of the Reformation*, Essay vii., Edinburgh, 1862; idem, *Historical Theology*, chap. xxv., Edinburgh, 1862; J. L. Girardeau, *Calvinism and Evangelical Arminianism compared*, Columbia, 1890; G. L. Curtiss, *Arminianism in History*, Cincinnati, 1894.

ARMITAGE, THOMAS: Baptist; b. at Pontefract (20 m. s.s.w. of York), Yorkshire, England, Aug. 2, 1819; d. at Yonkers, N. Y., Jan. 20, 1896. He became a Methodist preacher at the age of sixteen; emigrated to America in 1838; joined the Baptists in 1848 and was pastor of the Fifth Avenue Baptist Church, New York (then located on Norfolk Street and known as the Norfolk Street Church), from that year till Jan. 1, 1889. He was one of the founders of the American Bible Union (1850) and its president 1856–75. He published *Preaching, its Ideal and Inner Life* (Philadelphia, 1880); *A History of the Baptists Traced by their Vital Principles and Practices from the Time of our Lord and Saviour Jesus Christ to the Present* (New York, 1887; revised and enlarged ed., 1890).

ARMY. See WAR.

ARNAUD, är″nō′, **HENRI**: Waldensian; b. at Embrun (58 m. s.e. of Grenoble), Department of Hautes Alpes, France, Sept. 30, 1641; d. at Schönenberg near Dürrmenz (19 m. n.w. by w. of Stuttgart), Württemberg, Sept. 8, 1721. He studied at Basel, probably visited Holland, and continued his studies at Geneva; became pastor at Maneille in the valley of St. Martin, 1670, and later at an unknown place in Dauphiné; fled to La Torre, Piedmont, probably shortly after the revocation of the Edict of Nantes (October, 1685). He counseled resistance to the persecution of the Waldensians undertaken by Victor Amadeus II., Duke of Savoy, at the instigation of Louis XIV of France, and, when this failed, with the remnant of his people (about 3,000 in number) took refuge in Switzerland. There he was active in plotting for a return, and in August, 1689, he led about 900 of the exiles back to their old homes, where they maintained themselves against the French and Savoyard troops until political conditions (the influence of William of Orange and a breach with France) led the Duke to withdraw his opposition (1690). In the ensuing war with France he rendered good service to the duke, but resumed his spiritual duties in 1692. In 1698, on the renewal of persecution following a fresh alliance with France, he again went into exile in Switzerland, visited Germany, Holland, and England in the interest of his people, and in 1699 settled in Württemberg as pastor of the Waldensians living in and about Dürrmenz. He wrote *Histoire de la glorieuse rentrée des Vaudois dans leur vallées* (Cassel, 1710; later eds., Neuchâtel, 1845, Geneva, 1879; Eng. transl by H. D. Acland, London, 1827).

BIBLIOGRAPHY: For his life in German consult K. H. Klaiber, *Henri Arnaud, nach den Quellen*, Stuttgart, 1880; in Italian, E. Comba, Florence, 1889; Fr. ed. of the latter, abridged, with the addition of certain letters, La Tour, 1889.

ARNAULD: The name of a famous French family, known especially for their connection with Jansenism. The well-known lawyer **Antoine Arnauld** (1560–1619) foreshadowed the position of his children by defending the University of Paris against the Jesuits in 1594. Of his twenty children, ten died young; and nine of the others devoted themselves to religion. The most noteworthy are: The eldest, **Robert Arnauld (d'Andilly**; b. in Paris 1588; d. there Sept. 27. 1674), who held various positions in the government and at the court, but retired in 1640 to Port Royal and devoted himself to church history. He is best known by his translations into French, especially of Josephus and St. Augustine's "Confessions," and the *Vies des saints pères du désert* (2 vols., Paris, 1647–53; Eng. transl., 2 vols., London, 1757).—**Jacqueline Marie Arnauld** (known in religion as Marie Angélique de Ste. Madeleine; b. in Paris Sept. 8, 1591; d. Aug. 6, 1661) entered the abbey of Port Royal when only seven, and became abbess at eleven. Aroused to fervent devotion in 1609, she began a strict reformation of her abbey according to the Cistercian rule. She resigned the position of abbess in 1630 and introduced the custom of triennial elections. From 1626 to 1648 she was in Paris, at the new house known as *Port-Royal de Paris*.—**Henri Arnauld** (b. in Paris 1597; d. at Angers June 8, 1692) was at first a lawyer, but entered the priesthood, was elected bishop of Toul but declined the election since it had occasioned disputes, and became bishop of Angers in 1649. He was an earnest and zealous diocesan, and a decided Jansenist; he was one of the four bishops who refused to subscribe the bull *Unigenitus*, which condemned the *Augustinus* of Jansen. His *Négociations à la cour de Rome et en différentes cours d'Italie* was published after his death (5 vols., Paris, 1748).—**Antoine Arnauld** (b. in Paris Feb. 6, 1612; d. in Brussels Aug. 8, 1694), known as "the great Arnauld," like his brother Henri, studied law at first, but entered the Sorbonne in 1634, taking his doctor's degree and being ordained priest in 1641. In 1643 he published his work *De la fréquente communion*, written under St. Cyran's influence (see DU VERGIER DE HAURANNE, JEAN), with which he began a lifelong struggle against the Jesuits. Its cold and rigid severity was opposed to their system, and they attacked it bitterly. Arnauld carried the war into the enemy's country with his *Théologie morale des Jésuites* (n.p., 1643), and, though for thirty years from 1648 he lived in retirement at Port Royal, his pen was never idle. He defended the cause of Jansen, maintaining in his two famous letters to the Duc de Liancourt (1655) that the five condemned propositions were not found in the *Augustinus*. The Sorbonne condemned these writings, and in 1656 expelled him, with sixty other doctors who refused to submit to the decision, from its fellowship. He was obliged to go into hiding for a time, and, with Nicole, was sheltered by the Duchess de Longueville. But he was still, as he had been since the death of Saint Cyran (1643), the active head of the Jansenist party, working diligently to confirm the nuns of Port Royal in their opposition to the papal decrees, supplying Pascal with the material for his "Provincial Letters," and publishing numerous pamphlets and treatises against the Jesuits. When the "Peace of Clement IX." put a temporary end to the strife, Arnauld was able to turn his weapons against the Protestants, notably in the controversy with Claude on the Lord's Supper, which produced his *Perpétuité de la foi de l'église catholique touchant l'Eucharistie* (Paris, 1664). He still, however, continued to attack the Jesuits, and his defense of the "Gallican liberties" against the king in the controversy over the *Droit de régale* (see REGALE) brought him into such disfavor with the government that in 1679 he again went into hiding and soon after left France for Brussels, where the Spanish governor protected him. Here he wrote two works of special interest to English-speaking people, the *Apologie pour les catholiques* (2 vols., Liége, 1681–82), a defense of the English Roman Catholics against the charge of conspiracy, especially as brought by Titus Oates, and an attack on William of Orange (1689). Of more general interest is his controversy with Malebranche, which produced the *Traité des vraies et des fausses idées* (Cologne, 1683) and *Réflexions philosophiques et théologiques sur le nouveau système de la nature et de la grâce du Père Malebranche* (3 vols., 1685–86). During this period he collaborated with Quesnel in his translation of the New Testament, as he had previously with Nicole and other members of the Port Royal group in their educational works, especially the often-reprinted "Logic." He was a man of wide learning, acute penetration, eloquent style, and untiring diligence, but unbendingly obstinate and set in his own ideas, so that at Port Royal it was a rule never to contradict him, lest he should be unduly excited. His works were published at Lausanne (48 vols., 1775–83).—**Angélique (de Saint Jean) Arnauld,** daughter of Robert (b. in Paris Nov. 24, 1624; d. Jan. 29, 1684), entered the abbey of Port Royal in her nineteenth year under her aunt's training; became subprioress in 1653 and abbess in 1678. Her firmness of character, and undaunted courage made her the principal support of the nuns during the long and grievous persecution brought upon them by their adherence to Jansenist opinions. Of several works which she wrote, the most important is the *Mémoires pour servir à l'histoire de Port Royal* (3 vols., Utrecht, 1742).—For all the members of the Arnauld family see JANSEN, CORNELIUS, JANSENISM; PORT ROYAL.

ARNDT, ärnt, **AUGUSTIN:** German Jesuit; b. at Berlin June 22, 1851. He was educated at the universities of Berlin (1872-74), Breslau (1875), and Cracow (1880-84). He was professor of German at the Seminary of Vals, France, in 1878-80, and from 1883 to 1889 he was professor of theology at Cracow, while since the latter year he has been editor of the *Katholischer Sonntagsblatt für die Diözese Breslau.* He has written *Homer und Virgil, eine Parallele* (Leipsic, 1873); *Der Unsterblichkeitsglaube der Alten* (Gütersloh, 1873); *Blütenstrauss aus Luthers Werken* (Berlin, 1875); *Wo ist Wahrheit?* (Freiburg, 1875); *Fenelons ascetische Schriften* (3 vols., Regensburg, 1886–87); *Der heilige Stanislaus Kostka* (1888); *De præstantia Societatis Jesu* (Cracow, 1890); *De rituum relatione juridica* (Rome, 1895); *De libris prohibitis* (Regensburg, 1895); *Conferenzen über die Konstitutionen der Ursulinerinnen* (Breslau, 1897); *Betstunden für die ewige Anbetung* (1897); *Biblia Sacra: die heilige Schrift* (Regensburg, 1898); *Der Jubilaeumsbeichtvater* (1900); *Handbüchlein der Mässigkeitsbruderschaften* (Breslau, 1900); *Vorschriften über das Verbot der Bücher* (Trier, 1900); *Die kirchlichen Rechtsbestimmungen über die Frauenkongregationen* (Mainz, 1901); *Novizenbüchlein der grauen Schwestern* (Breslau, 1901); *Kandidatenbüchlein der grauen Schwestern* (1901); *Jubilaeumsbüchlein* (1901); *Die vier heiligen Evangelien* (Regensburg, 1903); *Das Neue Testament* (1903); and *Erlasse und Verordnungen* (1906) He has likewise written much in Polish, and is the author of numerous briefer contributions.

ARNDT, ärnt, **JOHANN:** German mystic; b. at Edderitz, near Ballenstedt (36 m. s.w. of Magdeburg), Anhalt, Dec. 27, 1555; d. at Celle (23 m. n. of Hanover), Hanover, May 11, 1621. He studied theology at Helmstedt, Wittenberg, Strasburg, and Basel and in 1583 became pastor at Badeborn in Anhalt. He was removed in 1590 by Duke Johann Georg because of his refusal to submit to the duke's order proscribing the use of images and the practise of exorcism. Summoned to Quedlinburg in the same year Arndt had to contend with the malice of a faction among the townspeople with whom his aggressive preaching found little favor, and in 1599 he followed a call to Brunswick. Here too, after some years of quiet, he came into conflict with his colleagues, largely because of the general opposition aroused by the appearance, in 1606, of the first part of his *Vom wahren Christenthum.* In 1609 he became pastor at Eisleben, but two years later received the important post of general superintendent at Celle and in this position remained till his death, exercising a lasting and beneficent influence on the constitution of the Lüneburg church system. In 1609 appeared three additional books of the *Wahre Christenthum* and in 1612 he published his no less famous *Paradiesgärtlein aller christlichen Tugenden.* The appearance of the *Wahre Christenthum* gave rise to a violent controversy. Steeped in the mysticism of the Middle Ages, Arndt asserted the insufficiency of orthodox doctrine toward the complete attainment of the true Christian life, and upheld the necessity of a moral purification made possible by righteous living and by bringing the soul into communion with God. Though he held fast, formally, to the doctrine of the Lutheran Church, he nevertheless became thus the great precursor of Pietism and his is the greatest name in the history of German mysticism after Thomas a Kempis. The first book of the *Wahre Christenthum* was translated into English in 1646, and complete translations were made by A. W Boehm in 1712 and by W. Jaques in 1815. An American edition appeared at Philadelphia in 1842, revised in 1868. The *Garden of Paradise* appeared in English in 1716.

(H. HÖLSCHER.)

BIBLIOGRAPHY: F. Arndt, *Johann Arndt*, Berlin, 1838; H. L. Pertz, *De Joanne Arndt ejusque libris*, Hanover, 1852.

ARNDT, JOHANN FRIEDRICH WILHELM: German Lutheran; b. at Berlin June 24, 1802;

d. there May 8, 1881. He began his theological studies at the University of Berlin in 1820, and in 1829 became assistant minister to the bishop of the province of Saxony. His sermons delivered in the cathedral of Magdeburg attracted large audiences and his influence was especially marked among the higher classes and the learned. Called to Berlin in 1833 as associate pastor, he succeeded to the office of head preacher in 1840, retiring in 1875 because of his dissatisfaction with the reorganization of the church system effected two years previously. During his long pastorate at Berlin, Arndt established his reputation as one of the most eloquent pulpit orators of his time, and his volumes of sermons, frequently issued, constituted highly important contributions to German homiletic literature. As at Magdeburg, his congregation included persons of great eminence, among them such theologians as Neander and Hengstenberg. Arndt's remarkable power in the pulpit consisted in an exceptional gift for psychological analysis and shrewd observation and an extremely forcible style. He did not, however, escape the danger of dogmatism, and doctrine and formulas constituted for him an important part of the Christian life. His thought shows little development throughout his long career and the attitude revealed in his earliest works is the same found in his later sermons. Of the numerous collections of these mention may be made of *Das christliche Leben* (Magdeburg, 1834); *Predigten über Davidis Leben* (1836); *Das Vaterunser* (1837); *Die Bergpredigt Jesu Christi* (1838). He also wrote *Das Leben Jesu Christi* (1850–55), and *Die gottesdienstlichen Handlungen der evangelischen Kirche* (1860). (Hans Kessler.)

ARNO OF REICHERSBERG: A younger brother of the more famous Gerhoh of Reichersberg; d. Jan. 30, 1175. The year of his birth is not known. He received his education from Gerhoh, whose "son in the Lord" he calls himself. A third brother, Ruodger, was dean at Augsburg, and later at Neuburg. After Gerhoh's death, Arno, then dean, was unanimously chosen provost of the collegiate church of Reichersberg on the Inn, in the diocese of Passau (June 29, 1169). He wrote his *Scutum canonicorum* (in *MPL*, cxciv. 1489–1528) under Eugenius III., and so earlier than 1153. It was called out by the jealousy existing between the monks and the canons, which Arno wholly condemns, pleading for fraternal unity between the two foundations with similar aims. At the same time he vigorously defends the canons' rule of life, considering them the true imitators of Christ and the apostles, especially because, unlike the monks, they occupy themselves directly with the service of their neighbors. He also wrote an apologetic treatise (ed. C. Weichert, Leipsic, 1888), defending the teaching of Gerhoh against Provost Folmar of Triefenstein, on a question of Christology—whether the man (*homo*) taken into God at the Incarnation is truly and strictly the Son of God. Arno vehemently asserts the affirmative, maintaining that all the qualities of the Godhead were communicated to the human nature, though veiled during the earthly life of Christ. As a corollary he condemns the prevailing view of a local heaven, in which Christ sits in bodily presence. Underneath his polemic against Folmar there is another, expressed or unexpressed, against a more important theologian, Peter Lombard; and in one place he also controverts Hugo of St. Victor. Among other contemporary theologians, he knows Bernard of Clairvaux and Rupert of Deutz. (A. Hauck.)

Bibliography: Wattenbach, *DGQ*, ii. 314, note 3; Hauck, *KD*, iv. 444 sqq.

ARNO OF SALZBURG: Archbishop of Salzburg 785–821. He seems to have been born in the diocese of Freising, where his name occurs in the records as deacon and as priest down to 776. After 782 he is found as abbot at St. Amand at Elnon in Hainault, which he retained even after his consecration as bishop of Salzburg, June 10, 785. He was sent to Rome in 787 to implore the help of the pope in reconciling Charlemagne with Tassilo, Duke of Bavaria, but failed, and Bavaria lost its independence the following year. Arno gained the confidence of the new ruler, however, and Charlemagne confirmed the church of Salzburg in its possessions (790). The bishop was employed as *missus dominicus* in Bavaria, and at the close of the war with the Avars, all the conquered lands were placed under the spiritual authority of Salzburg. When Pope Leo III. was driven out by the kinsmen of his predecessor, Arno was charged by Charlemagne with the task of restoring peace and order in Rome, and explaining to the pope the king's wishes for the settlement of ecclesiastical affairs in the eastern part of his realm (797). In deference to these wishes, Bavaria was included ecclesiastically as well as civilly in the Frankish kingdom, and Salzburg was raised to the dignity of a metropolitan see, Arno receiving the pallium April 20, 798. He visited Rome again in 799 to restore Leo III. once more, and in 800 for the coronation of Charlemagne. He was *missus dominicus* in Bavaria almost continuously from 802 to 806; he appears on the occasion of Charlemagne's making his will, and at the Council of Mainz in 813, after which he seems to have retired from public life. He was a friend of learning and art, and is said to have had more than 150 books copied.

(A. Hauck.)

Bibliography: Alcuin's letters to Arno are in Jaffé, *BRG*, vi., *Monumenta Alcuiniana*, Berlin, 1873; consult also Rettberg, *KD*, ii. 200, 237, 558; Wattenbach, *DGQ*, i. (1904) 166, 172, 175 sqq., 215, ii. 505; Hauck, *KD*, ii. passim.

ARNOBIUS, ār-nō'bi-us: A teacher of rhetoric at Sicca in proconsular Africa under Diocletian. At first he was a fierce opponent of Christianity, but he was converted and wrote seven books *adversus nationes*, in which he seeks to refute the charge of his contemporaries that Christianity was the cause of all misery in the world. To this point he devotes books i. and ii. The other books are a polemic against heathenism, showing in iii., iv., and v. the folly and immorality of the polytheistic mythology, while vi. and vii. speak of the heathen temple and sacrificial service. When the work was composed can not be stated exactly, but probably it was after 303. Arnobius was neither a clear thinker, nor a skilful writer (cf. Jerome, *Epist.*, lviii. 10). Where he tries to pose as philosopher, he betrays no deep study. His ideas conflict not seldom with Holy Scripture. Greek mythology he knows only from the "Preceptor" of Clement of Alexandria, and Roman mythology from the writings of Cornelius Labeo, whom he sometimes attacks. He had only a superficial knowledge of Christianity. His naive modalism is merely the expression of a very superstitious sentiment, and his notions concerning the origin, nature, and continuance of the soul have anything but a Christian-ecclesiastical color. G. KRÜGER.

BIBLIOGRAPHY: Arnobius's work is in *MPL*, iv. and was ed. by A. Reifferscheid, in *CSEL*, iv., 1875; Eng. transl. in *ANF*, vi. 405–543. Bibliography is in *ANF*, Bibliography, pp. 76–77. Consult *DCB*, i. 167; K. B. Francke, *Die Psychologie und Erkenntnislehre des Arnobius*, Leipsic, 1878; W. Kahl, in *Philologus*, supplementary vol. v., *Cornelius Labeo*, 717–807, Göttingen, 1889; A. Ebert, *Geschichte der Litteratur des Mittelalters im Abendland*, i. 64–72, Leipsic, 1889; A. Röhricht, *Die Seelenlehre des Arnobius*, Hamburg, 1893; idem, *De Clemente Alexandrino Arnobii in irridendo gentilium cultu auctore*, Hamburg, 1893; C. Stange, *De Arnobii oratione*, Saargemünd, 1893; Scharnagl, *De Arnobii majoris latinitate*, Görz, 1894–95; E. F. Schultze, *Das Uebel in der Welt nach der Lehre des Arnobius*, Jena, 1896; Krüger, *History*, 304–306; P. Spindler, *De Arnobii genere dicendi*, Strasburg, 1901.

ARNOBIUS THE YOUNGER: Reputed author of certain writings, concerning which scholars are not agreed except that they belong to the fifth century. They include: (1) *Commentarii in psalmos*, which are usually thought to be the work of a semi-Pelagian Gaul, though they may have been written in Rome; (2) *Adnotationes ad quædam evangeliorum loca*, which seems to have been used in the supposed gospel-commentary of Theophilus of Antioch (q.v.); (3) *Arnobii catholici et Serapionis conflictus de Deo trino et uno*; (4) The so called *Prædestinatus*, which may have been the work of this mysterious Arnobius (see PRÆDESTINATUS). G. KRÜGER.

BIBLIOGRAPHY: The works are in *MPL*, liii. Consult *DCB*, i. 170; T. Zahn, *Forschungen zur Geschichte des Kanons*, ii. 104–119, Erlangen, 1883; A. Harnack, in *TU*, i. 4, 152–153, Leipsic, 1883; S. Bäumer, in *Der Katholik*, ii. (1887) 398–406; A. Engelbrecht, *Patristische Analekten*, pp. 97–99, Vienna, 1892; B. Grundl, in *TQ*, lxxix. (1897) 555–568; G. Morin, in *Revue bénédictine*, xx., Maredsous, 1903; H. von Schubert, in *TU*, new ser., ix. 4, Leipsic, 1903.

ARNOLD OF BRESCIA.

Arnold of Brescia, church reformer of the twelfth century, was born at Brescia, but the year is not known; he was executed at Rome 1155. At an early age he devoted himself to the priesthood. Like many young Italians of his time he studied in France and became a pupil of Abelard. His scientific culture is particularly praised, and Abelard's keen criticism of tradition helped no doubt to loosen the bonds which connected

1. Life to 1139.

Arnold with the existing church authority. Some years later he appears again in his native city, having meanwhile been ordained priest. The *Historia pontificalis* calls him *canonicus regularis* and *abbas apud Brixiam*. The views to which he clung to his death were already fixed in his mind. The Church must resign worldly power and worldly possessions; priests, having worldly possessions, forfeit salvation; their necessary support they must obtain from the tithes, and the laity, who withheld from the priests what belonged to them, come in for a share of Arnold's criticism. His austere asceticism and powerful eloquence gained him great authority, which rendered his opposition formidable to Manfred, bishop of Brescia, and the latter accused him at a synod held in Rome in 1139. Arnold was banished from Italy and had to vow solemnly not to return without papal permission.

A revolution now took place in Brescia, and the "evil-minded consuls, hypocritical and heretical men," were expelled from the city by the knighthood. Arnold meanwhile had gone to France, where he assisted Abelard

2. Banished from Italy.

against Bernard of Clairvaux, and so the condemnation passed by Innocent II. in 1140 on Abelard concerned him likewise; they were to be separated and kept in monastic prisons. Arnold, however, remained unmolested for the time being, because of a conflict between the king and the curia. Bernard was at first against the king, but afterward he acted as mediator, and thus after a short time Arnold had to leave France. He went to Zurich, where he soon had a following. A letter of Bernard (cxcv.) to Bishop Herman of Constance [written 1140] caused his expulsion, but he soon found a safe refuge, for another letter of Bernard's (cxcvi.) to Cardinal Guido—probably the cardinal-deacon Guido who was active as papal legate in Bohemia and Moravia between 1142 and 1145—received Arnold into his retinue and honored him with his society. Arnold returned to Italy shortly after the death of Innocent (1143), and Eugenius III. (1145–53) received the fugitive again into the communion of the Church after a promise to do penance.

Rome was at that time the theater of great struggles. Toward the end of the life of Innocent II. the community had created a senate and appointed a patrician in place of the city-prefect dependent on the pope. Eugenius escaped these unpleasant relations by going to France, and Arnold developed great public activity. He attacked the cardinals, and even the

3. Political Activity in Rome.

pope. A new element now comes out in him according to the *Historia pontificalis*, which makes him say that those should not be tolerated who wish to enslave Rome, the mistress of the world, the source of liberty. He took up the idea of reclaiming for Rome her ancient powerful position in the world. He entered into close relations with the Roman community which had become a republic and had promised to protect him against every one. Eugenius sought to get possession of Rome by force of arms, and in their distress the Romans looked to King Conrad, who, however, had no thought of realizing their hopes, though he was in no position to help the pope in an effective manner. An agreement was made in

November, 1149, according to which Rome acknowledged the supremacy of the pope, but the government of the city remained in the hands of the senate. Arnold exercised his influence as before. When Frederick I. became ruler, Eugenius obtained his promise of a campaign against Rome. But the Arnoldists also applied to him in a writing, the strange contents of which may be regarded as an echo of Arnold's sermons. It declares that clerics who in spite of the gospel and the canonical rules claimed for themselves the right of confirming the emperor are successors of Julian the Apostate; the Donation of Constantine is a heretical fable, which even the every-day Roman ridicules; as the empire belongs to the Romans, who should hinder them from electing a new emperor? It is possible that such eccentric schemes repelled the more prudent elements. At the elections of Nov. 1, 1152, the Arnoldists seem to have been defeated, for the senate is soon found in negotiation with the pope, and he was enabled to make his entrance in December. A little later Frederick promised to subdue the Romans.

When Adrian IV. ascended the papal throne Dec. 5, 1154, he demanded of the senate the expulsion of Arnold, which for the time being was not heeded. But an attack made upon a cardinal gave opportunity, shortly before Palm Sunday, 1155, to pronounce an interdict on Rome,—a hitherto unheard-of proceeding.

4. Condemnation and Death.

The depression which already existed in the city was enhanced by this measure, and on Wednesday the senate appeared before the pope and obtained the removal of the interdict by swearing to expel Arnold and his adherents. Arnold's fate was now decided. Banished from Rome, he found indeed a refuge with the viscounts of Campagnatico, but, urged by the pope, Frederick induced them to hand him over to Adrian. The city-prefect, as Rome's criminal judge, delivered him to the gallows, had his body burned, and the ashes thrown into the Tiber. He died lamented even by men who, like Gerhoh of Reichersberg, by no means agreed with him. The great cause of his death was no doubt his opposition to the worldly power of the pope. But he was also regarded as a heretic. That he held false doctrines regarding baptism has not been substantiated; but he declared that the sacraments administered by priests not leading an apostolic life were invalid, and herein one could see a rejection of the official Church and hence a heresy. That Arnold left many followers is evident from the *Historia pontificalis*, and in the great bull of excommunication of Lucius III. (1184), Arnoldists are mentioned. Thenceforth only isolated notices concerning them are found; they were probably lost among the Waldensians.

S. M. DEUTSCH.

BIBLIOGRAPHY: Sources are: Otto of Freising, *De gestis Friderici*, i. 27–28, ii. 21, in *MGH*, *Script.*, xx. (1868) 338–491 and ed. G. Waitz in *Script. rer. Germ.*, Hanover, 1884; John of Salisbury, *Historia pontificalis*, xxxi., in *MGH*, *Script.*, xx. (1868) 515–545; Gunther, *Ligurinus*, iii., in *MPL*, ccxii.; Gerhoh of Reichersberg, *De investigatione antichristi*, xlii., in *MPL*, cxciv.; Boso, *Vita Hadriani IV.*, in J. M. Watterich, *Pontificum Romanorum vitæ*, ii. 324–325, Leipsic, 1862; *Gesta di Federigo I. in Italia* (Publications of the Istituto Storico Italiano), Rome, 1887. Consult also F. Odorici, *Storie Bresciane*, iv., Brescia, 1858; W. von Giesebrecht, *Arnold von Brescia*, Munich, 1895; idem, *Geschichte der deutschen Kaiserzeit*, iv., v., Brunswick, 1880–88; G. de Castro, *Arnold da Brescia*, Leghorn, 1875; W. Bernhardi, *Jahrbücher des deutschen Reichs unter Konrad III.*, Leipsic, 1883; E. Vacandard, *Arnauld de Brescia*, in *Revue des questions historiques*, xxxv. (1884) 52–114; A. Hausrath, *Arnold von Brescia*, Leipsic, 1891.

ARNOLD, CARL FRANKLIN: German Lutheran; b. at Williamsfield, O., Mar. 10, 1853. He was educated at the gymnasium at Bremen and the universities of Erlangen, Leipsic, and Königsberg (Ph.D., 1882). He was instructor in religion at the Wilhelms-Gymnasium in Königsberg from 1878 to 1888, when he was appointed professor of church history in the University of Breslau. Since 1898 he has also been ephorus of the Gräfliches Ledemtzky'sches Johanneum. In theology he is an advocate of positive union. He has written *Studien zur Geschichte der plinianischen Christenverfolgung* (Königsberg, 1887); *Die neronische Christenverfolgung* (Leipsic, 1888); *Auswahl aus J. G. Hamanns Briefen und Schriften* (Gotha, 1888); *Cæsarius von Arelate und die gallische Kirche seiner Zeit* (Leipsic, 1894); *Predigten des Cæsarius von Arelate in deutscher Uebersetzung* (1895); *Die Vertreibung der Salzburger Protestanten und ihre Aufnahme bei den Glaubensgenossen* (1900); *Die Ausrottung des Protestantismus in Salzburg unter Erzbischof Firmian und seinen Nachfolgern* (1901); *Protestantisches Leben in den Vereinigten Staaten* (1903). He edited the fifth and sixth editions of H. Weingarten's *Zeittafeln und Ueberblicke zur Kirchengeschichte* (1897, 1906).

ARNOLD, GOTTFRIED: Lutheran; b. at Annaberg (18 m. s. of Chemnitz), Saxony, Sept. 5, 1666; d. at Perleberg (75 m. n.w. of Berlin), Prussia, May 30, 1714. In 1685 he began the study of theology at Wittenberg but gave himself up to independent reading in early church history. Through the influence of Spener, then court preacher at Dresden, he became tutor in a noble family of that city in 1689, and later obtained a similar position at Quedlinburg. There he became identified with the most prominent exponents of mystic and separatist teachings and in 1696 published *Die erste Liebe* (ed. A. C. Lämmert, Stuttgart, 1844), a eulogy on the early Christian Church in which his hostility to dogma and ecclesiasticism led him to exalt the virtues of the primitive Church as opposed to the formulism of later orthodoxy. In 1697 he became professor of history at Giessen, but found himself out of sympathy with the practical nature of his duties and returned in the following year to Quedlinburg. In 1699–1700 he published his *Unparteiische Kirchen- und Ketzer-Historie* (4 vols.; new ed., Frankfort, 1729), which had a marked influence on church history. In studying heretical movements Arnold refused to accept as authority the evidence of hostile contemporaries and drew upon the writings of the sectaries themselves for his materials. In view of his constitutional opposition to orthodox doctrine this method naturally led to his assuming a position extremely favorable to the separatists of various ages and occasioned a vigorous controversy which plunged him deeper still into mysticism. From this period date his beautiful religious songs, of which a number have found a place in the evangelical hymnal. In 1704 he became pastor and inspector at Werben, in Prussia, and from that time may be dated his reconciliation with established theology. In 1707 he became inspector at Perleberg, bringing to the performance of his duties the utmost devotion and energy. Besides his church history, his writings number more than fifty, among them, *Geistliche Gestalt eines evangelischen Lehrers* (Halle, 1704) and *Wahre Abbildung des inwendigen Christenthums* (Frankfort, 1709). His hymns were edited by K. C. E. Ehmann (Stuttgart, 1856).

(F. W Dibelius.)

Bibliography: F. Dibelius, *Gottfried Arnold*, Berlin, 1873.

ARNOLD, MATTHEW: Church of England; b. at Laleham, near Chertsey (32 m. w.s.w. of London), Dec. 24, 1822, eldest son of Thomas Arnold (q.v.); d. in Liverpool Apr. 15, 1888. He studied at Winchester and Rugby schools, and at Balliol College, Oxford, and became fellow of Oriel 1845. In 1847 he became private secretary to the Marquis of Lansdowne, then president of the council and acting as minister of public instruction; by his influence was appointed in 1851 as inspector of schools, and held the position till 1886. He was professor of poetry at Oxford 1857–67 He was a zealous and able official and his reports upon continental schools, which he visited frequently, are valuable in educational literature. His poetry is of high rank; and as literary critic he was unrivaled in his generation. He possessed a subtle mind, a keen critical spirit, and a passionate love of truth, which, when applied to religious problems, found many defects in the current theology of the time, the chief being a disposition to rest on unprovable assumptions and to ignore the claims of reason. The greatest good he held to be progress toward perfection; and such progress could only be made by 'culture,' which meant acquaintance with the best that has been done and thought in the world. He declared that 'conduct is three-fourths of life,' characterized religion as 'morality touched with emotion,' originated the phrase 'the enduring power, not ourselves, which makes for righteousness,' and believed that 'miracles do not happen.' His works which bear on religious topics are: *Culture and Anarchy* (London, 1869); *St. Paul and Protestantism: with an introduction on Puritanism and the Church of England* (1870); *Literature and Dogma, an essay toward a better appreciation of the Bible* (1873); *God and the Bible, a review of objections to 'Literature and Dogma'* (1875); *Last Essays on Church and Religion* (1877). He also edited, with prefaces and notes, the two sections of the Book of Isaiah, *A Bible-Reading for Schools, the great prophecy of Israel's Restoration* [Isaiah xl.–lxvi.] (1872; new ed., 1875); *Isaiah of Jerusalem* [Isaiah i.–xxxix.] (1883). A complete edition of his works in 15 volumes was issued in London and New York, 1903–04. In accordance with his wish no authorized biography has been published, but his *Letters, 1848–88* (collected and arranged by G. W E. Russell, 2 vols., London, 1895) furnish an excellent substitute.

Bibliography: For life, *DNB*, Supplement, i. 70–75; G. W. E. Russell, *Matthew Arnold*, London, 1904. For his influence on the age, J. M. Robertson, *Modern Humanists*, London, 1891; W. H. Hudson, *Studies in Interpretation*, New York, 1896; J. Fitch, *Thomas and Matthew Arnold and their Influence on English Education*, London, 1897; G. White, *Matthew Arnold and the Spirit of the Age*, New York, 1898; G. Saintsbury, *Matthew Arnold*, London, 1899; W H. Dawson, *Matthew Arnold and his Relation to the Thought of our Time*, New York, 1904; J. M. Dixon, *Matthew Arnold*, New York, 1906 (on the religious side of his philosophy and poetry).

ARNOLD, NIKOLAUS: Reformed theologian; b. at Lissa (55 m. n.n.w. of Breslau), Poland, Dec. 17, 1618; d. at Franeker, Holland, Oct. 15, 1680. He studied under Amos Comenius, at Danzig (1635–41), and at Franeker, where Maccovius and Coccejus were his teachers. After visiting the academies of Groningen, Leyden, and Utrecht, and traveling in England, he was appointed minister at Beetgum, near Leeuwarden, Friesland, in 1645, and professor of theology at Franeker in 1651. He edited the works of Maccovius, and published, against Socinianism, *Religio Sociniana seu catechesis Racoviana major publicis disputationibus refutata* (Franeker, 1654); *Atheismus Socinianus* (1659); against the Roman Catholic Church, *Apologia Amesii contra Erbamannum*; against the prophecies of Comenius concerning the millennium, *Discursus theologicus contra Comenii prætensam lucem in tenebris* (1660).

ARNOLD, THOMAS: Master of Rugby and "Broad Church" leader; b. at West Cowes, Isle of Wight, June 13, 1795; d. at Rugby June 12, 1842. He studied at Warminster and Winchester schools and Corpus Christi College, Oxford, becoming a fellow of Oriel in 1815. He was ordained deacon in 1818, and in 1819 settled at Laleham, on the Thames near Staines, where he undertook to prepare a small number of young men for the universities. In 1828 he was ordained priest and appointed head master of Rugby; in 1841 he was made regius professor of modern history at Oxford, but delivered only one course of lectures. He is best known as one of the greatest of English schoolteachers; but he should be remembered no less as a keen-thinking and sharp-sighted leader of religious thought. Like Newman, Keble, and others of the reactionary High-church party, he was alarmed by the troubles political and otherwise, which appeared to be threatening the Church. But he sought safety by advocating that its doors should be opened so that all English Christians could find room within it. Differences of doctrine, constitution, and ritual he maintained were minor matters and should be disregarded; the essential thing in Christianity is practical godliness, manifesting itself in individual and social life. Church and State alike exist to help realize this ideal and each needs the other.[1] His views were expressed

[1] It is Thomas Arnold, if any one, who must be regarded as the pioneer of free theology in England. . . He was the first to show to his countrymen the possibility, and to make the demand, that the Bible should be read with honest human eyes, without the spectacles of orthodox dogmatic presuppositions, and that it can at the same time be

in two pamphlets, *The Principles of Church Reform* (London, 1833) and *Fragment on the Church* (1844); his religious writings also include six volumes of *Sermons*. His historical works comprise an edition of Thucydides (3 vols., 1830–35); the *History of Rome* (3 vols., 1838–43, unfinished); *History of the Later Roman Commonwealth* (2 vols., 1845); *Lectures on Modern History* (Oxford, 1842).

BIBLIOGRAPHY: A. P. Stanley, *Life and Correspondence of Thomas Arnold*, latest unabridged ed., London, 1901; Stanley collected also his *Miscellaneous Works*, 1845, and his *Travelling Journals*, 1852; *DNB*, ii. 113–117; J. Fitch, *Thomas and Matthew Arnold and their Influence on English Education*, London, 1897.

ARNOLDI (ɑr-nel'dî), **BARTHOLOMÆUS** (**Bartholomew of Usingen**): The teacher and later the opponent of Luther; b. at Usingen (17 m. n.n.w. of Frankfort) about 1464; d. at Würzburg Sept. 9, 1532. He entered the University of Erfurt probably in 1484, and was made master of arts in 1491. As teacher of philosophy and by his widely circulated writings he won the high esteem of both his colleagues and his pupils, among whom Luther seems to have been specially in close relations with him. When nearly fifty, and apparently in part owing to Luther's influence, he entered the Augustinian order, and later became professor of theology in the *studium generale* of the order at Erfurt. He was opposed to the later exaggerations of the scholastic methods, but without going as far in this direction as Luther, in whose rejection of philosophy he saw one of the sources of what he considered the reformer's later errors. He took a decided stand against the Wittenberg theses; after he had been deserted by his brethren of the Erfurt house he attacked the reforming movement in his first controversial treatise (1522), directed against the fiery preaching of Cuelsamer and Mechler. This was followed by many others covering the whole range of the controversy, and becoming more and more bitter as his old pupils scorned his exhortations. He was finally obliged to leave Erfurt, and in 1526 is found in the Augustinian house at Würzburg. He was not a great theologian nor even a good Latinist; but he seems to have been an honorable man who made a thorough study of his opponents' writings and learned to fight them with their own weapons. At Würzburg he was of great assistance to his bishop, Conrad von Thüngen, in the struggle with growing Protestantism, appeared with him at the Diet of Augsburg, and was among the theologians to whom the refutation of the Confession was committed.

(T. KOLDE.)

BIBLIOGRAPHY: G. Veesenmeyer, *Kleine Beiträge zur Geschichte des Reichstags zu Augsburg*, 105 sqq., Nuremberg, 1880; N. Paulus, *Der Augustiner Bartholomäus Arnoldi von Usingen*, in *Strassburger Theologische Studien*, i. 3, Freiburg, 1893.

ARNOLDISTS. See ARNOLD OF BRESCIA.

ARNOT, WILLIAM: Free Church, Scotland; b. at Scone, Perthshire, Nov. 6, 1808; d. in Edinburgh June 3, 1875. He studied at Glasgow, and in 1838 became pastor of St. Peter's Church in the same city; joined the Free Church movement in 1843; in 1863 succeeded Dr. Rainy as minister of the Free High Church, Edinburgh. He paid three visits to America, the last time as delegate to the meeting of the Evangelical Alliance in New York (1873). His chief publications were: *Life of James Halley* (Edinburgh, 1842); *The Race for Riches, and some of the Pits into which the Runners fall: Six Lectures applying the Word of God to the Traffic of Man* (London, 1851); *Laws from Heaven for Life on Earth: Illustrations of the Book of Proverbs* (2 vols., 1857–58); *The Parables of Our Lord* (1864); *Life of James Hamilton* (1870).

BIBLIOGRAPHY: *DNB*, ii. 119–120; *Autobiography, and Memoir by A. Fleming* (his daughter), London, 1877.

ARNULF OF LISIEUX: Bishop of Lisieux (90 m. w.n.w. of Paris) 1141–77 (or 81); d. in Paris Aug. 31, 1184. He was born in Normandy, accompanied Louis VII. of France to the Holy Land on the Second Crusade in 1147, was present at the coronation of Henry II. of England in 1154, and later tried unsuccessfully to mediate between Henry and Thomas Becket; he upheld the cause of Pope Alexander III. against Victor IV. at the Synod of Tours in 1163, and spent his last days in retirement in the abbey of St. Victor in Paris. His works are in *MPL*, cci. 1–200; most important are his letters (*Epistolæ ad Henricum II., regem Angliæ, Thomam archiepiscopum, et alios*), which are in *MPL*, ut sup., 17–152, and, ed. J. A. Giles, in *PEA*.

ARNULF, SAINT, OF METZ: Bishop of Metz; b. about 580; d. July 18 of an unknown year, according to Sigebert of Gembloux (*Chron.*, *MGH, Script.*, vi., 1844, p. 324) 640. He early distinguished himself in deeds of arms and affairs of state, but later devoted himself to an ecclesiastical career, and in 611 or 612 was made bishop of Metz. In this position he exercised considerable influence on the government of the Frankish kingdom, as a friend of Pepin of Landen, and enjoying the confidence of the Austrasian magnates. It was to him more than to any other that Clothair II. of Neustria owed his attainment of the dominion of Austrasia. Arnulf had been married as a young man, and through his son Ansegis, who married Pepin's daughter Begga, he became the ancestor of the

revered with Christian piety and made truly productive in moral life. He was the first who dared to leave on one side the traditional phraseology of the High-churchmen and the Evangelicals, and to look upon Christianity, not as a sacred treasure of the Churches and the sects, but as a divine beneficent power for every believer; not as a dead heritage from the past, but as a living spiritual power for the moral advancement of individuals and nations in the present. . He showed how classical and general historical studies may be pursued in the light of the moral ideas of Christianity, and how, on the other hand, a free and clear way of looking at things may be obtained by means of wide historical knowledge, and then applied to the interpretation of the Bible and the solution of current ecclesiastical questions. Thus he began to pull down the wall of separation which had cut off the religious life of his fellow countrymen, with their sects and Churches and rigid theological formulas and usages, from the general life and pursuits of the nation. It is also clear as day that, if longer life had been granted to him, the result of the further prosecution of his historical studies . . would have been further insight and courage to apply his historical and critical principles to the Bible. At all events, his work was subsequently further prosecuted in this direction by his friends and pupils.—Pfleiderer, *The Development of Theology in Germany since Kant and its Progress in Great Britain since 1825* (London, 1890), 367–368.

Carolingian house. Amid all his dignities, he longed for the peace of the contemplative life; probably in 627 he resigned his see and retired into the wilderness of the Vosges, where he lived as a hermit near his friend Romarich, the founder of the abbey of Remiremont. His body rests in the church at Metz which bears his name. (A. HAUCK.)

BIBLIOGRAPHY: *Vita*, by unknown author, in *MGH, Script. rer. Merov.*, ii. (1888) 426–446; and by another author in *MPL*, xcv. Consult Rettberg, *KD*, i. 488; Friedrich, *KD*, ii. 236; Bégel, *Histoire de S. Arnoul*, Bar-le-Duc, 1875; Wattenbach, *DGQ*, i. 144; Hauck, *KD*, i. 127, 161, 295, 316.

ARROWSMITH, JOHN: Puritan and Presbyterian; b. near Newcastle-on-Tyne Mar. 29, 1602; d. at Cambridge and was buried Feb. 24, 1659. He was educated at Cambridge, where he became fellow of St. Catherine's Hall (1623). He was successively incumbent of St. Nicholas's Chapel, King's Lynn (1631); master of St. John's College, Cambridge (1644); rector of St. Martin's, Ironmonger Lane, London (1645), and member of the sixth London classis; vice-chancellor of Cambridge University (1647); regius professor of divinity there (1651); master of Trinity College (1653). He sat in the Westminster Assembly of Divines (1643). Robert Baillie describes him as "a man with a glass eye in place of that which was put out by an arrow, a learned divine, on whom the Assembly put the writing against the Antinomians." He was on the committee to draw up a confession of faith, and preached thrice before Parliament, the sermons being published: *The Covenant-Avenging Sword Brandished* [Lev. xxvi. 25] (London, 1643, 4to, pp. 28); *England's Eben-ezer* [I Sam. vii. 12] (1645, 4to, pp. 34); *A Great Wonder in Heaven; or, a lively Picture of the Militant Church, drawn by a Divine Penman* [Rev. xii. 1, 2] (1647, 4to, pp. 44). While at Cambridge he published *Tactica sacra, sive de milite spirituali pugnante, vincente, et triumphante dissertatio* (Cambridge, 1657, 4to, pp. 363), containing also three *Orationes anti-Weigelianæ*. After his death there were published: *Armilla catechetica, A Chain of Principles; or, an orderly Concatenation of Theological Aphorisms and Exercitations, wherein the chief Heads of Christian Religion are asserted and improved* (Cambridge, 1659, 4to, pp. 490), an unfinished work designed to form a complete body of divinity in thirty aphorisms, only six of which were completed, covering for the most part the ground of the first twenty questions of the larger Westminster Catechism, in essentially the same order; also *Θεάνθρωπος or God-Man* (London, 1660, 4to, pp. 311), an exposition of the Gospel of John i. 1–18, discussing the divinity and humanity of Christ, and maintaining the Catholic doctrine against all heresies. C. A. BRIGGS.

ARSENIUS, är-sî'ni-us: **1.** Egyptian monk; d., nearly or more than one hundred years old, at Troe (Troja), near Memphis, about 450. He was a Roman of distinction, served as tutor to the sons of the emperor Theodosius, and retired into the desert of Scetis in Egypt under Arcadius. He is commemorated in the Greek Church on May 8 and in the Latin on July 19. He wrote a book of "Instruction and Exhortation" for his monks, and an exposition of Luke x. 25 (ed. A. Mai, *Classici auctores*, x., Rome, 1838, 553–557; *MPG*, lxvi. 1615–26). G. KRÜGER.

BIBLIOGRAPHY: *Vita*, in *ASB*, July, iv. 605–631; *DCB*, i. 172–174.

2. Patriarch of Constantinople 1255–67; d. 1273. On the death of the emperor Theodore Lascaris II. in 1259, Michael Palæologus usurped the throne, seized upon the legitimate heir, John Lascaris, a boy of six or seven years, and deprived him of his eyesight. Arsenius manfully espoused the cause of the young prince and was banished to an island in the Propontis in consequence. He had followers who for a number of decades remained in irreconcilable opposition and formal schism against the government. His will, in which he anathematized the emperor and his helpers, is in *MPG*, cxl. 947–958. G. KRÜGER.

BIBLIOGRAPHY: *KL*, i. 1447–50.

ART AND CHURCH.

There is nothing in the nature of Christianity which excludes art, although in the Apostolic Age, under the prevalence of the purely religious contemplation of life and life's problems, the knowledge and cultivation of it naturally receded. But when Christianity entered into the world of Greco-Roman culture, it soon became evident that it had great receptivity for art. If the Church allowed artistic decoration in the solemn resting-places of the dead, the catacombs, as early as the end of the first century, the conclusion is justified that art had also a place in the house of worship. Herein the fundamental position of the Church is clearly expressed; and the steady growth of artistic activity during the second and third centuries indicates not only a tacit permission, but even an active promotion on the part of the Church, though no definite statement to that effect is found. Nevertheless, some doubts were felt. The existing art was intimately connected with the cult of the gods and was thus defiled by heathenism. With this in mind, and knowing that Christian artists manufactured idols, Tertullian attributed to the devil the introduction into the world of artificers of statues and likenesses (*De idololatria*, iii.). But herein he does not touch upon the fundamental question, having in mind only art stained by idolatry. Clement of Alexandria is of much the same opinion, yet he adds "let art receive its meed of praise, but let it not deceive man by passing itself off for truth" (*Protreptikos*, iv.). The judgment of both Tertullian and Clement was warped by the ascetic ideal. Again the Old Testament prohibition of likenesses of living things had influence, and prevented all portraiture of God in human form till the second half of the fourth century. The Spanish synod at Elvira about 313 (see ELVIRA, SYNOD OF) declared that "pictures ought not to be in churches, nor that which is worshiped and adored to be depicted on the

1. Art in the Early Church.

walls" (canon xxxvi.). The same considerations influenced Eusebius of Cæsarea, as may be seen from his letter to the empress Constantia; and, to a still greater degree, Epiphanius, who tore down a curtain adorned with a picture in a Palestinian village church, because it was contrary to Holy Writ (*Epist. ad Joh. Hieros.*, ix.). The fear that the masses just emancipated from heathenism might transfer the heathen image-worship to the Christian was not groundless. But the general view of the Church was not expressed by these voices. Men esteemed for knowledge and the Christian life take note of works of art (Augustine, Gregory of Nyssa), encourage artists (Basil the Great), or express pleasure in artistic creations (Gregory of Nazianzus). Still more explicit is the language of the monuments of art. From the time of Constantine ecclesiastical architecture, representative art, and the minor arts made rapid progress. Not only the houses of worship but the holy vessels, vestments, and the like received decoration. Even an ascetic like St. Nilus planned a magnificent church (cf. Augusti, ii. 88 sqq.), and everywhere throughout Christendom bishops were eager to build (cf. Schultze, 31 sqq.). There was less reason for denying the admissibility of art, since it was believed that more than one picture had originated by divine miracle (cf. E. von Dobschütz, *Christusbilder*, Leipsic, 1899) and even the evangelist Luke was regarded as a painter (cf. T. Zahn, *Einleitung in das Neue Testament*, ii., Leipsic, 1899, 337).

2. The Romanesque and Medieval Periods. In the Carolingian and Romanesque periods the clergy and monks were the creators of ecclesiastical art. The Benedictines long stood at the head. The Gothic also developed under church influence, although in it the lay element had a greater part. Art-loving prelates are met with throughout the entire medieval period (cf. Otte, ii. 24–25). In the Greek Church of the Middle Ages, Church and art are even more closely connected, and the influence of the Church was greater. The freedom of art, in so far as it was taken into the ecclesiastical service, was more limited, but the current assumption that dead formalism and conventionality ruled in the Byzantine Church is an error. There was a glorious revival in the ninth century. The iconoclastic controversy had a destructive influence, but its outcome is proof of the inseparable connection of art and Church.

3. The Renaissance. The Renaissance brought a change. As it emphasized the rights of the individual and called for independence and personal responsibility, so it delivered art from ecclesiastical domination and tutelage. Free apprehension of nature took the place of the former more or less conscious dependence on tradition (J. Burckhardt, *Die Kultur der Renaissance in Italien*, Leipsic, 1885; idem, *Geschichte der Renaissance in Italien*, Stuttgart, 1890). In Michelangelo this freedom comes out the grandest. The Church itself, carried away by the powerful stream of the new culture, was first moved by it without reflection, but its true ideas characterize not so much the Renaissance popes, Julius II. and Leo X., as an Adrian VI. Hence the disenchantment which soon followed.

4. Since the Reformation. With the restoration of Roman Catholicism after the convulsions of the Reformation, commences the renunciation of the free art of the Renaissance and a return to the ecclesiastical ideals of the Middle Ages. Romanticism strengthened this impulse by similar tendencies, and modern ultramontane Roman Catholicism carried it out to the utmost. The inability of Roman Catholic ethics to appreciate the phenomena of the secular life influences also the judgment of the Church of Rome on the essence and purpose of art. It regards secular art as on a lower level than ecclesiastical. Protestantism, on the other hand, continues the conception of the Renaissance. The standards of valuation of a work of art are not to be taken from dogmatics and ethics, but from the character of art itself. No fundamental difference between secular and religious art is recognized. With this the possibility of an unlimited, free relation between Church and art is obtained. The two branches of Protestantism are here in perfect agreement. They perceive in art something which is permitted to the Christian as the use of secular culture in general. But the two confessions differ in that the Lutheran Church not only opened its houses of worship to art but asserted for it therein a necessary place; whereas the Reformed Church, strongly influenced in its ethics, as in other respects, by an Old Testament legalistic view, excluded art as much as possible from the culture and religious service in general. From this Protestantism has wrongly been suspected of being an adversary of art. But this rigor has been somewhat weakened, or wholly abandoned in modern times. From the position of Protestantism toward art follows its perfect independence of the ecclesiastical tradition. Much as it demands a religious and ecclesiastical art, it abstains from laying down canonical enactments with reference to its development, while constantly and properly insisting that such art shall be really promotive of its avowed lofty purpose.

VICTOR SCHULTZE.

BIBLIOGRAPHY: J. C. W. Augusti, *Beiträge zur christlichen Kunstgeschichte*, 2 vols., Leipsic, 1841–46; A. N. Didron, *Christian Iconography; or, the History of Christian Art in the Middle Ages*, transl. from the Fr., London, 1851; A. Lenoir, *Architecture monastique*, Paris, 1852; C. J. Hemans, *History of Ancient Christianity and Sacred Art in Italy*, Florence, 1866; idem, *History of Mediæval Christianity and Art in Italy*, vol. i., Florence, 1869, vol. ii., London, 1872; F. Piper, *Einleitung in die monumentale Theologie*, Gotha, 1867; W. Lübke, *Ecclesiastical Art in Germany during the Middle Ages*, London, 1870; R. St. J. Tyrwhitt, *Art Teaching of the Primitive Church*, London, 1872; H. Otte, *Handbuch der kirchlichen Kunstarchäologie des deutschen Mittelalters*, 2 vols., Leipsic, 1883–85; A. Jameson, *Sacred and Legendary Art*, 2 vols., Boston, 1886; M. Stokes, *Early Christian Art in Ireland*, London, 1888; J. von Schlosser, *Schriftquellen zur Geschichte der karolingischen Kunst*, Vienna, 1892; idem, *Quellenbuch zur Kunstgeschichte des abendländischen Mittelalters*, Vienna, 1896; E. L. Cutts, *Early Christian Art*, London, 1893; V. Schultze, *Archäologie der altchristlichen Kunst*, Munich, 1895; F. X. Kraus, *Geschichte der christlichen Kunst*, 2 vols., Freiburg, 1896–1900; W. Lowrie, *Monuments of the Early Church*, New York, 1901; E. M. Hurll, *The Life of our Lord in*

Art, with some Account of the Artistic Treatment of the Life of St. John the Baptist, Boston, 1898; T. Beaudoire, *Genèse de la cryptographie apostolique et de l'architecture rituelle*, Paris, 1903; A. Michel, *Hist. de l'art depuis les premiers temps chrétiens*, vols. i.–ii., New York, 1906; and the general works on Christian art and archeology.

ART, HEBREW: The ancient Israelites accomplished practically nothing in the realm of art. They lacked the necessary natural gifts, constructive power, and creative imagination. In the ancient time, when images of gods were indispensable to worship, their native incapacity was supplemented by no outside influence, and the old Israelitic images were of the rudest kind. After contact with more artistic neighbors had given them technical skill, the peculiar hostility of their religion to representative art prevented its development. To such an extent was this hostility carried that all likenesses of living creatures, whether human or animal, were forbidden. Such a prohibition—which survives in Islam to-day—was manifestly possible only among a people of no artistic tastes or powers; it is inconceivable among the Greeks. There is no mention of Israelitic sculpture. The complete silence concerning statues or stone ornamentation of any kind in Solomon's buildings indicates that nothing of the sort was found there. Stone sarcophagi, such as the Phenicians and Egyptians made, were not used. The *maggebhoth*, the cultic pillars of stone, make the nearest approach to statuary; but while among other nations the stone pillars developed into true statues of gods, among the Israelites they always remained mere pillars. Such an expression as "goodly images" in Hos. x. 1 probably indicates that sometimes, as among other Semitic peoples, rude forms were chiseled on the pillars. Wood carving seems to have been practised. The teraphim certainly had something like a man's head (I Sam. xix. 13). There were two cherubim of olive wood in Solomon's temple (I Kings vi. 23), and in Ezekiel's time the temple doors and walls were adorned with carving (Ezek. xli. 17–26; cf. also the later additions to the description of Solomon's temple, I Kings vii. 18, 29, 35). Doorposts and the wainscoting of houses and articles of furniture, such as divans, tables, and chairs, were thus decorated in the time of the later kings. But it is noteworthy that the masterpiece of such work, Solomon's throne (I Kings x. 18–20), was made by Phenician workmen. Metal work also developed under Phenician influence. Solomon had to send to Tyre for an artist to do the casting necessary for the temple (I Kings vii. 13–46). The art of overlaying with metal seems to have been better understood and to date from an earlier time. The ephod may have been made of wood or clay overlaid with gold or silver (see EPHOD), and the calves of Dan and Bethel (I Kings xii. 28–29) were doubtless constructed in this way. A knowledge of gem cutting is ascribed to the time of the Exodus (Ex. xxviii. 21), and the patriarchs are said to have had seals (Gen. xxxviii. 18),—which proves at least that the art was familiar and old when the narratives were written. There is mention of an iron graving tool with diamond point (Jer. xvii. 1). Israelitic seals which have been preserved resemble the Phenician so closely that they can be distinguished only when they bear a distinctively Israelitic name (see DRESS AND ORNAMENT, HEBREW, § 6). Hebrew pottery also has the same form as the Phenician; some of the specimens which have been found may be Phenician work. They are painted with geometric patterns (see HANDICRAFTS, HEBREW). Manifestly there can be no thought of a Hebrew style in any of the departments described, distinct from that prevailing in Phenicia and all Syria, and this was not original, but borrowed from Assyria and Egypt. I. BENZINGER.

BIBLIOGRAPHY: G. Perrot and C. Chipiez, *Histoire de l'art dans l'antiquité*, iv., Paris, 1887, Eng. transl., *History of Art in Sardinia, Judea, Syria, and Asia Minor*, 2 vols., London, 1890; Benzinger, *Archäologie*, 249–271; Nowack, *Archäologie*, i. 259–268.

ARTAXERXES, ār"tax-erk'sīz: The name of a Persian king mentioned in Nehemiah and Ezra, where, however, the word occurs in the form of Artachshashta, by which is doubtless meant Artaxerxes I. Longimanus, 465–425 B.C. In the Persian cuneiform inscriptions the name is written Artakhshathra, "righteous" or "sublime ruler." In Ezra iv. 7, Artaxerxes Longimanus is meant, not the Pseudo-Smerdis; so also Ezra vii. 1, 11 where, following Josephus *Ant.*, XI. v. 1, Xerxes has been read. In the twentieth year of Artachshashta or Artaxerxes, that is, in the year 445–444 B.C. Nehemiah, the cup-bearer of the king, went as governor to Jerusalem. See PERSIA. (B. LINDNER.)

ARTEMON (ār'tĭ-men) or **ARTEMAS**: A heretic of the third century, founder of a small sect called the Artemonites. Nothing is known of him except what may be gathered from brief references in Eusebius, Epiphanius, Theodoret, and Photius; it seems certain that he shrank from applying the name God to Jesus, and he is probably to be classed with the dynamistic Monarchians (see MONARCHIANISM); he was living at Rome, but separated from the Church and without influence, about 270. Paul of Samosata adopted and developed his views.

ARTHUR, WILLIAM: Methodist; b. at Kells (18 m. n.w. of Belfast), County Antrim, Ireland, Feb. 3, 1819; d. at Cannes, France, March 9, 1901. He began to preach at the age of sixteen, was accepted as a candidate for the ministry by the Irish Conference in 1837, and spent the next two years as a student at the Theological Institution at Hoxton, London. In 1839 he went to India, and opened a new mission station at Gutti, Mysore, but returned to England in 1841, completely broken down in health. His eyesight, in particular, was much impaired, and from this affliction he never fully recovered. He was stationed at Boulogne, 1846, in Paris, 1847–48; preached in London, 1849–50; was appointed one of the secretaries of the Wesleyan Missionary Society, 1851; first principal of the Belfast Methodist College, 1868; honorary missionary secretary, 1871. In 1888 he retired and thenceforth lived chiefly in southern France. In 1856 he was made a member of the legal committee of his Church, and from that time on was prominent in all connectional committees and conference proceedings. He was president of the Conference in 1866. During the Civil War in America he championed the Union cause and wrote a series of able articles in its support for *The London Quarterly Review*—a periodical which he helped to found in 1853 and to which he contributed regularly for thirty years. His books are numerous and some of them had an enormous sale. They include: *A Mission to the Mysore, with Scenes and Facts Illustrative of India, its People and its Religion* (London, 1847: ed., with introduction, notes, and appendix, H. Haigh, 1902); *The Successful Merchant, Sketches of the Life of Mr. Samuel Budgett* (1852); *The People's Day, an Appeal to the Right Hon. Lord Stanley against his Advocacy of a French Sunday* (1855); *The Tongue of Fire, or the True Power of Christianity* (1856); *Italy in Transition, Public Scenes and Private Opinions in the Spring of 1860* (1860); *The Modern Jove, a Review of the Collected Speeches of Pio Nono* (1873); *The Life of Gideon Ouseley* (1876); *The Pope, the Kings, and the People* (2 vols., 1877; ed. W B. Neatley, 1903); *On the Difference between Physical and Moral Law*, the Fernley lecture for 1883 (1883); *Religion without God and God without Religion*, a criticism of the philosophical systems of Frederic Harrison, Herbert Spencer, and Sir Fitzjames Stephen (3 parts, 1885–87).

BIBLIOGRAPHY: Consult *The Methodist Recorder*, xlii, 11–16, London, Mar. 14, 1901, for biographical sketch.

ARTICLES, IRISH, LAMBETH, THIRTY-NINE, ETC. See IRISH ARTICLES, LAMBETH ARTICLES, THIRTY-NINE ARTICLES, ETC.

ARUNDEL, ar'un-dl, **THOMAS:** Archbishop of Canterbury; b. at Arundel Castle (55 m. s.w. of London), Sussex, 1353; d. at Canterbury Feb. 19, 1414. He was the third son of the Earl of Arundel, and the family influence secured his promotion to the bishopric of Ely when only twenty-one; he was made Archbishop of York in 1388, of Canterbury in 1396, this being the first instance of a translation from York to Canterbury. He was active in the turbulent times of Richard II, and incurred the resentment of the king; in 1397, with his brother, the Earl of Arundel, he was impeached of high treason; the Earl was executed and the Archbishop was banished. He went to Rome, but the Pope, Boniface IX, at the request of Richard, transferred him to St. Andrews which in effect deprived him of a see, as Scotland adhered to the rival pope, Benedict XIII. He joined Henry of Lancaster on the continent, returned with him to England, 1399, crowned him king, Oct. 13, and was reinstated as Archbishop of Canterbury. He was five times Lord Chancellor of England, twice under Richard II (1386–89 and 1391–96), and three times under Henry IV Arundel was a shrewd and far-sighted prelate in the performance of what he understood to be his duty. He spent his wealth freely upon the churches in which he was interested. In his later years he entered heartily into the persecution of the Lollards and was especially conspicuous in the prosecution of Lord Cobham. He procured a prohibition of the vernacular translation of the Scriptures.

BIBLIOGRAPHY: W. F. Hook, *Lives of the Archbishops of Canterbury*, iv, London, 1865; *DB*, ii, 137–141.

ASA, ē'sa: Third king of Judah, son and successor of Abijah. He is said to have reigned forty-one years, contemporary with Jeroboam, Nadab, Baasha, Elah, Zimri, Omri, and Ahab of Israel. His dates, according to the old chronology, are 955–914 B.C.; according to Hommel, 911–871; according to Duncker, 929–872; according to Kamphausen, 917–877. Although in I Kings xv, 10, Maachah, the daughter of Abishalom, is mentioned as his mother, who, according to verse 2, was the mother of Abijah (called "Abijam" in I Kings; see ABIJAH), he was probably not the latter's brother, but his son, as is stated in verse 8. Maachah was probably the name of both his mother and his grandmother, and "daughter of Abishalom" is erroneously inserted in verse 10 from verse 2. Asa tried to uproot idolatry, and deposed his mother "because she had made an idol in a grove" (I Kings xv, 13, A. V.; R. V., "because she had made an abominable image for an Asherah;" the object in question may have been a phallic image). He drove the Sodomites from the land, and destroyed the idols. The high places, however, were not removed. At the suggestion of the prophet Azariah (according to the Chronicler) he caused his people to renew their vows to Yahweh at a great festival. He is said to have built cities and performed mighty deeds, but no details are given.

What is told of Asa's conduct in the war with Israel does not redound to his glory (I Kings xv, 16 sqq.). When Baasha fortified Ramah on the frontier between Israel and Judah, Asa could think of no better way to retaliate than to hire Ben-hadad, king of Syria, to invade Israel. The expedient accomplished its immediate purpose by forcing Baasha to retire from Ramah; but the ultimate outcome was the hundred years' war between Israel and the Arameans, which brought misfortune upon both lands and even involved Judah. The Chronicler states that the prophet Hanani was sent to rebuke Asa for his conduct, and was imprisoned for his boldness. The Chronicler further relates that in the eleventh year of Asa's reign "Zerah the Ethiopian" invaded Judah and met a great defeat. The event is not mentioned in the Book of Kings, and some regard the narrative as unhistorical. Those who accept it have not succeeded in identifying Zerah the Ethiopian. In his old age Asa suffered from a disease of the feet, perhaps gout. [The Chronicler characteristically remarks "yet in his disease he sought not to Yahweh, but to the physicians".] Asa's history is in I Kings xv, 9–14; II Chron. xiv–xvi. (W LOTZ.)

The most probable dates for Asa are 912–872 B.C. J. F. M.

BIBLIOGRAPHY: Consult the works mentioned under AHAB, and, in addition, for Zerah the Ethiopian, H. Winckler, *Alttestamentliche Untersuchungen*, pp. 160 sqq., Leipsic, 1892.

ASAPH. See PSALMS.

ASBURY, az'ber-i, **FRANCIS:** The first Methodist bishop ordained in America; b. at Hamstead Bridge, parish of Handsworth (a northern suburb of Birmingham), Staffordshire, England, Aug. 20, 1745; d. at Spottsylvania, Va., Mar. 31, 1816. He became a local preacher at the age of sixteen, and an itinerant minister in 1767; at his own request he was sent by Wesley as a missionary to America in 1771, landing at Philadelphia with his companion, Richard Wright, Oct. 27; in 1772 he was appointed Wesley's "general assistant in America," with supervisory power over all the Methodist preachers and societies in the country, but the next year was superseded by Thomas Rankin. On the outbreak of the Revolutionary War Rankin returned to England, but Asbury chose to remain. Like most of the Methodist preachers, he was a nonjuror (that is, he had conscientious scruples concerning oaths, and refused to take the oath of allegiance required by the authorities), and he suffered some annoyance from the officials during the war. After the close of the war the Methodists were organized into an independent Church, Thomas Coke (q.v.) and Asbury being chosen joint superintendents at the Christmas Conference at Baltimore, 1784, and Asbury ordained by Coke Dec. 27. The remainder of his life he devoted to the Church with tireless energy and unflagging zeal.[1]

Asbury was fearless in the discharge of duty, possessed a keen wit and uncommon shrewdness, was far-sighted and a good organizer. He never married; and his salary was sixty-four dollars a year. His early education was defective; but in later life he acquired some knowledge of Greek and Hebrew. In 1785 he laid the foundation of the first Methodist college, and he formed a plan of dividing the country into districts with an academy in each. His journal from the date of sailing for America to 1780 was published before his death, and the remaining years were transcribed and published by F. Hollingworth in 1821; it has been often reprinted (cf. *The Heart of Asbury's Journal*, ed. E. S. Tipple, New York, 1905).

Bibliography: E. L. Janes, *Character and Career of Francis Asbury*, New York, 1870 (the standard biography); W C. Larrabee, *Asbury and His Coadjutors*, 2 vols., Cincinnati, 1853; W. P. Strickland, *The Pioneer Bishop; or, the Life and Times of Francis Asbury*, ib. 1858; F. W. Briggs, *Bishop Asbury: a Biographical Study for Christian Workers*, London, 1874; J. F. Hurst, *History of the Christian Church*, ii, 894, 905, New York, 1900. For Wesley's views on the assumption by Asbury of the title "bishop" consult R. D. Urlin, *Churchman's Life of Wesley*, pp. 168–170, London, n.d.

ASCENSION, FEAST OF THE: In Acts i, 3 the fortieth day after the resurrection is designated as that of Christ's ascension. The Epistle of Barnabas (xv), on the other hand, grounds the observance of Sunday on its having been the day marked by both the resurrection and the ascension. If this is to be reconciled with the Acts, it can only be by the assumption that Luke counts four weeks as four decades, just as later ecclesiastical usage numbers the Sundays before Lent in this loose way as Septuagesima, Sexagesima, and Quinquagesima; but the "forty days" of the Acts sounds too definite for this hypothesis to be accepted. The Christian Church has observed this commemoration on the Thursday of the sixth week after Easter since it has been observed at all, which could only be after the festivals of Easter and Pentecost were firmly established. Origen does not know the festival (*Contra Celsum*, viii, 23). It is mentioned, however, in the *Apostolic Constitutions* (v, 19, viii, 13); and Chrysostom has a homily for it, besides referring to it in another place. Socrates (*Hist. eccl.*, vii, 26) mentions, under the year 390, that the people celebrated it as an established custom in a suburb of Constantinople. In the West its observance has been thought to be attested by an obscure canon of the Council of Elvira (306); in any case, Augustine knows it as an old one (*Epist. liv. ad Januarium*). Its celebration was specially solemn. The paschal candle, lighted at Easter to symbolize the resurrection of the Light of the World, is extinguished after the Gospel in the high mass of that day throughout the Roman Catholic Church, signifying the departure of Christ from earth. The Lutheran Reformation in Germany retained the feast as Scriptural; and it is observed as one of the principal festivals in the Anglican communion.

(Georg Rietschel.)

Perhaps the earliest reference to the feast extant is that of the *Peregrinatio Etheriæ* (c. 380), which states that a feast of the Ascension was celebrated in Jerusalem toward the close of the fourth century, coinciding with the festival of Pentecost and observed on the same day. The feast marks the close of the paschal season and is a holyday of obligation in the Roman Catholic Church. In the Latin liturgy the term "ascension" is used exclusively of our Lord. J. T. C.

Bibliography: A. Baillet, *Les Vies des saints, avec l'histoire des fêtes mobiles*, Paris, 1701; F. Probst, *Brevier und Breviergebet*, § 93, Tübingen, 1868; *DCA*, i, 145–147; N. Nilles, *Kalendarium manuale utriusque ecclesiæ*, ii, 364, Innsbruck, 1881.

ASCENSION OF PAUL. See Apocrypha, B, IV

ASCETICISM.

The term "asceticism" (Gk. *askēsis*) originally meant "practise," especially the training of an athlete. In philosophical language it denotes moral exercise and discipline (e.g., Epictetus, *Dissertationes*, iii, 12; Diogenes Laertius, VIII, viii, 8), and in this sense passed into ecclesiastical language (Eusebius, *Hist. eccl.*, II, xvii, 2; *Martyres Palæstinæ*, x, 2, xi, 2, 22). In the history of almost all religions, as well as in ancient moral

[1] He visited Massachusetts 23 times after 1791 . the state of New York 56 times, New Jersey 62 times, Pennsylvania 78 times, Delaware 33 times, Maryland 80 times, North Carolina 63 times, South Carolina 46 times, Virginia 84 times, Tennessee and Georgia each 20 times, and other states or territories with corresponding frequency. In his unparalleled career he preached about 16,500 sermons, or at least one a day, and travel d about 270,000 miles, or 6,000 a year, presiding in no less than 224 annual conferences, and ordaining more than 4,000 preachers.—Janes, p. 5. When he came to America the Methodists numbered 10 preachers and 600 members; when he died, after forty-five years of work, they had 695 preachers and 214,235 members.

philosophy, asceticism plays an important part, evidenced by phenomena like self-mutilation, circumcision, tattooing, fasting, flagellations, penance, etc., and by the ethics of the Buddhists, Stoics, Pythagoreans, and Neoplatonists. The Old Testament manifests, on the whole, few tendencies toward outward asceticism; but later Judaism, in its Pharisaic as well as in its Hellenistic form, cultivated it, especially in the practise of fasting (cf. Dan. x, 3; Tobit xii, 8; Matt. vi, 16, ix, 14; Luke xviii, 12).

1. New Testament Teaching. Primitive Christianity kept free from this externalizing asceticism. The custom of fasting was retained (Matt. iv, 2; Acts xiii, 2, xiv, 23, xviii, 18, xxi, 24, xxvii, 9; II Cor. xi, 27), but, as in the Old Testament, it was only auxiliary to prayer (Esther iv, 16; Dan. ix, 3; Tobit xii, 8; Luke ii, 37; Acts x, 30, xiii, 2, xiv, 23), and no merit was attached to it. In place of a legal and meritorious asceticism the Lord demands watchfulness, sobriety, and prayer (Matt. xxiv, 42, xxv, 13; Mark xiii, 37; cf. Acts xx, 31; I Cor. xvi, 13; II Cor. vi, 5, xi, 27; Eph. vi, 18; Col. iv, 2; I Thess. v, 6, 8; I Pet. i, 13, v, 8; II Pet. iii, 11–12; Rev. iii, 3, xvi, 15), as well as a readiness to resign everything to follow him and to take up the cross (Matt. viii, 21–22, x, 38–39, xvi, 24, xix, 21; Mark viii, 34, x, 28, 39; Luke ix, 57–58, xiv, 27). In the morals of Jesus everything depends upon the disposition and free deed. Thus Matt. vi, 17–18, ix, 15, xix, 12, are not to be understood as outward, ascetic regulations. The thoughts of Paul move along the same lines. In the moral struggle one must become master of the old man who has been put off (Rom. vii, 23, xiii, 14; Gal. v, 17; Eph. vi, 12–18; Col. iii, 5–8; I Tim. vi, 12), and discipline is also necessary to bring the body into subjection (I Cor. ix, 25–27). This is the true notion of asceticism as expressed in I Tim. iv, 7, 8. Remarks like I Cor. vii, 5, 8, 25–40 have not the value of generally received ethical laws; the legalism of Jewish life, the contempt of marriage, the worshiping of angels, and neglect of the body are all rejected (Gal. ii, 12–16; Col. ii, 16–23; I Tim. iv, 3). The New Testament, therefore, offers the following thoughts as bases for the notion of asceticism: the obligation of the Christian to crucify the flesh; the demand to bear the cross, to be sober and ready; and the exhortation to "exercise" the body and to fashion it into an organ fit for the ends of the Christian.

Hellenistic and Jewish influences worked together to introduce, with "moralism," in the old catholic time an ascetic order of life.

2. Asceticism in the Early Church. The institution of certain fast-days, fixed hours of prayer, the restricted use of food, abstinence from marriage, withdrawal from the world, characterize this tendency. Asceticism, no less than "knowledge," came to be considered as belonging to Christianity (Clement, *Strom.*, vi, 12). At an early period ascetics are found who retire into the desert and leave the Church from moral considerations (Irenæus, *Hær.*, III, xi, 9; IV, xxvi, 2, xxx, 3, xxxiii, 7). As ascetic tendencies enter more deeply into the Church (cf. the case of Origen, Eusebius, *Hist. eccl.*, vi, 2), and as the Church comes to know the world more intimately, it becomes easier to understand the origin of ascetic societies (cf. the pseudo-Clementine Epistles, *De virginitate;* Hieracas, in Epiphanius, *Hær.*, lxvii, 13; Athanasius, *Vita Antonii*, iii, 14; Cyril, *Catecheses*, iv, 24, v, 4, xii, 33; Methodius, *Convivium*, vii, 3; Aphraates, *Hom.*, vi). Here was the beginning of the later anchoretic and monastic system (see MONASTICISM).

On this road the Middle Ages proceeded. The ascetic practises were extended more and more, and their extension naturally produced among the monks a state of dulness. There are two things especially which mark the history of medieval asceticism: the institution of penance with its works of satisfaction, and the idea of imitating the poverty and suffering of Jesus. The first shows a descending evolution, but the second an ascending one, tending to introspection, as in the circle of the Friends of God. The way of asceticism was considered as the way of perfection. The Augsburg Confession (art. xxvi, 8) says of the medieval period: "Christianity was thought of as consisting solely of the observance of certain holy days, rites, fasts, attire."

3. Attitude of the Reformers. On the other hand, the Reformation abolished on principle the medieval estimate of asceticism, because the solemn ascetic works are not enjoined by God, but by worthless human commandments (art. xxiii, 6 sqq., 19 sqq., xxvi, 18; *Apol.*, xxiii, 6, 60, xxvii, 42–57), and can even be regarded as suicide and tempting of God (Luther, *Werke*, Erlangen ed., iv, 380, vii, 40, ix, 289, xi, 104). The ascetic system is also abolished by the concept of righteousness by faith which is opposed to meritorious works, which are therefore to be rejected (*Augs. Con.*, xx, 8, 9 sqq., xxvi, 1 sqq., 8, xxvii, 3, 44; *Apol.*, xv, 6 sqq.; *Art. Schmal.*, iv, 14; Luther, xx, 250, xvii, 8, xlii, 262, xliii, 193, lxv, 128, xxi, 330). Thus it is asserted that the ascetic works answer not the will of God and are not meritorious. For "Christian perfection" ascetic works are not necessary; indeed, moral conduct is the more certain evidence of God's presence (*Augs. Con.*, xvi, 4 sqq., xxvi, 10, xxvii, 10 sqq., xv, 49, 57; *Apol.*, xv, 25–26, xvii, 61; Longer Catechism, precept iv, 145). But asceticism is hereby not done away with. The "mortification of the flesh" ever remains a Christian duty (*Augs. Con.*, xxvi, 31 sqq.). But by this is not meant a weakening and destruction of the natural powers, but the self-discipline by which the natural powers are made subject to the soul, thus becoming fit for serving God. Outward fast-regulations are therefore very useful, but should never become a law (Luther, xliii, 197–199, lxv, 128). The Protestant view is briefly this: "Every one can use his own discretion as to fasting and watching, for every one knows how much he must do to master his body. Those, however, who think to become pious through works have no regard for fasting, but only for the works and, imagining that they are pious when they do much in that direction, sometimes break their heads over it and ruin their bodies over it" (Luther, xxvii, 27, 190, xliii, 199,

201, x, 290, xxi, 240, x, 250). It is useless to continue the historical review, since no essentially new types of asceticism have appeared in the Church. The Roman Catholic Church adheres on principle to the medieval conception, yet in the Jesuitic "Spiritual Exercises" the purely sensual asceticism strongly recedes, and there is accommodation to the modern spirit. Mysticism and pietism in evangelical Christendom have demanded renunciation and seclusion in a one-sided manner (cf. C. E. Luthardt, *Geschichte der Ethik*, ii, Leipsic, 1893, 154 sqq., 248 sqq., and the histories of pietism by Ritschl and Schmid; see PIETISM).

4. True Value and Uses of Asceticism.

Asceticism is a special moral act. Christian moral acts are free, devoted to the acquisition of the highest good or the realization of the kingdom of God. They have for their object the reformation of one's own personality (conversion and sanctification), as well as the influence on the surrounding conditions to be realized by this personality. The Christian life is a continual fight with sin, but is to overcome it by virtue of the effects of grace. This task can not in itself be called an "exercise," since it rather denotes the self-preservation of the Christian. To effect this self-preservation in the struggle against sin the Christian must indeed exercise and stretch his powers for the struggle. The object of morality is opposition to sin and the positive exemplification of the good. To bring this about it is necessary to have the mastery over the natural gifts and powers of man, which is obtained by attention to self, by watchfulness, and by accustoming one's own nature to subjection to the moral will. Asceticism is not directly a struggle against sin and realization of the Christian good, but it aims at such a rule over the natural powers that one is qualified to follow the good will readily in the struggle against sin and in the positive moral exemplification. The typical forms of asceticism (fasting, self-denial, etc.) show that the question is not directly the overcoming of sin or of doing good works, but the training of the natural powers for both. This is the specifically evangelical conception of asceticism. On the other hand, the Roman Catholics define asceticism as a direct moral act and as "the summary of all which serves to promote moral perfection" (Pruner, in *KL*, i, 1460); or asceticism is explained as that part of theology which "develops the principles of Christian perfection and points out the practical rules which bring about the soul's elevation to God" (J. Ribet, *L'Ascétique chrétienne*, Paris, 1888). Here the various exercises of asceticism are moral self-interest and good works, whereas, according to evangelical conception, asceticism is self-discipline to make one fit for good works; in this subordination it is a moral deed itself. Asceticism is therefore self-control in the true sense of the word.

Upon a closer examination the point here is this: (1) The task is to exercise nature in patience, watchfulness, self-denial, and sobriety, so that it becomes fit to bear the sufferings of the cross sent by God as a blessing. These are given to man from God for "the mortifying of the flesh"; the question is not of self-mortification and invited martyrdom. The cross is not to incite the Christian to sin, but to restrain the sinful lust. From this point of view the Christian is to consider the suffering and be affected by it. (2) Our nature in consequence of the sinfulness of man is exercised and ready to walk the ways pointed out by the evil will. In concrete things it exemplifies chiefly the dominion of the sensual desires over the spiritual will. Over against this, it is a Christian duty to accustom nature to subjugation under the spiritual will, to the regulation of the desires, to regularity and propriety of life, to steadfastness in useful work, to the proper relation between labor and recreation. Here one has to deal with moral gymnastics, which are to fit human nature to obey the good moral will imparted by grace. (3) For each man exist certain thoughts and incentives which in themselves are morally indifferent, but, as experience teaches, may become a temptation to the individual. To restrain these is the further object of asceticism; and herein it includes fasting in the ardent sense, e.g., with reference to society, eating and drinking, matrimony, sexual intercourse, novel-reading, the theater, dancing, total abstinence, etc. The question here is of a moral dietetics. With this the field of asceticism is circumscribed. Only it should be added that the ascetic practical proof must never become a law; it calls only for individual self-restraint. This, however, as little precludes ascetic habits in the individual as ascetic customs in communities. It must also be emphasized that the question can not be as to the meritorious character of asceticism; for, in the first place, this thought has no place in evangelical ethics; in the second place, because the necessity of ascetic exercises proves not man's moral maturity, but immaturity. Finally, it must be remarked that in the concrete life the ascetic practical proof can not be separated from sanctification and the moral struggle.

R. SEEBERG.

BIBLIOGRAPHY: G. Nitsch, *Praxis mortificationis carnis*, Gotha, 1725; E. Kist, *Christliche Ascetik*, 2 vols., Wessel, 1827–28; O. Zöckler, *Kritische Geschichte der Askese*, Erlangen, 1863 (contains a bibliography); idem, *Askese und Mönchtum*, 2 vols., Frankfort, 1897; *DCA*, i, 147–149; Schaff, *Christian Church*, i, 387–414; J. Mayer, *Die christliche Ascese*, Freiburg, 1894; R. Seeberg, in *GGA*, clx (1898), 506 sqq.; C. E. Hooijkaas, *Oudchristelijke Ascese*, Leyden, 1905; a detailed treatment of asceticism, Jewish and Christian, of the latter in all periods, is given in Neander, *Christian Church*, consult the Index; also the works on ethics and Christian morals, such as those of Reinhard, Rothe, Dorner, Martensen, Harless, Vilmar, Oettinger, Frank, H. Schultz, Luthardt, Wutke, and Smyth, and see ETHICS, and MONASTICISM.

ASCHHEIM, ash'haim, **SYNOD OF:** A synod held in a village of what is now Bavaria, a little to the east of Munich. The church there is mentioned in the seventh century. The year of the synod is not definitely named; but since Tassilo is mentioned as prince, and as still very young, and since its decrees are evidently influenced by those of the Frankish synod of Verneuil (July 11, 755), it must have been held either in the latter half of that year or in 756. Its canons are directed partly to the regulation of various ecclesiastical relations (ii, for the security of churches, and iv, of church property; v, payment of tithes; xiii, recognition of the canonical law as to marriage) and partly to the affirmation of the rights of the episcopate (iii, power over church property; vi, subordination of the clergy, and viii, ix, of monks and nuns; xiv, xv, spiritual oversight in courts of justice).

A. HAUCK.

BIBLIOGRAPHY: The *Capitula* are in *MGH, Leg.*, iii (1863), 457–459; ib. *Concil.*, ii (1904), 56–58. Consult Hefele, *Conciliengeschichte*, iii, 597–602; Hauck, *KD*, 1890, ii, 399.

ASHERAH (pl. *asherim;* in Judges iii, 7, II Chron. xix, 3, xxxiii, 3, *asheroth*): The transliteration of a Hebrew word which in the A. V. of the English Bible (following the LXX and Vulgate) is rendered "grove" or "groves" (see GROVES AND TREES, SACRED); in the A. V. the word is transferred ("Asherah") without attempt at translation. In explaining its meaning two entirely different senses in which it is employed must be distinguished: (1) as a sacred tree-stem or pole; (2) as the name of a Canaanitic goddess. There is now no doubt of the general meaning when the word is used in the former sense. Exactly what the latter refers to is still a matter of much debate. There are only three passages (Judges iii, 7; I Kings xviii, 19; II Kings xxiii, 4) in which the word (used with *ba'al*) clearly refers to a goddess; or, rather, only two, for in Judges the reading should be *'ashtaroth* (pl. of *'ashtoreth;* see ASHTORETH) as in similar early statements with regard to forbidden cults. The passage I Kings xv, 13, often supposed to refer to the worship of a goddess, should be translated as in the R. V. "made an abominable thing for (i.e., as) an asherah." The other two passages in Kings are regarded by recent conservative commentators as interpolations (cf. R. Kittel, *Die Bücher der Könige*, Göttingen, 1900, pp. 143, 300), and certainly justify the conclusion that at a late period *asherah* was used as another name for Ashtoreth. How this came about may be explained from the history of the asherah in Israel.

Two Distinct Meanings.

In preexilic times an asherah was not a divine companion or concurrent of a baal or the baals at all. It was, however, an indispensable part of the normal baal-worship. A "high-place," or shrine of the baal (*bamah*) consisted of an altar (with or without a "sanctuary"), a *maẓẓebhah* or stone pillar, and an *asherah* (see ALTAR; HIGH PLACE; MEMORIALS AND SACRED STONES). The pillar was a survival of the old stone-worship; that is to say, the adoration of the local deities or *numina*, who had their abode in sacred stones (cf. the *bethel* of Gen. xxviii, 19 and elsewhere). The *asherah* or sacred pole was in like manner a survival of the old tree-worship, that is, of the cult of sacred trees whose sanctity is a marked feature of the early histories (e.g., Gen. xii, 6, R. V.; Judges ix, 37, R. V.). In the Hebrew text of Deut. xi, 30; Judges ix, 6 (cf. R. V.) the sacred tree and the sacred stone appear standing side by side. One step further in the inevitable syncretism was the combination of both of these with the cult of the baal, the presiding divinity or "proprietor" of the district, who gave fertility to its soil and all consequential blessings to its inhabitants (cf. Hos. ii, 5, 8; see BAAL). Whatever other factors may have contributed to this cherishing of the *asherim*, these are the most important. At first the *asherim* were probably the stems of trees rudely chopped and stripped; afterward they were conventionalized into a shapely pole or mast, just as the "pillars" or *maẓẓebhoth* were at first roughly hewn blocks of stone.

The Preexilic Asherah.

At a later stage the *asherah* became transfigured into a goddess and naturally took the place of the old Ashtoreth in the imagination of the Hebrews, who, after the Exile, followed no longer the old Canaanitic rites. The fact that the worship of Ashtoreth had been combined with that of the baals, or rather absorbed into it, doubtless helped toward the substitution. The deification of an outward object of worship is a familiar phenomenon in nearly all religions, and in the present field of inquiry is actually paralleled by the conversion of a *bethel* or *bait-ili* (a god-inhabited stone) into a god, Baitulos, among the Phenicians and elsewhere (cf. Schrader, *KAT*, pp. 437–438).

Transformed into a Goddess.

Whether the fact that there was an old Canaanitic goddess *Ashirtu*, with a Babylonian namesake, aided in the confusion, in the Hebrew literature, of the two senses of *asherah*, is not quite clear. It is, at any rate, practically certain that in the time of the active idolatrous worship of Israel the *asherah* was not a goddess. See ASHTORETH.

J. F McCURDY.

BIBLIOGRAPHY: B. Stade, in *ZATW*, i (1881), 343–346, iv (1884), 293–295, vi (1886), 318–319; T. K. Cheyne, *The Prophecies of Isaiah*, ii, 291–292, London, 1882; G. Hoffmann, in *ZATW*, iii (1883), 123; idem, *Phönikische Inschriften*, in *Abhandlungen der Göttinger Gesellschaft der Wissenschaften*, xxxvi (1889), 26–28; M. Ohnefalsch-Richter, *Kypros, die Bibel, und Homer*, pp. 144–206, Berlin, 1893; Smith, *Rel. of Sem.*, pp. 187–190, 469–479

ASHIMA, a-shai'ma: A deity of the Hamathites, whose capital, originally called Hamath, afterward Epiphania, was on the Orontes, north of the Anti-lebanon. They were transported into Samaria by Shalmaneser to replete that depopulated district (II Kings xvii, 30). The deity was therefore Aramean, and was regarded by the Septuagint as feminine, but since nothing is known of it beyond what is told in II Kings, all suggestions as to its identity are mere conjectures.

ASHTORETH.

Ashtoreth is the name of a goddess whose worship, mostly associated with that of Baal or the baals, figured largely in the history of idolatry in ancient Israel. This divinity is especially marked as a goddess of the "Sidonians" or Phenicians (I Kings xi, 5, 33; II Kings xxiii, 13). She had also a temple among the Philistines at Ascalon, probably the same as that mentioned by Herodotus (i, 105). East of the Jordan her worship was rife in Moab, combined with that of the national god, Ashtar-Chemosh being named on the Moabite Stone in the ninth century B.C.; and the place names Ashtaroth (Deut. i, 4 and elsewhere), Ashteroth-Karnaim (Gen. xiv, 5), and Be-eshterah (Josh. xxi, 27) indicate its prevalence in the country of Bashan. That it was of ancient date in southern Syria is proved by Egyptian references to the goddess "Ashtart of the Hittite land." The most widely attested of these branches of the general cult among Canaanitic or Hebraic peoples is the Phenician, which is commemorated by many inscriptions both in the home country and in the western colonies.

1. The Cult in Palestine and Syria.

This famous goddess is also widely known as Astarte, which is the Greek form of the Phenician *'Ashtart*. The name Ashtoreth itself in the original Hebrew texts was *'Ashtareth*, the Masoretic form being a change made by using the vowels of *bosheth*, "the shameful thing," a nickname of Baal (q.v.). The Phenician *'ashtart* clearly points to the correct reading, as also does the Hebrew plural *'Ashtaroth*. The Babylonian and Assyrian form *Ishtar* is modified from *'Ashtar*, according to a regular phonetic law, through the influence of the initial guttural. *'Ashtar* is identical with the South Arabian *'Athtar* and Aramaic and North Arabian *'Atar* (from *'Athtar*), the former being a god and the latter apparently a goddess. Of the Arabian cult very little is known. When more has been learned of South Arabian mythology, much of the mystery which surrounds the origin of the universal Semitic worship of Ishtar-Ashtoreth will be cleared up.

2. Significance of the Related Names.

The following are the most important of the facts which may be regarded as established or practically certain: The cult originated in Babylonia and spread northward to Assyria, northwestward to Mesopotamia, thence to Syria and Palestine, and thence through the Phenicians to all of the Mediterranean peoples; south and southwestward it spread to Arabia, and thence across the sea to Abyssinia.

3. Extension of Ishtar Worship.

Both the name and the dominant forms of the cult were of Semitic and not of "Turanian" or Sumerian origin. There was a goddess Nana (q.v.) at Erech in South Babylonia, who was held to be identical with Ishtar simply because she had been worshiped there by a non-Semitic people, and, having attributes akin to those of Ishtar, was replaced by the latter when the Semites took over the ancient shrine. A similar syncretism took place under the same conditions in the interest both of Ishtar herself and of other Semitic divinities which she absorbed and superseded. The word *Ishtar* is a Babylonian verbal noun of the ifteal stem though the etymology is still unsettled.

4. The Early Ishtar Cult.

The worship of Ishtar was of very complex origin, both in its primary and in its secondary sources. When in greatest vogue as a principal Semitic religion it was, as above indicated, a composite or syncretism of many related cults, non-Semitic as well as Semitic. Of these some left deep traces of their original distinctive features and remained in part practically separate cults. Such, for example, was the worship of Ishtar of Arbela, in which the divinity appears as a war-goddess—an attribute probably suggested by the very natural conception of the planet Venus being the leader of the starry hosts. Ishtar was in fact primarily and chiefly identified with this most beautiful of celestial objects, especially as the evening star. This conception spread from Babylonia through the other Semitic lands to the Phenician settlements, and thence mainly by way of Cyprus, to the Greeks and Romans as the cults of Aphrodite and Venus. Among its primary sources, therefore, the worship of Ishtar was in large part astral, and Venus was its favorite celestial object. This combination was not of late origin, but is known to have been made in very early times (cf. Schrader, *KAT*, pp. 424 sqq.). The moon in the Ishtar cult never took the place of Venus; for the moon among the Semites was a male deity, whose worship was older than even that of Ishtar and was centered in Sin, the moon-god *par excellence*. Hence Ishtar in the inscriptions is represented not only as the daughter of Anu, the great heaven-god, but also as the daughter of Sin. It was as impossible that "the queen of heaven" of Jer. vii, 18 and other passages could be a name of the moon among the Hebrews in Palestine or Egypt as it could be among the Babylonians. The identification of Ishtar with the fixed star Sirius and with the constellation Virgo (perhaps through its beautiful star Spica), though comparatively early, was of secondary origin.

5. Dominant Types of Ishtar Worship. Its Astral Significance.

From the terrestrial side the primary motive of the worship of Ishtar was the impulse to deify sensuousness and sensuality. Of the resulting worship Ishtar-Venus became the celestial patron. She not only legitimated the sexual indulgences which marked her cult in Babylonia, Phenicia, Palestine, and the Semitic world generally, but she was naturally taken as the authoress of the sexual passion and therewith of all derivative and associated sentiments. This accounts for the part played by Ashtoreth or Astarte as the female counterpart of the Phenician Baal and of the local Canaanitic baals, and also for the wide-spread and influential myth of her relations with her lover Tammuz or Adonis (Ezek. viii, 14); see TAMMUZ.

6. The Sensual Development.

Linked with these primary attributes in the most remarkable and instructive ways was the worship of Ishtar as the fountain of the tenderest and most sacred human sentiments, also of imaginative conceptions of external nature, and even experiences of the inner moral and spiritual life (on the process of transition cf. J. F. McCurdy,

7. The Worship as Spiritualized.

History, Prophecy, and the Monuments, iii, New York, 1901, §§ 1184 sqq.). The best illustrations are afforded by the Babylonian hymns to Ishtar as the great mother-goddess, as the creator of the animate universe generally (cf. the exordium of Lucretius, *De rerum natura*), and as the helper of men, freeing them from sickness and the curse of sin and guilt.

Though we learn nothing directly from the Old Testament as to the character of the service of Ashtoreth in Palestine, the connections in which the word occurs make it clear that, whatever else may have been here and there included, the lowest forms of Ishtar worship were ordinarily exhibited. The regular association in the singular with "the baal" and in the plural ('*Ashtaroth*) with "the baals" indicates the predominance of the sexual aspects of the many-sided cult. Its popularity and seductiveness are also manifested in the use of the plural (exactly as in Babylonian) as an equivalent of goddesses in general (Judges ii, 13, x, 6; I Sam. vii, 3, 4, xii, 10) in passages which, it is true, proceed from later deuteronomic editing, but are therefore all the more indicative of the prevailing tendency.

3. Tendency of the Cult in Israel.

A comprehensive historical view of the whole subject helps to understand the fascination of Astarte worship as a seductive and formidable obstacle to the service of Yahweh. See ASSYRIA, VII; ATARGATIS; ASHERAH; BAAL; BABYLONIA, VII, 2, § 7; 3, § 5.

J. F. MCCURDY.

BIBLIOGRAPHY: J. Selden, *De dis Syris*, ii. 2, London, 1617; F. Münter, *Die Religion der Carthager*, pp. 62-86, Copenhagen, 1821; F. C. Movers, *Die Phönizier*, i, 559-650, Bonn, 1841; E. Schrader, *Die Höllenfahrt der Istar*, Giessen, 1874; idem, *KAT*, pp. 436 sqq.; P. Berger, *L'Ange d'Astarté*, Paris, 1879; F. Hitzig, *Biblische Theologie des Alten Testaments*, pp. 17 sqq., Carlsruhe, 1880; P. de Lagarde, *Astarte*, in *Nachrichten von der Gesellschaft der Wissenschaften zu Gottingen*, 1881, pp. 396-400; C. P. Tiele, *La Deesse Istar surtout dans le mythe Babylonien*, Leyden, 1884; F. Baethgen, *Beiträge zur semitischen Religionsgeschichte*, pp. 31-37, 218-220, Berlin, 1889; Collins, *'Ashtoreth and the 'Ashera*, in *PSBA*, xi (1888-89), 291-303; A. Jeremias, *Die babylonisch-assyrischen Vorstellungen vom Leben nach dem Tode*, pp. 4-45, Leipsic, 1887; idem, *Izdubar-Nimrod*, pp. 57-66, 68-70, ib. 1891; P. Jensen, *Die Kosmologie der Babylonier*, pp. 117-118, 135, 227 sqq., Strasburg, 1890; *Ashtoreth and Her Influence in the O. T*, in *JBL*, x (1891), 73 sqq.; G. A. Barton, *The Semitic Ishtar Cult*, in *Hebraica*, ix (1892-93), 131-165, x (1893-94), 1-74. For the "Queen of Heaven" consult: B. Stade, in *ZATW*, vi (1886), 123-132, 289-339; E. Schrader, in *Sitzungsberichte der Berliner Akademie*, 1886, pp. 477-491; idem, in *ZA*, iii (1888), 353-364; iv (1889), 74-76; J. Wellhausen, *Heidenthum*, pp. 38 sqq.; A. Kuenen, *De Melecheth des Hemels*, Amsterdam, 1888 (Germ. transl. in *Gesammelte Abhandlungen*, pp. 186-211, Freiburg, 1894).

On the connection between Aphrodite and Astarte consult: J. B. F. Lajard, *Recherches sur le culte de Vénus*, Paris, 1837; W. H. Engel, *Kypros*, ii, 5-649, Berlin, 1841; L. F. A. Maury, *Histoire des religions de la Grèce antique*, iii, 191-259, Paris, 1859; F. Hommel, *Aphrodite-Astarte*, in *Neue Jahrbücher für Philosophie und Pädagogie*, cxxv (1882), 176; Ohnefalsch-Richter, ut sup., pp. 269-327; *DB*, i, 165, 167-171; M. Jastrow, *The Religion of Babylonia and Assyria*, Boston, 1898 (cf. Index under *Ishtar*); *EB*, i, 330-333, 335-339; G. A. Barton, *A Sketch of Semitic Origins*, pp. 106, 246-268, New York, 1902; Schrader, *KAT*, pp. 436-438.

ASH WEDNESDAY (Lat. *Dies cineris, feria quarta cinerum*): The first day of Lent, the beginning of the forty days' fast before Easter in the Western Church. The name is not simply a general allusion to the repentance in sackcloth and ashes of which the prophets speak in the Old Testament, but refers more directly to a rite which marks the observance of the day in the Roman Catholic Church. The palm-branches blessed on the Palm-Sunday of the previous year are burned to ashes, and these ashes are placed in a vessel on the altar before the beginning of mass. The priest, wearing a violet cope (the color of mourning), prays that God will send his angel to hallow the ashes, that they may become a salutary remedy to all penitents. Then follows the prayer of benediction, which explains the symbolical meaning of the use of ashes still more clearly. The ashes are then thrice sprinkled with holy water and censed, after which the celebrant kneels and places some of them upon his own head. The congregation then approach the altar and kneel, while the sign of the cross is made upon their foreheads with the blessed ashes; to each one are said the words *Memento, homo, quia pulvis es et in pulverem reverteris* ("Remember, O man, that dust thou art and unto dust shalt thou return").

It is impossible to determine accurately the date at which the imposition of ashes, which originally formed a part of the public penance for grievous sinners, became a custom applicable to all the faithful. It is demonstrably at least as old as the synod of Beneventum in 1091, which expressly commands it for clergy and laity alike. In the Anglican communion the day is marked by a special service known as the "commination service," (q.v.) or at least by a special collect and Scripture lessons; and the Irvingite liturgy also contains prayers for it. See CHURCH YEAR.

BIBLIOGRAPHY: Bingham, *Origines*, book xviii, chap. ii. § 2; G. Bevinet, *History of the Reformation of the Church of England*, ii, 94, London, 1681; J. Kutschker, *Gebräuche*, pp. 91-152, Vienna, 1843.

ASIA MINOR IN THE APOSTOLIC TIME.

I. The Name: The term "Asia Minor" is not found in the New Testament; it is said to occur first in Orosius, i, 2 (400 A.D.). In the apostolic period "Asia" denoted the continent, Asia Minor, and the Roman province of Asia. Paul no doubt understood by Asia, the Roman province (I Cor. xvi, 19; II Cor. i, 8; II Tim. i, 15). The Apocalypse includes also the Phrygian Laodicea; and the provincial district is doubtless meant in I Pet. i, 1, where Asia stands after Pontus, Galatia, and Cappadocia and before Bithynia, though it is uncertain whether the author was informed of the political character of these designations. How far the Roman provincial demarcations had become familiar to the people it is difficult to tell. There are passages in the New Testament in which the term Asia is used in a narrower sense. In the time of Paul the country was still in a stage of development.

II. The Province of Asia: When Attalus III of Pergamos in 133 B.C. willed his country to the Romans, it was declared a province, though the real organization was not effected until 129. The main parts were the maritime districts Mysia, Lydia, and Caria. With these Cicero (*Pro Flacco*, xxvii, 65) mentions Phrygia, which belonged to the province after 116. Under the emperors Asia was a senatorial province ruled by a proconsul, whose seat was at Ephesus. The diet of the province, to which representatives (Gk. *asiarchai*; cf. Acts xix, 31) were sent, met annually in different cities. Its powers and duties culminated in the imperial cult; and hence it was presided over by the *sacerdos provinciæ* or, Greek, *archiereus tēs Asias*, who offered the sacrifices and pronounced the vow for the emperor and his house. This office changed annually and the years were dated accordingly.

III. The Imperial Cult: The empire as the guaranty of peace and the source of all blessings of culture appeared to the people as a divine power. From his point of view the author of the Apocalypse (xiii, 3–8) describes this worship of the empire by the world. He is convinced that the empire owes its success to a supernatural power, but not to the God of heaven—rather to the devil. The Jews as a rule enjoyed religious liberty throughout the empire, and were not required to take part in the imperial cult. What Cæsar had granted to them was confirmed by Augustus and Claudius. The sufferings of the Christians of Asia Minor, mentioned in the First Epistle of Peter, were not caused by their refusal to take part in this worship (cf. ii, 13 sqq.). It is true that the populace hated and persecuted the Christians, but not because they refused to honor the emperor; the name of this new *superstitio* was distrusted and outlawed as at Rome in the time of Nero (Tacitus, *Annales*, xv, 44).

IV. Cities: The number of free cities was steadily reduced under the emperors; and immunity from taxation was granted in place of autonomy. An edict of Antoninus Pius divided the cities into three classes according to size and importance. Pliny (*Hist. nat.*, V, xxix, 105 sqq.) mentions nine cities which possessed a court of justice, viz.: Laodicea ad Lycum, Synnada, Apamea, Alabanda, Sardis, Smyrna, Ephesus, Adramyttium, and Pergamos. **Ephesus**, at the mouth of the Cayster, often called on inscriptions "the first and greatest metropolis of Asia," was the seat of the proconsul. Another title of the city is "temple-keeper" (i.e., of Diana; cf. Acts xix, 35, R. V.; the Greek is *neōkoros*, the usual word for the custodian of a temple). A college of virgin priestesses ministered to Diana, presided over by a eunuch called Megabysos. It was no exaggeration of Demetrius when he said that the Ephesian Artemis was worshiped not only by all Asia, but by the whole world (Acts xix, 27); for through Ephesus flowed the commerce between the East and the West. Among the strangers residing there were many Jews, who had a synagogue (Acts xviii, 19, 26, xix, 8) and enjoyed special privileges, especially those who were Roman citizens, as may be seen from documents contained in Josephus and Philo. Ephesus was a member of the confederation of the thirteen Ionian cities, of which Miletus was the head.

A great road led from Ephesus to **Magnesia**, where was another temple of Artemis which Strabo places on a par with the Ephesian. Christianity came to Magnesia from Ephesus; among the epistles of Ignatius, that to the Magnesians immediately follows that to the Ephesians. After Magnesia, Strabo mentions **Tralles** (also mentioned by Ignatius), once a wealthy city, called Cæsarea under Augustus. Jews also dwelt there; and it is possible that the Gospel was brought thither from Ephesus (Acts xix, 10). It seems that special missionary attention was devoted to the cities along the Meander-Lykos road; for one meets with the three closely connected Phrygian congregations Laodicea, Hierapolis, and Colossæ, of which **Laodicea** was the most important and is alone mentioned in the Apocalypse. The Christian community seems to have shared in the wealth of the city (Rev. iii, 17). Laodicea never had an emperor's temple. Polycrates of Ephesus mentions among the "great lights" of Asia a bishop and martyr with the Phrygian name Lugaris as buried at Laodicea (Eusebius, *Hist. eccl.*, IV, xxiv, 5). In 165 there was "great strife concerning the Passover there" (ib. IV, xxvi, 3). **Colossæ**, an important city of Phrygia, was long the seat of a bishop. More important than Colossæ was **Hierapolis**, the native place of the philosopher Epictetus, and the place in which the apostle Philip lived and died. Papias was bishop of Hierapolis, as was also Claudius Apollinaris. **Apamea** was founded by Antiochus Soter and was the seat of a *conventus juridicus*. That many Jews lived here is known from Cicero (*Pro Flacco*, xxviii); they had their own constitution, a "law of the Jews."

The Lydian **Philadelphia** was sparsely populated on account of the frequent earthquakes. The Gospel was brought thither from Ephesus. Philadelphia is one of the seven churches of Asia mentioned in the Apocalypse (iii, 7–13); among its inhabitants Jews are mentioned (iii, 9). Ignatius addressed an epistle to the Philadelphians; and Eusebius (*Hist. eccl.*, V, xvii, 3) mentions a prophetess Ammia of Philadelphia. **Sardis** was the ancient city of the Lydian kings. Jews lived there, having their own jurisdiction. The Church at Sardis, one of the seven mentioned in the Apocalypse (iii, 1–6), was the episcopal see of Melito in the time of Antoninus Pius. Two famous roads led from Sardis: one to Pergamos by way of Thyatira, the other to Smyrna. All three cities are mentioned among the seven Churches of the Apocalypse. **Thyatira** was known especially for its gild of dyers. The Lydia mentioned in Acts xvi, 14, called a "seller of purple," had probably come to Philippi with wool which had been dyed at home. Thyatira plays an important part in the history of Montanism (Epiphanius, *Hær.*, li, 33). Taking a western road from Thyatira one comes to **Smyrna**, where in 195 B.C. a temple was built in honor of the *dea Roma*. Tiberius allowed a temple to be erected here to himself, his mother, and the senate. Politically Smyrna was not as important as Ephesus; but it had the reputation of being the most beautiful city of Asia. Jews in Smyrna are mentioned in Rev. ii, 9 and in the *Martyrium Polycarpi*, xii, 2, and both times as enemies of the Christians. Paul does not seem to have done missionary work there; but that the congregation was founded by John is not a necessary inference. By the "angel of the church in Smyrna" (Rev. ii, 8) Polycarp might be meant, had not the epistles to the seven churches originated in a much earlier period than the final redaction of the Apocalypse. From Smyrna the road leads by way of Cyme, Myrina, and Elæa to Pergamos, where it meets the road to Thyatira. **Pergamos,** the ancient royal city of the Attalides, was still famous under the Roman empire. In the time of Augustus (29 B.C.) the first provincial temple was erected here, and by the side of Ephesus Pergamos seems to have been the most prominent city in Asia. It was famous for the cult of Æsculapius. Although the Jews had influence, they were not the cause of the animosities mentioned in Rev. ii, 12–17 Though they are called in the Apocalypse a "synagogue of Satan" (ii, 9), it is most unlikely that they are meant by the words: "I know where thou dwellest, where Satan's seat is" (ii, 13); the language points to a more concrete phenomenon, which might be thought of as an embodiment of Satan, and no doubt refers to the worship of Æsculapius. This "savior," whose symbol was the serpent, and who, according to Justin (*Apologia*, i, 21, 22), looked much like Christ, could easily appear as a devilish caricature of the Son of God. The words "hast not denied my faith" imply that in the days of Antipas the population made an effort to force the worship of Æsculapius upon others.

From the seaport **Adramyttium,** where there was a *conventus juridicus*, following the north coast of the Adramyttian bay the road leads to **Assos,** where Paul seems to have been active (Acts xx, 13–14). It was the birthplace of Cleanthes the Stoic. **Troas,** or rather **Alexandria,** became famous under Roman sway. Augustus made it a colony. It was the seaport from which Paul went to Macedonia (Acts xvi, 11). It is perhaps characteristic of the Roman citizen, that, besides Ephesus, Troas is the only city of the province of Asia where Paul labored in person (Acts xx, 5–7; II Cor. ii, 12; II Tim. iv, 13). The Church of Troas is not mentioned in the Apocalypse, but is referred to by Ignatius in his epistles to the Philadelphians (xi, 2) and Smyrnæans (xii, 2). **Abydus, Lampsacus,** and **Cyzicus** were not included in Paul's mission.

V. The Islands of the Ægean Sea belonged in great part to the province of Asia. **Tenedos** was opposite Alexandria Troas; **Lesbos,** with the capital Mytilene, or as the later form reads in Acts xx, 14, **Mitylene,** was the first station on the passage from Assos. Thence Paul sailed (Acts xx, 15) to **Chios,** opposite the Ionic peninsula. On the following day he reached **Samos.** According to the reading of Codex D, he seems not to have tarried on the island itself in the city of Samos, but in the town of **Trogyllium** on a little isle of like name before the cape, mentioned by Strabo. South of Samos lay the small island of **Patmos.** Following the route of Paul (Acts xxi, 1) one comes to **Coos** and **Rhodes.** During the last decades before Christ, Rhodes was a center of culture; it was the native place of the Stoic Panætius, whose work "On Duty" Cicero used in his *De officiis*; in Rhodes, too, labored his pupil Posidonius (about 90–50 B.C.); the rhetorician Apollonius Molon, the teacher of Cicero and Cæsar; and Theodore of Gadara, the teacher of Tiberius.

VI. The Province Pontus-Bithynia: When King Nicomedes III, Philopator, of Bithynia bequeathed in 74 B.C. his country to the Romans, the governor of Asia made it a province, and it was extended toward the east in 64 B.C. by annexing north Paphlagonia and Pontus. After the separation of Pontus Galaticus, which was joined to Galatia, the new province with the double name Pontus (and) Bithynia comprised the entire coast region east of the Rhyndacus, north of Mt. Olympus, extending beyond the Halys to the city of Amisus. As a senatorial province it was ruled by proconsuls with a legate, a questor, and six lictors. Pliny the Younger was an extraordinary governor, who was sent to the province (111–112 A.D.) to regulate its finances. The domestic conditions in Bithynia are described not only in the correspondence of Pliny the Younger with Trajan, but also in the speeches of the sophist Dio Chrysostomus of Prusa, which have much of interest to the investigator of early Christianity (ed. H. von Arnim, 2 vols., Berlin, 1893–96; cf. also idem, *Dio von Prusa*, ib. 1898). The most noteworthy of the cities of Pontus and Bithynia were **Apamea, Chalcedon, Byzantium,** and **Prusa.** A court of judgment was also at **Nicæa** (see NICÆA, COUNCILS OF), where there was a temple of the *dea Roma* and of the *divus Julius*, whereas the provincial temple was at Nicomedia. In Pontus were **Amastris, Sinope, Amisus, Abonuteichus,** and **Comana.** Concerning the Jews in Pontus and Bithynia cf. Acts ii, 9, xviii, 2. The spread of Christianity in Pontus is attested by Pliny (*Epist.*, xcvi, 9).

VII. The Province Galatia has a complicated history. Its boundaries were often changed. It derived its name from the Celtic tribes which migrated to Asia Minor in the third century B.C., and, according to Strabo, occupied the eastern part of Phrygia. Without going into details, it can be assumed that in the New Testament "Galatia" means not the seat of the three Celtic tribes, but the Roman province including Pisidia and Lycaonia, therefore the territory of the first Pauline missionary journey. The question is of interest whether by "the Churches of Galatia" (Gal. i, 2) Paul understood only those of the first missionary journey. He shows an inclination to address his Churches according to provinces, following the Roman provincial divisions. When he addresses a Church with reference to its special needs, he naturally speaks to Corinthians, Thessalonians, Philippians; but where he overlooks his missionary territory as a whole, he uses the provincial names. There is no reason to believe that "the Churches of Galatia" means anything else than the Churches of the Roman province. Since the Epistle to the Galatians was not addressed to one Church, but to a number of Churches, Paul had to select a name expressive of all; and the designation "Churches of Galatia" was quite natural and appropriate for the Roman citizen, to whom the political divisions of the empire were no fortuitous arrangement, but a moral good. In the time of Paul there were no Galatians in the old sense; and the name means subjects of the Roman emperor belonging to the province of Galatia. Similarly Tychicus and the Ephesian Trophimus (Acts xxi, 29) are said to be of Asia (xx, 4); and Gaius and Aristarchus are called Macedonians (xix, 29, xxvii, 2; cf. II Cor. ix, 2, 4), although Gaius was certainly no Macedonian by birth. Of the Galatian cities **Ancyra** was the seat of the governor, having the provincial temple of Augustus and of the *dea Roma*, on the walls of which the deeds of Augustus were inscribed (the so-called *monumentum Ancyranum*). From Ancyra the road leads eastward to **Tavium**, the ancient capital of the Trocmæ. The capital of the Tolistobogi was **Pessinus**, famous for the rich temple dedicated to Cybele, whom the natives called Agdistis. North of Pessinus was **Germa**, a colony founded by Augustus (*Julia Augusta Fida Germa*). For military purposes a direct connection must have existed with **Antioch in Pisidia** (Acts xiii, 14), where Augustus had established a military colony under the name of Cæsarea, not mentioned in the New Testament. It was the center of a system of military settlements which the emperor established to protect the province against the mountain tribes of Pisidia and Isaurica. It is possible that Paul went to **Iconium** by way of Antioch. According to Strabo, Iconium belonged to Lycaonia; but in Acts xiv, 6 it seems not to be reckoned among the Lycaonian cities; the population was Phrygian. The Jews had a synagogue and in the *Acts of Paul and Thecla* a proconsul is erroneously mentioned in **Iconium**. Another city was **Lystra**, which was a Roman colony and had a temple of Jupiter. Another colony was **Derbe** at the south end of the province.

VIII. The Province Lycia-Pamphylia was organized by Claudius in 43 A.D. and again under Vespasian. Till 135 it was governed by the emperor; afterward, by the senate. Among the six larger cities of Lycia which are mentioned by Strabo are the two maritime towns **Patara** and **Myra**, through which Paul passed on his journeys (Acts xxi, 1–2, xxvii, 5–6). **Phaselis**, with three ports, did not belong to the Lycian confederacy in the time of Strabo, but was independent. The Jews in Phaselis are mentioned in I Macc. xv, 23. Of the Pamphylian cities **Attalia** is of special interest, because Paul on returning from his first missionary journey went thither to sail to Antioch (Acts xiv, 25–26). Ramsay suggests that the same vessel which brought the apostle from Paphos took him to Perga also.

IX. The Province Cilicia varied in extent at different times. Under Cicero's administration (51–50 B.C.), besides Cilicia, Pamphylia, Pisidia, Isaurica, and Lycaonia, the districts of Laodicea, Apamea, Synnada, and Cyprus, afterward joined with Asia, belonged to it. Through the organization of the provinces of Galatia (25 B.C.), Pamphylia (43 A.D.), and Cyprus (22 B.C.), the territory of the province was reduced to Cilicia proper. The western part of it, *Cilicia Aspera*, was given by Augustus to Archelaus of Cappadocia (25 B.C.), with Elaiussa-Sebaste as capital; and Caligula gave it to Antiochus IV of Commagene. Under Vespasian it was restored to the province of Cilicia. Considering the small extent which the province had under the first emperors, it no doubt was under the jurisdiction of the procurator of Syria. Under Hadrian Cilicia Campestris and Aspera became one imperial province. Under Domitian the seat of government was Antioch, otherwise **Tarsus** was the metropolis. From the time of Antony it was an *urbs libera*, densely populated and wealthy; it was the home of the Stoic philosopher Athenodorus, son of Sandon, the honored teacher of Augustus, perhaps also of Strabo. According to Cicero (*Ad Atticum*, XVI, xi, 4, xiv, 4), he helped him in the preparation of the *De officiis*. A rival of Tarsus was **Anazarbus, called also Cæsarea,** native city of the physician and author Dioscorides, who lived under Nero, and whose work, *De materia medica* (ed. C. Sprengel, Leipsic, 1829), Luke is said to have perused (cf. P. de Lagarde, *Psalterium juxta Hebræos Hieronymi*, Leipsic, 1874, pp. 165 sqq.; W. K. Hobart, *The Medical Language of St. Luke*, Dublin, 1882; Zahn, *Einleitung*, ii, 384, 435). From Tarsus the highroad leads over the Cilician Taurus to Cappadocia. On the road from Tarsus to Issus and Alexandria was **Mopsuestia,** the episcopal see of Theodore.

X. Cyprus: After a temporary union with Cilicia the province of Cyprus was separated in 22 B.C. and organized as a senatorial province, ruled by a *proprætor pro consule* with a legate and questor. Many Jews lived in Cyprus, and Cyprian Jewish Christians brought the Gospel to Antioch (Acts xi, 20); Barnabas was from Cyprus (Acts iv, 36). In **Salamis** there were many synagogues. In the revolt under Trajan the Jews killed 240,000 non-Jews, and completely devastated the city of Salamis. For a punishment they were all banished from the island. The Acts of the Apostles mention the two seaports Salamis in the east, and **Paphos; Soli**, on the southern coast, had a sanctuary of Aphrodite and Isis; **Citium** was the birthplace of the Stoic Zeno.

XI. The Province Cappadocia: In the year 17 A.D. Cappadocia, after the death of the last king Archelaus, was made a province, governed by a procurator who, as in Judea, was under the governor of the province of Syria in military matters. In the year 70 Vespasian united it with Galatia, but it was afterward again separated. Pontus Galaticus with Amasia and Pontus Polemoniacus, which had belonged to Galatia, Trajan joined to Cappadocia, to which was added Armenia Minor and Lycaonia with Iconium. Cappadocia had very few cities of importance. That Paul did no missionary work there is very intelligible; hence it is also improbable that he should have traveled through Cappadocia (Acts xviii, 23). The road would have brought him within three days from the Cilician gates to **Tyana,** the birthplace of Apollonius, a Roman colony after Caracalla; from thence perhaps to **Mazaka-Eusebea,** called **Cæsarea,** the most important and still flourishing city in Cappadocia, the metropolis of the province, the birthplace of Basil the Great. **Nazianzus** and **Nyssa,** the episcopal sees of the two Gregorys, were places of no importance.

(JOHANNES WEISS.)

BIBLIOGRAPHY: The article *Kleinasien in der Apostolischen Zeit*, in Hauck-Herzog, *RE*, 3d. ed., x, 535–563, is a scholarly and comprehensive treatment of the subject, and should be consulted for further information and titles of works dealing with particular localities and special topics. Ritter, *Erdkunde*, xviii, xix, 2, Berlin, 1858–59, and Sievers, *Asien*, pp. 78–86, 556–562, Leipsic, 1893, give a general description. For the history: G. F. Hertzberg, *Die Geschichte Griechenlands unter der Herrschaft der Römer*, vol. ii, Halle, 1868; T. Mommsen, *Römische Geschichte*, vol. v, Berlin, 1904, available for the English reader in the transl. by T. T. Dickson, *Provinces of the Roman Empire*, i, chap. vii, New York, 1887; J. Marquardt, *Römische Staatsverwaltung*, i, 333–349, Leipsic, 1881. A complete collection of inscriptions from Asia Minor has been undertaken by the Vienna Academy, of which vol. i, containing the inscriptions in the Lycian language, has been issued (1900). Of great value in English are W. M. Ramsay, in *Classical Review*, iii (1889), 174 sqq., *The Historical Geography of Asia Minor*, in *Supplementary Papers of the Royal Geographical Society of London*, vol. iv, 1890; idem, *The Church in the Roman Empire before A.D. 170*, London, 1893; idem, *The Cities and Bishoprics of Phrygia*, 2 vols., ib. 1895–97; idem, *St. Paul as Traveller and Roman Citizen*, ib. 1899; idem, *Letters to the Seven Churches of Asia*, ib. 1904; articles on the several cities in *DB* and *EB*. The article in Ruggiero, *Dizionario Epigrafico di Antichità Romane* is highly commended. On the political history of the provinces the best monograph is V. Chapot, *La province romaine proconsulaire d'Asie*, Paris, 1904.

ASINARII, as-i-nê'ri-ai: Originally a nickname of the Jews, because they were said to worship an ass (see Ass); afterward applied also to the Christians, of whom the same story was told. It is not impossible that the Jews were the first to shift the reproach from themselves to the Christians. Tertullian (*Ad nationes*, i, 14; *Apologia*, xvi) tells how an apostate Jew, bitterly hostile to the Christians, exhibited in Carthage a picture representing a god with ass's ears and a hoof on one foot, clad in a toga and holding a book, with the inscription DEUS CHRISTIANORUM ONOKOIHTHΣ ["Onokoietes, the God of the Christians;" the meaning of "Onokoietes" is not very clear; it has been explained as "ass-priest" or "ass-worshiper"; another reading is ONOKOITHΣ, "lying in an ass's manger" (?); perhaps there is a ribald implication]. More offensive to the Christians was the "travesty crucifixion" which the Jesuit Garrucci discovered in 1856 in the ruins of a building on the southern declivity of the Palatine, which was possibly a school for the imperial pages. In that case it was probably sketched in an idle moment by one of these lads, in mockery of the religion of his Christian comrades. It represents a man's body with an ass's head, not strictly hanging on a cross, since the feet are supported by a platform, but with the arms outstretched and fastened to the transverse piece of a T-shaped cross. To the left is a smaller figure, raising one hand in an attitude of adoration, and under it is the inscription ΑΛΕΞΑΜΕΝΟΣ ΣΕΒΕΤΕ [i.e., σέβεται] ΘΕΟΝ ("Alexamenos worships his god"). It is now in the Museo Kircheriano in Rome.

In 1870 Visconti discovered another inscription in the same building, with the words ΑΛΕΞΑΜΕΝΟΣ FIDELIS. Both of these probably belong to the beginning of the third century. That there is nothing improbable in a Christian having been among the imperial pages at that time is shown by Tertullian (*Apologia*, xxxvii) and by an inscription of the year 217, given by Rossi.

(A. HAUCK.)

BIBLIOGRAPHY: Older treatments of the subject, still useful, are Morinus, *De capite asinino deo Christiano*, Dort, 1620; H. Heinsius, *De laude asini*, p 186, Leyden, 1629; T. Hasæus, *De calumnia olim Judæis et Christianis impacta*, Erfurt, 1716. Later discussions are, P. Garrucci, in *Civilta cattolica*, series 3, vol. iv (1856), 529; *DCA*, i, 149. For the "travesty crucifixion," cf. F. Becker, *Das Spottcrucifix der römischen Kaiserpaläste*, Breslau, 1866; P. Garrucci, *Storia della arte Christiana*, plate 483, vi, 135, Prato, 1880; F. X. Kraus, *Das Spottcrucifix vom Palatin und neuentdecktes Graffito*, Freiburg, 1872; *DCA*, i, 516.

ASMODEUS, as″mo-di′us (in the Talmud, *Ashmedai*): An "evil spirit," first mentioned in the apocryphal book of Tobit (iii, 8), as loving Sara, the daughter of Raguel at Ecbatana, and causing the death of her seven successive husbands on the bridal night. But Tobias, the eighth, escaped, under the direction of Raphael, by burning "the ashes of the perfumes" with the heart and liver of a fish which he had caught in the Tigris. When Asmodeus smelled the fumes, he fled to Upper Egypt, and was bound there by Raphael (Tobit viii, 1–3). The figure of this demon is taken from the Persians who greatly influenced later Jewish angelology and demonology. He is Parsee in origin, and to be identified with Æshma of the Avesta, the impersonation of anger (the primary meaning) and rapine.

Once adopted by the Jews, Asmodeus, thanks to rabbinic fancies, took on greater dimensions. Thus he is said to have been implicated in Noah's drunkenness and to be the offspring of the incest of Tubal-cain with his sister Naamah; he is reputed to have driven Solomon from his kingdom, but later Solomon forced him to serve in building the Temple, which he did noiselessly by means of the worm Shamir, whose whereabouts he revealed to Solomon.

BIBLIOGRAPHY: J. A. Eisenmenger, *Entdecktes Judenthum*, i, 351–361, 823, Frankfort, 1700; A. F. Gfrörer, *Geschichte des Urchristenthums*, i, 378–424, Stuttgart, 1838; T. Benfey and M. A. Stern, *Ueber die Monatsnamen*, p. 201, Berlin, 1836; F. H. H. Windischmann, *Zoroastrische Studien*, ed. F. Spiegel, pp. 138–147, ib. 1863; Kohut, *Ueber die jüdische Angelologie und Dämonologie in ihrer Abhängigkeit vom Parsismus*, in *Abhandlungen fur die Kunde des Morgenlandes*, iv (1866), 72–86; F. Spiegel, *Eranische Alterthumskunde*, ii, 131–133, Leipsic, 1873; Grünbaum, *Beiträge zur vergleichenden Mythologie aus der Haggada*, in *ZDMG*, xxxi (1877), 215–224; consult also commentaries on Tobit.

ASMONEANS. See HASMONEANS.

ASPERSION WITH HOLY WATER: A rite of frequent use in the Roman Catholic Church. It has a place in the administration of baptism and extreme unction, in the nuptial blessing, and in the ceremonies of sepulture, as well as in the consecration of objects for divine worship and in blessings of all kinds. Persons entering or leaving a church make the sign of the cross with holy water. A solemn form of aspersion, practised in parish churches every Sunday before the high mass, is called the Asperges, from the first word of the antiphon usually intoned by the officiating priest. The explanation of the use of holy water in aspersions is found in the prayer said at the time when it is blessed,—that, wherever it is sprinkled, the invocation of God's name may drive away all evil spirits and every temptation, and that the Holy Spirit by his presence may comfort all who implore the divine mercy. See HOLY WATER.

JOHN T. CREAGH.

ASS: The wild ass (Heb. *pere*, poetic *'arodh; asinus onager* or *hemippus*) is often mentioned in the Old Testament, and appears to have been found in earlier times more frequently in Syria than is now the case. It is described as dwelling in the wilderness (Isa. xxxii, 14; Jer. ii, 24); and to the poet it is a type of unbridled love of freedom (Job xi, 12, xxxix, 5-6), and a picture of the wandering Bedouin (Gen. xvi, 12; Job xxiv, 5). Hosea (viii, 9) compares Ephraim wilfully running after Assyria, to a wild ass separated from the herd. It feeds on the vegetation of the salt steppe (Job vi, 5; Jer. xiv, 6). The animal is larger and more beautiful and graceful than the common ass; it is famous for its swiftness, and is hard to catch.

The tame ass has been from ancient times one of the most important domestic animals in the East, whence it was introduced into Greece and Italy (cf. V. Hehn, *Kulturpflanzen und Haustiere*, Berlin, 1894, pp. 130-131). The Oriental ass is larger, quicker, more enduring, and more intelligent than the European. As in older times, the light-gray asses or white asses are still preferred, which the Sleb Bedouins rear in the desert; the usual color is reddish-brown (hence the name *ḥamor*). All classes used them for riding, for which purpose the females were preferred (Num. xxii, 11; Judges x, 4; II Sam. xvii, 23, xix, 26; I Kings xiii, 13; II Kings iv, 24; cf. Matt. xxi, 2-9). In the time of David, mules were used (II Sam. xiii, 29; xviii, 9; I Kings i, 33). The driver went alongside or behind (Judges xix, 3; II Kings iv, 24). The ass was also used as a beast of burden (Gen. xlii, 26, xlix, 14; I Sam. xxv, 18; Neh. xiii, 15), for plowing (Deut. xxii, 10; Isa. xxx, 24, xxxii, 20), and for grinding. Being an unclean animal, it could not be sacrificed (Ex. xiii, 13, xxxiv, 20), nor could its flesh be eaten (but cf. II Kings vi, 25). With other nations, as the Egyptians, it was sacred, and with this may probably be connected the fable circulated by Greek and Roman writers that the Jews worshiped the ass as God (see ASINARII).

I. BENZINGER.

BIBLIOGRAPHY: An early treatment still valuable is by S. Bochart, *Hierozoicon*, i, 148-149, ii, 214-215, London, 1663; C. von Lengerke, *Kenaan*, i, 140-141, 146, 165, Königsberg, 1844; J. G. Wood, *Wild Animals of the Bible*, London, 1887; *DB*, i, 173-174; *EB*, i, 343-344.

ASS, BROTHERS OF THE (*Ordo asinorum*). See TRINITARIANS.

ASS, FEAST OF THE: A popular entertainment provided by the Church in the Middle Ages in several cities of France. The aim, as in the miracle-plays, mysteries, moralities, and many minor points of the ritual, was to impress the facts of Bible history upon the minds of the ignorant, and to give general religious instruction. At Rouen a drama was presented at Christmas-tide, in which the prophets, Moses, Aaron, John the Baptist and his parents, Simeon, Nebuchadnezzar, Vergil, and the Sibyl appeared in appropriate dress and announced the coming of a redeemer. The story of Balaam was one of the scenes, and the ass was made to speak by the help of a priest concealed between the legs. At Beauvais a young woman with a child in her arms, and mounted on an ass, was led in procession through the streets on Jan. 14, in commemoration of the flight to Egypt. Mass was then said, during which "hinham" was substituted for certain of the usual responses. There was a similar festival at Sens, and an ass's feast at Madrid on Jan. 17, in the course of which the story of Balaam's ass was recited. In the fifteenth century these feasts were forbidden because abuse had crept in and they had become a scandal. The ass naturally figured frequently in Palm Sunday processions, and a picture of an ass was often introduced in the churches at that time. See BOY-BISHOP; FOOLS, FEAST OF.

BIBLIOGRAPHY: S. du Tilliot, *Mémoires pour servir à l'histoire de la fête des fous*, p. 14, Lausanne, 1741; C. F. du Cange, *Glossarium*, s.v. "Festum asinorum."

ASSEBURG, äs'se-burg, **ROSAMUNDE JULIANE VON:** Religious enthusiast; b. at Eigenstedt, near Aschersleben (30 m. n.w. of Halle), Prussia, 1672; d. in Dresden Nov. 8, 1712. She might have been forgotten long ago, if the well-known millenarian, Johann Wilhelm Petersen (q.v.), had not called attention to her, and been followed in the study of her case by such men as Spener, Löscher, and Leibnitz. According to her own statement, she received divine revelations and had glorious visions when only seven years old, and was regarded in the neighborhood of her home as an inspired prophetess. She asserted that Christ himself had appeared to her, and that an angel had received her tears in a golden vessel. At first these revelations were confided only to the circle of her friends; but they obtained wider currency when she removed to Magdeburg and became acquainted with Petersen who published a treatise on her case in 1691, discussing the question whether God might be supposed still to reveal himself in direct apparitions. Löscher, at Dresden, and Johann Friedrich Meyer, at Hamburg, warned against believing her; Spener, asked for his opinion by the electress of Saxony, expressed himself with great caution; Leibnitz supported her, and compared her visions to those of St. Bridget and other holy women of the Middle Ages. Petersen received her at Lüneburg, where her mental excitement increased to such a degree as to cause disturbance in the town and to call for an official investigation. Petersen's deposition from the office of superintendent and banishment followed in 1692, and implied the condemnation of his friend She followed him to Wolfenbüttel and to Magdeburg; later she lived in Berlin, and in the house of a Saxon countess, where Petersen used to call and visit her as late as the year 1708. It is said that she died in Dresden Nov. 8, 1712, and was buried at Schönfeld near Pillnitz. Her poem euch gegeben, is included in some modern German hymn-books. (F. W Dibelius.)

Bibliography: J. W. Petersen, *Lebensbeschreibung*, Frankfort, 1719 (reproduced in Eng., in the work by J. W P., *A Letter to Some Divines Concerning the Question whether God, since Christ's Ascension doth any more Reveal Himself to Mankind by the Means of Divine Apparitions? With an Exact Account of what God hath Bestowed upon a Noble Maid . written in High-Dutch and Now Set Forth in Eng.*, London, 1695).

ASSEMANI, as-sê-mā'nî (Italianized from the Arabic *al-sama'aniyy*, "the Simeonite"): The name of several learned Maronites who came to Rome from the Lebanon.

1. Joseph Simonius Assemani: The oldest and best known; b. at Hasrun (35 m. n.e. of Beirut, near the cedar-grove at the foot of Jabal Makmal); d., eighty years old, at Rome Jan. 13, 1768. He was educated at the Maronite college in Rome, and is said to have learned thirty languages. In 1715 Pope Clement XI sent him to the East to look for manuscripts, and he was there again from 1735 to 1738 in behalf of the Roman Catholic Christians of the Lebanon. He published numerous works, of which the first, and perhaps the most important, was the *Bibliotheca orientalis Clementino-Vaticana in qua manuscriptos codices Syriacos, Arabicos, Persicos, Turcicos, Hebraicos, Samaritanos, Armenicos, Æthiopicos, Græcos, Ægyptiacos, Ibericos, et Malabaricos bibliothecæ Vaticanæ addictos recensuit digessit J S. Assemani.* Twelve volumes were planned, of which four were published (Rome, 1719–28). For Cardinal Quirini's edition of the works of Ephraem Syrus he prepared the three Greek volumes (1734–46), and in 1751–53 issued four volumes of *Italicæ historicæ scriptores*, a supplement to Muratori; four more volumes were planned. Six volumes of *Kalendaria ecclesiæ universæ* appeared in 1755; six more were planned and partially completed, but were destroyed by fire in the Vatican library in 1768. The *Bibliotheca juris orientalis canonici et civilis* (5 vols., 1762–66) is now very rare. The archives of the Propaganda and of the Inquisition contain more than 100 volumes of treatises by Assemani. Many of the works which he planned should be taken up by organized scholarly research. A list of his manuscript remains is given in Mai, *Nova collectio*, ii, 2 (Rome, 1828), 166–168.

2. Joseph Aloysius Assemani: A younger brother of the preceding; b. about 1710; d. at Rome Feb. 9, 1782. He was professor of Oriental languages in Rome. His chief work was *Codex liturgicus ecclesiæ universæ in xv. libros distributus* (13 vols., Rome, 1749–66). Most copies of the last volume were burned, but it (as well as the entire work) is accessible in anastatic reprint. Besides minor dissertations, he published *De catholicis seu patriarchis Chaldæorum et Nestorianorum commentarius historico-theologicus* (1755). His Latin translation of the *Collectio canonum* of Ebed Jesu and of the *Nomocanon* of Barhebræus is in Mai, *Nova collectio*, vii (1838).

3. Stephan Evodius Assemani: A cousin of the preceding two; b. 1707; d. Nov. 24, 1782. He was titular bishop of Apamea and member of the Royal Society of Great Britain. He published *Bibliothecæ Mediceæ Laurentianæ et Palatinæ codicum mss. orientalium catalogus* (Florence, 1742), containing in twenty-three plates the illustrations of Bible history from the Syriac codex of Rabulas; the three Syriac volumes of the works of Ephraem Syrus in the edition mentioned above; *Acta sanctorum martyrum orientalium et occidentalium in duas partes distributa : adcedunt acta S. Simeonis Stylitæ* (2 vols., Rome, 1748); and with J. S. Assemani, *Bibliothecæ apostolicæ Vaticanæ codicum manuscriptorum catalogus in tres partes distributus*, of which 3 volumes (Hebrew and Syriac manuscripts) had appeared (1756 sqq.), as well as eighty pages of the fourth (Arabic manuscripts), when the fire in the Vatican library destroyed the remainder.

4. Simon Assemani: A great-nephew of Joseph Simonius and Joseph Aloysius Assemani; b. in Rome Feb. 19, 1752, according to G. P. Zabeo, *Orazione in funere di Assemani* (Padua, 1821); others say in Tripolis, and give the date as Feb. 20, 1752, and Mar. 14, 1749; d. in Padua, where he was professor of Arabic, Apr. 7, 1821. His publications were chiefly on Arabic subjects, as *Museo cufico Naniana* (Padua, 1788); *Su la Setta Assissana* (1806).

E. Nestle.

Bibliography: J. S. Ersch and J. G. Gruber, *Allgemeine Encyclopädie*, vol. vi, Leipsic, 1821 sqq.; *Nouvelle biographie générale*, vol. iii, Paris, 1854.

ASSEMBLY, GENERAL: The highest court of the Presbyterian churches (see Presbyterians). The name is from Heb. xii, 23.

ASSER: Bishop of Sherborne; d. 909 or 910. He was a Briton, a monk of Menevia (St. David's), and related to the bishop of that see. His repute for learning was such that about 885 King Alfred asked him to enter his service, and an arrangement was ultimately made whereby the monkish scholar agreed to spend half of each year with the English king and half in his own home. Alfred gave him very substantial rewards, including a grant at Exeter and its district in Saxonland and Cornwall. He became bishop of Sherborne (in Dorsetshire) before 900. He wrote a life of Alfred (*De rebus gestis Ælfridi*), which is a chronicle of English history from 849 to 887, with a personal and original narrative of Alfred's career to the latter year. It betrays the author's Celtic birth in many passages, and in existing manuscripts has been much interpolated. The best editions are by F. Wise (Oxford, 1722), in Petrie's *Monumenta historica Britannica* (London, 1848), and by W H. Stevenson (Oxford, 1904, Eng. transl. by A. S. Cook, Boston, 1906).

Bibliography: T. Wright, *Biographia Britannica literaria*, i, 405–413, London, 1842 (questions Asser's authorship of the *De rebus gestis*); R. Pauli, *König Ælfred und seine Stelle in der Geschichte Englands*, Berlin, 1851 (shows that Wright's objections are unfounded).

ASSHUR: 1. City of Assyria. See Assyria, IV, § 1. **2.** Assyrian God. See Assyria, VII, § 2.

ASSHURBANIPAL. See Assyria, VI, 3, §§ 14–15.

ASSISTANTS IN PUBLIC WORSHIP: The historical functions of those whose place it is to assist the principal minister in divine service belong largely to the development of the various orders (see ORDERS, HOLY). In the modern Roman Catholic Church the celebrant at high mass is assisted by a deacon and subdeacon who are usually priests. The minor functions are performed by acolytes, usually laymen and boys. A priest is not allowed to celebrate even a low mass without at least one person to make the responses. In the Anglican prayer-book the clergymen who read the epistle and gospel are designated not deacon and subdeacon, but epistoler and gospeler. See also LAY-READER.

ASSMANN, äs'män, **JOHANN BAPTIST MARIA:** German Roman Catholic; b. at Branitz (80 m. s.e. of Breslau) Aug. 26, 1833. He was educated at the University of Breslau, and after his ordination to the priesthood in 1860 was assistant in Katscher from 1861 to 1864, and a mission priest and military chaplain in Kolberg in 1865–68. From the latter year until 1882 he was divisional chaplain at Neisse, and was then provost of St. Hedwig's, Berlin, and delegate of the prince-bishop for six years. In 1882 he was consecrated titular bishop of Philadelphia, and since the same year has been field provost of the Prussian army and navy, being also the recipient of numerous orders and decorations.

ASSOCIATE CHURCH OF NORTH AMERICA. See PRESBYTERIANS.

ASSOCIATE REFORMED SYNOD OF THE SOUTH. See PRESBYTERIANS.

ASSUMPTION, FEAST OF THE: A festival of the Roman Catholic Church, commemorating the assumption, or corporal translation, of the Virgin Mary into heaven after her death. This doctrine, which the Greek Church also teaches (Synod of Jerusalem, 1672), has never been made the object of a dogmatic papal definition, but the attitude of the Church toward it and the general teaching of theologians class it among those truths which it would be rash to deny; at the Vatican Council over two hundred bishops desired a decree making the Assumption an article of faith. The Assumption can not be proved from Holy Scripture, and is based entirely upon tradition, though the scriptural prerogatives of Mary are invoked to prove the propriety of such an occurrence. About the year 600 the emperor Maurice ordered the celebration of the feast on Aug. 15; and at about the same time Gregory the Great fixed the same date for the West, where it had previously been observed on Jan. 18, for a reason which can not now be ascertained. The Gallican Church held to Jan. 18 down to the ninth century. The most that can be said for the antiquity of the feast is that its general solemn observance in East and West at the end of the sixth century would seem to justify the belief that its beginnings date from at least a century earlier. The word "assumption," at one time applied generally to the death of saints, especially martyrs, and their entry into heaven, has come to have an exclusive application to the Blessed Virgin. See MARY, THE MOTHER OF JESUS.

JOHN T. CREAGH.

ASSUMPTION, AUGUSTINIANS OF THE (known popularly as **Assumptionists**): A religious congregation of men, founded at Nîmes in 1845 by Emmanuel d'Alzon (1810–80), and finally approved by the pope in 1864. The rule is that of St. Augustine, supplemented by special constitutions. The purpose of the society is the sanctification of its members, devotion to God, to the Blessed Virgin, and to the Church, and zeal for souls. The activity of the Assumptionists has been displayed in many fields. A large part of their energy has been devoted to the poor and working classes, in asylums, schools, and technical institutions. In 1864 the Little Sisters of the Assumption were organized to assist in this work, and later, to secure still more effectively the spiritual and material relief of the needy, three pious confraternities of laywomen were affiliated to the Oblates—the Servants of the Poor, the Sisterhood of Our Lady, and the Daughters of St. Monica. In 1863 Father d'Alzon was sent by Pius IX to Constantinople to take up missionary work, and to-day about 350 members of the society are laboring in Turkey, Bulgaria, Asia Minor, and Palestine, in schools, seminaries, hospitals, and general missionary work. The demands of this field led to the founding of the Oblate Sisters of the Assumption. Perhaps the best known work of the Assumptionists is the *Oeuvre de la Bonne Presse* for the dissemination of good literature. This undertaking which was attended by a remarkable degree of success, resulted in numerous newspapers and magazines, and almost countless other publications. *La Croix du Dimanche* had a circulation of 510,000. Dissolved by a decree of the Court of Appeal of Paris, Mar. 6, 1900, the Assumptionists were doomed to exile or dispersion, but still maintain their corporate existence, with a central house at Rome, and establishments in Belgium, Spain, Italy, England, Australia, Chile, and the United States. They count at the present time about 1,000 members. The habit is a black robe with long, flowing sleeves, a black cape and cowl, and a leathern cincture.

JOHN T. CREAGH.

ASSURANCE: The doctrine that those who are truly converted know beyond doubt that they are saved (cf. Col. ii, 2; Heb. vi, 11; x, 22).

The doctrine may easily be made to contribute to spiritual pride. The degree of its objectionableness depends upon the interpretation placed upon it. It is particularly objectionable when it assumes to deny a state of salvation to those who are troubled by doubts, and in its exaggerated form easily leads to Antinomianism (q.v.). The doctrine was taught by both Luther and Calvin, and has been generally held in Protestantism. Indeed, the Westminster Assembly was the first Protestant synod to declare assurance not to be of the essence of faith. In connection with the belief in unconditional election, the doctrine in Calvinism (cf. *Westminster Confession*, art. xviii) takes the form of assurance of final salvation (see PERSEVERANCE OF THE SAINTS). In Methodism it means full confidence of present, not eternal, salvation. In this form the doctrine was advocated by Wesley, who connected it with the witness of the Holy Spirit; and it is still generally held by Methodist theologians (see METHODISTS).

ASSYRIA.

I. The Name: The original form seems to have been *a-usar* ("water-plain"), which was assimilated to or confused with the name of the god Anshar ("Host of Heaven"), softened into Asshar, and Asshur. The country appears in both Assyrian and Hebrew as *Asshur* and "land of Asshur"; to the Greeks it was *Assyria;* in the Aramaic the name became *Athur* and *Athuriya*.

II. The Country: In the case of a land the extent of which fluctuated so greatly at different periods, and the name of which connoted very different areas, some convention is necessary. Accordingly, following the datum of original size rather than of subsequent development, historians regard as Assyria that portion of territory lying along the Tigris, mainly to the east of it, north of the confluence of the Lower (or Little) Zab on the south to the foothills of the mountains of Armenia on the north, and on the east from the Zagros Mountains to just beyond the Tigris on the west. This demarcation coincides with a change in the topographical character of the country at its southern limit. Below the Lower Zab the country becomes alluvial; above that it is rolling or mountainous; while the desert lies to the west. Since this is in accord with native characteristics of the people to be noted later, for which it helps to account, the boundaries given above are assumed for this article.

1. Geographical Position and Extent.

Topographically the Tigris is the chief feature, the character of which is best understood by comparison with the Euphrates (q.v.). It rises only a few miles south of the course of the Euphrates and at about the same level, but on the south side of the mountains. The Euphrates, therefore, has to skirt the north side of the range and break through on its much longer journey south. The general course of the Tigris is quite consistently southeast; and the two rivers reach the same level about opposite Bagdad. The consequence is that to make the difference in level of about 1,000 feet between the source and the alluvium, the Tigris, having a much shorter distance to go, makes a more rapid descent than the Euphrates, and its current is swifter. A second and noteworthy difference is that while the Euphrates receives only two important tributaries after turning south, the Tigris continues to receive all the way to its mouth streams which drain the mountain regions and basins to the east. While, therefore, the Euphrates loses much of its water to the thirsty soil through which it passes, the Tigris swells its torrent as it proceeds.

2. The Tigris.

Another characteristic of the country is its partial isolation. Mountains make it difficult of access from the north and east; and the desert does the same on the west. Its only easy approach is from the south by the rivers, where settled populations in ancient times guarded it from the nomadic hordes in that direction. Still one more note should be made. The country is not alluvial like the great and marvelously fertile plain of Babylonia. It is rolling or hilly, harder therefore to cultivate, and, being more northerly in situation, its returns to the cultivator are less generous. All these facts have their bearing upon the character of the people. Further still, the land to the west of the river being prevailingly desert, the population of Assyria was almost entirely to the east of it; and there, with a single exception, the great cities were situated.

3. Influence of Topography on History.

In its temperature and its sufficiently abundant rainfall Assyria was fortunate: it was much cooler and moister than its southern neighbor. Of course, the temperature was lower in proportion to elevation and to distance north. In the hills the winters were severe. The fauna was very extensive. In the earlier periods the elephant was known about the middle Euphrates. Of beasts of prey, there were the black-maned and another species of lion, the bear, panther, lynx, wild-cat, wolf, fox, jackal, and hyena. Of other animals, the porcupine, beaver, wild ass, wild boar, wild sheep, wild goat, ibex, gray deer, spotted

4. Climate, Fauna, Flora, and Minerals.

deer, and hare may be named, while the great wild ox was not yet extinct. Of birds of prey or carrion, the eagle, vulture, and various hawks were known. Birds suitable for food were the bustard, swan, goose, duck, partridge, grouse, and plover. The common domestic animals were employed, while dogs were trained for the chase. The pine, poplar, plane, oak, sycamore, and walnut abounded. Under cultivation, though some of them were importations, were the date (of inferior quality), orange, lemon, pomegranate, apricot, mulberry, fig, and grape. Assyrian citrons were famous; melons were abundant; while cucumbers, onions, the grains—wheat, barley, and millet—and the leguminous plants were food staples. Under the careful and extensive system of irrigation in use, the agriculturist reaped a good return for his labors. Mineral resources were abundant and conveniently at hand in the shape of iron, lead, copper, alum, salt, and bitumen, while alabaster of a fine quality, limestone, and sandstone were in close proximity to the cities or easily reached from the Tigris, on which they were floated down to the places where they were required.

III. Exploration and Excavation: It may appear somewhat inconsequent that excavations in Assyria and Babylonia should be the result of the discovery and partial decipherment of inscriptions from a locality so distant as Persepolis. Yet the discovery that these were neither mere ornamentation nor arbitrary signs influenced greatly the patient toil and research which have recovered in large part the history of nations once forgotten, and have carried history back into the fifth pre-Christian millennium. The steps leading to these results are as follows.

1. The Persepolis Inscriptions. The ruins at Persepolis had been mentioned in 1320 by Odoric, and the inscriptions in 1611 by the friar Antonio de Gouvea; they were first described by the Spanish ambassador of Philip III to Shah Abbas, Don Garcia Sylva Figueroa, in 1621; the guess that they read from left to right was first made in 1677 by Thomas Herbert; they were first called cuneiform in 1700 by Thomas Hyde; first decided to be in three forms of writing in 1774 by Carsten Niebuhr; declared to be in three languages in 1798 by Olaf Tychsen; and first really translated, in part, in 1815 by Georg F. Grotefend, whose work was the climax which finally stimulated to direct effort upon Assyrian and Babylonian mounds. While discussion had been going on over the Persepolis inscriptions, bits of inscriptions in the cuneiform character had been collected by the surveyors who had been observing, locating, and plotting the mounds in Assyria and Babylonia. A relationship had been asserted between these scraps and the Persepolis writing; and Niebuhr had urgently advised excavation in Babylonia and had predicted rich results.

The site of Nineveh had been correctly located as early as 1160 by the rabbi Benjamin of Tudela. Desultory digging had been done in Babylonia at various sites by Claudius Rich of the East India Company, in some cases missing by only a foot or two walls which must have led him to investigate farther and have anticipated by over a quarter of a century the real discovery of the lost empires.

2. Preliminary Exploration. Rich and Porter. That was in 1811; he visited Nineveh in 1820 and there turned up a few bricks with characters on them and bought others from the natives, all of which were sent home and found place in the British Museum. A visit of the artist and archeologist Sir R. K. Porter to the region, particularly to the mounds at Hillah in Babylonia, under the guidance of Rich, led to the publication in 1821-22 of a sumptuous work by Porter illustrated by his own brush. The interesting and even brilliant description of what was to be seen and inferred aroused anew the interest of Europe; so that the years which followed, as well as those which preceded his visit, were years of exploration. The sites of the mounds were visited and plotted and described until localities and names, with conjectures as to their history, became almost commonplace. The era of excavation, however, was still to come.

In 1842 a French consulate was established at Mosul, across the river from the site of Nineveh, and Paul Emil Botta was appointed consul. Botta had served in Egypt, Arabia, and Syria, and had so become well acquainted with the Arabs and their methods of working, as well as with French procedure in archeological investigation. He had met a German scholar named Julius Mohl, who had visited Babylonia and had been impressed with the opportunities which it was not in his power to grasp. By him Botta was urgently advised not to be content with mere explorations and plotting of sites, but to dig. Accordingly Botta at once began at Kouyunjik, but with results so scanty that he transferred his operations to Khorsabad,

3. Botta at Khorsabad. where speedily so large a number of bas-reliefs and well-preserved inscriptions were discovered in the uncovered palace of Sargon, that upon his sober report of the facts the French government made a grant of 3,000 francs to continue the work. The local pasha meanwhile had procured an order for the cessation of the operations; but the arrival of a firman soon enabled Botta to resume, the result being the nucleus of the magnificent collection now in the Louvre, made between 1842 and 1846. In the latter year Botta was transferred, and his work as an excavator came to an end; but the results were published by the French government in five magnificent volumes which are even yet almost high-water mark.

While Botta was engaged in digging, and after some of his successes had been gained, he was visited by Austen Henry Layard, whose early reading had given him a decided bent toward archeology. Layard told the story of the mounds to Lord Stratford, who had secured the Halicarnassus marbles for the British Museum; and in 1845 the latter made a contribution of £60 which Layard was to use in excavating. Layard returned to Mosul, kept his plans from the local pasha, and began excavating at Nimrud (Calah) at two different points. His first day's work led him into two chambers, belonging to two palaces, lined with alabaster slabs bearing inscriptions. Further effort resulted in the uncovering of colossi which created sensation first among his Arab laborers and then in England, in the latter case so pronounced that the apathetic British government made a parsimonious grant for the continuance of the work. The local pasha had closed the trenches; but authority from the Porte was obtained which overruled opposition. The palace of Shalmaneser II was excavated, and the black obelisk unearthed with its sunken panels of relief and its 210 lines of inscription and the mention of Jehu of Israel, along with many other inscriptions. Layard had the benefit of Hormuzd Rassam's skill in managing natives, since Rassam was himself of the country, but educated in England. In 1847 Kalah-Shergat was attacked; and among other finds was the great inscription of Tiglath-Pileser I. An interval of two years was employed partly in writing his first books, and then Layard returned as the agent of the British Museum and excavated at Nimrud, Kalah-Shergat, Nebi Yunus, and Kouyunjik, at the latter place uncovering Sennacherib's palace. In 1851 his transference to the diplomatic service at Constantinople brought his work as an excavator to an end. He had identified Calah and Nineveh, had discovered eight palaces, and had recovered part of the great royal library, many historical inscriptions, the great collection of seals and seal impressions, the great slab, 21 ft. by 16 ft. 7 in., the monolith and statue of Asshurnasirpal, and great numbers of bronze and copper vessels, implements, and arms. Meanwhile his books, written in most pleasing style and using with telling effect Biblical passages referring to Assyria and Babylon, had thoroughly awakened England to the importance of the operations. While his active work in digging ceased, his diplomatic post afforded him the opportunity of facilitating the efforts of others by preventing much of the local bigoted and fanatical or avaricious obstruction which had impeded his own success.

4. Layard and Rassam.

In the year 1852 Rassam, who had contributed so much to Layard's success, was commissioned by the British Museum to continue the work of excavating, under the direction of Sir Henry Rawlinson. He unearthed at Kouyunjik the palace of Asshurbanipal with its "chamber of the lion hunt" and the record chamber with its heaps of inscribed tablets, including the Deluge Tablets, the richest discovery yet made. At Nimrud he found E-zida, the temple of Nebo, six statues of the god, the stele of Shamshi-Ramman IV, and the fragments of the black obelisk of Asshurbanipal II. At Kalah-Shergat the two intact prisms of Tiglath-Pileser I with their 811 lines of inscription were the prizes. His work was followed by that of Loftus and Boutcher, which produced less spectacular but equally solid values, while Hilmi Pasha, who had displaced the unscrupulous Mohammed Pasha, recovered at Nebi Yunus some winged bulls, a number of bas-reliefs, and other important material.

5. Rassam, 1852.

Meanwhile the French government had made an appropriation of 70,000 francs, by which Victor Place was enabled during 1851–55 to carry on investigations at Khorsabad and Kalah-Shergat. The plan of the former was thoroughly worked out, while fourteen cylinders, a magazine of pottery, another of glazed tiles, and the bakery and wine cellar of the palace were uncovered. Unfortunately the materials gathered by this expedition and the one of the same period at Birs Nimrud in Babylonia were lost by the capsizing of the raft on which they were being conveyed down the river for shipment.

6. Place.

The joint results of these labors being a mass of unread inscriptions, it is hardly surprising that a tacit understanding supervened to suspend excavations until decipherment should decide the value of the documents. Progress was rapid; Assyrian and Babylonian, Vannic and Sumerian yielded their secrets; and the reading of part of the material proved its great importance (see INSCRIPTIONS).

A new start was taken in the year 1872. George Smith had discovered among Rassam's tablets obtained from Asshurbanipal's palace the fragments of the deluge story. The possible, even certain, illumination of the Bible by these documents, guaranteed by the reading of the names of several of the Hebrew kings, stimulated to new effort. The popular demand became urgent for new discovery; yet the government's action was so tardy, under the restrictions of routine, that private enterprise was evoked and the London *Daily Telegraph* offered £1,000 to defray the expenses of an expedition, if Smith would lead it and send reports of progress. The start was made in January of 1873; Kouyunjik was the site chosen for work; and three new fragments of the deluge series were recovered, along with a number of historical inscriptions. With this success the *Telegraph* was satisfied and recalled Smith. The same year he was sent back by the British Museum, and secured some 3,000 inscriptions, many of which filled gaps in the material already at hand. In 1875 he was again sent out; but Turkish opposition intervened, and when that had been overcome, his death had occurred.

7. George Smith.

During the period 1877–82 Rassam was the agent in the field; and he unearthed at Balawat (fifteen miles from Mosul) the beautiful bronze plates of the gates of Imgur-Bel, a city which was the site of a palace of Asshurnasirpal II. Kouyunjik was more thoroughly explored, 2,000 pieces, some of them exceedingly fine, being the reward. But the rich finds of previous years made these results seem meager; and the consequence was a cessation of excavation in Assyria which has not yet been resumed, the southern region of Babylonia being more promising and offering greater rewards.

8. Rassam, 1877–82.

The difficulties which have to be overcome by excavating archeologists in these regions are fourfold. (1) Financial. The French and German governments have established a fine record of support of scientific research; the record of the British is not so clear; the United States has done nothing. Consequently expeditions from the United States have to rely upon private enterprise.

9. Obstacles in Excavating. It is a pity that some great fund is not available that shall make appeal for special resources unnecessary: the result would be more thorough work and not the kind which looks for spectacular effects and leaves on the ground material as valuable as that recovered. (2) Governmental. This is in the shape either of refusal or delay, at the Sublime Porte, to grant permission to dig, or at the field in the case of bigoted or obstinate pashas. The only remedy in the former case is timely application supported by suitable diplomatic effort. If the pasha on the ground is inclined to interpose obstructions, the display of a firman should be sufficient. (3) Popular. The suspicion and superstition of the Arabs can be overcome only by the exercise of great patience and diplomacy. Their confidence once gained, the Arabs are loyal to their employers, as is amply proved by experience. The assistance of one trained in dealing with them is, however, a necessity. (4) Natural. The ruins of the country and of its system of irrigation, the resulting stretches of marshes with their miasmatic fevers, the heat of the sun, and the scorching winds and dust-storms, are obstacles which can not be overcome. Their effects may be palliated by proper precautions, which, unfortunately, the excavator too often neglects in the ardor of his pursuit of knowledge.

IV. The Cities: According to the best reading of Gen. x, 11 (R. V. margin), "out of Shinar went forth Asshur, and builded Nineveh, Rehoboth-Ir, and Calah, and Resen." By excepting from these Rehoboth-Ir (which is now regarded as a mistake for *Rehoboth-Nina*, either the place where Mosul now is, or the "open places," i.e., "squares," of Nineveh itself), and by adding Asshur, Arbela, and Dur-Sharrukin, a list of the known cities belonging to Assyria proper is completed.

Asshur, the modern Kalah-Shergat, on the west side of the Tigris, rather below the middle point of the places where the Upper and

1. Asshur. the Lower Zab join the Tigris, was the chief city of Assyria until the reign of Asshur-bel-kala, son of Tiglath-Pileser I, c. 1090 B.C. It never attained as frequent mention or description as Nineveh in contemporary records, though the inscriptions record the frequent rebuilding and repair of the great temple of Asshur which bore the name of E-karsag-kurkurra. That it was eclipsed by its rival Nineveh is due perhaps to two causes: (1) The more healthful and pleasant situation of the latter; and (2) The location of Asshur in the zone of danger from Babylonian attack. But the return of quite late kings to it as their capital shows the hold the old city had upon the sentimental regard of those rulers.

Nineveh (Assyr. *Nina* or *Ninua;* Hebr. *Ninweh* or *Nineweh;* LXX, *Nineui*), the modern Kouyunjik on the north and Nebbi Yunus on the south of the Choser, named probably, like the southern city of the same name, from Nin, daughter of Ea and identified with Ishtar of Nineveh, stood on the left bank of the Tigris, about twenty miles north of the confluence of the Upper Zab with the Tigris. Its walls enclosed about 1,800 acres, and were about seven and one-half miles in circumference (approximately two miles square). Herodotus describes them as being 380 feet high and 80 feet thick, though in all probability the height given is an exaggeration; but Layard's plans make them, at one of the principal gates, where they were doubtless reinforced, 110 feet thick. The gates were flanked with towers for their defense. The eastern wall

2. Nineveh. was protected by a moat filled with water from the Choser. The time and circumstances of the founding of the city are unknown, though its Semitic origin seems implied by its name. The last datum is not quite conclusive, since it might have been pre-Semitic and renamed by its Semitic possessors. As it lay on the Indo-Mediterranean caravan route, its early origin and importance are assured. Gudea (see BABYLONIA, VI, 3, § 3) left an inscription referring to the building of a temple in Nineveh which may (and probably does) refer to the Babylonian city. Similarly precarious is the identification of the Assyrian Nineveh with the one mentioned by Dungi, second king of Ur (c. 2700 B.C.), as the place where he built a temple to Nergal. The fact that Shalmaneser I made gifts to such a temple in Nineveh does not, considering the diffusion of the worship of Nergal, make the identification secure. The conjecture of Jeremias that it once belonged to a kingdom called Kisshati has little to support it. About 1450 B.C. it was possibly under control of the (Hittite?) state of Mitanni, since Tushratta, king of Mitanni, lent an image of Ishtar of Nineveh to the contemporary Pharaoh. It is named twice in the Amarna Tablets (q.v.), both times in connection with Ishtar. The first Assyrian who made his residence there was Asshur-bel-kala, mentioned above. It was neglected for a number of centuries, and finally under Sennacherib was made perhaps the richest and best adorned city of the times. He tore down the old palace and built a double one, one part in the Assyrian style and one in the Syrian. He also conducted thither a water-supply drawn from the upper reaches of the Choser. Esarhaddon and Asshurbanipal added great structures, and it became the foremost city of the world, a great center of commerce and enormous wealth. Under the last-named king, it became a repository also of Babylonian culture.

Calah (Assyr. *Kalhu*) was the city next in importance, really a suburb of Nineveh, twenty miles south, in the fork of the Upper Zab

3. Calah. and the Tigris. It was apparently founded by Shalmaneser I (c. 1300 B.C.) and used as his capital in place of Asshur. It was then neglected until the time of Asshurnasirpal (c. 880 B.C.), who rebuilt it, fortified it with a massive wall, brought a water-supply from the Zab, and made of it a garden city, adorned with foreign trees and shrubbery. His palace was one of great beauty, and the bas-reliefs found there by Layard, George Smith, and Rassam are in the British Museum. Shalmaneser II built another palace, one of the adornments of which was the famous

Black Obelisk; and this palace was occupied also by Tiglath-Pileser III. Esarhaddon destroyed it and used the materials to construct his own palace. For these different structures a great platform was built of bricks and faced with stone, forty feet high, to guard against floods.

4. Resen, Arbela, and Dur-Sharrukin. Of Resen ("fountain-source") little is known except its location between Nineveh and Calah, and that it is identified with the Larissa of Xenophon's *Anabasis* (III, iv, 7). Arbela ("[The City of the] Four Gods"), the modern Erbil, is never noticed in the early inscriptions, yet must have had an important though quiet life, and long outlived its more pretentious and magnificent sister cities. It was situated in the mountains between the Upper and Lower Zab, and was the seat of worship of one of the Ishtars, next in prominence to her of Nineveh. Dur-Sharrukin ("Sargon's Fort"), the modern Khorsabad, the site of the palace of Sargon (707 B.C.) and of the necessary adjuncts thereto, was north of Nineveh, near the sources of the Choser and on the slopes of the hills. It was much smaller than the capital, its walls being 3,820 yards in circumference. Two mountain streams flowed past it. Only in Sargon's time did it have much importance.

V. The People, Language, and Culture: The people belonged to the so-called Northern Semites, and were related consequently most closely to the Semitic Babylonians, Arameans, Hebrews, and Phenicians. They were sturdy in physique, and their physiognomy, clearly portrayed in their many bas-reliefs, is of a pronounced Semitic type.

1. National Character. Their character is traceable partly to their origin, partly to their environment. Their isolation preserved or intensified their native qualities, and prohibited the mellowing influences of contact with other peoples as well as the toleration which comes with admixture of blood. Their country was less attractive to marauders, besides being out of the beaten track of the migrations. The mountaineers to the east and north served as buffers against the great waves from the northeast, until they were subdued or denationalized by forced colonization. Thus, in contrast with the Babylonians, who became a much mixed people, the Assyrians preserved the purity of their race and consequently its primitive characteristics, among them that of fierceness (Isa. xxxiii, 19). This quality of a new people is illustrated in the case of two other Semitic peoples. The ferocity of the Chaldeans (c. 600 B.C.) is attributable to the fact that they, too, were a "new people," only recently from their Arabian habitat; and the fanaticism of the Mohammedan hosts is a matter of history, due not merely to religious causes. The isolation of the Assyrians is in nothing more remarkably illustrated than in the fact that their literature was of late importation from the south, subsequent to their great military operations, much of it in the days of Asshurbanipal (669–626 B.C.). Another trait of this people is a national self-consciousness lacking to most Semites. The larger cities of Assyria do not appear as self-governing units bearing impatiently the sway of the overlord. Assyria appears almost without exception as united; and the exceptions come from dissensions in the royal family in disputes about the succession.

The occupations of the people are largely included in the two words "war" and "commerce."

2. Occupations. The early Assyrian contract tablets found in Cappadocia bear testimony to a commercial enterprise which prophesied of the wars of the future. It has been correctly concluded by several historians that the object of campaigns was not alone extension of territory, but that security and enlargement of trading operations had their part in the purposes of the warring kings. This finds warrant not so much in the express words of the inscriptions as in indirect hints such as are found in the Amarna Tablets (q.v.) and in the usages of the times as represented by Ahab and Ben-hadad (I Kings xx, 34). Of other occupations, agriculture has already been assumed (see II, § 4, above), as also the handicrafts in the mention of the metals. Casting was known, and there has been found a mold for arrow-heads of accurate construction, in four parts, in which three heads could be cast at the same time. The representations of siege operations show ingenuity in the mechanical construction of implements of offensive warfare.

The language belongs also to the North Semitic group, and is very close to the Babylonian, differing only dialectically.

3. Language. The expression of it in the cuneiform was inherited directly from the Babylonians, indirectly from the pre-Semitic inhabitants of Babylonia, but developing as a consequence of the fact that writing is the expression of a living force, speech.

The culture of Assyria was borrowed. In nothing is this clearer than in their methods of building.

4. The Culture not Native. Although they lived in a land where stone was easily procured, the principal building material was sun-dried brick, in the more pretentious structures faced with burnt brick and sometimes with stone. Even the choice of sites, near the rivers where platforms had to be erected to avoid floods, was probably due to early habit acquired in Babylonia or imitated. To this method and material of building were due the constant repetition of building operations on the great temple-structures and the narratives of the same in the annals of both countries. Roof-making was, from a structural point of view, evidently most imperfectly developed. When once the roof was broken, and the elements had access to the unburnt brick, swift collapse of a structure was inevitable. Yet to this very fact in most cases is attributable the preservation of the libraries and records unearthed; for the superincumbent clay sealed hermetically the chambers used as repositories. In the way of literature nothing creative appears to have come from the Assyrians except the mere narratives of the campaigns. The tablets containing the portions of the epics are known to be copies from the south. The elegant style of Asshurbanipal's annals suggests that the formative period of Assyrian literature was just beginning, but the speedy collapse of the empire prevented any ripening into creative work.

VI. The History.—1. **Chronology:** The crucial datum is the mention of an eclipse in the eponymate of Pur-shagali in the month Sivan (May–June). A total eclipse occurred at Nineveh, June 15, 763 B.C., thus fixing the year of Pur-shagali's eponymate. The bearing of this on Assyrian chronology appears below. Other data are afforded by the *Eponym Canon*, found in the library of Asshurbanipal, a sort of calendar in which succeeding years are named respectively for officers of state. There are several sets of these, all incomplete, but often overlapping each other, and in these synchronistic parts showing that they are not replicas of each other, but in some cases independent documents. They cover consecutively the period 902–667 B.C. and give the succession of the kings as well as of the eponyms, often including a short statement of the principal events of the year. In a succession like this, if the date of one is fixed, that of the rest follows; the eclipse just mentioned furnishes the desired fixed date. On these two sets of data hangs nearly all of Assyrian and Babylonian chronology, as well as that of some of the contemporary nations. The *Canon of Ptolemy* (Greek), is an appendix to the astronomical work of Claudius Ptolemæus, based on solar and lunar eclipses and using Babylonian sources. This was successfully employed to indicate the order in which the *Eponym Canon* should be arranged. The *Synchronistic History of Babylonia and Assyria* (cuneiform) gives an enumeration of Babylonian kings and contemporary Assyrian monarchs, and covers the periods 1400–1050 and 900–800 B.C. The *Babylonian Chronicle* (cuneiform) covers the period 744–668 B.C., during the Assyrian dominance, and therefore throws light on Assyrian chronology or corroborates results otherwise obtained. For the early periods dependence must be placed upon isolated data. Thus, Sennacherib, in the rock inscription at Bavian (Schrader, *KB*, ii, 116 sqq.) alleges that he restored to the temple E-kallati images carried off to Babylon by Marduk-nadin-ahi 418 years earlier in the days of Tiglath-Pileser I. This is practically corroborated by the Babylonian king's statement that in his tenth regnal year he gained a victory over Assyria. The date of restoration was 689 B.C., putting the date when the images were carried off at 1107 B.C., making the coronation year of the Babylonian 1117 B.C., and establishing the contemporaneity of the kings. Sennacherib mentions another fact which (though in round numbers and therefore slightly suspicious) places Tiglath-Nindar (or Ninib), son of Shalmaneser I, about the year 1289 B.C. Similarly, Tiglath-Pileser I (dated above) records a fact which places the death of his great-grandfather Asshur-Dan c. 1175 B.C. He also gives the date of the rebuilding of a temple by the patesi (see BABYLONIA) Shamshi-Ramman as 641 years earlier, thus placing the latter c. 1815 B.C. Further data are obtained by mention of the ancestors of different monarchs. When Ramman-Nirari calls himself son of Pud-il, grandson of Bel-nirari, great-grandson of Asshur-Uballit, he serves a useful purpose by naming a succession of four kings. Tiglath-Pileser I announces that the Shamshi-Ramman whom he dates was son of Ishmi-Dagan, and that both were patesis of Assyria. This datum shows also that in their time Assyria was not independent, since *patesi* is not the title of an independent ruler. These data give results upon which in most cases agreement is reached by scholars within the margin of a year.

1. Sources and Results.

2. **Ethnological Data:** Gutium (Assyr. *Kutu*) was situated northeast from Nineveh, and stretched from the headwaters of the Upper Zab to Lake Urumiah. It is probably referred to in Gen. xiv. The *Namri* occupied the southern part of the Zagros mountain range, between Media and Assyria, east of the Lower Zab. The *Madai* and *Manda*, later known as the *Umman-Manda*, were Aryan tribes beyond the Namri to the east of the mountains and toward the Caspian. The *Kasshi*, sometimes confused in the Old Testament (the unpointed Hebrew is the same) with Cush (Ethiopia), were northeastern neighbors of the Elamites and gave a long-lived dynasty to Babylonia. The *Kaldu*, later known as the Chaldeans, occupied the territory north and west of the head of the Persian Gulf and became rulers of Babylonia when the Assyrian empire fell. The *Manni* or *Minni* inhabited the territory between lakes Van and Urumiah, and were sturdy foes of the Assyrians. The *Urartu* or Armenians dwelt in the Armenian mountains and valleys northwest of Lake Van, and partly controlled the plains at the foot. They were perhaps the most difficult foes the Assyrians had to meet. The *Mitanni*, during the rise of Assyria, held Upper Mesopotamia c. 1400 B.C., and are supposed to have been a Hittite power. By their position they controlled the trade route between the Upper Tigris, the Mediterranean, and the West. *Gozan*, later *Gauzanitis*, was a district on the upper waters of the Chabur. *Bit-Adini* was the Aramean state north of the confluence of the Chabur with the Euphrates. *Kummuḫ* was a state considerably to the north of Bit-Adini on the southern spurs of the Taurus Mountains. In the northeastern part of Syria, north of where Antioch was situated later, not quite contemporary with each other were the Aramean states of *Patin*, *Unki*, *Samal*, *Gurgum*, and *Yaudi*—the latter for many years mistaken by Assyriologists for Judah, particularly as it had a king named *Azriyahu* nearly contemporary with Azariah of Judah. It lay between Samal and Unki (cf. Winckler, *Altorientalische Forschungen*, i, 1893). *Kue* was the name of the eastern part of the coast of Cilicia. Northeast from Kue was the *Muṣri* of Asia Minor (confused in I Kings x, 28 and II Kings vii, 6 with Egypt, though mentioned in connection with Syria and the Hittites in both passages; in the former passage the name *Kue* is perhaps concealed in the word *ma-koh*). Still farther to the north were the

1. Peoples and Places Named in Assyrian Annals.

Mushke, known to the Greeks as *Moschi*. The Phenicians, the Syrians of Aleppo, Hamath, Arpad, and Damascus are all frequently mentioned in the inscriptions, as are the Hebrew kingdoms, Edom, Moab, Ammon, and Philistia. Arabia was known as *Arabi*, *Arubu*, and *Aribi*. In North Arabia the cuneiform makes known a district called *Muṣri* or *Miṣr*, also mistaken in the Hebrew of I Kings xi. 17, for *Miṣraim*, Egypt. It was subdued by Tiglath-Pileser III. South Arabian inscriptions also name the locality. In the same region was a district called *Cush*, sometimes confused with Ethiopia. *Meluḫḫa*, the *Ma'in* of the Old Testament, was in North Arabia. *Saba*, the Sheba of I Kings x, 1, *Minaea*, rediscovered by Glaser, and *Yaman*, probably the modern Yemen, are all noted in the annals of the kings. Northeast Arabia was known as *Magan*.

3. The Story of Assyria: The history of Assyria before 1800 B.C. is veiled. Gen. x, 11 (R. V margin) affirms the Babylonian background of this people, and all evidence from archeology, language, and cultural remains, supports the affirmation. The date of colonization is unknown, but it was before 2300 B.C. Asshur was the first city. The connection with the parent country was close c. 2000 B.C. Hammurabi of Babylon (c. 2250 B.C.) had Assyrian soldiers in his army. No ruler earlier than Ishmi-Dagan (c. 1850 B.C.) is known, and he bore the title of *patesi* (or *isshaku*), a term that implied political dependence. In the time of his son, Shamshi-Ramman, Nineveh was already in existence; for he restored a temple of Ishtar there. Between his time and that of Asshur-bel-nisheshu only a few names are known. Igur-kapkapu (or Bel-kapkapu or Bel-bani) and his son Shamshi-Ramman II, Kallu and his son Irishum are all, but of the first it is known that a tablet exists dated in his reign, and (from it) that he bore the title of king. Assyrian contract tablets belonging to the period 1800–1500 B.C. have been found in Cappadocia, indicating commercial, and perhaps a beginning of territorial, expansion. At the time when Thothmes III of Egypt was most active, the Assyrian king sent him a gift of "a great stone of lapis-lazuli" which Thothmes interpreted as a sign of submission, and so recorded it. If Assyria really feared Egypt, that fear did not last long, for the Hittites were soon active, and Egyptian aggression did not threaten the Tigris.

1. Early History and Names, to 1500 B.C.

2. The Winning of Independence, 1500–1300 B.C.

The independence of Assyria, won soon afterward, was due, not to Assyria's strength, but to the weakness of the parent power. Internal strife gave the Kasshites the opportunity to conquer Babylonia, but they were too busy cementing their own power to attack Assyria, and the boundary was settled under Asshur-bel-nisheshu and Puzu-Asshur in treaties to which the Kasshite Karaindash of Babylon was one of the parties. This implies independence. About 1400 B.C., fifty years later, the Babylonian Burnaburiash claimed Assyria for his territory. The probable dependence of Nineveh upon Tushratta of Mitanni has been noted above (IV. § 2). Assur-uballit wrote to Amenophis IV as an independent monarch; and indeed the claim of Assyria to Babylon began in the same reign. The Assyrian's daughter had married Kara-kardash of Babylon, and the latter's son had succeeded his father and then been murdered by his subjects. Asshur-uballit intervened, subjected Babylon, and placed another grandson on the throne. In the same reign and the next the Assyrian arms were carried to the borders of Elam, which led to war between Kurigalzu II of Babylon and Bel-nirari in which the northern cause was successful. Ramman-nirari I (c. 1345–30 B.C.) reconquered the lands already overrun, and located cities for their government. He extended his sway beyond the Euphrates, and had a successful essay against Mitanni. New troubles with Babylonia arose over the conquest of Gutium; both sides claimed the victory, but the Assyrian boundary was advanced. Ramman's inscription is the earliest one of Assyria that is dated, and in it he calls himself king, not of Asshur, but of *Kisshati*, "the world."

3. Shalmaneser I–Tiglath-Pileser I, 1300–1100 B.C.

Shalmaneser I (c. 1300 B.C.) left on his successors an impression of greatness. He crossed the Euphrates and pushed his conquests as far as Muṣri, which probably means that the territory up to the river at least was added to Assyrian territory. Asshur was abandoned as the capital, and Calah was built. The temple of Ishtar at Nineveh was also reconstructed, and Harran was added to the possessions of the king. Shalmaneser's son, Tiglath-Ninib, invaded Babylonia, captured and plundered Babylon, partly destroyed the wall, carried north with him the image of Marduk, governed the south from his own capital, and assumed the titles borne by Sargon the Great (see BABYLONIA), king of Sumer and Akkad, as well as of Kisshati and Asshur. But he could not sustain himself, and lost his life in a rebellion headed by his son. For a time the Assyrian star declined. It is very likely that to this decline the Hittites had contributed; for the dash to the Mediterranean must have aroused them and certainly have included in its scope some of their cities. The Babylonians became the aggressors, and the next king, Asshurnasirpal I had difficulty in repelling them. Under the next four reigns Assyria's territory shrank to about its original extent. Then Assur-Dan I (c. 1210–1181 B.C.) began to regain territory south of the Lower Zab. His grandson, Asshur-rish-ishi, cleared the way to Babylon by conquering foes on the southeast, and then defeated Nebuchadrezzar I of Babylon. He rebuilt the Ishtar-temple in Calah. With Tiglath-Pileser I began a new era for Assyria. The celebrated eight-sided prism contains a part of his record. That full information of his predecessors' activity is not at hand is shown by his having in the very beginning of his reign to subdue people so distant as the Mushke. He won a victory over them among their hills, destroyed 14,000 out of the 20,000 engaged, and pursued the plan of subduing the territory by destroying the fighting forces. Tribute was exacted from the rest. During the next three years he carried his arms into the mountain regions northeast, northwest, and southeast with the uniform result of success and immense booty. A confederation of twenty-three kings from the neighborhood of Lake Van was overcome, and heavy tribute imposed. Muṣri was once more subdued, and Babylonia had to submit. At the end of his fifth year Tiglath-Pileser claimed to have subdued "forty-two countries with their rulers." Mention of the Hittites first occurs in his reign.

At this point it is well to note, in explanation of the preceding and of much that follows, a characteristic of early Semitic rule.

4. Semitic Rule Unstable.

Constant reconquest of subjected territory was necessary The order of events was: subjection and a light tribute if submission had been ready, a heavy one if strong opposition had been offered; this was invariably followed by rebellion at the first seeming opportunity, and a change in the ruler was always considered an opportunity; then new subjection and a heavier tribute; when rebellion again arose, the case of the rebels was desperate, and further revolt was eliminated by almost complete desolation of the refractory territory. The creation of an empire by unifying peoples under a beneficent rule had not yet been conceived. On the other side was the inherent tendency to segregation, which was a characteristic of the Semites. An invader could reduce city after city, throwing against it the force of his united army, while other cities awaited their fate in trembling. Confederations invariably fell apart. Assyria was the one Semitic power thoroughly unified; and this unity was the cause of its victorious progress until the wars of centuries had sapped its strength.

Tiglath-Pileser's activities were not all warlike; he rebuilt Asshur, restored its temples and palaces, and fostered agriculture and arboriculture.

5. A Time of Quiescence, 1100–950 B.C.

He was followed by two of his sons in succession, who removed the capital to Nineveh once more, restoring its great Ishtar-temple. A new period of quiescence or of exhaustion for Assyria had come, and its enemies organized themselves for new resistance. This resistance coincides with that of the expansion of the Hebrew kingdom. The Arameans had settled in Mesopotamia and fallen heir to the Hittite possessions including Hamath, Aleppo, and Damascus. They were traders, and, holding the caravan routes, directly menaced Assyrian commerce. The Phenicians, too, had been making of their cities strong fortresses. Between Tiglath-Pileser I and II were several rulers whose names are known and little else, while there is also a gap in the known succession. But the period was not the time of entire weakness generally supposed; the outburst of vigor which followed and continued with little intermission for three and one-half centuries proves it a time of development of power which was used in a series of campaigns which have not ceased to astonish since knowledge of them has been regained.

Tiglath-Pileser II (c. 950 B.C.) began a succession of kings, all of whose names are known, though of what either he or his son Asshur-Dan II (c. 930 B.C.) did, little is certain. During the next reign, that of Ramman-nirari II (911–891 B.C.), the

6. Tiglath-Pileser II, 950 B.C.–Asshurnasirpal III, 885–860 B.C.

struggle with Babylonia was renewed, the latter losing territory to its opponent. Tiglath-Ninib (890–885 B.C.) placed under tribute the highlands of the north from Urumiah to the Mediterranean. Asshurnasirpal III (885–860 B.C.), son of the foregoing, carried forward the work of conquest. One of the finest inscriptions extant is his, on alabaster in 389 lines, corroborated by other texts. His first campaign in Armenia was so savage that with a single exception, severely punished, all tribes in his line of march hastened to submit. While on a campaign against Kummuh, he heard of the rebellion of an Aramean community at Bit-Kalupe on the Euphrates. He at once countermarched, took and plundered the city, cut off the legs of the officers engaged in the rebellion, flayed the nobles and stretched their skins on a pile built for the purpose, and sent the rebel governor to Nineveh to be flayed. The result was immediate submission of the district and of all in his line of march. While he was thus engaged in the west, rebellion broke out in the east and southeast, was crushed, broke out again, and was again put down with plundering, devastation, and slaughter. Sedition among the Arameans, fomented and assisted by Nabupaliddin of Babylonia, was overcome, and Suru, the capital, destroyed. The fomenter of the trouble in turn found work in repelling the Aramean hordes and occupation in rebuilding the temple of Shamash at Sippar. Continued rebellion among the Arameans revealed the fact that the little state of Bit-Adini, the *Bene-'Edhen* of II Kings xix, 12, was the cause of the rising. This the Assyrians assailed and destroyed, and showed that they would permit no strong state on the Euphrates. The Mediterranean coast was next visited; tribute was received from the Phenicians; wood was gathered for the new works at Calah; and a memorial was left on the rocks at Nahr-el-Kalb (near Beirut). Asshurnasirpal made the Assyrian name a synonym for ferocity and savagery. Yet war was not his whole occupation. Calah had fallen into ruins while Asshur had been the capital. He rebuilt it, erected there a great palace, and conducted to the city a water-supply from the Lower Zab.

With Shalmaneser II (860–824 B.C.) began contact of the Assyrians with the Hebrews. In the Black Obelisk and the Monolith

7. Shalmaneser II, 860–824 B.C.

texts this king has left some of the finest inscriptions known. These with supplementary records show a personal leadership by the king of his armies for twenty-six consecutive years. Under him began that battering at the gates of Damascus which continued from his time till the city fell in 732 B.C., and then was directed against the Hebrews, Arabs, and Egyptians till about 660 B.C. The three prominent Syrian powers at the time were centered at Hamath, Patin, and Damascus.

A coalition of these with their allies, including Israelites (Ahab furnished a contingent of 2,000 [?] chariots and 10,000 men), Arabs, and Ammonites, was met and defeated at Karkar. The quality of the victory claimed by Shalmaneser is doubtful, since in three inscriptions (the Black Obelisk, Monolith, and Bull; cf. Schrader, *Keilschriftforschung*, p. 47) the number of killed varies from 14,000 to 25,000, and no statement is made of tribute imposed. The victory was barren. There was revealed here a force which might have stayed the advance of Assyria could it have been held together. Six campaigns were made in this region during 854–839 B.C., none decisive in itself, but contributing in the end to the isolation of Damascus. Jehu of Israel sent tribute to divert from himself the attacks of Damascus. With reference to his campaigns in Armenia, Shalmaneser describes himself as "trampling down the country like a wild bull." But there, too, results were indecisive, and the region remained a menace to the dominant power. Media was invaded in a mere booty-snatching expedition. Internal conflict in Babylonia resulted in the reestablishment of Assyrian power there, and in checking the northward march of the Kaldu. The later years of the king were harassed by rebellions at home, led in one case by his sons, and due in part probably to utter weariness at the constant drain caused by the perpetual wars.

8. Shamshi-Ramman IV and his Successors, 824–745 B.C.

This legacy of civil war was left to the son Shamshi-Ramman IV (824–812 B.C.), who used two years in defeating his brother and in repressing the general rebellion of the provinces. A coalition of Babylonians, Elamites, Southern Arameans, and Kaldu was met and defeated and quiet restored after two campaigns. Payment of tribute was forced in different regions only by the presence of the army. His son, Ramman-nirari III (812–783 B.C.), who called himself a descendant of Igur-(Bel-)kapkapu, reduced Damascus to tributary relationship. The entire eastern coast of the Mediterranean contributed to his exchequer. A series of eight campaigns against the Medes took this king to the Caspian, and the south to the Persian Gulf was tributary. He made an attempt to weld religiously Babylonia and Assyria by the introduction of Babylonian cults into Nineveh, while Babylonia was treated as an Assyrian province. With the next king, Shalmaneser III (783–773 B.C.), began a period of decadence which continued for three reigns. Campaigns to enforce payment of tribute are mentioned, but Armenia in the mean time gained in power. Under Asshur-Dan III (773–755 B.C.) the story of rebellion and disaster grows. The eclipse of the sun, 763 B.C., and pestilence in 759 and 754 were events of this reign. Asshur-nirari II (755–745 B.C.) left fewer notices, but enough to make evident that warlike attempts were not altogether discontinued. In an uprising at Calah he disappeared, and with him the dynasty which had ruled at least since Tiglath-Pileser II.

9. Tiglath-Pileser III, 745–727 B.C.

Under the great Tiglath-Pileser III (745–727 B.C.), the Pul of II Kings xv, 19, Assyria recovered at a bound her greatest former eminence and surpassed it. The origin of the new king is unknown, for in his numerous inscriptions he never mentions his ancestry. His vigor and boldness of conception and swiftness of execution were unparalleled even in Assyrian history. Babylonia, during the period of Assyria's weakness, had been unable to take advantage of relief from pressure, owing to attacks by the Arameans. Tiglath-Pileser invaded the country, repelled the Arameans, reorganized the government, and conciliated the inhabitants by paying homage to the chief deities. The districts east were reconquered, and a new policy carried out of settling disaffected subjects in a distant part of the empire. Urartu, under a king named Sarduris II, had completely demolished Assyrian supremacy in the north. A single sweeping victory over him changed all this, and his allies paid their tribute to the conqueror. Arpad fell in 740 B.C., and with it the northwest was pacified. A new coalition of states of Syria, Asia Minor, and Palestine was formed; but at the appearance in the field of the Assyrian forces, it fell apart, Menahem of Israel paid tribute, the states north of Israel were put under a governor, their inhabitants deported, and colonists brought in from other parts. A rebellion near Nineveh was suppressed by the governors, who had been made responsible for good order. They deported the rebellious subjects to Syria and settled Syrians in their places. Armenia was crippled in a campaign which reached the capital on Lake Van, but did not capture it. Tiglath-Pileser began next to clear the road to Egypt, just then weakened by attacks from Ethiopia. Syria was effectually overawed, Phenicia paid tribute, and Gaza was captured and held as an outpost. To offset this, Israel and Damascus had determined to force Judah into an alliance against the Assyrian. Ahaz was thoroughly alarmed, and all the efforts of Isaiah were insufficient to restrain him from throwing himself into the arms of Assyria. Tiglath-Pileser listened to the appeal, ravaged Israel, had Hoshea made king (II Kings xv–xvi), assailed Damascus, destroyed its dependencies, and finally captured it in 732 B.C. While engaged in the west, the king heard of rebellion in Babylonia. This was punished; and Merodach-baladan, who proved almost a perennial rebel, submitted. The Assyrian appointed governors from the north instead of leaving native princes to rule, did homage to the gods of the land, in 726 B.C. "took the hands of Bel," the annual right and duty of the rightful king of Babylon, and assumed the name Pul with the old title "King of Sumer and Akkad and of Babylon" (see BABYLONIA). Tiglath-Pileser's death occurred the next year. His achievements in war and in government were the greatest the world had yet known. The Semitic crescent of territory from the Persian Gulf to the border of Egypt was his without dispute; tribute was sent from Arabia as far south as Sabæa, from Armenia, from Elam, and from the states on the Mediterranean. The policy of exchanging populations of chronically rebellious states had made the empire more homogeneous by putting seditious nations where circumstances did not favor risings.

Of Tiglath-Pileser's successor, Shalmaneser IV (727–722 B.C.), but little is known, not even his relationship to his predecessor. Under

10. Shalmaneser IV, 727–722 B.C. him Hoshea was led into what proved the final rebellion of the northern Israelitic kingdom, and the episode narrated in II Kings xvii occurred. In this chapter Hoshea is represented as sending messengers to "So, king of Egypt." So has been erroneously identified with Shabak. Sargon mentions a *Shabi* of the Arabian Muẓri; *Shabi* in Assyrian would represent the Hebrew word *So* pointed to read *Seve;* and modern scholars are inclined to follow Winckler (*Mittheilungen der vorderasiatischen Gesellschaft,* i, 5) and see a double confusion in *Miẓraim* ("Egypt") for *Muẓri,* and in *So* for *Seve.* It is to the point that this Shabi furnished no little trouble for Sargon, Shalmaneser's successor. From him, then, Hoshea expected help and rebelled, when Shalmaneser attacked, defeated, and captured him, and invested Samaria. The city held out for three years. Meanwhile Shalmaneser died and was succeeded by Sargon (722–705 B.C.). Samaria was captured in 721; and the Israelitic kingdom ceased to exist.

Sargon's ancestry is very doubtful: he claimed no royal lineage, nor did his son for him; but his grandson, Sennacherib, connected him

11. Sargon, 722–705 B.C. with the Igur-kapkapu mentioned above. He reproduced the traits of the great Tiglath-Pileser III—self-confidence, vigor in plan and action, and great military and administrative ability. In Babylonia the determined rebel Merodach-baladan seized Babylon with the help of the Elamites; Sargon claimed the victory in the battle which ensued, but Merodach retained his crown. In the west Hamath raised the flag of rebellion, and Shabi of Musri and Hanno of Gaza engaged to support Hamath; but Sargon attacked the town before the allies could come in, then marched south, and defeated Shabi at Raphia. The next rising was in the north, with Urartu as the backbone of the movement. But Assyria was still able to conquer; and, soon after, the old Hittite center, Carchemish, was destroyed. Campaigns in Media, eastern Asia Minor, and Arabia kept the armies moving. Finally peace was secured in the north by the ending of the kingdom of Urartu, which had for centuries defied Assyria and proved its most dangerous foe. A new uprising in Palestine, Philistia, Edom, and Moab, involving Hezekiah of Judah and evidently fomented by Egypt (Isa. xx), necessitated the sending of Sargon's tartan with an army, who occupied the Philistine cities, deported the inhabitants, and crushed the rebellion. The other states seem to have escaped punishment. Only Babylon was needed to round out the empire. Merodach-baladan had foreign military forces in support; but he had alienated the native priests, the most influential class of his subjects. They called in the Assyrians, who put the Chaldeans to flight; and Sargon was acclaimed the deliverer of the city of Babylon. He performed sacrifice and took office as viceroy (not king), and restored the temple-worship in the great religious centers. In the northwest, boundaries were pushed back, and even Cyprus sent tribute. Sargon built Dur-Sharrukin with its magnificent palace, but occupied it only a year.

Sargon was succeeded by his son Sennacherib (705–681 B.C.). The change in succession was followed by another attempt of Mero-

12. Sennacherib, 705–681 B.C. dach-baladan to possess Babylonia. It is likely that the embassy to Hezekiah (II Kings xviii, 13) occurred here. If so, its motive is plain: he was fomenting a revolt in the west to create a diversion while he settled himself in the south. But Sennacherib marched south at once, defeated the rebel, captured Babylon, rifled the palace, and then punished severely the Aramean supporters of the Kaldu, appropriating immense booty and removing, according to the Taylor cylinder, over 200,000 people and settling them in the Median mountains after a successful campaign there. The rebellion fomented by Merodach (if the suggestion above be correct) had gathered headway, with Hezekiah leading the movement, the latter having seized Philistia. The revolt must have been general; for Sennacherib first visited Phenicia, captured Sidon, set up his appointee as king, and apportioned him a fair kingdom. The coalition fell apart before his army, though several of the Philistine towns held out and were reduced. An army from Egypt was defeated, Ekron captured, and its chiefs impaled. Then Sennacherib turned on Judah, captured forty-six towns, deported 200,150 inhabitants, and gave the district to his governors in Philistia to manage. Hezekiah submitted and paid tribute, to gather which he was compelled to strip palace and temple. Sennacherib, either at this time or later, sent a small force to demand the surrender of Jerusalem. Beyond question the reason for this was that the conquest of Egypt was projected, and the Assyrian did not care to leave so strong a fortress as Jerusalem in his rear. The surrender was refused; the forces were withdrawn; a new campaign in Babylonia against the irrepressible Merodach-baladan was successfully carried through; and Asshur-nadin-shum, son of Sennacherib, was put on the throne of Babylon. The next eleven years were spent mainly in the south against the Elamites and Kaldu under Merodach-baladan. After holding the country for some time the allies were defeated in 691 B.C. after a terrible conflict. Babylon was taken, sacked, burned to the ground, the waters of the Euphrates turned upon the site, and the statue of Marduk taken to Asshur. A final expedition against Egypt was probably undertaken near the end of his life by Sennacherib. Tirhakah of Egypt advanced to meet him, perhaps as far as Pelusium. There Sennacherib experienced a severe check, variously explained. II Kings ix, 35 tells of a pestilence which destroyed in a single night 185,000 men; Tirhakah claimed credit for a great victory; Herodotus (ii, 141) was told by the Egyptians that field-mice gnawed the bow-strings and quivers of the Assyrians and left them defenseless before the Egyptians; and the *Babylonian Chronicles* suggest the necessity for return in a rebellion in that region. Sennacherib was killed in 681 B.C. by one (*Babylonian Chronicle*) or two (II Kings xix, 36–37) of his sons. He had removed the seat of government from Calah to Nineveh, and built there the "peerless" palace, and had provided the city with a system of water-works.

13. Esar-haddon, 681–668 B.C.

Esar-haddon (681–668 B.C.), Sargon's son, who succeeded him, reversed the policy toward Babylonia. He assumed the title of viceroy of Babylon, and almost at once set about rebuilding the city in a style of greater grandeur. By restoring the gods carried away by his father he regained the good-will of the people. His first care, however, was to avenge the death of Sennacherib and to secure his own position in Nineveh, whence his brothers, the murderers, who had seized the throne, fled on his approach. The extreme south, again in rebellion, was subdued and the projected invasion of Egypt was undertaken. But first the rebellion of Phenicia had to be quelled, in which three years were occupied, when Sidon was destroyed, a new city built and settled by colonists. Tyre was assailed; but its sea-gate enabled it to hold out. In 783 B.C. Tirhakah was enabled to repel the first attack on Egypt; but Esar-haddon renewed the attempt three years later, was successful in three battles, and occupied Memphis. The land was parceled out for government, and no great opposition was offered by the people, to whom the disaster seemed beyond repair. Northeastern Arabia was then subdued that it might no longer afford assistance to the recurrent rebellions of Palestine. New troubles were by that time affecting the northern boundaries. The Indo-European migration, generally known as the Cimmerian or Scythian, had begun. This was split into two bodies, one of which pressed down into Persia and Media and settled there, and the other passed westward. The former occupied a part of what had been Assyrian territory, and later formed a part of the force which captured Nineveh. The latter passed through Armenia; but its forces were prevented by Esar-haddon from penetrating southward. In 668 B.C. the king was called to Egypt by rebellion there. Before leaving, he had one son proclaimed his successor in Assyria (Asshurbanipal) and another in Babylon (Shamash-shum-ukin). He died the same year, and before reaching Egypt, having extended Assyrian domination farther than it had yet reached. He was fond of building, and constructed the great arsenal at Nebi-Yunus, the materials for which were contributed by twenty-two kings and princes, ten of them in Cyprus. The name of Manasseh of Judah appears in this list of tributaries.

14. Asshur-banipal, 668–626 B.C.

The events of the reign of Asshurbanipal (668–626 B.C.; Greek, *Sardanapalus*, Aram. *Osnappar*, Ezra iv, 10) are hard to make out, not because of paucity of material, for it is abundant, nor because of roughness or carelessness, for the annals are elegant and polished, but because the chronological clue is not given. It is clear, however, that his first movement was to the border-land between Elam and Babylonia, where his presence prevented serious trouble. A new invasion of Egypt was made necessary by Tirhakah's return, the Assyrian forces being gathered partly on the Mediterranean coast. Tirhakah was defeated, and the country occupied this time as far south as Thebes. A new rising which took place almost immediately was as quickly punished in ruthless fashion, and enormous booty was sent home. A third insurrection under the son of the now dead Tirhakah was futile. Tyre had finally submitted and sent tribute. But the story continues of revolts in different parts of the empire which presage its speedy fall. The king was occupied in desperate attempts to maintain himself. Participation in these led to the conquest of Elam up to the very walls of Susa. Even his brother on the throne of Babylon revolted; but Asshurbanipal's movements were swift and sure. Babylon, Borsippa, Sippara, and Cutha were beset; Shamash-shum-ukin in despair burned himself in his own palace; and people from the captured towns were settled in Samaria. A new challenge from Elam was accepted; and finally Susa was taken with immense booty. The usual success attended the king's final campaign in Arabia. The results of this long succession of successful wars was the heaping up of enormous wealth in the cities of Assyria, particularly in Nineveh. The end of a victorious campaign was the transportation of precious metals, works of art, flocks, and herds, and, in the later reigns, of people as slaves to Assyria. The great works of the Assyrian kings were doubtless in great part the product of the toil of captives. And the captors of Nineveh fell heir to this immense wealth. Asshurbanipal's wars were not his only interest. Apart from the palace which he built, the walls of which were lined with sculptured reliefs, he was fond of the hunt, and his contests with lions are frequently portrayed. Most significant for modern times was his interest in literature. His library, uncovered by George Smith, was amassed by the copying of tablets from libraries in the south, and contained works on history, ethics, science, religion, and linguistics.

15. Asshur-banipal's Successors, 626–606 B.C.

Asshurbanipal was succeeded by his son Asshur-etil-ilani, of whom it is known that he built or restored the temple E-zida in Calah, and that during his fourth year he claimed the title of king of Sumer and Akkad. Whether a Sin-shum-lishir next reigned is not known; but mention of him as a king of Assyria has been found. A Sin-shar-ishkun is known from three tablets from Sippar and Erech. In his seventh year he was still king of a part of Babylonia, though not of Babylon, over which Nabopolassar had established himself. Upon an invasion of Babylonia by the Assyrian, Nabopolassar invoked the aid of the Umman-Manda, and Sin-shar-ishkun was forced to retreat, Nabopolassar securing the provinces as the former evacuated them. It seems that one branch of the Scythians were allies of the Assyrians at this time and actually defeated the armies of the assailants, thus prolonging the life of Nineveh. The rush of the Scythians, which so terrified western Asia and elicited the prophecies of Nahum and Zephaniah (Driver, *Introduction*, 5th ed., 1894, pp. 314–320), is to be explained by their alliance with Assyria and a desire to attack Egypt, the king of which, Psammetichus, had assailed Philistia. Their sudden disappearance is as remarkable as their unheralded coming.

The Umman-Manda returned soon to Nineveh. The story of the siege is unknown; but the city fell 607–606 B.C., and its vast treasures became the nucleus of the tremendous wealth of the later Persian empire. With it fell the empire which twenty-five years earlier had controlled all southwestern Asia.

VII. The Religion: From the relationship of Assyrians and Babylonians set forth in the preceding it would be expected that both resemblances and differences would be found to exist in the two religions. The resemblances are as follows: (1) The general character of the cults is the same; the liturgies, prayers, psalms are often identical, as are some of the deities. (2) The goddesses are of minor importance in Assyria, appearing hardly as prominent as in the southern land. Theoretically the gods had consorts; practically these are but shadows and a name. (3) The great exceptions to this in both countries were the Ishtars; to the extent exhibited below, the pantheons were the same, at least in theory (see BABYLONIA). The dissimilarities are: (1) Asshur assumes the character of a national god as far back as he can be traced. (2) His aloofness is a new feature; he in particular seems ever without consort and family. (3) The next difference needs stating at some length. In their annals the Babylonians laid great stress upon their temple-building, even more than upon wars and the construction of palaces. From the emphasis laid upon religion, and the care taken to house the divinities and provide for their maintenance, the country seems priest-ridden, with the kings devoted first of all to religion. The Assyrians, on the other hand, while indeed they often built or restored temples, devoted much less space to the recital of their operations and put far less emphasis on the story of this activity than on that attending their wars and the construction of their palaces. They seemed less absorbed in their religion, though not less devout when worshiping. It is a case of correctly reading in a lesser abundance of matter a lower quality of intensity. Religion seemed less on the Assyrian's mind. (4) The pantheon was much smaller. Tiglath-Pileser I, one of the most pious of Assyrian monarchs, names Asshur, Bel (rarely named elsewhere), Sin, Ramman, Ninib, and Ishtar. Shalmaneser II mentions on the obelisk, in addition to the gods of Tiglath-Pileser I, Anu, Ea, Marduk, Nergal, Nusku, and Belit. It is just the deities mentioned here which were most generally disregarded; and their notice by this king is doubtless to be traced to his attempt to fuse more closely the north and the south. Asshurbanipal omits Anu, Ea, Marduk, and Belit, but mentions two Ishtars and adds Nebo. But a caveat should be entered here, which is justified by knowledge of facts existing in other lands where a similar civilization had been attained; as in Oriental countries generally, so in Assyria there were an aristocratic or official cult and a popular and democratic cult. The pantheon of the kings, particularly of Tiglath-Pileser, represented the former; the peasant and farmer worshiped the gods and spirits of field, tree, and fountain, and these did not get into the inscriptions.

1. Relation to Babylonian Religion.

The chief of the Assyrian pantheon, not found in the pantheon of Babylonia, was Asshur. His derivation and origin are obscure, though there is some plausibility in the suggestion that he was ultimately derived from Anu, the heaven-god of Babylonia. But it is possible that Asshur the city was not originally Semitic, and that the local god was adopted by the Semitic colonists. As that city was for a long period the capital, he became the chief deity. The great triad of the south was entirely subordinated and lost; Anu, Bel, and Ea find scanty mention in the god-lists of the kings. The significance of Asshur is that he stands for nationalism. His position from the first seems more elevated, his attitude has in it more of aloofness and abstraction than even Marduk ever attained in the south. Moreover, he never appears to be chained to a locality. Whatever city was the capital, there he made his abode. His symbol or representation was not an image, but a winged disk surmounted by the figure of an archer discharging his shaft. This served also as a military standard, and accompanied the armies in their campaigns. While individual kings could and did choose what may be called individual patrons among the gods, Asshur was always the nation's guardian and protagonist, the unquestioned chief. Yet it must be noted that in spite of this reverence, even when Assyria most completely dominated Babylonia, there was no attempt to displace Marduk or Shamash or any other of the southern deities by Asshur; his domain was his own country, and there was honor among the gods, precluding one from usurping the due of another. Sayce was the first to point out that in this deity and the conceptions about him there was the possibility of all the greatness of a monotheism such as developed in the conception of Yahweh. Asshur's position was unique, without wife or family, a consideration which doubtless had much to do with the elevation of the conception which was formed of his being. There seems every reason to assume that he was originally a sun-deity, but this feature is not prominent in the original records in which he figures. The other gods form, after a fashion, his retinue or court, but even this feature is far less pronounced than in the case of Marduk.

2. Asshur.

Ishtar was in Assyria never one, but at least three; she of Nineveh, of Arbela, and of Kitmur (a city of which almost nothing is known). The first two were the most prominent; and both appear to have been above all goddesses of battle. Ishtar of Kitmur ruled in the domain of love. In the south this goddess reached her eminence by absorbing

3. Ishtar.

or assimilating the beings, functions, and rites of local goddesses, such as Nana of Erech, Nina and Bau of Shirpurla, Sarpanit of Babylon, and Anunit. In neither place was she originally a moon-deity; this function appears in late times, and generally in the west after she had become associated, often as consort, with Baal as sun-god. In some cases religious prostitution was associated with her cult: but it was not, as is so often supposed, exclusively or primarily her rite. The origin of name and goddess is obscure. Nearly, if not quite, all Semitic peoples had a deity of the name, though Athtar of South Arabia was male. The hypothesis of non-Semitic origin seems out of court, in view of the universality of her cult among Semites; and yet no satisfactory Semitic etymology has been found. If she was a loan-goddess, she was borrowed in the prehistoric age of the Semitic peoples. The Ishtar of Nineveh ranked next to Asshur in estimation, was to the Assyrians Belit ("the Lady"), as Asshur was Bel ("the Lord"); yet, as is implied in the foregoing, she was never his consort. "Goddess of Battle," "Princess of Heaven and Earth," "Queen of All," are titles given her. In the religious literature she is invoked as the "gracious mother of creation, the giver of plenty, hearer of the supplications of the sinner," and as the goddess of fertility. It was partly out of this latter conception that the debasing worship grew which attended her as the Oriental Aphrodite. The functions of the various Ishtars were quite the same; and there is more of the primitive attachment to locality than in the case of Asshur. (See Ashtoreth.)

4. Ramman.

The deity who seemed to rank third, at any rate if one may judge by the frequency with which his name was used in the formation of proper names, was Ramman, the thunderer, god of storms, and probably in consequence of this, also of fertility and fruitfulness. He was identified with Hadad or Adad, a deity of Syria, one of whose principal seats was Aleppo. There has always been considerable doubt whether his name, which in the cuneiform is represented by the sign IM, should be read *Ramman* or *Hadad*. The name has been found in the region of Van in the cuneiform written phonetically *Hadad*, so that it is settled that at least the form common in Syria was known in Assyria and used there. But it is not a necessary conclusion that the sign IM is always to be read *Hadad* and never *Ramman*.

5. The Sun-gods Shamash, Ninib, and Nergal.

Doubtless the cults of Asshur, Ishtar, and Ramman were those characteristic of Assyria. But the student of religions will always be alert for signs of sun-worship; and, since Asshur, if he was indeed originally a sun-deity, had been disassociated from that relationship, it would be expected that other deities would represent that phase of early worship. There were three sun-gods in Assyria who had a more or less prominent position, were derived from the south, and were known in both lands as Shamash, Ninib, and Nergal. The first was *par excellence* the sun-god (cf. the Hebr. *shemesh*, "sun"); and the splendor and fervor and inspiration of his ritual almost equals that of Asshur. It is practically certain that he had temples in every city. Ninib became connected among the Assyrians with hunting and sports, and then with war. Nergal represented rather the maleficent, destructive power of the sun; he was, therefore, associated with war as the destroyer, with pestilence, and also with the chase.

6. Sin, the Moon-god. Nusku, the Fire-god.

A religion which derived its elements in large part from a people to whom the moon had been an eminent power would be expected to retain clear traces of that cult. Accordingly Sin, called also Nannar, the pre-Semitic EN-ZU, god of wisdom, who had early seats in Ur and Harran, both connected by the Hebrews' tradition with the father of their race, Abraham, had his seats of worship also in Assyria. The diffused character of his worship will be partly realized when it is remembered that he gave his name to the peninsula of Sinai. He was always closely associated with the endowment of mankind with wisdom. Nusku was a fire-god, then the deity of charms and incantations, a night deity, and also associated with the impartation of knowledge.

7. Rivalry of Babylonia and Assyria.

Other deities had little place in the worship and regard of the people. Mention of them seems rather perfunctory, a sort of parade of piety, or a diplomatic measure of conciliation toward the south, rather than an acknowledgment of their importance for the country or the religion. A factor that swayed mightily the selection of the members of the pantheon—a selection which was instinctive rather than deliberative and planned—was the persistent rivalry of Babylonia and Assyria. It was impossible for the god Marduk to become domiciled in Nineveh or Asshur or Calah, for he was the god of the rival city. Even if he had been more mobile, had the native Babylonian conception of deity been more favorable to a change of residence of the god than it was, the fact mentioned would have impeded his adoption of a seat in the north. But, as has been noted above, even when the arms and star of the Assyrians were thoroughly dominant in the south, no attempt was made to demand that Asshur take his place at the head of the southern pantheon. The image of Marduk was carried to Assyria as a sign of his subjection; but that of Asshur was not installed in his place, so far as any hint goes in the annals accessible. So that the Assyrian recognition of Marduk conveys simply the impression of assent to his lordship in his own land. It is not beyond suspicion that the tendency to favor Nebo was not because he was especially revered, though as the god of oracles he became less chained to a locality and more eligible to general worship than others; more probably he was used by Ramman-nirari and Asshurbanipal to diminish the prestige of the almost hostile god Marduk.

The background and undercurrent of Assyrian religion was thoroughly animistic. Omens of all sorts were consulted; magic of formulas and of material, sympathetic and simple, was everywhere;

sorcery was a constant peril and device; spirits evil and good, maleficent and beneficent, swarmed. The diagnosis of disease was recognition of obsession or infliction of suffering or prevention of health by spirits or deities who must be driven out or exorcised or placated in order to lighten or abolish the suffering or to secure health. The formulas of magic were numerous and potent, the medicine-man or *shaman* as well as the priest thrived. While for king, nobility, army, and priesthood the great gods were supreme, there are hints even in the annals of the kings, and more decided proof in the collections of magical texts, of apprehensions of the lower powers, of hopes that rested not on the gods. Of incantation tablets a whole series give a ritual of "the evil demons." Parts of the body had their appropriate ritual for their preservation from disease and to banish the spirits which chose them as the spheres of their operations. The formulas arose and became fixed because the occasion which produced them appeared to be recurrent. And, as elsewhere in early religion, the exact letter, word, and intonation were essential to success in using them.

8. Magic.

The idea of sin as transgression against the will of the gods was highly developed; and some of the penitential psalms, with the polytheistic expressions eliminated, would fitly express the most pious sentiments of devout Christians in worship of today. The notion of communion between god and man is involved in the elaborate system of omens and oracles which obtained. For ideas of eschatology, the underworld, and future life, see BABYLONIA.

GEO. W. GILMORE.

BIBLIOGRAPHY: On the explorations and discoveries: R. W Rogers, *History of Babylonia and Assyria*, vol. i, New York, 1900; H. V. Hilprecht, *Explorations in Bible Lands*, pp. 1–578, Philadelphia, 1903 (very full and fresh); A. H. Layard, *Nineveh and Its Remains*, 2 vols., London, 1848 49 (an old classic and good for geographical and topographical detail), and as a companion piece, H. Rassam, *Asshur and the Land of Nimrod*, New York, 1897.

On the language: F. Delitzsch, *Assyrische Grammatik*, Leipsic, 1906, Eng. transl., 1889; J. Menant, *Les Langues perdues de la Perse et de l'Assyrie*, Paris, 1885; A. H. Sayce, *Primer of Assyriology*, New York, 1895 (deals with the people, the language, and the whole subject).

For sources: H. C. Rawlinson, *Cuneiform Inscriptions of Western Asia*, 5 vols., London, 1861–84; *Assyriologische Bibliothek*, begun by C. Bezold, continued by F. Delitzsch and P. Haupt, Leipsic, 1886 sqq.; Schrader, *KB*; H. Winckler, *Sammlung von Keilinschriften*, Leipsic, 1893 sqq.; J. A. Craig, *Assyrian and Babylonian Religious Texts*, 2 vols., ib. 1895–97; C. Johnston, *Epistolary Literature of Assyrians and Babylonians*, Baltimore, 1898; R. F. Harper, *Assyrian and Babylonian Letters*, 5 vols., Chicago, 1900–05; idem, *Assyrian Literature*, New York, 1901.

On chronology: A. Kamphausen, *Die Chronologie der hebräischen Könige*, Bonn, 1883; B. G. Niebuhr, *Die Chronologie Babyloniens und Assyriens*, Leipsic, 1896.

On the history the best for the English reader is R. W Rogers, *History of Babylonia and Assyria*, ii, New York, 1900; other works are: F. Hommel, *Geschichte Babyloniens und Assyriens*, Berlin, 1885; C. P. Tiele, *Babylonisch-assyrische Geschichte*, 1886–88; F. Mürdter and F. Delitzsch, *Geschichte von Babylonien und Assyrien*, Stuttgart, 1891; H. Winckler, *Geschichte Babyloniens und Assyriens*, Leipsic, 1892; idem, *Die Völker Vorderasiens*, and *Die politische Entwickelung Babyloniens und Assyriens*, in *Der alte Orient*, I, i, II, i, ib. 1899–1900; G. Maspero, *Dawn of Civilization*, New York, 1894; idem, *The Struggle of the Nations*, 1897; idem, *The Passing of the Empires*, 1900; J. F. McCurdy, *History, Prophecy and the Monuments*, 3 vols., ib. 1894–1901 (gives the parallel development of Israel and the contemporary nations); F. Kaulen, *Assyrien und Babylonien nach den neuesten Entdeckungen*, Freiburg, 1899; L. B. Paton, *Early History of Syria and Palestine*, New York, 1901 (involves the history of Assyria); G. S. Goodspeed, *History of Babylonians and Assyrians*, New York, 1902 (popular).

On special subjects: G. Smith, *History of Assurbanipal*, London, 1871; W. Lotz, *Die Inschriften Tiglath-Pilesers I.*, Leipsic, 1880; E. Schrader, *Die Keilinschriften am Eingange der Quellgrotte des Sebeneh-Su*, Berlin, 1885 (on the reliefs of Tiglath-Pileser I, Tiglath-Ninib, and Asshurnasirpal III at Sebneh); S. A. Smith, *Die Keilschrifttexte Assurbanipals*, Leipsic, 1887–89; H. Winckler, *Die Keilschrifttexte Sargons*, ib. 1889; idem, *Die Inschriften Tiglat-Pilesers I.*, ib. 1893; idem, *Die Keilschrifttexte Assurbanipals*, ib. 1895; B. Meissner and P. Rost, *Die Bauinschriften Sanheribs*, ib. 1893; P. Rost, *Die Keilschrifttexte Tiglat-Pilesers III.*, ib. 1893; D. G. Lyon, *Die Keilschrifttexte Sargons II.*, in *Assyriologische Bibliothek*, I, iv, ib. 1883; H. Winckler, *Altorientalische Forschungen*, 1st series, ib. 1893 97, 2d series, 1898–1901, 3d series, 1902, in progress (I, i, 1893, on Yaudi; I, iv, 1896, on Muzri; I, vi, 1897, on the Cimmerians; II, i, on Esarhaddon; II, ii, 1898, on Tiglath-Pileser III); O. Weber, *Sanherib König von Assyrien*, n *Der alte Orient*, ib. 1905; L. W. King, *Records of the Reign of Tukulti-Ninib I., King of Assyria*, London, 1904; F. Delitzsch and P. Haupt, *Beiträge zur Assyriologie*, ib. 1890–1906 (contains a series of treatises on special topics); on Muzri, Meluhha, and Main, cf. H. Winckler, in *Mitteilungen der vorderasiatischen Gesellschaft*, i and iv, 1898, Schrader, *KAT*, i, 140 sqq., and Winckler, *Geschichte Israels*, i, 150–153, 2 vols., Leipsic, 1895–1900.

On the religion: M. Jastrow, *Religion of Babylonia and Assyria*, Boston, 1898 (revised ed., in German, issued in parts and still in progress, Berlin); J. A. Knudtzon, *Assyrische Gebete an den Sonnengott*, Leipsic, 1894; G. Tanks, *Alttestamentliche Theologie*, Hanover, 1904; A. S. Geden, *Studies in Comparative Religion*, London, 1898.

On the relations of Assyriology to the Old Testament: Schrader, *KAT*, and *COT*; B. T. A. Evetts, *New Light on the Holy Land*, ib. 1891; H. Winckler, *Alttestamentliche Untersuchungen*, Leipsic, 1892; A. H. Sayce, *Higher Criticism and the Monuments*, London, 1894; C. J. Ball, *Light from the East*, ib. 1899; T. G. Pinches, *The Old Testament in the Light of the History . of Assyria and Babylonia*, ib. 1902; H. Winckler, *Keilinschriftliche Textbuch zum Alten Testament*, Leipsic, 1903; J. Jeremias, *Das Alte Testament im Lichte des alten Orients*, ib. 1904; F. Delitzsch, *Babel und Bibel*, Leipsic, 1902, Eng. transl., Chicago, 1906.

Journals of note containing valuable material are: *ZA*; *Revue d'Assyriologie et d'Archéologie Orientale*, Paris; *Orientalische Litteraturzeitung*, Berlin; *American Journal of Semitic Languages and Literatures*, Chicago; *Journal of the Royal Asiatic Society*, London; *Transactions* and *PSBA*, ib. Consult also the literature under BABYLONIA.

ASTARTE. See ASHTORETH.

ASTERIUS, as-tî're-us: Name of twenty-five writers mentioned in Fabricius-Harles (*Bibliotheca Græca*, ix, Hamburg, 1804, 513–522). The following are the more important:

1. Asterius Urbanus: Montanist, editor of a collection of oracles used by the anti-Montanist mentioned in Eusebius, *Hist. Eccl.*, V, xvi, 17.

G. KRÜGER.

BIBLIOGRAPHY: *ANF*, vii, 333–337 (contains introduction and Eng. transl. of fragments); cf. Eusebius, *Hist. Eccl.* by McGiffert, *NPNF*, 2d series, i, 232, note 27.

2. Asterius of Cappadocia: A teacher of rhetoric, converted from paganism to Christianity. He relapsed in the persecution under Maximianus (c. 305), and, notwithstanding the support of the semi-Arian party, could not afterward attain to ecclesiastical dignities. Theologically he was a disciple of Lucian of Antioch (see LUCIAN THE MARTYR) and represented Arianism in a mild form. According to Jerome (*De vir ill.*, xciv) he wrote commentaries on the Epistle to the Romans, the Gospels, and the Psalms. G. KRÜGER.

BIBLIOGRAPHY: T. Zahn, *Marcellus von Ancyra*, pp. 38 sqq., Gotha, 1867.

3. Bishop of Petra in Arabia. He was originally a follower of Eusebius, but renounced the party at Sardica in 343, and was banished to Libya. In 362 he took part in the synod held at Alexandria. G. KRÜGER.

BIBLIOGRAPHY: *DCB*, i. 177-178.

4. Bishop of Amasia in Pontus from 378; d. before 431. He was a famous pulpit orator of the ancient Greek Church; of his homilies, which have historical importance, twenty-one are wholly extant, and extracts from six others are given by Photius (codex 271). They are in *MPG*, xl. G. KRÜGER.

BIBLIOGRAPHY: K. F. W. Paniel, *Pragmatische Geschichte der christlichen Beredsamkeit*, i, part 2, 562-582, Leipsic, 1841; L. Koch, in *ZHT*, xli (1871), 77-107; *DCB*, i. 178; Krüger, *History*, p. 367.

ASTIE, ās"tī', JEAN FRÉDÉRIC: Swiss Protestant; b. at Nérac (65 m. s.e. of Bordeaux), Lot-et-Garonne, France, Sept. 21, 1822; d. at Lausanne May 20, 1892. He studied at Geneva, Halle, and Berlin, went to the United States, and was pastor of a French church in New York from 1848 to 1853; from 1856 till his death he was professor of philosophy and theology in the Free Faculty at Lausanne. From 1868 he was joint editor of the *Revue de Théologie et de Philosophie*, published at Geneva and Lausanne. Besides polemical pamphlets, he wrote *Louis Fourteenth and the Writers of His Age*, lectures in French delivered in New York, translated by E. N. Kirk (Boston, 1855); an account, in French, of the religious revival in the United States in 1857-58 (Lausanne, 1859); a history of the United States (2 vols., Paris, 1865); *Esprit d'Alexandre Vinet* (2 vols., 1861); *Les Deux Théologies nouvelles sans le sein du Protestantisme français* (1862); *Explication de l'Évangile selon Saint-Jean* (3 vols., Geneva, 1864); *Théologie allemande contemporaine* (1874); *Mélanges de théologie et de philosophie* (Lausanne, 1878); and published an edition of the *Pensées* of Pascal (2 vols., Paris, 1857; 2d ed., 1882).

ASTROLOGY AND ASTRONOMY. See STARS.

ASTRUC, ās"trūc', JEAN: Roman Catholic; b. at Sauve (20 m. w.n.w. of Nîmes, department of Gard), Languedoc, Mar. 19, 1684; d. in Paris May 5, 1766. He was carefully educated by his father, who had been a Protestant pastor, but had been converted to Roman Catholicism; he studied also at Montpellier, where he received the degrees of M.A. and M.D. (1703), lectured at Montpellier, became professor on the medical faculty at Toulouse (1710), and at Montpellier (1717). In 1729 he became physician to King Augustus III of Poland, returned to France in 1730 as physician to Louis XV, was professor at the royal college in Paris from 1731, and member of the medical faculty there from 1743. He was eminent in his profession and published several medical treatises of value. The study of skin diseases led him to consider the Pentateuchal laws of the clean and the unclean; and this occasioned the work which entitles him to mention in a theological encyclopedia, a work which is regarded by many modern scholars as pointing out the true path of Pentateuchal investigation. It appeared anonymously (12mo, Brussels, 1753), with the title, *Conjectures sur les mémoires originaux dont il paroit que Moyse s'est servi pour composer le livre de la Génèse. Avec des remarques qui appuient ou qui éclaircissent ces conjectures*, and consists of a preface (pp. 1-2), preliminary remarks (pp 3-24), the Book of Genesis and chapters i and ii of Exodus in French translation from the Geneva folio edition of 1610 arranged according to the supposed *mémoires* (pp. 25-280), the "conjectures" proper (pp. 281-495), closing with an index of twenty-eight pages

That the Pentateuch is based upon older documents was no new idea. Astruc's originality consisted rather in his assumption that these sources had not been recast, but had been pieced together, and in his attempt to reproduce the sources, following as a clue the varying use of *Elohim* and *Yahweh* for the divine name. He thought that he discovered traces of twelve documents, and made naive guesses at their authorship; as Amram the father and Levi the great-grandfather of Moses for Ex. i-ii, and what immediately precedes, respectively; Joseph for his own story; Levi for the Dinah narrative (Gen. xxxiv); etc. He rightly perceives that his hypothesis explains the two expressions for the divine name, as well as repetitions and chronological difficulties. He also thinks that it vindicates Moses from the reproach of careless workmanship, since it is probable that originally he arranged the material in columns like the work of Origen or a harmony of the Gospels, and that negligent or ignorant copyists put it in consecutive form. The Mosaic authorship, Astruc considered established beyond possibility of doubt by passages such as John i, 45, v, 46. The fear that freethinkers would misuse his work deterred him from publishing it till his seventieth year; and he issued it then only on the assurance of a man "learned and very zealous for religion" that "far from being injurious to the cause of religion, it could only be helpful to it, because it would remove or clear up several difficulties which arise in reading the book and with the weight of which commentators have always been burdened" (Preface, p. 1). The title-page bears the motto *Avia Pieridum peragro loca nullius ante trita solo* ("Free through the muses' pathless haunts I roam, where mortal feet have never strayed," Lucretius, iv, 1). A German translation of the *Conjectures*, abridged, appeared at Frankfort in 1782, with the title *Mutmassungen in Betreff der Originalberichte deren sich Moses wahrscheinlicherweise bei Verfertigung des ersten seiner Bücher bedient hat, nebst Anmerkungen wodurch diese Mutmassungen theils unterstützt theils erläutert werden*. As a guaranty of his soundness in the faith, Astruc published immediately after the *Conjectures* a *Dissertation sur l'immortalité et sur l'immatérialité de l'âme* with a *Dissertation sur la liberté* (Paris, 1755). His *Mémoires pour servir à l'histoire de la Faculté de médecine de Montpellier* were edited after his death with an *Éloge historique* by A. C. Lorry. (F. Böhmer†.)

Bibliography: A. C. Lorry, *Vie d'Astruc*, in his ed. of Astruc's *Mémoires pour servir à l'histoire de la Faculté de médecine de Montpellier*, Paris, 1867; A. Westphal, *Les Sources de la Pentateuque*, I. *Le Problème littéraire*, p. 111 sqq., Paris, 1888; C. A. Briggs, *Study of Holy Scripture*, pp. 246, 250, 278 sqq., New York, 1899.

ASYLUM, RIGHT OF: Among practically all nations is found an early belief that places dedicated to the service of divine beings acquire a sanctity which makes them inviolable places of refuge for people pursued by their enemies. Specific prescriptions for the carrying out of this principle are found in the Mosaic law (Ex. xxi, 13; Deut. xix, 7–10). Certain temples among the Greeks had the same quality; and in Rome, where originally only special temples had been places of refuge for slaves, under the empire statues of the emperor were considered as affording protection, which the law definitely recognized in the case of slaves. In early Christian times the bishops possessed the privilege of interceding for accused persons or condemned criminals, who accordingly fled to the churches; but these were not considered inviolable asylums either by the ecclesiastical or by the imperial law. On the contrary, the latter definitely provided against abuses which had grown up in connection with this practise.

The right of asylum first received legal recognition for the West in 399; this was made more definite in 419, extended by Valentinian III (425–455), and regulated by Leo I in 466. But Justinian restricted it in 535; and the final shape assumed by the Roman law was that certain defined classes of persons who might have taken sanctuary in the churches could not be removed against their will, while the bishops had the right, but not the duty, of allowing them to remain there. In the Germanic kingdoms forcible violation of an asylum was indeed forbidden; but the fugitive had to be surrendered, though he was exempted from the penalty of death or mutilation. In the Frankish kingdom the *Decretio Chlotharii* (511–558) took a position in harmony with that of the Synod of Orleans (511); the surrender of the fugitive was only required on an oath being given to renounce the penalties just mentioned; but no secular punishment was provided for the violation of sanctuary, and the Carolingian legislation did away with this oath, while it denied the right of asylum altogether to those condemned to death. Under the influence of the *Decretum Gratiani* and other collections of decretals, the right of asylum was considerably extended; and this extension has been partly confirmed, partly revised by various papal decisions since the sixteenth century.

In general the right may be said to attach to churches and other buildings directly connected with them, to a certain amount of adjacent ground, to the whole enclosures of monasteries, to hospitals and similar pious institutions, and to episcopal palaces. The fugitive, whether judicially condemned or not, and even if he has escaped from prison, may not be repulsed or removed, even with his consent, by state officers. He may only be surrendered when what he has done comes under the head of a *casus exceptus*, such as murder, treason, robbery of churches, etc. The violation of sanctuary is sacrilege, and incurs excommunication *ipso facto*. The right of asylum, however, provoked a secular reaction after the sixteenth century, which in the eighteenth went as far as total abolition in some countries. This is now everywhere the case, though the Church holds to the right in principle.

(E. Friedberg.)

Bibliography: The fundamental book is Rittershusius, Ἀσυλία, *hoc est, de jure asylorum*, Strasburg, 1624, reprinted in *Critici Sacri*, i, 249 sqq., best ed., Amsterdam, 1698; S Pegge, in *Archæologia*, vol. viii (published by the Society of Antiquaries, London, 1770 sqq., gives history of Asylum in Great Britain down to James I); Bingham, *Origines*, book viii, chap. xi; J. J. Altmeyer, *Du Droit d'asile en Brabant*, Brussels, 1852; A. Bulwincq, *Das Asylrecht in seiner geschichtlichen Entwickelung*, Dorpat, 1853; C. R de Beaurepaire, *L'Asile religieux dans l'empire romain et la monarchie française*, Paris, 1854; J. J E Proost, *Histoire du droit d'asile religieux en Belgique*, Brussels, 1870; A Stöber, *Recherches sur le droit d'asile*, Mülhausen, 1884; J. F. Stephen, *History of Criminal Law*, vol. i, chap xiii, London, 1883; A P Riessel, *The Law of Asylum in Israel*, Leipsic, 1884; A. Gengel, *Asylrecht und Fürstenmord*, Frauenfeld, 1885; H. Lammasch, *Auslieferungspflicht und Asylrecht*, Leipsic, 1887; P. Hinschius, *Kirchenrecht*, iv, 380, Berlin, 1888; N. M. Trenholm, *Right of Sanctuary in England*, University of Missouri, 1903.

ATARGATIS, at-ār-gē'tis: A word which does not occur in the canonical Scriptures; but in II Macc. xii, 26 mention is made of "a temple of Atargatis" (*Atargateion*) as a place of refuge sought by the Arabians and Ammonites who were defeated by Judas Maccabæus. This temple was situated in Carnion (cf. I Macc. v, 43–44), which is probably the same as the Ashteroth-Karnaim of Gen. xiv, 5. The supposition is natural that the place was an old seat of Astarte-worship, and some have even identified Atargatis directly with Astarte.

Support has been found for this view in the fact that a principal seat of the cult of Atargatis was Ascalon, and that Herodotus (i, 105) places there a temple of "the heavenly Aphrodite." This is not conclusive, for there may have been shrines of both goddesses in the same city, or—which is far more probable—the Aphrodite of the days of Herodotus may have been succeeded by Atargatis. She had there a famous shrine for several centuries before and after the Christian era. Mabug or Hierapolis, on the Euphrates, was an equally famous seat of her worship.

In connection with both temples fishes were kept sacred to the goddess, and at Ascalon she was represented as a sort of mermaid—a woman with the tail of a fish (Lucian, *De dea Syria*, xiv; cf. xlv). Various reasons are given for these customs. According to one form of the legends in Greek and Roman writers, Derceto (the name Atargatis modified), having thrown herself into the water, was saved by a fish (Hyginus, *Astronomia*, ii, 30); according to another version she was turned into a fish (Diodorus Siculus, ii, 4). The dove, which was sacred to Astarte, Aphrodite, and Venus, also figures in the same legends.

The only question of present importance is the connection between the cult of Atargatis and that of Astarte. That the connection was close is indicated *prima facie* by the fact that the *Atar* of

Atargatis is the contracted form of *'Athtar*, the Aramaic equivalent of Ishtar or Astarte (see Ashtoreth, § 2). Presumably *Atar* is here confounded with the name of another deity. A certain Palmyrene god *Ati* or *Atah* is supposed to be the one in question, but his attributes are not sufficiently known to make the combination certain.

Although a wholly satisfactory explanation of the compound name is lacking, a plausible hypothesis as to the leading motive of the complex cult may be offered. After the political extinction of Semitism, and the consequent depreciation of Ishtar-Astarte (along with the decline of the complementary Baal-worship), it was found necessary to perpetuate some of the leading features of such a wide-spread and deep-rooted cult. The fertility and life-giving power of water was one of the most familiar of the conceptions of the world of thought and fancy of which Astarte was the center. This idea was in large measure suggested by the mysterious origin and fecundity of fish, the chief of water animals. These consequently figure very largely, along with other elements, in the cult of Atargatis, which replaced but did not supersede the worship of Astarte. See Ashtoreth.

J. F McCurdy.

Bibliography: J. Selden, *De dis Syris*, ii. 3, London, 1617; F. C Movers, *Die Phonizier*, i. 584–600, Bonn, 1841; K. B. Stark, *Gaza und die philistaische Kuste*, pp. 250–255, Jena, 1852; *Derceto the Goddess of Ascalon*, in the *Journal of Sacred Literature*, new series, vii (1865), 1–20; P. Scholz, *Gotzendienst und Zauberwesen bei den alten Hebräern*, pp. 301–333, Regensburg, 1877; J. P. Six, in the *Numismatic Chronicle*, new series, xviii (1878), 102 sqq.; Hauvette-Besnault, in *Bulletin de correspondance hellénique*, vi (1882), 470–503; L. Preller, *Römische Mythologie*, vol. ii, Berlin, 1883; W. Robertson Smith, in the *English Historical Review*, ii (1887), 303–317; F. Baethgen, *Beiträge zur semitischen Religionsgeschichte*, pp. 68–75, Berlin, 1889; R. Pietschmann, *Geschichte der Phönizier*, pp. 148 149, Berlin, 1889; Schürer, *Geschichte*, ii, 23–24, Eng. transl., II, i, 13–14 and iii, 91–92; *DB*, i. 194–195; *EB*, i. 379; Smith, *Rel. of Sem.*, 172–176.

ATHANASIAN CREED.

The so-called Athanasian Creed (*Symbolum Athanasianum*, also called, from its first word, *Symbolum Quicunque*) is an exposition of the catholic faith which, from the Carolingian period, in some places earlier than in others, began to be sung at prime every day throughout the Western Church. It was not then called a "symbol" or creed; the passage in Theodulf of Orleans (*De spiritu sancto*, *MPL*, cv, 247) which was supposed so to designate it is corrupt, and Hincmar's reference to "Athanasius speaking in the creed" (*De prædestinatione*, *MPL*, cxxv, 374) has been shown to refer, not to this, but to the so-called *fides Romanorum* (see below, II, § 5).

I. Title not Justified: None of the manuscripts of the ninth or tenth century, no certain quotation of this date, none of the old commentaries, call it a creed And even later, Thomas Aquinas expressly says that Athanasius wrote his exposition not in the manner of a creed but rather in that of a teacher's lesson (*Summa*, IIb, 1, 10, 3). And he is right Nothing was originally considered a creed, strictly speaking, but the baptismal profession of faith, and only a composition of similar structure could be accounted a creed, or more properly, a form of the creed.

1. Not an Ecumenical Creed. The *Quicunque* can not come under this head; it is a theological exposition of the doctrines of the Trinity and the Incarnation found in the creed. It is natural, however, that its use in public worship should approximate it in the popular mind to the Apostles' Creed used at baptism, and the Nicene used in the mass. As late as 1287, it is true, a diocesan synod at Exeter refers to the "articles of faith as they are contained in the psalm *Quicunque vult* and in both symbols;" but in the thirteenth century the name of creed was not seldom applied to it. Durandus (d. 1296) says "the creed is threefold;" and Alexander of Hales in like manner, writing in England about 1230, says, "there are three symbols, one of the apostles; one of the Fathers, which is sung in the mass; and the third, the Athanasian, which is sung at prime." Accordingly the Reformers, when their time came, had learned to receive these old confessions as "the three creeds" of catholic Christendom. They did not know that the Greek Church had neither the Apostles' nor the Athanasian, and the later Lutherans included all three as a universal heritage in their *Corpus doctrinæ*. So also Zwingli, the French and Belgic Confessions, and the Anglican Thirty-nine Articles expressly accepted the three creeds as ecumenical. But the Eastern Churches do not know the Athanasian as an authority, in spite of the assertion of the Russian theologian Macarius. Of the Reformed Churches, those which accept the Westminster Confession, while agreeing with its general teaching, do not accept it formally; the American Episcopal Church has dropped it from the prayer-book; the Churches of Puritan origin and the Methodists do not use it; so also the Swiss and French Reformed, to say nothing of the antitrinitarian bodies.

But the Athanasian Creed is not only not ecumenical; it is not even Athanasian. Since Gerhard Voss demonstrated this in 1642, the Athanasian origin of it has been practically abandoned by scholars, even those of the Roman Catholic Church.

2. Not Athanasian. There are decisive grounds against it: it was composed in Latin—the Greek forms, which can be shown to be as late as the thirteenth century, are mere translations; Athanasius himself, as well as his biographers, know nothing of it—the Greeks mention it first about 1200; and it expresses things of later origin, such as the final settlement of not only the Trinitarian but the Apollinarian and Christological controversies, the dogmatic formulas of Augustine, and the doctrine of the double procession of the Holy Spirit. The evidence of the manuscripts, too, is insufficient. Several of them give it without any author's name, and of the seven oldest commentaries only two mention Athanasius in the title and one in the introduction. Besides all this, it is not difficult to account for its attribution to Athanasius.

II. History of Discussion: But, however generally these facts are recognized, there is little positive agreement as to any other origin. The period of study of the subject which reaches from Voss to 1870 produced a bewildering variety of hypotheses. Voss himself conjectured that it grew up on Frankish soil under Pepin or Charlemagne, as a consequence of the controversies over the *filioque;* his contemporary, Archbishop Ussher, attributed it to an unknown author before the middle of the fifth century; and Quesnel to Vigilius of Thapsus (c. 500), in which he was followed by Cave, Du Pin, and many others. Antelmius was for Vincent of Lerins (c. 430); Muratori for Venantius Fortunatus (d. c. 600); Lequien doubtfully suggested Pope Anastasius I (d. 401); Waterland, whose book is the most learned and authoritative of the older discussions, favored Hilary of Arles (d. 449); and Speroni referred it to Hilary of Poitiers (d. 367).

1. Theories of Origin.

A new period in the study of the subject opened with 1870, the impulse coming from England, where the creed is publicly recited in the Anglican liturgy on certain days, not without opposition. The commission for the revision of the Prayer-book in 1689 had recommended the insertion of a note explaining away the "damnatory clauses," and the question of its retention came up again before the Ritual Commission appointed in 1867, with no practical result except to stir up fresh interest in the creed and advance its study. Ffoulkes tried in 1871 to assign it to Paulinus of Aquileia (d. 802); Swainson published a learned, if not uniformly satisfactory, book in 1875, coming to the conclusion that it was a composite product, which assumed its present form between 860 and 870. Lumby's book, published in 1873, was in substantial agreement with Swainson, dating the crystallizing process between 813 and 870. The theory of two sources was also accepted, with notable modifications, by Harnack in his *Dogmengeschichte*. He saw in the Trinitarian section an exposition of the Nicene Creed, growing up by degrees in Gaul from the fifth century and assuming its present form in the sixth; to this was added perhaps in the eighth or ninth the second half, about whose origin nothing can be certainly said except that it is older than the ninth century. Ommanney and Burn added new material but no new results. An independent French investigation by Morin urged the claims of Pope Anastasius II (496–498).

Of these hypotheses, those which point to Anastasius I and II do not deserve serious consideration, even if they receive a specious attractiveness from the fact that some of the manuscripts (though the later ones) give the name, and a thirteenth century compilation treats "of the third symbol, that of Pope Anastasius"; but Morin himself admits that without this no one would ever have thought of the theory, which has really no other support than the stupidity of medieval copyists.

2. Facts as to Manuscripts.

In order to form an opinion of the other theories, it is necessary to glance at the facts as to the manuscripts. Down to 1870 eight were named as ancient, viz.: (1) a psalter in the Cottonian Library, which Ussher put in the time of Gregory the Great; (2) the *Psalterium Aethelstani* in the same collection, dated by Ussher 703; (3) the *Codex Colbertinus* 784, dated by Montfaucon c. 750; (4) the *Sangermanensis*, about the same age; (5) the *Codex regius* 4908, c. 800; (6) the *Codex Colbertinus* 1339, called *Psalterium Caroli Calvi ;* (7) the *Codex Ambrosianus*, which Muratori in 1697 thought to be over a thousand years old; (8) a psalter in Vienna, presented by a Frankish king Charles to a pope Adrian, thought by Waterland to belong to the first year of Adrian I (772). Recent investigations have altered the status of several of these. That supposed to be the oldest, the one named first above, lost after Ussher's time and rediscovered in 1871 in the so-called Utrecht Psalter, is now believed by experts to be of the ninth century, and thus not much older than (6), which was certainly written between 842 and 869. The second is now known to be a compilation of three pieces, that containing the creed being later than the ninth century. The fourth can no longer be used as a basis for argument, since it is lost. The fifth may not be older than (6); and (8) is considered to belong to the time of Charles the Bald and Adrian II (867–872) Of all these manuscripts, then, only that numbered (7) above can be shown to be older than 800 as not only Muratori, Waterland, and Montfaucon believed it to be, but also such modern scholars as Ceriani, Reifferscheid, and Krusch have maintained. Yet this is not the only one to place the origin further back, if only a little further, than 800. Two more must now be added: (9) *Paris.* 13,159, a psalter from Saint-Germain-des-Prés, not the same as (4), assigned on strong grounds to c. 795; and (10) *Paris.* 1451, a collection of canons dated with apparent probability 796. The manuscripts, then, place the date of the *Quicunque* at least as early as the end of the eighth century

3. Ancient Commentaries.

The same evidence is given by the oldest commentaries. Waterland and the older students of the question knew of only one commentary older than that attributed to Bruno of Würzburg (d. 1045)—the so-called *Expositio Fortunati*. The latter, first published by Muratori from the *Codex Ambrosianus* 79 (eleventh or twelfth century), was ascribed by most of the earlier investigators to Venantius Fortunatus (d. c. 600), and regarded as the oldest evidence of the existence of the *Quicunque*. At present there are sixteen extant manuscripts of this *Expositio*, besides three codices which give the bulk of it in the form of glosses Its ascription to Fortunatus, resting only on the comparatively late authority of the *Codex Ambrosianus*, and easily to be explained there by the fact that the codex begins with his exposition of the Apostles' Creed, has now been abandoned. The only other author's name is offered by a lost manuscript from St. Gall, printed by Melchior Goldast in 1610, which calls it *Euphronii presbyteri expositio*. Morin identified this Euphronius with the bishop of Tours of that name (555–572), who was well known to Venantius Fortunatus. Burn is inclined to see its author in Euphronius of Autun, who built the church of St. Symphorian there about 450. But this positive criticism is very hazardous in view of the number of anonymous manuscripts, to say nothing of the frequency of the name Euphronius in Gaul. A more important question is that of its date. An attempt has been made to decide this from the fact that the author explains the words *in sæculo* in section 31 of the creed (Schaff, *Creeds*, ii, New York, 1887, 68) by "that is, in the sixth millennium [*sextum miliarium*] in which we now are." This has been supposed to indicate 799 as the *terminus ante quem*; but no stress can be laid on this; people spoke of the *sextum miliarium*, with Augustine, after 799 as well as before it. Just as little can be made of its supposed dependence on Alcuin for a *terminus post quem*, as Ommanney has shown. The only sure limit of date might be supposed to be given by the fact that the oldest manuscript (*Bodleian. Junius* 25) belongs to the ninth century —probably the beginning—were it not that a whole group of other ancient commentaries allow us to put the *terminus ante quem* further back. Ommanney has rendered a signal service to the investigation by the discovery of these, and Burn has followed independently. These are, in the order of the dates given by Burn: (2) the *Expositio Parisiensis*, certainly written between Gregory the Great and 900; (3) the *Expositio Trecensis*, assigned by Ommanney to the seventh, by Burn to the end of the eighth century; (4) the *Expositio Oratorii*, found in the same manuscript, dated by Ommanney about 700, by Burn a century later; (5) the *Stabulensis*, ninth century according to Burn; (6) the *Buheriana*, based on (4), and written, according to Ommanney, in the first half of the eighth century, to Burn, in the ninth; and (7) the *Aurelianensis*, first published in 1892 by Cuissard, who attributes it to Theodulf of Orleans, while Burn is for an author of the middle or end of the ninth century. Now, of all these commentaries, only the *Expositio Fortunati* and the *Trecensis* (which in its first part is very dependent on the former), do not evidence a knowledge of the entire *Quicunque*. To be sure, Burn's dates—to say nothing of Ommanney's—are by no means certain. But none the less these commentaries are of great importance as helps to a decision of the difficult problem under discussion. The last-named, one of the latest (because dependent on three or four of the others), is preserved in a manuscript which Delisle assigns to the ninth century; and the *Trecensis*, used in the compilation of this, presupposes in its turn the *Expositio Fortunati*. This being so, it is not too bold a conclusion that the latter, everything about which shows it to be the oldest of them all, belongs to the period before 799. If this is granted, one may go a little further, and point out that since its author says nothing about the approaching end of the *sextum miliarium*, he did not live very near that date.

Both the *Expositio Fortunati* and the *Expositio Trecensis* leave certain verses of the *Quicunque* without mention. Are we to conclude that the whole of it was not known to their authors? We have seen how far the testimony of the manuscripts supports the theses of Ffoulkes, Swainson, and Lumby; our *Quicunque* was definitely in existence before the end of the eighth century.

4. The Theory of Two Sources.

But that does not in itself militate against the acceptance of the theory of two sources; Harnack considers it possible that both halves of our present creed were found in conjunction in the eighth century, or even earlier. We must therefore look further into that theory. Its main support is the manuscript referred to above as (3), the *Codex Colbertinus* 784 (now known as *Paris.* 3836), which all authorities agree to place in the eighth century, Swainson dating it as early as 730. In this manuscript the Christological portion of the Athanasian Creed (though with noteworthy verbal variants) is found under the rubricated caption *Hæc invini treveris in uno libro scriptum sic incipiente Domini nostri Jesu Christi fideliter credat et reliqua.* Now, assuming that the scribe copied exactly what he found in the Treves manuscript, Swainson, Lumby, and Harnack see in this text, which goes well back into the eighth century (possibly to 730), distinct documentary evidence for the separate existence of the Christological half of the *Quicunque*. But it does not seem to have been observed that the manuscript will not sustain this contention. The copyist put down in red ink, as his introduction, words which actually form a part of the verse which makes, in the complete creed, the transition from the Trinitarian to the Christological section. The "Treves fragment" is thus really a fragment—part of a whole whose first half stood in the same relation to our *Quicunque* as the extant second half. There is nothing surprising in this conclusion. That a preacher (and Swainson himself has noticed that this fragment is clearly a fragment of a sermon) should have undertaken to set forth "the faith," and then have spoken only of the Incarnation and not of the Trinity, would have been much more surprising. But the conclusion, if not surprising, is none the less weighty; for it takes both halves of the creed distinctly further back than any of the manuscripts described above. We do not know how old the Treves manuscript was when the writer of *Paris.* 3836 copied it in 750 or 730; but there is room for a logical train of reasoning which leads to valuable results. It is obviously improbable that a copyist with a complete manuscript before him should copy only the last part, beginning in the middle of a sentence; therefore the Treves manuscript (or its original) must have been defective. This train of thought gains in force when we notice that the "fragment" represents exactly a third of our *Quicunque*. On the assumption that the two first pages of the original went down to *incarnationem quoque*, the third beginning with *Domini nostri Jesu Christi*, the loss of the first part would fully explain the condition of *Paris.* 3836. It follows further that the *Codex Trevirensis*, already defective about 750, was more probably than not relatively old then, and the manuscript evidence actually confirms the supposition that the Treves fragment must originally have been preceded by something answering to the first section of the present *Quicunque*. The theory of two sources breaks down, therefore, at its strongest point—for the other arguments, from both external and internal evidence, are very weak.

But the interest of the *Codex Paris.* 3836 is not exhausted by its decisive evidence against the two-source theory, or by the remarkable text which it offers. It brings up the question whether the *sermo* contained in the *Codex Trevirensis* was taken from the *Quicunque*, or whether the latter in some way grew out of this and other like sermons. The Apostles' Creed in its simplicity was the standard of faith for the Western Church at least, long after the Trinitarian and Christological controversies had carried dogmatic development far beyond its simple words. Popular misconceptions of the meaning of those words had called for more precise definitions in numerous sermons on the creed still extant. To supply these is Augustine's aim in his *Sermones de traditione symboli* (212, 213, 214), which contain expressions reminding of the *Quicunque*. The same is true of the pseudo-Augustinian 244, attributed by the Benedictine editors and some modern scholars to Cæsarius of Arles; and whether or not he wrote it, it is a product of the Lerins school, in which similar formulas were current. Thus Vincent himself recalls our phrases in his *Commonitorium* (434), and other parallels are found in Faustus of Riez, abbot of Lerins 433–462, and in Eucherius of Lyons, who was a monk there from 416 to 434. But parallels of thought are to be expected wherever those traditional theologians discussed the Trinity or the Incarnation; and we need only mention here those authors who offer us not merely a parallel of thought but a close resemblance in phrasing outside of the consecrated formulas of definition. Besides Augustine, to whom, as has long been recognized, not a few phrases go back, and Vincent of Lerins, those who deserve especial mention are Vigilius of Thapsus (or the author who passes under his name), Isidore of Seville, and Paulinus of Aquileia. In the writings more or less doubtfully ascribed to Vigilius, especially the three books against Varimadus and the twelve on the Trinity, we find at least three sections (13, 15, 17) almost word for word, and a confession of faith—the so-called *fides Romanorum* —which touches the *Quicunque* rather in general structure than in details. Isidore, writing on the rule of faith, uses these similar expressions directly as an exposition of the Apostles' Creed. The oration of Paulinus at the Council of Friuli has led to his identification by Ffoulkes as the original author; in it expressions parallel to no less than twelve verses of the *Quicunque* occur. The fact that Paulinus was addressing a council reminds us that many synodal confessions of faith had a life and an influence far beyond their original purpose, being adopted and copied as happy formulations of the faith. Thus the Council of Arles (813) adopted the Confession of Toledo (633), and many more examples might be given. The two most important of these confessions for our subject are those described in the newer investigations as *fides Romanorum* and *symbolum Damasi*. The latter (included under this obviously misleading title among the works of Jerome) is specially interesting not only because it reminds in several places of the *Quicunque*, and because it is closely related to the Toledan confession of 633, but also because a resemblance may easily be traced here and there to the *Expositio Fortunati*. Still more important is the other, which, under the title *Fides catholica ecclesiæ Romanæ*, can be traced in manuscript to the sixth century. It was cited as Athanasian by Hincmar and by Ratramnus in passages which used to be thought to refer to the *Quicunque*; its whole structure is worth notice—it begins with a Trinitarian section, reminding us of our subject, and this is followed by a Christological one, which, exactly as in the *Quicunque* and in the Toledan confession of 633, goes down to the last judgment.

5. Parallels to the Athanasian Creed.

III. Present Status: The question whether such expositions of the faith, or any of them, presuppose the existence of the *Quicunque* is the real question at the present stage of the discussion. If they do, its author must have lived very early; if they do not, its development forms only a part of the varied development of these expository formulas down through the ages. The decision for the first alternative would be easy if any of the theologians named above, before Paulinus, could be shown to have been acquainted with our *Quicunque*. But this acquaintance is, for various reasons, not probable in the cases of Paulinus, of Cæsarius of Arles, of Vincent of Lerins, of Vigilius of Thapsus, or of Isidore. Many reasons, for which there is not space here, go to make us think further that the same thing applies to the writer of the Treves fragment; and, after all, the weight of evidence seems in favor of the second alternative mentioned. A long-continued and gradual process, in which the *sermo Trevirensis* is but one stage, seems the inevitable conclusion. Much remains to be done before the various steps of the process can be determined. But one of the most important data for this further research is the famous canon of the Council of Autun: "If any priest, deacon, subdeacon, or cleric does not receive the creed which has been handed down from the Apostles as inspired by the Holy Spirit and the creed of bishop St. Athanasius without criticism, he is to be condemned by his bishop." Waterland and the older investigators had reason to doubt its authenticity, which, however, modern research has confirmed. The council was demonstrably held under the presidency of Leodegar, bishop of Autun 659–683, but its date is not positively known; the best we can do is to assign it roughly to 670, as the middle of Leodegar's episcopate.

1. Attempted Conclusion.

If, then, the *Quicunque* was ascribed to Athanasius about 670, a still earlier date for the conclusion of its formation may well be looked for. The question how much earlier this may be involves the question of its birthplace—for productions were possible in seventh century Italy and Spain which were impossible in the contemporary Merovingian north. Italy is excluded by the fact that the copyist of the *Codex Paris.* 3836 was not familiar with the *Quicunque;* nothing speaks for Africa; and against Spain may be urged the fact that it seems to have been unknown there at a period later than that at which the canon of Autun shows it had begun to play an important part in the Frankish regions. Besides this negative evidence for a Gallic origin, there is the positive one of the frequent echoes of it in the fifth century theologians of southern Gaul. But if it grew up in France at all, it was not the Merovingian theologians who could give it its final shape; the place of this development is to be sought in the south of France, between c. 450 and 600—so that the *sermo Trevirensis* may very well belong to the fifth century. The new importance and significance which the document assumed in the Carolingian period does not require belief in a late authorship; it is sufficiently explained by the fact that the Carolingian culture knew how to make full use of this heritage of the past, which had remained isolated and inoperative in Gaul during the confusion of the Merovingian period. The *Quicunque* is no product of the early Middle Ages; it is a precipitate resulting from the early western development of expositions of the creed. But its history shows how in this process the theologians' exposition of the faith has been confounded with the faith itself to such an extent as to preclude its acceptance as a final authority by evangelical Christians. (F. Loofs.)

2. Controversy in Anglican Church.

The Athanasian Creed is ordered to be recited at morning prayer in the Church of England, in place of the Apostles', on a number of greater festivals. In the antidogmatic period when the American revision of the Prayer-book was made, it was wholly omitted; and the same sort of tendency to avoid positive expressions of strong belief, which might give offense to those who held different views, has caused attempts to be made at different times since 1867, if not to remove it from the English Prayer-book, at least to render its recitation optional, to omit the so-called "damnatory clauses," or by a retranslation to avoid the very possible misconstruction which might be placed upon them. Of this movement Dean Stanley was one of the principal leaders, and Canon Liddon, supported by a large number who dreaded any tampering with the standards of faith, was one of the principal opponents. The opposition has been so determined and vigorous that all propositions for a change have thus far been defeated.

Bibliography: The text in six variant forms is in *MPG*, xxviii; in the *Utrecht Psalter*, London, 1875 (a facsimile ed. of the codex); cf. T. Hardy, *Reports on the Athanasian Creed in Connection with the Utrecht Psalter*, ib. 1873; and is edited by A. E. Burn, *The Athanasian Creed and its Early Commentaries*, in *TS*, vol. iv, part 1, Cambridge, 1896; also to be found in Schaff, *Creeds*, ii, 66-71. For the history of the creed consult: G. D. W. Ommanney, *Dissertation on the Athanasian Creed*, London, 1897 (critical and historical); D. Waterland, *Critical History of the Athanasian Creed*, Cambridge, 1723, revised ed. by J. R. King, London, 1870 (the fullest discussion, but in part antiquated); E. S. Ffoulkes, *The Athanasian Creed*, ib. 1871 (historical); C. A. Heurtley, *Harmonia Symbolica*, Oxford, 1858; idem, *The Athanasian Creed*, ib. 1872; Schaff, *Creeds*, i, 34-42; idem, *Christian Church*, iii, 689-698; G. Morin, *Les Origines du Symbole Quicunque*, in *Revue des questions religieuses*, v (1891), No. 9; Harnack, *Dogma*, iv, 133 sqq., 156, v, 302-303, vii, 174. For the debate in the Anglican Church consult: A. P. Stanley, *The Athanasian Creed*, London, 1871 (adverse to the use of the creed); J. S. Brewer, *Origin of the Athanasian Creed*, ib. 1872 (defensive); *Memorials to the Primates and Petition to Convocation . . . for Some Change either in the Compulsory Rubric or in the Damnatory Clauses*, Chester, 1872; G. A. Willan, *The Athanasian Creed not Damnatory*, London, 1872; *The Athanasian Creed; Suggestions . . . by a lay Member of the General Synod*, Dublin, 1876; C. A. Swainson, *The Nicene and Apostles' Creed . . . with an Account of . . . "The Creed of St. Athanasius,"* London, 1894 (historical and critical, but bearing on the Anglican discussion); F. N. Oxenham, *The Athanasian Creed: Should it be Recited? and is it True?* ib. 1902.

ATH'A-NA'SIOS PA-RI'OS: Dogmatician of the Greek Church; b. on the island of Paros 1725; d. at Chios June 24, 1813. He studied in the Athos academy under Eugenius Bulgaris, and from 1792 till 1812 was director of the school at Chios, which is the period of his most important activity. He belongs to the most prominent and fertile theological writers of the Greek Church of his time, and was also an able philosopher. A pupil of Bulgaris, in his opposition to the West he surpassed his master; he attacked with great energy not only the Roman Church and her scholasticism, and the Protestants, but also the western rationalism—the worst representative of which, in his eyes was Voltaire—particularly in its opposition to positive Christianity and monasticism. This explains his opposition to the desire of his people for liberty. Yet his historical judgment was so far influenced by Bulgaris, that in theology he recognized the more recent teachers of his Church, even Koressios, as "fathers," and seemingly made concessions to Biblical criticism. But Western science he used only when he attacked his opponents. His polemical disposition sometimes placed him in opposition to his own Church. By his connection with the Athos community he became involved in the Kolyba-controversy (see Athos), and wrote his "Exposition of the Faith" in 1774. In 1776 he was excommunicated, but the ban was removed in 1781. His principal work is an "Epitome or Summary of the Holy Dogmas of the Faith" (Leipsic, 1806), in which he shows his dependence on Bulgaris, but at the same time so much independence of thought that this epitome may be regarded as one of the most important dogmatic efforts of the Greek Church of the eighteenth century. The sources of doctrine are, according to him, the Holy Scripture, written tradition, and the teaching of the Church as fixed by the synods. The work of Christ he treats under the headings of king, priest, lawgiver, and judge. In the doctrine of the Lord's Supper he accepts transubstantiation. He opposes rationalism in his "Christian Apology" (Constantinople, 1797), attacking especially the false freedom and the false equality of the French, and renouncing all sympathy with the Greek struggles for freedom. Against Voltaire especially he directed the "Antidote for Evil," which was published after his death (Leipsic, 1818). Of his hagiographical works the most noteworthy were lives of Gregorios Palamas (Vienna, 1785), and of Marcus Eugenicus (1785), which have little independent value. In the "New Limonarium" (Venice, 1819) he gives many marvelous stories and biographies of modern saints. Very interesting is a treatise at the beginning of the book, in which he tries to show that those who were condemned as Christians because of a renunciation of Islam are just as much martyrs as those of the ancient time. Athanasios was also active as a preacher. A discourse on Gregorios Palamas, printed after the *Logoi* of Makarios Chrysokephalos (Vienna, 1797?) is a brilliant combination of popular eloquence and fanatical rhetoric. PHILIPP MEYER.

BIBLIOGRAPHY: A biography, trustworthy in the main, with a list of his writings, by his pupil, A. Z. Mamukas, is given in C. N. Sathas, Νεοελληνικὴ φιλολογία, Athens, 1868; consult also P. Meyer, *Die Haupturkunden der Athosklöster*, pp. 76 sqq., 236 sqq., Leipsic, 1894.

ATH''A-NA'SIUS.

Athanasius, bishop of Alexandria, was born apparently at Alexandria 293; d. there May 2, 373. His fame is due solely to his unswerving and self-sacrificing opposition to the Arian heresy, and some account of his life, with a statement of his views, is given in the article ARIANISM. A few facts will be added here, and an account of his literary activity attempted.

I. Life: The principal sources for the biography of Athanasius are the numerous documents bearing on the great Arian controversy which have been preserved, and his own works, which are rich in biographical material,—especially his "Apologies" ("against the Arians," "to Constantine," and "for his Flight") and his "History of the Arians for Monks."

1. Sources. The oration on Athanasius by Gregory Nazianzen (xxi, *NPNF*, 2d ser., 269–280; dating from 380?) is a mere panegyric without much biographical value. The biographies prefixed to the Benedictine edition of his works are later than the fifth century historians and quite worthless. Of greater importance are two sources not known to the seventeenth century editor of his works. These are the fragment published by Maffei (1738) of the so-called *Historia acephala*, written between 384 and 412, and the preface to the "Festal Letters" of Athanasius which are preserved in a Syriac version (ed. Cureton, Mai). Both of these come apparently from a single older source, and are very careful in their chronology, so that since they have been known the dates given by Socrates and Sozomen have often to be corrected.

Some difficulties still remain; but a careful comparison of these authorities enables us with reasonable security to fix the date of Athanasius's consecration at 326, and, with the help of a recently discovered fragment of a Coptic "Encomium," written by a contemporary of Bishop Theophilus of Alexandria (d. 412), to put his birth back to 293. Of his life up to 326, however, we still know very little. He seems to have been an Alexandrian; that his parents were Christians is not proved. The traditional story of his playing at "church" as a boy and, in the character of a bishop, so correctly baptizing some catechumens that Bishop Alexander (313–326) recognized the validity of the baptism, and took the lad under his care, is worthy of its first narrator, Rufinus; the chronology is sufficient to condemn it.

2. Early Life. Chosen Bishop 326. Devoting himself, however, to a clerical life, he served (according to the Coptic "Encomium") six years as reader; by the outbreak of the Arian controversy he was already a deacon, and in close relations with the aged bishop Alexander, perhaps as his amanuensis. This would account for Alexander's taking him to the Council of Nicæa, and perhaps for Sozomen's story that he designated him as his successor. At any rate, Athanasius was chosen to this office on Alexander's death (326), and was received with enthusiasm by the great majority of his flock. His opponents early asserted that he was chosen bishop by a minority and consecrated secretly; but this is disproved by the evidence of the Egyptian bishops assembled in council in 339.

The position was by no means an easy one. The Meletian schism (see MELETIUS OF LYCOPOLIS) had rent the Egyptian Church in two; and, although the Nicene decisions had opened the way for a termination of the schism, the manner in which this came about did not preclude the continuance of strife as to the validity of the orders of the Meletian clergy. Athanasius had scarcely been consecrated when these disturbances broke out anew, complicated by the enmities aroused by his decided anti-Arian attitude.

3. The Arian Controversy. First Exile. At the instance of Eusebius of Nicomedia, the leader of the semi-Arians (see EUSEBIUS OF NICOMEDIA AND CONSTANTINOPLE), the emperor demanded the readmission of Arius into the Church; but Athanasius stoutly refused his consent, and immediately the storm broke (see ARIANISM, I). He was summoned before the emperor, who was at that time in Nicomedia, and accused of conspiring to prevent the export of grain from Egypt to Constantinople. Only after long and wearisome exertions did he succeed in proving his innocence. Immediately after his return, new accusations were brought against him; it was said that he had killed a Meletian bishop, Arsenius, and used his bones for magical arts. An investigation was ordered, and a synod summoned to meet at Cæsarea (334). Athanasius refused to appear; and the investigation came to a natural end on the discovery that Arsenius was alive. Eusebius, however, still had the emperor's ear, and Athanasius was summoned to appear at a synod in Tyre. He left Alexandria July 11, 335, but found at Tyre that the council had made up its mind to condemn him, and repaired to Constantinople, where he succeeded in convincing the emperor of the unfairness of the synod. Constantine saw in him, none the less, an obstacle to peace, the maintenance of which seemed the most desirable thing, and banished him to Treves toward the end of the year. Constantine died May 23, 337, and Athanasius's first exile ended with his return to his diocese, Nov. 23 of the same year, his entrance into the city being, according to Gregory Nazianzen, "more triumphal than had ever an emperor."

The opposition and intrigues still continued, however; the enemies of Athanasius accused him of having sold and employed for his own use the corn which the late emperor had destined for the poor widows of Egypt and Libya. A synod of African bishops declared in his favor, but as Constantius was influenced by Eusebius of Nicomedia, and as the prefect of Egypt, Philagrius, wanted the see for a countryman of his own, Gregory of Cappadocia, he was driven into his second exile March 19, 339, and Gregory was installed by military force at Easter. Athanasius went to Rome, where he was well received by Pope Julius, and later to Gaul to confer with Hosius, whom he accompanied to Sardica to take part in the famous council held there (343?). After spending some time at Naissus in Dacia, at Aquileia, and in Gaul (where he met Constans, whose influence with his brother was exerted in his favor), he finally appeared once more before Constantius, and obtained permission to return. Gregory died June 25, 345, and was not replaced; and Athanasius was able to resume his jurisdiction Oct. 21, 346. After the death of Constans (Jan., 350), his position once more became unsafe; and the end of a long series of intrigues and machinations was that the "Duke" Syrianus surrounded the church of St. Theonas with 5,000 soldiers to arrest him on the night of Feb. 8, 356. He escaped, and fled the next day, finding refuge during this his third exile among the monks and hermits of the desert, though for a part of the time he lay concealed within the city, and by his writings continued to encourage his faithful followers. On Feb. 24, 357, another Cappadocian, George, was made bishop, and as many as possible of the ecclesiastical offices were filed by Arians. George, however, was able to maintain himself for only eighteen months, and then, after a three years' absence, was imprisoned three days after his return, and put to death in the disturbances which followed the death of Constantius. The new emperor, Julian the Apostate (361–363), issued an edict permitting the exiled bishops to return to their sees, hoping thus to increase the confusion in the Church, to the profit of the paganism which he was bent on restoring. The third exile of Athanasius thus ended Feb. 21, 362.

4. Second and Third Exiles.

But a fourth exile followed shortly. The new emperor's counselors found Athanasius too dangerous a man for their plans, and Julian issued a special edict commanding him, as he had returned to Alexandria without personally receiving permission, to leave it at once (Oct. 24, 362). He remained in concealment in the deserts of the Thebaid until he heard of Julian's death (June 26, 363), when he returned to Alexandria (Sept. 5), though only to pass through on his way to see the new emperor, Jovian, at Antioch. Jovian received him kindly, and his fourth exile was definitely terminated by his return on Feb. 20, 364. Jovian's death after only eight months brought fresh trouble to the orthodox. An edict of Valens (May 5, 365) reversed Julian's recall of the exiled bishops; and on Oct. 5 the prefect Flavianus broke into the church of St. Dionysius and compelled Athanasius to flee once more. He remained at a villa in the neighborhood of the city, until Valens found the discontent in so important a place as Alexandria dangerous, and made a special exception in favor of Athanasius, who was able to return Jan. 31, 366. The last seven years of his episcopate were undisturbed.

5. Fourth and Fifth Exiles.

The refuge of Athanasius among the monks and hermits of the desert during his third and fourth periods of exile leads up to a point which needs special mention—his relations with monasticism. Athanasius was not only the father of orthodoxy in the East, but also the first bishop to take an active part in encouraging the monastic life. This assertion is so far from being founded on the "Life of Anthony" alone that it would still be demonstrable if his authorship of that work were less certain than it is. From an early period he was in close relations with Egyptian monasticism. When the assembled bishops in 339 designate him as "one of the ascetics" (referring to the motives which led to his election), it may mean no more than that he belonged to the large number in the Christian community who practised the ascetic life in varying degrees, without retiring from the world. We can not say whether his personal intercourse with Anthony (d. 356) occurred altogether after he was a bishop or partly before. But he came early in his episcopate into contact with Pachomius (d. 345), who came out with his brethren to greet their new bishop when he undertook a visitation of the Thebaid between the Easters of 328 and 329. Lasting relations with this colony were kept up by means of the yearly visits of deputations of the monks to Alexandria for the purpose of making necessary purchases. Pachomius is reported to have said that there were three sights specially pleasing to the eyes of God in the Egypt of his time—Athanasius, Anthony, and his own community of monks. Athanasius knew Theodore, the successor of Pachomius, and visited him in his desert retreat at Phboou—probably in 363, for which year we have evidence of a journey as far south as Antinoë and Hermopolis. So well known were these relations that an imperial officer sent by Constantius to apprehend him in 360 searched for him, though in vain, at Phboou. When Theodore died (368), Athanasius

6. Relations with Monasticism.

wrote his successor a letter of warm sympathy. These long and intimate relations with Egyptian monasticism support the assertion of Jerome (*Epist.*, cxxvii) that the Roman lady Marcella first heard through Athanasius, in 341, of Anthony, Pachomius, and the ascetic communities of the Thebaid. If, however, he rendered monasticism a service by calling to it the attention of the western world, he did even more for it by successfully combating the tendency which it showed at first to form a caste apart from, and to some extent in rivalry with, the clergy; he was also the first (at least in the Church of the empire) to promote monks to the episcopate—a point of great importance to the later development of the Eastern Church.

II. Writings: Athanasius ranks high as an author—though it may be doubted whether he would have attained so high a place had it not been for the epoch-making war which he waged upon Arianism. Of pure learning he had not much, or else it was put in the background by the more absorbing interests of his life. His most important works were written for some special purpose of the moment; and they may therefore be best considered in their chronological order, the more that any classification of them is practically impossible. The editors of his works place first the two connected treatises "Against the Heathen" and "On the Incarnation." These have until recently been considered as a product of Athanasius's youth (c. 318); but some recent critics (Schultze, Dräseke) have attempted to deny his authorship and to assign them to the middle of the fourth century. The grounds given for this opinion are unconvincing, although the date may be brought down as late as 325. Next follow the oldest of the "Festal Letters" (329–335 and 338–339); of the later ones only short fragments have been preserved, either in Greek or Syriac—among them part of the 39th, which is important for its bearing on the New Testament canon. Up to 348 the only things that can be surely dated are the "Encyclical Letter," written soon after Easter, 339, and the discussion of Matt. xi, 27 (probably incomplete), belonging to a time before the death of Eusebius of Nicomedia. But with the collection of documents known as the "Apology against the Arians" (between 347 and 351) begins a long series of works more important for the history of the period, and at the same time more certainly to be dated. These are the "Defense of the Nicene Council" (probably 351); the "Defense of Dionysius" soon after; the "Letter to Dracontius" (Easter, 354 or 355); the "Letter to the Bishops of Egypt and Libya" (between February of 356 and the same month of 357); the "Apology to Constantius" (probably summer of 357); the "Apology for his Flight," a little later; the "History of the Arians for Monks" (end of 357 or beginning of 358); the "Letter to Serapion on the Death of Arius" (358); the four "Letters to Serapion," decisive for the doctrine of the consubstantiality of the Holy Ghost (during the third exile); "On the Synods of Ariminum and Seleucia" (end of 359); the "Book to the Antiochians" (362); the "Letter to Jovian" (364); the "Letter to the Africans" (probably 369); and about the same time, after the Roman synod of 369 or 370, the "Letters to Epictetus," "to Adelphus," and "to Maximus the Philosopher," so weighty for the controversies of the fifth century. We have not mentioned in this enumeration a few important works whose date can not be certainly determined, as well as a large number of smaller letters, sermons, and fragments. To the former class belong the "Life of Anthony," whose genuineness has been disputed of late years on insufficient grounds; the "Four Orations against the Arians," which have by many been considered the dogmatic masterpiece of Athanasius (usually dated in the third exile, but for various reasons more probably to be assigned to a much earlier date, say, 338 or 339); the fragmentary "Longer Sermon on the Faith," and the "Statement of Faith," both of which seem fairly assignable to the earliest period of Athanasius's authorship. Owing to his fame, it is not to be wondered at that a large number of works were ascribed to him which have since been classed as doubtful or certainly not his. For the famous exposition of the doctrines of the Trinity and Incarnation which passes under his name, see ATHANASIAN CREED.

1. His Works in Chronological Order.

As to the teaching of Athanasius, especially in regard to his Christology, consult the article ARIANISM; some further discussion of his views on the human nature of Christ, which deserve a more thorough examination than they have ever received, will be found under NESTORIUS. It is the opinion of Harnack that the doctrine of Athanasius is identical with that of Alexander and underwent no development. But it would be difficult to prove that the teaching of the two is really identical, at least on the basis of the writings of Athanasius from the "Defense of the Nicene Council" on; and perhaps as hard to show that his views did not develop as time went on. It is more probable (though the question needs more thorough investigation) that he began by simply accepting Alexander's teaching, and then struck out a path of his own. His terminology, in questions of Christology, demonstrably changes. The earlier works, like those of Alexander, do not use the word which became the crucial test of orthodoxy, *homoousios;* even in the main thesis of the "Statement of Faith" *homoios tōi patri* is found, though *homoousios* occurs in the explanations, but with an express caution against a Sabellian meaning. The same impression is strengthened by the "Orations against the Arians," written after he had spent some time in banishment at Treves; it is probably an already visible effect of his contact with western thought that we get a slightly different terminology—but the influence of the older phrases, which he gave up later, is still clearly marked; he employs the word *homoousios*, which his opponents rejected as unscriptural, only once in passing, and uses *homoios* several times to denote the generic identity of substance between the Father and the Son. In short, in these "Orations" Athanasius's terminology is in a transitional stage, not free from uncertainty. Later,

2. His Teaching.

he got over his concealed dread of the term *homoousios*, though without giving up the assimilation of *ousia* and *hypostasis*, as to which he was evidently uncertain in the "Orations." In fact, his later *homoousios* is scarcely distinguishable from *monoousios*, and the earlier *homoios* [*tēs ousias*] no longer sufficed him. If we ask the origin of this change between 339 and 348–352, it will be obvious that we can not neglect to think of his sojourn in the West from 339 to 346, and his intercourse with Marcellus. Further evidences of development may be found in his teaching as to the manhood of Christ. If, however, his change of attitude toward the Homoousians, his condemnation of Basil of Ancyra, etc., show that he was capable of development, it need not be taken as a reproach. He knew better than many of his contemporaries how to separate the fact, as to which he never wavered, from the formulas employed to describe it; his convictions were fixed early, but to the end of his life he never obstinately asserted the completeness of the phrases he had chosen to express them. Through evil report and good report, through the many changes of a long and eventful career, he maintained indisputably his title to the respect which we give to love of truth and honesty of mind. (F. Loofs.)

Bibliography: The Benedictine ed. of the works was printed in 4 vols., at Padua, 1677; again at Paris, 1699, ed. B. de Montfaucon; in *MPG*, xxv–xxviii; and in A. B. Caillau. *Patres Apostolici*, xxx–xxxii, Paris, 1842–43. The dogmatic treatises are accessible in the ed. of J. E. Thilo, Leipsic, 1853. Editions or translations of selected works are: *Historical Tracts and Treatises in Controversy with the Arians*, in *Library of the Fathers*, viii, ix, xiii, and xxviii, 1843; *Contra Gentes*, ed. H. von Hurter, in *Collectio opusculorum sanctorum patrum*, xliv, Innsbruck, 1874; *Select Treatises*, transl. by J. H. Newman, 2 vols., London, 1881; *Historical Writings ed. from the Benedictine Text*, by W. Bright, Oxford, 1881; *Dialogue of Athanasius and Zacchæus*, ed. F. C. Conybeare, in *Anecdota Oxoniensia*, part 8, ib. 1882; *Orations Against the Arians*, ed. W. Bright, with a life, ib. 1873, reissued in *Ancient and Modern Library of Theological Literature*, 1887; *Select Writings and Letters*, transl. with prolegomena, in *NPNF*, iv; and *De Incarnatione Verbi Dei*, transl. with notes by T. H. Bindley, London, 1903. Especially noteworthy is the edition of the long lost *Festal Letters*, by W. Cureton from a Syriac manuscript, London, 1853, Eng. transl. by H. Burgess, Oxford, 1854. His life, from early sources, is in *ASB*, May, i, 186–258, cf. 756–762 and vii, 546–547; consult the biographies by P. Barbier, Paris, 1888; R. W Bush, London, 1888; and H. R. Reynolds, ib. 1889 ("lucid and able"). For his writings and teaching consult J. A. Moehler, *Athanasius der Grosse und die Kirche seiner Zeit*, Mainz, 1844 (Roman Catholic); H. Voigt, *Die Lehre des Athanasius*, Bremen, 1861; F. Boehringer, *Athanasius und Arius, oder der erste grosse Kampf der Orthodoxie und Heterodoxie*, Stuttgart, 1874 (Protestant, in his familiar series); E. Fialon, *St. Athanase, Étude littéraire*, Paris, 1877; L. Atzberger, *Die Logoslehre des Athanasius, ihre Gegner und Vorläufer*, Munich, 1880; G. A. Pell, *Lehre des Athanasius von der Sünde*, Passau, 1888 (Roman Catholic, "difficulties not always faced"); W. Bright, *Lessons from the Lives of Three Great Fathers*, New York, 1891; P. Lauchert, *Die Lehre des heiligen Athanasius*, Leipsic, 1895; K. Hoss, *Studien über Schrifttum und Theologie des Athanasius*, Freiburg, 1899; Harnack, *Dogma*, passim (consult Index), 7 vols., Boston, 1895–1900 (important, very detailed); L. L. Paine, *Critical History of the Evolution of Trinitarianism*, Boston, 1900 (brilliant, deals with the position of Athanasius respecting homoousianism); W. F. Fraser, *A Cloud of Witnesses to Christian Doctrine*, third series, *Against Arianism*, part 1, *St. Athanasius*, London, 1900; L. H. Hough, *Athanasius; the Hero*, Cincinnati, 1906.

ATHEISM: A term employed with some variety of connotation. Sometimes it is taken purely negatively and applied to every point of view which does not distinctly assert the existence of God, or order the life in view of his claims upon it. In this application it is broad enough to include not only such systems as Agnosticism and Secularism (qq.v.), but even that simple forgetfulness of God which is commonly known as "practical atheism." Sometimes, on the other hand, it is given a distinctly positive sense, and made to designate the dogmatic denial of the existence of God. Even when it is so understood, however, it has a wider and a narrower application, dependent on the meaning attached to the term "God," the denial of which constitutes its differentiation. In its narrowest sense, it is confined to those theories which deny the existence of all that can be called God, by whatever extension or even abuse of that term. In this sense it stands over against Pantheism or Fetishism, as truly as over against Theism; and takes its place alongside of this whole series of terms as designating a distinct theory of the universe. In its widest sense, on the contrary, it receives its definition in contrast with, not a vague notion of the divine, but the specific conception of Theism, and designates all those systems, differing largely in other respects, which have in common that they are antagonistic to a developed Theism. In this application, Atheism is synonymous with Antitheism, and includes not only Pantheism (q.v.), but even Polytheism, and, with some writers, Deism itself,—all of which fail in some essential elements of a clear Theism. Most commonly the term is employed by careful writers either in its narrowest sense, or else in the somewhat broadened sense of the denial of a personal God. Between these two definitions choice is not easy. All depends on our definition of God, and what we are prepared to admit to involve recognition of him. From the point of view of developed Theism all that can be thought God is denied when a living personal God, the creator, preserver, and governor of all things is disallowed; it is inevitable, therefore, that from the standpoint of Theism, Atheism should tend to receive one of its more extended connotations. It may be truer to the historical sense of the term, however, to take it in its narrowest sense and to treat it as designating only one of the Antitheistic theories, and as standing as such alongside of the others, from which it is differentiated in that it denies the validity of the notion of God altogether, while the others allow the possible or actual existence of the divine in one or another sense of that term.

Different Uses of the Word.

The question which has been much discussed, whether Atheism is possible, depends for its solution very much upon its definition. That negative Atheism, especially in the form of "practical atheism," is possible, is evident from its persistent appearance in the world. Whether men may be totally ignorant of God or not, they certainly can very completely ignore him. And if the great atheistic systems like Buddhism and Confucianism have not been able to preserve the purity of their Atheism, no more have the great theistic systems—Mohammedanism, Judaism, Christianity itself—been able to eliminate "practical atheism" from among their adherents. **The Possibility of Atheism.** It is equally idle to deny the possibility of positive Atheism in its wider sense, in the face of the great part which has been played in the world by the various forms of Pantheism, which not only underlies whole systems of religion but is continually invading with its leaven the most austere and complete systems of Theism. It is only in its narrowest sense, in which it is the denial of all that is called God or that is worshiped, that the possibility of Atheism can be brought into question, and then only when we regard it, not in its outward expression, but in the most intimate convictions of the heart. No one can doubt that portentous systems of reasoned Atheism have flourished in the bosom of the most advanced culture. As little can it be denied that, among the backward races, a very low order of religious conception may sometimes be discovered. It may well be contended, however, that even the most thoroughly compacted system of atheistic thought only overlies and conceals an instinctive and indestructible "sense of the divine," just as the most elaborated system of subjective idealism only insecurely covers up an ineradicable realism; and that it is this innate "sense of the divine" which we see struggling in the conceptions of low savages to express itself in the inadequate forms which alone a low stage of culture can provide for it. If this is all that is meant, Atheism is, no doubt, a condition impossible to man. Man differs from the lower creations, not in being less dependent than they, but in being conscious of his dependence and responsibility; and this consciousness involves in it a sense of somewhat, or better, some one, to which he is thus related. The explication of this instinctive perception into an adequate conception is a different matter; and in this explication is wrapped up the whole development of the idea of God. But escape from the apprehension of a being on whom we are dependent and to whom we are responsible is no more possible than escape from the world in which we live. God is part of our environment.

History of Atheism. The history of reasoned Atheism is as old as the history of thought. There can be no right thinking unless there be thinking, and it is incident to thinking among such creatures as men that some may think awry. In all ages, accordingly, the declaration has found its verification that those who have not liked to retain God in their knowledge he has given over to a reprobate mind. India and China both early gave birth to gigantic atheistic systems. The materialism of classical antiquity found its expression especially in the Atomists—Democritus, Epicurus, Lucretius. The unbelief of the eighteenth century ran to seed in the French Encyclopedists—De la Mettrie, D'Holbach, Diderot, Lalande—and embodied itself in that *Système de la Nature* which Voltaire called the Bible of Atheism. In the nineteenth century the older materialism strengthened itself by alliance, on the one hand, with advancing scientific theory, and, on the other, with the increasing social unrest; and Atheism found expression through a series of great systems—Positivism, Secularism, Pessimism, Socialism. The doctrine of Evolution (q.v.), which was given scientific standing by Darwin's *Origin of Species* (1859), became almost at once the prime support and stay of the atheistic propaganda. In every department of thought "evolution" is supposed to account for everything, while itself needing no accounting for. Men as widely unlike in everything else as Feuerbach, Strauss, Flourens, Czolbe, Duehring, Vogt, Buechner, Moleschott, Mailänder, Haeckel, Nietzsche, have united in a common proclamation of dogmatic Atheism; and probably in no period since the advent of Christianity has positive Atheism been proclaimed with more confidence or accepted more widely.

BENJAMIN B. WARFIELD.

BIBLIOGRAPHY: R. Flint, *Antitheistic Theories*, Edinburgh, 1880 (gives literature in Appendix 4); J. Beattie, *Evidences of the Christian Religion*, 2 vols., Edinburgh, 1786 (contains a bibliography); J. Buchanan, *Faith in God and Modern Atheism Compared*, Edinburgh, 1855; *Modern Atheism under its Forms of Pantheism, Materialism, Secularism; Development and Natural Laws*, Boston, 1856; Paul Janet, *Le Matérialisme contemporain*, Paris, 1864; Félix Dupanloup, *L'Athéisme et le péril social*, Paris, 1866; É. Méric, *Morale et athéisme contemporaine*, Paris, 1875; J. S. Blackie, *Natural History of Atheism*, London, 1877 (keen and discriminating); J. Cairns, *Unbelief in the Eighteenth Century*, London, 1881; E. Naville, *Le Père Céleste*, Geneva, 1865, Eng. transl., *Modern Atheism or the Heavenly Father*, London, 1882 (philosophical); F. W. Hedge, *Atheism in Philosophy*, Boston, 1884; W. H. Mallock, *Atheism and the Value of Life*, London, 1884; H. H. Moore, *Anatomy of Atheism in the Light of the Laws of Nature*, Boston, 1890; A. Egger, *Der Atheismus*, Einsiedeln, 1901 (evangelical); F. le Dantec, *L'Athéisme*, Paris, 1906.

ATHENAGORAS, ath″e-nag′o-ras: Reputed author of two Greek treatises of the time of the Antonines, one on the resurrection, the other an apology for the Christians. He is entirely unknown to the tradition of the Church. Eusebius, Jerome, and their successors are silent, and, as the survey which Eusebius gives of the apologetic literature of the second century is very complete, his silence could not fail to attract attention. Very early the existence of an apologist of the name was doubted and the work was ascribed to Justin (cf. Baronius, *Annales*, ii, ad an. 179, chap. xxxix). This supposition, however, is from internal reasons untenable. The first testimony, and the only one from the third century, to the existence of the apology and the name of its author, is a quotation by Methodius, found (1) in the ancient Bulgarian translation (ed. Bonwetsch, i, 293); (2) in Epiphanius, *Hær.*, lxiv, 20, 21; (3) in Photius, *Bibl. cod.* 234 (cf. Athenagoras, *Supplicatio*, xxiv, p. 27 B). Certain notices by an unknown scribe (*Cod. Barocc.* 142, fol. 216) quoting from the "Christian History" of Philippus Sidetes (early in the fifth century) state that Athenagoras was an Athenian by birth, and first director of the catechetical school of Alexandria; he lived in the time of Hadrian and Antoninus Pius; like Celsus, he was occupied with searching the Scriptures for arguments against Christianity, when he was suddenly converted. Most of these notices, however, are palpably erroneous. Yet, in spite of the entire absence of tradition and the close resemblance to the apology of Justin, the date of the work must be placed somewhere in the second century. It is addressed to the emperors Marcus Aurelius and Lucius Aurelius Commodus, and various passages indicate the period between 176 and 178. After an introduction (i–iii) the author refutes the chief calumnies urged against the Christians in that day, viz., that they were atheists (iv–xxx), and that they ate human flesh and committed the most horrible crimes in their assemblies (xxxi–xxxvi). In the treatise on the resurrection, Athenagoras argues in its favor from the goodness, wisdom, and power of God, together with the natural constitution of man. (A. HARNACK.)

BIBLIOGRAPHY: The text of Athenagoras is given in *MPG*, vi; the best editions are by J. C. T. Otto, in *Corpus apologetarum Christianorum*, vol. vii, Jena, 1876, and E Schwarz, in *TU*, iv, 2, Leipsic, 1891; a handy ed. is by F. A. March, New York, 1876; an Eng. transl. is to be found in *ANF*, ii, 125–162. Consult Harnack, *Litteratur*, i. 256–258, ii, 317–319; Krüger, *History*, pp. 130–132; L. Arnould, *De Apologia Athenagoræ*, Paris, 1898 A full bibliography up to 1886 is in *ANF*, Bibliography, 36–38.

ATHENS. See GREECE, I., § 2.

ATH'OS: The easternmost of the three tongues of land projecting into the Ægean Sea from the Chalcidian peninsula. It is about 35 miles long and culminates at the southern extremity in Mt. Athos proper, 6,780 feet high. Grand forests, murmuring brooks, clear air, and charming combination of rocks and sea, make it one of the most beautiful spots of Europe. By the Orthodox Greeks it is always called "the Holy Mount." According to the legend, the Holy Virgin Christianized Mt. Athos and Constantine the Great founded the first monasteries there. But the Athos monasticism does not appear in church history before the middle of the ninth century. At that time the monks formed a laura of the old fashion, with its center at Karyas, presided over by a *prōtos* appointed by the emperor in Constantinople. With the founding of the Laura of St. Athanasius, the first great monastery there, in 963, Athos rises in historical importance.

The Various Monasteries.

The founder of this monastery (which still bears his name) and of the whole monastic life on Mt. Athos, belonged to a noble family in Trebizond. Through Michael Maleinos, the famous hegumenos of Mt. Kyminos in Asia Minor, where he himself lived at first as monk, he became acquainted with the future emperor, Nicephoras II (Phocas). The two men became good friends and the laura was founded at the instance of the emperor. Ever after Athos enjoyed imperial favor and monasteries were founded in rapid succession. To the tenth century belongs the founding of Iveron, Vatopedi, and Philotheu; to the eleventh, Xeropotam, Esfigmenu, Dochiariu, Agiu Paulu, Karakallu, and Xenophontos; to the twelfth, the two important Slav monasteries, Russiko and Chilandari; to the thirteenth, Zografu; and to the fourteenth, Pantokratoros, Simopetra, Dionysiu, and Gregoriu. The most recent is Stauronikita, founded in 1542. There were others which long ago disappeared, such as a Latin monastery of the Amalfines.

Until the fifteenth century all the monks lived together, according to rules laid down by Athanasius in his three writings, the

The Monastic Life to the Fifteenth Century.

Kanonikon, the *Diathēkē*, and the so-called *Diatypōsis* (cf. Meyer, *Haupturkunden*). Any man of unblemished character could be received; but women, children, beardless youths, and people of royal descent were forbidden entrance. After a three years' probation admission into the holy company of the brethren took place and the tonsure was received. At the head of the monastery stood the *hēgoumenos*, assisted by a council of "the chosen," i.e., the higher monastic officers and the priest-monks. Two ephors, generally a noble layman outside of Athos and a monk not belonging to the monastery, formed a non-resident directorate. Approved monks could live by themselves, and received a special dwelling (Gk. *kellion*), whence they were called kelliotes, or after their mode of living, ascetics or hesychasts, but were dependent on the monastery. The relation of the monasteries to each other and the entire constitution of the holy mount was regulated at that period by the typica of 975, 1045, and 1394 (printed in Meyer). The *prōtos* stood at the head, by his side the *synaxis*, consisting of the representatives of the monasteries, which as before met at Karyas. At first the life during this period was austere, but in the eleventh century it relaxed, and at one time nomads with wives and children were sheltered at Athos (Meyer, 163 sqq.). The Latin rule at Constantinople was an especially sad time for the monasteries. In the Hesychastic controversy (1341–51) western science was rejected especially through the influence of the Athos monks and quietistic mysticism was received into the teachings of the Greek Church (see HESYCHASTS).

With the fifteenth century a new period commences in the constitution of the holy mount, which by degrees transformed the entire life. The idiorrhythmic life begins, which consisted in the abolition of the common life in the monasteries and the adoption of a plan whereby every monk, sometimes with a few friends, lived by himself. The common roof and the church

Changes after 1500.

alone are common to all. Since every one lived at his own expense, the power of the hegumenos was soon crippled. But the influence of idiorrhythm went still further. As the monasteries following it soon became worldly, the stricter tendency, which was by no means extinct, reacted upon the monks and new places of earnest asceticism were established outside of the monasteries, such as the *skētai*, monastic villages, the first of which was founded by St. Anna in 1572. Here one could live an ascetic life after the old fashion. Such sketes were dependent on their monasteries; their rights are set forth in separate collections of canons (cf. Meyer, 248). The last regulation of the rights of the kelliotes, who still remained, and of the sketists took place in 1864 (Meyer, 251). The influence of idiorrhythm was ultimately of such a character on the general constitution of the holy mount, that the office of protos was abolished and the entire constitution became democratic. The last typicon is of 1783 (Meyer, 243). In the nineteenth century half of the monasteries returned to the common life, but the old constitution was retained. Down to the eighteenth century the religious and moral life was of a low type. After 1750 there seems to have been a revival. At that time Eugenios Bulgaris (q.v.) was teacher in the academy of Vatopedi. At the end of the eighteenth century there were certain lively religious controversies on Mt. Athos, among others the so-called **kolyba** controversy—whether the memorial days of the dead could be celebrated on Sunday instead of Saturday.

On the whole the life on Athos has remained unchanged, and is still a remnant of pure medievalism. The great number of manuscripts and documents there offer to the scholar a rich field of activity. The student of art finds all that Byzantine art produced gathered together. The student of religion can study the Eastern piety of all Christian centuries, for each period has left behind distinct remains. It is to be hoped that the struggle of the nationalists, especially the struggle of Panhellenism against Panslavism, will not deprive the Athos monachism of its universality.

PHILIPP MEYER.

BIBLIOGRAPHY: The *Historiæ Byzantinæ* of Nicephoras Gregoras, book xiv, in *MPG*, cxlviii, and of John Cantacuzenus, book iv, in *MPG*, cliv, 15-370, passim; John Comnenus, Προσκυνητάριον τοῦ ἁγίου ὄρους, Venice, 1701, and often; J. P. Fallmerayer, *Fragmente aus dem Orient*, Stuttgart, 1845; M. I. Gedeon, ὁ Ἄθως, Constantinople, 1885; Porphyrius Uspensky, *Geschichte des Athos und seiner Klöster* (in Russian), 3 vols., Kiev and Moscow, 1845-92; Philipp Meyer, *Die Haupturkunden für die Geschichte der Athosklöster*, Leipsic, 1894; A. Schmidtke, *Das Klosterland des Athos*, Leipsic, 1903; H. Gelzer, *Vom heiligen Berge und aus Macedonien*, Leipsic, 1904; H. Brockhaus, *Die Kunst in den Athosklöstern*, Leipsic, 1891. Catalogues of the documents are given in V. Langlois, *Le Mont Athos et ses monastères*, Paris, 1867; J. Müller, *Slawische Bibliothek*, Vienna, 1851; and in the Περιγραφικὸς Κατάλογος, published at Constantinople in 1902 at the instance of the patriarch Joachim III. A catalogue of the manuscripts in most of the libraries is given in S. Lampros, Κατάλογος τῶν ἐν ταῖς βιβλιοθήκαις τοῦ ἁγίου ὄρους Ἑλληνικῶν κωδίκων, 2 vols., Cambridge, 1895-1900. Many documents have been published in Greek and Russian periodicals. A new collection has been begun by Regel, Χρυσόβουλλα καὶ γραμμάτια τῆς ἐν τῷ Ἁγίῳ Ὄρει μονῆς τοῦ Βατοπεδίου, St. Petersburg, 1898. For special literature, consult Krumbacher, *Geschichte;* the English works of R. Curzon, *Visits to Monasteries in the Levant*, London, 1849, 1865, and A. Riley, *Athos or the Mountain of the Monks*, London, 1887, may also be mentioned.

ATKINS, JAMES: Methodist Episcopalian; b. at Knoxville, Tenn., Apr. 18, 1850. He was educated at Emory and Henry College (B.A., 1872) and entered the ministry in the Holston Conference of the Methodist Episcopal Church, South, in 1872, in which he held various pastorates until 1879. He was president of Asheville Female College, 1879-89 and 1893-96, and of Emory and Henry College, 1889-93. Since 1896 he has been the Sunday-school editor of the Methodist Episcopal Church, South. He is president of the Board of Missions of the Western North Carolina Conference, and vice-president of the General Board of Missions of the Methodist Episcopal Church, South, and was also a member of the commission which effected the union of the Methodist Episcopal Churches of Japan in 1906. He is the author of *The Kingdom in the Cradle* (Nashville, 1905).

ATMIYA SABHA. See INDIA, III, 1.

ATONEMENT.

I. Significance and History of the Doctrine: The replacement of the term "satisfaction" (q.v.), to designate, according to its nature, the work of Christ in saving sinners, by "atonement," the term more usual at present, is somewhat unfortunate. "Satisfaction" is at once the more comprehensive, the more expressive, the less ambiguous, and the more exact term. The word "atonement" occurs but once in the English New Testament (Rom. v, 11, A. V., but not R. V.) and on this occasion it bears its archaic sense of "reconciliation," and as such translates the Greek term *katallagē*. In the English Old Testament, however, it is found quite often as the stated rendering of the Hebrew terms *kipper, kippurim*, in the sense of "propitiation," "expiation." It is in this latter sense that it has become current, and has been applied to the work of Christ, which it accordingly describes as, in its essential nature, an expiatory offering, propitiating an offended deity and reconciling him with man. In thus characterizing the work of Christ, it does no injustice to the New Testament representation.

1. The New Testament Presentation. The writers of the New Testament employ many other modes of describing the work of Christ, which, taken together, set it forth as much more than a provision, in his death, for canceling the guilt of man. To mention nothing else at the moment, they set it forth equally as a provision, in his righteousness, for fulfilling the demands of the divine law upon the conduct of men. But it is undeniable that they enshrine at the center of this work its efficacy as a piacular sacrifice, securing the forgiveness of sins; that is to say, relieving its beneficiaries of "the penal consequences which otherwise the curse of the broken law inevitably entails." The Lord himself fastens attention upon this aspect of his work (Matt. xx, 28, xxvi, 28); and it is embedded in every important type of New Testament teaching, —as well in the Epistle to the Hebrews (ii, 17), and the Epistles of Peter (I, iii, 18) and John (I, ii, 2), as currently in those of Paul (Rom. viii, 3; I Cor. v, 7; Eph. v, 2) to whom, obviously, "the sacrifice of Christ had the significance of the death of an innocent victim in the room of the guilty" and who therefore "freely employs the category of substitution, involving the conception of imputation or transference" of legal standing (W. P. Paterson, art. *Sacrifice* in *DB*, iv, 343–345). Looking out from this point of view as from a center, the New Testament writers ascribe the saving efficacy of Christ's work specifically to his death, or his blood, or his cross (Rom. iii, 25–59; I Cor. x, 16; Eph. i, 7; ii, 13; Col. i, 20; Heb. ix, 12, 14; I Pet. i, 2, 19; I John i, 7, v, 6–8; Rev. i, 5), and this with such predilection and emphasis that the place given to the death of Christ in the several theories which have been framed of the nature of our Lord's work, may not unfairly be taken as a test of their scripturalness. All else that Christ does for us in the breadth of his redeeming work is, in their view, conditioned upon his bearing our sins in his own body on the tree; so that "the fundamental characteristic of the New Testament conception of redemption is that deliverance from guilt stands first; emancipation from the power of sin follows upon it; and removal of all the ills of life constitutes its final issue" (O. Kirn, art. *Erlösung* in Hauck-Herzog, *RE*, v, 464; see REDEMPTION).

The exact nature of Christ's work in redemption was not made the subject of scientific investigation in the early Church. This was due partly, no doubt, just to the clearness of the New Testament representation of it as a piacular sacrifice; but in part also to the engrossment of the minds of the first teachers of Christianity with more immediately pressing problems, such as the adjustment of the essential elements of the Christian doctrines of God and of the person of Christ, and the establishment of man's helplessness in sin and absolute dependence on the grace of God for salvation. Meanwhile Christians were content to speak of the work of Christ in simple scriptural or in general language, or to develop, rather by way of illustration than of explanation, certain aspects of it, chiefly its efficacy as a sacrifice, but also, very prominently, its working as a ransom in delivering us from bondage to Satan. Thus it was not until the end of the eleventh century that the nature of the Atonement received at the hands of Anselm (d. 1109) its first thorough discussion. Representing it, in terms derived from the Roman law, as in its essence a "satisfaction" to the divine justice, Anselm set it once for all in its true relations to the inherent necessities of the divine nature, and to the magnitude of human guilt; and thus determined the outlines of the doctrine for all subsequent thought. Contemporaries like Bernard and Abelard, no doubt, and perhaps not unnaturally, found difficulty in assimilating at once the newly framed doctrine; the former ignored it in the interests of the old notion of a ransom offered to Satan; the latter rejected it in the interests of a theory of moral influence upon man. But it gradually made its way. The Victorines, Hugo and Richard, united with it other elements, the effect of which was to cure its one-sidedness; and the great doctors of the age of developed scholasticism manifest its victory by differing from one another chiefly in their individual ways of stating and defending it. Bonaventura develops it; Aquinas enriches it with his subtle distinctions; Thomist and Scotist alike start from it, and diverge only in the question whether the "satisfaction" offered by Christ was intrinsically equivalent to the requirements of the divine justice or availed for this purpose only through the gracious acceptance of God. It was not, however, until the Reformation doctrine of justification by faith threw its light back upon the "satisfaction" which provided its basis, that that doctrine came fully to its rights. No one before Luther had spoken with the clarity, depth, or breadth which characterize his references to Christ as our deliverer, first from the guilt of sin, and then, because from the guilt of sin, also from all that is evil, since all that is evil springs from sin (cf. T. Harnack, *Luther's Theologie*, ii, Leipsic, 1886, 16–19, and Kirn, ut sup., 467). These vital religious conceptions were reduced to scientific statement by the Protestant scholastics, by whom it was that the complete doctrine of "satisfaction" was formulated with a thoroughness and comprehensiveness of grasp which has made it the permanent possession of the Church. In this, its developed form, it represents our Lord as making satisfaction for us "by his blood and righteousness"; on the one hand, to the justice of God, outraged by human sin, in bearing the penalty due to our guilt in his own sacrificial death; and, on the other hand, to the demands of the law of God requiring perfect obedience, in fulfilling in his immaculate life on earth as the second Adam the probation which Adam failed to keep; bringing to bear on men at the same time and by means of the same double work every conceivable influence adapted to deter them from sin and to win them back to good and to God,—by the highest imaginable demonstration of God's righteousness and hatred of sin and the supreme manifestation of God's love and eagerness to save; by a gracious proclamation of full forgiveness of sin in the blood of Christ; by a winning revelation of the spiritual order and the spiritual world; and by the moving example of his own perfect life in the conditions of this world; but, above all, by the purchase of the gift of the Holy Spirit for his people as a power not themselves making for righteousness dwelling within them, and supernaturally regenerating their hearts and conforming their lives to his image, and so preparing them for their permanent place in the new order of things which, flowing from this redeeming work, shall ultimately be established as the eternal form of the Kingdom of God.

2. Development of the Doctrine.

Of course, this great comprehensive doctrine of "the satisfaction of Christ" has not been permitted to hold the field without controversy Many "theories of the atonement" have been constructed, each throwing into emphasis a fragment of the truth, to the neglect or denial of the complementary elements, including ordinarily the central matter of the expiation of guilt itself (cf. T. J. Crawford, *The Doctrine of Holy Scripture Respecting the Atonement*, Edinburgh, 1888, pp. 395–401; A. B. Bruce, *The Humiliation of Christ*, Edinburgh, 1881, lecture 7; A. A. Hodge, *The Atonement*, Philadelphia, 1867, pp. 17 sqq.). Each main form of these theories, in some method of statement or other, has at one time or another seemed on the point of becoming the common doctrine of the Churches. In the patristic age men spoke with such predilection of the work of Christ as issuing in our deliverance from the power of Satan that the false impression is very readily obtained from a cursory survey of the teaching of the Fathers that they predominantly conceived it as directed to that sole end. The so-called "mystical" view, which had representatives among the Greek Fathers and has always had advo-

3. Various Theories.

cates in the Church, appeared about the middle of the last century almost ready to become dominant in at least Continental Protestantism through the immense influence of Schleiermacher. The "rectoral or governmental theory," invented by Grotius early in the seventeenth century in the effort to save something from the assault of the Socinians, has ever since provided a half-way house for those who, while touched by the chilling breath of rationalism, have yet not been ready to surrender every semblance of an "objective atonement," and has therefore come very prominently forward in every era of decaying faith. The "moral influence" theory, which in the person of perhaps the acutest of all the scholastic reasoners, Peter Abelard, confronted the doctrine of "satisfaction" at its formulation, in its vigorous promulgation by the Socinians and again by the lower class of rationalists obtained the widest currency; and again in our own day, its enthusiastic advocates, by perhaps a not unnatural illusion, are tempted to claim for it the final victory (so, e.g., G. B. Stevens, *The Christian Doctrine of Salvation*, New York, 1905; but cf. per contra, of the same school, T. V. Tymms, *The Christian Idea of Atonement*, London, 1904, p. 8). But no one of these theories, however attractively they may be presented, or however wide an acceptance each may from time to time have found in academic circles, has ever been able to supplant the doctrine of "satisfaction" either in the formal creeds of the Churches, or in the hearts of simple believers. Despite the fluidity of much recent thinking on the subject, the doctrine of "satisfaction" remains to-day the established doctrine of the Churches as to the nature of Christ's work of redemption, and is apparently immovably entrenched in the hearts of the Christian body (cf. J. B. Remensnyder, *The Atonement and Modern Thought*, Philadelphia, 1905, p. xvi).

II. The Five Chief Theories of the Atonement: A survey of the various theories of the Atonement which have been broached, may be made from many points of view (cf. especially the survey in T. G. Crawford, ut sup., pp. 385–401; Bruce, ut sup., lecture 7; and for recent German views, F. A. B. Nitzsch, *Lehrbuch der evangelischen Dogmatik*, Freiburg, 1892, §§ 43–46; O. Bensow, *Die Lehre von der Versöhnung*, Gütersloh, 1904, pp. 7–156; G. A. F. Ecklin, *Erlösung und Versöhnung*, Basel, 1903, part 4). Perhaps as good a method as any other is to arrange them according to the conception each entertains of the person or persons on whom the work of Christ terminates. When so arranged they fall naturally into five classes which may be enumerated here in the ascending order.

1. Theories which conceive the work of Christ as *terminating upon Satan*, so affecting him as to secure the release of the souls held in bondage by him. These theories, which have been described as emphasizing the "triumphantorial" aspect of Christ's work (Ecklin, ut sup., pp. 113 sqq.) had very considerable vogue in the patristic age (e.g., Irenæus, Hippolytus, Clement of Alex-

1. The "Triumphantorial Theory."

andria, Origen, Basil, the two Gregories, Cyril of Alexandria, down to and including John of Damascus and Nicholas of Methone; Hilary, Rufinus, Jerome, Augustine, Leo the Great, and even so late as Bernard). They passed out of view only gradually as the doctrine of "satisfaction" became more widely known. Not only does the thought of a Bernard still run in this channel, but even Luther utilized the conception. The idea runs through many forms,—speaking in some of them of buying off, in some of overcoming, in some even of outwitting (so, e.g., Origen) the devil. But it would be unfair to suppose that such theories represent in any of their forms the whole thought as to the work of Christ of those who made use of them, or were considered by them a scientific statement of the work of Christ. They rather embody only their author's profound sense of the bondage in which men are held to sin and death, and vividly set forth the rescue they conceive Christ has wrought for us in overcoming him who has the power of death.

2. Theories which conceive the work of Christ as *terminating physically on man*, so affecting him as to bring him by an interior and hidden working upon him into participation with the one life of Christ; the so-called "mystical theories." The fundamental characteristic of these theories is their discovery of the saving fact not in anything which Christ taught or did, but in what he was. It is upon the Incarnation, rather than upon Christ's teaching or his work that they throw stress, attributing the saving power of Christ not to what he does for us but to what he does in us. Tendencies to this type of theory are already traceable in the Platonizing Fathers; and with the en-

2. "Mystical Theories" and their Advocates.

trance of the more developed Neo-platonism into the stream of Christian thinking, through the writings of the Pseudo-Dionysius naturalized in the West by Johannes Scotus Erigena, a constant tradition of mystical teaching began which never died out. In the Reformation age this type of thought was represented by men like Osiander, Schwenckfeld, Franck, Weigel, Boehme. In the modern Church a new impulse was given to essentially the same mode of conception by Schleiermacher and his followers (e.g., C. I. Nitzsch, Rothe, Schöberlein, Lange, Martensen), among whom what is known as the "Mercersburg School" (see MERCERSBURG THEOLOGY) will be particularly interesting to Americans (e.g., J. W Nevin, *The Mystical Presence*, Philadelphia, 1846). A very influential writer among English theologians of the same general class was F. D. Maurice (1805-72), although he added to his fundamental mystical conception of the work of Christ the further notions that Christ fully identified himself with us and, thus partaking of our sufferings, set us a perfect example of sacrifice of self to God (cf. especially *Theological Essays*, London, 1853; *The Doctrine of Sacrifice*, Cambridge, 1854; new ed., 1879). Here, too, must be classed the theory suggested in the writings of the late B. F. Westcott (*The Victory of the Cross*, London, 1888), which was based on a hypothesis of the efficacy of Christ's blood, borrowed apparently directly from William Milligan (cf. *The Ascension and Heavenly Highpriesthood of our Lord*, London, 1892) though it goes back ultimately to the Socinians, to the effect that Christ's offering of himself is not to be identified with his sufferings and death, but rather with the presentation of his life (which is in his blood, set free by death for this purpose) in heaven. "Taking this blood as efficacious by virtue of the vitality which it contains, Dr. Westcott holds that it was set free from Christ's body that it might vitalize ours, as it were, by transfusion" (C. H. Waller, in the *Presbyterian and Reformed Review*, ii, 1892, p. 656). Somewhat similarly H. Clay Trumbell (*The Blood Covenant*, New York, 1885) looks upon sacrifices as only a form of blood covenanting, i.e., of instituting blood-brotherhood between man and God by transfusion of blood; and explains the sacrifice of Christ as representing communing in blood, i.e., in the principle of life, between God and man, both of whom Christ represents. The theory which has been called "salvation by sample," or salvation "by gradually extirpated depravity," also has its affinities here. Something like it is as old as Felix of Urgel (d. 818; see ADOPTIONISM), and it has been taught in its full development by Dippel (1673–1734), Swedenborg (1688–1772), Menken (1768–1831), and especially by Edward Irving (1792–1834), and, of course, by the modern followers of Swedenborg (e.g., B. F. Barrett). The essence of this theory is that what was assumed by our Lord was human nature as he found it, that is, as fallen; and that this human nature, as assumed by him, was by the power of his divine nature (or of the Holy Spirit dwelling in him beyond measure) not only kept from sinning, but purified from sin and presented perfect before God as the first-fruits of a saved humanity; men being saved as they become partakers (by faith) of this purified humanity, as they become leavened by this new leaven. Certain of the elements which the great German theologian J. C. K. von Hofmann built into his complicated and not altogether stable theory—a theory which was the occasion of much discussion about the middle of the nineteenth century—reproduce some of the characteristic language of the theory of "salvation by sample."

3. Theories which conceive the work of Christ as *terminating on man, in the way of bringing to bear on him inducements to action;* so affecting man as to lead him to a better knowledge of God, or to a more lively sense of his real relation to God, or to a revolutionary change of heart and life with reference to God; the so-called "moral influence theories." The essence of all these theories is that they transfer the atoning fact from the work of Christ to the response of the human soul to the influences or appeals proceeding from the work of Christ. The work of Christ takes immediate effect not on God but on man, leading him to a state of mind and heart which will be acceptable to God, through the medium of which alone can the work of Christ be said to affect God. At its highest level, this will mean that the work of Christ is directed to leading man to repentance and faith, which repentance and faith secure God's favor, an effect which can be attributed to Christ's work only mediately, that is, through the medium of the repentance and faith it produces in man. Accordingly, it has become quite common to say, in this school, that "it is faith and repentance which change the face of God;" and advocates of this class of theories sometimes say with entire frankness, "There is no atonement other than repentance" (Auguste Sabatier, *La Doctrine de l'expiation et son évolution historique*, Paris, 1903, Eng. transl., London, 1904, p. 127).

3. "Moral Influence Theories." The Essential Thought.

Theories of this general type differ from one another, according as, among the instrumentalities by means of which Christ affects the minds and hearts and actions of men, the stress is laid upon his teaching, or his example, or the impression made by his life of faith, or the manifestation of the infinite love of God afforded by his total mission. The most powerful presentation of the first of these conceptions ever made was probably that of the Socinians (followed later by the rationalists, both earlier and later,—Töllner, Bahrdt, Steinbart, Eberhard, Löffler, Henke, Wegscheider). They looked upon the work of Christ as summed up in the proclamation of the willingness of God to forgive sin, on the sole condition of its abandonment; and explained his sufferings and death as merely those of a martyr in the cause of righteousness or in some other non-essential way. The theories which lay the stress of Christ's work on the example he has set us of a high and faithful life, or of a life of self-sacrificing love, have found popular representatives not only in the subtle theory with which F. D. Maurice pieced out his mystical view, and in the somewhat amorphous ideas with which the great preacher F. W Robertson clothed his conception of Christ's life as simply a long (and hopeless) battle against the evil of the world to which it at last succumbed; but more lately in writers like Auguste Sabatier, who does not stop short of transmuting Christianity into bald altru-

4. Various Forms of These Theories.

ism, and making it into what he calls the religion of "universal redemption by love," that is to say, anybody's love, not specifically Christ's love,—for every one who loves takes his position by Christ's side as, if not equally, yet as truly, a savior as he (*The Doctrine of the Atonement in its Historical Evolution*, Eng. transl., ut sup., pp. 131–134; so also Otto Pfleiderer, *Das Christusbild des urchristlichen Glaubens in religionsgeschichtlicher Beleuchtung*, Berlin, 1903, Eng. transl., London, 1905, pp. 164–165; cf. Horace Bushnell, *Vicarious Sacrifice*, New York, 1865, p. 107: "Vicarious sacrifice was in no way peculiar"). In this same general category belongs also the theory which Albrecht Ritschl has given such wide influence. According to it, the work of Christ consists in the establishment of the Kingdom of God in the world, that is, in the revelation of God's love to men and his gracious purposes for men. Thus Jesus becomes the first object of this love and as such its mediator to others; his sufferings and death being, on the one side, a test of his steadfastness, and, on the other, the crowning proof of his obedience (*Rechtfertigung und Versöhnung*, iii, §§ 41–61, 3d ed., Bonn, 1888, Eng. transl., Edinburgh, 1900). Similarly also, though with many modifications, which are in some instances not insignificant, such writers as W Herrmann (*Der Verkehr des Christen mit Gott*, Stuttgart, 1886, p. 93, Eng. transl., London, 1895), J. Kaftan (*Dogmatik*, Tübingen, 1901, pp. 446 sqq.), F. A. B. Nitzsch (*Evangelische Dogmatik*, Freiburg, 1892, pp. 504–513), T. Häring (in his *Ueber das Bleibende im Glauben an Christus*, Stuttgart, 1880, where he sought to complete Ritschl's view by the addition of the idea that Christ offered to God a perfect sorrow for the world's sin, which supplements our imperfect repentance; in his later writings, *Zu Ritschl's Versöhnungslehre*, Zurich, 1888, *Zur Versöhnungslehre*, Göttingen, 1893, he assimilates to the Grotian theory), E. Kühl (*Die Heilsbedeutung des Todes Christi*, Berlin, 1890), G. A. F. Ecklin (*Die Heilswerth des Todes Jesu*, Gütersloh, 1888; *Christus Unser Bürge*, Basel, 1900; and especially *Erlösung und Versöhnung*, 1903, which is an elaborate history of the doctrine from the point of view of what Ecklin calls in antagonism to the "substitutional-expiatory" conception, the "solidaric-reparatory" conception of the Atonement,—the conception, that is, that Christ comes to save men not primarily from the guilt, but from the power of sin, and that "the sole satisfaction God demands for his outraged honor is the restoration of obedience," p. 647). The most popular form of the "moral influence" theories has always been that in which the stress is laid on the manifestation made in the total mission and work of Christ of the ineffable and searching love of God for sinners, which, being perceived, breaks down our opposition to God, melts our hearts, and brings us as prodigals home to the Father's arms. It is in this form that the theory was advocated (but with the suggestion that there is another side to it), for example, by S. T. Coleridge (*Aids to Reflection*), and that it was commended to English-speaking readers of the last generation with the highest ability by John Young of Edinburgh (*The Life and Light of Men*, London, 1866), and with the greatest literary attractiveness by Horace Bushnell (*Vicarious Sacrifice*, New York, 1865; see below, § 7; see also article BUSHNELL, HORACE); and has been more recently set forth in elaborate and vigorously polemic form by W N. Clarke (*An Outline of Christian Theology*, New York, 1898, pp. 341–367), T. Vincent Tymms (*The Christian Idea of Atonement*, London, 1904), G. B. Stevens (*The Christian Doctrine of Salvation*, New York, 1905), and C. M. Mead (*Irenic Theology*, New York, 1905).

In a volume of essays published first in the *Andover Review* (iv, 1885, pp. 57 sqq.) and afterward gathered into a volume under the title of *Progressive Orthodoxy* (Boston, 1886), the professors in Andover Seminary made an attempt (the writer here being, as was understood, George Harris) to enrich the "moral influence" theory of the Atonement after a fashion quite common in Germany (cf., e.g., Häring, ut sup.) with elements derived from other well-known forms of teaching. In this construction, Christ's work is made to consist primarily in bringing to bear on man a revelation of God's hatred of sin, and love for souls, by which he makes man capable of repentance and leads him to repent revolutionarily; by this repentance, then, together with Christ's own sympathetic expression of repentance God is rendered propitious. Here Christ's work is supposed to have at least some (though a secondary) effect upon God; and a work of propitiation of God by Christ may be spoken of, although it is accomplished by a "sympathetic repentance." It has accordingly become usual with those who have adopted this mode of representation to say that there was in this atoning work, not indeed "a substitution of a sinless Christ for a sinful race," but a "substitution of humanity *plus* Christ for humanity *minus* Christ." By such curiously compacted theories the transition is made to the next class.

4. Theories which conceive the work of Christ as *terminating on both man and God, but on man primarily and on God only secondarily*. The outstanding instance of this class of theories is supplied by the so-called "rectoral or governmental theories." These suppose that the work of Christ so affects man by the spectacle of the sufferings borne by him as to deter men from sin; and by thus deterring men from sin enables God to forgive sin with safety to his moral government of the world. In these theories the sufferings and death of Christ become, for the first time in this conspectus of theories, of cardinal importance, constituting indeed the very essence of the work of Christ. But the atoning fact here too, no less than in the "moral influence" theories, is man's own reformation, though this reformation is supposed in the rectoral view to be wrought not primarily by breaking down man's opposition to God by a moving manifestation of the love of God in Christ, but by inducing in man a horror of sin, through the spectacle of God's hatred of sin afforded by the sufferings of Christ,—through which, no doubt, the contemplation of man is led on to

5. "Rectoral or Governmental Theories."

God's love to sinners as exhibited in his willingness to inflict all these sufferings on his own son, that he might be enabled, with justice to his moral government, to forgive sins.

This theory was worked out by the great Dutch jurist Hugo Grotius (*Defensio fidei Christianæ de satisfactione Christi*, etc., Leyden, 1617; modern ed., Oxford, 1856; Eng. transl., with notes and introduction by F. H. Foster, Andover, 1889) as an attempt to save what was salvable of the established doctrine of satisfaction from disintegration under the attacks of the Socinian advocates of the "moral influence" theories (see GROTIUS, HUGO).

6. Advocates of These Theories. It was at once adopted by those Arminians who had been most affected by the Socinian reasoning; and in the next age became the especial property of the better class of the so-called supranaturalists (Michaelis, Storr, Morus, Knapp, Steudel, Reinhard, Muntinge, Vinke, Egeling). It has remained on the continent of Europe to this day, the refuge of most of those, who, influenced by the modern spirit, yet wish to preserve some form of "objective," that is, of Godward atonement. A great variety of representations have grown up under this influence, combining elements of the satisfaction and rectoral views. To name but a single typical instance, the commentator F. Godet, both in his commentaries (especially that on Romans) and in a more recent essay (published in *The Atonement in Modern Thought* by various writers, London, 1900, pp. 331 sqq.), teaches (certainly in a very high form) the rectoral theory distinctly (and is corrected therefor by his colleague at Neuchâtel, Prof. Gretillat, who wishes an "ontological" rather than a merely "demonstrative" necessity for atonement to be recognized). Its history has run on similar lines in English-speaking countries. In Great Britain and America alike it has become practically the orthodoxy of the Independents. It has, for example, been taught as such in the former country by Joseph Gilbert (*The Christian Atonement*, London, 1836), and in especially well worked-out forms by R. W. Dale (*The Atonement*, London, 1876) and Alfred Cave (*The Scriptural Doctrine of Sacrifice*, Edinburgh, 1877; new ed. with title, *The Scriptural Doctrine of Atonement and Sacrifice*, 1890; and in *The Atonement in Modern Thought*, ut sup., pp. 250 sqq.). When the Calvinism of the New England Puritans began to break down, one of the symptoms of its decay was the gradual substitution of the rectoral for the satisfaction view of the Atonement. The process may be traced in the writings of Joseph Bellamy (1719–90), Samuel Hopkins (1721–1803), John Smalley (1736–1820), Stephen West (1735–1819), Jonathan Edwards, Jr. (1745–1801), Nathanael Emmons (1745–1800); and Edwards A. Park was able, accordingly, in the middle of the nineteenth century to set the rectoral theory forth as the "traditional orthodox doctrine" of the American Congregationalists (*The Atonement: Discourses and Treatises by Edwards, Smalley, Maxcy, Emmons, Griffin, Burge, and Weeks, with an Introductory Essay by Edwards A. Park*, Boston, 1859; cf. Daniel T. Fiske, in the *Bibliotheca Sacra*, Apr., 1861, and further N. S. S. Beman, *Sermons on the Atonement*, New York, 1825, 2d ed., 1846; N. W Taylor, *Lectures on the Moral Government of God*, New York, 1859; Albert Barnes, *The Atonement in its Relation to Law and Moral Government*, Philadelphia, 1859; Frank H. Foster, *Christian Life and Theology*, New York, 1900; Lewis F. Stearns, *Present Day Theology*, New York, 1893). The early Wesleyans also gravitated toward the rectoral theory, though not without some hesitation, a hesitation which has sustained itself among British Wesleyans until to-day (cf., e.g., W B. Pope, *Compendium of Christian Theology*, London, 1875; Marshall Randles, *Substitution, a Treatise on the Atonement*, London, 1877; T. O. Summers, *Systematic Theology*, 2 vols., Nashville, Tenn., 1888; J. J. Tigert, in the *Methodist Quarterly Review*, Apr., 1884), although many among them have taught the rectoral theory with great distinctness and decision (e.g., Joseph Agar Beet, in the *Expositor*, Nov., 1892, pp. 343–355; *Through Christ to God*, London, 1893). On the other hand, the rectoral theory has been the regnant one among American Methodists and has received some of its best statements from their hands (cf. especially John Miley, *The Atonement of Christ*, New York, 1879; *Systematic Theology*, ii, New York, 1894, pp. 65–240); although there are voices raised of late in denial of its claim to be considered distinctively the doctrine of the Methodist Church (J. J. Tigert, ut sup.; H. C. Sheldon, in *AJT*, viii, 1904, pp. 41–42).

The final form which Horace Bushnell gave his version of the "moral influence" theory, in his *Forgiveness and Law* (New York, 1874; made the second volume to his revised *Vicarious Sacrifice*, 1877) stands in no relation to the rectoral theories; but it requires to be mentioned here by their side,

7. Horace Bushnell. because it supposes like them that the work of Christ has a secondary effect on God, although its primary effect is on man. In this presentation, Bushnell represents Christ's work as consisting in a profound identification of himself with man, the effect of which is, on the one side, to manifest God's love to man and so to conquer man to him, and, on the other, as he expresses it, "to make cost" on God's part for man, and so, by breaking down God's resentment to man, to prepare God's heart to receive man back when he comes. The underlying idea is that whenever we do anything for those who have injured us, and in proportion as it costs us something to do it, our natural resentment of the injury we have suffered is undermined, and we are prepared to forgive the injury when forgiveness is sought. By this theory the transition is naturally made to the next class.

5. Theories which conceive the work of Christ as *terminating primarily on God and secondarily on man*.

8. "Theories of Reconciliation." The lowest form in which this ultimate position can be said to be fairly taken, is doubtless that set forth in his remarkably attractive way by John McLeod Campbell (*The Nature of the Atonement and its Relation to Remission of Sins and Eternal Life*, London, 1856; 4th ed., 1875), and lately argued out afresh with even more than Campbell's winningness and far more than his cogency, depth, and richness, by the late R. C. Moberly (*Atonement and Personality*, London, 1901). This theory supposes that our Lord, by sympathetically entering into our condition (an idea independently suggested by Schleiermacher, and emphasized by many continental thinkers, as, for example, to name only a pair with little else in common, by Gess and Häring), so keenly felt our sins as his own, that he could confess and adequately repent of them before God; and this is all the expiation justice asks. Here "sympathetic identification" replaces the conception of substitution; "sodality," of race-unity; and "repentance," of expiation. Nevertheless, the theory rises immeasurably above the mass of those already enumerated, in looking upon Christ as really a Savior, who performs a really saving work, terminating immediately on God. Despite its insufficiencies, therefore, which have caused writers like Edwards A. Park, and A. B. Bruce (*The Humiliation of Christ*, ut sup., pp. 317–318) to speak of it with a tinge of contempt, it has exercised a very wide influence and elements of it are discoverable in many constructions which stand far removed from its fundamental presuppositions.

The so-called "middle theory" of the Atonement, which owes its name to its supposed intermediate position between the "moral influence" theories and the doctrine of "satisfaction," seems to have offered attractions to the latitudinarian writers of the closing eighteenth and opening nineteenth centuries. At that time it was taught in John Balguy's *Essay on Redemption* (London, 1741), Henry Taylor's *Apology of Ben Mordecai* (London, 1784), and Richard Price's *Sermons on Christian Doctrine* (London, 1737; cf. Hill's *Lectures on Divinity*, ed. 1851, pp. 422 sqq.). Basing on the conception of sacrifices which looks upon them as merely gifts designed to secure the good-will of the King, the advocates of this theory regard the work of Christ as consisting in the offering to God of Christ's perfect obedience even to death, and by it purchasing God's favor and the right to do as he would with those whom God gave him as a reward. By the side of this theory may be placed the ordinary Remonstrant theory of *acceptilatio*, which, reviving this Scotist conception, is willing to allow that the work of Christ was of the nature of an expiatory sacrifice, but is unwilling to allow that his blood any more than that of "bulls and goats" had intrinsic value equivalent to the fault for which it was graciously accepted by God as an atonement. This theory may be found expounded, for example, in Limborch (*Theologia Christiana*, 4th ed., Amsterdam, 1715, iii, chaps. xviii–xxiii). Such theories, while preserving the sacrificial form of the Biblical doctrine, and, with it, its inseparable implication that the work of Christ has as its primary end to affect God and secure from him favorable regard for man (for it is always to God that sacrifices are offered), yet fall so far short of the Biblical doctrine of the nature and effect of Christ's sacrifice as to seem little less than travesties of it.

9. Certain "Sacrificial Theories."

The Biblical doctrine of the sacrifice of Christ finds full recognition in no other construction than that of the established church-doctrine of satisfaction. According to it, our Lord's redeeming work is at its core a true and perfect sacrifice offered to God, of intrinsic value ample for the expiation of our guilt; and at the same time is a true and perfect righteousness offered to God in fulfilment of the demands of his law; both the one and the other being offered in behalf of his people, and, on being accepted by God, accruing to their benefit; so that by this satisfaction they are relieved at once from the curse of their guilt as breakers of the law, and from the burden of the law as a condition of life; and this by a work of such kind and performed in such a manner, as to carry home to the hearts of men a profound sense of the indefectible righteousness of God and to make to them a perfect revelation of his love; so that, by this one and indivisible work, both God is reconciled to us, and we, under the quickening influence of the Spirit bought for us by it, are reconciled to God, so making peace—external peace between an angry God and sinful men, and internal peace in the response of the human conscience to the restored smile of God. This doctrine, which has been incorporated in more or less fulness of statement in the creedal declarations of all the great branches of the Church, Greek, Latin, Lutheran, and Reformed, and which has been expounded with more or less insight and power by the leading doctors of the Churches for the last eight hundred years, was first given scientific statement by Anselm (q.v.) in his *Cur Deus homo* (1098); but reached its complete development only at the hands of the so-called Protestant Scholastics of the seventeenth century (cf., e.g., Turretin, *The Atonement of Christ*, transl. by J. R. Willson, New York, 1859; John Owen, *The Death of Death in the Death of Christ*, 1650, Edinburgh, 1845). Among the numerous modern presentations of the doctrine the following may perhaps be most profitably consulted. Of Continental writers: August Tholuck, *Lehre von der Sünde und von der Versöhnung* (Hamburg, 1823); F. A. Philippi, *Kirchliche Glaubenslehre* (Stuttgart, 1864–82), IV, ii, 24 sqq.; G. Thomasius, *Christi Person und Werk* (3d ed., Leipsic, 1886–88), vol. ii; E. Böhl, *Dogmatik* (Leipsic, 1887), pp. 361 sqq.; J. F. Bula, *Die Versöhnung des Menschen mit Gott* (Basel, 1874); W Kölling, *Die Satisfactio vicaria* (2 vols., Gütersloh, 1897–99); Merle d'Aubigné, *L'Expiation de la croix* (Geneva, 1868); A. Gretillat, *Exposé de théologie systématique* (Paris, 1892), iv, pp. 278 sqq.; A. Kuyper, *E Voto Dordraceno* (Amsterdam, 1892), i, pp. 79 sqq., 388 sqq.; H. Bavink, *Gereformeerde Dogmatik* (Kampen, 1898), iii, pp. 302–424. Of writers in English: The appropriate sections of the treatises on dogmatics by C. Hodge, A. H. Strong, W. G. T. Shedd, R. S. Dabney, and the following separate treatises: W Symington, *On the Atonement and Intercession of Jesus Christ* (New York, 1852; defective, as excluding the "active obedience" of Christ); R. S. Candlish, *The Atonement, its Efficacy and Extent* (London, 1867);

10. The Doctrine of "Satisfaction."

A. A. Hodge, *The Atonement* (Philadelphia, 1867; new ed., 1877); George Smeaton, *The Doctrine of the Atonement as Taught by Christ Himself* (Edinburgh, 1868; 2d ed., 1871); idem, *The Doctrine of the Atonement as Taught by the Apostles* (1870); T. J. Crawford, *The Doctrine of the Holy Scriptures Respecting the Atonement* (London, 1871; 5th ed., 1888); Hugh Martin, *The Atonement in its Relations to the Covenant, the Priesthood, the Intercession of our Lord* (London, 1870). See SATISFACTION.

BENJAMIN B. WARFIELD.

BIBLIOGRAPHY: The more important treatises on the Atonement have been named in the body of the article. The history of the doctrine has been written with a fair degree of objectivity by Ferdinand Christian Baur, *Die Christliche Lehre von der Versöhnung in ihrer geschichtlichen Entwickelung*, Tübingen, 1838; and with more subjectivity by Albrecht Ritschl in the first volume of his *Rechtfertigung und Versohnung*, 3d ed., Bonn, 1889, Eng. transl. from the first ed., 1870, *A Critical History of the Christian Doctrine of Justification and Reconciliation*, Edinburgh, 1872. Excellent historical sketches are given by G. Thomasius, in the second volume of his *Christi Person und Werk*, pp. 113 sqq., 3d ed., Leipsic, 1888, from the confessional, and by F. A. B. Nitzsch, in his *Lehrbuch der evangelischen Dogmatik*, pp. 457 sqq., Freiburg, 1892, from the moral influence standpoint. More recently the history has been somewhat sketchily written from the general confessional standpoint by Oscar Benson as the first part of his *Die Lehre von der Versöhnung*, Gütersloh, 1904, and with more fulness from the moral influence standpoint by G. A. F. Ecklin, in his *Erlösung und Versöhnung*, Basel, 1903. Consult also E. Ménégoz, *La Mort de Jésus et le Dogme de l'Expiation*, Paris, 1905. The English student of the history of the doctrine has at his disposal not only the sections in the general histories of doctrine (e.g., Hagenbach, Cunningham, Shedd, Harnack) and the comprehensive treatise of Ritschl mentioned above, but also interesting sketches in the appendices of G. Smeaton's *Doctrine of the Atonement as Taught by the Apostles*, Edinburgh, 1870, and J. S. Lidgett's *The Spiritual Principle of the Atonement*, London, 1898, from the confessional standpoint, as well as H. N. Oxenham's *The Catholic Doctrine of the Atonement*, London, 1865, 3d ed., 1881, from the Roman Catholic standpoint. Consult also: J. B. Remensnyder, *The Atonement and Modern Thought*, Philadelphia, 1905; D. W. Simon, *The Redemption of Man*, London, 1906; C. A. Dinsmore, *Atonement in Literature and Life*, Boston, 1906; L. Pullan, *The Atonement*, New York, 1906. An interesting episode is treated by Andrew Robertson, *History of the Atonement Controversy in the Secession Church*, Edinburgh, 1846.

ATONEMENT, DAY OF: The great Hebrew and Jewish fast-day, occurring annually; called in Lev. xxiii, 27–28 *yom ha-kippurim*, in the Talmud simply *yoma*, "*the* day"; in vulgar Hebrew *yom kippur*. The legal provisions are given in Lev. xvi (cf. Ex. xxx, 10); xxiii, 26–32; Num. xxix, 7–11. Since these enactments, in spite of their relative differences, are not sufficient to define the very important ritual in all details, a supplementary tradition became necessary; the Mishnaic treatise *Yoma* is devoted to the celebration of the day during the Second Temple. According to

Institution and Ritual.

Lev. xvi, 29, xxiii, 27, Num. xxix, 7, the day fell on the tenth of the seventh month (Tishri); it was to be a sabbath of rest ("sabbath of sabbaths," Lev. xvi, 31), on which all labor was prohibited, and the congregation had to meet in the sanctuary (Lev. xxiii, 27–28). A general fast—the only one enjoined in the Mosaic law—was prescribed for the day. By this fast, the "afflicting of the soul," the members of the congregation were to bring themselves into a penitential mood appropriate to the serious atonement act. The day is therefore called sometimes simply "the fast-day" (Josephus, *Ant.*, XIV, iv, 3, where, however, as in XIV. xvi, 4, the "third month" causes some difficulty; Philo, *De septenario*, 296 M) or "the fast" (Philo, 278 M; Acts xxvii, 9); by the rabbis also "the great fast" to distinguish it from the fast-days which were introduced after the Exile. The stranger who dwelt in the land was also obliged to rest from work, but he was not obliged to fast (Lev. xvi, 29).

The rite to be performed in the sanctuary is described in Lev. xvi, 3–28. Aaron (i.e., the high priest), attired in plain priestly clothing is to offer, first for himself and his house, a young bullock for a sin-offering. He is to bring its blood into the Holy of Holies and sprinkle with it the *Kapporeth*, the expiatory covering of the ark. In the same manner he has to deal with the blood of the goat, appointed as a sin-offering for the people. With this blood the other vessels of the sanctuary also were afterward sprinkled. Two goats were presented before God for the people, and the high priest cast lots, designating the one goat "for Yahweh" as a sin-offering, the other "for Azazel" (A. V. "scapegoat;" see AZAZEL); on this second goat the high priest laid his hands and confessed the sins of the people, which the goat was to carry away into the wilderness. Thither it was led by a man, so that it could not return (with the two goats compare the two birds, Lev. xiv, 4–7). The sin is to remain in the territory of the unclean desert-demon Azazel (cf. Zech. v, 5–11). When this act was over the burnt offering for the high priest and the people and other offerings were brought. The great importance of this day is seen from the fact that the high priest officiates personally, and his functions are mostly performed in the Holy of Holies, which he could enter only on this day; furthermore, from the purpose of the whole, to purify priest and congregation, and the habitation of God and its vessels, from all defilement. On this account this day is also referred to as a type in the New Testament (cf. especially Heb. ix, 7, 11 sqq., 24 sqq.; also the Epistle of Barnabas vii).

The antiquity of this fast-day, its Mosaic origin, and even its preexilic existence, is denied by Vatke (*Biblische Theologie*, i, Berlin, 1835, 548), George (*Feste*, Berlin, 1835, 200 sqq.), Graf, Wellhausen, Kuenen, Reuss, and others. It is indeed strange that this important festival is nowhere mentioned in preexilic writings except in the Law. But this may be accidental. At all events it is a rash inference that so solemn a festival must be of late origin, because the old festivals of the Hebrews were of a joyous character. In favor of the higher antiquity of this usage is the fact that

Date of Origin.

the entire action takes place by the ark of the covenant, which did not exist after the Exile and of whose absence nothing is said in the Law. The desert-demon Azazel (for which in later times one would rather expect Satan as opposed to Yahweh) also points back to the Mosaic time of the abode in the wilderness. It may, however, rightly be inferred from the fact that the Day of Atonement is not mentioned in preexilic literature that it did not pass into the consciousness and life of the people, like the three great festivals, Passover, Pentecost, and Feast of Tabernacles. It was a festival connected mainly with the priesthood and sanctuary, hence it was more strictly observed at the center of the legitimate worship. There came a change in the postexilic time, in which the Temple at Jerusalem exercised greater influence upon the people. But even then we see that in spite of the prescribed self-mortification the people knew how to indulge in joyful recreation; from the Mishnah (*Taanit* iv, 8) we learn that on the Day of Atonement (no doubt in the evening, after the high priest had returned to his home), the maidens all went forth, arrayed in white garments, into the vineyards around Jerusalem, where they danced and sang, inviting the young men to select their brides (cf. Delitzsch, *Zur Geschichte der jüdischen Poesie*, Leipsic, 1836, 195–196). The Gemara finds such joy perfectly legitimate on a day when atonement was made for Israel. After the destruction of Jerusalem the celebration of the Day of Atonement was continued, although the sacrificial rites could no more be performed. The grand festival with its solemn earnestness had so deeply impressed itself upon the people, that it could not be wholly dispensed with. (For the later usages see *Orach Chayim*, translated by Löwe, 150 sqq.; Buxtorf, *Synagoga Judaica*, chaps. xxv–xxvi.) In general the penitential prayers in the synagogue have taken the place of the atoning temple-sacrifices. Nevertheless, the cessation of the sacrifice is deplored; in some places the house-father takes a cock, the mother a hen, which are killed as a substitute for the sacrifice.

C. von Orelli.

The late date of the origin of the festival would seem to be made certain by the following considerations: (1) Its absence from the list of feasts given in the earlier books can not be accidental, especially in view of the radical character of its practical prescriptions. (2) These prescriptions and their moral sanction were not in keeping with the spirit of the earlier laws, in which there is no suggestion of fasting and contrition. (3) Transition stages between the prophetic and the priestly legislation are indicated in the ideal conception of Ezekiel, the prophet-priest, with its two single days of atonement (xlv, 18–20), also in the intervening institution by Ezra of a general fast on the twenty-fourth day of the seventh month, with no mention of the tenth day of the priestly code. (4) The old festivals of the Hebrews were of a joyous character, while the Levitical Day of Atonement was one of great solemnity. J. F. M.

Bibliography: The Mishna tract *Yoma*, translated into Latin with notes by R. Sheringham, London, 1648; the same, ed. H. L. Strack, Leipsic, 1904; an Eng. transl. is in J. Barclay, *The Talmud*, London, 1878; the Tosephta on this tract and Jerusalem Gemara in Ugolini, *Thesaurus*, xviii, 153 sqq.; Maimonides, *Yad ha-Ḥazaḳah*, transl. by F. Delitzsch, *Hebräerbrief*, pp. 749 sqq., Leipsic, 1857; J. Lightfoot, *Ministerium templi*, chap. xv, in *Opera*, i, 671–756, Rotterdam, 1686; J. G. Carpzov, *Apparatus historico-criticus antiquitatum sacri codicis*, pp. 433 sqq., Frankfort, 1748; J. Lund, *Jüdische Heiligthümer*, pp. 1161 sqq., Hamburg, 1738; J. H. Otho, *Lexicon rabbinico-philologicum*, pp. 182 sqq., Geneva, 1675; J. Meyer, *De temporibus sacris Hebræorum*, in Ugolini, *Thesaurus*, vol. i; C. W. F. Bähr, *Symbolik des mosaischen Cultus*, ii, 664 sqq., Heidelberg, 1839; M. Brueck, *Pharisäische Volkssitten und Ritualien*, Frankfort, 1840; H. Kurtz, *Der alttestamentliche Opferkultus*, pp. 335 sqq., Berlin, 1862; B. Wechsler, *Zur Geschichte der Versöhnungsfeier*, in *Jüdische Zeitschrift*, ii (1863), 113–125; Nowack, *Archäologie*, ii, 183–194; Benzinger, *Archäologie*, pp. 200, 398, 401, 427; the works on Old Testament theology, and the commentaries to Lev. xvi, particularly Driver's *Leviticus*, in *SBOT*, 1898. On the critical question consult Franz Delitzsch, in *ZKW*, i (1880), 173–183. For the later Judaism, consult J. F. Schröder, *Satzungen und Gebräuche des talmudisch-rabbinischen Judenthums*, 130 sqq., Bremen, 1851; S. Adler, in *ZATW*, ii (1882), 178 sqq., 272; L. Dembitz, *Jewish Services in Synagogue and Home*, Philadelphia, 1898; M. Jastrow, in *AJT*, i (1898), 312 sqq.

ATRIUM: In the church architecture of the earlier centuries, an open space in front of the entrance to the church, surrounded by porticos, and provided with a fountain, or at least a large vessel containing water. Here the penitents who were not allowed to enter the church assembled, and begged the faithful to pray for them.

ATTERBURY, FRANCIS: English Jacobite bishop; b. at Milton or Middleton Keynes (about 45 m. n.w. of London), Buckinghamshire, England, March 6, 1662; d. at Paris Feb. 22, 1732. He studied at Christ Church, Oxford, and received holy orders about 1687. His brilliant success as a controversialist, and his powerful eloquence in the pulpit, soon attracted attention; he was made chaplain to William and Mary in 1692, dean of Carlisle in 1704, dean of Christ Church in 1711, and bishop of Rochester and dean of Westminster in 1713. He was a Tory in politics, and in ecclesiastical affairs his sympathies were with the High-churchmen. The succession of George I at the death of Queen Anne was unfavorable to his ambition, and, as a Tory, being coldly received by the new king, he took his place in the foremost ranks of the opposition, refused in 1715 to sign the paper in which the bishops declared their attachment to the House of Brunswick, and began in 1717 to correspond directly with the Pretender, and carried on his intrigues so skilfully that his most intimate friends did not suspect him. But in 1722 his guilt was manifested; he was committed to the Tower, and by an act of Parliament was banished for life in March, 1723, and all British subjects were forbidden to hold communication with him except by the royal permission. He went to the continent, and lived most of the time in Paris, in more or less constant correspondence with the Pretender, for whose sake he had suffered so much. Ill health and the death of a devoted daughter added to his afflictions. Atterbury was a man of restless and pugnacious disposition, with many striking qualities, and one of the foremost preachers and orators of his time. He had little learning, however, his talents were superficial, and his judgment was rash. In private life he is said to have been winning and amiable, and he counted among his friends most of the literary men of the day as well as many influential personages. He had much popular sympathy in his banishment. At his death his body was carried to England and buried privately in Westminster Abbey.

The most important of Atterbury's controversial writings were: *An Answer to Some Considerations on the Spirit of Martin Luther and the Original of the Reformation* (Oxford, 1687), in reply to an attack upon the Reformation by Obadiah Walker; *An Examination of Dr Bentley's Dissertations on the Epistles of Phalaris and the Fables of Æsop* (London, 1698); *Rights and Privileges of an English Convocation Stated and Vindicated* (1700). Selections from his sermons have been many times printed and a collected edition in four volumes appeared in London, 1723–37. His *Epistolary Correspondence, Visitation Charges, Speeches, and Miscellanies* were edited by J. Nichols (5 vols., London, 1783–90).

Bibliography: The standard life is by T. Stackhouse, *Memoirs of the Life, Character, Conduct, and Writings of Francis Atterbury*, London, 1727; his biography by Macaulay is in the *Encyclopædia Britannica*; consult also F. Williams, *Memoirs and Correspondence of Francis Atterbury*, 2 vols., London, 1869; *DNB*, ii, 233–238; W. H. Hutton, *English Church (1625–1714)*, pp. 273, 278, 280, London, 1903.

ATTERBURY, WILLIAM WALLACE: Presbyterian; b. at Newark, N. J., Aug. 4, 1823. He was educated at Yale College (B.A., 1843) and Yale Divinity School (1847). He held Presbyterian pastorates at Lansing, Mich., from 1848 to 1854 and at Madison, Ind., from 1854 to 1866. He traveled in Europe and the East and acted as a supply for various pulpits at Cleveland, O., and other cities from 1866 to 1869, when he was chosen secretary of the New York Sabbath Committee. In 1898 he was relieved of much of his work in this capacity by the appointment of an assistant, to whom he relinquished his regular duties two years later. He has also been an active member of the United States branch of the Evangelical Alliance, and was its secretary in 1875. His writings, which are generally brief, are devoted chiefly to the various aspects of the Sunday question.

AT'TICUS: Patriarch of Constantinople 406–425 (or 427). He was born at Sebaste in Armenia, repaired early to Constantinople, and was one of the party opposed to Chrysostom (q.v.), who was expelled from Constantinople in June, 404; his successor, Arsacius, an old man of eighty years, died the following year, and after a few months Atticus was elevated to the patriarchate. He is described as a man of but moderate learning, whose sermons were not thought worth preserving, but possessed of much skill in affairs, and esteemed for charity and piety. He restored the name of Chrysostom to the diptychs in 412. Two of his letters with a fragment of a third, and two fragments of a homily on the birth of Christ are preserved; consult *MPG*, lxv, 637–652.

ATTO: The name of three churchmen.

1. Bishop of Basel. See Haito.

2. Archbishop of Mainz. See Hatto.

3. Bishop of Vercelli 924–961. If his will (preserved with his works in *MPL*, cxxxiv, 9–916) is to be taken as genuine, he came of the family to which Desiderius, the last Lombard king, belonged; and this would account for his remarkable education, which included not only a knowledge of the Bible and the principal western Fathers, but Greek as well, with at least some works of the eastern ecclesiastical writers. He was especially well read in legal history, knowing the Roman, Lombard, and canon law. He was ordained at Milan, where he became archdeacon, and in 924 was advanced to the see of Vercelli. Among the productions of his episcopal career is his *Capitulare*, a series of instructions for the clergy, which shows him to have been a foe to superstition and a friend of popular education. His other extant works are a commentary on the Pauline epistles, following the older exegesis; eighteen sermons; nine letters; the treatise *De pressuris ecclesiasticis*, which pleads for the exemption of the clergy from the jurisdiction of secular tribunals and protests against lay interference with ecclesiastical elections and the alienation of church property; the *Polypticum*, which contains a philosophical presentation of the affairs of Italy from the accession of King Hugh (926) down to the repeated intervention of Otto I. Atto is an outspoken opponent of the Germans, and a partizan of Berengar of Ivrea. This work exists in two forms, of which the shorter is undoubtedly the authentic one, the other being a version edited with a view of removing some of its obscurities.

(A. Hauck.)

Bibliography: The *Opera* were edited by C. Buroutius, 2 vols., Vercelli, 1768, and are in Mai, *Veterum scriptorum nova collectio*, vi, 2, pp. 42 sqq., Rome, 1832, and in *MPL*, cxxxiv. Consult J. Schultz, *Atto von Vercelli*, Göttingen, 1885; A. Ebert, *Geschichte der Literatur des Mittelalters*, iii, 368 sqq., Leipsic, 1887.

ATTRIBUTES OF GOD. See God, II, § 3.

ATTRITION. See Penance.

ATWATER, LYMAN HOTCHKISS: Presbyterian; b. at Hamden, Conn., Feb. 23, 1813; d. at Princeton, N. J., Feb. 17, 1883. He was graduated at Yale 1831; was tutor there and student of divinity 1833–35; pastor of the First Congregational Church, Fairfield, Conn., 1835–54; professor (at first of mental and moral philosophy, after 1869 of logic and moral and political science) at Princeton College, 1854 till his death. He was also lecturer in Princeton Seminary and acting president of the college. He contributed many articles to the religious reviews and was one of the editors of the *Biblical Repertory* (1869–71) and its continuation (from 1872), the *Presbyterian Quarterly and Princeton Review*. He published a *Manual of Elementary Logic* (Philadelphia, 1867).

ATWILL, EDWARD ROBERT: Protestant Episcopal bishop of Kansas City; b. at Red Hook, N. Y., Feb. 18, 1840. He was educated at Columbia College (B.A., 1862) and the General Theological Seminary (1864), and was successively rector of St. Paul's, Burlington, Vt. (1867–80), and Trinity, Toledo, O. (1881–90), until he was consecrated first bishop of the newly organized diocese of Kansas City in 1890.

ATWOOD, ISAAC MORGAN: Universalist; b. at Pembroke, N. Y., Mar. 24, 1838. He was educated at Yale, but did not graduate. He was a tutor in Ferguson Boys' School in 1859 and principal of Corfu Classical Institute in 1859–60. In the following year he entered the Universalist ministry and until 1879 held various pastorates in New York, Maine, and Massachusetts. He then became president of the Canton (N. Y.) Theological School, where he remained until 1899. Since 1898 he has been general superintendent of the Universalist Church in the United States and Canada, of which he was also appointed secretary in 1905. He lectured before the St. Lawrence University Divinity School in 1900–06 and before the Lombard College Divinity School in 1906. He was vice-president of the Universalist General Convention in 1880–85 and is a member of the Advisory Board of the New York State League of Churches and of the committee on churches in the Religious Education Association. From 1867 to 1874 he edited the *Christian Leader*, of which he has since been associate editor, while in 1886–89 he was a staff-contributor to the *Independent* and in 1892–94 was on the editorial staff of the *Standard Dictionary*. He is also a member of the American Social Science Association and of the New York Economic Club. In theology he holds firmly to the cardinal doctrine of the Universalist denomination. His principal writings are: *Have We Outgrown Christianity?* (Boston, 1870); *Latest Word of Universalism* (1879); *Walks About Zion* (1880); *Episcopacy* (1885); *Revelation* (1893); and *Balance Sheet of Biblical Criticism* (1896).

ATZBERGER, LEONHARD: Roman Catholic; b. at Velden (a village near Vilsviburg, 42 m. n.e. of Munich) July 23, 1854. He was educated at the Gymnasium and Lyceum of Freising and at the University of Munich. He was ordained to the priesthood in 1879, and three years later became privat-docent at Munich, where he was university preacher in 1886. In 1888 he was appointed associate professor of theology at the same university, and was promoted to full professor in 1894. He has written *Die Logoslehre des heiligen Athanasius* (Munich, 1880); *Die Unsündlichkeit Christi* (1883); *Christliche Eschatologie in den Stadien ihrer Offenbarung im Alten und Neuen Testament* (Freiburg, 1890); *Der Glaube* (1891); *Geschichte der christlichen Eschatologie in der vornicänischen Zeit* (1896); and *Handbuch der katholischen Dogmatik* (1898–1903; being the fourth volume of the work of the same title by M. J. Scheeben).

AUBERLEN, au'ber-len, **KARL AUGUST:** Theologian; b. at Fellbach, near Stuttgart, Nov. 19, 1824; d. at Basel May 2, 1864. He studied in the seminary of Blaubeuren 1837–41, and theology at Tübingen 1841–45; became repetent in theology at Tübingen 1849, and professor at Basel 1851. As a young man he was attracted by the views of Goethe and Hegel and enthusiastic for the criticism of Baur; but he later became an adherent of the old Württemberg circle of theologians—Bengel, Oetinger, Roos, etc. He published *Die Theosophie Oetingers* (Tübingen, 1847); *Der Prophet Daniel und die Offenbarung Johannis* (Basel, 1854; Eng. transl., by Adolph Saphir, *The Prophecies of Daniel and the Revelation*, Edinburgh, 1874; 2d German ed., 1857); *Die göttliche Offenbarung* (i, Basel, 1861; Eng. transl., with memoir, Edinburgh, 1867). A volume of sermons appeared in 1845; a volume of lectures on the Christian faith in 1861.

AUBERTIN, ō''bār''tan', **EDME:** French Reformed clergyman; b. at Châlons-sur-Marne (90 m. e. of Paris) 1595; d. at Paris Apr. 5, 1652. He became minister at Chartres 1618, and at Charenton (Paris) 1631. To prove that the doctrine of the Reformed Church concerning the Eucharist was the same as that of the ancient Church, he wrote *Conformité de la créance de l'Église avec celle de St. Augustin sur le sacrement de l'Eucharistie* (Paris, 1626), afterward enlarged and entitled *L'Eucharistie de l'ancienne Église* (1629). The work attracted attention and caused much controversy.

AUBIGNÉ, JEAN HENRI MERLE D'. See MERLE D'AUBIGNÉ.

AUBIGNÉ, ō''bī''nyê', **THÉODORE AGRIPPA D':** Huguenot soldier and writer; b. at St. Maury, near Pons (50 m. n. of Bordeaux), in Saintonge, Feb. 8, 1552; d. at Geneva Apr. 29, 1630. He grew up under influences which tended to make him a strong partizan in the religious disputes of the time; studied for a period under Beza at Geneva, but ran away to join a Huguenot regiment at the age of fifteen; fought with distinction through the wars which ended in the accession of Henry IV, and, notwithstanding his rough manners and unpolitic candor, retained the friendship of the king till his death. After the abjuration of Henry he retired from the court, and devoted the later years of his life to literary work. In 1620 to escape threatening persecution he took refuge in Geneva. One of his sons was the father of Madame de Maintenon. His most important work was the *Histoire universelle depuis 1550 jusqu'à l'an 1601* (3 vols., Maillé, 1616–20; new ed., by A. de Ruble, 9 vols., Paris, 1886–98). The *Tragiques* (1616; ed. C. Read, 2 vols., Paris, 1896), a long epic poem, treats in bad verse of the same subject as the *Histoire universelle*. These works, little read when published, and almost forgotten during the eighteenth century, in modern times have come to be regarded as valuable sources of French history. His complete works have been edited by E. Réaume and F. de Caussade (6 vols., Paris, 1873–92).

BIBLIOGRAPHY: His autobiography was published by L. Lalaune, *Mémoires de T. A. d'Aubigné*, Paris, 1889. Consult further E. Prarond, *Les Poètes historiens; . d'Aubigné sous Henri III.*, Paris, 1873; P. Morillot, *Discours sur la vie et les œuvres d'Agrippa d'Aubigné*, Paris, 1884; A. von Salis, *Agrippa d'Aubigné*, Heidelberg, 1885; G. Guizot, *Agrippa d'Aubigné*, Paris, 1890.

AUBURN DECLARATION: An incident of the Old and New School controversy in the Presbyterian Church in 1837. The General Assembly of that year, controlled by the Old School party, "exscinded" the synods of Utica, Geneva, and Genesee, in New York, and Western Reserve, in Ohio, declaring them to be "neither in form nor in fact a part of the Presbyterian Church." On the 17th of the following August a convention of about two hundred clergymen and a number of prominent laymen, representing all the presbyteries in these synods, met in Auburn, N. Y., to repel the charge of unsoundness in the faith and set forth the views they actually held. A declaration was adopted, consisting of sixteen articles, corresponding to a similar list of sixteen heresies alleged to be held by the New School churches, which had been presented to the Assembly and had been the basis of its action. Replying to the first of the charges, that it was taught "that God would have been glad to prevent the existence of sin in our world, but was not able without destroying the moral agency of man; or that, for aught that appears in the Bible, sin is incidental to any wise, moral system," the members of the convention declared that they believed that "God permitted the introduction of sin, not because he was unable to prevent it consistently with the moral freedom of his creatures, but for wise and benevolent reasons which he has not revealed" (art. i). In replying to the other charges, the convention pronounced fully in the sense of the Westminster Symbols. With a perhaps unconscious supralapsarianism, they put the doctrine of election first in order, and all the other facts in the process of redemption after it; so the arrangement suggests that it was the primary purpose of God to save a definite number of men out of a race to be thereafter created; that in pursuance of this purpose man was formed, the fall decreed, and an atonement provided sufficient to meet the case of that predestined number, and no others. No affirmation of the universality of the atonement is found among these sixteen propositions. Original sin, total depravity, vicarious atonement, Christ's intercession for the elect previous to their conversion, absolute dependence upon irresistible divine grace for the renewal of the heart, instantaneous regeneration, etc., all these dogmas are emphatically affirmed. "All who are saved are indebted from first to last to the grace and spirit of God and the reason why God does not save all is not that he wants the power to do it, but that in his wisdom he does not see fit to exert that power further than he actually does" (art. xiii). In short, the Auburn Declaration rises well up to the high-water mark of the Calvinistic theology and was indorsed by the General Assembly (Old School) in 1868 as containing "all the fundamentals of the Calvinistic Creed."

BIBLIOGRAPHY: For full text of the declaration consult Schaff, *Creeds*, iii, 777–780; consult also E. D. Morris, *The Presbyterian Church, New School, 1837–1869*, pp. 77 sqq., Columbus, O., 1905.

AUDIANS: The followers of a certain Audius, according to Epiphanius (*Hær.*, lxx; followed by Augustine, *Hær.*, 1), Theodoret (*Hist. eccl.*, iv, 10; *Hær. fab.*, iv, 10), and Ephraem Syrus (*Serm.*, xxiv, *Adv. hær.*), who state that Audius was a Mesopotamian, a layman who lived "in the time of Arius," that he declaimed against the worldly conduct of the clergy, founded an ascetic sect, and, in his old age banished to Scythia, did successful missionary work among the Goths. When Epiphanius wrote (c. 375) the sect was practically extinct in its original home. He praises the orthodoxy of Audius and his exemplary life, but blames him and his followers for holding anthropomorphic views of God and for being quartodecimans. G. KRÜGER.

BIBLIOGRAPHY: C. W. F. Walch, *Entwurf einer vollständigen Historie der Ketzereien*, iii, 300–321, Leipsic, 1766; G. Hoffmann, *Auszüge aus syrischen Akten persischer Märtyrer*, pp. 122, Leipsic, 1880; J. Overbeck, *S. Ephraemi Syri Rabulæ opera*, p. 194, Oxford, 1865; L. E. Iselin, in *JPT*, xvi (1890), 298–305.

AUDIENTIA EPISCOPALIS: The name given by the code of Justinian to the bishop's power of hearing and deciding judicial cases. This power in the early Church was based upon such passages of Scripture as Matt. xviii, 18–16 and I Cor. vi, 1–6. The *Didache* testifies to the exercise of this power by the presbyters, or by the college of presbyters with the bishop at their head; and the Apostolic Constitutions forbid Christians to go to law, even with the heathen, before a pagan tribunal. Small differences are to be adjusted by the deacons; the more important are to be laid before the bishop sitting in judgment with his clergy every Monday; he is to decide after careful investigation and orderly examination of witnesses, by a procedure following closely that of the secular tribunals. The enforcement of his sentence by the civil power could, of course, only follow when the act took on the form of a stipulation, which could be brought before the courts. But with the public recognition of Christianity, Constantine gave the bishops a real judicial power. The first of his three edicts on this subject is lost, and there have been many controversies about the other two, of 321 and 333. Either party might appeal to the bishop at any stage in the proceedings, and his decision was final, though it required enforcement by the civil tribunals, for even Constantine gave the bishop no *imperium*. This privilege was abolished by Arcadius for the East (398) and by Honorius for the West (408); the regulations established by Valentinian III in 452 provide that no one shall be forced to appear before the episcopal tribunal, and reduce the power to something more like its original limits. In the form then fixed, it remained in Justinian's code. The bishops attempted, in virtue of their disciplinary authority over their clergy, to compel the latter to submit even their civil differences to episcopal judgment; this Justinian approved, and extended to suits by laymen against clerics. The representatives of the ecclesiastical tendency in the Frankish kingdom went back to the edicts of Constantine. Thus Florus of Lyons, in his commentary on the constitutions published later by Sirmond, disregarded the facts that these had been reversed by Constantine's successors, and that in any case the edicts of Roman emperors were no authority for the Frankish kingdom; and Benedictus Levita wrote an introduction to the law of 333 in which he asserted that Charlemagne had proclaimed this as the law of his empire. Regino only quotes one passage from the edict of 333; but later collections down to that of Gratian include the whole of what is given by Benedictus Levita; and Innocent III (1198–1216) relied upon it as the basis of his *Denunciatio evangelica* (see JURISDICTION, ECCLESIASTICAL). But the later development of systematic ecclesiastical judicature absorbed the function of the bishop as arbiter. (E. FRIEDBERG.)

BIBLIOGRAPHY. B. Schilling, *De origine jurisdictionis ecclesiasticæ in causis civilibus*, Leipsic, 1825; Jungk, *De origi-*

nibus et progressu episcopalis judicii in causis civilibus laicorum usque ad Justinianum, Berlin, 1832; Turck, *De jurisdictionis civilis per medium ævum . . . origine et progressu*, Münster, 1832; B. Matthiass, *Die Entwicklung des römischen Schiedsgerichts*, pp. 130 sqq., Rostock, 1888. There is an Eng. transl., with introduction and notes, of the *Institutes* of Justinian, by T. C. Sanders, London, 1888.

AUDIN, ō''dan' (JEAN MARIE), VINCENT: French Roman Catholic; b. at Lyons 1793; d. at Paris Feb. 21. 1851. He studied theology at the seminary of l'Argentière, then studied law, but in 1814 went to Paris and lived thenceforth as bookseller and author. He wrote *Histoire de la Saint-Barthélemy* (2 vols., Paris, 1826); *Histoire de Luther* (2 vols., 1839; Eng. transl., Philadelphia, 1841); *Histoire de Calvin* (2 vols., 1841); *Histoire de Henri VIII* (2 vols., 1847; Eng. transl., London, 1852); *Histoire de Léon X* (2 vols., 1844). His work has been criticized as prejudiced and unscholarly.

Bibliography: J. Barbey d'Aurevilly, *Notice sur J. M. Audin*, Paris, 1856.

AUDREY, SAINT. See Etheldreda, Saint.

AUFKLÄRUNG, THE. See Enlightenment, the.

AUGER, ō''zhê', EDMOND: Jesuit preacher; b. at Alleman, near Troyes, France, 1530; d. at Como June 17, 1591. He made a pilgrimage to Rome, and, while filling a menial position, attracted the notice of Loyola, who admitted him to the novitiate; sent back to France as mission preacher, he is said to have converted more than 40,000 Huguenots to the Church of Rome. He became court preacher and confessor to Henry III in 1575, and founded the Congregation of the Penitents of the Annunciation of the Virgin Mary, 1583. He wrote ascetical and controversial works, but is best known by his *Catéchisme français*, written in Lyons, 1563 (published at Paris, 1568).

Bibliography: For his life consult N. Bailly, Paris, 1652; Dorigny, Avignon, 1828; M. A. Pericaud, Lyons, 1828.

AUGSBURG, BISHOPRIC OF: The origin of the Augsburg bishopric is lost in obscurity, but there is no doubt that it goes back to the days of the Roman empire. The importance of the colony of Augusta Vindelicorum is sufficient to account for the early introduction of Christianity there. That it was evangelized from the north of Italy is probable from the fact that it originally formed a part of the ecclesiastical province of Aquileia. It survived the downfall of the empire, the Alemannic conquest, and the subjection of the Alemanni in their turn to Frankish rule. The early boundaries of the diocese, including not only Suabian but also Bavarian and Frankish territory, give further evidence that it was in existence before the establishment of Teutonic dominion. The present diocese has lost a few Austrian districts and those parts which are now in Württemberg, but has retained so much of the old diocese of Constance as is now Bavarian. From the foundation of the archbishopric of Mainz, Augsburg was a suffragan see under its jurisdiction until the reorganization of 1817 transferred it to the newly founded province of Munich. The secular jurisdiction which the bishops of Augsburg had exercised for more than a thousand years was taken from them in 1802 and transferred to the Elector of Bavaria. (A. Hauck.)

Bibliography: P. I. Braun, *Geschichte der Bischöfe von Augsburg*, 4 vols., Augsburg, 1813–15; A. Steichele, *Das Bistum Augsburg . . . beschrieben*, 6 vols., Augsburg, 1864–1901; consult also Rettberg, *KD*; Friedrich, *KD*; and Hauck, *KD*.

AUGSBURG CONFESSION AND ITS APOLOGY.

Origin of the Confession (§ 1).
Its Character and Contents (§ 2).
Origin of the Apology (§ 3).
History of the Confession and the Apology (§ 4).

On Jan. 21, 1530, the Emperor Charles V issued letters from Bologna, inviting the German diet to meet in Augsburg Apr. 8, for the purpose of discussing and deciding various important questions. Although the writ of invitation was couched in very peaceful language, it was received with suspicion by some of the Evangelicals. The far-seeing Landgrave of Hesse hesitated to attend the diet, but the Elector John of Saxony, who received the writ Mar. 11, on Mar. 14 directed Luther, Jonas, Bugenhagen, and Melanchthon to meet in Torgau, where he was, and present a summary of the Protestant faith, to be laid before the emperor at the diet. This summary has received the name of the "Torgau Articles." On Apr. 3 the elector and reformers started from Torgau and reached Coburg on Apr. 23. There Luther was left behind. The rest reached Augsburg May 2. On the journey Melanchthon worked on an "apology," using the Torgau articles, and sent his draft to Luther at Coburg on May 11, who approved it. Several alterations were suggested to Melanchthon in his conferences with Jonas, the Saxon chancellor Brück, the conciliatory bishop Stadion of Augsburg, and the imperial secretary Alfonso Valdez. On June 23 the final form of the text was adopted in the presence of the Elector John of Saxony, the Landgrave Philip of Hesse, the Margrave George of Brandenburg, the Dukes Ernest and Francis of Lüneburg, the representatives of Nuremberg and Reutlingen, and other counselors, besides twelve theologians. After the reading the confession was signed by the Elector John of Saxony, Margrave George of Brandenburg, Duke Ernest of Lüneburg, the Landgrave Philip of Hesse, the Prince Wolfgang of Anhalt, the representatives of Nuremberg and Reutlingen, and probably also by the electoral prince John Frederick and Duke Francis of Lüneburg. During the diet the cities of Weissenburg, Heilbronn, Kempten, and Windesheim also expressed their concurrence with the confession. The emperor had ordered the confession to be presented to him at the next session, June 24; but when the evangelical princes asked that it be read in public, their petition was refused, and efforts were made to prevent the public reading of the document altogether. The evangelical princes, however, declared that they would not part with the confession until its reading should be allowed. The 25th was then fixed for the day of its presentation. In order to exclude the people, the little chapel of the episcopal palace was appointed in place of the spacious city hall, where the meetings of the diet were held. The two Saxon chancellors Brück and Beyer, the one with the Latin copy, the other

1. Origin of the Confession.

with the German, stepped into the middle of the assembly, and against the wish of the emperor the German text was read. The reading lasted two hours and was so distinct that every word could be heard outside. The reading being over, the copies were handed to the emperor. The German he gave to the imperial chancellor, the Elector of Mainz, the Latin he took away. Neither of the copies is now extant.

2. Its Character and Contents. The history of its origin shows that the document presented at Augsburg was confession and apology at the same time, destined to serve the cause of peace and to refute the charge of deviating from the ancient doctrine of the Church and of having communion with sectaries; and the entire first part (*Articuli præcipui fidei*, arts. i–xxi) was intended to prove that the Evangelicals agreed with the Catholic teaching, and wherever they differed from the transmitted form of doctrine they wished to restore the original, genuine teaching of the Church. The second part (*Articuli in quibus recensentur abusus mutati*, xxii–xxviii) treats of abuses and proves how certain general abuses must be abolished for the sake of conscience and that such action was not only supported by Scripture but also by the practise of the ancient Church and the acknowledged teachers of the Church.

[The first part of the Confession, which treats of the chief articles of faith, speaks of the following subjects: art. i, of God; ii, of original sin; iii, of the Son of God; iv, of justification; v, of the ministry of the Church; vi, of the new obedience; vii, of the Church; viii, what the Church is; ix, of baptism; x, of the Lord's Supper; xi, of confession; xii, of repentance; xiii, of the use of sacraments; xiv, of ecclesiastical orders; xv, of ecclesiastical rites; xvi, of civil affairs; xvii, of Christ's return to judgment; xviii, of free will; xix, of the cause of sin; xx, of good works; xxi, of the worship of saints. The second part recounts the abuses which have been corrected: art. i, of both kinds in the Lord's Supper; ii, of the marriage of priests; iii, of the mass; iv, of confession; v, of the distinction of meats and of traditions; vi, of monastic vows; vii, of ecclesiastical power.]

3. Origin of the Apology. The hope that the opponents of the Confession would make a profession of their faith was not fulfilled. They refused to be considered as a party. Nevertheless, it was decided to have the Confession examined by intelligent and unprejudiced scholars, who were to acknowledge that which was correct and to refute that which was against the Christian faith and the Christian Church (Ficker, *Die Confutation des Augsburger Bekenntnisses*, Leipsic, 1891, pp. 15 sqq.). Among the twenty scholars selected by Campeggi were some of the most malicious opponents of Luther, like Eck, Faber, Cochlæus, Dietenberger, and Wimpina, and their refutation (reprinted by Ficker) was of such a character that it was rejected by the emperor and the estates siding with Rome. A revision, however, was accepted, and as *Responsio Augustanæ confessionis* it was read on Aug. 3, 1530, in the same room in which the Confession had been read. Since this reply, the *Confutatio pontifica*, as it afterward came to be known (the Latin text in Kolde, 141 sqq.), was adopted by the emperor as his own and conformity to it was demanded, the Protestants thought necessary to refute it. No copy of the confutation was given to the Evangelicals, and, as negotiations led to no result, Melanchthon and others were requested to prepare an "Apology of the Confession," that is to say, a refutation of the charges of the *Confutatio*, and the same was approved by the Evangelical estates. In the circular for dismissing the diet which was presented to the estates, Sept. 22, the remark was found that the evangelical confession "had been refuted." This remark was contradicted by the chancellor Brück in the name of the Evangelicals, who presented at the same time Melanchthon's apology. But the emperor, to whom Ferdinand had whispered something, refused to accept it. This is the so-called *Prima delineatio apologiæ*, first made known in Latin by Chyträus (*Historia Augustanæ confessionis*, Frankfort, 1578, 328 sqq.; best edition of the Latin and German text in the *Corpus reformatorum*, xxvii, 275 sqq.). Subsequently Melanchthon received a copy of the Confutation, which led to many alterations in the first draft of the Apology. It was then published in 1531 under the title *Apologia confessionis Augustanæ*. It follows the articles of the Augustana (i.e., the Augsburg Confession), and on account of its theological exposition is rather a doctrinal work than a confession.

4. History of the Confession and the Apology. Although the emperor prohibited the printing of the evangelical confession without his special permission, during the diet six German editions and one in Latin were published (cf. *Corpus reformatorum*, xxvi, 478 sqq.). Their inaccuracy and incorrectness induced Melanchthon to prepare an edition to which he added the Apology. Thus originated the so-called *editio princeps* of the Augustana and Apology, which was published in the spring of 1531. This edition was regarded as the authentic reproduction of the faith professed before the emperor and empire. Whereas the first recension of the Apology was composed in behalf of the evangelical states, the edition now issued by Melanchthon was evidently a private work to which he attached his name as author, which is not the case with the Augustana. Nevertheless, the Apology was accepted everywhere and the German translation of Justus Jonas made it accessible to the laity. In 1532 the Apology was officially accepted at Schweinfurt by the evangelical estates as an "apology and exposition of the confession along with the confession." Ever since the Augustana and Apology have been regarded as the official principal confessions of the nascent Evangelical church. Their recognition was a condition of membership in the Schmalkald League; both were adopted in the Concord of Wittenberg of 1536 and again at Schmalkald in 1537. Meanwhile Melanchthon worked continually to improve the text. The German edition of the Augustana published in 1533 shows changes in arts. iv, v, vi, xii, xv, xx, which are of no doctrinal consequence. The same is the case with subsequent editions. More important was the new Latin edition of 1540, where the apology is said to have been *diligenter recognita*. But the Augustana appears here in such a form, especially in art. x, that it afterward received the name *variata*. Although attention had been called in 1537 to Melanchthon's changes in the text, and the Elector John Frederick criticized them as arrogant (*Corpus reformatorum*, iii, 366), we find that the "Variata" when published gave no offense. The assertion that Luther condemned it, can not be confirmed (cf. Köllner, *Symbolik*, i, Hamburg, 1837, 239). The new edition was used freely, as a new edition is preferable to an older; even such strict Lutherans as Johann Brenz praised Melanchthon for it (*Corpus reformatorum*, iv, 737). Even the fact that Johann Eck at the Worms Colloquy in 1541 mentioned the change of the original text (*Corpus reformatorum*, iv, 34 sqq.; Ranke, *Deutsche Geschichte*, iv, 176) had so little effect upon the contemporaries and Melanchthon, that when a new edition became necessary in 1542 the latter introduced other changes. After the death of Luther, when dogmatic controversies widened the chasm between Melanchthonians and the strict Lutherans and the edition of 1540 became the party-symbol of the former and later also of the Crypto-Calvinists, it naturally became an object of suspicion to the stricter Lutherans and it was but natural that in preparing the Book of Concord the original text was adopted. The Latin text represents the *editio princeps* of 1531, whereas the German was made from a Mainz copy.

(T. KOLDE.)

BIBLIOGRAPHY: The best text of the Confession in Lat. and Germ. is by Tschackert, Leipsic, 1901; given also by T. Kolde, Gotha, 1896, cf. the ed. by F. Rausch, *Die ungeänderte augsburgische Confession*, Dresden, 1874; the Lat. with Eng. transl. by C. B. Krauth is in Schaff, *Creeds*, iii, 3-73; the Krauth transl. of the Confession and Eng. transl. of the Apology by H. E. Jacobs are in the latter's *Book of Concord*, i, 69-302, Philadelphia, 1893, while full information as to the history of these documents is given in the same, ii, 24-41. For early history and collections of sources consult D. Chyträus, *Historie der Augsburger Confession*, Rostock, 1576, and often; J. J. Müller, *Historie von der evangelischen Stände Protestation wie auch von dem zur Augsburg übergebenen Glaubensbekenntnisse*, Jena, 1705; E. S. Cyprian, *Historie der Augsburger Confession*, Gotha, 1730; C. A. Salig, *Vollständige Historie der Augsburger Confession*, 3 vols., Halle, 1730; G. G. Weber, *Kritische Geschichte der Augsburger Confession, aus archivalischen Nachrichten*, 2 vols., Frankfort, 1785. For history of the text consult *CR*, xxvi, 280; G. W. Panzer, *Die unveränderte augsburgische Confession*, Nuremberg, 1782 (Germ. and Lat.); G. P. C. Kaiser, *Beitrag zu einer kritischen Literärgeschichte der Melancthonschen Originalausgabe*, ib. 1830. For the sources consult C. E. Förstemann, *Urkundenbuch zur Geschichte des Reichstags zu Augsburg, 1530*, Halle, 1830; idem, *Archiv für die Geschichte der kirchlichen Reformation*, vol. i, part 1, Halle, 1831; Luther's *Briefe*, ed. M. L. de Wette, vol. iii, Berlin, 1826; *CR*, ii; T. Kolde, *Analecta Lutherana*, pp. 119 sqq., Gotha, 1883; F. Schirrmacher, *Briefe und Akten zur Geschichte des Religionsgesprächs und des Reichstags zu Augsburg*, ib. 1876. On the history and interpretation consult G. L. Plitt, *Einleitung in die Augustana*, 2 vols., Erlangen, 1867-68; O. Zöckler, *Die augsburgische Confession als symbolische Lehrgrundlage*, Frankfort, 1870; C. P. Krauth, *The Conservative Reformation and its Theology as represented in the Augsburg Confession*, Philadelphia, 1871; L. von Ranke, *Deutsche Geschichte*, iii, 172 sqq., Leipsic, 1881; J. Ficker, *Die Konfutation des augsburgischen Bekenntnisses, ihre erste Gestalt und ihre Geschichte*, ib. 1891; H. E. Jacobs, *Book of Concord*, ut sup. (the best edition for English readers); T. Kolde, *Martin Luther*, ii, 324 sqq., Gotha, 1893; Schaff, *Christian Church*, vi, 706-718; J. W. Richard, *Philip Melanchthon*, pp. 190-218, New York, 1898; J. Köstlin, *Martin Luther*, ii, 192 sqq., Berlin, 1903.

AUGSBURG, INTERIM OF. See INTERIM.

AUGSBURG, RELIGIOUS PEACE OF: A convention concluded in a diet at Augsburg Sept. 25, 1555, intended to settle the religious question in Germany. After his victory over the Schmalkald League (1547), the Emperor Charles V thought he was near his goal, the religious and ecclesiastical unity of the empire. But the desertion of Duke Maurice of Saxony, and the Treaty of Passau (1552) changed the situation, because by the latter public recognition was given to the Lutheran faith as among the ecclesiastical institutions of the empire. Such recognition meant a complete rupture with the ecclesiastical and political development inherited from the Middle Ages, and a peace on the basis of the equal recognition of both religions was highly unacceptable to the emperor. As he could not prevent it, he withdrew from the negotiations and transferred all power to his brother Ferdinand, who felt like himself, but was ready to accept the inevitable. When the diet at Augsburg was finally opened Feb. 5, 1555, Ferdinand's endeavor was directed more toward strengthening the peace of the country than to religion. But the Protestants insisted upon settling the question of the religious peace first, without regard to a council. The opposite party yielded reluctantly. With the exception of the Augsburg cardinal, Otto von Truchsess, the spiritual princes agreed that "there should be concluded and established a continual, firm, unconditional peace lasting forever," between the professors "of the old religion and the estates belonging to the Augsburg Confession." The stipulations of the peace were as follows: All adherents of the Augsburg Confession were to be included, without regard to its various editions (see AUGSBURG CONFESSION AND ITS APOLOGY), those sects alone being excluded which had been condemned by decrees of the diet, as already provided in the Treaty of Passau. Spiritual jurisdiction in Protestant territory was to be suspended, but the chapters were not to be expelled from Protestant cities. Confiscated spiritual estates, which did not belong to those immediately subject to the emperor and which at the time of the Treaty of Passau or later were no longer in the possession of the clergy were to remain in the hands of the Evangelicals. To the secular estates alone was unrestricted freedom of religion granted, and they were masters of the religion of their subjects, for "where there is one Lord, there should be one religion." The conversion of a spiritual prince to the Augsburg Confession, according to the *reservatum ecclesiasticum* added by the king, carried with it the loss of his spiritual dignity and his office as well as of the imperial fief. The imperial chamber, to which Protestants were now admitted, was to watch over the continuance of the peace. Considered all in all, the success of the Protestants was small. Protestantism was deprived of the chance to spread, by the *reservatum ecclesiasticum*, a large part of Germany was permanently assigned to Catholicism, and the Lutheran reformation, which had hardly begun, was broken off, not to be resumed. The little that had been gained was established, but the immediate effect was the outbreak of the internal doctrinal controversies and the rise of the official Church.

(T. Kolde.)

In Austria and its dependencies Lutheranism profited greatly by the peace. Many nobles having become Protestant claimed and exercised the right to promote the Protestant cause in their possessions. To be sure, the Hapsburgs claimed for themselves the exclusive right to determine the religion of the people in all their dependencies; but they found it impossible to enforce their views upon the nobles.

A. H. N.

Bibliography: Lehenmann, *De pace religionis acta publica et originalie*, Frankfort, 1631; L. von Ranke, *Deutsche Geschichte*, vol. v, book x, Leipsic, 1882; M. Ritter, *Deutsche Geschichte im Zeitalter der Gegenreformation*, i, 79 sqq., Stuttgart, 1889; G. Wolff, *Der Augsburger Religionsfriede*, ib. 1890; F. von Bezold, *Geschichte der deutschen Reformation*, p. 866, Berlin, 1890; G. Egelhaaf, *Deutsche Geschichte im sechszehnten Jahrhundert*, ii, 587 sqq., Stuttgart, 1891.

AUGUSTI, au″gūs′tî, **JOHANN CHRISTIAN WILHELM**: Theologian and archeologist: b. at Eschenberga, Saxe-Coburg-Gotha, Oct. 27, 1772; d. at Coblenz Apr. 28, 1841. He studied theology at Jena and became professor of philosophy there 1800, of Oriental languages 1823; professor of theology at Breslau 1812, at Bonn 1819, where he represented the older school of theology by the side of younger teachers such as Lücke, Gieseler, and Nitzsch; in 1828 he became councilor of the consistory of Coblenz, in 1835 president. Among his works are *Denkwürdigkeiten aus der christlichen Archäologie* (12 vols., Leipsic, 1817–31); *Lehrbuch der christlichen Dogmengeschichte* (1805; 4th ed., 1835); *Einleitung in das Alte Testament* (1806; 2d ed., 1827). The most widely used of his works was the *Handbuch der christlichen Archäologie* (3 vols., 1836–37); he also assisted de Wette in translating the Bible into German (1809–14). Adaptations of his works on archeology were published in English by J. E. Riddle (London, 1839) and L. Coleman (Andover, 1841).

AUGUSTINA, SISTER. See Lasaulx, Amalie von

AUGUSTINE OF ALVELDT: German Franciscan; b. at Alfeld (27 m. s. of Hanover), Prussia, c. 1480; d. probably in Halle after 1532. He first appears in Leipsic, where he was a reader in theology at a convent. He is the Minorite to whom Erasmus refers in the *Spongia*. He is known chiefly as an opponent of Luther. On Jan. 20, 1522, he engaged in a public disputation at Weimar with Johann Lange in defense of cloister-life. He became guardian of the Franciscan cloister at Halle about 1523. His works have now no value, except as curiosities.

AUGUSTINE (AUSTIN), SAINT, OF CANTERBURY: The apostle to the English and first archbishop of Canterbury; d. at Canterbury May 26, 604 or 605. When first heard of he was *præpositus* (prior) of the monastery of St. Andrew, founded by Gregory the Great in Rome, and was sent by Gregory in 596 at the head of a mission of forty monks to preach to the Anglo-Saxons. They lost heart on the way and Augustine went back to Rome from Provence and asked that the mission be given up. The pope, however, commanded and encouraged them to proceed, and they landed on the Island of Thanet in the spring of 597 They found the way not unprepared as Bertha, daughter of Charibert of Paris and wife of Ethelbert, king of Kent, was a Christian and was allowed to worship God in her own way. Ethelbert permitted the missionaries to settle and preach in his town of Canterbury and before the end of the year he was converted and Augustine was consecrated bishop at Arles. At Christmas 10,000 of the king's subjects were baptized. Augustine sent a report of his success to Gregory with certain rather petty questions concerning his work, which do not indicate a great mind. In 601 Mellitus (q.v.) and others brought the pope's replies, with the pallium for Augustine and a present of sacred vessels, vestments, relics, books, and the like. Gregory directed the new archbishop to ordain as soon as possible twelve suffragan bishops and to send a bishop to York, who should also have twelve suffragans,—a plan which was not carried out, nor was the primatial see established at London as Gregory intended. More practicable were the pope's mandates concerning heathen temples and usages; the former were to be consecrated to Christian service and the latter, so far as possible, to be transformed into dedication ceremonies or feasts of martyrs, since "he who would climb to a lofty height must go up by steps, not leaps" (letter of Gregory to Mellitus, in Bede, i, 30). Augustine reconsecrated and rebuilt an old church at Canterbury as his cathedral and founded a monastery in connection with it. He also restored a church and founded the monastery of St. Peter and St. Paul outside the walls. His attempts to effect a union with the old British Church in Wales failed. See Anglo-Saxons, Conversion of the; Celtic Church in Britain and Ireland.

Bibliography: The important sources are Bede, *Hist. eccl.*, i, 23–ii, 3 and the letters of Gregory the Great (in Haddan and Stubbs, *Councils*, iii, 5–38). The thirteenth centenary of Augustine's mission in 1897 called forth a number of publications, including an edition of the chapters of Bede, with introduction, by A. Snow, O. S. B., London, 1897, and *The Mission of St. Augustine to England according to the Original Documents*, ed. A. J. Mason, Cambridge, 1897, which gives everything of importance in Latin and English (cf. also Haddan and Stubbs, ut sup., iii. 3–60). Monographs of a more popular character were issued by G. F. Browne, *Augustine and his Companions*, London, 1895; E. L. Cutts, *Augustine of Canterbury*, ib. 1895; Brou, S. J., *St. Augustin de Canterbury et ses compagnons*, Paris, 1897, Eng. transl., London, 1897; F. A. Gasquet, *The Mission of St. Augustine*, ib. 1897; W. E. Collins, *Beginnings of English Christianity: Coming of St. Augustine*, ib. 1898 (brief but scholarly); mention may be made also of *DNB*, 1885, ii, 255–257; W. Hook, *Lives of the Archbishops of Canterbury*, vol. i, London, 1860; E. Bassenge, *Die Sendung Augustins zur Bekehrung der Angelsachsen*, Leipsic, 1890; A. P. Stanley, *Historical Memorials of Canterbury*, pp. 19–55, London, 1883; G. F. Maclear, *Apostles of Mediæval Europe*, pp. 87–98, London, 1888; W. Bright, *Early English Church History*, pp. 40–109, Oxford, 1897. The life of Augustine is included in Cardinal Newman's *Lives of the English Saints*, London, 1845.

AUGUSTINE, SAINT, OF HIPPO.

I. Life: 1. Formative Period: Augustine, bishop of Hippo (Lat. *Augustinus;* the prænomen Aurelius given by Orosius, Prosper, and others, has no evidence in his own writings, or in letters addressed to him), is not only the most important of the Fathers of the early Church, but at the same time the one best known through a variety of specially full and useful sources. He was one of the most fertile writers of the early period, and the multiplication of his manuscripts has allowed his works to come down relatively complete in number. Among these, the *Confessiones* and the *Retractationes* have a unique value for the history of primitive church life, while others are full of biographical details. Moreover, a countryman of his, Possidius, Bishop of Calama, who was in close relations with him for forty years and present at his death, has given us a life which deserves a place of honor in early hagiography. We have thus remarkably satisfactory sources both as to Augustine's life and as to his literary work. He himself, in his *Confessiones* (written between 397 and 400), has described the events of his first thirty-three years; and for the rest of his life we have both the treatises and letters, which begin about the time when the *Confessiones* stop, as well as the biography by Possidius. For the historical understanding of his works, as well as for their dates and criticism, Augustine himself has left in the *Retractationes* (completed at the end of 427) a unique guide. In this review he takes up each one of his writings, except the letters and sermons, in chronological order, with the purpose of explaining things which might be misconstrued or of restating them in a better way; and Possidius has given us also a comprehensive and systematic list of all the writings, as an appendix to his biography.

1. Sources for a Biography.

Augustine is the first ecclesiastical author the whole course of whose development can be clearly traced, as well as the first in whose case we are able to determine the exact period covered by his career, to the very day. He informs us himself that he was born at Thagaste (Tagaste; now Suk Arras), in proconsular Numidia, Nov. 13, 354; he died at Hippo Regius (just south of the modern Bona) Aug. 28, 430. [Both Suk Arras and Bona are in the present Algeria, the first 60 m. w. by s. and the second 65 m. w. of Tunis, the ancient Carthage.] His father Patricius, as a member of the council, belonged to the influential classes of the place; he was, however, in straitened circumstances, and seems to have had nothing remarkable either in mental equipment or in character, but to have been a lively, sensual, hot-tempered person, entirely taken up with his worldly concerns, and unfriendly to Christianity until the close of his life; he became a catechumen shortly before Augustine reached his sixteenth year (369–370). To his mother Monnica (so the manuscripts write her name, not Monica; b. 331, d. 387) Augustine later believed that he owed what he became. But though she was evidently an honorable, loving, self-sacrificing, and able woman, she was not always the ideal of a Christian mother that tradition has made her appear. Her religion in earlier life has traces of formality and worldliness about it; her ambition for her son seems at first to have had little moral earnestness and she regretted his Manicheanism more than she did his early sensuality. It seems to have been through Ambrose and Augustine that she attained the mature personal piety with which she left the world. Of Augustine as a boy his parents were intensely proud. He received his first education at Thagaste, learning to read and write, as well as the rudiments of Greek and Latin literature, from teachers who followed the old traditional pagan methods. He seems to have had no systematic instruction in the Christian faith at this period, and though enrolled among the catechumens, apparently was near baptism only when an illness and his own boyish desire made it temporarily probable.

2. Boyhood. Parental Influences.

His father, delighted with his son's progress in his studies, sent him first to the neighboring Madaura, and then to Carthage, some two days' journey away. A year's enforced idleness, while the means for this more expensive schooling were being accumulated, proved a time of moral deterioration; but we must be on our guard against forming our conception of Augustine's vicious living from the *Confessiones* alone. To speak, as Mommsen does, of "frantic dissipation" is to attach too much weight to his own penitent expressions of self-reproach. Looking back as a bishop, he naturally regarded his whole life up to the "conversion" which led to his baptism as a period of wandering from the right way; but not long after this conversion, he judged differently, and found, from one point of view, the turning-point of his career in his taking up philosophy in his nineteenth year. This view of his early life, which may be traced also in the *Confessiones*, is probably nearer the truth than the popular conception of a youth sunk in all kinds of immorality. When he began the study of rhetoric at Carthage, it is true that (in company with com-

3. Schooling and Early Marriage.

rades whose ideas of pleasure were probably much more gross than his) he drank of the cup of sensual pleasure. But his ambition prevented him from allowing his dissipations to interfere with his studies. His son Adeodatus was born in the summer of 372, and it was probably the mother of this child whose charms enthralled him soon after his arrival at Carthage about the end of 370. But he remained faithful to her until about 385, and the grief which he felt at parting from her shows what the relation had been. In the view of the civilization of that period, such a monogamous union was distinguished from a formal marriage only by certain legal restrictions, in addition to the informality of its beginning and the possibility of a voluntary dissolution. Even the Church was slow to condemn such unions absolutely, and Monnica seems to have received the child and his mother publicly at Thagaste. In any case Augustine was known to Carthage not as a roysterer but as a quiet honorable student. He was, however, internally dissatisfied with his life. The *Hortensius* of Cicero, now lost with the exception of a few fragments, made a deep impression on him. To know the truth was henceforth his deepest wish. About the time when the contrast between his ideals and his actual life became intolerable, he learned to conceive of Christianity as the one religion which could lead him to the attainment of his ideal. But his pride of intellect held him back from embracing it earnestly; the Scriptures could not bear comparison with Cicero; he sought for wisdom, not for humble submission to authority.

4. Comes Under Manichean Influences.

In this frame of mind he was ready to be affected by the Manichean propaganda which was then actively carried on in Africa, without apparently being much hindered by the imperial edict against assemblies of the sect. Two things especially attracted him to the Manicheans: they felt at liberty to criticize the Scriptures, particularly the Old Testament, with perfect freedom; and they held chastity and self-denial in honor. The former fitted in with the impression which the Bible had made on Augustine himself; the latter corresponded closely to his mood at the time. The prayer which he tells us he had in his heart then, "Lord, give me chastity and temperance, but not now," may be taken as the formula which represents the attitude of many of the Manichean *auditores*. Among these Augustine was classed during his nineteenth year; but he went no further, though he held firmly to Manicheanism for nine years, during which he endeavored to convert all his friends, scorned the sacraments of the Church, and held frequent disputations with catholic believers.

5. Teaches at Thagaste.

Having finished his studies, he returned to Thagaste and began to teach grammar, living in the house of Romanianus, a prominent citizen who had been of much service to him since his father's death, and whom he converted to Manicheanism. Monnica deeply grieved at her son's heresy, forbade him her house, until reassured by a vision that promised his restoration. She comforted herself also by the word of a certain bishop (probably of Thagaste) that "the child of so many tears could not be lost." He seems to have spent little more than a year in Thagaste, when the desire for a wider field, together with the death of a dear friend, moved him to return to Carthage as a teacher of rhetoric.

6. Rejection of Manicheanism. Removal to Rome.

The next period was a time of diligent study, and produced (about the end of 380) the treatise, long since lost, *De pulchro et apto*. Meanwhile the hold of Manicheanism on him was loosening. Its feeble cosmology and metaphysics had long since failed to satisfy him, and the astrological superstitions springing from the credulity of its disciples offended his reason. The members of the sect, unwilling to lose him, had great hopes from a meeting with their leader Faustus of Mileve; but when he came to Carthage in the autumn of 382, he too proved disappointing, and Augustine ceased to be at heart a Manichean. He was not yet, however, prepared to put anything in the place of the doctrine he had held, and remained in outward communion with his former associates while he pursued his search for truth. Soon after his Manichean convictions had broken down, he left Carthage for Rome, partly, it would seem, to escape the preponderating influence of his mother on a mind which craved perfect freedom of investigation. Here he was brought more than ever, by obligations of friendship and gratitude, into close association with Manicheans, of whom there were many in Rome, not merely *auditores* but *perfecti* or fully initiated members. This did not last long, however, for the prefect Symmachus sent him to Milan, certainly before the beginning of 385, in answer to a request for a professor of rhetoric.

7. Life Under Ambrose at Milan.

The change of residence completed Augustine's separation from Manicheanism. He listened to the preaching of Ambrose and by it was made acquainted with the allegorical interpretation of the Scriptures and the weakness of the Manichean Biblical criticism, but he was not yet ready to accept catholic Christianity. His mind was still under the influence of the skeptical philosophy of the later Academy. This was the least satisfactory stage in his mental development, though his external circumstances were increasingly favorable. He had his mother again with him now, and shared a house and garden with her and his devoted friends Alypius and Nebridius, who had followed him to Milan; his assured social position is shown also by the fact that, in deference to his mother's entreaties, he was formally betrothed to a woman of suitable station. As a catechumen of the Church, he listened regularly to the sermons of Ambrose. The bishop, though as yet he knew nothing of Augustine's internal struggles, had welcomed him in the friendliest manner both for his own and for Monnica's sake. Yet Augustine was attracted only by Ambrose's eloquence, not by his faith; now he agreed, and now he questioned. Morally his life was perhaps at its lowest point. On his betrothal, he had put away the mother of his son; but neither the grief which he felt at this parting nor regard for his future wife, who was as yet too young for marriage, prevented him from taking a new concubine for the two intervening years. Sensuality, however, began to pall upon him, little as he cared to struggle against it. His idealism was by no means dead; he told Romanian, who came to Milan at this time on business, that he wished he could live altogether in accordance with the dictates of philosophy; and a plan was even made for the foundation of a community retired from the world, which should live entirely for the pursuit of truth. With this project his intention of marriage and his ambition interfered, and Augustine was further off than ever from peace of mind.

8. Attracted to Neoplatonism.

In his thirty-first year he was strongly attracted to Neoplatonism by the logic of his development. The idealistic character of this philosophy awoke unbounded enthusiasm, and he was attracted to it also by its exposition of pure intellectual being and of the origin of evil. These doctrines brought him closer to the Church, though he did not yet grasp the full significance of its central doctrine of the personality of Jesus Christ. In his earlier writings he names this acquaintance with the Neoplatonic teaching and its relation to Christianity as the turning-point of his life, though in the *Confessiones* it appears only as a stage on the long road of error. The truth, as it may be established by a careful comparison of his earlier and later writings, is that his idealism had been distinctly strengthened by Neoplatonism, which had at the same time revealed his own will, and not a *natura altera* in him, as the subject of his baser desires. This made the conflict between ideal and actual in his life more unbearable than ever. Yet his sensual desires were still so strong that it seemed impossible for him to break away from them.

9. Conversion to Christianity.

Help came in a curious way. A countryman of his, Pontitianus, visited him and told him things which he had never heard about the monastic life and the wonderful conquests over self which had been won under its inspiration. Augustine's pride was touched; that the unlearned should take the kingdom of heaven by violence, while he with all his learning, was still held captive by the flesh, seemed unworthy of him. When Pontitianus had gone, with a few vehement words to Alypius, he went hastily with him into the garden to fight out this new problem. Then followed the scene so often described. Overcome by his conflicting emotions he left Alypius and threw himself down under a fig-tree in tears. From a neighboring house came a child's voice repeating again and again the simple words *Tolle, lege,* "Take up and read." It seemed to him a heavenly indication; he picked up the copy of St. Paul's epistles which he had left where he and Alypius had been sitting, and opened at Romans xiii. When he came to the words, "Let us walk honestly as in the day; not in rioting and drunkenness, not in chambering and wantonness," it seemed to him that a decisive message had been sent to his own soul, and his resolve was taken. Alypius found a word for himself a few lines further, "Him that is weak in the faith receive ye;" and together they went into the house to bring the good news to Monnica. This was at the end of the summer of 386.

10. Baptism. Ordination in Africa.

Augustine, intent on breaking wholly with his old life, gave up his position, and wrote to Ambrose to ask for baptism. The months which intervened between that summer and the Easter of the following year, at which, according to the early custom, he intended to receive the sacrament, were spent in delightful calm at a country-house, put at his disposal by one of his friends, at Cassisiacum (Casciago, 47 m. n. by w. of Milan). Here Monnica Alypius, Adeodatus, and some of his pupils kept him company, and he still lectured on Vergil to them and held philosophic discussions. The whole party returned to Milan before Easter (387), and Augustine, with Alypius and Adeodatus, was baptized. Plans were then made for returning to Africa; but these were upset by the death of Monnica, which took place at Ostia as they were preparing to cross the sea, and has been described by her devoted son in one of the most tender and beautiful passages of the *Confessiones*. Augustine remained at least another year in Italy, apparently in Rome, living the same quiet life which he had led at Cassisiacum, studying and writing, in company with his countryman Evodius, later bishop of Uzalis. Here, where he had been most closely associated with the Manicheans, his literary warfare with them naturally began; and he was also writing on free will, though this book was only finished at Hippo in 391. In the autumn of 388, passing through Carthage, he returned to Thagaste, a far different man from the Augustine who had left it five years before. Alypius was still with him, and also Adeodatus, who died young, we do not know when or where. Here Augustine and his friends again took up a quiet, though not yet in any sense a monastic, life in common, and pursued their favorite studies. About the beginning of 391, having found a friend in Hippo to help in the foundation of what he calls a monastery, he sold his inheritance, and was ordained presbyter in response to a general demand, though not without misgivings on his own part.

11. Presbyterate at Hippo.

The years which he spent in the presbyterate (391–395) are the last of his formative period. The very earliest works which fall within the time of his episcopate show us the fully developed theologian of whose special teaching we think when we speak of Augustinianism. There is little externally noteworthy in these four years. He took up active work not later than the Easter of 391, when we find him preaching to the candidates for baptism. The plans for a monastic community which had brought him to Hippo were now realized. In a garden given for the purpose by the bishop, Valerius, he founded his monastery, which seems to have been the first in Africa, and is of especial significance because it maintained a clerical school and thus made a connecting link between monasticism and the secular clergy. Other details of this period are that he appealed to Aurelius, bishop of Carthage, to suppress the custom of holding banquets and entertainments in the churches, and by 395 had succeeded, through his courageous eloquence, in abolishing it in Hippo; that in 392 a public disputation took place between him and a Manichean presbyter of Hippo, Fortunatus; that his treatise *De fide et symbolo* was prepared to be read before the council held at Hippo October 8, 393; and that after that he was in Carthage for a while, perhaps in connection with the synod held there in 394.

12. Beginnings of Polemic Activity. The intellectual interests of these four years are more easily determined, principally concerned as they are with the Manichean controversy, and producing the treatises *De utilitate credendi* (391), *De duabus animabus contra Manichæos* (first half of 392), and *Contra Adimantum* (394 or 395). His activity against the Donatists also begins in this period, but he is still more occupied with the Manicheans, both from the recollections of his own past and from his increasing knowledge of Scripture, which appears, together with a stronger hold on the Church's teaching, in the works just named, and even more in others of this period, such as his expositions of the Sermon on the Mount and of the Epistles to the Romans and the Galatians. Full as the writings of this epoch are, however, of Biblical phrases and terms,—grace and the law, predestination, vocation, justification, regeneration—a reader who is thoroughly acquainted with Neoplatonism will detect Augustine's old love of it in a Christian dress in not a few places. He has entered so far into St. Paul's teaching that humanity as a whole appears to him a *massa peccati* or *peccatorum*, which, if left to itself, that is, without the grace of God, must inevitably perish. However much we are here reminded of the later Augustine, it is clear that he still held the belief that the free will of man could decide his own destiny. He knew some who saw in Romans ix an unconditional predestination which took away the freedom of the will; but he was still convinced that this was not the Church's teaching. His opinion on this point did not change till after he was a bishop.

2. Work as Bishop: The more widely known Augustine became, the more Valerius, the bishop of Hippo, was afraid of losing him on the first vacancy of some neighboring see, and desired to fix him permanently in Hippo by making him coadjutor-bishop,—a desire in which the people ardently concurred.

1. Election to the Bishopric. Augustine was strongly opposed to the project, though possibly neither he nor Valerius knew that it might be held to be a violation of the eighth canon of Nicæa, which forbade in its last clause "two bishops in one city" (Hefele, *Conciliengeschichte*, i, 407 sqq., Eng. transl., i, 409–410); and the primate of Numidia, Megalius of Calama, seems to have raised difficulties which sprang at least partly from a personal lack of confidence. But Valerius carried his plan through, and not long before Christmas, 395, Augustine was consecrated by Megalius. It is not known when Valerius died; but it makes little difference, since for the rest of his life he left the administration more and more in the hands of his assistant.

A complete narration of Augustine's doings during the thirty-five years in which he was the glory of the little diocese would require a history of the African, almost of the whole Western, Church. Here we can do no more than briefly discuss some things which constitute his importance to later Christianity, and mention a few important biographical facts. Further details will be found in the articles DONATISM, PELAGIUS, SEMIPELAGIANISM, MONASTICISM, NORTH AFRICAN CHURCH. The life of Augustine by his friend Possidius shows that

2. Possidius's View of Augustine's Services. its author was possessed by the desire to erect a suitable memorial to a man who was destined to have a lasting importance in the history of the Church; it is much more than a mere product of hagiography. He considers Augustine first as an author who has left so many works in refutation of heresy and encouragement of piety that few even of diligent students can master them all; and he feels himself therefore bound to include a brief account of his subject's literary activity. Then he deals with the services which Augustine rendered to the peace and unity of the Church by his labors against the Donatists; and finally he attributes to Augustine's encouragement of monasticism much of its growth, together with an actual regeneration of the clerical life. His view on the two latter points, if colored a little by the local point of view, is still the respectable opinion of a contemporary; but it does not altogether agree with the deliberate historical judgment of posterity. The Vandal invasion, which came like a spring frost upon the young life of the African Church, and the Mohammedan conquests, both prevented Augustine's labors from having their full effect in Africa. Leaving aside for the moment the influence of his writings, one may really say that the condemnation of Pelagianism was the only permanant result of his work.

But his writings have continued to exert such an influence, by no means confined to the time of the early Church nor to African soil, as no other Father before or since has ever attained.

3. Doctrinal Importance of Augustine. If we look to the posthumous effects they have had, we may agree with the verdict of Possidius, and carry it further than was possible to a contemporary. Augustine is practically the father of all western Christianity after his time. It is true that Catholicism has never officially accepted his doctrine of grace in its entirety; but this fact is of relatively slight importance when we think of the colossal influence which his writings have had upon the gradual shaping of the Church's doctrine as a whole—there is scarcely a single Roman Catholic dogma which is historically intelligible without reference to his teaching. And it is not only the dogmas of the Western Church over which he has exerted an unparalleled influence; its hierarchical and its scientific development both derive from him. The great struggle between the rival chiefs of medieval Christendom, the pope and the emperor, is explicable in its deepest meaning, intelligible in its course, only from his *De civitate Dei;* when medieval theology was most active, then it was most under his influence, and the scholastic movement was determined, not only in its speculations but in its very method, by him. From him, again, medieval mysticism, in both its authorized and its heretical forms, received its most decisive impulse; Augustinian influences must be taken into account in the study of all the so-called precursors of the Reformation. When, however, we have called him the father of medieval Catholicism, we have not yet said all. The effect of his teaching in the East has been, to be sure, slight and indirect; but the Reformers made an ally of him. The characteristic notes of what are specifically called the Reformed Churches, in contradistinction to the Lutheran, are especially founded upon Augustinian tradition. In the history of philosophy, too, he has been a force far beyond the Middle Ages; in both Descartes and Spinoza his voice may be distinctly heard.

Space forbids any attempt to trace all the causes of these abiding effects; and in what remains to be said, biographical interest must be largely our guide. We know a considerable number of events in Augustine's episcopal life which can be surely placed—the so-called third and eighth synods of Carthage in 397 and 403, at which, as at those still to be mentioned, he was certainly present; the disputation with the Manichean Felix at Hippo in 404; the eleventh synod of Carthage in 407; the conference with the Donatists in Carthage, 411; the synod of Mileve, 416; the African general council at Carthage, 418; the journey to Cæsarea in Mauretania and the disputation with the Donatist bishop there, 418; another general council in Carthage, 419; and finally the consecration of Eraclius as his assistant in 426. None of these events, however, marks a decisive epoch in his life, which flowed on quietly and evenly during the whole time of his episcopate, except the last few months. Thus it will require careful study to determine the epochs in his intellectual development during this period.

4. Events of His Episcopate.

II. Theology: His special and direct opposition to Manicheanism did not last a great while after his consecration. About 397 he wrote a tractate *Contra epistolam [Manichæi] quam vocant fundamenti;* in the *De agone christiano,* written about the same time, and in the *Confessiones,* a little later, numerous anti-Manichean expressions occur. After this, however, he only attacked the Manicheans on some special occasion, as when, about 400, on the request of his "brethren," he wrote a detailed rejoinder to Faustus, a Manichean bishop, or made the treatise *De natura boni* out of his discussions with Felix; a little later, also, the letter of the Manichean Secundinus gave him occasion to write *Contra Secundinum,* which, in spite of its comparative brevity, he regarded as the best of his writings on this subject. In the succeeding period, he was much more occupied with anti-Donatist polemics, which in their turn were forced to take second place by the emergence of the Pelagian controversy.

1. His Anti-Manicheanism.

It has been thought that Augustine's anti-Pelagian teaching grew out of his conception of the Church and its sacraments as a means of salvation; and attention was called to the fact that before the Pelagian controversy this aspect of the Church had, through the struggle with the Donatists, assumed special importance in his mind. But this conception should be denied. It is quite true that in 395 Augustine's views on sin and grace, freedom and predestination, were not what they afterward came to be. But the new trend was given to them before the time of his anti-Donatist activity, and so before he could have heard anything of Pelagius. What we call Augustinianism was not a reaction against Pelagianism; it would be much truer to say that the latter was a reaction against Augustine's views. He himself names the beginning of his episcopate as the turning-point. Accordingly, in the first thing which he wrote after his consecration, the *De diversis quæstionibus ad Simplicianum* (396 or 397), we come already upon the new conception. In no other of his writings do we see as plainly the gradual attainment of conviction on any point; as he himself says in the *Retractationes,* he was laboring for the free choice of the will of man, but the grace of God won the day. So completely was it won, that we might set forth the specifically Augustinian teaching on grace, as against the Pelagians and the Massilians, by a series of quotations taken wholly from this treatise. It is true that much of his later teaching is still undeveloped here; the question of predestination (though the word is used) does not really come up; he is not clear as to the term "election"; and nothing is said of the "gift of perseverance." But what we get on these points later is nothing but the logical consequence of that which is expressed here, and so we have the actual genesis of Augustine's predestinarian teaching under our eyes. It is determined by no reference to the question of infant baptism—still less by any considerations connected with the conception of the Church. The impulse comes directly from Scripture, with the help, it is true, of those exegetical thoughts which he mentioned earlier as those of others and not his own. To be sure, Paul alone can not explain this doctrine of grace; this is evident from the fact that the very definition of grace is non-Pauline. Grace is for Augustine, both now and later, not the *misericordia peccata condonans* of the Reformers, as justification is not the alteration of the relation to God accomplished by means of the *accipere remissionem.* Grace is rather the *misericordia* which displays itself in the divine *inspiratio,* and justification is *justum* or *pium fieri* as a result of this. We may even say that this grace is an *interna illuminatio* such as a study of Augustine's Neoplatonism enables us easily to understand, which restores the connection with the divine *bonum esse.* He had long been convinced

2. His Anti-Pelagianism.

that "not only the greatest but also the smallest good things can not be, except from him from whom are all good things, that is, from God;" and it might well seem to him to follow from this that faith, which is certainly a good thing, could proceed from the operation of God alone. This explains the idea that grace works like a law of nature, drawing the human will to God with a divine omnipotence. Of course this Neoplatonic coloring must not be exaggerated; it is more consistent with itself in his earlier writings than in the later, and he would never have arrived at his predestinarian teaching without the New Testament. With this knowledge, we are in a position to estimate the force of a difficulty which now confronted Augustine for the first time, but never afterward left him, and which has been present in the Roman Catholic teaching even down to the Councils of Trent and the Vatican. If faith depends upon an action of our own, solicited but not caused by vocation, it can only save a man when, *per fidem gratiam accipiens*, he becomes one who not merely believes in God but loves him also. But if faith has been already inspired by grace, and if, while the Scripture speaks of justification by faith, it is held (in accordance with the definition of grace) that justification follows upon the *infusio caritatis*, —then either the conception of the faith which is God-inspired must pass its fluctuating boundaries and approach nearer to that of *caritas*, or the conception of faith which is unconnected with *caritas* will render the fact of its inspiration unintelligible and justification by faith impossible. Augustine's anti-Pelagian writings set forth this doctrine of grace more clearly in some points, such as the terms "election," "predestination," "the gift of perseverance," and also more logically; but space forbids us to show this here, as the part taken in this controversy by Augustine is so fully detailed elsewhere (see PELAGIUS; SEMIPELAGIANISM). An enumeration of his contributions to this subject must suffice.

3. Anti-Pelagian Writings.

They are as follows: *De peccatorum meritis et remissione* (412); *De spiritu et litera* (412); *De natura et gratia contra Pelagium* (415); *De perfectione justitiæ hominis* (about 415); *De gestis Pelagii* (417); *De gratia Christi et de peccato originali* (418); *De nuptiis et concupiscentia* (419 and 420); *De anima et ejus origine* (about 419), which does not bear directly on Pelagianism, but answers a Pelagianizing critic of Augustine's reserve on the question of traducianism and creationism; *Contra duas epistulas Pelagianorum ad Bonifatium, romanæ ecclesiæ episcopum* (about 420); *Contra Julianum* (about 421); *De gratia et libero arbitrio* (426 or 427); *De correptione et gratia* (426 or 427); *De prædestinatione sanctorum* (428 or 429); *De dono perseverantiæ* (428 or 429); and the *opus imperfectum* written in the last years of his life, *Contra secundam Juliani responsionem*.

In order to arrive at a decision as to what influence the Donatist controversy had upon Augustine's intellectual development, it is necessary to see how long and how intensely he was concerned with it. We have seen that even before he was a bishop he was defending the catholic Church against the Donatists; and after his consecration he took part directly or indirectly in all the important discussions of the matter, some of which have been already mentioned, and defended the cause of the Church in letters and sermons as well as in his more formal polemical writings.

4. Activity Against Donatism.

The first of these which belongs to the period of his episcopate, *Contra partem Donati*, has been lost; about 400 he wrote the two cognate treatises *Contra epistulam Parmeniani* (the Donatist bishop of Carthage) and *De baptismo contra Donatistas*. He was considered by the schismatics as their chief antagonist, and was obliged to defend himself against a libelous attack on their part in a rejoinder now lost. From the years 401 and 402 we have the reply to the Donatist bishop of Cirta, *Contra epistulam Petiliani*, and also the *Epistula ad catholicos de unitate ecclesiæ*. The conflict was now reaching its most acute stage. After the Carthaginian synod of 403 had made preparations for a decisive debate with the Donatists, and the latter had declined to fall in with the plan, the bitterness on both sides increased. Another synod at Carthage the following year decided that the emperor should be asked for penal laws against the Donatists. Honorius granted the request; but the employment of force in matters of belief brought up a new point of discord between the two sides. When these laws were abrogated (409), the plan of a joint conference was tried once more in June, 411, under imperial authority, nearly 300 bishops being present from each side, with Augustine and Aurelius of Carthage as the chief representatives of the catholic cause. In the following year, the Donatists proving insubordinate, Honorius issued a new and severer edict against them, which proved the beginning of the end for the schism. For these years from 405 to 412 we have twenty-one extant letters of Augustine's bearing on the controversy, and there were eight formal treatises, but four of these are lost. Those which we still have are: *Contra Cresconium grammaticum* (about 406); *De unico baptismo* (about 410 or 411), in answer to a work of the same name by Petilian; the brief report of the conference (end of 411); and the *Liber contra Donatistas post collationem* (probably 412). After this date, though he occasionally touched on the question in letters and sermons, he produced practically no more literary polemics in regard to it; we know of one lost anti-Donatist treatise of about 416, and still possess one written for a special occasion *Contra Gaudentium, Donatistarum episcopum*, about 420; but these are all.

The earliest of the extant works against the Donatists present the same views of the Church and its sacraments which Augustine developed later. The principles which he represented in this conflict are merely those which, in a simpler form, had either appeared in the anti-Donatist polemics before his time or had been part of his own earlier belief. What he did was to formulate them with more dogmatic precision, and to permeate the ordinary controversial theses with his own deep thoughts on *unitas, caritas,* and *inspiratio gratiæ* in the Church, thoughts which again trace their origin back to his Neoplatonic foundations. In the course of the conflict he changed

5. Development of His Views.

his opinion about the methods to be employed; he had at first been opposed to the employment of force, but later came to the "Compel them to come in" point of view. It may well be doubted, however, if the practical struggle with the schismatics had as much to do with Augustine's development as has been supposed. Far more weight must be attached to the fact that Augustine had become a presbyter and a bishop of the catholic Church, and as such worked continually deeper into the ecclesiastical habit of thought. This was not hard for the son of Monnica and the reverent admirer of Ambrose. His position as a bishop may fairly be said to be the only determining factor in his later views besides his Neoplatonist foundation, his earnest study of the Scripture, and the predestinarian conception of grace which he got from this. Everything else is merely secondary. Thus we find Augustine practically complete by the beginning of his episcopate—about the time when he wrote the *Confessiones.* It would be too much to say that his development stood still after that; the Biblical and ecclesiastical coloring of his thoughts becomes more and more visible and even vivid; but such development as this is no more significant than the effect of the years seen upon a strong face; in fact, it is even less observable here—for while the characteristic features of his spiritual mind stand out more sharply as time goes on with Augustine, his mental force shows scarcely a sign of age at seventy. His health was uncertain after 386, and his body aged before the time; on Sept. 26, 426, he solemnly designated Eraclius (or Heraclius) as his successor, though without consecrating him bishop, and transferred to him such a portion of his duties as was possible. But his intellectual vigor remained unabated to the end. We see him, as Prosper depicts him in his chronicle, "answering the books of Julian in the very end of his days, while the on-rushing Vandals were at the gates, and gloriously persevering in the defense of Christian grace." In the third month of the siege of Hippo by the barbarian invaders, he fell ill of a fever, and, after lingering more than ten days, died Aug. 28, 430. He was able to read on his sick-bed; he had the Penitential Psalms placed upon the wall of his room where he could see them. Meditating upon them, he fulfilled what he had often said before, that even Christians revered for the sanctity of their lives, even presbyters, ought not to leave the world without fitting thoughts of penitence.

He left no property behind him but the books which he had procured for the library of the church, among which, according to Possidius, corrected copies of his own works were some of the most valuable. They constitute, in fact, Augustine's legacy to the Church at large. Certain parts of it which have not been enumerated above may be mentioned here. He himself divided his writings into three classes: the 232 treatises (*libri*) discussed in the *Retractationes;* the letters; and the "popular tractates, which the Greeks call homilies" (he calls them *sermones ad populum* in another

6. Additional Writings.

place). He had intended to review the two latter classes as he did with the *libri* in the *Retractationes,* but death prevented him. In so far, therefore, as the index of Possidius fails us—and this is often the case, owing to the uncertainty of titles and the great number of letters and sermons—a critical study of these classes of writings is much more difficult to make than of the *libri.* The edition published by the Benedictines of St. Maur (Paris, 1679–1700) in eleven folio volumes affords a useful working basis; it includes 217 letters, though the classification is not always justified, and a few more have come to light since. The sermons comprise a much larger number. Augustine must be considered, although his preaching did not please himself, as the greatest Western preacher of the early Church. He did not memorize his sermons, but after saturating himself with his subject, spoke from the inspiration of the moment; some of them he himself dictated for preservation after preaching them, while others were taken down by his hearers. Among those for which he is responsible are the series on the Gospel of John, dogmatically among his most interesting works (about 416), and the comments on the Psalms, partly preached (between 410 and 420).

Of works not yet mentioned, those written after 395 and named in the *Retractationes,* may be classified under three heads—exegetical

7. Miscellaneous Works.

works; minor dogmatic, polemical, and practical treatises; and a separate class containing four more extensive works of special importance. The earliest of the minor treatises is *De catechizandis rudibus* (about 400), interesting for its connection with the history of catechetical instruction and for many other reasons. A brief enumeration of the others will suffice; they are: *De opera monachorum* (about 400); *De bono conjugali* and *De sancta virginitate* (about 401), both directed against Jovinian's depreciation of virginity; *De divinatione dæmonum* (between 406 and 411); *De fide et operibus* (413), a completion of the argument in the *De spiritu et litera,* useful for a study of the difference between the Augustinian and the Lutheran doctrines of grace; *De cura pro mortuis,* interesting as showing his attitude toward superstition within the Church; and a few others of less interest. We come now to the four works which have deserved placing in a special category. One is the *De doctrina christiana* (begun about 397, finished 426), important as giving his theory of scriptural interpretation and homiletics; another is the *Enchiridion de fide, spe, et caritate* (about 421), noteworthy as an attempt at a systematic collocation of his thoughts. There remain the two doctrinal masterpieces, the *De trinitate* (probably begun about 400 and finished about 416) and the *De civitate Dei* (begun about 413, finished about 426). The last-named, beginning with an apologetic purpose, takes on later the form of a history of the City of God from its beginnings, before the world was, to the time when it looks upward, beyond the world, to its heavenly goal. The closing years of his life, after the completion of the *Retractationes* in 426–427, were busy ones. Besides works already named, he wrote four others in these years: three against heresies, and the *Speculum de scriptura sacra*, a collection of the ethical teaching of the Scripture for popular use. We can not now tell whether the last paragraph of the *Opus imperfectum* or the latest of the letters were the last words he wrote; but the close of the letter is eminently characteristic of him: "That we may have a quiet and tranquil life in all piety and love, let this be your prayer for us (as it is ours for you), wherever you are; for, wherever we are, there is no place where he is not whose we are."

(F. Loofs.)

Bibliography: The earliest printed ed. of the collected works was by Amerbach, 9 vols., Basel, 1506, reprinted Paris, 1515, lacking, however, the *Epistolæ*, *Sermones*, and *Enarrationes in Psalmos*, of the original edition; an ed. by Erasmus was published in 10 vols., Basel, 1529, often reprinted there, at Venice, and at Lyons; the next ed. by the theologians of the University of Louvain was in 10 vols., Antwerp, 1577, often reproduced (a great advance on both the others); the Benedictine ed., still the best, came next, 11 vols., Paris, 1679–1700 (the article *Augustine* in *DCB*, i. 222–224 gives the contents of this ed., volume by volume); other editions are by Leclerc, 12 vols., Antwerp [Amsterdam], 1700–03, Gaume, 11 vols., Paris, 1836–39, Antonelli, 14 vols., Venice, 1858–60, *MPL*, xxxii-xlvii; in *CSEL* fifteen volumes have appeared, 1887–1905 (this will be the definitive edition). An Eng. transl. of the most important works is in *NPNF*, 1st series, vols. i-viii (vol. i contains *St. Augustine's Life and Work* by P. Schaff. This edition reproduces in revised form the fifteen volumes of the Edinburgh edition, Marcus Dods editor, and the three volumes on the New Testament and the six on the Psalms in the Oxford *Library of the Fathers*, with treatises not previously translated, making it superior to all previous translations). Of individual works editions that are noteworthy or convenient are the following: *Civitas Dei*, *Opuscula selecta de ecclesia*, *De gratia et libero arbitrio*, *De prædestinatione*, *De dono perseverantiæ*, *De trinitate*, *In Joannem*, and *Confessiones* are all in the Teubner series; *Civitas Dei*, Lat. text and Eng. transl., by H. Gee, 2 vols., London, 1893–94, and Lat. text with Fr. transl., 3 vols., Paris, 1846; *Select Anti-Pelagian Treatises*, Lat. text with introduction by W. Bright, Oxford, 1880. Translations of separate treatises worthy of mention are, in English: *Confessions*, by W. Watts, London, 1631, republished by W. G. T. Shedd, Andover, 1860, by W. H. Hutchings, London, 1883, by A. Smellie, ib. 1897, and by C. Bigg, ib. 1898; *Letters*, selected and translated by Mary H. Allies, ib. 1890; *Homilies on John*, by H. F. Stewart, ib. 1902; *City of God*, by J. Healey, 3 vols., ib. 1903; in German: *Confessiones* by A. Rapp, Bremen, 1889, by W. Bornemann, Gotha, 1889, and by E. Pfleiderer, Göttingen, 1902; *Meditationes*, by A. Dreier, Steyl, 1886; in French: *La Cité de Dieu*, by E. Saisset, 4 vols., Paris, 1855; *Méditations*, by Pelissier, ib. 1853; *Lettres*, by J. J. F. Poujoulat, 4 vols., ib. 1858; *Les Confessions*, by P. Janet, ib. 1857, and by C. Douais, ib. 1893. For the life of Augustine the chief sources are his *Confessiones*, *Retractationes*, and *Epistolæ*, and the *Vita Augustini* by his pupil Possidius, the latter ed. A. G. Cramer, Kiel, 1832, from which are culled the accounts in L. S. Tillemont, *Mémoires ecclésiastiques*, vol. xi, Paris (1706 (Eng. transl., 2 vols., London, 1733–35), and in *ASB*, Aug. vi, pp. xxviii, 213–286. Modern accounts to be mentioned are: F. A. G. Kloth, *Der heilige Kirchenlehrer Augustin*, 3 vols., Aachen, 1839–40; J. J. F. Poujoulat, *Histoire de St. Augustin*, 3 vols., Paris, 1843; C. Bindemann, *Der heilige Augustinus*, 2 vols., Leipsic, 1844–55 (a standard work); F. Böhringer, *Aurelius Augustinus, Bischof von Hippo*, Stuttgart, 1878; U. J. C. Bourke, *Life and Labours of St. Augustine*, Dublin, 1880; R. W. Bush, *St. Augustine, his Life and Times*, London, 1883; C. H. Collette, *St. Augustine; his Life and Writings as affecting his Controversy with Rome*, ib. 1883; *Histoire de St. Augustin*, 2 vols., Paris, 1886 (by a member of the Augustine Order); P. Schaff, *Studies in Christian Biography, St. Chrysostom and St. Augustine*, New York, 1891; C. Wolfsgruber, *Augustinus. Auf Grund des kirchengeschichtlichen Nachlasses von Kardinal Rauschen*, Paderborn, 1898; A. Hatzfeld, *St. Augustin*, Paris, 1902 (Eng. transl. of earlier ed., London, 1898); J. Hudson, *St. Augustine, Bishop of Hippo*, ib. 1899; J. McCabe, *St. Augustine and his Age*, New York, 1903 (a brilliant book); G. W. Osmun, *Augustine, the Thinker*, Cincinnati, 1906. For discussions of various phases of his activities and influence consult: J. C. F. Bähr, *Geschichte der römischen Literatur*, supplement volume, part 2, 3 parts, Carlsruhe, 1836–40; G. F. Wiggers, *Versuch einer pragmatischen Darstellung des Augustinismus und Pelagianismus nach ihrer geschichtlichen Entwickelung*, Hamburg, 2 vols., 1821–33, Eng. transl., *An Historical Presentation of Augustinism and Pelagianism from the Original Sources*, Andover, 1840 (a standard work); J. B. M. Flottes, *Études sur St. Augustin, son génie, son âme, sa philosophie*, Montpellier, 1861; Nourisson, *La Philosophie de St. Augustin*, 2 vols., Paris, 1866; Ferraz, *De la psychologie de St. Augustin*, ib. 1869; A. Naville, *Étude sur le développement de sa pensée jusqu'à l'époque de son ordination*, Geneva, 1872; A. Dorner, *Augustinus, sein theologisches System und seine religionsphilosophische Anschauung*, Berlin, 1873; J. H. Newman, *Augustine and the Vandals*, and *Conversion of Augustine*, in vol. iii of *Historical Sketches*, London, 1873; J. B. Mozley, *The Augustinian Doctrine of Predestination*, London, 1878; A. F. Théry, *Le Génie philosophique et littéraire de St. Augustin*, Amiens, 1878; J. Storz, *Die Philosophie des heiligen Augustinus*, Freiburg, 1882, K. Werner, *Die augustinische Theologie*, Vienna, 1882; S. Angus, *Sources of the First Ten Books of Augustine's De civitate Dei*, Princeton, N. J., 1906; H. Reuter, *Augustinische Studien*, Gotha, 1887; G. J. Seyrich, *Die Geschichtsphilosophie Augustins nach seiner Schrift De civitate Dei*, Leipsic, 1891; J. Specht, *Die Lehre von der Kirche nach dem heiligen Augustinus*, Paderborn, 1891; W. Heinzelmann, *Augustins Ansichten vom Wesen der menschlichen Seele*, Erfurt, 1894; O. Scheel, *Die Anschauung Augustins über Christi Person und Werk*, Tübingen, 1901. Besides the foregoing the various histories of the church and of Christian doctrine may be consulted with profit.

AUGUSTINIANS: The general name for a number of orders and congregations of both men and women living according to the so-called Augustinian rule. It is true that St. Augustine composed no monastic rule, for the hortatory letter to the nuns at Hippo Regius (*Epist.*, ccxi, Benedictine ed.) can not properly be considered such; nevertheless three sets have been attributed to him (texts in Holstenius-Brockie, *Codex regularum monasticarum*, ii, Augsburg, 1759, 121–127), the longest of which, a medieval compilation from certain pseudo-Augustinian sermons in 45 chapters, is the one commonly known as the *regula Augustini*, and served as the constitution of the Regular Canons of St. Augustine and many societies imitating them, as, for example, the Dominicans (see Chapter; Dominic, Saint, and the Dominican Order).

The Hermits of St. Augustine (who are generally meant by the name "Augustinians;" known also as "Austin Friars;" the order to which Martin Luther belonged) were the last of the four great mendicant orders which originated in the thirteenth century. They owed their existence to no great personality as founder, but to the policy of Popes Innocent IV (1241–54) and Alexander IV (1254–61), who wished to antagonize the too powerful Franciscans and Dominicans by means of a similar order under direct papal authority and devoted to papal interests. Innocent IV by a bull issued Dec. 16, 1243, united certain small hermit societies with Augustinian rule, especially the Williamites, the John-Bonites, and the Brictinans (qq.v.). Alexander IV (admonished, it was said, by an appearance of St. Augustine) called a general assembly of the members of the new order under the presidency of Cardinal Richard of St. Angeli at the monastery of Santa Maria del Popolo in Rome in Mar., 1256, when the head of the John-Bonites, Lanfranc Septala, of Milan, was chosen general prior of the united orders. Alexander's bull *Licet ecclesiæ catholicæ* of Apr. 13, 1256, confirmed this choice. The same pope afterward allowed the Williamites, who were dissatisfied with the new arrangement, to withdraw, and they adopted the Benedictine rule. The new order was thus finally constituted. Several general chapters in the thirteenth century (1287 and 1290) and toward the end of the sixteenth (1575 and 1580), after the severe crisis occasioned by Luther's reformation, developed the statutes to their present form (text in Holstenius-Brockie, ut sup., iv, 227–357; cf. Kolde, 17–38), which was confirmed by Gregory XIII. A bull of Pius V in 1567 had already assigned to the Hermits of St. Augustine the place next to the last (between Carmelites and Servites) among the five chief mendicant orders. In its most flourishing state the order had forty-two provinces (besides the two vicariates of India and Moravia) with 2,000 monasteries and about 30,000 members. The German branch, which until 1299 was counted as one province, was divided in that year into four provinces: a Rheno-Swabian, Bavarian, Cologne-Flemish, and Thuringo-Saxon. To the last belonged the most famous German Augustinian theologians before Luther: Andreas Proles (d. 1503), the founder of the Union or Congregation of the Observant Augustinian Hermits, organized after strict principles; Johann von Paltz, the famous Erfurt professor and pulpit-orator (d. 1511); Johann Staupitz, Luther's monastic superior and Wittenberg colleague (d. 1524).

Reforms were also introduced into the extra-German branches of the order, but a long time after Proles's reform and in connection with the Counter-reformation of the sixteenth and seventeenth centuries. The most important of these later observant congregations are the Spanish Augustinian tertiary nuns, founded in 1545 by Archbishop Thomas of Villanova at Valencia; the "reformed" Augustinian nuns who originated under the influence of St. Theresa after the end of the sixteenth century at Madrid, Alcoy, and in Portugal; and the barefooted Augustinians (Augustinian Recollects; in France *Augustins déchaussés*) founded about 1560 by Thomas a Jesu (d. 1582). O. Zöckler†.

Bibliography: Helyot, *Ordres monastiques*, iii, 1–72; T. Kolde, *Die deutsche Augustinerkongregation und Johann von Staupitz*, Gotha, 1879; Heimbucher, *Orden und Kongregationen*, ii, 388, 443 sqq.; Currier, *Religious Orders*, pp. 310–315, 669–772.

AURELIAN: Roman emperor 270–275. He was of humble origin but through his talents as a soldier rose to a high position under the emperors Valerian and Claudius and by the latter was nominated Cæsar at the wish of the army. Upon the death of Claudius (270), Aurelian succeeded to the principate at a time when the integrity of the empire was threatened by the barbarians and the appearance of numerous pretenders within its bounds. His talent and energy in restoring order and repelling invasion won him the title of Restorer of the Commonwealth. He was victorious on the Danube and in Italy, but is best known in connection with the overthrow of the Syrian kingdom of Palmyra and its celebrated queen Zenobia. He was assassinated in Thrace by one of his own officers while preparing to set out on an expedition against the Persians.

Aurelian, according to an old tradition in the Church, originated the ninth of the ten great persecutions of the Christians spoken of by the early writers; but this tradition seems to rest on a misunderstanding of the texts. Orosius (vii, 23) speaks of Aurelian as a persecutor of the Christians, but attributes to him only the inception of a plan of persecution without stating that it was put into effect. The author of the *De mortibus persecutorum* (vi) is authority for the statement that an edict hostile to the Christians was promulgated, but that before it could reach the border provinces the death of the emperor intervened. Eusebius (*Hist. eccl.*, vii, 30), to whom all other accounts may be referred as the source, says that toward the end of his reign Aurelian experienced a change of view with regard to the Christians and for the worse, but that before he could proceed to the execution of his hostile designs he was overtaken by the divine vengeance. Eusebius speaks neither of the actual issue of an edict nor of its execution, and this accords with the known character of the emperor and the conditions prevailing in the empire. Aurelian was first of all a soldier and was occupied almost entirely with military affairs during his reign. It is highly improbable that in a time of foreign danger and internal unrest he would risk further disturbances by organizing a general persecution of the Christians; and, though he was devoted to the pagan faith and even to its superstitions, he would recognize that Christianity had held, since the time of Gallienus, a publicly guaranteed position in the State. (August Klostermann.)

Bibliography: Gibbon, *Decline and Fall*, chap. xi; T. Mommsen, *Provinces of the Roman Empire*, i, 180, 268–269; ii, 117–120, New York, 1887; V. Duruy, *History of Rome*, vii, 283–323, Boston, 1890; and other histories of the period.

AURICULAR CONFESSION (From Lat. *auricula*, "the external ear"): Confession into the ear of a priest in private, enjoined by Leo the Great (440–461) as a substitute for public confession. The twenty-first canon of the Fourth Lateran Council (1215), under Innocent III, makes it obligatory every year upon all Catholics, on pain of excommunication, and consequently the loss of Christian burial. See Confession of Sins.

AURIFABER, au-ri-fā'ber (**GOLDSCHMID**), **ANDREAS:** German physician and theologian, best known in connection with the Osiandrian controversy in Prussia; b. at Breslau 1514; d. at Königsberg Dec. 12, 1559. He began his studies at

Wittenberg in 1527 and there gained the friendship of Melanchthon. In 1529 he became rector of the Latin school at Danzig and two years later accepted a similar post at Elbing. The bounty of Duke Albert of Prussia enabled him to pursue the study of medicine at Wittenberg and in Italy, and after 1545 he was physician to the Duke and professor of physics and medicine in the newly established university at Königsberg, issuing, in the performance of his duties, a number of treatises on physics and physiology. In 1550 he married a daughter of Osiander and thus became involved in the bitter controversy aroused by the latter's views on justification and grace (see OSIANDER, ANDREAS). After Osiander's death in 1552, Aurifaber, who in the preceding year had been made rector of the university, became the leader of the Osiandrian party and made use of his office and his influence over the duke to crush the rival faction in Prussia, driving its adherents from the university in 1554. In pursuance of the same object he traveled extensively throughout Germany and by his activity aroused the bitter hatred of the conservatives, who assailed him with extreme virulence. Aurifaber, however, retained his influence till his death, which occurred suddenly, in the antechamber of the duke. (G. KAWERAU.)

AURIFABER, JOHANNES, OF BRESLAU (*Vratislaviensis*): German reformer and church administrator, younger brother of Andreas Aurifaber; b. at Breslau Jan. 30, 1517; d. there Oct. 19, 1568. He began the study of languages and philosophy at Wittenberg in 1534, and later turned to theology, forming an intimate friendship with Melanchthon, whose lifelong friend and adviser he remained. He became a member of the philosophical faculty in 1540, and in 1545 was dean. In 1547 he became rector of a school at Breslau but returned in the following year to Wittenberg, leaving again in 1550 to assume the position of professor of theology at the University of Rostock, secured for him through Melanchthon's intercession. In 1551–52 he took a leading part in the drafting and promulgation of the Mecklenburg church order. Through the influence of his brother Andreas he was summoned to Königsberg in 1554 as professor of theology and inspector of the churches within the see of Samland, where it was hoped that his reputation for mildness and the conciliatory character of his theology would be instrumental in allaying the bitter dissensions aroused by the teachings of Osiander. Aurifaber devoted himself to the task of pacification and in September, 1554, presided over a general synod called for the purpose of arriving at a compromise between the factions. The parochial clergy, however, regarded with mistrust the advent of an outsider who was not wholly free from suspicion of the Osiandrian taint and the synod failed to effect a compromise. Aurifaber was nevertheless appointed president of the see of Samland. Persisting in his efforts at conciliation he summoned a second synod at Riesenburg in 1556 and succeeded in obtaining from the Osiandrian faction a recantation of their extreme doctrines, without, however, satisfying either party. His unpopularity increased as a result of the publication, in 1558, of the new Prussian church order, with the preparation and editing of which Aurifaber was closely concerned and in which his opposition to the practise or exorcism in baptism found expression. Many of the clergy refused to subscribe to the new ordinances and recourse was had to imprisonment and expulsion, measures which were repugnant to Aurifaber and made his office irksome. In 1565 he resigned and returned to Breslau, where he became two years later pastor and inspector of schools and churches. (G. KAWERAU.)

AURIFABER, JOHANNES, OF WEIMAR (*Vinariensis*): German Lutheran divine, best known as a collector and editor of the writings of Luther; b. probably in the county of Mansfeld in 1519; d. at Erfurt Nov. 18, 1575. He began his studies at the University of Wittenberg in 1537, where he attached himself closely to Luther. From 1540 to 1544 he acted as tutor to the young count of Mansfeld and in the following year made the campaign against the French as field chaplain. In 1545 he went to live with Luther as his *famulus* and remained with him till the great reformer's death in the following year. In 1550 he became court preacher at Weimar and for the next ten years took a very prominent part in the internal quarrels of the followers of Luther, distinguishing himself as a zealous adherent of the so-called Gnesio-Lutheran faction. His extreme views caused his dismissal from the court of Weimar in 1561 and he removed to Eisleben where he began his series of Luther publications. In 1566 he became pastor at Erfurt, where he passed the rest of his life engaged in almost incessant strife with his colleagues. Aurifaber began collecting Lutherana as early as 1540 and by 1553 he claimed to be in possession of 2,000 letters of the master. From 1553 to 1556 he was coeditor on the Jena edition of the works of Luther. In the latter year he published a volume of Latin letters by Luther and followed this with a second volume in 1565. In 1566 appeared his celebrated *Tischreden und Colloquia D. M Luthers*, of which part only, that dealing with the last days of the reformer, was based on notes taken by Aurifaber. The great mass of the work followed closely a collection of Luther's Table Talk prepared by Lauterbach as early as 1538 and subsequently revised by him. With Lauterbach's material Aurifaber incorporated much from other sources, displaying, however, little care in the collation of his texts or even in the logical arrangement of the sources. His compilation, therefore, has the value only of a secondary authority except for the memoranda of his own preservation. Without attempting deliberate falsification of his texts Aurifaber showed little hesitation in modifying the tone of Luther's discourse, so that his work should not be read without caution. It is more than probable that in many places he has sought to intensify Luther's characteristic homeliness of expression, with the result of lending to the book a spirit of gratuitous coarseness. Aurifaber derived great profit from the sale of collections of Luther's writings to the Protestant princes of Germany.

(G. KAWERAU.)

BIBLIOGRAPHY: On the *Table Talk* consult W. Meyer, *Ueber Lauterbachs und Aurifabers Sammlungen der Tischreden Luthers*, Göttingen, 1896. Consult further Von Popowsky, *Kritik der handschriftlichen Sammlung des Johann Aurifaber*, Königsberg, 1880.

AUSO'NIUS, DECIMUS MAGNUS: Latin poet and rhetor; b. at Burdigalia (Bordeaux) about 310; d. there about 393. His family was of Celtic origin and the poet numbered among his near ancestors members of the Druid class. He received his education at Tolosa and, returning to his native city about 327, established himself as a teacher of grammar and rhetoric, attaining in a career of more than thirty years the reputation of one of the greatest professors of his time. About the year 364 Ausonius probably declared himself formally a Christian, for in the following year he was summoned to Treves as tutor of the young Gratian, eldest son of the Emperor Valentinian I, a post which would have scarcely have been open to him if he had continued to profess the pagan faith. The sincerity of his conversion or rather the depth of his new belief has been made the subject of a long controversy, his writings offering evidence in support of different views. Thus his *Versus paschales pro Augusto*, falling between the years 367 and 371, express an undoubted adherence to the formulas of the Nicene Creed, while about the year 378 in the *Precatio consulis designati* he turns once more to the heathen gods, invoking Janus among them. Over Gratian, Ausonius exercised unbounded influence and when the former ascended the throne of the Western Empire in 375 his tutor attained an important position in state affairs and was powerful enough to bestow the highest offices on members of his own family. He made use of his influence to further the cause of education in Gaul by instituting schools of rhetoric in the principal cities and he was active in saving the monuments of the ancient civilization from the iconoclastic fury of the early Christians In 378 he was made prefect of Gaul and in the following year became consul. This was the climax of his career and was followed by the speedy disappearance of his influence over the emperor, who was now completely under the sway of the great Ambrose. Ausonius felt deeply the loss of power and it has been conjectured that his animosity against Ambrose finds expression in his *Mixobarbaron*, which some would have to be a travesty in form and matter upon the hymns of the bishop of Milan. Whether his views upon Christianity also underwent an unfavorable change with the decline of his fortunes is uncertain. A poem of the year 379 in which Ausonius commends himself to the aid of Christ as his master, would be decisive on this point were it not for the fact that in the first collection of his poems which he prepared in 383 the Christian element appears as unimportant, while verses quite in the nature of the old pagan hedonism find a very conspicuous place. After the death of Gratian, Ausonius gave himself up to literary work, leading a life of luxurious ease in his native city or on his estates in Aquitania. From this period date the family poems, *Parentalia*, and the biographic *Commemoratio professorum Burdigalensium*, which, though far inferior in literary value to his exquisite masterpiece, the *Mosella*, are of value as sources for the life and thought of his times. It is in this period, too, that Ausonius appears in his most interesting aspect as the representative of the classic spirit and culture battling in vain against the rising spirit of asceticism, which under the inspiration of men like Martin of Tours was rapidly transforming the character of West European civilization. Among the most devoted followers of St. Martin was Paulinus of Nola, a former pupil of Ausonius, and in the letters which passed between the two men this conflict between the old and new finds eloquent expression. Possibly the nearest approximation to the poet's real views on Christianity may be obtained by considering him solely in the character of a literary craftsman, to whom, by temperament, religion was a more remote influence than art, and who, while lending adherence to the formulas of the Christian faith, continued to find in the old beliefs inspiration and grateful material for the use of his poetic gifts. (F. ARNOLD.)

BIBLIOGRAPHY: The *opuscula* of Ausonius have been edited by C. Schenkl, *MGH, Auct. ant.*, v, 2, 1883, and by R. Peiper, in *Bibliotheca Teubneriana*, Leipsic, 1886; they are also in *MPL*, xix. An excellent edition of the *Mosella*, with French translation, is that of H. de la Ville de Mirmont, Bordeaux, 1889; consult also idem, *De Ausonii Mosella*, Paris, 1892; A. Ebert, *Geschichte der Litteratur des Mittelalters*, i, 294 sqq., Leipsic, 1889; M. Manitius, *Geschichte der christlichen lateinischen Poesie*, pp. 105 sqq., Stuttgart, 1891; C. Jullian, *Ausone et Bordeaux*, Bordeaux, 1893; J. W. Mackail, *Latin Literature*, pp. 265–267, New York, 1895; S. Dill, *Roman Society in the Last Century of the Western Empire*, especially pp. 141–156, London, 1898.

AUSTIN: A syncopated form of Augustine, used especially for St. Augustine of Canterbury (q.v.); also used for the adjective Augustinian; as, an Austin friar.

AUSTIN, JOHN: English Roman Catholic; b. at Walpole (65 m. n. of London), Norfolk, 1613; d. in London 1669. He studied at St. John's, Cambridge, and remained there until about 1640, when, having embraced the Roman Catholic religion, he found it necessary to leave the university; he studied law and lived in London, and for some time during the civil war was a private tutor in Staffordshire. Under the pseudonym of William Birchley he published *The Christian Moderator; or persecution for religion condemned by the light of nature, law of God, evidence of our own principles* (part i, London, 1651; parts ii–iv, 1652–61), aiming to vindicate the Roman Catholic beliefs against popular misconceptions and pleading for the rights and privileges accorded to other religious bodies. He also wrote *Devotions; First Part, in the Ancient Way of Offices, with psalms, hymns, and prayers for every day in the week and every holy day in the year* (2d ed., Rouen, 1672; place and date of 1st ed. not known), a work which in various forms has passed through many editions (4th ed., 1685; "reformed" by T. Dorrington, 1687, 9th ed., 1727; by Mrs. Susanna Hopton, with preface by Dr. George Hickes, commonly known as "Hickes's Devotions," 1701, 5th ed., 1717, reprinted, 1846). *The Harmony of the Holy Gospels Digested into one History, reformed and* *improved by J. Bonnel* (London, 1705) is thought to have been originally published as the second part of the *Devotions*.

Bibliography: A. à Wood, *Athenæ Oxonienses*, iii, 149, 150, 1226, 1227, Oxford, 1692; C. Butler, *Historical Memoirs, of English . . . Catholics*, iv, 459, London, 1822; *DNB*, ii, 263-264; J. Gillow, *Biographical Dictionary of English Catholics*, i, 87-90, London, 1885.

AUSTRALIA.

Australia is a continent and a federal commonwealth that includes, for administrative purposes, the island of Tasmania; it consists of five states, with a population of about 3,670,000 in 1901, in addition to the 172,000 inhabitants of Tasmania. In 1788 Sydney, in the present state of New South Wales, was founded, chiefly as a penal settlement, but the immigration of freemen continued side by side with that of criminals until 1840, while after 1835 the latter class of settlers entered the colony in considerable numbers. In the present Western Australia and Queensland penal settlements were established at King George Sound and Brisbane in 1825 and 1826, while Adelaide and South Australia were settled in 1836. In consequence of the rich discoveries of gold Victoria was formed into a new colony in 1851, and Queensland was separated from New South Wales eight years later. These districts enjoyed the utmost independence, especially after 1855, but the need of union was increasingly felt, so that on Jan. 1, 1901, a confederation of all the colonies and Tasmania was formed under the name of the Commonwealth of Australia. The administration consists of the Governor-General, seven ministers, a senate of six members from each of the allied states, and a house of seventy-six representatives. In addition to this, each state has its own parliament and president.

1. History.

The legal bond of Australia with the mother country is extremely loose, since the power of the English Governor-General is restricted to a temporary veto with regard to foreign affairs. On the other hand, by far the greater majority of the population recognize themselves as united with the mother country by descent, language, and religion, so that Australia and England are knit together by internal bonds other than political. The import and export trade, moreover, is carried on chiefly with England, which is also the principal creditor of the national debt of Australia. The immigrants naturally transplanted their ecclesiastical tendencies and institutions into their new home, and the religious communities of Australia are vitally connected with those of the mother country as well as with other British colonies, thus further cementing the internal union of Australia and England.

2. Relation to England.

An external union of Church and State was long maintained in Australia, the state finances paying the greater part of the salaries of the clergy and contributing largely to the building of churches and parish expenses until the seventh decade of the nineteenth century. The dissolution of this relation, begun by New South Wales in 1862, brought little disadvantage to the larger denominations, and of the smaller sects only the Lutherans (chiefly Germans) suffered severely by the change.

3. Church and State. General Statistics.

The following table gives results of the census of 1901, to which figures for 1891 are added for comparison:

	New South Wales.	Queensland.	South Australia.	Tasmania.	Victoria.	West Australia.
Anglicans, 1901	623,200	185,050	107,000	83,850	424,000	75,650
" 1891	503,000	142,600	89,300	76,100	417,200	24,800
Presbyterians, 1901	132,700	57,650	18,400	11,550	192,000	14,750
" 1891	109,400	45,850	18,200	9,800	167,050	2,000
Methodists, 1901	137,700	46,600	90,000	25,000	182,000	24,600
" 1891	110,150	30,900	60,850	17,200	158,050	4,600
Congregationalists and Independents, 1901	24,900	9,800	13,400	5,600	17,200	4,450
1891	24,120	8,600	11,900	4,510	22,210	1,580
Lutherans, 1901	7,400	25,550	26,200	400	14,100	1,750
" 1891	7,950	23,400	23,350	1,100	9,400	950
Baptists, 1901	16,650	12,300	22,000	4,800	33,000	2,950
" 1891	13,150	10,300	17,600	3,300	27,900	1,000
Total, 1901	942,550	338,950	277,000	131,200	862,300	124,150
" 1891	767,770	261,450	221,200	112,010	801,810	34,980

To the figures for 1901 are to be added 1,240 Quakers, 3,100 Unitarians, 22,050 who reported themselves simply as Protestants (the majority probably Germans), 11,660 "Christians," and 24,200 adherents of smaller bodies. The Salvation Army numbered 31,150. The sum total of the Protestant population of the Commonwealth is therefore in the neighborhood of two and three-quarter millions.

The Roman Catholics are also strong in Australia, as is shown by the following table:

	New South Wales.	Queensland.	South Australia.	Tasmania.	Victoria.	West Australia.
1901	347,160	120,700	52,200	30,350	260,050	40,800
1891	286,950	92,800	47,200	25,800	240,300	12,500

Adding 6,200 who designated themselves simply as "Catholics," the sum total is 857,450.

The ecclesiastical jurisdiction of the religious bodies naturally conforms to the political boundaries of the states, although, as in case of the states, unions, either temporary or permanent, have been formed. The oldest and most prominent Protestant body in Australia is the Anglican Church, with a membership of 1,498,750. Services were held as early as 1788, although the bishopric of Australia (including Tasmania and New Zealand) was not created until 1836. In 1847 three new bishoprics were created and the former bishop of Australia became bishop of Sydney and metropolitan of

4. Anglican Church.

Australia and Tasmania. In 1897 the incumbent was made archbishop of Sydney and he has the title of primate of Australia. He is elected by the Australian bishops, but must be confirmed by the archbishop of Canterbury. At present the province of New South Wales includes, besides the primatial see of Sydney, the dioceses of Bathurst (founded 1869), Goulburn (1863), Grafton and Armidale (1867), Newcastle (1847), and Riverina (1883). The province of Victoria comprises the dioceses of Ballarat (1875), Bendigo (1902), Gippsland (1902), Melbourne (1847), and Wangaratta (1902). The province of Queensland includes the dioceses of Brisbane (1859), North Queensland (1878), Rockhampton (1892), New Guinea (1896), and Carpentaria (1900). Further, there are the independent dioceses of Tasmania, with seat at Hobart (1842); Adelaide, for South Australia (1847); Perth (1857) and Bunbury (1903), in West Australia. Each bishopric manages its own affairs, diocesan conventions being convened from time to time by the bishop and attended by both clergy and laity. The chief business of these conventions concerns finance, the education of clergy, and relations to other ecclesiastical bodies. In 1872 a regular organization was adopted which unites the dioceses of the present Commonwealth under the primate of Sydney. Clerical and lay representatives of these sees assemble every five years at Sydney for general conference and legislation. In education the Anglican Church is important chiefly through a number of colleges under its supervision.

The Presbyterians, who numbered 427,000 in the Commonwealth in 1901, belong to several branches. Their first minister was installed at Sydney in 1823. The synod of each state and the general assembly meet annually. The Australian Methodists in 1901 were 506,000 strong. After the census of that year, which showed seven branches of Methodists in New South Wales, the union of the entire denomination was effected by the establishment of the "Methodist Church of Australia," first in three colonies, and in 1902 in the remainder. The first Wesleyan service in Australia was held in 1821, but a Methodist conference was not established until 1854; it was at first affiliated with the British conference, becoming independent in 1876. An annual conference is held in each colony, and the general conference meets triennially, while every ten years the Australian Methodists take part in the international Methodist Ecumenical Conference. The Baptists of Australia numbered 91,700 in 1901, although they did not begin to increase rapidly until after 1852, their gains being due primarily to their missionary activity in cooperation with the larger denominations already mentioned. The Congregationalists, including the Independents, numbered 75,350 in 1901, but can scarcely be considered a united and influential religious community on account of their basal principle.

5. Other Protestants.

The Roman Catholic Church in the Commonwealth, with 857,450 members, is divided into five provinces. Although Roman Catholic priests were in Australia as early as 1803, it was not until 1820 that the Church came to a vigorous development with the aid of State subvention of clergy and buildings. In 1834 Sydney became the seat of a vicar apostolic with twenty-five priests, and eight years later was elevated into an archbishopric and the seat of a metropolitan for Australia and the islands, Hobart and Adelaide being suffragan sees, although they did not remain in the province of Sydney, which now includes Maitland (1847), Armidale (1862), Goulburn (1862), Bathurst (1865), Lismore (formerly Grafton; 1887), and Wilcannia (1887). The second oldest archbishopric is Melbourne, which was created a diocese in 1847 and elevated to an archdiocese in 1874. To it belong the bishoprics of Sandhurst (1874), Ballarat (1874), and Sale, the southeastern part of Victoria (1887). In 1887 Adelaide and Brisbane (founded as bishoprics in 1842 and 1859) were made archbishoprics. The province of the former comprises the dioceses of Perth (1845); Victoria, formerly Palmerston, in the north, opposite Melville Island (1847); Port Augusta, on Spencer Gulf (1887); and Geraldton (1898); also the abbacy of New Norcia (founded on Moore River in 1867) and the apostolic vicarship of Kimberley (1887). Brisbane includes the bishopric of Rockhampton (1881) and the apostolic vicarships of Cooktown (founded in 1876 and placed for the most part in the charge of the Augustinians for missionary purposes) and Queensland (1887). The fifth province is Hobart (Tasmania), founded as a bishopric in 1842, raised to metropolitan rank in 1888. Many of these dioceses contain but few Roman Catholics, and were poor in ecclesiastical institutions and churches at the time of their creation. With the rapid increase of immigration after the seventh decade of the nineteenth century, however, and in the determination to resist the propaganda of Protestant denominations, orders and congregations were brought to Australia at an early period, and were particularly active in missions and parochial schools. The most extensive settlements were those of the Jesuits, the Marists, the Dominicans, and the Brothers of the Christian Schools, although the Benedictines were the first to arrive. The most active female orders are the Sisters of Charity, the Sisters of the Good Shepherd, and the Sisters of St. Joseph. Roman Catholic associations flourish in all the cities, and schools of all kinds, especially intermediate, are under ecclesiastical control, while Roman Catholic newspapers and weeklies promote the interests of this Church. Synods of the Roman Catholic clergy of Australia have thrice been held, the first being in 1844.

6. Roman Catholics.

The number of Jews in Australia is relatively small; there were in 1901 only 14,850, of whom 6,450 were in New South Wales and 5,910 in Victoria. Mohammedans, chiefly from India and the Sunda Islands, numbered scarcely 4,500, chiefly in Queensland. Confucians and Buddhists were not carefully distinguished in every colony, as is clear from the grave discrepancy between the number of Chinese immigrants and

7. Non-Christian Religions.

the figures assigned to Confucianism and Buddhism. The majority of Buddhists live in New South Wales, while the most of the Confucians are found in Queensland and Victoria. The estimated number of the latter in the Commonwealth is between 15,000 and 16,000, and that of the former more than 7,000.

Polytheists and fetish-worshipers come from the islands of the Pacific, the Philippines, and the Sunda Islands; it is uncertain how large a proportion of this category is made up of the aborigines. By far the greater number of Australian blackfellows have been converted to Christianity by missionary activity in their behalf, although the precarious conditions of life and the poverty of nature in the interior render it extremely difficult to reach the natives in that region, and the obstacles are augmented by their spiritual and moral degradation. Nevertheless, not only the larger denominations, but also the smaller, such as the Lutherans and the Quakers, are engaged in missionary activity among the aborigines. There are, in addition, special societies under the auspices of the Anglican Church and unions of several denominations, such as the Aborigines' Protection Mission, the Society for the Propagation of the Gospel, the Free Mission (in New South Wales), and the Australian Board of Missions (in Victoria). The missions of the Roman Catholic Church are chiefly in the north. The number of unconverted Australian aborigines is estimated between 10,000 and 20,000. Several missions have also been established for workmen in the gold mines.

8. Missions Among Aborigines.

The number of those who profess to be without a religion, such as freethinkers and the like, is inconsiderable, the census returning less than 24,000 of this class; to this group, however, should doubtless be added many of those who declined to answer the question concerning their religion, so that the number can probably be doubled.

9. Education.

The public schools of Australia underwent an important change in the eighth decade of the nineteenth century, when obligatory gratuitous instruction was introduced into all the colonies. While many schools are still maintained by religious denominations, all citizens contribute to the support of the public schools. The intermediate schools, on the other hand, are, for the most part, under denominational control and of denominational origin. Popular Christian education is also furthered by the Sunday-schools, which are well attended. WILHELM GOETZ.

BIBLIOGRAPHY: G. W. Rusden, *History of Australia*, 3 vols., London, 1883; T. A. Coghlan, *Statistical Account of the Seven Colonies of Australia*, Sydney, 1891; R. R. Garran, *The Coming Commonwealth; a Handbook of Federal Government*, ib. 1897; P. F. Moran, *Hist. of the Catholic Church in Australasia*, ib. 1897; W Westgarth, *Half a Century of Australian Progress*, London, 1899; *Australian Handbook*, ib. 1902; W. H. Moore, *Constitution of the Commonwealth of Australia*, ib. 1902; *Encyclopædia Britannica, Supplement*, s.v.

AUSTRIA.

Austria is an empire of southern Europe, forming with the kingdom of Hungary (which is not included in the present article; see HUNGARY) the Austro-Hungarian Monarchy. Excluding also the former Turkish provinces of Bosnia and Herzegovina (q.v.), the area is 115,903 square miles, the population (1900) 26,107,304.

I. The Roman Catholic, Greek, and Armenian Churches: During the period of the Reformation, Protestantism made much progress among the people and gave rise to a considerable number of sects, especially in Bohemia. But the government remained Roman Catholic and by force and law freed the Church from heresy and then began to rule it. Long before the reign of Joseph II (1780–90) Gallican and Jansenist teachings were introduced and were intensified by Febronianism (see HONTHEIM, JOHANN NIKOLAUS), and Joseph transformed the Austrian Church into a body which was almost schismatic. An ecclesiastical government was formed which regulated the minutest details by state law, sparing scarcely any department of activity, legislation, or administration (see JOSEPH II).

A new period began with the concordat of 1855 (see CONCORDATS AND DELIMITING BULLS, VI, 2, §§ 6, 8). The imperial patent of Mar. 4, 1849, and the imperial enactments of Apr. 18 and 23, 1850, laid the foundation of the complete independence of the Church and in 1853 negotiations were begun with the Curia for carrying out the new provisions. The result was the concordat of Aug. 18, 1855, which was promulgated by a bull of the pope and by an imperial patent, both dated Nov. 5 of the same year. A definite agreement in regard to all ecclesiastical matters was enacted in thirty-six articles. The jurisdiction and administration of the Church, so far as its internal interests were concerned, were placed entirely under church control, in this category falling the relations between the bishops, the clergy, the laity, and the Holy See; the education and ordination of the clergy; diocesan administration; the arrangement of public prayers, processions, pilgrimages, funerals, provincial councils, and diocesan synods; the superintendence and giving of instruction to the Roman Catholic youth, and all religious instruction from the theological faculties to the public schools; the ecclesiastical right to censor books; jurisdiction

1. The Concordat of 1855.

over marriage; the discipline of the clergy; the right of patronage; ecclesiastical penalties inflicted on the laity; seizing of ecclesiastical property; and the internal administration of religious orders. The State retained control of marriage in its civil aspect, the civic position of the clergy, and the right to punish them. An agreement between Church and State was necessary for the creation or alteration of dioceses, parishes, and other benefices, the collation to livings and ecclesiastical offices, the appointment of professors of theology, catechists, the inspectors of schools, the introduction of orders and religious congregations, and the expenditure of religious funds.

The results of the concordat, though it was actually enforced in but few points, were especially noteworthy in two phases of public life. The marriage laws hitherto prevailing were subjected to a rigid scrutiny, and by the imperial patent of Oct. 8, 1856, the Roman Catholics received a new law corresponding in all respects to the decrees of the Council of Trent, placing divorce under the control of the newly created episcopal divorce court. Seminaries for boys were established in all dioceses, and received children of lawful birth

2. Effects of the Concordat.

immediately after they left the public schools, giving them, in addition to their gymnasium training, preparation for later theological studies, thus forming places of education for the future clergy. The expenses of these seminaries were partly covered by ecclesiastical funds and partly by the income from benefices. The influence of the State was limited to the supervision of their financial relations and the superintendence of instruction so far as it concerned the State. The result was an increase in the number of Roman Catholic theological students from 1,804 in 1861 to 3,286 in 1868, after which began a period of decline, due especially to the law of Dec. 5, 1868, which abrogated the previous exemption of theological students from military service, an additional factor being the school laws of 1868 and 1869, which made admission to study in a faculty conditional on the possession of a diploma from a gymnasium. The breach with the concordat widened steadily, and the law of May 25, 1868, repealed the imperial patent of Oct. 8, 1856. The former regulations concerning marriage were again enforced, divorces being referred to state tribunals and civil marriage being again permitted. Finally, by a despatch of July 30, 1870, Austria abrogated the concordat altogether.

The theological training of the Roman Catholic clergy is given partly by the faculties of the various universities and partly by the diocesan seminaries. Theological faculties exist in the uni-

3. Theological Education.

versities of Vienna, Graz, Innsbruck, Prague (two), Lemberg (for both the Latin and Greek rites), Czernowitz, and Cracow, in addition to two independent theological faculties, not affiliated with any university, in Salzburg and Olmütz. The course given by the diocesan seminaries corresponds essentially to that given by the university faculties, but they are forbidden to confer academic degrees and the bishop is in absolute control. Certain orders provide for the education of their own members in twenty monastic schools, yearly courses being given in successive years in different monasteries in the Tyrol. In 1895 the Roman Catholic Church had 16,132 priests, the Greek Catholic 2,649, and the Greek Oriental 475.

In cases where a living has no canonical claims to a definite income, the revenues of the Church, and even the State, come to its assistance. The claim to such an income, either from the property of the living or from the benefice, begins with ordination to the priesthood, but if religious foundations and monasteries desire to give a title to such income to one who does not belong to their own number, they are required to secure the consent of the government. The endowment of the Church has come from the monasteries secularized in the reign of Joseph II and later, abandoned churches, and suppressed communities, canon-

4. Revenues.

ries, benefices, and ecclesiastical feoffs. It is continually augmented, moreover, by the intercalaries (the income of vacant positions), the auxiliary taxes of dioceses and orders, and, in Bohemia, by a certain per cent. of the sale of salt. This fund, when the property has been sold, is invested in state bonds which belong to the ecclesiastical province or diocese, the income being administered by the government with the cooperation of the bishop or bishops. It is charged with the defrayal of certain expenses (the cathedral chapters of Budweis, Salzburg, Trent, and Brixen drawing their entire income from it), as well as with the payment of all other disbursements which are not obligatory on a third party. The revenues are devoted to the defrayment of patronage, the income and endowment of new parishes, the building of churches, the increase in the income of livings, the salary of chaplains, the making good of deficits, the support of mendicant orders, the salaries of teachers at the state schools, and the maintenance of theological faculties and seminaries. A second fund is that for students, which is derived from the estates of the Jesuit monasteries suppressed by Maria Theresa on Dec. 23, 1774, and is devoted to defraying the expenses of Roman Catholic education in intermediate and higher institutions of learning. Since the passage of the new school law, this fund is also used for undenominational public schools, since the estates of the Jesuit monasteries are not regarded as the property of the Church. For the value of the livings and the income of the religious orders no recent data are at hand, but in 1875 the former amounted in all parts of the empire to 7,644,611 florins, and the latter to 4,100,375 florins.

Austria is divided into nine ecclesiastical provinces as follows: (1) the archdiocese of Vienna for Upper and Lower Austria, with the two suffragan dioceses of St. Pölten and Linz; (2) Salzburg for Salzburg, Styria, Carinthia, Tyrol, and Vorarlberg, with the five suffragan dioceses of Seckau, Lavant, Gurk, Brixen, and Trent; (3) Görz for Carniola, Küstenland, and the island of Arbe, with the four suffragan dioceses of Laibach, Triest-Capo d'Istria, Parenzo-Pola, and Veglia-Arbe; (4) Prague for

Bohemia, with the three suffragan dioceses of Leitmeritz, Königgrätz, and Budweis; (5) Olmütz for Moravia and a portion of Silesia, with the suffragan diocese of Brünn; (6) the Austrian portion of the exempt diocese of Breslau for the remainder of Silesia; (7) the Austrian portion of the archdiocese of Warsaw, with the diocese of Cracow; (8) Lemberg for Galicia (excepting Cracow) and Bukowina, with the two suffragan dioceses of Przemysl and Tarnow; (9) Zara for Dalmatia (excepting Arbe), with the five suffragan dioceses of Sebenico, Spalato-Macarsca, Lesina, Ragusa, and Cattaro.

5. Archdioceses and Dioceses.

Austria, like Germany, has countless Roman Catholic societies, institutions, and foundations. In almost every parish there are brotherhoods and societies for prayer, associations of both sexes and all ages, societies of priests, congregations of Mary, Franciscan Tertiaries, the Society of the Holy Family (with 25,000 families in the diocese of Lavant alone), societies for pilgrimage and for the building and adornment of churches, church music, home missions, brotherhoods of St. Michael, political Roman Catholic societies, and general Roman Catholic social organizations with 40,000 members in the single province of Upper Austria. Children and youth are cared for in protectories, kindergartens, orphan asylums, refectories, boarding-schools, refuges, training-schools for apprentices, and the like, while the great Roman Catholic school-union has about 40,000 members. Popular education is promoted by reading clubs and societies for the dissemination of educational literature, as well as by reading-rooms and libraries for the clergy and laity, while Roman Catholic science, literature, and art are advanced by the *Leo-Gesellschaft*, the Czech society *Vlast*, and by various periodicals. Countless institutions are devoted to charity, including almshouses, memorial foundations, poor gilds, hospitals of the most various characters, and funds for the feeding of the poor in monasteries. There are likewise insurance societies for the protection of masters, partners, apprentices, peasants, workmen, credit and other purposes of economic nature, but clubs of Roman Catholic students are still only in embryo.

6. Societies and Charities.

There is a large number of Greek and Armenian Christians, some being Uniates and some non-Uniates. The Uniate Greeks, or Greek Catholics, form a special ecclesiastical province with the archdiocese of Lemberg and the suffragan diocese of Przemysl. The Uniates of the Armeno-Catholic rite also have an archbishopric of Lemberg, the archbishop likewise ruling over the non-Uniate Armenians of Galicia and Bukowina. The non-Uniate Greeks of the Greek Oriental rite have a patriarchate at Carlowitz with ten bishoprics or eparchies, of which seven are in Hungary, one in Czernowitz (Bukowina), one at Hermannstadt (Transylvania), and one at Sebenico (for Dalmatia and Istria), in addition to the community at Vienna. The patriarch is chosen by the national congress of Servia, which must remain in session sufficiently long for its candidate to receive the sanction of the emperor, after which the formal consecration takes place. The non-Uniate Armenians of the Armeno-Oriental rite control the Mekhitarist monastery in Vienna (see MEKHITARISTS) and are accordingly subject to the Uniate Armenian archbishop of Lemberg. The Old Catholics have three parishes at Vienna, Warnsdorf, and Ried, and in 1902 built two new churches at Schönlinde and Blottendorf. The Philippones, or Lippowanians, expelled from Russia, have formed scattered communities in Galicia and Bukowina.

7. Greek and Armenian Christians.

II. The Protestant Churches: Austria is essentially Roman Catholic, and the number of Evangelical Protestants in the Empire has declined from a tenth of the population at the time of their greatest expansion in the sixteenth century to a fiftieth. A patent of toleration was issued in their favor on Oct. 13, 1781, and the Protestant patent of Apr. 8, 1861, conferred upon them full equality before the law. At the same time the political, civil, and academic disabilities of the non-Catholics were removed, and they were no longer required to contribute to the support of another Church, while they were now permitted to adorn their churches, to celebrate their feasts, and to exercise pastoral care. On the day after the patent was issued (Apr. 9), a preliminary church constitution was drawn up, but one which was substituted on Jan. 6 (23), 1866, canceled important rights of self-government, and from this the present constitution of Dec. 9, 1891, differs only in minor details. The Evangelical Church, divided into parishes, seniories, superintendencies, and synods, is unrestricted in respect to its confession, its books, the creation of societies for ecclesiastical and educational purposes, and its relations to foreign religious bodies. It forms a national Church, of which the emperor may be regarded as the bishop, his prerogatives in its control being distinguished from the corresponding functions of the Roman Catholic German sovereigns in degree, not in kind. His position is due, however, to his constitutional relation to the Evangelical Church, and not, as in the case of the German princes, to his ecclesiastical relation. The lawful administration of Evangelical funds, as well as revenues and assessments, is guaranteed by the State.

1. The Evangelical Church and its Organization.

The Austrian Evangelical Church is divided into ten superintendencies, six of the Augsburg Confession, three of the Helvetic Confession, and one mixed. Those of the Augsburg Confession are: (1) Vienna, with the seniories of Lower Austria, Triest, Styria, the region south of the Drave in Carinthia, and the region north of the Drave and in the Gmünd valley in Carinthia; (2) Upper Austria, with an upper and a lower seniory; (3) Western Bohemia; (4) Eastern Bohemia; (5) Asch (also in Bohemia); (6) Moravia and Silesia, with the seniories of Brünn, Zauchtl, and Silesia. The superintendencies of the Helvetic Confession are: (1) Vienna, (2) Bohemia, with the seniories of Prague, Chrudim, Podiebrad, and Czaslau; and

RELIGIOUS STATISTICS.—AUSTRIA-HUNGARY, DEC. 31, 1900.

Provinces.	Roman Catholics.	United.		Old Catholics.	Oriental.		Evangelicals.		Moravians.	Anglicans.	Mennonites.	Unitarians.	Philippones.	Jews.	Mohammedans.	Other Confessions.	Without Confession.	Total.
		Greeks.	Armenians.		Greeks.	Armenians.	Augsburg Confession.	Helvetic Confession.										
Lower Austria	2,864,222	3,215	96	1,054	4,285	119	58,052	7,408	5	552	7	84	6	157,278	801	265	2,954	3,100,493
Upper Austria	790,178	88	4	193	47	4	18,148	240	....	12	....	5	......	1,260	....	4	58	810,246
Salzburg	191,223	7	....	7	14	....	1,211	73	....	11	....	....	......	199	....	1	17	192,763
Styria	1,339,240	117	....	284	850	2	12,675	484	....	35	1	....	4	2,283	362	9	148	1,356,494
Carinthia	346,598	65	....	9	31	....	20,100	383	....	10	....	....	......	212	....	1	14	367,324
Carniola	506,916	357	1	3	289	....	285	128	1	14	1	....	......	145	....	....	11	508,150
Triest and territory	169,921	41	2	10	1,378	47	1,346	456	2	134	....	1	......	4,954	4	22	291	178,599
Görz and Gradiska	322,139	9	....	....	59	....	269	85	....	15	....	....	......	295	....	3	22	232,597
Istria	343,815	61	1	....	389	....	290	187	....	2	1	1	......	285	....	3	17	345,060
Tyrol	848,157	100	....	15	54	....	2,806	426	....	87	....	....	......	1,008	5	6	46	852,712
Vorarlberg	127,544	7	....	8	3	2	946	589	....	2	1	1	......	117	....	1	8	129,237
Bohemia	6,065,213	1,784	15	10,351	369	23	72,922	71,738	483	155	....	5	......	92,745	2	973	1,894	6,318,697
Moravia	2,325,057	513	4	910	184	1	26,606	37,760	53	25	....	....	1	44,255	1	50	252	2,437,706
Silesia	576,099	397	1	10	38	....	91,264	477	6	3	1	2	....	11,988	....	12	126	680,422
Galicia	3,350,512	3,104,103	1,532	69	2,233	110	40,055	5,327	....	45	383	....	4	811,371	1	15	219	7,315,990
Bukowina	86,656	23,388	439	10	500,262	381	18,383	889	1	....	....	1	3,544	96,150	8	49	40	730,195
Dalmatia	496,778	187	1	4	96,278	....	153	29	....	2	2	....	......	334	12	....	2	593,784
Total	20,660,279	3,134,439	2,096	12,967	606,764	698	365,505	128,567	556	1,104	418	104	3,559	1,224,899	1,281	1,414	6,149	26,150,759
Figures for 1890	18,934,166	2,814,072	2,611	8,240	544,739	1,275	315,828	120,524	368	1,296	490	147	3,218	1,143,305	81	745	4,308	
Absolute change	−1,726,113	+320,367	−515	+4,697	+62,025	−577	+49,677	+8,033	+188	−192	−72	−43	+341	+81,594	+1,200	+669	+1,841	
Per cent. change	+9.12	+11.38	−19.72	+57.00	+11.39	−45.26	+15.73	+6.67	+51.09	−14.81	−14.69	−29.25	+10.60	+7.14	+1,481.48	+89.80	+42.73	

(3) Moravia, with a western and an eastern seniory. The superintendency of mixed confession is that of Galicia and Bukowina, with three seniories of the Augsburg Confession, western, middle, and eastern, and one of the Helvetic Confession, Galicia. There is also a small Anglican parish in Triest, under the control of the Helvetic superintendency of Vienna. The number of ministers and vicars in 1900 was 299, and there were 640 places of worship.

2. Changes of Confession. While in the last decade of the nineteenth century the increase of Roman Catholics was but 9.12 per cent, the Evangelicals of the Augsburg Confession showed an increase of 15.17 per cent, as against 9.28 in the preceding decade; and the Helvetic Confession a gain of 6.67 per cent, as contrasted with the more rapid accretion of 9.05 in the ten years previous. In Bohemia the Evangelical gain was 20.06 per cent, in Styria 25.9 per cent, and in Lower Austria 37.01 per cent. In Silesia and Galicia alone the increase of Evangelicals failed to keep pace with the gain in population, this being due to the increasing emigration from the German districts of West Silesia and the German colonies in Galicia, an additional factor being the immigration of Galician workmen to Silesia to work in the coal mines.

No statistics are available for a classification of the Austrian Protestants according to language, nor are the figures sufficiently complete to afford a safe basis to determine the changes caused by immigration and emigration. The *Los von Rom* movement, which began in 1898, resulted by 1900 in the loss of more than 40,000 members to the Roman Catholic Church, some 30,000 becoming Evangelicals, several thousand Old Catholics, an undetermined number joining the Moravians and Methodists, while some broke entirely with denominational Christianity. Many, however, returned to the Roman Catholic Church. A hundred new chapels were erected, and seventy-five preachers, chiefly from Germany, entered upon the work (see Los von Rom).

3. Schools. Religious instruction is given in the primary and secondary schools by the minister of the parish, or, in certain cases, by secular teachers of religion, either in the school or in "stations." By a law of June 17, 1888, an allowance was given or a special teacher of religion was appointed in the higher classes of primary or secondary schools of more than three classes, and more than 160 teachers of this description are active in over 560 "stations." The Church also provides for religious instruction in normal and intermediate schools, although state aid is given only when the total number of Evangelical scholars in such an institution is more than twenty. National, district, and local school boards are entrusted with the administration and supervision of normal and intermediate schools in each province, and in almost all the boards the Evangelical Church has a vote (at least advisory) and representatives. In consequence of the rivalry of the state undenominational schools, however, the Evangelical schools tend to become more or less ultramontane, and are gradually decreasing as a result of the double taxes levied on the Evangelicals. In 1869 there were 372 Evangelical schools, a number which has since decreased by two-thirds. An Evangelical normal school exists in Bielitz for the training of Evangelical teachers, while in Czaslau there is a Czech Evangelical Reformed seminary for Bohemia and Moravia.

4. Theological Education. The education of the Evangelical clergy is confined to the Evangelical theological faculty maintained at the expense of the State in Vienna. Though desired by the estates for this purpose in the sixteenth century, it was first founded as a theological institute after the separation of the empire from Germany and the prohibition to attend German universities (Apr. 2, 1821). On Oct. 8, 1850 (July 18, 1861) it was made a faculty with the right to confer degrees, but although the only Evangelical theological school in all Austria, clerical intrigues, Protestant narrowness, and the disfavor and indifference of the Liberals have prevented it from being incorporated with the university and securing the rooms allotted to it in the new buildings. The school consists of six professors and two privatdocents, teaching Augsburg and Helvetic dogmatics separately. The course of study is at least six semesters, two of which must be spent at Vienna. Since the formation of the dual monarchy in 1861, which denies to Hungary all Austrian subventions, and as a consequence of the Hungarian legislation and the national excitement, the number of students at the theological school has diminished. In 1904–05, however, fifty-one were studying there, although the meager salaries attached to the majority of the parishes gives little hope of an increased student body. In 1901 a small national denominational Utraquist home was established at Vienna by private contributions for the aid of students without means, and is conducted by an inspector and an ephor.

5. Financial Status of the Evangelicals. In view of the necessity of maintaining their churches, schools, and charitable organizations, the congregations have the right to claim State aid, but this is asked reluctantly, despite the heavy debts of most of the congregations, especially in Galicia. Outside assistance is, therefore, absolutely necessary. The oldest and most generous benefactor is the *Gustav Adolf Verein* (q.v.) which has spent millions of florins, and which is divided in Austria into a main society with fifteen branch societies, in addition to thirty societies for women, forty-nine for children, and 324 local organizations. This is followed by the *Lutherischer Gotteskasten* and, more recently, by the *Evangelischer Bund* (see Gotteskasten, Lutherischer; Bund, Evangelischer), as well as by many societies and private benefactors in Switzerland and Holland. The property of the individual superintendencies is administered by committees of the districts concerned, while the foundations and funds of the superintendencies and seniories are controlled by committees appointed from these bodies, and also by the supreme church council and the *Gustav Adolf Verein.* These funds are devoted to many purposes, such as general ecclesiastical interests, the support of ecclesiastical officials and their widows and orphans, candidates for the ministry and theological students, general educational objects, teachers with their widows and orphans, religious instruction, charities, and burials. The Evangelical Church likewise provides pensions for superannuated pastors and teachers, as well as for their widows and orphans.

6. Societies and Charities.

Societies and charitable organizations are extremely numerous among the Evangelicals of Austria. Women's clubs exist in many city congregations, and institutions for those intending to be confirmed are also popular. Orphan asylums exist at Biala, Bielitz, Goisern, Graz, Krabschitz, Russic, Stanislau, Teleci, Ustron, Weikersdorf (Gallneukirchen), Waiern, and Vienna (St. Pölten). Summer homes are provided by the *Erster Evangelischer Unterstützungsverein für Kinder,* while the *Oberösterreichischer Evangelischer Verein für Innere Mission* cares for the sick, maintaining in Gallneukirchen, in addition to a house of deaconesses, asylums for the sick and insane, as well as homes for convalescents. The deaconesses trained at Gallneukirchen find employment at Gablonz, Graz, Hall, Marienbad, Meran, and Vienna, while in Aussig and Teplitz they have been placed in charge of the municipal hospital after the expulsion of the nuns. Closely connected with this society is that of the *Verein für die Evangelische Diakonissensache in Wien* with its home, summer sanitarium, and hospital. In 1901 a third house of deaconesses was established at Prague, and a number of other Evangelical homes and hospitals also exist. Provision is made for the dead and their survivors by the *Evangelischer Leichenbestattungsverein* in Vienna and by the *Sterbekasse für Evangelische Pfarrer und Lehrer Oesterreichs.* Educational institutions abound, while devotion is fostered by libraries of various types, "evenings at home," church concerts, Sunday-schools, Young Men's Christian Associations, and young women's societies. The Czech "Comenius Society," the "Evangelical Literary Society of the Augsburg Confession," and the "Comenium," as well as the German *Evangelischer Volksbildungverein,* the first three at Prague and the last at Teschen, are literary in character. The only scientific Evangelical magazine, however, is the *Jahrbuch der Gesellschaft für die Geschichte des Protestantismus in Oesterreich,* founded in 1879 for the investigation and presentation of the history of Evangelical Protestantism.

7. Minor Denominations and Non-Christians.

Among other Protestant denominations, State recognition is accorded only to the Moravians, beginning with 1880. Baptists, Irvingites, Mennonites, Methodists, Congregationalists, the Scotch New Free Church in Vienna, and the Free Evangelical Church in Bohemia are regarded as undenominational, and are allowed to worship only in private. The Jews are now represented in all provinces of Austria, although previous to 1848 no Jew was allowed to reside in Salzburg, Styria, Carinthia, Carniola, Istria, Tyrol, and Vorarlberg. The Mohammedans in the army thus far have places of worship only in the barracks.

8. Religious Distribution and Statistics.

With regard to the distribution of various confessions in Austria, it may be said that the Greek Uniates are found chiefly in Galicia, the Armenian Uniates in Galicia and Bukowina, the Greek Catholics of the Oriental rite in Bukowina and Dalmatia, the Armenian Catholics of the Oriental rite in Bukowina and Galicia, the Jews in Lower Austria, Galicia, and Bukowina. The Evangelicals of the Augsburg Confession are far more evenly distributed than those of the Helvetic Confession, who are centered chiefly in Bohemia and Moravia. Almost half of those professing no creed are in Lower Austria. The religious statistics of the empire on the basis of the census of Dec. 31, 1900, are summarized on page 381. GEORG LOESCHE.

BIBLIOGRAPHY: K. Kuzmany, *Lehrbuch des allgemeinen und österreichischen evangelisch-protestantischen Kirchenrechtes,* Vienna, 1856; J. A. Ginzel, *Handbuch des neuesten in Oesterreich geltenden Kirchen-Rechtes,* 3 vols., Vienna, 1856–62; *Sammlung der allgemeinen kirchlichen Verordnungen der kaiserlichen kirchlichen evangelischen Oberkirchenrates* (published continuously since 1873); *Statistische Monatschrift* (published at Vienna by the Central Commission for Statistics since 1875); M. Baumgarten, *Die katholische Kirche unserer Zeit und ihre Diener in Wort und Bild,* 3 vols., Munich, 1897–1902; G. A. Skalsky, *Zur Geschichte der evangelischen Kirchenverfassung in Oesterreich,* Vienna, 1898; G. Loesche, *Jahrbuch der Gesellschaft für die Geschichte des Protestantismus in Oesterreich* (published since 1883 in Vienna); *Oesterreichische Statistik* (edited under the Central Commission for Statistics, in Vienna), especially vols. lxii–lxiii, 1902; the *Quellen und Forschungen zur österreichischen Kirchengeschichte* has begun publication under the care of the Leo-Gesellschaft in Vienna, 1906.

AUTHORITY, ECCLESIASTICAL (*Potestas ecclesiastica*): The vested power of the Church over its members, by virtue of a divine commission (*mandatum divinum*) in the foundation of the Church.

Pre-Reformation and Roman Catholic View.

According to the pre-Reformation view and according to the same view as conserved by the Roman Catholic Church to-day, this authority is vested only in the pope and the bishops; so that any others can exercise it merely in their name, as their commissioned agents. Indeed, strictly regarded, according to the sense of the curia, it devolves exclusively upon the pope, so that even the bishops possess none but a derivative power from him; and in so far as this conception of the matter is fundamental to the Vatican, it must accordingly be regarded as the sense which officially obtains in the Roman Catholic Church to-day.

Intrinsically, to be sure, the power of the Church is a salutary and spiritual power even according to the pre-Reformation doctrine. But the commission also carries with it everything which appears expedient in the sight of the commissioned themselves, with reference to the interests and cure of souls, toward the appertaining regulation of external conduct. Within limits affecting the cure of souls, then, the Church is also empowered with civil functions and prerogatives. In this respect, the pre-Reformation doctrine distinguishes two sides or directions of ecclesiastical authority: an internal power (*potestas ordinis* or *sacramentalis*) and an external (*potestas jurisdictionis* or *jurisdictionalis*), the former acting upon the so-called *forum internum*, the latter upon the *externum*.

Protestant View. The Evangelical Church, Lutheran and Reformed alike, puts a narrower construction upon ecclesiastical authority, interpreting the *potestas ecclesiastica* exclusively as the power of administering the word and sacraments in the widest sense of the term; which includes the cure of souls under these instrumentalities, but not at all the external regulation of conduct by the exercise of legal compulsion. The exclusion of the ungodly from the congregation is to be brought about without human power, solely through the word of God; and so this jurisdiction is only an act of verbal execution. Not infrequently in the Evangelical confessional writings, ecclesiastical authority is mentioned comprehensively as the "power of the keys" (see KEYS, POWER OF THE). As such it is attributed not to a single estate in the Church, but to the Church as a whole. The power of the Church is thus committed immediately to the Church; intermediately and for practical operation the persons thereunto adopted receive it from the Church.

Thus the Evangelical conception of ecclesiastical authority assigns to the secular powers, or as modernly expressed, the State, a different province in relation to the control of church affairs, from that of pre-Reformation times and likewise that of the Roman Catholic Church to-day. The Schwabach articles of 1528 declare "the power of the Church is only to choose ministers and to exercise the Christian ban," and to provide for the care of the sick; "all other power is held either by Christ in heaven, or by temporal powers on earth." The reiterated expressions of Luther and other Reformers, to the effect that this temporal power has no ecclesiastical jurisdiction and may not

Views of Luther and Other Reformers. interfere in church government, mean consistently this alone, that the temporal power has no spiritual jurisdiction and may not intermeddle with the cure of souls. The matter of control in the external affairs of the Church, that is, what we nowadays call church government, was deferred by Luther even so early as his tract to the German nobility, and at a later period constantly so, to the temporal powers directly; and the same is true of the other German Reformers. In particular, they claim for the Church no manner of legislative prerogative; the Reformation ecclesiastical law subsists rather, in so far as it was formulated by new legislation, entirely upon State enactments (see CHURCH ORDER). Only since the established reformation Church has come to be superseded more and more by the organized union Church on a presbyterial-synodical basis, has the latter, apart from the absolute administration of word and sacraments, been also empowered by the State with the *jus statuendi;* and this it exercises within forms and limits determined by the State; as it also exercises the right of independent church government according to its constitutional latitude under this organization. In both instances, however, this is done not upon any fundamentally intrinsic ground, but solely on historic grounds; and therefore, in so far as no unwholesome ideas come into play, without conflict with the State authorities. E. SEHLING.

In the free Churches of Great Britain, in the British colonies, and in the United States, there is no assumption of ecclesiastical authority by the civi government, its sole function being to protect the Churches in their right to hold property and to carry on their work. In many cases church property and in some communities where an income tax prevails ministers' salaries are exempted from taxation. Individuals are protected by the civil courts from injustice at the hands of a Church. Ministers may, e.g., sue for their salaries or for wrongful dismissal, and excommunicated members for malicious or unjust treatment; but even in such cases, the courts are careful to interfere as little as possible with the authority of the Churches. In each religious body the question of authority is determined by its polity. In episcopal bodies much authority is vested in individual bishops and boards of bishops, in presbyterial bodies in synods, in congregational bodies in the local church. See CHURCH GOVERNMENT; POLITY. A. H. N.

AUTHORIZED VERSION OF THE ENGLISH BIBLE. See BIBLE VERSIONS, B, IV, 6.

AUTO DA FÉ (Portuguese, "Judgment [Judicial Decision] of the Faith," from Latin, *actus fidei*): The public announcement and execution of the judgment of the Inquisition upon heretics and infidels; also called *sermo publicus*, or *generalis, de fide*, because a sermon on the Catholic faith was delivered at the same time. It was not to take place on Sunday or in a church, but on the street. At sunrise of the appointed day, those condemned with the hair shaved off, and variously dressed, according to the different degrees of punishment, were led in a solemn procession, with the banners of the Inquisition at the head, to some public place. When the secular authorities, whose duty it was to be present, had sworn to stand by the Inquisition, and execute its orders, the sermon was delivered, and then judgments against the dead as well as the living were pronounced. Next the backsliders, and those who refused to recant, were expelled from the Church and given over to the secular authorities for punishment, and then the procession again began to move. The bones of the dead who had been condemned were carried on sledges to the place of execution. Those condemned to death rode on asses, between armed men, and wore coats and caps, called in Spanish *sanbenito*, painted over with devils and flames. Not only the mob and the monks, but also the magistrates, and sometimes even the king and the court were present at the spectacle. There were, however, differences in the solemnization of autos da fé in Southern France, in Spain, in Italy, and in the Portuguese colonies in India. After the middle of the eighteenth century they disappeared, and the verdicts of the Inquisition were executed in private.

BIBLIOGRAPHY: Exhaustive articles are to be found in P. Larousse, *Grand dictionnaire universel*, i, 980–981, Paris, 1866, and in Bertholet, *La Grande Encyclopédie*, iv, 756–758; consult also H. C. Lea, *History of the Inquisition*, i, 389–391, ii, 200, New York, 1888; L. Tanon, *Histoire des tribunaux de l'inquisition de France*, Paris, 1893. The article in *JE*, ii, 338–342, is very full and is most valuable for the abundant literature there cited.

AUTPERTUS, AMBROSIUS: Abbot of St. Vincent at Benevento; d. probably in 781, though the date 778 has generally been accepted. He is chiefly memorable for his comprehensive commentary on the Apocalypse, which also gives the most reliable information as to his life. The brief autobiography which terminates it states that he was born in the province of Gaul, and that he began and finished his commentary in the days of Pope Paul I (757–767), Desiderius, king of the Lombards, and Arichis II, duke of Benevento. In this work, for which he obtained the special protection of Stephen III (752–757) against the attacks of the ignorant, he follows the Fathers, especially Augustine and Jerome; his principal purpose is the attempt to discover the mystical sense of the apocalyptic imagery. He is as much attracted by the method of spiritual interpretation offered by the Donatist Ticonius as was his predecessor, the "obscure" Primasius (q.v.), in working over this heretic in an orthodox sense; Ticonius's seven rules [cf. *DCB*, iv, 1026], especially the sixth, *de recapitulatione*, governed the ecclesiastical exegesis of the time. But Autpertus added moral and devotional considerations of his own, and aimed at imitating the transparent clearness of Gregory the Great. The commentary as a whole made such an impression on Alcuin that in his own exposition of the Apocalypse he scarcely attempted to do more than make extracts from it. An uncritical eleventh century biography of Autpertus, contained in the *Chronicon Vulturnense*, mentions a number of other writings—commentaries on Leviticus, the Psalms, and the Song of Solomon, a treatise *De conflictu vitiorum*, homilies on the Gospels, and lives of the founder and first abbots of his monastery; these lives are poor in historical material, and are really an ideal picture of monastic life as a stimulus to the zeal of his fellow monks. Autpertus's own rule as abbot did not last long. His election provoked a schism in the monastery; he was the choice of the Frankish monks, while one Potho was elected by the Lombards. The contest was referred to Charlemagne through an accusation of treason brought against Potho. The king asked Adrian I to decide, and both competitors were summoned to Rome; Autpertus died on the way, and Potho was acquitted. Both the letters written by Adrian to Charles on the subject are addressed "*nostro spiritali compatri*," which seems to fix their date after Adrian had baptized Charles's youngest son in Rome (April 15, 781), and thus to place the death of Autpertus later than the date given by the *Chronicon Vulturnense*, July 19, 778. His works are in *MPL*, lxxxix. (J. HAUSSLEITER.)

BIBLIOGRAPHY: C. U. J. Chevalier, *Répertoire des sources historiques du moyen-âge*, pp. 96–97, Paris, 1877; *Histoire littéraire de France*, iv, 141–161; J. C. F. Bähr, *Geschichte der römischen Litteratur im karolingischen Zeitalter*, pp. 191–192, 293–295, Carlsruhe, 1840; Hauck, *KD*, ii, 133, 138.

AUTUN, ō″tūn′: A town of France, department of Saône-et-Loire, 160 m. s.e. of Paris. It is the old Bibracte, the capital of the Ædui in Cæsar's time, whose name was changed under the emperors to Augustodunum. It was one of the principal towns of Gallia Lugdunensis; its walls had a circumference of over two miles. The few inscriptions preserved from its early Christian period show that the Greek language was used in the Christian community there, side by side with the Latin, as late as the fourth century. The first bishop of whom we have certain knowledge was Reticius, who was present at the First Synod of Arles (316). In the seventh century Bishop Leodegar held a provincial synod there, whose decrees have only in part survived. The first canon contains one of the earliest distinct mentions of the Athanasian Creed; the fifteenth shows the progress already made in the Frankish kingdom by the Benedictine rule. (A. HAUCK.)

BIBLIOGRAPHY: *MGH, Legum*, Sectio III, *Concilia*, vol. i, *Concilia ævi Merovingici*, i (1893), 220; Hefele, *Conciliengeschichte*, iii, 113, Eng. transl., iv, 485.

AUXERRE, ō″sār′, **SYNOD OF:** A diocesan synod held by Bishop Aunachar in the Burgundian city of Auxerre, the old Autessiodorum or Altisiodorum in Gallia Lugdunensis, 105 m. s.s.e. of Paris. Thirty-four priests, three deacons, and seven abbots were present. Its date can be only approximately fixed, since all we know of Aunachar is that he took part in the Synod of Paris in 573 and the two Synods of Mâcon in 583 and 585. It must accordingly have been held between 570 and 590. Forty-five canons were passed, which have a certain importance as contributing to our knowledge of the pagan superstitions still surviving at the period and condemned in several canons. (A. HAUCK.)

BIBLIOGRAPHY: *MGH, Legum*, Sectio III, *Concilia*, vol. i, *Concilia ævi Merovingici*, i (1893), 178; Hefele, *Conciliengeschichte*, iii, 42–47, Eng. transl., iv, 409 414.

AUXIL′IUS: German clerical author; d. after 911. He went to Rome in the pontificate of Formosus (891–896) to receive holy orders from him, as, he tells us, was common custom at the time. He remained in Italy, perhaps at first in Rome, but probably later in or near Naples, with whose bishop Stephen and archdeacon Peter he appears in relation. It is at least not impossible that he finally became a monk at Monte Cassino. We still possess four treatises of his, which all bear directly or indirectly on the controversy about Pope Formosus (q.v.). That *In defensionem sacræ ordinationis papæ Formosi*, written in 908 or 909, describes the events leading up to the pontificate of Formosus, to show that these afford no ground for contesting the legitimacy of his episcopate, and those which followed his death, to prove how unjust was the sentence upon him. The aim of Auxilius is to prove the validity of orders conferred by Formosus, and the object of the three other treatises is the same. The second, *Libellus in defensionem Stephani episcopi*, gives not a little information about the checkered career of the Stephen mentioned, proving the validity of his Neapolitan episcopate, though he was enthroned by Benedict IV (900–903), who was or-

dained by Formosus. The third and fourth bear directly upon the validity of these ordinations. The works are in *MPL*, cxxix, 1053–1100, and E. Dümmler, *Auxilius und Vulgarius* (Leipsic, 1866), pp. 59–116. The *Liber cujusdam requirentis et respondentis*, in *MPL*, cxxix, 1101–12, is not genuine.
(A. HAUCK.)

BIBLIOGRAPHY: Watttenbach, *DGQ*, i (1894), 305.

AVA: The first German poetess; d. at Melk (on the Danube, 50 m. w. of Vienna), or a neighboring convent of Lower Austria, Feb. 8, 1127. A number of poems are ascribed to her, of which the most important and most certainly genuine is described in one of the manuscripts as treating of "the life, passion, and resurrection of the Lord, and of the Holy Spirit, according to the gospels; of the Last Judgment and Antichrist, and of the delights of heaven."

A later manuscript includes the life of John the Baptist. Two sons are said to have helped in its composition, who are thought to have been two poets known from other works, named Hartmann and Heinrich. The former was educated for the priesthood at Passau, became prior of St. Blasien in 1094, then abbot of Göttweih, founded the monastery of Lambrecht in 1096, and died in 1114. The latter was a layman and probably survived Hartmann. Ava was a *reclusa*, but conjectures as to her sinful early life and later ascetic practises are based upon the doubtful works and are hardly justified by these. The poem as preserved is not composite. It displays real poetic gifts and, in the choice of incidents as well as in their treatment, indicates that the author was a woman, with no trace, however, of feminine enthusiasm. The material is drawn from the gospels and the Acts, for the presentation of Antichrist and the Last Judgment from Rev. xvii–xx. The aim seems to have been to present a simple narrative in poetic form of the great deeds of God in the new covenant similar to treatments of Genesis, Exodus, and other parts of the Pentateuch which are known to have been already in existence. There is no homiletical coloring, and moral reflections and allegory are avoided. The separation of the good and the bad at the Last Judgment gives opportunity for a brief but instructive picture of social conditions of the time, which indicates personal familiarity with the sins of the higher classes. The time of composition was probably about 1120. A. FREYBE.

BIBLIOGRAPHY: J. Diemer, *Deutsche Gedichte des xi und xii Jahrhunderts, aufgefunden im regulierten Chorherrenstifte zu Vorau in der Steiermark*, Vienna, 1849; W. Scherer, *Geistliche Poeten der deutschen Kaiserzeit*, ii, in *Quellen und Forschungen zur Sprache und Culturgeschichte der germanischen Völker*, vii, pp. 73–77, Stuttgart, 1875; and especially A. Langguth, *Untersuchungen über die Gedichte der Ava*, Budapest, 1880.

AVARS, THE: A tribe related to the Huns, who from the middle of the sixth century came into contact with the Christian nations—first with the Byzantine empire, and then with the Frankish kingdom; but they learned Christianity from neither of these. Virgil of Salzburg seems to have been the first to attempt their conversion, and Charlemagne supported him. Duke Tassilo of Bavaria summoned them to Germany as allies against him; in 788 they attacked the Frankish kingdom from two sides, but were repulsed on both, and the struggle ended with their complete subjugation in 796, when they accepted Christianity as one of the conditions of peace. The territory thus won for Charlemagne and Christian missions extended from the Enns and the slopes of the Styrian Alps to the Danube. It was divided between the dioceses of Aquileia, Salzburg, and Passau. The Avars, however, soon afterward disappeared from history, probably being absorbed by the Slavic population which formed a majority in their territory. (A. HAUCK.)

BIBLIOGRAPHY: Schiefner, *Versuch über das Awarische*, St. Petersburg, 1862; Hauck, *KD*, ii, 419.

AVE MARIA. See ROSARY.

AVE MARIA BRETHREN. See SERVITES.

AVENARIUS, JOHANNES. See HABERMANN, JOHANN.

AVENGING OF THE SAVIOR. See APOCRYPHA, B, I, 7.

AVERCIUS, a-ver'shius **(AVIRCIUS, ABERCIUS), OF HIEROPOLIS** (in the Glaucus valley, not Hierapolis-on the Lycus): A Phrygian, the inscription on whose gravestone is preserved in a legendary life, written probably about 400, and was found, in part, on a portion of the actual stone by W. M. Ramsay in 1883 at the warm baths near Hieropolis. The inscription, with restorations, may be rendered as follows:

I, the citizen of a noble city, have made this (monument) in my lifetime that I might have here a resting-place in the eyes of men for my body, Avercius by name, the servant of a holy shepherd who pastures flocks of sheep upon the hills and meadows; whose eyes are large and all-seeing; for he taught me . . writings worthy of faith. To Rome he sent me that I might see the king and the queen in golden apparel with sandals of gold. But I saw a people there bearing a shining seal. I saw likewise the plains of Syria and all its cities (as well as) Nisibis, after I had crossed the Euphrates. But everywhere I had a companion, for Paul sat in the chariot with me. And Faith led the way (as guide) and in all places set before me as food a fish from the spring, gigantic, pure, which a holy virgin had caught. And this (fish) he (Faith) gave at all times as food to friends,—(Faith) who has good wine, giving mixed drink and bread. This have I, Avercius, while I stood by, ordered to be written down; seventy-two years old was I when it was done. You who understand the meaning of this, pray for Avercius, every one that is of the same mind. In my grave let no one lay another. But if any one do so, he shall pay to the treasury of the Romans 2,000, and to the loved native city Hieropolis 1,000, pieces of gold.

From this wording G. Ficker concludes that Avercius was a priest of Cybele, while Harnack would make him out the member of a sect partially Gnostic, partially heathen, wherein pagan mysteries were combined with one of the mysteries of the Christian faith, namely, the Lord's Supper. The weight of authority, however, is in favor of the Christian character of the inscription. It must be dated somewhere about 200,—a time when it was not safe to make too open profession of Christian faith; hence Avercius phrases his confession in mysterious language which has a double meaning, yet is easily intelligible to one "who understands." The life already referred to supports this view, being based apparently on a well-established local legend corroborative in many details of the writing on the tombstone. Possibly the author may have been the Avercius Marcellus, a native of Phrygia, to whom a work against the Montanists was dedicated about the year 193 (Eusebius, *Hist. eccl.*, v, 16). As internal evidence, are cited the unmistakable allusion to the Lord's Supper, to baptism (the "shining seal"), and the reference to Paul, which may be taken to mean either that Avercius had the works of the apostle with him on his travels or compared his own journey to that of Paul from Damascus to the west. The inscription is now in the Lateran museum at Rome. (T. ZAHN.)

BIBLIOGRAPHY: The life is in *MPG*, cxv. Consult J. B. Pitra, *Spicilegium Solesmense*, iii, 532–533, Paris, 1855; idem, *Analecta sacra*, ii (1884), 180–187; W. M. Ramsay, in the *Journal of Hellenic Studies*, iv (1883), 424–427; idem, in *The Expositor*, ix (1889), 156–180, 253–272; idem, *The Cities and Bishoprics of Phrygia*, vol. i, part 2, 709–715, 722–729, Oxford, 1897; G. B. de Rossi, *Inscriptiones Christianæ*, ii, pp. xii–xxv, Rome, 1888; J. B. Lightfoot, *The Apostolic Fathers*, ii, part 1, 493–501, London, 1889; T. Zahn, *Forschungen*, v, 57–99, Leipsic, 1892; G. Ficker, in *Sitzungsberichte der Berliner Akademie*, 1895, 87–112; A. Harnack, *TU*, xii, 4, Leipsic, 1895.

AVES, HENRY DAMEREL: Protestant Episcopalian bishop of Mexico; b. in Huron Co., O., July 10, 1853. He was educated at Kenyon College, Gambier, O. (Ph.B., 1878), the Cincinnati Law School (1879–80), and the theological seminary attached to Kenyon College (B.D., 1883). He was then rector successively at St. Paul's, Mt. Vernon, O. (1883–84); St. John's, Cleveland (1884–92); and Christ Church, Houston, Tex. (1892–1904). In 1904 he was consecrated bishop of Mexico.

AVIGNON, ɑ̄''vī''nyōn': The capital of the department of Vaucluse, southern France, situated on the Rhone, about 400 m. s.s.e. of Paris, and 50 m. n.n.w. of Marseilles. It became the papal residence in 1309, at which time it was under the rule of the kings of Sicily (the house of Anjou); in 1348 Pope Clement VI bought it from Queen Joanna I of Sicily for 80,000 gold gulden, and it remained a papal possession till 1791, when, during the disorders of the French Revolution, it was incorporated with France. Seven popes resided there,—Clement V, John XXII, Benedict XII, Clement VI, Innocent VI, Urban V, and Gregory XI; and during this period (1309–77; the so-called Babylonian Captivity of the popes) it was a gay and corrupt city. The antipopes Clement VII and Benedict XIII continued to reside there, the former during his entire pontificate (1378–94), the latter until 1408, when he fled to Aragon. Avignon was the seat of a bishop as early as the year 70, and became an archbishopric in 1476. Several synods of minor importance were held there, and its university, founded by Pope Boniface VIII in 1303 and famed as a seat of legal studies, flourished until the French Revolution. The walls built by the popes in the years immediately succeeding the acquisition of Avignon as papal territory are well preserved. The papal palace, a lofty Gothic building, with walls 17–18 feet thick, built 1335–64, long used as a barrack, is now to be turned into a museum.

AVILA, ɑ̄'vī-lɑ̄, **JUAN DE:** Ascetic writer, called the apostle of Andalusia; b. at Almodovar del Campo (16 m. s.w. of Ciudad Real) in the archdiocese of Toledo, between 1494 and 1500; d. in Montilla (18 m. s.e. of Cordova) May 10, 1569. In 1516 he entered the University of Salamanca to study law, but soon retired to his home and lived a strict ascetic life for three years. Then he studied theology at Alcala under Domingo de Soto. Having been admitted to orders, he continued his ascetic life and won fame as a preacher in different places. Through envy he was brought before the Inquisition and refused to defend himself, but was acquitted for his exemplary life. At the age of fifty he went into retirement, broken in body by his exertions in preaching and ascetic practises; thenceforth he addressed smaller circles and devoted himself to writing. He declined a profferred appointment as canon in Grenada, as well as the bishopric of Segovia and the archbishopric of Grenada. His tomb in the Jesuits' Church at Montilla bears the inscription, *Magistro Johanni Avilæ, Patri optimo, Viro integerrimo, Deique amantissimo, Filii ejus in Christo, Pos-[uerunt]*. His writings were collected in nine volumes at Madrid, 1757; the chief were *Audi filia* and the *Cartas espirituales* (in vol. xiii of the *Biblioteca de Autores Españoles*, Madrid, 1850).

K. BENRATH.

BIBLIOGRAPHY: Life in Spanish by Luis de Grenada (d. 1588) in vol. iii, pp. 451–486, of his works, Madrid, 1849; N. Antonio, *Bibliotheca Hispana nova*, i, 639–642, Madrid, 1783; L. degli Oddi, *Life of the Blessed Master John of Avila*, transl. from the Italian, *Quarterly Series*, vol. xcvii, London, 1898.

AVITUS, ɑ-vai'tʊs, **ALCIMUS ECDICIUS:** Bishop of Vienne; d. Feb. 5, 518. He was born of a distinguished Romano-Gallic family, connected with the Emperor Avitus (455–456); his father, Hesychius, was bishop of Vienne, where the son seems to have been educated, probably in the involved and fanciful rhetorical style of Sapaudus, who was then teaching there. In 494 we find him mentioned as his father's successor in the see; and until the death of Gundobad (516) he exercised a predominant influence on the Church of Burgundy, and through it on the civil government. He induced Gundobad's son, Sigismund, to renounce Arianism, and the old king himself listened gladly to Avitus and seemed disposed to follow this example. In the contest over boundaries between the metropolitan sees of Vienne and Arles, Avitus won a decisive victory under Pope Anastasius II (496–498). He was a zealous supporter of the close connection between the south of Gaul and the Roman see which was restored in 494, and did his best to promote the power of the latter. His political influence was far from salutary, since it was exercised mainly for ecclesiastical ends. His theology was dominated by his opposition to Arianism and other kindred heresies; otherwise he appears to have been chiefly interested in questions of ritual and church law. His last great success was to call and preside over the Burgundian council at Epao in 517, some of whose canons show his authorship, even in their wording. His prose writings consist partly of sermons, partly of letters, which, as was customary at that time, attain the dimensions of complete tractates. These have some historical value, which would be greater if we could establish a more secure chronology for them. The most famous is Epist. xlvi (xli), addressed to Clovis in the beginning of 497. Epist. xxxiv (xxxi) is important for the light which it throws upon his attitude in regard to ecclesiastical polity. Here he speaks for the Gallic episcopate in relation to the Roman contest arising out of the charges against Pope Symmachus. This noteworthy manifesto unfolds an entire ultramontane programme, addressed to the senators Faustus and Symmachus, probably at the end of 501. Some of his oratorical productions are interesting, but more important is his poetical work, an epic dealing with the origin of the human race, and a didactic poem. The former is called by Ebert "at least in regard to its plan, the most significant contribution to the poetical treatment of the Bible in early Christian literature." It seems to have been composed in the last decade of the fifth century, and consists of 2,522 hexameter verses, divided into five books which carry the history of the world from its creation through the fall of man (in which Satan is drawn as an imposing figure reminding of Milton) to the Flood and the Exodus. It is much more than a bald transcript of the Biblical text, and frequently goes off into long typological trains of thought. (F. Arnold.)

Bibliography: The works are in *MPL*, lix, and ed. R. Peiper in *MGH*, *Auct. Ant.*, vol. vi, part 2, 1883; also, *Œuvres complètes de St. Avit*, ed. U. Chevalier, Lyons, 1890. Consult A. Charaux, *St. Avite sa vie, ses œuvres*, Paris, 1876; P. Parizel, *St. Avite, sa vie et ses écrits*, Louvain, 1859; A. Ebert, *Geschichte der Litteratur des Mittelalters*, i, 393–402, Leipsic, 1889; W. S. Teuffel, *Geschichte der römischen Literatur*, p. 1219, No. 5, Leipsic, 1890; C. F. Arnold, *Cæsarius von Arelate und die gallische Kirche seiner Zeit*, pp. 191 sqq., 202–215, 578, Leipsic, 1894.

AVIZ, ā''vîz', ORDER OF: An association of knights founded about 1145 by King Alfonso I of Portugal to extend his dominions into Moorish territory to the south. They were originally called *nova militia*; when Alfonso captured Evora from the Moors (1166) he gave it to the knights as their seat and they took the name "Brethren of St. Maria of Evora," and after 1211, when Alfonso II gave them the town of Aviz (75 m. n.e. of Lisbon), they were known as the "Brethren (or Knights) of Aviz." Their constitution, which, besides the three customary vows, imposed also the obligation to fight against the infidels, was prepared in its main outlines by the Cistercian abbot Johannes Civita about 1162. Like the Order of Alcantara (q.v.) the Knights of Aviz were for a time dependent upon the Order of Calatrava (q.v.), but at the beginning of the fifteenth century they obtained their independence, and successfully resisted an attempt of the Council of Basel to restore the supremacy of the Calatrava Order. Toward the end of the Middle Ages they received dispensation from the vow of celibacy and were allowed to marry once. In 1789 the order was changed into one of military merit and the ecclesiastical vows were abolished. O. Zöckler†.

Bibliography: Helyot, *Ordres monastiques*, vi, 65–69; G. Giucci, *Iconografia storica degli ordini religiosi e cavallereschi*, i, 61–63, Rome, 1836; P. B. Gams, *Die Kirchengeschichte von Spanien*, iii, 57–58, Regensburg, 1876.

AWAKENING: A term which in recent times has occasionally been mentioned in Protestant dogmatics as a member of the *ordo salutis* (see Order of Salvation). Elsewhere the term is used, especially in the language of the Pietists and Methodists, to designate the great commotion produced in the heart, especially by preaching. To this usage corresponds also the popular conception which understands by the term "awakening" specifically the stirring of strong religious feelings, such as at times accompany the beginning of the Christian estate. In this sense books or sermons are characterized as "awakening," and periods of history in which there is a rapid change of religious feeling are called "times of awakening."

So far as the Biblical basis for the conception is concerned, the sources are quite meager. Only Rom. xiii, 11 and Eph. v, 14 come into consideration. In both passages the act of awakening is placed in close connection with the light or illumination. He who is brought into the sphere of the light, does not continue to sleep, but awakes out of his sleep and then by the awaking is illuminated by the light. If the work of grace be considered as an enlightenment, then its first effect in man is that of awaking. According to the Biblical usage, therefore, we are to think neither of a special divine act of "awaking" nor of a condition, having temporal duration, of "awaking" or "becoming awake." There are, however, some recent dogmaticians who take these positions (e.g., C. I. Nitzsch, *System der christlichen Lehre*, Bonn, 1851, pp. 298, 304–305; I. A. Dorner, *Glaubenslehre*, vol. ii, part 2, Berlin, 1881, 725–728; F. Reiff, *Christliche Glaubenslehre*, ii, Basel, 1873, 349; F. Nitzsch, *Lehrbuch der Dogmatik*, Freiburg, 1892, p. 593). Calling (q.v.) is then divided into illumination (q.v.), which aims to give a knowledge of salvation, and awakening, which directs the will to the salvation. Others, on the contrary, emphasize more the subjective condition of the awakening. It is the introduction to regeneration; the awakened is "mightily moved by grace"; it is a "condition of religious suffering," for as yet there is no self-determination (Martensen, *Die christliche Dogmatik*, Berlin, 1870, pp. 361–362); it is "a moment in which the soul is more profoundly seized by grace," "the birth throes of the new man," where "there is still too much being built upon feeling and sensibility" (Thomasius, *Lehre von Christi Person und Werk*, ii, Leipsic, 1888, 377, 384; cf. Luthardt, *Kompendium der Dogmatik*, Leipsic, 1893, p. 264; Wacker, *Die Heilsordnung*, Gütersloh, 1898, pp. 33, 34). Of special interest is the representation of "awakening" given by the dogmatician of German Methodism, A. Sulzberger (cf. *Die christliche Glaubenslehre*, ii, Bremen, 1876, 368 sqq.). But in spite of these and other efforts to give the term "awakening" a place in dogmatics, the necessity of the conception can not be maintained. Objectively, it adds nothing to "calling," and, subjectively, it has no specific connotation as against the first beginnings of faith and "conversion" in the old dogmatics. Here as in general, the undue subdividing of the *ordo salutis* is to be opposed. R. Seeberg.

AWAKENING, THE GREAT. See REVIVALS OF RELIGION.

AXEL. See ABSALON.

AYER, JOSEPH CULLEN, JR.: Protestant Episcopalian; b. at Newtonville, Mass., Jan. 7, 1866. He was educated at Harvard University and the universities of Berlin, Halle, and Leipsic (Ph.D., 1893), and at the Episcopal Theological School, Cambridge, Mass., from which he was graduated in 1887. He was honorary fellow at Johns Hopkins in 1899–1900, and in the following year was appointed lecturer on canon law in the Cambridge Theological School. In 1905 he was chosen professor of ecclesiastical history in the Divinity School of the Protestant Episcopal Church in Philadelphia. His theological position is that of a conservative Broad-churchman or a liberal High-churchman. In addition to numerous briefer studies on canon law, music, and painting, in various reviews, and, besides contributions to the second, third, and fourth volumes of *The World's Orators* (New York, 1900), he has written *Die Ethik Joseph Butlers* (Leipsic, 1893) and *The Rise and Development of Christian Architecture* (Milwaukee, 1902).

AYLMER, él-mer (ELMER), JOHN: Bishop of London; b. at Aylmer Hall, parish of Tivetshall St. Mary (15 m. s. of Norwich), Norfolk, England, 1521; d. in London June 3, 1594. He studied at Cambridge (B.A., 1541) and was tutor to Lady Jane Grey; was made Archdeacon of Stow in 1553. During the reign of Mary he retired to Strasburg and Zurich, and wrote there a reply to John Knox's *Monstrous Regiment of Women* (Geneva, 1558), under the title *An Harborowe* [Harbor] *for Faithful and True Subjects against the late blown blast concerning the government of women* (Strasburg, 1559). He returned to England shortly after the accession of Elizabeth (1558) and was made archdeacon of Lincoln in 1562, bishop of London in 1577. He was a somewhat narrow-minded man, of arbitrary and arrogant temper, and as bishop displayed a harshness toward Puritans and Roman Catholics which brought upon him much unpopularity and exposed him to the biting satire of the Marprelate tracts (q.v.); yet he was a man of learning and a patron of scholars. Besides the volume already mentioned he left sermons and devotional works.

BIBLIOGRAPHY: The best book is by J. Strype, *Historical Collections of the Life and Acts of John Aylmer*, Oxford, 1821; S. R. Maitland, *Essays on the Reformation in England*, London, 1849; J. Hunt, *Religious Thought in England*, i, 73–76, London, 1870; *DNB*, ii, 281–283.

AZARIAH, az"a-rai'ā: King of Judah. See UZZIAH. For the apocryphal "Prayer of Azariah," see APOCRYPHA, A, IV, 3.

AZAZEL a-zê'zel or a-zā'zel (Heb. *'aza'zel*): The word translated "scapegoat" in the A. V., found only in Lev. xvi, in the legislation concerning the Day of Atonement, where the high priest is directed to take two goats as sin-offering for the people, to choose by lot one of them "for Yahweh" and the other "for Azazel" (ver. 8), and to send the latter forth into the wilderness (ver. 10, 21–22; see ATONEMENT, DAY OF). The meaning of the word has occasioned much discussion. Starting from the fact that "for Yahweh" and "for Azazel" stand in opposition (ver. 8), many think that it is the name of a being opposed to Yahweh,—a desert-monster, a demon, or directly Satan. Such as attempt an etymological interpretation then explain it as characterizing the demon or Satan as removed or apostatized from God, or a being repelled by men (*averruncus*), or one which does things apart and in secret (from *azal*, "to go away"). Others conceive of Azazel, not as a proper name, but as an appellative noun and modified reduplicated form of a root *'azal*, "to remove, retire," signifying *longe remotus* or *porro abiens*. The sense of verses 8, 10, and 26, then, is that the goat is designated by the lot as an azazel, i.e., something which is to go far away, and is sent into the wilderness as such; and the idea is expressed symbolically that with the sending away of the goat, sin has also been removed from the people for whom atonement has been made, and they regard themselves as freed and released from their sins. The contrast between "for Yahweh" and "for Azazel," however, in ver. 8 favors the interpretation of Azazel as a proper noun, and a reference to Satan suggests itself. It has been urged that nowhere else in the Pentateuch is Satan mentioned, and that afterward, when the idea of Satan comes out more fully in the consciousness of the Old Testatment congregation, the name Azazel is not found. But it may be that Azazel—whatever its meaning may be—was the name of an old heathen idol or of one belonging to Semitic mythology and thought of as the evil principle, which older Judaism made the head of the demons as later Judaism used the name of the Philistine Baal Zebub. A definite explanation, satisfactory to all, can hardly be looked for. The name of Azazel, like Belial and Beelzebub, is transferred from the Old Testament language into the Book of Enoch as designation of a power of evil. W. VOLCK†.

BIBLIOGRAPHY: H. Schultz, *Old Testament Theology*, i, 403–406, Edinburgh, 1892; Diestel, *Set-Typhon, Asasel, und Satan*, in *ZHT*, 1860, pp. 159 sqq.; G. H. A. von Ewald, *Die Lehre der Bibel von Gott*, ii, 191–192, Leipsic, 1874; Oort, in *ThT*, x (1876), 150–155; S. R. Driver, in *Expositor*, 1885, pp. 214–217; Nowack, *Archäologie*, ii, 186–187; Benzinger, *Archäologie*, p. 478; *DB*, i, 207–208; *EB*, i, 394–398; consult also the commentaries on Leviticus. For ethnic analogies cf. J. G. Frazer, *Golden Bough*, ii, 18–19, London, 1900.

AZYMITES, a-zim'aits (Gk. *azymitai*, from *a*-privative and *zymē*, "leaven"): An epithet given by the Greek Church to the Latin Church from the eleventh century, because the latter uses unleavened bread in the Lord's Supper. Michael Cerularius, Patriarch of Constantinople (q.v.), in 1053 attacked the practise of the Western Church, declaring their Eucharist worthless because unleavened bread was lifeless and powerless. A hot contest ensued in which the Latins maintained that either leavened or unleavened bread could be used; they retaliated upon their opponents with the epithets *fermentarii* or *fermentacei* (from Lat. *fermentum*, "leaven") and *prozymitai* (from Gk. *pro*, "for," and *zymē*). The Council of Florence (1439) decreed that each Church must follow its own custom, and for the Latin Church to change would be grievous sin. See LORD'S SUPPER.

B

BAADER, bä'der, **FRANZ XAVER VON:** Roman Catholic philosopher; b. at Munich Mar. 27, 1765; d. there May 23, 1841. He studied and practised medicine, afterward became a mining engineer, and, after a visit to England (1791–96), held official positions in the Bavarian department of mines. In 1826 he became professor of philosophy and speculative theology at Munich. In 1838, having opposed the interference of the Church in civil affairs, he was forbidden to lecture on religion and thenceforth confined himself to psychology and anthropology. He was an original and suggestive thinker, and exercised considerable influence on his own and the succeeding generation, although the aphoristic and paradoxical form in which he presented his thought often makes it difficult to understand him. He sought for a deep and true understanding of Christianity, always with the conviction that "the legitimate organs had lost the key." A tendency toward individual judgment caused the Roman Catholics to reject him as one of their philosophers; he considered the papacy an equivocal institution not essential to the Church, and contrasted the Eastern and Western Churches unfavorably to the latter (in *Der morgenländische und der abendländische Katholicismus*, Stuttgart, 1841). At the same time he was a theosophist rather than a philosopher or theologian, and sought the lost key in the mystical speculations of Eckhart, St. Martin, and Böhme; hence he was equally out of sympathy with the rationalistic tendencies of nineteenth century theology. His system is set forth in his *Fermenta cognitionis* (parts i–v, Berlin, 1822–24; part vi, Leipsic, 1825) and *Vorlesungen über spekulative Dogmatik* (part i, Stuttgart, 1828; parts ii–v, Münster, 1830–38). His works, collected and edited by his scholars (Franz Hoffmann, Hamberger, Emil von Schaden, Lutterbeck, von Osten, Schlüter), appeared in 16 vols., Leipsic, 1851–60; vol. xv contains a biography by Hoffmann.

Bibliography: C. P. Fascher, *Zur hundertjährigen Geburtsfeier F. von Baadern*, Leipsic, 1865; J. Hamberger, *Cardinalpunkte der baaderschen Philosophie*, Stuttgart, 1855; idem, *Fundamentalbegriffe von F. Baaders Ethik, Politik und Religionsphilosophie*, ib. 1855; C. A. Thilo, *Beleuchtung des Angriffs des F. Baader*, in *Theologisirende Rechts- und Staatslehre*, Leipsic, 1861; G. Goepp, *Essai sur F. de Baader*, Strasburg, 1862.

BAAL.

Baal is frequently mentioned in the Old Testament as a god of the idolatrous Israelites, as well as of the Phenicians, Philistines, and Moabites (?). The name also occurs in a proper name of the Edomites, in Phenician and Aramaic inscriptions, in Greek and Roman authors (*Baal, Bal*), in the Septuagint and writings dependent on it, and in Josephus. Greek and Latin writers for the most part speak of *Bēl, Bēlos, Bel* as a Babylonian as well as a Syrian and Phenician god. The form *Bal* is more frequently found in composite Phenician proper names as Abibalos, Hannibal, etc., according to which the Phenicians pronounced the name of the god *ba'l* (cf. P. Schröder, *Die phönizische Sprache*, Halle, 1869, p. 84). The Phenicians carried their religion wherever they went, and thus the worship of Baal was very widely spread. Even the Semitic Hyksos in Egypt, according to Egyptian testimony, worshiped the god *Bar* (= *Ba'al*; cf. E. Meyer, *Set-Typhon*, Leipsic, 1875, p. 47, and *ZDMG*, xxxi, 1877, p. 725; W Max Müller, *Asien und Europa nach altägyptischen Denkmälern*, Leipsic, 1893, p. 309).

1. Various Forms of the Name.

There can be no doubt of the identity of the names *Ba'al* and *Bel*, the Babylonian god mentioned in the Old Testament, the *Bēl* or *Bēlos* of the Greeks, i.e., the Assyrian *Belu* (*Bilu*) contracted from *Be'el*, which is modified from *Ba'al* by the influence of the guttural. In an Esarhaddon inscription *Ẓil-Bel* ("Baal is protection") is the name of a king of Haziti, i.e., of Gaza (E. Schrader, *Keilinschriften und Geschichtsforschung*, Giessen, 1878, pp. 78–79), where *Bel* is evidently used for the Canaanitic Baal. The "*bol*" in the names of the Palmyrene deities Aglibol and Yaribol (and "*bel*" in Malakbel) may be still another form of Baal.

The Hebrew word *ba'al* means "owner" or "lord," also "husband," as possessor of the wife. The names of Semitic divinities all set forth the idea of power, and thus present a conception different from that of the Aryan divinities (cf. A. Deissman, in *The Expository Times*, xviii, 205 sqq.). Furthermore, it has been disputed whether *ba'al* in the sense of "lord" was an epithet of honor attached to divinity in general, or was given as a proper name to a definite local god. In favor of the latter supposition is the fact that there was a Baal of Tyre, a Baal of Sidon, a Baal of Harran, a Baal of Tarsus, and so on. When in later times many such local deities were worshiped in close proximity, the name "Baal" designated the principal god of a place; for he alone could there be called the owner or lord. From this can be explained the later confusion between the Canaanitic Baal and the Babylonian Bel, also the fact that Baal was called Zeus by the Greeks and Jupiter by the Romans. When *ba'al* occurs in the Old Testament with the article, this does not prove that there was a special god called Baal; it shows only that *ba'al* appears in the Old Testament not as a proper name but rather as an appellative noun. The use of the article in the Old Testament can be explained from this, that in cases where the Old Testament speaks of an actual Baal-cult, some one Baal among the many is meant; the later Old Testament usage, especially that of Jeremiah, employed "the baal" in the sense of "the idol."

2. Meaning and Use of the Name.

If Baal were merely the designation of some god

as owner of a place of worship or the honorary title of a god, an inquiry into the common meaning of the word would not be necessary. But such an inquiry is suggested by the statements concerning the Baals of different places. From the Arabic appellative meaning of the word *ba'l* it has been supposed that in places naturally irrigated the deity was worshiped as the Baal of that place.

3. The Conception of Baal. According to Hosea (ii, 15), the idolatrous Israelites imagined that the gods worshiped by them, whom the prophet otherwise calls "the Baals," were the authors of the good things of nature. Sacred springs are also found in places where the Tyrian Heracles was worshiped. But this does not necessarily imply that some special terrestrial notion must be connected with Baal. It is easy to understand how among an agricultural people like the Cananites the god of heaven could be conceived as god of agriculture, for the field can not produce without the blessing of heaven. But it is possible that in different Baal-cults a terrestrial idea and the conception of Baal as heaven-god, at first distinct and separate, afterward grew together, as in the case of Astarte (see ASHTORETH). It is erroneous to assert that every individual god who had the name of Baal was worshiped as lord of heaven; still more so to hold that each was specially worshiped as a sun-god, or that Baal was everywhere and at all times so represented.

While there is no evidence of the solar meaning of Baal, it is certain that the Phenicians at times attributed to their Baal or Baals some solar characteristics. As generally in the Phenician deities, beneficent and destructive powers were not separated but were represented as being combined in one and the same deity, so it was with Baal, so far at least as both powers were thought of as proceeding from heaven or more particularly from the sun. That Baal bestows natural blessing, has been seen above. Names like *Hannibal* "grace of Baal," *Asdrubal* "Baal helps," *Baal-shama* "Baal hears," *Baal-shamar* "Baal keeps," and the like, designate him as a benevolent god. That human sacrifices were offered to Baal can not be inferred from the Old Testament. The passages Jer. xix, 5; xxxii, 35 speak of children who were offered to Moloch, and the Baal mentioned there is only a general designation of the idol. That the Baal-prophets cut themselves in the service of their god (I Kings xviii, 28) can not be regarded as a substitute for human sacrifice. The representative animal of Baal was the bull, which also represented the ancient god of the Hebrews.

Certain Baals are named in the Old Testament with epithets which designate them more exactly: (a) *Baal-Berith*, worshiped by the Shechemites (Judges ix, 4; cf. verse 46; viii, 33), denotes probably the protector of a definite covenant or "the Baal before whom agreements are made." (b) *Baal-Peor* (Num. xxv, 3, 5; Deut. iv, 3; Hos. ix, 10; Ps. cvi, 28), also simply Peor (Num. xxv, 18; xxxi, 16; Josh. xxii, 17; cf. the name of a Moabite city Beth-Peor, "temple of Peor," Deut. iii, 29; iv, 46; xxxiv, 6; Josh. xiii, 20), was a god of the Moabites (Num. xxv, 1–5) or of the Midianites (Num. xxv, 18, xxxi, 16), worshiped on Mount Peor, where the Israelites committed whoredom with the daughters of Moab (Num. xxv, 1) or Midian (Num. xxv, 8). (c) *Baal-Zebub*, see BEELZEBUB. Certain place-names compounded with Baal (not necessarily all, cf. II Sam. v, 20) were originally god-names, the word *beth* ("temple") being understood in the place-name.

4. Special Baals in the Old Testament. Baals known from such place-names are: (d) *Baal-Gad* (Josh. xi, 17; xii, 7; xiii, 5), the "fortune-bringing Baal." *Gad* (Isa. lxv, 11; perhaps also Gen. xxx, 11) occurs independently as a name of a deity (see GAD). (e) *Baal-Hermon* (Judges iii, 3; I Chron. v, 23), usually identified with Baal-Gad, the designation of the Baal worshiped on Mount Hermon. (f) *Baal-Meon* (Num. xxxii, 38; Ezek. xxv, 9; I Chron. v, 8), the god of a Moabite (Reubenite) city, the full name of which reads Beth-Baal-Meon (Josh. xiii, 17), contracted into Beth-Meon (Jer. xlviii, 23), i.e., "temple of the Baal of Meon." (g) It is possible that *Baal-Zephon* (Exod. xiv, 2, 9; Num. xxxiii, 7), the name of a station of the Israelites on the Red Sea, belongs here. Zephon, or more correctly Zaphon, is known as a god-name from Egyptian, Phenician, Carthaginian, and Assyrian inscriptions. Baal-Tamar, a place mentioned in Judg. xx, 33, may also be derived from the name of a god, and Baal-Hamon (Song of Sol. viii, 11), Baal-Hazor (II Sam. xiii, 23), Baal-Perazim (II Sam. v, 20), and Baal-Shalisha (I Sam. ix, 4; II Kings iv, 42) were probably designations of local deities, of whom nothing is known.

There can be no doubt that, in ancient times, the Hebrews called their god the Baal, whether they used this name to designate Yahweh, or a special Baal worshiped beside him.

5. The Baal-cult in Israel. The latter can not be proved; the former is indicated by names of the Davidic time compounded with Baal. The worship of the Canaanite Baals in opposition to the Yahweh-worship had many adherents among the Israelites as early as the time of the Judges (Judges ii, 11, 13; iii, 7; vi, 25 sqq.; x, 6; I Sam. vii, 4; xii, 10). There is no proof that the Hebrews upon their settlement in Canaan adopted the Baal-cult practised there, but the fact can hardly be doubted. The earliest certainty comes from the time of King Ahab of Israel, who, influenced by his Phenician wife, introduced the Phenician Baal-worship, erecting a Baal-temple in Samaria and appointing a numerous priesthood (I Kings xvi, 31–32; xviii, 19). Elijah (q.v.) vigorously opposed this idolatrous cult (I Kings xviii). Jehoram, Ahab's son, put away a Baal-column erected by his father (II Kings iii, 2), but did not extirpate the cult. Jehu abolished the worship of the Phenician god (II Kings x, 21–28). But in the eighth century the prophet Hosea speaks of Baal-worship as existing in Israel without stating which "Baal" or "Baals" are meant. Of the Baal-cult in Judah we know only that it was abolished under the influence of Jehoiada the priest (II Kings xi, 18). Probably under the influence of Athaliah, grandmother of Joash and daughter of the Phenician

Jezebel, Baal-worship had been introduced into Judah (cf. II Chron. xxiv, 7); this Baal was no doubt Melkart of Tyre. Not much reliance can be placed upon the statement (II Chron. xxviii, 2) that Ahaz worshiped the Baals (but cf. II Kings xvi, 3-4). In the statement (II Kings xxi, 3) that Manasseh reared up altars "for Baal" (better "for the Baals"), Baal may be a general term for idol. Whenever Jeremiah speaks of the Baal (ii, 8; vii, 9; xi, 13; xxii, 29), he generally means "the idol" (so also II Kings xvii, 16), which is especially evident from II Kings xi, 13 (cf. "the Baals," ii, 23; ix, 14). In Zephaniah, too (i, 4), in "the remnant of Baal" the word Baal is equivalent to "idolatry." In the time of Jeremiah the idolatrous Judeans worshiped the sun, the moon, and the host of heaven. All these powers Jeremiah calls "the Baal" or "the shameful thing" (Jer. xi, 13). The name Baal was so obnoxious to the later scribes that they substituted for it the word *bosheth*, "shame," a word used as early as Jeremiah; and the Alexandrian Jews, as Dillmann has shown, read in their Greek text the word *aischynē* instead of *Baal*, which explains the use of the feminine article before *Baal* (cf. Dillmann, *Ueber Baal mit dem weiblichen Artikel*, in the *Monatsberichte der Akademie der Wissenschaften zu Berlin, phil.-hist. Klasse*, 1881).

For the mode of worship in Israel reference can be made only to those passages of the Old Testament in which Baal-worship is undoubtedly to be understood as the cult of the Phenician god. He was worshiped with sacrifices and burnt offerings (II Kings x, 24) especially of bullocks (I Kings xviii, 23), and by kissing his images (I Kings xix, 18). In the Baal-temple of Samaria the pillar of Baal was of stone (II Kings x, 27). Usually a Baal was worshiped in conjunction with Astarte (Judges ii, 13; x, 6; I Sam. vii, 4; xii, 10). A Baal-altar with an Asherah is mentioned in Judges vi, 25. According to II Chron. xxxiv, 4, the *ḥammanim* or sun images stood on or beside the altars of Baal. When the statement is made that incense was offered upon the roofs to the Baal (Jer. xxxii, 29; cf., on the "burning of incense" to the Baal in general, Jer. vii, 9; xi, 13), not Baal-worship, but worship of the stars is meant (Jer. xix, 13; Zeph. i, 5; cf. II Kings xxiii, 12). In the time of Ahab there were many priests and prophets (about 450) of Baal (II Kings x, 19; I Kings xviii, 19). The prophets worshiped the god by leaping around the altar (I Kings xviii, 26) and by cutting themselves with knives and lances (verse 28). The leaping appears to have been a means of inducing the trance-state (verse 29), it may also have been a part of the cult. The "vestry" mentioned II Kings x, 22 probably belonged to the royal palace, and was not intended for the official robes of the priests. See ASHERAH; ASHTORETH; HIGH PLACE.

6. Ceremonies of the Baal-worship.

BIBLIOGRAPHY: Smith, *Rel. of Sem.*, pp. 93-113 (best); J. Selden, *De dis Syris*, London, 1617; F. Münter, *Religion der Karthager*, pp. 5-61, Copenhagen, 1821; F. C. Movers, *Die Phönizier*, i, 169-190, 254-321, 385-498, Bonn, 1841; R. Rochette, *L'Hercule Assyrien et Phénicien*, in *Mémoires de l'académie des inscriptions et belles-lettres*, new series, vol. xviii, part 2 (1848), 9-374; D. Chwolsohn, *Die Ssabier*, ii, 165-171, Leipsic, 1856; L. Diestel, i *Jahrbücher für deutsche Theologie*, 1860, pp. 719-734; H. Oort, *The Worship of Baalim in Israel*, from the Dutch by Colenso, London, 1865; E. Schrader, *Baal und Bel*, in *TSK*, 1874, pp. 335-343; W. W. Baudissin, *Jahve et Moloch*, pp. 14-41, Leipsic, 1874; B. Stade, in *ZATW*, vi (1886), 303-306; F. Baethgen, *Beiträge zur semitischen Religionsgeschichte*, pp. 17-29, Göttingen, 1888; R. Pietschmann, *Phönizier*, 182 sqq., Berlin, 1889; Benzinger, *Archäologie*, consult Index; Nowack, *Archäologie*, ii, 301-305; E. Sachau, *Baal-Harran in einer altaramäischen Inschrift*, in *Sitzungsberichte der Berliner Akademie*, 1895, pp. 119-122; F. Vigouroux, *Les Prêtres de Baal*, in *Revue Biblique*, part 2, 1896, 227-240; *DB*, i, 209-211; *EB*, i, 401-409; H. Gunkel, *Elias, Jahve, und Baal*, Tübingen, 1907.

On Baal-Peor: E. Kautzsch and A. Socin, *Die Aechtheit der moabitischen Alterthümer geprüft*, pp. 69-77, Strassburg, 1876; W. Baudissin, *Studien zur semitischen Religionsgeschichte*, ii, 232, Leipsic, 1878; F. Baethgen, *Beiträge zur semitischen Religionsgeschichte*, pp. 14-15, 261, Göttingen, 1888. On Aglibol and Malachbel: Lajard, *Recherches sur le culte de Cyprès*, in *Mémoires de l'académie des inscriptions et belles-lettres*, new series, vol. xx, part 2 (1854), 39-40; Levy, in *ZDMG*, xviii (1864), 99-103; M. de Vogüé, *Syrie centrale, inscriptions sémitiques*, 1868, pp. 62-65. On Baal in Hebrew proper names: Geiger, in *ZDMG*, xvi (1862), 728-732; E. Nestle, *Die israelitische Eigennamen und ihre religionsgeschichtliche Bedeutung*, Leipsic, 1876; G. B. Gray, *Studies in Hebrew Proper Names*, London, 1896.

BAALBEK, bāl′′bek′: A city of Cœle-Syria, celebrated for its magnificence in the first centuries of the Christian era, and famous ever since for its ruins. It is situated on a plain near the foot of the Anti-Lebanus range, about forty miles northwest of Damascus, and 3,800 feet above sea-level. Its earlier name was Baalbek, "City of Baal," changed under the Seleucidæ to Heliopolis. In Egypt there was a Heliopolis (also called On; see ON), and the plausible supposition has been offered that these two places were of common origin. In proof, the saying of the author of *De dea Syria*, that in the great temple of Heliopolis an antique idol was worshiped which had been brought from Egypt, is quoted, and also the statement of Macrobius in his *Saturnalia*, that the statue of Jupiter Heliopolitanus came from Egypt. Supporting this is the judgment of C. A. Rich, quoted below, that the substructure of the ruins at Baalbek is Egyptian, at least in part. It was only after Baalbek was made a Roman colony, under the name *Colonia Julia Augusta Felix Heliopolitana*, that it became a place of importance. It can not be identified satisfactorily with any Bible locality. It is mentioned by Josephus (*Ant.*, XIV, iii, 2), Pliny (*Hist. nat.*, v, 22), and Ptolemy; and coins of the city have been found of almost all the emperors from Nerva to Gallienus.

Location and History.

Baalbek contains ruins of three temples: of the sun, of Jupiter, and a small one of Venus; also of a Christian basilica. The first is attributed to Antoninus Pius (138-161) by John Malala (c. 525-600); only six columns and their entablature and the substructure remain. The walls of the temple of Jupiter are standing, but the roof is gone. C. A. Rich, who examined the ruins in 1894, says (*American Architect*, xlvii, 1895, pp. 3 sqq.) that the substructure of the whole, at least in part, is Egyptian, while the

The Ruins.

beveled masonry under the peristyle of the temple of the sun is Phenician. The Germans, who have in hand the examination of Baalbek, have made out that a great altar, thought at first to be cut from the living rock and pieced out with masonry, but subsequently discovered to be wholly of masonry, is the center of the entire group. This was surrounded by a series of walls built up so as to allow the superposition of a platform level with the base of the altar, forming the floor of the great court. On the east, west, and north sides, these walls were employed to make passages and chambers beneath the platform. To the east of the platform was a hexagonal court, giving access to the great court, while to the west was the great temple of the sun.

The temple of Jupiter is to the south of the west end of the great court, distant about fifty feet from the south wall of the latter. Around this court on three sides, also around the hexagonal court, was carried a lofty peristyle on a stylobate of three steps. Four sides of the hexagonal court held chapels, the other two sides being given to the entrances to the courts. The north and south sides of the great court held each three chapels and two niches, most richly elaborated, the east side having two, one on each side of the entrance. On the floor of the great court on the north and the south sides of the altar were two large basins, unfinished, two and a half feet deep, with walls paneled on the outside, the panels decorated with genii and festooned flowers. Clear traces of a Christian basilica have been found on the great platform, the great altar being the center, while the line of the eastern wall of the temple of the sun is conterminous with the west wall of the basilica. The floor of the latter was seven and a half feet above the court pavement, thus preserving intact the great altar, which was built over.

Of the temple of the sun the two most marked features, long known, were the six great columns with their entablature and the three megaliths at the west end, two of the latter measuring sixty-three feet long by thirteen square, and sixty-four feet long by fourteen square. Another stone still lies in the quarry near-by cut out from the rock, and measures sixty-nine and a quarter feet long by fourteen square. The columns, of which there were originally fifty-eight, nineteen at each side and ten at each end, were seventy-five feet in height with a diameter of seven and a quarter feet, and the entablature was fourteen feet in height. These columns supported the roof. The use of the megaliths was only recently discovered. It now appears that they were carried around the south side of the base of the temple, and it is possible that they will be found on the other sides as well. It appears that the temple was built on an artificial mound of earth, and that the great stones were employed to sustain this mass. The order of architecture is the Corinthian, with all the elaboration to which that style so easily lends itself. The floor area of the temple of the sun was approximately 290 feet by 160.

The Great Stones.

The temple of Jupiter, also of the Corinthian order, 227 by 117 feet, was surrounded by a peristyle of forty-two plain columns, while ten fluted ones were in the vestibule. The entablature was of very profuse and rich ornamentation.

The whole was reached from the east by a magnificent flight of steps no longer standing, 150 feet in breadth. The scope of the entire group of structures may be judged from the fact that from the east porch of the hexagonal court to the west wall of the temple of the sun is 900 feet, while the breadth of the great court was 400 feet.

In connection with recent study of these ruins two interesting questions have been answered. On the soffit of the temple of the sun, now hidden by the braces sustaining it, is a figure in relief of an eagle carrying in his talons a caduceus and in his beak a garland, the ends of which are held by two putti. It is believed that the eagle represents Jupiter, the caduceus Mercury, and the putti represent the evening and morning star, i.e., Venus, all of whom received worship at the place. Mr. Rich in the article cited shows that great masses like the megaliths were moved by a sort of crane, V-shaped, socketed on metal, to one end of which was attached a cradle in which stones were put until the mass to be moved was counterbalanced.

GEO. W. GILMORE.

BIBLIOGRAPHY: Wood and Dawkin, *The Ruins of Balbec*, London, 1757 (still very valuable); E. Robinson, *Later Biblical Researches*, 505–527, New York, 1856; W. M. Thomson, *The Land and the Book*, iii, New York, 1886; H. Frauberger, *Die Akropolis von Baalbek*, Frankfort, 1892; C. A. Rich, in *American Architect*, xlvii (1895), 3 sqq.; M. M. Alouf, *Geschichte Baalbeks*, Prague, 1896; *Jahrbuch des kaiserlichen deutschen archäologischen Instituts*, xvi (1901), 133–160, xvii (1902), 87–123; *Biblia*, March, 1903, 387–393; *American Journal of Archæology*, new series, vi (1902), 348–349, vii (1903), 364, viii (1904); *PEF, Quarterly Statements*, Jan., 1904, 58–64, July, 1905, 262–265.

BAASHA, bê'a-sha: Third king of Israel, 952–930 B.C., according to the old chronology; 925–901, Duncker; 909–886, Hommel; 914–891, Kamphausen. He was the son of Ahijah of the tribe of Issachar, apparently of a family of little repute, but probably rose to be a commander in the army. When Nadab, king of Israel, was besieging the Philistine city of Gibbethon, Baasha conspired against him, slew him, and then proceeded to establish himself on the throne by a massacre of the entire house of Jeroboam. His residence was at Tirzah, where he was also buried. He undertook to fortify Ramah, on the frontier between Israel and Judah, two hours north of Jerusalem, thus menacing the southern kingdom, but desisted on hearing that Benhadad of Damascus had invaded northern Israel instigated by Asa, king of Judah (q.v.). Whether he resisted Benhadad or made terms with him is not stated, but the cities which the latter is said to have captured were later in Israel's possession (II Kings xv, 29). The religious condition of Israel under Baasha remained as under his two predecessors. His history is found in I Kings xv, 16–22, 27–34; xvi, 1–6.

(W LOTZ.)

BIBLIOGRAPHY: Consult the works mentioned under AHAB.

BABA; BABA BATRA; BABA KAMMA; BABA MEZIA. See TALMUD.

BABCOCK, MALTBIE DAVENPORT: Presbyterian; b. in Syracuse, N. Y., Aug. 3, 1858; d. in Naples, Italy, May 18, 1901. He was graduated at Syracuse University, 1879, and from Auburn Theological Seminary, 1882; he became pastor of the First Presbyterian Church, Lockport, N. Y., 1882, of the Brown Memorial Presbyterian Church, Baltimore, Md., 1887, and of the Brick Presbyterian Church, New York, 1900. In the following spring he went on an excursion to the Holy Land, on his way back contracted Mediterranean fever and died in a hospital in Naples. His comparatively brief life made a deep impression because he consecrated his remarkable powers and attainments to the public service. His sermons were of unusual effect. They were unconventional, sincere, and fervid, glowed with a spiritual light, and held the attention of even the most indifferent. His loving heart went out to all whom he met and his single desire was to do them good. As pastor and preacher he will long be remembered and spoken of in unmeasured terms of praise. In Baltimore he was counted one of the first citizens and in New York he bade fair to repeat his personal and professional triumph. Book-making was not his aim in life and the publications which bear his name were posthumous; they are: *Thoughts for Every Day Living* (New York, 1901), a volume of selections; *Letters from Egypt and Palestine* (1902), written to the Men's Association in the Brick Church; *Three Whys and their Answer* (1902); *Hymns and Carols* (1903); and *The Success of Defeat* (1905).

Bibliography: C. E. Robinson, *Maltbie Davenport Babcock*, New York, 1904.

BABISM.

Babism, the system of a mystic Mohammedan sect, which originated in Persia about the middle of the nineteenth century, is said to have more than 1,000,000 adherents to-day and is still spreading, and offers in its history some striking parallels to the origin and early development of Christianity. Mohammedanism is a religion sharply defined, even iron-bound in its doctrinal precision, dogmatic to the last degree in its essentials; and yet it has manifested the greatest elasticity in politics, in social life, in philosophy, and in religious beliefs (see Mohammed, Mohammedanism). Material and expressed in material terms, its theology has nevertheless embraced the abstractions of Greek philosophy, Persian mysticism, and Hindu pantheism and incarnation among the doctrines held by its adherents. Babism and its precursors most completely illustrate these anomalies. The roots of the sect lie in the early doctrine known as Shiah, which has flourished most prolifically and almost solely on Persian soil. The foundation of Shiah teaching is the doctrine concerning the Imam. According to this system, the Imamate or Califate is not elective nor is it to be usurped; it is of divine right and altogether spiritual; Ali, through Ayesha's guile thrice defeated for succession to Mohammed and finally assassinated, was the first Imam. The essence of the Imamate is a light which passed directly from Mohammed to Ali and passes from one Imam to the next. By virtue of this light the Imam becomes impeccable, omniscient, divine, an incarnation of deity. A philosophic ground of this doctrine is that even an infallible book like the Koran to be effective requires an infallible exponent, which is furnished by the Imamate. But the Imamate, though it is a succession, is not unlimited, and of the two main branches of Shiites one reckons six and the other twelve Imams. Both branches hold the mystical doctrine that the last Imam did not die, but lives "concealed" in one of the Arabic utopias, Jabulka or Jabulsa. A corollary is that he is to reappear, e.g., as the Mahdi "the Guided," who is to "fill the earth with justice"—a prophecy and a hope which naturally lead to repeated attempts at their fulfilment and realization (see Mahdi). It is further held that there were two degrees of "concealment" or "occultation," the minor and the major. During the former, communication with the faithful was made by intermediaries who were called *Abwab* or "Gates" (singular *bab*). When the last of the Abwab died (1021) without naming a successor, the major occultation began in the entire cessation of communion between the Imam and the faithful. Naturally the Shiites have ever since been expecting the reopening of communication with the Imam and a period of enlightenment in his revealing.

1. Antecedents of Babism.

The immediate precursors of the Babis were the Shaikhis, followers of Shaikh Ahmad (1753–1826), a Shiite mystic, ascetic, and thinker. His special teaching was that the Imams were personifications of divine attributes and that of these personifications Ali was chief. He gathered around him a great company of believers, the leadership of whom passed after his death to Hajji Sayyid Kazim, still a young man, but reserved, mysterious, and ascetic to a degree, under whom the sect multiplied in numbers and came to include many of the nobility. Just before his death (1843) Sayyid Kazim forbade his followers to mourn and declared that it was good that he should go in order that "the true one should appear." He died without appointing a successor. Among his disciples had been a certain Mirza Ali Mohammed, a native of Shiraz, who was only twenty-three years of age when Sayyid Kazim died. Mirza Ali was met by Mullah Husain, one of the searchers for a successor to the dead leader, and claimed to be the sought one, the "true one who was to appear" and the Bab or "Gate." He also claimed inspiration, established his right to the place of leader by revealing undiscovered meanings in the Koran, and convinced the searchers that their quest was ended. This claim was the more easily allowed because the year in which it was made was reckoned as the one thousandth from that of the disappearance of the last Imam. Millenarianism of a certain kind is as potent in its influence over Mohammedans as it was in Christendom in the year 1000 of the Christian era. Adherents came in

2. Mirza Ali Mohammed, the Bab.

by the hundred when the news that the Bab had appeared was spread abroad, as it soon was in the manner peculiar to the East. To the personal attractiveness of the young leader and the agreement of his pantheistic teachings with the mysticism held by most Shiites there was added as a compelling force driving to association with his following the great evils of a tyrannous civil and religious administration, so that the Babis soon became a large and important body.

The next year (1843) the Bab made the pilgrimage to Mecca, returning confirmed in his opposition to the mullahs or clergy. He attacked them in his preaching, and when they sent their ablest debaters to confute him and his claims, these partizans were either silenced or convinced. They then secured his arrest and attempted to assassinate him, but were prevented since he was under the protection of the governor. When the latter died (1847), Mirza Ali was thrown into prison in Maku and finally taken to Tabriz, where his confinement was daily made more rigorous. All the time he was exceedingly prolific in a literary way, claiming indeed as evidence of his inspiration the ability to produce 1,000 lines of poetry a day. His mildness and gentleness won the hearts even of his jailers, and converts were increased as accounts of his sufferings were made public. The most notable conversion was that of a famous, learned, and very beautiful woman to whom the Bab gave the name Jenab-i-Tahira, "Her Excellency the Pure." She was permeated with mysticism, and by her devotion and persuasiveness during her life and still more by her martyrdom (1852), she gained large numbers as adherents of the faith. Meanwhile in 1848 the late Shah was crowned, and selected as his prime minister a violent opponent of Babism. Under the persecution immediately instituted, some of the Babis seized arms and proclaimed the Bab sovereign, a proceeding which he discountenanced. The prime minister then had the Bab executed, July 8, 1850, expecting that his death would cause the dissolution of the sect. But Mirza Ali had nominated Mirza Yahya his successor and head of the nineteen councilors, and continuity was secured. On assuming leadership, the latter took the names of Sub-i-Ezel and Hazrat-i-Ezel, "Dawn and Holiness of Eternity."

3. Persecution and Death of the Bab.

The execution of the Bab exasperated his followers, and some of them attempted to assassinate the Shah. This involved the sect in new persecutions and in wholesale executions in public in which the most execrable atrocities were perpetrated (Count Gobineau has described some of the scenes in *Les Religions et les philosophies*, pp. 301–303, quoted in Renan, *Les Apôtres*, p. 378, Eng. transl., p. 201). As a result there was a great exodus of the adherents of the sect to Bagdad, whence, upon Persian official protest against their continued residence so near to the Persian territory, the Turkish government removed them to Adrianople. The leader secluded himself very persistently, conducting affairs through his half-brother Beha. The latter suddenly proclaimed himself the one foretold by the Bab as "the one whom God shall manifest," drew after himself most of the following, and split the sect into the "Ezelites" and the "Behaites." Between the two parties hostilities so bitter broke out that the Turks sent Beha to Acre, which became the headquarters of the Behaites and the center of their propaganda. Ezel was removed to Cyprus, and his following has become almost extinct. Beha was almost as prolific a writer as the Bab, and his works are extant in a Bombay edition. He died in 1892, and his son Abbas Effendi took his place and is the present leader. The number of Babis is estimated at over 1,000,000, and they carry on a propaganda in the United States (described in *AJT*, Jan., 1902). See BEHAISM.

4. Doctrines.

The doctrines of the Babis rest on two bases: (1) The general system of Shiah in its pantheistic and mystical phases; and (2) the assumption that no revelation is final, but represents only the measure of truth the stage of human progress has rendered man capable of receiving. Hence, as the revelation of Moses was superseded by that of Jesus, and his by Mohammed's, and his in turn by the Bab's, so the latter's is superseded by Beha's. But Abbas Effendi has tried to throw a log under the car of progress by declaring that "whoever lays claim to a revelation before 1,000 full years have passed is a lying impostor." The explicit teachings are (1) the veneration of the Imams; (2) the fact of their concealment and the doctrine of intermediaries; (3) the reappearance of the Imam as a reincarnation; (4) the non-finality of any revelation; (5) the incarnation of deity as an avatar from time to time to give instruction (Adam, Noah, Abraham, Moses, David, Jesus, Mohammed, and the Bab were such avatars, alike rejected by their hearers); (6) the possibility of an achievement, like that of the Buddhist Nirvana, of unity of the individual with True Being; (7) the fact of a final judgment; (8) the system of numbers based on nineteen: the year consists of nineteen months, of nineteen days, of nineteen hours, of nineteen minutes; the Bab had eighteen associates, he making the nineteenth and being the point of unity; the square of nineteen is the symbol of the universe; the Bab and his disciples represent God and, each of these having nineteen under him, make up the square which represents perfection. Commended for practise by the Babis are: abolition of religious warfare, friendly intercourse with all sects and people, obedience to the ruler, submission to law, confession of sin to God, acquisition of all knowledge which contributes to human good, and mastery of some trade or profession. Prayer is three times (not five times) a day, and the believer turns his face toward Acre, not toward Mecca. The Babi fast is not the month of Ramadhan, but the last month of the Babi year and lasts nineteen days. There is evident in all this a determination to mark the separation of the sect from Mohammedanism.

The Bab's dictum on worship is worthy of quotation: "So worship God that if the recompense of thy worship of him were to be the fire, no alteration of thy worship would be produced. If you worship from fear, that is unworthy of the threshold of the holiness of God, nor will you be accounted a believer; so also, if your gaze is on Paradise and you worship in hope of that, for then you have made God's creation a partner with him."

Geo. W Gilmore.

Bibliography: The best descriptions of Babism are in the writings or translations of E. G. Browne, who gives material gained from first-hand knowledge and in sympathetic vein, as follows: *Traveller's Narrative, written to illustrate the Episode of the Bab*, 2 vols., Cambridge, 1893; *A Year among the Persians*, London, 1893; *Mirza Husayn of Hamadan, Tarikh-i-Jadid, or the New History of Mirza Ali Muhammad the Bab*, transl. by E. G. B., New York, 1892 (diffuse, but full; a native account with condensed narrative and valuable notes); *Babism*, in *Religious Systems of the World*, pp. 189 sqq.; *Literary History of Persia*, passim, New York, 1902. Other accounts are in: J. A. de Gobineau, *Les Religions et les philosophies dans l'Asie Centrale*, pp. 141 sqq., Paris, 1865 (detailed and sympathetic; one of his pathetic descriptions of the persecution is quoted in E. Renan, *Les Apôtres*, pp. 378 sqq., Paris, 1866, Eng. transl., pp. 201–202, London, n.d.); G. N. Curzon, *Persia and the Persian Question*, i, passim, especially pp. 496–504, 2 vols., London, 1892; A. S. Geden, *Studies in Comparative Religion*, pp. 291 sqq., ib. 1898 (concise but clear); E. Sell, *Essays on Islam*, pp. 46 sqq., ib. 1901 (deals with the antecedents of the sect); *AJT*, Jan., 1902 (describes the American propaganda); J. E. Carpenter, in *Studies in Theology*, by J. E. C. and P. H. Wicksted, London, 1903; M. H. Phelps, *The Life and Teachings of Abbas Effendi*, New York, 1903 (gives one of the later phases of the development); Beha-Ullah, *Les Préceptes du Béhaisme*, Paris, 1906.

BABYLONIA.

Babylonia designates the country extending from the head of the Persian Gulf to about 34° north latitude (approximately the latitude of Beirut; c. 75 m. n. of Bagdad) and lying between the rivers Tigris and Euphrates or immediately adjacent to them.

I. The Names. Importance of Babylonia: Babylonia was the Greek name for the country, derived from the name of the capital city Babylon, this last also a Grecized form from the Semitic *Bab-ilu*, Heb. *Babel*, "Gate of God." By the earliest inhabitants known the whole land was called *Edin*, "the Plain." In Gen. x, 10 the name given it is *Shinar*, the derivation of which is in dispute. The most probable origin is from *Sungir*, a variant reading of *Girsu*. The *g* in Sungir represents the Semitic ghayin which could be represented in Hebrew only by ayin; the word would then be transliterated *Sn'r* and could be pronounced Shinar. The land was known to the Hebrews also as *Ereẓ Kasdim*, "Land of the Kasdim," the second word a variation for *Kaldu*, Hebraized *Kaldim*. From this last came the Greek form Chaldea. The Kaldu were the race which controlled the country about 610–538 B.C. A name used by the early inhabitants now called Sumerians or Akkadians was *Kengi-Uri*, Semitized by Sargon and others into *Sumeru-Akkad*, "Sumer and Akkad." Another name, derived from a Kasshite source and appearing in the Amarna Tablets, is *Karduniyash*.

The reasons for the great interest in Babylonia are twofold, cultural and Biblical. In that country have been revealed the certain traces of the earliest advanced civilization yet discovered as well as that which had the longest continuous existence. The highest estimates place the beginnings of this civilization between 8000 and 10000 B.C.; at a moderate reckoning it seems that evidences of culture are in sight dating from 5000 B.C. The Biblical interest centers about two facts: first, that in Genesis the origin of Abraham is traced to Ur, one of the oldest cities in Babylonia; and, second, the fact that Babylonia was the land of Israel's exile and became to Israel a second home, where many Israelites settled permanently. But there is a third reason for interest. One of the lessons a comparative study of history teaches is that Babylonia represents a principle very different from that which underlies Assyrian history. Assyria stood for Semitic materialism, for fighting ability, and conquest by force of arms. Babylonia, on the other hand, represented culture, civilization, literature, and the all-controlling power of religion. Its force in this respect is notable especially for the way in which its civilization subdued even its conquerors. Its Elamitic, Kasshite, and even Assyrian masters came under the sway of its religious moods and its literary methods. Kasshite and Chaldean kings forgot to write of their wars and transmitted almost solely the accounts of the erection and adornment of temples and the making of canals.

1. Reasons for Interest.

II. The Land: Geologically, Babylonia is almost wholly alluvial. The thirty-fourth parallel of latitude cuts across the line of demarcation between the limestone and the alluvium, leaving in the northeast a slight stretch of the latter to the north of the parallel, and on the southwest a little region of limestone east of the Euphrates to the south. The alluvium on the west is nearly conterminous with the Euphrates, except in the extreme south; to the east the soil made by the rivers stretches to the foothills of the Persian mountains. Its narrowest part is where the rivers make their nearest approach to each other; from that point northward the alluvium is only between the rivers, while below it immediately widens beyond the Tigris eastward and thence to the Persian Gulf maintains its width. The account just given involves the statement that in prehistoric times the Persian Gulf stretched north to a point just beyond the thirty-fourth parallel, and that before the deposit of the rivers, its waters have receded a distance of 425 miles. The rate of this deposit is known for a part of this period. The town known as Spasinus Charax in the time of Alexander the Great was then one mile from the Gulf. In 1835 Mohammera, recognized as the site of the town just mentioned, was forty-seven miles away. Thus forty-six miles of land had been made in 2,160 years, or at the rate of over 110 feet a year. It is interesting that this ascertained rate, supposing it to have been uniform during the historic period, corroborates the chronology gained from other sources.

1. Alluvial.

To the character of the land as alluvium, to its subtropical position, and to the elaborate system of irrigation and careful agriculture, and the abundant moisture, was due its wonderful fertility, second only, if it were second, to that of the Nile valley. To these characteristics were due many important consequences, notable among them the structure and material of the buildings and the kind of governmental and popular activities. It was inevitable that an alluvial land, inundated by two rivers, the periods of overflow of which were not quite synchronous but in part successive (see ASSYRIA), should abound in marshes; and that to relieve this condition, distribute the waters, and drain the land, canals, and many of them, should be constructed. And the extent of country thus to be redeemed being large, the making of canals became a governmental function. Again, an alluvial district provides neither stone nor wood for building. The clay of the land must therefore be utilized as building material; and it is almost inevitable that most of the bricks be sun-dried, since fuel for burning them is scarce and expensive. Once more, it is evident that since the inundations were annual, some method of putting human habitations beyond the reach of the waters would be required, and it is found that the cities were built upon platforms of bricks. Thus Babylonia became a land of mounds and of canals, the construction of the latter being one of the chief activities of the rulers. The "rivers of Babylon" were a feature of the landscape, and the mounds are abundantly in evidence.

2. Influence on Life and Activities.

Of the fertility varying accounts have been transmitted. Herodotus (i, 193) gives the increase of cereals as 200 to 300 fold; Theophrastus (*Hist. plantarum*, viii, 7) as fifty to 100; Strabo (xvi) as by report 300 fold; and Pliny as 150 fold. Herodotus was notoriously credulous, Strabo and Pliny got their reports at second hand. The statement of Theophrastus is not beyond belief.

Knowledge of early climatic conditions is in part a matter of observation in modern times under conditions which differ greatly from earlier conditions, and in part of inference from known effects. The temperature reported by the excavators runs in June and July as high as 120° F. in the shade. And this heat is made more oppressive by the hot winds brought by the sandstorms of the desert. That the conditions were not so severe during the palmy days of Babylonia is almost certain, since the abundant canals of flowing water must have reduced the temperature and so have modified the atmospheric depressions caused by rarefaction. The fauna and flora differed little from those of Assyria (q.v.). Of grains, wheat, barley, millet, sesamum, oats, and perhaps rice, were grown; wheat and barley were probably indigenous. The gourd family was abundant, leguminous plants were in great variety, and the leeks numerous. Of trees the apple, fig, apricot, pistachio, almond, walnut, cypress, tamarisk, plane, acacia, and above all the palm, were cultivated. The waters abounded in fish, the carp being especially plentiful. The water fowl were naturally the most numerous, the swan, goose, duck, pelican,

3. The Climate, Fauna, and Flora.

crane, stork, heron, and gull being known. Of land birds the ostrich, bustard, partridge, quail, pigeon, turtle-dove, and ortalon are still found. Birds of prey are the hawk and the eagle.

III. Exploration and Excavation: Antiquarian interest in Babylonia had always been greater than in Assyria, perhaps because the region had oftener been visited and described. Bricks with inscriptions had been seen and sent to England by the East India Company's agents at Bassorah; these, however, were not the result of excavation but of purchase or of superficial search of the mounds. They served, none the less, to awaken and maintain interest in the country. For the background of Babylonian excavation see ASSYRIA, III.

1. Rich and Mignan. The first excavator in Babylon was Claudius James Rich, who in Dec., 1811, visited Babil, had some Arabs dig at the top of the mound, found layers of inscribed bricks, and purchased others from the natives, which when sent home proved to carry writing of the same general character as that of the Persepolitan inscriptions. In 1826–28 Capt. Robert Mignan was attached to the East India Company's station at Bassorah, in command of the military escort. He was interested in exploratory work and particularly in the region between Bagdad and Bassorah. In his travels in the district he made some small researches, as for instance at Kassr, where he put thirty men at work, found a platform of inscribed bricks, a number of seal cylinders, and a barrel cylinder, the first ever found by a European, and some remains of the Greek age.

2. Loftus. Attached as geologist to the Turko-Persian Frontier Commission (1850–54) was William Kennett Loftus. In the course of a ride from Bagdad to Mohammera he had picked up or bought a number of small antiquities, and proposed to excavate for more at Warka. Permission from his commanding officer was obtained, and in 1850 Loftus set to work. A number of "slippered" coffins were secured whole, and by the ingenious device of pasting thick layers of paper inside and out three were kept intact and sent to the British Museum. In 1854 Loftus excavated a number of buildings, recovered many inscribed bricks but no works of art, in which he was most interested. The finds of Botta at Nineveh (see ASSYRIA, III, 3) seemed so great in comparison with his own that he became discouraged even with his success in finding mortuary remains, tablets and vases, and a considerable number of contract tablets of different periods. He removed his operations to Senkereh, discovered there the temple of Shamash, found bricks that brought Hammurabi into light and recovered the records of King Ur-gur (2700 B.C.) and other objects relating to the period between him and Nabonidus (539 B.C.). Work at other mounds, as at Tell-Sifr, was productive of inscriptions dated under the first dynasty of Babylon, and of utensils of copper belonging to the third pre-Christian millennium. During this same period Layard and Rassam made an essay at Tell-Mohammed near Bagdad, but found little of interest and importance. Excavations at Babil, Kassr, and elsewhere were also resultless. At Niffar little besides the slipper coffins rewarded the workers, and Layard was led to abandon as unpromising the site from which half a century later the great finds of the expedition of the University of Pennsylvania were recovered.

3. Fresnel and Oppert. The French expedition under Fulgence Fresnel and Jules Oppert began work at Kassr, Tell-Amran, and elsewhere near Babylon in 1852. There were considerable results from the gleanings of the next three years, the most valuable being the marble vase of Naram-Sin. Unfortunately the whole was lost in the Tigris with the finds which had come from Assyria. Under the direction of Rawlinson, the British vice-consul at Bassorah undertook work at Mugheir. It was speedily determined that the temple there, which had never wholly collapsed, belonged to the moon-god Sin, which comprised the results of building operations from the time of Ur-gur (2700 B.C.) to that of Nabonidus, and the inscriptions of the latter recording his work of restoration were found. Sufficient was unearthed to carry the history of the place as far back as 4000 B.C., but the site still awaits systematic excavation. Abu-Shahrein was examined and found to be unique in the quantity of stone used on the great structures, and evidences were also discovered which implied pre-Sargonic date. It is a promising site for future work. At Birs Nimrud examination of the ruins was undertaken, and the experience of Rawlinson enabled him to point out the exact place where cylinders would be found (which proved to be those of Nebuchadrezzar), in the corners of the temple of Nebo.

4. De Sarzec. For about twenty years systematic operations were suspended while scholars at home were examining the material accumulated. Meanwhile Ernest de Sarzec had been appointed vice-consul for the French at Bassorah. He secured the good-will of Nasir Pasha, then the real ruler of the district, and began a series of campaigns at Telloh which covered the period between 1877 and 1900, the year before his death. The net results of the work there were the discovery of Gudea's bricks and of the temple which he built; nine diorite statues in the highest form of Babylonian art yet discovered, headless indeed, but inscribed; two cylinders with the longest inscriptions in Sumerian yet discovered; and, in 1894, a treasure of 30,000 tablets, thousands of which were stolen by the Arabs because De Sarzec was unable to care for them. The temple of Nin-Girsu or Ninib, god of Lagash, was uncovered, also the celebrated stele of vultures which represents the birds carrying away from Gishku parts of the bodies of the slain enemies of King Eannatum, art objects of the highest finish in the shape of round trays of onyx, the silver vase of Entenema, beautifully chased, and votive statues. The tablets recovered were mainly commercial and administrative, the series running from c. 4000 B.C. to about 2550 B.C. The additional fact was developed that by 4000 B.C. the writing had already passed beyond the stage of picture-writing.

Between 1878 and 1882 Rassam conducted excavations for the English at Borsippa and in the region of Babylon, and among the tablets unearthed were those of the Egidi firm of bankers. Over 60,000 were discovered, but unfortunately most of them were ruined by moisture. In general they were of a business character, though a number were literary, mythological, and religious, and one was the cylinder of Cyrus describing his conquest of the city of Babylon. Sippar was identified with Abu-Habba, where the celebrated tablet of the sun-god was recovered; in this place alone Rassam uncovered 130 chambers. The result of German excavations at Surghul and El-Habba in 1887 was a large collection of mortuary remains and more exact knowledge of methods of disposing of the dead.

5. Rassam.

6. The University of Pennsylvania Expedition.

The next noteworthy attempt at excavation was made by an American expedition sent out by the University of Pennsylvania (see below, IV, 9). In 1884 an association of scholars in America was formed to forward research in Babylonia, and the same year the Wolfe expedition under Dr. Ward, Mr. Haynes, and Dr. Sterrett sailed to make a preliminary survey and recommend a site for systematic excavation. Niffar was chosen, and there, beginning in 1888, the most systematic work has been done and consequently permanently valuable results have been there obtained. Aside from the recovery of over 50,000 tablets and art objects of various sorts, perhaps the most significant consequence is the approximate determination of the period of occupation of the site, which was accomplished by means of the depth of the débris. The Parthian fortress was seventeen to nineteen feet above the pavement of Naram-Sin, and the interval between the early ruler and the Parthians was about 3,500 years. From the pavement to the virgin soil was about thirty feet, for twenty-five of which continuous evidences of human activity were found in the shape of constructive works, urns, and seal impressions. A low estimate would place the city's beginnings then as early as 6000 B.C.

A German expedition has been working since 1899 on the mounds which cover the old city of Babylon and has identified Kasr with Nebuchadrezzar's palace, and Tell-Amran with E-sagila.

IV. The Cities: Two facts differentiate Babylonian from Assyrian cities. (1) The former received character rather from their temples than from their palaces, from their religion than their temporalities. (2) They were not arbitrary creations like most of the Assyrian cities. Investigations at Nippur and careful examination of the evidence (as by C. S. Fisher, *Babylonian Expedition of the University of Pennsylvania*, part 1, Philadelphia, 1905) proves that the location of the centers of life, culture, and worship were the results of the usual play of natural circumstances. With the plain subject to periodical inundations, the highest spots were occupied by the earliest inhabitants, reed huts were built, and a shrine was erected. The character of the materials used invited frequent conflagrations with loss of life, which explains the beds of ashes next to virgin soil and the human remains found wherever excavation is carried far enough. With increase of population came systematic effort to escape the inundations by elevating the original mound, further elevation through the decay of the structures, which was hastened by the character of the materials used as the people advanced to the use of sun-dried and burned bricks, and finally the governmental erection of platforms on which the larger cities were built.

1. Origin and Development.

It is necessary for even an elementary appreciation of the history of Babylonia, to recognize the early existence of two groups of cities, one in the south in the district represented by the general name of Sumer, and one in the north covered by the term Akkad. Midway between was the city of Nippur. At the opening of history strife between the north and the south is in evidence. Whether this was due to the incoming of Semites at that early age is not yet certain, though the possibilities are that way. A difference in the language is evident in that early time, and they of the south claimed the purer speech. The cities of the south were Eridu, Ur, Erech, Girsu, Larsa, Shirpurla, and Lagash, and, much later, in the extreme south, Bit-Yakin. North of Nippur were Kish, Cutha, Agade, Sippar, and in later days Babylon and Borsippa. Of these, Eridu, Ur, Erech, Larsa, Nippur, and Sippar retained their eminence almost throughout history because of the celebrity of the shrines and of their deities. Shirpurla, Girsu, Isin, Kish, and Agade dropped out of sight in the later period; Babylon achieved its predominance in the middle period and maintained it to the end.

Eridu, Sumerian *Eri-dugga*, "Holy City," the modern Abu-Shahrain, "Father of two Mouths," was the southernmost city of early Babylonia, situated then on the Persian Gulf, now 130 miles inland. This fact, on the basis of the data given for the rate of deposition of silt by the rivers in the historical period, indicates an antiquity of close to 6000 B.C. That the ruins contain the remains of the famous temple E-sagil is certain, since the city was the home of the god Ea, who was said to come each day out of the sea to teach its inhabitants the useful arts. This deity remained in the pantheon till the last. Among the reasons for the interest in this site is the fact that it was never, so far as known, a political center. It was the home of the Adapa legend, the fisherman myth found in the Amarna tablets (cf. Boscawen, *First of Empires*, London, 1903, pp. 69–77). See below VII, 2, § 3, 3, § 3.

2. Eridu.

Ur, Sumerian *Uru* or *Urima*, the modern Mugheir (30 m.n.e. of Eridu), is on the right bank of the Euphrates. The ruins form a rude oval 1,000 yards by 800. Its position made it probably the greatest mart of those early times. It was located (1) on the river, easy therefore of access from the Gulf and from the entire north; (2) at the entrance of a wadi which leads straight into the heart of Arabia and marks the caravan route; (3) at the starting-point of the road across the desert to Egypt and Africa, a route early provided with wells; (4) just a little below where the Shatt-al-Kahr, the continuation of the Shatt-al-Nil, entered the Euphrates, thus giving access to central Babylonia; (5) a little above the Shatt-al-Hai, which gave it a waterway to the Tigris. Besides these great advantages as a commercial site, Ur was the locus of a pilgrim shrine. It was also at times the center of political movements, and gave several dynasties to the land. As the home of Sin, with his celebrated temple E-gishshirgal, "House of Great Light," and as the home of the goddess Nin-gal, its religious significance was hardly less than its commercial importance.

3. Ur.

Larsa, the Ellasar of Gen. xiv, the modern Senkereh, was situated 15 miles e. of Erech, probably on the Shatt-al-Nil. It was a home of the sun-god whose temple took its Semitic name, *Bit-Shamash*, Sumerian *E-babar*, "House of Light," from the god himself. This temple, built or restored by Ur-gur and Dungi, was restored by other kings at frequent intervals. Not much is known of the city except that it was the head of a small state and was the last city to submit to Hammurabi when he unified the country, c. 2250 B.C.

4. Larsa.

Erech, Sumerian *Unu* or *Unug*, "Seat," Semitic *Uruk* or *Arku*, the modern Warka and the Greek Orchoe, probably the home of the Archevites of Ezra iv, 9, was situated between the Shatt-al-Nil and the Euphrates, 30 miles n. of Ur. The ruins are about six miles in circumference, indicating a large population. Erech was Sumerian in origin, one of the most sacred of Babylonian cities from early times, and continued to stand high in the esteem of the people. The two goddesses, Ishtar and Nana or Nina or Anunit, had their seat there in the two temples *E-ulmash*, "House of the Oracle," and *E-Ana*, "House of Heaven." Besides the two temples Erech had the seven-staged ziggurat *E-zipar-imina*. It was a walled city, intersected by canals, and has yielded to the spade of the excavator evidences of the activities of early kings of the Ur dynasty, Dungi and Ur-Bau. It was a seat of learning also, the source of part of the library of Asshurbanipal, the locus of the Gilgamesh epic and of a creation story, the place of abode of the wailing priestesses of Ishtar who celebrated the Ishtar-Tammuz episode. It was therefore rich in those possessions which were dearest to the Babylonians. Later it fell into decay and was used as a necropolis.

5. Erech.

Shirpurla, the modern Telloh, was situated east of Erech. In the opinion of modern scholars it was originally two cities, Shirpurla and Lagash. It was the home of two celebrated kings, Ur-Bau and Gudea. The fish-goddess Nina had a home there, and the temple of *Nin-sungir* was also located in the place. It may have been the Babylonian Nineveh. Its inscriptions are wholly in Sumerian, and the ceremonies at the founding of temples are best known from discoveries made at this city

6. Shirpurla and Lagash.

Isin or Nisin is one of the lost cities, its site not yet having been recovered or at least identified. It was in all probability a little north of the middle of the line joining Erech and Shirpurla. It contained the ziggurat-temple *E-kharsag-kalama*, "Mountain of the World," belonging to Ishtar-Nina.

7. Isin or Nisin.

Girsu is another of the lost cities; possibly the modern Tell-Id covers it. At any rate its location is sought a few miles northeast of Erech. It was very early a seat of government but was soon dwarfed by its more prosperous neighbors, abandoned, and then lost to sight.

8. Girsu.

Nippur, the modern Niffar (35 m. s.e. of Babylon), revered in ancient times as the home of En-lil, the earliest Bel of Babylonia, and the locus of his great temple *E-kur*, "Mountain House," was on the Shatt-al-Nil which ran through the city. It is the site of the epoch-making excavations of the University of Pennsylvania through which more of light on early conditions has come than from any other single source. It contained the chief sanctuary of the land in the early and middle period, and its possession was always coveted by the rulers because of the prestige which accrued, but its prestige was purely religious. Kings of the north and of the south and of united Babylonia vied in doing honor to its god, placing there votive offerings to Bel. Even after Babylon had attained its predominance and Marduk had seized the position and attached the name of Bel, the Sumerian En-lil still received his meed of worship. The topography of Nippur has been investigated by the help of a native map dated about 3000 B.C. found on the site (cf. C. S. Fisher, *Babylonian Expedition of the University of Pennsylvania*, part 1, Philadelphia, 1905). Ur, Erech, and Nippur remained for millenniums the triad of most holy cities of the land.

9. Nippur.

North of Babylon and Borsippa are Kish and Cutha, a few miles apart and related to each other as were Borsippa and Babylon. Cutha is represented by the modern Tell-Ibrahim (15 m. s.e. from Sippar and the same distance n.e. from Babylon). It was the seat of the god Nergal and the site of his temple *E-shidlam*, "House of Shadow." Its neighbor Kish, possibly the modern Al-Ohaimer, appears in the records belonging to the very dawn of history. Not improbably, it was one of the early seats of the Semitic settlers. Its king Lugal-zaggisi in the fifth pre-Christian millennium claimed dominion from the "Lower Sea" (Persian Gulf) to the "Upper Sea" (Mediterranean or Lake Van?), and it was again prominent in the time of Hammurabi, who had a palace there, and built the ziggurat called *E-mitiursag*, "House of Warrior's Adornment."

10. Kish and Cutha.

Akkad and Sippar must also be treated together, for it is believed that they were not two but one. Akkad, Sumerian *Agade*, was the city of Sargon I and the capital in his time of the region of Akkad (the Sumerian *Uri*), and is mentioned Gen. x, 1. Sippar was almost certainly a dual city, located at the modern Abu-Habba. The Hebrew dual form *Sepharvaim* has by some been referred to this city. The displacement of Ishtar of Akkad by Anunit goes well with the hypothesis of the oneness of Akkad and Sippar, and equally concordant is the long continuance in importance of Sippar and the utter loss of Akkad as a city. Akkad had no great claims to importance outside of its eminence politically under Sargon; and its political eminence was utterly lost when Babylon assumed the leadership in Babylonia. On the other hand, Sippar always had claims to importance on account of its deity Shamash, and this importance would easily permit it to assimilate and absorb its less important neighbor. Thus Sippar lived on, its temple of Shamash, *E-barra*, "House of Brilliance," and its temple of Anunit, *E-ulbar*, securing its fame.

11. Akkad and Sippar.

Babylon bore also the name *Tin-tir*, "Seat of Life." In Gen. x, 10 it is named as one of the four cities of Shinar. The description which has been current in Christendom goes back to the narrative of Herodotus (i, 178-179; transl. in Rogers, *History of Babylonia and Assyria*, i, 389-391, where is given also the India House inscription of Nebuchadrezzar describing the defenses he added to the city). According to Herodotus, Babylon was a great square fifty-four miles in circuit, enclosed by a moat of running water and by a rampart 300 feet in height and seventy-five broad. Ctesias gives only forty-one miles for the circuit. The mounds called by modern Arabs Jumjuna, Amran, Kassr, and Babil are recognized as covering parts of the old city. The origin of Babylon as a city is unknown, as it does not appear in history till just before the time of Hammurabi, 2250 B.C., and it then figures as his capital. The prowess of that king elevated it to the supreme political position, which it maintained till Persian times. From Hammurabi's days "king of Babylon" was one of the proudest titles of the monarchs of Western Asia. Though destroyed by Sennacherib Babylon was restored by Esarhaddon in a style of still greater magnificence, but it was Nebuchadrezzar who elevated it to its pinnacle of greatness. It was he who completed its two great walls, the outer *Nimitti-Bel*, "Dwelling of Bel," and its inner, *Imgur-Bel*, "Bel is Gracious," and dug the moat of which Herodotus tells. He finished the two great streets, which he elevated and paved. The walls enclosed spaces not occupied by dwellings, asserted to be large enough to raise crops ample to support the inhabitants during a siege, making Babylon, with its great external defenses, impregnable against a foe on the outside. Its great temple for Marduk, *E-sagila*, "House of the Lofty Head," and its ziggurat *E-temenanaki*, seven stages in height, are described by the proud builder and beautifier of them. The temple was a compound of sanctuaries, the principal one, of course, Bel's, containing the splendid statue by taking the hands of which year by year the kings of Babylon confirmed their right to the title. Nebuchadrezzar's palace was also there, built new from the foundations. Hardly less famous than walls and temples and palace were the great gateways, closed by massive bronze-covered doors guarded by huge colossi. And another temple or z ggurat, *E-kur*, "Mountain House" was also located in the city. This king might well have exclaimed: "Is not this great Babylon which I have built for the royal dwelling-place, by the might of my power and for the glory of my majesty?" (Dan. iv, 30; cf. D. W McGee, *Zur Topographie Babylons auf Grund der Urkunden Nabopolassars und Nebukadnezars*, in *Beiträge zur Assyriologie*, iii, 524-560.)

12. Babylon.

Borsippa, the modern Birs Nimrud, is of importance only as the suburb of Babylon and the home of Nebo, the prophet-god of the country. There are some signs that its origin antedated that of Babylon, as for instance the fact that on his yearly visit to Marduk Nebo was accompanied by Marduk part way on the return journey, and this is interpreted as an indication of a former precedence which was abolished when Marduk became supreme. This is corroborated by the relationship assigned to Nebo as the son of Marduk, a fiction of late date. The famous temple of the place was named *E-zida*, "Established House," sacred to Nebo. The temple of the Seven Spheres of Heaven and Earth was also located there.

13. Borsippa.

Bit-Yakin was a city in the extreme south, the capital of the Kaldu before they became masters of Babylonia. It had been the home of Merodach-Baladan, and belonged to the kingdom of the Sea Lands.

14. Bit-Yakin.

V. The People, Language, and Culture: Careful discrimination with respect to periods must be made in describing the population. The fertility and the wealth and culture existent in the country made it the natural focus of efforts at subjugation. Different races came in and settled in the land, but the old population was able to assimilate the new elements which made the region their home. The Babylonians of later periods were consequently a people of very mixed origin. The earliest inhabitants were a non-Semitic race, almost certainly Mongolian, using an agglutinative language which differed in its vocabulary, its root forms, and its grammar from the Semitic type (see below, §§ 3 5). This earliest population, dating back to the beginning of the fifth pre-Christian millennium, is shown by statues from Telloh now in the Louvre to have been short of stature and thick set, brachycephalic, with high cheek bones, flat face, broad nose, and almond-shaped eyes, and to have been either beardless or to have had the head and face shaven. Other statues of the same period seem to represent a mixed race with the characteristics just noted somewhat toned down. With these is to be contrasted the type shown in later reliefs and statues, a dolycephalic race, typically slender, with aquiline features, and hair and beard that were long and wavy.

1. The Earliest Inhabitants Mongolian.

Upon the earlier Sumerians, as the Mongolic people is named, before 4000 B.C., came in the

Semites as conquerors of part of the land, which after some hundreds of years was wholly under their control. Thus a second element was added to the population. Somewhere about 2500 B.C. a second Semitic immigration reenforced the first and marked the completeness of Semitic domination. Elamites and Kasshites, both probably predominantly Mongolian, and then Semites again followed each other at intervals. Still another Semitic addition to the population is to be added in the conquest by the Kaldu; while the Assyrian and Chaldean periods added other elements in the colonists forcibly introduced from subjected countries. In the Chaldean period, therefore, the population had become exceedingly heterogeneous in respect to origin.

2. Semitic Immigrations.

Modern knowledge of the tongues of Babylonia has come entirely from a study of native sources, viz.: The inscriptions on bricks out of which structures were built or streets or squares paved, on door-sockets, on votive offerings of various materials, on record-tablets of clay or stone, on statues, on cylinders of varying form, on cones, vases, and bowls (see INSCRIPTIONS). The writing in which these records were made is called cuneiform or wedge-shaped, from the form of the simple elements of which most of the characters are composed. It exists in two varieties, concerning which two theories have been stated and defended. One is that the earlier form is not a language in the sense of a distinct speech, but is a cryptic or artificial method of writing, corresponding loosely with the hieratic of Egypt. Along with this may go the hypothesis that there was no pre-Semitic race in Babylonia, and that the whole civilization was Semitic in origin and development. The second theory is that this method of writing was a distinct tongue, belonging to a non-Semitic family, akin to the Mongol-Tataric group. For a number of years modern students of Babylonian inscriptions were in two camps nearly equally divided in numbers and authority. But within the last twenty-five years the advocates of the second theory have become the more numerous, until at the present day Halévy in France, McCurdy in Canada, and Price and Jastrow in the United States are the only scholars of high rank who support the first theory. A reason for the long debate is that the cuneiform is exceedingly complex and its acquisition difficult. The signs are conventional, not natural. Different forms exist for the same sound, and the same character may have different values, syllabic or ideographic, and may therefore be pronounced in a number of ways and may also carry more than one meaning.

3. The Language. Two Forms.

The facts which have abundantly established the reality of a Sumerian-Akkadian language may be summed under two heads: (1) The character of the writing. As already noted above, the Sumerian differs in vocabulary, root-forms, and grammar from the Semitic type. It has not the triliteral, triconsonantal roots of the latter, lacks the accidence of gender, is not inflectional, is fond of compounded words, has a unique numeral system, uses postpositions instead of prepositions, while dependent clauses precede major clauses and causal particles follow their clauses. (2) Facts in history. The existence of two languages is presupposed by the ethnology of the land, a Mongolian people gradually conquered by a Semitic. Hammurabi entrusted his records to both methods of writing, this proceeding being exactly what would be expected of a king ruling a dual realm whose subjects were of different races and tongues. The texts are often bilingual in alternate lines, and Sumerian-Semitic dictionaries or syllabaries are found. Moreover, religious formulas, ritualistic and magical, are in the Sumerian language and persist so down to the latest times. This is in accord with the universal law of religions, according to which ritual and other formulæ are retained in use long after the language has ceased to be understood. Further, the employment of the Sumerian language was provincial; its home was in the south and there it lingered longest. This tallies with what is but the other face of the same fact, viz., that the south was the region latest subdued by the conquering Semites. Moreover, the antagonism between the north and the south which study of the history discloses is in part explained by difference in race, which in this case accompanies difference in speech. Add to the foregoing that a tablet in the Semitic tongue mentions by name the Akkadian, stating that in a "great tablet house" (library) the "tongue of Akkad is in the third [room]." Akkadian and Sumerian were dialectical varieties of the same speech.

4. The Sumerian-Akkadian Language.

The other language, the Assyrio-Babylonian, was of the common Semitic type, inflectional, its roots were triliteral and triconsonantal, and it belonged to the north Semitic branch which included the Aramaic, Phenician, and Hebraic families. It presents few difficulties to the average scholar in Semitic, apart from those offered in the reading of the character itself. The twofold method of writing goes back to about 4000 B.C. But after the final conquest by the Semites, c. 2250 B.C., the use of the Sumerian tongue was almost entirely confined to matters religious or magical. To the world-speech it has given one word at least of value, "Sabbath."

5. The Assyrio-Babylonian Language.

In one or the other, sometimes in both, of these languages the literature of Babylonia was written. In the earliest period, and in the south down to the middle period, records were entirely in the Sumerian. The substance of the literature is very varied. It may be comprised under six heads: historical, diplomatic, scientific, religious, commercial, and legal. (1) The historical material includes the record of the operations of government. Noticeable is the fact that the records of the kings of the land deal largely with temple-building or the excavation of canals or beautification of cities—a striking contrast to the record of martial exploits which so nearly fill Assyrian annals. (2) Diplomatic intercourse is suggested by the Amarna correspond-

6. The Literature.

ence (see AMARNA TABLETS). (3) The scientific writings include books on history, geography, astrology, astronomy, medicine, mathematics, and linguistics. (4) Religious texts include the epics, myths, folk-tales, and the ritual of prayer, psalmody, incantation, and magic. (5) The commercial texts, forming by far the greatest bulk of the inscriptions recovered, are usually inventoried under the name "contract tablets," a term which is far too narrow to describe accurately the great variety of these documents. They are oftener records of transactions completed than statements of agreements to be carried out. They cover every phase of social, even of family, life, and deal with marrying and purchase, renting of land and hiring of persons, with crops and merchandise and handicrafts. (6) For the legal literature see HAMMURABI AND HIS CODE.

The writing of this literature was often microscopic and had to be read with the help of a magnifying-glass. It is interesting to note in this connection that a lens (of crystal) evidently used for such a purpose is now in the British Museum. Long works appeared on a series of tablets, and the order in the series was indicated by marginal notes such as are made on modern sheets intended as copy for the printer or as employed in commercial correspondence. Copying of old tablets was often most faithfully done, and some late documents exist which record that in the exemplar followed by the scribe there was a hiatus in the text. The poetry, like that of the Hebrews, was characterized by parallelism, and the strophical structure is often evident.

Nippur is the only place where systematic excavations have been carried down to the stratum manifesting the beginning of the city in the collection of inflammable reed huts so often burned down with evident loss of life Written records began much later. According to the chronology assumed by this article, the earliest documents date back to about 4500 B.C At that time there were cities which possessed an advanced civilization, where the social fabric was already complex, and where the strife for empire was already violent. Public works were carried on by the government, and division of labor had been accomplished. The condition was such that a long antecedent development is necessarily assumed. Thus it is known that Nippur had four navigable canals, possibly one of them the regular channel of the Euphrates of the time. It was not so very long before the two great canals, the Shatt-al-Nil (probably the Chebar of Ezekiel) and the Shatt-al-Hai were in existence. The former branched off from the Euphrates above where Babylon stood later, struck out toward the interior of the country and, after running south over 100 miles, joined the same river nearly opposite Ur. The Shatt-al-Hai started from the Euphrates a little below Ur and crossed the country in a northeasterly direction till it joined the Tigris. In the extreme north, just below Sippar, another canal united the two rivers. Besides these great channels others are known to have existed and in many cases their courses may still be traced. By 3000 B.C. these works had made Babylonia the land of many waters. As a further evidence of the advance of civilization it is shown that as early as 4000 B.C., tin and antimony were used to harden copper and to make it more fusible. Another indication of culture are the many testimonies to an early commerce which embraced probably all Arabia, the Sinaitic peninsula, Egypt, and the Mediterranean coast region; and a remarkable fact is startling to learn, namely, that the Nippur arch is placed by Hilprecht prior to 4000 B.C. (*Nippur*, p. 399) The corbeled arch shown in the same work (p. 420) is not a true arch, but is similar to the Mycenæan gateways formed of stones beveled so as to meet at the top. This period, therefore, was one of regulated commerce, advanced public works, and large international intercourse. Cadastral surveys were made by the government in the fifth pre-Christian millennium as a basis for taxation and for the regulating of sales of land. Civilized methods of government were therefore employed.

7. The Civilization.

The legal provisions are also of value in revealing the type of civilization. Slavery is in evidence during all periods. Slaves were of two classes, private and public; in the latter case they might belong to the government or to the temples. Public slaves were doubtless employed on the great public works; temple slaves were used in the usual menial offices about the temples, and also in tilling the temple lands. Even in Sumerian times the law protected the slave from ill-treatment. The servitor was often apprenticed to a handicraft that his labor might be more profitable to his owner. But he might engage in trade on his own account and, if fortunate, even purchase his freedom. Records are known where a slave lent his master money and at the usual interest. The whole impression given by usages respecting slavery is therefore that of a mild and comfortable culture. This impression is heightened by the tendency of law and custom respecting marriage. While the usage was theoretically polygamous, the many protections thrown around the wife and her dower, the hindrances to divorce and the penalties for it, and the mutual agreements contrary to polygamy indicate that the practise was predominatingly monogamous. Not opposed to this general appearance is the showing made by the status of woman. She could hold property, could trade, and might maintain and defend actions at law. Partnership of man and wife in conduct of business is often in evidence. The freedom of woman is one of the noteworthy features of Babylonian life.

8. Slavery and the Status of Women.

In full accord with the indications already given is the diversity of the activities of the early population. Besides the agriculturist and shepherd, there were weavers and fullers and dyers—Babylonian garments in a later period were in high repute—brickmakers and potters, smiths of various sorts and carpenters and stonecutters, goldsmiths and jewelers and carvers in wood and ivory. The learned professions included, besides the priests who gave tone to society, scribes who acted as

9. Occupations.

teachers and librarians and publishers and notaries, physicians and astronomers and musicians. Gold, silver, copper, and ivory, and later bronze, glass, and lapis lazuli, were worked and employed in the useful and ornamental arts.

10. Science. It is not improbable that the high scientific attainments of the first pre-Christian millennium have been mistakenly read back into much earlier times. Doubtful is the claim that eclipses were correctly predicted before the Assyrian age; though by that time the periodicity of these events was well known and records of eclipses and obscurations were kept at Borsippa and Sippar. Science was inaccurate, the fallacy of *post hoc propter hoc* being characteristic of this as of all early civilizations, most evident in the doctrine of omens.

The civilization thus described is Sumerian-Akkadian, not Semitic, as the preponderating weight of scholarship now affirms. The Semites came in upon this civilization and adopted and adapted it so that its ideals became theirs,—even the theology was taken over and remolded in the Semitic consciousness.

VI. History. 1. Chronology: Babylonian chronology rests upon the same general facts as that of Assyria (q.v.). The absolute datum is the eclipse of the year 763 B.C. The other dates depend upon synchronisms, either stated or computed by means of comparison of native documents such as the King-list or the Babylonian Chronicle, or upon individual statements respecting date, genealogy, and the like. Besides these data, the form of the characters in the documents often gives a clue to the relative age of certain documents and therefore of the maker. The King-list gives the names of kings c. 2400–625 B.C. A second King-list gives the first and second dynasties of Babylon. The Babylonian Chronicle refers to members of the first, fifth, sixth, and seventh dynasties, and another Chronicle gives parts of three dynasties, furnishing a check upon the first. The most important isolated data are the following.

1. The Data. A king named E-(dingir)nagin calls himself a son of Akurgal; Entena is named son of En-anna-tum and descendant of Ur-Nina, while En-anna-tum II is son of Entena; and the daughter of Ur-Bau is called the wife of Nammaghani. These items give the succession in a dynasty. Burnaburiash is shown by the Amarna Tablets (q.v.) to have been a contemporary of Thothmes III and IV of Egypt, and he is stated by Nabonidus to have reigned 700 years after Hammurabi. This datum places Hammurabi about 2100 B.C., which comes within a century of the date obtained from other sources. A king named Shagarakti-buriash is placed by Nabonidus c. 800 years before his own time, a date which agrees well with the character of the name and with other indications. A boundary-stone of the fourth regnal year of Bel-nadin-apli (1118 B.C.) asserts that from Gulkishar, king of the Sea Lands, to Nebuchadrezzar I, was 696 years, which item locates Gulkishar c. 1818 B.C. Sennacherib asserts that 418 years before 689 B.C., Marduk-nadin-ahi of Babylon carried off two images from Assyria; this datum fixes the year of the victory as 1107 B.C., while the beginning of Marduk-nadin-ahi's reign is settled as 1117 by a stone telling of a victory over Assyria in his tenth regnal year. Asshurbanipal relates that in a certain year (known to be 640 B.C.) he brought back from Elam an image carried thither 1,635 years earlier by Kudur-nanhundi, an Elamite, thus placing the Elamite invasion c. 2275 B.C. This fits in exceedingly well with the datum about the date of Hammurabi referred to above. Nabonidus states in the inscription in which he dates Shagarakti-buriash (ut sup.) that he found the corner-stone of the temple of Shamash at Nippur laid by Naram-Sin 3,200 years earlier, thus placing Naram-Sin about 3750 B.C., and giving the date by which to locate early events.

There have been in recent years attempts to reduce the age of Sargon and Naram-Sin by from 318 to about 1,000 years. For the shorter reduction alone is there positive indication, the fact being that a dynasty which reigned 318 years is sometimes repeated, and it is supposed that Nabonidus included in his reckoning this doubled period. The round numbers which appear in Nabonidus's statements are also the objects of suspicion. But there

2. Value of Nabonidus's Dates. are certain facts which lead to the conclusion that Nabonidus was not far out of the way. In the first place, he was very much the antiquarian, very little the king. His very care in going to the foundations of buildings he was engaged in restoring and his evident pride in recording his archeological discoveries is a *prima facie* testimony to his good faith. Moreover, the statements he makes are, in general, consistent with each other and with the results from other sources. Throwing light upon antiquarian methods in the time of this king is a squeeze of a tablet of Sargon I, i.e., an impress with raised letters reading backward. It is an example of scientific work done about 550 B.C. Moreover, as suggesting sources for the calculations of this king in records preserved till his time, there was found at Nippur a collection of tablets of different periods from the assumed date of Sargon to 615 B.C., this collection sealed up in a jar. It is not beyond the bounds of probability, therefore, that Nabonidus had access to documents similar to these upon which he based his calculations. Inasmuch as there is no positive evidence against the date for Sargon furnished by Nabonidus, and objections to it come principally from a distrust of statements involving high antiquity, and taking into account the indications derived (a) from depth of débris, (b) from the changes in the character of the writing, and (c) from allusions to Eridu as once situated on the Gulf, the probability is suggested that no great change is likely to be required in the general system of dates now adopted tentatively for early Babylonia.

2. The Pre-Sargonic Age, 4500-3800 B.C. History opens with the mention of *En-shag-kush-anna,* who names himself king of *Kengi,* the name for South Babylonia or Sumer. He also calls himself *patesi* * of En-lil of Nippur. He is doubtless a Sumerian, as is shown both by his name and his region; but that the Semite is already **1. En-shag-kushanna.** in the land and even among the king's subjects is clear. With this first of the known kings of the land comes also knowledge of the strife between North and South. Other cities are in existence, and the relations are not friendly. Girsu and Kish are named, and hostilities had been carried on by En-shag-kush-anna with the latter, for he names it "the wicked of heart"; and he must have conquered it, for he presented spoil from it at Nippur. Not far from the time of this king another is heard of from Shirpurla whose name is Uru-kagina, and his title of king indicates that his city was then **2. Uru-kagina.** the head of the district. He is known by several inscriptions, which reveal him building temples and digging canals. The preeminence of the south is still indicated, for soon after the ruler of Kish is the patesi *U-dug*, perhaps contemporary with *En-ge-gal*, who is called king of Girsu. Yet how quickly the fortune of war changes is shown by the fact that the next ruler of Kish is Mesilim, named as lord paramount, who intervenes to fix the boundaries between two cities, Gishban and Shirpurla, while the ruler of the latter receives the title patesi. That the lordship of Mesilim was more than **3. Mesilim.** nominal appears from the mention of Ush who is patesi of Gishban, while the ruler of Girsu has the same title; and that the hegemony was not temporary is proved by the fact that the succeeding ruler of Kish, named Lugal-da-ag (?), bore the title king. But with the names which appear next the leadership reverts to the south with the dynasty of Shirpurla in control. Of the names of eight persons connected with this dynasty the first two, Gursar and Gunidu, seem only ancestors of the later rulers. The rest follow in the order Ur-Nina, Akurgal, father of **4. Ur-Nina, Akurgal, Eannatum, Entemena.** Eannatum and Enannatum I, the latter the father of Entemena and grandfather of Enannatum II. The third, fourth, and fifth of these had the title king, the others were patesis. Ur-Nina is known as a constructor of temples and canals, bringing wood for his temples from Arabia, suggesting either conquest or commerce. His time and that of his son Akurgal seem peaceful; but with his grandson the Semites are once more aggressive. It is from Eannatum that the celebrated stele of vultures comes, recording his victory over the Semites, from whom he delivered Ur and Erech. The results were so great and the confidence gained so decided that Eannatum invaded Elam and made Sumerian supremacy seem assured. From his nephew Entemena comes the celebrated silver vase, the most beautiful of the objects of high antiquity.

* The term "patesi" is used in different ways: a man may be a patesi of a god, of a city, of a king, of men, and of a festival. These different ways of using the word seem to be equivalent, respectively, to the words priest, subordinate ruler, viceroy, shepherd, and director. It indicates subordinate rank, therefore, and seems to be used politically in contradistinction to the term king; though the king of the land may be at the same time the patesi of a god.

After the reign of Enannatum II there is a gap, and the next ruler of Shirpurla claims only the title patesi.

From his time down to about 3850 B.C. a number of Semitic kings of Kish are known, the last of whom, Alusharshid, claimed to be "king of the world." This king invaded Elam and presented at the temples of Nippur and Sippar the "spoil of Elam" in the shape of inscribed **5. Alusharshid.** marble vases. The Semites are thus shown advancing to control. The Semitic wedge meantime had been driven as far as Gutium, while a Semitic kingdom of *Lulubi* is known in the mountain regions of the lower Zab. These notes are interesting as showing the course and development of the growing power of the people from Arabia. Their entry must have been made into the region between the two rivers about the point where the Tigris and Euphrates make their nearest approach. There the wedge was inserted, the point penetrating beyond the Tigris. Semitic power developed both to north and to south, the latter the locality which resisted longest and where the Sumerian civilization remained unsubdued.

About 4000 B.C. the patesi Ukush of Erech had a son Lugal-zaggisi (the names are Sumerian) who became king of Kish and Gishban, and seems to have made Erech the capital of a **6. Lugal-zaggisi, Lugal-kigubnidudu, Lugal-kisalsi.** united Babylonia. He lauded En-lil as bestower of the kingship of the world, and claimed rule from the rising of the sun to its setting, from the "lower sea" (Persian Gulf) to the "upper sea" (Mediterranean or Lake Urumiah?). About 3900 B.C. there was a king of Erech named Lugal-kigub-nidudu, known to be earlier than Sargon because the latter used his blocks at the gates, but what part he and his son Lugal-kisalsi took is unknown. The names of a number of rulers of other cities of this period appear in inscriptions as diggers of canals or builders of temples, or as making offerings to the gods, and as bearing title either of king or patesi. The pre-Sargonic period therefore reveals the Semites in Northern Babylonia, striving for control of the whole land, at times achieving it only to be pushed back. Meanwhile they record their victories in the Sumerian tongue. The land had already become a region of canals, commerce had won its empire, and communication with the far west seems already established.

3. Sargon to Hammurabi, 3800–2250 B.C. Sargon's name was till about a decade ago the high mark of antiquity. This king is best known by the name just given, though he appears on the inscriptions as *Shargani-shar-ali*. An eighth century tablet, claimed to be a copy of an early one, **1. Sargon.** tells his life-story to the effect that he was born of poor parents, that his mother put him in an ark of reeds and bitumen and committed him to the river which brought him to one Akkil, an irrigator, who reared him as a gardener, and that Ishtar made him king. Another tablet asserts that he mastered the Elamites and conquered Martu or Syria. His historical character, once seriously questioned, is now beyond doubt, and his name is linked with that of his son, Naram-Sin, in journeys of conquest as far as the Mediterranean, while both brought back wood from Lebanon for their temples. Sargon speaks of forming all countries into one, by which is doubtless meant an attempt at organizing the whole realm so that the alternations of government which had been the rule should cease. The capital was Akkad or Agade. His son was as famous as himself, both as warrior and builder. Nippur owed to him its great wall eighteen feet wide, laid on foundations in trenches that were sunk fifteen feet for security and built of bricks that bore his name. He claimed to be king of Sumer and Akkad and of "the four quarters of the world," a title often assumed by later rulers. Confirming the claim to control of the region is the fact that Lugal-ushum-gal appears as contemporary of both Sargon and his son, and is patesi (not king) of Shirpurla. He it is who calls Naram-Sin "the mighty god of Agade," and a seal from far-away Cyprus seems to indicate that even during his life Naram-Sin was deified. During this period Syria was under a governor named Uru-malik (a Canaanitic name), who ruled for the Babylonian overlord. A post was instituted, and literature was encouraged. Sargon had books of omens and of history compiled. In spite of the promise this Akkad dynasty seemed to show, after the reign of Sargon's grandson, Bingani-shar-ali, it sank out of sight. Its significance was its dominance for the time and its testimony to the ability of the Semites to carry on campaigns in as distant points as Elam and the Mediterranean.

2. Naram-Sin.

With the fall of Akkad, Shirpurla once more comes into prominence, but the exact period can not be fixed within 300 years. Between 3500 and 3200 B.C. appears Ur-Bau with the title patesi, followed by a son-in-law Nammaghani, also patesi, and he, after an interval, by Gudea. The first- and last-named of these were the rulers for whom were made the beautiful statues of diorite mentioned above. The inscriptions, particularly those of Gudea, tell of his building operations in which he was inspired by the goddess Nina. His statues show the hands clasped in reverential attitude and in one case he is studying the plan of a building which is represented on a tablet placed on his knees. From Magan and Meluhha he brought dolerite and gold and gems, from Amanus cedar logs 105 feet long, and choice building stones from other regions. Here again is the suggestion of great commercial operations or else of widely extended powers.

3. Ur-Bau and Gudea.

Who held the leadership in the time of these patesis is not known, but their successors recognized the suzerainty of the kings of Ur. Besides them a number of rulers of Shirpurla are known, but the succession is not completely made out. Gudea's successor was Ur-Ningirsu, then at intervals Akurgal II, Lukani, and Galalama, the date of the last being about 3100 B.C. The significance of this period is the renascence of Sumerian power. Ur shows the next attempt for supremacy, and the dating here also is still *sub judice*. The question is whether there were two pairs of kings bearing the names of Ur-gur and Dungi; if so they must be put about 450 years apart. Then Ur-gur I and Dungi I must be placed c. 3200–3150 B.C. and Ur-gur II and Dungi II 2700–2650 B.C. An accumulation of indications suggest four of these kings and not two. The period under Ur-gur I was evidently one of Semitic decline similar to those seen in Assyria, for this king not only left monuments of himself in the shape of temples at Ur, Erech, Larsa, and Nippur, but he was in control of North Babylonia. Dungi calls himself king of the four quarters, implying complete mastery. It is once more characteristic that of the wars which must have been waged to construct this empire, not a word is said; the inscriptions deal with peaceful matters, mainly religious. The length of this dynasty is not known. A new aspirant for honors appears in the city of Isin under a Semitic dynasty, the kings whose names are certain being Ur-Ninib, Libit-Anunit, Bur-Sin, and Ishme-Dagan. It will be noted that the second element in each of these names is the name of a deity. Reversal comes with the son of Ishme-Dagan, Enannatum, who acknowledges himself a vassal of the king of Ur. But his predecessors had control of Ur, Eridu, Erech, and Nippur, the great religious centers, as well as of Cutha, the temples in all these places being restored by either Ur-gur or Dungi.

4. Ur-gur and Dungi.

The "second Ur dynasty" is a matter of grave debate. Radau names Gungunu and Ur-gur II, in which he is alone; generally accepted are Dungi II, Bur-Sin II, Gamil-Gin, and Ine-Sin; but Radau interjects a Dungi III after the second of the name, and Ur-Bau II after him, and Idin-Dagan after Ine-Sin. The decision must wait. The old title of Sargon is still in use, "king of the four quarters," and the Mediterranean region was visited either in trade or hostility.

The downfall of this dynasty brought Larsa to the fore, the kings of which signified their supremacy by using the customary title of Sargon. Only two kings appear here, Nur-Ramman and his son Siniddina, the latter a contemporary of Hammurabi. Temples in Ur and in Larsa, the wall and a canal for the latter city are among their constructive achievements. The supremacy of this city was cut short by an invasion of the Elamites, the mention by Asshurbanipal of the theft of the idol placing this raid about 2285 B.C.

5. Nur-Ramman and Siniddina.

4. The Supremacy of Babylon, 2250–1783 B.C. Even if the Elamitic raid had not taken place, another cause would have shortened the control by Larsa. A new people, of Arabian origin, had come to reenforce Semitic control. Under them Babylon had been growing in power, and was ready to assert itself. The attack of the Elamites undoubtedly made easier the assault of the Semites. The leader of the former was Kudur-Mabug, "a prince of the Western land" Anshan, which centuries later was to foster Cyrus. He established himself in South

1. The Elamites. Kudur-Mabug and Eri-aku.

Babylonia, conciliated the religious by erecting a temple for Sin at Ur, and commended to that deity his son, who succeeded him, whose name is read *Eri-aku* and *Rim-Sin*, the two names being exact equivalents (see ELAM). Gen. xiv is right in making Arioch the contemporary of Hammurabi (Amraphel?)*. Over this Arioch Hammurabi claims a victory as well as over the king of Western Elam, which is the indication of a united Babylonia and marks the end of the political importance of the Sumerians. From this time on it is not the rivalry of different cities which is responsible for the clash of arms in the region, but the attempt of nations to possess it. The first dynasty of Babylon, to which Hammurabi (c. 2250 B.C.) belonged, numbered eleven kings, five before and five after him. The city had taken no part in large politics. Its rulers had doubtless been cementing their position, but no sign of it has come down. The only thing suggestive is the fortification of the city by Sumu-la-ilu, the second of the dynasty, while Zabu, his successor, had built a temple in Sippar to Anunit. For the reign of Hammurabi and his code see HAMMURABI. From his successors little has come down. His son carried on the usual building operations in Nippur and elsewhere; of the remaining four kings the only records are incidental references in commercial tablets, but they imply peace and prosperity in the land.

2. The First Babylonian Dynasty. Hammurabi.

The account of the next or second dynasty of Babylon (2250–1783 B.C.) found in the King-lists is under grave suspicion on account of the length of the reigns assigned to the different kings. One is given sixty regnal years, another fifty-six, another fifty-five, and a fourth fifty. From the period as yet not a single document has come to light. The King-lists give only the names. Hommel once held that the dynasty did not exist, but he now accepts as historical the first six kings.

3. The Second Babylonian Dynasty.

5. The Kasshite Period, 1783–1207 B.C. The next dynasty was foreign and came from the East. They are known as Kasshites or Kosshites, and their home was the hill country north of Elam and between Babylonia and what became Persia. The movement which brought them into the land seems like an immigration of new peoples, virile and active, subduing a people used to peace, agriculture, and commerce in a quietude won for them by the great Hammurabi. Concerning this whole period little is known. There is only one inscription of any length belonging to these times, and the name of the king there mentioned is not given in the King-lists, which, in the part covering this period, are much mutilated. There is a votive tablet from the first known of the rulers, named Gandish, and some fragmentary inscriptions. The seventh ruler was probably Agum-kakrime, one of whose inscriptions was copied for Asshurbanipal's library. He called himself "king of Kasshu and Akkad, king of the broad land of Babylon." Other titles show that he claimed a very large empire, from the frontiers of Persia to the borders of Syria. He restored the images of Marduk and Sarpanit, which had been carried away by a people in the northeast. That the sway of religion had lost none of its power to enchant and enchain is shown by the active building operations which he carried on. By about 1500 B.C. light breaks again, and Karaindash appears as a ruler who is devoted to the deities of the land and arranges his titles in Babylonian fashion. The Synchronistic History throws light on the period and reveals friendly relations with the young Assyrian empire. The two nations appear as equals, making treaties and settling boundaries. Only a little later a king is known as Kallima-Sin (or, as it is proposed to read his name, Kadashman-Bel), and he is found corresponding with Amenophis IV (see AMARNA TABLETS). It is interesting to find in that correspondence discussion of a commercial treaty and of the customs duties to be exacted. It is also worth noting that a very close chronology is attainable here through the triple synchronisms from Babylonia, Assyria, and Egypt. Kurigalzu I (c. 1410 B.C.) followed Burnaburiash I, son of Kallima-Sin, using the titles "king of Sumer and Akkad, king of the four quarters." Burnaburiash II, correspondent of the Pharaoh Amenophis IV in the Amarna series, was next, but only the general peace of the world appears in his times. About 1370 Karahardash succeeded, and his queen was the daughter of Asshur-uballit of Assyria. His son succeeded him, carried on a war with the Sutu, a nomadic people in the northwest, and on his return was killed by rebellious Kasshites. The principal events which followed are given in the article on Assyria. Kurigalzu II was placed on the throne, invaded Elam and captured Susa, as a votive tablet declares, and followed up the victory by defeating Bel-nirari of Assyria. A new conflict with the northern power was thus begun, in which the Assyrians were superior and for a time held Babylonia, 1285–69 B.C. Under Ramman-shum-usur the latter began to recover its own, and by 1211 B.C. was reestablished in all its former territory. Four years later the Kasshite dynasty came to an end.

1. Agum-kakrime.

2. Later Kasshite Kings.

6. The Isin and Assyrian Periods, 1207–625 B.C. The nominal rulers of the land in the next period were the members of a dynasty of eleven kings known from the King-list as the dynasty of Isin. Whether this city was the one active in politics 1,700 years earlier, or whether it was a part of the city of Babylon, is yet under debate. The names of the first five kings are lost, the sixth was Nebuchadrezzar I, c. 1135 B.C. The period was marked by Assyrian attacks. Even Nebuchad-

*The identification of Eri-aku, Kudur-Lagamar, and Hammurabi with the Arioch, Chedorlaomer, and Amraphel of Gen. xiv has been made to do illegitimate service in supporting that chapter. The inscription in which the names were thought to occur belongs to the period of the Arsacidæ and does not contain the name of Chedorlaomer. But the "Tidal" of Gen. xiv is probably the *Tud-ḳula* of the tablet in question, and "Arioch of Ellasar" of Genesis is probably Eri-aku, son of Kudur-Mabug. The probability is now acknowledged that Gen. xiv is drawn from very late sources, of which this tablet may have been one.

rezzar was twice defeated, though he was a warrior of great ability who carried his arms to Syria on the west and to Elam on the east. He was followed by Bel-nadin-apal and he by Marduk-nadin-ahi. The latter made a successful attack upon Assyria which was punished later by the capture of Babylon and subjection of the whole country by Tiglath-Pileser I, c. 1100 B.C. The King-list gives a succession of five dynasties, one that of the "Sea Lands," the place from which the Chaldeans were later to issue, a second of "Bazi," another of Elam, a fourth of Babylon, and still another of the Far South, of which the noted Merodach-baladan was a member. But all of these held the throne either by sufferance or appointment of Assyria or assumed it during the temporary quiescence of that power.

1. Nebuchadrezzar I and his Successors.

7. The Kaldu or Chaldean Period, 625–538 B.C. The many attempts made by Merodach-baladan to gain control of Babylon (see ASSYRIA) were important, not in themselves so much, as for the foreshadowing of the rising supremacy of the Chaldeans. The kingdom of the Sea Lands had formed around the headwaters of the Persian Gulf, and its dominant people, fresh from Arabia, were feeling their way to world empire. The decay of the Assyrian power was their opportunity. Nabopolassar made himself king of Babylon. While he was absent attacking the outskirts of his kingdom in Mesopotamia, the Assyrian Sin-shar-ishkun invaded Babylonia, probably 610–609 B.C., and Nabopolassar was cut off from his base. The Umman-Manda, an aggregation of tribes gathered about a Median nucleus, brought about the fall of Assyria, and Nabopolassar was left free to establish himself. Already great numbers of his tribesmen had entered Babylonia, and the possession of the capital gave him the needed prestige to rally them around him. The native Babylonians were ready to receive him because of their hatred to the Assyrian oppressor, so he succeeded as the head of Semitic Asia. Another fact had doubtless much to do with the ease with which he assumed power. The religious interest of Babylonia seems to have absorbed his attention, and he acted like a son of the soil whose heart was fully in accord with Babylonian ideals. This is illustrated by the fact that though the events of his reign must have been stirring and important, the three inscriptions he left are concerned with building of temples and digging of canals. Among the great events was the defeat of the Egyptian Necho by his son and general, Nebuchadrezzar. Necho had already seized the western appanages of Assyria, against which doubtless Nabopalassar was intending to operate in his Mesopotamian campaign, and had led forth a great army in hope of gaining a still larger share of the defunct Assyrian empire. The two armies, Egyptian and Chaldean, met at Carchemish, the Egyptians were defeated and pursued to the very border of Egypt by the victorious Nebuchadrezzar. The latter there received tidings of the death of his father, and the very newness of the kingdom required his instant presence at home.

1. Nabopolassar.

Nebuchadrezzar II (604–562 B.C.) has left many inscriptions, which, like his father's, tell little of battles and campaigns and much of his constructive labors on the city of Babylon, his pride. The story of his campaigns comes largely from other sources, partly Biblical. The refusal of Jehoiakim to pay tribute caused Nebuchadrezzar to let loose on him the neighboring hostile tribes, and paved the way for the campaign in 597 B.C. in which Jerusalem was taken and its inhabitants in part deported. Renewed rebellion stirred up by the new Pharaoh, Hophra, led to a reoccupation of Palestine; Hophra was defeated, Jerusalem taken, and its defenses destroyed in 586 B.C. Tyre was assailed and a siege of thirteen years resulted, after which terms were made. Civil war in Egypt gave Nebuchadrezzar his opportunity, the country was invaded and plundered as a punishment for its intrigues in Palestine and Syria. There can be little doubt that the alliance of the Chaldean with the house of Media in his marriage of Amuhia, daughter of Cyaxares, did much to cement his power. It hardly seems an accident that the force of Media should have been spent in the north, westward into Asia Minor, while Nebuchadrezzar's operations covered the regions southward. Something of Nebuchadrezzar's building operations has been told in the description of Babylon (see above, IV, § 12), but how extensive these were can be appreciated only in the light of Rawlinson's statement that he examined the ruins of not less than one hundred places in the vicinity of Babylon and in very few were there not found traces of Nebuchadrezzar's activity. In a land whose kings were all builders not one of the rulers had approached him in the extent, variety, completeness, and magnificence of his buildings.

2. Nebuchadrezzar II.

Of Nebuchadrezzar's son, Amil-Marduk (562–560 B.C.), only II Kings xxv, 27 (where he is called Evil-merodach) and Berosus give any information. The one records an act of mercy, the other asserts that he reigned lawlessly. He was assassinated and the chief conspirator, Neriglissar (560–556 B.C.) seized the throne. Temples and canals absorbed his interest, and he was succeeded by Labashi-Marduk who reigned nine months and was assassinated. Nabonidus (555–538 B.C.) was the last Semitic king of Babylon. He was a pietist, an antiquarian, and a temple-builder, with but little aptitude for the cares of State and little interest in them. How he contributed to present knowledge has been told in the section on chronology in this article and that on Assyria. He resided most of the time at Tema, a place not otherwise known. His son Belshazzar may have been associated as regent with him, though there is no authority in the inscriptions for calling him king. Between the time of Nebuchadrezzar and Nabonidus relations with the Medes had been broken off. Cyrus, the king of Anshan, had enlarged his realm, and finally, having defeated Astyages, had assumed the title, king of Persia. He had overthrown Crœsus, and all Asia Minor at once fell into his hands. His

3. Nabonidus and Belshazzar. The Fall of Babylon.

next move would obviously be southward to Babylonia, but Nabonidus made no preparation for the crisis that was coming. When the war finally broke out, he collected the statues of the gods of Babylon, left the command of the army to Belshazzar, and when the latter was defeated fled into Babylon. Gobryas led the victorious army against the capital, where a sturdy and indeed successful defense might have been expected. The walls and gates which might have defied the best that Cyrus could do proved no protection, and though there is no proof that such is the fact, historical probability can offer no explanation of the speedy capture of the city other than that Nabonidus's worst enemy was within, and that from within the gates swung open to admit the captor. Thus the rule of Asia passed from the Semites to the Aryans to hold until at the end of a millennium Arabia should once more discharge its hordes and in the Mohammedan conquest make a new era. See Cyrus the Great; Persia.

VII. The Religion. 1. Historical Development: The survey of the political geography and history of Babylonia shows it to have been as early as 4500 B.C. what it continued to be, a land of cities. History shows also that even at that early date there was a tendency toward what later became nationalization, in the effort of one or another city to control the whole land. These two features are reproduced in the religion. Each city had a deity who claimed the worship of the inhabitants; frequently there were two, generally in that case a god and a goddess, originally in all probability not spouse and consort, but independent. And in the pre-Sargonic period there are clear evidences that one of the gods of one of the cities had attained an eminence, not indeed of kingship over the gods, but of position among them. The general disposition of kings who took their titles from cities other than Nippur to devote their spoil to En-lil and to deposit it in his temple, suggests for him a general recognition not accorded to other deities, even to Ea of Eridu. While no specific claim of lordship over the gods was made for En-lil, not only was he practically the chief of the gods, but a theoretical headship is implied in the theological fiction by which later Marduk's definite claim to preeminence was supported, viz., that En-lil had transferred to the deity of Babylon the leadership among the gods because of the latter's victory over Tiamat, the demon of chaos, though, of course, the real reason of Marduk's supremacy was the hegemony of Babylon. The principle of centralization, of nationalization, was clearly at work in the sphere of religion as well as of politics. But this was limited by another principle, that preeminence among the gods did not involve supersession of other gods in their own seats of worship. En-lil was ever localized only in Nippur, Marduk had his seat only in Babylon, just as Asshur never set up his throne and temple in Babylon even during the Assyrian period. The political strife between Sumerian and Semite was also reflected in the religion. There can be no doubt of two facts: first, the Sumerians had a decided favoritism for female deities; second, Semitic female deities were, with the single exception of Ishtar, but the pale reflection of the gods. While then in the earliest periods the goddesses were numerous and prominent, in later times they either faded out of existence, were made the consorts of the gods and so became eclipsed, or were identified with Ishtar.

1. Political Factors.

In the development of the religion, besides the political principle, there became operative also a philosophical-priestly activity. Out of this grew the semidetachment of certain gods from extreme localization and connections were formed for them having cosmic meaning. Noticeable here is the formation of the two principal triads: Anu heaven-god, Bel or En-lil earth-god, Ea water-god, and Sin of the moon, Shamash of the sun, and Ramman (Adad) of the storm or cloud. While worship of these gods still centered at definite temples, in invocations they were addressed more generally. Their association with larger phenomena made them accessible to a larger clientele, just as Nebo's association with prophecy made him the object of a larger circle of worshipers than was rightly his in his position as god of Borsippa. And the philosophical principle worked also in the reduction of the number of the deities, particularly of the goddesses. The notion of identification was particularly insistent, so that many of the Sumerian goddesses were in time pronounced the same as Ishtar, and that deity made her way to her unique position as the one great goddess of Babylonia.

2. The Philosophical-Priestly Factor.

This reduction in number of deities is completely proved. In the period from c. 2250 B.C. on, besides the eight great gods already named, only Marduk, Ninib, Nergal, and Nusku have any prominence. Tammuz might perhaps be added, but it is possible to maintain that in his worship Ishtar was the central figure. Yet in earlier times the number of the deities was very much greater. Manirtusu, an early king of Kish, mentions about fifty deities. The incantation texts, coming from an earlier stratum of thought and practise, increase the number greatly, one series alone giving 150 god-names. There can be no doubt that the sun-gods of the various cities were originally separate, though the priestly philosophy regarded them as the same; this can be said also of the moon-deities, who became one in Sin.

3. Decrease in the Number of Deities.

Etymology enables the investigator to go still farther back and posit for earliest Babylonia an animistic worship when spirits were numerous, some of whom rose to high position and became great gods. This is demonstrable in the cases of En-lil ("Lord of Spirits"), Ea, and Damkina, the consort of Ea, and is practically certain in several other cases. Secondly, the entire system of magic and incantation is the surest proof that animism preceded polytheism in old Babylonia. To illustrate the belief in spirits, mention may be made of the Sumerian *zi*, "the living thing," having about the same connotation as "spirit" in animistic usage. The *lil* were ghosts, subter-

4. The Earliest Religion Animistic.

ranean spirits of the darkness and storm, sexless, attended by vampires. *En-lil* means "Lord of Ghosts," and he was the destroyer in the deluge. *Utukku* meant "demon," a ghost escaped from the dead; and another name for demon was *ekimmu*, a being which took delight in obsessing the living. The demons were numberless, had their dwelling in the desert, and were malign in their activities, working harm in all relations of life. So of other spirits it might be said that they swarmed—on the earth, in the air, under the earth, in the waters; there were spirits for every sort of existence and they controlled or might affect for good or ill every deed, even the thoughts and dreams, of men. The actions of even the good spirits might be inimical; the bad spirits must ever be guarded against. Hence there had grown up in the earliest times known an empirical magic, a routine of enchantment, a ritual of spells, the forms and practise of which are vouched for by hundreds of tablets. Since sickness, disease, and misfortune were often believed to be due to the malignity of evil powers, self-determined or directed by the evilly disposed among men, the means of release lay in charms or enchantments which included the employment of formulas, or which used fire, water, herbs, or metals without magical sayings. Series of incantation rituals have been discovered, named from the demons they aim to foil or from the parts of the body affected by illness, or from the means used in the exorcism. And these remained potent throughout the existence of Babylonia as a realm and then continued their power in the West whither they were transplanted. Other signs of the animism once existent are found in the animal forms of the gods, while the ritual of worship led the worshiper to figure forth his relationship to the god by assuming raiment which typified animal or other forms of life. This is Sumerian; the development under Semitism was anthropomorphic. On the other hand, man was himself deified—this was the case with Naram-Sin, while Gudea and Gimil-Sin erected temples to their own godhead.

5. Spirits and Demons.

6. Magic.

The transition to polytheism never involves complete dissolution of the prior animism. Survivals of the older faith ever perpetuate ancient practise. The gods of Babylonia evolved from the spirits; in some cases the process can almost be measured, but the spirits lived on. By 4500 B.C., however, there were already great deities whose majesty was acknowledged beyond their own cities.

2. The Gods: The deities who were earliest grouped in a triad were Anu, Bel (En-lil), and Ea. Of these Anu (Sumerian *Ana*), or Bel-shamayim, "Lord of heaven," as he came to be considered, appears to have been first localized at a place called Der, not otherwise known, and subsequently worshiped at Erech. He was the nearest to an abstraction of all Babylonian deities and the first to be disassociated from local connections and universalized (fourth millennium B.C.). Perhaps because of this disassociation he was the oftener invoked in prayer and incantation. The assignment of a supramundane region of control marks the beginning of priestly philosophy. Lugal-zaggisi claimed to be Anu's priest, and it was this king who first, so far as is yet known, united in a triad the three gods just mentioned. Anu was often known as *ilu*, the god *par excellence*, with whom other deities took refuge. He was called the father of Ishtar, and his consort was Antum (Semitic *Anat*), perhaps remembered in the birthplace of Jeremiah, Anathoth.

1. Anu.

Of Bel or En-lil, god of Nippur, much has already been said. His commanding position, compelling homage from hostile kings, was gained before the making of the first records which have so far been recovered. Bel's Sumerian ideograph represents the ram (suggesting a totemistic connection), while the meaning of his name, "Lord of Spirits," or "demons," has already been noted. In an inscription of Enshagkushanna Bel is named "King of the Lands," the one explicit statement of his eminence among the gods. In accordance with his name he was lord of the underworld, and as such was especially concerned with incantations. His consort was the Sumerian goddess Nin-harsag, the "Lady of the Mountain" (Semitic *Belit*), and his temple was E-kur, "Mountain-House." The preeminence he had was lost to Marduk when Babylon became the chief city and its god assumed the principal place in the pantheon.

2. Bel.

The third member of the triad and god of Eridu, Ea (Sumerian *En-ki*, "Lord of the Country"), had the waters as his division of the universe. The earliest traditions connect him with the Persian Gulf, whence he used to emerge daily to instruct his people in the civilizing arts. As associated with the deep, he became god of the river Euphrates, and then of the river which, according to Babylonian cosmography, encircled the earth. As a water-deity he was a god of knowledge, therefore of culture, light, beneficence, and healing. And by these same attributes he was also a god of cunning and beguiled the first man out of immortality. His oracles came by the roar of the surf on the shore. He was depicted also as half man, half fish, and his worshipers are pictured in robes which mimic the skin of a fish, again suggesting totemism, an indication not lessened by the fact that his ideograph stands also for "antelope." As god of wisdom it was inevitable that Ea should have part in incantations. His attitude toward humanity is generally beneficent, and he is called the creator of men. His consort, Damkina, a Sumerian deity, was originally independent. They are credited with a son Asari, with whom Marduk was identified in order to legitimate his claim to the chief place among the gods. Each of the three deities associated with Eridu can be traced backward to animistic origins.

3. Ea.

The second triad consisted of Shamash (sun-god), Sin (moon-god), and Ramman or Adad (thunder- or cloud-god). That the sun could not escape worship in such a land as Babylonia is a foregone conclusion, and that the deity of the sun should take different names was almost as inevitable. So of sun-gods there were, e.g., Utu in Larsa, Shamash in Sippar, Nergal in Cutha, Za-mal-mal in Kish. Marduk was originally solar. That the sun's activity should be viewed in different ways is also natural, hence some of the deities mentioned remained distinct. But that gods of different cities having similar aspects should be identified was to be expected in accordance with the laws of religious evolution.

4. Solar Deities. Shamash.

So Shamash came to be worshiped in different centers, the sun-deities of those places being identified with him, while others like Ninib and Nergal were differentiated and given special functions as sun-gods of the morning and springtime or of noon and summer. The powers attributed to Shamash in his two principal seats of Sippar and Larsa were such as belonged to the kindly god of light,—powers of healing and revelation, as well as of protection by detection and punishment of crime. He was given as consort Nin-A, a Sumerian deity originally male, who under Semitic misunderstanding was made to change his sex. Another explanation, less probable, is that the change of sex is a sign of subordination of the Sumerian to the Semitic god.

5. Lunar Deities. Sin.

If the worship of sun-deities was notable, not less so was that of moon-gods. Both Semites and Sumerians encouraged the cult, but there are many signs that among the latter it was a favorite. So En-zu, "Lord of Wisdom," and Nan-nar, "Giver of Light," were names the Sumerians bestowed on this deity. Nan-nar's principal seat was at Ur, connected with Abraham in the Biblical narrative. As Sin, a Semitic deity, he was located at Harran, also associated with Abraham, and he gave its name to the mountain and peninsula of Sinai. It is noteworthy that at Harran the god's image took the form of a conical pillar, and this suggests another phase of animism, that of the phallic cult. With Nannar-Sin also was connected the attribute of imparting wisdom, giving knowledge, particularly of measures.

6. Adad or Ramman.

The third member of this triad was Adad (also read *Ramman*, the Rimmon of Syria), god of storms. This is the one deity whose localization never seems to have been effected. He seems to have developed out of the storm-spirits. His nature led him to be regarded both as beneficent and malevolent. The rains brought destruction, and also fertilization, to the fields. So he was invoked to bring blessing to friends and misfortune to foes. Perhaps this led to his association with Shamash in the function of punishing evil-doers. His consort was Shala, never an important deity, and her ideograph could represent also a milch-goat.

7. Ishtar.

A deity sometimes displacing Adad as third member of this triad was the great Ishtar. In Arabia and Moab Athtar was male. In one case in Babylonia a male god was identified with her, and androgyny is there in sight. She was patroness of Erech, and had shrines in many towns. She was too strong a personality to be the mere consort of a deity. The attempt was made to wed her; but it involved either that her consort should be subordinate because of her greatness, a thing unthinkable for Semites, or that she should be reduced to passivity, which that same greatness forbade. She is noted for the absorption and comprehension in her being of all the noted goddesses of old Babylonia. Ninharsag of Erech (the great mother), the war-deity Nana of Erech, Nina of Shirpurla, Anunit (Sumerian *Anuna*) of Sippar, all yielded up their personalities to Ishtar as she grew in greatness, and her name came to be a synonym for "goddess." She even disdained the feminine termination *ah* in her name, and she was the *Belit*, "Mistress," as Marduk was *Bel*, "Lord," of the land. At her principal temple at Erech impure worship was a part of her ritual.

8. Nergal.

Nergal, already mentioned as personifying the sun's destructive action, was worshiped at Cutha in the temple E-shidlam, "House of Shade," at least from the time of Dungi till c. 700 B.C. He was a god of the dead in conjunction with Allatu, this flowing naturally from his office as destroyer. He, too, absorbed other deities (e.g., Ira, a fire-god) and took others as his servitors (e.g., Namtar, the plague-god). His consort as god of the dead was Eresh-Kigal, as a god of the living Laz. The pantheon of the dead was a late scholastic development.

9. Ninib, Girru, and Tammuz.

Ninib and Girru (Assyrian *Nusku*) were two deities who had absorbed a number of earlier gods. The former was connected with agriculture and war, the latter with the sun and with fire. Girru was also a victor over demons, and as such was much invoked in incantations. Tammuz (Sumerian *Dumu-zi*) was originally a sun-god, son of Ea and bridegroom of Ishtar, a culture god of Eridu, of note chiefly because of his being the cause of Ishtar's descent into Hades which is the theme of one of the epics. In Syria he was Adonai, "my lord," and gave the Greeks their Adonis (cf. on the name Ninib, J. D. Prince, in *JBL*, xxiv, 1905, part 1, p. 54).

10. Marduk.

Marduk, the youngest of Babylonian deities, supreme in Bablyonia from c. 2250 till the fall of the Semitic power, owed his position first to the political preeminence of Babylon, secondly to priestly ingenuity which connected him with En-lil and then manufactured the fiction that because of Marduk's victory over Tiamat En-lil resigned to him his supremacy. To clear the way, Marduk was identified with Asari, son of En-lil. He was probably a sun-god, though his name seems to come from *Amar-duggu*, "good heifer," a title of Asari. Hammurabi seems to have been the first to declare his supremacy. Nabonidus appears to have attempted to carry this supremacy a step further and to have been thwarted by the priesthood. As it was, Marduk was never to Babylonia what Zeus was to Greece.

Nebo (from the same root as Hebrew *nabhi*, "prophet"; Sumerian *Dim-sar*, "Wise Scribe"), god of Borsippa, originally superior to Marduk, was subjected to the latter by being made his son. He was god of utterance, wisdom, revelation, writing, and culture. There appears to have been a connection with Ea of Eridu, but exactly what is not yet made out. As the god of wisdom Nebo

11. Nebo.

was readily dissociated from local connections, and was even adopted in Assyria. Indeed he took on universal functions as the god of prophecy. As such he was kindly, and none of the dread which attached to thoughts of other deities appears in mention of him.

3. The Priests and the Epics: The type of worship has already been indicated in the article on Assyria. Among the kingly functions sacrifice continued. The priests were numerous, and though they appear little in the texts, their influence can always be read between the lines. The ill-starred attempt of Nabonidus to make Marduk more than

1. Influence of the Priests.

he had been, to set him in a place like that of Asshur's in Assyria, was doubtless frustrated by priestly opposition. As the scribes, the teachers, the molders of theology and myth, in a country so devoted to a religion of set forms, the priests had an influence which can hardly be exaggerated. The cosmogony which is most in evidence is manifestly of their make and postdates the rise of Babylon to preeminence, since in it Marduk is conqueror of the rebellious *Tiamat*, "chaos," and out of her rent body creates the universe and then human kind.

The three epics contain earlier material and doubtless took form before Semitism laid its hands upon them. The Gilgamesh epic is the earliest which contains the world-wide thought of a means of escape from death. In this case it is a tree, and

2. The Gilgamesh Epic.

after obtaining a scion and curing his own mortal illness Gilgamesh lost the scion while on his way home, it being stolen from him by a serpent as he was drinking from a spring. Here occur elements of comparison with the Genesis tree of life in the midst of the garden (not the tree of knowledge of which the first pair ate), and the serpent is also in evidence. A further point for comparison is that Gilgamesh was in opposition to deity in the person of Ishtar, not indeed by eating of the fruit of the tree but by slaying of a sacred bull. The eleventh tablet of the series contained the Babylonian deluge narrative (see Noah). A second epic connected

3. The Adapa Epic.

with Eridu tells the story of the first man, Adapa (which name it has been proposed to read *Adamu*, cf. *Expository Times*, June, 1906, p. 416–417), and how he too just missed immortality through the guile of Ea. He was summoned to heaven to answer for breaking the wings of the south wind. Ea warned him not to partake of food while there, and by his obedience he failed of the immortality that the "food of life," which was offered him, would have bestowed (see Adam, II, § 5). The third epic,

4. Marduk and Chaos.

dealing with Marduk's contest with the demon, Chaos, has two points of interest: first, it bears upon its face its date, not earlier than Hammurabi, under whom it probably took form; second, it is manifestly a plagiarism from a much earlier story in which Ea was the hero who vanquished Apsu, "the deep," and then became creator and protector of men. A fourth narrative, which hovers between epic

5. Ishtar's Descent Into Hades.

and ritual, concerns the bereaval of Ishtar in the loss of her bridegroom Tammuz, to recover whom she descends into Hades. This narrative is late, its description of the environment of the underworld exhibiting the refinements of Semitic elaboration. Geo. W. Gilmore.

Bibliography: The works cited under Assyria (q.v.) generally deal also with Babylonia and should be consulted. General works are F. Lenormant, *Études cunéiformes*, 5 parts, Paris, 1878–80; J. Menant, *Nineveh et Babylon*, ib. 1887; H. Hilprecht, *Assyriaca. Eine Nachlese auf dem Gebiete der Assyriologie*, Halle, 1894; C. Fossey, *Manuel d'Assyriologie*, vol. i, Paris, 1904 (on explorations, decipherment, and origin and history of the cuneiform); B. Meissner, *Assyriologische Studien*, 1–3, Berlin, 1903–05. Additional sources are: P. Haupt, *Die sumerischen Familiengesetze*, Leipsic, 1879; J. Halévy, *Documents religieux de l'Assyrie et de la Babylonie*, Paris, 1882; vol. iii of E. Schrader's *Keilinschriftliche Bibliothek*, Berlin, 1890–92, contains historical inscriptions from Urukagina to Cyrus; H. Hilprecht, *Babylonian Expedition of the University of Pennsylvania, Series A, Cuneiform Texts*, vol. i, parts 1–2, vol. ix, Philadelphia, 1893–98; L. W. King, *Letters and Inscriptions of Hammurabi . and other Kings of the First Dynasty of Babylon*, 3 vols., London, 1898–1900 (vol. iii contains translations); J. A. Craig, *Assyrian and Babylonian Religious Texts*, vols. i, ii, *Prayers, Oracles, Hymns*, Leipsic, 1895–97; idem, *Astrological-Astronomical Tablets*, ib. 1899; I. M. Price, *The Great Cylinder Inscriptions A and B of Gudea transliterated and translated*, Leipsic, 1899; F. Martin, *Textes religieux Assyriens et Babyloniens*, Paris, 1900 (contains transcription, transl., and commentary); V. Scheil, *Textes élamites*, 3 vols., ib. 1901–04; C. H. W. Johns, *An Assyrian Doomsday Book or Liber censualis*, Leipsic, 1901; idem, *Babylonian and Assyrian Laws, Contracts and Letters*, Edinburgh, 1904; R. F. Harper, *Assyrian and Babylonian Letters*, Chicago, 1902–04; G. A. Barton, *Haverford Library Collection of Cuneiform Tablets . from . Telloh*, Philadelphia, 1905; S. Langdon, *Building Inscriptions of the Neo-Babylonian Empire*, part 1, *Nabopolassar and Nebuchadrezzar*, Paris, 1905 (transliteration, transl., and introduction).

On exploration consult the works of Rogers (vol. i) and Hilprecht (*Explorations*) mentioned under Assyria, that of Fossey, ut sup., and J. P. Peters, *Nippur; or, Explorations and Adventures on the Euphrates*, 2 vols., New York, 1897; A. Billerbeck, *Geographische Untersuchungen*, Berlin, 1898.

On the people: G. Hüsing, *Elamische Studien*, Berlin, 1898; H. Ranke, *Die Personnamen in den Urkunden der Hammurabidynastie*, Munich, 1902; H. Winckler, *Die Völker Vorderasiens*, Leipsic, 1899. On the cuneiform writing: J. Menant, *Le Syllabaire Assyrien, exposé des éléments*, 2 vols., Paris, 1869–73; T. Nöldeke, *Some Characteristics of the Semitic Race*, in *Sketches from Eastern History*, New York, 1892; F. Delitzsch, *Die Entstehung des ältesten Schriftsystems*, 2 parts, Leipsic, 1897–98; F. Thureau-Dangin, *Recherches sur l'origine de l'écriture cunéiforme*, part 1, *Formes archaïques*, Paris, 1898; F. E. Peiser, *Studien zur orientalischen Altertumskunde. Das semitische Alphabet*, Berlin, 1900; A. Amiaud et L. Mechineau, *Tableau comparé des écritures Babylonienne et Assyrienne*, 2d ed., Paris, 1902. For lexicography consult: Fr. Delitzsch, *Assyrisches Wörterbuch*, Leipsic, 1888–90; R. E. Brunnow, *Classified List of Ideographs*, Leiden, 1889; E. Scheil, *Syllabaire, Recueil de signes archaïques* , Paris, 1898; J. D. Prince, *Materials for a Sumerian Lexicon*, Leipsic, 1905. On grammar consult J. Menant, *Manuel de la langue Assyrienne*, Paris, 1880. On the Sumerian question: E. de Chossat, *Répertoire Sumérien*, Lyons, 1882; F. Hommel, in *Journal Royal Asiatic Society*, 1886; idem, *Sumerische Lesestücke*, Munich, 1894; J. Halévy, *Notes Sumériennes*, in *Revue sémitique*, i x (1893 1902); F. H. Weissbach, *Die sumerische Frage*, Leipsic, 1898; T. G. Pinches and C. P. Tiele, *Akkadian and Sumerian*, in *Journal Royal Asiatic*

Society, xxxii (1900), 75–96, 343–344, 551–552; E. Babelon, *La Langue sumérienne*, in *Annales de philosophie Chrétienne*, vii, 35–57, 171–189.

On the civilization and its influences consult: F. S. Peiser, *Skizze der babylonischen Gesellschaft*, Berlin, 1896; A. S. Palmer, *Babylonian Influence on the Bible and Popular Beliefs. . . a Comparative Study of Gen. i–ii*, London, 1897; A. H. Sayce, *Babylonian and Assyrian Life and Customs*, New York, 1899; I. M. Price, *The Monuments and the O. T.*, Chicago, 1900; H. Zimmern, *The Babylonian and the Hebrew Genesis*, London, 1901; H. Winckler, *Die babylonische Kultur in ihren Beziehungen zu unsrigen*, Leipsic, 1902; H. Zimmern, *Keilinschriften und Bibel*, Berlin, 1903; F. Küchler, *Beiträge zur Kenntnis der . . Medizin*, Leipsic, 1904; C. F. Lehmann, *Babylonien's Kulturmission*, ib. 1905; W. St. C. Boscawen, *Prehistoric Civilization of Babylonia*, in *Journal Anthropological Institute*, vii, 21–36; and the literature in the "Babel-Bibel" controversy.

For the history books available are: C. Niebuhr, *Die Chronologie . . 2000–700 vor Christus*, Leipsic, 1896; H. Winckler, *Die babylonische Kassitendynastie*, ib. 1894; idem, *Die politische Entwickelung Babyloniens und Assyriens*, ib. 1900; F. Hommel, *Ancient Hebrew Tradition*, London, 1897; G. S. Goodspeed, *History of Babylonians . . .*, New York, 1902; H. Radau, *Early Babylonian History*, New York, 1900 (of the very highest value, based on first-hand study of texts); W. St. C. Boscawen, *First of Empires*, New York, 1905 (suggestive, but slovenly in its references); T. Friedrich, *Altbabylonische Urkunden aus Sippara*, Leipsic, 1906 (fresh, instructive). Special subjects related to the history are treated in: J. N. Strassmaier, *Inschriften von Nabonidus*, 4 parts, Leipsic, 1887–89; C. F. Lehmann, *Shamashshumukin*, ib. 1892; B. Meissner, *Beiträge zum altbabylonischen Privatrecht*, ib. 1893; H. Winckler, *Altorientalische Forschungen*, vi and viii, 2, ib. 1899 (deal with Nebuchadrezzar); I. M. Price, *Some Literary Remains of Rim-Sin (Arioch), c. 2285*, Chicago, 1904; Nebuchadrezzar inscriptions are found in *PSBA*, x, 87–129, 358–368, and in Schrader, *KB*, iii, part 2, 10–45; *Assyrian and Babylonian Literature, Selected Translations*, New York, 1901, contains inscriptions of both Nebuchadrezzars, Nabupalidin, Nabopolassar, Nabonidus, the Synchronous History, the Babylonian chronicle, most of the epical fragments, magical and other texts, prayers, hymns, penitential psalms, laws, and proverbs.

On the Religion: A. Jeremias, *Die babylonisch-assyrischen Vorstellungen vom Leben nach dem Tode*, Leipsic, 1887; idem, *The Babylonian Conception of Heaven and Hell*, in *Ancient East*, No. 4, London, 1902; H. Zimmern, *Babylonische Busspsalmen*, Leipsic, 1885; idem, *Beiträge zur Kenntnis der babylonischen Religion*, 3 parts, ib. 1896–1900; G. A. Barton, *Semitic Ishtar Cult*, in *Hebraica*, Apr.–July, 1893, Oct., 1893–Jan. 1894; J. A. Knudtzon, *Assyrische Gebete an den Sonnengott*, 2 vols., ib. 1893; L. W King, *Babylonian Religion and Mythology*, London, 1899; F. Hrozny, *Sumerisch-babylonische Mythen von dem Gotte Nimrag* (Ninib), Berlin, 1903; by far the best treatise on the religion is by Jastrow, in *DB*, Supplementary Volume, pp. 531–584. On Magic: A. Laurent, *La Magie et la divination chez les Chaldéo-Assyriens*, Paris, 1894; L. W King, *Babylonian Magic and Sorcery*, London, 1896; *Reports of the Magicians and Astrologers of Babylon*, vol. i, *Text*, vol. ii, *Transl.*, ib. 1900; C. Fossey, *La Magie Assyrienne*, Paris, 1902. On the epics: P. Haupt, *Babylonische Nimrodepos*, 2 parts, Leipsic, 1884–91; M. Jastrow, *A Fragment of the Babylonian "Dibarra" Epic*, Philadelphia, 1891; A. Jeremias, *Izdubar-Nimrod*, Leipsic, 1891; P. Jensen, *Assyrisch-babylonische Mythen und Epen*, in *KB*, Berlin, 1900–01; idem, *Das Gilgamesh-Epos in der Weltliteratur*, vol. i, Strassburg, 1906; L. W. King, *Seven Tablets of Creation . .* , London, 1902; B. Meissner, *Ein . . . Fragment des Gilgamosepos*, Berlin, 1902.

BABYLONIAN EXILE: 1. Of the Hebrews. See Israel. **2.** Of the popes. See Avignon.

BACCANARISTS. See Paccanari, Nicolo.

BACH, bɑн, JOHANN SEBASTIAN: Musician; b. at Eisenach Mar. 21, 1685; d. at Leipsic July 28, 1750. He belonged to a family which through several generations had distinguished itself by musical talent; lost his parents early, and had, from his fourteenth year, to provide for his own education. In 1703 he was appointed court-musician in Weimar; and in 1723, already one of the most celebrated musicians of the time, he was made cantor and director of church music at Leipsic. His celebrity during his lifetime he owed mainly to his skill as an organist and pianist; his compositions were not appreciated till a later age. They consist chiefly of church music, oratorios, masses, etc., for organ and orchestra, for instruments as well as for the human voice; after his death the manuscripts were divided among his sons, and remained unnoticed till the time of Mendelssohn. See Music, Sacred.

Bibliography: P. Spitta, *Johann Sebastian Bach*, 2 vols., Leipsic, 1873–80, Eng. transl., 3 vols., London, 1884–86; C. F. A. Williams, *Bach*, in *Master Musicians* series, New York, 1900; H. Barth, *Johann Sebastian Bach, ein Lebensbild*, Berlin, 1902; A. Pirro, *Johann Sebastian Bach, the Organist, and his Works, from the French*, New York, 1903; A. Schweitzer, *J. S. Bach, le musicien poète*, Leipsic, 1905; Philipp Wolfrum, *Johann Sebastian Bach*, Berlin, 1906.

BACH, JOSEPH: Roman Catholic; b. at Aislingen (22 m. n.w. of Augsburg), Bavaria, May 4, 1833; d. at Munich Sept. 22, 1901. He studied philosophy and theology in the University of Munich; became privat-docent there, 1865; professor extraordinary of theology, 1867; ordinary professor of philosophy of religion and pedagogics, and university preacher, 1872. He wrote: *Die Siebenzahl der Sacramente* (Regensburg, 1864); *Meister Eckhart* (Vienna, 1864); *Propst Gerhoch von Reichersberg* (1865); *Die Dogmengeschichte des Mittelalters vom christologischen Standpunkte, oder die mittelalterliche Christologie vom 8. bis 16. Jahrhundert* (2 vols., 1873–75); *Joseph von Görres* (Freiburg, 1876); *Des Albertus Magnus Verhältniss zur Erkenntnisslehre der Griechen, Lateiner, Araber, und Juden* (Vienna, 1881); *Ueber das Verhältniss des Système de la Nature zur Wissenschaft der Gegenwart* (Cologne, 1884); *Der heilige Rock zu Trier* (Frankfort, 1891); *Die Trierer Heiligtumsfahrt im Jahre 1891* (Strasburg, 1892).

Bibliography: A. Schmid, *Lebens-Bild des . . . Joseph Bach*, Kempten, 1902.

BACHER, bɑн'er, WILHELM: Hungarian Jewish Orientalist; b. at Liptó-Szent-Miklós (65 m. s.w. of Cracow), Hungary, Jan. 12, 1850. He was educated at the Evangelical Lyceum of Pressburg, and the universities of Budapest, Breslau, and Leipsic (Ph.D., 1870). He was graduated from the Jewish Theological Seminary of Breslau as rabbi in 1876 and was appointed to the rabbinate of Szegedin. In the following year, however, the Hungarian government chose him to be one of the professors of the new *Landesrabbinerschule* at Budapest, where he has since taught on a great variety of subjects. In 1878 he was a field-chaplain in the Austro-Hungarian army of occupation in Bosnia. Seven years later he was appointed director of the Talmud Torah school in Budapest, an institution with which he is still connected. In 1894 he was one of the founders of the Jewish literary society *Izraelita Magyar Irodami Társulat*, of which he was elected vice-president four years later. His chief works, in addit on to numerous contributions to scientific periodicals and various encyclopedias, are *Nizâmi's Leben und Werke, und der zweite Theil des Nizâmi'schen Alexanderbuches* (Leipsic, 1871); *Muslicheddin Sa'adi's Aphorismen und Sinngedichte, zum ersten Male herausgegeben und übersetzt* (Strasburg, 1879); *Die Agada der babylonischen Amoräer* (1878); *Die Agada der Tannaiten* (2 vols., 1884–90); *Leben und Werke des Abulwalîd Merwân ibn Ganâḥ und die Quellen seiner Schrifterklärung* (1885); *Die Agada der palästinischen Amoräer* (3 vols., 1892–99); *Die hebräische Sprachwissenschaft vom zehnten bis zum sechzehnten Jahrhundert* (Treves, 1892); *Die Bibelexegese der jüdischen Religionsphilosophen des Mittelalters vor Maimûni* (Strasburg, 1892); *Die Anfänge der hebräischen Grammatik* (1895); *Die Bibelexegese Maimûni's* (1896); *Die älteste Terminologie der jüdischen Schriftauslegung* (2 vols., 1899–1905); *Ein hebräisch-persisches Wörterbuch aus dem vierzehnten Jahrhundert* (1900); and *Aus dem Wörterbuch Tanchum Jeruschalmi's* (1903). In 1884 he and Joseph Bánóczi founded the *Magyar Zsidó Szemle*, which they edited for seven years, and which is still the only Jewish review in Hungary.

BACHIARIUS, bak-i-ā'ri-us: An author, presumably a monk (cf. Gennadius of Marseilles, *Script. eccl.*, xxiv), to whom are ascribed two writings: (1) a *Liber de fide*, in which he defends his orthodoxy against attacks, probably of the Priscillianists (cf. Priscillian, ed. G. Schepss, *CSEL*, xviii, 1889, index, p. 167); and (2) a *Liber de reparatione lapsi ad Januarium*, in which he takes the part of a monk whose offenses against morality had been treated with extreme rigor by his abbot.

G. Krüger.

Bibliography: The works are in *MPL*, xx. Consult Fessler-Jungmann, *Institutiones patrologiæ*, vol. ii, part 1, 418–427 Innsbruck, 1892; S. Berger, *Histoire de la Vulgate*, p. 28, Nancy, 1893; G. L. Hahn, *Bibliothek der Symbole*, § 208, Leipsic, 1897; F. Kattenbusch, *Das apostolische Symbol*, i–ii, passim, Leipsic, 1894–1900.

BACHMANN, bāH'mān **(GEORG), PHILIPP:** German Protestant; b. at Geislingen (34 m. s.e. of Stuttgart) Oct. 13, 1864. He was educated at the University of Erlangen (Ph.D., 1887) and the seminary for preachers at Munich (1888). He was a lecturer at Erlangen in 1888–90, and pastor at Urfersheim in 1890–92, after which he was a teacher of religion at Nuremberg until 1902, when he was appointed professor of systematic theology at Erlangen. He has written *Die persönliche Heilserfahrung* (Leipsic, 1889); *Die augsburgische Confession* (1900); *Sittenlehre Jesu* (1904); and *Kommentar zu I Korinther* (1905).

BACHMANN, JOHANNES FRANZ JULIUS: Lutheran; b. at Berlin Feb. 24, 1832; d. at Rostock Apr. 12, 1888. He studied at Halle and Berlin, became privat-docent at Berlin, 1856, ordinary professor of theology at Rostock, 1858, also university preacher, 1874. In his student days Tholuck and Hengstenberg attracted him most, and it was in large measure the learning, ingenuity, and firmness of the latter in defending tradition which influenced Bachmann to devote himself especially to the investigation of the Old Testament. His theological position may be thus characterized: The conception of prophecy seemed to him determined by the mode of its fulfilment; for this reason he believed that the spiritual, not the literal, exposition of the Old Testament should be followed. Nevertheless, he tried to avoid the one-sided spiritualism which Hengstenberg espoused in his earlier works. His scholarship in his chosen field is evident in two works, *Die Festgesetze des Pentateuchs aufs neue kritisch untersucht* (Berlin, 1858), in which he endeavors to prove, against Hupfeld, the harmonious unity of the festival laws of the Pentateuch; and in his unfinished commentary on the Book of Judges (Berlin, 1868), upon which he had spent years of labor. Of this work George F. Moore remarks (*Commentary on Judges*, New York, 1895, 1): "By far the fullest recent commentary on Judges is that of J. Bachmann, which was unfortunately never carried beyond the fifth chapter. The author's standpoint is that of Hengstenberg, and he is a stanch opponent of modern criticism of every shade and school; but in range and accuracy of scholarship, and exhaustive thoroughness of treatment, his volume stands without a rival." Bachmann also wrote with reverence and learning a biography of his teacher Hengstenberg (2 vols., Gütersloh, 1876–80).

E. König.

Bibliography: H. Behm, *Johannes Bachmann*, Rostock, 1888 (by his son-in-law).

BACILIERI, bā"chî-lî-ê'ri, **BARTOLOMEO:** Cardinal-priest; b. at Breonio (near Verona), Italy, Mar. 28, 1842. He was educated at Verona and the Collegio Capranica, Rome, and after long service in the priesthood, was consecrated titular bishop of Nyssa in 1888, at the same time being appointed bishop coadjutor of Verona. Three years later he became bishop of the latter see, and in 1901 was created cardinal-priest of San Bartolomeo all'Isola. He is a member of the congregations of the Index and of Indulgences and Relics.

BACON, BENJAMIN WISNER: Congregationalist; b. at Litchfield, Conn., Jan. 15, 1860. He was graduated at Yale in 1881 and the Yale Divinity School 1884, and held successive Congregational pastorates at Old Lyme, Conn. (1884–89), and Oswego, N. Y. (1889–96). In 1896 he became instructor in New Testament Greek in the Yale Divinity School, and in 1897 Buckingham professor of New Testament criticism and interpretation. In addition to numerous briefer contributions and a translation of Wildeboer's *Het Ontstaan van den Kanon des Ouden Verbonds* (Groningen, 1889) under the title *The Origin of the Canon of the Old Testament* (London, 1895), he has written *The Genesis of Genesis* (Hartford, 1891); *Triple Tradition of the Exodus* (1894); *Introduction to the New Testament* (New York, 1900); *The Sermon on the Mount* (1902); and *The Story of St. Paul* (Boston, 1905).

BACON, FRANCIS: English philosopher and statesman; b. in London Jan. 22, 1561, son of Sir Nicholas Bacon (b. 1509; d. 1579), Lord Keeper of the Great Seal under Elizabeth; d. at Highgate, near London, Apr. 9, 1626. He studied at Trinity College, Cambridge, 1573-75, and in 1576 was admitted to Gray's Inn. He entered parliament in 1584, became one of the leading lawyers of England, and rose through various posts in the public service until he reached the Lord Chancellorship in 1618. The same year he was raised to the peerage as Baron Verulam, and three years later was made Viscount St. Albans. In 1621 he was charged with accepting bribes, and was tried and found guilty; his offices were taken from him, he was sentenced to a fine of £40,000, to imprisonment during the king's pleasure, and was disabled from sitting in parliament and coming within twelve miles of the court. Feeling his disgrace keenly, he went into retirement and devoted the remainder of his life to study and literary work. The parliamentary sentence, however, was not imposed, for the king (James I) practically remitted his fine and in 1622 he was allowed to come to London.

Life.

As philosopher and man of letters Bacon's fame is in bright contrast to his sad failure in public life. His philosophy is contained chiefly in the various parts and fragments of a work which he called *Instauratio magna* and which he left incomplete; the most important part is the *Novum organum* (published 1620). His philosophy is a method rather than a system; but the influence of this method in the development of British thought can hardly be overestimated. As Luther was the reformer of religion, so Bacon was the reformer of philosophy. Luther had claimed that the Scripture was to be interpreted by private judgment, not by authority. The problem of Bacon was to suggest a method of interpreting nature. The old method afforded no fruits. It "flies from the senses and particulars" to the most general laws, and then applies deduction. This is the "anticipation of nature." To it Bacon opposes the "interpretation of nature." Nature is to be interpreted, not by the use of the deductive syllogism, but by the induction of facts, by a gradual ascent from facts, through intermediate laws called "axioms," to the forms of nature. Before beginning this induction, the inquirer is to free his mind from certain false notions or tendencies which distort the truth. These are called "Idols" (*idola*), and are of four kinds: "Idols of the Tribe" (*idola tribus*), which are common to the race; "Idols of the Den" (*idola specus*), which are peculiar to the individual; "Idols of the Market-place" (*idola fori*), coming from the misuse of language; and "Idols of the Theater" (*idola theatri*), which result from an abuse of authority. The end of induction is the discovery of forms, the ways in which natural phenomena occur, the causes from which they proceed. Nature is not to be interpreted by a search after final causes. "Nature to be commanded must be obeyed." Philosophy will then be fruitful. Faith is shown by works. Philosophy is to be known by fruits.

Bacon's Philosophy.

In the application of this method in the physical and moral world, Bacon himself accomplished but little. His system of morals, if system it may be called, is to be gathered from the seventh and eighth books of his *De augmentis scientiarum* (1623; a translation into Latin and expansion of an earlier English work, the *Advancement of Learning*, 1605), and from his *Essays* (first ed., 10 essays, 1597; ed. with 38 essays, 1612; final ed., 58 essays, 1625). Moral action means action of the human will. The will is governed by reason. Its spur is the passions. The moral object of the will is the good. Bacon, like the ancient moralists, failed to distinguish between the good and the right. He finds fault with the Greek and Roman thinkers for disputing about the chief good. It is a question of religion, not of ethics. His moral doctrine has reference exclusively to this world. Duty is only that which one owes to the community. Duty to God is an affair of religion. The cultivation of the will in the direction of the good is accomplished by the formation of a habit. For this Bacon lays down certain precepts. No general rules can be made for moral action under all circumstances. The characters of men differ as their bodies differ.

Ethics.

Bacon separates distinctly religion and philosophy. The one is not incompatible with the other; for "a little philosophy inclineth man's mind to atheism, but depth in philosophy bringeth men's minds about to religion." Bacon has been sometimes regarded as a defender of unbelief, because he opposed the search after final causes in the interpretation of nature. But it is one thing to discourage the search after final causes in science, it is another thing to deny the existence of final causes. "I had rather believe," he says, "all the fables in the Legend and the Talmud and the Alcoran than that this universal frame is without a mind" (*Essay on Atheism*). The object of scientific inquiry should be the "form," not the final cause.

Relation Between Philosophy and Religion.

While philosophy is not atheistic it does not inform religion. Tertullian, Pascal, and Bacon agree in proclaiming the separation of the two domains. Tertullian and Pascal do it to save religion from rationalism; Bacon does it to save philosophy from the "Idols." *Credo quia absurdum* is expressed in the following words: "But that faith which was accounted to Abraham for righteousness was of such a nature that Sarah laughed at it, who therein was an image of natural reason. The more discordant, therefore, and incredible, the divine mystery is, the more honor is shown to God in believing it, and the nobler is the victory of faith" (*De augmentis*, bk. ix). Religion comes, therefore, not from the light of nature, but from that of revelation. "First he breathed light upon the face of the matter, or chaos, then he breathed light into the face of man, and still he breatheth and inspireth light into the face of his chosen" (*Essay on Truth*). One may employ reason to separate revealed from natural truth, and to draw inferences from the former; but we must not go to excess by inquiring too curiously into divine mysteries, nor attach the same authority to inferences as to principles. If Bacon was an atheist, as some claim, his writings are certainly not atheistic. He must, in that case, have been a hypocrite in order to be a flatterer, and, if a flatterer, a most foolish one. Yet the inductive method has given natural theology the facts which point most significantly to God.

Bibliography: Bacon's religious works are thus enumerated by Prof. Thomas Fowler: (1) the *Meditationes sacræ* (published with the *Essays*, 1597); (2) *A Confession of Faith* (written before 1603, published 1648); (3) a *Translation of Certain Psalms into English Verse* (composed during a fit of sickness 1624, published 1625); (4) three prayers, *The Student's Prayer*, *The Writer's Prayer*, and a third composed during his troubles (1621). The most complete and best edition of Bacon's *Works* is by J. Spedding, R. L. Ellis, and D. D. Heath, 7 vols., London, 1857–59, new ed., 1870, which is supplemented by Spedding's *Letters and Life*, 7 vols., 1861–74; abridged ed., 2 vols., 1878. Of numerous editions of special works, mention may be made of *The Advancement of Learning* by W. Aldis Wright, 4th ed., Oxford, 1891; the *Essays* by Archbishop Whately, London, 1856, 6th ed., 1864; by W. Aldis Wright, Cambridge, 1862; and by E. A. Abbott, 2 vols., London, 1876; and the *Novum organum*, translation and text by G. W. Kitchin, Oxford, 1855; text with introduction, notes, etc., by Thomas Fowler, 2d ed., ib. 1889. For the life of Bacon and criticism, consult Macaulay's famous essay (handy ed., by Longmans, 1904), which, however, is considered incorrect and unfair; Thomas Fowler, *Francis Bacon*, in the series of *English Philosophers*, London, 1881; idem, in *DNB*, ii, 328–360 (the best summary); R. W. Church, in the *English Men of Letters*, London, 1884; E. A. Abbott, *Francis Bacon: Account of his Life and Works*, ib. 1885; J. Nichol, *Francis Bacon, his Life and Philosophy*, 2 vols., ib. 1888–89, reissued, 1901.

BACON, LEONARD: Congregationalist; b. in Detroit, Mich., Feb. 19, 1802; d. in New Haven, Conn., Dec. 24, 1881. He was graduated at Yale in 1820, studied theology at Andover, became pastor of the First (Center) Church in New Haven in 1825, and retained his connection with the church during his life, after 1866 as pastor emeritus. He was instructor in revealed religion in the Yale Divinity School, 1866–71, and lecturer on church polity and American church history, 1871 till his death. He was one of the founders and early editors of *The New Englander* (1843) and of *The New York Independent* (1848). His published books include a life and selections from the works of Richard Baxter (2 vols., New Haven, 1830); *Thirteen Historical Discourses on the Completion of Two Hundred Years from the Beginning of the First Church in New Haven* (1839); *Slavery Discussed in Occasional Essays from 1833 to 1846* (New York, 1846); *The Genesis of the New England Churches* (1874). He possessed a marked individuality of character and was an able and influential leader in his denomination. He was prominent in the slavery contest, and was a prolific writer and frequent speaker upon all topics of social and political reform.

BACON, LEONARD WOOLSEY: Congregationalist; b. at New Haven, Conn., Jan. 1, 1830; d. at Assonet, Mass., May 12, 1907. He was educated at Yale (B.A., 1850); he studied theology at Andover and Yale (1854), and medicine at Yale (M.D., 1855). He was pastor of St. Peter's Presbyterian Church, Rochester, N. Y., in 1856–57 and of the Congregational Church at Litchfield, Conn., in 1857–60. He was missionary at large for Connecticut in 1861–62, and then held successive pastorates at Stamford, Conn. (1863–65), Brooklyn, N. Y. (1865–70), and Baltimore, Md. (1871–72). From 1872 to 1877 he was in Europe, and after his return to the United States was pastor at Norwich, Conn. (1878–82), Philadelphia (1883–86), and Augusta, Ga. (1886–88). Since 1901 he has been pastor of the Congregational Church at Assonet, Mass. He has edited *Congregational Hymn and Tune Book* (New Haven 1857); *The Book of Worship* (New York, 1865); *The Life, Speeches, and Discourses of Father Hyacinthe* (1872); *The Hymns of Martin Luther Set to their Original Melodies, with an English Version* (1883); and *The Church Book: Hymns and Tunes* (1883). He has also written *The Vatican Council* (New York, 1872); *Church Papers: Essays on Subjects Ecclesiastical and Social* (1876); *The Simplicity that Is in Christ* (1885); *Irenics and Polemics* (1898); *History of American Christianity* (1898) and *Story of the Congregationalists* (1904).

BACON (BACO), ROGER: The famous Franciscan theologian, called *doctor mirabilis*; b. at or near Ilchester (31 m. s. of Bristol), Somersetshire, 1214; d. at Oxford June 11, 1294. He studied first at Oxford, then at Paris, where he took the degree of doctor of holy scripture in 1248 and joined the order of St. Francis,—probably immediately after receiving his degree. In taking this step, he followed, it is said, the advice of the famous bishop of Lincoln, Robert Grosseteste (q.v.); but it is more probable that his countryman Adam of Marsh (*de Marisco*) from Bath, himself a Franciscan and professor of philosophy at Oxford (d. about 1260), induced him to join that order (cf. J. Felten, *Robert Grosseteste*, Freiburg, 1887, 94 sqq.). Bacon now taught in Oxford and Paris, though it can not be stated how long he stayed in either place.

On account of his deep insight into the realm of natural science, which was then little known, and because of the astonishing effects which his physical experiments produced upon pupils and other contemporaries, he was suspected of being a "magician" and astrologer, busying himself with illicit arts. Some accidental remarks of his on the influence of the stars upon human destiny may have furnished occasion for this surmise. There is no doubt that he was himself the scholar of whom he narrates that he was fined for making a burning-glass (*Op. maj.*, iii, 116). The many vexations which he experienced, especially at the hands of the friars, induced him to write to Pope Clement IV (formerly Guido Foulques), who as cardinal-legate in France and England had shown a friendly disposition toward him. Clement answered from Viterbo (Aug. 22, 1266) in a kindly manner, and requested Bacon to send some of his works. Accordingly he sent his *Opus majus* to Rome, and between 1266 and 1268 also the *Opus minus* and *Opus tertium*. A pupil of Bacon, the London magister John, seems to have taken an important part at that time in interpreting these works to the pope, and probably also produced and explained some instruments made by

Suspected and Persecuted as a Magician.

his teacher. The first investigation was favorable to the genial scholar, but a renewed charge which was brought against him by the general of the Franciscans, Jerome of Ascoli, during the pontificate of Nicholas III (1277–81), especially on account of the treatise *De vera astronomia*, ended with Bacon's imprisonment in a monastery either in Paris or at some other place in France. Ten years he thus spent behind the walls, but when Jerome had become Pope Nicholas IV, Bacon obtained his liberty through the recommendation of influential friends and was permitted to return to England.

Bacon belongs to those scientists of the Middle Ages who approached modern methods. On this account he criticizes sharply the scholastic method of instruction. In his *Compendium studii philosophiæ* he speaks disparagingly of Aristotle, Albert the Great, and Thomas Aquinas, whose "boyish" learning and effort he censures, also of the great Franciscan theologian Alexander of Hales. The attacks upon the latter explain in part the hostilities which he experienced from his fellow friars. In the *Opus majus* (treating in six sections "of the hindrances of philosophy; of the relation between theology and philosophy; of the study of languages; of mathematics; of optics; of experimental knowledge") his decidedly antischolastic standpoint is also evident.

Anticipation of Modern Methods and Discoveries. No less do we find this in his *Opus minus*, which endeavors to reproduce the contents of the *Opus principale* in an abbreviated form, and in the *Opus tertium*, in which the principal theses of both works are reproduced in a more aphoristic form (clothed in a more elegant diction to make their understanding easier and more acceptable to his papal protector Clement IV). In his theological works, of which two only have been preserved, Bacon also appears as representative of an antischolastic tendency. The *Epistola de laude Scripturæ Sacræ* (ed. Wharton, in Ussher's *Historia dogmatica de Scripturis*, London, 1699) is permeated by a reformatory spirit. He emphasizes the sentence: *Tota scientia in Bibliis contenta est principaliter et fontaliter;* he insists upon the reading of the Bible in the original (and, if possible, also by the laity); he emphasizes in a critical spirit the need of correcting the Vulgate and cautions against the implicit confidence of the expositors in the authority of the Church Fathers. In the last of his works, the *Compendium studii theologici* (composed in 1292), he appears rather as a representative of church tradition, and denounces the "gross errors" of a Parisian theologian, the sententiarian Richardus Cornubiensis. The advanced character of hi theological thought and teaching is evident also in his works on natural philosophy; for example, he speaks in the *Opus minus* of the "seven principal sins" in theological study, including the neglect of the original languages of the Holy Scripture, the corruption of the traditional text, and the wrong confidence in the authority of the Fathers. With regard to the future progress and triun hs of natural science, Bacon, in bold anticipatio , foresaw and predicted many things, which as ure to him the repute of a prophet, just as he discovered the principles of the telescope and microscope, was able to outline the laws of refraction and reflection, and penetrated more deeply into the laws of cosmology than any other scholar of the Middle Ages. His proofs that the Julian calendar needed correction, and the ways and means which he indicated to accomplish this end, and for which he was praised by Copernicus, must also be mentioned.

Of Bacon's writings the most are philosophical, or rather physical. The most important works of this class, especially the *Opus majus*, remained in manuscript till toward the end of the eighteenth century. The *Opera chemica Rogeri Baconis*, which was published in folio in 1485, was followed by a few minor writings pertaining to alchemy and mathematics. Of these the most interesting is the tractate on the secret powers of art and nature (first published at Paris, 1541, under the title, *De mirabili potestate artis et naturæ;* often issued since the beginning of the seventeenth century with the title: *De secretis operibus artis et naturæ*).

Writings. His principal work, *Opus majus ad Clementem IV*, was first published in the eighteenth century by Samuel Jebb (London, 1733), and not before 1859 were his philosophical and physical works, which supplement his main work, issued (*Fr. R. Baconis opera quædam hactenus inedita, scil. Opus tertium, Opus minus, Compendium studii philosophiæ, De nullitate magiæ, De secretis naturæ operibus*, ed. J. F. Brewer, Rolls Series, No. 15). Two other works followed this publication: the tractate *De philosophia morali*, which Bacon composed as part vii of his *Opus majus* (Dublin, 1860), and *De multiplicatione specierum*, which was published in 1897 as an addition to J. H. Bridges's new edition of the *Opus majus* (*The Opus majus of R. Bacon, edited with introduction and analytical table*, 2 vols., Oxford, 1897), which gives for the first time the complete text, including also the seventh part, of moral-philosophical contents. His *Greek Grammar and a Fragment of his Hebrew Grammar*, edited from the manuscript, with notes by E. Nolan and S. A. Hirsch, appeared in 1902 (London), and a Greek tragedy was first published in the same year by the Cambridge press. In manuscript are still the *Computus naturalium* (3 books pertaining to the calendar and chronology), the *Communia naturalium*, and the *Communia mathematica*.

O. ZÖCKLER†.

BIBLIOGRAPHY: For the life Jebb's preface to his edition of the *Opus majus*, ut sup.; M. le Clerc, in the *Histoire littéraire de la France*, vol. xx, Paris, 1842; E. Charles, *Roger Bacon, sa vie, ses ouvrages, ses doctrines*, Paris, 1861 ("a model of industry, skill, and intelligence"); L. Schneider, *Roger Bacon, eine Monographie zur Geschichte der Philosophie des dreizehnten Jahrhunderts*, Augsburg, 1873; *DNB*, ii, 374–378; J. H. Bridges, in the introduction to his edition of the *Opus majus*, ut sup. (this and Charles are the best sources); H. Hurter, *Theologia catholica tempore medii ævi*, pp. 310–312, Innsbruck, 1899. On Bacon as scientific investigator consult: K. Werner, *Die Psychologie, Erkenntnisslehre und Wissenschaftslehre des Roger Baco*, and *Die Kosmologie und allgemeine Naturlehre des Roger Baco*, both Vienna, 1879. For his significance as forerunner of the evangelical doctrine of scripture and as Bible-critic, F. A. Gasquet, *English Bible Criticism in the Thirteenth Century*, in *The Dublin Review*, cxxii (1898), 1–22.

I.—27

BADEN, bä'den: A grand duchy in the southwestern part of the German Empire, bounded on the north by Hesse and Bavaria, on the east by Württemberg and Hohenzollern, on the south and west by the Rhine, which separates it from Switzerland, Alsace, and the Rhine Palatinate (Rhenish Bavaria); area, 5,281 square miles; population (1900), 1,867,944, of whom 1,131,639 (60.6%) are Roman Catholics; 704,058 (37.7%), Evangelical Protestants, partly Lutherans, and including some of the Reformed communion, especially near the Swiss border, and several flourishing Methodist congregations, which have received help from America; 5,563, other Christians; 26,132 (1.4%), Jews; and 552, otherwise classified. In late years, owing to immigration and emigration, the number of Roman Catholics has decreased, while that of Protestants has increased.

In the eye of the law the Evangelical and Roman Catholic Churches are public corporations with the right of holding public divine services. Other bodies are restricted to privileges specially granted. Congregations manage their own affairs and the right of patronage is unknown. Ecclesiastical property is administered by Church and State jointly. No religious order can be introduced without consent of the government. Invested funds for the benefit of the sick and the poor, as well as for education, have generally been withdrawn from ecclesiastical boards.

The Evangelical Protestant Established Church is a union of diverse elements, consequent upon territorial changes, accomplished in 1821. As now constituted the grand duke is at the head. All permanent residents of a parish are regarded as members of the congregation, and the active members choose a representative committee, which has a voice in the selection of the pastor and important financial questions, and selects the Church Council. The latter with the pastor has the general charge of the congregation. Congregations are united into dioceses, and diocesan synods, consisting of all pastors and an equal number of elders meet yearly. Diocesan affairs are in the hands of a dean and a diocesan committee of two clerical and two lay members elected by the synod. A general synod meets every five years; it consists of the Prelate, seven members named by the grand duke, and one clerical and one lay delegate from each synod. It cooperates in ecclesiastical legislation, approves the church budget, has the right of complaint against the Upper Church Council, and chooses a synodal committee to work with the latter. The Upper Church Council is appointed by the grand duke. Church revenues are supplemented, when necessary, by taxation, equal sums being appropriated for the Evangelical and Roman Catholic Churches, although the latter has declined such aid under the condition imposed binding the bishop to accept all laws and ordinances of the State. Ministers receive salaries ranging from 1,600 to 4,000 marks, graded according to years of service. Religious instruction is obligatory in all schools and a (Protestant) theological faculty is maintained at Heidelberg.

The Roman Catholic Church of Baden belongs to the province of the Upper Rhine and forms the archbishopric of Freiburg. The relations between Church and State, particularly the questions of the position of the bishops, the appointment of priests, the maintenance of independent Roman Catholic schools, the right of establishing religious societies and institutions, and the management of church property, have been in almost continual dispute between the government and the curia, and protracted negotiations have not led to a permanent settlement. WILHELM GOETZ.

BADEN (IM AARGAU), CONFERENCE OF: An early attempt to check the Reformation in Switzerland. It met at Baden in Aargau, May 21, 1526, and closed June 8. The assembly was large and brilliant, the cities, with the exception of Zurich, having very generally sent their delegates and theologians. The chief speakers for the Reformation were Œcolampadius and Berthold Haller; for the Roman Catholics Eck, Faber, and Murner. The entire conduct of the assembly was in the hands of the opponents of the Reformation and its decision against the latter was a foregone conclusion. Its decrees, however, had little influence on the popular mind, and indiscreet efforts to give them practical effect brought them still further into disfavor. The acts were published by Murner (Lucerne, 1527).

BIBLIOGRAPHY: Schaff, *Christian Church*, vii, 98–102, New York, 1892.

BADEN (IN BADEN), CONFERENCE OF, 1589. See PISTORIUS.

BADER, bä'der, **JOHANN:** Leader of the Reformation at Landau in the Palatinate (18 m. n.w. of Carlsruhe); b., probably, at Zweibrücken (50 m. w. of Speyer), Rhenish Bavaria, about 1470; d. at Landau shortly before Aug. 16, 1545. Of his early years almost nothing is known. He seems to have studied at Heidelberg in 1486 and succeeding years and then appears as chaplain in Zweibrücken, where he was also tutor to Duke Ludwig (b. 1502). In 1518 Bader was called as minister to Landau, where he labored till his death. From 1522 he openly opposed Roman abuses and especially auricular confession. Called to appear before the spiritual court at Speyer, he followed the summons and, after many proceedings, was bidden, July 17, 1523, to preach in future the holy gospel only and to obey the imperial mandates. As he believed that he had been preaching the pure gospel, he did not feel called upon to change his former manner, and, upheld by the confidence of his congregation, he opposed the teachings of the Church the more, and openly attacked the doctrine of purgatory, mass for the dead, invocation of the saints, monastic vows, and fasts. For this he was again summoned to Speyer, Mar. 10, 1524. His proposal, to prove his teachings from the New Testament, was rejected, and he was excommunicated. Not in the least intimidated, he appealed to a future council, published his appeal with all the documents, and, supported by the city-council, steadfastly continued his reformatory work. He devoted great care to the instruction of the youth, and assembled the "young people" of the city and instructed them in the Christian faith. About Easter, 1526, he published his *Gesprächsbüchlein*, which may be regarded as the oldest evangelical catechism. In this he gives an exposition of the Lord's Prayer, the Apostles' Creed, the doctrine of baptism, and the ten commandments. In 1527 he opposed the Anabaptists, but afterward he was strongly influenced by Schwenckfeld, as appears especially in his *Katechismus* published in 1544, a new edition of his earlier work, containing a treatment of the Lord's Supper not found in the *Gesprächsbüchlein*. He states that where the principal requisite for a true celebration of the Lord's Supper—a church of true believers—is lacking, it is better not to celebrate. And indeed, after 1541, Bader could no more be induced to celebrate the Lord's Supper at Landau, because he did not regard the congregation there as sufficiently holy.

JULIUS NEY.

BIBLIOGRAPHY: J. P. Gelbert, *Magister Johann Baders Leben und Schriften*, Neustadt, 1868. For a full account of the debate on infant baptism at Landau, Jan. 20, 1527, between Hans Denk and Bader, cf. Bader's *Brüderliche Warnung für den newen Abgöttischen Orden der Widertäuffer* (1527), of which copies are to be found in Munich and in the library of the University of Rochester. Bader strongly opposed Denk at the time, but later he adopted most of his views; cf. L. Keller, *Ein Apostel der Wiedertäufer*, pp. 196–200, Leipsic, 1882.

BAENTSCH, bêntsh, **BRUNO JOHANNES LEOPOLD**: German Lutheran; b. at Halle Mar. 25, 1859. He was educated at the gymnasium and university of his native city, and held successive pastorates at Rothenburg on the Saale (1886–88) and Erfurt (1888–93). In 1893 he became privat-docent of Old Testament science at the University of Jena, where he was appointed associate professor in 1899 and full professor two years later. In theology he is an adherent of the historico-critical school. He has been a member of the *Königliche Akademie gemeinnütziger Wissenschaften* since 1891, and has written *Das Bundesbuch, Ex. xx, 22–xxiii, 33* (Halle, 1892); *Die moderne Bibelkritik und die Autorität des Gotteswortes* (Erfurt, 1892); *Das Heiligkeitsgesetz, Lev. xvii–xxvi, eine historisch-kritische Untersuchung* (1893); *Geschichtsconstruction oder Wissenschaft?* (Halle, 1896); *Die Bücher Exodus, Leviticus, Numeri übersetzt und erklärt* (2 vols., Göttingen, 1900–03); *H. St. Chamberlains Vorstellungen über die Religion der Semiten* (Langensalza, 1905); and *Altorientalischer und israelitischer Monotheismus* (Tübingen, 1906).

BAERWINKEL, FRIEDRICH WILHELM RICHARD: German Lutheran; b. at Dallmin (a village near Perleberg, 77 m. n.w. of Berlin) July 3, 1840. He was educated at the universities of Bonn and Halle from 1859 to 1862 (Ph.D., Jena, 1864), and after passing his theological examinations in 1862 and 1865, being at the same time a private tutor, was a teacher in a real-school in Halle from 1863 to 1868. Since the latter year he has been pastor of the Reglerkirche in Erfurt, where he is also superintendent and senior of the Evangelical Ministerium, as well as a member of the local academy of sciences since 1891, being likewise a member of its senate since 1905. He has been, moreover, a member of the governing board of the *Evangelischer Bund* since its establishment in 1886, and is a member of the synodical council of the Prussian General Synod, besides being president of several ecclesiastical committees. He is a mediating theologian, and an advocate of the "modern theology of the ancient faith." He has written *Luther in Erfurt* (Erfurt, 1868); *Ueber den religiösen Wert von Reuter's "Ut min Stromtid"* (1876); and *Im Garten Gottes* (1900), as well as many briefer pamphlets, particularly in the *Flugschriften des evangelischen Bundes*.

BAETHGEN, bêth'gen, **FRIEDRICH WILHELM ADOLF**: Protestant theologian; b. at Lachem (a village near Hameln, 25 m. s.w. of Hanover) Jan. 16, 1849; d. at Rohrbach (a village near Heidelberg) Sept. 6, 1905. He studied at Göttingen and Kiel, and served in the German army in the war against France, 1870–71. He was in Russia, 1873–76; in Berlin, 1876–77, and in the British Museum, 1878. He became privat-docent at Kiel in 1878, and associate professor of theology in 1884. From 1881 to 1884 he was also *adjunctus ministerii* in Kiel. In 1888 he was called to Halle in the same capacity, but in the following year was appointed regular professor of theology at Greifswald, where he also became counselor and member of the Pomeranian consistory. In 1895 he was called to Berlin. He was the author of *Untersuchungen über die Psalmen nach der Peschita* (Kiel, 1878); *Sindban oder die sieben weisen Meister* (Leipsic, 1879); *Syrische Grammatik des Mar Elias von Tirhan herausgegeben und übersetzt* (1880); *Anmuth und Würde in der alttestamentlichen Poesie* (Kiel, 1880, a lecture); *Fragmente syrischer und arabischer Historiker herausgegeben und übersetzt* (Leipsic, 1884); *Evangelienfragmente: der griechische Text des Cureton'schen Syrers wiederhergestellt* (1885); *Beiträge zur semitischen Religionsgeschichte: der Gott Israels und die Götter der Heiden* (Berlin, 1888); *Die Psalmen, übersetzt und erklärt* (Göttingen, 1897); and *Hiob übersetzt* (1898); in addition to preparing the second edition of Riehm's *Handwörterbuch des biblischen Altertums* (2 vols., Bielefeld, 1893–94).

BAGSHAWE, EDWARD GILPIN: Roman Catholic titular archbishop of Seleucia Trachea; b. at London Jan. 12, 1829. He was educated at London University College School and at St. Mary's College, Oscott, near Birmingham (B.A., London University, 1848). In 1849 he joined the Congregation of the Oratory of St. Philip Neri, London, and in 1852 was ordained priest by Cardinal Wiseman. After a priesthood of twenty years he was consecrated Roman Catholic bishop of Nottingham by Archbishop Manning (Nov. 12, 1874), but resigned in 1901. In the following year he was appointed titular bishop of Hypæpa, and in 1904 was elevated to the titular archdiocese of Seleucia Trachea. In addition to a number of briefer pamphlets, he has written *Notes on Christian Doctrine* (London, 1896; originally a series of lectures delivered before the Hammersmith Training College for Teachers); *The Breviary Hymns and Missal Sequences in English Verse* (1900); *The Psalms and*

Canticles in English Verse (1903); and *Doctrinal Hymns, with the Life of Our Lord in the Mass* (1906).

BAHRDT, bārt, **KARL FRIEDRICH:** A caricature of the vulgar rationalism of the eighteenth century; b. at Bischofswerda (20 m. e.n.e. of Dresden), Saxony, Aug. 25, 1741; d. at Halle Apr. 23, 1792. He was the son of a Lutheran pastor who afterward became professor at Leipsic, and commenced his studies at Leipsic when quite young. In spite of his many pranks he was promoted as magister and appointed catechist at St. Peter's. Being devoted to Biblico-exegetical studies under the influence of the learned Ernesti, he was made extraordinary professor in Biblical philology 1766, but was dismissed in 1768 for immoral life. At the same time he abandoned the orthodox standpoint, which he probably never had held seriously. From now on his life is that of a dissolute adventurer. He appears first at Erfurt, afterward at Giessen (1771), where he managed to obtain a theological professorship. Here he published (1772) a silly "Musterrevision" of the Bible, entitled *Neueste Offenbarungen Gottes in Briefen und Erzählungen*, which even Goethe ridiculed (in his *Prolog zu den neuesten Offenbarungen Gottes*). The enlightener was dismissed from his office in Giessen in 1775. He then tried his luck as director of a *philanthropicum* in the Grisons, then as superintendent-general in the Palatinate, finally as privat-docent at Halle. That he was received here, was due to the liberal government of King Frederick II of Prussia, whose free-thinking minister of ecclesiastical affairs and of public instruction, Zedlitz, procured for Bahrdt the *venia legendi*. He attracted great attention, not so much by his lectures as by his surprisingly prolific literary productivity. With reckless brutality he attacked every kind of belief in revealed religion. His *System der moralischen Religion* (Berlin, 1787) advocates open naturalism; Christ is to him the greatest naturalist. Having ruined his religious and moral reputation, he finally opened an inn in a vineyard near Halle, and thus sought to attract the interest of students of the university. Meanwhile the Prussian government had taken a different course; Frederick II was succeeded by the reactionary Frederick William II (1786-97), whose minister of worship, Wöllner, in 1788 endeavored to restore orthodoxy. Bahrdt did not hesitate to ridicule (anonymously) Wöllner's religious edict in a comedy. For this he was imprisoned in the fortress of Magdeburg in 1789. During the year which he spent here he wrote smutty stories and his autobiography, a mixture of falsehood, hypocrisy, and impudent self-abasement. In 1790 he again opened his inn fell ill in 1791, and died of disease induced by a too free use of mercury in the attempt to effect a self-cure. In Halle the report was spread that he died of an unclean disease. Highly gifted, Bahrdt never yielded to moral discipline, and thus sunk into the deepest baseness; in his later years he seems to have lost every trace of decency; the flood of writings which he sent out into the world is altogether worthless; he is in every respect merely a representative of a wholly demoralized rationalism. PAUL TSCHACKERT.

BIBLIOGRAPHY: D. Pott, *Leben, Meinungen und Schicksale des C. F. Bahrdt, aus Urkunden gezogen*, 4 parts, Berlin, 1790-91; G. Frank, in *Raumers Historische Taschenbuch*, ser. 4, vol. vii, 1866, 203-370, especially 346 sqq.

BAIER, bai'er, **JOHANN WILHELM:** Lutheran theologian of the seventeenth century; b. at Nuremberg Nov. 11, 1647; d. at Weimar Oct. 19, 1695. He studied philology, especially Oriental, and philosophy at Altdorf from 1664 to 1669, in which year he went to Jena and became a disciple of the celebrated Musæus, the representative of the middle party in the syncretistic controversy, whose daughter he married in 1674. Taking his doctor's degree the same year, he became in 1675 professor of church history in the university, and lectured with great success on several different branches of theology. In 1682 he was chosen to represent the Protestant side in the negotiations with the papal legate Steno, bishop of Tina, for reunion of the Churches. He was three times rector at Jena before he was called by the elector Frederick III, in 1694, as professor and provisional rector to the new university of Halle. Here his devotion to strict orthodoxy brought him into conflict with some of his colleagues, and the pietistic movement also gave him trouble, so that after a year he was glad to accept the combined positions of chief court preacher, superintendent, and pastor at Weimar—which, however, he held only a few months. He left a name in the history of theology, especially by his dogmatic compendium, which still preserves the early Protestant traditions among High Lutherans, especially in America. The Jena theologians, and Musæus in particular, had been asked by Ernest the Pious to draw up such a work, to take the place of the antiquated Hutter, and Musæus urged his son-in-law to do it. The first edition appeared in 1686, the second, enlarged, in 1691, and it has been frequently reprinted since. It was commended for general use as a text-book by its method, its conciseness, and its absence of mere polemics. It was obviously, however, intended by its author as a vindication of the Jena theology, which had been sharply attacked from Wittenberg, and lay under some suspicion of syncretism. Its dependence upon Musæus is really the distinguishing feature of the book, which is largely a compilation from him. Baier's other works include polemical writings against Erbermann, a convert to Roman Catholicism and a Jesuit, and against the Quakers; and three other compendiums, published after his death (1698), one of exegetical, and one of moral theology, as well as one of the history of dogma. His real significance lies in the fact that he handed on and popularized the theology of Musæus; and his work was continued by Buddeus, whom he left at Halle as professor of moral philosophy.

(JOHANNES KUNZE.)

BIBLIOGRAPHY: G. A. Will, *Nürnbergisches Gelehrtenlexikon*, i, 47-53, v, 39, Nuremberg, 1755; W. Schrader, *Geschichte der Friedrichsuniversität zu Halle*, i, 49-50, Berlin, 1894; C. Stange, *Die systematischen Prinzipien in der Theologie des Musäus*, Halle, 1895.

BAIER, JOHANNES: German Roman Catholic; b. at Hetzles (a suburb of Erlangen) Oct. 16, 1852. He was educated at the Lyceum of Bamberg and the University of Munich (D.D., 1885), and was ordained to the priesthood in 1877. From that year until 1882 he was a tutor in the archiepiscopal seminary for boys at Bamberg and also assistant lecturer in dogmatics at the lyceum of the same city, besides being assistant parish priest at Bamberg and Nuremberg in the summer of 1877 and at Hersbruck in 1879–80. In 1882–86 he was a teacher of religion at the normal school at Bamberg, where he became *Oberlehrer* and tutor in the latter year, and where he has been professor since 1901. Since 1906 he has been headmaster of the same institution, and in the same year was made an honorary Austin friar. In theology "he belongs to the conservative party and is a friend of rational sound progress." Besides many contributions to theological and philosophical periodicals, and in addition to numerous poems, he has written, frequently under the pseudonym of Dr. Johannes Scholasticus, *Die Naturehe* (Regensburg, 1886); *Die religiöse Unterweisung in der Volksschule* (Würzburg, 1890); *Der heilige Bruno, Bischof von Würzburg, als Katechet* (1891); *Das alte Augustinerkloster in Würzburg* (1894); *Die Stellung der Religionsunterricht zur Philosophie Herbarts* (1895); *Dr. Martin Luthers Aufenthalt in Würzburg* (1895); *Die Geschichte des Cisterzienserklosters Langheim mit den Wallfahrtsorten Vierzehnheiligen und Marienweiher* (1895); *Die Geschichte der beiden Karmelitenklöster und des Reurerinnenklosters im Würzburg* (1900); *Sailers Buch über Erziehung für Erzieher* (Freiburg, 1901); *Analyse und Synthese im Religionsunterricht* (Würzburg, 1902); *Sailer in seinem Verhältnis zur modernen Pädagogik* (1904); *Die Willensbildung* (Kempten, 1905); and *Methodik des Religionsunterrichts in Volks- und Mittelschulen* (Leipsic, 1906).

BAILEY, HENRY: Church of England, canon of St. Augustine's, Canterbury; b. at North Leverton (13 m. n.w. of Lincoln), Notts., Feb. 12, 1815. He was educated at St. John's College, Cambridge (B.A., 1839). He was Crosse University Scholar in 1839 and Tyrwhitt Hebrew University Scholar, 1st class, two years later, while he was elected fellow of his college in 1842 and Hebrew lecturer in 1848. From 1850 to 1878 he was warden of St. Augustine's College, of which he has been honorary fellow since 1878, and after 1863 was honorary canon of Canterbury. He was also rector of West Tarring, Sussex, from 1878 to 1892 and was rural dean of Storrington in 1886–92. He was twice appointed Select Preacher at Cambridge and was Proctor in Convocation in 1886–92. Since 1888 he has been canon of St. Augustine's. He has written *Rituale Anglo-Catholicum* (London, 1847); *Manual of Devotion for Clergy* (1890); and *Gospel of the Kingdom* (1902).

BAILLET, bα''yē', ADRIEN: Roman Catholic; b. at Neuville, near Beauvais (54 m. n.n.w. of Paris), June 13, 1649; d. in Paris Jan. 21, 1706. He was educated in the Seminary of Beauvais; became a priest 1675 and obtained a small vicarage; in 1680 he was appointed secretary to Lamoignon, president of the Parliament of Paris, and spent the rest of his life in unremitting devotion to study. His most important works were: *Jugements des savants sur les principaux ouvrages et auteurs* (9 vols., Paris, 1685–86); *Les vies des saints* (3 vols., 1695–1701); *Vie de Descartes* (2 vols., 1691); *Histoire de Hollande*, a continuation of Grotius (4 vols., 1693). He was favorable to the Jansenists and has been called hypercritical. A monograph, *De la dévotion à la Sainte Vierge et du culte qui lui est dû* (1693) was thought to attack the doctrine and practise of the Church and put upon the Index, and a like fate befell the first and second volumes of the *Vies des saints*, which were said to contain remarks little short of slanderous. The first volume of the Amsterdam edition (1725) of the *Jugements des savants* contains an *Abrégé* of his life.

BAILLIE, ROBERT: Presbyterian; b. at Glasgow 1599; d. there July, 1662. He studied at his native city, and was made professor of divinity there in 1642, and principal of the university in 1661. He was a fine scholar and took an active part and wrote much in all the church controversies in his time. His *Letters and Journals* (ed. David Laing, 3 vols., Edinburgh, 1841–42, with a notice of his writings and a description of his life) are of great historical interest. To him we owe a graphic description of the Westminster Assembly of Divines, to which body he was sent as one of the five Scotch clergymen in 1643, and sat in it for three years.

BIBLIOGRAPHY: *Biographia Britannica*, ed. A. Kippis, i. 510–515, London, 1778; T. Carlyle, *Baillie the Covenanter*, in *Westminster Review*, xxxvii. 43, reprinted in his *Miscellanies* (a remarkable paper); *DNB*, ii, 420–422.

BAIRD, CHARLES WASHINGTON: Presbyterian; b. at Princeton, N. J., Aug. 28, 1828, son of Robert Baird (q.v.); d. at Rye, N. Y., Feb. 10, 1887. He was graduated at the University of the City of New York, 1848, and at Union Theological Seminary, 1852; was chaplain of the American Chapel at Rome, Italy, 1852–54; agent of the American and Foreign Christian Union in New York 1854–55; pastor of the Reformed (Dutch) Church on Bergen Hill, Brooklyn, 1859–61; of the Presbyterian Church at Rye, N. Y., 1861–87. He published *Eutaxia, or the Presbyterian Liturgies* (New York, 1855; revised and reprinted as *A Chapter on Liturgies*, with preface, and appendix, *Are Dissenters to Have a Liturgy?* by Thomas Binney, London, 1856); *A Book of Public Prayer compiled from the authorized formularies of worship of the Presbyterian Church as prepared by the Reformers Calvin, Knox, Bucer, and others* (New York, 1857); *A History of Rye, Westchester County, N Y* (1871); *A History of the Huguenot Emigration to America* (2 vols., 1885, new ed., 1901; left incomplete at his death).

BAIRD, HENRY MARTYN: Presbyterian, author of the authoritative history of the Huguenots; b. at Philadelphia, Pa., Jan. 17, 1832, son of Robert Baird (q.v.); d. at Yonkers, N. Y., Nov. 11, 1906. He was educated at New York University (B.A., 1850), the University of Athens, Greece (1851–52),

Union Theological Seminary (1853–55), and Princeton Theological Seminary (1856). After being tutor in the College of New Jersey from 1855 to 1859. he was appointed professor of the Greek language and literature in the University of the City of New York, and became professor emeritus in 1902. He was corresponding secretary of the American and Foreign Christian Union in 1873–84, and was the first vice-president of the American Society of Church History, in addition to being a member of the board of the Société de l'Histoire du Protestantisme Français, honorary member of the Huguenot Society of America, honorary fellow of the Huguenot Society of London, and a member of various historical associations. He published *Modern Greece* (New York, 1856); *Rise of the Huguenots of France* (2 vols., 1879); *The Huguenots and Henry of Navarre* (2 vols., 1886); *The Huguenots and the Revocation of the Edict of Nantes* (2 vols., 1895); and *Theodore Beza, the Counsellor of the French Reformation* (1899).

BAIRD LECTURES: A lectureship on a foundation established by Mr. James Baird (d. 1876), a wealthy Scotch ironmaster, member of Parliament 1851–57 who was greatly interested in religious and educational affairs. While the Baird Lectures had their inception in 1871, their realization was made possible when in 1873 Mr. Baird established the "Baird Trust" and gave into its care £500,000 to be used for aggressive Christian work. A part of the income of this fund provides for a series of lectures each year at Glasgow and also, if required, at one other of the Scotch university towns. Each course must consist of not fewer than six lectures and must be delivered by a minister of the Church of Scotland, who may be reappointed. Since 1883 each lecturer has held the position for two years with the exception of Rev. William Milligan, who lectured in 1891 only. The most noteworthy contributions are the series by Professor Robert Flint in 1876–77 on *Theism* and *Anti-Theistic Theories* (Edinburgh, 1877–79), and that by J. Marshall Lang in 1901–02 on *The Church and its Social Mission* (1902). A full list of the lecturers and their subjects may be found in L. H. Jordan, *Comparative Religion* (New York, 1905), pp. 565–566.

BAIRD, ROBERT: Presbyterian; b. near Uniontown, Fayette County, Pennsylvania, Oct. 6, 1796; d. at Yonkers, N. Y., Mar. 15, 1863. He was graduated at Jefferson College, Canonsburg, Penn., 1818, and at Princeton Seminary in 1822; was ordained in 1828 and thenceforth devoted his life to the cause of total abstinence, education, and the effort to spread Protestantism in Roman Catholic countries. He resided in Europe as agent of the French Association and of its successor, the Foreign Evangelical Society, from 1835 to 1843, and continued in the service of the society in the United States 1843–46; from 1849 to 1855 he was corresponding secretary of the American and Foreign Christian Union and again, 1861 to his death; his ninth mission to Europe was made in 1861. He wrote *Histoire des sociétés de tempérance des États-Unis d'Amérique* (Paris, 1836); *Religion in the United States of America* (Glasgow 1844); *Sketches of Protestantism in Italy* (Boston 1845).

Bibliography: H. M. Baird, *Life of Rev. Robert Baird*, New York, 1866 (by his son).

BAJUS, bā'yus, **MICHAEL (MICHEL DE BAY)**: Theologian of Louvain; b. at Melin (arrondissement of Ath, 14 m. n.w. of Mons), Hainault, 1513; d. at Louvain Sept. 15, 1589. He was educated in the University of Louvain, where he became magister 1535, head of the Standonck college and member of the faculty of arts 1540, and doctor of theology 1550. When four Louvain professors were summoned to Trent at the reopening of the council there in 1551 Bajus and his like-minded colleague Johannes Hessels (q.v.) filled the vacancies by lecturing on the Holy Scriptures. Bajus was soon appointed professor in ordinary.

Being convinced that the questions of faith which were started by the Reformation could not be sufficiently answered by the scholastic method, Bajus endeavored to found the study of theology more upon the Scriptures and the Fathers, especially upon Augustine, whose works he is said to have read nine times. But soon a great controversy arose, and in 1560 his opponents secured the condemnation by the Sorbonne of eighteen propositions extracted from the lectures of Bajus. Bajus defended himself, complained of unfair treatment, and declared that he was ready to submit to the holy see and the council. After a few years the controversy began anew caused by a number of dogmatic tractates, the first of which (*De libero arbitrio, De justitia, De justificatione*, and others) were published in the beginning of 1563, others (*De meritis operum, De prima hominis justitia, De virtutibus impiorum, etc.*) in 1564, and a general collection (*Opuscula omnia*) in 1566.

The Controversy Concerning Bajus's Orthodoxy.

Bajus's opponents induced the new pope, Pius V, in 1567 in the bull *Ex omnibus afflictionibus* to condemn seventy-nine propositions from his writings as heretical, false, suspicious, bold, scandalous, and offensive to pious ears, without stating, however, which of the propositions deserved the one or the other epithet, and without mention of Bajus's name. The bull, written in the usual form without punctuation, says: *Quas quidem sententiæ stricto coram nobis examine ponderatas quanquam nonnullae aliquo pacto sustineri possent in rigore et proprio verborum sensu ab assertoribus intento hæreticas erroneas damnamus, etc.* If a comma be inserted after *intento*, as was done by the Louvain theologians and afterward by the Jansenists, the bull contains the concession that some propositions in the strict sense intended by the authors are perhaps permissible; but if, with the Jesuits, the comma is put after *sustineri possent*, the contrary meaning is imparted, that some propositions which may perhaps be interpreted in an orthodox sense, are nevertheless condemned as meant by their authors. Hence arose the later controversy about the *comma Pianum*. A papal brief (May 13, 1569) sustained the condemnation, and Bajus submitted and was absolved. In his lectures (Apr. 17, 1570) he expressed himself once more in the sense of his apology. The bull against him was now first made public. The Louvain faculty made explanations, which were satisfactory in form, but the majority still adhered to the Augustinian system. Bajus remained in his prominent position, and was made chancellor of the University and dean of the Collegiate Church of St. Peter in 1575. He founded in the university a *Collegium Sancti Augustini*, to which his nephew Jacob, who acted as his executor, gave the name of *Collegium Baianum*.

His Doubtful Teachings.

The propositions of Bajus which were attacked and condemned by the papal bull rest entirely on the fundamental Augustinian idea of the entire depravity of man through original sin, of the absolute moral inability of the fallen man to do good, and of utterly unconditional and irresistible grace. To retain and carry out the Augustinian idea, he believed it necessary to oppose the scholastic (and Tridentine) notion of the original state of man. He will not admit that the original nature of man consisted in the so-called *pura natura*, to which came as an additional gift (*donum superadditum, supernaturalia dona*) the *justitia originalis*, which lifts man above his nature and qualifies him for salvation. He thinks that the *status puræ naturæ est impossibilis*. According to Scripture, Christ first brought grace. From this point of view the state of fallen man appears as essential corruption of human nature according to the Augustinian presentation, which especially precludes free will in the sense of power of choice. *Liberum arbitrium hominis non valet ad opposita*. There exists indeed a certain freedom of choice with reference to things which are not under consideration, but no condition of religio-moral indifference. Finally Bajus follows Augustine as a matter of course in the assertion that in the justified person original sin does indeed not rule as concupiscence, but still acts, and adopts the *manet actu, præterit reatu*. As the whole man is corrupted by sin, so also is all humanity.

Relation to the Reformers.

In all these points Bajus coincides very closely with the Augustinianism of the Reformers, and only in a few points does he make a not very successful effort to explain away certain harsh expressions (e.g., concerning determinism) and charge them to the Reformers only. But he stops far short of making the decided deviation which the Reformers made from Augustine with regard to the doctrine of justification. Grace justifies man. Since no man on earth can attain active perfection in this life, our righteousness will rest more upon the forgiveness of sins than upon our virtue. It is characteristic how the forgiveness of sins comes in here like a makeshift. *Si proprie loqui velimus, remissio peccatorum justitia non erit, quia justitia proprie legis obedientia est sive intus in voluntate sive foris in opere. Sed in scripturis sacris peccatorum remissio ideo etiam nomine justitiæ intelligitur, quia licet proprie non sit, tamen apud deum pro justitia reputatur*. Justification means to make righteous and have forgiveness of sins; but it is the former above all.

The bull against Bajus is very instructive for the history of doctrinal theology, because the Augustinian theology is here censured with all plainness. Thus, condemnation is pronounced upon the following propositions: that every sin deserves everlasting punishment (20); that all works of the unbelievers are sin (25); that the will without the help of grace can only sin (27); that concupiscence, even where it acts unwillingly, is sin (51); that the sinner is not animated and moved by the absolving priest but only by God (58); that the merit of the redeemed is given to them freely (8); that temporal sins can not be atoned for by one's own doings *de condigno*, but that their abolition, like the resurrection, must be ascribed in a proper sense to the merit of Christ (77, 10).

R. SEEBERG.

BIBLIOGRAPHY: *Michael Baii opera: cum bullis pontificum et aliis ipsius causam spectantibus collecta . . ., studio A. P. theologi* [G. Gerberon], Cologne, 1696; J. B. P. du Chesne, *Histoire du Bajanisme*, Douai, 1731; F. X. Linsenmann, *Michael Bajus und die Grundlegung des Jansenismus*, Tübingen, 1867; L. E. du Pin, *Nouvelle bibliothèque*, xvi; R. Seeberg, in Thomasius, *Dogmengeschichte*, vol. ii, part 2, 718 sqq., Leipsic, 1889; A. Harnack, *Dogmengeschichte*, iii, 628 sqq., Freiburg, 1890, Eng. transl., vii, 86–93.

BAKER, DANIEL: Presbyterian; b. at Midway, Liberty County, Ga., Aug. 17, 1791; d. at Austin, Texas, Dec. 10, 1857 He studied at Hampden Sidney College, Va., 1811–13 and was graduated at Princeton, 1815; was licensed (1816) and ordained (1818) in Virginia; was pastor in Washington, 1822–28; in Savannah, 1828–31; after a noteworthy revival season in his church there, resigned and spent the rest of his life, with the exception of brief pastorates, traveling through the southern States as evangelist and missionary; became general missionary in Texas of the Board of Missions in 1848, was one of the founders of Austin College (Presbyterian), at Huntsville, Texas, in 1849, and agent of the college till his death. While in Washington he published *A Scriptural View of Baptism*, afterward revised and enlarged as *A Plain and Scriptural View of Baptism* (Philadelphia, 1853); he also published two series of *Revival Sermons* (1854–57).

BIBLIOGRAPHY: W. M. Baker, *Life and Labors of Rev. Dan. Baker*, Philadelphia, 1858.

BAKER, SIR HENRY WILLIAMS: Hymnologist; b. in London May 27, 1821; d. at Monkland, near Leominster, Herefordshire, Feb. 12, 1877. He took his B.A. degree at Cambridge (Trinity College) 1844; became vicar of Monkland 1851; succeeded his father, Vice-Admiral Sir Henry Loraine Baker, as baronet 1859. He wrote certain tracts and prayers, and hymns of no slight merit (including the version of Psalm xxiii, *The King of Love my shepherd is*). He was one of the most prominent compilers of *Hymns, Ancient and Modern* (London, 1861; *Appendix*, 1868; revised and enlarged edition, 1875), one of the most successful of modern hymnals, to which he contributed some twenty-five hymns, original and translated.

BIBLIOGRAPHY: S. W. Duffield, *English Hymns*, p. 77 et passim, New York, 1886; Julian, *Hymnology*, p. 107; *DNB*, iii, 11.

BALAAM, bê'lam: A non-Israelitic prophet or soothsayer, son of Beor, from Pethor (Assyrian *Pitru*, cf. E. Schrader, *KAT*, i. 38; F Delitzsch, *Wo lag das Paradies*, Leipsic, 1885, p. 269; J. Halévy, *Mélanges d'Épigraphie et d'Archéologie Sémitiques*, Paris, 1874, p. 77; Max Müller, *Asien und Europa nach altägyptischen Denkmälern*, Leipsic, 1893, p. 291), a city of northern Mesopotamia, not far from the Euphrates. He seems to have been known as a sorcerer throughout a wide region, and according to Num. xxii, 5 sqq., was engaged by Balak, king of the Moabites, to curse Israel in the name of the God whom Israel served. But the God in whose name Balaam practised his magical arts, is a living God who could interfere with and govern Balaam's doings. And such an interference took place when Balak called Balaam. By this means his divination became real prediction.

The Biblical Narrative.

Balaam, moved by desire for reward, accepted Balak's invitation, which aroused Yahweh's anger. That he accepted the invitation gladly may be seen from the anger which seized him as his animal suddenly shied on the way and refused to proceed. His own eyes were held so that he did not perceive the apparition in his path. He would have seen it if he had gone with the disposition of a prophet of Yahweh, for he would then have had an eye open to that which his God sent him. The irrational animal which carried him became the instrument to set him right. Its resistance changed into intelligible speech. For the animal spoke in the same manner as the wife of the first man heard the serpent speak. In neither case need one think of an act of divine omnipotence, granting to the speechless animal the momentary function of human organs of speech. The act concerned rather the ear of the prophet and for him the animal's plaintive tone became articulate utterance. The prophet could be brought to his senses and aroused from a mental disposition intent only upon gain by something extraordinary, which was the reason why the animal refused to proceed. Now he also saw the apparition which had startled his beast, and the horror of it made him even willing to turn back, still more to speak only that which should offer itself to him as God's word.

After Balaam had arrived in the mountainous part of Moab, near the sources of the Arnon between the Arnon and the Jabbok, Balak, after offering sacrifices to predispose Yahweh in his favor, three times assigned to Balaam a station (Num. xxii, 41; xxiii, 14, 28), that from the high place he might curse Israel which was encamped before his eye. But three times, overcome by Yahweh's spirit, the prophet blessed the people (Num. xxiii, 7–10; 18–24; xxiv, 3–9), first giving the reason which made it impossible for him to curse Israel, viz., that it differed entirely from other nations, being richly favored by God; he then expanded the blessing briefly indicated in this first parable, and in a third deliverance finally described the glorious prosperity of Israel and its dominion as well as the fearful power of this people which should crush all enemies, having been set for a curse and a blessing to the nations. Balak was greatly enraged and dismissed the seer who, according to Num. xxiv, 15–24, spoke to the king more fully of the future which awaited Israel during its rule, and of the mighty commotions which should destroy nations. Under the figure of a star and scepter he sees in the distant future a king coming forth from Israel, whose glorious power none may resist, and the ruin of the world-powers one after the other and one through the other.

It can not be denied that there is something strange in Balaam's utterances foretelling world-historical events to a remote future. But to have recourse to the expedient that we have here a prophecy after the event, or that the originally transmitted prophecy of Balaam has been enlarged in later time in accordance with the course of history, is to deprive Balaam's whole appearance of its essential meaning in connection with Old Testament prophecy.

Significance of Balaam's Prophecies.

Balaam's importance consists in just this, that from the time when Israel first appeared among the nations, the future of the nations and world-powers was disclosed not to one of its own prophets but to one outside of it. And the knowledge of the history of future centuries which was there communicated to the people served to comfort them in the midst of threatening world-movements till Daniel's revelations came and continued the knowledge of the future from the point where Balaam left it. The great importance of Balaam's prophecy finds its expression also in this, that whenever the Israelitic prophets of later times speak of the relations of Israel to the world-nations, we hear his words ringing through their utterances. As a matter of course, this reference of the origin of the oracles of Balaam to Mosaic times applies only to the essential contents, not to the form of expression as it now exists. The latter must be attributed to the narrator.

Balaam's condemnation in the New Testament (II Pet. ii, 15–16; Rev. ii, 14) is founded upon the notice Num. xxxi, 16, according to which he advised Balak to seduce Israel to the sensual cultus of Baal-Peor. The contradiction in which this later and additional notice seems to stand with Num. xxiv, 25, which passage at the first glance every one understands to mean that Balaam, after his parting-word concerning Israel, returned to his home, is easily reconciled by the supposition that Balaam actually left Balak, but stayed with the Midianites, who were allied to the Moabites (Num. xxii, 4, 7), in order to serve Israel's enemies and to await the success of his plan to lead them astray. In the war of revenge which broke out against Midian (Num. xxv, 16–19), the divine punishment overtook him (Num. xxxi, 8; Josh. xiii, 22). His giving to the Midianites the advice so fatal to Israel in its consequences can be explained from the irritation which took hold of him when he found himself deprived of the reward which he desired. W. Volck†.

The fascinating and somewhat perplexing story of Balaam as given in Numbers becomes less puzzling when it is analyzed and traced to its sources. The whole story is an episode of the history of the tribes of Israel at the close of their wanderings after the Exodus. The main continuous narrative, as we now have it, is found in Num. xxii–xxiv and contains two well-defined elements: a prose portion or the narrative proper, and a poetical portion comprising four oracles uttered by the hero of the story.

The incidents are in brief as follows: Balak, king of Moab, alarmed at the numbers and strength of the Hebrews, sends for the noted seer and wizard, Balaam of Pethor (Assyrian *Pitru*) on the Euphrates in Mesopotamia, to bring a curse upon them. Balaam would not answer the messengers till he had consulted God as to what he should do. God at first forbade him to go; but after he was again approached by an embassy from Balak with greater gifts and more urgent appeals, he was granted permission upon the condition that he should utter only God's direct message (Num. xxii, 5–21). He at once sets out for Moab with the princes of the embassy, and on meeting Balak he assures him that at best he can act only as God's mouthpiece (Num. xxii, 35–38). Then Balak takes him to Bamoth-Baal EV, "the high places of Baal"), not far south of the Arnon. Here elaborate sacrifices were prepared, and, when Balaam retired for consultation, God appeared to him and gave him a message which foretold the greatness and blessedness of Israel (Num. xxii, 39–xxiii, 10). After a bitter remonstrance from Balak a similar transaction took place upon the summit of Pisgah followed by an oracle in which Israel's purity of worship and its valor are extolled (Num. xxiii, 11–24). Balaam was next transferred by Balak to Peor—apparently another height of Nebo, commanding a specially good view of the Dead Sea desert (Jeshimon), where Israel was encamped. At this stage Balaam, instead of going into the solitude, uttered his oracle from immediate inspiration (as "the spirit of God came upon him") with a glowing description of the beauty and fertility of the promised land and a forecast of the military triumphs of Israel (Num. xxiii, 25–xxiv, 9). Finally Balak in anger dismisses the prophet, who without the advantages of the prescriptive sacrifices spontaneously delivers himself of a prophecy in which Israel is pictured as victorious over Moab itself as well as over the peoples to the south of Palestine. Balaam then returns to his distant home (Num. xxiv, 10–25). Embedded in this main narrative is the story of Balaam's being confronted by the angel of Yahweh, when on his way to Moab, and of the speaking she-ass who sees this divine messenger invisible to the prophet (Num. xxii, 22–34).

The Narrative Analyzed.

A reference to the last-named section may best introduce a brief analysis of the sources. It is evident at a glance that this section contradicts the preceding part of the present narrative. Verse 22a directly contravenes verse 20a, and verses 22 sqq., which make Balaam to have traveled privately, are inconsistent with verse 20b (cf. verses 35 and 36, where the main story is resumed). Moreover, the incident of the angel and the clairvoyant and speaking ass is out of place and inconsequent. There was no occasion that Balaam should learn that it was useless to resist the will of Yahweh (cf. verse 32) since it was in accordance with the divine command that he had entered upon his journey. The marvel of an animal endowed with human speech has many parallels in folk-lore from the earliest times, and adds nothing to the dignity and force of the narrative but rather detracts from it. In fact, if chap. xxii, 22–35 be removed we have a consistent and instructive allegory of the historico-prophetic order.

Its Inconsistencies.

This single and separate episode of the journey to Moab belongs to J, and the rest of the narrative in chap. xxii belongs to E. Chaps. xxiii and xxiv are probably the work of a redactor using materials from both of these great sources. More particularly, it is apparent that the oracles of chap. xxiii bear, on the whole, an Elohistic and those of chap. xxiv a Jehovistic stamp. In the narrative proper E predominates throughout. Indeed the journey episode is almost all that we have from J in the prose portions of the story. Hence it is now impossible to say what his conception was of the original attitude of Balaam toward his mission. The variations of the story, however, do not obscure the essence of it as far as it concerns the personality and doings of Balaam. In the remote background there appears the figure of a famous Aramean seer of the twelfth century B.C. who among the contending tribes and peoples of Palestine discerned special elements of greatness and power in the Hebrew tribes and in the religion of Yahweh, and had some prevision of their future, to which he gave official utterance. There is no reason why such a belief may not have had a foundation in fact. It must be remembered that the chief proximate ancestors of the Hebrews were Aramean (Deut. xxvi, 5), and that no small portion of the narrative of Genesis consists of cherished traditions of Aramean associations. Moreover, the twelfth century was the epoch-making period of emigration and travel from western Mesopotamia across the Euphrates and southward.

The Sources.

The oracles are of course the significant element of the Balaam story. Their underlying motive is to vindicate the rightful predominance of Israel over its rivals to the east and south. It is this motive which has diverted the tradition of Balaam from its original scope and employed it to justify the remorseless border wars waged by southern Israel in the days of the monarchy. In the nature of the case the poems were composed not more than a very few generations after the events. Now since the oracles of chap. xxiii are essentially Elohistic and had their origin in the northern kingdom, the events which suggested them took place before the schism, not later than the warlike days of David. Indeed it is generally agreed that the subjugation of Moab and Edom (cf. xxiv, 17, 18), which took place in his time, formed the central point of practical interest for the whole series. The literary period of Solomon may have been the starting-point. But the process of enlargement and

The Oracles. Their Motive and Date.

refinement in the individual poems must have lasted till the eighth century.

An appendix to the oracles is found in chap. xxiv, 20–24, which must have been composed originally at a late date, since deportations by the Assyrians are referred to (verse 22), and perhaps also even the Macedonian conquests of the fourth century (verse 24). This poem should of course be separated from the others in our texts.

The Story in P and Later Literature.

Quite apart from the main current of tradition and its idealization is the use made of the Balaam story by the priestly writer in Num. xxxi, 8, 16. He connects the prophet with the Midianitish seductions described (also by P) in Num. xxv, 6–18. The statement that Balaam suggested the corruption of Israel by sensual allurements and suffered death in the ensuing holy war, is out of harmony with the original conception of the prophet, which is retained throughout the older accounts. The notion, however, gained continually in popularity, and is recalled in the later literature even in New Testament times (cf. II Pet. ii, 15, Jude 11; Josephus, *Ant.*, IV, vi, 6). Prejudice is already shown in Josh. xxiv, 9; Deut. xxiii, 4, 5; but a more just sentiment is displayed in Mic. vi, 5. A historical example of the influence of the tradition may be seen in Neh. xiii, 1, 2.

J. F. McCurdy.

Bibliography: For review of literature up to 1887 consult F. Delitzsch, *Zur neuesten Literatur über den Abschnitt Bileam*, in *ZKW* 1888. On the general subject F. A. G. Tholuck, *Die Geschichte Bileams*, in his *Vermischte Schriften*, i, 406–432, Hamburg, 1839; E. W. Hengstenberg, *Geschichte Bileams und seine Weissagungen*, Berlin, 1842; H. Oort, *Disputatio de Num. xxii–xxiv*, Leyden, 1860; G. Baur, *Geschichte der alttestamentlichen Weissagungen*, pp. 329 sqq., Giessen, 1861; A. Kuenen, in *ThT*, xviii (1884), 497–540; A. Dillmann, consult on the passage his commentary in *Kurzgefasstes exegetisches Handbuch zum Alten Testament*, Strasburg, 1887; A. H. Sayce, *Balaam's Prophecy, Num. xxiv. 17–24, and the God Seth*, in *Hebraica*, iv (1887), 1–6; A. van Hoonacker, *Observations critiques sur les récits concernant Bileam*, in *Le Muséon*, Lyons, 1888; J. Halévy, in *Revue Sémitique*, 1894, 201–209; *DB*, i, 232–234; *EB*, i, 461–464; T. K. Cheyne, in *Expository Times*, 1899, 399–402. Bishop Butler's celebrated sermon on the character of Balaam is in vol. ii of his works, Oxford, 1844.

BALAN, bā'lan, PIETRO: Roman Catholic church historian; b. at Este (17 m. s.s.w. of Padua), Italy, Sept. 3, 1840. He was educated in the seminary at Padua, where he was appointed professor in 1862. He was director of the Venetian *La Libertà Cattolica* in 1865 and of the Modenese *Diritto Cattolico* in 1867. In 1879 he became subarchivist of the Vatican, but retired on account of ill health four years later, and has since resided at Pregatto in the province of Bologna. He was nominated chamberlain by Leo XIII in 1881, and domestic prelate in the following year, while in 1883 he was appointed referendary of the Papal "segnatura." In the latter year he was also created a commander of the order of Francis Joseph. He is the author of *Studi sul Papato* (Padua, 1862); *Tommaso Becket* (1864); *Storia di S. Tommaso di Cantorbery e dei suoi tempi* (2 vols., Modena, 1867); *I Precursori del razionalismo moderno fino a Lutero* (2 vols., Parma, 1867–68); *Romani e Longobardi* (Modena, 1868); *L'Economia, la Chiesa e gli umanitari* (1869); *Pio IX, la Chiesa e la Rivoluzione* (2 vols., 1869); *Dante ed i Papi* (1870); *Chiesa e Stato* (1871); *Sulle Legazioni compiute nei paesi nordici da Guglielmo vescovo di Modena nel secolo XIII* (1872); *Il Vescovo di Modena Alberto Boschetti* (1872); *Storia di Gregorio IX e dei suoi tempi* (3 vols., 1872–73); *Storia d'Italia dai primi tempi fino al 1870* (7 vols., 1875–86); *Storia del pontificato di Papa Giovanni VIII* (1876); *Storia della Lega Lombarda, con documenti* (1876); *Memorie storiche di Tencarola nel Padovano con documenti inediti* (1876); *Storia della Chiesa Cattolica durante il pontificato di Pio IX* (3 vols., Turin, 1876–86); *Memorie della B. Beatrice I di Este* (1877); *Roberto Boschetti e l'Italia dei suoi tempi* (2 vols., 1878–84); *Discorsi tenuti nel quinto Congresso Cattolico in Modena* (Bologna, 1879); *Sull'Autenticità del diploma di Enrico II di Germania a Papa Benedetto VIII* (Rome, 1880); *S. Catterina da Siena e il Papato* (1880); *La Politica italiana dal 1863 al 1870, secondo gli ultimi documenti* (1880); *La Storia d'Italia e gli archivi segreti della Santa Sede* (1881); *Le Relazioni fra la Chiesa Cattolica e gli Slavi meridionali* (1881); *I Papi e i vespri siciliani, con documenti* (1881); *Il Processo di Bonifazio VIII* (1881); *La Politica di Clemente VII fino al sacco di Roma* (1884); *Roma capitale d'Italia* (1884); *Monumenta reformationis Lutheranæ ex tabulariis Sancti Sedis secretis, 1521–25* (Regensburg, 1884); and *Clemente VII e l'Italia del suo tempo* (Milan, 1887).

BALDACHIN: A canopy-like ornament in stone or bronze over the altar in some Roman Catholic churches, designed originally to protect the Eucharist from objects that might fall on it from above. The name is derived from *Baldacco*, an old Italian form of Bagdad, and owes its use in this connection to the fact that Bagdad was a rich source of the precious cloths which were frequently employed in decorating the protecting ornament over altars. In spite of legislation of the Congregation of Rites requiring a baldachin over every altar, the contrary practise is common everywhere at the present day, even in Rome. Formerly the baldachin was called a ciborium because the ciborium or vessel containing the Eucharist was suspended from it. A splendid example of the baldachin is seen in the bronze masterpiece of Bernini over the main altar of St. Peter's in Rome. A portable baldachin is held over the sacrament of the altar when it is borne in procession or, in some places, when it is carried to the sick. A baldachin should be erected also over a bishop's throne.

John T. Creagh.

BALDE, bāl'da, JAKOB: German Jesuit, distinguished as a scholar, poet, and preacher; b. at Ensisheim (55 m. s.s.w. of Strasburg), Alsace, Jan. 4, 1604; d. at Neuburg (29 m. n.n.e. of Augsburg), Bavaria, Aug. 9, 1668. He was destined for a legal career, and was educated by the Jesuits in his native town, at Molsheim, and at Ingolstadt. In 1624 he renounced the world and entered the Society, still continuing his classical studies, and teaching rhetoric at Munich and Innsbruck. In 1633 he was ordained; from 1635 to 1637 he was professor of rhetoric in the University of Ingolstadt; and from 1638 to 1640, after the death of Jeremias Drexel, court preacher to Maximilian I in Munich. Here he remained as historiographer of the duchy for ten years longer, but won more renown by the poetical compositions of the years 1637-46. His work in this period was lyrical (*Lyrica*, Munich, 1638–42; *Sylvæ*, 1641–45), but after 1649 he turned rather to satire and elegy. His health forced him to leave Munich in 1650, and after three years at Landshut and one at Amberg, he settled at Neuburg on the Danube, where he spent his last years in the peaceful dignity of the office of chaplain to the count palatine Philip William. His memory, which had to a great extent died out, was revived at the beginning of the nineteenth century by Herder, Orelli, and others, and his name has since been increasingly honored, especially by the efforts of the Munich society, founded in 1868, which bears it. He well deserves this renown from more than one point of view. He was a great classical scholar, a positive reincarnation of Roman antiquity. As a Latin poet (his small body of vernacular work is far inferior) he displays a wonderful array of excellent qualities —vivid imagination, depth of thought and feeling, brilliant invention and composition, and mastery of the most difficult forms. The characteristic universal scholarship of his age is best shown in his *Urania Victrix* (1663), which touches every branch of knowledge. Besides the works already mentioned, and some epics belonging to his first period, his *Philomela* (1645), full of devotion to the Crucified, his *Elegiæ variæ* (1663), and his amusing satires on quack doctors and other impostors in *Medicinæ gloria* (1649) may be named.

(F. List.)

Bibliography: His collected works were first published in complete form at Munich, 1729, the earlier editions at Cologne, 1660 and 1718, being defective; his *Carmina lyrica* appeared, ed. B. Müller, Regensburg, 1884. Consult L. Brunner, *J. Balde, le grand poète de l'Alsace. Notice historique et littéraire*, Guebwiller, 1865; J. Bach, *Jacob Balde, der neulateinische Dichter des Elsasses*, Strasburg, 1885; F. Tauchert, *Herder's griechische und morgenländische Anthologie und seine Uebersetzungen von J. Balde*, p. 176, Munich, 1886.

BALDENSPERGER, WILHELM: German Protestant; b. at Mülhausen (63 m. s.s.w. of Strasburg), Alsace, Dec. 12, 1856. He was educated at the universities of Strasburg, Göttingen, and Paris, and in 1880 was appointed supply at Strasburg. Two years later he was chosen assistant pastor and secretary of the editorial board of the *Journal du Protestantisme français* at Paris, where he remained until 1884. From 1886 to 1890 he was vicar at Mundolsheim (a suburb of Strasburg) and Strasburg, but in the latter year was appointed associate professor of New Testament exegesis at the University of Giessen, becoming full professor two years later. He was created a knight of the first class of the Order of Philip the Magnanimous in 1904. In addition to many briefer studies and his contributions to the Brunswick edition of the works of Calvin, he has written *Das Selbstbewusstsein Jesu im Lichte der messianischen Hoffnung seiner Zeit* (Strasburg, 1888); *L'Influence du dilettantisme artistique sur la morale et la religion* (1890); *Karl August Credner, sein Leben und seine Theologie* (Leipsic, 1897); *Der Prolog der vier Evangelien* (Giessen, 1898); and *Das spätere Judenthum als Vorstufe des Christenthums* (Giessen, 1900).

BALDWIN: Archbishop of Canterbury; d. at Acre Nov. 19, 1190. He was born at Exeter in humble circumstances, but received a good education; became archdeacon of Exeter, but resigned to enter the Cistercian monastery of Ford, Devonshire, and within a year was made abbot; became bishop of Worcester, 1180, archbishop of Canterbury, 1184. He engaged in a quarrel with the monks of Canterbury, and successfully asserted his preeminence among the bishops of England; with King Henry II he had much influence; he crowned Richard I in 1189, and attended him to the Holy Land the next year. His works (edited by B. Tissier) are in the *Bibliotheca patrum Cisterciensium*, v (Paris, 1662), from which they are reprinted in *MPL*, cciv.

BALE, JOHN: English polemical writer of the Reformation period; b. at Cove, near Dunwich, Suffolk (25 m. n.e. of Ipswich), Nov. 21, 1495; d. at Canterbury Nov. 1563. He was educated in the Carmelite monastery at Norwich, and at Jesus College, Cambridge; embraced the Reformation, married, and had to seek refuge in Germany in 1540; returned under Edward VI, was made Bishop of Ossory, in Ireland, 1552, and tried to introduce reformed doctrines and practise with an intemperate zeal; fled to the Continent after the accession of Mary, and lived for some years at Basel; returned under Elizabeth, and was made prebendary of Canterbury in 1560. He wrote much and with a coarseness and bitterness in controversy which gained him the name of "Bilious Bale." His principal work is *Illustrium majoris Britanniæ scriptorum summarium* (Ipswich, 1548; enlarged editions, Basel, 1557 and 1559); he also became noted as a writer of miracle plays in which he violently attacked the Roman Church. His play *Kynge Johan* has been published by the Camden Society (1838); and the Parker Society has published a selection of his works (1849), with biographical notice by H. Christmas.

Bibliography: The fullest account of his life is in C. H. Cooper, *Athenæ Cantabrigienses*, London, 1858.

BALL, JOHN: Puritan and Presbyterian; b. at Cassington (5 m. n.w. of Oxford) Oct. 1585; d. at Whitmore (4 m. s.w. of Newcastle-under-Lyme), Staffordshire, Oct. 20, 1640. He was educated at Brasenose College and St. Mary's Hall, Oxford, and in 1610 became minister at Whitmore. He was one of the fathers of Presbyterianism in England, and, as Richard Baxter says, "deserving as high esteem and honor as the best bishop in England." His *Small Catechism containing the Principles of Religion* (London) reached an eighteenth impression in 1637; and his larger catechism, entitled *A Short Treatise, containing All the Principal Grounds of Christian Religion*, a fourteenth impression in 1670. They were published anonymously. His *Treatise of Faith* (London, 1631; 3d edition, corrected and enlarged 1637, with an introduction by Richard Sibbs) is divided into two parts, the first showing the nature, and the second the life of faith. It is an exceedingly valuable and complete discussion. But his chief work was published after his death by his friend Simeon Ashe, with an introduction signed by five Westminster divines, entitled *A Treatise of the Covenant of Grace* (1645). This is of great importance as exhibiting that view of the covenants which found expression in the Westminster symbols. Important also is *A tryall of the New-Church way in New England and in Old* (1644). According to Thomas Blake, " his purpose was to speak on this subject of the covenant all that he had to say in all the whole body of divinity. That which he hath left behind gives us a taste of it." In this he anticipated Cocceius and the Dutch Federal Theology, but his view of the covenants is somewhat different from theirs. Simeon Ashe also issued several other works of Ball of a practical and controversial character.

C. A. Briggs.

Bibliography: A. à Wood, *Athenæ Oxonienses*, ii. 670, ed. P. Bliss, 4 vols., London, 1813–20; *DNB*, iii. 74–75.

BALLANCHE, ba''lɑ̄nsh', **PIERRE SIMON:** French theocratic philosopher of the Restoration, an intimate member of the circle which gathered around Chateaubriand and Madame Récamier; b. at Lyons Aug. 4, 1776; d. in Paris Aug. 7, 1847. His great work, the *Palingénésie sociale* (Paris, 1830), is an attempt to construct the philosophy of history on the basis of revelation; only the first of three parts projected was completed; a fragment of the third part, the *Vision d'Hébal* (1841), attempts in a vague way to predict the future. Ballanche's thought was unsystematic and his style obscure. He was elected to the Academy in 1841. A collected edition of his works was begun in 1830, but only four volumes of the nine planned appeared.

Bibliography: Sainte Beuve, *Portraits contemporains*, vol. ii. Paris, 1846; J. J. Ampère, *P. Ballanche*, Paris, 1848; G. Frainnet, *Essai sur la philosophie de P. S. Ballanche*, Paris, 1902.

BALLANTINE, bal'an-tain, **WILLIAM GAY:** Congregationalist; b. at Washington, D. C., Dec. 7, 1848. He was graduated at Marietta College, Marietta, O. (1868), and Union Theological Seminary (1872). He studied at Leipsic in 1872–73, and in the following year was a member of the American Palestine Exploring Expedition. He was then successively professor of chemistry and natural science in Ripon College (1874–76), assistant professor of Greek in the University of Indiana (1876–78), professor of Greek and Hebrew in the same institution (1878–81), and professor of Old Testament language and literature in Oberlin Theological Seminary (1881–91). From 1891 to 1896 he was president of the latter institution, but resigned and studied in Greece until in 1897 he was appointed instructor in Bible at the International Y. M. C. A. Training School, Springfield, Mass. He was an editor of the *Bibliotheca Sacra* in 1884–91, and has written *Philippians, the Model Letter* (New York, 1898); *Christ in the Gospel of Mark* (1898); *Inductive Bible Studies, Mark and Acts* (1898); *Luke and John* (1899); and *Matthew* (1900).

BALLARD, ADDISON: Congregationalist; b. at Framingham, Mass., Oct. 18, 1822. He was educated at Williams College (B.A., 1842), and was successively principal of Hopkins Academy, Hadley, Mass. (1842–43), tutor in Williams College (1843–44), and principal of the academy at Grand Rapids, Mich. (1845–46). In 1846–47 he was a home missionary in Grand River Valley, Mich., and was then professor of Latin in Ohio University (1848–54), professor of rhetoric in Williams College (1854–55), and professor of mathematics, natural philosophy, and astronomy at Marietta College (1855–57). He has held successive pastorates at the First Congregational Church, Williamstown, Mass. (1857–65), the Congregational Church at North Adams, Mass. (1865–66; stated supply), and the First Congregational Church, Detroit, Mich. (1866–72). He was professor of Christian Greek and Latin and of moral philosophy and rhetoric at Lafayette College in 1874–93, and of logic in New York University from 1894 to 1904. He is an honorary member of the London Society of Science, Letters, and Art, and in theology is an advocate of the doctrine of justification by faith. He has written *Arrows, or the True Aim in Teaching and Study* (Syracuse, N. Y., 1890); *From Talk to Text* (New York, 1904); *Through the Sieve* (1907).

BALLE, bal'le, **NICOLAI EDINGER:** Bishop of Zealand; b. at Vestenskov, near Nakskov (on the w. coast of the island of Laaland, 80 m. s.w. of Copenhagen), Denmark, Oct. 12, 1744; d. in Copenhagen Oct. 19, 1816. He studied at Copenhagen, Leipsic, Halle, and Göttingen; in 1770–71 he gave lectures at Copenhagen on church history and philology, and then accepted a pastorate in the bishopric of Aalborg; in 1772 he returned to the university, was made court preacher and doctor of theology in 1774, first professor of theology in 1777, assistant to Bishop Harboe of Zealand in 1782, and finally his successor in 1783; he resigned as bishop in 1808. Balle lectured and wrote on almost all theological branches, but church history was his specialty, and in 1790 he published a *Historia ecclesiæ Christianæ*, reaching to the Reformation. His *Theses theologici* (1776), the last work on dogmatics written in Denmark in the Latin tongue, was used at the universities of Kiel and Wittenberg. He opposed rationalism and free-thinking, and when the candidate Otto Horrebow started a publication, *Jesus og Fornuften* (" Jesus and Reason "), Balle replied with *Biblen forsvarer sig selv* (" The Bible Defending Itself "). He introduced weekly Bible readings in the capital, advocated the public school, and believed in special training for teachers. In 1791 he published a primer, which contains supranaturalistic as well as rationalizing views, and in 1798 a new hymn-book. Both these works served their time, but were finally superseded on the revival of Christian and church life in Denmark. Balle's position among the bishops of Denmark is an important and honorable one. In recognition of his labors, the citizens of Denmark presented to him in 1798 a gold medal with the inscription: "To the friend of religion, to the friend of the State, Matt. x, 32." The pastors of Zealand erected a monument over his grave, and a bas-relief in the garrison church where he explained the Bible represents him with the Bible in his hand. (F. NIELSEN.)

BIBLIOGRAPHY: L. Koch, *Bishop N. E. Balle*, Copenhagen, 1876; F. Nielsen, *Bidrag til den evangelisk-kristelige Psalmebogs Historie*, ib. 1895.

BALLERINI, bal"la-rî'nî, **PIETRO** and **GIROLAMO**: Brothers, of Verona, distinguished by their joint labors in church history and canon law; b., the former, Sept. 7, 1698, the latter, Jan. 29, 1702; d., Pietro, Mar. 28, 1769, Girolamo, Apr. 23, 1781. Both were educated in the Jesuits' school in Verona and became secular priests. Pietro for a time was at the head of the *Accademia delle belle lettere* in Verona and spent eighteen months in Rome (1748–50) as counselor to the Venetian ambassador there, during which time he made good use of exceptional opportunities for investigation. Both brothers devoted the greater part of their lives to studies in common and produced, with other works, editions of the *Sermones* of St. Zeno of Verona (Verona, 1739; in *MPL*, xi); of the *Summa theologica* of St. Antoninus of Florence (4 vols., Verona, 1740); of the *Summa de pœnitentia* of St. Raymond of Pennaforte (1744); of the *Opera* of Pope Leo the Great (3 vols., Venice, 1753–57; *MPL*, liv–lvi), one of the most important pieces of editorial work of the eighteenth century, with an appendix on the collections of canons before Gratian; and of the *Opera* of Ratherius, Bishop of Verona (Verona, 1765; *MPL*, cxxxvi). Pietro also participated in literary controversies of his time and defended the absolute papacy with learning and zeal. His two last works, *De potestate ecclesiastica sanctorum pontificum et conciliorum generalium contra opus J. Febronii* (1765) and *De vi ac ratione primatus pontificum* (1766), have been edited by E. W. Westhoff (Münster, 1845–47), and an appendix to the former on papal infallibility was translated into German by A. J. Binterim (Düsseldorf, 1843). K. BENRATH.

BIBLIOGRAPHY: G. M. Mazzuchelli, *Gli Scrittori d'Italia*, vol. ii, part 1, 178–185, 6 parts, Brescia, 1753–65; L. Federici, *Elogi istorici de' più illustri ecclesiastici Veronesi*, iii, 69–120, Verona, 1819.

BALLOU, ba-lū', **HOSEA**: American Universalist; b. at Richmond, N. H., Apr. 30, 1771; d. at Boston June 7, 1852. He was the son of a poor Baptist minister and had to struggle for an education; began to preach at the age of twenty, and was ordained at the Universalist convention of 1794; settled at Dana (then called Hardwick), Mass., the same year; removed in 1803 to Barnard, Vt., in 1809 to Portsmouth, N. H., in 1815 to Salem, Mass., and in 1818 to Boston, where he took charge of the Second (School Street) Universalist Society. In 1819 he assisted in founding and became editor of the *Universalist Magazine* (later called *The Trumpet, The Universalist*, and *The Christian Leader*), the first Universalist newspaper in America; in 1831, of *The Universalist Expositor* (afterward *The Universalist Quarterly Review*). He wrote *Notes on the Parables* (Randolph, Vt., 1804); *A Treatise on the Atonement* (1805); *Examination of the Doctrine of Future Retribution* (Boston, 1834); and several volumes of sermons.

BIBLIOGRAPHY: M. M. Ballou, *Life Story of Hosea Ballou, for the Young*, Boston, 1854; T. Whittemore, *Life of Hosea Ballou*, 2 vols., ib. 1854; O. F. Safford, *Hosea Ballou; a Marvellous Life Story*, ib. 1889.

BALLOU, HOSEA, 2d: American Universalist, grand-nephew of Hosea Ballou; b. at Guilford, Vt., Oct. 18, 1796; d. at Somerville, Mass., May 27, 1861. He assisted his uncle in school-teaching at Portsmouth; was first settled as pastor at Stafford, Conn., in 1821 was called to Roxbury, Mass., and in 1838 to Medford; in 1853 became first president of Tufts College. He helped the elder Hosea Ballou as editor of denominational periodicals and wrote *The Ancient History of Universalism* (Boston, 1829).

BIBLIOGRAPHY: H. S. Ballou, *Hosea Ballou 2d, first President of Tufts College; his Origin, Life, and Letters*, Boston, 1896.

BALM: The rendering in both English versions of the Hebrew *ẓori* (Gen. xxxvii, 25 and xliii, 11, where R. V. has "mastic" in the margin; Jer. viii, 22; xlvi, 11; li, 8; Ezek. xxvii, 17). An important product of Palestine, particularly of the East-Jordan country, is evidently referred to, and the transparent, yellowish-white, fragrant gum of the mastic-tree (*Pistacia lentiscus*, L) is probably meant. Pliny mentions the Judean mastic (*Hist. nat.*, xiv, 122 sqq.). The substance was prized by the ancients as a medicine (Pliny, xxiv, 32 sqq.). The identification of *ẓori* with balsam by Jewish tradition is not correct; such a tropical or subtropical product would hardly be found on the mountains of Gilead. In Song of Sol. v, 1, *basam* may be the true balsam (so R. V., margin; text and A. V., "spice"; cf. "bed of spices," v, 13; vi, 2). It grew in the Ghor, and the balsam gardens of Jericho were famous (Josephus, *Ant.*, IX, i, 2; XIV, iv, 1, and many others). Pompey is said to have carried it thence to Rome, and Josephus thought the Queen of Sheba brought it to Palestine (*Ant.*, VIII, vi, 6; cf. I Kings x, 10). There are several varieties, of which the chief is the *Amyris Gileadensis*, L, the true Arabian or Mecca balsam. It is a low, berry-producing tree, with small blossoms, and imparipinnate leaves. The balsam exudes from the ends of the twigs. Myrrh also belongs to the balsamodendra and probably bdellium; see MYRRH; BDELLIUM. I. BENZINGER.

BALMES, bal"mês', **JAIME (LUCIANO)**: Spanish politico-religious writer; b. at Vich (37 m. n.n.e. of Barcelona), Catalonia, Aug. 28, 1810; d. there July 9, 1848. He studied at his native place and at the University of Cervera, and was ordained priest 1833; became teacher of mathematics at Vich 1837. After 1840 he acted as associate editor of *La Civilizacion* and sole editor of *La Sociedad*, journals of Barcelona, in which he had opportunity to express his political views; visited France and England 1842, and after returning to Spain settled in Madrid, where from Feb., 1844, to Dec. 31, 1846, he published *El Pensamiento* *de la Nacion* in the interest of the Catholic party. He hailed the accession of Pius IX and the last thing he published was a brilliant work in his praise (*Pio IX*, Madrid, 1847). He gained his greatest fame by his *Protestantismo comparado con el Catolicismo en sus relaciones con la civilizacion europea* (4 vols., Barcelona, 1842–44; Eng. transl., from the French, by C. J. Hanford and R. Kershaw, *Protestantism and Catholicity Compared in their Effects on the Civilization of Europe*, London, 1849; 31st American edition, Baltimore, 1899), a work modeled on Guizot's *History of Civilization*, and an able presentation from the Roman Catholic point of view. He also wrote *La Religion demostrada al alcance de los niños* (Barcelona, 1841, Eng. transl., by Canon Galton, *The Foundations of Religion Explained*, London, 1858); *Cartas á un esceptico en materia de religion* (Madrid, 1845; Eng. transl., by W M'Donald, *Letters to a Skeptic on Religious Matters*, Dublin, 1875); *El Criterio* (Madrid, 1845; Eng. transl., *Criterion: or how to detect error and arrive at truth*, New York, 1875); *Filosofia fundamental* (4 vols., Barcelona, 1846; Eng. transl., by H. F Brownson, 2 vols., New York, 1856); *Curso de Filosofia elemental* (4 vols., Madrid, 1847). He published a collected edition of his political writings at Madrid, 1847

BIBLIOGRAPHY: B. Garcia de los Santos, *Vida de Balmes, estracto y analisis de sus obras*, Madrid, 1848; A. de Blanche-Raffin, *Jacques Balmès, sa vie et ses ouvrages*, Paris, 1849.

BALOGH, FERENCZ: Hungarian Reformed; b. at Nagy Várad (140 m. s.e. of Budapest) Mar. 28, 1836. He was educated at the gymnasium of his native city and at the Reformed theological seminary of Debreczin (1854–58), where he remained nine years in various capacities. He visited Paris, London, and Edinburgh for the purpose of further study in 1863–65, and in 1866 was appointed professor of church history in the Reformed theological seminary of Debreczin, where he has since remained and of which he has been rector five times. He has been an elder in the session of the Reformed Church since 1860, and an ecclesiastical councilor for life in the Transtibiscan superintendency of the same religious denomination since 1883. He was a delegate of the Hungarian Reformed Church to the general councils of the Presbyterian Alliance at Edinburgh (1877) and London (1888), and was a member of the national synod of Debreczin in 1881–82. He has been a member of the committee of the Hungarian Protestant Literary Society since 1890, and an honorary member of the British and Foreign Bible Society since 1904. In theology he is a strict adherent of the Helvetic Confession. His numerous works include the following in Hungarian: "Peter Melius, the Hungarian Calvin" (Debreczin, 1866); "History of the Hungarian Protestant Church" (1872); "General Church History to the Present Time" (5 vols., 1872–90); "History of Dogma up to the Reformation" (1877); "Principal Points of Modern Theology" (1877), a polemic against the German Evangelical Union; "Literature of Hungarian Protestant Church History" (1879); "Specific Illustrations of the most Recent Unitarian History" (1892); "Phenomena of the History of Dogma in the Eighteenth and Nineteenth Centuries" (1894); and "History of the Reformed College of Debreczin" (1905). He likewise wrote in English *History of the Creeds*, which appeared in the *Report of the Proceedings of the Presbyterian Alliance* (Philadelphia, 1880), and is the author of numerous minor contributions in Hungarian, French, and German, while in 1875 he founded at Debreczin the Hungarian weekly "Evangelical Protestant Gazette," which he conducted for three years in a successful crusade against the Budapest "Protestant Union."

BALSAM. See BALM.

BALSAMON, bal'sa-men, **THEODOROS:** Greek writer on church law; b. in Constantinople; d. there about 1200. He was chosen patriarch of Antioch in 1193, but, as the patriarchate was in the hands of the Latins, remained in Constantinople. The most important of his writings is the commentary on the *Nomocanon* and *Syntagma* of Photius, in which he helped to make general the view that in matters of the Greek canon law, not the Justinian compilation, but the Basilica were authoritative. Balsamon's "Answers" to the patriarch Mark of Alexandria and his eight "Dissertations" (Gk. *meletai*) are of great importance for the canon law of the Greeks. PHILIPP MEYER.

BIBLIOGRAPHY: The best edition of his juridical writings is found in Rhalles and Potles, Σύνταγμα τῶν θείων καὶ ἱερῶν κανόνων, 6 vols., Athens, 1852–59; Krumbacher, *Geschichte*, passim.

BALTHAZAR, bal'tha-zar, **OF DERNBACH AND THE COUNTERREFORMATION IN FULDA:** Balthazar of Dernbach, abbot of Fulda 1570–1606, was born about 1548; d. at Fulda Mar. 15, 1606. He came of an old Hessian family, and though his parents were Protestants, took the Catholic side as a boy. In 1570, young as he was, he was elected prince-abbot of Fulda, and became the leading champion of the Counterreformation there. The territory under his jurisdiction, adjoining Protestant Hesse and Saxony, seemed practically lost to Rome. The chapter, jealous of its rights, was willing rather to join with the enemies of the Church than to support a strict, determined abbot; the upper classes were striving for both temporal and spiritual independence; the citizens stood by the Augsburg Confession. Balthazar took a decided stand against all three classes. His first task was the enforcement of ecclesiastical discipline, the appointment of Catholic officials, and the suppression of popular demands for the appointment of a Lutheran preacher and the erection of a Protestant school. He called the Jesuits to his aid; in 1571 they started a school and the next year a college. The chapter were much annoyed by the privileges granted to the newcomers, and as a movement hostile to the abbot grew, Protestant princes took a hand. As selfish motives actuated the chapter and the gentry, so they played a part with the Landgrave of Hesse, who joined the Elector of Saxony and the Margrave of Brandenburg-Ansbach (Oct., 1573) in sending an embassy to demand the expulsion of the Jesuits and the abandonment of anti-Protestant measures.

The demands did not move the abbot, though they strengthened his opponents; a formal alliance was made between the chapter and the gentry. Balthazar gained time by politic delays, and found support from his fellow Catholics; the Curia and Duke Albert of Bavaria sought to influence the emperor in his favor. After some hesitation, Maximilian took his side, and rebuked the princes (Feb., 1574) for their interference. Dissensions sprang up between the allies; and the chapter finally made peace with their abbot. He proceeded more diligently than ever to assert his jurisdiction and to keep down the new faith. In 1576 the three classes joined once more in opposition, and this time the chapter were willing to consider the deposition of their chief. Bishop Julius of Würzburg was destined as his successor, and justified the part he played as the only means of saving Roman Catholicism in the district. He promised religious freedom to the country gentry, while refusing it to the towns, and observance of all the rights, both of the gentry and the chapter—practically the restoration of the conditions previous to 1570. Balthazar was in Hammelburg, supervising the restoration of Catholicism there, which had been previously unsuccessful. On June 20 the forces of his opponents entered the town, followed the next day by Bishop Julius. They numbered about 200 horsemen, and Balthazar had made no provision for defense. On the 23d he was forced to abdicate; compensation in both money and benefices was offered to him, on condition that he would write to the emperor and other princes, assuring them that the proceedings had been freely agreed to by him. A few days later, Julius was formally chosen administrator of Fulda. But it was not possible long to conceal the real facts. The emperor immediately addressed a stern mandate to Julius, annulling the agreement, and Balthazar recalled his forced consent. Julius lost the support of the Roman Catholic princes when the facts were known, and the Protestants had little confidence in him. Long legal proceedings followed. The Diet of Regensburg provided a temporary administrator, who was, however, a vassal of the Bishop of Würzburg. Yet from 1579 onward Catholicism made steady progress, largely through the tireless labors of the Jesuits, which Balthazar, living at Bieberstein near Fulda, supported to the extent of his power. To him also was owing the erection of a seminary at Fulda in 1584. When, therefore, in 1602 the final decision was rendered in his favor, his return in December met with no opposition from the new generation, and the Counterreformation made still more rapid strides during the remaining four years of his activity, until at his death the Roman Catholic faith was restored in practically the whole district, with the exception of the country gentry. This earliest case of the successful resistance of a minority to the Reformation had a great importance as showing what could be done and inspiring the Catholic party to take the offensive in reconquering territory which they seemed to have lost. WALTER GOETZ.

BIBLIOGRAPHY: Komp, *Fürstabt Balthazar von Fulda und die Stiftsrebellion von 1576*, in *Historisch-politische Blätter*, lvi, 1865 (contains rich collection of sources); H. Egloffstein, *Fürstabt Balthazar von Dernbach und die katholische Restauration im Hochstifte Fulda, 1570–1606*, Munich, 1890; H. Moritz, *Die Wahl Rudolfs II, der Reichstag zu Regensburg und die Freistellungsbewegung*, pp. 26, 347, 411 sqq., Marburg, 1895; K. Schellhass, *Nuntiaturberichte*, iii, 3, Berlin, 1896; W. E. Schwarz, *Nuntiaturkorrespondenz Groppers*, Paderborn, 1898.

BALTIMORE COUNCILS: A name given to ten assemblies of the Roman Catholic Church in the United States held during the nineteenth century. The first independent episcopal see of the Church created in the American Republic was that of Baltimore (erected in 1790), and the same diocese was made the first metropolitan see of the United States in 1808. On account of this priority in point of time the archdiocese of Baltimore enjoys a quasiprimatial dignity conferred upon it by the pope, and hence that city has been the place of meeting of the various assemblies of the American hierarchy. The first of these assemblies was held under the presidency of Most Rev. James Whitfield, fourth archbishop of Baltimore, in Oct., 1829. This council and the six following ones, held respectively in 1833, 1837, 1840, 1843, 1846, and 1849, belong to the category designated canonically as provincial councils; i.e., assemblies of all the bishops of a territory known as an ecclesiastical province, and presided over by the metropolitan or archbishop. Three other Baltimore Councils (held in 1852, 1866, and 1884) are called plenary or national, by which is meant an assembly of all the bishops of a country, convoked and presided over by the primate or some other dignitary commissioned thereto by the pope. At the time of the first council, the province of Baltimore was the only one in the United States, comprising, besides its own see, the sees of Boston, New York, Bardstown (Kentucky), Charleston, and Cincinnati, and only the incumbents of these dioceses with their coadjutors constituted the voting members of the council. The decrees drafted were thirty-seven in number, and they were confirmed by a papal rescript of Oct. 16, 1830. They embody the earliest attempt at a uniform legislation in church matters in the United States, and they deal with the most urgent needs of a time when church forces were scattered and without organization. Thus, among other things, means are taken to regularize the credentials and the ministrations of the small number of available clergy, and to obviate the abuses arising from lay interference in ecclesiastical matters, particularly that known as "trusteeism." The Douai version of the English Bible was recommended, and various regulations were formulated with reference to the administration of the sacraments, because in the generally prevailing circumstances, it was impossible to carry out in full the prescriptions of the Roman ritual. The six succeeding councils, which continued to frame, as circumstances required, the local canonical legislation of the Roman Catholic Church in the United States, were similar in purpose, form of procedure, and general results.

The First Plenary Council of Baltimore was held in May 1852, and was presided over by Archbishop Kenrick, who had been appointed to that function by Pope Pius IX. There were present six archbishops and twenty-four bishops with a large number of theologians and canonists, who acted as consultors. The decrees of the former councils of Baltimore were confirmed and extended to all parts of the country; certain enactments were made concerning the canonical administration of dioceses, the publication of marriage banns, the establishment of ecclesiastical seminaries, etc. The council suggested to the Roman authorities the erection of a metropolitan see in San Francisco and the establishment of ten new dioceses in various parts of the country. The suggestion was acted upon by Pius IX who confirmed the decrees of the council by a rescript dated Sept. 26, 1852.

The Second Plenary Council of Baltimore was held in Oct., 1866, under the presidency of the Most Rev. M. J. Spalding, archbishop of Baltimore; there were present seven archbishops, thirty-eight bishops, three mitered abbots, and 120 theologians. The motives for calling the council and the topics discussed were in the main the same as those pertaining to the previous assemblies, but in particular it was deemed useful, "at the close of the great national crisis which had acted as a dissolvent upon all sectarian ecclesiastical organizations, to reaffirm solemnly the bond of union existing between the Catholics of all parts of the republic, and to deliberate on the measures to be adopted in order to meet the new phase of national life which the result of the war had just inaugurated." Besides, it was felt to be an urgent duty on the part of the heads of the Church to discuss the future status of the newly emancipated yet very dependent negro. Among the results of the council may be mentioned the erection of ten new dioceses and the drafting of a scheme for the selection of bishops, which, having been approved in Rome, remained in force until amended in the Third Plenary Council.

This last and most important of the Baltimore Councils was held Nov. 9–Dec. 7, 1884, under the presidency of the Most Rev. James Gibbons, who had been appointed to that office by Pope Leo XIII. The number of prelates who took part in the council was fourteen archbishops, sixty bishops, five visiting bishops from Canada and Japan, seven mitered abbots, one prefect apostolic, eleven monsignors, eighteen vicars-general, twenty-three superiors of religious orders, twelve rectors of ecclesiastical seminaries, and ninety theologians. The object of the council was to provide efficient means of organization for the needs of the rapidly growing Church of the United States, and to prepare the way for the gradual introduction of the more useful elements of canon law into the administration of religious affairs in this country. The decrees of the council, which were approved by Pope Leo, Sept. 10, 1885, comprise eleven *tituli* or sections, and each one of these is divided into several chapters. This body of legislation touches successively upon the prerogatives and duties of bishops and the inferior members of the clergy, on divine worship, the administration of the sacraments, the training of the clergy, Catholic schools, ecclesiastical courts, church property, etc. Since the promulgation of these decrees in 1885 they constitute the norm of ecclesiastical law as applied within the jurisdiction of the Roman Catholic Church in the United States.

James F Driscoll.

Bibliography: *Concilia provincialia Baltimori habita ab anno 1829 usque ad annum 1840*, Baltimore, 1842; *Concilium plenarium totius Americæ septentrionalis fœderatæ habitum anno 1852*, ib. 1853; *Concilii plenarii Baltimorensis II. acta et decreta*, ib. 1868, 2d ed., 1877; *Third Plenary Council of Baltimore, 1884*, New York, 1885; *Memorial Volume of the Third Plenary Council of Baltimore*, Baltimore, 1885; *Acta et decreta concilii plenarii Baltimorensis*, ib. 1886; J. G. Shea, *Hist. of the Catholic Church in the United States*, vols. iii–iv, New York, 1892; T. O'Gorman, *American Church History Series*, ix, 340 sqq., New York, 1895.

BALTUS, bȯl″tüs′, JEAN FRANÇOIS: French Jesuit; b. at Metz June 8, 1667; d. at Reims, as librarian of the college, Mar. 19, 1743. He joined the Jesuits in 1682, and taught in several schools in France; became censor of books in Rome, 1717. He distinguished himself by a number of literary and theological works, of which the most important are, *Réponse à l'histoire des oracles de M. de Fontenelle* (2 vols., Strasburg, 1707; Eng. transl., London, 1708), in which he maintains that the ancient oracles were not mere frauds on the part of the priests, but utterances under demoniacal influence; and *Défense des Saints Pères accusés de platonisme* (Paris, 1711), in which he vindicates the originality of the Fathers and their complete independence of the ancient philosophy.

BALTZER, JOHANN BAPTISTA. See Hermes, Georg.

BALUZE, bā″lüz′, ÉTIENNE: Roman Catholic canonist and historian; b. at Tuile (*Tutela Lemovicum*, 45 m. s.s.e. of Limoges), in Limousin, France, Nov. 23, 1630; d. at Paris June 28, 1718. He belonged to a family of famous jurists and studied first with the Jesuits at Tulle. In 1646 he was sent to Toulouse, where he remained till 1654, attending the philosophical lectures at St. Martial, the Jesuit college there. While still in school he showed an inclination for old parchments and historical documents. As his father made him study civil law, he could only devote himself in secret to his favorite studies in the library of Charles of Montchal, bishop of Toulouse. Exceptional acumen and persevering application made his critical method a safe one and he soon became known among the scholars of his time. His studies made it necessary for him to become either a monk or a priest, or to enter the service of some ecclesiastical dignitary. He received the tonsure and looked for a patron, whom he found in the successor of Montchal, Peter of Marca, afterward archbishop of Paris, who also showed him how to utilize his extensive historical studies for the canon and civil law. After Marca's death (1652) different bishops and archbishops tried to attach him to themselves. For a short time he remained with the Archbishop of Auch, and Le Tellier, the chancellor, who appointed him canon of Reims. In 1667 the minister J. B. Colbert made him his librarian, and Baluze occupied this position until compelled to resign by advanced age after thirty-three years' service. He collected hundreds of documents from abbeys and monasteries and copied a large number. In 1707 Louis XIV appointed him inspector of the *Collège royal*, where he had been professor of canon law since 1689. In this position he corresponded and had personal intercourse with scholars of different countries. A history of the house of Auvergne, which he edited during this time with the help of Cardinal Bouillon, obliged him to leave Paris after the flight of his ambitious protector (1710). Though eighty years of age, Baluze was obliged to go from place to place and finally settled at Orléans, where he remained till 1713. The family of Bouillon being received again by the king after the Peace of Utrecht, Baluze was able to return to Paris. Deprived of all means, he was obliged to devote himself entirely to literary activity, and he died without completing his history of Tulle. He wrote: *Regum Francorum capitularia* (1677; new edition by de Chiniac, 3 vols., fol., 1780); *Epistolæ Innocentii papæ III* (1682); *Conciliorum nova collectio* (1683, fol.); *Vitæ paparum Avenionensium* (1693); *Historia Tutelensis* (1717); *Cypriani opera* (1726); *Bibliotheca Baluziana* (1719); *Miscellanea* (7 vols., 1677–1713).

G. Bonet-Maury.

Bibliography: His autobiography is in the *Bibliotheca Baluziana*, Paris, 1719. Consult L. E. Du Pin, *Bibliothèque des auteurs ecclésiastiques*, xix, 1–6, 47 vols., Paris, 1686–95; Niceron, *Mémoires*, i, 459–471; Vitrac, *Éloge de Baluze*, ib. 1777; M. Deloche, *É. Baluze, sa vie et ses œuvres*, ib. 1856; L. Delisle, *Le Cabinet des manuscrits de la Bibliothèque Nationale*, i, 364–367, 445–475, ib. 1868; *Bulletin de la société des lettres de la Corrèze*, iii (1881), 93 and 457, iv (1882), 513, v (1883), 160, vi (1884), 645, ix (1887), 100–163, x (1888); A. Lefranc, *Histoire du Collège de France*, Paris, 1893; E. Fage, *É. Baluze, sa vie, ses ouvrages, son exile, sa défense*, ib. 1899.

BAMBERG, BISHOPRIC OF: A see founded in 1007 by King Henry II in the city (*civitas Papinberc*) which Otho II had given to Henry's father, Duke Henry of Bavaria, in 973. As Henry II had no children, his idea was to leave this possession to God, at the same time aiding in the final conquest of paganism in the district. But the territory of the Wends on the upper Main, the Wiesent, and the Aisch had belonged to the diocese of Würzburg since the organization of the Middle German bishoprics by St. Boniface, so that no new diocese could be erected without the consent of the occupant of that see. He raised no objection to parting with some of his territory, especially as the king promised to have Würzburg raised to an archbishopric and to give him an equivalent in Meiningen. The consent of Pope John XVII was obtained for this arrangement, but the elevation of Würzburg to an archbishopric proved impracticable, and its bishop withdrew his consent. The king persisted, however, and had the erection of the new diocese confirmed at the great Synod of Frankfort, subsequently naming his chancellor, Eberhard, the first bishop. [The next seven bishops were named by the emperors, after which free canonical election was the rule. Eberhard's immediate successor, Suidger of Morsleben, became pope in 1046 as Clement II. At the beginning of the thirteenth century the diocese gradually became a territorial principality, and its bishops took secular precedence next after the archbishops. The fortieth bishop, George III of Limburg (1505–22), was inclined toward the Reformation, which caused a violent social outbreak under his successor Weigand (1522–56), and the city suffered severely in the Margraves' War (1552–54), as well as in the Thirty Years' War, when it was placed under the jurisdiction of Bernard, the new Duke of Franconia. At the Peace of Westphalia (1648), the bishops recovered their possessions; but these were overrun by the French revolutionary armies, and in 1802 annexed to Bavaria. From 1808 to 1817 the diocese was vacant]; but by the Bavarian Concordat of the latter year it was made an archbishopric, with Würzburg, Speyer, and Eichstädt as suffragan sees. The present diocese comprises Upper Franconia and the northern half of Middle Franconia.

(A. Hauck.)

Bibliography: Adalbert, *Vita Heinrici*, ed. G. H. Pertz, in *MGH, Script.*, iv (1841), 787 sqq.; A. Ussermann, *Episcopatus Bambergensis*, Blaise, 1802; P. Jaffé, *Monumenta Bambergensia*, Berlin, 1869; *KL*, i, 1915–28 (very full); J. Looshorn, *Geschichte des Bistums Bamberg*, 6 vols., Munich, 1886–1906 (an exhaustive history); Hauck, *KD*, iii, 418–428.

BAMPTON LECTURES: A series of eight lectures or sermons instituted at the University of Oxford by the Rev. John Bampton, M.A., of Trinity College, Canon of Salisbury (b. 1689; d. 1751), who left his entire estate for the purpose. By the terms of the founder's will they shall be preached on Sunday mornings in Term, "between the commencement of the last month in Lent Term [the day before Palm-Sunday] and the end of the third week in Act Term [the day before Whitsunday—the Saturday after the first Tuesday in July, or later, if continued by Congregation], upon either of the following subjects—to confirm and establish the Christian Faith, and to confute all heretics and schismatics—upon the divine authority of the holy Scriptures—upon the authority of the writings of the primitive Fathers, as to faith and practise of the primitive Church—upon the Divinity of our Lord and Savior Jesus Christ—upon the Divinity of the Holy Ghost—upon the Articles of the Christian Faith, as comprehended in the Apostles' and Nicene Creeds." The publication of the lectures is obligatory. The lecturer is chosen by the heads of colleges and must be at least a master of arts of Oxford or Cambridge; no one can be selected a second time. The first course was given in 1780; since 1895 lectures have been suspended in alternate years because of diminution in the income provided by the endowment fund. At present the estate produces £120 to each lecturer.

A list of lecturers and subjects is given in *The Historical Register of the University of Oxford* (Oxford, 1900); also, down to 1893, in J. F. Hurst, *Literature of Theology* (New York, 1896); the continuation from the latter date is as follows:

1894. Rev. John Richardson Illingworth, *Personality, Human and Divine*, pp. xv, 274, 8vo, London, Macmillan, 1895.

1895. Very Rev. Thomas Banks Strong, *Christian Ethics*, pp. xxvii, 388, 8vo, London, Longmans, 1896.

1897. Rev. Robert Lawrence Ottley, *Aspects of the Old Testament*, pp. xix, 448, 8vo, London, Longmans, 1897.

1899. Rev. William Ralph Inge, *Christian Mysticism*, pp. xv, 380, 8vo, London, Methuen, 1899.

1901. Rev. Archibald Robertson, *Regnum Dei*, pp. xix, 402, 8vo, London, Methuen, 1901.
1903. Rev. William Holden Hutton, *The Influence of Christianity upon National Character, illustrated by the Lives and Legends of the English Saints*, pp. xiv, 12, 385, 8vo, London, Wells, Gardner, Darton & Co., 1903.
1905. Rev. Frederick William Bussell, *Christian Theology and Social Progress*, London, Methuen, 1907.

BAN: In the civil law of the old German Empire, a declaration of outlawry; in the twelfth century adopted by the church as the common name for a declaration of excommunication (q.v.).

BANCROFT, RICHARD: Archbishop of Canterbury; b. at Farnworth, Lancashire, 1544; d. in Lambeth Palace, London, Nov. 2, 1610. He was educated at Cambridge (B.A., 1567; D.D., 1585), was made rector of Teversham, near Cambridge, 1576, and rose steadily till he became Bishop of London in 1597 and Archbishop of Canterbury in 1604. He was a High-churchman, asserting that the episcopal authority is based upon a divine right, and most violently opposed to the Puritans, whom he often attacked in his sermons. As president of the Convocation, he presented for adoption the Book of Canons now in force, and as Archbishop he was "the chief overseer" of the authorized version of the Bible, which he had opposed as a Puritan proposition at the Hampton Court Conference (1604). His literary remains are unimportant.

BANES, bā″nês′, **DOMINGO:** Spanish theologian; b. either at Mondragon (65 m. s.e. of Bayonne, France), Biscaya, or at Valladolid Feb. 28, 1528; d. at Medina del Campo Oct. 21, 1604. He studied at Salamanca; joined the Dominicans 1544; lectured on theology at Avila, Alcala, Valladolid, and Salamanca. At Avila he became the confessor of St. Theresa and remained her friend till his death. He was one of the greatest of the expounders and defenders of Thomism (see THOMAS AQUINAS, SAINT) and contributed much to the condemnation of Molina. His chief work was his commentary on the *Summa theologiæ* of Thomas Aquinas (4 vols., Salamanca, 1584–94).

BANGORIAN CONTROVERSY. See HOADLEY, BENJAMIN.

BANKS, JOHN SHAW: English Wesleyan; b. at Sheffield Oct. 8, 1835. He was educated at King Edward's School, Birmingham, and, after being a missionary in southern India from 1856 to 1864, was a minister of his denomination in Plymouth, Dewsbury, London, Manchester, and Glasgow until 1880. Since the latter year he has been professor of theology in Headingley College, Leeds. He was president of the Wesleyan Conference in 1902, and has written *Three Indian Heroes: Missionary, Statesman, Soldier* (London, 1874); *Martin Luther, the Prophet of Germany* (1877); *Our Indian Empire, its Rise and Growth* (1880); *Manual of Christian Doctrine* (1887); *Scripture and its Witnesses, Outlines of Christian Evidence* (1896); *The Tendencies of Modern Theology* (1897); *Development of Doctrine in the Early Church* (1899); *Development of Doctrine from the Early Middle Ages to the Reformation* (1901), in addition to translating F. A. Philippi's "Commentary on St. Paul's Epistle to the Romans" (2 vols., Edinburgh, 1878–79); D. G. Monrad's "The World of Prayer" (London, 1879); and I. A. Dorner's "System of Christian Doctrine" (in collaboration with A. Cave, 4 vols., Edinburgh, 1880–82), as well as a number of less important German theological works.

BANKS, LOUIS ALBERT: Methodist Episcopalian; b. at Cornwallis, Ore., Nov. 12, 1855. He was educated at Philomath College, Philomath, Ore., and Boston University, but did not take a degree. He has held pastorates at the Hall Street Church, Portland, Ore., Vancouver and Seattle, Wash., Boisé City, Ida., Trinity Church, Cincinnati, O., First Church, Cleveland, O., Hanson Place Church, Brooklyn, N. Y., St. John's Church and First Church, Boston, Mass., Grace Church, New York City, and Trinity Church, Denver, Col. He was Prohibition candidate for governor of Massachusetts in 1893, and is now an evangelist for the American Antisaloon League. In theology he is an orthodox Methodist. He has written *The People's Christ* (Boston, 1891); *The White Slaves* (1892); *The Revival Quiver* (1893); *Anecdotes and Morals* (New York, 1894); *Common Folks' Religion* (Boston,. 1894); *Honeycomb of Life* (New York, 1895); *Heavenly Trade Winds* (1895); *The Christ Dream* (1896); *Christ and his Friends* (1896); *Paul and his Friends* (1896); *The Saloon-Keeper's Ledger* (1896); *The Fisherman and his Friends* (1897); *Seven Times around Jericho* (1897); *Hero Tales from Sacred Story* (1897); *The Christ Brotherhood: Heroic Personalities* (1898); *The Unexpected Christ* (1898); *Immortal Hymns and Their Story* (Cleveland, 1898); *Sermon Stories for Boys and Girls* (New York, 1898); *Immortal Songs of Camp and Field* (Cleveland, 1899); *The Great Sinners of the Bible* (New York, 1899); *A Year's Prayer Meeting Talks* (New York, 1899); *Chats with Young Christians* (Cleveland, 1900); *David and his Friends* (New York, 1900); *The Lord's Arrows* (1900); *Fresh Bait for Fishers of Men* (Cleveland, 1900); *Poetry and Morals* (New York, 1900); *Hidden Wells of Comfort* (1901); *The Great Saints of the Bible* (1901); *Unused Rainbows* (Chicago, 1901); *The Motherhood of God* (1901); *The King's Stewards* (New York, 1902); *Life of Rev. T. DeWitt Talmage, D.D.* (1902); *Youth of Famous Americans* (1902); *Windows for Sermons* (1902); *The Healing of Souls* (1902); *The Great Portraits of the Bible* (1903); *Soul-Winning Stories* (1903); *Thirty-one Revival Sermons* (1904); *The Religious Life of Famous Americans* (1904); and *Great Promises of the Bible* (1905).

BANNS: A public announcement of an intended marriage, made in church during service. The word is a plural of ban, meaning an authoritative proclamation. The singular in the modern sense occurs in the fifteenth century; since then the plural only is found. Banns really have no connection either with the *professiones* of the early Church, alluded to by Ignatius and Tertullian, or with the provision made in the Carolingian capitulary of 802 for investigation by the clergy and *seniores* in order to avoid incestuous marriages.

The public announcement seems to have become customary first in France, then in England (where the Synod of Westminster, 1200, decreed that no marriage should be contracted without banns thrice published in the church), and were prescribed for the whole Church by Innocent III in the Lateran Council of 1215. According to the provisions of the Council of Trent the proclamation must be made in the place of residence of both parties on three consecutive Sundays or feasts of obligation. The bishop may dispense from this rule, and in case of need the parish priest may disregard it; in any case its observance does not affect the validity of the marriage. The evangelical churches of Germany retained this custom, as involving investigation of possible impediments and intercession of the congregation for the couple, and most secular laws, where marriage in church is required, have also sanctioned it, as a preliminary to ecclesiastical marriage. [In the Church of England the Prayer-book requires the publication of banns on three successive Sundays, after the second lesson at morning or evening prayer. This may be avoided by the procuring of a special licence from the Archbishop of Canterbury. In the United States banns are published only in the Roman Catholic Church and certain minor denominations.]

(E. Friedberg.)

Bibliography: Bingham, *Origines*, book xxii, chap. ii, § 2; E. Martène, *De antiquis ecclesiæ ritibus*, book ii, chap. ix, art. v, 3 vols., Antwerp, 1736–37; J. Fessler, *Der Kirchenbann und seine Folgen*, Vienna, 1862; Schilling, *Der Kirchenbann nach kanonischen Recht*, Leipsic, 1859.

BAPTISM.

I. Biblical Doctrine.—1. Origin and Practise: Conybeare has tried to prove that the original text of Matt. xxviii, 19 did not contain the baptismal command or the Trinitarian formula, which were interpolated, according to him, at the beginning of the third century. But since the investigations of Riggenbach, the ordinary reading may be considered the original. Jesus, however, can not have given his disciples this Trinitarian order of baptism after his resurrection; for the New Testament knows only baptism in the name of Jesus (Acts ii, 38; viii, 16; xix, 5; Gal. iii, 27; Rom. vi, 3; I Cor. i, 13–15), which still occurs even in the second and third centuries, while the Trinitarian formula occurs only in Matt. xxviii, 19 and then only again Didache vii, 1 and Justin, *Apol.*, i, 61. It is unthinkable that the Apostolic Church thus disobeyed the express command of the Lord, which it otherwise considered the highest authority. Occurrences like those of Acts xix, 1–7 ought to have shown that the prescribed formula of baptism could not have been shortened to "the name of the Lord Jesus," if the character of baptism was to be retained as commanded. Judging from I Cor. i, 14–17, Paul did not know Matt. xxviii, 19; otherwise he could not have written that Christ had sent him not to baptize, but to preach the gospel. Moreover, had it been known at the Apostolic Council, the missionary spheres could not have been so separated that Peter was recognized as the apostle of the circumcision, Paul and Barnabas as apostles of the heathen (Gal. ii, 7–8); rather would the original apostles have claimed the universal apostolate for themselves. Finally, the distinctly liturgical character of the formula Matt. xxviii, 19 is strange; it was not the way of Jesus to make such formulas. Nevertheless this baptismal command contains the elements which constitute Christian baptism; for the activity of the Son in baptism implies the immediate cooperation of the Father; and from the beginning Christian baptism has been considered the mediating agency of the Holy Spirit. Therefore while the formal authenticity of Matt. xxviii, 19 must be disputed, it must still be assumed that the later congregations recognized as the will of their Lord that which they experienced as the effect of baptism and traced it back to a direct word of Jesus.

If Matt. xxviii, 19 can not be considered as a baptismal command, we have no direct word of Jesus which institutes baptism; for Mark xvi, 16 belongs to the spurious appendix of the Gospel and is dependent upon Matt. xxviii, 19. But from the very beginning the Christian Church has universally practised baptism (Acts ii, 38; viii, 36, 38; x, 48; I Cor. xii, 13; Gal. iii, 27; Eph. iv, 5; John iii, 5), and must therefore have been convinced that it was acting according to the will of the Lord. The origin of baptism may perhaps be explained as follows: the word of Jesus in Acts i, 5 repeats John the Baptist's prophecy of spiritual baptism (Mark i, 8). Moreover, the farewell discourses in John and the expression *epangelia tou pneumatos*, which occurs like a technical term in Acts ii, 33; Gal. iii, 14; Eph. i, 13, postulate an utterance of Jesus concerning the gift of the Spirit to the disciples. But Jesus had spoken of baptism as a symbol of the gift of the Spirit. Being filled with the Spirit was for him the antitype of the baptism of John. When the disciples, after the completion of the Messianic work, took up again the baptismal rite which they had formerly practised at his command (John iii, 22; iv, 1, 2) as a preparation for admission into the Messianic congregation, and the Holy Spirit descended upon the baptized, they came to the conviction that they were acting according to the will of their Master and now combined the abovementioned words concerning the Spirit and Christian baptism. Christian baptism has its real root in the baptism of John, not in the sphere of mysterious initiations and lustrations of Greek religious societies, or in the great wave of Babylonian baptism which poured over the civilized countries of that time from the East.

2. Significance of Christian Baptism: The Greek phrase *baptizein en* or *epi tōi onomati Iēsou* means that the act of baptism takes place with the utterance of the name of Jesus; *baptizein eis to onoma Iēsou* means that the person baptized enters into the relation of belonging to Christ, of being his property. All three formulas are alike in so far as the baptized are subjected to the power and efficacy of Jesus, who is now their Lord. According to Paul (Rom. vi, 1–11; Col. ii, 11, 12; Gal. iii, 26, 27; I Cor. xii, 13; vi, 11; Eph. v, 26; Tit. iii, 5), baptism secures purification from sins, the putting off of the sinful body of the flesh, mortification of sin, renewal of life, regeneration, the power of the Holy Spirit, communion with the life of Christ, incorporation into the mystical body of Christ, the Church. Everywhere baptism is represented as the mediating agency of real objective effects, with God as their cause, and not as a merely symbolical act. Paul's teaching on baptism is not a transition from pagan cults, but his mystical doctrine concerning Christ and the Spirit are to be explained from his religious experience, which he objectifies in a manner conditioned by the history of his time. The Book of Acts does not contain theological reflections on baptism like those of Paul's epistles, but simple views of the congregations, and the connection with the baptism of John is here plainer (Acts xxii, 16; ii, 38) than in Paul. It is true, we find also in Acts the relation of the gift of the Spirit to baptism (Acts ii, 38; viii, 13–17; xix, 6; in ix, 17–18; x, 44–48 the gift of the Spirit precedes baptism), but this connection is looser than in Paul, and in some passages (viii, 13–17; xix, 6) it is only external. Baptism is mentioned in the New Testament also in I Pet. iii, 21; Heb. x, 22; vi, 2; John iii, 5; xiii, 10. The act was often performed immediately after the recognition of the Messiahship of Jesus and the decision to join the Messianic congregation without further preparation (Acts ii, 41; viii, 38; ix, 18; x, 33–48; xvi, 33). A detailed baptismal profession of faith was still wanting; but baptism in the name of Jesus was equivalent to such a profession.

P. Feine.

II. Church Doctrine.—1. Patristic Teaching: The expressions of the Fathers on the subject are very indefinite, the symbolical and realistic features not clearly distinguished. It is perhaps not to be taken seriously when Justin (*I Apol.*, lxi) compares regeneration by the water of baptism with natural generation as its proper counterpart; but with Tertullian speculation concerning the general cosmic signification of the water, its inner natural relation to the spirit of God (Gen. i, 2), goes so far that he undoubtedly thinks of some sort of real connection of the Spirit with the water of baptism. He probably imagines that the Holy Spirit after the invocation of God makes his "abode" in the water (*De baptismo*, iii–v). But it is not clear how God or the Spirit is supposed to act upon man through the water or out of the water, how far through the agency of the body or how far through will and thought.

1. Primitive Period.

Since the earliest days two ideas have been characteristic of the estimate of baptism—the view that it forms the sure, and, as a rule, the only entrance to the congregation of Christ and its blessings, i.e., to salvation; and the belief that while its effects may be lost, it can not be repeated. To the former view there was only one exception, the belief that martyrdom, the baptism of blood, could replace baptism with water. Baptism of blood was even to be preferred in so far as it admitted directly and irrevocably into the heavenly congregation of Christ. Why it was considered impossible to repeat baptism with water is not quite intelligible. It is certain, however, that this view was soon felt to be a heavy burden. The more highly baptism was valued, the more was the loss of its grace dreaded, and thus a tendency grew up to postpone it to the end of life. None the less, as early as the second century the custom developed of baptizing children, if not infants in arms at least those of "tender age" (see below, IV, 2). Tertullian disapproved of this, being of the opinion that baptism should be postponed to the period of a fuller development. He is also the first to mention the institution of sponsors (see below, III, 7). All the blessings of the Church are brought into connection with baptism—forgiveness of sins, renewal of life (regeneration), reception of the Holy Spirit, proper knowledge of God ("illumination"), assurance of eternal life (incorruptibility of soul and body). In course of time, the different acts of baptism were separated—the immersion in water from the anointing and laying on of hands, which had been added, it is uncertain how early. It was then thought that immersion or ablution signified purification from sin, and the other acts equipment with the Spirit and bestowal of eternal life. In practise, however, these theoretical distinctions were never strictly kept apart. Tertullian required that as a rule only the bishop, or a presbyter or deacon delegated by him, should perform the act of baptism; only in case of necessity was a layman authorized to perform it (*De baptismo*, xvii). Cyprian goes so far as to say that a priest (*sacerdos*) "must" (*oportet*) "purify and hallow" the water (*Epist.*, lxx, 1).

2. Fourth Century. In the fourth century the doctrine of baptism was treated by Cyril of Jerusalem in his third catechetical lecture (*MPG*, xxxiii, 425 sqq.), by Gregory Nazianzen in his "Discourse on Holy Baptism" (*Orat.*, xl, *MPG*, xxxvi, 360 sqq.), and by Gregory of Nyssa ("Greater Catechetical Oration," xl, *MPG*, xlv, 101; and "Address to those who Postpone Baptism," *MPG*, xlvi, 1). Both Gregory of Nyssa and Gregory Nazianzen desire an "early" baptism, at any rate no "procrastination." Baptism is here spoken of as a power of prime importance as an aid to man in his temptations. It is so necessary that even a child can not be saved without it. Gregory Nazianzen "recommends" that a child shall be baptized in the "third year of his life." That, in spite of the opposition to which Tertullian witnesses, baptism of children became soon more and more a general custom, is evident from the fact that Origen ("On Romans," bk. v) considers it an apostolic tradition. The motive for its enforcement differs with different authors. In fact, the general notions as to the meaning of baptism vary so widely that there was evidently not yet any recognized "church doctrine" in the strict sense of the word. Not a few ideas from the analogous rites of pagan mysteries crept into the teaching of theologians.

3. Augustine. The first who developed a really dogmatic theory of baptism was Augustine, under the stress of his controversy with the Donatists (see HERETIC BAPTISM). His most important early writing on the subject is the comprehensive work *De baptismo contra Donatistas libri vii* (*MPL*, xliii), with which may be coupled the smaller treatise *De unico baptismo contra Petilianum* (ibid.). He makes a sharp distinction between *sacramentum* and *res sacramenti*. It is possible, according to him, to obtain the *sacramentum* without the *res*, the grace of which the sacrament is a sign. He also taught originally that one might obtain the *res* without the *sacramentum*, but later he abandoned this view, at least in regard to baptism. The older he grew, the more firmly he was convinced that baptism was indispensable for salvation, since men could be saved only within the Church, to which baptism was the only entrance. It is true, he was thinking in this connection primarily of adults; but even in their case he was of the opinion that God would be gracious if by any chance a catechumen should die without baptism by no fault of his own. Later, however, he believed that even children dying unbaptized could not be saved, although they would meet only the smallest degree of condemnation (cf. *De peccatorum meritis et remissione et de baptismo parvulorum libri iii*, *MPL*, xliv). In the controversy with Pelagius, Augustine had frequent occasion to develop and justify his views on the baptism of children (cf. especially his *Epist. ad Dardanum*, *Epist.*, clxxxvii, *MPL*, xxxiii). It was Augustine especially who developed the theory that baptism had reference to original sin. It is true he laid more emphasis originally on sin in general than on original sin as the obstacle to be removed by baptism. But the more the idea of the baptism of children began to occupy his mind, so much the more original sin became the central point of his interest, coupled with the question of the importance to be attached to faith in connection with baptism. He taught not that the children themselves had faith, but that the faith of the Church benefited them. Since the Church presents the children to God in baptism, making a confession of faith in their stead, God grants them real forgiveness and power for a real "conversion of the heart" when they grow older (cf. especially his *Epist. ad Bonifacium*, *Epist.*, xcviii, *MPL*, xxxiii). But at this point his views on predestination come in, and with them his distinctions within the sacrament, according to which baptism does not suffice for salvation if one is not predestined.

2. Roman Catholic and Eastern Teaching:

1. Scholasticism and Later Roman Catholicism. Scholasticism on the whole only elaborated and systematized the doctrine of Augustine (cf. Peter Lombard, *Sent.*, IV, dist. iii–vii, and Thomas Aquinas, *Summa*, III, quæst. lxvi–lxxi). The views expressed in the *Catechismus Romanus* (part II, chap. ii) and in Bellarmine's treatise *De baptismo* (*Disputationes de controversiis Christianæ fidei*, II, ii, 1) rest upon the same basis. It became customary among the scholastics to explain the doctrine of the sacraments by the distinction of the conceptions *materia* and *forma*. Everything in the sacrament rests upon divine institution and therefore can not be altered even by the authority of the Church. The Church can not abolish a sacrament, and is bound to observe its matter and form, but may be assured of possessing and transmitting everything that the sacrament ought to contain and offer according to the divine will. If matter and form are properly connected, the sacrament produces its effects *ex opere operato*. The matter of baptism is water only; its form is the words, "I baptize thee in the name of the Father and of the Son and of the Holy Ghost." In baptism all sins are forgiven, in the child original sin, in adults actual sins also. With special reference to original sin Thomas teaches that it is taken away only *reatu*, i.e., in regard to its guilt (which is great enough to exclude one from the bliss of heaven), but not *actu*. The latter expression means that "concupiscence" still remains as a "tinder" (*fomes*) from which at any moment sin may be kindled into flame. Peter Lombard emphasizes the idea that natural concupiscence is "weakened." The Council of Trent (*Sessio V*) teaches that it is not sin in the proper sense. Real conversion follows baptism, but rests partly upon the grace which it bestows and which only needs to be used by our free will. Great significance is attached to the teaching of Thomas especially concerning the "character" which baptism confers. This also goes back to Augustine, who touches this idea briefly in order to establish the validity of the baptism of heretics. Baptism incorporates us with Christ under all circumstances. It confers the "character" of belonging objectively to Christ, to his "body," the Church. This character is indelible, and depends only upon the due administration of the sacrament as to matter and form. Thus baptism brings every one into actual contact with the flow of grace emanating from Christ. Whoever "interposes an obstacle" by not receiving baptism in the subjectively right disposition (for instance, as a heretic) does not experience this immediate contact with grace as justification until he subsequently removes the obstacle (as, in the case supposed, by returning to the faith of the Church). The character conferred in baptism carries with it the right and capacity to receive the other sacraments, and at the same time involves the duty of obedience to the Church. In practise it is the sacrament of penance which subsequently makes the character of the baptized heretic or hypocrite efficacious for salvation. On the basis of its theory of character, the Roman Church acknowledges "in principle" the baptism of Protestants, but practically is often in doubt whether the Protestant Churches perform baptism with due regard to matter and form. Converts are thus, where any uncertainty exists, baptized hypothetically with the form, "If thou art not already baptized, I baptize thee," etc. In one essential point scholasticism differed from Augustine, at least from the Augustine of the later, stricter period, by acknowledging not only the "baptism of blood," but the "baptism of the Holy Spirit" or "of desire" as conveying grace. According to Peter Lombard and especially Thomas Aquinas, an adult may even before baptism anticipate in faith the effects of baptism upon the heart (*conversio* in the proper sense); he may so efficaciously desire salvation as to be incorporated with Christ *mentaliter* and possess the *res sacramenti* without the *sacramentum*, so that if he should die suddenly, the *votum sacramenti* would be sufficient to secure him salvation. The Roman Church still denies salvation to unbaptized infants; the whole tradition on that point was so firmly established that scholasticism did not dare to think differently. According to this doctrine unbaptized infants do not go to hell, but they do not get into heaven; they remain in a special place, the *limbus infantium* (see LIMBUS).

Not much need be said of Eastern teaching in medieval and modern times. The later Greek mind seems to have found other "mysteries," not indeed more important, but more interesting and more in need of exposition. Of course, however, this sacrament could not be omitted from the considerations of mystagogic theology (q.v.). From the time of Cyril of Jerusalem and the pseudo-Dionysius the baptismal ceremonics have had their fixed place in these discussions; but a much larger place is given, especially in the Byzantine period, to the Eucharist. The most exhaustive treatment of the subject after the Areopagite is that of Nikolaos Kabasilas, metropolitan of Thessalonica (d. 1371), particularly in his treatise "On Life in Christ." The Greeks emphasize the ideas of regeneration and illumination, and conceive both under such aspects as are attainable by specific philosophical (Aristotelian) methods. The notion of a new birth is carried through by means of the terms "matter" and "form"; and the doctrine of a transference from the kingdom of darkness or sin into that of light or truth is easily illustrated by the relation long supposed to exist between darkness and matter, between light and form or the true "idea" or image of God in man. The conception of original sin was current also among the later Greeks. The theologians of the seventeenth century considered Protestant views a corruption of the truth, which they found in an unconditional realism as to the value of the baptismal ceremony. Baptism to them is not merely the forgiveness, but the abolition, the extinction, of sin—although it is sometimes hard to seize the precise shade of meaning intended to be conveyed by their rhetorical expressions. They require, in opposition alike to Rome and to Protestantism, a threefold immersion, although the Russian Church has formally abandoned the practise of rebaptizing Westerns. They teach that children dying without baptism can not be saved, although Mesoloras, for example, lays stress upon the lightness of the penalty in their case.

2. The Eastern Church.

3. Teaching of the Reformers: In order to understand correctly Luther's attitude toward baptism, it is necessary to grasp his idea of grace, which forms the central distinction between the conception of the sacraments in Protestantism and Roman Catholicism. Luther defined grace no longer in the sense of divine power (*virtus*), but as a sign or token of the divine disposition—in the older Latin sense as the divine favor. He also considered baptism necessary for salvation, believing unconditionally in the command of Christ, Matt. xxviii, 19. He did not seek for the reason of this command, for its "necessity" in a rational sense, seeing in it simply an expression of the love of Christ, who desires to convince us through baptism of God's favor and thereby to awaken "faith" (*fides* in the sense of *fiducia*). In baptism we experience the actual bestowal of the favor of God, which, without it, does not, or at least does not indubitably, descend on man. Luther does not understand the necessity of baptism for salvation in the sense that the grace of God is included in the sacrament in an objective sense, but that while one can not be entirely certain of grace without the sacrament, in virtue of it one may be "always" assured of the grace of God in faith. The preaching of the gospel addresses itself too much to humanity in general; the sacrament applies itself to the individual as such, and thus gives him the assurance of grace, and in case of doubt it is the only full guaranty that he is in God's favor. Luther does not follow the Roman idea of "character" as conferred by baptism, but applies his new definition of grace to the content

1. Lutheran.

of baptism in order to establish the fact that baptism possesses validity for the whole life, validity as a real offer of grace. He seeks in baptism nothing but grace. Throughout the whole life that is realized which God in baptism makes known to us as his will through the *signum*, the act performed by means of water. Luther's idea of baptism was identical with his idea of the sacraments in general—that they make plain and confirm the "Word." Like the Word, baptism can only be efficacious if it finds faith or establishes faith by its power. But in faith one can always look back on it, in order to know that he possesses God's grace.

As in regard to Luther's view of the sacraments in general, three periods may be distinguished in his exposition of baptism, which, however, are characterized by their mode of expression rather than by a development of thought. From the first period originated the "Sermon on the Sacrament of Baptism" (1519; "Works," Erlangen ed., xxi, 229–244). Here he distinguishes especially between the "sign" and that which it "signifies," to establish the fact that it is faith which appropriates to man what the sign signifies. Immersion in water in the name of God denotes death to sin and resurrection to grace. The second period begins in 1520 and is characterized especially by the work *De captivitate Babylonica* ("Works," Erlangen ed., *Opera varii argumenti*, v, 55 sqq.). Here he puts all the emphasis upon the "promise" which the order of baptism contains. In reality, the Word is everything in the sacrament, immersion in the water is only the seal which confirms the Word and makes it fully certain. In the third period also, that of his controversy with the fanatics, Luther emphatically proclaimed that the Word is the principal thing in the sacrament. He maintained, at times almost in the spirit of the law, that baptism is based upon a "command" of Christ. On the other hand, he enthusiastically pointed to the fact that through the Word the water becomes a "divine, heavenly, sacred" element. This must be understood in the same way as his attribution of a divine character to parents and authorities. In the last analysis he only wishes to establish firmly and show plainly the unconditional authority of baptism as a representation of the divine will over us. His words are not to be understood in the sense of a theosophical speculation. To the last period belongs the Larger Catechism, the treatise *Von der Wiedertaufe, an zwei Pfarrherrn* (1528; "Works," Erlangen ed., xxvi, 254 sqq.), and a number of sermons on baptism, especially that of 1535 ("Works," 2d Erlangen ed., xix).

Melanchthon's doctrine is identical with Luther's. He says that God inscribes "by means of the water his promise" in a certain sense "upon our bodies." The Reformers were convinced that children must be baptized in order to be saved; for on account of original sin they also need pardoning and renovating grace. But if baptism must awaken faith in order to save the children, it was a great problem, at least for Luther, whether that could really be said to take place. He believed that it might, in consideration of the almightiness of the Word of God, which could even change the heart of the impious, and *a fortiori* could bring a child to faith. The different representatives of Lutheranism differed in the form of their teachings concerning baptism, especially the baptism of children, but in the matter itself they agreed (cf. H. Heppe, *Dogmatik des deutschen Protestantismus im 16. Jahrhundert*, iii, Gotha, 1857). In the orthodox period of Lutheranism baptism was always understood as a kind of representation of the Word (*verbum visibile*), in accordance with the statement of the Apology of the Augsburg Confession (vii) that the sacraments have no other content and therefore no other effect than the Word. But the doctrine was no longer sustained by the vivid intuition of Luther. When he spoke of the Word, he always had before his eyes the living personality of Christ as the incarnate Word of God; he "saw" in the Spirit how God graciously inclines to man. For the theologians of the orthodox period, on the other hand, the Word of God was simply the Bible, and the sacrament a constituent part of the Word because it represents a scriptural institution. They were sure that it was an especially powerful "word"; but they were no longer able to explain in what its power consisted and how it produced its effects. Quenstedt made regeneration and renovation, including that of children, dependent upon baptism. Regeneration was for him transposition into the state of adoption which is brought about by God's bestowing in baptism the power of faith (*vires credendi*). Since the baptized person, in virtue of this power, turns to God, he is also enabled to assume the *vires operandi* and to enter thereby on the process of moral "renovation," which continues throughout the whole life.

2. Reformed.

Zwingli and Calvin also devoted much of their thought to the question of baptism. Zwingli, who became interested in it especially through the Anabaptists, wrote several special treatises on it. According to him, it is not the function of baptism to mediate grace, since that could be accomplished only internally and immediately through the Spirit of God; but baptism has its value as a means of setting children apart for God, and as a sign for them that they belong to the congregation of Christ and are bound to his service. Calvin was influenced more than any other Reformer by Augustine's distinction of *sacramentum* and *res sacramenti*, because, like Augustine, he always has predestination in mind, especially in connection with the baptism of children. In regard to the elect he believes, with Luther, in a real "bestowal" or "sealing" of grace through baptism. The sacrament signifies for them the beginning of the development of the "new life" in the Church. It is a peculiarity of Calvin that he rejects private baptism. The other Reformers hardly touched this subject; its position was established from ancient times. But Calvin thought that baptism, like all ecclesiastical functions, was a matter of the *ministerium ecclesiasticum*. A child, numbered among the elect, who dies without baptism, suffers no harm in God's sight. It is evident that Calvin counts baptism only among the normal means of grace which bind the elect to the Church, as they undergo their development on earth; but his reason can not be clearly seen. The orthodox dogmaticians of the Reformed Church continued the thoughts of Calvin (cf. A. Schweizer, *Die Glaubenslehre der evangelisch-reformirten Kirche*, ii, Zurich, 1847; H. Heppe, *Dogmatik der evangelisch-reformirten Kirche*, Elberfeld, 1861).

3. Modern Developments.

The age of pietism and rationalism showed no interest in baptism. Schleiermacher (*Der christliche Glaube*, §§ 136–138) treats baptism as the solemn act of reception into the "community of believers," in which alone the individual can attain real communion with Christ. Baptism of children, according to him, has no meaning unless Christian education follows, and it is only an "incomplete" baptism if it does not lead to a later act of confession of faith (confirmation). In the course of the nineteenth century the reawakened life of Lutheranism produced new, but on the whole not healthy tendencies in the doctrine of baptism. Scheel distinguishes three tendencies. The first is one which tries to give to the sacraments as a whole and to baptism especially a special import apart from the Word. Some small beginnings of this tendency may be noticed even in the old orthodoxy, especially in the teachings of Leonhard Hutter. In our modern time it is represented by Norwegian (Danish) and German Lutheran theologians, among the former especially by G. W. Lyng and Krogh-Tonning, among the latter chiefly by the Erlangen theologians Höfling, Thomasius, and others. Baptism is here explained as a natural power of the spirit which by means of the body renovates and "regenerates" the whole man. Theosophical speculations on the relation of body and soul form the background of this theory. Quite different is the second tendency, which is represented especially by H. Cremer of Greifswald and P. Althaus of Göttingen. In opposition to the former theory, the stress is here again laid upon the Word in the sacrament. Here also baptism is considered a bath of regeneration, but it is explained as neither natural nor "moral," but as purely religious or "soteriological." Baptism is a "transposition" into a new life, into the real life. It is assurance of grace, and as such salvation from the judgment and death which we have deserved. Its moral effects follow as a natural result of justification. Faith is produced in the degree in which man becomes conscious of what God has done for him and assured him in baptism. In the child baptism denotes exactly the same thing as in the adult. It is necessary because the Lord has instituted it and made the effects of grace dependent upon it. The third tendency is chiefly represented by A. von Oettingen (Dorpat) and takes a middle ground between the two other tendencies. Here baptism is thought of as not only "convincing" like the preaching of the Word, but in an especial manner as both "generating" through assurance of grace and also, through a "realistic" transformation of the nature of man, "regenerating." Emphasis is once more laid upon the thought of Luther that baptism, as distinguished from the general preaching of the gospel, assures the individual as such of his salvation. It is true, in baptism it is the "Word" which produces all effects, but it produces them in a hidden and often mysterious manner.

Among recent works on baptism is that of Gottschick, who, impelled by certain events in Bremen, investigated the doctrine of the Reformers with a view to determining how far the Trinitarian formula is a constituent part of baptism. Scheel concludes his work also with a detailed dogmatic discussion. These writers, with M. Kähler (*Die Sacramente als Gnadenmittel. Besteht ihre reformatorische Schätzung noch zu Recht?* Leipsic, 1903), are nearly related to each other in their interpretation of baptism. They go back to the living intuition of Luther, who saw the whole Christ standing behind the order of baptism, thus considering it not merely as of legal authority. Scheel shows especially that the proper act or rite of baptism can not be fully appreciated dogmatically, but only from the standpoint of the psychology of religion. Dogmatically he considers baptism only as the presentation of the Word or gospel. All three regard baptism of children as an arbitrary, but blameless custom, which is removed alike from dogmatic justification and from dogmatic criticism; the empirical efficacy of the "Word," they say, is incalculable. F. KATTENBUSCH.

III. Liturgical Usage.—1. General Development to the Reformation: The origin of Christian baptism seems closely connected with the Jewish custom of baptizing proselytes, which was based on the wide-spread idea of attaining ritual purity by ablutions, found in practically all the ancient religions. Whether Christian baptism be founded on a specific command of Christ or not (see above, I, 1), there is no doubt that it soon became a universal Christian custom.

1. Original Forms.

If there had been no other reason, it would have seemed obviously fitting, in the interest both of the community and of the new converts, that their entrance should be marked by a special rite. As soon as definite sacramental ideas were connected with the rite—and this must have been very early—it spread throughout the Christian organizations. It is an attractive theory, supported by Cyprian's express statement (*Epist.*, lxiii, 17), that the Jews and the Gentiles in the apostles' time had a different manner of baptizing; that among the Jewish Christians a single immersion was the rule, in the name of Christ alone, on the analogy of the Jewish proselyte baptism, while the threefold immersion in the threefold name, which had its counterpart in the heathen lustrations, was the rule among the Gentile Christians. It is uncertain whether the later rite with which Jewish proselyte baptism was performed (see PROSELYTE) was in existence at the foundation of the Christian Church; but if so, it is most likely that the Christian rite was a free adaptation of it. It is possible that the analogy of the reading of the commandments and the proselyte's promise to keep them suggested the similar vow on the part of the Christian catechumen (Clement, *Hom.*, xiii, 10; Justin, *I Apol.*, lxi; Tertullian, *De spectaculis*, iv), although, of course, it may have originated independently.

The early course of the development made out of

a simple symbolic action a complex ritual consisting of various ceremonies, quite in accord with the natural tendency of a sacramental conception. The first step was to add the laying on of hands. Baptism must not only signify entrance into the Christian fellowship and communion with Jesus, the forgiveness of sins and liberation from the power of evil, but also confer the gift of the Holy Spirit, imparted, indeed, by baptism itself, but more surely and definitely by the imposition of hands. The Didache and Justin do not mention this rite, but that does not prove that it did not exist. The importance attached to it is shown by the fact that in the two places in the Acts where it is mentioned (viii, 16; xix, 6) it is performed by apostles. According to the entire mental attitude of the period, it was undoubtedly looked upon as not merely symbolic but sacramental.

2. The Subapostolic Age.

For the subapostolic age the main authorities are Justin (*I Apol.*, lxi, 2; lxv, 1) and the Didache (vii), the former representing the practise of Rome, the latter that of western Syria. Yet they agree in all essentials. For both baptism is a complete immersion in the open air; if the Didache permits still water to be used in place of running, and affusion in place of immersion, the local conditions are obviously taken into account—the probably frequent scarcity of water in a Syrian summer. Both have the Trinitarian formula, which involves a threefold dipping or pouring. It is clear from the Didache and probable from Justin that laymen were authorized to administer the rite. Both agree in requiring the candidate to be fasting, in which other brethren specially interested are to join. It is a safe assumption from both that baptism was immediately followed by participation in the Lord's Supper. Thus by the middle of the second century the administration of baptism would seem to have been alike in essentials throughout the whole Church. The laying on of hands may not have been universal (Heb. vi, 2 shows that it was known in places outside of Rome and Syria); and here and there a formal profession of faith may have been in use. Nothing is yet heard of any consecration of the water, or of fixed seasons for baptism.

3. In Tertullian.

The first completely developed baptismal ritual appears in Tertullian. The forms already seen in Justin and the Didache are clearly to be recognized, but it is likely that not a few customs sprang up about the middle of the second century for which the earliest evidence is found in Tertullian. The most striking of these is the renunciation of the devil, which was a solemn ceremony full of meaning, and practically an essential feature in the territory of the Gentile Church. To judge from Tertullian's most detailed account in the *De baptismo*, there was a period of preparation, marked by frequent prayers, fasting, vigils, and confession of sin. The baptism proper begins with the invocation of the Holy Spirit upon the water (see EPIKLESIS); next follows apparently the renunciation, and then the threefold immersion in the name of the Father and of the Son and of the Holy Ghost, with a profession of faith in the form of answers to the interrogations of the minister; then the anointing, and the laying on of hands with prayer. That the reception of the Eucharist still followed the baptism is clear from several passages; after this the newly baptized, clothed in white garments, join in prayer with the "brethren," and milk and honey are given them. For a week after baptism they abstain from the usual daily bath (*De corona*, iii).

4. Lines of Development.

Although this ritual gives the basis of the development of the next few centuries, it must not be forgotten that this development varied considerably in different parts of the Church. There is not space here to follow out the ways in which the East differed from the West, and one province from another. One main distinction between East and West is the greater richness of the rite in the former, while the latter held closely to primitive simplicity and even in course of time actually shortened the form—though later it was once more added to. This enrichment is to be explained along the lines of the preparation for the definite and final act of baptism by varied ceremonies of dedication and exorcism patterned after the ancient pagan mysteries (see EXORCISM). The catechumen was considered to have crossed the boundary which divided the kingdom of darkness from that of light with the first of these initiatory ceremonies. It is thus easily understood how the lines separating these preparatory ceremonies from baptism proper were fluctuating. On the one hand, things which had originally been part of the main rite were pushed back into the preparation, as in Jerusalem and Rome the renunciation and profession of faith took place in the outer court or vestibule, while the baptism proper began with the blessing of the water in the baptistery. On the other, the process which had once taken weeks was now compressed into an hour, and thus such things as the recitation of the creed, the giving of the name, the administration of salt, etc., became part of the baptismal ceremony. The close connection between baptism and the Eucharist made it possible for large sections of the latter service to be fused with the baptismal in places, as among the Nestorians, Copts, and Armenians. Thus, once more, certain actions originally part of the baptismal function gradually separated from it into independent rites, as the blessing of oil and water, and the unction after baptism, which developed into confirmation under hierarchical influence. The decisive elements in the development may be summed up in the following points: the increasing prevalence of infant baptism; the gradual decay of the catechumenate through this and through the large numbers coming to baptism; the tendency to imitation which brought in new customs, especially those followed by a dominant church with a definite ritual like Rome or Antioch; and finally the abbreviation of the ceremonies for the benefit of parents and sponsors.

2. Development of the Ritual in Various Parts of the Church: For eastern Syria (the territory of the Syriac language, with its center at Edessa in

Osrhoene), some information may be gained from the Acts of Thomas, which, although of heretical origin, probably do not differ from the orthodox rites on this point. These mention

1. Syria. imposition of hands and prayer, anointing with consecrated oil, baptism in the name of Father, Son, and Holy Ghost (under certain conditions by immersion only), the service closing with the celebration of the Eucharist. This Syrian Church appears to have maintained its liturgical independence until Bishop Rabbula of Edessa (d. 435) introduced the customs of the Greek churches, especially of Antioch; but there may have been earlier influences from that source; the later Syrian Jacobites have essentially the same baptismal rite as is found in the Eastern Church at large, especially Constantinople.

Coming to western Syria (with Antioch for its center) and Palestine (Greek-speaking districts), the primary authority for Cœle-syria is the Syriac *Didascalia* (third century), from which the following order may be deduced: possibly first the renunciation and profession of faith; anointing with imposition of hands; baptism proper; imposition of hands by the bishop and further anointing. This agrees with what may be inferred for Antioch from the Apostolic Constitutions (middle or latter half of the 4th cent.), in which the seventh book, dealing with baptism and undoubtedly derived from an older source, is of especial value. According to this the order is as follows: in the anteroom, or outside the baptistery, the renunciation, the act of allegiance to Christ, the Trinitarian confession of faith, recited by the candidate, the consecration of the oil, and the unction; in the baptistery, a prayer of thanksgiving and blessing of the water, baptism in the threefold name, blessing of the balsam, imposition of hands and unction, Lord's Prayer, and prayer of the newly baptized. In its essential points this ritual is found also in Cyril of Jerusalem (d. 386); the main differences are that the first anointing takes place, according to him, within the baptistery, and that he does not mention the blessing of the water (though there is reason to think that he knew it), the prayer of thanksgiving, or the Lord's Prayer. Thus it is clear that the type of baptismal rite in western Syria and Jerusalem was substantially the same in the fourth century, and relatively simple, which speaks for its antiquity. The next glimpse afforded by tradition, about a century later, is in Dionysius the Areopagite (*De hierarchia ecclesiastica*, ii–iii, *MPL*, iii, 393 sqq.). This is much more richly developed; the individual acts are in some cases repeated three times, the blessing of the water has more formality, and imposition of hands occurs after the profession of faith, while nothing is said of the second anointing.

In the territory including Asia Minor and Constantinople, between 350 and 450 a baptismal ritual must have grown up and spread widely which did not differ essentially from the present Eastern usage. That of the Syrian Jacobites agrees with it, not only in general structure but even in the text of prayers—and since they separated from the Church in 451 (finally in 519), they must have had it before their separation. The oldest version of this liturgy, which the Jacobites traced back to James the Apostle, is

2. Asia Minor and Constantinople. probably that which bears the name of Basil the Great, and it is possible that it originated with this liturgically active bishop. Both types agree in placing the act of reception of catechumens and the last exorcism before baptism, and the reading of the Scriptures comes before the actual baptism. Here again, as in the Apostolic Constitutions and Cyril, the first act of the real baptismal ceremony is the blessing of the water. The Byzantine liturgy has only one anointing with oil before baptism, while the Jacobite forms have two before and one with chrism after. Little is certainly known of the Nestorian and Armenian liturgies, but both have much less connection with the Greek than has that of the Syrian Jacobites.

The Egyptian liturgy has peculiarities which mark it off from the Syrian. It may be reconstructed from the prayer-book of

3. Egypt and Ethiopia. Bishop Serapion of Thmuis (c. 350) in the following form: blessing of the water; prayer for the catechumens, renunciation, prayer before anointing, anointing, confession of faith, prayer; presentation of catechumens by the deacon to the bishop, prayer, baptism, imposition of hands with prayer, consecration of chrism, anointing with it. The main differences between this and the rite of the Apostolic Constitutions, which originated about the same time, lie in the different positions assigned to the blessing of the water of the first unction and in the fact that the imposition of hands after baptism is distinguished from the anointing in the Egyptian, and closely connected with it in the Syrian. The later approximation of the two is attributable to the influence of the Syrian upon the Egyptian. The sixth century liturgy known under Baumstark's name places the blessing of the water (as well as of oil and chrism) within the main action instead of before it. Some later Egyptian liturgies place before the renunciation the anointing which formerly followed it. The Coptic liturgy ultimately had three unctions. That after the baptism separated into two—one by the priest immediately after baptism, the other by the bishop in the church (as in Rome). The later Egyptian liturgies (Baumstark's Alexandrian, the Coptic, and the Ethiopian) have a section at the beginning which is clearly the earlier reception of catechumens, containing the giving of a name, unction with the oil of catechumens, imposition of hands and exorcism, and wholly free from the Syrian influence.

For the investigation of the Western development, Rome is of the greatest importance, as tending to influence the provinces, which

4. Rome. at first had peculiarities of their own, though they agreed in general type. Unfortunately the information as to the early Roman development is very fragmentary. Justin's testimony has been already referred to; but there is no doubt that a more formal ritual existed than his words directly cover. That the Roman

Church had an anointing after baptism is perhaps the only thing to be safely concluded from Hippolytus. Two centuries later, under Innocent I (402-419), this anointing had been divided between the priest and the bishop, whether the latter was present at the time or not, and the bishop claimed the right of consecrating the chrism and imposition of hands. From Leo I (440-461) the following order may be worked out: renunciation, profession of faith in God, blessing of the water, threefold immersion, anointing with chrism, and signing with the cross. From the sixth century the rite known as the scrutinies developed in preparation for baptism, taking place in seven special masses in the last weeks before Easter, to which the catechumenate period had now been reduced. At this time the Sacramentary of Gelasius and the first Roman *Ordo* show no essential changes from the order under Leo I. After the last scrutinies have taken place in the vestibule of the baptistery, including renunciation and profession of faith, clergy and people enter the baptistery singing a litany, and the blessing of the water follows; the "symbol" is recited at the time of the actual baptism in the form of three questions and answers; then the presbyter anoints the candidate with chrism on the back; the procession moves to the *consignatorium*, where confirmation or consignation is administered by the bishop, consisting of signing with the cross on the forehead and imposition of hands; and another litany leads to the eucharistic celebration. This form may have been used until the ninth century; but finally a tendency sets in to fuse the acts belonging to catechumens and *competentes*, in a shortened form, with the baptism, while the confirmation is more completely separated from it. By the fusion of the *Ordo ad catechumenum faciendum* with the actual baptismal ceremony is formed the present Roman rite, which in its final form dates from Paul V (1614). It has two different rites, one for infants and one for adults. The latter, representing more closely the ancient system, has the following parts: preparation by the clergy in the church, the candidates waiting without, including reading of Psalm xli, perhaps a survival of the ancient reading of Scripture; at the church door, the giving of the name, renunciation and profession of faith, threefold blowing in the face, signing with the cross on forehead and breast, prayer, more signs of the cross, imposition of hands, blessing and administration of salt, another imposition of hands, and exorcism—distinct traces of the old catechumenate ceremonies; in the church, confession of faith, imposition of hands and exorcism, symbolic opening of the ears, renunciation, and anointing—the ancient *redditio symboli* with its consequent exorcism; in the baptistery, baptism proper and confirmation. Rome endeavored constantly to spread its baptismal liturgy and customs through the other provinces. The scrutiny-masses were introduced into Gaul and the Frankish kingdom in the seventh and eighth centuries. In Spain the Synod of Braga (561) made the Roman rite binding on a whole province; it probably, though not certainly, spread into Africa, and Milan showed a tendency to accept it. The question as to what rites were used in these provinces before the Roman can not be answered completely, but some important points may be set down.

5. Spain and Africa.

It would seem that the ancient customs survived longer in Spain than anywhere else in the West. The witnesses, however, are late, beginning with Isidorus Hispaliensis (d. 636), whose *De officiis ecclesiasticis* makes it possible to establish the following order: blessing of the water; renunciation, pronounced by the candidate standing in the water; confession of faith in three parts, probably in the form of question and answer; baptism in the threefold name, but probably by a single immersion; anointing with chrism and imposition of hands, performed only by the bishop. The rite is somewhat further developed as it appears in Toledo with the *De cognitione baptismi* of Ildefonsus (d. 667). Here the blessing of the water is more ceremonious (a wooden cross is used); the single immersion is clearly shown; and after the entire ceremony the Lord's Prayer is recited and thus delivered to the new-made Christian, as it was among the Syrian Jacobites. Another ancient rite preserved in Spain was the foot-washing after baptism (attested by the Synod of Elvira, 306); and many of these old customs were retained in the *missale mixtum* of the Mozarabic liturgy. For Africa we get substantially the same account in the earliest witness, Tertullian, as in Cyprian, in Optatus of Mileve, and in Augustine, showing that little change had come about in two centuries.

6. Milan and North Italy.

For Milan and North Italy, the principal source is the *De mysteriis*, still generally, though not certainly, ascribed to Ambrose. Here the order was: the symbolic opening of the ears and unction on ears and nose, in the antechamber; in the baptistery, renunciation, blessing of the water, profession of faith by the candidate standing in the water, in the form of three questions and answers, one immersion following each answer, unction on the head, foot-washing, clothing in white garments, probably imposition of hands, and the Eucharist. With this in the main agree the four addresses of Maximus of Turin to the neophytes (fifth century; *MPL*, lvii, 771), and the pseudo-Ambrosian *De sacramentis*. The latter, however, has an additional unction before the renunciation, which is retained in the later Milanese usage, as mentioned by Archbishop Odilbert (d. 814). This ritual is characterized by the combination of the ceremonies belonging to catechumens and *competentes* into one service with the baptism proper, and in general is closely allied to that of the Frankish Church of the ninth century and to the later Roman *ordo*.

7. Gaul.

In Gaul, according to the sacramentaries which are here the first definite authorities, the service began with a solemn blessing of the water in the absence of the candidates; in the antechamber followed the renunciation; in the baptistery, threefold confession and immersion; in another place, confirmation by the bishop, clothing in white, foot-washing—speaking generally, a simple and very ancient form of service. It contained only one unction, with chrism; but in the *Sacramentarium Gallicanum* a second is added, before the renunciation, with oil, on ears, nose, and breast, following an exorcism. This ancient ritual was either influenced or replaced by the Roman. The development reached by the time of Charlemagne is visible in the instructions sent by him to the bishops of his dominions in the last years of his reign, not later than 812, and obviously based on the Roman *ordo*. No absolute uniformity was, however, attained, so that even in the fifteenth and sixteenth centuries it is impossible to speak of one single baptismal ritual for Germany or for France; but they agree fairly closely in the prayers and in the formulæ for exorcism.

3. The Baptismal Service in the Reformation Churches: The transition stage was marked by simple translation of the current older ritual without essential alterations, as in the service put forth by Thomas Münzer in 1524, though made in the previous year, and that of Luther in his *Taufbüchlein verdeutscht*, also 1523. Luther omitted the exorcism of salt and the opening of the ears, shortened the initial exorcisms, omitted the profession of faith by the sponsors, and used the Lord's Prayer as a prayer, instead of the earlier usage of reciting it in the hearing of the newly baptized for their instruction. This service, comparatively little different from the Latin forms, was widely used or imitated. The first thorough recasting of the service was made at Strasburg in 1525, and in the next year appeared a new edition of Luther's book; these, with Zwingli's order of 1525, form the three points of departure for the later development. Luther's is divided into two parts. Outside the church or in the vestibule occurred an exorcism, signing with the cross on forehead and breast, prayers, another exorcism, reading of Mark x, 13–16, imposition of hands, and recitation of the Lord's Prayer. At the font: salutation, renunciation and profession of faith, request for baptism, also made by the sponsors, baptism by threefold immersion, giving of the chrisom-cloth. The exorcism, deliberately retained by Luther, aroused opposition and controversy even in the sixteenth century. The Strasburg ritual, drawn up under Butzer's influence, left much less of the pre-Reformation service. It was composed of an exhortation ending with a prayer, the Lord's Prayer, Apostles' Creed, reading of Matt. xix, pledge of sponsors to bring up the child in the Christian faith, baptism by pouring, and final prayers. Slight alterations were made in 1537 and later, but the service has remained in this essentially evangelical form. Zwingli's service consisted of an introductory formula, questions to sponsors, prayer, reading of Mark x, 13–16, request for baptism, baptism, giving of chrisom-cloth. It is thus obvious that the Zwinglian and Strasburg services differ from Luther's in the omission of the exorcisms and renunciation, considered as inappropriate to the baptism of a child of Christian parents, and in the substitution of pouring for immersion.

1. Three Main Types.

These three forms have had decisive influence on the development of the Evangelical Churches. Luther's was the standard for the old Lutheran established Churches, with the omission here and there of the signing with the cross and the exorcisms. That of Strasburg had a powerful influence, through the cooperation of Butzer and Hedio with Melanchthon, on the "Cologne Reformation" of 1543 and a number of other German services, and more than the Zwinglian on that of Calvin, so that it gradually influenced the entire Reformed community with the exception of German Switzerland, where Zwingli was followed. The Church of England service has features of both Lutheran and Reformed types, the former predominating.

2. Later Development.

The baptismal formularies of the German evangelical churches remained more or less on the old model until the age of rationalism, when the exorcisms (to which Spener had already objected) were removed together with the meaningless questions to the child, and in many places the renunciation; immersion was also generally discontinued. Even where the old service-books remained officially in force, the ministers frequently disregarded them and made use of private compositions, composed in thoroughly eighteenth century style, and unsuited to the taste of the nineteenth. The movement for the reform of the services which set in between 1810 and 1820 showed an inclination to return to the older formularies, not indeed restoring the exorcisms, but frequently including once more the questions to the child and the renunciation.

4. The Minister of Baptism: It would seem that the original system allowed any baptized person to baptize others; at least it is impossible to assert that only the apostles or those commissioned by them could administer the sacrament (cf. I Cor. i, 14–17; Acts vi, 5; viii, 12, 38). The same inference may be drawn from the Didache (vii) and Ignatius (*Ad Smyrnæos*, viii, 2). Tertullian allows lay baptism in the absence of a cleric (*De baptismo*, xvii), though the natural minister is the bishop—a view which became more and more prevalent, so that baptisteries were found only in episcopal sees. But the practical difficulty of enforcing this principle led bishops to commission others, especially presbyters. The natural right of the bishop was still expressed in the fact that it was he who consecrated the oils used, and gave the unction and laying on of hands after baptism. The scholastic theologians supplied a theory to fit this already ancient practise, asserting that the right belonged to the bishop, but that he might delegate it. The right of the priest was dogmatically declared, following Thomas Aquinas (*Summa*, III, lxvii, 2), by Eugenius IV: "the minister of this sacrament is the priest, who has *ex officio* the right to baptize" (*Decretum pro instructione Armeniorum*, 1439). The *Catechismus Romanus* (II, ii, 18) asserts that priests exercise this function *jure suo*, so that they may baptize even in the presence of the bishop. Deacons, however, were only allowed to baptize by commission of a bishop or priest.

Yet, although thus the right to baptize was appropriated to officials of the Church, the old practise of lay baptism was maintained by the doctrine of the necessity of baptism to salvation. The validity of lay baptism is dogmatically asserted by Augustine (*Contra Parmenianum*, II, xiii, 29; *Epist.*, cexxviii), but only, of course, in the absence of a presbyter and in danger of death. The Synod of Elvira (306) decreed (canon xxxviii) that on a journey by sea or in any case where no church is accessible, a layman, so long as he had not lost his baptismal grace by apostasy or bigamy, might baptize a catechumen in mortal illness, though the bishop was afterward to give the laying on of hands, if possible. These principles (with the exception of the restriction as to the moral quality of the baptizer) became generally accepted. Both the *Catechismus Romanus* and the *Rituale Romanum* permit both men and women, even unbelievers or heretics, to administer baptism in case of necessity, provided they use the proper formula. The Lutheran Church recognizes lay baptism as permissible in case of necessity. The Reformed Churches, on the other hand, denying the necessity of baptism to salvation, forbid it as a usurpation of the ecclesiastical ministry.

The right of women to baptize has a separate history. There is no evidence that they baptized in the primitive age, though it is conceivable that the right was conceded to prominent women. Tertullian recognizes no such right (*De baptismo*, xvii), condemns the Gnostics who had the custom, and protests energetically when a woman appears in Carthage teaching and baptizing. In the acts of the martyrs, however, there are some cases of both teaching and baptizing by female martyrs, such as Domitilla and Chryse; and nothing but the existence of pushing women who claimed both this right and that of administering the Eucharist would explain protests like those in the Apostolic Constitutions (iii, 9) and Epiphanius (*Hær.*, lxxix). That women, especially "clerical" women (widows and deaconesses) assisted at baptisms, especially in the unction of female candidates is evident from the Syriac *Didascalia*; but this did not involve the concession of the right to baptize. The modern Roman Catholic custom can scarcely, then, be a survival of ancient practise, as it is first sanctioned by Urban II (1088–99; cf. *MPL*, cli, 529). Thomas Aquinas justifies it on dogmatic grounds (*Summa*, III, lxvii, 4); but it is only permitted now in the absence of a man. The Lutheran Church retained the practise, Luther expressly declaring such baptism valid, and the Lutheran agenda giving the right especially to midwives.

5. The Time for Baptism: No special season was observed in the apostolic age, nor is such limitation ever mentioned in the oldest Christian literature. But before the end of the second century Easter must have been recognized as the appropriate time. The fixing of a special season was the natural consequence of the great number of candidates and of the catechumenate system, which led up through common instruction to common reception of the sacrament. The choice of Easter was determined not only by the feeling that heavenly grace was more abundant at that time, but also by Paul's connection of baptism with the death and resurrection of Christ (Rom. vi, 3; Col. ii, 12; iii, 1). The increasing number of candidates led to the addition of Pentecost, for which again there was an intrinsic appropriateness. These two seasons were widely adopted, and the popes enforced them zealously against innovators (e.g., Siricius, 385, *MPL*, xiii, 1134; Celestine I, *MPL*, l, 536; Leo I, 429, *MPL*, liv, 696, 1209; Gelasius I, *MPL*, lix, 52; Gregory II, *MPL*, lxxxix, 503, 533; Nicholas I, *Ad consulta Bulgarorum*, lxix). The oldest of these papal utterances passed into the collections of decretals and thus gained universal sanction. The first break in the practise came from the East, where it became customary to baptize at the Epiphany also; Leo I asserts that in Sicily more people were baptized then than at Easter. The second Irish synod under Patrick (canon xix, Hefele, *Conciliengeschichte*, ii, 678) puts the Epiphany on a level with Easter and Pentecost. Then it became customary to baptize also at Christmas, the evidence for which goes back to the sixth century, and on the feasts of martyrs, apostles, and John Baptist. Infant baptism made it all the more impossible to adhere to the few ancient days. Even Pope Siricius had admitted that children and the sick might be baptized at any time. Attempts were made to enforce the old restriction in the ninth century (synods at Paris, 829; Meaux or Paris, 845, 846; Mainz, 847); but in the tenth it began to disappear. Thomas Aquinas, though he still prefers Easter and Pentecost for adult baptism, recommends that infants shall be baptized immediately after birth. The *Rituale Romanum* speaks of the vigils of Easter and Pentecost as the most fitting times for the solemn administration of the sacrament; but almost the only trace of the ancient custom is the blessing of the baptismal font on those two days as part of the regular ceremonies. From the eleventh century no more attention was paid in the East to the old seasons.

6. The Place of Baptism: Primitive Christianity had complete freedom also in regard to the place. Running or sea water was, indeed, preferred; and the open air was the usual place (Victor I, d. 202, still presupposes this as the norm, *MPG*, v, 1485). But perhaps even while this was still the custom, the atrium was used for the ceremony which conferred entrance to the Church, until finally special baptisteries began to be built in connection with the episcopal churches (see BAPTISTERY). The restriction of baptism to the *ecclesiæ baptismales* was frequently attempted, but with diminishing success. By the present Roman Catholic and Greek usage, baptism in private houses is permitted only in case of necessity. The same rule was laid down by the Reformers, but in the seventeenth century the custom of baptizing healthy infants at home came up, and in the eighteenth became the normal practise in some Lutheran communities, especially among the upper classes, who considered it a distinction of rank; and the Reformed and Roman Catholic practise was partially influenced by this tendency. The Anglican Prayer-book requires children who have been privately baptized to be brought to their parish church as soon as possible thereafter for a solemn ceremony of formal "reception into the Church."

7. Sponsors: The institution of godfathers and godmothers is not coeval with infant baptism, but originated in the custom of requiring an adult pagan unknown to the bishop to be accompanied, when he came to seek baptism, by a Christian who could vouch for him, and who was also bound to watch over his preparation and instruction. It is worth noting that in the Eleusinian mysteries the candidate to be initiated had a similar sponsor, known as *mystagogos.* The date of the Christian function is unknown. Since Tertullian is the first witness for sponsors at infant baptism (*De baptismo*, xviii), the custom must have been established before his time; and its existence may possibly be inferred from Justin (*I Apol.*, lxi, 2). But the duties attached in modern times to the office of sponsor are rather those which would be connected with infant baptism. The sponsor was obliged to represent the child, since the oldest baptismal formularies, drawn up for adults, were used without change for infants, who could not answer questions, make the renunciation, or recite the profession of faith. This is clearly brought out in the oldest Egyptian baptismal ritual, where the parents are regarded as the most natural sponsors. Augustine takes the same view (*Epist.*, xcviii, 6); but he also contemplates the bringing of children of slaves by their masters and of orphans or foundlings by other benevolent persons. Attempts have been made to prove that the sponsorship of parents continued the usual custom down to the eighth century, and that an innovation is represented by the Synod of Mainz (813); but it is usually the case that such synodal decisions have a long previous history and raise to the rank of laws things already established as customs. Thus the seventh Roman *Ordo* speaks simply of godfathers and godmothers, and mentions the parents only in connection with the oblation, and then in addition to the sponsors. Cæsarius of Arles speaks clearly of the spiritual relationship into which the sponsors enter with the child in a way which, taken in connection with Augustinian ideas, would soon tend to exclude the parents from this office. Another consequence of the notion of spiritual affinity was the prohibition of marriage between sponsors, which appears as early as the Code of Justinian (V, iv, 26). The Trullan Council (canon liii) absolutely forbids marriage between a child's godfather and its mother. By the thirteenth century this view had extended so far as to prohibit marriages between the baptizer and the baptized or the latter's parents, between the sponsors themselves, between them or their children and the baptized person, or even between a godfather's widow and the godson or his natural parent. The Council of Trent diminished these restrictions, so that, according to the *Catechismus Romanus* (II, ii, 21), marriage is now forbidden only between baptizer or sponsor and the baptized person, and between the sponsors and parents.

The close relation between sponsors and child was considered to lay a grave responsibility upon the former. Having renounced the devil and professed the faith on the child's behalf, they were bound to see that these vows were carried out. This is emphasized in the instructions of Cæsarius of Arles and in those issued for the Frankish mission, where Charlemagne insisted that the sponsors should know the creed and the Lord's Prayer thoroughly. This insistence tended to diminish, though Thomas Aquinas still presupposed the instruction of children by their godparents (*Summa*, III, lxxi, 4); but the *Catechismus Romanus* complains that "nothing more than the bare name of this function remains," and attempts to enforce its duties.

Originally there was but one sponsor, but with the admission of parents to the office this principle was broken through. A tendency to increase the number as much as possible is attested by synodal decrees of the early Middle Ages, which place the proper number at two, three, or four. The Council of Trent allows only one sponsor of the same sex as the candidate, or at most two of different sexes. According to Roman Catholic law, a sponsor must have been baptized and preferably confirmed; the *Rituale Romanum* excludes infidels and heretics, those laboring under excommunication or interdict, notorious criminals, the insane, and those ignorant of the rudiments of the faith; monks and nuns, since their separation from the world makes it difficult for them to perform the duties, are not supposed to undertake them.

The institution of sponsors was retained, with infant baptism, by the Evangelical Churches at the Reformation. Though parents were still excluded, the notion of spiritual affinity was dropped, and any baptized Christian is now, though it was not usual at first, permitted to take the office without regard to his creed—a latitude which would be illogical if the function carried with it the duty of religious instruction, as it does not at present. Some among those who recognize that it is practically an empty form are in favor of abolishing it altogether, while others would have it reformed and made once more a living reality. [The Anglican baptismal office (which contemplates two godfathers and one godmother for a boy, and vice versa) contains a solemn charge to them as to their duties, including spiritual instruction and bringing the child to confirmation at the proper time.]

(P. Drews.)

IV. Discussion of Controverted Points.—1. The Argument against the Necessity of Immersion: In the view of those who do not practise immersion, baptism is a "washing with water in the name of the Father, and of the Son, and of the Holy Ghost," in which the "dipping of the person into the water is not necessary;" but it may be "rightly administered by pouring or sprinkling water upon the person" (*Westminster Shorter Catechism*, Q. xciv, and *Confession*, xxviii, 3). "We must bear in mind," said Walafrid Strabo a thousand years ago (*De rebus eccl.*, xxvi, *MPL*, cxiv, 959), "that many have been baptized not only by immersion but by affusion, and may yet be so baptized if necessary." "Whether the person who is baptized," says John Calvin (" Institutes," IV, xv, 19 end), " be wholly immersed, or whether thrice or once, or whether water be only poured or sprinkled upon him, is of no importance." " The mode of applying water as a purifying medium," says Charles Hodge (*Systematic Theology*, iii, 526), " is unessential."

This is the position occupied also by Thomas Aquinas, *Summa*, III, lxvi, 7; *Catechismus ex decreto Concilii Tridentini*, Leipsic ed., 1853, p. 136 (Eng. transl. by J. Donovan, London, 1833, p. 155); Dominicus a Soto, *Distinc.*, III, i, 7; Durandus, *In sententias*, IV, iii, 4; William Lyndwood, *Provinciale*, iii, 25; Giovanni Perrone, *Prælectiones theologicæ*, vi, 10; C. Pesch, *Prælectiones theologicæ*, vol. vi, Freiburg, 1900, pp. 150–151; T. M. J. Gousset, *Théologie dogmatique*, vol. ii, Paris, 1850, p. 412; H. von Hurter, *Theologiæ dogmaticæ compendium*, vol. iii, p. 210, § 324; P. Minges, *Compendium theologiæ dogmaticæ specialis*, part ii, Munich, 1901, p. 45; J. Dalponte, *Compendium theologiæ dogmaticæ specialis*, Trent, 1890, VII, i, 814, p. 565; R. Owen, *Dogmatic Theology*, London, 1887, p. 405; Darwell Stone, *Holy Baptism*, Oxford, 1899, pp. 135 sqq.; H. E. Jacobs, *Summary of Christian Doctrine*, Philadelphia, 1905, pp. 329 sqq.; H. L. J. Heppe, *Dogmatik der evangelisch-reformirten Kirche*, Elberfeld, 1861, p. 441; B. de Moor, *Commentarius in J. Marckii compendium theologiæ*, 7 parts, Leyden, 1761–78, XXX, ix, vol. v, p. 413; J. J. van Oosterzee, *Christian Dogmatics*, New York, 1874, p. 749; H. Bavinck, *Gereformeerde Dogmatiek*, vol. iv, Kampen, 1901, p. 273; A. Grétillat, *Exposé de théologie systématique*, vol. iv, Neuchâtel, 1890, p. 493; R. L. Dabney, *Syllabus and Notes*, p. 764; E. D. Morris, *Theology of the Westminster Symbols*, Cincinnati, 1901, pp. 678 sqq.; R. V. Foster, *Systematic Theology*, Nashville, 1898, pp. 749 sqq.; W. B. Pope, *Compendium of Christian Theology*, vol. iii, London, 1879, p. 322; Miner Raymond, *Systematic Theology*, vol. iii, Cincinnati, 1877, p. 359; John Miley, *Systematic Theology*, vol. ii, New York, 1894, p. 397; N. Burwash, *Manual of Christian Theology*, vol. ii, London, 1900, p. 359; H. C. Sheldon, *System of Christian Doctrine*, Cincinnati, 1903, pp. 520 sqq.; J. W. Etter, *Doctrine of Christian Baptism*, Dayton, Ohio, 1888, p. 121; J. Weaver, *Christian Theology*, Dayton, Ohio, 1900, p. 250.

It is important to keep in mind the exact point which is in debate. This is not whether the Greek word which was adopted to designate this sacrament, and which has passed into English as " to baptize," means " to immerse." Nor is it whether the early Christians, or even the apostles, baptized by immersion. It is whether so slender a circumstance as the mode of applying the water can be so of the essence of baptism that nothing can be baptism except an immersion.

The contention that immersion alone can be baptism is usually based on the presumption that baptism was originally administered by immersion. It does not appear, however, that, granting the fact, the inference from it is stringent. Its assumption throws baptism out of analogy with all other Christian usages, with the sister sacrament of the Lord's Supper, and with itself in other particulars.

1. Immersion, even if the Original Form, a Circumstantial Detail.

Probably no one imagines that the validity of the Lord's Supper depends upon painfully conforming in the mode of its celebration to all the circumstantial details of its first celebration. The Lord's Supper was instituted at an evening meal, as a part of a household feast which was itself the culminating act of an annual festival, from which it derived deep significance; in a private gathering, of men alone, who received the elements in a reclining posture. No one seeks to reproduce any of these things in the manner of its celebration. Even the use of unleavened bread, which might be thought a more intimate circumstance, is treated as a matter of indifference by a large part of Christendom. If primitive baptism were by immersion, it will scarcely be doubted that it was administered to completely nude recipients. The Jews, in their parallel rite of proselyte baptism, insisted upon this to such an extent that " a ring on the finger, a band confining the hair, or anything that in the least degree broke the continuity of contact with the water, was held to invalidate the act " (C. Taylor, *The Teaching of the Twelve Apostles*, Cambridge, 1886, pp. 51, 52). The allusions of the early Fathers imply a like nudity in their method of celebrating the Christian rite (Bingham, *Origines*, XI, xi, 1; *DCA*, i, 160). Few would demand that this usage should be imitated. In the midst of so much freedom in the circumstantials of Christian ordinances, it is not obvious that the mode of applying the water must be treated as of the essence of the sacrament.

Nor is it easy to be sure what the mode of applying the water employed by the apostles was; or whether indeed it was uniform.

2. The Apostolic Practise not Certain.

No mode of applying the water is prescribed in the New Testament. In the record the New Testament gives of acts of baptism, the mode in which the water was applied is never described. It is never even implied with a clearness which would render differences of interpretation impossible. Nor does what we may think the most natural suggestion seem in all instances to be to the same effect. If we are inclined to fancy the phrase " to baptize in water " (Gk. *baptizein en hydati*, Matt. iii, 11; John i, 26, 31, 33) suggestive of immersion, we can not fail soon to recall that it may just as well mean " with water " and that it is varied, even in parallel passages, to the simple dative of cause, manner, means, or instrument (Mark i, 8; Luke iii, 16; Acts i, 5; xi, 16). If " baptizing in the river Jordan " (Matt. iii, 6; Mark i, 5), varied even to what some unidiomatically render "baptizing into Jordan" (Mark i, 9), strikes us as intimating immersion, we are bound to bear in mind that both phrases may just as well be translated " at Jordan " (Thayer's *Lexicon*, s.v. *ἐν*, I, 1,c; cf. esp. Luke xiii, 4, and F Blass, *Grammar of New Testament Greek*, Eng. transl., London, 1898, p. 122); just as we are bound to bear in mind of those passages which, in our English Bible, speak of going " down into the water " to be baptized and coming " up out of the water " after baptism (Mark. i, 10; Acts viii, 38, 39), that they may just as well be rendered going " down to the water " and " coming up from the water "; and just as we are bound to bear in mind in the presence of all such passages that there are other manners of baptizing besides immersion, which require for their accomplishment going into and coming out of the water. If we read of a locality being selected for baptizing " because there was much water," or, possibly better, " because there were many waters," that is, numerous pools, or springs, or rivulets there (John iii, 23), we read also of the administration of baptism in circumstances in which there is no likelihood that "much water" was available—for example, in a private house (Acts x, 47, where the water almost seems to have been something to be brought and expended in the act; cf. Acts ix, 18; xxii, 16), or even in the noisome jail at Philippi (Acts xvi, 33). Candor would seem to compel the admission that not only is there no stress laid in the New Testament on the mode of applying the water in baptism, but that all the allusions to baptism in the New Testament can find ready explanation on the assumption of any of the modes of administration which have been widely practised in the Churches.

In these circumstances it is not strange that appeal should be made to subsidiary lines of investigation, in the hope that by their means at least a probable judgment may be reached as to the mode in which baptism was administered in apostolic times. Of these, most frequent appeal has been made to these three: the philology of the term employed in the New Testament to designate baptism; the archeology of the rite as practised in the Churches; the inherent symbolism of the sacrament. It must be confessed that the results of this threefold appeal are less decisive than could have been wished.

3. Philological Considerations.

It is of course true that the term "to baptize" goes back to a root which bears the sense of "deep" (cf. W. W Skeat, *Etymological Dictionary of the English Language*, Oxford, 1882, p. 733, no. 89). Its immediate primitive, the Greek verb *baptein*, from which it is formed by adding the termination *-izein*, which gives it a repetitive or intensive meaning (cf. Jelf's *Greek Grammar*, i, 331, § 330), naturally, therefore, has the sense "to dip," while "baptize" itself would primarily mean "to dip repeatedly" or "to dip effectively." Even the primitive verb, *baptein*, of course, acquired secondary senses founded on its fundamental implication of "dipping," but ultimately leaving it out of sight. Thus, as iron is tempered by dipping, when applied to iron *baptein* came to mean "to temper"; as garments are dyed by dipping, *baptein* came to mean, when applied to garments, "to dye"; and it soon passed on to mean simply, without any implication of the mode by which it is accomplished, "to temper," "to dye," "to steep," "to imbue," and the like. When, for example, the Greek bully threatened his fellow that he would "dye [*baptein*] him with the dye of Sardis"—a place famous for its red dye—he meant precisely what the English bully means when he threatens his fellow "to give him a bloody coxcomb," and was as far as possible from implying that the effect would be produced by a process of dipping. So when we read in the common Greek version of Dan. iv, 30 (35); v, 21, that Nebuchadnezzar was "wet [*baptein*] with the dew of heaven," there is no implication whatever of the mode of the application of the dew to his person. The derivative, *baptizein*, of course, lent itself even more kindly to the development of these secondary senses, because, as an intensive form, it naturally emphasized the effect. Accordingly it is rarely used more literally than of the sinking of ships by storm or by war, with the implication, of course, of their destruction; or of the bathing of persons (Eubulus, *Nausicaa*, 1), with the implication, of course, of their cleansing. It passes freely over into such metaphorical usages as when a drunkard is spoken of as baptized with wine, a profligate as baptized with debt, a city as baptized with sleep, a hapless youth as baptized with questions, or as when the prophet (Isa. xxi, 4, LXX) is made to say he is baptized with iniquity; the English equivalent in such cases being something like "overwhelmed," "steeped," or the like. Such a term obviously lay close at hand for application to the Jewish ceremonial lustrations, in which, not the mode, but the effect of the application of the water receives the stress. In the Greek Old Testament it has not yet, indeed, obtained the position of the technical designation of these lustrations. But the beginnings of such a usage are already traceable there (Ecclus. xxxi, 30 [xxxiv, 25]; Judith xii, 7; cf. II Kings v, 14); and by the time the New Testament was written it seems to have supplanted the term commonly employed in the Greek Old Testament [*louesthai*] for this purpose (cf. Cremer, s.v., and J. A. Robinson, in *JTS*, Jan., 1906, vii, 26, 187–189). At least that term occurs in the New Testament only once of a ceremonial lustration, and then only in connection with *baptizein* as explaining its effects, while *baptizein* occurs quite naturally in this sense (Mark vii, 4; Luke xi, 38; Heb. ix, 10) and is the term adopted, probably from such a preceding use, to designate the symbolical washing proclaimed by John the Baptist, and the Christian rite which is called "baptism." In these circumstances it seems very rash to assume that the word was applied to the Christian rite in its primitive meaning of "to dip"; or indeed that any implication of that primitive meaning still clings to it in this application. The presumption is very strong that even in its preliminary use of the Jewish lustrations, it had already "lost its earlier significance of 'dipping,' or 'immersing'" and "acquired the new religious significance of 'ceremonial cleansing by water'" (J. A. Robinson, ut sup.; cf. *EB*, i, 473; *DB*, i, 238). In any event the stress of the word in its application to the Christian rite is not upon the mode in which the water is applied in it, but to its effect as a symbolical cleansing. The etymology of the word, in short, throws no clear light on the mode of applying the water in baptism in the usage of the apostles.

Nor does archeology lend much more aid. It is, indeed, true that the present divergences in the practise of the Churches are the result of growth, and that behind them lies what without much straining may be called a universal usage of at least theoretical immersion. And it is true that the earliest clear intimation which has come down to us of the manner in which Christians baptized, belonging probably to about the middle of the second century (found in the seventh chapter of the Didache), contemplates normal baptism as by immersion. But it is equally true that throughout the whole patristic period no one ever doubted the entire validity of baptism administered in other modes of applying the water. The Didache makes provision for baptism by affusion whenever water in sufficient quantity for immersion is not at hand (cf. A. Harnack, *Lehre der zwölf Apostel*, Leipsic, 1884, pp. 23–24; F. X. Funk, *Doctrina duodecim apostolorum*, Tübingen, 1887, p. 3); and Cyprian (*Epist.*, lxxv [lxix], 12–14; *ANF*, v, 401) argues the whole case out with respect to the baptism of the sick by affusion. No contrary voice is ever raised; but in various ways a full body of testimony is borne to the unhesitating acceptance, throughout the early Church, of baptism by affusion as equally valid with that by immersion. And despite the consentient testimony of the literature of the period to immersion as normal baptism, the entire testimony of the monuments is to the opposite effect (cf. C. F. Rogers, *Baptism and Christian Archæology*, in the Oxford *Studia Biblica et Ecclesiastica*, IV, v; also *Bibliotheca Sacra*, Oct., 1896, pp. 601–641). This monumental evidence comes, it is true, from only a single section of the Church,—that which had its center at Rome; but it makes it clear that from the second century down to a comparatively late date baptism as actually administered, in that region at least, was not an immersion but an affusion, although ordinarily apparently affusion upon a nude recipient standing in shallow water. When we realize that this was the actual mode of baptism in the early Roman Church, we catch apparent allusions to it in the literature of other portions of the Church also, and begin to suspect it may have been prevalent elsewhere too. Indeed, we are deterred from confidently ascribing it to the Apostolic Church itself chiefly by the gulf of a century's width which separates the Apostolic Church from our earliest evidence, literary or monumental. This is not a century over which we may lightly leap. During its course the church usages for which we have both first and second century evidence changed greatly; and all the conditions for a development of new usages with respect to the mode of baptism were present in the circumstances of the times. Nor can we be helped over the gulf by the analogy of the Jewish proselyte baptism. For, in the first place, the points of departure of the two usages were different. The Jewish rite was rooted specifically in the bath preliminary to sacrifice; the Christian took hold through the command of our Lord and the baptism of John of the entire lustration system and tradition. And in the next place, the Jewish usage, just because a development of the presacrificial bath, owed its elaboration into a separate rite, to the cessation of the sacrifices, which threw the bath into an importance it could not have had in their presence; it is therefore too late in its origin to have served as a model for Christian baptism

4. Archeological Considerations.

We are left, therefore, to the essential symbolism of the rite to indicate how it must needs be administered, and how, therefore, the apostles must have administered it. If, indeed, it could be established that the essential symbolism of the rite is burial and resurrection with Christ, an application of the water in such a manner as to suggest this might well be thought necessary to its proper administration. There are many who take this view, and seek support for themselves in the connection instituted between baptism and dying and rising again with our Lord in Rom. vi, 3–5; Col. ii, 12. The Church Fathers from a comparatively early date (certainly from the fourth century—Cyril of Jerusalem, Basil, Gregory of Nyssa, Chrysostom) were accustomed to speak familiarly of the Christian enacting in baptism the drama of redemption through death and burial and resurrection. But the Church Fathers never lost sight of the fact that the fundamental symbolism of the rite was cleansing; to them it was before all else the bath in which sins were washed away. And certainly the passages cited from the New Testament can scarcely be fairly adduced as implying that in its very mode of administration baptism signified for the Apostolic Church burial and resurrection with Christ. Their reference is not to the mode of baptism but to its effects. So little does Paul depend upon the very mode in which baptism is administered to suggest burial and resurrection with Christ, that he actually labors to make his readers connect their baptism with the death and resurrection of Christ by the aid of another mediating thought; viz., that their baptism was with respect to Christ's death for their sins. He repeats the heavy clause, "through baptism unto death" (Rom. vi, 4) in order to prevent them from missing a point which, if baptism in its very mode symbolized burial and resurrection with Christ, they could not in any event miss. This may not prove that baptism as known to Paul was not by immersion. But it seems to indicate that its symbolism to him was not burial and resurrection with Christ. And, indeed, it is hard on other grounds to maintain that this is the inherent symbolism of immersion as a religious rite. Few will maintain that this is the inherent symbolism of the Jewish lustrations. Few will maintain even that the baptism of John the Baptist, which most advocates of immersion as the only valid form of baptism will suppose to have been by immersion, was charged with this symbolism. It seems clear enough that baptism, the matter of which is nature's great detergent, has as its essential symbolism just cleansing. And this being so, there seems nothing in the essence of the sacrament to demand one mode of applying the water above another, within the limits of this symbolism. And we can not forget that our Lord Jesus himself said on a memorable occasion: "He that is bathed needeth not save to wash his feet, but is clean every whit"; and that the Lord Jehovah declared through his prophet that he would "sprinkle clean water upon his people and they should be clean" from all their filthiness. From which we may perhaps infer that out of the circle of ideas of neither the Old Testament nor the New Testament would it be imaginable that a complete bath were necessary in order to symbolize a complete cleansing.

5. Considerations from Symbolism.

It would hardly appear probable that the mode of applying the water in baptism can enter into the very essence of the sacrament, when it is so difficult to obtain certainty as to what that mode was in the hands of the apostles. Each of us may properly cherish an opinion of his own as to what that mode was.

6. The Mode of Applying the Water Unessential.

The opinion of the writer of this article is that it was probably by pouring water on the head of the recipient, standing, ordinarily perhaps, but apparently not invariably, in a greater or less depth of water. But he would not like to insist that no mode of administering baptism but this is valid. Certainly the New Testament lays no stress on the mode of applying the water; and even were it established that it was rather by immersion that the apostles were accustomed to administer it, it is not apparent that no other modes of administering it are valid. It might even be granted that the term "baptism" means nothing but "immersion," and that it was applied to this rite because it meant "immersion," and just in order to describe it as a rite of "immersion"; and still it would not follow that the rite can be validly administered only by "immersion." As in the case of the sister sacrament of the Lord's Supper, in which the term "supper," in its English form and in the Greek of the Lord's time, means an evening meal and was given to this ordinance because it meant an evening meal and to signalize the fact that the feast at which it was instituted was an evening meal, so in the case of baptism, it may be altogether conceivable that the name of the ordinance is derived from a prominent external circumstance connected with its first administration, and yet as far as possible from forming an integral element of the sacrament itself. Whatever may have been the primitive meaning of the term which was adopted to designate it, and however the rite was customarily administered in the first days of its use, the thing is a washing with water for the sake of cleansing to symbolize the cleansing of the sinner by the blood of Jesus Christ. And the main matter is therefore not the mode of washing, but the fact of washing.

Benjamin B. Warfield.

2. The Baptism of Infants: A large section of Protestant Christendom, especially in the United States, dissents from the practise of infant baptism. It includes the various denominations of Baptists, Disciples of Christ, the Dunkers, Mennonites, Winebrennerians, and other Christian bodies. These Christians and their sympathizers in pedobaptist denominations, ground

1. Arguments against Infant Baptism.

their dissent (1) upon the absence of a positive command of Christ, or of any account of apostolic procedure which expressly favors the practise; (2) they hold infant baptism to be a violation of the very idea of baptism, since baptism presupposes conversion and an intelligent profession of faith, which can not be expected from infants.

To these arguments it is replied in general that, while no positive command for baptizing infants is given by Christ or his apostles, the pages of the New Testament offer a strong probability that infants were baptized from the beginning; and the testimonies of Irenæus, Origen, and Tertullian confirm this impression. The argument in detail is as follows: (1) The general command to baptize all nations, naturally interpreted, includes

2. Arguments in Reply.

the baptism of infants; and the mention of the baptism of whole households (Acts x, 48; xvi, 15, 33; I Cor. i, 16; xvi, 15) implies the presence of children; at least their presence in some households is far more probable than their absence in all. If to these considerations be joined the reiterated assertion that the promise of the remission of sins and of the Holy Spirit was to the believers and their *children* (Acts ii, 38; cf. iii, 25), we have a strong probability, to say the least, that infants were baptized by the apostles. (2) Christ's treatment of children, whom he blessed and pronounced to be members of the kingdom of heaven (Matt. xviii, 3; xix, 14) shows that children are fit subjects for the kingdom of heaven; are they not then also fit recipients of the initiatory rite, which is baptism with water? All baptism is in idea an infant baptism, and requires to begin life anew in a truly childlike spirit, without which no one can enter the kingdom of God. (3) The analogy of circumcision, which began with adult Abraham and then extended to all his male children, favors the baptism of infants. Baptism is the initiatory rite of introduction into the Christian Church, and the sign and seal of the new covenant, as circumcision was the sign and seal of the old covenant (Rom. iv, 11). The blessing of the old covenant was to the seed as well as to the parents; and the blessing of the new covenant can not be less comprehensive. Infant baptism rests upon the organic relation of Christian parents and children (I Cor. vii, 14). It is a constant testimony to the living faith of the Church, which descends, not as an heirloom, but as a vital force, from parent to child.

No time can be assigned for the beginning of the practise of infant baptism. If it had been an innovation, it seems likely that it would

3. Origin of Infant Baptism.

have provoked a violent protest. No traces of this can be found except in Tertullian, who, alone in the early Church, denies the expediency of infant baptism. The requirement of repentance and faith, which the apostles made a condition of baptism, was to be expected when it is remembered that their exhortations were addressed to adults. This will always be the mode of procedure when the gospel is first preached to a people. Adult baptism always comes first in every missionary Church. Infant baptism, it is reasonable to assume, arose naturally from the very beginning, as Christianity took hold of family life and training.

The three earliest witnesses to the prevalence of infant baptism are Irenæus, Origen, and Tertullian. The testimony of Irenæus, though not unequivocal, leans strongly in favor of the apos-

4. Patristic Testimony.

tolic usage. Born probably between 120 and 130, a disciple of Polycarp, one of John's disciples, he was surely an excellent witness. He says, "Christ came to save through means of himself all who through him are born again [regenerated] to God, *infants,* and children, and boys, and youths, and old men" (*Hær.*, II, xxii, 4). The phrase "born again to God" refers plainly to baptism; in Irenæus's usage (cf. I, xxi, 1) baptism is "being born to God," and (III, xvii, 1) "the power of regeneration unto God." Origen, who was himself baptized in infancy, distinctly derives the custom from the apostles. "The Church," he says (on Rom. v, 9), "has received the tradition from the apostles to give baptism to little children." He also speaks of infant baptism as a "custom of the Church" (*Hom.*, on Lev. viii, *MPG*, ii, 496). The opponents of the practise make much use of Tertullian (close of the second century). In his *De baptismo* (xviii) he counsels delay of baptism, particularly in the case of infants. But, when the passage is investigated, it is found that his motive is not the impropriety, but the inexpediency of infant baptism, on the ground that it involved the great risk of forfeiting forever the remission of sins in the case of relapse. The very argument proves not only the existence, but the prevailing practise of infant baptism. Tertullian does not even hint at its being a postapostolic innovation. His opposition is due to his peculiar theory of the magical effect of baptism in washing away the guilt of past sins, and is by no means antipedobaptist. Loofs (*Dogmengeschichte*, Halle, 1893, p. 137) sententiously sums up the early historic evidence in these words: "The rite of infant baptism can be traced in Irenæus, was contested by Tertullian, and was for Origen an apostolic usage."

The practise of the third century is uncontested. Cyprian (d. 258) says (*Epist.*, lxiv) an infant should be in no case denied grace and baptism. The Synod of Carthage in 252 rejected the opinion that baptism should, like circumcision, be deferred to the eighth day after birth (cf. Hefele, *Conciliengeschichte*, i, 115). But that the custom was not universally followed is evident from the cases of Augustine, Gregory Nazianzen, and Chrysostom, who had Christian mothers, but were not baptized till they were converted in early manhood; and Constantine the Great put off his baptism till his death-bed. Gregory Nazianzen recommended that the baptism of children be put off till they were three years old, unless there was danger of death. This delay was recommended by church teachers because of the prevailing doctrine of the effects of baptism, which was regarded as washing away original sin and all actual transgressions committed before the administration of the rite.

The Schoolmen, following the later Fathers, taught that children are proper subjects of baptism because they are under the curse of Adam, and baptism washes away the guilt of original sin. As the mother nourishes her offspring in the womb before it can nourish itself, so in the bosom of mother Church infants are nourished and receive salvation through the act of the Church. It is not a question of faith but of the definite sponsorial and fostering act of the Church; so Thomas Aquinas (*Summa*, III, lxviii, 9, ed. Migne, iv, 646: "Children receive salvation not of themselves but by act of the Church") and Bonaventura (*Breviloquium*, vii, ed. Peltier, vii, 320A). A child can not be baptized before it is born, but if its head appear it may be baptized, for the head is the seat of the immortal agent (Peter Lombard, *Sent.*, IV, vi, 2; Thomas Aquinas, *Summa*, III, lxviii, 11). Thomas Aquinas (*Summa*, III, lxviii, 10) and most of the Schoolmen pronounced it unlawful to baptize the children of Jews and infidels without their parents' consent, but Duns Scotus took the opposite view (cf. R. Seeberg, *Duns Scotus*, Leipsic, 1900, p. 364). The baptism of infants was expressly commended by the Council of Trent (Session vii, *de baptismo*, canon xiii). It was also commended by the Protestant Confession of the Reformation period: the Augsburg Confession (art. ix, with an anathema against the Anabaptists); the Second Helvetic Confession (xx, 3, also with an anathema against the Anabaptists); the Heidelberg Catechism (question lxxiv); the Gallican Confession (xxxv); the Belgic Confession (xxxiv); the Thirty-nine Articles (xxvii); the Scotch Confession (xxiii); and the Westminster Confession (xxviii).

5. The Schoolmen and the Reformation Period.

It must be admitted that adult baptism was the rule and infant baptism the exception in the apostolic age, and not until the fifth century, when the Church was widely established in the Roman Empire, was infant baptism general. It continued to be the universal rule, with some exceptions, as in the case of the Cathari, until the Protestant Reformation, when "believers' baptism" came to be insisted on by some leaders in Switzerland, Holland, etc. Infant baptism has no meaning apart from the Christian family and without the guaranty of Christian education. Hence the Church has always insisted on catechetical instruction, and most Churches practise confirmation as a subjective supplement to infant baptism. Compulsory infant baptism was unknown in the ante-Nicene age; it is a profanation of the sacrament, and one of the evils of the union of Church and State, against which Baptists have a right to protest.

(Philip Schaff†) D. S. Schaff.

3. The Baptist Position Concerning Immersion and Infant Baptism: The Greek word *baptizein* means "to dip," "to submerge." When we read in the Septuagint (II Kings v, 14) that Naaman went down into the Jordan and "baptized himself" (Gk. *ebaptisato*), we are compelled to understand a dipping; and there is cited from Greek literature not a single instance of the use of the word in which the idea of submersion is not involved.

1. True Baptism a Burial in Water.

Wherefore it is held that the rite of baptism as spoken of in the New Testament was always a burial in water and that the command to baptize is a command to immerse. The burial in water has always been the practise of the Greek Church, its older patriarchates holding that there is no other baptism (Stanley, *Eastern Church*, Lecture i). The Baptists and some other bodies in Western Christendom hold rigidly to this view. Immersion is the only catholic act of baptism, the only one whose validity is recognized *semper et ubique et ab omnibus*. The burial in water continued to be the standard usage of the Roman Church for more than a thousand years. Thomas Aquinas speaks of it as "the more common" usage. It was the practise in Britain till the reign of Elizabeth, and is still demanded in the order of the Church of England for the baptism of infants unless the parents shall certify that the child is weak. Though pouring or sprinkling is now employed rather as a matter of convenience, affusion was for many centuries resorted to only in case of necessity.

The first extended discussion of the question is found in the epistle of Cyprian to Magnus written about the middle of the third century. Being asked whether those can be deemed *legitimi Christiani*, "Christians in full standing," who, being converted in sickness are *non loti sed perfusi*, "not immersed in the water but having it simply poured over them," he gives an affirmative opinion but does so with the very greatest hesitation. His words are: "So far as my poor ability comprehends the matter;" and "I have answered your letter so far as my poor and small ability is capable of doing;" and "So far as in me lies I have shown what I think." He disclaims any intention of saying that other officials should recognize affusion as baptism and even goes so far as to suggest that those who have thus received affusion may on their recovery from sickness be immersed. But, citing various sprinklings in the Mosaic ritual, he gives the view, that *necessitate cogente*, immersion being out of the question, those who have been poured upon may be comforted by being told that they have been truly baptized (*Cypriani epist.*, lxxv [lxix], 12–14; *ANF*, v, 400–401). This epistle makes it clear beyond all controversy that in the third century the ordinary baptism was immersion, and that even in the Latin Church there were those who declared it the only baptism. It further appears with equal clearness that affusion was never practised in the Apostolic Church, for had the apostles resorted thereto even in a single instance Cyprian would certainly have known the fact and would never have presented so mild an apology for a usage which had apostolic precedent, nor indeed would any one have taken exception to the practise.

2. The Testimony of Cyprian.

For a thousand years the resort to the use of affusion was justified only on the ground of necessity. And the supposed necessity existed in the idea that baptism was essential to salvation and so that when immersion, the established rite, was out of the question, something must be put in its place or the soul would be lost. The use of affusion would never have been thought of except for the idea that water baptism was essential to salvation. But those who deny that salvation is conditioned on baptism, who regard baptism as merely a token of a salvation already wrought, see no necessity for a resort to affusion. They will continue to administer immersion whenever it is practicable, and where it is not they will let the convert die without any water baptism whatever. They condemn the use of affusion not only as unnecessary but as based on a gross superstition.

3. Origin of Affusion.

To the declaration that baptism is simply a washing, it is answered that Jesus's baptism of suffering was not a washing but a submersion beneath the tide of wo and that the baptism of the Holy Spirit is a whelming in the waves of divine influence, while many of the Fathers regarded the baptism of fire, not as a purification, but as a swallowing up of the wicked in waves of burning. And granting that originally the immersion was but a lustration, the apostles point out in it another image; viz., that of burial and resurrection. The act of affusion contains nothing whatever of purely Christian symbolism, for simple lustration is found in the Mosaic and even in heathen ritual. The burial in water is the only distinctively Christian baptism, for it alone sets forth the death and resurrection of our Lord, which is the central fact of the Christian system. To the idea that the purpose of the "apostolic" immersion was simply a washing and that this can be attained just as well by a pouring or sprinkling, it may be added that the purpose of the pouring is simply a profession of faith, which can be given just as well by word of mouth, and thus that all use of water may be dispensed with. Those who abandon the "apostolic" immersion simply on the ground of convenience leave the way clear for the adoption of the position of the Society of Friends, the abandonment of water baptism entirely.

4. The Argument from Symbolism.

As to the subjects of the rite, the Baptists hold that it should be administered only on profession of faith. There is found in Scripture no instance of the baptism of an unconscious infant nor will a fair exegesis discover in any text the remotest reference to such a usage. On the contrary, it stands in direct antagonism to the New Testament idea of the Church. The baptism of infants arose from the idea that in baptism one is regenerated and christened, that is, made a Christian. But, as they grow up, no difference appears between the baptized child of Roman Catholic or Episcopalian and the unbaptized offspring of the pious Quaker or the Baptist, or indeed of the unbeliever.

5. Objections to Infant Baptism.

The Presbyterians baptize infants on the ground that the Church is to consist (*Westminster Confession*, xxv, 2), not of the converted alone, but of believers "together with their children." The sons of believers, however, may grow up unbelievers, even atheists, and thus the Church, the bride of Christ, come to be made up in part, possibly the greater part, of the unregenerate, perhaps the immoral. When a child is "dedicated" to Christ, to baptize it without awaiting its hoped-for conversion is not only as unreasonable as it would be to ordain the infant to the ministry on faith that he will yet be another Jonathan Edwards, but it is also to introduce an impenitent element into the Church. As well might the missionary baptize at the start the whole heathen tribe, who, he has faith to believe, will be converted.

If an infant may be baptized on the ground that it is pure and sinless, then, since the babe of Turk or pagan is as pure as the child of the Christian, there is no reason why all infants, even the whole race of man, should not be baptized into the Church. The Church is based on the idea that there is a difference between the disciples of Christ and men at large. But there is no theory of infant baptism which does not freely introduce the impenitent into the Church, thus wiping out all distinction between the Church and the world. The burden of John's preaching was that the new kingdom was not simply a continuance of the Jewish commonwealth, that though all could be circumcised and introduced into the latter who could say, "We have Abraham to our Father," baptism and membership in the former were given not on parental faith but only on personal repentance. That baptism was given on different grounds from circumcision is seen in the fact that the believing Jews continued to have their infants circumcised (Acts xxi, 20), that Timothy who had been baptized was nevertheless circumcised, and that it was demanded that the Gentile converts be circumcised though they had all been baptized.

NORMAN FOX†.

BIBLIOGRAPHY: On I: H. Holtzmann, in *ZWT*, xxii (1879), 401 sqq.; J. H. Scholten, *Die Taufformel*, Gotha, 1885; E. Haupt, *Zum Verständniss des Apostolats im N. T.*, pp. 38 sqq., Halle, 1896; A. C. McGiffert, *The Apostolic Age*, New York, 1897; P. Althaus, *Die Heilsbedeutung der Taufe im N. T.*, Gütersloh, 1897; F. C. Conybeare, in *ZNTW*, ii (1901), 275 sqq.; W. Heitmüller, *Im Namen Jesu*, Göttingen, 1903; idem, *Taufe und Abendmahl bei Paulus*, ib. 1903; idem, in *TSK*, lxxviii (1905), 461 sqq.; E. Riggenbach, *Die trinitarische Taufbefehl, Matt. xxviii, 19*, Gütersloh, 1903; E. von Dobschütz, in *TSK*, lxxviii (1905), i sqq.; F. M. Rendtorff, *Die Taufe im Urchristentum*, Leipsic, 1905 (gives the present status of the inquiry); A. Seeberg, *Die Taufe im N. T.*, Lichtenfelde, 1905; *DB*, i, 238–245; *EB*, i, 471–476; and the works on N. T. theology by Weiss, Beyschlag, and others.

On II–III, ,1: The history of baptism includes as a section which has created a literature of its own the treatment of baptism in the frescoes, etc., of the catacombs. On this consult: G. B. de Rossi, *Roma sotterranea*, 2 vols., Rome, 1861–67, reproduced in Eng. by Northcote and Brownlow, London, 1878–80; R. Garrucci, *Storia dell' arte cristiana*, 6 vols., Prato, 1872–81; *Bullettino di archeologia cristiana*, 1876; F. X. Kraus, *Realencyklopädie der christlichen Alterthümer*, "Taufe," "Neophyten," Freiburg, 1881–86; T. Roller, *Les Catacombes de Rome*, 2 vols., Paris, 1881; J. Strzygowski, *Ikonographie der Taufe Christi*, Munich, 1885; *Archæology of the Mode of Baptism*, in *Bibliotheca Sacra*, 1896, pp. 601–644; A. de Waal, *Die Taufe Christi auf constantinischen Gemälden der Katakombben*, in *Römische Quartalschrift*, 1896; J. Wilpert, *Die Malereien der Sakramentskapellen*, Freiburg, 1903; *Le Pitture delle catacombe*, Rome, 1903.

Further, on the archeology and the history of the rite consult: E. Martène, *De antiquis ecclesiæ ritibus*, vol. i, Antwerp, 1736; J. C. W. Augusti, *Archäologie der Taufe*, in *Denkwürdigkeiten*, vol. vii, Leipsic, 1825 (valuable, contains bibliography of older works); M. Schneckenburger, *Ueber das Alter der jüdischen Taufe*, Berlin, 1828; A. J. Binterim, *Denkwürdigkeiten*, i, part 1, ii, part 1, pp. 2–34, 7 vols., Mainz, 1837–41; J. W. Höfling, *Das Sakrament der Taufe*, 2 vols., Erlangen, 1846–48 (has great value, especially on the liturgical side); G. L. Hahn, *Die Lehre von den Sakramenten in ihrer geschichtlichen Entwickelung*, Breslau, 1864 (learned and useful); F. Probst, *Sakramente und Sakramentalien der 3 ersten Jahrhunderte*, Tübingen, 1872; S. M. Merrill, *Christian Baptism, its Subjects and Modes*, Cincinnati, 1876; J. Corblet, *Hist. . . du sacrement de baptême*, 2 vols., Paris, 1882; M. Usteri, in *TSK*, lv (1882), 205 sqq., lvi (1883), 155 sqq., 610 sqq., 730 sqq., lvii (1884), 417 sqq., 456 sqq. (these worthful articles set forth the doctrine of Zwingli, Oecolampadius, the Reformed Church, Calvin, Butzer, and Capito); P. Althaus, *Die historischen und dogmatischen Grundlagen der lutherischen Taufliturgie*, Hanover, 1893; idem, *Die Heilsbedeutung der Taufe im N. T.*, ib. 1897 (deals also with modern Lutheran orthodox doctrine); G. Anrich, *Das antike Mysterienwesen in seinem Einflusse auf das Christentum*, Göttingen, 1894; G. Wobbermin, *Die Beeinflussung des Christentums durch das antike Mysterienwesen*, Berlin, 1896; F. E. Warren, *Liturgy and Ritual of the Ante-Nicene Church*, London, 1897; A. Raschenbusch, *Die Entstehung der Kindertaufe im 3. Jahrhundert*, Hamburg, 1898; F. Wiegand, *Die Stellung des apostolischen Symbols im . Mittelalter*, vol. i, Leipsic, 1899; L. Duchesne, *Origines du culte chrétien*, pp. 294 sqq., Paris, 1903; V. Ermoni, *Le Baptême dans l'église primitive*, Paris, 1904; T. F. Fotheringham, in *Princeton Review*, 1905; O. Scheel, *Die dogmatische Behandlung der Tauflehre in der modernen positiven Theologie*, Tübingen, 1906 (learned and critical); the works on the History of Doctrine by Harnack, Seeberg, Loofs (4th ed., Halle, 1906); also W. Heitmüller, ut sup., 1.

On III, 2, §§ 1–7: *Apostolic Constitutions*, vii, 39–45 (latest ed., F. X. Funk, 2 vols., Paderborn, 1906); an anonymous form is reproduced in J. A. Assemani, *Codex liturgicus ecclesiæ*, i, 219 sqq., 13 vols., Rome, 1749–66, and in H. J. D. Denzinger, *Ritus Orientalium, Coptorum, Syrorum, Armenorum*, i, 267 sqq., 2 vols., Würzburg, 1863–64; the "Apostolic Baptismal Liturgy" of Severus of Antioch (Jacobitic), in Assemani, ii, 261 sqq., and in Denzinger, i, 302 sqq.; another ascribed to Severus of Antioch, in Denzinger, i, 309 sqq.; the liturgy of Jacob of Edessa, in Assemani, i, 240 sqq., ii, 226 sqq., iii, 152 sqq.; a liturgy translated into Syriac from Basil the Great, in Assemani, iii, 199 sqq., and Denzinger, i, 319 sqq.; Cyril of Jerusalem, in *MPG*, xxxiii, 331 sqq.; and Dionysius the Areopagite, *MPG*, iii, 393 sqq. For the Greek Orthodox liturgy consult: Assemani, i. 130 sqq., ii, 129 sqq., iii, 226 sqq.; H. A. Daniel, *Codex liturgicus*, iv, 492 sqq., Leipsic, 1854; J. Goar, *Euchologion*, pp. 274 sqq., 287 sqq., Venice, 1730; F. C. Conybeare, *Rituale Armenorum*, pp. 399 sqq., Oxford, 1905. For the Nestorians: Assemani, i,174 sqq., ii, 211 sqq., iii, 136 sqq.; Denzinger, i, 364 sqq.; G. P. Badger, *The Nestorians and their Rituals*, pp. 195–212, London, 1852; *Liturgia sanctorum apostolorum Adæi et Maris*, Urmia, 1890, Eng. transl. in *The Liturgy of the Holy Apostles Adai and Mari*, London, 1893; G. Diettrich, *Die nestorianische Taufliturgie*, Giessen, 1903. For the Armenians consult: Conybeare, ut sup., pp. xxxi sqq.; Assemani, i, 168 sqq., ii, 194 sqq., iii, 118 sqq.; Denzinger, i, 384 sqq.; and for another version, Assemani, ii, 202 sqq., iii, 124 sqq.; Denzinger, i, 391 sqq.; and for the Eng. transl., Conybeare, ut sup., pp. 86 sqq. For Egypt and Ethiopia consult: for the *Euchologium* of Serapion of Thmuis, *TU*, xvii (1899), 3b; Brightman, in *JTS*, i (1900), 88 sqq., 247 sqq.; F. X. Funk, *Didascalia et Constitutiones Apostolorum*, ii, 158 sqq., Paderborn, 1905. An Arabic liturgy is in *Oriens Christianus*, i, 32 sqq., Rome, 1901. The Coptic order is in Assemani, i, 141 sqq., ii, 150 sqq., iii, 82 sqq.; Denzinger, i, 192 sqq. The Ethiopic order is in *MPL*, cxxxviii, 929 sqq.; Denzinger, i, 222 sqq.; and the Baptismal Book of the same is in Trumpp, in *AMA*, Philosophisch-philologische Klasse, xiv (1878), 3, pp. 149 sqq.; cf. for another, G. Horner, *Statutes of the Apostles*, pp. 162 sqq., London, 1904. For the West: *Sacramentarium Gelasianum*, ed. Wilson, pp. 78 sqq., Oxford, 1894; *Sacramentarium Gregorianum*, J. Mabillon, *Museum Italicum*, ii, 26, sqq., 82 sqq.; *Rituale Romanum Pauli V.*, Regensburg, 1881; Daniel, ut sup., i, 171 sqq. For Spain, Isidore of Seville, *De officiis ecclesiasticis*, ii, 25; Ildephonsus of Toledo, *Adnotationes de cognitione baptismi*, *MPL*, xcvi, 111 sqq. For Milan, *Manuale Ambrosianum*, ed. Magistretti, i, 143 sqq., ii, 466 sqq., Milan, 1905. The early French ritual is found in the *Missale Gothicum*, *MPL*, lxxii, 274–275; *Missale Gallicanum*, ib. pp. 367 sqq.; *Sacramentarium Gallicanum*, ib. pp. 500–501; consult further: M. Gerbert, *Vetus liturgica Allemanica*, i, 80 sqq., ii, 1 sqq., St. Blas, 1776; A. Franz, *Das Rituale von St. Florian*, pp. 65 sqq., Freiburg, 1904. For the period of the Reformation, E. Sehling, *Die evangelischen Kirchenordnungen des 16. Jahrhunderts*, i, 470 sqq., Leipsic, 1902 (for the form of Münzer); Daniel, ut sup., ii, 185 sqq.; F. Hubert, *Die Strassburger liturgischen Ordnungen*, pp. 25 sqq., Göttingen, 1900 (for the Strasburg form); and Daniel, ut sup., iii, 112 sqq. (for the Zwinglian form).

On IV, 1–2: W. Wall, *Hist. of Infant Baptism*, new ed., London, 1862 (an old classic); J. W. Dale, *Inquiry into the Meaning and Usage of the Word Baptize*, 4 vols., viz.: *Usage of Classical Greek Writers*, Philadelphia, 1867; *Judaic Baptism*, Boston, 1873; *Johannic Baptism*, Philadelphia, 1872; *Christic and Patristic Baptism*, ib. 1874;

W. R. Powers, *Irenæus and Infant Baptism*, in *American Presbyterian and Theological Review*, 1867, pp. 239–267; W. Hodges, *Baptism Tested by Scripture and Hist.*, New York, 1874; J. A. Martigny, *Dictionnaire des antiquités chrétiennes*, "Baptême," "Fidèles," Paris, 1877; J. Corblet, *Histoire dogmatique, liturgique et archéologique du sacrement du baptême*, 2 vols., Paris, 1881–83 (contains a copious bibliography); H. M. Dexter, *The True Story of John Smyth the Se-Baptist*, Boston, 1881; A. P. Stanley, *Christian Institutions*, London, 1884; P. Schaff, *The Oldest Church Manual*, pp. 29–57, New York, 1886; C. W. Bennett, *Christian Archæology*, pp. 389–415, London, 1895; L. Duchesne, *Autonomies ecclésiastiques, Églises séparées*, p. 93, Paris, 1896; idem, *Les Origines du culte chrétien*, ib. 1898, Eng. transl., London, 1903; W. H. Whitsitt, *A Question in Baptist History*, Louisville, 1896; B. Dörholt, *Das Taufsymbolum der alten Kirche nach Ursprung und Entwicklung*, Paderborn, 1898; H. Marucchi, *Éléments d'archéologie chrétienne*, i, 282, Brussels, 1899; J. S. Axtell, *The Mystery of Baptism*, New York, 1901; C. F. Rogers, *Early Hist. of Baptism*, in *Studia Biblica et Ecclesiastica*, v, 4, Oxford, 1903; F. M. Rendtorff, *Die Taufe im Urchristentum*, Leipsic, 1905; Schürer, *Geschichte*, ii, 129 sqq., Eng. transl., II, ii, 319 sqq. (deals with Judaic baptism); *DCA*, i, 150–178 (condensed, but lucid); the works on church hist. and hist. of doctrine; Schaff, *Creeds*, vols. ii, iii (for credal statements).

On IV 3, the following may be cited: A. Carson, *Baptism in its Mode and Subjects*, Philadelphia, 1857 (an extended discussion with replies to various writers); T. J. Conant, *Meaning and Use of Baptizein*, New York, 1860 (an exhaustive list of passages in Greek literature); J. C. Chrystal, *Hist. of the Modes of Christian Baptism*, Philadelphia, 1861 (argues for trine immersion); R. Ingham, *A Handbook on Christian Baptism*, 2 parts, London, 1865–71; W. Cathcart, *The Baptism of the Ages*, Philadelphia, 1878 (citations from documents of different periods); H. S. Burrage, *The Act of Baptism*, ib. 1879 (collection from all the centuries showing the usage of each period); D. B. Ford, *Studies on the Baptismal Question*, Boston, 1879 (reviews Dale's works, ut sup.); N. Fox, *Rise of the Use of Pouring for Baptism*, in *Baptist Quarterly Review*, Oct., 1882; A. P. Stanley, ut sup., chap. 1; J. M. Frost, *Pedo-Baptism, is it from Heaven or of Men?* Philadelphia, 1889; A. H. Newman, *Hist. of Anti-Pedobaptism*, ib. 1896; A. Rauschenbusch, *Die Entstehung der Kindertaufe im 3 Jahrhundert und die Wiedereinführung der biblischen Taufe im 17 Jahrhundert*, Hamburg, 1898.

BAPTISM FOR THE DEAD: A custom mentioned by Paul in I Cor. xv, 29. It probably consisted in the vicarious baptism of a living Christian for a catechumen who had died unbaptized, the latter being thereby accounted as baptized and so received into bliss. It is doubtful if the custom was ever widely prevalent and it seems soon to have died out in the Church, although kept alive by Marcionites, Montanists, and other heretics (cf. Chrysostom, *Hom.*, xl, on I Cor.; Epiphanius, *Hær.*, xxviii, 6). The sixth canon of the Synod of Hippo in 393 forbade the practise. It is observed by the Mormons at the present day.

Objection is made to this interpretation on the ground that Paul would not have referred to such a practise with even a tacit approval, and that the practise is in sheer contradiction to Paul's doctrine of justification and baptism. Epiphanius, Calvin, Flacius, Estius, and others interpreted the Greek *huper tōn nekrōn* in the passage mentioned to mean "when about to die," "on their death-bed."

Another interpretation regards *tōn nekrōn* as referring to bodies, the baptism of which, on the supposition that they are mortal, would be useless. Another ingenious interpretation refers *huper tōn nekrōn* to the imminent danger of violent death at the hands of unbelieving persecutors incurred by those making a public profession of their faith in baptism. "What is the use of incurring such danger if there is to be no resurrection?"

Bibliography: R. J. Cooke, in *Methodist Review*, xlix (1889), 100; J. W. Horsley, in *Newbery House Magazine*, June, 1889; *DB*, i, 245, and the commentaries on I Cor. xv, 29.

BAPTISM BY HERETICS. See Heretic Baptism.

BAPTISM WITH THE HOLY GHOST AND WITH FIRE: A figurative expression used by John the Baptist (Matt. iii, 11; Luke iii, 16) and understood to refer to the descent of the Holy Spirit on the Day of Pentecost (Acts ii, 1 sqq.; cf. i, 5).

BAPTISMAL REGENERATION. See Regeneration.

BAPTISTERY: A building or a portion of a church used for administering baptism. The history and institution of baptisteries is naturally connected with the development of the baptismal form. Immersion, which was customary in the ancient Church, required a basin of the requisite depth, and the custom of solemn seasons for baptism made necessary a considerable space for the reception of the numerous neophytes. The atrium and impluvium of the antique dwelling, in which divine service was held for nearly two centuries (see Architecture, Ecclesiastical, I, § 2), appeared first of all as fit for it and were used in the beginning for the performance of the rite (cf. Schultze, p. 51). The neophyte, after having received baptism, was led from the atrium to the congregation assembled in the adjoining space. But when the atrium became merely the vestibule of the basilica, being an open court besides, buildings were erected as early as the fourth century exclusively for the administration of baptism (Gk. *baptistēria, phōtistēria*, Lat. *fontes, fontes baptisterii*). As a rule these buildings were near the choir (as in St. Sophia in Constantinople, and the baptisterium of the Lateran basilica), or toward the west (orthodox baptisterium at Ravenna), or on the west-front (Grado, Parenzo). Sometimes a location in the immediate neighborhood of the church was not considered necessary or could not be obtained from local reasons (Arian baptisterium at Ravenna). An open or covered gallery often connected the two buildings (Torcello, Aquileia, and elsewhere).

Early Baptisteries.

Baptisteries are almost exclusively buildings with central arrangement of circular or polygonal plan; the rectangular form is rare. The walls were supplied with recesses, or a lower passage-way surrounded an elevated central structure supported by columns and roofed with a dome. The development of the baptismal rite from the fourth century and practical considerations in general necessitated the addition of other rooms, as a vestibule (Gk. *proaulios oikos, esōteros oikos*, Lat. *atrium*; Lateran, Nocera), a dressing-room, and more especially, a school-room (Gk. *katēchoumenon*). In such rooms

Form and Structure.

episcopal meetings were occasionally held. An apse or complete choir was also sometimes supplied. In the center of the baptistery was the basin (Gk. *kolymbēthra*, Lat. *piscina*, *fons*), polygonal or circular, seldom cruciform, and artifically supplied with water (cf. J. von Schlosser, *Schriftquellen zur Kunstgeschichte der Karolingerzeit*, Vienna, 1892, no. 232). Low, ornamented barriers surrounded it, with openings for going down and coming up. Three steps—symbolically referring to the holy Trinity, in the name of which the baptism was performed—led down and up (*gradus descensionis*, and *ascensionis*). Curtains covered the basin and seats stood along the walls. The arts were employed chiefly in the mosaic decorations of the dome, but reliefs in stucco, marble ornamentation, and artistic pavements were also used. As subjects for pictorial representation the baptism of Christ and the hart panting after the water brooks (Ps. xlii, 1), representing the longing after baptism, commended themselves (cf. Schultze, pp. 205 sqq., 228 sqq., 240–241). Inscriptions were also not lacking, telling of the purpose of the building and the blessing of the baptismal grave (Holtzinger, pp. 219–220; Schlosser, u.s., no. 910).

Most of the extant baptisteries of early Christian time (which were freely dedicated to John the Baptist) are in Italy (cf. O. Mothes, *Die Baukunst des Mittelalters in Italien*, i, Jena, 1882, 125 sqq.). In the East some samples have recently been discovered and more may be looked for. In general the number was limited, since the right of baptism was connected with the episcopal churches (*ecclesiæ baptismales*), and was only gradually granted to the parochial churches. The discontinuance of the baptism of adults was not in itself a reason for the abolition of baptisteries; only the inner arrangement, as the form of the basin, was influenced thereby. However, for practical reasons, the tendency grew stronger to substitute for the detached building an addition, or rather a separate room in the church itself; during the Middle Ages the detached buildings became exceptional. In these baptismal chapels the font or basin took the place of the piscina. In the old plan of St. Gall belonging to the ninth century, the christening-font is already in the interior of the church (F. Keller, *Bauriss des Klosters von St. Gallen*, Zurich, 1884, plan and p. 18). Immersion, which was still customary during the Middle Ages, required a large basin (cf. the instructive illustrations from the ninth century in J. Strzygowski, *Iconographie der Taufe Christi*, Munich, 1885, plate viii, 4–7). The material was generally stone, but sometimes bronze or brass. The round or polygonal form may perhaps be looked upon as a survival of the antique piscina. As the latter was adorned by art, so also ornamentations and figurative representations are found on the outside of the baptismal fonts, such as the apostles executing the baptismal command of Christ and the baptism of Jesus. Sometimes the four rivers of Eden personified or lions served as supports; in Liége there were oxen, an imitation of the molten sea in the court of the priests of Solomon's temple. In the Gothic period the broad, massive form of the older time becomes more slender, and the architectural ornamentations occupy a larger space. Connected with the Roman Catholic rite of consecrating the baptismal water is the use of a covering, which in its artistic shaping is in harmony with the whole, and often develops into a high superstructure. In the Middle Ages enactments were passed by the Church concerning the material and other matters (*Rituale romanum, de sacramento baptismatis*, 30; cf. V. Thalhofer, *Handbuch der katholischen Liturgik*, i, Freiburg, 1883, 816 sqq.). When immersion ceased to be practised in the Roman Church the baptismal fonts became smaller.

Superseded by Baptismal Fonts.

The Protestant Church knows of no consecration of the baptismal water. In order to connect as closely as possible the two sacraments which were recognized, the baptismal font was at first placed near the altar,—a custom which in modern times has rightly been increasingly disregarded. As to baptism and baptisteries in the catacombs, nothing can be positively asserted, and all probability is against it. The water reservoirs which are sporadically found there, have no connection with baptism.

VICTOR SCHULTZE.

BIBLIOGRAPHY: H. Holtzinger, *Handbuch der altchristlichen Architektur. Form, Einrichtung und Ausschmückung der altchristlichen Kirchen, Baptisterien . . .*, Stuttgart, 1889; Bingham, *Origines*, book viii, chap. vii, §§ 1–4; E. Martène, *De antiquis ecclesiæ ritibus*, pp. i, 135, 153, Antwerp, 1736; *DCA*, i, 173-178; F. X. Kraus, *Real-Encyklopädie der christlichen Alterthümer*, art. *Taufkirche*, vol. ii, Freiburg, 1880–86; H. Otte, *Handbuch der kirchlichen Kunstarchäologie des deutschen Mittelalters*, ii, 303 sqq., Leipsic, 1883; V. Schultze, *Archäologie der altchristlichen Kunst*, pp. 75 sqq., 92 sqq., Munich, 1895; T. Beaudoire, *Genèse de la cryptographie apostolique et de l'architecture rituelle du premier au sixième siècle. Baptistères, basiliques . . .*, Paris, 1903.

BAPTISTINES (BATTISTINI, BATTISTINE): A religious order for both sexes, named after its patron saint, John the Baptist. The male branch (*Congregatio sacerdotum sæcularium missionariorum de S. Johanne Baptista*) was founded at Genoa by the pious priest Dominico Francesco Olivieri (d. 1766) and received papal approval from Benedict XIV in 1755. Its special purpose was to perform missionary work, which was carried on in Bulgaria, Rumelia, and China. The female order was instituted by Giovanna Maria Battista Solimani (d. 1758), who established a community at Moneglia (33 m. e.s.e. of Genoa) as early as 1730. Olivieri became their spiritual director. In 1736 they removed to Genoa and in 1744 were confirmed by Benedict XIV under the official name of Hermitesses of St. John the Baptist. Each member took the name Battista, whence arose the popular designation of *Battistine*. They followed a rigidly ascetic life, marked in particular by strict fasting, and devoted themselves to works of charity. The male Baptistines ceased toward the end of the eighteenth century, but the female branch continued in Genoa, Rome (where a convent was founded in 1755), and elsewhere in Italy till the middle of the nineteenth century.

O. ZÖCKLER†.

BIBLIOGRAPHY: G. Moroni, *Dizionario di erudizione storico-ecclesiastica*, s.v. *Battistæ*, Rome, 1831–32; Heimbucher, *Orden und Kongregationen*, ii, 307–308, 375.

BAPTISTS.

1. Origin of the Name. The use of the term "Baptist" as a denominational designation is of comparatively recent origin, first appearing about the year 1644. Its German equivalent (*Täufer*) was applied by Zwingli and others to the antipedobaptists of their time, expressing their opinion that the latter laid undue stress on believers' baptism; and the terms "Anabaptist" and "Katabaptist" (*Wiedertäufer* and *Widertäufer*) were used implying repetition and perversion or destruction of the infant baptism that for many centuries had been practised (see ANABAPTISTS). These designations were of course repudiated as opprobrious by antipedobaptists, who were content to call themselves "Christians," "Apostolic Christians," "Brethren," "Disciples of Christ," "Believing Baptized Children of God," etc. Early English antipedobaptists were stigmatized as "Anabaptists," with the worst continental implications, by their opponents, and were much concerned to disown this designation. In the earliest Particular (Calvinistic) Baptist confession of faith (1644) the churches concerned designate themselves as "those churches which are commonly (though falsely) called Anabaptists," and in the appendix to the confession (1646) they call themselves "Baptized Believers." In the confession of 1688 Baptist churches are designated "congregations of Christians baptized upon profession of their faith" and "baptized congregations." Other common designations (1654, etc.) are "Baptized Churches," "Baptized Christians," and "Churches of Christ in England, Scotland, and Wales." "Churches of Christ in London," "Churches of Christ in Ireland," etc., are expressions that occur in documents of 1653–57. As a sort of compromise between "Anabaptists" and "baptized believers," "baptized people," etc., the term "Baptists" was gradually adopted (1670 or earlier). In 1672 it is used in a royal license.

2. Precursors of the Baptists. Baptists have always professed to base their doctrine and practise exclusively upon New Testament precept and example. If they have failed to realize their aim, it has been due to imperfect understanding of the New Testament Scriptures or to the imperfection inherent in human nature. Baptists find their spiritual ancestry in all individuals and parties that during the early Christian centuries, the Middle Ages, and the Reformation time, in the spirit of obedience and loyalty to Christ, sought to stay the tide of incoming pagan and Judaizing error, or in times of general apostasy endeavored to restore Christianity to its primitive purity and simplicity. They find rejection of infant baptism and insistence on believers' baptism among the ancient, medieval, and modern Paulicians (Thondraki; see PAULICIANS), with the common (if not exclusive) practise of immersion and the most strenuous effort to realize regenerate membership, which so far identifies them with Baptists; but with their adoptionist Christology and sectarian exclusiveness modern Baptists have little sympathy. In the Petrobrusians of the twelfth century (see PETER OF BRUYS) Baptists find their principles almost completely embodied, but there is no indication that the former insisted upon immersion as the exclusively valid act of baptism.

Many of the Waldenses and the Bohemian Brethren (qq.v.) rejected infant baptism and practised believers' baptism, but they seem not to have disfellowshiped their pedobaptist brethren and laid no stress upon immersion; while in the rejection of judicial oaths, magistracy as allowable for a Christian, capital punishment, and warfare, they put an interpretation on the Scriptures that modern Baptists do not approve. The historical relations of modern Baptists to the Anabaptists of the sixteenth century are close and direct. English Puritanism and Brownism (see BROWNE, ROBERT), from which English Baptists sprang, were themselves products in part at least of the Anabaptist movement. A still more direct influence was exerted by the Mennonites of the Netherlands upon the English refugees that there became antipedobaptist (1609 onward). Anabaptists were the forerunners of modern Baptists in rejection of infant baptism and insistence on believers' baptism, in insisting on the sole authority of the Scriptures, in their efforts to secure and maintain regenerate church membership, in pleading for liberty of conscience and the separation of Church and State; but nearly all Anabaptists rejected oaths, magistracy, warfare, and capital punishment, all were anti-Augustinian in their anthropology, many were chiliastic, many were antitrinitarian, some were pantheistic and antinomian, many were communistic, and none (so far as is known) insisted on immersion as the exclusively valid act of baptism (see ANABAPTISTS).

I. The English Baptists.—1. Rise of the General Baptists: John Smyth (q.v.) became a Puritan as early as 1590 but continued in the Established Church until 1606, when he led in the organization of a separate congregation at Gainsborough, the members of which covenanted together "to walk in all his [God's] ways, made known or to be made known unto them, according to their best endeavors, whatsoever it might cost them, the Lord assisting them." In 1606 or 1607 they fled from persecution and settled in Amsterdam. They did not unite with the older Puritan church in Amsterdam, of which Francis Johnson and Henry Ainsworth (qq.v.) were pastor and teacher, but were on terms of fellowship with this body. In his reply to Richard Bernard's *Separatists' Schism*, published some months after his arrival, Smyth expressed the profoundest aversion to "Anabaptists," whom he classed with Papists, Arians, and "other heretics and anti-Christians," whose "prayers and religious exercises" could not be acceptable to God. By this time he had reached convictions in favor of pure congregationalism as against the presbyterial pracvise of Johnson. He soon took issue with "the Ancient Brethren of the Separation" as regards the use of the book [Bible] in reading, prophesying, and singing in church meetings, declaring it to be "no part of spiritual worship" and hence "unlawful"; he objected to the "triformed presbytery" (pastors, teachers, and rulers) as "none of God's ordinance but man's device"; and insisted that "in contributing to the church treasury, there ought to be both a separation from them that are without, and a sanctification of the whole action by prayer and thanksgiving." He is reported by some of his contemporaries to have objected to the use of translations of the Bible and to have insisted "that teachers should bring the originals, the Hebrew and Greek, and out of them translate by voice." He had evidently become hypersensitive regarding anything that savored of human additions to divine prescriptions.

1. John Smyth and his Congregation.

Prejudice against the Anabaptists seems for some time to have hindered the application of Smyth's principle to infant baptism, but late in 1608 or early in 1609 it was borne in upon him that if the Church of England was apostate (as his Separatist brethren agreed), then its ordinances were invalid, and that infant baptism was wholly without Scripture warrant and so in any case to be rejected. Accordingly he and his followers dissolved their church, disowned their baptism (Smyth repudiating also his ordination), resolved to introduce anew believers' baptism and to effect a completely new church organization with the New Testament as their only guide. Smyth seems to have first administered the ordinance to himself and then to the rest of the company. Then as baptized believers they effected a new organization with Smyth as pastor. They now felt impelled to protest against the church of Johnson and Ainsworth as "a false church, falsely constituted in the baptizing of infants, and their own unbaptized estate." When charged with inconsistency and changeableness, Smyth insisted that a change for the better is always in order, and that not to change so long as complete conformity to Scripture has not been attained "is evil simply; and therefore that we should proceed from the profession of Puritanism to Brownism, and from Brownism to true Christian baptism, is not simply evil and reprovable in itself, except it be proved that we have fallen from true religion." In answer to the charge of "Se-baptism" he claims that there is as much warrant for believers baptizing themselves as there is for setting up a true church (which his Separatist opponents professed to have done), inasmuch as a "true church can not be erected without baptism," and that "any man raised up after the apostasy of Antichrist" may "in the recovering of the church by baptism, administer it upon himself in communion with others." He further justifies self-administered baptism on the ground, among others, that "in the Old Testament every man that was unclean washed himself; every priest going to sacrifice washed himself. Every master of a family ministered the Passover to himself and all of his family." He adds: "A man can not baptize others into the church, himself being out of the church. Therefore it is lawful for a man to baptize himself together with others in communion, and this warrant is a plerophory for the practise of that which is done by us."

2. They Organize a New Church.

As Puritans, Separatists, and Mennonites practised affusion at this time and as no issue was raised in the controversial literature called out by this new movement among English Separatists or in the later negotiations between these English antipedobaptists and the Mennonites respecting the act of baptism, it seems highly probable that Smyth practised affusion. Deep-seated prejudice against Anabaptists, unfamiliarity with the Dutch language, and the attitude of aloofness assumed by the Mennonites, furnish a sufficient explanation of the failure of these English antipedobaptists to secure baptism at the hands of the Dutch brethren with whom they had so much in common.

Shortly before or shortly after the introduction of believers' baptism, in sympathy with the Arminian movement then current and with the Socinianized Mennonism of the time, Smyth adopted Socinian (Pelagian) views, denying original or hereditary sin and the redemption of infants by Christ. He also adopted the Mennonite view that Christ did not derive "the first matter of his flesh" from Mary, that "an elder of one church is an elder of all the churches in the world," and that "magistrates may not be members of Christ's church and retain their magistracy." Smyth's church, led by Thomas Helwys and John Murton, then excommunicated him and his followers because of their departure from the principles on which the church

3. Smyth Excommunicated by his Church.

had been constituted. These (thirty-three in number) now sought admission into the fellowship of the Mennonite church in Amsterdam of which Lubbert Gerrits was pastor. In their application they "confess this their error, and repent of the same, viz.: that they undertook to baptize themselves contrary to the order laid down by Christ," and express the desire "to get back into the true church of Christ as speedily as may be." Helwys and his associates besought the Mennonites to take "wise counsel, and that from God's word," how they should deal "in this cause betwixt us and those who are justly, for their sins, cast out from us. And the whole cause in question being succession, . consider, we beseech you, how it is Antichrist's chief hold, and that it is Jewish and ceremonial, an ordinance of the Old Testament, but not of the New." They cite the case of John the Baptist to prove that an unbaptized person may inaugurate baptism. They claim that "whosoever shall now be stirred up by the same Spirit to preach the same word, and men thereby being converted, may, according to John's example, wash them with water, and who can forbid? And we pray that we may speak freely herein, how dare any man or men challenge unto themselves a preeminence herein, as though the Spirit of God was only in their hearts, and the word of God now only to be fetched at their mouths, and the ordinance of God only to be had from their hands, except they were apostles? Hath the Lord thus restrained his Spirit, his word, and ordinances, as to make particular men lordly over them, or keepers of them? God forbid. This is contrary to the liberty of the gospel, which is free for all men, at all times and in all places. And now for the other question, that elders must ordain elders; or if this be a perpetual rule, then from whom is your eldership come? And if one church might once ordain, then why not all churches always?"

It might have been expected that the Mennonites of Amsterdam would receive with open arms these English brethren who were seemingly so thoroughly at one with them in doctrine and practise. Several considerations led them to hesitate. The connectional church order of the Mennonites made it necessary for the Amsterdam church to secure the approval of other churches in fellowship. An unwise

4. Attempts to Join the Mennonites.

act might easily rend the entire brotherhood, as unhappy experiences in the past had abundantly demonstrated. The Amsterdam Mennonite congregation found Smyth's party so thoroughly in accord with themselves that they were prompted to express to their brethren at Leeuwarden the opinion that "these English, without being baptized again, must be accepted." Yet, if the Leeuwarden brethren thought otherwise, Smyth and his associates were willing to accept and the Amsterdam brethren to administer a new baptism, if it could be proved from Scripture and reason to be necessary. The Leeuwarden brethren could not be induced to commit themselves as to the validity of Smyth's baptism or to assume any responsibility for what their Amsterdam brethren might do in the premises. One of the Mennonite brethren furnished Smyth's party with a meeting-place in the Great Cake House; but they were not received into full fellowship until 1615, three years after Smyth's death.

In 1611 Smyth and his followers put forth a declaration of their faith in one hundred articles. The confession sets forth just views as to the nature of saving knowledge of God as involving conformity in character to God's attributes. Arminian views are clearly and moderately set forth with respect to God's relation to the fall and to human sin. "Adam being fallen did not lose any natural power or faculty, . . and therefore . still retained freedom of will" (17). "Original sin" is declared to be "an idle term," there being "no such thing as men intend by the term, . because God threatened death only to Adam, not to his posterity, and because God created the soul" (18). It is accordingly maintained that "infants are conceived and born in innocency without sin" (20). It is asserted that "Adam being fallen, God did not hate him, but loved him still and sought his good" (22). "The new creature which is begotten of God needeth not the outward Scriptures, creatures, or ordinances of the church, . yet

5. Smyth's Declaration of Faith.

he can do nothing against the Law or Scriptures, but rather all his doings shall serve to the confirming and establishing of the Law" (61–63). "The outward church visible" is declared to consist "of penitent persons only, and of such as believing in Christ bring forth fruits worthy of amendment of life" (65). "All penitent and faithful Christians are brethren in the communion of the outward church, . though compassed with never so many ignorances and infirmities; and we salute them all with a holy kiss, being heartily grieved that we which follow after one faith, and one spirit, one Lord, and one God, one body, and one baptism, should be rent into so many sects and schisms: and that only for matters of less moment" (69). It is taught "that the outward baptism of water is to be administered only upon such penitent and faithful persons as are [aforesaid], and not upon innocent infants, or wicked persons" (70); that "in the outward supper which only baptized persons must partake, there is presented and figured before the eyes of the penitent and faithful that spiritual supper which Christ maketh of his flesh and blood: which is crucified and shed for the remission of sins . . and which is eaten and drunken . . only by those which are flesh of his flesh and bone of his bone, in the communion of the same spirit" (72); that "there is no succession in the outward church, but that all the succession is from heaven, and that the new creature only hath the thing signified and substance, whereof the outward church and ordinances are shadows, and therefore he alone hath power and knoweth aright how to administer in the outward church, for the benefit of others: yet God is not the author of confusion but of order and therefore we are in the outward church to draw as near the first institution as may be in all things; therefore it is not lawful for every brother to administer the word and sacraments" (81). The following declaration on liberty of conscience is especially noteworthy: "That the magistrate is not by virtue of his office to meddle with religion or matters of conscience, to force or compel men to this or that form of religion or doctrine, but to leave Christian religion free to every man's conscience. . That if the magistrate will follow Christ and be his disciple, he must deny himself, take up his cross, and follow Christ: he must love his enemies and not kill them, he must pray for them and not punish them, he must feed them and give them drink, not imprison them, banish them, dismember them, and spoil their goods " (84-85). Going to law before civil magistrates, marriage with unbelievers, and the taking of oaths are forbidden to Christians. Community of goods in times of need is recommended.

Smyth died in Aug., 1612, after a long period of decline during which he manifested a wonderful degree of charity toward all true believers. He expressed the profoundest regret for his bitterly censorious writings against the Church of England, the Separation, and Helwys, and showed the utmost aversion to everything controversial. In his *Retractation of his Errors and the Confirmation of the Truth*, published a year or two after his death, along with the confession of faith from which extracts have been given, and a brief account of his life and death, he restates the points at issue in the controversies in which he had been engaged, and in a thoroughly judicial and irenic spirit indicates what he is still constrained, without controversy, to maintain, as well as what he feels inclined to surrender. Helwys had been so intemperate as to charge him with sinning against the Holy Ghost in receding from the position he had reached regarding the independent inauguration of baptism and church organization. The point at issue was not the necessity of succession in the administration of baptism and the organization of churches, but whether "although there be churches already established, ministers ordained, and sacraments administered orderly, yet men are not bound to join these former churches established, but may, being as yet unbaptized, baptize themselves (as we did) and proceed to build churches of themselves, disorderly (as I take it)." Smyth points out that Helwys's contention would involve a recognition of the right of any two or three private persons (even women), in a community where rightly constituted churches abound, to disregard these churches and baptize and organize themselves. "Concerning succession, briefly thus much: I deny all succession except in the truth; and I hold we are not to violate the order of the primitive church, except necessity urge a dispensation; and therefore it is not lawful for every one that seeth the truth to baptize, for then there might be as many churches as couples in the world, and none have anything to do with other, which breaketh the bond of love and brotherhood in churches; but, in these outward matters, I dare not any more contend with any man, but desire that we may follow the truth of repentance, faith, and regeneration, and lay aside dissension for mint, comin, and annis seed." Helwys understood Smyth to deny with the Mennonites that Christ received his flesh from Mary. He now points out that while once inclined to distinguish between the first and second flesh of the infant in the womb and to hold that the former was not derived while the latter, the product of nourishment, was derived from Mary, he has now reached the conviction that it is better to attribute his flesh to Mary without going beyond the Scriptures in curious inquiry "whereof Christ's natural flesh was made." He thinks it far more important that "we should search into Christ's spiritual flesh, to be made flesh of his flesh, and bone of his bone, in the communion and fellowship of the same spirit."

6. His Last Utterances.

By 1611 Helwys and his associates reached the conviction that flight in persecution and voluntary exile were absolutely unjustifiable. Late in 1611 or early in 1612 they returned to England and settled in London. Helwys was not content to carry out, with his company, his own convictions; he published (1612) *A Short Declaration of the Mystery of Iniquity*, in which "in great confidence and passion" (Robinson) he held up to reproach all the English dissenting refugees in the Netherlands, charging that in seeking to avoid being "sheep in the midst of wolves" the false-hearted leaders had fled into strange countries to save their lives and had drawn other people after them, leaving the true believers who could not thus save their lives without leadership and leaving their native land without gospel testimony.

7. Helwys Returns to London.

In *A Declaration of Faith of English People Remaining at Amsterdam in Holland* (1611), set forth by Helwys and his associates, while Christ's righteousness is said to be imputed to all (general redemption), men are declared to be "by nature the children of wrath, born in iniquity, and in sin conceived even so now being fallen, and having all disposition unto evil, and no disposition or will unto any good, yet God giving grace, man may receive grace, or may reject grace. " It is further taught, "That God before the foundation of the world hath predestinated that all that believe in him shall be saved, and all that believe not shall be damned; all which he knew before. And this is the election and reprobation spoken of in the Scriptures, concerning salvation and condemnation; and not that God hath predestinated men to be wicked, and so to be damned, but that men being wicked shall be damned." It is taught "That man may fall away from the grace of God, and from the truth. That a righteous man may forsake his righteousness, and perish." Civil magistracy is recognized as "a holy ordinance of God" and magistrates "may be members of the church of Christ, retaining their magistracy." From this confession, as well as from Helwys's *Proof that God's Decree is not the Cause of any Man's Sin or Condemnation*, published the same year, it appears that Helwys held to a moderate type of Arminianism, while Smyth had become almost Socinian in his doctrine.

8. His Doctrines.

Little is known of the careers of Helwys, Murton,

and their associates after their repatriation. In 1614 a zealous, clear-headed antipedobaptist, Leonard Busher by name, addressed to King James and the High Court of Parliament a treatise entitled *Religious Peace: or A Plea for Liberty of Conscience*, the first work on the subject published in English. Among the more striking sentences are the following: "It is not only unmerciful, but unnatural and abominable; yea, monstrous for one Christian to vex and destroy another for difference and questions of religion." "I do affirm, that through the unlawful weed-hook of persecution, which your predecessors have used, and by your majesty and parliament is still continued, there is such a quantity of wheat plucked up, and such a multitude of tares left behind, that the wheat which remains can not yet appear in any right visible congregation." "With Scripture, and not with fire and sword, your majesty's bishops and ministers ought to be armed and weaponed." Having shown that even in the Old Testament time "the Lord would not have his offerings by constraint," he proceeds: "So now in the time of the gospel, he will not have the people constrained, but as many as receive the word gladly, they are to be added to the church by baptism. And therefore Christ commanded his disciples to teach all nations and baptize them; that is, to preach the word of salvation to every creature of all sorts of nations, that are worthy and willing to receive it. And such as willingly and gladly receive it, he hath commanded to be baptized in the water, that is, dipped for dead in the water." The last sentence would seem clearly to identify Busher with the Baptists as regards his conception of the subjects and mode of baptism; but whether he was a member of the little Helwys company or a disconnected antipedobaptist we are not informed. The following year (1615) there was published *Objections answered by way of Dialogue, wherein is proved that no man ought to be persecuted for his religion, so he testifie his allegiance by the Oath, appointed by Law, By Christ's unworthy Witnesses, His Majesty's faithful Subjects: Commonly (but most falsely) called Anabaptists* This somewhat elaborate and thoroughgoing plea for liberty of conscience proceeded from the Helwys company and has been attributed to John Murton, as has also *A Most Humble Supplication of many of the King's Majesty's Most Loyal Subjects who are persecuted (only for differing in religion), contrary to divine and human testimonies* (1620). According to an early tradition recorded by Roger Williams, the latter treatise was written with milk brought daily in a bottle with a fresh sheet of paper each day rolled up for a stopper and the written sheet returned as stopper of the empty bottle to be deciphered by a friend.

9. Baptist Publications.

Helwys seems to have died a few years after returning to England. Murton was thenceforth leader of the party. By 1624 or 1626, as is learned from correspondence of members of Murton's connection with the Mennonites of Amsterdam preserved in the archives of the latter (B. Evans, *Early English Baptists*, ii, London, 1862, pp. 21–22), there were, besides the congregation at Newgate, London, small congregations at Lincoln, Tiverton, Salisbury, and Coventry, aggregating about 150 members. Differences had by this time arisen among the brethren and a minority, led by Elias Tookey, had been excommunicated. Both sides sought the moral support and the fellowship of the Amsterdam Mennonite church. As usual, the Mennonite brethren were extremely cautious, and required to be accurately informed on many points before committing themselves to either party. Tookey failed to satisfy the Mennonites on a number of points: he and his party thought it right to celebrate the Supper in the absence of an ordained minister; were not willing to refuse oaths or military service; while none of them denied the deity of Christ, there was difference of opinion as to what was involved in his deity. They wished the Mennonites to write to Murton and his friends on their behalf "in order to augment peace and welfare." In 1626 two commissioners from the five churches of Murton's connection visited the Mennonites of Amsterdam with a view to fellowship. These also were disposed to defend oaths as almost necessary at the time in England and to insist that Christ had his flesh from Mary. Against the practise of the Mennonites they were strongly inclined to perpetuate the weekly celebration of the Supper. They acknowledge that the ministering of the sacraments is inseparably united with the ministering of the word, but insist that without ordination servants of the church may "preach, convert, baptize, and perform other public actions with the consent of the church, when the bishops are not present." They crave the indulgence of their Dutch brethren in a difference of opinion regarding the right of a Christian to exercise magistracy. They insist upon the right of Christians to bear arms for national and local defense. The Mennonites treated both parties kindly but refused to enter into organic union with either. Two letters addressed to the Mennonites in 1630–31, the one by the church at Lincoln, the other by that at Tiverton, in answer to letters of reproof occasioned by their overreadiness to exercise severe discipline even to the wasting and scattering of their constituencies, turn the tables upon their somewhat patronizing counselors, justify their efforts to purge themselves of evil by abundant citation of Scripture, rebuke the Mennonites for their laxity, which if they had known before they applied for union (1626) they would first have sought to reform, and blame them for refusing union on grounds that can not be shown to be Scriptural. One of the matters of complaint was that the English antipedobaptists disciplined members for attending the services of the Established Church. There is no indication of difference of opinion respecting the act of baptism.

10. Further Traces of Baptists in England.

John Murton seems to have died about 1630, when his widow returned to Amsterdam and united with the Mennonite church.

Somewhat vague traditions of the existence of Baptist churches about this time (in some cases considerably earlier) at Stony Stratford, Ashford, Biddenden, Eythorne, Hill Cliffe, Bocking, Canterbury, and Amersham are still current in England. Attempts to confirm these traditions by antiquarian research have so far failed. Some of the Baptist churches that claim early foundation may have grown out of Anabaptist, Lollard, or Separatist congregations of the earlier time. Little further is known of English antipedobaptist life until about 1640–42, when in common with the Calvinistic antipedobaptists, they became convinced that immersion alone is baptism.

2. Rise of the Particular (Calvinistic) Baptists: In 1616 Henry Jacob, a learned Puritan minister, who for some years had been pastor of an English congregation at Middelburg, Zealand, and who had published a number of works against the English establishment, after much conference with his Separatist brethren in the Netherlands and in England and much fasting and prayer with his associates, reached the conviction that duty required him to return to England and to "venture himself for the kingdom of Christ's sake." Such of his members as chose to return with him he organized anew at Southwark, London, all covenanting together "to walk in all God's ways as he had revealed or should make known to them." The congregation proceeded to choose and ordain Jacob pastor and "many saints were joined to them." After about eight years of heroic service and suffering, Jacob emigrated to America. After an interval, John Lathrop became pastor and with many of the members spent much of the time in prison. Finding it impossible to labor in England Lathrop also sailed for America (1634). In 1633, differences of opinion having arisen as to recognition of the parish churches, a number of the brethren were peaceably dismissed to form an independent congregation, "Mr. Eaton with some others receiving a further baptism." John Spilsbury's name does not appear among

1. Congregations in London.

the seceders of 1633, but some time between this date and the second secession of 1638 he had become the pastor of an antipedobaptist congregation; whether this was distinct from Eaton's congregation does not clearly appear. The record reads· "These also being of the same judgment with Sam Eaton and desiring to depart and not be censured, our interest in them was remitted with prayer made in their behalf, June 8, 1638, they having just forsaken us and joined with Mr. Spilsbury." Shortly before or shortly after this secession William Kiffin, then a young man of twenty-two, afterward till 1701 one of the most influential leaders of the Particular Baptists, united with Eaton. The learned and zealous Henry Jessey had become pastor of the Jacob-Lathrop church in 1637 In 1640 the conviction that "dipping the body into the water" is the only valid baptism forced itself upon a number of the members and the matter was much agitated in antipedobaptist circles. As a result of conferences on this matter Richard Blount, who understood Dutch, was sent to Holland where the Collegiants of Rhynsburg (see COLLEGIANTS) were practising immersion, and received baptism at the hands of J. Batte, a teacher among them. This party had arisen about 1619, but its immersion may have been derived from the Polish (Socinian) antipedobaptists. On his return Blount immersed Blacklock, and they two baptized large numbers (1641). The immersionist antipedobaptists had by this time formed themselves into two companies. Spilsbury insisted that "baptizedness is not essential to the administrator" of baptism and, with a number of adherents, discountenanced Blount's method of restoring baptism. As the agitation had been going on for some months before Blount's journey to Holland, it is not unlikely that Spilsbury and his adherents, including Kiffin, had some time before introduced immersion independently. Spilsbury's argument against the necessity of succession in baptism prevailed. In 1643 friendly discussion of the question of infant baptism was renewed in the congregation of which Jessey was pastor. Hanserd Knollys, a university graduate and Puritan preacher, who had spent some time in New England and had found himself out of harmony with the theocracy, was at this time a member of Jessey's church. According to the ancient records "H. K., our brother, not being satisfied for baptizing his child, after it had been endeavored by the elder and by one or two more, himself referred to the church then that they might satisfy him or he rectify them, if amiss therein, which was well accepted. Hence meetings were appointed for conference about it and each was performed with prayer and much love." An interesting outline of the arguments pro and con by Jessey and Knollys, in which other brethren (Kiffin among them) joined. is given in the record. A considerable number were convinced with Knollys against the baptism of infants, and the church after taking the advice of the elders and brethren of other churches (including Praisegod Barebone, Dr. Parker, Thomas Goodwin Philip Nye, Simpson, and Burrows). several of whom had recently returned from exile in the Netherlands and were to become prominent members of the Westminster Assembly, it was decided that inasmuch as the antipedobaptist brethren had absented themselves, not from obstinacy, but from tender conscience and holiness, and in order to avoid disturbing the proceedings of the church, that the church would not "excommunicate, no, nor admonish, which is only to obstinate. to count them still of our church and pray (for) and love them," and to "desire conversing together so far as their principles permit them." By this time Kiffin had become pastor of a church and some of those who left Jessey's church on this occasion joined with him, while others organized themselves into a new church with Knollys as pastor (1644).

By October 1644, the Calvinistic antipedobaptists of London who had adopted immersion as the exclusively valid form of baptism "had become seven churches." At this time, in order to defend themselves against charges of Arminianism, opposition to civil government, etc., usually associated with the name "Anabaptist" and slanderously urged against themselves, representatives of these churches united in a confession of faith in fifty-two articles, wherein along with Calvinistic teachings on theology, Christology, and anthropology, are set forth Baptist views of baptism and the Supper (the "dipping or plunging of the body" of the believer "under water," the Supper to be partaken of after baptism), magistracy, oaths, etc., and a vigorous statement of the doctrine of liberty of conscience. "But if any man shall impose upon us anything that we see not to be commanded by our Lord Jesus Christ, we should in his strength rather embrace all reproaches and tortures of men, to be stripped of all outward comforts, and, if it were possible, to die a thousand deaths, rather than do anything against the least tittle of the truth of God, or against the light of our own consciences." This confession was signed by fifteen brethren representing the seven churches. The name of Kiffin stands first, those of Spilsbury, Skippard, Gunne, Webb, Hobson, and Phelps, are first in the other groups. In the second edition (1646) a French church represented by Le Barbier and Le Duret is added, and the names of Hanserd Knollys, Benjamin Cox, and Thomas Holms appear for the first time.

2. Confession of 1644.

The following record, written apparently by Jessey, dates from 1644: "After that H. Jessey was convinced also, the next morning early after that which had been a day of solemn seeking the Lord in fasting and prayer (That if infant baptism were unlawful and if we should be further baptized, etc., the Lord would not hide it from us, but cause us to know it). First H. Jessey was convinced against pedobaptism and then that himself should be baptized (notwithstanding many conferences with his honored and beloved brethren Mr. Nye, Mr. Th. Goodwin, Mr. Burroughs, Mr. Greenhill, Mr. Cradock, Mr. Carter, etc., etc. .), and was baptized by Mr. Knollys, and then by degrees he baptized many of the church, when convinced they desired it." Several who had left the church to become Baptists now returned. Jessey long continued to minister to a mixed congregation, Baptists and pedobaptists mutually tolerating each other. In the general religious ferment which set in with the opening of the Long Parliament (Nov. 3, 1640) and the greater freedom which was then allowed, many who had doubted the propriety of infant baptism felt free to avow and propagate their principles.

3. General Baptists from 1641 Onward: It is probable that most or all of the antipedobaptist churches of the Helwys-Murton connection survived the Laudian persecutions and others may have arisen after 1632. Thomas Lamb was arrested at Colchester for disseminating heresy some time before 1640. After his release he resumed his ministry in London and is said to have become familiar with nearly every prison in London and its vicinity. At the beginning of this period he was pastor of a congregation in Bell-alley, which became a fruitful mother of churches. In 1643 he was reenforced by Henry Denne, who had been educated at Cambridge and was instrumental, with Lamb and several other zealous evangelists, in the conversion of multitudes in Huntingtonshire, Cambridgeshire, Lincolnshire, Kent, and elsewhere. Lamb's church became a missionary society which sent forth evangelists into various parts of England and into Wales. Between 1641 and 1649 about ten associations are supposed to have been established, with quarterly, half-yearly, or annual meetings, for edificatory, disciplinary, and missionary purposes. Possibly from early connection with the Mennonites, the General Baptists emphasized connectional church government rather than church independency. Several years before 1671 a General Assembly of the churches of the entire connection had been formed, which usually met in London. The General Baptist churches exercised a rigorous discipline over their membership in matters of doctrine and life. Persistence in Calvinistic teaching (as in denial of the universality of the atonement) was a ground of excommunication. Divisive controversies on church singing and on the imposition of hands occupied a large share of attention. Quakers and Ranters invaded the congregations and in some cases were responsible for decimating their membership. Divided congregations, churches at variance with neighboring churches, and even aggrieved individuals could appeal to the associations. The General Assembly became virtually a court of appeal from churches and associations. An aggrieved member of a church might appeal to two or more neighboring churches, which were under obligation to hear and judge the case. From such a judgment, appeal might be made to the association and from this to the General Assembly. Thus every local difficulty was likely to pervade the entire connection. Thus equipped with a system of graduated courts of appeal, the connection came to feel the need of general executive officers, and found the New Testament prototype of what they wanted in the apostolate. These officials were called "messengers" or "bishops." According to the *Orthodox Creed* (1678), "The bishops have the government of those churches that had suffrage in their election, ordinarily, as also to preach the word to the world." Thomas Grantham (in *Christianismus Primitivus*, London, 1678), a chief defender of Baptist episcopacy, thus defined the office: "1. To plant churches where there are none; 2. To set in order such churches as want officers to order their affairs; and 3. To assist faithful pastors or churches against usurpers and those that trouble the peace of particular churches by false doctrines." Grantham expressed the wish that representatives of all the baptized churches in the world might meet occasionally in a great consistory to consider matters of difference among them. The Lincolnshire Association in 1775 gave still more ample powers to the "messenger," who is said to have "full liberty and authority, according to the Gospel, to freely inquire into the state of the churches respecting both the pastor and people, to see that the pastors do their duty in their places, and the people theirs; he is to exhort, admonish, and reprove both the one and the other, as occasion calls for. In virtue of his office, he is to watch over the several flocks committed to his care and charge, to labor to keep out innovations in

1. Organization and Polity.

doctrine, worship, and discipline, and to stand up in defense of the Gospel."

The General Baptists were greatly prospered during the Civil War, in which they heartily participated, and during the Cromwellian period. Along with other dissenters they suffered severely under Charles II. After the Revolution (1688-89), owing in part to the disciplinary system already described and still more to the pervasive influence of Socinianism, disintegration set in. The process was accelerated by their resistance to the evangelical revival led by the Wesleys and Whitefield. By 1770 they had dwindled to small proportions and most of those that remained had become unitarian.

2. Revival at Barton.

In 1743 a religious revival occurred in the vicinity of Barton. After a time the converts became impressed with the importance of immersion and brought a large tub into the meeting-house for the dipping of infants. Without any knowledge of Baptists they became convinced (1755) that believers only should be baptized and they proceeded to introduce baptism anew, Donithrope baptizing Kendrick, who in turn baptized his baptizer, and the two baptized between sixty and seventy others. Those who did not feel the need of a further baptism were allowed to remain in communion. Their numbers multiplied until by 1770 six Baptist churches with near a thousand members and ten ordained pastors had resulted from the movement.

3. The New Connection.

In 1762 Dan Taylor (q.v.), a young man of twenty-four, who had recently been converted in the Wesleyan meetings and had been engaging successfully in evangelistic work in Yorkshire, became convinced independently of the unscripturalness of infant baptism, left the Wesleyans, and associated himself with four others who had had a similar experience at Heptonstall. Having reached Baptist convictions and having learned of some General Baptists in Lincolnshire, one hundred and twenty miles distant, Taylor journeyed in the midst of winter and was baptized by Jeffries, pastor of the Gamston church. Taylor proved himself a master workman and by 1770 he had founded or rescued from decay fifteen churches, which united in forming a "New Connection of General Baptist churches, with a design to revive experimental religion or primitive Christianity in faith and practise." The brief articles of faith combine evangelical Arminianism with insistence on believers' baptism (immersion) as indispensable. Socinian views of the person of Christ and hyper-Calvinistic antinomianism are explicitly condemned. The New Connection rigorously excluded from membership General Baptists of the older type who would not sign their confession and whose ministers failed to come up to their standard of personal religious experience. By the close of the eighteenth century the New Connection had an academy for the training of ministers, had engaged in Sunday-school work, and had started a magazine. Their membership had grown to about four thousand. It is probable that the General Baptist churches of the older type had about the same number of members at the same time.

4. In the Nineteenth Century.

During the nineteenth century the denomination grew in numbers, educational and literary enterprise, and in missionary activity. In 1816 they formed a missionary society and entered upon foreign work. Their most influential leader at this time was J. G. Pike. For many years the General Baptists had joined with the Particular Baptists in the Baptist Union and there had been a free interchange of pulpits and members. In 1891 a union of General and Particular Baptists was effected. Until recent times the General Baptists had almost uniformly practised restricted communion and rigorously excluded Calvinistic Baptists from the Supper. During the nineteenth century their views on this matter became assimilated to those of the great majority of the Particular Baptists.

4. Particular Baptists from 1644 Onward:

1. To the Restoration.

From the date of the signing of the confession of 1644–46, Baptists of the Calvinistic type went forward by leaps and bounds. Through the evangelistic efforts of John Myles and Vavasour Powell Baptists early gained a firm footing in Wales. In 1651 four churches met at Carmarthen to consider the questions of singing of psalms and the laying-on of hands, and a year earlier three of the churches had gathered for consultation on missionary business. The meeting of 1650 had voted that each church should raise ten pounds for the dissemination of the gospel. From this time onward the Welsh Baptists made much of associations and these were the prototypes of the Philadelphia Association in America (see below, II, 1, § 8). The London churches were active in evangelizing the provinces, leading ministers spending much time in this kind of work. Baptists of both types were soon numerous in the Parliamentary army, many of whose officers were of this persuasion (Fleetwood, Cromwell's son-in-law and Lord Deputy of Ireland, Major General Harrison, Col. Hutchinson, Major Paul Hobson, and others). Baptist officers were in several cases effective preachers and most of them gave every encouragement to Baptist preaching and the establishment of Baptist churches in the neighborhood of the camps. The efforts of the Westminster Assembly and of the Presbyterian Parliament to check the spread of Baptist principles proved ineffective, and Baptists and Independents became so powerful in the army that they were able to dissolve the Assembly and to cast out the Presbyterian members of Parliament. Baptists encouraged Cromwell to assume the headship of the state; but they soon grew weary of his military government. It seems well established that their determined opposition prevented Cromwell from accepting the royal title when it was pressed upon him by others. Harrison, who had been active in the trial and execution of Charles I, became Cromwell's bitter opponent. He embraced socialistic and millenarian ideas. John Milton advocated Baptist principles and was a stanch antipedobaptist, but there is no evidence that he was ever a member of a Baptist church. Among Cromwell's "Tryers," appointed to pass upon the qualifications of candidates for the pulpits of endowed churches were Henry Jessey, Daniel Dyke, and John Tombes, a highly educated collegian who wrote and disputed against infant baptism. These and about twenty-two other Baptist ministers thought it right to accept appointments as pastors of endowed churches, a majority of the parishioners in each case petitioning for their services. Hanserd Knollys and many other Baptist ministers protested against the Court of Tryers as too much like the High Commission Court of Laud's time. Besides being one of the most influential and devoted pastors of his time, William Kiffin was a successful man of affairs and by the liberal use of his wealth promoted the Baptist cause.

It has been noticed that the first Particular Baptist congregations were formed by peaceable withdrawal from a pedobaptist church and that Jessey remained pastor of a mixed church. Open communion was from the first practised by most of the churches. Controversy between Kiffin and Bunyan, in which the latter denied that differences of opinion and practise respecting an external rite should be allowed to hinder the manifestation of Christian love and brotherhood in the Supper, left the question an open one.

In 1653 several churches in Ireland that had been formed through the labors of London ministers addressed a letter to their brethren in London suggesting the desirability of "brotherly correspondence" with them and through them "with all the rest of the churches of Christ in England, Scotland, and Wales." They requested that two or more suitable brethren "visit, comfort, and confirm all the flock of our Lord Jesus that are, or have given up their names to be, under his rule and government, in England, Scotland, and Wales." The London brethren accepted the suggestion and messengers were sent out to visit the churches. Jessey "was sent by divers churches to visit about thirty-six congregations in Essex, Sussex, Norfolk, Middlesex." In the same year a circular letter was addressed by many churches in London, Wales, etc., to other churches, suggesting the sending of messengers to a meeting with a view to harmonizing doctrine and practise among the churches and arranging for the approval and sending out of teachers. The Western Association was formed the same year, the Midland Association in 1655. The Western Association in 1655 appointed and ordained Thomas Collier, its most influential leader, "General Superintendent and Messenger to all the Associated Churches." In 1656 this association adopted a confession of faith (the "Somerset") in which the duty of the churches individually and collectively to "preach the gospel to the world" is asserted, and special recognition is made of obligation to labor for the conversion of the Jews. It may be worthy of note that Henry Jessey, who was an enthusiastic Hebraist, was deeply interested in the Jews of his time and raised a considerable amount of money for the relief of the persecuted and distressed.

2. Cooperation and Union.

Particular Baptists as well as General, though probably not to so large an extent, suffered much from the intrusion of Familists, Seekers, Ranters, and Fifth Monarchy Men.

Baptists promoted the restoration of Charles II and accepted in good faith his assurances of toleration. The uprising of the Fifth Monarchy Men (q.v.), led by Henry Venner (1661), was the occasion of an outbreak of persecution. Twenty-six Baptist ministers who had held benefices under the Cromwellian régime were deposed through the execution of the Act of Uniformity (1662), the least regrettable of the results of the Restoration. These ministers, it will be remembered, had been educated in the Established Church and no doubt justified themselves in abetting a union of Church and State by the practical consideration that the funds were available for the support of a ministry and that it was bettter for them to do the service to which they were invited rather than to leave the people destitute or with inferior pastors. The Bill of Indulgence (1675) opened the way for efforts to strengthen the ministry of dissenting churches. In the same year the Particular Baptist ministers of London requested the churches in England and Wales to send representatives to meet in London the following May, with a view to taking measures for "providing an orderly standing ministry in the church, who might give themselves to reading and study, and so become able ministers of the New Testament." The meeting seems not to have occurred till 1677, when a confession of faith, that of the Westminster Assembly with necessary modifications, was adopted and formally promulgated. In 1689 (just after the Revolution and the promulgation of the Act of Toleration) representatives of about a hundred churches assembled for the expression of fellowship and the reaffirming of the confession of 1677. The meeting was most harmonious, scarcely a note of dissent being heard. A dearth of properly qualified pastors is lamented. During the Civil War and Commonwealth times many highly educated ministers from the Established Church had joined the Baptist ranks. This source of supply had failed. Failure "to make gospel-provision for their maintenance" is thought to be one of the reasons why so few competent men devote themselves wholly to the work. For remedying this defect it was decided to raise "a public stock or fund of money," "first by a free-will offering to the Lord; and secondly, by a subscription, every one declaring what he is willing to give weekly, monthly, or quarterly to it." "A general fast in all the congregations" was arranged for, a list of "evils to be bewailed and mourned over" is given, and special prayer is to be offered for the conversion of "the poor Jews." The assembly was careful to disclaim "superiority and superintendency over the churches" and determined that in future assemblies no differences between churches and persons should be debated. Nine London brethren were entrusted with the collection and the administration of the fund for the assistance of weak churches, the sending forth of missionaries, and the assistance of gifted and sound men "in attaining to the knowledge and understanding of

3. To 1717.

the languages, Latin, Greek, and Hebrew." The question of open or restricted communion was left to the churches, each to act in the matter "as they have received from the Lord." The assembly of 1691 was made up of representatives of a hundred churches belonging to twelve associations. In 1692 it was decided to divide the assembly, one portion to meet in London and the other in Bristol, at different seasons of the year, these assemblies not to be accountable to each other and each to send messengers to the other. At this time a grievous controversy was raging on the question "whether the praises of God should be sung in public assemblies," Kiffin, Keach, Cox, Steed, and other leading brethren being involved. It was decided to refer the matter to seven brethren appointed by the assembly, who administered a scathing rebuke to the offenders, which was taken in good part. The Bristol meeting prospered, but the London meeting declined. The Broadmead church, Bristol, was one of the earliest and strongest of the Particular Baptist Churches outside of London and the importance of Bristol as a Baptist center was greatly enhanced by the endowment left by Edward Terrill (d. 1686) with the Broadmead church for ministerial education, which became available in 1717. Out of this foundation grew the theological college that from its inception has been one of the chief factors in the progress of the denomination.

4. To 1775.

In 1717 the London ministers inaugurated another missionary fund. The great leaders of the past century had all passed away, and there had been a marked decline in the Baptist cause. The older assembly with its fund seems to have become extinct. Benjamin Stinton, pastor of one of the wealthier churches, and the Hollis brothers, wealthy business men, who while contributing liberally for the support of Baptist work regularly attended Presbyterian services, urged that General Baptists be invited to cooperate in the raising and administration of the fund and to participate in its use. This cooperation was refused, but there was in London at this time a strong sentiment in favor of Baptist union. The fund was to be administered by representatives of the contributing churches, to be appointed in numbers proportioned to their contributions, and individual contributors not members of contributing churches participated in the management. John Hollis was for years treasurer of the fund and left it a large legacy. It may be observed that to the Hollis family Harvard University was indebted for endowment and equipment. In opposition to this unionistic movement, a "Society of Ministers of the Particular Baptist Persuasion" was formed 1723-24, which for many years exerted a powerful and wide-spread influence. By way of reaction against the Socinian teachings that were pervading the Established Church and all the dissenting bodies, Particular Baptist theologians like John Gill and John Brine promulgated a high type of Calvinistic teaching that in the minds of the uncultured easily degenerated into fatalism and antinomianism. Many Particular Baptist ministers went to the extreme of considering it an impertinence to preach to the unregenerate or to pray for them, and many churches excluded from fellowship any who dissented from their fatalistic views. By 1753 there had been such a decline that John Ryland, who made a careful inquiry, could find only 4,930 Particular Baptists in England and Wales. They opposed the evangelical revival with almost fanatical zeal. In the London and Bristol centers there remained a number of more moderate pastors and churches. In general it may be said that pastors educated at Bristol rarely carried their doctrine and practise to the fatalistic and antinomian extreme.

5. Andrew Fuller. Missionary Enterprise.

The conversion of Andrew Fuller (q.v.) to evangelical views, chiefly through the reading of a pamphlet by Jonathan Edwards on the importance of a general union of Christians in prayer for a revival of religion, and through the influence of the evangelical revival in England, marks an epoch in the history of the Particular Baptists. For a few years before 1792 ministers of the Northamptonshire Association, under Fuller's leadership, held monthly prayer-meetings for the extension of the gospel. In May, 1792, William Carey (q.v.) having become deeply impressed with the destitution of the heathen and the duty of Christians to carry out the great commission, preached a sermon on the topic: "Expect great things from God; attempt great things for God," which made a profound impression and led to the organization, a few months later (Oct. 2), at Kettering (Fuller's church) of the Baptist Missionary Society. From this time onward Fuller devoted much of his time and effort to the diffusion of the missionary spirit throughout his denomination and among dissenters and churchmen. He visited from time to time all parts of Britain in the interest of Carey's mission. His popular but profound publications disseminated moderate Calvinistic views suffused with missionary enthusiasm. Not since the Cromwellian age were Baptist principles brought to the attention of the religious public in so acceptable a manner. Closely associated with Fuller was John Ryland (q.v.), who in 1783 became pastor of the Broadmead church, Bristol, and Principal of the Baptist College. For thirty years he exerted a wide-spread influence as pastor and teacher. Among the students that went forth from the college were John Foster and Robert Hall (qq.v.). Fuller's chief Baptist opponents were Abraham Booth, who from being a General Baptist became a Particular Baptist of the more rigorous type and wrote largely in defense of believers' baptism, restricted communion, and high Calvinism ("Reign of Grace"), and Alexander Maclean, leader of the Scotch Baptists. The successful inauguration of missionary work in India and Carey's achievements in the acquisition of Oriental languages and in Bible translation gave the denomination a prestige and popular acceptance that it had not before enjoyed. By 1801 the Particular Baptists had increased to 29,000.

The work of the denomination in Foreign Missions was greatly prospered, and commanded enthusiastic support. India, Ceylon, China, Palestine, Africa, the Bahamas, Trinidad, San Domingo, Turk's Island, and Italy are the present beneficiaries. At an earlier date Jamaica was evangelized by this body. The present annual income of the Foreign Missionary Society is about £100,000. It supports about three hundred missionaries and evangelists and has about 20,000 members in its mission churches.

About 1812 a conviction was expressed by a writer in the *Baptist Magazine* that, while numerically strong, the Baptists of England and Wales exerted little influence because of their lack of union. "Union of the most extensive, firm, and durable nature" was earnestly advocated by him. A number of brethren met in London the same year to plan for a union. Particular Baptists contended much more strenuously than General Baptists for church independency, and the recognition of the fullest independence of the local churches was indispensable. Among the principal promoters of the enterprise were Joseph Ivimey, the historian, Drs. Ryland and Rippon, of London, and James Hinton, of Oxford. The union did not at once take firm hold on the denominational life or become a marked success. But the great religious and political upheaval of the third and fourth decades of the nineteenth century (Reform bills, Catholic Emancipation, abolition of Corporation and Test Acts, Hampden Controversy, Tractarian Controversy, etc.) aroused Baptists anew to the importance of making their influence felt and the Union grew in importance. The determined and successful Romanizing propaganda of the Oxford school and the disruption (1843) of the Scottish Church encouraged English dissenters to believe that disestablishment was possible in England and led to concerted efforts for religious equality. At the formation of the Anti-State-Church Association (1844) Baptists were the only religious body represented. In the recent agitation against the education act, Dr. John Clifford (q.v.) was the recognized leader and to him and his free church coadjutors was largely due the victory of the Liberal party in 1906.

6. Baptist Union.

Through the enthusiastic advocacy of Robert Robinson and Robert Hall, and other favoring influences, open communion became widely prevalent in England early in the nineteenth century. In Wales, however, restricted communion has always prevailed. In 1845 a number of "Strict Baptist" churches formed the Baptist Evangelical Society under the leadership of Dr. John Stock. This society undertook missionary work in Germany and founded a theological college at Manchester. The most eminent English Baptist leaders of the present day carry their liberality so far as to practise open or mixed membership. Alexander Maclaren, the famous Manchester preacher was for many years pastor of a mixed church. The same is true of Dr. Clifford. F. B. Meyer, president of the Baptist Union, 1905–06, was for some years pastor of a pedobaptist congregation in London.

The coming of Charles Haddon Spurgeon to the pulpit of New Park Street Church, London, in 1854, marks an epoch in the history of British Baptists. Within a few years he became recognized as one of the greatest of preachers. That he built up a church of six thousand members, preached regularly in the Metropolitan Tabernacle to 7,000 people with a large overflow, that he reached through his published sermons millions of people throughout the world, represent only a small part of his beneficent activity. From his Pastor's College hundreds of young men went forth as pastors into all parts of Britain and throughout the world, and it is estimated that considerably over a hundred thousand have been added to churches pastored by Spurgeon's students. The Stockwell Orphanage founded by Spurgeon has set an example to Baptists and others in practical philanthropy. His Book Fund supplied the needs of multitudes of pastors. His magazine and his popular writings multiplied his influence. The last years of Mr. Spurgeon (1884–92) were somewhat embittered by a controversy in which he became engaged with the Baptist Union because of its toleration of liberal views on the Scriptures, the person of Christ, the atonement, future punishment, etc. His own Puritan convictions made him incapable of seeing anything but the abomination of desolation in less rigorous modes of thought that had become widely prevalent. When the Union refused to exclude from its fellowship those whose teachings he regarded as unsound he severed his connection with this body and was followed by many of his former students and the churches to which they ministered.

7. Charles Haddon Spurgeon.

The Baptists of Wales suffered much during the first half of the eighteenth century from hyper-Calvinism, but the religious fervor of the race was too great to be completely quenched. More promptly than the English Baptists, they responded to the quickening influences of the evangelical revival, especially to the Calvinistic phase of it represented by Whitefield. During the latter part of the century Sandemanianism and Socinianism made some headway among them. The teachings of Andrew Fuller finally prevailed, and the spirit of evangelism attained to a fervor among Welsh Baptist preachers rarely surpassed. Christmas Evans (q.v.) was from 1791 onward by far the greatest evangelizing force. Anglesea was the chief scene of his labors, but he is said to have traversed Wales forty times on preaching tours and to have preached one hundred and sixty-three associational sermons. Many other men of power carried forward throughout Wales the work in which Evans was the chief prophet. Pontypool College (1836) grew out of earlier efforts at ministerial education. Haverfordwest College was founded in 1839 and Llabollen College in 1862. Like the English denominational colleges these are small institutions in which two or three teachers instruct twenty or thirty students for the ministry. The Welsh churches, while retaining for home work a liberal share of scholarly ministers, have sent to England and America many of their brightest and best. The Philadelphia Association has profited largely by Welsh talent and consecration. The Welsh Baptists at present num-

8. The Welsh Baptists.

ber nearly 150,000, nearly 30,000 having been added within the past year and a half as a result of the great revival of 1904–05.

The Baptist churches planted in Ireland in the Cromwellian time by Thomas Patient and other London Baptists either became entirely extinct or survived in a very feeble way. About 1803 Alexander Carson (q.v.), who had been graduated a few years before from the University of Glasgow and was pastor of a Presbyterian church at Tubbermore with ample state support, reached convictions in favor of congregational church government and believers' baptism so strong that he gave up his living and the prospect of a Glasgow professorship. With a few like-minded believers he organized a Baptist church which during his forty years of service grew to a membership of 500. His best-known work is his treatise on baptism, but his doctrinal and controversial writings are numerous. He is said to have contributed the scholarship to Haldane's commentary on Romans. He was closely associated with the Haldanes. Like the Scottish Baptists, Carson practised weekly communion. He also followed the Scriptural injunction "salute one another with a holy kiss," himself kissing one of the deacons, and others following his example. After the sermon the brethren were encouraged to exhort. He was frequently called to Scotland and England for sermons and addresses. Since Carson's time English Baptists have devoted much effort to the propagation of Baptist principles in Ireland with small numerical results.

9. Alexander Carson and the Irish Baptists.

In Scotland also the Baptist movement that flourished in Cromwell's time failed of maintenance. In the eighteenth century Sir William Sinclair of Keiss, Caithness, who had been baptized while visiting England, gained a number of adherents in his own neighborhood, whom he baptized and organized into a church (about 1750). This is the oldest Baptist church in Scotland. In 1765 Robert Carmichael, a Sandemanian minister of Glasgow, was baptized in London by John Gill. He baptized several members of his former church and organized them into a Baptist church. Archibald McLean, who had been a member of Carmichael's church in Glasgow, joined his former pastor in Edinburgh, was baptized by him, became his colaborer, and succeeded him (1769) with Dr. Robert Walker as coelder. McLean was a vigorous and somewhat voluminous writer, and his works (published in seven volumes, 1805) have exerted a profound influence on Scottish Baptist life and thought. By far the most important factor in the history of Scottish Baptists was the conversion to evangelical principles, and then to Baptist views, of Robert and James Alexander Haldane (qq.v.). The former was deeply interested in religious and philanthropical matters from 1793 onward, and in fifteen years spent $350,000 in educating and supporting evangelists, building chapels, circulating religious literature, etc. In 1799 James became pastor of an Independent church in Edinburgh and in 1801 his brother built for the church a large tabernacle in which he ministered for fifty years. In 1808 both became avowed Baptists, and from this time onward, while conducting their work on somewhat broad lines, were highly influential in the propagation of Baptist principles. Christopher Anderson was converted under the ministry of James Haldane (1799). Through the influence of English Baptist students at the University of Edinburgh he became a Baptist, and was excluded therefor from Haldane's church. He was persuaded by Andrew Fuller to enter the ministry and in 1806 led in the founding of a regular Baptist church in Edinburgh, where he soon preached to overflowing congregations. His ministry of thirty years greatly strengthened the Baptist cause in Scotland. Anderson's church practised restricted communion and did not, like most Scottish Baptist churches, have plurality of elders or weekly communion. Among the most noted preachers of the Scottish Baptist churches, some of whom labored exclusively in Scotland while others did so in England, may be named Drs. Patterson, Landels, Culross, and Alexander Maclaren. Scottish Baptists have never gained great numerical strength, their present membership being less than 21,000. The Baptists of Great Britain number at present about 500,000, which, in view of the constant drain upon the membership by emigration, is a very creditable showing. This estimate takes account of about 400 unassociated churches. One of their greatest achievements was the raising of the £250,000 Twentieth Century Fund for home and foreign work.

10. Scotch Baptists. The Haldanes.

II. Baptists in the United States.—1. To 1740: About March, 1638, Roger Williams (q.v.), having been banished from Massachusetts two years before because of agitation against the charter, advocacy of extreme Separatist views, insubordination on conscientious grounds to the theocratic authorities, etc., and having settled on Narragansett Bay, felt it his duty, in cooperation with a dozen like-minded men and women who had followed him from Massachusetts, to introduce believers' baptism anew and to organize independently a new church on the apostolic model. Ezekiel Holliman first baptized Williams, who in turn baptized Holliman and the rest of the party. Winthrop attributes Williams's antipedobaptist views to the influence of the wife of Richard Scott, a sister of Mrs. Anne Hutchinson, the antinomian agitator (see ANTINOMIANISM AND ANTINOMIAN CONTROVERSIES, II, 2). He was already familiar with the opinions of the Mennonites and probably also with those of the followers of Smyth and Helwys and the contemporary Calvinistic antipedobaptists of London. He had reached the conviction that the ordinances and church order of the apostolic time had been lost by apostasy and, for the time, he was persuaded that a company of true believers had the right to restore them; but he did not long rest in this conviction. To the end of his life he maintained that true churches could only be constituted of regenerate members baptized upon a profession of their faith, and on many occasions expressed the conviction that in doctrine and practise the

1. Roger Williams.

Baptists were nearer than others to the apostolic norm; yet after a few months of experience he became so doubtful as to the warrantableness of what he had done, that he felt constrained to withdraw from the fellowship of the church he had founded and to spend the rest of his life as a "Seeker" (q.v.). Nothing short of a miraculously given commission to restore the ordinances would thenceforth meet his requirement. It was after he had assumed this position that he gained immortality of fame as an advocate of liberty of conscience and as, in cooperation with John Clarke (q.v.), the founder of a state in which this doctrine was embodied to an extent never before known.

For some years little is known of the career of the little church. The principle of individualism was so emphasized in the Providence community that complete harmony among the members of the church could hardly have been expected. Within a few years several who had been members of antipedobaptist churches in England (probably of the Arminian type) seem to have reenforced the constituent members and to have introduced elements of discord. Among the Arminian members, afterward to become somewhat prominent, were William Wickenden, Gregory Dexter, and Chad Brown, who, like many of the English General Baptists insisted upon the laying-on of hands after baptism as a Christian ordinance and an indispensable qualification for church-fellowship. Williams himself regarded the laying-on of hands as an ordinance of Christ. Thomas Olney, one of the constituent members, probably succeeded Williams in leadership, and by 1652 was coelder along with the brethren named. By this time diversities of opinion as to the extent of Christ's redemptive work and the laying-on of hands had become so pronounced as to occasion a schism. Olney led the faction that opposed the laying-on of hands as an ordinance and probably insisted on limited redemption, while Brown, Wickenden, and Dexter, on the basis of Heb. vi, 1–2, led the party, probably a majority, that insisted on the laying-on of hands as one of the "Six Principles." The fact that Olney's party did not survive as a church has led to the claim on behalf of the Newport church, organized some years later than the original Providence church, of priority among surviving churches. But the party led by Brown and the others seems equally entitled to be regarded as the original church. Wickenden extended his labors to New York State, where he was imprisoned (1656) for baptizing and administering the Lord's Supper. By 1669 his Arminianism had developed into Socinianism greatly to the alarm of Williams. He died in 1670. Gregory Dexter, who had printed Williams's *Key to the Indian Language* (1643) in London, removed to Providence about 1644. He was probably a General Baptist before his emigration. He became one of the most prominent men in the colony (President, 1653). Brown was for about twenty-five years a pillar among the Providence Baptists. He is of special interest as the ancestor of the Browns who gave their name to the first Baptist College in America and have done so much for its endowment and equipment (see below, II, 2, § 3).

2. The Providence Church.

The First Baptist Church of Newport owes its origin to John Clarke (q.v.), an educated Englishman who arrived at Boston in Nov., 1637, and cast in his lot with a company of Antinomians (Anne Hutchinson, Wheelwright, Coddington, and others), who were leaving Massachusetts for conscience' sake and who through Williams's good offices secured from the Indians the island of Aquidneck (Rhode Island), where they organized a colony (Mar., 1638) with recognition of Jesus Christ as King of Kings and Lord of Lords. The first agreement was theocratic, but in 1641 a distinctly democratic constitution with full provision for liberty of conscience was adopted. Clarke was equally prominent with Williams in the later political history of the united colonies that became Rhode Island, and, like Williams, spent much time in England in the public interest. As early as the year 1638 Governor John Winthrop designated Clarke as "a physician and preacher to those of the island." By 1640–41 strife had arisen between Clarke, Lenthall, Harding, and others, and Easton, Coddington, Coggeshall, and others, the latter maintaining the antinomian views of Anne Hutchinson, the former repudiating these views and probably at this time objecting to the baptism of infants. Winthrop wrote of the presence of "professed Anabaptists" on the island in 1641. There is no direct proof of the organization of Clarke's followers on a Baptist basis until 1644 or a little later. Mark Lukar, who was among those baptized by Blount and Blacklock in London in 1641–42, was for many years one of the most influential members of the Newport church. The date of his arrival has not been ascertained. If he arrived in 1644, as seems probable, he may have been a constituent member and have led in the introduction of believers' baptism. Samuel Hubbard, a friend of Roger Williams and a man of intelligence and force of character, removed from Connecticut in 1648, where he had adopted antipedobaptist views and was baptized into the fellowship of the church. In 1665 Stephen Mumford, an English Seventh-Day Baptist, became a member of this church and won to his views Hubbard, Hiscox, and others. Failing to carry the majority of the church for Sabbatarianism, they withdrew in 1671 and formed a separate congregation. In 1649 Obadiah Holmes of Seekonk, Mass., near the Rhode Island border, was baptized into the fellowship of the church and with a number of other persons attempted to carry on Baptist work in the Seekonk neighborhood. Civil interference with their meetings led them to remove to Newport. In 1651 Clarke, Holmes, and Crandall visited Lynn, Mass., to minister to some antipedobaptists there. They were imprisoned, heavily fined, and Holmes, for refusing on principle to pay the fine, was cruelly whipped. In 1652 Clarke published in England *Ill News from New England*, a full account of this act of persecution with a somewhat elaborate argument for liberty of conscience. The division of sentiment among the Providence Baptists on the laying-on

3. The Newport Church.

of hands extended to the Newport church, which had been strictly Calvinistic. William Vaughan, a member of the church, went to Providence in 1652 and submitted to the rite. Wickenden and Dexter accompanied him to Newport and a number were convinced in favor of the "Six Principles." In 1656 a division occurred. From this time onward until the Great Awakening Baptist progress in New England was almost confined to the General (Six Principles) type. Several churches were formed in Rhode Island, Connecticut, and southern Massachusetts, and associational meetings were held among them early in the eighteenth century.

In Massachusetts a rigorous law was enacted (1644) against "Anabaptists," whose presence was supposed to imperil civil and religious order, banishment being the penalty for openly condemning or opposing the baptism of infants or secretly propagating Anabaptist principles. The law was put into execution in a number of cases before the persecutions at Seekonk and Lynn mentioned above. In 1646 Winslow stated that in one of the churches of the Plymouth settlement (presumably that of Chauncy at Scituate) the pastor "waiveth the administration of baptism to infants." Remonstrance on the part of the synod seems to have led to the resumption of infant baptism, though this future president of the college at Cambridge continued to insist upon immersion. About 1652 or 1653 Henry Dunster, the highly efficient first president of the college at Cambridge (1640 onward), became so profoundly impressed against infant baptism that he did not feel at liberty longer to keep his views in abeyance, and after many conferences with the overseers and ample warning he was obliged at great sacrifice of sentiment and material good to relinquish his position. The patience of the authorities and their willingness for him to continue in the office provided he would cease to agitate against infant baptism speak well for their tolerant spirit. The influence of Dunster is clearly manifest in the movement for the founding of the First Baptist church of Boston under the leadership of Thomas Gould (1655). In 1663 John Myles, a Welsh Baptist minister who had acted as one of Cromwell's Tryers for Wales, driven from his post by the Act of Uniformity (1662), came with his congregation to Massachusetts and secured a tract of land in Rehoboth, near the Rhode Island border. Partly because of their remoteness from churches of the standing order and partly perhaps because they were less aggressive than most Baptists in their condemnation of the union of Church and State, they suffered little molestation until 1667 and even then they were permitted to continue their worship on condition of holding their meetings at a greater distance from the Rehoboth congregational meeting-house. Myles proved himself a man of power and built up at Swansea in Rehoboth a vigorous church of the Calvinistic type. He also gave valuable assistance to the Boston brethren after they had secured a measure of toleration. Organization was not effected by the Boston antipedobaptists until 1665, when Thomas Gould and three others were baptized and joined with Richard Goodall and four others who had been baptized in England. In spite of persecution this faithful body grew to considerable size. Even after the Act of Toleration (1689) had come into force in England, intolerance held sway in Boston. In 1680 John Russel, an officer of the church, published in London, with an "Address to the Christian Reader" by Kiffin, Dyke, Collins, Knollys, Harris, and Cox, *A Brief Narrative of some considerable passages concerning the first gathering and further progress of a Church of Christ, in Gospel Order, in Boston in New England, commonly (though falsely) called by the name of Anabaptists, for clearing their innocency from the scandalous things laid to their charge* (reprinted in Wood's *History of the First Baptist Church in Boston*). English Congregationalists, and English Baptists, protested in vain against the intolerance of the Massachusetts authorities in dealing with the Boston Baptists, partly because of the justification that it would seem to furnish to the home government for the persecution of non-conformists. A Six Principle church was formed at Swansea in 1693, and in 1732 a Baptist church was formed in Rehoboth by John Comer, the able pastor of the original Newport church, who had left his charge because of his adoption of the doctrine and practise of laying-on of hands, but had remained a Calvinist. Indian Baptist churches were formed by 1694 on Martha's Vineyard and Nantucket Island through the labors of Peter Foulger, of the First Baptist church of Newport, and others. In 1735 through the influence of Comer a church was organized at Sutton, Mass., from which, by friendly division, the Leicester church was formed in 1738. The Brimfield, Mass., church was gathered and organized through Ebenezer Moulton in 1736.

4. Baptists in Massachusetts.

In 1682 some members of the Boston church who had settled at Kittery, Me., sought and obtained the cooperation of the church in the organization of a new church at that place. The leaders were Humphrey Churchwood and William Screven. The latter was approved as a minister by the parent church and became pastor of the new body. Persecution soon broke up the Kittery church. In 1683 or 1684 Screven made his way to South Carolina, accompanied or followed by several of the members, and settled on the Ashley river, a short distance from the place where Charleston was about to be founded. About 1683 a colony of Britons, among whom were several Baptists, had settled on Port Royal island. At about the same time a large company from Somersetshire, England, including several Baptists of intelligence and social rank (Lady Blake and Lady Axtell), settled in the Charleston neighborhood and became members of the church at Somerton with Screven as pastor. In 1693 the church was removed to Charleston, which was assuming commercial importance. Screven died in 1713 leaving the church with a membership of nearly a hundred. Through his zeal, preaching stations had been established at a number of points and something practical had been done for the evangelization of the negro slaves. In 1733 a schism occurred that resulted in the

5. In South Carolina.

organization of a General Baptist church, and in 1736 members residing in the Ashley river community withdrew to form a church of their own. This greatly weakened the Charleston church and by the close of the present period it had become almost extinct. In 1737 a company of Welsh Baptists from Welsh Tract, Pa. (now Delaware), settled on the Peedee river, S. C., and formed the Welsh Neck church.

6. In Virginia, North Carolina, and Connecticut. In 1714, in response to an appeal from some Baptists in Isle of Wight County, Va., Robert Nordin was sent out by the General Baptists of London. He succeeded in organizing a church at Burleigh and another in Surrey county. In 1727 a Baptist church was formed in northern North Carolina under the leadership of Paul Palmer, who had been a member of the Welsh Tract church and who was presumably Calvinistic. In Connecticut, through the labors of Valentine Wightman, Stephen Gorton, and others, General (Six Principles) Baptist churches were constituted at Groton (1705), New London (1726), Wallingford (1735), and Farmington (now Southington) a little later. These were closely associated with the General Baptist churches of Providence, Newport, South Kingston, and Dartmouth, R. I.

7. In New York. In 1643 Lady Moody, who had become a zealous antipedobaptist, left Massachusetts and settled at Gravesend, N. Y. On her way she spent some time in New Haven, where she won to her views the wife of Theophilus Eaton, first governor of the colony and daughter of an English bishop. For many years religious services were held by Lady Moody without regular church organization. Francis Doughty, driven from Massachusetts on account of antipedobaptist views, labored for a while at Flushing and left for Virginia in 1656 without effecting a church organization. In 1656 William Wickenden, of Providence, preached, baptized, and celebrated the Lord's Supper at Flushing, but was driven away after imprisonment and an attempt to collect from him a heavy fine. From 1711 onward Valentine Wightman, of Connecticut (General Baptist), frequently visited New York on the invitation of Nicholas Eyres, a prosperous brewer, who with others was baptized by Wightman in 1714. Eyres became pastor of the congregation. He was ordained and the church recognized by brethren from Rhode Island and Connecticut in 1724. This church became involved in debt and controversy (Arminianism vs. Calvinism) and was extinct before the close of this period. At Oyster Bay, L. I., there were Baptists from 1700 onward. A Baptist church (probably General) was constituted a little later.

8. In the Quaker Colonies. The Quaker colonies furnished an attractive field for Baptist effort. The first Baptist church founded in this section was that at Cold Spring (1684) through the labors of Thomas Dungan, an Irish minister who had been a member of the First Church, Newport. This church became extinct by 1702. The Lower Dublin, or Pennepek, church followed in 1688. Several families of Welsh Baptists, with one Irish and one English Baptist, had settled in the neighborhood two years earlier. Elias Keach, the prodigal son of the famous Benjamin Keach, of London, was converted while practising imposture upon the brethren and became a preacher of power. Under his leadership the Pennepek church was organized in 1688, and in a few years through his evangelistic efforts baptized believers were to be found at the Falls, Cold Spring, Burlington, Cohansey, Salem, Penn's Neck, Chester, Philadelphia, and other places, who continued to be members of the Pennepek church enjoying occasional preaching services and gathering quarterly at different places for evangelistic services and communion. Keach returned to England in 1692. Here also controversy arose respecting the laying-on of hands and occasioned Keach's withdrawal in 1689 from the pastorate of the church. The laying-on of hands became the common practise of the churches of the Philadelphia Association, but was never a term of communion. Churches were formed in the following places: Piscataqua, N. J. (1689), Middletown, N. J. (1688), Cohansey, N. J. (1691), Philadelphia (1698), Welsh Tract, Del. (1703), Great Valley, Pa. (1711). The Welsh element prevailed, but many of the members of the churches were English and not a few had had New England experience. Many Mennonites settled in this region and reenforced the antipedobaptist life; so also the Dunkers. Baptists in Philadelphia were considerably strengthened (1692–1700) by the conversion to their views of a number of Keithian Quakers. Some of these were constituent members of the church and in 1707 the Keithians invited the Baptists to share the use of their meeting-house. Seventh-Day Baptists early appeared in this region and churches were organized by them at Piscataqua (1705), Newtown (1700), and Shiloh (1737). In 1707 churches which from the beginning had held general meetings together joined in organizing the Philadelphia Association, than which no agency has been so potent in the unification and extension of the denominational life. The adoption, with modifications, by the Association of the English Particular Baptist Confession of Faith of 1689 tended to fix the doctrinal type of what was long the most aggressive aggregation of Baptists in America. Before the Great Awakening the Baptists of the Philadelphia Association were carrying on successful missionary work.

2. From 1740 to 1821: A Socinianized Arminianism long before the beginning of this period had wrecked a number of the older Calvinistic Baptist churches. As in England, so in America, evangelical religion was at a low ebb during the first third of the eighteenth century. The Great Awakening (see Revivals of Religion) found the Baptists wholly unprepared to cooperate. The Arminian Baptists were repelled by the Calvinistic teachings of the great evangelists, while Baptists of all parties had suffered so much at the hands of pedobaptists that they would have been disinclined to join heartily in any general Christian movement. Yet no denomination profited more largely by the revival of religion. A considerable number of "New Light" churches which had been formed by way of separation from churches of the standing order that opposed the revival, or in new communities from the products of the new evangelism, came to feel that the practise of infant baptism was inconsistent with their demand for regenerate membership. In many cases "New Light" churches were divided in opinion respecting infant baptism and mutual toleration of each others' opinions was agreed upon. Convictions proved too strong to allow mixed churches long to persist and separation proved inevitable. Among the most valuable accessions to the Baptist ranks from this source was Isaac Backus (d. 1806), who was for many years the champion of the denomination in the cause of religious equality and wrote a meritorious history of the New England Baptists. Hezekiah Smith (d. 1805) after his graduation at Princeton (1762) wrought as an evangelist in South Carolina and more largely in New England. While pastor of the Haverhill (Mass.) church he devoted a large share of his time to evangelistic effort and to the collection of funds for the support of Rhode Island College. The First Church of Boston, under the influence of Jeremy Condy (pastor 1739–65), had become Arminian (Socinian) in sentiment and strongly opposed the revival. Under the well-educated and eloquent Samuel Stillman (pastor after 1765) the church regained its evangelical zeal and its high standing among the churches. In 1760 the membership of the church was more than doubled. Under the influence of the Great Awakening a number of brethren led by Ephraim Bound formed a second Baptist church (1743). Valentine Wightman, one of the very few Baptists of the older sort who had entered heartily into the revival movement, assisted in the ordination of Bound. The Swansea and Rehoboth churches held resolutely aloof from the revival movement and would have no fellowship with the New Light brethren until 1771 when several hundred were added to their membership through evangelistic effort. Some of the converts formed a new church at Rehoboth which practised open communion. At about the same time the "New Light" Congregational church of Rehoboth suffered schism, Elhanan Winchester, a baptized evangelist, becoming pastor of the antipedobaptist party which organized on an open communion basis. Winchester refused to administer the Supper to any but baptized believers and was excommunicated. He afterward became a Universalist leader. A third open communion church was formed in this region in 1777.

1. The Great Awakening.

The churches of the Philadelphia Association had reached a position of assured strength that enabled them to assert their principles with the utmost decision while maintaining the most friendly relations with their brethren of other denominations. The growth of the churches of Pennsylvania and New Jersey during this period was only normal. The Philadelphia Association, being long the only body of the sort among the Calvinistic Baptists, had by 1762 extended its influence so as to embrace churches in New England, New York, Virginia, and Maryland. At this time the association comprised only twenty-nine churches with a membership of 1,318. The territory of the association was covered by the evangelizing activity of the Tennents and the Presbyterian discipline was so effective that few of the converts became Baptists. In 1756 measures were taken by the association for the establishment of a grammar-school under the care of Isaac Eaton, at Hopewell, N. J.

2. The Philadelphia Association.

About 1762, members of the association under the leadership of Morgan Edwards began to agitate and plan for the establishment of a Baptist College. The graduation of James Manning and Hezekiah Smith at this time from Princeton and the availability of the former for educational work may have brought the matter to an issue. Rhode Island was selected as the most promising location for a college because of its men of eminence, its central position, its lack of a college, and its devotion to civil and religious liberty. In 1663 Manning was sent to Rhode Island to confer with leading brethren there. In 1764 a charter was secured, which, while giving control to the Baptists, provided for the participation in the government of the institution of Quakers, Congregationalists, and Episcopalians. The charter provides: "Into this liberal and catholic institution shall never be admitted any religious tests. But, on the contrary, all the members hereof shall forever enjoy full, free, absolute, and uninterrupted liberty of conscience; and the places of professors, tutors, and all other officers, the president alone excepted, shall be free and open for all denominations of Protestants and that sectarian differences shall not make any part of the public and classical instruction." The trustees and fellows included the most prominent men of the various denominations. Morgan Edwards visited England on behalf of the college and Hezekiah Smith made a canvass of the South. It was arranged that pending the raising of funds Manning should minister to a few Baptist families at Warren and conduct there a grammar-school (1764). In 1765 Manning was appointed president and in 1769 seven young men received the bachelor's degree—the first academic degrees ever conferred by a Baptist institution. In 1804 Rhode Island College became Brown University and under this name has steadily grown in equipment and influence. Among its presidents have been Francis Wayland, Barnas Sears, Alexis Caswell, E. G. Robinson, E. B. Andrews, and W. H. P. Faunce.

3. Rhode Island College (Brown University).

As a result of the influence of the Baptists of the Philadelphia Association, the Warren Association was formed in 1767. The moving spirits were James Manning and Hezekiah Smith. Only four churches participated in its organization, Isaac Backus and many of the "New Light" brethren as well as all of the older churches holding aloof from fear lest the body should "assume any jurisdiction over the churches." The influence of the Warren Association was soon felt and became mighty in favor of education, evangelization, and religious liberty.

In 1749 Oliver Hart from the Philadelphia Association went to Charleston, S. C., where he was influential in reviving the Baptist cause and in forming the Charleston Association after the model of the Philadelphia. From 1742 onward members of the Philadelphia Association (Gano, Vanhorn, Miller, Thomas) visited the scattered and unorganized Baptists of Virginia and North Carolina, won some Arminians to Calvinism, introduced better church discipline, and secured the organization (1765) of the Kehukee Association, composed of churches in Virginia and North Carolina. Through the labors of David Thomas, also a gift of the Philadelphia Association, several churches were constituted in the Northern Neck of Virginia and in 1766 formed the Ketokton Association with the approval and cooperation of the Philadelphia. This association adopted the Philadelphia Confession, with its requirement of the laying on of hands.

4. Southern Associations.

Of momentous importance for the diffusion of Baptist principles throughout the South was the enthusiastic evangelism of Shubael Stearns and Daniel Marshall, "New Light" Baptists from New England (1754 onward). Stearns had become a Baptist in New England (1751) and had felt an irresistible impulse to devote his life to missionary work in the South. Marshall was led to Baptist views after his arrival in Virginia from contact with Baptists of the Philadelphia Association type. Within the next thirty years multitudes were converted and accepted Baptist views through their ministry, and churches were organized in Virginia, North Carolina, South Carolina, and Georgia. The Sandy Creek (N. C.) church was organized by Stearns in 1755 and in a few years it had over 600 members. In 1758 the Sandy Creek Association was formed, which for years embraced all the churches of the Separate type in the South. In seventeen years the connection had grown to forty-two churches with 125 ministers. The evangelism of Stearns and Marshall was characterized by an enthusiasm that verged upon fanaticism. Many new converts, without previous educational equipment or subsequent training, entered zealously upon the work of evangelization and the people heard with gladness their uncouth but earnest testimony to the power of the Gospel.

5. Evangelistic Work of Stearns and Marshall.

Because of their fiery enthusiasm and their unwillingness to take out licenses and conform to the Colonial conditions of toleration the Separate Baptists of Virginia suffered much persecution in genuine martyr fashion and thereby won for themselves great popular acceptance and made the episcopal establishment highly odious. Virginia Baptists of the older type conformed to the laws and suffered little persecution, and looked with disfavor upon the Separate Baptists as unduly enthusiastic and as allowing untrained and untried men (and even women) freely to evangelize. Stearns was disposed to lay more stress on the interdependence than the independence of the numerous and widely scattered churches of the Sandy Creek Association. Under his influence overtures from the Regular Baptists for the union of Regulars and Separates were rejected (1767) by a small majority. By 1770 many churches and ministers of the association had become dissatisfied with the rigorous ruling of Stearns and insisted upon the division of the body into three associations. The result was the formation of the General Association of Separate Baptists, for Virginia, and the Rapid-Ann Association, for South Carolina. From 1770 onward the Separate Baptists increased in Virginia from 1,335 in 1771 to 3,195 in 1773. In 1774 it was determined by the General Association to restore the office of apostle, and Samuel Harris, the most successful of the Virginia evangelists, was appointed apostle for the southern district, and a little later John Waller and Elijah Craig became apostles for the northern district. In 1775 the question of general and particular redemption was debated in the General Association, and by a small majority particular redemption prevailed. The three apostles withdrew by way of protest and disruption seemed inevitable. But better counsels prevailed and mutual toleration was agreed upon. Arminian tendencies gradually disappeared and in 1783 the Philadelphia Confession was adopted with provision against its too strict construction.

6. Separate Baptists in Virginia.

Virginia Baptists were among the earliest and stanchest supporters of the Revolution and led in the struggle for religious equality. The General Association in 1776 appointed a committee on grievances, which zealously devoted itself to the abolition of dissenters' disabilities until the establishment itself was abolished, the glebe lands confiscated, and absolute separation of Church and State secured. Not content with being chiefly instrumental in securing religious equality in Virginia, Virginia Baptists watched closely the forming of the Federal Constitution and were instrumental in procuring the insertion of art. i, which prohibits Congress from taking any cognizance of religion. From 1883 onward Regular Baptists of Virginia joined hands with the Separates in the struggle for religious equality and the separation of Church and State and in 1787 the two parties united, agreeing to bury in oblivion the names Regular and Separate, and adopting the name "United Baptist Churches of Christ in Virginia." In New England the struggle for religious liberty on the part of the Baptists was no less heroic, but it was far less successful. In Virginia the Episcopal clergy were corrupt and oppressive and were bitterly opposed to the Revolution, and Baptists had the cooperation of leading statesmen, of the patriotic masses, and (in most measures) of the Presbyterians; while in New England the clergy and members of the standing order were leaders in the cause of Colonial independence and Baptists became unpopular by agitating their grievances and threatening to appeal to England for their redress at the very time when resistance to British authority was being determined upon. This difference of attitude of the Established Churches in the two sections accounts for the fact that the

7. Baptists and Religious Liberty.

Baptists of Virginia not only led in the struggle for religious liberty but multiplied in numbers during the Revolution and after, while Massachusetts and Connecticut Baptists failed to secure religious liberty and made little progress during the Revolution. In 1812 there were in Virginia, North Carolina, South Carolina, Georgia, Kentucky, and Tennessee 108,843 Baptist communicants, while those of Maine, New Hampshire, Massachusetts, Rhode Island, and Connecticut numbered 32,372, and those of New York, New Jersey, Pennsylvania, Delaware, and Maryland, 26,852. In Virginia alone there were 35,655 Baptist church members.

3. From 1812 to the Present Time: While Baptists had by the beginning of this period attained to a numerical strength of nearly 200,000, they were deficient in culture and had made almost no provision for an educated ministry. Brown University was still the only institution for higher education, and this provided no theological course. In Boston, Providence, Newport, New York, Philadelphia, and Charleston, and in a number of other churches in the Philadelphia, Warren, and Charleston Associations there was considerable culture. The Charleston Association had established (1791) an Education Fund, and by 1813 had aided nineteen young ministers in securing an education, some under private tutorship, some at Brown University, and some in other institutions. In 1812 the Baptist Education Society of the Middle States was constituted and Dr. William Staughton, of Philadelphia, began to instruct students for the ministry on its behalf. The vast majority of American Baptists at this time regarded ministerial education as an impertinent human effort to exercise the divine prerogative of calling and equipping ministers, and looked with disfavor upon the paying and receiving of ministerial salaries as introducing a commercial element where the Holy Spirit should work unimpeded. A large proportion of Baptist preachers owned their farms and were self-supporting. Many of them without scholastic advantages acquired considerable education and were men of power. The tendency was to neglect the towns, where the self-supporting method was impracticable and where enthusiastic but illiterate ministers were less acceptable. Some able ministers who could have afforded to minister in towns and cities resolutely refused to leave their country homes and work. Churches like those of Boston, New York, and Philadelphia found the utmost difficulty in supplying their pulpits when vacancies occurred. The only periodical publication in circulation at the time was the *Massachusetts Baptist Missionary Magazine*, the first number of which was published in 1803 and the twelfth in 1808. Under the editorship of Dr. Thomas Baldwin, of Boston, it exerted a strong but not very wide-spread influence in favor of missions, education, and better methods of denominational work. The Lake Baptist Missionary Society (afterward called the Hamilton Missionary Society) was formed in Central New York (1807) for domestic evangelization. From the beginning of the century (or earlier) Baptists of Boston, New York, Philadelphia, and Charleston joined with other denominations in contributing toward the support of the missionary work of Carey and his associates in India. In 1812 Philadelphia Baptists began to hold monthly union meetings and larger quarterly meetings "for the spread of the gospel."

1. Lack of an Educated Ministry.

The conversion to Baptist views of Adoniram Judson and Luther Rice (qq.v.), as they were about to open up missionary work in India under the auspices of the American Board of Commissioners for Foreign Missions, marks an era in the history of American Baptists. Judson announced his conversion to American Baptists through Thomas Baldwin, of Boston, and L. Bolles, of Salem, and threw himself and his missionary enterprise upon the liberality and enlightened zeal of the denomination. The more intelligent Baptist communities rejoiced that so glorious a responsibility had been providentially thrust upon the denomination and began at once to organize local missionary societies for the diffusion of the missionary spirit and the raising of funds. "The Baptist Society for Propagating the Gospel in India and other Foreign Parts" was formed at Boston in 1813 with Baldwin as president and Daniel Sharp as secretary. Rice returned to America (summer of 1813) for the purpose of arousing American Baptists to a sense of their obligation and opportunity. Through his efforts local missionary societies were formed from Maine to Georgia and considerable money was raised. In May, 1814, thirty-three leading brethren from eleven States met in Philadelphia and organized the "General Missionary Convention of the Baptist Denomination in the U. S. A. for Foreign Missions," to meet triennially. Richard Furman, of Charleston, was chosen president and Thomas Baldwin secretary. The Convention appointed a Board of Commissioners as an executive with Baldwin as president and Philadelphia (from 1826 onward, Boston) as headquarters. William Staughton of Philadelphia was the first corresponding secretary. By 1817 Rice and other leaders had become convinced that provision for the education of ministers was absolutely essential to the progress of denominational work at home and abroad, and the Triennial Convention of 1817 approved of the raising of funds for this purpose. In 1818 a theological institution was opened in Philadelphia, with William Staughton and Irah Chase as instructors. As early as 1815 Rice had reached profound conviction regarding the necessity of missionary work in the newly settled regions of the West, and in 1817 the Triennial Convention decided to enter upon this work. Two zealous and well educated ministers, J. M. Peck and J. E. Welsh, were appointed home missionaries. The work of the former proved apostolic and was of momentous importance. From 1817 onward Rice labored with consuming zeal for the establishment in Washington of a National Baptist University. Columbian College was opened in 1822 and has done a noble work. The theological work inaugurated in Philadelphia was transferred to Washington in 1821. As a means of promoting

2. Missionary and Educational Work.

the missionary and educational work Rice began (1816) the publication of *The Latter Day Luminary* and (1822) *The Columbian Star*.

By 1826 the college had become inextricably involved in debt. The situation became so desperate that the mission funds were drawn upon to meet pressing claims. From the beginning the great mass of the Baptists had shown themselves indifferent or hostile to the missionary and educational enterprises. It was easy for ignorant and illiberal pastors to persuade their still more ignorant and illiberal parishioners that the introduction of commercialism into religion was of the devil and that they were doing God service in resisting all efforts at exploitation on the part of the money-gatherers. In many cases associations excluded churches, and churches members, for contributing to the funds of the enterprises fostered by the Triennial Convention. State Conventions were formed as bonds of union for those who were alive to the importance of united effort.

3. Opposition and Difficulties.

Massachusetts Baptists had effected a State organization in 1802. South Carolina followed in the year 1821. In a few years nearly every State had organized a convention made up exclusively of cooperating churches, associations, and individuals. In the States of Ohio, Tennessee, and Kentucky, the missionary movement was well-nigh overwhelmed by the antieffort party. In Ohio, Baptists contributed for Foreign Missions in 1820, $547 From 1821 to 1828 nothing was given, while $10 constituted the contribution in 1829 and $5 that of the following year. In Tennessee, missionary societies were dissolved and associations rescinded all resolutions favorable to the schemes of the Triennial Convention. Not till after 1840 could the cause of missions get a hearing. The most influential leader of the movement was Daniel Parker, an illiterate enthusiast, who held to an extreme type of supralapsarianism and wrought up his followers to a fanatical hatred of all organized effort. It was in the regions occupied by this perverse type of Baptists that Alexander Campbell (q.v.) worked so successfully, combining, as he did, with his bitter denunciation of human institutions, vigorous antagonism to hyper-Calvinistic theology.

In 1825, owing in part to the financial difficulties of Columbian College, and the willingness of New England Baptists to provide for its support, the theological work was transferred to Newton Theological Institution at Newton Center, Mass., with Irah Chase as president. In 1819 the Baptists of New York laid the foundations for Colgate University at Hamilton, N. Y., with its literary and theological departments. In 1826, for reasons above suggested, the Triennial Convention left Columbian College to its own resources, retaining only the right to nominate fifty brethren from whom its Board should be chosen. The Baptists in the various States have been too much occupied in founding and building up local colleges to give adequate support to Columbian, and recently its Board have thought it best to declare it undenominational and to change its name to George Washington University. Ample provision has been made by the denomination for ministerial education by the establishment, in addition to the institutions already mentioned, of Rochester Theological Seminary (1850), at Rochester, N. Y., Southern Baptist Theological Seminary (1859, Louisville, Ky.), Divinity School of the University of Chicago (Baptist Union Theological Seminary, Morgan Park, Ill., 1867), Crozer Theological Seminary (1868, Upland, Penn.), Pacific Coast Baptist Theological Seminary (1890, Berkeley, Cal.), Baylor Theological Seminary (1901, connected with Baylor University, Waco, Tex.), Kansas City Theological Seminary (1901), and the Theological Department of Union University (1867, Richmond, Va.). These institutions have property and endowments aggregating about $7,000,000, over 100 instructors, and over 1,200 students.

4. Theological Seminaries.

The denomination maintains about 100 universities and colleges of various grades with property and endowments aggregating about $45,000,000, nearly 2,000 instructors, and 30,000 students. The most important of these are the University of Chicago, Chicago, Ill. (founded 1891, with assets of $20,000,000); Brown University, Providence, R. I. (1764, $5,500,000); Colgate University, Hamilton, N. Y. (1819, $2,500,000); Bucknell University, Lewisburg, Penn. (1846, $1,700,000); Baylor University, Waco, Tex. (1845, $600,000); Colby College, Waterville, Me. (1818, $700,000); Denison University, Granville, O. (1831, $1,050,000); Stetson University, Deland, Fla. (1887, $600,000); Mercer University, Macon, Ga. (1838, $550,000); Richmond College, Richmond, Va. (1832, $1,065,000); Rochester University, Rochester, N. Y. (1850, $1,370,000); Wake Forest College, Wake Forest, N. C. (1834, $500,000); William Jewell College, Liberty, Mo. (1849, $550,000); Kalamazoo College, Kalamazoo, Mich. (1833, $431,000); Vassar College, Poughkeepsie, N. Y. (1861, $1,660,000). A score of other institutions with less ample resources are doing good work along chosen lines. There are more than 100 academic institutions under the auspices of the denomination, with nearly 20,000 students and nearly $5,000,000 worth of property.

5. Universities, Colleges, and Schools.

By 1832 the domestic missionary work of the Triennial Convention had reached such proportions that the need of a separate Board and a separate appeal for funds was apparent. At this time the American Baptist Home Mission Society was organized. The Society has always made New York City its headquarters. Its missionary work on the frontiers, among the Indians, negroes, and foreign populations, in Canada, Mexico, Cuba, and Porto Rico, employs at present over 1,500 missionaries and teachers. There are twenty-five schools and colleges for colored people supported by it wholly or in part. It has nearly $1,500,000 of permanent funds for various purposes, and mission and school properties valued at $1,300,000. Since its organization nearly 200,000 persons have been baptized by its missionaries and nearly 6,000 churches organized.

6. The Home Mission Society.

The demand for an agency for the publication and circulation of denominational and other religious literature led to the organization of the Baptist General Tract Society in 1824. Its headquarters were at Washington and it was under the general direction of Luther Rice. The complications that arose in connection with Columbian College and the superior publishing and distributing facilities offered by Philadelphia led to a change of location in 1826. In 1840 a revised constitution with the name American Baptist Publication Society was adopted. The society has formed an important factor in the growth of the denomination and it has kept abreast of its needs. The annual receipts of the publishing department at present amount to nearly $900,000 and in its missionary and Bible departments to about $200,000. Its net assets amount to about $1,600,000. The refusal of the American Bible Society to appropriate funds for the publication of a Burmese version in which the words for "baptize" and "baptism" were translated by words equivalent to "immerse" and "immersion" (see BIBLE SOCIETIES, III, § 2) led to the organization of the American and Foreign Bible Society (1836). The refusal of this society to secure the publication of an English version in which "immersion" should supplant "baptism" led to the formation of the American Bible Union (1850), which employed Thomas J. Conant, H. B. Hackett, and others to prepare a new version of the Bible with critical apparatus and notes. The New Testament and portions of the Old were completed. Hostility between the American and Foreign Bible Society and the American Bible Union was crippling to both and in 1883 both were compelled by a great denominational gathering to relinquish the field, the Missionary Union assuming responsibility for the publication and circulation of the Scriptures in foreign languages in its fields and the Publication Society undertaking to complete and circulate the Bible Union and the Anglo-American Revised versions, as well as the King James version.

7. The Publication Society.

Before 1840 the slavery question was agitated in Baptist circles. Many Southern Baptists, including leading ministers, were slaveholders, and nearly all were very sensitive to Northern abolitionist utterances. In 1843 the neutrality of the Foreign Mission Board was reaffirmed. With a view to making continued cooperation practicable, Richard Fuller, an eminent Southern Baptist, offered a resolution in the Triennial Convention for 1844 for the elimination from the consideration of the body of all matters foreign to the object designated in the constitution and declaring cooperation in the proper work of the body not to involve or imply concert or sympathy as regards other matters. This resolution was withdrawn in favor of one whereby the body disclaimed all sanction of slavery or of antislavery and left each individual free in a Christian manner and spirit to express and promote his own views on these subjects. Notwithstanding the adoption of this resolution the Foreign Mission Board was thought to have procured the resignation of an Indian missionary who was a slaveholder. Southern Baptists were convinced that thenceforth slaveholders would be discriminated against and that future sessions of the Convention would be rendered tumultuous by attacks on slavery and rejoinders. A literary controversy between Francis Wayland, President of Brown University, and Richard Fuller awakened much interest and demonstrated the impossibility of harmony between Northern and Southern Baptists. Conciliatory measures were attempted on both sides; but the conviction had become overmastering among Southern leaders that the Baptists of the South could work more successfully with separate Convention and Boards. This policy was carried into effect in May, 1845, by 370 messengers from the various Southern States. Home and Foreign Mission Boards were at once constituted, and both these departments of work have been vigorously prosecuted. The Foreign Mission Board (Richmond) has for years conducted successful missionary work in Italy, Brazil, Argentina, Mexico, Africa, China, and Japan, and has attained to an annual income of about $300,000. The total membership of native churches under the Board is reported (1905) as 11,423. The Home Mission Board (Atlanta) expends nearly $200,000 a year within the bounds of the Convention, in Cuba, and in the insular possessions of the United States. The Sunday-school Board (Nashville), besides furnishing Sunday-school papers and other requisites, publishes a number of books, and fosters Sunday-school work through a professorship in the Southern Baptist Theological Seminary and through district secretaries who labor throughout its constituency. Its annual receipts are about $125,000. The Southern Baptist Theological Seminary is cherished by the Convention, which nominates brethren from whom the members of its Board are chosen and receives its annual report.

8. The Southern Baptists.

After the formation of the Southern Baptist Convention, the Foreign Mission Board of the Triennial Convention became the American Baptist Missionary Union, which has since had annual meetings in connection with the American Baptist Publication Society, the American Baptist Home Mission Society, etc. Women's auxiliary societies cooperate with the Northern and Southern Boards.

The Baptist Congress is not strictly a denominational organization; but is supported by subscribing members and holds an annual meeting for the free discussion of current questions of doctrine, polity, and life. Its annual reports furnish the public with the most advanced thought. The Baptist Young People's Union of America (1891 onward) seeks to promote Christian activity, intelligence, and denominational spirit among the Baptist young people of the United States and Canada.

9. The Baptist Congress and Young People's Union.

Baptist owners of slaves were by no means indifferent to their spiritual welfare. It is estimated that there were 400,000 negro Baptists in the United States at the close of the Civil War. Most of these were members of the churches of their masters; but in the towns and cities many negro churches had been constituted. The first of these on record is that in Savannah, Ga. (1788) of which Andrew Bryan was for many years pastor. The largest negro Baptist church before emancipation was that in Richmond, Va., of which for twenty-five years Robert Ryland, president of Richmond College, was pastor. In many churches controlled by the whites a majority were negroes. After emancipation they everywhere effected separate church organization. Associations were almost immediately formed, State Conventions soon followed, and in 1880 a National Convention was organized with its Home Mission, Foreign Mission, Education, Publishing, and Baptist Young People's Union Boards. Besides the University, Theological Seminary, and Colleges founded and fostered by the American Baptist Home Mission Society, they have established, own, and control scores of institutions of higher and lower grades. Over 15,000 students are in attendance at these schools. While hundreds of their ministers have enjoyed educational advantages and are in a position to elevate those under their ministry, thousands are illiterate and incapable of wise leadership. Since emancipation they have increased in number fivefold, the present membership, according to the statistician of the National Baptist Convention (1905) being 2,189,000.

10. Colored Baptists.

The first to gather German Baptist churches in America was Conrad Fleischmann, a Swiss, who in 1841 organized three churches in Pennsylvania. By 1851 there were eight small churches with 405 members. The present membership is about 25,000. They have seven annual Conferences and a triennial General Conference. Their publishing house is located in Cleveland and their training-school for ministers is organically connected with the Rochester Theological Seminary. Educational and missionary work among the Germans of the United States and Canada has been from the first generously assisted by American Baptists.

11. German Baptists.

The first Scandinavian Baptist church in America was formed in Illinois in 1848. At present there are about 5,000 Dano-Norwegian Baptists with eighty-six churches, whose representatives meet annually in seven Conferences. Their ministers are educated in the Dano-Norwegian Department of the Divinity School of the University of Chicago. Swedish Baptists (first church organized 1853) are far more numerous, having at present over 300 churches and nearly 25,000 members. The education of their ministers is provided for in the Divinity School of the University of Chicago. Scandinavian Baptists are most numerous in Wisconsin, Illinois, Minnesota, Dakota, Iowa, and Nebraska.

12. Scandinavian Baptists.

4. Minor Baptist Parties in the United States: (*a*) The Six-Principles Baptists are a survival of the General Baptists that prevailed in Rhode Island and Connecticut in the early time. They still contend for the laying-on of hands as an indispensable ordinance. They have at present less than a score of churches with less than a thousand members.

(*b*) The first Seventh-Day Baptist church was organized at Newport, R. I., in 1671. As the name indicates, they make the celebration of the Jewish Sabbath as the day of rest and worship rather than the Lord's Day an essential, and devote much of their attention to showing the error of adopting another day and the evil consequences that flow from this perversion. They have institutions of learning at Milton, Wis., and Alfred Center, N. Y., and circulate considerable literature through their publishing house at the latter place. They have ninety-seven churches with a membership of less than 9,000, scattered over twenty-four States. For the so-called Seventh-Day Baptists, German, see COMMUNISM, II, 5.

(*c*) The Free-Will Baptists originated in New Hampshire in 1780 under the leadership of Benjamin Randall who left the Congregationalist body to become an anti-Calvinistic and open communion Baptist. The Arminian teaching was no doubt due to Methodist influence. Free-Will Baptists took an active part in the antislavery agitation (1835 onward) and thus closed the South against their influence. They were reenforced in 1841 by 2,500 Free-Communion Baptists of New York State; but the Adventist movement a little later deprived them of a large number. From 1845 to 1857 their numbers declined from 60,000 to 49,000, but by 1870 they regained this loss. They have lost about 1,500 members since 1890; the present membership (1905) is 86,322. They have 1,543 churches distributed over thirty-three States. They early adopted quarterly and annual conferences, the former made up of delegates of churches, the latter of delegates from the former. The system is overtopped by the General Conference composed of delegates from the local annual conferences. The quarterly meeting may discipline churches, the annual meeting quarterly meetings, and the General Conference annual meetings. Ministers are first licensed by the quarterly meeting and after probation are ordained by the council appointed by the same body. Women are eligible for ordination to the ministry. Negotiations looking to the union of the Free-Will Baptists with the Regular Baptists of the North are pending with good prospects of success.

(*d*) It has been noted that the General Baptists from Virginia first introduced Baptist teaching into North Carolina. Some of the churches formed under this influence refused to amalgamate with the Separate and Regular Baptists. After a time they adopted the name Original Free-Will Baptists to distinguish themselves from the more numerous body mentioned above. They differ from the Free-Will Baptists in practising foot-washing, anointing the sick with oil, restricting the ministerial office to men, and having ruling elders for the settlement of controversies. Annual conferences may silence unworthy preachers, disown elders, and settle church difficulties. They have three Conferences, 167 churches, and less than 12,000 members, all in North Carolina and South Carolina.

(*e*) A number of General Baptist churches of the older English type failed to amalgamate with the more popular Baptist parties of the nineteenth century. The first association of this party was formed in Kentucky in 1824. This association adopted open communion in 1830. A General Association was formed in 1870 to embrace all the churches of the connection. Unlike most of the smaller Baptist bodies, this had increased from 8,000 members in 1870 to 21,362 in 1890. More recent statistics are not available. Their confession of faith indicates closer agreement with Regular Baptists in doctrine and in practise than does that of the Free-Will Baptists. They have about 400 churches in Missouri, Indiana, Kentucky, Illinois, Arkansas, Tennessee, and Nebraska.

(*f*) A few churches in Indiana have retained the name Separate Baptists. They are in general agreement with Free-Will Baptists. They seem to be confined to Indiana, where they have an association with 24 churches and about 1,600 members.

(*g*) In the union of Regular and Separate Baptists in Kentucky in 1801 a doctrinal basis not strictly Calvinistic was adopted. About 200 churches in Kentucky, Tennessee, Missouri, Alabama, and Arkansas, with a membership of over 13,000, still call themselves United Baptists and hold aloof from the great Baptist body. They are moderately Calvinistic, practise restricted communion, and insist upon foot-washing as an ordinance to be practised by all baptized believers. They have several associations.

(*h*) Mention has already been made of the bitter opposition that arose in many Baptist communities to the missionary and educational enterprises that centered in the Triennial Convention (1814 onward). The Chemung Association (N. Y. and Penn.) seems to have been the first (1835) to disfellowship other associations that had departed from the simplicity of the doctrine and practise of the gospel by "uniting themselves with the world and what are falsely called benevolent societies founded upon a monied basis." This example was speedily followed by many other associations, especially in the South and Southwest. Besides holding to extreme necessitarian (supralapsarian) doctrine in accordance with which human agency in the conversion of men is absolutely ineffective and the attempt to employ it impertinent, they practise foot-washing as an ordinance and utterly repudiate missionary, Bible, tract, Sunday-school, and temperance societies, State conventions, theological schools, and similar organizations. The United States census of 1890 brought to light 121,-347 Baptist communicants of this type, with churches in twenty-eight States and the District of Columbia. They are most numerous in Georgia, Alabama, Tennessee, North Carolina, Kentucky, and Virginia, but are found all the way from Maine to Texas and from Nebraska to Florida. They call themselves Primitive Baptists; they are commonly called "Hardshells" and Anti-Mission Baptists by their opponents.

(*i*) The followers of Daniel Parker, the most virulent opponent of the organized work of the denomination (b. in Georgia, ordained in Tennessee in 1806, active in Illinois 1817–36, and in Texas after 1836), are known as the Old Two-Seed-in-the-Spirit Predestinarian Baptists. They still persist in twenty-four States and had in 1890 nearly 500 churches with nearly 13,000 members. They derive their name from the peculiar doctrine of Parker set forth in certain pamphlets (1826–29) on the doctrine of Two Seeds. This was a fantastic dualistic account of the introduction and perpetuation of evil in mankind, reminding of Gnostic speculations. God created Adam and Eve and infused into them particles of himself so that they were wholly good. The devil corrupted them by infusing particles of himself. It was predetermined by God that Eve should bring forth a certain number of good offspring, the seed of God, and that her daughters should do likewise. The evil essence infused by the serpent led to an additional brood of offspring, the seed of Satan or the serpent. For the former the Atonement was absolute, they will all be saved. The Atonement did not apply to the seed of the serpent, who are hopelessly lost. The doctrine of Parker was absolutely fatalistic and was in the worst sense antinomian. His followers go beyond the other Primitive Baptists in their uncompromising hostility to "human institutions."

(*k*) The Baptist Church of Christ came into separate existence by way of reaction against the antinomian hyper-Calvinism of the churches led by Daniel Parker. They teach general redemption along with perseverance of the saints. Like most of the minor Baptist parties they practise foot-washing as an ordinance. This, more than anything else, prevents their union with the great Baptist body; but, like the Primitive Baptists, they seem to object to organized denominational missionary and educational work. The chief strength of the body is in Tennessee, but congregations are found in Arkansas, Alabama, Mississippi, Missouri, North Carolina, and Texas. In 1890 the party had 152 churches with a total membership of 8,254.

The Dunkers (q.v.) have much in common with Primitive Baptists, and, with the Church of God founded in Pennsylvania in 1830 by John Winebrenner (see CHURCH OF GOD, 1), are more worthy to be classed with Baptists than some of the above parties. The River Brethren (q.v.) and the Mennonite body known as the Brüder-Gemeinde (see MENNONITES) have much in common with Baptists. The Disciples of Christ (q.v.), originally an offshoot from the Baptists, agree with the latter in insisting upon immersion as the only valid baptism and in their recognition of the sole authority of the Scriptures in matters of faith and practise. They differ from Baptists in a number of important matters, but there is more in common between progressive Disciples and the great Baptist body than there is between the latter and several of the minor parties that bear the Baptist name. The body who call themselves "Christians," frequently known as the Christian Connection (see CHRISTIANS) also regard immersion of believers as the only true baptism. They practise open communion and admit to membership those who do not agree with them respecting immersion. In England they would pass for satisfactory Baptists.

III. Baptists in the British Possessions.—1. The Dominion of Canada: The Maritime Provinces were the first to receive Baptist influence. In 1752 a Dutch Baptist named Andres is said to have settled in Lunenburg and to have disseminated his principles there. In 1763 Ebenezer Moulton of Massachusetts organized a church at Horton, N. S., of Baptists and Congregationalists, which soon became wholly Baptist. Just before, during, and after the Revolutionary War, a considerable number of New England Baptist loyalists found their way to Nova Scotia, New Brunswick, and Prince Edward Island. In 1880 an association was formed which adopted the English Particular Baptist Confession of 1689. In 1846 the Baptist Convention of Nova Scotia, New Brunswick, and Prince Edward Island was formed with a constituency of 14,177. Acadia University (chartered 1840, successor to Horton Academy, 1828) at Wolfville, N. S., was adopted by the Convention and has educated a large number of leaders not only for the Maritime Provinces, but for Western Canada and the United States. It now has endowment and equipment worth about $500,000. The Convention has its domestic and foreign mission boards and has engaged zealously and successfully in every line of denominational work. About 17,000 Free-Will Baptists have united with the Regulars on the basis of a brief doctrinal statement that avoids strict Calvinistic phraseology and insistence on restricted communion. The Maritime Baptists number at present about 67,000.

1. The Maritime Provinces.

Baptist loyalists in small numbers during the later years of the eighteenth century found their way into what is now Ontario and Quebec, and by the beginning of the nineteenth century about six small churches had been organized in three widely separated localities. These were fostered by missionary effort from the United States and reenforced by further immigration of their fellow countrymen. Later a considerable number of English Baptists of open communion antecedents came in and were the occasion of discord. In 1816 a company of Scotch Highlanders, who had become Baptists in connection with the Haldane movement, settled in the Ottawa region. Most of these became advocates of restricted communion; but several of the most eminent (notably John Gilmour) favored open communion. A society was formed in England (1836) for fostering Baptist work in Canada. The Upper Canada Missionary Society refused to cooperate fully with the educational and missionary work that centered in Montreal and was conducted under English open communion auspices. The Canada Baptist College established in Montreal in 1838 died of inanition in 1849, although it had at its head such scholars as Benjamin Davis and J. M. Cramp. Dissension prevented the success of further efforts to provide the denomination with educational facilities until 1860, when the Canadian Literary and Theological Institute was opened at Woodstock with R. A. Fyfe as Principal. Fyfe proved a leader of the first rank and exerted a strong unifying influence upon the denomination. By this time the denomination in Ontario and Quebec had a membership of about 13,000. After cooperating with the American Baptist Missionary Union in foreign mission work for a number of years, the Baptists of Ontario and Quebec organized an independent Foreign Mission Society, whose work has steadily grown until at present $40,000 are expended annually on its missions in India and Bolivia. In 1881 Toronto Baptist College was founded as a theological seminary by Senator William McMaster. This institution developed into McMaster University as a result of the bequest of nearly $1,000,000 by the founder. In 1888 the organization of the denomination was completed in a new constitution and charter, which commits to the Convention made up exclusively of delegates of churches the election of Home Mission, Foreign Mission, Publication, and Education Boards. Baptists in Ontario and Quebec now number about 47,000.

2. Ontario and Quebec.

Baptist work in the Canadian Northwest began about 1873. It has grown to large proportions and has enjoyed the support of Baptists in the older Provinces, in Great Britain, and in the United States. A Convention was organized in 1881, and Brandon College, at Brandon, Man., was established in 1899. The college already has equipment and endowment worth about $150,000. The Baptist cause in British Columbia has not yet attained to very large dimensions. During the earlier years Baptist churches in this region worked in connection with the American Baptist Home Mission Society. In 1897 they formed a Convention of their own and since that time they have depended for help chiefly upon the Baptists of the older Provinces. Baptists in Manitoba and the Northwest Territories now number about 7,000; in British Columbia, 2,000.

3. The Northwest and British Columbia.

2. Australia, Tasmania, and New Zealand: In these colonies Baptists were among the earliest British settlers, and Baptist churches were organized from 1834 onward. The several British types of Baptist life have been represented and some controversy has had place regarding communion, Calvinism and Arminianism, etc.; but the ordinary English open communion type has prevailed. There are still about a dozen churches of the old Particular Baptist antimissionary type. Most of the churches of the various provinces are grouped in seven Unions, which correspond with each other and support in common a religious journal. The Baptist College of Victoria in affiliation with the University of Melbourne was conducted from 1890 to 1900 and then abandoned. Some Foreign Mission work is being accomplished in India in connection with the English Baptist Society. There are at present in Australasia sixty-eight churches and about 21,000 members. Progress for the past few years has been very slow.

3. The British West Indies, Central America, and Africa: English Baptists commenced missionary work among the negroes of Jamaica in the year 1814. The way had been prepared somewhat by Moses Baker, an American negro Baptist. In fifteen years there were 10,000 Baptists on the island. A negro insurrection in 1831 led to the destruction of much of their church property and to the persecution of the leaders; but sympathy was awakened in Britain and the losses were made good. The work was extended to the Bahamas, Trinidad, Honduras, San Domingo, etc. The Jamaica Baptists have at present nearly 200 churches and nearly 34,000 members; in Haiti there are 12 churches with nearly 2,000 members; in Cuba (through American Baptist effort) there are 31 churches with nearly 4,000 members; in the Bahamas nearly 4,000 members; and in Central America 10 churches with nearly 700 members. In Africa, through American, English, and German missionary effort there are 81 Baptist churches with 11,388 members, mostly in British territory, the Kongo, and the Kamerun.

4. India, Ceylon, Burma, and Assam: In these British possessions, through English, American, and Canadian missionary effort 1,244 churches have been organized with a membership of over 126,000. A very large proportion of the converts have been won by missionaries from the United States and Canada.

IV. Baptists in Mission Lands: In China there are about 13,000 Baptist church members almost equally divided among the English, Northern, and Southern Baptist missions. In Japan there are about 2,500 Baptist church members of whom over 2,000 belong to the American Baptist Missionary Union and the rest to the missions of the Southern Baptist Convention. In Mexico missions of the Southern Baptist Convention have nearly 1,400 church members to their credit, while those of the American Baptist Home Mission Society, with twenty-six laborers, have a far smaller number. In Brazil the missions of the Southern Baptist Convention have established sixty-nine churches with a membership of over 4,000, and in Bolivia Canadian Baptist missionaries have organized three churches with 115 members.

V. Baptists on the Continent of Europe.—1. Germany and German Missions: The first Baptist church of the modern type organized in Germany was formed in Hamburg in 1834 under the leadership of J. G. Oncken (q.v.), who several years before had reached Baptist views from independent study of the New Testament. In his youth Oncken had spent some years in England and had been sent (1823) by an English evangelical society as a missionary to Germany. Oncken and six others availed themselves of the presence of Barnas Sears, of the United States, afterward famous as an educational leader, to receive baptism at his hands. Oncken proved a leader of heroic type and with the aid of American Baptists carried on for many years wide-spread and fruitful missionary labors and raised up like-minded ministers who are still carrying forward the work throughout German-speaking Europe and beyond. In 1880 a theological seminary was established near Hamburg that has given educational equipment to hundreds of earnest and self-sacrificing young men. The present membership in Germany is about 34,000. They sustain a mission in the Kamerun with over 2,000 converts. The German Baptist Union for the spread of the gospel in foreign parts includes churches in Austria (648 members), Hungary (10,500 members), Switzerland (796 members), the Netherlands (1,396 members), Rumania (277 members), and Bulgaria (74 members). The Russian Baptist churches, which have resulted chiefly from the activity of German Baptists of the Oncken type, have now a membership of about 25,000 and a Union of their own; but they still cooperate with the German Union in the raising and use of missionary funds. Through the missionary labors of German Baptists a few Lithuanians were brought into the Baptist fold (1857 onward). A more successful work was done among the Letts, and about 7,000 of the Russian Baptists are Lettish. From the same source Baptist influence was brought to bear upon the Esthonians, of whom over 1,000 are now Baptist church members. The Finns received Baptist teaching from the Swedish Baptists (1868 onward) and now have over 2,000 Baptist church members.

2. Scandinavia: From Germany Baptist influence also extended into Scandinavian lands. Julius Koebner, one of Oncken's early converts and colaborers, was a Dane and on a visit to his native land won to his faith a company of Christians that had become dissatisfied with Lutheranism. The first church was organized in Copenhagen in 1839. Persecution impeded the progress of the Baptist cause and religious freedom was not gained until 1850. A considerable number of ministers trained in the Scandinavian Department of the Divinity School of the University of Chicago have assisted in carrying forward the work in Denmark as well as in Sweden and Norway. In 1895 the Danish Baptists established a small theological school of their own. They have not made rapid progress and their present membership is only about 4,000. German Baptist influence entered Norway not later than 1840. The first church was organized two years later. At present Norwegian Baptists have over 30 churches with a membership of about 3,000. A Danish Baptist named Foerster labored in Sweden in 1848 and baptized five persons near Gothenburg. The Baptist cause has greatly prospered here, so that at present there are 40,000 members and nearly 600 churches. Since 1866 they have had a theological seminary at Stockholm. They are thoroughly organized for missionary and educational work and have reached a degree of influence and recognition enjoyed by Baptists nowhere else on the Continent of Europe.

3. France and Italy: In France, Belgium, and French Switzerland there are about 40 churches with a membership of 2,272, due in large measure to English Baptist missionary enterprise. In Italy there are 55 churches and about 1,500 members, the result, in almost equal measure, of the missionary endeavors of the English Baptist Missionary Society and of the Southern Baptist Convention. The latter body sustains a theological college.

Two highly significant events, indicating the desire of Baptists everywhere to draw closer together and to cooperate in the world-wide dissemination of their principles, were the formation of the General Baptist Convention (St. Louis, May, 1905) to embrace the entire continent of North America and its islands and to hold triennial meetings, and the Baptist World Congress (London, July, 1905), in which Baptists from all parts of the world gathered and organized a Baptist World Alliance, to meet every five years in different parts of the world. The union of the Free Baptists in the Maritime Provinces of Canada and the Regulars (1905) and the steps taken toward union between the Free Baptists of New England and the Regulars in the same year show that the tendency is in the direction of union rather than of further division.

Counting all nominally Baptist bodies throughout the world, the present number of Baptists is about 6,000,000. If to these other bodies of antipedobaptist immersionists be added, the number is increased to about 7,500,000.

A. H. Newman.

Bibliography (Only volumes derived from independent sources are here mentioned): I. English Baptist History: T. Crosby, *Hist. of the English Baptists*, 4 vols., London, 1738–40; J. Ivimey, *A Hist. of the English Baptists*, ib. 1811–30; A. Taylor, *History of the English General Baptists*, 2 vols., ib. 1818; B. Evans, *The Early English Baptists*, 2 vols., ib. 1862; R. Barclay, *The Inner Life of the Religious Societies of the Commonwealth*, ib. 1879 (not on Baptists exclusively, but gives their genesis in England in an authoritative way; an excellent volume); D. Masson, *Life of John Milton, and History of his Times*, 6 vols., ib. 1859–80 (a work of great learning and authority. Milton was an antipedobaptist, but, so far as is known, not a member of a Baptist Church); J. Clifford, *The English Baptists*, ib. 1881 (the work of different contributors, but edited by the chief English Baptist leader); J. C. Carlile, *The Story of the English Baptists*, ib. 1905.

II. English and American Baptist History: T. Armitage: *A History of the Baptists*, New York, 1887 (contains a full history); H. C. Vedder, *A Short History of the Baptists*, Philadelphia, 1892 (authoritative); idem, *The Baptists*, New York, 1902.

III. American Baptist History: I. Backus, *A History of New England, With Particular Reference to the Denomination of Christians called Baptists*, 3 vols., Boston, 1777–96, new ed., with notes by David Weston, 2 vols., Newton, Mass., 1871; H. S. Burrage, *A History of the Baptists in New England*, Philadelphia, 1894; H. C. Vedder, *A History of the Baptists in the Middle States*, ib. 1898; B. F Riley, *A History of the Baptists in the Southern States East of the Mississippi*, ib. 1898; J. A. Smith, *A History of the Baptists in the Western States East of the Mississippi*, ib. 18—; L. Moss, *A History of the Baptists in the Trans-Mississippi States*, ib. 19—; A. H. Newman, *A History of the Baptist Churches in the United States*, New York, 1898; idem, *A Century of Baptist Achievement*, ib. 1901 (the work of different persons); C. H. Mattoon, *Baptist Annals of Oregon, 1844–1900*, McMinnville, Oregon, 1905.

IV. Biographies of Baptists (all clergymen except two): *M. B. Anderson*, by A. C. Kendrick, Philadelphia, 1895; *Isaac Backus*, by A. Hovey, Boston, 1859; *George Dana Boardman*, by A. King, ib. 1834; *Edmund Botsford*, by C. D. Mallary, Charleston, 1832; *James Pettigru Boyce*, by J. A. Broadus, New York, 1893; *J. A. Broadus*, by A. T. Robertson, Philadelphia, 1901; *R. C. Burleson*, by H. Haynes, Waco, 1891; *Alexander Campbell*, by R. Richardson, 2 vols., Philadelphia, 1868–70; *William Colgate* (layman), by W. W. Everts, ib. 1881; *Nathaniel Colver*, by J. A. Smith, Boston, 1875; *Spencer Houghton Cone*, by Livermore, New York, 1856; *John Price Crozer* (layman), by J. W. Smith, Philadelphia, 1868; *E. W. Dodson*, by J. H. Farmer, Toronto, 1903; *J. Denovan*, by O. C. S. Wallace, ib. 1901; *Henry Dunster*, by J. Chaplin, Boston, 1872; *The Dunster Family*, by S. Dunster, ib. 1876; *Richard Fuller*, by J. H. Cuthbert, New York, 1879; *R. A. Fyfe*, by J. E. Wells, Toronto, 1882; *H. B. Hackett*, by G. H. Whittemore, Rochester, 1876, *Adoniram Judson*, by F. Wayland, 2 vols., Boston, 1853, and by E. Judson, New York, 1883; *Jacob Knapp* (autobiography), ib. 1868; *D. A. McGregor*, by A. H. Newman, Toronto, 1891; *P. H. Mell*, by P. H. Mell, Jr., Louisville, 1895; *Jesse Mercer*, by C. D. Mallary, New York, 1844; *John Mason Peck*, by R. Babcock, Philadelphia, 1864; *Luther Rice*, by J. B. Taylor, Baltimore, 1840; *Adiel Sherwood*, by S. Boykin, Philadelphia, 1884; *William Staughton*, by S. W. Lynd, Boston, 1834; *Baron Stow*, by J. C. Stockbridge, ib. 1894; *James Barnett Taylor*, by G. B. Taylor, Philadelphia, 1872; *Francis Wayland*, by F. and H. L. Wayland, 2 vols., New York, 1868; *Roger Williams*, by J. D. Knowles, Boston, 1834; also by W. Gammell, ib. 1844; and H. M. Dexter, ib. 1879; and O. S. Strauss, New York, 1894; *Elhanan Winchester*, by E. M. Stone, Boston, 1836; *Daniel Witt*, by I. B. Jeter, New Orleans, 1875; *Carey, Marshman and Ward*, by J. C. Marshman, London, 1859; *Virginia Baptist Ministers*, by J. B. Taylor, New York, 1860.

BARADAI, JACOB (JACOBUS BARADÆUS). See Jacobites.

BARAITA. See Talmud.

BARBARA, SAINT: A saint whose career belongs to the domain of legend; her name is not found in the *Martyrologium Hieronymianum* or in Bede. According to the traditional story, she was a maiden of great beauty, who, having been early converted to Christianity, was given up by her own father to the authorities, and beheaded by the *præses* of the province, Martinianus, steadfastly refusing to deny Christ. Her father is said to have been killed by lightning at the scene of the execution, which is stated to have been Nicomedia (in Bithynia), Tuscia (i.e., Etruria), and Heliopolis in Egypt; the time was either under Maximinus (235–238) or sixty or seventy years later under Maximianus or Galerius. In Roman Catholic countries she is popularly considered to give protection against fire and tempest, and she is also the patron saint of the artillery. She is invoked by the dying in consequence of the story of Henry Kock at Gorkum, in Holland, in 1448, who, being nearly burnt to death, called on her and was preserved alive long enough to receive the last sacraments. Her feast falls on Dec. 4.

Bibliography: Célestin, *Histoire de Ste. Barbe*, Paris, 1853; Villemot, *Histoire de Ste. Barbe, vierge et martyre, patronne de l'artillerie de terre et de mer et des mineurs*, Besançon, 1865.

BARBAULD, ANNA LETITIA: Poetess; b. at Kibworth (10 m. s.e. of Leicester), Leicestershire, June 20, 1743; d. at Stoke Newington (a suburb of London) Mar. 9, 1825. She was the daughter of the Rev. John Aikin, a Presbyterian minister and school-teacher, and was carefully educated by her father; married the Rev. Rochemont Barbauld (d. 1808), a Unitarian minister, in May, 1774; with her husband she conducted a very successful school at Palgrave, Suffolk, till 1785; thereafter lived at Hampstead and Stoke Newington. At the solicitation of her brother (Dr. John Aikin) she published her first volume of *Poems* in 1773 and four editions were sold within a year. In the same year appeared *Miscellaneous Pieces in Prose by J [ohn] and A. L. Aikin*; in 1775 *Hymns in Prose for Children* and *Early Lessons for Children* (written for her pupils), and *Devotional Pieces Compiled from the Psalms of David*. Her later writings are of a general and critical character and include political pamphlets, an edition of Collins (1797), of Akenside (1808), the *British Novelists* (50 vols., 1810), with essay and biographical and critical notices, etc. Perhaps her best-known hymns are "Come, says Jesus's sacred voice," "How blest the righteous when he dies," and "Awake, my soul, lift up thine eyes."

Bibliography: *The Works of A. L. Barbauld, with a Memoir*, by her niece, Lucy Aikin, 2 vols., London, 1825; Mrs. A. L. Le Breton, *Memoir of A. L. Barbauld, with Letters and Notices*, ib. 1874; Mrs. G. A. Ellis, *Memoir of A. L. Barbauld, Letters and Selections from Poems and Prose Writings*, Boston, 1874; S. W. Duffield, *English Hymns*, pp. 76, 225, 459, New York, 1886; Julian, *Hymnology*, pp. 113–114.

BARBER, HENRY HERVEY: Unitarian; b. at Warwick, Mass., Dec. 30, 1835. He was educated at Deerfield (Mass.) Academy and Meadville Theological School (1861). He held successive pastorates at Harvard, Mass. (1861–66), Somerville, Mass. (1866–84), and Meadville, Pa. (1884–90), while from 1884 to 1904 he was professor of philosophy and theology at Meadville Theological School. Since 1904 he has been professor emeritus. He is a member of the American Historical Association and of the American Economic Association, and from 1875 to 1884 was editor of the *Unitarian Review*.

BARBER, WILLIAM THEODORE AQUILA: Wesleyan; b. at Jaffna (190 m. n. of Colombo), Ceylon, Jan. 4, 1858. He was educated at London University (B.A., 1882) and Caius College, Cambridge (M.A., 1883). He was assistant professor in the Wesleyan Theological Missionary College, Richmond, from 1882 to 1884, when he became headmaster of Wuchang Missionary High School, Central China. Eight years later he returned to England, and until 1896 was a preacher in the Leeds (Brunswick) Circuit. In 1896 he was appointed general secretary of the Wesleyan Missionary Society, but two years later was chosen headmaster of the Leys School, Cambridge, where he had already been assistant master in 1877–80. He was secretary of the General Missionary Conference, Shanghai, 1890, and since 1902 has been a member of the Legal Hundred of the Wesleyan Conference. In theology he is a broad Evangelical. He has written *The Land of the Rising Sun* (London, 1894); *David Hill, Missionary and Saint* (1898); *Raymond Lull, the Illuminated Doctor* (1903); and *David Hill, an Apostle to the Chinese* (1906).

BARBEYRAC, bār"bē"rāc', **JEAN:** French writer on law; b. at Béziers (44 m. s.w. of Montpellier), Languedoc, Mar. 15, 1674; d. at Groningen Mar. 3, 1744. He fled with his parents into Switzerland after the revocation of the Edict of Nantes, 1685; studied at Lausanne, Geneva, and Frankfort-on-the-Oder; became teacher in the College of the Reformed Congregation at Berlin, 1697; and, in 1710, was appointed professor of law and history in the Academy of Lausanne, and in 1716 in the University of Groningen. He translated Puffendorf's *De jure naturæ et gentium* into French (2 vols., Amsterdam, 1706), and added a valuable preface and notes; he also translated other works of Puffendorf and Grotius, wrote a *Traité du jeu* (2 vols., 1709), maintaining that games of chance are not immoral, and a *Traité de la morale des Pères de l'Église* (1728). He was a moderate Calvinist, and refused to sign the Helvetic *Formula Concensus*, which disapproved of the doctrines of Amyraut and the other Saumur theologians.

Bibliography: Gardes, *Oratio funebris in obitum J. Barbeyrac*, Groningen, 1744 (by his colleague); G. Laissac, *Notice biographique sur Barbeyrac*, Montpellier, 1838.

BARCKHAUSEN-VOLKMANN CONTROVERSY: A discussion of the question of predestination and grace which was carried on with much ardor in Germany early in the eighteenth century. In the Reformed Church of Brandenburg particularly many things tended to start troublesome questions on these points. The *Confessio Sigismundi* of 1614 had followed the Augsburg Confession with "revision and improvements," whereby it became not merely universalistic, but synergistic, and, in its exposition of predestination, approximated to the "Reformed Evangelical Churches." As a matter of fact it taught both the absolute election of every believer and universal grace. The need of making concessions to the Lutherans led to some modifications, as in the *Colloquium Lipsiense* of 1631, the *Declaratio Thoruniensis* of 1645 (see Leipsic, Colloquy of; Thorn, Conference of), and an edict of the Great Elector in 1664 (in C. O. Mylius, *Corpus constitutionum Marchicarum*, i, Berlin, 1737, 382 sqq.). The Brandenburg Church was thus separated from orthodox Calvinism, while still adhering to the Reformed type, and this the more as a large number of French congregations bound to Calvin's *Confessio Gallicana* were settled in the country.

The Barckhausen-Volkmann controversy began with the publication (Cologne, 1712) of the *Theses theologicæ* of Paul Volkmann, rector of the Joachimsthal gymnasium at Berlin; it was a complete presentation of the Reformed dogmatics, maintaining universal grace and conditional election. Konrad Heinrich Barckhausen, a native of Detmold and colleague of Volkmann in Berlin (in 1715 rector of the Friedrich Werder gymnasium), came forward as protagonist against Volkmann's views. Under the pseudonym Pacificus Verinus he published in 1712 an *Amica collatio doctrinæ de gratia* and followed it the next year with a coarse German writing *Mauritii Neodorpii Calvinus orthodoxus, d. i. ein kurzes Gespräch worin bescheiden untersucht wird ob und wie weit die Lehre der Universalisten mit der Lehre der ersten reformirten Lehrer übereinkommen*. A Berlin preacher, Stercki by name, took up the discussion on Volkmann's side and Philippe Naudé (q.v.) replied. The controversy was growing hotter when the Prussian king, Frederick William I, in 1719 issued an edict commanding both sides to keep silence (Mylius, ut sup., 534–535). (E. F. Karl Müller.)

Bibliography: J. G. Walch, *Einleitung in die Religionsstreitigkeiten . ausser der evangelisch-lutherischen Kirche*, i, 457, iii, 746 sqq., 5 vols., Jena, 1733–36; Hering, *Beiträge zur Geschichte der evangelisch-reformirten Kirche in den preussisch-brandenburgischen Ländern*, i, 57 sqq., Berlin, 1784; A. Schweizer, *Die protestantischen Centraldogmen*, ii, 816 sqq., Zurich, 1854 sqq.

BARCLAY, ALEXANDER: English scholar of the Renaissance period; b. probably in Scotland about 1475; d. at Croydon (9 m. s. of London), Surrey, 1552. He is believed to have studied at one, or perhaps both, of the English universities; traveled on the continent; was made chaplain in the collegiate church at Ottery St. Mary, Devonshire; afterward became a monk in the Benedictine monastery of Ely: in 1546 became vicar of Great Baddow, Essex, and of Wokey, Somersetshire; in 1552 also rector of All Saints in Lombard Street, London. His chief works were the *Ship of Fools* (London, 1509), a translation, with some additions, of Sebastian Brandt's *Narrenschiff;* and the *Eclogues* (n.d., probably 1514).

Bibliography: A full account of Barclay and valuable list of references is given in *DNB*, iii, 156-161; consult also for list of his writings and his life the edition of the *Ship of Fools*, by T. H. Jamieson, 2 vols., Edinburgh, 1874.

BARCLAY, JOHN: Minister of the Church of Scotland and founder of the Barclayites or Berœans; b. at Muthill (35 m. n.w. of Edinburgh), Perthshire, 1734; d. at Edinburgh July 29, 1798. He was graduated M.A. at St. Andrews; was assistant minister at Errol, Perthshire, 1759–63, being dismissed in the latter year for teaching obnoxious doctrine; assistant at Fettercairn, Kincardineshire, 1763–72, where he was popular and admired, but continued to promulgate views inacceptable to the ministers. In 1773 the General Assembly sustained his presbytery (Fordoun), which had inhibited him from preaching. His followers then formed independent congregations at Edinburgh and Fettercairn, and Barclay became minister of the former. He also preached and founded a society in London. His adherents took the name Berœans (from Acts xvii, 11), professing to build their system of faith and practise upon the Scriptures alone, without regard to any human authority whatever. They denied natural religion, maintaining that knowledge of God is from revelation alone; considered faith in Christ and assurance of salvation as inseparable and the same; held that the sin against the Holy Ghost is unbelief; and interpreted a great part of the Old Testament prophecies and the whole of the Psalms as typical of Christ and not applicable to the experiences of private Christians. In other respects their views were those of ordinary Calvinism. They originally had several churches in Scotland and a few in America. Eadie (*Ecclesiastical Cyclopedia*, London, 1862) characterizes them as "a small and diminishing party of religionists."

Bibliography: A collected edition of Barclay's *Works*, with brief memoir and statement of the views of his followers, was published in Glasgow, 1852; cf. *DNB*, iii, 164-166, and literature mentioned there.

BARCLAY, JOSEPH: Third Anglican-German Bishop of Jerusalem; b. near Strabane (15 m. s. by w. of Londonderry), County Tyrone, Ireland, Aug. 21, 1831; d. at Jerusalem Oct. 23, 1881. He studied at Trinity College, Dublin (B.A., 1854; M.A., 1857); was ordained curate at Bagnalstown, County Carlow, Ireland, 1851; becoming interested in the work of the London Society for Promoting Christianity among the Jews, he offered himself as a missionary in 1858, and was sent to Constantinople; was incumbent of Christ Church, Jerusalem, 1861–70; curate of Howe, Lincolnshire, 1871, of St. Margaret's, Westminster, 1871–73; was consecrated bishop of Jerusalem July 25, 1879, and took up his residence in the city the following January. He preached in Spanish, French, and German, was a good Hebrew scholar, and acquainted with Turkish and Arabic. He published *The Talmud*, a translation of select treatises of the Mishnah, with introduction and notes (London, 1878), a work which has been generally criticized by Jewish scholars as prejudiced.

Bibliography: A critical biography was published anonymously at London, 1883, giving extracts from his journals and letters; cf. also *DNB*, iii, 167.

BARCLAY, ROBERT: Scotch Quaker; b. at Gordonstown (28 m. n.w. of Aberdeen) Dec. 23, 1648; d. at Ury (14 m. s.w. of Aberdeen) Oct. 3, 1690. He was descended from an ancient Scottish family and his father was Col. David Barclay of war celebrity in Germany and Sweden. After a careful home training he was sent to his uncle, Robert Barclay, rector of the Scotch College in Paris, for further education, and so came under Roman Catholic influences and inclined toward that communion. But in 1664 he was called home and in 1667 followed his father into the Society of Friends. He was zealous with voice and pen in the advocacy of their faith and in consequence was in prison for five months during 1676–77, and was again under arrest in 1679. If he had not had aristocratic and influential friends it might have gone much worse with him. He traveled through Great Britain and also in Holland and Germany. He was the most remarkable theologian the Quakers have produced. Besides a *Catechism and Confession of Faith* (1673; repeatedly reissued; translated into Latin, French, Danish, and Dutch), he prepared controversial works. The treatise upon which his great fame rests is *An Apology for the true Christian divinity, as the same is held forth, and preached by the people, called, in scorn, Quakers.* He had previously published fifteen theological theses for a debate and they were so favorably received that he translated them into Latin and accompanied them with an exposition in the same language, prefaced them with a remarkably faithful epistle to Charles II, dated Nov. 25, 1675, and issued the volume at Amsterdam in 1676. He says that he did this "for the information of strangers." In 1678 he published, probably in Aberdeen, his own translation of the *Apology*, and it has become a classic. An edition, the fourteenth, was published at Glasgow in 1886, and other editions have appeared in Philadelphia; there are translations of it in German, French, Dutch, Spanish, and Danish. In 1692 William Penn brought out an edition of it, with other works, under the title *Truth Triumphant through the spiritual warfare, Christian labours and writings of that able and faithful servant of Jesus Christ, Robert Barclay.*

Bibliography: R. B. Barclay, *Genealogical Account of the Barclays of Urie*, Aberdeen, 1740, ed. H. Mill, London, 1812; W. Armistead, *Memoir of R. Barclay*, Manchester, 1850. For full list of books by and on Robert Barclay consult Joseph Smith, *Descriptive Catalogue of Friends' Books*, 2 vols., London, 1867, and *Supplement*, 1893. The sketch in *DNB*, iii, 167–170 is also valuable; also *Reliquiæ Barclaianæ, a Collection of Letters privately printed*, 1870 (lithographed).

BAR COCHBA. See Bar Kokba.

BARDENHEWER, BERTRAM OTTO: German Roman Catholic; b. at München-Gladbach (16 m. w. of Düsseldorf) Mar. 16, 1851. He was educated at the universities of Bonn (Ph.D., 1873) and Würzburg, and in 1879 became privat-docent of theology at the University of Munich. In 1884 he accepted a call to Münster as professor of New Testament exegesis and Biblical hermeneutics, and two years later returned in the same capacity to Munich, where he still remains. He has been a member of the *Deutsche morgenländische Gesellschaft* since 1873, and of the papal Bible Committee since 1903. He was rector of the university in 1906, and has written *Hermetis Trismegisti qui apud Arabes fertur de castigatione animæ libellus* (Bonn, 1873); *Des heiligen Hippolytus von Rom Kommentar zum Buche Daniel* (Freiburg, 1877); *Polychronius, Bruder Theodors von Mopsuestia und Bischof von Apamea* (1879); *Die pseudo-aristotelische Schrift über die reine Gute, bekannt unter dem Namen Liber de causis* (1882); *Patrologie* (1894); and *Geschichte der altkirchlichen Literatur* (2 vols., 1902–03). Since 1895 he has edited *Biblische Studien* at Freiburg.

BARDESANES, bɑr″de-sê′nîz **(BAR-DAISAN):** Gnostic; b. of Persian parents (Nuhama and Nasiram; cf. *Chron. Edess.*, ed. L. Hallier, *TU.* ix, 1, Leipsic, 1892, 90; Michael Syrus), at Edessa, on the Daisan, on the 11th day of Tammuz (July), 154; d. there 222 (Moses of Chorene, *Hist. Armen.*, ii, 63; Michael Syrus). He was educated with the princes at the court (Epiphanius, *Hær.*, lvi, 1) and won distinction as well by his bodily excellences as for versatility of mind and the linguistic and scientific knowledge which he acquired. With his parents he went to Mabug (Hieropolis), where he became acquainted with Kuduz, a priest of the Dea Syra, who adopted him and taught him the doctrines of his cult. When twenty-five years of age, the priest sent him to Edessa, where he heard the preaching of the Christian bishop Hystaspes, was instructed by him, and baptized. He soon interested the Abgar of Edessa (Bar-Manu, c. 179–216) in the new religion. When Caracalla took Edessa (216–217), Bardesanes fled into Armenia, where he spent his time in writing and preaching, but returned afterward to Edessa.

Of his writings, Eusebius (*Hist. eccl.*, iv, 30) and Theodoret (*Hær. fab.*, i, 22) mention dialogues against the teachings of Marcion; Eusebius and Epiphanius (l.c.) mention also an apology. An Armenian church history, composed in his exile, was used as source by Moses of Chorene. Ephraem Syrus (*Serm. adv. hær.*, liii) knew of a book of 150 psalms or hymns. By their hymns Bardesanes and his son Harmonius became the creators of the Syriac church hymn. Whether the hymns (e.g., the hymn on the destinies of the soul) preserved in the so-called Acts of Thomas (cf. W Wright, *Apocryphal Acts of the Apostles*, i, London, 1871, 247) are to be traced to Bardesanes, is doubtful. Eusebius, Epiphanius, and Theodoret mention also a work of Bardesanes "On Fate," which is extant under the title "The Book of the Laws of the Countries," though apparently revised by one of his disciples. Finally, George, Bishop of the Arabians, quotes a passage from a work of Bardesanes on "The Mutual Synodoi of the Stars of Heaven."

It is impossible to assign to Bardesanes in the present state of knowledge the place which he occupies in Gnostic speculation. Some affinity with Valentinianism can be established from the work which has been preserved, which, however, reproduces the views of Bardesanes in a revised form. But there can be no doubt as to his connection with the Babylonian Gnosis. He was certainly greatly influenced by Chaldean mythology and astrology. His cosmogonic speculations, which Hort (*DCB*, i, 254) rightly calls "strange Mesopotamian heathenism," contain no special originality when compared with the Mandæan and Ophitic fancies. It is noteworthy that he retained the unity of the divine principle against the Marcionites, which does not preclude his speaking of an "eternal matter." His "Christ" is that of the Docetæ (who had no real body and did not really suffer). He denied the resurrection of the flesh. He made a mysterious connection between the soul and the celestial spirits. But in this determinism he saw only a natural limitation which did not preclude the free volition of man. For the rest, he explained his speculations only in narrower circles and seems to have kept silent about them in the presence of the congregation. Church history must not forget that Bardesanes won Edessa for Christianity. His influence was still strong in the time of Ephraem, who opposed him vigorously and hated him as *the* head of the three-headed monster, Marcion, Mani, Bardesanes. Nevertheless the people took pleasure in Bardesanes's fantastic religious poetry. Ephraem substituted orthodox hymns for the heretical, but retained the meter. The celebrated Rabulas (q.v.; d. 435) seems to have been the first to put an end to Bardesanism in Edessa. But it was not confined to Edessa; it spread to the Southern Euphrates, to Khorasan, even to China. In the West it seems to have been without influence, and to the real West it never penetrated. G. Krüger.

Bibliography: His *Book of the Laws of Divers Countries* is given in Eng. transl., *ANF*, viii, 723–734; a rich bibliography will be found in *ANF*, Bibliography, p. 108. Consult A. Merx, *Bardesanes Gnosticus*, Halle, 1863; A. Hilgenfeld, *Bardesanes, der letzte Gnostiker*, Leipsic, 1864; idem, *Ketzergeschichte des Urchristenthums*, Leipsic, 1884; *DCB*, i, 250–260 (especially noteworthy); Harnack, *Litteratur*, i, 184–191, ii, part 2, 128–132; Krüger, *History*, pp. 75–77; F. Nau, *Une Biographie inédite de Bardésane l'astrologue* (from the chronicle of Michael Syrus), Paris, 1897; idem, *Le Livre des lois des pays* (Syriac and French), Paris, 1899; F. C. Burkitt, *Early Eastern Christianity*, London, 1904. On the use of his hymns by Ephraem Syrus consult H. Burgess, *Hymns and Homilies of Ephraem Syrus*, pp. xxviii–xl, London, 1853.

BAREFOOTED MONKS AND NUNS: The popular name for members of various religious orders who go without any foot-covering whatever or with sandals in place of shoes. They are also called "discalced" (Lat. *discalceati*, "unshod"), but this name is more properly restricted to those who wear sandals and is used especially of the "discalced Carmelites." It is said that the custom was introduced in the West by St. Francis of Assisi (q.v.), who, with his companions, in 1209 discarded shoes in supposed obedience to Matt. x, 10, and thenceforth went wholly barefoot. There have been barefooted or discalced members of many orders,—the Clarenines, Recollects, Capuchins, Poor Clares, Minimites, Augustinians, Camaldolites, Servites, Carmelites, Cistercians (Feuillants), Trinitarians, Passionists, and others. It is usually the stricter divisions of the order who adopt the practise.

BARHAM, RICHARD HARRIS: Church of England; b. at Canterbury Dec. 6, 1788; d. in London June 17, 1845. He studied at Brasenose College, Oxford, took orders in 1813, and in 1817 became curate of Snargate, Kent. In 1821 he removed to London as minor canon of St. Paul's and thenceforth resided in London, where he held different livings and positions. He was esteemed for his exemplary life, and his sound sense and kind heart made him a good counselor and valued friend. His fame rests upon the *Ingoldsby Legends*, written under the pseudonym "Thomas Ingoldsby" for *Bentley's Miscellany* and *The New Monthly Magazine*, collected in book form 1840; a second series was published in 1847 and a third, edited by the author's son, the same year (many later editions). In this work Barham proved the possession of humorous powers of a high order and produced what is perhaps the best collection of rimed mirth in the English tongue; his extraordinary command of language appears also in passages of much lyric beauty; and the satire of theological and church tendencies which have not yet passed away give the work more serious value than that of merely promoting amusement.

Bibliography: *Life and Letters of the Rev. R. H. Barham, with a Selection from his Miscellaneous Poems*, edited by his son, R. H. D. Barham, 2 vols., London, 1880.

BAR HEBRÆUS. See Abulfaraj.

BARING-GOULD, SABINE: Church of England; b. at Exeter Jan. 28, 1834. He was educated at Clare College, Cambridge (B.A., 1854), was ordered deacon in 1864, and was ordained priest in the following year. He was then successively curate of Horbury, Yorkshire (1864-66), vicar of Dalton, Yorkshire (1866-71), and rector of East Mersea, Essex (1871-81). He inherited the family estates of Lew-Trenchard in 1872 and since 1881 has been rector of Lew-Trenchard, Devonshire. His numerous works include *The Path of the Just* (London, 1854); *Iceland, its Scenes and Sagas* (1862); *Post-Mediæval Preachers* (1865); *Book of Were-Wolves* (1865); *Curious Myths of the Middle Ages* (2 vols., 1866-68); *The Origin and Development of Religious Belief* (2 vols., 1869-70); *The Golden Gate* (1870); *The Silver Store, Collected from Mediæval Christian and Jewish Mines* (1870); *Legendary Lives of Old Testament Characters* (2 vols., 1871); *One Hundred Sermon Sketches for Extempore Preachers* (1871); *Village Conferences on the Creed* (1873); *The Lost and Hostile Gospels* (3 vols., 1874); *Yorkshire Oddities* (1874); *Some Modern Difficulties* (1875); *Village Sermons for a Year* (1875); *The Mystery of Suffering* (1877); *Germany, Present and Past* (1879); *Sermons to Children* (1879); *The Preacher's Pocket* (1880); *The Village Pulpit* (2 vols., 1881); *Church Songs* (1884); *The Seven Last Words* (1884); *The Passion of Jesus* (1885); *The Nativity* (1885); *The Resurrection* (1888); *Our Inheritance, a History of the Holy Eucharist in the First Three Centuries* (1888); *Historic Oddities and Strange Events* (2 vols., 1889-91); *Old Country Life* (1889); *In Troubadours' Land* (1890); *Conscience and Sin* (1890); *History of the Church in Germany* (1891); *Songs of the West* (1891); *The Tragedy of the Cæsars* (2 vols., 1892); *Curious Survivals* (1892); *The Deserts of Southern France* (2 vols., 1894); *A Garland of Country Song* (1894); *Old Fairy Tales Retold* (1894); *Old English Fairy Tales* (1895); *Napoleon Bonaparte* (1896); *A Study of St. Paul* (1897); *The Sunday Round* (1898); *Book of the West* (2 vols., 1899); *Book of Dartmoor* (1900); *Virgin Saints and Martyrs* (1900); *Brittany* (1902); *Book of North Wales* (1903); *Book of Ghosts* (1904); *Book of South Wales* (1905); *Book of the Riviera* (1905); and *Memorial of Horatio, Lord Nelson* (1905). He has likewise written a number of novels, and edited the *Lives of the Saints* (17 vols., London, 1872-77).

BAR KOK'BA: The name traditionally assigned to the leader of the great insurrection of the Jews in Palestine against the Romans under the emperor Hadrian in the years 132-135 (see Israel). The Roman historians Spartian and Dio Cassius, however, give no name and do not even speak of one single prominent leader; nor does the name occur on the coins struck during the revolt, or, according to Derenbourg (p. 423), in the rabbinical authorities. It rests on Christian tradition beginning with Justin Martyr, an author likely to be well informed. In his larger "Apology" (xxxi) he speaks of the leader of the rising as *Barchochebas*, saying that he inflicted severe penalties on the Christians (regarded as apostate Jews). Eusebius (*Hist. eccl.*, IV, viii, 4) reproduces this passage, with the variant spelling *Barchōchebas*, and confirms it in IV, vi, 2, where he says that the leader won his authority over the ignorant by basing on his name (meaning "star" or "son of a star") the claim to have been sent directly by God as a light to the oppressed. Beyond this Eusebius appears to know nothing of him except that in the last decisive battle, at the present Bittir (7 m. by rail s.w. of Jerusalem), in the eighteenth year of Hadrian (134-135), he suffered the penalty of his deeds.

That the Jews had a native leader in this rising is clearly proved by the coins, both those which are adapted to Jewish use from coins of Vespasian and Trajan, and must thus belong to this period, and those which on account of similarity of treatment are evidently of the same date (cf. F. W Madden, *History of Jewish Coinage*, London, 1864, 203 sqq., and *Coins of the Jews*, 1881). The inscriptions of these give on the reverse sometimes "in [the year of] the freedom of Israel" alone, sometimes the same with the number 2 for the year, or "year 1 of the deliverance of Israel"; on the obverse sometimes "Eleazar the priest" (who must not be confounded with the uncle of Bar Kokba, the scribe Eleazar), sometimes "Jerusalem," claiming the right of coinage for the city, and sometimes "Simeon, prince of Israel." That the leadership of Simeon coincided with the priesthood of Eleazar is shown by a distinct variety which names Eleazar the priest on the obverse and Simeon, without any title, on the reverse. According to the coins, therefore, during the time of the revolt, Israel had a secular head of the name of Simeon; which leads to the hypothesis that the same man who inspired the people by the name of Bar Kokba was really called Simeon. This theory finds support in certain coins which show the letters of the name of Simeon on both sides of a temple portico above which is a star. Moreover, the Jewish accounts are consistent with it. The *Seder 'Olam* mentions the three and a half years of a native ruler as the epoch following the wars of Vespasian and Quietus, calling this ruler, however, "Bar Kozeba." And the Talmudic explanations to the Mishnah treatise *Ma'aser sheni*, when they forbid the payment of tithes with money coined by rebels or otherwise unauthorized, give as examples that of "Ben Kozeba" or the "coins of Kozeba" and the "coins of Jerusalem." By the analogy of the latter, the former might also be a local designation (cf. I Chron. iv, 22); but the variant form first given makes it much more probable that it is from the name of the ruler; and there is no difficulty in identifying this ruler with the Simeon already mentioned, especially as Jewish tradition, quoting (in the Talmud on *Ta'anit*) from Rabbi Akiba, shows how easy was the transformation of the name of Ben Kozeba into the form Bar Kocheba (or Bar Kokba), with its encouraging reference to the prophecy of Balaam (Num. xxiv, 17).

Not much can be safely asserted of Bar Kokba's personality and achievements, for the Jewish sources mentioned above tell nothing trustworthy about him which is not already known from Dio Cassius, with the exception of his relations to Akiba and to Eleazar, whom, on suspicion of treachery, he is said to have killed with a kick. The immense number of his adherents (200,000 men, who had pledged themselves to the conspiracy by cutting off a finger), the fabulous size of his citadel of Bittir, and the awful bloodshed there, are merely imaginative projections from the natural facts of such a rising. As a consequence of his failure, Bar Kokba has lived in Jewish memory as a deceiver; but one who could bring about so vigorous and stubborn a revolt and dominate it to its close must have been a man of great power and determination, who had made the nation's cause his own.

(AUGUST KLOSTERMANN.)

BIBLIOGRAPHY: The principal source is Dio Cassius, *Historia Romana*, book lxix, chaps. 12-14, ed. F. G. Sturz, 9 vols., Leipsic, 1824-43; the *Samaritan Book of Joshua*, ed. Juynboll, Leyden, 1848, may be used cautiously. Consult J. Hamburger, *Realencyklopädie für Bibel und Talmud*, vol. ii, Leipsic, 1891; J. Derenbourg, *Essai sur l'histoire et la géographie de la Palestine*, Paris, 1867; idem, *Notes sur la guerre de Bar Kozeba*, in *Mélanges de l'École des Hautes Études*, ib. 1878; H. Grätz, *Geschichte der Juden*, iv, 137 sqq., Leipsic, 1893; Schürer, *Geschichte*, i, 682-685, 695-696, 765-772, Eng. transl., I, ii, 297-301, 311; A. Schlatter, *Die Tage Trajans und Hadrians*, Gütersloh, 1897; *JE*, ii, 506-509.

BARLAAM. See HESYCHASTS.

BARLAAM AND JOSAPHAT (or JOASAPH): The abbreviated title of a Greek religious romance commonly ascribed, without adequate reasons, to John of Damascus (q.v.; d. about 754). The fuller title is "History of the Soul-profiting of Barlaam and Josaphat (or Joasaph)." The popularity of the story is manifest from the fact that it was translated into Arabic, Ethiopic, Armenian, and Hebrew, as well as Latin, Icelandic, English, and other European languages. Research has proved that the work is based upon an Indian story (the *Lalitavistara*, composed 76 A.D.), in which Buddha (transformed into Josaphat) is the hero. Josaphat is represented as son of Abenner, an Indian king bitterly opposed to the Christian religion. His future conversion to a new faith and fame as a religious leader are predicted at the time of his birth by astrologers. Every effort is made by his father to enthral him in pleasures, to conceal from him the miseries of the world, and to shield him from all influences calculated to impress him with a sense of obligation to the world. At last, weary of pleasure and ease, Josaphat goes forth to see the world, is driven to despair by its misery, and is converted by Barlaam, a Christian hermit. To overthrow his son's convictions the king arranges a disputation in which Nachor, a court sage, is to impersonate Barlaam and by a feeble defense of Christianity to discredit it. By special divine interposition Nachor makes a noble defense of Christianity, which leads to his own conversion, and that of the king and his people. Barlaam and Josaphat secured places in the Roman Catholic calendar as saints. It was discovered a few years ago by Prof. J. A. Robinson, by a comparison of the defense of Christianity in the Greek story with the newly discovered Syriac text of the long-lost "Apology" of Aristides (see ARISTIDES, MARCIANUS), that the former, modified to some extent to suit the purpose for which it was employed, is the original of the "Apology." The Greek text is in *MPG*, xcvi, 860 sqq. A. H. NEWMAN.

The story of Barlaam and Josaphat forms the subject of the chief poem of Rudolf of Ems, a Middle High German poet (d. between 1250 and 1254), composed in 1220-23. It was based on a Latin book received from Abbot Guido of Cappel, which is said to have been a translation of the Greek legends of John of Damascus, already rendered by a certain Bishop Otho in the twelfth century. Rudolf, however, was unaware of this version or of another, which seems to have been made in the first half of the thirteenth century, and of which only a few fragments have been preserved. The story of the ascetic life of Buddha was highly attractive to a Christian ascetic, and Rudolf was the more drawn to the theme since he wished to atone for the frivolity of his earlier writings, declaring that this poem was no romance of knighthood, love, adventure, or the summertide, but a complete and sincere war upon the world, whereby men and women might be made better and purer.

Rudolf's "Barlaam and Josaphat" contains about 16,000 verses, and describes the victory of Christianity over heathen teachings. It thus summarizes the Middle Ages, and accordingly rises far above the level of a mere revamping or even amplification of an original source. In the poem Josaphat is the son of a heathen Indian king named Avernier. Astrologers foretell the conversion of the prince, who is accordingly confined by his father in a palace built especially for him. Surrounded by every luxury, he is kept from all knowledge of age, disease, and death. Permitted, after a time, to leave the palace, Josaphat sees a lame man and a blind man, and on a second excursion meets a man weighed down with all the infirmities of age. When sobered by reflection on these sights, God sends him Barlaam, a hermit from the island of Sennaar, who appears in the presence of the prince disguised as a jewel-merchant. Only to the pure in heart, however, can he show the most precious gem, which, he at last tells Josaphat, is Christianity. He then describes the life of Christ, so that Josaphat asks concerning baptism, whereupon Barlaam tells him of baptism, eternal life, the chief doctrines of Christianity, and the lives of the saints and martyrs who renounced the vanity of the world. At the request of Josaphat, Barlaam baptizes him, administers the sacrament to him, and urges him to remain pure in word and thought. The king seeks in vain to win his son back to heathenism, but the priests are refuted, the magician Theodas is converted, and temptations to sensuality are overcome. Avernier then offers Josaphat the half of his kingdom, and his administration manifests the omnipotence of Christianity, while the glory of his father gradually wanes, and his councilors bow before the ethical power of the new faith. Meanwhile Josaphat prays to God to turn his father's heart, and in answer to these petitions the king takes counsel how he may atone for his former iniquity. His councilors advise him to follow the example of his son, whereupon he writes a pathetic letter to Josaphat, full of lamentations and self-accusations. Father and son met, Avernier was instructed by Josaphat, received baptism together with all his councilors, surrendered the entire kingdom to the prince, and lived as a hermit the remaining four years of his life. After his father's death, Josaphat appointed Barachias as his successor and became an anchorite, finding his teacher Barlaam again. He bravely resisted all manner of fleshly temptations, and lived with Barlaam in fasting and prayer until his teacher died. Josaphat buried him, and himself died at the age of sixty. (A. Freybe.)

Bibliography: A collection of titles will be found in V Chauvin, *Bibliographie des ouvrages Arabes*, vol. iii, Paris, 1898. A Lat. transl. of John of Damascus' story is in *MPL*, lxxiii, 443–606; and the version of Rudolf of Ems was edited by F. Pfeiffer, Leipsic, 1843. Consult *Barlaam und Josaphat; französisches Gedicht des dreizehnten Jahrhunderts von Gui de Cambrai*, ed. H. Zotenberg and P. Meyer, Stuttgart, 1864; E. Cosquin, in *Revue des questions historiques*, xxviii (1880), 579–600; E. Braunholtz, *Die erste nichtchristliche Parabel des Barlaams und Josaphat*, Halle, 1884; H. Zotenberg, *Notice sur le livre de Barlaam et Josaphat*, Paris, 1886; A. Krull, *Gui de Cambrai: eine sprachliche Untersuchung*, Göttingen, 1887; F. Hommel, *Die älteste arabische Barlaam-Version*, Vienna, 1888; *Two Fifteenth Century Lives of St. Barlaam*, ed. J. Jacobs, London, 1893 (contains discussion of the influence of Buddhist legend on Western medieval literature); E. Kahn, *Barlaam und Josaphat: bibliographisch-literargeschichtliche Studie*, Munich, 1893; K. S. Macdonald, *Introduction to the Story of Barlaam and Joasaph*, 1895; idem, *Story of Barlaam and Joasaph* [London], 1895; *Story of Barlaam and Joasaph: Buddhism and Christianity*, ed. J. Morrison, Calcutta, 1895; A. Krause, *Zum Barlaam und Josaphat des Gui von Cambrai*, 2 vols., Berlin, 1899–1900. See also the literature under Aristides, Marcianus.

BARLETTA: More correctly Gabriel of Barletta (on the e. coast of Italy, 33 m. w.n.w. of Bari), a Dominican of the fifteenth century. About 1480 he preached in different cities of northern Italy. His sermons (first collected at Brescia, 1497; often reprinted in the following century) have the usual scholastic form of the time, but are enlivened by an originality of ideas, a lively wit, and a sense of humor often grotesque, which gave rise to the adage, "He knows not how to preach who knows not how to barlettize." The moral seriousness of the sermons and their striking descriptions of the distress of the country and its lost greatness made them influential and powerful. In a history of popular preachers Barletta must have a chief place (cf. *Zeitschrift für praktische Theologie*, vii, 1885, 30 sqq.; viii, 1886, 227 sqq.). K. Benrath.

BARNABAS: The companion of the Apostle Paul, himself called an apostle in Acts xiv, 4, 14. According to Acts iv, 36, he was a Levite born in Cyprus, his original name was Joses, and he was surnamed by the apostles (in Aramaic) *Barnebhuah*, which is explained by the Greek *huios paraklēseōs* ("son of exhortation," not "of consolation," cf. Acts xi, 23) and denotes a prophet in the primitive Christian sense of the word (cf. Acts xiii, 1; xv, 32). Like his aunt, the mother of John Mark (Col. iv, 10), Barnabas seems to have been living in Jerusalem, and he sold his property, after having joined the Christian congregation in the first year of its foundation, for the benefit of needy coreligionists (Acts iv, 37; xii, 12). He soon occupied a leading place in the community.

Authentic History.

Of his activity the Book of Acts records that he introduced the still distrusted Saul to the Jerusalem church after his return from Damascus (ix, 27). When the news of the spread of Christianity to Antioch came to Jerusalem Barnabas was sent to the former city (xi, 22–24). From Antioch he went to Tarsus to meet Paul and with him worked for an entire year in the Antioch church (xi, 25–26). Both were sent to Jerusalem with a contribution for the Christians of Judea (44 A.D.) and returned to Antioch with John Mark (xi, 27–30; xii, 25). The three were sent on a missionary journey to Cyprus, Pamphylia, Pisidia, and Lycaonia (xiii, 1 sqq.). In the narrative of this journey Paul occupies the first place from the point where the name "Paul" is substituted for "Saul" (xiii, 9). Instead of "Barnabas and Saul" as heretofore (xi, 30; xii, 25; xiii, 2, 7) "Paul and Barnabas" is now read (xiii, 43, 46, 50; xiv, 20; xv, 2, 22, 35); only in xiv, 14 and xv, 12, 25 does Barnabas again occupy the first place, in the first passage with recollection of xiv, 12, in the last two, because Barnabas stood in closer relation to the Jerusalem church than Paul. Paul appears as the preaching missionary (xiii, 16; xiv, 8–9, 19–20), whence the Lystrans regarded him as Hermes, Barnabas as Zeus (xiv, 12). After this journey follows a long stay in Antioch (xiv, 26–28) until they became involved in a controversy with the Judaizers and were sent to the Apostolic Council at Jerusalem, where the matter was settled (xv, 1–29; Gal. ii, 1–10; see APOSTOLIC COUNCIL AT JERUSALEM). According to Gal. ii, 9–10 Barnabas was included with Paul in the agreement made between them, on the one hand, and James, Peter, and John, on the other, that the two former should in the future preach to the heathen, not forgetting the poor at Jerusalem. Having returned to Antioch and spent some time there (xv, 35), Paul asked Barnabas to accompany him on another journey (xv, 36). Barnabas wished to take John Mark along, but Paul did not, as he had left them on the former journey (xv, 37–38). An unhappy dissension separated the two apostles; Barnabas went with Mark to Cyprus (xv, 39) and is not again mentioned in the Acts; but from Gal. ii, 13 a little more is learned about him, and his weakness under the taunts of the Judaizers is evident; and from I Cor. ix, 6 it may be gathered that he continued to labor as missionary.

Legendary History. Legends begin where authentic history ends. Barnabas is brought to Rome and Alexandria. The "Clementine Recognitions" (i, 7) make him preach in Rome during Christ's lifetime, and Clement of Alexandria (*Stromata*, ii, 20) makes him one of the seventy disciples. Not older than the third century is the tradition of the later activity and martyrdom of Barnabas in Cyprus, where his remains are said to have been discovered under the emperor Zeno (474–491). The Cyprian church claimed Barnabas as its founder in order to rid itself of the supremacy of the Antiochian bishop, just as did the Milan church afterward, to become more independent of Rome. In this connection, the question whether Barnabas was an apostle became important, and was often treated during the Middle Ages (cf. C. J. Hefele, *Das Sendschreiben des Apostels Barnabas*, Tübingen, 1840; O. Braunsberger, *Der Apostel Barnabas*, Mainz, 1876). The statements as to the year of Barnabas's death are discrepant and untrustworthy.

Tertullian and other Western writers regard Barnabas as the author of the Epistle to the Hebrews. This may have been the Roman tradition—which Tertullian usually follows—and in Rome the epistle may have had its first readers. But the tradition has weighty considerations against it. According to Photius (*Quæst. in Amphil.*, 123), Barnabas wrote the Book of Acts, and a gospel is ascribed to him (cf. T. Zahn, *Geschichte des neutestamentlichen Kanons*, ii, 292, Leipsic, 1890).

Alleged Writings. Of more interest is the tradition which makes Barnabas author of an epistle in twenty-one chapters, contained complete in the *Codex Sinaiticus* at the end of the New Testament. A complete Greek manuscript was discovered by Bryennios at Constantinople, and Hilgenfeld used it for his edition in 1877. Besides this there is a very old Latin version (now in the imperial library at St. Petersburg), in which, however, chaps. xviii–xxi are wanting. Toward the end of the second century the epistle was in great esteem in Alexandria, as the citations of Clement of Alexandria prove. It is also appealed to by Origen. Eusebius, however, objected to it and ultimately the epistle disappeared from the appendix to the New Testament, or rather the appendix disappeared with the epistle. In the West the epistle never enjoyed canonical authority (though it stands beside the epistle of James in the Latin manuscripts). The first editor of the epistle, Menardus (1645) advocated its genuineness, but the opinion to-day is, that Barnabas was not the author. It was probably written in Alexandria in 130–131, and addressed to Christian Gentiles. The author, who formerly labored in the congregation to which he writes, intends to impart to his readers the perfect gnosis that they may perceive that the Christians are the only true covenant people, and that the Jewish people had never been in a covenant with God. His polemics are, above all, directed against Judaizing Christians. In no other writing of that early time is the separation of the Gentile Christians from the patriotic Jews so clearly brought out. The Old Testament, he maintains, belongs only to the Christians. Circumcision and the whole Old Testament sacrificial and ceremonial institution are the devil's work. According to the author's conception, the Old Testament, rightly understood, contains no such injunctions. He is a thorough anti-Judaist, but by no means an antinomist. The main idea is Pauline, and the apostle's doctrine of atonement is more faithfully reproduced in this epistle than in any other postapostolic writing. The author no doubt had read Paul's epistles; he has a good knowledge of gospel-history but which of the gospels, if any, he had read, can not be asserted. He quotes IV Esdras (xii, 1) and Enoch (iv, 3; xvi, 5). The closing section (chaps. xviii–xxi), which contains a series of moral injunctions, is only loosely connected with the body of the epistle, and its true relation to the latter has given rise to much discussion.

(A. HARNACK.)

BIBLIOGRAPHY: A list of editions and discussions is in *ANF*, Bibliography, pp. 16–19. The *editio princeps*, Paris, 1645, was preceded in 1642 by an edition of Usser, Oxford, 1642, which, however, was consumed by fire in 1644, cf. J. H. Barkhouse, *The Editio princeps of the Epistle of Barnabas*, Oxford, 1883; the epistle was edited also by J. G. Müller, Leipsic, 1869; A. Hilgenfeld, ib. 1866, 2d ed., 1877 (containing the material discovered by Bryennios); W. Cunningham, London, 1877; in *Patrum apostolicorum opera*, ed. Gebhardt and Harnack, Leipsic, 1875, 2d ed., 1878 (contains a list of titles up to the year 1878); Funk, 1887, *ANF*, i, 133–149 contains an Eng. transl. and an introduction. Consult *DCB*, i, 260–265 (discusses the earlier literature on the subject); S. Sharpe, *Epistle of Barnabas, from the Sinaitic MS*, London, 1880; Völter, in *JPT*, xiv (1888), 106–144; J. Weiss, *Der Barnabasbrief, kritisch untersucht*, Berlin, 1888; Harnack, *Litteratur*, i, 58–62; G. Salmon, *Historical Introduction to the Study of the Books of the New Testament*, pp. 513–519, London, 1892; Krüger, *History*, pp. 18–21; (Barnabas), *Brief an die Hebräer*, ed. F. Blass, Halle, 1903.

BARNABITES (*Clerici regulares S. Barnabæ*): A congregation of regular clerics founded in the city and diocese of Milan in 1530 by a nobleman of Cremona, Antonio Maria Zaccaria (b. 1502;

educated at Padua and a physician by profession; ordained priest, 1528; d. 1539), with the help of his friends, Giacomo Antonio Morigia and Bartolomeo Ferrari, and two priests, Francesco Lucco and Giacomo Caseo. The region was then suffering severely from the wars between Charles V and Francis I, and the purpose was stated in the constitution to be the promotion of a love of divine service and the true Christian life by means of preaching and the frequent administration of the sacraments. The original and official name was *Clerici regulares S. Pauli decollati*, which is found in the brief of Clement VII (1533) confirming the congregation as well as in the edict of Paul III (1535) which exempted the society from episcopal jurisdiction. In 1538 the grand old monastery of St. Barnabas by the city wall of Milan was given to the congregation as their main seat, and thenceforth they were known as the Regular Clerics of St. Barnabas. After the death of Zaccaria they were favored and protected by Archbishop Carlo Borromeo of Milan and later by Francis of Sales because of their successful missionary work in Upper Italy. They entered France under Henry IV in 1608, and Austria under Ferdinand II in 1626. In the last-named country they still have six monasteries, the chief being at Vienna. In Italy their houses are larger and more numerous (twenty in all), and that connected with the Church of S. Carlo a' Catanari in Rome is the most prominent and richest. The Order can boast of eminent scholars, as Gavanti, Niceron, Gerdil, Lambruschini, and Vercellone in the past, and Savi, Semeria, and others in the present. O. Zöckler†.

Bibliography: Helyot, *Ordres monastiques*, iv, 100–116; *KL*, i, 2030–34; J. Hergenröther, *Allgemeine Kirchengeschichte*, iii, 276–277, Freiburg, 1886; Heimbucher, *Orden und Kongregationen*, i, 490, 519–520, ii, 256 sqq. On the life of the founder consult F. S. Bianchi, *Breve vita A. M. Zaccaria*, Bologna, 1875.

BARNARD, JOHN: Congregational minister; b. at Boston Nov. 6, 1681; d. at Marblehead Jan. 24, 1770. He was graduated at Harvard in 1700; accompanied the expedition to Port Royal as chaplain in 1707; was ordained minister at Marblehead in 1716, where he developed a great activity both for the moral and the material welfare of his flock. He published *A New Version of the Psalms of David* (Boston, 1752), and some sermons which show an incipient deviation from Calvinism.

Bibliography: His autobiography, written in his 86th year, is published in the *Collections of the Massachusetts Historical Society*, 3d series, vol. v, Boston, 1836.

BARNES, ALBERT: Presbyterian; b. at Rome, N. Y., Dec. 1, 1798; d. at West Philadelphia Dec. 24, 1870. He was graduated at Hamilton College, Clinton, N. Y., in 1820, and at Princeton Theological Seminary, 1823; was ordained pastor of the Presbyterian church at Morristown, N. J., 1825; was pastor of the First Presbyterian Church, Philadelphia, 1830–67, when he resigned and was made pastor emeritus. He was an advocate of total abstinence and the abolition of slavery and worked actively in the Sunday-school cause. In 1835 he was brought to trial for heresy by the Second Presbytery of Philadelphia upon ten specifications (given in E. H. Gillett, *History of the Presbyterian Church*, revised ed., ii, Philadelphia, n.d., pp. 473–474), but was acquitted. Appeal was then made to the Synod of Philadelphia (1835) and he was suspended from the ministry until he should repent of his errors. He appealed to the General Assembly of 1836 and the decision of the Synod was reversed. The agitation still continued and the trial was one of the active causes of the disruption of the Presbyterian church in the United States in 1837 (see Presbyterians) and Mr. Barnes was a leader of the New School party; yet he lived to rejoice in the reunion in 1870. His *Notes* on the entire New Testament and on portions of the Old (*Notes Explanatory and Practical on the New Testament*, 11 vols., Philadelphia, 1832–53; revised edition, 6 vols., New York, 1872; *Isaiah*, 2 vols., 1840; *Job*, 2 vols., 1844; *Daniel*, 1853; *The Book of Psalms*, 3 vols., 1868), designed originally for his congregation in Philadelphia, were eminently fitted for popular use and more than one million copies were sold; they are not original, but show much patient and conscientious labor. Other publications were *Scriptural Views of Slavery* (Philadelphia, 1846); *The Church and Slavery* (1857); *The Atonement in its Relation to Law and Moral Government* (1859); *The Way of Salvation* (1863); *Lectures on the Evidences of Christianity in the Nineteenth Century* (New York, 1868); *Prayers for the Use of Families* (1870); *Life at Three Score and Ten* (1871).

BARNES, ARTHUR STAPYLTON: Roman Catholic; b. at Kussouli (20 m. s.w. of Simla), India, May 31, 1861. He was educated at Eton (1874–77), Royal Military Academy, Woolwich (1877–78), and University College, Oxford (B.A., 1883), and was a lieutenant in the Royal Artillery in 1877–79. He later studied theology and was ordained to the Anglican priesthood. In 1889 he became vicar of St. Ives, Hunts, with Woodhurst and Oldhurst, and was vicar of the Hospital of St. Mary and St. Thomas, Ilford, from 1893 to 1895, when he entered the Roman Catholic Church. He then studied at Rome for the priesthood and was engaged in diocesan work at Westminster until his appointment as Roman Catholic chaplain to Cambridge University. He has also been a Private Chamberlain to the Pope since 1904. In addition to numerous briefer studies, he has written *The Popes and the Ordinal* (London, 1896) and *St. Peter at Rome* (1899).

BARNES, ROBERT: Church of England; b. at or near Lynn (26 m. n.e. of Ely), Norfolk, 1540; d. at the stake as a Protestant martyr, London, July 30, 1540. He studied at Cambridge, where he became an Augustinian friar, and at Louvain, where he proceeded doctor of divinity. Returning to Cambridge, he rose to be master of the house of the Augustinians. In 1526 he began to advocate Protestant views with great boldness, and so quickly got into trouble. Though treated leniently he was imprisoned from 1526 to 1528, when he escaped to the Continent, where he lived till 1531, and called himself Antonius Anglus. He enjoyed the friendship of the German Reformers. In Wittenberg in 1530 he published his first book, a collection of passages from the doctors of the Church—all in Latin—which supported, as he claimed, the Protestant position. In 1531 a German translation of these passages appeared in Nuremberg. In that year he returned to England and was employed on diplomatic journeys by Henry VIII and Thomas Cromwell, for instance to arrange the marriage between Henry and Anne of Cleves. He was always outspoken, and showed more zeal than prudence in propagating his Protestant views. So at last he was cast into prison in the Tower and, although no definite charge was laid against him, was burnt at Smithfield as a heretic. In 1573 John Foxe printed his English works (London) which display his courage, clearness, and comprehensiveness; selections were issued by Legh Richmond in his *Fathers of the English Church* (London, 1807)—in both the account of Barnes reprinted from Foxe's *Monuments* will be found.

BIBLIOGRAPHY: Sources for his life are in the *Calendar of Letters and Papers ... of Henry VIII*, vol. v, ed. J. S. Brewer and J. Gairdner, in *Rolls Series*, 11 vols., 1862–88. Luther's Preface to Barnes's *Confession* in Luther's works, Erlangen ed., lxiii, 396–400. Consult the biography in *DNB*, iii, 253–256.

BARNES, WILLIAM EMERY: Church of England; b. at London May 26, 1859. He was educated at Peterhouse, Cambridge (B.A., 1881), and was ordered deacon in 1883 and ordained priest in the following year. He was curate of St. John's, Waterloo Road, Lambeth, in 1883–85, assistant theological lecturer at Clare College, Cambridge, in 1885–94, and assistant tutor at Peterhouse in 1891–1904. Since the latter year he has been Hulsean professor of divinity at Cambridge. He has also been chaplain of Peterhouse since 1885 and fellow since 1889, as well as examining chaplain to the bishop of London since 1903. In addition to numerous briefer contributions and his work as editor of the *Journal of Theological Studies* from 1899 to 1904, he has written *Canonical and Uncanonical Gospels* (London, 1893); *The Peshitta Text of Chronicles* (1897); *Chronicles with Notes*, in *The Cambridge Bible for Schools* (1899); *Isaiah Explained*, in *The Churchman's Bible* (1901); *The Psalms in the Peshitta Text* (1904); and *The Creed of St. Athanasius* (1905).

BARNETT, SAMUEL AUGUSTUS: Church of England; b. at Bristol Feb. 8, 1844. He was educated at Wadham College, Oxford (B.A., 1865), and was ordered deacon in 1867 and priested in the following year. He was curate of St. Mary's, Bryanston Square, London, in 1867–72, vicar of St. Jude's, Whitechapel, in 1872-93, and curate of the same church in 1897–1903. In 1884 he founded Toynbee Hall, Whitechapel, of which he has since been warden, as well as chairman of the Whitechapel Board of Guardians, of the Children's Country Holiday Fund, and of the Pupil Teachers' Scholarship Fund. In 1893 he was appointed a canon of Bristol Cathedral, and was also select preacher at Oxford in 1896–97 and at Cambridge in 1900. In addition to minor contributions, he has written *Practicable Socialism* (in collaboration with his wife, London, 1893) and *The Service of God* (1895).

BARNUM, HENRY SAMUEL: Presbyterian; b. at Stratford, Conn., Aug. 13, 1837. He was educated at Yale College (B.A., 1862) and Auburn Theological Seminary, from which he was graduated in 1867. In the same year he was ordained to the Presbyterian ministry, and for five years was a missionary of the American Board of Commissioners for Foreign Missions at Harpoot, Turkey. Since 1872 he has been a missionary of the same organization at Van, Turkey, and since 1884 has also edited a weekly in Armenian and Turkish. He has likewise written a number of commentaries in Armenian.

BARO (BARON), PETER: Anti-Calvinist; b. at Étampes (35 m. s.s.w. of Paris) Dec., 1534; d. in London Apr. 17, 1599. He studied law at Bourges, and began in 1557 to plead in the court of the Parliament of Paris, but retired in 1560 to Geneva, where he studied theology and was ordained by Calvin. In 1572 he returned to France, but soon fled from persecution to England and in 1574 was appointed Lady Margaret professor of divinity at Cambridge. He fell out with the rigid Calvinists; and a sermon on the Lambeth articles, preached Jan. 12, 1596, gave so much offense that he was compelled to renounce his chair in the university and retire to London. Among his works are *In Jonam prophetam prælectiones* (London, 1579); *Summa trium de prædestinatione sententiarum* (Hardwyck, 1613), translated in Nichols's *Works of James Arminius*, i (London, 1825), 92–100.

BIBLIOGRAPHY: His autobiography is found abridged in R. Masters, *Memoirs of the Life and Writings of T. Baker*, pp. 127–130, Cambridge, 1784. Consult C. H. Cooper, *Athenæ Cantabrigienses*, ii, 274–278, London, 1861; *DNB*, iii, 265–267.

BARO'NIUS, CÆSAR (Cesare de Barono): The father of church history among Roman Catholics since the Reformation; b. at Sora (56 m. e.s.e. of Rome), in the kingdom of Naples, Oct. 31, 1538; d. in Rome June 30, 1607. His family was ancient and distinguished for piety. He was educated first at Veroli, then at Naples, where he studied theology and law. He went to Rome in 1557, just at the time when Paul IV was attempting to restore the papacy to its medieval splendor and dominion; but he felt less attraction to public policy than to a life of scholarly retirement. This he found in the new Congregation of the Oratory under Philip Neri (q.v.) whose system prepared the young man, without his knowledge, for the great work he was to do. The Oratorians were directed by their founder to occupy the morning hours with studies in ecclesiastical matters, but in a manner which should conduce to instruction as well as to edification. More and more attracted by the study of church history thus required, Baronius began diligently to collect and compare materials for its prosecution, and worked for thirty years amidst the vast mass of unpublished material which the Vatican archives contained. He had apparently no far-reaching literary plans until he was called upon by his superior, by Cardinal Caraffa, and by other friends to utilize his stores of knowledge in the defense of the Church against the powerful

Life.

attack which had been made upon it in the "Magdeburg Centuries" (q.v.) and to provide a complete Roman Catholic church history such as did not then exist,—a desideratum which his *Annales ecclesiastici* supplied with no small credit to the author, considering the conditions of historical writing in the sixteenth century. The fame which he acquired by the execution of his task drew him unwillingly from his retirement. He was made prothonotary of the apostolic see and later, by Clement VIII in 1596, a cardinal, as well as librarian of the Vatican. At both the papal elections which occurred in 1605 he was a candidate against his will, and came near being chosen. But the exhausting labor involved in the completion of his huge work really caused his death two years later.

The Annales Ecclesiastici.

The *Annales ecclesiastici* begin with the birth of Christ and come down to 1198. In form they resemble the ordinary medieval chronicle, the events of each year being grouped together under the date without regard to any other connection. This form would have been well adapted to the author's purpose of offering the great mass of historical material to the reader as sources arranged in order, if it had been carried out with strict application of critical principles and the utmost exactness. Baronius tried, indeed, to meet these requirements; but with all his pains he did not altogether succeed. To say nothing of the limitations inseparable from his fundamental beliefs and polemical attitude, the errors in non-contentious points, such as dates, are so numerous as to make great care necessary in using the *Annales*. Nevertheless they are a storehouse of learning. Though the work was occasioned by the appearance of the "Magdeburg Centuries," it is not directly controversial. The opposition appears rather in the simple fundamental conception that true history can only be written by the aid of the documents to which he had access, guaranteed by the authority of the Roman Church, and that it is only necessary for these documents to be known in order to secure universal recognition of the claims of that Church. He agrees with the Centuriators as to the purity of the Church of the first six centuries; but while they endeavor to show that the Christianity of the Middle Ages was an actual apostasy from that happy state, Baronius does his best to demonstrate the continuity of Catholicism and the early existence of a distinctively Roman character in Christianity. His other writings are of far secondary importance.

The first edition of the *Annales* appeared in 12 volumes at Rome, 1588–1607; the Mainz edition, 1601–05, was revised by Baronius himself; that of Antwerp, 1597–1609, is noteworthy because Philip III suppressed vol. xi within his dominions because of the *Tractatus de monarchia Siciliæ* contained in it [separately printed, Paris. 1609]. The *Annales* have been continued (1) from 1198 to 1565 by Abraham Bzovius (8 vols., Rome, 1616 sqq.; 9 vols., Cologne, 1621–30); (2) from 1198 to 1640 by Henricus Spondanus (Paris, 1640 sqq.; Leyden, 1678); (3) from 1199 to 1565 by the Oratorian Odoricus Raynaldus (9 vols., Rome, 1646–77; Cologne, 1693–1727; 14 vols., Lucca, 1740 sqq.), the best continuation; (4) from 1566 to 1571 by Jacobus Laderchius (3 vols., Rome, 1728–37; Cologne, 1738 sqq.); (5) from 1572 to 1583 by Augustin Theiner (3 vols., Rome, 1856 sqq.). The *Critica historico-chronologica in universos Cæsaris Baronii annales* of F. Pagi (4 vols., Antwerp, 1705 sqq.; 1724) are an indispensable companion to the work. The most convenient edition is that of Mansi (38 vols., Lucca, 1738–57), which has Pagi's emendations appended to the text, the continuation of Raynaldus, and three volumes of valuable indices. The most recent edition (incomplete), with all continuations, appeared, vols. i–xxviii at Bar-le-Duc, 1864–75, vols. xxix–xxxvii at Paris, 1876–83.

(Carl Mirbt.)

Bibliography: Sarra, *Vita del . . . Cesare Baronio*, Rome, 1862. On his history consult F. C. Baur, *Die Epochen der kirchlichen Geschichtsschreibung*, pp. 72–84, Tübingen, 1852; P. Schaff, *History of the Apostolic Church*, pp. 56–57, New York, 1874; C. de Smedt, *Introductio generalis in historiam ecclesiasticam*, pp. 461 sqq., Ghent, 1876; H. Hurter, *Nomenclator literarius recentioris theologiæ catholicæ*, i, pp. 209–212, Innsbruck, 1892; J. F. Hurst, *History of the Christian Church*, i, 42, 52, 723, 751, ii, 568, New York, 1900; *Cambridge Modern History, The Renaissance*, p. 609, London, 1902.

BARRETT, BENJAMIN FISK: Swedenborgian; b. at Dresden, Me., June 24, 1808; d. at Germantown, Penn., Aug. 6, 1892. He was graduated at Bowdoin, 1832, and at the Harvard Divinity School, 1838; became a Swedenborgian, 1839; was pastor of the New Church Society, New York, 1840–48; in Cincinnati 1848–50; after a temporary retirement because of ill health became pastor in Philadelphia; president and corresponding secretary of the Swedenborg Publishing Association, Philadelphia, 1871. He was editor of *The Swedenborgian*, 1858–60, and of *The New Church Monthly*, 1867–70 (when it was merged in *The New Church Independent*). He compiled and edited *The Swedenborg Library*, giving the substance of Swedenborg's theological teachings (12 vols., Philadelphia, 1876–81). His books include a *Life of Emanuel Swedenborg* (New York, 1841); *Lectures on the Doctrines of the New Church* (1842; title afterward changed to *Lectures on the New Dispensation*); *Beauty for Ashes, or the old and new doctrine concerning the state of infants after death contrasted* (1855); *The Golden Reed, or the true measure of a true church* (1855); *The Question concerning the Visible Church* (1856; new ed., with title *The Apocalyptic New Jerusalem*, Philadelphia, 1883); *Catholicity of the New Church* (1863); *The New View of Hell* (1870); *The Golden City* (1874); *The New Church, its nature and whereabouts* (1877); *Swedenborg and Channing* (1879); *The Question* [what are the doctrines of the New Church?] *Answered* (1883); *Heaven Revealed* (1885).

Bibliography: J. R. Irelan, *From Different Points of View: B. F. Barrett, Preacher, Writer, Theologian, and Philosopher*, Germantown, 1896.

BARRIÈRE, JEAN DE LA. See Feuillants.

BARROW (BARROWE), HENRY: English Separatist; hanged at Tyburn, London, Apr. 6, 1593. He came of good family in Norfolk, studied at Clare Hall, Cambridge, 1566–70, studied law, and was admitted a member of Gray's Inn in 1576. He belonged to the court circle and is said to have led a dissolute life until converted by a chance sermon. Probably through the influence of John Greenwood (q.v.) he adopted the views of the Brownists. After Greenwood's arrest, Barrow visited him in prison and was himself illegally detained, Nov., 1586, and kept in confinement thenceforth till his execution. While in prison, in collaboration with Greenwood, he wrote several books and pamphlets, including *A True Description out of the Word of God of the Visible Church* (1589; cf. W. Walker, *Creeds and Platforms of Congregationalism*, New York, 1893, 28-40) and *A Brief Discovery of the False Church* (1590). Dr. Dexter's suggestion (*Congregationalism of the Last Three Hundred Years*, New York, 1880, 192-202) that he wrote the Marprelate Tracts (q.v.) has not met with general acceptance. He differed from Robert Browne in placing the government of the Church in the hands of elders rather than the entire congregation, fearing too much democracy. See CONGREGATIONALISTS, I, 1, § 3. After the erratic leader of the Separatists had submitted to the Church, he turned his invectives against Barrow and Greenwood, who remained Separatists consistently to the end (see BROWNE, ROBERT).

BIBLIOGRAPHY: *Egerton Papers*, ed. J. P. Collier for Camden Society, pp. 166-179, London, 1840; *DNB*, iii. 297-298 (has excellent list of references); Champlin Burrage, *The True Story of Robert Browne*, pp. 48-60, Oxford, 1906.

BARROW, ISAAC: Church of England; b. in London Oct., 1630; d. there May 4. 1677. He studied at Trinity College, Cambridge; traveled in Europe and the East, 1655-59, residing for more than a year in Turkey; was ordained on his return to England, and after the Restoration was made professor of Greek at Cambridge; became professor of mathematics in 1663, but resigned in 1669 in favor of his famous pupil, Isaac Newton, and devoted himself to theology. Charles II made him his chaplain and in 1673 appointed him master of Trinity; in 1675 he was made vice-chancellor of the university. His reputation is deservedly high as a scholar, mathematician, and scientist; his *Treatise of the Pope's Supremacy* (London, 1680) shows much skill in controversy; his sermons are elaborate and exhaustive, but ponderous in style and inordinately long. His theological works edited by John Tillotson appeared in four volumes at London, 1683-87; they have been several times reissued, the best edition being that by A. Napier (9 vols., Cambridge, 1859).

BIBLIOGRAPHY: The best account of his life is by W. Whewell, prefixed to vol. ix of Barrow's works, ut sup.; a critical account is given *DNB*, iii, 299-305. His *Treatise of the Pope's Supremacy* has been reprinted by the Cambridge University Press and the S. P. C. K.

BARROWS, JOHN HENRY: Congregationalist; b. at Medina, Mich., July 11. 1847; d. at Oberlin, Ohio, June 3, 1902. He was graduated at Olivet College, Michigan, 1867; studied theology at the Yale Divinity School and Union Theological Seminary, New York, 1867-69, and at Andover, 1874-75; was ordained pastor of the Eliot Congregational Church, Lawrence, Mass., 1875; was pastor of Maverick Church, East Boston, 1880-81; of the First Presbyterian Church, Chicago, 1881-96; president of Oberlin College, Jan., 1899, till his death. He was chairman of the committee on religious conferences of the Columbian exposition of 1893, organized the Parliament of Religions at Chicago in that year, and published an account of it (2 vols., Chicago, 1893); his Haskell lectures at the University of Chicago, 1895, were repeated, with many other addresses, in India and Japan the following year and were published under the title *Christianity the World Religion* (1897); in 1898 he was Morse lecturer at the Union Theological Seminary upon the topic *The Christian Conquest of Asia* (New York, 1899).

BIBLIOGRAPHY: Mary E. Barrows, *John Henry Barrows, a Memoir*, New York, 1905 (by his daughter).

BARROWS, SAMUEL JUNE: Unitarian; b. in New York City May 26, 1845. After being for a time a journalist and stenographer, he studied theology at Harvard Divinity School (B.D., 1875) and studied for a year at Leipsic. He was pastor of the First Church (Unitarian), Dorchester, Mass., from 1876 to 1880, and was editor of the *Christian Register* from 1881 to 1897. He has been since 1896 the United States representative on the International Prison Commission, and since 1900 the corresponding secretary of the Prison Association of New York. In 1897-99 he was a member of Congress for the tenth district of Massachusetts. His writings include: *Life and Letters of Thomas J Mumford* (Boston, 1879); *The Doom of the Majority of Mankind* (1883); *Ezra Abbott* (Cambridge, 1884); *A Baptist Meeting House* (Boston, 1885); and *Isles and Shrines of Greece* (1898).

BARRUEL, AUGUSTIN: French politico-religious writer; b. at Villeneuve-de-Berg (95 m. n.w. of Marseilles), Ardèche, Oct. 2, 1741; d. at Paris Oct. 5, 1820. He was teaching in the Jesuit college in Toulouse when the order was suppressed in France (1764), and thereupon undertook extensive travels in Europe; returned to France in 1774 and wrote against the infidelity of the age as associate editor of the *Année littéraire*, after 1788 as editor of the *Journal ecclésiastique*, and in his book, *Les Helviennes ou lettres provinciales philosophiques* (5 vols., Amsterdam, 1784-88). In August, 1792, he fled from the Revolution to England and remained there till 1800. He published at London an *Histoire du clergé pendant la Révolution française* (2 vols., 1793); *Mémoires pour servir à l'histoire du Jacobinisme* (5 vols., Amsterdam, 1796-99; Eng. transl., 4 vols., 1798); *L'évangile et le clergé français* (1800). After his return to France he published *Du pape et de ses droits religieux* (2 vols., Paris, 1803), which gave the Ultramontanes occasion to say that he had sold himself to Bonaparte. His work in general is marked by exaggeration and bitterness and he goes to an absurd extreme in opposition to the freemasons and secret societies.

BIBLIOGRAPHY: Dussault, *Notice sur la vie et les ouvrages de Barruel* Paris, 1825.

BARRY, ALFRED: Church of England, suffragan bishop in West London; b. at London Jan. 15, 1826. He was educated at King's College, London, and Trinity College, Cambridge (B.A., 1848), where he was elected fellow in 1849. He was subwarden of Trinity College, Glenalmond, in 1849–54, headmaster of Leeds Grammar School in 1854–62, principal of Cheltenham College in 1862–68, and principal of King's College, London, in 1868–83. Having been ordained deacon in 1850 and priest in 1853, he was canon of Worcester in 1871–81 and of Westminster in 1881–84, in addition to being chaplain to the queen in 1875–84. In 1884 he was consecrated bishop of Sydney and primate of Australia, but resigned in 1889, and until 1891 was suffragan bishop in the diocese of Rochester. He was then appointed canon of Windsor, and was rector of St. James's, Piccadilly, from 1895 to 1900. He was consecrated suffragan bishop in West London in 1897. In addition to numerous volumes of sermons, he has written *Introduction to the Old Testament* (London, 1850); *The Atonement of Christ* (1871); *What is Natural Theology?* (Boyle Lectures for 1876); *The Manifold Witness for Christ* ((Boyle Lectures for 1877–78); *Teacher's Prayer Book* (1882); *First Words in Australia* (1884); *Parables of the Old Testament* (1889); *Christianity and Socialism* (1891); *Light of Science on the Faith* (Bampton Lectures for 1892); *England's Message to India* (1894); *Ecclesiastical Expansion of England* (Hulsean Lectures for 1894–95); *The Position of the Laity* (1903); and *The Christian Sunday* (1904).

BARRY, WILLIAM FRANCIS: English Roman Catholic; b. at London Apr. 21, 1849. He was educated at St. Mary's College, Oscott, English College, Rome, and Gregorian University, Rome (D.D., 1873). He was ordained to the priesthood at St. John Lateran, Rome, in 1873, and from that year until 1877 was vice-president and professor of philosophy at the Birmingham Diocesan Seminary. He was then appointed to the professorship of theology at St. Mary's College, Oscott, where he remained until 1880. From 1881 to 1883 he was curate at Snow Hill, Wolverhampton, and since the latter year has been rector of St. Birinus, Dorchester, Oxfordshire. He was a delegate to the Temperance Convention at the Chicago World's Fair in 1893, and lectured before the Royal Institution, London, in 1896. Since 1889 he has been a member and lecturer of the Catholic Truth Society, and in 1897 was elected vice-president of the Irish Literary Society of London. In addition to numerous briefer studies and contributions to periodicals, he has written *The New Antigone* (London, 1887); *The Two Standards* (1899); *Arden Massiter* (1900); *The Wizard's Knot* (1901); *The Papal Monarchy* (1902); *The Day Spring* (1903); *Cardinal Newman* (1903); *Perils of Revolt* (1904); *Ernest Renan* (1905); and *The Tradition of Scripture* (1906; put upon the Index).

BARSU'MAS: 1. Archimandrite or abbot of a Syrian monastery, adherent of Eutyches and his doctrine. At the Robber Synod of Ephesus (449) he appeared at the head of a thousand rough and turbulent monks, and took part personally in the tumults which disgraced that assembly (see EUTYCHIANISM). Two years later he presented himself at the Council of Chalcedon but was refused admittance. He continued to work for Eutychianism till his death in 458. By the Jacobites he is honored as a saint and miracle-worker.

2. Bishop of Nisibis 435–489. See NESTORIANS.

BARTH, bärt, **CHRISTIAN GOTTLIEB:** Pastor and friend of missions; b. in Stuttgart July 13, 1799; d. at Calw (20 m. w. of Stuttgart) Nov. 12, 1862. He studied theology at Tübingen, became pastor of Möttlingen, near Calw, in 1824, but retired in 1838 to Calw, and devoted himself entirely to the missionary cause. He founded the missionary society of Württemberg, and brought it in active cooperation with Basel and all the great missionary societies of the Christian world. He wrote some of the best German missionary hymns. He edited the *Calwer Missionsblatt* and wrote a great number of works of practical Christianity, and stories for children and youth, some of which met with an almost unparalleled success. Several were translated into English, e.g., *The Autobiography of Thomas Platter* (London, 1839); *Bible Stories for the Young* (1845); *Stories for Christian Children* (2 series, 1851 and 1854).

BIBLIOGRAPHY: K. Werner, *C. G. Barth, nach seinem Leben und Wirken gezeichnet*, 3 vols., Calw, 1865–69; G. Weitbrecht, *Dr. Barth nach seinem Leben und Wirken*, Stuttgart, 1875; W. Kopp, *C. G. Barth's Leben und Wirken*, Calw, 1886.

BARTH, JACOB: Judeo-German Semitic scholar; b. at Flehingen (a village of Baden) Mar. 3, 1851. He was educated at the universities of Leipsic, Strasburg, and Berlin, and since 1874 has taught Hebrew, exegesis, and the philosophy of religion at the rabbinical seminary in Berlin, and has also lectured for many years on Semitic and Jewish literature at the Veitel Heine Ephraim Institute in the same city. In 1880 he was appointed associate professor of Semitic languages in the University of Berlin. He has written *Beiträge zur Erklärung des Buches Hiob* (Berlin, 1876); *Maimonides Commentar zum Tractat Makkoth* (1880); *Beiträge zur Erklärung des Jesaja* (1885); *Die Nominalbildung in den semitischen Sprachen* (2 vols., Leipsic, 1889–91); *Etymologische Studien zum semitischen, insbesondere zum hebräischen Lexikon* (1893); *Wurzeluntersuchungen zum hebräischen und aramäischen Lexikon* (1902); and a large number of contributions to various learned periodicals. He has also edited the *Kitab al-Faṣiḥ* of Thalab (Leyden, 1876); the first two parts of the Leyden edition of the "Annals" of al-Tabari (1879-81); and the *Diwan* of al-Kutami (1902).

BARTH, MARIE ÉTIENNE AUGUSTE: French Lutheran; b. at Strasburg Mar. 22, 1834. He was educated at the Collège Royal and the academy of his native city, being graduated from the latter in 1855. From 1856 to 1861 he was professor of rhetoric and philosophy at the college of Buchsweiler, Alsace, but has since lived as a private scholar in Paris. He is a chevalier of the Legion of Honor, a grand officer of the Royal Order of Cambodia, and a Commander of the Dragon of Annam. He is a member of learned societies in France, Holland, Russia, Great Britain, and the United States, and in addition to numerous contributions to Oriental and scientific periodicals in France, has written *Les Religions de l'Inde* (Paris, 1879; Eng. transl., *The Religions of India*, by J. Wood, London, 1882); *Inscriptions sanscrites du Cambodge* (Paris, 1885); and *Inscriptions sanscrites du Cambodge et de Campu* (1894).

BARTHOLOMEW (Gk. *Bartholomaios*, Aram. *Bar-Talmai*, "Son of Talmai"): One of the twelve Apostles, mentioned in Matt. x, 3; Mark iii, 18; Luke vi, 14; Acts i, 13. Nothing is told in the New Testament of his work as an apostle. According to Eusebius (*Hist. eccl.*, v, 10) and Jerome (*De vir. ill.*, xxxvi), he preached the Gospel in India—that is, in what is called India to-day, not, as some have argued, Arabia Felix. Other Asiatic countries have been named as the scenes of his labors, especially Armenia, where he is said to have been flayed alive and crucified with his head down. Legend narrates that his body was miraculously conveyed to the island of Lipari, and thence to Benevento. His feast-day is usually the 24th of August; at Rome, however, it is celebrated on the 25th. An old and wide-spread theory (though Augustine, for example, did not accept it) identifies Bartholomew with Nathanael of Cana in Galilee (John i, 45–51; xxi, 2). That John counted Nathanael as an apostle is probable because in the former of these passages he represents him as joining the company of Jesus with the earlier and later apostles, and in the latter passage he mentions him in the company of apostles. In support of the theory, it is noticed that in the lists of the apostles in the synoptic Gospels (though not in the Acts) he is mentioned next to Philip, while Nathanael was brought to Jesus by Philip; and John nowhere mentions Bartholomew, while the synoptists do not mention Nathanael. But, on the other hand, it is remarkable that the synoptists do not give the other name for Bartholomew, if he is the same, while John speaks of Nathanael as if the reader would know at once who he was. (K. SCHMIDT.)

BARTHOLOMEW OF BRAGA (known also as *Bartholomæus de Martyribus* from the church in Lisbon in which he was baptized): Archbishop of Braga 1558–82; b. at Lisbon 1514; d. at Viana (on the coast of Portugal, 40 m. n. of Oporto) July 16, 1590. He belonged to the Dominican order and took part in the Council of Trent, the decisions of which he introduced into Portugal. He founded the first clerical seminary in Portugal and won well-deserved renown by establishing hospitals and hospices. In 1582 Pope Gregory XIII allowed him to resign his office, and thenceforth he lived as simple monk in the monastery of Viana, giving instruction and performing works of mercy. He wrote Biblical commentaries, a Portuguese catechism, and a *Compendium doctrinæ spiritualis* (Lisbon, 1582; many later editions). An edition of his works, with life, by Malachias d'Inguimbert appeared in two volumes at Rome, 1727.

K. BENRATH.

BARTHOLOMEW OF BRESCIA: A canonist of the thirteenth century. Little is known with any certainty of his life. He was born about the beginning of the century at Brescia, studied Roman and canon law in Bologna under Laurentius Hispanus, and afterward taught canon law there. He is principally remembered for his commentary on the *Decretum Gratiani* (about 1240), but he wrote several other works on canon law, which are usually not much more than revised editions of earlier works. (E. FRIEDBERG.)

BARTHOLOMEW'S DAY, THE MASSACRE OF SAINT. See COLIGNY.

BARTHOLOMITES: 1. A society founded at Genoa in 1307 by certain Armenian Basilian monks who had fled thither from persecution in their native land. They built there a church to the Virgin and St. Bartholomew, whence their name. Pope Clement V (1305–14) allowed them to follow their Eastern rite and customs, but in course of time they conformed to Western usages, and in 1356 Innocent VI allowed them to choose a general. They existed at Genoa and in other places in Italy till 1650, when Innocent X suppressed the order.

2. A congregation of secular priests founded at Salzburg about 1643 by Bartholomäus Holzhauser, canon of Salzburg (b. at Langenau, near Ulm, 1613; d. at Bingen May 20, 1658). Their statutes, confirmed by Innocent XI in 1680 (complete text in Holstenius-Brockie, *Codex regularum*, vi, Augsburg, 1759, 543–595), regulated their life on communistic principles, whence their official name, *Institutum clericorum sæcularium in communi viventium*, and their popular designation as "Communists." For a time the society flourished in the dioceses of South Germany as well as in Hungary, Poland, and Spain, but with the suppression of their last house, at Landshut, in 1804, they went out of existence.

O. ZÖCKLER†.

BIBLIOGRAPHY: 1. Heimbucher, *Orden und Kongregationen*, i, 48. 2. Helyot, *Ordres monastiques*, viii (1719), 119–126; Heimbucher, *Orden und Kongregationen*, ii, 363–366; J. F. L. Gaduel, *Vie du Barthélemy Holzhauser*, Orléans, 1892 (contains also a study of the order).

BARTLET, JAMES VERNON: English Congregationalist; b. at Scarborough (37 m. n.e. of York), Yorkshire, Aug. 15, 1863. He was educated at Exeter College, Oxford (B.A., 1886), and at Mansfield College (1886–89), where in 1889 he was appointed fellow and began to lecture on church history, remaining senior tutor in residence until 1900. In the latter year he was appointed professor of church history in the same institution, and still holds this position. In addition to numerous briefer contributions, he has written *Early Church History* (London, 1894); *The Apostolic Age* (Edinburgh, 1900); *Commentary on Acts* (in *The Century Bible*, 1901); and *The Earlier Pauline Epistles* (in *The Temple Bible*, 1901); and was joint author of *The New Testament in the Apostolic Fathers* (1905).

BARTLETT, SAMUEL COLCORD: Congregationalist; b. at Salisbury, N. H., Nov. 25, 1817; d. in Hanover, N. H., Nov. 16, 1898. He was graduated at Dartmouth 1836, and at Andover Theological Seminary 1842; was ordained 1843, and was pastor at Munson, Mass., 1843–46; professor of intellectual philosophy and rhetoric in Western Reserve College, Hudson, O., 1846–52; pastor at Manchester, N. H., 1852–57; in Chicago 1857–59; was one of the founders of the Chicago Theological Seminary (Congregational) and professor of Biblical literature there 1858–77; president of Dartmouth 1877–92, and lecturer on the relation of the Bible to science and history and instructor in natural theology and evidences of Christianity, 1892–98. Besides many articles in the periodicals and addresses, he published *Life and Death Eternal, a refutation of the doctrine of annihilation* (Boston, 1866; 2d ed., 1878); *Sketches of the Missions of the A. B. C. F. M.* (1872); *Future Punishment* (1875); *From Egypt to Palestine through Sinai* (New York, 1879), an account of a journey to explore the desert of the Exodus; *Sources of History in the Pentateuch* (1883); *The Veracity of the Hexateuch* (Chicago, 1897).

BARTOL, CYRUS AUGUSTUS: Unitarian; b. at Freeport, Me., April 30, 1813; d. in Boston Dec. 16, 1900. He was graduated at Bowdoin, 1832, and at the Harvard Divinity School, 1835; in 1837 he was ordained as assistant pastor to Dr. Charles Lowell at the West Church (Unitarian), Boston; after Dr. Lowell's death in 1861 he became pastor, and served till 1888. He was a member of the Transcendental Club and published a number of volumes, chiefly sermons and addresses, among them being *Discourses on the Christian Spirit and Life* (2d ed., revised, Boston, 1850); *Discourses on the Christian Body and Form* (1853); *Pictures of Europe* (1855); *Church and Congregation* (1858); *Radical Problems* (1872); *The Rising Faith* (1873); *Principles and Portraits* (1880); *Spiritual Sacrifice* (1884).

BARTOLI, bār″tō-lī′, **DANIELLO:** Italian Jesuit; b. at Ferrara Feb. 12, 1608; d. at Rome Jan. 13, 1685. He entered the Society of Jesus in 1623; was a distinguished preacher and teacher of rhetoric in different cities of Italy; in 1650 he became historian of his order at Rome. He wrote biographies, moral and ascetical works, and books upon physical science. His *Istoria della compagnia di Gesù* (5 vols., Rome, 1653–73), especially the part devoted to Asia, is replete with curious information; as an introduction to this work he wrote the *Vita e istituto di S. Ignazio* (Rome, 1650; Eng. transl., 2 vols., New York, 1856). His collected works were edited by H. Marietti (34 vols., Turin, 1823–44). The life of Ignatius and the moral and ascetical works have been published at Piacenza (9 vols., 1821) and at Milan (3 vols., 1831).

BARTON, ELIZABETH: English impostor of the reign of Henry VIII; b., according to her own statement, in 1506; beheaded in London April 20, 1534. In 1525, while a servant at Aldington, Kent, her ravings in consequence of some nervous disorder gained for her a local reputation as one divinely inspired. She recovered her health after a few months, but her fame remained, and certain monks, notably one Edward Bocking, made use of her to attempt to check the advance of the Reformation. Instructed by them she continued her alleged prophesyings. In 1527 she was taken to the priory of St. Sepulchre at Canterbury, and under the title of the " Nun " or " Holy Maid of Kent " her fame went far and wide and she seems to have been partly or fully believed in by persons of intelligence and influence. When the divorce from Catharine of Aragon was proposed she inveighed against it and ultimately went so far in her threats against the king that she and certain of her abetters were arrested and brought to trial in 1533. Under torture Elizabeth and Bocking confessed to fraud; with two friars and two priests they were beheaded at Tyburn, the Nun repeating her confession on the scaffold. Sir Thomas More, Bishop Fisher, and others were implicated and narrowly escaped suffering at the same time.

Bibliography: The sources for a biography are indicated in the long and critical notice in *DNB*, iii, 343–346.

BARTON, GEORGE AARON: Friend; b. at East Farnham, Canada, Nov. 12, 1859. He was educated at Haverford College, Haverford (B.A., 1882), and Harvard University (Ph.D., 1891). He was teacher of mathematics and classics at the Friends' School, Providence, R. I., in 1884–89, and lecturer on Bible languages in Haverford College in 1891–95, while in 1891 he was appointed professor of Biblical literature and Semitic languages at Bryn Mawr College, a position which he still holds. He has been a member of the American Oriental Society since 1888, of the Society of Biblical Archeology, London, since 1889, of the Society of Biblical Literature and Exegesis since 1891, of the Archeological Institute of America since 1900, of the Vorderasiatische Gesellschaft, Berlin, since 1899, of the Victoria Institute, London, since 1902, and of the Orients-Gesellschaft, Berlin, and the Egypt Exploration Fund since 1904. He was president of the Oriental Club of Philadelphia in 1898–99, and a member of the council of the Society of Biblical Literature and Exegesis in 1900–03, and in 1903–04 was one of the executive committee of the American School of Oriental Research in Palestine, of which he was director in the previous year. He was also a delegate to the Inter-Church Conference in 1905, and since 1879 has been an acknowledged minister of the Society of Friends (orthodox). In theology he is in general agreement with the so-called " new theology." In addition to briefer studies and contributions to various religious encyclopedias, he has written *The Religious Use of the Bible* (Philadelphia, 1900); *The Roots of Christian Teaching as Found in the Old Testament* (1902); *A Sketch of Semitic Origins, Social and Religious* (New York, 1902); *A Year's Wandering in Bible Lands* (Philadelphia, 1904); and *The Haverford Library Collection of Cuneiform Tablets or Documents from the Temple Archives of Telloh* (1905).

BARTON, WILLIAM ELEAZAR: Congregationalist; b. at Sublette, Ill., June 28, 1861. He was educated at Berea College (B.S., 1885) and Oberlin Theological Seminary (B.D., 1890). He was ordained to the Congregational ministry at Berea, Ky., in 1885, and has held successive pastorates at Robbins, Tenn. (1885–87), Litchfield, O. (1887–90), Wellington, O. (1890–93), Shawmut Congregational Church, Boston, Mass. (1893–99), and First Congregational Church, Oak Park, Ill. (since 1899). He is a corporate member of the American Board of Commissioners for Foreign Missions and of the Chicago Society of Biblical Research; a director of the Congregational Educational Society, of the Chicago Theological Seminary, of the Illinois Home Missionary Society, and formerly of the similar society in Massachusetts; a trustee of Berea College; and vice-president of the Congregational Sunday-school and Publication Society and of the American Peace Society. He is lecturer on applied practical theology at the Chicago Theological Seminary, and was a delegate to the Triennial National Congregational Council in 1895, 1898, and 1904, and to the International Decennial Council of the same denomination in 1899. In theology he is a progressive conservative Congregationalist. He is associate editor of the *Bibliotheca Sacra*, and his writings, in addition to numerous sermons and works of fiction, include: *The Psalms and Their Story* (Boston, 1898); *Old Plantation Hymns* (1899); *The Improvement of Perfection* (Portland, Me., 1900); *Faith as Related to Health* (Boston, 1901); *Consolation* (1901); *An Elementary Catechism* (1902); *The Old World in the New Century* (1902); *The Gospel of the Autumn Leaf* (Chicago, 1903); *A Shining Mark* (Philadelphia, 1903); and *Jesus of Nazareth, His Life and the Scenes of His Ministry* (Boston, 1904).

BARUCH, APOCALYPSE OF. See Pseudepigrapha, Old Testament, II, 10–11. **Book of.** See Apocrypha, A, IV, 5.

BASCOM, HENRY BIDLEMAN: Bishop of the Methodist Episcopal Church, South; b. at Hancock, Delaware County, New York, May 27, 1796; d. at Louisville, Ky., Sept. 8, 1850. He was licensed to preach 1813; was appointed chaplain to Congress 1823; was president of Madison College, Uniontown, Pennsylvania, 1827–29; agent of the American Colonization Society, 1829–31; elected professor of moral science in Augusta College, Kentucky, 1832, president of the Transylvania University, Kentucky, 1842, bishop 1850. He was prominent in the organization of the Methodist Church, South, and from 1846 to 1850 he edited the *Southern Methodist Quarterly Review*. He published sermons and lectures and a volume upon *Methodism and Slavery*. His collected works were printed at Nashville (4 vols., 1850–56).

BASCOM, JOHN: Congregationalist; b. at Genoa, N. Y., May 1, 1827. He was educated at Williams College (B.A., 1849) and Andover Theological Seminary (1855). He was a tutor in Williams College in 1852–53 and professor of rhetoric in the same institution from 1855 to 1874. In the latter year he was chosen president of the University of Wisconsin, where he remained until 1887. He then returned to Williams College as lecturer on sociology, and four years later was appointed professor of political science, holding this position until 1903. He is an adherent of the new theology of the Congregational type, and has written: *Political Economy* (Andover, 1859); *Æsthetics* (New York, 1862); *Philosophy of Rhetoric* (1865); *Principles of Psychology* (1869); *Science, Philosophy, and Religion* (1871); *Philosophy of English Literature* (1874); *Philosophy of Religion* (1876); *Growth and Grades of Intelligence* (1878); *Ethics* (1879); *Natural Theology* (1880); *Science of Mind* (1881); *Words of Christ* (1883); *Problems in Philosophy* (1885); *Sociology* (1887); *The New Theology* (1891); *Historical Interpretation of Philosophy* (1893); *Social Theory* (1895); *Evolution and Religion* (1897); *Growth of Nationality in the United States* (1899); and *God and His Goodness* (1901).

BASEDOW, bā'ze-dō" **(BASSEDAU), JOHANN BERNHARD:** German rationalist and innovator in educational methods; b. at Hamburg Sept. 11, 1723; d. at Magdeburg July 25, 1790. After a wilful boyhood he studied theology at Leipsic (1744–46), but followed his studies in very irregular fashion and hampered by poverty; he was tutor to a noble family of Holstein 1749–53; became teacher at the academy of Sorö, Denmark, in 1753, and at the gymnasium of Altona in 1761; he was forced to retire from both of these positions because of his unorthodox views freely and offensively expressed in various publications (*Praktische Philosophie für alle Stände*, Copenhagen, 1758; *Philalethie: neue Aussichten in die Wahrheiten und Religion der Vernunft*, 2 vols., Altona, 1763–64; *Theoretisches System der gesunden Vernunft*, 1765; *Grundriss der Religion welche durch Nachdenken und Bibelforschen erkannt wird*, 1764). After 1767 he abandoned theology for education. Influenced by Rousseau's *Émile*, he sought to devise a system that should be according to nature and dispense with the exercise of authority on the part of the teacher and with the necessity for work on that of the pupil. His views are set forth in his *Vorstellung an Menschenfreunde und vermögende Männer über Schulen, Studien, und ihren Einfluss in die öffentliche Wohlfahrt, mit einem Plane eines Elementarbuches der menschlichen Erkenntniss* (Hamburg, 1768; new ed., Leipsic, 1894) and his *Elementarwerk* (4 vols., 1774). He had remarkable success in enlisting sympathy and gaining patrons, and in 1774 was able to open an institution for the realization of his ideas, the "Philanthropin" at Dessau (described in *Das in Dessau errichtete Philanthropinum*, Leipsic, 1774). After four years he retired, having shown himself, by loose management and personal bad habits, utterly unfitted for the position. He spent the rest of his life in literary work and private teaching. His writings on theological and educational subjects number more than sixty; the former are crude and coarse, and grossly rationalistic; the latter ill-considered and impracticable, although some of his ideas as developed by others have been productive of good. He was well characterized by Goethe as a man who undertook to educate the world, but himself had no education at all.

Bibliography: *ADB*, ii, 113–124 (by his great-grandson, Max Müller); R. Diestelmann, *J. B. Basedow*, Leipsic, 1897.

BA'SEL, BISHOPRIC OF: The origin of this diocese probably goes back into the Roman period. Just above Basel, at the present Kaiseraugst, lay the Roman city of Augusta Rauricorum, which retained its importance well into the fourth century. Historical analogy justifies the supposition that Christianity was not unknown there. By the end of the fourth century the town must have sunk into decay, since the *Notitia provinciarum Galliæ* does not mention it. As, however, in the seventh century we hear of a bishop Ragnachar of Augusta, we are led to infer the retention of an older title; and when we find him also designated as Bishop of Augusta and Basel, we are able to understand this by the supposition that the see was transferred from the old decayed town to the rising city of Basel, which is mentioned as early as 374 by Ammianus Marcellinus. Apparently, then, Christianity in this region survived all the storms which raged there in the fifth and sixth centuries. After the establishment of Frankish rule, the diocese included the Alemannic districts between the Rhine and the Aar, the Alsatian Sundgau, the Burgundian Sorengau, and the northeastern part of the Elsgau. Its boundary, accordingly, was formed partly by the two rivers, partly by a line drawn from the Aar to the Doubs, thence to the southern slope of the Vosges, then along their crest, then to the Rhine at Breisach. [The Benedictine monk Hatto or Haito (q.v.), bishop c. 805–822, was a trusted counselor of Charlemagne and his envoy to the emperor Nicephorus at Constantinople. At the end of the tenth century the bishopric developed into an imperial principality. It was at Basel that in 1061 Cadalus of Parma was elected by the imperialists as antipope against Alexander II (see HONORIUS II, ANTIPOPE); and Bishop Burkhard of Hasenburg (1071–1107) was one of the most influential counselors of Henry IV. Under the Hohenstaufen emperors also, the bishops of Basel were usually on the imperial side. After the council (see BASEL, COUNCIL OF), the next important event in the history of the diocese is the outbreak of the Reformation, which occurred in the episcopate of the wise and pious Christopher of Utenheim (1502–27), and in spite of his efforts led to much turbulence and the ultimate suppression of the Roman Catholic religion in 1529. The university was suspended, and most of the professors left the town with Erasmus and Glarean. The bishop went to Pruntrut and the chapter to Freiburg, whence it did not return to the diocese until 1678. A succession of zealous prelates strove to undo the work of the Reformation (see JACOB CHRISTOPHER, BISHOP OF BASEL). The territory of the diocese was incorporated with the French Republic, and at the Congress of Vienna with the cantons of Bern and Basel. In 1828 the see was reerected, and at present includes the Roman Catholic population of the cantons of Basel, Solothurn, Bern, Aargau, Zug, Lucerne, Schaffhausen, and Thurgau; the bishop resides in Lucerne.]

(A. HAUCK.)

BIBLIOGRAPHY: The *Series episcoporum Basiliensium* to 1060 A.D. is in *MGH*, *Script.*, xiii (1881), 373–374; *Monuments de l'histoire de l'ancien évêché de Bâle*, ed. Trouillat, Basel, 1858; J. J. Merian, *Geschichte der Bischöfe von Basel*, Basel, 1862; E. Egli, *Kirchengeschichte der Schweiz*, Zurich, 1893.

BASEL, CONFESSION OF: A confession of faith submitted to the citizens of Basel for their acceptance on Jan. 21, 1534. It was prepared by Myconius on the basis of a briefer formula put forth by Œcolampadius in his address at the opening of the synod in September, 1531. It is simple and moderate, occupying an intermediate position between Luther and Zwingli. Until 1826 it was read in the pulpits on Wednesday of Holy Week, but then was made binding on the clergy only; in 1872 it was set aside entirely. The confession was also accepted at Mühlhausen and is sometimes called the Mylhusiana; the first Helvetic confession is also called the Second Confession of Basel, because it was written there (see HELVETIC CONFESSIONS).

(R. STÄHELIN†.)

BIBLIOGRAPHY: The best reprint is given by K. R. Hagenbach, in his *J. Oekolampad und O. Myconius*, pp. 465–470, cf. 349–530, Elberfeld, 1859. Consult Schaff, *Creeds*, i, 385–388, where the literature is given.

BASEL, COUNCIL OF: The last of the "reforming councils" of the fifteenth century. By the decree *Frequens* of the Council of Constance (q.v.), a periodical repetition of ecumenical synods was enjoined. The first synod held accordingly at Pavia and Sienna, 1423–24 (see PAVIA, COUNCIL OF; SIENNA, COUNCIL OF), had passed without accomplishing anything. After the execution of John Huss, his victorious and uncompromising followers (see HUSS, JOHN, HUSSITES) greatly embarrassed the Roman Church and the German empire, and Pope Martin V felt obliged to convene a new ecumenical council to meet in a German city. Basel was selected. The pope died shortly after, but his successor, Eugenius IV, a Venetian, had to confirm the convocation. His legates opened the council at Basel Aug. 27, 1431. But when it became known that the pope thought of dissolving it at once, as he expected nothing good from it, distrust of the pope filled the members of the council. On Feb. 15,

Attitude Toward the Pope.

1432, the council declared itself to be a continuation of that of Constance and therefore an ecumenical one, representing the Holy Catholic Church, and deriving its authority immediately from God; therefore it could only dissolve itself of its own free will. In fixing the order of business, that of the Council of Constance, where the members were grouped according to nationality, was discarded; and four committees were formed: (1) on matters of faith, (2) on political affairs, (3) on ecclesiastical reforms, and (4) on general business. These committees met separately, each having its own president. The agreement of three of them was necessary to bring a question before a general session. The council was at first presided over by Cardinal Cesarini, or some other cardinal designated by the pope. But much was lacking to make the work of the council effective; the pope distrusted the Fathers of Basel and these distrusted the pope; both were ruled by party-hatred and passion; the highest aim of the council was the subjection of the pope to it. On Apr. 29, 1432, the pope and his cardinals were invited to come to Basel. As the former did not come, a process was instituted (Sept. 6) against him for contumacy. The council stood at that time in the zenith of its power, since it was recognized by most states, and Eugenius had to yield and expressly recognize the council Aug. 1, 1433.

Relations with the Hussites.

In the mean time the authority of the council had increased through its negotiations with the Hussites. On Jan. 4, 1433, the Hussites Procopius, the terror of Christendom, and John Rokyczana, the learned and fanatic orator, together with a numerous and brilliant retinue, rode into Basel, not as penitent heretics, but with proud and fierce mien, as guests of the council. The negotiations with them resulted in an agreement in 1434 by which the so-called Compactata of Prague (see HUSS, JOHN), embodying their principal demands, among others the use of the cup in the celebration of the Lord's Supper, were granted with modifications.

Church Reform.

Beginning in 1435, the council considered and issued a number of decisions, which concerned the reform of the Church in its head and members and the introduction of a better discipline, but these measures were dictated by hatred to the curia, rather than by enthusiasm for reform. The annates, the pallium-money, the tax on the papal confirmation of ecclesiastical promotion, the judicial authority of the pope, the richest source of the revenues of the curia, were abolished and declared to be simony. Prospects of a compensation were held out, but not fixed. As concerns the spiritual offices the canonical chapter-election was reinstated in its full right, the papal reservations, with a few exceptions, were abolished, and strict provisions were made concerning the moral worthiness of those to be elected. The troublesome appeals to Rome were limited, also the election and number of the cardinals and their prebends. But the restriction of the sources of power of the curia when it needed revenues the most, excited the fierce opposition of the whole army of officials. In the council a small but strong party arose which wished to avoid a breach with the curia, a party of legates, headed by Cardinal Cesarini.

Proposed Union with the Greek Church.

Another matter, however, brought about a complete breach. The Greek emperor John Palæologus had addressed himself to both the pope and the council with a view of obtaining help against the menacing Turks through a union of the Greek and Roman Churches. The pope would not concede that the glory of having brought about a union with the Greeks should belong to the members of the council; he and the minority at Basel wished the negotiations with the Greeks to be carried on in a city of Italy, whereas the antipapal majority at Basel wished the negotiations to be carried on there. The party of the legates left the council in 1437 and outwardly also sided with the pope. Of the cardinals only Louis d'Allemand (q.v.) remained and the vacant seats of the bishops were filled by clerics of lower order. The council became more and more democratic. All regard for the pope now ceased; the council opened the process against him and the cardinals and on Jan. 24, 1438, he was suspended. The pope declared the council to be a company of Satan, excommunicated its members, and convened a countercouncil at Ferrara, which he soon removed to Florence, where he met the Greek emperor and his spiritual and secular retinue (see FERRARA-FLORENCE, COUNCIL OF). He brought about the so-called Florentine union, which in itself was delusive and unreal, but greatly enhanced the fame of the pope in the eyes of his contemporaries, while the council at Basel deposed him June 25 as a backsliding heretic.

Decline and End of the Council.

The governments took advantage of the differences of both parties. In France, the Synod of Bourges (1438) incorporated the decrees of the Council of Basel with the laws of the kingdom, the so-called pragmatic sanction of Bourges (see PRAGMATIC SANCTION). Germany declared in 1439 that it would keep neutral, and observed the neutrality for some time to the great detriment of the curia. Ultimately, however, almost all European governments sided with Eugenius. The council at Basel persisted in its opposition under the direction of Allemand. On Nov. 5, 1439, it elected an antipope in the person of the Duke Amadeus of Savoy, who took the name of Felix V (q.v.) and was crowned at Basel with great pageantry. He did not satisfy the expectations of the Fathers at Basel and was not recognized by the princes and nations. The German king, Frederick III, was especially averse to him, and the cunning secretary of the king, Æneas Sylvius Piccolomini (see PIUS II, POPE) secretly influenced the German church policy in favor of Eugenius, who lived to know, though dying, that the German king and most of the German princes had declared for him Feb. 7, 1447. Great concessions had indeed been wrung from the pope; they were afterward modified or not regarded at all. The tolling of bells and bonfires announced the victory of Rome. The German king withdrew his support of the council, and it decreed June 25, 1448, to meet at Lausanne, where Pope Felix V had his residence. Ten months later the king of France induced the pope to resign, and the council, tired of the unending conflict, made Nicolas V his successor, whom the cardinals at Rome had appointed after the death of Eugenius. In this way it meant to preserve at least a semblance of authority, and in its last session, Apr. 25, 1449, it decreed its own dissolution. In spite of the failure of the council the belief that the Church needed reformation persisted.

PAUL TSCHACKERT.

BIBLIOGRAPHY: The sources for a history are in the Acts of the Council, to be found in Mansi, *Concilia*, vols. xxix xxxi, and Harduin, *Concilia*, vols. viii–ix; also in Æneas Sylvius, *Commentarius de rebus Basileæ gestis*, used in C. Fea, *Pius II. a calumniis vindicatus*, Rome, 1823; *Monumenta conciliorum generalium seculi xv, Concilium Basiliense, Scriptorum*, i, ii, iii, Vienna. 1857–94; and *Concilium Basiliense; Studien und Quellen zur Geschichte des Concils von Basel*, ed. J. Haller, G. Beckmann, R. Wackernagel, G. Coggiola, Basel, 1896–1904 (reports on the MSS. still preserved in Basel and Paris, and criticism of Æneas

Sylvius, Ragusa, and Segovia). Consult J. Lenfant, *Histoire de la guerre des Hussites et du Concile de Basle*, Amsterdam, 1731; I. H. von Wessenberg, *Die grossen Kirchenversammlungen des fünfzehnten und sechszehnten Jahrhunderts*, vol. ii, 4 vols., Constance, 1840; J. Aschbach, *Geschichte des Kaiser Sigmunds*, vol. iv, Hamburg, 1845; G. Voigt, *Enea Sylvio Piccolomini als Papst Paul II*, vol. i, Basel, 1856; O. Richter, *Organisation und Geschäftsordnung des Basler Concils*, Leipsic, 1877; A. Bachmann, *Die deutsche Könige und die kurfürstliche Neutralität*, Vienna, 1888; P. Joachimsohn, *Gregor Heimburg*, Munich, 1891; J. F. Hurst, *History of the Christian Church*, i, 785–786, ii, 69, 93, 341, New York, 1897–1900; Hefele, *Conciliengeschichte*, vol. vii; *KL*, i, 2085–2110; Pastor, *Popes*, i, 280–338; Creighton, *Papacy*, iii, 1–45.

BASHAN, bē'shun: The northeastern part of trans-Jordanic Palestine. The name occurs in the Old Testament in prose and sometimes in poetry with the article (" the Bashan "), indicating that *bashan* was originally a common noun, and its signification is made evident by the Arabic *bathanah*, " a fertile plain free from stones." The Greeks had the name in the forms *Basan*, *Basanaitis*, the LXX has *Basanitis*, and Josephus *Batanaia* and *Batanea* (cf. Eusebius and Jerome, *Onomasticon*). The location of the district is clearly noted in the Old Testament as the northern third of the plateau to the east of the Jordan (Deut. iii, 8; Joshua xiii, 11–12), with Gilead (the Yarmuk) as the southern boundary, Hermon on the north, and Salcah on the east.

As soon as the traveler going east from the Sea of Tiberias crosses the Nahr-al-Allan, eighteen miles away, he may note the abrupt change of the structure of the plain. The numerous hillocks, a peculiarity of the Jaulan, disappear, as do the great lava blocks, and in their place one sees a great plain of mellowed, red-brown, fertile soil stretching away east, north, and south. The boundary of this on the northeast is the volcanic, wooded heights of Al-Kunetra and the base of Mt. Hermon, on the north the district of Wadi al-Ajam, on the east the Lejjah and Jebel Druz or Jebel Hauran, and on the south the plateau of Al-Hamad, with the stony Jaulan in the west. It is divided by two great wadies (Dahab and Zadi), which empty into the Yarmuk. Ruins abound, and on some of the hillocks are the graves of the former leaders and chiefs of the districts.

The spongy, easily worked soil is a mixture of disintegrated lava, ashes, and sand from Jebel Hauran. To this composition is due the extraordinary fertility of the region, yielding half crops even in seasons of drought. The plain is almost treeless, the only exceptions being the old terebinths which stand by Arabic holy-places or villages. The slope of the southern part, which is the granary of Syria, is quite sharp from east to west, while from north to south the altitude is about the same. The boundaries already noted (the steppe of Hamad and the Druz mountains) are prominent. The last are the " Salmon " of Ps. lxviii, 14–15. The region formed part of the kingdom of Og (Joshua xii, 5). It is celebrated in the Old Testament for its cattle (Deut. xxxii, 14; Ezek. xxxix, 18), and in these times probably served better a pastoral than a nomadic population. The " oaks of Bashan " (Isa. ii, 13; Ezek. xxvii, 6) have disappeared except on the foothills of the Hauran and Hermon mountains, where there are small groves, and along the Yarmuk.

The following cities of Bashan are mentioned in the Old Testament: (1 and 2) Ashtaroth and Edrei, capitals of Og (Deut. i, 4, iii, 1; Joshua xii, 4); (3) Ashteroth Karnaim (Eusebius and Jerome, *Onomasticon*), not far from Job's grave [an Arab sanctuary], and near Shaikh Sad, until 1903 the seat of government; (4) Bozrah (I Macc. v, 26), at the southwest of the Hauran, containing ruins dating from Roman times; (5) Golan (Joshua xxi, 7), one of the Levitical cities of refuge, probably the modern Saham al-Jolan on the western edge of the plateau; (6) Karnain (I Macc. v, 26, perhaps Amos vi, 13, A. V. " horns "), not located; (7) Salcah, modern Salkhad, east from Bozrah, on the watershed, with a castle built in an old crater. These places are all on the edge of the plateau, as are the modern cities.

The Old Testament mentions also the district Argob in Bashan, which had sixty cities (I Kings iv, 13; Deut. iii, 4), a possession of Jair (Deut. iii, 14, but cf. Judges x, 3 sqq., I Kings iv, 13), and in the eastern part of the Jaulan. (H. GUTHE.)

BIBLIOGRAPHY: J. L. Porter, *Giant-Cities of Bashan*, New York, 1871; id., *Five Years in Damascus*, London, 1855; J. G. Wetstein, *Reisebericht über Hauran und die Trachonen*, Berlin, 1860; idem, *Das batanäische Giebelbirge*, Leipsic, 1884; C. J. M. de Vogüé, *La Syrie centrale, inscriptions sémitiques*, 2 vols., Paris, 1868–77; R. F. Drake and C. F. T. Drake, *Unexplored Syria*, 2 vols., London, 1872; G. Schumacher, *Across the Jordan*, pp. 20–40, 103–242, ib. 1886; idem, *The Jaulan*, p. 125, ib. 1888; idem, *Das südliche Basan zum ersten Male aufgenommen und beschrieben*, Leipsic, 1897; W. M. Thomson, *The Land and the Book*, 3 vols., New York, 1886; F. Buhl, *Geographie von Palästina*, Freiburg, 1896; G. A. Smith, *Historical Geography of the Holy Land*, pp. 542, 549–553, 575 sqq., 611 sqq., London, 1897; D. W. Freshfield, *The Stone Towns of Central Syria*, New York, n.d.

BASHFORD, JAMES WHITFORD: Methodist Episcopal bishop; b. at Fayette, Wis., May 25, 1849. He was educated at the University of Wisconsin (B.A., 1873), the Theological School of Boston University (B.D., 1876), the School of Oratory in the same institution (1878), and Boston University (Ph.D., 1881). He was tutor in Greek at the University of Wisconsin in 1873–74, and held successive pastorates at Harrison Square Methodist Episcopal Church, Boston (1875–78), Jamaica Plain, Boston (1878–81), Auburndale, Mass. (1881–84), Chestnut Street, Portland, Me. (1884–87), and Delaware Ave., Buffalo, N. Y. (1887–89). He was president of Ohio Wesleyan University in 1889–1904, and in the latter year was chosen bishop, and in this capacity went to Shanghai, China. In theology he is distinctly liberal, believing that Christianity can be better interpreted from the point of view of evolution than from the older standpoint, and being confident that higher criticism, if used with sound scholarship, will not endanger the fundamentals of Christianity. He has written: *Science of Religion* (Delaware, O., 1893); *Wesley and Goethe* (Cincinnati, 1903); and *Methodism in China* (1906).

BASIL OF ACHRIDA: Archbishop of Thessalonica. He came from Achrida (on the n.e. shore of the modern Lake Ochrida, 100 m. n. of Janina, in Albania) in Macedonia and became archbishop in 1146. His importance lies in the fact that he wrote and spoke against the union of the Greek Church with the Roman. He wrote a letter on the subject to Pope Adrian IV in 1154. To about the same time belong his dialogues with Anselm of Havelberg, ambassador of Frederick Barbarossa, published by J. Schmidt in *Des Basilius aus Achrida bisher unedirte Dialoge* (Munich, 1901). Another dialogue with Henry of Benevento is still in manuscript. Vasiljewskij has published an address of Basil's on the death of Irene, first wife of the Emperor Manuel Comnenos, in *Vizantijskij Vremnik*, 1894, 55–132. His earlier printed writings are in *MPG*, cxix. PHILIPP MEYER.

BIBLIOGRAPHY: Krumbacher, *Geschichte der byzantinischen Litteratur*, pp. 88, 466, Munich, 1897.

BASIL (BASILAS) OF ANCYRA: A physician, born at Ancyra, and bishop there from 336, succeeding Marcellus (q.v.). He was deposed by the Synod of Sardica in 343, reinstated by Constantius in 350, and, with George of Laodicea (q.v.), became the leader of the homoiousian middle party. In 360 he was banished to Illyria, and died in exile. With George he composed a dogmatic memoir and, according to Jerome, also a writing against Marcellus, a treatise on virginity, and "some other things." The sources are Socrates, *Hist. eccl.*, ii, 26, 42; iii, 25; Jerome, *De vir ill.*, lxxxix; Sozomen, *Hist. eccl.*, iv, 24; Philostorgius, v, 1; Epiphanius, *Hær.*, lxxiii, 12–22. See ARIANISM. G. KRÜGER.

BIBLIOGRAPHY: J. Schladebach, *Basilius von Ancyra*, Leipsic, 1898; *DCB*, i. 281–282.

BASIL, SAINT, THE GREAT: Bishop of Cæsarea in Cappadocia; b. at Cæsarea, of a wealthy and pious family, c. 330; d. there Jan. 1, 379. He was somewhat younger than his friend, Gregory Nazianzen, and several years older than his brother, Gregory of Nyssa, who, with him, are known as the three great Cappadocians. The first years of his life Basil spent on a rural family estate under the guidance of his grandmother, Macrina (q.v.), whom he always remembered with gratitude. He received his literary education at first in Cæsarea, then at Constantinople, finally at the great school in Athens, where he became intimate with Gregory and the future emperor Julian. The practical ideal of pure Christianity, the elevation of the soul above sensuality, the flight from the world, and the subjection of the body were already apparent in him. The family tendency to an ascetic life proved decisive after his return to Cæsarea (c. 357). For a time, indeed, he acted as rhetor, but he resisted exhortations to devote himself to the education of youth. At this time he seems to have received baptism, and, after being received into the Church, he visited the famous ascetics in Syria, Palestine, and Egypt. To the dogmatic controversies which stirred the Church he paid no attention, though he deplored them. Upon his return to Cæsarea he distributed his property among the poor and withdrew to a lonely romantic district, attracting like-minded friends to a monkish life, in which prayer, meditation, and study alternated with agriculture. Eustathius of Sebaste (q.v.) had already labored in Pontus in behalf of the anchoretic life and Basil revered him on that account, although the dogmatic differences, which then estranged so many hearts, gradually separated these two men also. Siding from the beginning and at the Council of Constantinople in 360, with the Homoiousians, Basil went especially with those who overcame the aversion to the homoousios in common opposition to Arianism, thus drawing nearer to Athanasius (see ARIANISM). He also became a stranger to his bishop, Dianius of Cæsarea, who had subscribed the Nicene form of agreement, and became reconciled to him only when the latter was about to die.

Earlier Life.

In 364 Basil was made a presbyter of the Church at Cæsarea and as such opposed the new bishop Eusebius, who was not favorably disposed toward asceticism. For a time he again withdrew to solitude, but the increasing influence of Arianism induced him to devote his undivided strength to ecclesiastical affairs. He now appears as the real leader of the Church of Cæsarea, and in directing the church discipline, in promoting monachism and ecclesiastical asceticism, and especially by his powerful preaching, his influence grew. His successful exertions during the famine in the year 368 are especially praised. After the death of Eusebius (370), Basil was elected bishop of Cæsarea in spite of much opposition on dogmatic and personal grounds; even his friend Gregory felt offended. Occupying one of the most important episcopal sees of the East, Basil's influence on public affairs was now great. With all his might he resisted the emperor Valens, who strove to introduce Arianism, and impressed the emperor so strongly that, although inclined to banish the intractable bishop, he left him unmolested. To save the Church from Arianism Basil entered into connections with the West, and with the help of Athanasius, he tried to overcome its distrustful attitude toward the Homoiousians. The difficulties had been enhanced by bringing in the question as to the essence of the Holy Spirit. Although Basil advocated objectively the consubstantiality of the Holy Spirit with the Father and the Son, he belonged to those, who, faithful to Eastern tradition, would not allow the predicate homoousios to the former; for this he was reproached as early as 371 by the orthodox zealots among the monks, and Athanasius defended him. His relations also with Eustathius were maintained in spite of dogmatic differences and caused suspicion (see EUSTATHIUS OF SEBASTE). On the other hand, Basil was grievously offended by the extreme adherents of Homoousianism, who seemed to him to be reviving the Sabellian heresy. The end of the unhappy factional disturbances and the complete success of his continued exertions in behalf of Rome and the East, he did not live to see. He suffered from liver complaint and excessive asceticism made him old before his time and hastened his early death. A lasting monument of his episcopal care for the poor was the great institute before the gates of

Presbyter and Bishop of Cæsarea.

Zeitfracht Medien GmbH
Ferdinand-Jühlke-Straße 7
99095 Erfurt, Deutschland
produktsicherheit@kolibri360.de